DRUNK DRIVING DEFENSE

DRUNK DRIVING DEFENSE

Fifth Edition

LAWRENCE TAYLOR, J.D.
Long Beach, California

Member, California and Washington Bars
Former Deputy Public Defender, Los Angeles
Former Deputy District Attorney, Los Angeles
Former Fulbright Professor of Law, Osaka University

ASPEN LAW & BUSINESS
A Division of Aspen Publishers, Inc.
Gaithersburg New York

Printed in the United States of America

ISBN 0-7355-1146-2

3 4 5 6 7 8 9 0

Library of Congress Cataloging-in-Publication Data

Taylor, Lawrence, 1942-
Drunk driving defense / Lawrence Taylor. — 5th ed.
p. cm.
Includes bibliographical references and index.
ISBN 0-7355-1146-2
1. Drunk driving defense — United States. 2. Defense (Criminal procedure) — United States. I. Title.
KF2231.T39 1999
345.73′0247 — dc21 99-41726
CIP

Fifth Edition

About Aspen Law & Business

Aspen Law & Business — comprising the former Prentice Hall Law & Business and Little, Brown and Company's Professional Division, and Wiley Law Publications — is a leading publisher of authoritative treatises, practice manuals, services, and journals for attorneys, financial and tax advisors, corporate and bank directors, and other business professionals. Our mission is to provide practical solution-based how-to information keyed to the latest legislative, judicial, and regulatory developments.

We offer publications in the areas of banking and finance; bankruptcy; business and commercial law; construction law; corporate law; pensions, benefits, and labor; insurance law; securities; taxation; intellectual property; government and administrative law; matrimonial and family law environmental and health law; international law; legal practice and litigation; and criminal law.

Other Aspen Law & Business products treating criminal and litigation issues include:

ASPEN LAW & BUSINESS
A Division of Aspen Publishers, Inc.
A Wolters Kluwer Company
www.aspenpublishers.com

SUBSCRIPTION NOTICE

This Aspen Law & Business product is updated on a periodic basis with supplements to reflect important changes in the subject matter. If you purchased this product directly from Aspen Law & Business, we have already recorded your subscription for the update service.

If, however, you purchased this product from a bookstore and wish to receive future updates and revised or related volumes billed separately with a 30-day examination review, please contact our Customer Service Department at 1-800-234-1660, or send your name, company name (if applicable), address, and the title of the product to:

ASPEN LAW & BUSINESS
A Division of Aspen Publishers, Inc.
7201 McKinney Circle
Frederick, MD 21704

To Judy

ABOUT THE AUTHOR

Lawrence Taylor is nationally recognized as one of the foremost authorities on DWI/DUI litigation in the United States. A graduate of the University of California (Berkeley) and UCLA Law School, former prosecutor, and Fulbright Professor of Law, he is the author of the standard textbooks in the field: *Drunk Driving Defense, 5th ed.* (New York: Aspen Law & Business, 2000) and *California Drunk Driving Defense, 2d ed.* (San Francisco: West/Bancroft-Whitney, 1996). He has also written over 30 articles on the subject. His web site (www.duicenter.com) is considered the premier drunk driving research source on the Internet.

Over the past 20 years, Mr. Taylor has proven a popular lecturer on DUI trial techniques at over 200 CLE seminars in 38 states. He has appeared on numerous television and radio programs, and has been featured in such publications as *The Wall Street Journal, USA Today, The National Law Journal,* and *Lawyer's Weekly, USA.* He serves on the Board of Regents of the National College for DUI Defense in Atlanta, Georgia, and was elected dean of the College for 1995–1996.

Mr. Taylor continues to limit his Los Angeles/Orange County practice to the defense of drunk driving cases.

SUMMARY OF CONTENTS

III

PRE-TRIAL

IV

TRIAL

CONTENTS

3.

THE ADMINISTRATIVE LICENSE SUSPENSION 105

II

EVIDENCE

4.

FIELD EVIDENCE 161

III

PRE-TRIAL

8.

9.

10.

DISCOVERY 637

11.

SUPPRESSION OF EVIDENCE 713

IV

TRIAL

12.

13.

14.

THE DEFENSE 1065

15.

CLOSING 1119

TABLE OF CHECKLISTS

TABLE OF FORMS

TABLE OF PLEADINGS

PREFACE

Driving under the influence of alcohol, or "drunk driving," is by far the most commonly encountered offense in the courts today. Yet it has always been one of the most difficult charges to defend, involving as it does more esoteric areas of science and law than most felonies, while affording increasingly fewer constitutional safeguards. The difficulties, however, have become much greater since the first edition of *Drunk Driving Defense* was published in 1981. The substantive, evidentiary, and procedural aspects of DUI litigation have grown immeasurably more complex in this period of time, while at the same time the stakes for the client have been raised. In fact, the entire DUI scene has undergone a change in recent years that may accurately be described as revolutionary.

These radical changes are attributable to a heightened national awareness of the drunk driving problem. Spurred on by constant media attention and such lobbying groups as Mothers Against Drunk Driving (MADD), legislators across the country have stumbled over each other to provide prosecutors with tougher weapons. It falls upon the defense attorney, of course, to understand and counter these new weapons with weapons of his own.

The most noticeable element in the prosecution's new arsenal is the so-called per se law. Since 1982, the vast majority of states have enacted statutes that created a new offense: driving while having an excessive blood-alcohol level (commonly .08 or .10 percent). This crime, which is usually charged along with the traditional DUI offense, is completely unconcerned with whether the driver was intoxicated or not: the crime is a biological one. Thus the prosecutor's job is made considerably easier — and the defense attorney's considerably more difficult.

New and more sophisticated analytical devices have been introduced to prove the accused's blood-alcohol content. Once considered "state-of-the-art," the Breathalyzer 900 and 900A are now looked on as the simplistic "Model T"s of the breath testing scene. Infrared spectroscopic instruments have taken over the field, with such units as the Intoxilyzer 5000 offering three-band analysis, internal computerization, acetone detection, and radio frequency interference options. Most recently, Draeger has offered its new Alcotest 7110, combining fuel cell technology with an improved infrared wavelength. Blood and urine samples are analyzed less commonly with traditional methods and more frequently with headspace gas chromatography.

But as the methods of analysis become more complex, the possibilities for error grow — and the problem becomes more difficult for counsel to handle. The phenomenon has created difficulties across the full spectrum of chemical analysis. Thus, for example, the spread of infrared analysis requires counsel to become familiar with lightwave theory and such potential defects as nonspecific analysis and the effects of acetone and acetaldehyde. Similarly, the theory and fallacies of retrograde extrapolation must be understood if counsel expects to effectively attack any method of blood-alcohol analysis. The defense attorney must be able to expose the weaknesses of the computer programming in the newer breath machines, such as the "assumed" alveolar air ratio used in computing blood-alcohol levels. As these instruments become ever more sophisticated, they are also increasingly susceptible to false readings caused by radio frequency interference. Counsel must become familiar with this phenomenon and with the admissions by the federal government and the manufacturers themselves as to its effects. Quite simply, the defense attorney who does not familiarize himself with recent developments in blood-alcohol analysis is lost.

Chemical analysis has not been the only arena to experience radical evidentiary changes. Even traditional "field sobriety tests" have witnessed innovations. The "horizontal gaze nystagmus" test, for example, has spread rapidly across the country and can be devastating evidence — if defense counsel is unprepared to expose its foundational and physiological defects. And new models of hand-held preliminary breath-testing devices are becoming increasingly common among patrol officers.

As the new laws, procedures, and forms of evidence have been introduced, so the courts have kept pace, with a seemingly unending stream of appellate decisions. In one short period, for example, the U.S. Supreme Court rendered a series of DUI decisions: self-incrimination was the subject in *South Dakota v. Neville* (1983); blood-alcohol discovery was dealt with in *California v. Trombetta* (1984); the application of *Miranda* in drunk driving was defined in *Berkemer v. McCarty* (1984). A few years later, the Court addressed the right to jury trial in DUI cases in *Blanton v. North Las Vegas* (1989); the validity of sobriety checkpoints in *Michigan Department of State Police v. Sitz* (1990); double jeopardy in drunk driving cases in *Grady v. Corbin* (1990); and questioning as part of field sobriety testing in *Pennsylvania v. Muniz* (1990). At the state level, courts across the country have busily churned out contradictory decisions concerning such diverse subjects as DUI roadblocks, foundational requirements for blood-alcohol analysis, right to counsel, admissibility of refusal evidence, and double jeopardy in administrative license suspension cases.

Concurrent with these changes is a marked increase in the severity of sentences rendered in drunk driving cases. Whereas in the past an offender could expect a fine, probation, and perhaps attendance at a "drunk driving school," he is now increasingly faced with loss of his driver's license and mandatory jail sentences — and, in cases of repeat offenders, with long terms or even felony status.

Underlying this recent rash of developments has been a growing federal presence in the DUI field. Through a "carrot-and-stick" approach using federal highway funds, and with the ominous threat of the Commerce Clause, federal authorities are successfully bringing pressure on states to meet federal guidelines concerning per se laws, intoxication levels, blood-alcohol analysis, sentencing standards, standardized field sobriety tests, "zero tolerance" laws for drivers under 21, etc. As federal involvement continues, the laws, evidence, and procedures in states across the country will continue to become even more uniform.

What does all of this mean to the attorney representing a client charged with driving under the influence? It means that education and preparation are more important than ever. The field of DUI litigation has always been a difficult one: Its complexity has probably doubled in recent years. At the same time, the damage that can be suffered by the client has been increased substantially.

Yet despite the vastly more sophisticated nature of drunk driving litigation, the client accused of this offense is likely to be defended by counsel who normally does not handle criminal matters; the crime is unique in that it is committed primarily by individuals who are respectable citizens and who often turn to their business or family lawyer for help. As a result, this highly complex case is handled routinely by attorneys with insufficient knowledge of the extensive scientific, evidentiary, procedural, and tactical considerations involved. And the result is too often predictable.

This text offers in as compact a format as possible the material necessary to prepare counsel for effectively defending — or prosecuting — the drunk driving case. It deals with, among many other subjects: the *corpus delicti;* the lawyer-client relationship; chemical evidence presumptions; pre-trial investigation; discovery; obtaining defense analysis of chemical evidence; implied consent laws; plea bargaining techniques; jury selection; cross-examination of the police officer, eyewitness, and chemical expert; field sobriety tests; urine, blood, and breath analysis; constructing a defense; jury instructions; sentencing; probation violations; and license suspension hearings.

In covering these and other aspects of the drunk driving case in this fifth edition, even greater use is made of practice-oriented materials. Checklists offering quick reference to the most critical aspects of the case (such as examination of the arresting officer, finding fault in the field sobriety test, and specific flaws in various methods of blood-alcohol analysis) are supplied. Forms used by police and other agencies are also provided. These include arrest reports, breath instrument operational instructions, and license suspension notices. Sample legal motions are presented. The book contains examples of motions successfully used by experienced defense counsel for discovery, appointment of chemical experts, suppression of blood-alcohol evidence, etc. Finally, the text includes actual examinations to serve as an illustration — verbatim cross and direct of the various witnesses with whom counsel will be confronted in trial — as well as specific suggestions for use in jury voir dire, opening statement, and closing argument.

The substantive and procedural details of a drunk driving charge, of course, vary slightly from state to state. However, the general principles remain the same: The Intoxilyzer used in Alabama is the same instrument used in Wyoming; the "walk-the-line" test employed by the California Highway Patrol is similar to that administered by the Detroit Police Department; the discovery possibilities in Oregon are substantially the same as in Texas. The knowledge gained from this text will prepare counsel for representing a drunk driving client anywhere in the United States. In fact, most of the evidentiary material is applicable worldwide.

Drunk driving is a deceptively difficult type of case to deal with, and the risks to the client are much higher than are generally appreciated. This text provides the extensive knowledge and skills necessary for counsel to competently defend against such a charge. Armed with that knowledge, counsel will often find himself the only person in the courthouse who fully understands the vast complexities of the drunk driving case. And that translates into obtaining better results for the client.

Lawrence Taylor

September 1999

ACKNOWLEDGMENTS

The author wishes to thank the following individuals and organizations who have generously permitted for use of their materials and information: Michael E. Cantrall, Executive Director of the California Public Defender's Association, for use of materials contributed by C. John Landry, Michael Bleauvelt, Dr. Herschel Frye, and the National Jury Project, published by the Association; Flem Whited III; Douglas Cowan; J. Gary Trichter; Jonathan Artz; James Farragher Campbell; Phillip B. Price, Sr.; Dr. Harvey J. Cohen; Dr. James Feldman; J. Michael Flanagan; Dr. Herschel Frye; Stephen J. Heiser; Dr. Michael P. Hlastala; Dr. Richard E. Jensen; James Kaster; Bruce R. MacDonald; Richard Hutton; Dr. Randall C. Baselt; William C. Head; Richard Essen; John Tarantino; Jon Fox; Mary C. McMurray; Anne ImObersteg; Barry Simons; Michael J. Snure; Robert W. Chestney; William Giguiere; Howard J. Weintraub; Les Hulnick; Reese Joye; Kimberly de la Garza; and Don Nichols.

COMMENT

Defense lawyers familiar with the increasingly convoluted drunk driving laws and their rationalizations may appreciate the following quote, excerpted from the April 2, 1990, column of Mike Royko of the Chicago Tribune. The quote, taken verbatim from the conclusions of a 600-page report on alcohol abuse commissioned by Congress, represented the latest thinking of this nation's "experts" on alcohol and the law:

> To put it simply, people who drink a lot have many problems, but few people drink a lot. People who only drink a little have fewer problems, but there are a great many people who drink a little.
>
> Therefore, the total number of problems experienced by those who drink a little is likely to be greater than the total number experienced by those who drink a lot, simply because more people drink a little than a lot.

I

CRIME AND PUNISHMENT

"Have you a criminal lawyer in this burg?" "We think so, but we haven't been able to prove it on him."

CARL SANDBURG
THE PEOPLE, YES

1

THE OFFENSE

§1.0 *The Nature of the Crime*

> Solon used to say that . . . laws were like cobwebs, for that if any trifling or powerless thing fell into them, they held it fast; while if it were something weightier, it broke through them and was off.
>
> DIOGENES

Driving under the influence of alcohol, or "drunk driving" as it is usually called, is the most commonly committed crime in the United States. Yet it is almost always committed by a noncriminal — that is, by an otherwise respectable citizen who has never been in trouble with the law. Consequently, representation of the defendant often is attempted by attorneys not versed in criminal law. Typically, the defendant's business or family lawyer will undertake to represent him "as a favor." Drunk driving, the lawyer tells himself, is merely a glorified traffic offense. Certainly it is not as serious or complex as a "real" crime, and therefore cannot call for any particular expertise.

This is invariably a tragic mistake.

Any lawyer representing a client charged with drunk driving should be aware of certain preliminary facts:

1. Though the most common of all offenses, drunk driving is one of the most complex to understand and defend properly.
2. The stakes are high — higher in the long run than for most other crimes.

3. A unique system of legal standards and procedures exists in drunk driving cases, a system geared to facilitate a conviction.

Once the defense lawyer is fully aware of these facts, he can proceed to competently represent his client.

Common though drunk driving is in our courts, it represents one of the most difficult criminal offenses to understand and to litigate. Consider first the nature of other crimes: If the client is charged with petty theft, for example, the issue is usually simply a question of whether he was really seen taking something; if burglary is the charge, perhaps fingerprints represent the most esoteric area involved (if even that); and, in a rape charge, semen analysis may be the only subject requiring any special expertise. In fact, in the majority of crimes, the trial hinges solely on one issue: Did the eyewitnesses see what they testified they saw? Even in circumstantial evidence cases, rarely is anything more exotic than handwriting analysis or ballistics evidence involved.

Now, consider only superficially what the primary issues are in a drunk driving case: What was the concentration of alcohol in the defendant's blood an hour or so prior to the analysis of a breath sample? To what extent was alcohol chemically affecting the brain tissue of the defendant in such a way as to "appreciably" impair his "judgment," his motor reactions, and his coordination? In other words, the basic issue is to define chemically what was going on in the client's brain and body at the time of arrest. Even brain surgeons do not yet fully understand how the human brain functions. Yet, in an attempt to determine the biochemical conditions within his client's body at a remote moment, counsel must be knowledgeable in chemistry, physiology, photochemical and infrared analyses, gas chromatography, etc. And what is meant by "appreciably" impaired? How does one define "judgment"? How is individual tolerance to alcohol measured? What effects do various drugs and medical conditions have on the digestion and/or elimination of alcohol? These issues can continue seemingly without end.

Make no mistake: Drunk driving is one of the most complex of all criminal charges, and undertaking to defend a client on such a charge without extensive preparation constitutes nothing short of malpractice.

The second misconception commonly held by both clients and attorneys is that the punishment for drunk driving is only minor. After all, drunk driving is only a step removed from a traffic citation.

Again, consider the probable consequences if your client were arrested for, say, petty theft, solicitation, or assault. Since it would probably be his first offense, and since he has probably led a sterling life, he will probably not receive jail time. Instead he will be fined perhaps $300 and placed on informal probation for approximately two years. In many jurisdictions, he can come back into court after a probationary period and have the conviction expunged — that is, erased from his record. End result: a few hundred dollars, inconvenience, and attorney's fees. In fact, statistics indicate that the majority of defendants convicted of felonies end up serving no time in custody; the majority are placed on probation, often without even having to pay a fine.

What does the citizen arrested for drunk driving face? Depending on the jurisdiction, of course, the first offender may be fined $1,000 and also placed on probation, as a beginning. In addition, the court may take his driver's license, a license that may be critical to operating his business or performing his job. His car may be impounded or have ignition "interlocks" placed in it. He may have to attend special schools on alcoholism or drunk driving, occasionally for a "fee" of hundreds of dollars. According to one somewhat dated study, a convicted first offender's average cost for bail, an attorney, treatment programs, and fines exceeds $5,000 — assuming no accident. Auto Club News (Southern California), October–November 1989. That figure is considerably higher today. And he may well serve time in jail; many jurisdictions now impose mandatory jail sentences for first offenders. On his second conviction he will almost certainly spend time in custody. This is not time served by a hardened con but by a terrified citizen totally unfamiliar with the callous penal system.

Already the client has suffered more punishment than the majority of convicted felons do. But there is more: A convicted defendant will end up paying thousands of dollars over the next few years in increased auto insurance premiums. He probably is required by law to carry automobile insurance, but he is now a convicted drunk driver who falls into a high risk category; his premiums will be far higher than those of a bank robber or hatchet murderer. Further, the client may be suffering from alcoholism. In effect, he may be criminally prosecuted and punished for having what is now recognized to be a medical (and possibly genetic) condition.

If there is any doubt about the clear trend around the country as to sentencing in drunk driving cases, consider the case of a defendant in Los Angeles. In an article appearing in the *Los Angeles Times* it was reported that this defendant had been arrested in Hollywood for DUI. He had three other DUI cases pending, though none of the four incidents involved personal injury or property damage; he was also on probation for drunk driving. In proceedings that the Times reporter said "resembled those for a notorious murder," bail was set at $500,000. The defendant subsequently pleaded guilty. His sentence for these consolidated misdemeanors? The judge imposed a jail term of *nine years and 220 days!* Three years later, a Louisiana jury topped that by sentencing a defendant convicted of drunk driving with three prior convictions to *11 years at hard labor.*

So the stakes are high. Never underestimate the damage that a drunk driving conviction can do to a client.

The third misconception commonly held about drunk driving is that the usual criminal safeguards apply. Quite simply, they do not.

Consider for a moment a situation in a homicide case where the prosecution introduces a revolver used in the killing together with opinion testimony that the fingerprints on it are probably the defendant's. Thereafter, the jury might be instructed that, because of this opinion evidence, the defendant is *presumed* to be guilty unless he introduces sufficient evidence to overcome this presumption. Again, consider an extortion case where evidence of a voice analysis machine indicates that it was probably the defendant who made the threatening phone call. The judge might tell the jurors that they *must* convict the defendant unless he successfully proves his innocence. Finally, consider a drunk driving case where the prosecutor offers the results of an Intoxilyzer test into evidence. The jury may be instructed that the defendant is legally *presumed* to have been under the influence of alcohol.

Are these instructions a violation of the constitutional presumption of innocence? Are they a denial of the Fifth Amendment right against requiring the defendant to testify at trial? Are they reversible error? Of course, in a murder or an extortion trial, these instructions violate the Constitution and are reversible error. But under the present laws of most states, such instructions in a drunk driving case are totally proper and, in fact, required. And in almost all of the remaining states, such chemical evidence as an Intoxilyzer test sets up, at the very least, a prima facie case for the prosecution. The defense will be required to produce evidence to overcome the factual presumption.

Quite simply, a criminal defendant is presumed to be innocent until proven to be guilty beyond a reasonable doubt — except in drunk driving cases. There, because of blood-alcohol evidence no different in nature — and, in fact, often less reliable — than any other scientific evidence, the presumption is reversed.

"Intent" is another aspect of drunk driving that should be clearly understood: None is required. Neither the intent to become intoxicated nor the intent to operate a motor vehicle is necessary to the *corpus* of the crime. Drunk driving is, quite simply, an absolute liability offense.

Perhaps even more interesting, the *corpus* itself is vague and literally impossible to accurately determine. What is meant by "under the influence"? By statute, it is usually described along the lines of having reached that state of intoxication at which the reflexes and judgment have been impaired so much that the driver cannot safely operate a vehicle in the manner of a normally prudent and sober person. But how does one determine this *corpus* — that is, how is this physical-mental state determined? It is impossible, at least with the present state of medical knowledge, actually to go inside a person's brain, nerves, and muscles and directly observe their condition. Proof can only come through circumstantial evidence, indirect measurements, and opinion testimony.

Even the relatively recent so-called per se laws present problems. Statutes now make it an offense to drive while the blood-alcohol level is in excess of .08 or .10 percent, depending on the jurisdiction. The crux of such a statute is that the question of whether the driver was actually under the influence is irrelevant: The law is satisfied by proof of blood-alcohol level alone. Typically, the new per se law exists side by side with the traditional "under the influence" statute — and the defendant will probably be charged with both (he cannot be sentenced for both, however; see §2.3.1). These statutes are clear in defining the offense: Quite simply, it is a crime to drive while having more than a given blood-alcohol level. But how is an individual to *know* what his blood-alcohol level is? How can a driver know if his level is an innocent .09 or a guilty .10 percent? For without the benefit of constant blood-alcohol analysis, it is impossible for any person to accurately predict the percentage of alcohol in his blood at any point in time.

Unlike most crimes involving the occurrence of an incident of some sort, drunk driving concerns not an *event* but a *condition.* And unlike condition offenses such as being under the influence of narcotics, which offense involves the simple issue of presence or nonpresence of drugs that can be accurately determined by simple tests, the offense of drunk driving occurs only when the individual crosses over that vague and arbitrary line separating the drinker from the drunk. The definition of *drunk* hinges on a difference of a hairline. The presumption that any driver with an Intoximeter reading of .07 percent is not under the influence but that one with a reading of .08 percent is, may appear to be patently ridiculous. But such is the law.

Drunk driving cases are, oddly, analogous to pornography cases. Uniquely, neither crime requires any specific intent, and neither consists of a definable offense. The Supreme Court struggles with concepts of "redeeming social value," "prurient interests," and "contemporary community standards," and upholds a ban on a book in one state while the book is permitted legally in another. The Court permits the showing of motion pictures that would clearly have been criminal a few years earlier. How *does* one specifically and predictably describe what is obscene? And how does one specifically determine the inner workings of the accused drunk driver's body and brain at a remote point in time? In pornography cases, at least the ultimate issue goes to the jury, which weighs the opinion testimony of various experts. In drunk driving cases, on the other hand, most states have "solved" the problem by instructing the jury that if the prosecution's chemical evidence indicates that the blood-alcohol level was .08 percent or higher, the defendant is presumed to be guilty. Or, even more expediently, the defendant is simply charged with the per se offense, and he *is* guilty if his blood-alcohol level was that high.

How did all this come about?

There is no question that drunk driving is an increasingly serious problem in the United States and, indeed, throughout the world. There are more cars on the road than ever before; at the same time, the pressures of modern civilization continue to push the figures on alcoholism and per capita alcohol consumption ever higher. The inevitable by-product of this combination is a never ending slaughter on the highways. And it doesn't take many front-page photographs of mangled six-year-old children to cause a public uproar and stir demands for tougher penalties for drunk drivers. The legislatures and courts of the states, being essentially political in nature, have been consistently responsive to these public outcries for crackdowns on drunk driving. The courts make sentences more severe; legal procedures are made "more efficient"; police departments pour money into the latest scientific methods of establishing guilt.

The increasingly severe terms of drunk driving legislation are based, of course, on the premise that tougher provisions will serve a deterrent effect — that is, the more harsh the law, the fewer drunk drivers. Yet the National Highway Traffic Safety Administration estimates that only one arrest is being made for every 1,500 to 2,000 drunk drivers on the road today — too few to represent a real deterrent.

The experiences of various jurisdictions that have cracked down on drunk drivers in the past are interesting. Between 1971 and 1976, for example, the federal government spent $88 million on Alcohol Safety Action Programs (ASAP), including an experimental enforcement blitz in Virginia. This attack on drunk driving resulted in the yearly arrests in one area increasing from 171 to 3,000, and involved stiffer legislation and more streamlined courtroom procedures. Yet after an investigation of the results of this program in 1974 by the Insurance Institute for Highway Safety, the conclusion was reached reluctantly that there were "no reductions in drunk driving fatalities unique to the ASAP areas. . . . It is only possible to conclude scientifically that ASAP's as large-scale programs have been ineffective." Status Report, Insurance Institute for Highway Safety, July 8, 1974.

One of the more publicized crackdowns occurred in Chicago between December 1970 and June 1971: A traffic court judge publicly announced that those convicted on DUI charges would receive a minimum sentence of seven days in jail and a one-year license suspension. After the six-month experiment was completed, the judge announced that holiday deaths were reduced by more than 60 percent.

A group of university statisticians decided to investigate the judge's claims. After considerable study they discovered that, contrary to his assertions, there was only a chance slight variation in holiday deaths from the preceding five years. They also noted that in nearby Milwaukee there was a much sharper drop in the rate of fatalities over the same six-month period — despite the absence of a crackdown in that city. Robertson, et al., Jail Sentences for Driving While Intoxicated in Chicago: A Judicial Action That Failed, 8(1) Law and Society Review 56 (1973).

In 1972, judges in Phoenix began their own "get tough" program, handing out one-day jail sentences to first offenders. The success of the program was applauded in an article that appeared in Reader's Digest. Unfortunately, however, the results were again not those claimed. A report by the National Highway Traffic Safety Administration reluctantly concluded that "overall, court backlogs increased, court expenses rose dramatically, and the intended effect of a severe penalty was nullified." Most important, the new policy resulted in no reduction in drunk driving accidents or deaths. Alcohol Countermeasures Status, NHTSA (1981).

Advocates of tougher legislation and sentencing are fond of pointing to the Scandinavian countries as examples of harsh treatment resulting in reduced alcohol-related traffic fatalities. The truth is, however, that there has been no greater correlation in those countries than in the United States.

In 1975, Professor H. Laurence Ross of the University of Denver engaged in an extensive study of drunk driving legislation and sentencing requirements in Norway and Sweden, comparing them with accident statistics in those countries. In an article entitled The Scandinavian Myth: The Effectiveness of Drinking-and-Driving Legislation in Sweden and Norway, IV(2) Journal of Legal Studies 285 (June 1975), Professor Ross concluded that "the impression that there is strong and convincing evidence to believe that the Scandinavian laws have deterred drinking and driving is false." In Sweden, for example, strict per se laws were passed that reduced blood-alcohol levels and mandated a one-month prison term for first-offense drunk drivers, plus loss of license for a year. After studying traffic fatality statistics in Sweden before and after these legislative and judicial approaches were instituted, Professor Ross concluded that "neither the 1941 introduction of per se legislation nor the 1957 reduction in the legal (blood alcohol) limit is associated with any marked change in fatalities."

Yet the nationwide crackdown on drunk drivers continues. Unfortunately, the wrongly accused are also caught up in this legal dragnet.

The result of this "get tough" policy has been twofold: First, the stakes for a client charged with driving under the influence of alcohol or drugs are now higher than ever. And, second, the procedural safeguards have been streamlined at the expense of the defendant.

So the deck in a drunk driving case is stacked. Counsel taking on such a case should be fully aware of this simple fact. But he should also be aware of the deceptive complexity of drunk driving litigation — for in that very complexity lies salvation for the defense attorney. As counsel will see in the pages to follow, evidence produced during a drunk driving trial is incredibly involved beneath the misleading surface. Very few lawyers — prosecution or defense — are even superficially acquainted with the intricacies of drunk driving evidence and tactics. The average prosecutor, not understanding half of what is being said, puts his witnesses on the stand and simply turns them loose.

For the few lawyers who learn the involved art of drunk driving defense, then, the field is wide open.

§1.1 The Corpus

> It is a very easy thing to devise good laws; the difficulty is to make them effective. The great mistake is that of looking upon men as virtuous, of thinking that they can be made so by laws.
>
> HENRY ST. JOHN BOLINGBROKE

The traditional crime of "drunk driving" is commonly considered to be driving a motor vehicle on a road or highway while under the influence of intoxicating liquor (DUI). In a few states (notably Texas), the offense is defined in terms of driving while intoxicated (DWI). Some states (Oregon, for example) use the term "operating'' (OUI or OUII — operating under the influence of intoxicants), while still others refer to being in ''actual physical control'' of the vehicle. The newer so-called *per se* offense, on the other hand, consists of driving/operating/being in control of a vehicle on a road or highway with an excessive blood alcohol concentration — either .08 or .10 percent, or greater, depending upon the state. Absent additional factors, these offenses are generally considered to be misdemeanors. In most states, both offenses will be charged where the evidence supports it.

The *corpus delecti*, then, consists of three elements. For the traditional DUI/DWI offense, that *corpus* is:

1. Driving or operating or being in control of a motor vehicle;
2. On a road or highway (or anywhere within the state);
3. While under the influence of alcohol (or while intoxicated/inebriated).

The new *per se* offense simply alters one of those elements:

1. Driving or operating or being in control of a motor vehicle;
2. On a road or highway (or anywhere within the state);
3. With a blood-alcohol concentration of .08 percent (or .10 percent) or higher.

In the initial analysis of any drunk driving case, counsel should be particularly careful to consider the possibility that the prosecutor's *corpus* is not complete. All too often, the prosecutor — and defense counsel — immediately concentrate on that portion of the *corpus* that is the only contention in the vast majority of such cases: whether the defendant was under the influence of alcohol or had an excessive blood-alcohol level. And, all too often, the prosecutor and defense counsel overlook the simple fact that the defendant was not observed driving. A common situation is the discovery of an intoxicated defendant sitting in a car that is wrapped around a telephone pole. The conclusion that the defendant was driving — particularly if the car is registered to him — may be logical, even automatic, but it may not be legally sufficient.

Nothing should be assumed: the prosecution case should always be checked against the three-point *corpus,* rather than just against the question of intoxication.

For a discussion of the admissibility of a defendant's statements that he was driving without independent evidence of that driving, see §11.3.2

§1.2 *What Constitutes "Driving"?*

> Lost is our old simplicity of times,
> The world abounds with laws,
> And teems with crimes.
>
> ANONYMOUS

While some states use the word *driving* in their statutes, others use such terms as *operating* or being in *physical control.* The differences in definition and application can be significant. To confuse matters, court decisions may use terminology like "being in actual physical control" to define a statutory word like "driving" or "operating." To further confuse matters, what constitutes "driving" or "operating" or "being in control" varies from one jurisdiction to another — and, not uncommonly, within a given jurisdiction. And to make things completely confusing, what constitutes the element of driving for purposes of the criminal offense may be different from what constitutes that element for administrative license suspension purposes.

The following is an example of one appellate court's attempt to clarify the terminology for that state, at least in the criminal context:

> The words "operating" and "driving" are not synonymous; they have well-recognized statutory distinctions. Of the two terms, the latter is generally accorded a more strict and limited meaning. The term "driving" is generally used to mean, in this connection, steering and controlling a vehicle while in motion; the term "operating," on the other hand, is generally given a broader meaning to include starting the engine or manipulating the mechanical or electrical devices of a standing vehicle. . . .
>
> One may not drive a vehicle without operating it; but one may

operate the engine or devices of a vehicle without driving it. [*McDuell v. State,* 231 A.2d 265 (Del. 1967).]

The language of the statute, then, can be critical — and should be clearly understood by counsel.

The Uniform Vehicle Code §11-902(a) (1968), which has been adopted in many states, uses the phrase to "drive or be in actual physical control." While most of the adopting states follow the language of the Code, some of them have not included the "physical control" aspect in their statutes, and many have combined references to drugs with those relating to alcohol or intoxicating liquor. Some states do not follow the precise Code language. For example, some jurisdictions refer to driving "while in an intoxicated condition." Other legislation relates to persons operating vehicles under the influence of "alcohol" or "alcoholic liquor," while still other states simply refer to "intoxicants."

What constitutes driving or operating in an individual case has been the subject of numerous and inconsistent judicial decisions. And despite attempts by appellate courts to encompass any type of conduct in a vehicle within the statute's definition, the argument that the client's conduct did not fall within the ambit of the statute should be made in any case not involving actual in-motion driving behind the wheel.

Some appellate courts have attempted to enumerate a list of factors to be considered in determining from their totality whether a defendant was driving/operating or in control of a vehicle for purposes of the drunk driving statute. A Nevada court, for example, set forth the following criteria:

1. The defendant's position in the vehicle;
2. Was the engine running or not;
3. Was the defendant conscious or unconscious;
4. Where the keys were located (ignition, defendant's pocket, on the floor, etc.);
5. Were the headlights on or off (if at night);
6. Was the defendant trying to move the vehicle;
7. Was the vehicle parked on private or public property; and
8. Do circumstances indicate that the defendant had to drive the vehicle to the location.

Rogers v. State, 773 P.2d 1226 (Nev. 1989). Similarly, in *State v. Love,* 897 P.2d 626 (Ariz. 1995), the Arizona Supreme Court adopted a "totality of the circumstances" test to determine whether ther was actual physical control. In rejecting a rigid ignition on/off rule, the court used many of the same factors as the Nevada court to determine whether the vehicle was merely being used as a temporary shelter:

1. Was the driver awake;
2. Was the engine running or the ignition on;
3. Where were the keys;
4. Where was the driver located;
5. Were the headlights on;
6. What time of day or night was it;
7. Was the vehicle legally parked or was it on a road;
8. Was the heater or air conditioner on;
9. Were the windows up or down;
10. What was the defendant's version of events.

See also, *Richfield City v. Walker,* 790 P.2d 87 (Utah 1990), where additional factors were considered such as (1) the position of the vehicle, (2) whether the defendant was the sole occupant, (3) whether the defendant had the apparent ability to start the vehicle.

These factors suggest certain factual scenarios concerning the issue of driving/operating/control, which occur in drunk driving cases with some frequency. Thus, for example, counsel will likely be confronted at some time with some of the following situations:

1. The client was asleep or unconscious behind the wheel;
2. The client was awake but the ignition was turned off;
3. The engine was on but there was no actual "driving" — i.e., movement of the vehicle;
4. The vehicle had run out of gas or was otherwise inoperable;
5. The vehicle was coasting or being pushed or towed;
6. The client was using the vehicle as temporary shelter.

Asleep or unconscious behind the wheel (engine off). Whether an unconscious defendant found behind the wheel of a vehicle is sufficient to constitute driving, operating, or being in control may depend upon the surrounding circumstances — commonly, upon whether the engine was running or not. Generally, the courts tend to view unconsciousness behind the wheel with the engine off as insufficient for proof of driving/operating.

In *State v. Zavala,* 666 P.2d 456 (Ariz. 1983), the court was confronted with a situation where the defendant was unconscious behind the wheel of a vehicle whose engine was off. The facts relevant to the issue of whether there was "actual physical control" of the vehicle were as follows:

> A patrolman was alerted to the presence of a pickup truck in the emergency or parking lane off the traveled portion of Interstate Highway 10 near Picacho Peak. The officer arrived at the location, which he had passed some twenty minutes earlier, to discover the defendant hanging partially from the window on the driver's side of the truck. The defendant was unconscious, and the appearance of his mouth and the front of his shirt indicated that he had recently vomited. The officer noted the strong odor of alcohol beverage on the defendant and in the truck. The key to the ignition was in the off position, and the truck's motor was not running. The hood of the truck was warm, but it was September at noontime.
>
> The officer tried to rouse the defendant by shaking him, to no avail. The officer then administered an ammonia inhalant and more shaking until the defendant regained consciousness. [666 P.2d at 457.]

The court began its analysis by reviewing a previous decision that had sought to define "actual physical control." In *State v. Webb,* 78 Ariz. 8, 274 P.2d 338 (1954), the court had found the defendant to be in actual physical control of a motor vehicle. The *Webb* court focused on two circumstances: The truck's engine was running and the truck was sitting in the lane of traffic. Because in *Zavala* the defendant's ignition was off and the truck was entirely in the emergency lane of the highway, the court came to the opposite conclusion and went on to discuss the basis for holding that there was no actual physical control:

> Admittedly, state courts are not in complete agreement as to the definitions of "actual physical control," see, e.g., *Key v. Town*

> *of Kinsey,* 424 So. 2d 701, 704 (Ala. Crim. App. 1982); *McGuire v. City of Seattle,* 31 Wash. App. 438, 442, 642 P.2d 765, 768 (1982); *City of Cincinnati v. Kelley,* 47 Ohio St. 2d 94, 97–98, 351 N.E.2d 85, 87–88 (1976), *cert. denied,* 429 U.S. 1104, 97 S. Ct. 1131, 51 L. Ed. 2d 554 (1977); *State v. Ruona,* 133 Mont. 243, 247–48, 321 P.2d 615, 618 (1958). We agree, however, with the Utah Supreme Court that the element of actual physical control is shown where a defendant has "the apparent ability to start and to move the vehicle," distinguishing this circumstance from the situation where a defendant is "physically unable to start the car, as would be the case with an unconscious or sleeping motorist." *Garcia v. Schwendiman,* 645 P.2d 651, 654, n.3 (1982); cf. *State v. Bugger,* 25 Utah 2d 404, 483 P.2d 442 (1971) (sleeping defendant found off travelled portion of highway with non-running engine not in actual physical control).

The court then set forth an important public policy consideration, which counsel should bear in mind when presenting arguments in such cases:

> In the instant case the defendant was not in "control of a vehicle while not actually driving it or having it in motion" as contemplated in *State v. Webb,* supra, and defendant may not be convicted of being "in actual physical control" pursuant to the statute. The interpretation we place on the legislature's imprecise language is compelled by our belief that it is reasonable to allow a driver, when he believes his driving is impaired, to pull completely off the highway, turn the key off and sleep until he is sober, without fear of being arrested for being in control. To hold otherwise might encourage a drunk driver, apprehensive about being arrested, to attempt to reach his destination while endangering others on the highway.

In another case involving an unconscious defendant behind the wheel, however, a contrary result was reached by a Minnesota court, which held that whether the engine was running or not was not determinative. In *State Department of Public Safety v. Juncewski,* 308 N.W.2d 216 (Minn. 1981), a defendant was held to be in "physical control" of his vehicle where he was found seated behind the wheel of his pickup truck with his head up against the steering wheel, with the key in the ignition but the engine presumably not running. The Minnesota Supreme Court ruled that the fact that the engine was or was not running is not determinative of whether a person is in "physical control": "The real purpose of the statute is to deter individuals who have been drinking intoxicating liquor from getting into their vehicles, except as passengers. . . ." Id., citing *State v. Ghylin,* 250 N.W.2d 252 (N.D. 1977).

It should be noted that *Juncewski* was a license revocation case. However, the Minnesota Court of Appeals has since affirmed a DWI conviction where a defendant had been found alone in the front seat of a car that had been resting in a ditch for two hours before he was discovered by the arresting officer. *State v. Thurman,* 348 N.W.2d 776 (Minn. 1984). Yet the same Court of Appeals subsequently reversed another conviction where a defendant was found asleep in his own car parked in his own driveway, holding that "the facts in this case do not support the conclusion that appellant exercised the necessary physical control." *State v. Pazderski,* 352 N.W.2d 85 (Minn. 1984).

Asleep or unconscious behind wheel (engine on). Where the defendant is unconscious behind the wheel and the engine is running, counsel may have a more difficult time attacking the sufficiency of the evidence. One court may find this to be sufficient circumstantial evidence of driving (e.g., *People v. Johnson,* 40 Ill. App. 3d 982, 353 N.E.2d 130 (1976)), while another may decide that driving requires the driver to be conscious and/or the vehicle to be in motion (e.g., *State v. Graves,* 269 S.C. 356, 237 S.E.2d 584 (1977)).

In *Reddie v. State,* 736 S.W.2d 923 (Tex. App. 1987), however, an appellate court reversed a conviction where the defendant was found slumped over the wheel of a car idling in the middle of a street. The court held that there was insufficient evidence of "driving," noting that the "evidence must show that while intoxicated he exerted *personal effort* to cause the vehicle to function." 736 S.W.2d at 927 (emphasis added). Similarly, the court in *Hiegel v. State,* 538 N.E.2d 265 (Ind. App. 1989), consulted Webster's Third International Dictionary and Black's Law Dictionary to determine that a defendant asleep in his vehicle with the engine running and the lights on was *not* "operating" it: "In normal usage, 'operate' means to perform a function, or operation, or produce an effect. . . . Therefore, the word 'operate' requires effort, the doing of something, by the operator." 538 N.E.2d 267. Accord *Corl v.*

State, 544 N.E.2d 211 (Ind. App. 1989). And in *Bullock v. Department of Motor Vehicles,* 775 P.2d 225 (Nev. 1989), a defendant was found asleep in his vehicle in a parking lot with the engine running and the parking lights on. The court reasoned that "he had become a passive occupant" who did not attempt to "operate" the vehicle.

In *Warman v. Motor Vehicles Department,* 745 P.2d 270 (Colo. App. 1987), the defendant had been found unconscious in the driver's seat of a parked car; the engine was running and the headlights were on. The appellate court concluded that this did not constitute sufficient evidence that he had been driving or actually had been in physical control. In *State v. Kenney,* 534 A.2d 681 (Me. 1987), the defendant similarly had been found asleep in the driver's seat of his truck, parked in the middle of the road; the engine was running and the lights were on. However, the court found this sufficient to constitute operating a vehicle. A similar result was arrived at in *Matter of Clayton,* 748 P.2d 401 (Idaho 1988), where the defendant was observed slumped forward in the driver's seat with the engine running. In *Phillips v. State,* 363 S.E.2d 283 (Ga. 1987), the defendant was held to be in physical control of a truck parked in the middle of the road; he was found passed out behind the wheel. And in *Gore v. State,* 536 A.2d 735 (Md. App. 1988), the defendant was found to be "driving" when he was found asleep behind the wheel where the car key was in the ignition in the "on" position, the alternator/battery light was lit, the transmission was in the "drive" position, and the engine was warm to the touch.

Defendant conscious behind wheel but vehicle is inoperable. The majority of courts will find that sitting behind the wheel of a vehicle that is inoperable (due to accident; mechanical problem, or lack of gasoline) does not constitute driving/physical control. See, e.g., *City of Columbus v. Seabolt,* 607 N.E.2d 61 (Ohio App. 1992), in which the defendant was found behind the wheel of her car with the engine running but with the vehicle stuck in mud with two blown tires.

In the case of *State v. Lane,* 673 S.W.2d 874 (Tenn. 1983), the Tennessee Court of Criminal Appeals affirmed a conviction in a case involving a defendant steering an incapacitated vehicle being pushed off the road by another vehicle. However, a Florida appellate court came to an opposite conclusion. In *Jones v. State,* 510

So. 2d 1147 (Fla. App. 1987), the defendant had been found by police slumped over the steering wheel. She explained that it had quit running while her sister had been driving it and attempted to demonstrate for the officers how it would not start. Florida's DUI statute provides that "(a) person is guilty of the offense of driving under the influence . . . if such person is driving *or in actual physical control* of a vehicle . . ." (emphasis added). On appeal, the court held that since the statute did not require operability of the vehicle, the prosecution was not required to prove that it was operable in order to prove "actual physical control." However, the court also held that "The fact of inoperability *may be a defense* and as such may be raised by the defense," 510 So. 2d at 1149, and reversed the conviction:

> It readily appears that a person ought not to be convicted of having a vehicle under his or her control while intoxicated when in fact the vehicle was inoperable, the intoxicated person did not operate the vehicle prior to its becoming disabled, and the vehicle's mechanical problems were such that it could not under any reasonable circumstances have been operated by the person accused. [Id. at 1149.]

Key v. Town of Kinsey, 424 So. 2d 701 (Ala. 1982), involved the question of whether a defendant was in "actual physical control" of a vehicle that had run out of gas. The facts as related in the opinion were as follows:

> Kinsey Police Chief Franklin D. Sopuch testified that while on patrol on May 2, 1981, he saw an automobile parked on a median strip between the north and south bound lanes of U.S. 431. The appellant was alone, sitting on the driver's side of the front seat, leaning across the passenger's side of the automobile. Appellant was removed from the vehicle and taken to the Houston County Jail, where Chief Sopuch administered an approved test of assessing intoxication, which recorded appellant's alcohol level in his blood as .19.
>
> Appellant admitted that he had been drinking, but denied operating the automobile. He testified that the car was out of gas, and that his son, the driver, had walked to get gasoline at the nearest open service station. He testified that his son had the keys to the car and that the car would not operate without keys.

> The police chief acknowledged that the appellant had no keys to the car at the time of his arrest, and that he at no time saw the car being driven by the appellant.
>
> There was no evidence presented that any attempt was made to start the car. It was impounded and towed by a wrecker later that night. [424 So. 2d at 702.]

The court reversed the conviction of the defendant and, in the process, defined the term "actual physical control":

> "Actual physical control" is exclusive physical power, and present ability, to operate, move, park, or direct whatever use or non-use is to be made of the motor vehicle at the moment. *State v. Purcell,* 336 A.2d 223 (Del. Super. Ct. 1975).
>
> Using the term in its composite sense, it means "existing or present bodily restraint, directing influence, domination or regulation." *Parker v. State,* 424 P.2d 997 (Okla. Crim. App. 1967); *State v. Ruona,* 133 Mont. 243, 321 P.2d 615 (1958).
>
> We conclude that the following are the necessary elements to establish that one is in physical control of a vehicle under the provisions of Code §32-5A-191, supra:
>
> 1. Active or constructive possession of the vehicle's ignition key by the person charged or, in the alternative, proof that such a key is not required for the vehicle's operation;
> 2. Position of the person charged in the driver's seat, behind the steering wheel, and in such condition that, except for the intoxication, he or she is physically capable of starting the engine and causing the vehicle to move;
> 3. A vehicle that is operable to some extent. [Id. at 703.]

Defendant was conscious and behind the wheel, the engine was on — but there was no actual movement of the vehicle. A number of courts have held that there must be some actual movement of the vehicle for the facts to constitute driving or operating; this position may be weaker in jurisdictions where only "physical control" is required. In *Mercer v. Department of Motor Vehicles,* 53 Cal. 3d 753 (1991), for example, the California Supreme Court was confronted with a case where the defendant was unsuccessfully attempting to put his running vehicle in gear. The court held that there must be some actual volitional movement of the vehicle by the defendant to amount to "driving." And in *Commonwealth v.*

Byers, 650 A.2d 468 (Pa. Super. 1994), a Pennsylvania court held that attempting to start a vehicle is insufficient evidence by itself to prove "actual physical control."

The vehicle was coasting, being pushed or towed. Appellate courts have varied also in their approach to how much "control" a defendant has over a vehicle that is moving but without power. In *State v. Brister,* 514 So. 2d 205 (La. App. 1987), the defendant was shown to be in the car when it rolled forward 15 feet. The appellate court found this to be insufficient to constitute operating, saying that there must be some evidence that the defendant "exercised some control or manipulation over the vehicle."

Some courts go to extremes in efforts to crack down on drunk drivers. For example, operation of a motor vehicle has been found to have occurred where the defendant was seen sitting behind the wheel of a car being *towed*! In *State v. Dean,* 733 P.2d 105 (Or. App. 1987), an Oregon appellate court reasoned:

> A person can be in actual physical control of a motor vehicle even though the vehicle is not being propelled by its own motive power. While a vehicle is being towed, the person behind the wheel assumes responsibility for steering and braking the vehicle in a safe manner. [Id. at 106.]

See also, *Williams v. State,* 884 P.2d 167 (Alaska App. 1994).

The vehicle was being used as temporary shelter by defendant. In *State v. Willard,* 660 A.2d 1086 (N.H. 1995), the New Hampshire Supreme Court held that a defendant found asleep in a vehicle with the engine running was not in actual physical control. The court reasoned that the main focus should be on whether the vehicle was being used as a temporary shelter against the weather or whether it was reasonable to assume that there was an imminent danger he was about to drive.

Much of the judicial ruling on the reach of drunk driving statutes is attributable to whether the language uses the phrase "driving," "operating," or "actual physical control." As mentioned earlier, "operating" generally has a broader meaning than "driving." "Actual physical control" has an even wider meaning as applied by the courts and has been interpreted to mean "present bodily restraint, directing influence, domination or regulation" (*State v. Ruona,* 133 Mont. 243, 321 P.2d 615 (1958)); under this broad definition, *preventing* a vehicle from operating or moving — such as by locking the doors — would constitute an act of "actual physical control."

Nevertheless, the inconsistencies in rulings between — and certainly within — jurisdictions cannot be entirely attributed to differences in statutory language. More important to such decisions are undoubtedly the traditional policy considerations: fairness to a defendant versus extending protection of the public from drunk drivers generally.

Whether the defendant was "driving," "in control," or "operating" is, of course, a question of fact for the jury. Nevertheless, judges continue to give instructions such as: "If you find that the defendant was located behind the wheel of a motor vehicle, operable or not, with the keys in the ignition and the motor running, you *will* find that he is in actual physical control of a motor vehicle." *Hodge v. State,* 766 S.W.2d 619 (Ark. App. 1989). On appeal, the appellate court held that the instruction improperly removed the issue from the jury's consideration. In reply to the State's contention that the instruction was based on specific fact situations in appellate decisions, the court replied:

> None of those cases, however, hold that proof of those circumstances establishes that element of the offense as a matter of law. They hold only that proof of such facts constitutes substantial evidence to support such a finding, i.e., that a jury may infer from those facts that the accused person was in actual physical control of the vehicle. [766 S.W.2d 621.]

For a discussion of the necessity of evidence of driving in the officer's presence to constitute a lawful arrest, see §11.2.

§1.2.1 Putting the Defendant Behind the Wheel

A second, and closely related, issue is the question of the sufficiency of evidence as to whether the *defendant* was in fact the individual driving, operating, or in control of the vehicle. This must be distinguished from the question of whether his conduct *constituted* driving, operating, or controlling.

Proof that the defendant was at some time driving the vehicle is usually accomplished through testimony of the arresting officers, commonly from their observations of a traffic violation or erratic driving. Sometimes, particularly after an accident with another car, testimony of civilian witnesses is used to "put the defendant behind the wheel." Occasionally, there is no direct eyewitness evidence available, and the prosecution must attempt to prove the driving by circumstantial evidence. The most common situation involves an automobile illegally parked or smashed against some obstruction such as a traffic light, with the defendant being found in the car or nearby.

In such circumstantial evidence cases, the first thing counsel must remember is that admissions by the defendant will not supply the missing element of the *corpus delicti:* The prosecution must establish at least a prima facie case that the defendant was driving the vehicle. And this must be done *independently of any admissions* (e.g., *Allen v. State,* 314 So. 2d 154 (Fla. 1975)). Of course, the *corpus* need not be established beyond a reasonable doubt; the prosecution need only produce enough evidence to corroborate the admissions. Nevertheless, it is a common practice of prosecutors — whether by design or ignorance — to attempt to establish the fact that a defendant was driving solely through the introduction of his statements to the police or witnesses.

The defendant's driving may be established by circumstantial evidence. But this must be evidence of such a nature as "to exclude every other reasonable hypothesis save that of the guilt of the accused" (*Brown v. State,* 584 P.2d 231 (Okla. Cr. App. 1978)). Unfortunately, in their desire to validate drunk driving convictions the courts have a marked tendency to overlook this rule. Nevertheless, defense counsel should be aware of the applicable standards in this area and insist on their observance.

Finally, counsel must be aware of any weaknesses in eyewitness identification. If there is some question as to the certainty of a witness's identification of the client as the person driving the vehicle, counsel should take appropriate steps to ensure a fair in-court identification. One method, if permitted by the court, is to have the client sit in the audience during the witness's testimony. At the least, the defendant should appear in an in-court lineup.

The effect of pre-trial identification of the client should not be overlooked. The suggestive and reinforcing effect on an emotionally upset witness of seeing the client in a police lineup, in a mug shot display, or in a one-on-one field identification, possibly at the scene of the accident, cannot be overstated. After such pretrial identification procedures, the witness is often unintentionally identifying the defendant in trial on the basis of having seen him in an earlier lineup, mug shot, or field identification — not as the driver of a car.

§1.2.2 "Vehicle"

"Vehicle" or "motor vehicle," as used in the drunk driving statutes, clearly encompasses automobiles, trucks, and motorcycles. Rarely will counsel be confronted with an issue of whether the contraption driven by his client fits within the meaning of the word *vehicle.* But it does happen.

The California courts have determined that a "moped" (a motor-assisted bicycle) is a "motor vehicle" within the meaning of the statute (*People v. Jordan,* 75 Cal. App. 3d Supp. 1, 142 Cal. Rptr. 701 (1977)). Similarly, driving a tractor has been held to constitute operation of a motor vehicle (*State v. Green,* 251 N.C. 141, 110 S.E.2d 805 (1959)). (Of course, the operation of the tractor must have been on a road or highway to constitute a criminal offense.) A horse-driven carriage, operated on public streets, however, does not fit within the definition of a "motor vehicle" (*People v. Szymanski,* 63 Misc. 2d 40, 311 N.Y.S.2d 120 (1970)); query, however, whether it would be considered a vehicle, as opposed to a *motor* vehicle.

The Louisiana Court of Appeals has held that a *bicycle* is not a vehicle under the state's drunk driving statute. *State v. Guidry,* 467 So. 2d 156 (La. App. 1985). The statute defined *vehicles* as including "other means of conveyance," but the court ruled that this referred only to *motorized* vehicles. However, an Ohio court has taken a different view, holding that a bicycle is a "vehicle" for purposes of the DUI statute but not a "motor vehicle" for purposes of the license suspension statute. *State v. Hilderbrand,* 531 N.E.2d 775 (1987). Accordingly, the court upheld the defendant's conviction but ordered his license reinstated.

As an example of the extent to which the courts are increasingly going in their "war on drunk driving," consider a May 6,

1999, Associated Press story in which a man in Arkadelphia, Arkansas, was arrested and charged with DUI — on a lawn mower.

§1.2.3 "Highway"

The second element of the *corpus* requires that the driving be done on certain types of roads to constitute an offense. The statute will usually specify where drunk driving or operating is prohibited: on "any public highway," on any "way open to the public," on "highways and elsewhere throughout the state." Some statutes are silent as to where the offense is proscribed.

Generally, a broadly worded statute such as those proscribing drunk driving anywhere in the state leaves little room for interpretation. The statute will apply no matter where within the jurisdiction it occurs, and its application to conduct on private property has been held constitutional by at least one state decision (*Cook v. State,* 20 Ga. 463, 139 S.E.2d 383 (1964)). A number of states, however, have held that terms such as "within the state" do not apply to private property. See, e.g., *State v. Day,* 638 P.2d 546 (Wash. 1981); *State v. Haws,* 869 P.2d 849 (Okla. 1994); *Pahl v. Commissioner of Public Safety,* 398 N.W.2d 67 (Minn. App. 1984).

If, on the other hand, the statute is worded in terms of driving or operating "on a highway," the question must be asked as to just what constitutes a "highway." And, as usual, the courts have been reluctant to constrict the meaning, preferring to broaden the reach of the statute as much as possible. However, it would be stretching the definition to include private roads, at least those not open to the public. Similarly, operating a vehicle on a privately owned parking lot — even one open to the public, such as a shopping center — has been held to be beyond the purview of the drunk driving statute (see *State v. Cole,* 238 S.E.2d 849 (W. Va. 1977)). Nor would driving under the influence on the driveway of a private residence appear to be unlawful (see *Application of Hendrix,* 539 P.2d 1402 (Okla. 1975)).

A New York appellate court has ruled that a public parking lot located at a shopping center is not a highway, private road, public highway, or roadway within the meaning of the New York Vehicle and Traffic Law. *People v. Wormuth,* 438 N.Y.S.2d 455 (1981). Other courts have reached the same conclusion when faced with similar facts. In *State v. Ball,* 264 S.E.2d 884 (W. Va. 1980), the West Virginia Supreme Court of Appeals ruled that a private parking lot was not a public highway within the meaning of that state's statutory provision (W. Va. Code §17C-5-2 (1976)). And an appellate court in Connecticut has held that a parking lot open for the use of employees and customers was nevertheless not "open to the public" and thus not within the language of the drunk driving statute. *State v. Boucher,* 528 A.2d 1165 (Conn. App. 1987).

The definition of what constitutes a "public highway" may be different for the implied consent statute than for the criminal DUI statute — with different legal results.

In *State v. Zachery,* 601 So. 2d 27 (La. App. 1992), the defendant was arrested for drunk driving in the parking lot of a McDonald's restaurant; after advisement under the implied consent law, he was given a breath test. Under existing Louisiana law, a driver *could* be convicted for drunk driving in a parking lot. The defendant, however, argued that the *implied consent* law was not triggered by driving in a private parking lot; rather than arguing for dismissal, therefore, he asked for suppression of the breath test results. The trial court agreed and ordered the results suppressed.

The appellate court upheld the suppression, holding that the state's implied consent provisions authorizing breath testing applied only to situations where the driver was observed on a "public highway." The provisions of the implied consent statute defined "highway" as an area that is "publicly maintained"; the McDonald's lot was privately maintained. Thus, although the officer could *arrest* the defendant for driving in the parking lot, the officer could not invoke the implied consent statute to require the defendant to submit to chemical testing.

In *People v. Montelongo,* 504 N.E.2d 936 (Ill. App. 1987), the Appellate Court of Illinois held that the state's DUI statute applied to parking lots but that its implied consent statute did not. The drunk driving statute proscribed driving "any vehicle within this state" while under the influence of alcohol. The implied consent statute, on the other hand, provided that consent for blood-alcohol testing is presumed any time a person drives a vehicle "upon the public highways of this state." The court therefore reversed a lower court decision suspending the appellant's driver's license.

Clearly it is important for counsel to carefully consider the exact language used in his state's criminal statute — and, in a license suspension case, the state's implied consent statute. As the *Montelongo* case shows, it should not be presumed that the statutes use similar language.

In *State v. Day,* 638 P.2d 546 (Wash. 1981), the Supreme Court of Washington refused to extend its drunk driving law to a situation where the defendant was observed driving a truck rapidly around in circles in a field owned by his parents. The court based its decision on the fact that "defendant was not on or near a public road, was never observed driving on a public road or driving on property where the public had a right to be." Id. at 546–547. Pursuant to Washington statute, a person can be convicted of driving while intoxicated for operation of a motor vehicle anywhere "within the state." Wash. Rev. Code §46.61.005(2). In reviewing the facts, however, the court relied on two prior cases in reaching its determination that the purpose of the statute was an "effort to reduce the hazard the drunk driver presents to the traveling public." *Fritts v. Department of Motor Vehicles,* 6 Wash. App. 233, 241, 492 P.2d 558, 563 (1971); see also *State v. Moore,* 79 Wash. 2d 51, 483 P.2d 630 (1971); Initiative 242 (codified as Wash. Rev. Code 46.20.092, 46.20.308, 46.20.311, 46.20.911, and 46.61.506, effective in 1975).

In Texas a driver was able to obtain a reversal of her conviction for driving while intoxicated based on the state's failure to show that she had been driving on a public road. *Nelson v. State,* 628 S.W.2d 451 (Tex. Crim. App. 1982). The defendant's automobile was found in a ditch, and the defendant was found outside of her car in an extremely intoxicated condition. While there was no real issue as to who was operating the car at the time it ran into the ditch, the court of appeals reversed the lower court's conviction of the defendant, stating that the prosecution "failed to show that appellant was driving upon a public road or highway." Id. at 453. The fatal defect in the state's case was the failure to establish "that access to the ditch was possible only from the public road." Id.

Those statutes that fail to specify where the conduct is prohibited have tended to be interpreted, predictably, as broadly as possible. The New Jersey courts, for example, have applied the statute to a private parking lot by reasoning the legislative failure to include limiting geographic language must reflect an intention to punish drunk driving wherever it took place (*State v. McColley,* 157 N.J. Super. 525, 385 A.2d 264 (1978)). On the other hand, the New York courts have ruled that a private parking lot was beyond the reach of a statute silent as to location, on the reasonable grounds that a penal statute must be strictly construed in favor of the defendant (*Craig v. Melton,* 89 Misc. 2d 449, 391 N.Y.S.2d 265 (1976)).

One final possible issue should be brought to the attention of defense counsel in a drunk driving case. Where the client is not observed actually driving on the highway but rather is seen in a private alley, parking lot, or driveway connected to a highway, it may become necessary for the prosecution to prove by circumstantial evidence that he had, in fact, driven earlier on the public road. For example, the police may have observed the defendant driving across a shopping center parking lot and parking. Proof of drunk driving on a nearby highway would entail evidence that the parking lot was surrounded by public highways, that the defendant was alone in his own car, that he lived and worked outside of the shopping center, etc. On the other hand, defense counsel is free to suggest or offer evidence that the inebriation took place in a bar or restaurant within the shopping center.

§1.3 Under the Influence of Alcohol

> Great is the power of steady misrepresentation.
>
> CHARLES DARWIN

The question of intoxication is, of course, the essence of the drunk driving charge. While factual questions of driving or location may occur on occasion, in the vast majority of DUI cases there will be but a single issue for opposing counsel to litigate: Was the defendant under the influence of alcohol? (In the per se case, of course, the issue will also be whether the defendant had a blood-alcohol concentration of .08 or .10 percent or higher.)

The term *under the influence,* should, at the outset, be distinguished from the offense of "plain drunk" or "drunk in public." Properly speaking, the phrase "drunk driving" is a misnomer, for there is a considerable legal difference between "drunk" and driving while "intoxicated" or "under the influence." The concept of *drunk,* as used in public drunk statutes, refers to a person who is so inebriated that he is incapable of caring for his own safety. This is a considerably greater degree of inebriation than "intoxicated" or "under the influence." This latter condition is often legally defined as that physical state in which the liquor has so far affected the nervous system, brain, or muscles as to impair the ability to operate a vehicle in a manner like that of an ordinarily prudent and cautious person under like conditions in the full possession of his faculties using reasonable care.

This third element of the offense of drunk driving is usually phrased statutorily as "under the influence of intoxicating liquor" (DUI). In a few states, however, the statute refers instead to driving in an "intoxicated condition," or, just simply, "driving while intoxicated" (DWI). Still others refer to "operating under the influence of intoxicants" (OUII). Whether these phrases are merely different ways of stating the same thing is yet another area of disagreement. Some states hold that "under the influence" and "intoxicated" refer to the same condition (*Morad v. Wyoming Highway Department,* 66 Wyo. 12, 203 P.2d 954 (1949)), while others have ruled that "intoxicated" requires the prosecution to prove a greater degree of inebriation (e.g., *Clowney v. State,* 97 So. 2d 316 (Fla. 1957)).

Another variation in this type of legislation has its roots in Canadian Criminal Code §285(4)a, which for many years has prohibited "driving while ability [is] *impaired* by alcohol," in addition to "driving while under the influence." Some states, such as New York (N.Y. Veh. and Traf. Law §1192(1)) have adopted this concept and made "driving while impaired" a lesser degree of the offense. The existence of two standards affords leeway to law enforcement agencies in making arrests in those cases where there may be some doubt about convicting the defendant of the more serious charge.

Obviously, it is incumbent on counsel to examine the precise statutory language of the jurisdiction involved as well as the judicial interpretations of the drunk driving statute in that jurisdiction. There almost always will be problems of interpreting the statutory language.

Whether we say "intoxication" or "under the influence," we

are basically talking about the degree to which alcohol has impaired the defendant's ability to drive. And, once again, the jurisdictions differ in the degree of impairment that they will require the prosecution to establish in order to justify a conviction. These standards are reflected in the jury instructions approved for use in the various jurisdictions.

At one end of the scale, impairment need not even be proven; simply being under the influence of liquor is enough (*City of Milwaukee v. Richards,* 269 Wis. 570, 69 N.W.2d 445 (1955)). Not far removed from this standard, Missouri law requires only a showing of "any intoxication that in any manner impairs the ability of a person to operate" a vehicle (*State v. Laws,* 547 S.W.2d 162 (Mo. 1977)); Colorado is satisfied if the driver is affected "in the slightest degree" by alcohol (*Snyder v. City of Denver,* 123 Colo. 222, 227 P.2d 341 (1951)). In California, on the other hand, the prosecution must establish impairment "to an appreciable degree" (*People v. Mead,* 126 Cal. App. 2d 164, 271 P.2d 619 (1954)).

The Supreme Court of Montana has reversed a DUI case and remanded for new trial where the trial court gave the previously approved jury instruction requiring only a finding of impairment "in the slightest degree." In *City of Helena v. Davis,* 723 P.2d 224 (Mont. 1986), the jury was instructed that "If the ability of the driver of an automobile has been lessened in the slightest degree by the use of alcohol, then the driver is deemed to be under the influence of alcohol." This is an instruction commonly given in a number of states, and one that had previously been approved by the Montana Supreme Court.

The defendant, however, argued that this instruction was at variance with statutory language defining the offense. That statute defined the offense as follows: "It is unlawful . . . for any person who is under the influence of . . . alcohol and any drug *to a degree that renders him incapable of safely driving a vehicle* to drive or be in actual physical control of a vehicle within this state." Mont. Code Ann. §61-8-401 (emphasis added).

The Supreme Court agreed that the statute did not define the offense as impairment "in the slightest degree," but rather required impairment "to a degree that renders him incapable of safely driving a vehicle." But see *State v. Grimes,* 773 P.2d 227 (Ariz. App. 1989).

In a similar case, a Massachusetts court reversed a DUI

conviction because of the giving of a jury instruction that misinterpreted the statutory phrase "under the influence." In *Commonwealth v. Marley,* 486 N.E.2d 715 (Mass. 1985), the trial court instructed the jury as follows:

> Being under the influence means that the Defendant at the time was influenced in some perceptible, some noticeable, degree by the intoxicating liquor that he had taken, and that's about all it does mean. It doesn't mean that he could not drive his car and drive it safely. . . . [S]uch a violation does not require proof that liquor adversely influenced or affected the operation of the vehicle. If you find that the Defendant operated the vehicle at a time when he was perceptibly affected by intoxicating liquor, regardless of the effects of such liquor on his operation, then you should find him guilty of the offenses charged in the complaint. [Id. at 718.]

The appellate court reversed, holding that "the Commonwealth must prove beyond a reasonable doubt that the defendant's consumption of alcohol diminished the defendant's *ability* to operate a motor vehicle safely" (emphasis by court).

Similarly, there is conflict between the jurisdictions as to whether the intoxication must affect the ability to drive "safely." New Jersey, for example, specifically rejects the necessity of showing inability to safely operate a vehicle; slight impairment of general mental or physical ability is enough (*State v. Johnson,* 42 N.J. 146, 199 A.2d 809 (1964)). Kansas, however, requires impairment sufficient to affect safe driving (*State v. Sauvage,* 201 Kan. 555, 441 P.2d 861 (1968)).

Of course, all of these definitions are to some degree meaningless to a jury. For all practical purposes, the fine differences in language will be lost. For the jury the question will be a simple one: Had the defendant drunk too much liquor? And that will lead to another question: What kind of evidence determines whether he had too much?

Basically, the courts now permit three kinds of evidence to be introduced to determine when a defendant has consumed "too much" liquor: evidence of observed symptoms, opinion testimony, and results of biochemical tests.

Evidence of observed symptoms is usually offered in the form of observations by the arresting officer such as erratic driving, alcoholic breath, flushed face, slurred speech, staggering, inability to perform field sobriety tests, and so on. Occasionally, such testimony will be offered by lay witnesses instead of, or in addition to, police testimony. These observations have a dual thrust. They tend to indicate how much alcohol has been consumed, and they are evidence of the degree of impairment of judgment, reflex, and coordination — factors constituting the legal definition of "under the influence."

In most cases, the officer will be asked his *opinion* of the defendant's condition. Whether this is objectionable may depend on the jurisdiction's approach to the issue of "ultimate issue" testimony and on the form of the opinion.

It should be noted that most jurisdictions do not require proof of impairment of both mental and physical abilities; proof of impairment of either is usually sufficient for conviction. Typical of most standards is that of Ohio:

> . . . being "under the influence" of alcohol or intoxicating liquor means that the accused must have consumed some intoxicating beverage, whether mild or potent, and in such quantity, whether small or great, that the effect thereof on him was to adversely affect his actions, reactions, conduct, movements or mental processes, or to impair his reactions, under the circumstances then existing, so as to deprive him of that clearness of the intellect and control of himself which he would otherwise possess. [*State v. Steele,* 95 Ohio App. 107, 117 N.E.2d 617 (1952).]

Evidence of observed symptoms, then, tends to establish directly what is proscribed by statute — that the defendant's mental and/or physical capabilities were faulty.

The third form of evidence normally offered by the prosecution, however, is of a secondary nature. The *results of chemical tests* — in the form of blood analysis, urinalysis, or, most commonly, breath analysis — tend to establish only what percentage of the defendant's total blood volume is composed of alcohol at the time of testing. This figure is then compared to a chart based on averages, and a conclusion about impairment is drawn. Most important, the jury is instructed about the burden of proof or presumption of guilt based on this figure. Yet, as will be seen in later chapters, this figure is often unreliable; it is based on potentially faulty testing equipment or procedures, premised on often erroneous assumptions, and calculated on the presumption that all human beings are biologically identical.

This third form of evidence is particularly insidious. Because of its "scientific" nature, the jury is more inclined to accept it as the ultimate evidence. The jury tends to reject the testimony of mortal men when it conflicts with the "scientific." Yet, chemical tests are often the least reliable form of evidence, and the least relevant. They indicate — all too often erroneously — only how much alcohol is in the system. They do not indicate anything concerning the ultimate issue — that is, whether the defendant was actually impaired in his functions.

In the rare case, counsel may confront the issue of what constitutes "liquor." Is cough syrup an "intoxicating liquor"? Can a person be legally "under the influence of alcohol" if the source of that alcohol is a medicine or other substance not designed for drinking as an alcoholic beverage? Yes, according to the Court of Appeals of Alaska. In *Tambert v. Alaska,* 694 P.2d 791 (Alaska App. 1985), the defendant appealed his conviction on the grounds that he had been under the influence of "medicinal" versus "recreational" alcohol. He admitted having taken Nyquil and terpin hydrate for an illness; expert testimony at trial established that Nyquil is 25 percent alcohol, and terpin hydrate 41 percent.

The Alaska DUI statute refers only to "intoxicating liquor." The defendant argued that this phrase was unconstitutionally vague, that it did not put him on notice that cough syrup came within its definition, and that the judge's instruction to the jury that the alcohol in Nyquil is the same as in beer or liquor was in error. In rejecting the arguments, the appellate court held that since Nyquil and terpin hydrate contain alcohol, "they are therefore intoxicating liquors."

The prosecution must allege in its complaint what substance caused the defendant's condition. That is, the pleadings must be specific enough to put the defendant on notice as to the exact theory of the charge. In *Garcia v. State,* 720 S.W.2d 655 (Tex. App. 1986), the defendant was charged with driving "a motor vehicle . . . while intoxicated, when the defendant did not have the normal use of his mental and physical facilities." On appeal, he argued that the complaint did not allege the manner or means of intoxication. Furthermore, the lack of specificity could permit a later prosecution for the same offense. The appellate court agreed, reversing his conviction for error in denying his motion to quash, reasoning that the pleadings failed to inform the defendant whether his intoxication was caused by alcohol, drugs, narcotics, or a combination of these.

There is one last consideration concerning proof of intoxication: The prosecution must establish the defendant's condition *at the time he was driving.* Evidence of the amount of alcohol in his system at the time a blood sample was taken at a hospital two hours after the arrest is relevant only insofar as a conclusion can be made as to the probable amount at the time of driving, based on figures for alcohol "burn off" for "average humans." By itself, the test figure will only tend to indicate the defendant's condition at the time the blood sample was drawn. This is collateral to the issue of his condition while driving. Obviously, such a test figure is yet one further step removed from the ultimate fact and thus that much more unreliable — and dangerous. For a discussion of *retrograde extrapolation* — estimating earlier blood alcohol levels — see §5.2.

§1.3.1 Presumption of Intoxication from Blood-Alcohol Analysis

All 50 states now have some kind of law or laws establishing statutory presumptions from the results of chemical tests given to drunk driving suspects. Many of these states have patterned their statutes after the Uniform Vehicle Code §11-902.1 (Supp. II 1976):

> (b) Upon the trial of any civil or criminal action or proceeding arising out of acts alleged to have been committed by any person while driving or in actual physical control of a vehicle while under the influence of alcohol, the amount of alcohol in the person's blood at the time alleged as shown by chemical analysis of the person's blood, urine, breath, or other bodily substance shall give rise to the following presumptions:
>
> 1. If there was at that time 0.05 percent or less by weight of alcohol in the person's blood, it shall be presumed that the person was not under the influence of alcohol.
>
> 2. If there was at that time in excess of 0.05 percent but less than 0.10 percent by weight of alcohol in the person's blood, such fact shall not give rise to any presumption that the person

> was or was not under the influence of alcohol, but such fact may be considered with other competent evidence in determining whether the person was under the influence of alcohol.
>
> 3. If there was at that time 0.10 percent or more by weight of alcohol in the person's blood, it shall be presumed that the person was under the influence of alcohol.

The Code does not limit the introduction of other evidence on the issue of intoxication and specifically provides that, for the presumption to apply, the chemical analysis must have been performed "according to the methods approved by the State Department of Health" (see §11.6.8). This, of course, permits the defense two avenues of attack despite the operation of a legal presumption. First, the defense can produce evidence supportive of the client's sobriety. While the jury will be instructed that the defendant is presumed guilty, sufficient contradictory evidence may serve to rebut the presumption. Second, the basis for the presumption can be brought into question. As the presumption depends on the validity of the chemical testing, the procedures used in taking and analyzing the blood, breath, or urine samples can be cross-examined for any flaws. In short, if the test was administered improperly, the jury is free to disregard the results.

The majority of states have adopted the Uniform Vehicle Code's recommended blood-alcohol presumptive levels — that is, a presumption of intoxication at .10 percent or more of alcohol in the blood by weight. Some states have gone further, adopting the English and Canadian standard of .08 percent at which a presumption of intoxication applies.

The purpose and effect of the statutory presumption is to ease the burden on the prosecutor of proving beyond a reasonable doubt that the defendant was under the influence. The presumption created by the statute is not an absolute one but is rebuttable. In effect, the presumption operates to shift the burden of proof at least to some extent to the defendant to show that he was not under the influence of alcohol.

There has been some confusion as to what exactly such presumptions legally mean and precisely how they affect the burden of proof. A few courts have incorrectly referred to the presumption as being "conclusive," requiring the defendant to prove his innocence; others have held that the burden of proof on the prosecution remains the same throughout the trial regardless of presumptions. (See *People v. Guilford,* 245 N.Y.S.2d 781 (1964).) A Vermont court dealt with the question of whether the presumption that a person is under the influence of an intoxicant based on his blood-alcohol reading violates the rule in criminal cases that a defendant is presumed innocent unless proven guilty beyond a reasonable doubt. In *State v. Dacey,* 138 Vt. 491, 418 A.2d 856 (1980), the Vermont Supreme Court held that the trial court's instruction to the jury misled them into believing that they had to find the defendant to be under the influence if they believed the blood-alcohol test evidence. In addition, it determined that the instruction placed on the defendant at least the burden of producing evidence, which he could not be compelled to do. The court added that the inference of the statute can only be based on evidence of defendant's blood-alcohol concentration "at the time of operation," according to the exact language of the statute. Therefore, for the inference to be raised properly, expert testimony must relate the blood-alcohol test results back to the time of operation.

The Supreme Judicial Court of Massachusetts has addressed the question of the constitutionality of blood-alcohol presumptions. In *Commonwealth v. Moreira,* 385 Mass. 792, 434 N.E.2d 196 (1982), the court reversed a drunk driving conviction where a jury had been instructed that "if [blood-alcohol] evidence is that such percentage was ten one-hundredths or more there shall be a presumption that such defendant was under the influence of intoxicating liquor." The jury, which had evidence that the defendant registered .12 percent on the Breathalyzer, was then further instructed in accordance with Instruction 4.10 of the Model Jury Instructions for Criminal Offenses in the District Courts of Massachusetts:

> So if you are convinced beyond a reasonable doubt that the test administered to the defendant is scientifically accurate and was properly and competently administered, then you are bound to follow the presumptions of the test, or the statute. However, if you have a reasonable doubt as to the accuracy of the test, either because it is scientifically invalid or that it was not properly or com-

> pletely administered, or if you find that the presumptions raised by the statute have been overcome by other competent evidence, then you should disregard the test and find the defendant innocent or guilty based on the remaining evidence in the case. [434 N.E.2d at 198.]

In accepting the defendant's argument on appeal that the totality of the instructions operated to shift to him the burden of proof on the issue of intoxication, the court rejected the prosecutor's argument that the instructions, at most, constituted only a permissible presumption — not mandatory — and simply shifted the burden of producing evidence. Said the court:

> We note first that it is constitutionally impermissible to shift to a defendant the burden of disproving an element of a crime charged. [Cites.] It follows that it is prohibited to shift the burden of proof to a defendant by means of a presumption. . . .
>
> The Commonwealth contends that the language of the instruction, when considered in its entirety . . . could not admit of a construction that would make the presumption mandatory to a reasonable juror. We disagree.
>
> [A] jury cannot be instructed that if the defendant failed to introduce evidence to gainsay the breathalyzer test, they are required to find the fact that the defendant was under the influence of intoxicating liquor. The jury should have been instructed that they could draw reasonable inferences from the results of the breathalyzer test in this case, but that the test is merely evidence of the defendant's being under the influence of liquor and does not necessarily dictate such a conclusion.
>
> General language in the judge's charge to the effect that the Commonwealth shoulders the burden of proving the defendant's guilt beyond a reasonable doubt and that the defendant has no duty to establish his innocence does not save the charge here. The test is what a reasonable juror *could* have understood the charge to mean, not what he was likely to understand. . . . The [instruction] could have led a reasonable juror to believe that he had to find that the defendant was under the influence of liquor unless the defendant persuaded him otherwise. [Cites.] [434 N.E.2d at 198–200.]

The Colorado Supreme Court has similarly addressed the constitutionality of a commonly encountered jury instruction that explains the effect of the DUI presumption. In *Barnes v. People,* 735 P.2d 869 (Colo. 1987), the trial court had given a standard instruction that "Unless the presumption is rebutted by evidence to the contrary, you must accept the presumption as if it had been factually established by evidence." The relevant DUI statute set forth the common and seemingly mandatory presumption that if the defendant's blood-alcohol level was .10 percent or higher, "it *shall* be presumed that the defendant was under the influence of alcohol."

The Supreme Court reversed and remanded, holding that such an instruction violated the presumption of innocence and shifted the burden of proof from the state to the defendant. Recognizing that the statute appeared to create a mandatory presumption, the court simply said that constitutional limits required that it be read as creating only a permissible inference. The fact that the trial court had read other instructions that appeared to contradict the mandatory effect and clarify the constitutional rights did not solve the problem: Where "one of the instructions is an incorrect and clearly prejudicial statement of law, the fact that the other instruction contains a correct statement of law cannot cure the error." 735 P.2d at 874.

The Wisconsin Supreme Court was faced with a related issue in *State v. Vick,* 104 Wis. 2d 678, 312 N.W.2d 489 (1981), in which a trial court's instruction was deemed only a permissive presumption and did not shift the burden of proof or attempt to create a mandatory presumption. The issue before the court was whether an unconstitutional presumption was created by the trial court's instruction that if it were proven defendant was under the influence at the time of *testing,* then he was under the influence of an intoxicant at the time he was *operating* his vehicle. 312 N.W.2d at 494. The court used the test set forth in *Ulster County v. Allen,* 442 U.S. 140, 157 (1979):

> Because this permissive presumption leaves the trier of fact free to credit or reject the inference and does not shift the burden of proof, it affects the application of the "beyond a reasonable doubt" standard only if, under the facts of the case, there is *no rational way* the trier could make the connection permitted by the inference. For only in that situation is there any risk that an expla-

> nation of the permissible inference to a jury, or its use by a jury, has caused the presumptively rational fact finder to make an erroneous factual determination. [312 N.W.2d at 497.]

Employment of the *Ulster* test precipitated the court's conclusion that the inferred fact of driving while intoxicated flowed more likely than not from the proven fact of the Breathalyzer results based on all the evidence presented in that case.

In *State v. Bence,* 29 Wash. App. 233, 627 P.2d 1343 (1981), the jury was instructed that a blood-alcohol reading of .10 percent or more permitted them to presume that defendant was under the influence of intoxicating liquor. The defendant contended that the test was too remote from the critical time (of his driving on the freeway) to assist the jury in its function of resolving the basic issue in the case. The court, citing *State v. Dacey,* supra, held that when evidence indicates substantial consumption of alcohol after termination of driving and prior to administration of the test, the presumption from the basic fact to the presumed fact may lack a rational foundation. The Washington court went on to state that a Breathalyzer test administered an hour after the accused stopped driving could be considered as circumstantial evidence that his blood-alcohol content was at that level or higher while he was driving.

Whether a presumption arising from a blood-alcohol test is enough by itself to sustain the prosecution's burden of proof is a subject of further disagreement among the jurisdictions. Generally, as has been noted, the presumption is merely that — an operative presumption, insufficient to sustain the prosecutor's burden of proof beyond a reasonable doubt. (See, e.g., *State v. Jent,* 270 N.C. 652, 155 S.E.2d 171 (1967); *People v. Fink,* 238 N.Y.S.2d 847 (1963); *State v. Bailey,* 184 Kan. 704, 339 P.2d 45 (1959); *State v. Williams,* 245 Iowa 401, 62 N.W.2d 241 (1954).) Other states have held that such a presumption is sufficient if accompanied by even the slightest corroboration, such as the testimony of an expert witness. (*People v. Markham,* 153 Cal. App. 2d 260, 314 P.2d 217 (1957).) Still others, however, have taken the position that no corroboration is necessary and that the results of the chemical test are sufficient to sustain the prosecution's burden of proof beyond a reasonable doubt. (*Helmly v. State,* 142 Ga. App.

577, 236 S.E.2d 540 (1977); *State v. Myers,* 88 N.M. 16, 536 P.2d 280 (1975).)

Regardless of fine definitions, the statutory presumptions are generally rebuttable. The language of the statute usually provides that the defendant is not to be limited in his introduction of any competent evidence relevant to the question of whether he was under the influence of alcohol. Thus, he may offer his own testimony, the testimony of other lay or expert witnesses, the results of additional chemical tests, or any other relevant evidence to overcome the initial presumption that he was intoxicated at the time of driving. Counsel may also wish to enlist the prosecution's expert witness in rebutting the presumption by asking them to review, before testifying, studies or articles such as Baylor, Layne, et al., Effects of Ethanol on Human Fractionated Response Times, 23 Drug and Alcohol Dependency 31 (1989), in which researchers found that a BAC of .10 percent caused no impairment in reaction time.

Of course, the jury must be clearly instructed that the presumption is rebuttable. In *Spurlin v. State,* 505 So. 2d 1287 (Ala. Crim. App. 1988), a drunk driving conviction was reversed when the trial judge failed to instruct the jury that the .10 percent presumption of intoxication was rebuttable. See also *Yost v. State,* 542 So. 2d 419 (Fla. App. 1989).

Finally, counsel should read his state's presumption statute very carefully if he is confronted with a *felony* drunk driving charge or a vehicular homicide, manslaughter, or murder charge arising out of drunk driving: The presumption may not apply. In *State v. Shaw,* 530 A.2d 653 (Conn. App. 1987), for example, the statutory language was held to mean that the presumption applied only to the basic drunk driving offense.

In *Shaw,* the presumption language appeared in the text of the basic drunk driving statute. A different result would presumably apply where, for example, the Uniform Vehicle Code's §11-902.1 was adopted because this language specifically states that the presumption applies "[u]pon the trial of *any* civil or criminal action or proceeding arising out of acts alleged to have been committed by any person while driving or in actual control of a vehicle while under the influence of alcohol . . ."

All states have now passed new drunk driving laws that go

further than simply imposing a presumption as the result of blood-alcohol test results. These so-called per se laws (which commonly coexist with the traditional drunk driving statutes) create a new offense of having a certain amount of alcohol in the blood, commonly .08 or .10 percent, while driving. Thus the question of whether the accused was actually under the influence of alcohol is irrelevant: Guilt lies simply in having the alcohol in the system (see §1.4).

Clearly, such laws are much more easily enforced than traditional drunk driving laws. Just as clearly, individuals whose abilities to operate a motor vehicle are not impaired and whose only crime is one of chemistry will be convicted of criminal offenses.

Faced with such a charge, defense counsel should realize that the validity of the blood-alcohol reading is still subject to question. All of the normal grounds for attacking the test results (see infra) still should be pursued in an attempt to invalidate the blood-alcohol reading. And if the court permits, counsel should introduce evidence of sobriety to rebut the validity of the test result; every effort should be made to convince the jury that the client exhibited no symptoms that would be associated with the blood-alcohol level obtained. If handled correctly, defense counsel can succeed in shifting the jury's focus to the issue of intoxication and away from the issue of what the blood-alcohol level was.

§1.4 Over .08 or .10 Percent Blood Alcohol

> Since the masses are always eager to believe *something,* for their benefit nothing is so easy to *arrange* as facts.
>
> CHARLES MAURICE DE TALLEYRAND-PÉRIGORD

As part of the crackdown on drunk drivers across the country, state legislatures have passed so-called *per se* drunk driving statutes. These statutes do not simply treat the results of blood-alcohol tests as evidence from which a rebuttable presumption of intoxication is drawn: the *offense* is having a designated amount of alcohol in the blood, commonly .08 or .10 percent, while driving. (As of January 1999, all but one state — South Carolina — and the District of Columbia had adopted per se laws; fifteen of these use .08

percent as the legal standard.) Thus this new brand of drunk driving law is completely unconcerned with whether the individual is, in fact, under the influence of alcohol. The crime consists of driving with alcohol in the blood — that is, the evidence becomes the crime itself.

Obviously, this new type of statute greatly facilitates the prosecutor's job — and makes it even more imperative for defense counsel to be able competently to attack the validity of the blood-alcohol testing procedure. The only defenses to such a charge are three: (1) the defendant was not driving; (2) the test results, though accurate, do not reflect the blood-alcohol content at the time he was driving; or (3) the test results are inaccurate or were not administered according to legally mandated procedures.

These new per se statutes usually coexist with the traditional drunk driving statute, and, in fact, the defendant may be charged with violation of both offenses (although, of course, he can only be punished for one). Thus, the prosecutor is given a powerful new weapon. If the suspect registers over .10 percent on the blood-alcohol test, he can be charged with violation of the per se statute — and easily convicted. If the suspect refuses to take the test, he can still be charged with the traditional statute that makes it criminal to drive while under the influence of alcohol; the testimony of the arresting officer and/or civilian witnesses is sufficient to uphold a conviction. Similarly, if the test results are below .10 percent, or if the jury rejects the blood-alcohol evidence, the prosecutor can still proceed under the old statute and obtain a conviction.

An example of this new statutory approach is found in the laws of the state of Washington:

> R.C.W. §46-61.502. Driving While Under the Influence of Intoxicating Liquor or Drug — What Constitutes.
>
> A person is guilty of driving while under the influence of intoxicating liquor or any drug if he drives a vehicle within this state while:
>
> 1. He has 0.10 percent or more by weight of alcohol in his blood as shown by chemical analysis of his breath, blood or other bodily substance made under R.C.W. §46-61.506 as now or hereafter amended; or

2. He is under the influence of or affected by intoxicating liquor or any drug; or
3. He is under the combined influence of or affected by intoxicating liquor and any drug.

Thus under Washington's laws a drunk driving arrestee can be charged with subsection (1) if he registers .10 percent or higher on the blood-alcohol test; if the results are lower, or if he refuses to submit to such a test, he may be convicted of subsection (2). And in most cases, he can — and probably will — be charged with both.

This statute was quickly challenged on the grounds that it created an irrebuttable presumption of intoxication, thus unconstitutionally shifting the burden of proof from the prosecution to the defendant. In *City of Seattle v. Urban,* 648 P.2d 922 (Wash. 1982), the state supreme court rejected this argument and held that the statutory language did not designate a presumption but rather set out alternative methods of committing the crime of driving while under the influence.

In 1986, the Washington legislature changed its per se statute by substituting "alcohol in his *blood*" with "*breath,*" thus making the relationship of breath alcohol to blood alcohol irrelevant. (See §6.0.1, Breath-Blood Partition Ratio.) The state's supreme court subsequently ruled that this modified version of the statute was also constitutional. *State v. Brayman,* 751 P.2d 294 (Wash. 1988). In doing so, the court acknowledged that a breath test was a less direct method of measuring blood-alcohol content, but concluded that it was nevertheless a reasonable indication of impairment. The court also rejected an equal protection argument — that is, that the new standard discriminated against those with blood-breath ratios below 2100:1 — by finding that the record failed to define a class of individuals who had been discriminated against.

California's statutory scheme is very similar to Washington's — as are most states'. Vehicle Code §23152(b) makes it a misdemeanor for a person to drive a vehicle with .08 percent or more alcohol in his blood. Section 23152(a) retains the old law, which makes it a misdemeanor to drive a vehicle while under the influence of alcohol and/or drugs.

Interestingly, on passage of the new statute, the city attorney for the city of Los Angeles — the official responsible for prosecuting probably more drunk driving cases than any other official in the country — immediately instructed his deputy prosecutors to refuse to file complaints under this per se approach. Instead, City Attorney Ira Reiner told his staff that they were to continue to charge drunk drivers under the old statute. The problem, according to Reiner, is that the Los Angeles police department forensic experts advised him that they could not accurately determine what a suspect's blood-alcohol level was at the time of driving based on tests taken later at the police station. "The department's Scientific Investigation Division told us that without any evidence of the pattern of drinking," Reiner was quoted as saying, "they would not be able to express any opinion as to the level of blood-alcohol at the time of driving." (See §5.2, Retrograde Extrapolation.) Reiner suggested that the "fatal flaw" in the new per se statute could be cured by providing that the blood-alcohol content refer to the time of testing rather than to the time of driving.

An appellate court soon struck down the new per se law as unconstitutionally vague. In *People v. Alfaro,* 144 Cal. App. 2d 683 (1983), the court observed that "we deal with a law which allows persons to drink and drive, but gives no reasonably ascertainable means of knowing when such conduct becomes 'criminal.'" The California Supreme Court, however, quickly upheld the constitutional validity of the new per se law. In *Burg v. Municipal Court,* 673 P.2d 732 (Cal. 1983), the court held:

> One who drives a vehicle after having ingested sufficient alcohol to approach or exceed the level proscribed in neither "innocent" nor is he without "fair warning." The very fact that he has consumed a quantity of alcohol should notify a person of ordinary intelligence that he is in jeopardy of violating the statute. [673 P.2d at 741.]

The Court agreed that it is impossible for a motorist to determine whether his or her blood-alcohol level is at a legal .07 percent or an illegal .08 percent. But, the opinion continued, due process principles require only that a person be given "fair notice":

> Those who drink a substantial amount of alcohol within a relatively short period of time are given clear warning that to avoid possible criminal behavior they must refrain from driving. Consid-

> ering also today's heightened level of public awareness regarding the problem, we cannot believe that any person who drives after drinking would be unaware of the possibility that his blood-alcohol level might equal or exceed the statutory standard. [Id.]

In a series of footnotes, however, the court noted that a blood-alcohol test is not conclusive evidence of a defendant's guilt: "The defendant remains free to challenge the accuracy of the test result, the manner in which it was administered and by whom." Id. at 737 n. 10.

If the client is charged with a violation of a per se statute — that is, the prosecution has accused him of driving with a blood-alcohol level in excess of the statutory amount (.08 or .10 percent) — then an analysis of the state's case consists primarily of a close look at the blood-alcohol evidence. This will involve extensive use of discovery to determine whether there are any weaknesses in the procedures used to collect and analyze the client's blood, breath, or urine sample. Can the results of the test be successfully attacked in pre-trial motions to suppress? If not, can a jury be persuaded that the results are not sufficiently reliable? The subjects of discovery, motions to suppress, and blood-alcohol analysis are discussed in following chapters.

§1.4.1 Drivers Under 21

Responding to accelerating pressure from MADD and federal authorities, many states are adopting special drunk driving laws for drivers under a certain age — typically, targeting those under 21. These may be criminal or license-suspension provisions; often there will be two statutes that co-exist — criminal and suspension — with application of the adult criminal statute.

California offers an example of this approach. If a driver under the age of 21 is arrested and found to have a blood-alcohol concentration of, say, .06 percent, he will be exposed to three separate — and concurrent — statutory schemes. First, his license will be immediately confiscated under the state's "zero tolerance" law providing for a one-year suspension where the blood-alcohol concentration is .01 percent or greater. Second, he will still be subject to the adult misdemeanor statute (Vehicle Code §23152a) of driving under the influence of alcohol (the prosecution could also charge him with the adult .08 percent charge on a retrograde extrapolation theory). Third, he can also be charged with a criminal infraction (i.e., less than a misdemeanor) for driving with .05 percent BAC or higher. This charge arises out of a new and very confused (and arguably unconstitutional) §23140 of the that state's Vehicle Code:

> (a) It is unlawful for a person under the age of 21 years who has 0.05 percent or more, by weight, of alcohol in his or her blood to drive a vehicle.
> (b) A person may be found to be in violation of subdivision (a) if the person was, at the time of driving, under the age of 21 years and under the influence of, or affected by, an alcoholic beverage regardless of whether a chemical test was made to determine that person's blood-alcohol concentration and if the trier of fact finds that the person had consumed an alcoholic beverage and was driving a vehicle while having a concentration of 0.05 percent or more, by weight, of alcohol in his or her blood.

Apparently, proof of a .05% BAC is not limited to cases where evidence of blood, breath, or urine is available. It is unclear, however, just what alternative forms of evidence are acceptable — and this would, seemingly, render the statute subject to a constitutional challenge for vagueness.

Note that the under-21 statute is more *specific* than Veh C §23152, and thus a driver under the age of 21 cannot be charged with this "adult" version of the drunk driving statute.

Vehicle Code §23140 is a more specific statute than Veh C §23152, and should thus preclude prosecution for the more general Veh C §23152. This conclusion would seem to be reenforced by the legislative intent reflected, for example, in the provisions for special alcohol education programs designed for minors (Veh C §§23141 et seq.). However, Veh C §23142 provides that:

> If any person is found to have violated Section 23140 and is also found to have violated Section 23152 or 23153, in addition to, and not as an alternative to, the requirements of Section 23154 or any other provision of Article 2 (commencing with Section 23152), that person shall be required to participate in the alcohol education program or the alcohol rehabilitation program required by this article.

Although there is an argument that this constitutes multiple punishment, the intent would seem to be that a driver under 21 can be "found" to have (that is, convicted of having) committed all three offenses.

§1.4.2 Commercial Drivers

As with youthful drivers, most states now have enacted special DUI provisions for commercial drivers. These may involve criminal standards or license suspensions or both. Typically, a lower blood-alcohol concentration is required for violation, and whether the accused was driving a commercial vehicle or a private vehicle at the time may be determinative.

To again use the state that has often pioneered new DUI legislation as an example, California's relevant statute (Vehicle Code §23152d) provides:

> It is unlawful for any person who has 0.04 percent or more, by weight, of alcohol in his or her blood to drive a commercial motor vehicle, as defined in Section 15210.

Additional portions of the "Commercial Motor Vehicle Safety Act" provide for a six-month suspension of all driving privileges and a one-year prohibition of operating a commercial vehicle; the prohibition is for life upon a second conviction. The Act further requires commercial drivers to notify an employer of any convictions/suspensions.

The Act further provides that commercial drivers must be "ordered out of service for 24 hours if the BAC is found to be .01% or higher"; violation, however, constitutes only an infraction.

It can be expected that the increasingly expanded presence of the federal government in the drunk driving arena generally will first see increased federal legislation in this area, under the constitutional authority of the Commerce Clause. In fact, 18 USCS §342 already makes it a federal felony to operate a common carrier under the influence of alcohol or drugs.

§1.4.3 Presumption of BAC at Time of Driving

The majority of states have enacted statutes which "relate back" the blood-alcohol concentration at the time of testing to the BAC at the time of driving. In other words, the blood-alcohol level at the time the test was administered is *presumed* to be the same as the level at the time the defendant was driving. Thus the legislature have given the prosecution yet another valuable weapon: *retrograde extrapolation* as a matter of law. (For a discussion of retrograde extrapolation, see §5.2.)

California's statute is typical:

> In any prosecution under this subdivision, it is a rebuttable presumption that the person had 0.08 percent or more, by weight, of alcohol in his or her blood at the time of driving of the vehicle if the person had 0.08 percent or more, by weight, of alcohol in his or her blood at the time of performance of a chemical test within three hours after the driving.

The presumption is, of course, rebuttable: a conclusive presumption would conflict with the presumption of innocence, *Morissette v. United States,* 342 U.S. 246 (1952); and see *McLean v. Moran,* 963 F.2d 1306 (9th Cir. 1992), where the court held that Nevada's three-hour presumption was unconstitutionally applied as a mandatory presumption.

Thus the defense must offer evidence to rebut this presumption — that is, evidence that the defendant's blood-alcohol level at the time he was driving was *lower* than the level at the time he was tested. This can be done, for example, by showing recent alcohol consumption, causing a *rising BAC curve* (see §5.2.4). For a discussion of blood alcohol generally, see Chapter 5.

§1.4.4 Lay Expertise

The state supreme court decisions upholding the per se laws against attack on vagueness/notice grounds are not without value to the defense. These decisions are basically premised on the theory — as they must be to survive challenge — that all drivers are presumed to *know* what their blood-alcohol levels are. In the words of the California Supreme Court:

> Charts are readily available to the public that show with reasonable certainty the number of different alcoholic beverages necessary for a particular individual to reach a blood-alcohol level of 0.10 percent. [*Burg v. Municipal Court,* 673 P.2d 732, 742 (1983).]

Since the premise of per se statutes is that a driver is competent to assess his blood-alcohol level at the time he is driving, then this judicially recognized fact should apply at trial. In other words, the defendant should be competent to *testify* about his blood-alcohol concentration — over the anticipated objection of the prosecutor that he lacks expertise. And the defendant should be entitled to an instruction advising the jury that he is, in fact, competent to estimate his own blood-alcohol level.

Furthermore, if blood-alcohol concentration "charts" provide sufficient notice to uphold the statute from a "void-for-vagueness" challenge, the same "charts" should be competent evidence at trial, even in the hands of a lay person.

A proposed jury instruction in cases where the driver has testified concerning his blood-alcohol concentration might read:

> You are instructed that a lay person who consumes alcoholic beverages can detect with reasonable probability whether or not his or her blood alcohol level exceeds. 10 percent. Such a lay person can testify competently to his or her blood alcohol level at the time of arrest.

§1.4.5 Admissibility of Non-Impairment Evidence

If the client has manifested symptoms that appear contrary to what would be expected of an individual with his indicated level of blood alcohol, counsel should consider introducing evidence of those symptoms in a per se prosecution. For example, if a breath test indicates a blood-alcohol concentration of .14 percent, but the client was pulled over only for speeding, exhibited few of the usual symptoms of intoxication, and performed relatively well on the field sobriety tests, these facts should be developed for the jury to contradict the chemical test results. In other words, the police officer's observations of the defendant's behavior would be contrary to those expected of a person with the indicated BAC.

The various jurisdictions have split on whether lack-of-impairment evidence is relevant in a per se prosecution. In some states (e.g., Alaska, Arizona, Virginia, and Oregon), such evidence is admissible to contradict the expected symptoms from the indicated blood-alcohol concentration. In others (e.g., Alabama,

Minnesota, and Pennsylvania), such evidence is considered to be irrelevant.

Thus, for example, in *Davis v. Commonwealth,* 381 S.E.2d 11 (Va. App. 1989), the trial court ruled that defense evidence of the defendant's condition at the time of a traffic accident was irrelevant and inadmissible: the blood-alcohol test result was "conclusive proof of the offense" of driving with a BAC of .10 percent or more. On appeal, this view was soundly rejected, the appellate court holding that the test result was merely "an evidentiary fact which creates a rebuttable presumption that the measurement accurately reflects the blood-alcohol concentration at the time of driving."

In *State v. Horning,* 511 N.W.3d 27 (Minn. App. 1994), however, an appellate court held such evidence was *not* relevant, emphasizing the distinction between the subjective nature of the DUI statute and the objective nature of the per se statute.

An Idaho court has taken a middle ground. In *State v. Edmunson,* 867 P.2d 1006 (Idaho App. 1994), the defendant in a per se prosecution had attempted to introduce audio tapes recorded by the officers as well as the results of field sobriety tests he had taken. The court held that lack-of-impairment evidence is admissible for the purpose of impeaching the accuracy of the chemical test results. However, the court added, a foundation must be laid, normally consisting of expert testimony concerning symptoms reasonably to be expected from the indicated BAC.

§1.5 Under the Influence of Drugs

> Justice is open to everybody in the same way as the Ritz Hotel.
>
> JUDGE STURGESS

Driving under the influence of drugs or narcotics is, in most jurisdictions, treated similarly to driving under the influence of alcohol. Some states have statutes dealing exclusively with this offense, while others cover it with alternative language in comprehensive drunk driving statutes.

Counsel may find that the criminal complaint filed against his client reads in the alternative, despite the fact that there is no evidence of drug usage. Charging in the alternative is a common tactic used by prosecutors and accomplishes three things. First, it does away with the necessity of having to amend the complaint in midstream if evidence of drug usage surfaces during pre-trial investigation. Second, it avoids problems of variance if testimony concerning drugs surfaces unexpectedly during trial. And third, it offers the unethical prosecutor the opportunity to plant the seed of possible drug usage in the jurors' minds — regardless of lack of evidence and regardless of any instructions from the court.

A second type of drug-related driving offense involves operating a motor vehicle under the combined effects of drugs and alcohol. Usually, this is proscribed in alternative language in a comprehensive drunk driving statute. On the other hand, it may be dealt with by separate statute or by case law interpreting one or more statutes. (See, e.g., *State v. Thomas,* 79 Idaho 372, 318 P.2d 592 (1957), holding that impairment from combined influence justifies a conviction for driving under the influence of alcohol.) Here, a low blood-alcohol reading will prove of relatively little help to a defendant, for it is the *combined* influence of drugs and alcohol that is in issue. Where, for example, a driver has had one drink and one "downer" (barbiturate), neither would necessarily be sufficient to cause intoxication, even if the separate known reactions are added together. In combination, however, due to the chemical reaction between certain drugs and alcohol within the body, the cumulative impairment will probably be greater than would be expected. This is a case of one plus one equalling three.

What if the amount of a drug is *de minimus* — that is, insufficient to have any appreciable effect: Can the prosecution nevertheless introduce evidence of the presence of the drug in a case where the defendant is charged with driving under the influence of alcohol? In *State v. McClain,* 525 So. 2d 420 (Fla. 1988), the defendant was charged with vehicular manslaughter while intoxicated; a blood test indicated .14 percent blood alcohol — and a trace of cocaine. His motion to exclude evidence of the cocaine was granted after an expert at the suppression hearing testified that the amount of cocaine was almost undetectable; the expert further testified that he could not say whether the amount of cocaine present could have affected the defendant's driving.

The Supreme Court of Florida affirmed the suppression, holding that the evidence was not relevant — that is, the considerable prejudicial impact outweighed the minimal probative value.

Defense counsel representing a client charged with driving under the combined influence of alcohol and drugs should consider challenging the constitutionality of the statute. The Supreme Court of Alaska considered the constitutionality of Alaska Stat. §28.35.030(a)(3) (1982), which proscribed driving "while . . . under the combined influence of intoxicating liquor and another substance." See *Williford v. State,* 674 P.2d 1329 (Alaska 1983). In particular, the Alaska court considered a challenge by a convicted driver who argued that the foregoing statutory language was "void for vagueness."

In analyzing the driver's argument, the Alaska Supreme Court began by reviewing the findings of the lower appellate court:

> In rejecting Williford's argument that "another substance" is unconstitutionally vague, the court of appeals substituted the word "drug" for "substance": "Although the outer limits of the statute might not be entirely clear, it was designed to prevent a person from driving while intoxicated when she has knowingly consumed alcohol and a *drug.* The statute certainly gives adequate notice of that intention." 653 P.2d at 341 (emphasis added). "Substance" is not defined under the driving while intoxicated laws. The dictionary defines "substance" in part as "the physical matter of which a thing consists: . . . matter of a particular kind or chemical composition." *Webster's New World Dictionary* 1420 (2d college ed. 1980). "Drug" is defined in part as "any substance used as a medicine or as any ingredient in a medicine." Id. at 429. Thus, "substance" is not synonymous with "drug," but is a much broader term, encompassing all matter, not just medicinal substances. We believe that the term is vague because a person is given no notice as to what substances, when used in combination with alcohol, are prohibited. In this sense, the prohibition of driving while under the combined influence of alcohol and another substance "forbids . . . the doing of an act in terms so vague that men of common intelligence must necessarily guess at its meaning." *Connally v. General Construction Co.,* 269 U.S. at 391, 70 L. Ed. at 328. [674 P.2d at 1331.]

The Court held that Alaska Stat. §28.35.030(a) (3) did not give adequate notice of what constitutes "the combined influence of intoxicating liquor and another substance,'' and found the statute to be unconstitutionally vague.

A third type of offense that counsel may encounter is the driving of a motor vehicle by an individual *addicted* to dangerous drugs or narcotics. In such a case, the question of impairment is irrelevant. The sole issue is one of status or condition: Was the defendant addicted at the time he was driving? In some states, individuals participating in a recognized methadone program are exempted from prosecution for this offense. Again, defending such a case involves special knowledge concerning ''reading'' hypodermic needle marks, pupil reaction, etc., which is beyond the purview of this text.

Counsel should be aware that the drug or narcotic being used by the client at the time of driving need not be illegal: It can be an over-the-counter drug, or it can be a restricted drug lawfully prescribed by a physician. As with driving under the influence of alcohol, it is the *effect* of the drug on driving that is the point of the legislation, not its legal status. The use of a properly prescribed drug can result in a criminal offense if it impairs the driver's ability to safely operate a vehicle. Obviously, sedatives such as barbiturates can have a marked effect on driving ability; less obviously, insulin (taken for diabetes) has been held to be a drug that can impair driving (*People v. Keith,* 184 Cal. App. 2d Supp. 884, 7 Cal. Rptr. 613 (1960)).

It should also be kept in mind that being under the influence of certain drugs or narcotics without a prescription can constitute an offense regardless of driving status. If, for example, there are no witnesses to a client's having been the driver of a just-wrecked vehicle, the police may nevertheless arrest the driver simply for being under the influence of a dangerous drug or narcotic, an offense that in some jurisdictions, oddly enough, carries harsher penalties than driving under the influence of drugs.

Counsel may be able to present a defense on the theory that the client was not aware of the effects of drugs he had consumed. In *Commonwealth v. Wallace,* 14 Mass. App. 358, 439 N.E.2d 848 (1982), the defendant offered evidence that his intoxication was due to taking a lawfully prescribed drug (Librium), that he was unaware of the intoxicating effects that this medication was having on him, and that no warnings about the effects had been given to him. The trial court refused to admit this evidence, and the defendant was convicted of driving under the influence of drugs and of operating a vehicle negligently. In reversing the conviction and remanding for a new trial, the Massachusetts Appeals Court held:

> [I]t was error to preclude the defendant from introducing evidence that he did not know of the possible effects of the medication on his driving ability, that he did not receive warnings as to its use, and that he had no reason to anticipate the effects which the drug induced. His failure to receive warnings from his physician and pharmacist, if there is evidence of such failure, is relevant both to the charge of driving under the influence of drugs . . . and to the charge of negligence. . . . [439 N.E.2d at 852.]

Likening the situation to one of involuntary intoxication, the court reasoned that

> such circumstances . . . differ substantially from those of a person who drives after voluntarily consuming alcohol or drugs whose effects are or should be known. The law recognizes the differences, and authorities have characterized as "involuntary intoxication by medicine" the condition of a defendant who has taken prescribed drugs with severe unanticipated effects. See La Fave and Scott, *Criminal Law* §45, at 348 (1972); Perkins, *Criminal Law* 897 (2d ed. 1969). . . .
>
> Although there are few cases involving unanticipated effects by prescription drugs on a defendant's driving ability, and although each case depends on the specific statutory provision involved, the concept of "involuntary intoxication" has been applied to motor vehicle violations of this type under consideration in the present case. Authorities elsewhere indicate that such a nonvoluntary taking of a drug excuses certain motor vehicle offenses [citing cases in New York, Kentucky, Washington, Minnesota, Maine, Oklahoma, and North Carolina]. [Id. at 850–851.]

Counsel should consider the question of *tolerance* when confronted with a case involving driving under the influence of marijuana. At least one scientific study has concluded that experienced marijuana users develop the ability to compensate for the effect of the drugs on their driving performance. Marks and MacAvoy, Divided Attention Performance in Cannabis Users and Nonusers. Following Alcohol and Cannabis Use Separately and in

Combination, 99 Psychopharmacology 3 (1989). The researchers concluded that experienced users "develop tolerance to cannabis and cross-tolerance to alcohol or are able to compensate for the effects of drug and alcohol intoxication."

This text will not attempt to go into the lengthy and complex subjects of proof of drug consumption, identity of drugs or narcotics and their symptoms, etc. Counsel should realize that, although many of the same considerations of driving under the influence of alcohol apply to driving under the influence of drugs, defense of the latter requires its own expertise. However, when confronted with a case in which his client is charged with driving under the influence of drugs, or under the combined influence of drugs and alcohol, the following brief summary of symptoms of the more commonly used drugs may prove helpful in reviewing the officer's crime report.

Amphetamines: A stimulant, the most common forms of which are Benzedrine, Dexedrine, and methamphetamine. Common effects: pupil dilation, increased pulse rate and blood pressure, heightened alertness, nervousness, excitability, and talkativeness.

Barbiturates: A sedative/depressant. Symptoms: drowsiness, mental confusion, slow movement, and impaired coordination and motor function — similar to symptoms for alcohol intoxication, but without any odor of alcohol.

Cocaine: A stimulant/narcotic. Effects: dilated pupils, which react slowly to light, and increased pulse rate and blood pressure; nostrils are often red from sniffing the drug.

Marijuana: Possible symptoms: dilated pupils, bloodshot eyes, slowed reactions, disorientation, and relaxed inhibitions.

Methaqualone: A depressant. Symptoms: dilated pupils, slurred speech, weak and rapid pulse, staggering walk, and impaired coordination.

Phencyclidine (PCP): Causes effects that resemble stimulants, depressants, *and* hallucinogens: poor balance, muscle rigidity, disorientation, agitated state, blank expression, memory loss, aggression, strange behavior, and nystagmus (horizontal *and* vertical).

The Los Angeles Police Department, using the results of research sponsored by the National Highway Traffic Safety Administration, has devised a battery of field sobriety tests designed to detect drivers impaired by drugs — in fact, to detect the *specific* drug involved. Studdard, DWI Countermeasure: Testing the Impaired Driver, Police Chief (July 1984).

The battery involves eight tests: one-leg-stand, finger-to-nose, walk-the-line, standing steadiness, nystagmus, pupil reaction, pupil size, and pulse rate. The officer is also supposed to look for skin marks, apathy, drowsiness, and hyperactivity. Using this combination of tests and observations, an experienced officer theoretically can determine what type or class of drug the suspect has consumed. Obviously, the effectiveness of a test is completely dependent upon the experience and expertise of the officer.

§1.6 Felony Drunk Driving: DUI with Injury

> One method of delivery alone remains to us; which is simply this: we must lead men to the particulars themselves; and their series and order; while men on their side must force themselves for awhile to lay their notions by and begin to familiarize themselves with facts.
>
> Francis Bacon

As the national crackdown on drunk driving continues, prosecutors, legislators, and the courts are increasingly looking toward expansion of the limits on a driver's criminal and civil liability. One method that has seen much recent favor is to drastically increase the punishment by simply interpreting the conduct as fitting a more serious type of crime. Thus under certain circumstances the misdemeanor offense of driving under the influence of alcohol will be treated as a felony — punishable by incarceration in state prison. The most ominous manifestation of this trend is the growing use of murder statutes where drunk driving results in a death.

Drunk driving can have felony status when the driving results in an injury to another party. Where there is "bodily injury" or "substantial bodily harm," depending on the jurisdiction's statutory language, the charge in most states will be what is commonly referred to as "felony drunk driving." California's felony drunk driving statute is fairly typical:

> Any person who, while under the influence of intoxicating liquor, or under the combined influence of intoxicating liquor and any drug, drives a vehicle and when so driving does any act forbidden by law or neglects any duty imposed by law in the driving of such vehicle, which act or neglect proximately causes bodily injury to any person other than himself, is guilty of a felony. . . . [Cal. Veh. Code §23101(a).]

Thus three further elements have been added to the *corpus delicti:*

1. violation of a statute
2. bodily injury
3. proximate causation

As to these three additional elements, counsel should be aware of two possible sources of error in the prosecution's pleading or in his proof. First, the prosecution cannot "bootstrap" the first of the new requirements: The violation of law must be of a statute other than the drunk driving statute. Commonly, the violation will consist of some traffic offense such as speeding or running a traffic light. Second, the bodily injury must be proximately caused by the client's violation of the statute. If there is an independent source of causation, the elements of the *corpus* are not satisfied. For an extreme application of this requirement, see *People v. Weems,* 54 Cal. App. 4th 854 (1997), where the defendant's passengers were not wearing seat belts — sufficient, according to the court, to satisfy the neglect of duty requirement of the felony DUI statute: The injuries were proximately caused by the failure of the defendant to ensure that they were belted in.

As an example of a prosecutorial "over-filing" of a drunk driving case, there is the situation in which the client was driving his vehicle while under the influence and rammed into another vehicle proceeding more slowly in front of him, causing the driver of that vehicle to be hospitalized. The inexperienced or overly zealous prosecutor may automatically think of the equation, ''drunk driving *plus* injury *equals* felony drunk driving.'' However, absent additional facts, there are two essential elements missing in this situation: There is no evidence of an independent violation of a statute, nor, therefore, is there any evidence that the injuries were caused by a violation.

Can a driver be charged with *assault with a deadly weapon* where there was no intent and the ''weapon'' was his vehicle? Apparently so, at least according to one appellate decision in Texas. In *Roberts v. State,* 766 S.W.2d 578 (Tex. App. 1989), the defendant caused an accident while fleeing police, resulting in the death of one person and injury to two others. He was charged with and convicted of aggravated assault with a deadly weapon and aggravated assault resulting in serious bodily injury. On appeal, the court found that the car qualified as a ''deadly weapon,'' and that the defendant's conduct amounted to an assault even though it was reckless rather than intentional.

§1.6.1 Multiple Prior Convictions ("Three Strikes")

One of many recent developments in the ongoing ''war'' on drunk driving (i.e., politicians' attempts to appease MADD) is greatly increased sentencing for multiple offenders. While the imposition of more severe punishment for the repeat offender has been standard for many years, this new approach elevates the offense to felony or state-prison status where the requisite number of prior convictions exist. Commonly, this involves two or three ''priors'' — hence, the nickname ''three strikes'' DUI — usually within a period of five or seven years of the new offense (some states, however, are considering legislation making prior offenses chargeable for the lifetime of the offender).

A proper defense in such a case would, of course, involve investigating and moving to ''strike'' any or all of the prior convictions as unconstitutional. See Chapter 9, Prior Convictions. If any one prior can be knocked out, the pending charge reverts to a misdemeanor. Obviously, the existence of such pretrial motions to strike might motivate the prosecution to accept a plea bargain wherein one prior conviction is dropped from the complaint and the client pleads to an amended complaint charging a misdemeanor with priors.

Should the matter go to trial, of course, counsel should either be sure to demand bifurcation of trial (§9.2) or admit the priors so that evidence cannot be offered (since they are no longer in issue) and a jury will not be prejudiced (see §9.0).

§1.6.2 Manslaughter

A second and even more serious type of felony occurs when there is a death that is caused by driving under the influence of alcohol. The various jurisdictions call such an offense manslaughter, "vehicular homicide," or even murder.

Again, California's statute is illustrative, defining "manslaughter in the driving of a vehicle" as either a misdemeanor or a felony, depending on the circumstances. It is a felony if the death occurred

> [i]n the commission of an unlawful act, not amounting to felony, with gross negligence; or in the commission of a lawful act which might produce death, in an unlawful manner, and with gross negligence. [Cal. Penal Code §192(3)a.]

The manslaughter will be treated as a misdemeanor if the death occurred

> [i]n the commission of an unlawful act, not amounting to felony, without gross negligence; or in the commission of a lawful act which might produce death, in an unlawful manner, but without gross negligence. [Cal. Penal Code §192(3)b.]

The statute concludes by specifically requiring that the homicide resulting from the driving must have been proximately caused by the commission of the unlawful act or of the inherently dangerous lawful act in an unlawful manner.

In other jurisdictions, driving under the influence that results in the death of another individual is described as involuntary manslaughter, usually under a theory similar to California's; the offense is seen as engaging in gross negligence or committing an unlawful act. (See, e.g., *Whitman v. State,* 97 Fla. 988, 122 So. 567 (1929); *People v. Townsend,* 214 Mich. 267, 183 N.W. 177 (1921).)

Still other states, however, consider the offense to constitute the more serious charge of voluntary manslaughter. In such cases, the elements usually consist of reckless, wanton, or grossly negligent operation of a vehicle on a highway in such a manner as is likely to injure others using the highway, proximately causing the death of another. (See, e.g., *Rainey v. State,* 245 Ala. 458, 17 So. 2d 687 (1944).) Again, driving under the influence would constitute the "reckless, wanton, or grossly negligent" requirements. Although there is no actual intention to kill, the law's premise is that a person intends the natural consequences of his acts.

Can the fact of intoxication constitute "gross negligence"? Previous California cases had seemed to say that intoxication was, by itself, sufficient to constitute the requisite "gross negligence" for manslaughter in a DUI case. In *People v. McNiece,* 226 Cal. Rptr. 733 (Cal. App. 1986), however, the court held that the fact of intoxication was not sufficient of itself to support a finding of gross negligence, saying "something in addition" must be shown. And in *People v. Stanley,* 187 Cal. App. 3d 1048, 232 Cal. Rptr. 22 (1986), the court specifically held that the facts supporting gross negligence must arise from the nature of the driving.

In *People v. Conlin,* 282 Cal. Rptr. 646 (Cal. App. 1991), however, another California appellate court appears to have done some "backsliding." That case involved a situation in which the defendant had been drinking all day. When he left in his car with a friend, he was involved in a head-on collision; the friend and two others were killed. A subsequent chemical test indicated the defendant had a blood-alcohol level of .23 percent, and he was charged with three counts of vehicular manslaughter. At trial, the jury was given an instruction explaining that it must "determine from the overall circumstances of the defendant's intoxication or the manner in which he drove, or both, whether his conduct constituted gross negligence." Id.

On appeal from convictions on all three counts, the defendant contended that gross negligence must be predicated upon the facts surrounding the driving only, citing *Stanley* and *McNiece.*

The court initially acknowledged the holding in *McNiece* that "something in addition" to intoxication must be shown to constitute the requisite gross negligence. That "something in addition,'' however, could be shown by the ''overall manner in which the defendant operated the vehicle, including the circumstances of the defendant's intoxication.'' Id. at 653. Factors to be considered, among others, could be the level of intoxication, defendant's speed in relation to the maximum safe speed, and ignored advice from others not to drive.

Query: In effect, is not the *Conlin* court simply paying lip service to the *McNiece* and *Stanley* rulings? If the prosecution must prove ''something in addition'' to intoxication, and that something must concern operation of the vehicle, is it not circuitous to say that gross negligence can be established by showing ''circumstances of the intoxication,'' such as the ''level of intoxication''?

In *People v. Thinel,* 417 N.W.2d 585 (Mich. App. 1987), on the other hand, the trial court instructed the jury that driving a vehicle while intoxicated constituted gross negligence; the defendant was convicted of involuntary vehicular manslaughter. The appellate court reversed and remanded, holding that the instruction was error: The finding of gross negligence was properly for the jury to determine — that is, a reasonable jury could find no gross negligence even though they believed the defendant to have been intoxicated.

The California Supreme Court subsequently went even further, holding in a gross vehicular manslaughter case that a defendant's *subjective* state of mind is admissible on the admittedly objective issue of gross negligence.

In *People v. Ochoa,* 6 Cal. 4th 1199, 26 Cal. Rptr. 23 (Cal. 1993), the prosecution offered evidence of the defendant's prior conviction for drunk driving, his probationary status at the time of the offense, and his attendance at an alcohol-awareness class. Over the defendant's objection that state of mind was not relevant to the objective issue of gross negligence, the trial court admitted all of this. The appellate court reversed.

Supreme Court Chief Justice Lucas, writing the majority opinion reversing the lower court, initially conceded that the test was an objective one:

> Gross negligence is the exercise of so slight a degree of care as to raise a presumption of conscious indifference to the consequences. . . . The test is objective: whether a reasonable person in

> the defendant's position would have been aware of the risk involved.

The Chief Justice then went on to conclude that state of mind was nonetheless relevant:

> [I]f the evidence showed that the defendant *actually appreciated the risks* involved in a given enterprise, *and nonetheless proceeded* with it, a finding of gross negligence (as opposed to simple negligence) would be appropriate whether or not a reasonable person in defendant's position would have recognized the risk. [Emphasis in original.]

Justice Panelli's dissent in *Ochoa* may offer some useful strategy to counsel representing a client in a vehicular manslaughter case where state of mind is in issue:

> Having thus tipped its hat to precedent, the majority then essentially ignores it. . . . The end result is a test that is no longer truly objective. Rather than evaluating the nature of the defendant's *conduct,* the majority actually evaluates his *subjective awareness of the risk,* as evidenced by his prior conviction for driving under the influence, the terms of his probation, and the warnings he received at an alcohol-awareness class. . . .
>
> In any event, because the majority have declared that a defendant's subjective awareness of the risk is relevant to a charge of vehicular manslaughter with gross negligence, it necessarily follows that a defendant may introduce evidence to show that he was not subjectively aware. To deny the defendant the right to present relevant evidence would create serious problems under the due process clause.

Yet another example of how far the courts are willing to go in obtaining DUI convictions can be found in the recent case of *People v. Smith,* 279 Cal. Rptr. 184 (Cal. App. 1991). In that case, the defendant struck a pedestrian, killing him; the defendant's blood-alcohol level was .17 percent. At the defendant's vehicular manslaughter trial, the judge permitted the admission into evidence of a card that set forth the defendant's conditions of probation for a prior drunk driving offense. On appeal, the court affirmed the conviction, holding that the evidence tended to show his knowledge that he was not supposed to drive after drinking — and that this was relevant to the issue of gross negligence.

As with felony drunk driving, a charge of manslaughter requires a causal connection to be pleaded and proven. Thus, for example, in *State v. McGill,* 326 S.E.2d 345 (N.C. App. 1985), the defendant was convicted of involuntary manslaughter and appealed on the grounds that the prosecution had failed to show a sufficient causal connection between his intoxication and the accident resulting in the deaths of the two victims. The court agreed with the defendant:

> Evidence of driving while intoxicated standing alone will not support an involuntary manslaughter conviction [cites]. . . . [W]hile it is clear that driving while impaired is culpable negligence, in order to convict an impaired driver of involuntary manslaughter based upon his impairment, the state must show that while driving impaired defendant violated some other rule of the road, and that this violation was the proximate cause of the accident. [Id. at 346, 347.]

In *Nugent v. State,* 749 S.W.2d 595 (Tex. App. 1988), the defendant's affirmative defense to the involuntary manslaughter charge was that the conduct of the deceased driver of the other car was a *concurrent cause* of the accident. On appeal, he claimed that the jury instruction contained only an abstract definition of concurrent cause, without any effort to apply this legal concept to the facts of the case. The appellate court reversed and remanded for a new trial:

> We hold that the trial court should have applied the law of concurrent causation to the facts in this case and charged the jury that if they found [decedent's] conduct clearly sufficient to cause the accident and Nugent's clearly insufficient to cause the accident, they should acquit the defendant. [749 S.W.2d at 598.]

In another case addressing the question of admissibility of the conduct or condition of the victim in a vehicular homicide, a Wyoming court held that such evidence properly goes to the issue of causation. *Buckles v. State,* 830 P.2d 702 (Wyo. 1992).

In that case, defendant was convicted of aggravated vehicular homicide after he crashed into the victim's car in an intersection, killing him; the defendant's BAC was .24 percent. On appeal, he argued that the trial judge improperly refused to let him offer evidence that a urinalysis performed on the victim indicated the presence of cocaine. Further, the judge would not permit defense evidence that the victim was waving to a pedestrian and not watching where he was driving. All of this, said the judge, was irrelevant; he instructed the jury that "any negligence on the part of the victim is not a defense."

The appellate court reversed, agreeing with the defendant that such evidence goes to the question of *causation*. The state was required to show beyond a reasonable doubt that the defendant's drunk driving proximately caused the victim's death; while contributory negligence was not a defense to the charge, the victim's inattention and use of cocaine were relevant to the question of whether the defendant caused the death. As the court observed by way of illustration:

> Suppose that [the defendant] had been killed in this collision and [the victim] had survived. After taking him to the hospital, a sample of [the victim's] urine had been taken with the results of the test disclosing the presence of cocaine metabolites. Had [the victim] been charged with aggravated vehicular homicide, the relevancy of this evidence would have been clear. In that scenario, it seems equally clear that the evidence of [the defendant's] intoxication would not have been excluded. [Id. at 706.]

§1.6.3 Murder: DUI with Inferred Malice

Finally, there are those jurisdictions that will view homicide proximately caused by drunk driving as murder — and, conceivably, murder in the first degree.

Some states have enacted statutes providing that murder in the second degree is committed where a death is caused by a "wanton or reckless act," the normally required mental element of malice being inferred from the act. Yet others, however, have gone so far as to designate the offense as first degree murder (e.g., *Norman v. State,* 121 Tex. Crim. 433, 52 S.W.2d 1051 (1932)); usually, the drunken driver must have acted with "utter recklessness or wantonness." Again, this is probably a legal redundancy when dealing with driving while intoxicated. However, the California

Supreme Court has affirmed a prosecutor's right to charge an intoxicated driver involved in a fatal accident with second degree murder. In *People v. Watson,* 30 Cal. 3d 290, 627 P.2d 279 (1981), the court held that the vehicular manslaughter statute was not intended to establish gross negligence as the ceiling for culpability in traffic fatality cases. The requisite *mens rea* of malice, it held, can be implied from the facts where the driver "does an act with a high probability that it will result in death and does it with a base antisocial motive and with a wanton disregard for human life." The court, citing *Taylor v. Superior Court,* 598 P.2d 854 (1979), then commented that

> one who willfully consumes alcoholic beverages to the point of intoxication, knowing that he must operate a motor vehicle, thereby combining sharply impaired physical and mental facilities with a vehicle capable of great force and speed, reasonably may be held to exhibit a conscious disregard of the safety of others. [179 Cal. Rptr. 43, at 50.]

However, the court went on to say that "we do not suggest that the . . . facts conclusively demonstrate implied malice. . . . Moreover, we neither contemplate nor encourage the routine charging of second degree murder in vehicular manslaughter cases."

What constitutes "malice" for purposes of "DUI murder"? One California court has distinguished it from gross negligence by observing that second degree murder (malice) requires "conscious disregard for life," while vehicular manslaughter (gross negligence) requires only a "conscious indifference to the consequences."

> Phrased in everyday language, the state of mind of a person who acts with conscious disregard for life is, "I know my conduct is dangerous to others, but I don't care if someone is hurt or killed." The state of mind of the person who acts with conscious indifference to the consequences is simply, "I don't care what happens." [*People v. Olivas,* 218 Cal. Rptr. 567, 569 (Cal. App. 1985).]

The court found the difference "subtle but nevertheless logical," reasoning that only in the first case is the individual actually aware of the risk created. Query the validity of this distinction.

Trying to apply the reasoning of *Watson* and *Olivas,* a California appellate court in *People v. Mays,* 243 Cal. Rptr. 444 (Cal. App. 1988), held that proof of intoxication and reckless driving does not automatically constitute the "wanton disregard for human life" required for a second degree murder conviction in California. Despite evidence that the defendant had been speeding and passing in an unsafe manner, had crashed with another vehicle after going over the center line, and had tested at .09 and .10 percent, the court ruled that the requisite state of mind had not been proven and accordingly reduced the conviction to the lesser-included offense of vehicular manslaughter.

A disturbing aspect of this trend toward overcharging in the continuing crackdown on drunk driving is the possible use of otherwise inadmissible *prior convictions* to prove the requisite malice. In the case of *People v. McCarnes,* 224 Cal. Rptr. 846 (1986), for example, the prosecution successfully introduced evidence of four prior DUI convictions. The trial judge determined that the highly prejudicial nature of this evidence was substantially outweighed by its probative value on the question of malice. The judge reasoned that the priors were relevant to the issue of whether the defendant "did possess the knowledge that his conduct would endanger the lives of others as well as . . . that he consciously and deliberately disregarded such knowledge." The resulting conviction was affirmed on appeal, the appellate court approving the admission into evidence of the prior convictions on the question of malice.

How far can all of this go? In *People v. Brogna,* 248 Cal. Rptr. 761 (1988), the prosecution was permitted to offer evidence not only of two prior convictions but of the fact that the defendant had attended Alcoholics Anonymous meetings and drunk driving educational programs — all "relevant to prove the accused's awareness of the life threatening risks caused by his conduct."

A note entitled People v. Watson: Drunk Driving Homicide — Murder or Enhanced Manslaughter?, 71 California Law Review 1298 (1983), examines the *Watson* case. The note addresses the issue of when malice should be inferred in a drinking/driving case and makes a convincing argument that drinking and driving ordinarily should not be a basis for inferring malice:

Prior to *Watson,* California law generally did not allow vehicular homicides to be prosecuted as murder, absent application of the felony murder rule or a showing of intent to kill or injure. The reason for this was that an automobile does not ordinarily pose a serious enough threat to human life to warrant inferring malice. In the absence of an intent to injure, only an instrument likely to cause death, such as a weapon, could be the basis for inferring malice. At first this seems illogical, given the fact that 50,000 automobile fatalities occur annually, with about 5,000 of those occurring in California. A look at some statistics however, reveals that use of an automobile does not always give rise to a high probability of causing death.

Approximately one-half of all automobile fatalities are alcohol-related. The probability of a fatal accident occurring rises dramatically as a driver's blood alcohol level increases. "A person with a blood alcohol level of 0.08% poses four times the risk of causing a fatal accident as a person who has not been drinking; at 0.15% the risk is twenty-five times as great." Problem drinkers are involved in two-thirds of the alcohol-related automobile fatalities; the other one-third are caused by social drinkers. Seven percent of all drivers are problem drinkers; sixteen percent are social drinkers. Thus, seven percent of the driving public — the problem drinkers — account for roughly one-third of all automobile fatalities. Excessive speed and reckless driving also contribute to the likelihood of a fatal accident. Because force at impact increases geometrically with a vehicle's speed; excessive speed increases the likelihood that an accident will be fatal; the greater the force the greater the risk of death. Similarly, reckless driving increases the chance that an accident will occur.

While the chances of fatal injury increase drastically as intoxication increases, the actual probability of such injury resulting from a single episode of drunk driving may still be quite small. For example, sober drivers traveled approximately 165.1 billion miles in California in 1981 with "only" 2500 fatalities. Assuming that the average driver covers 12,000 miles per year, the chance of a sober driver becoming involved in an automobile fatality in any one year is approximately two hundredths of one percent. So a driver with a blood alcohol level of 0.15%, who has a chance of being involved in a fatal accident twenty-five times greater than a sober driver, has about a one-half of one percent chance of causing a fatality during any one year. While other factors such as rate of speed, manner of driving, time of day, location, and weather conditions obviously in-

> fluence this probability, the likelihood of inflicting death in any one drunk driving episode may be quite low. The high volume of alcohol-related traffic fatalities is more the result of the large number of drunk drivers, than a high probability of most drunk drivers causing a fatality. [71 California Law Review 1307–1309 (footnotes omitted).]

Counsel should also bear in mind that the death need not have been inflicted on a pedestrian or driver or occupant of another car. The law is quite clear that, for example, should the intoxicated client crash into a telephone pole and kill his own passenger, he could be criminally liable under the manslaughter-murder statutes.

Voluntary intoxication may negate the element of express or implied malice in a vehicular murder charge. In *People v. Whitfield,* 11 Cal. App. 4th 1045, 15 Cal. Rptr. 2d 4 (Cal. App. 1992), review granted, March 8, 1993, for example, the defendant struck another vehicle head-on, killing its driver; his blood-alcohol concentration was .24 percent. At his trial for second degree murder, the defendant offered evidence that individuals with his BAC may lose consciousness. The trial court, however, refused to give a jury instruction on unconsciousness ("If you find that a defendant, while unconscious as a result of voluntary intoxication, killed another human being without intent to kill and without malice aforethought, the crime is involuntary manslaughter").

The appellate court affirmed, holding that evidence of voluntary intoxication is admissible only to negate a specific intent crime — and second degree murder, based upon implied malice, was a general intent offense.

The California Supreme Court affirmed, but held that the lower court misinterpreted the statutory law. "Evidence of voluntary intoxication is admissible with regard to the issue of whether a defendant harbored either express or implied malice," the supreme court said. However, the fact that a driver was unconscious at the time of driving "does not preclude a finding that the defendant harbored malice, because malice may have been formed prior to that time." In Whitfield's case, the jury could properly have concluded from the facts that he acted prior to any unconsciousness with knowledge of the dangerousness of his conduct and a conscious disregard of that knowledge.

§1.7 Civil Liability

> Good laws lead to the making of better ones; bad ones bring about worse.
>
> JEAN JACQUES ROUSSEAU

Normally, operating a motor vehicle in violation of the applicable drunk driving statute will constitute negligence per se and thus establish civil liability if the injuries are proven to be proximately caused by the unlawful conduct. Introduction of proof of violation of a drunk driving statute creates, in most jurisdictions, a rebuttable presumption of negligence. In other words, such proof establishes, without the necessity of producing further evidence, a prima facie case of negligence. (See, e.g., *Temple v. DeMirjian,* 51 Cal. App. 2d 559, 125 P.2d 544 (1942).)

Of course, the reverse does not hold true: Because of the differences in burden of proof — preponderance of the evidence versus proof beyond a reasonable doubt — evidence of civil verdicts of liability premised on drunk driving are not admissible in the course of a criminal prosecution. (See 30 Am. Jur. 2d, Evidence §981, and 46 Am. Jur. 2d, Judgments §620.)

As to independent introduction of proof of intoxication in a civil trial, many of the same considerations that will be discussed in the remainder of the text will hold true. Generally speaking, however, the standards for introduction of evidence of intoxication will tend to be less restrictive in a civil than in a criminal trial; any evidence that is relevant and has a proper foundation probably will be admitted. Whereas chemical evidence may be suppressed in a criminal trial due to constitutional or statutory defects, for example, the same evidence may be held admissible in a civil trial.

A finding of intoxication may have certain effects in civil litigation aside from the issue of establishing negligence. Many jurisdictions have some form of "guest statute" — although the Supreme Court has limited these to situations where the owner-passenger is suing the guest-driver for damages. In such cases, the guest statute's bar against recovery can be avoided if the guest-driver is civilly proven to have engaged in "wilful misconduct." However, the word *wilful* means no more than intentional — done either with knowledge that serious injury probably will result or with a wanton and reckless disregard of the possible results. The mere consumption of liquor would not, of itself, be sufficient to establish wilfulness, but intoxication as defined by the applicable drunk driving statutes would probably constitute such wilfulness.

A second possible effect of establishing intoxication may be the awarding of punitive damages. Some jurisdictions permit an exemplary award over and above the award of general and special damages where the plaintiff has been successful in proving that the defendant was so intoxicated as to act with reckless and wanton disregard for life.

If the party bringing the action for damages was under the influence of alcohol, contributory or comparative negligence will apply. But the defendant's intoxication does not furnish an excuse for his own negligence, nor does it relieve him from exercising the same degree of care required of a sober person under the same circumstances. (See, e.g., *McIntosh v. Standard Oil,* 89 Kan. 289, 131 P. 151 (1913).)

§1.8 Inchoate and Accomplice Liability

> "Write that down," the King said to the jury, and the jury eagerly wrote down all three dates on their slates, and then added them up, and reduced the answer to shillings and pence.
>
> LEWIS CARROLL
> *Alice's Adventures in Wonderland*

Reflecting the continuing DUI "crackdown," a very few jurisdictions have begun to expand criminal liability beyond the act of driving while under the influence or with .08 (or .10) percent blood alcohol. Sanctions are now being sought for *attempting* to commit these offenses or for *aiding and abetting* their commission. Whether this is a trend that will spread to other states, as did the per se laws, remains to be seen.

There is, of course, a positive aspect to the recognition of these new versions of drunk driving: the potential for plea bargaining. In most jurisdictions, an attempt to commit an offense is not punishable in the same way as the commission of the completed offense; the same is usually true for aiding and abetting.

In any event, the statutory language requiring such dire consequences as mandatory jail time and/or license suspension usually refers to the completed offense; an attempt to commit the offense may not trigger these provisions. Bearing this in mind, a negotiated plea to attempted DUI (or to being an accomplice) may be a mutually acceptable alternative to the harsh consequences of a plea "straight up."

§1.8.1 Attempted Drunk Driving

Can an individual be convicted of *attempted* drunk driving? Although it would appear improbable, there is appellate authority upholding such a conviction. In *People v. Garcia,* 214 Cal. App. 3d Supp. 1, 262 Cal. Rptr. 915 (1989), the arresting officer found the defendant sitting behind the wheel of her car, stopped in the fast lane with the flashers on. When the car started to roll backwards, she tried to start the engine; the engine was turning over as the car rolled backwards. She finally stopped the car by shifting into "park." Convicted of attempted DUI, the defendant appealed, arguing that no such crime existed in California. The Appellate Department of the Los Angeles Superior Court disagreed, holding that the provisions of California's statute regarding attempt applied to drunk driving offenses. The court added, however, that it was "not unmindful that there might be some troublesome questions which will have to be resolved in later cases." One of these "troublesome questions" involves the fact that DUI is a *general* intent crime, while an attempt requires a *specific* intent. Thus one troublesome result could be that the specific intent could be negated by the very intoxication in issue — that is, an individual could be too drunk to attempt to drive under the influence, yet be sober enough to accomplish the completed act.

§1.8.2 Accomplice to Drunk Driving

Can an individual be charged with being an *accomplice* to drunk driving? In *State v. Stratton,* 591 A.2d 246 (Me. 1991), the defendant and a friend were drinking together at a bar. When they left, the defendant had his friend drive since the friend was less intoxicated. The two were stopped by the police, and the defendant was taken to a police station where he refused to take a breath test because he had not been driving. He was subsequently charged with operating or attempting to operate a motor vehicle under the influence. At trial, the jury found him guilty as both a principal and an accomplice. On appeal, the court held that the accomplice statute applied to drunk driving offenses, and that the evidence was sufficient for a jury to find both the intent and the solicitation necessary for accomplice liability.

Query: Assuming for the moment the validity of an accomplice theory in drunk driving cases, could not the defendant's intoxication negate the specific intent required to be an accomplice?

§1.9 Affirmative Defenses

> Law, says the judge as he looks down his nose,
> Speaking clearly and most severely,
> Law is as I've told you before,
> Law is as you know I suppose,
> Law is but let me explain it once more,
> Law is The Law.
>
> WYSTAN HUGH AUDEN

The drunk driving offenses — driving under the influence of alcohol and driving with an excessive blood-alcohol concentration — generally have not lent themselves well to the traditional criminal defenses. Lack of intent, for example, is usually held to be irrelevant in view of the strict liability nature of the offenses: specific intent is not required and general intent cannot, perhaps for policy reasons, be negated by voluntary intoxication (this reasoning may not, however, apply in the various felony DUI offenses). Other defenses, such as necessity, duress, or entrapment, are commonly held inapplicable for reasons which can be explained only by the oft-encountered double standard in the drunk driving field.

Nevertheless, counsel will encounter fact patterns which at least arguably fit one of the recognized defenses and he should raise them. One of the most commonly encountered situations, for example, involves the possible defense of *mistake of fact* in a per se prosecution: The defendant honestly and reasonably believed that his BAC was below the prescribed level. See §1.9.4. Yet the defense — an absolute one — is rarely raised or even recognized.

The area of traditional defense doctrines is one that requires the DUI practitioner to be creative and maintain a fresh outlook. The simple fact is that drunk driving is an offense which has only recently emerged from the status of a "glorified traffic ticket" to one of a serious offense with considerable complexity. Counsel must break through the "old thinking," both by revising his own approach to these cases and by educating the judiciary.

§1.9.1 Necessity

In the rare case, counsel may encounter facts constituting the affirmative *defense of "necessity."* Also known as the *"choice of evils" defense,* this involves a situation in which the defendant chooses to commit a crime in order to prevent imminent harm to life or property. Applied to the drunk driving case, this would involve a person who knowingly drives a vehicle while under the influence of alcohol or drugs in order to save someone's life or property from immediate danger. For the defense to apply, the danger must be *immediate;* there must be no viable *alternative* course of action; the defendant usually must *admit* committing the offense; and the driving must occur before the danger has passed. The defense usually raises issues of fact, and these go to the jury for determination.

A California court has set forth what it feels to be the requisites for a defense of necessity in a drunk driving case:

> (1) (Defendant) must have driven while drunk to prevent a significant evil, (2) with no adequate alternative, (3) the harm flowing from intoxicated driving was not disproportionate to the harm avoided, (4) he had a good faith belief it was necessary to expose the public and property to the significant risk of harm inherent in a high speed chase of an intoxicated driver to prevent a greater harm, (5) his objective belief was reasonable under all the circumstances, and (6) he did not substantially contribute to creating the emergency. [*People v. Slack,* 258 Cal. Rptr. 702 (Cal. App. 1989).]

Additionally, the court quoted the United States Supreme Court: "Under any definition of these defenses one principle remains constant: if there was a reasonable, legal alternative to violating the law, 'a chance both to refuse to do the criminal act and also to avoid the threatened harm,' the defenses will fail." *United States v. Bailey,* 444 U.S. 394, 410 (1980).

The defendant in *Slack* claimed he was fleeing across the Mexican border from Tijuana police who had physically abused him in the past. Calling this account "absolutely bizarre," the court held that the facts did not support the defense as a matter of law: The defendant did not adequately show there was no alternative to drunk driving, or that the "emergency" was not the result of his own acts. Additionally, "the risk of vehicular destruction is so great that even the risk of physical assault to the intoxicated person pales in comparison."

On the other hand, an Illinois appellate court in *People v. Allcorn,* 539 N.E.2d 813 (Ill. App. 1989), affirmed a trial court's recision of a license suspension on the grounds that the driver was transporting his fiancée to a dentist's office because of a medical emergency.

For a discussion of the necessity defense as it applies to drunk driving situations, see Yaworsky, Driving While Intoxicated: 'Choice of Evils' Defense That Driving Was Necessary to Protect Life or Property, 64 A.L.R.4th 298 (1988). For another example of the application of the doctrine to a drunk driving case, see *Reeve v. State,* 764 P.2d 324 (Alaska App. 1988).

§1.9.2 Duress

The defense of duress is, like all affirmative defenses in DUI trials, a factual rarity and difficult to use successfully. Somewhat similar to the defense of *necessity* (§1.9.1), establishing a duress defense requires different elements:

1. The defendant drove under the influence of alcohol (or over .08 or .10 percent BAC) in order to avoid serious injury or death;
2. There existed no other alternative;
3. The harm avoided by driving was greater than the harm created;

4. The defendant had a reasonable *and* good faith belief that he had to commit the offense in order to avoid the harm; and
5. The situation of risk was not created by defendant.

§1.9.3 Entrapment

Suppose a police officer asks (or even impliedly forces) an individual to drive a vehicle, and that individual is subsequently arrested for DUI. Would the affirmative defenses of *entrapment* or *duress* be available?

This issue was presented to the New Jersey Supreme Court, with the "double standard" results so common in drunk driving cases. In *State v. Fogarty*, 607 A.2d 624 (N.J. 1992), the defendant asked his brothers at a wedding reception to drive him home because he was intoxicated. In the parking lot, however, the brothers got into a fight, attracting the attention of local police. One of the arriving officers struck a brother with his nightstick; when the defendant asked him to treat his brother less harshly, the officer told him to leave the parking lot. When the defendant did not comply, the officer repeated the order, still wielding his nightstick, and escorted the defendant to his truck. The defendant got in, started the engine — and backed into a police car. He was arrested for drunk driving and was tested at .12 percent BAC.

At trial, the court ruled that the defendant had failed to prove entrapment by a preponderance of the evidence, and the defendant was convicted. On appeal, however, the conviction was reversed and remanded on a theory of "*quasi-entrapment*" — that is, the defendant should be acquitted if he could show that *but for* the officer's order he would not have driven.

Incredibly, the state's supreme court reversed. The statutory defense of entrapment, said the court, applied only to offenses listed under the Criminal Code. Turning to the common-law defense of entrapment, the court held that this was unavailable as well.

The court noted that there are two forms of entrapment: subjective and objective. Subjective entrapment focuses on the mental state of the defendant; it requires a showing that the defendant was not predisposed to commit the offense and that the police planted the idea in his mind. Objective entrapment, in contrast, looks to the conduct of the police: their behavior must be so egregious as to compromise the integrity of the conviction.

According to the facts before the court, the police officer did nothing to plant a criminal plan in the defendant's mind. As to the question of objective entrapment (on which the lower court reversal was based), the supreme court found that the lower court had altered the defense by injecting a "but for" test and injecting the defendant's state of mind into the formula. Not only was this irrelevant to the question of police behavior, but it "opened the door" to fabricated excuses: "Obviously, if the law were to permit [drunk drivers] to offer as a defense that they drove only because they reasonably feared that telling the police that they were drunk might lead to arrest, the invitation to offer a pretext would be clear." 607 A.2d at 629.

The court concluded its analysis by observing that driving under the influence was a strict liability offense: state of mind was not relevant. In an exhibition of twisted logic, the court reasoned that state of mind was likely to be impaired in a DUI case anyway. To allow a defendant to decide whether he should drive is absurd: The more intoxicated he is, the more likely he is to decide that it is reasonable to drive.

The court then (probably correctly) characterized the defendant's claim as more akin to a *duress* defense than one of entrapment — and dismissed that as well:

> [N]o one ordered the defendant to get drunk and no one ordered defendant to drive drunk. The police did not coerce defendant into driving his vehicle through use or threats of violence. The police officer merely ordered defendant to get in his truck and leave the scene of the fight. That does not constitute duress. [Id. at 631.]

See also *State v. Fletcher,* 792 S.W.2d 395 (Mo. App. 1990), where the court held that entrapment was not available as a defense "as to any crime which involves . . . placing in danger a person other than the person perpetuating the entrapment." The court reasoned that the defendant placed the general public in danger by driving while intoxicated. Query, however, the logic of the court's abstract conclusion: Cannot the commission of most crimes — robbing a store, for example, or selling dangerous drugs — be said to be potentially dangerous to the general public? A reasonable application of the concept would seem to be that the defense of entrapment is not available where there is an identifiable danger to a *specific* person.

In *Adams v. State,* 585 So. 2d 161 (Ala. 1991), the defense of entrapment failed because the defendant was unable to prove that the officer knew he was intoxicated and that the defendant would not have driven if it were not for the officer's actions. But see *State v. Lechti,* 367 N.W.2d 138 (Neb. 1985), where the court held that a defendant who drives in response to the lawful order of a law enforcement officer engages in privileged conduct and may not be prosecuted for his actions.

§1.9.4 Mistake of Fact

In an appropriate case involving a per se charge, counsel should consider asking for a *mistake of fact* jury instruction. Such a case would exist where the defendant honestly and reasonably believed that his blood-alcohol concentration was below the legal limit.

This is particularly true where the trial court has denied counsel's request for an instruction that the defendant is competent to assess his own BAC: If he is *not* competent, then he could easily be mistaken about the blood-alcohol level. In fact, both instructions should be requested in a per se case, since even a person competent to determine such matters can make a good faith mistake.

Mistake of fact is, of course, generally considered to be a complete defense to criminal conduct. The prevailing law is as follows:

> It may be stated as a general rule (subject, however, to exceptions in certain cases) that mistake of fact will disprove a criminal charge if the mistaken belief is (a) honestly entertained, (b) based upon reasonable grounds and (c) of such a nature that the conduct would have been lawful and proper had the facts been as they were reasonably supposed to be. [R. M. Perkins and R. N. Boyce, Criminal Law 1045 (3d ed. 1982).]

Certainly, the defendant who honestly believes he has not consumed enough alcohol to have over .10 percent alcohol in his blood would qualify: The belief is probably a reasonable one, unless he has admitted to drinking large amounts of liquor, and his conduct would not have been in violation of the per se law "had the facts been as they were reasonably supposed to be."

The following instruction is taken from California Jury Instructions, Criminal 138 (1979). Although it is a general use instruction, there appears to be no reason why it could not be used in a per se drunk driving case.

> IGNORANCE OR MISTAKE OF FACT
>
> An act committed or an omission made under an ignorance or mistake of fact which disproves any criminal intent is not a crime.
>
> Thus a person is not guilty of a crime if he commits an act or omits to act under an honest and reasonable belief in the existence of certain facts and circumstances which, if true, would make such act or omission lawful.

The instruction can, of course, be rephrased to fit the facts of a per se trial.

§1.9.5 Involuntary Intoxication

What if an individual drinks from a punch bowl at a party — not knowing that the punch has been secretly "spiked" by a prankster — and is later pulled over by a police officer? What if another person takes a medication prescribed by his doctor — without being told that it will cause impairment of his driving abilities — and is subsequently arrested for driving under the influence of drugs? Are these people guilty of DUI — or can they assert the affirmative defense of *involuntary intoxication*?

The various states have taken different approaches to the applicability of the involuntary-intoxication defense to DUI. Some take the position that this is a "strict liability" offense. See, e.g., *State v. Pistole,* 476 N.E.2d 366. Others permit the involuntary-intoxication defense only where the intoxication was caused by use of force or threat of force from a second party. A few, however, recognize the defense on the grounds that some *mens rea* must exist in any crime. See, e.g., *State v. Wallace,* 439 N.E.2d 851.

For an interesting discussion of the defense, see noted Miami DUI attorney Richard Essen's article, Involuntary Intoxication: A Viable DWI Defense?, 3(9) DWI Journal 1 (Sept. 1998).

§1.9.6 Insanity (Alcohol Abuse)

Is insanity a defense to a drunk driving charge? At least one defendant has successfully argued that chronic alcohol abuse resulted in a form of mental disease that rendered him unable to resist drinking. *State v. Chapman,* 418 N.W.2d 659 (Mich. App. 1987). But this is very clearly a minority view. See, *State v. Burroughs,* 729 S.W.2d 571 (Mo. App. 1987); *Crusoe v. State,* 239 So. 2d 147 (Fla. App. 1970).

The defense may depend upon the jurisdiction's definition of insanity. If the defendant suffered from organic brain damage caused by alcoholism such that he was no longer able to distinguish right from wrong, the defense may lie in a state applying the traditional *McNaughten* standard. Similarly, if acute alcoholism constituted an addiction such that the defendant was unable to resist a compulsion to drink, the defense might apply in an "irresistable impulse" jurisdiction — assuming, perhaps, proof of a coexistent inability to refrain from driving.

2

THE SENTENCE

§2.0 *Sentencing in the DUI Case*

> Only the man who has enough good in him to feel the justice of the penalty can be punished; the others can only be hurt.
>
> WILLIAM ERNEST HOCKING

Punishment in drunk driving cases has become both more severe and more complex in recent years, particularly when viewed in the context of parallel driver's license suspension/revocation proceedings. Sentence enhancements now exist for prior convictions, refusal to submit to chemical testing, excessive speed, unusually high blood-alcohol levels, and the presence of children in the vehicle, to name the most common examples. New approaches to mandatory "rehabilitative" alcohol education are being tried. Many states, spurred on by the federal government, are requiring the mandatory installation of *ignition interlock devices.* Some jurisdictions have passed laws permitting or requiring the temporary impound of a defendant's vehicle or, in some cases, its confiscation and sale. So-called "stop-and-snatch" laws have been widely enacted, permitting the arresting officer to immediately confiscate the driver's license and serve a notice of suspension (the suspect is apparently presumed to be guilty).

At the same time, for better or worse, the increasing imposition of federal standards has resulted in sentencing that is gradually becoming more uniform throughout the states. Counsel can expect to see their local sentencing guidelines change in coming years as federal presence in the field increases.

In most drunk driving cases, the provisions of a sentence will involve at least some or all of the following:

1. Fine
2. Jail time
3. Suspension, restriction, or revocation of license
4. Attendance at drunk driving classes
5. Probation (supervised or informal)

The defendant probably will be most concerned with the possibility of having to serve a jail sentence, if even for only a day or two. Secondarily, he will be worried about the effects on his job of losing his driver's license. (The third most important effect of a guilty plea may be one not involving the courts: increased insurance premiums.)

Should counsel decide that entering a plea in a given case is preferable to the risks of trial, he should make every effort to determine, prior to the plea, what sentence the judge intends to impose. In this way, counsel can prepare his client for what is coming, avoiding the shock of having it handed down from the bench in open court. Further, the client will have made the necessary preparations at home and at his workplace should a short jail sentence be imposed.

In most cases, the judge will advise counsel of his intended sentence should a plea be entered, if for no other reason than to encourage counsel to enter a guilty plea rather than take the court's time with motions and trial. There are, however, those judges who will refuse to commit themselves. With these individuals, counsel may be forced to play a game of Russian roulette. Even these judges may buckle when confronted with the alternative of time-consuming motions and a possible trial; having such a choice tactfully presented by defense counsel, the judge may well offer to divulge the intended sentence.

Still other judges will refuse to commit themselves to a sentence until they have had an opportunity to review a report from the probation department, setting forth the details of the offense, the defendant's record, and intimate details of his present and past private and professional life. Again, there is some risk involved in pleading blindly in this manner. Of course, counsel will have a pretty good idea of how favorable or unfavorable such a report will turn out, and he certainly should contact the probation officer and ensure favorable input of information, letters of reference, etc. The end result, however, still remains an unknown.

There are two possible ways of avoiding this risk. First, counsel should consider requesting a *pre-plea* probation report — that is, having the court order a probation department investigation and report before a plea is entered. Once the court has considered the report, it may be willing to commit itself as to sentencing before taking the plea. To entice the court into such a procedure, counsel should represent to the court that his client would plead guilty should the court's intended sentence after reading the report involve, for example, no jail time.

The second possible procedure is similar: Counsel enters a plea of guilty after obtaining an agreement with the court that, should it decide to impose jail time, for example, after reading the report, counsel would be free to withdraw the previously entered plea and proceed to trial. In both instances, both counsel's client and the judge are protected: The client avoids the blind chance of a harsh sentence, and the court avoids sentencing too leniently through lack of information.

It is not uncommon to find oneself in the awkward position of representing a client who is being interviewed by a probation officer or other individual for a pre-sentence or pre-plea report. If it is a pre-plea report, the client should be instructed to make no incriminating statements to the probation officer *unless* there is an agreement with the court that no such statements will be used in any way should the matter proceed to trial.

But what if the interview takes place *after* a plea? Is the defendant required to make statements that could result in a more severe sentence? An Illinois appellate court has held that a defendant convicted of drunk driving could refuse a court order to cooperate in an "alcohol evaluation" interview. In *People v. Baker,* 511 N.E.2d 219 (Ill. App. 1987), the court held that the privilege against self-incrimination protected the defendant from giving "testimony which is relevant to imposing sentence for an offense of which he has already been found guilty." 511 N.E.2d at 221. Furthermore, because it would be burdensome to separately adjudicate the Fifth Amendment aspects of each and every question asked at the alcohol evaluation, the court held that the defendant may simply refuse to take part in the procedure at all as long as he asserts his privilege against self-incrimination as the reason.

In the majority of cases, the sentences in similar circumstances within a given jurisdiction will be fairly uniform, and counsel will understand and be able to predict a given court's practices. A first offender, for example, may be fined $1,000 and placed on probation for three years. If a non-injury accident was involved or there was an altercation with the arresting officer, 10 days of jail may be added. If the defendant is a second offender, 5 days may be tacked on; if a third offender, 30 days, and so on. This practice ensures uniformity of treatment, facilitates court procedures, and avoids the necessity for counsel to subject his client to the risks of an unknown sentence. On the other hand, this blanket sentencing also ignores the individual differences from case to case, resulting in expediency at the expense of justice.

Counsel should be thoroughly familiar with any legislative provisions relevant to the possible sentence that could apply to his client. Most states have mandatory provisions for repeat offenders, for example. These laws typically provide that an accelerating number of days of jail *must* be imposed on each successive conviction for drunk driving. On the other hand, a few states have recognized that repeat offenders are often alcoholics and should not be treated as criminals; appropriate treatment is statutorily authorized in lieu of jail time. Similarly, the applicable laws relevant to driver's license suspension or revocation should be studied; if a "point-count" system is used, the defendant's prior driving record must be reviewed.

§2.0.1 Ignition-Interlock Devices

One of the many recent innovations in the DUI field is the "ignition interlock," a device that prevents a driver from starting a vehicle without first breathing into a primitive breath analyzing device and getting a negative reading. Many courts are now beginning to require the installation and use of these instruments as a condition of probation after a drunk driving conviction.

As ignition interlocks become increasingly popular across the country, a number of manufacturers are beginning to produce the devices. The first of these were the Guardian Interlock and the Autosense Breath Alcohol Analyzer. These have recently been followed by the Safety Interlock (Safety Interlock, Inc., Carmel, California), the Lion Analytics VBM (Lion Analytics Limited, New South Wales, Australia), and the Lincoln Co-Driver (Lincoln Research Limited, Auckland, New Zealand); in addition, two prototypes have recently undergone testing — the Soberlyzer and the Alcohol Breath Ignition Controller.

How effective are these new devices? According to a study conducted by the National Highway Traffic Safety Administration, most of these products are not very accurate at low (.05 percent) and moderate (.08 percent) blood-alcohol levels. See Workshop on In-Vehicle Alcohol Test Devices, NHTSA DOT HS-807-145 (Sept. 1986).

California instituted a statewide "Mandatory Ignition Interlock Device" (IID) program as of July 1, 1993. Under the provisions of the program, individuals convicted of drunk driving within seven years of a previous drunk driving conviction are required to install one of the devices on any vehicle he owns or operates. The device, which costs up to $700, is installed on the dashboard; it will permit the vehicle to start only if there is a captured breath sample of less than .02 percent.

There are exceptions to the IID requirement, the broadest being where installation would not be "in the interests of justice." If the person cannot afford the installation, he may be given community service to perform instead. Another exception exists where the defendant has a physician's report indicating that a medical problem precludes sufficient breath strength for a valid sample.

If an individual must drive a vehicle as part of his job and the vehicle is wholly owned and controlled by the employer, an IID is not required. However, the employer must be notified by the individual that his license has been restricted and the individual must carry proof of that notification while driving.

§2.0.2 Vehicle Impound or Forfeiture

A small but increasing number of states are enacting legislation permitting the temporary impounding of the vehicle used by a convicted drunk driver — or even its confiscation and eventual sale.

The impound is typically for a period of 30 days, with the

costs of storage paid by the defendant. California's statute, for example, gives the court discretion to impound the car at the defendant's expense for up to 30 days as an additional punishment; if a prior conviction is proven or admitted, however, the court *must* order it impounded — unless "the interests of justice" dictate otherwise. This latter escape hatch, commonly employed in that state, is applied to situations where the loss of the car would cause loss of employment or other severe hardship.

The more drastic step of confiscation and sale is often couched in terms of declaring the vehicle a *nuisance*. Again, as an example, California's applicable statute provides that the sentencing judge *may* declare the car a nuisance and have it seized and sold at auction where the defendant is the registered owner and the offense involves (1) vehicular manslaughter, (2) drunk driving with two prior convictions, or (3) felony drunk driving with one prior conviction.

These new and draconian measures raise a host of questions that have yet to be addressed. What of the interests of joint owners? Of a spouse's community property interest in the vehicle? Can the car be sold if it is worth more than the maximum fine authorized by law? Is there a violation of equal protection: Are not defendants who owned the vehicles being treated more harshly than defendants who were renting or borrowing them? Why should one defendant be "fined" a new Mercedes-Benz, while another is "fined" a worthless old Volkswagen? Where is the connection to culpability?

Another possible issue where a vehicle has been impounded after a DUI arrest is *double jeopardy* (see §3.0.1 relating to double jeopardy in the context of license suspensions). If the impoundment appears punitive in nature — if it is subject to being returned to the arrestee after release from custody, for example, or if specific periods of time are authorized — then it would seem to follow that the individual has already been punished once (i.e., placed in jeopardy) for the offense. This may occur in the context of a DUI arrest and/or an arrest for driving with a suspended license.

These and other questions will undoubtedly be argued as the constitutionality of these confiscation statutes are challenged. And, undoubtedly, legislatures will continue to fall over themselves in the rush to show voters how tough they are on drunk drivers.

§2.0.3 Deportation Consequences

Counsel should be aware of the possible consequences of a DUI conviction should his client not be a citizen of the United States — at least, if the charge is a felony or punishable by at least one year incarceration.

Federal law currently requires the mandatory deportation of any non-citizen who is convicted of an "aggravated felony." 8 U.S.C. §1101(a)(42)(F). The deportation will occur regardless of the legal status of the non-citizen, and it will be permanent: The individual is barred from ever re-entering. These deportation provisions were amended in 1996 to redefine "aggravated felony" to include any "crime of violence . . . for which the term of imprisonment [is] at least one year." 18 U.S.C. §16 defines "crime of violence" to include a felony that "involves a substantial risk that physical force against the person or property of another may be used in the course of committing the offense." And a 1996 amendment made actual imprisonment unnecessary: A suspended sentence of one year or more is enough.

In 1998, the Board of Immigration Appeals rendered a decision in which it addressed the issue: Is a felony DUI conviction an "aggravated felony"? The case involved a permanent resident who was convicted of DUI while his license was suspended — a felony under Arizona law — and sentenced to four months in jail; a subsequent probation violation resulted in a two-and-one-half-year prison sentence. In *In re Magallanes-Garcia* (No. 3341), the Board ruled that this constituted an "aggravated felony," citing media reports that drunk drivers cause over 25,000 deaths a year, and ordered permanent deportation.

Responding to this decision, the Immigration and Naturalization Service immediately instituted "Operation Last Call" and arrested over 500 individuals in Texas for deportation based upon past DUI convictions.

This raises serious concerns for the attorney representing any client charged with *any* drunk driving offense. Initially, it should not be automatically assumed that the client is an American citizen; the failure to make inquiry could be malpractice grounds. Once it is determined that the client is a non-citizen, the following questions should be considered:

1. If a plea or conviction is for a felony, is it possible to get a sentence of less than one year? Would the judge and/or prosecutor consider a 364-day sentence — which may be preferable to the client than a two-year suspended sentence.
2. What is the likelihood of the client being convicted in the future for drunk driving, possibly triggering a "three-strikes" felony (see §1.6.1)? He should at least be advised of this possible consequence before any plea bargain is concluded.
3. If the jurisdiction can impose a sentence of one year or more on a misdemeanor (in Minnesota, for example, an "enhanced gross misdemeanor" can be punished by two years in prison), can this expose the client to deportation? It is unclear whether such a misdemeanor would qualify as a "crime of violence," as the definition of that offense may mean it has to be a felony under federal law, not state law.

§2.1 *Statutory Enhancements: Refusal, Speed, and Other Factors*

> We must not make a scarecrow of the law,
> Setting it up to fear the birds of prey,
> And let it keep one shape, till custom make it
> Their perch and not their terror.
>
> William Shakespeare
> *Twelfth Night*

The constantly accelerating (and politically popular) DUI "crackdown," together with the increasing carrot-and-stick presence of the U.S. Department of Transportation, has resulted in a wave of new and ever-harsher approaches to punishment in drunk driving cases. Fines and jail terms have been raised for the basic offense of driving under the influence of alcohol and/or driving with .08 or .10 percent blood-alcohol concentration. License restrictions, suspensions, and revocations are more extensive and easier to obtain. The impact of prior convictions has raised terms of incarceration to felony levels.

One facet of this "get tough" approach has been a proliferation of sentence *enhancements:* statutes providing for increased penalties where specific criteria exist. While this varies from jurisdiction to jurisdiction, there are a number of such enhancing grounds that appear likely to continue to spread across the country. These include:

High blood-alcohol concentration. Commonly, there is a mandatory higher jail sentence where the BAC is .20 percent or higher.

Refusal to submit to chemical testing. The increased jail term for refusing is often in addition to the administrative suspension for refusing. (Note: If the jurisdiction punishes refusal as a substantive offense, it cannot also use the refusal as an enhancement in the DUI/per se case, as this would constitute multiple punishment.)

Speeding and/or reckless driving. This enhancement involves driving in excess of a specified speed while under the influence of alcohol or over .08/.10 percent BAC. California, for example, imposes the enhancement where the defendant drove 20 mph over the speed limit on a surface street or 30 mph over the limit on a freeway.

Child endangerment. Increased penalties are imposed where there is a minor passenger in the vehicle at the time of the drunk driving. Commonly, this is defined as an individual under the age of 14.

Accident or injury. In many jurisdictions, the existence of property damage can trigger a more severe sentence; in others, it will define a different offense. Where there is personal injury involved, most jurisdictions elevate the offense to felony status (see §1.6).

The prosecution must, of course, *plead* the enhancements and do it with specificity — that is, with specifically alleged facts, rather than merely in the statutory language. And the facts must be independently proven beyond a reasonable doubt; in a jury trial this is usually done with special findings of fact.

Where the enhancement has the potential to emotionally bias the jury against the defendant on the drunk driving charge itself, and proof appears to be easily accomplished, counsel should consider admitting the allegation. Thus, for example, where there is an easily proven prior conviction or where there is a small child in the vehicle, the allegation should be admitted prior to trial. Since the fact is no longer in issue, it can be argued, admission of evidence concerning the allegation should not be permitted.

It may be that the defendant wishes to plead guilty to the drunk driving charge, but contest the enhancement(s). This can be accomplished in a number of ways, such as by submitting the matter on the arrest report or by an evidentiary hearing. Where the alleged enhancement is for excessive blood alcohol, for example, counsel may wish to plead to the per se offense but contest the issue of whether the BAC was over .20 percent at the time of driving.

This procedure, of course, suggests possibilities for plea bargaining. Dropping an enhancement in exchange for a plea to the drunk driving charge is the obvious approach. But in many cases the prosecution, for perhaps political reasons, is unwilling to be seen as "soft" on DUI. In this situation, counsel might consider an arrangement with the prosecutor and the judge: a plea of guilty, with the enhancement submitted on the arrest report — and an implicit understanding that the court will find insufficient evidence to sustain the allegation. This can have particularly beneficial consequences for the client where the enhancement involves facts that give rise to an administrative license suspension: A judicial finding on that fact should be binding on the motor vehicle agency (see discussion of *collateral estoppel* in §3.1.2).

§2.1.0 Prior Convictions

In many cases, counsel will be confronted with a client charged with drunk driving who has had an earlier conviction for the same offense. In such situations, almost all states have statutes that provide for increased penalties — mandatory jail time, suspension of driver's license, higher fines, formal probation, etc. These statutory mandates for subsequent convictions significantly raise the stakes in defending a client against a charge of driving under the influence of alcohol: Loss of a license can result in the loss of a job, and a period of time in jail can be a traumatic experience for someone not hardened to the system.

At trial, counsel will have to make a difficult decision. Either he must admit the prior conviction charged in the complaint, thus ensuring a more severe sentence should his client be convicted of the pending charge, or he must deny the prior conviction and have the damaging evidence of earlier drunk driving presented to the jury.

There is, however, a procedure available to defense counsel whereby the risks at trial and the harsh mandatory sentencing provisions can be avoided: moving to strike the prior conviction as having been unconstitutionally obtained. This pre-trial motion to have the prior convictions declared unconstitutional has generally been limited to convictions obtained as the result of a plea. If, however, the conviction was obtained as a result of a trial wherein significant constitutional rights of the client were violated, there is no reason why this may not be asserted as a ground for striking the prior conviction, independent of any appeals or lack of appeals from that conviction.

Counsel should be aware not only of the *dates* of the priors and the time requirements of the applicable statutes, but also whether they refer to *commission* or *conviction*. Thus, for example, in *Hewitt v. Commonwealth*, 541 A.2d 1183 (Pa. Commw. 1988), a driver's license was revoked on "habitual offender" grounds — that is, he had three priors. On appeal, the driver claimed that the period of time between his first and third convictions exceeded the statutory five years. However, the appellate court held that "habitual offender status is attained when the *commission* of three specified offenses occurs within the statutory five-year period, even if the date of *conviction* for one of the offenses falls outside that period."

For a discussion of motions to strike prior convictions as unconstitutionally obtained, see §§9.0.1 *et seq.*

§2.2 *Alternative Sentencing*

> It is one thing to show a man he is in error, and another to put him in possession of the truth.
>
> JOHN LOCKE

The legislatures of many states are beginning to recognize that the drunk driver is often simply an alcoholic, an individual suffering from a condition that is increasingly recognized as a disease. Treating such a person as a criminal is neither fair to him nor beneficial to society. The harsh sentence — including the possible loss of his job through the loss of his driver's license or his absence from work due to a jail sentence — may only aggravate the person's need for alcohol, increasing the risks to society of another drunken driving incident. In recognition of this, some states have passed laws offering rehabilitation programs of various types as an alternative to the usual penal sanctions. These programs avoid the normal imposition of jail sentences and/or suspension or revocation of driver's licenses.

In fact, the failure of the court to consider alternative sentencing schemes may constitute an abuse of judicial discretion. In an interesting West Virginia case, for example, a DUI defendant was sentenced to six months in jail and thereafter petitioned the circuit court for an alternative sentence of work release and/or electronically monitored confinement at home. The petition was denied. On further appeal, the state supreme court reversed and remanded for a reconsideration of the sentence because the trial judge had not adequately considered less restrictive alternatives to incarceration. The court reasoned that sentencing statutes were remedial in nature and should be construed liberally to accomplish the purpose for which they were enacted. *State v. Kerns,* 394 S.E.2d 532 (1990).

Even if there are no statutes providing for rehabilitative programs in counsel's state, every effort should be made in an appropriate case to convince the court that a rehabilitative sentence would be more productive to society than a punitive one. The majority of judges will be receptive to such a suggestion when it is properly presented, particularly where effective programs are functioning in the area (and there are few places where Alcoholics Anonymous, at least, is not operating). If no such programs are available, counsel should consider the possibility, again in appropriate cases, of individual psychiatric counseling. The possibilities are endless for formulating rehabilitative programs; in fact, the primary limitation is the creativity of counsel himself.

Many attorneys will object to pursuing rehabilitation for their clients, arguing that they are not social workers but attorneys: Their job is to either win an acquittal or gain the best possible sentence, and the client's personal problems are his own. This attitude is archaic, denies the ethical obligation of an attorney to his client, and ignores the fact that the best possible sentence may be a rehabilitative program. Counsel can render a far greater service to his client by arranging such a program than by simply negotiating a plea bargain or even by winning an acquittal. If the client is truly an alcoholic, he undoubtedly will be arrested for drunk driving again, perhaps after running down a child on a bicycle.

The types of formal programs designed specifically for drunk driving offenders vary widely. The "first offender" programs, for example, are geared to just that: the individual who has never been arrested or convicted before for the offense. The programs proceed on the assumption that no alcoholism is involved and are geared to an educational format: classroom lectures, "scare visits" to alcoholic wards and/or automobile accident wards of hospitals, etc. The "multiple offender" programs, on the other hand, are usually oriented more toward dealing with a serious drinking problem and may involve group rap sessions, individual counselling, or even medical treatment.

The procedures for qualifying for an existing program will vary. Unless a statute provides for general application of the program, there will be some screening process, usually in the form of a questionnaire or an interview. For first offender programs, the problem drinker will be identified and declared ineligible. For the repeat offender programs, the procedure is usually designed to screen out individuals who are resistant to rehabilitation — that is, who are not willing to *try* to solve their drinking problem.

The legal ramifications of the programs must be understood clearly by the defendant and by his attorney. In most cases, the defendant will have pleaded guilty, and attendance at the program will be a condition of probation; if he fails to complete the program satisfactorily, he can be held to be in violation of probation and resentenced accordingly. In other cases, the program envisions a suspension of the charges pending the defendant's attendance at the program. Successful completion of the program, which may involve a year or even longer, will result in a dismissal of the drunk driving charges; failure to complete the program will mean the defendant will find himself back at the arraignment stage again, possibly having been required to admit his guilt during, or as a condition of obtaining, the program.

Counsel therefore should understand clearly what the possible consequences of such programs can be. He should assess the likelihood of his client's successful completion of the course as well as the chances that the client will be arrested for drunk driving before the probationary period is over. If a client is unlikely to complete the program successfully he may be better off simply pleading guilty and taking a 5-day jail sentence than risking a 60-day sentence for failing in the program.

Another factor to consider is the time and expense involved in going through a rehabilitation program. Each program varies, of course, but some can be quite expensive and time-consuming. The more elaborate ones can cost over $1,000 and involve many days of attendance over an extended period. Quite simply, the client may prefer the penal alternatives.

Do such probationary supervision or educational programs decrease the likelihood that a convicted drunk driver will be arrested again? In an article entitled Rehabilitative Sanctions for Drunk Driving: An Experimental Evaluation, appearing in the Journal of Research in Crime and Delinquency 55 (January 1983), the results of a probation follow-up project in Tennessee were analyzed. Over 4,000 persons arrested for DWI in Memphis were classified either as social or problem drinkers and randomly assigned to one of four treatments: no treatment (control group), probation supervision, education/therapy, or supervision plus education/therapy. Each client was followed for at least two years after referral to the project. The purpose of the follow-up was to find out whether the type of treatment received affected the number of rearrests for DWI or for other misdemeanors and felonies. The programs selected were clearly intended to rehabilitate offenders and not to punish them. However, previous studies had shown that even treatments designed to rehabilitate may be perceived as punishment and that any treatment that is so perceived *is* punishment.

The persons selected had no prior DWI convictions and were

residents of Shelby County (Memphis) so that they would be available for follow-up. The sample group excluded individuals with serious health problems, including health problems associated with alcohol. Offenders were placed by the court on either diversion or probation, and participation in the treatment assigned by the project was a mandatory condition of either probation or diversion. A person with no prior convictions for any misdemeanor or felony was qualified for the diversion program.

The hypothesis of the study was that clients receiving probation supervision (either with or without education/therapy) should have fewer arrests for non-DWI offenses as well as for DWI offenses if probation supervision is an effective means of preventing criminal recidivism.

For social drinkers, the group having the lowest rate of recidivism was the control group that had received no treatment or supervision. For problem drinkers, the group having the lowest rate of recidivism was the group that received supervision and education/therapy, closely followed by the control group that had received no treatment or supervision. Another startling discovery was a significant increase in DWI arrests for social drinkers on diversion who were assigned to supervised groups.

The author of the article, Robert T. Holden, concludes that the supervision and education/therapy programs were not effective in reducing recidivism. He states several possible reasons for that conclusion: (1) The programs clearly were inappropriate for a large proportion of the project's clients; (2) many of the project's clients appeared to drive while drunk as part of a general pattern of criminal deviance; (3) the treatment programs were too weak to have any effects on recidivism; and (4) randomly assigned treatments have been a relatively unimportant aspect of the sanctioning process. He concludes, thus, for persons with no prior arrest experience, that the procedural sanctions may have had a much greater effect than any of the treatment programs could have had. For experienced offenders, neither the procedural sanctions nor the treatment programs could be expected to have had much effect. In either case it would have made little difference which treatment was assigned.

No clear direction for future policy emerges from this study. If only cost-effectiveness is considered, the control treatment (release following conviction) is superior to the other treatments because it costs essentially nothing. Otherwise many education programs, particularly those developed in Memphis, are relatively inexpensive and can be financed by a fee charged to the participants. Another alternative is to try more punitive sanctions, but, according to Holden, evaluation of highly punitive sanctions is difficult. A final thought from the authors: "The best solution to the drunk driving problem does not lie in post-conviction treatments at all, but rather in education of the public."

Counsel may wish to consider suggesting to the court the possibility of community work as an alternative to a jail sentence or license suspension. He may, for example, argue that donating 50 hours of the defendant's time to the local Red Cross or YMCA as a condition of probation will provide a greater benefit to the community than the harsher, and more expensive to the taxpayers of the community, alternative of incarceration. This can be made particularly attractive where the defendant has a skill that can be of use to local agencies, such as carpentry, athletics, medicine, plumbing, teaching, etc. Again, counsel will often find that he is limited primarily by his own creativity in trying to structure a sentence that is both helpful to his client and acceptable to the court.

As yet another alternative to the increasingly prevalent jail sentence, counsel might also consider an innovative approach used in Oregon to alleviate crowded jail conditions. Rather than incarcerating certain individuals convicted of drunk driving, the court orders them to stay in their homes under "house arrest." This restriction is monitored by electronic surveillance: A five-ounce signaling device, attached to the individual's leg, will signal a central computer if he goes more than 200 feet from a monitor. The computer can be programmed to accommodate specific schedules — for example, to permit the subject to go to his job at specific times, or to attend alcohol treatment sessions.

§2.3 *Multiple Punishment*

> Extreme justice is extreme injustice.
>
> MARCUS CICERO

Many jurisdictions have enacted laws prohibiting a prosecuting agency from punishing a defendant for separate violations arising out of one act or a single course of conduct. For example, an overzealous prosecutor might try to charge a defendant not only with driving for two or three blocks under the influence of alcohol but also with speeding, reckless driving (i.e., driving while intoxicated), weaving across a center lane marker, making an unsafe lane change (i.e., weaving), and having an open container of alcoholic beverage in the vehicle.

The issue of multiple punishment should be distinguished from that of *double jeopardy*. Although the issues are obviously related, and courts continue to confuse the two in applying legal concepts, they are different. Multiple punishment concerns a single act that is concurrently prosecuted and punished as two separate criminal offenses; double jeopardy is generally understood to refer to *consecutive* prosecution (see §8.3.2).

Unfortunately, there appears to be no uniform standard that can be applied to determine whether the defendant is being punished repeatedly for what amounts to one offense. The issue to be decided by the court is whether the charges can be separated into distinct acts or whether they constitute a single act or continuing course of criminal conduct. To put it another way: Is there a substantial relationship between the conduct constituting each separate offense?

Each case must be assessed on its own facts and by applying the jurisdiction's case law. In *State v. Johnson,* 273 Minn. 394, 141 N.W.2d 517 (1966), for example, the court concluded that a defendant could not be charged with both drunk driving and having crossed a center line while engaged in that drunk driving. And in *People v. Moore,* 20 Cal. App. 3d 444, 97 Cal. Rptr. 601 (1971), it was held that a defendant could be charged with only one count of felony drunk driving despite the fact that he had injured or killed a number of individuals.

In *State v. Adams,* 744 P.2d 833 (Kan. 1987), the defendant was convicted of DUI and involuntary manslaughter. On appeal, the DUI conviction was reversed: All of the elements of DUI were involved in proving the charge of involuntary manslaughter. In *State v. Hoffman,* 416 N.W.2d 231 (Neb. 1987), the defendant was convicted of drunk driving, motor vehicular homicide, and assault. The drunk driving conviction was reversed as constituting double jeopardy, since it was a lesser-included offense of motor vehicle homicide; the assault conviction was affirmed as it required proof of different elements.

In *Hoag v. State,* 511 So. 2d 401 (Fla. App. 1987), the defendant left the scene of the accident after driving into a group of pedestrians, killing one and injuring four. He was subsequently convicted of manslaughter by driving while intoxicated *and* of manslaughter by culpable negligence. On appeal, the court vacated the culpable negligence conviction, holding that the multiple conviction constituted double jeopardy. The court also vacated four out of five counts of leaving the scene of an accident with injuries on the same grounds.

In *Pennsylvania v. Hernandez,* 488 A.2d 2983 (Pa. 1985), the defendant collided with another vehicle, killing its driver. He was subsequently charged with and convicted of involuntary manslaughter and "homicide by vehicle," and sentenced to 2½-to-5 years for each, to be served consecutively. On appeal, the court vacated the "homicide by vehicle" conviction, holding that it was included in the involuntary manslaughter conviction.

In *Dunlop v. Alaska,* 696 P.2d 687 (Alaska App. 1985), an Alaska appellate court faced the issue of the constitutionality of a state statute authorizing separate punishment for each death arising out of a single criminal incident. The defendant had been convicted of two counts of manslaughter after he hit two pedestrians with his car, killing them both; he was sentenced to consecutive terms of five years on each count. The court held that the statute was in violation of the double jeopardy provision of the Alaska Constitution.

A related problem arises where a defendant is charged with multiple offenses arising out of one act or a single continuing course of conduct. For example, consider the defendant who was arrested for drunk driving after hitting a parked car and running a red light: May he be charged separately, and punished separately, for drunk driving, reckless driving, running a red light, and hit-and-run? Or is it all one continuing act, for which the prosecution can charge only one or two offenses, and for which the defendant can only be punished once?

In most states he can be multiply convicted and punished. In some jurisdictions there exist statutes precluding multiple prosecution and multiple punishment for a single act that is made punishable by different statutes. The question remains, however, as to what constitutes a single act or course of conduct. And once again, the case decisions in this area offer little in the way of uniform guidelines. Each situation apparently must be considered on the basis of its own facts. For what it is worth, the courts tend to speak in terms of "singleness of the conduct" (*State v. Johnson,* 273 Minn. 394, 141 N.W.2d 517 (1966)), "necessarily included offenses" (*People v. Knowles,* 35 Cal. 2d 175, 217 P.2d 1 (1956)), and "singleness of intent and objectives" (*Neal v. California,* 55 Cal. 2d 11, 357 P.2d 839 (1960)). (See also *Fugate v. New Mexico,* 101 N.M. 58, 678 P.2d 686; 101 N.M. 82, 678 P.2d 710 (1984), *aff'd mem.,* 105 S. Ct. 1858 (1984).)

It should be kept in mind that even where multiple convictions for multiple counts in a single prosecution are permitted, mandatory joinder statutes may require the prosecutor to "take all of his shots" at once. Thus subsequent prosecutions for related offenses would be barred.

§2.3.1 Punishment for Both DUI and .08 or .10 Percent Offenses

One recurrent problem with the new per se statutes stems from the common prosecutorial practice of charging a defendant with both the traditional and the per se offenses. Although the defendant may not be punished for both offenses, many jurisdictions have permitted him to be *convicted* of both.

A California case, *People v. Cosko,* 152 Cal. App. 3d 54, 199 Cal. Rptr. 289 (1984), discusses the issue of whether the defendant could be convicted twice under separate subdivisions of the California Vehicle Code. The driver's argument was presented as follows:

> Appellant contends that he was improperly convicted of two counts of driving under the influence, one for violating Vehicle Code section 23153, subdivision (a), and another for violating subdivision (b) of the same section based on one incident. We conclude that the Legislature added the 0.10 percent blood alcohol offense subdivision (subd. b) to facilitate proof of driving under the influence and that it did not intend a single driving under the influence incident to result in two driving under the influence convictions under Vehicle Code section 23153.
>
> We are not concerned with the question of double charging, which is within the prosecutor's discretion, or with double punish-

> ment, which is clearly prohibited by Penal Code section 654. The question of double conviction, however, requires analysis of the legislative intent behind the addition of the 0.10 percent subdivision. [Id. at 290.]

The court concluded that the legislature did not intend that routine driving under the influence convictions would result in two convictions. The court based this opinion on an examination of the legislative history and the sentencing scheme of the statute. The court therefore held:

> The general rule in the case of an improper combination of convictions is that the less serious offense is vacated while the more serious stands. (E.g., *People v. Cole,* supra, 31 Cal. 3d at p.582.) Since neither the under the influence offense nor the 0.10 percent offense is more serious than the other, the determination which conviction should stand is a discretionary matter. [Id. at 291–292.]

The *Cosko* decision was subsequently ordered by the California court not to be published. However, a later case was published. In *People v. Duarte,* 161 Cal. App. 3d 438 (1984), a California appellate court held that a defendant may be convicted under both statutes. However, he may only be punished for one; the judge must choose which one. Technically, punishment for the second conviction is temporarily stayed until after completion of sentence on the first — at which time the stay is made permanent. Also, only one of the convictions may be used as a prior conviction for purposes of enhanced punishment on future DUI convictions.

In *Sering v. State,* 488 N.E.2d 369 (Ind. App. 1986), an Indiana appellate court was faced with a case in which the defendant had been charged with, convicted of, and sentenced for violation of both the state's DUI statute and its .10 percent per se statute.

The court first addressed the issue of whether cumulative punishment had been unconstitutionally imposed, applying the standard of *Blockburger v. United States,* 284 U.S. 299 (1939):

> The applicable rule is that where the same act or transaction constitutes a violation of two distinct statutory provisions, the test to be applied to determine whether there are two offenses or only

> one, is whether each provision requires proof of a fact which the other does not. [*Sering,* 488 N.E.2d at 374.]

The court concluded that the two charges did not constitute the same offense, since the per se statute "has a specific BAC as an element that distinguishes it from the offense of operating a vehicle while intoxicated."

However, the court then turned to Indiana statutes to decide if one offense was necessarily included within the other so that conviction of both would constitute impermissible cumulative conviction and punishment:

> We conclude . . . that operating a vehicle with BAC of .10 percent is a lesser included offense of operating a vehicle while intoxicated because the former offense differs from the latter offense in that a less serious risk of harm to the public interest is required to establish its commission. . . .
>
> [W]e find the legislature did not intend the imposition of cumulative convictions and punishments when the same act constitutes a violation of the two relevant statutory provisions. Therefore, we order the cause remanded with instructions to vacate Sering's conviction and sentence for operating a vehicle with BAC .10 percent. [Id. at 376.]

In *People v. Pena,* 524 N.E.2d 671 (Ill. App. 1988), the defendant was convicted of (1) DUI; (2) driving with .10 percent blood alcohol; (3) reckless driving; (4) eluding a police officer; and (5) three counts of speeding. The appellate court ordered one of the two drunk driving convictions vacated, holding that the defendant could not be convicted of both. The court also ordered the three speeding convictions reduced to one, as they were "based on a single course of conduct."

A Georgia appellate court has taken a similar approach, holding that a defendant could neither be punished for, nor convicted of, both the DUI statute and the per se statute. *Fudge v. State,* 362 S.E.2d 147 (Ga. App. 1987). However, another Georgia court took the opposite approach at almost the same time. In *Tomlin v. State,* 362 S.E.2d 489 (Ga. App. 1987), it was held that the defendant *could* be found guilty of both the DUI charge and the .12 percent charge — although he could only be sentenced on one.

§2.4 Probation Violation Hearings

> If we take habitual drunkards as a class, their heads and their hearts will bear an advantageous comparison with those of any other class. There seems ever to have been a proneness in the brilliant and warm-hearted to fall into this vice. The demon of intemperance ever seems to have delighted in sucking the blood of genius and generosity.
>
> ABRAHAM LINCOLN

Counsel inevitably will be confronted with representing a client at a hearing to determine whether he has violated the terms and conditions of probation imposed in an earlier drunk driving case. Unfortunately, a defendant's rights at such a hearing are considerably less than they would be at a trial. Although he is granted the right to be represented by counsel and to produce evidence in his favor, he may not be given the right to cross-examine the witnesses against him. The procedures and applicable legal safeguards in counsel's jurisdiction should be checked, of course, but in some jurisdictions the court may find a probationer in violation simply on the basis of written reports. Recent rulings, however, should result in this procedure's being considered as a denial of due process.

Another debilitating factor in a probation hearing is that the judge need not find the alleged facts of violation to be true beyond a reasonable doubt. The technical standards vary, but they will usually relate to language such as "preponderance of the evidence" or "substantial likelihood" of truth. And, of course, the trier of fact is the judge, usually the judge who earlier had imposed the probation. There is no right to a jury trial on the issue.

For these reasons, counsel is at a tremendous disadvantage when representing a client at a probation violation hearing: The odds are stacked heavily against him. But there are procedures that can help the situation.

First, violation hearings are often just as amenable to plea bargaining as the drunk driving charge was originally. Counsel is in a weaker position, certainly, but there is room to negotiate and to discuss with the judge the possibilities of alternatives to remanding the client to jail. Here, again, counsel must use his imagination in trying to present to the court an acceptable alternative to a jail sentence, stressing the benefits to society of such an alternative, not to mention the benefit to the court of not having to take the time of conducting a hearing on the violation issue. Extending the probationary period for a year might be suggested, for example, together with imposition of a fine or community service.

A second procedure involves the typical case where the violation consists of the defendant's having been again arrested for drunk driving. There is nothing that requires the judge sitting on the violation to wait until the pending charges on the second drunk driving case are resolved before finding the probationer in violation. The judge is free to find the defendant in violation of the terms of probation and sentence him accordingly long before the trial on the pending charges from which the violation arises. In fact, due to the difference in the legal standards involved, the judge could find the defendant in violation even after an acquittal on the new charges.

To avoid a quick determination of probation violation, and at the same time to effectively convert the "preponderance of the evidence" standard into the more difficult "proof beyond a reasonable doubt" standard, counsel should make every effort to get the probationary judge to suspend proceedings until after the resolution of the pending charges — that is, until after the defendant has either pleaded guilty to the second case or has been acquitted or convicted. The argument should be made that to hold the probation hearing first is simply unfair and a denial of due process in that it coerces the defendant into plea bargaining and adversely affects his ability to prepare for trial. Furthermore, there is a constitutional right to a speedy trial, but no such right to a speedy violation hearing; it would seem to follow that the priority for determination and hearing is more properly the trial first, with the probationary hearing to follow.

Perhaps the best argument that can be made is to appeal to the court's selfish interests by pointing out that inconsistent and embarrassing results can be avoided by holding off the hearing until after resolution of the new case. It could be awkward, after all, for the defendant to be found in violation of probation due to the truth of the allegations in the new charges and then to be acquitted of those charges or have the charges subsequently dismissed by the prosecutor.

Counsel may encounter a so-called sweat-patch test in a probation violation hearing. The sweat-patch test is a method of measuring alcohol consumption over a period of up to three days. A watertight adhesive patch is attached to the skin and absorbs perspiration at a steady rate. The concentration of alcohol in the collected perspiration varies with the amount of alcohol consumed. Over time, the mean blood-alcohol concentration can be determined for the test period.

The sweat-patch test has potential applications in alcohol treatment programs and in court-supervised probation. One drawback to the use of the test, however, has been the difficulty in obtaining an alcohol concentration reading in time to provide rapid feedback to the test subject.

As originally proposed, the sweat-patch test required removal of the patch, placement in a sealed container, and transportation to the laboratory. In the laboratory, the patch would be centrifuged in a hermetically sealed tube, and the extracted perspiration would be assayed for alcohol content by gas chromatography.

An alternative method for assaying the alcohol in the sweat-patch was proposed in an article by Dr. Michael Phillips entitled Sweat-Patch Test for Alcohol Consumption: Rapid Assay with an Electrochemical Detector, 6 Alcoholism: Clinical and Experimental Research 532–534 (Fall 1982). This alternative method uses the Alco-Sensor III, a battery-operated pocket-sized device distributed by Intoximeters, Inc., of St. Louis, Missouri.

Although the Alco-Sensor III is designed primarily for measurement of breath alcohol, the technique described in the above-cited article utilizes a 16-gauge, 1½-inch needle affixed to the inlet, with a plastic gasket between the inlet and the needle to provide an airtight fit. The technique requires a 30-minute incubation period and the use of at least three standard ethanol solutions that are run simultaneously. It does, however, provide a relatively rapid means of providing feedback to the test subject.

The sweat-patch test suggests itself as a useful method to determine whether a person has consumed alcohol during a given period of time. This information may be valuable in circumstances where a person is undergoing outpatient alcohol treatment or is subject to conditions of probation requiring abstinence from alcohol. The validity of such tests, however, depends on the ability to maintain the integrity of the adhesive patch.

3

THE ADMINISTRATIVE LICENSE SUSPENSION

§3.0 Implied Consent

> Those who have conducted prosecutions on police evidence know the appalling risks which arise when the police approach a case with a preconceived notion of the guilt of the accused.
>
> F. E. SMITH

A defendant charged in a criminal complaint with drunk driving will also, in most jurisdictions, be facing parallel administrative or civil proceedings. These proceedings, usually requested by the driver, are held for the purpose of deciding whether to uphold a suspension or revocation of his driver's license, either for (1) refusing to take a blood-alcohol test, or (2) for taking one that reflects a blood-alcohol concentration of at least .08 or .10 percent. That suspension is usually imposed — and the license confiscated — by the arresting officer.

In effect, these latest examples of the double standard prevalent in the DUI field constitute a presumption of guilt. But, as with sobriety roadblocks, they are being upheld by the state courts. Due process, apparently, is afforded by the fact that the individual is given a temporary license, usually good for 30 days, and a written notice that he has the right to an administrative hearing on the issue if he so demands within a given period of time.

These relatively new summary suspensions are authorized by so-called *implied consent* laws, which are the direct result of the federal government's successful "carrot-and-stick" attempt to get the states to adopt relatively uniform laws on drunk driving. Incorporated into the Alcohol-Impaired Driving Countermeasures Act of 1991, the summary license suspension proceedings reflect the "new philosophy" imposed upon the states of implied consent laws. The previous implied consent laws of the various states were aimed solely at the driver refusing to submit to blood-alcohol testing, and were theoretically designed to discourage such lack of cooperation. The new federal approach, however, abandons that view and emphasizes instead the immediate removal of the driver from the highways — and a circumvention of the cumbersome criminal justice system. In effect, it creates a dual-track system of punishment (although the courts, to avoid nagging double jeopardy issues, like to refer to the suspensions as "administrative sanctions" rather than punishment). As of January 1999, first-offense administrative license suspensions ranged from as low as seven days (Virginia) to as high as one year (Georgia); ninety days appeared to be the most common period.

Although the original implied consent statutes passed decades ago were subject to procedural infirmities, today's statutes have largely survived broad constitutional attacks. Thus, for example, the admissibility of a refusal to submit to chemical testing has been held not a violation of the Fifth Amendment. *South Dakota v. Neville,* 459 U.S. 553, 103 S. Ct. 916, 74 L. Ed. 2d 748 (1983). The Sixth Amendment right to counsel has been held not to apply to proceedings where there is no risk of imprisonment. *Argersinger v. Hamlin,* 407 U.S. 25, 92 S. Ct. 2006, 32 L. Ed. 2d 520 (1972). For a discussion of the Fifth Amendment double jeopardy issue, see §8.3.2.

Fourteenth Amendment due-process challenges have usually been rejected so long as license suspension proceedings provide at a minimum:

1. A lawful arrest;
2. A sworn report from the officer;
3. A hearing if requested; and
4. A temporary license until the hearing is provided.

See *Mackey v. Montrym,* 443 U.S. 1, 99 S. Ct. 2612, 61 L. Ed. 2d 321 (1979); *Schutt v. MacDuff,* 205 Misc. 43, 127 N.Y.S.2d 116 (Supp. 1954). There are, however, isolated cases that have viewed DUI implied consent hearings as "quasi-criminal" in nature, thus requiring somewhat more than the usual minimal administrative safeguards. See, e.g., *Heles v. State of South Dakota,* 530 F. Supp. 646 (D.S.D. 1982). The Supreme Court of Alaska has ruled that "the same procedural safeguards apply in civil driver's license revocation proceedings for driving while intoxicated as apply in criminal prosecutions for that offense." *Barcott v. Department of Public Safety,* 741 P.2d 226, 228 (Alaska 1987).

In that case, the appellant faced revocation of his license if his blood-alcohol level was .10 percent or higher. At the hearing, however, he had been precluded from offering evidence concerning the accuracy of the breath machine. In holding that it was a violation of due process to keep him from presenting such evidence, the Supreme Court reasoned that "A driver's license is an important property interest, and the driver has a constitutional right to a meaningful hearing before the state can suspend his license." Id. at 133.

The California Supreme Court, in *Berlingheri v. DMV,* 33 Cal. 3d 392 (1982), has recognized that the continued possession of one's license is a vested, fundamental right that is protected by the United States Constitution through the Fourteenth Amendment. The court noted:

> In determining whether the right [to drive] is fundamental the court [does] not alone weigh the economic aspect of it, but the effect of it in human terms and the importance of it to the individual in the life situation.

The court then went on to say:

> We conclude that the decision to suspend a driver's license has a substantial effect on a right which, for the purpose of judicial review of an administrative decision, can only be considered as fundamental. . . . [T]he basic consideration in determining whether a right is "fundamental" focuses upon the importance of the affected right to the individual who stands in jeopardy of losing it.

The United States Court of Appeals for the Ninth Circuit has gone further and held that the revocation of one's driver's license involves a deprivation of a federal "liberty" right. The court, in discussing that the revocation procedures of the DMV satisfy due process, stated:

> We find such a federal right by adopting the analysis of the First Circuit which held that the use of a motor vehicle is a "liberty" interest protected by due process. [citations] Therefore, the application and suspension of such a motor vehicle license must comport with the due process requirements of the Fourteenth Amendment of the Federal Constitution. *Schuman v. California,* 584 F.2d 868 (1978).

Although the basic standards for implied consent suspensions are similar across the country, the nature of the procedures used vary greatly. Thus, in one state the hearing may be conducted by a sitting judge, in another by an administrative law judge, and in a third by a lay employee of the motor vehicle department. The prosecutor may be a deputy attorney general, a local prosecutor, or a DMV employee. Procedural due process ranges all the way from full discovery, confrontation, rules of evidence, findings of fact, appeal, etc., to the abysmal situation presently existing in California. Hearings in that state are presided over by a lay employee of the DMV; this employee is also the prosecutor, and so rules on his (and his opponent's) own objections and offers of evidence; if confrontation is desired, the licensee is required to subpoena the officer and pay his salary; when the DMV employee, as judge, decides that he, as prosecutor, has won the hearing, the licensee can appeal — to the DMV. To make matters worse, hearings are often not held or decided until after license has already served the entire suspension (four months for a first offense).

This section will discuss the initial legal issues which should be considered by counsel representing a client in such administrative proceedings. Regardless of whether the suspension is for a refusal or for a per se offense, the officer's initial conduct must be reviewed. Did he have probable cause to stop, detain, and arrest? Given probable cause to arrest, was the arrest a lawful one — that is, did the officer have the *authority* to make the arrest? Where a choice of chemical tests is authorized in the jurisdiction, was the defendant given such an option? If not, what if any are the legal consequences?

Later sections will deal with the unique issues involved in the two different kinds of suspensions. The refusal and issues of implied consent require particular attention from the practitioner.

These substantive areas are followed by a discussion of the procedural aspects of administrative suspension hearings, including discovery, format, and evidentiary rules.

Finally, the connection between the administrative proceedings and the criminal courts will be considered. What remedies exist for judicial review? Do findings by the administrative agency act as *collateral estoppel* on the criminal prosecution — or vice versa? Does punishment imposed in one proceeding act as *double jeopardy* in the other?

§3.0.1 Double Jeopardy: Criminal and Administrative Punishment

The usual procedure in drunk driving cases is to proceed against the accused on two separate fronts: criminal prosecution and administrative license suspension. The end results, however, are similar: The client is punished. Does a criminal prosecution following an administrative license suspension (or vice versa) constitute *double jeopardy*?

The traditional view has been that it does not. This is usually rationalized on the pretext that license suspension, unlike criminal sentencing, is not punitive in nature. Thus, for example, in *Ellis v. Pierce,* 282 Cal. Rptr. 93 (Cal. App. 1991), the defendant was charged with drunk driving — and one week later his license was suspended for six months for refusing to submit to chemical testing. On appeal from the suspension hearing he argued that the suspension constituted double jeopardy because of the previously filed DUI complaint.

The appellate court held that a person who had already been criminally prosecuted could not be subjected to a second civil sanction — unless that sanction was *not punitive.* The court then looked at the nature of a refusal license suspension and observed that since it could not be characterized as retribution, deterrence, or compensation to any party for a loss, it was not punitive.

This approach, similar to the old view that driving is a privilege rather than a right, is simply unrealistic and unfair. The simple fact is that the individual is being prosecuted and punished twice. And in an appropriate case counsel should consider a plea or defense of "once in jeopardy."

Note, however, that the court in *Ellis* was dealing with a case where the individual's license was suspended for *refusing to submit to chemical testing*. In such a case, the person is not being prosecuted and punished twice *for the same conduct:* he is criminally prosecuted for drunk driving and civilly "prosecuted" for refusing to take a test. In a test, In an administrative per se suspension, however, a very different situation exists: His license is being suspended for the very same conduct for which he is being (or has been) criminally prosecuted.

Thus the focus in an administrative per se suspension, at least, should be on what constitutes "punishment." For if a license suspension is punishment, then clearly a plea or defense of double jeopardy would be appropriate.

Until a few years ago, civil sanctions did not constitute punishment. See *United States v. One Assortment of 89 Firearms,* 465 U.S. 354 (1984). However, that position was clearly abandoned in *United States v. Halper,* 490 U.S. 435, 109 S. Ct. 1892, 104 L. Ed. 2d 487 (1989). In that drug forfeiture case, the Supreme Court held that "the labels 'criminal' and 'civil' are not paramount in determining whether a sanction constitutes punishment for double jeopardy purposes":

> The notion of punishment, as we understand it, cuts across the division between the civil and the criminal law, and for the purposes of assessing whether a given sanction constitutes multiple punishment barred by the Double Jeopardy Clause, we must follow the notion where it leads. [490 U.S. 447–448.]

The Supreme Court then adopted a new test for determining whether a nominally civil sanction constitutes "punishment" for double jeopardy purposes:

> A civil sanction that cannot fairly be said solely to serve a remedial purpose, but rather can only be explained as also serving either retributive or deterrent purposes, is punishment . . . [Id. at 448.]

The Supreme Court reaffirmed this position four years later, emphasizing again that a sanction which is designed even in part to deter or punish will constitute punishment, regardless of whether it also has a remedial purpose. See *Austin v. United States,* 509 U.S. 602, 113 S. Ct. 2801, 125 L. Ed. 2d 488 (1993). Under *Austin,* in order to determine whether a forfeiture constitutes 'punishment,' it is necessary to consider the entire scope of the statute rather than just the characteristics of the property to be forfeited. The Court provided a three-prong approach to determining whether a civil sanction constitutes punishment:

1. "[T]he historical understanding of forfeiture as punishment" weighs heavily in favor of the conclusion that forfeiture continues to serve punitive purposes. [113 S. Ct. 2812.]
2. Is there discernible a punitive purpose from *a "clear focus of [the statute] on the culpability of the individual*"? [Id.; emphasis added.]
3. Had the legislative body passing the statute "understood those provisions as serving to deter and punish"? [Id.] Evidence of this is that the body "has chosen to *tie forfeiture directly to the commission of*" *the criminal offense.* [Id. at 2811; emphasis added.]

The following year, the U.S. Supreme Court rendered a key decision in this area. *Department of Revenue of Montana v. Kurth Ranch,* 521 U.S. —, 128 L. Ed. 2d 767, 114 S. Ct. 1937 (1994), involved a "marijuana tax" imposed by the state of Montana. The Court held that it violated double jeopardy for a defendant to be tried criminally for selling marijuana and then to be charged civilly for a failure to pay the tax. The fact that one proceeding was civil and one was criminal did not matter, the Court said, so long as *they both involved the same offense and both were intended as punishment.*

Shortly after *Kurth Ranch,* the Ninth Circuit extended this reasoning to civil forfeiture. In *United States v. $405,089.23 U.S. Currency, et al.,* 33 F.3d 1210 (9th Cir. 1994), the U.S. Court of Appeals was confronted with the question of whether the federal government violated the Double Jeopardy provisions of the Fifth Amendment by pursuing parallel proceedings against defendants for one course of conduct: (1) criminal prosecution for money laundering and conspiracy to manufacture drugs, and (2) civil forfeiture of property based on the same violations of law. The Court concluded:

> There can be little doubt that this case implicates the core Double Jeopardy protection. . . . The forfeiture complaint in this case was based on precisely the same conduct addressed in the claimant's criminal case, and it sought to forfeit title to the claimants' property on the basis of precisely the same violations of the same statutes. In short, this civil forfeiture action and the claimant's criminal prosecution addressed the identical violations of the identical laws; the only difference between the two proceedings was the remedy sought by the government.

Obviously, there is a clear parallel between the civil forfeiture of property in the discussed federal case and the civil "forfeiture" of a driver's license in the case herein. In both cases, the government is attempting to punish the individual in the two different proceedings for the exact same conduct (in the instant case, for driving with .08 percent blood alcohol; the only evidence offered at D.M.V. suspension hearings consists of the identical police reports relied on by the prosecution in filing the criminal charges).

After considerable litigation — and contradictory rulings — on the issue across the country, the U.S. Supreme Court finally dealt a near-fatal blow to the double jeopardy defense in administrative-criminal cases. In *Hudson v. United States,* — U.S. — (1997), defendants appealed convictions for using their positions as bank officers to secure fraudulent loans — three years after paying civil fines to a federal government agency for the same conduct. They based their double jeopardy claim on *United States v. Halper.* Chief Justice Rehnquist, writing for the majority, stated:

> We believe that *Halper*'s deviation from longstanding double jeopardy principles was ill-considered. As subsequent cases have demonstrated, *Halper*'s test for determining whether a particular sanction is "punitive," and thus subject to the strictures of the Double Jeopardy Clause, has proved unworkable.

Rehnquist then approved the traditional approach of considering (1) the expressed intent of the legislature, and (2) whether there is clear proof that a civil sanction is so punitive as to be criminal in nature.

The United States Supreme Court has refused to accept an ALR-DUI double jeopardy case for reasons not given. *Jones v. Maryland,* No. 95-1131, *cert. denied* (March 18, 1996).

§3.1 The Administrative Hearing

> The law hath not been dead, though it hath slept.
>
> WILLIAM SHAKESPEARE
> *Measure for Measure*

It has now generally been recognized that a driver's license in today's society is more than just a privilege; at least one federal court has referred to it as a "liberty interest" protected by the Fourteenth Amendment (see §3.0). Whether considered a "liberty interest," a "property right," or a "privilege," it is widely accepted that this valuable document cannot be suspended or revoked without affording due process.

In most jurisdictions, due process will consist of an administrative hearing, commonly conducted by the department of motor vehicles. Such hearings differ radically from court proceedings, of course, and it is important that counsel representing a client before such an agency familiarize himself with the rules and procedures.

The hearing officer, for example, may not have any legal background and may not be entirely familiar with even those evidentiary issues that apply to such hearings. He may also be wearing two hats, acting as the "prosecutor" in presenting the evidence, then switching to his role as administrative judge to rule on objections and decide the outcome. This obvious conflict of interests can be particularly frustrating. And, in fact, some of those jurisdictions employing this system are attempting to separate the two functions. Nevertheless, counsel should be prepared for a simple fact of life in many jurisdictions: The hearing may be conducted by the very agency that has suspended, or is trying to suspend, the license. As a result, there is a strong inclination on the part of the agency and its hearing personnel to achieve this purpose — to confirm that grounds for the suspension exist.

A second major difference from court proceedings is that

hearsay is admissible, though it may not be sufficient of itself to support a finding. This often means that the agency's entire case will consist of the arresting officer's report and, possibly, a record of the blood, breath, or urine test; the officer may never appear to give testimony.

Thus, for example, the Supreme Court of Wyoming has held that the officer's "implied consent form" constitutes an acceptable exception to the hearsay rule as a "public record." *Department of Revenue and Taxation v. Hill,* 751 P.2d 351 (Wyo. 1988). Furthermore, such a document was sufficient of itself to support a license suspension. The court concluded that "the right to confrontation and due process is protected and sustained provided that the accused driver is afforded an opportunity *at his election and expense* to subpoena the arresting officer for cross-examination." 751 P.2d at 357 (emphasis added). See also *Gray v. Adduci,* 532 N.E.2d 1268 (N.Y. 1988), permitting hearsay evidence to be the basis of an administrative license revocation; *People v. Johnson,* 542 N.E.2d 1226 (Ill. App. 1989), holding that the officer need not appear at the suspension hearing unless subpoenaed by the driver. But see *Nieman v. Department of Transportation,* 452 N.W.2d 203 (Iowa App. 1989), holding that an officer's signed implied consent form was hearsay and constituted insufficient grounds for proving probable cause to arrest.

It should again be noted that in most administrative hearings, hearsay is admissible but cannot be the basis for any finding of fact on a central issue, unless the evidence would be admissible over objection in court. The motor vehicle department often circumvents this by relying upon the "official documents" exception to the hearsay rule, by adopting the police report as an official document of the agency. Further, the agency will use governmental presumptions of authenticity and accuracy. The end result is that defense counsel may be confronted with an agency case consisting entirely of paper — and nothing to cross-examine.

Most jurisdictions, however, permit counsel to subpoena witnesses to the hearing; certainly, due process and the right of confrontation, if not simple fair play, would seem to demand this. In most cases, the agency will issue civil subpoenas which counsel must have served. And it is this power of subpoena that can prove invaluable in representing the client before both the agency and the courts. Of course, the officer's testimony provides the opportunity to contest the issues before the agency. But it also provides another critical — and commonly overlooked — benefit: an otherwise unobtainable *deposition* of the officer in advance of the criminal trial.

Since the issues before the agency usually involve factual determinations of blood-alcohol concentration, circumstances of refusal and/or probable cause to stop, detain, and arrest the client for driving while intoxicated, the entire spectrum of the officer's expected trial testimony can be examined. And, as with a deposition, the hearing provides the opportunity to commit the officer to testimony that can later be used to impeach him in trial. Note: If the testimony at the hearing is not being taken down by a shorthand reporter or tape recorded, counsel should consider bringing his own tape recorder and later having it transcribed.

This de facto discovery opportunity is not limited to the officer. Counsel may wish to consider serving civil subpoenas on the individual responsible for maintaining and calibrating the breath machine, or the technician who conducted the blood or urine analysis.

The more conventional method of discovery in suspension hearings is usually by means of a formal or informal request for discovery, or through the submission of interrogatories. For an example, see the Respondent's Interrogatories to Petitioner at the end of the section.

The issues at the administrative hearing will commonly include the following:

1. Did the officer have reasonable cause to believe the licensee had been driving under the influence? (See §3.2.3.)
2. Was the licensee driving a motor vehicle? (See §3.2.2.)
3. Was the licensee placed under lawful arrest? (See §3.2.3.)

If the hearing is for an administrative per se suspension:

4. Did a valid chemical test indicate a blood-alcohol concentration of .08 percent (or .10 percent) or greater?

If the suspension is for refusing to submit to chemical testing:

5. Was the licensee properly advised of the implied consent provisions? (See §§3.3.2 and 3.3.3.)
6. Did he refuse to submit to testing? (See generally §3.3.1.)

Although such legal issues as probable cause are usually in issue, some jurisdictions take the position that the license suspension hearing is a civil proceeding and that the exclusionary rule simply does not apply. In *James v. Director of Revenue,* 767 S.W.2d 604 (Mo. App. 1989), for example, the court dealt with the issue of the admissibility of a breath test result where a denial of counsel by the officer was alleged. The court simply held that "the exclusionary rule did not apply to civil proceedings." See also *Green v. Director of Revenue,* 745 S.W.2d 818 (Mo. App. 1988); *Westendorf v. Department of Transportation,* 400 N.W.2d 553 (Iowa 1987). Yet it would appear that the United States Supreme Court has held to the contrary. See *Welsh v. Wisconsin,* 466 U.S. 740 (1984).

Finally, an adverse determination by the hearing officer is usually subject to judicial review, commonly by filing a writ (e.g., *mandamus* or *prohibition*) in the appropriate court. There may, however, be a requirement that administrative remedies first be exhausted before relief can be obtained from the courts. If the motor vehicle department has provision for an administrative review, this will probably have to be pursued before filing the writ. See the sample Request for Administrative Review, plus Interrogatories, at the end of this section.

The following represents sample Interrogatories, followed by a sample pleading for seeking administrative review of a license revocation, reproduced here with the permission of Don Nichols of Minneapolis, Minnesota:

(Title of Court and Cause)

RESPONDENT'S
INTERROGATORIES TO
PETITIONER

TO: Special Assistant Attorney General

PLEASE TAKE NOTICE that Respondent in the above-entitled action requests Answers within thirty (30) days to the following Interrogatories, under oath, in compliance with Rules 26 and 33 of the *(state)* Rules of Civil Procedure. Please note that these Interrogatories shall be deemed to be continuing so as to require supplemental answers if you, your attorney, or any other person acting on your behalf obtains further information, in which case such further information shall be immediately conveyed to the undersigned.

With regard to the incident that resulted in the proposed revocation of the respondent's *(state)* driving privileges pursuant to *(state statute)* please state the following:

1. The name and the governmental agency of the peace officer(s) making the arrest.
2. Describe the facts leading up to the arrest of the respondent.
3. Did the officer making the arrest observe the respondent's behavior? If so, describe such behavior.
4. Where did the peace officer(s) park the patrol car in relation to the respondent's vehicle?
5. Where did the respondent sit in the patrol car?
6. Were the patrol car windows rolled up?
7. Did the respondent smoke in the squad car?
8. What did the respondent say while he was in the patrol car? Describe in detail the conversations between peace officer(s) and the respondent.
9. Was the respondent's vehicle towed away, and, if so, did the respondent and the peace officer(s) wait for the tow truck, and how long did they wait for the tow truck to arrive?

10. Did the patrol car go directly to the jailhouse? If not, describe the route the patrol car took.
11. Where did the patrol car park in relation to the police station or courthouse?
12. Who opened the door for the respondent?
13. What side did the respondent get out on?
14. Did the peace officer(s) touch the respondent's body at any time?
15. Did the peace officer(s) walk in front of the respondent or behind the respondent to the jail or courthouse?
16. Did the peace officer(s) bump against the respondent or did the respondent bump against the peace officer(s) at any time?
17. Did the peace officer(s) say anything to the respondent while he was being accompanied to jail or while he was in jail?
18. Were there any passengers in the respondent's vehicle when it stopped or before it was stopped? Please answer in detail.
19. Was a *Miranda* warning given to the respondent? If so, when?
20. Please describe in detail any statements made by the respondent to the peace officer(s).
21. Please describe in detail any statements made by the respondent to others, when given, and to whom.
22. Was the respondent's vehicle searched? If so, give details and result of search.
23. Describe in detail any questions asked by peace officer(s) of respondent.
24. What blood-alcohol tests were offered to the respondent?
25. What dexterity tests were given to the respondent, by whom were they given, and what were the results of such tests?
26. How was the respondent dressed at the time of the alleged offense?
27. Was the respondent wearing glasses at the time of arrest?
28. Was the respondent advised of his right to take another test? If so, when and by whom?
29. Was the respondent advised of his right to have his physician take an additional test?

30. Was the respondent advised of his right to refuse the test?
31. Was the respondent advised of his right to telephone an attorney before choosing to take the test? If so, when and by whom?
32. Was the respondent advised of his right to consult in private with an attorney before choosing to take the test?
33. Did the respondent telephone an attorney before refusing to take the test? If so, when and whom did he call?
34. Did the respondent consult with an attorney in private before refusing to take the test? If so, when and with whom?
35. Where was the peace officer(s) coming from prior to the respondent's arrest?
36. What time did the peace officer(s) come on duty on the day the respondent was arrested?
37. Where did the peace officer(s) go after the respondent was arrested?
38. How many arrests did the peace officer(s) make on the day the respondent was arrested?

Dated this _____ day of ___________, 19____.

____

Attorneys for Respondent

(Title of Court and Cause)

REQUEST FOR
ADMINISTRATIVE REVIEW

As the attorney for ______________________, I hereby request administrative review of the implied revocation on the following bases:

1. That the officer did not have probable cause that _____ ______________________ was driving while under the influence of alcohol or a controlled substance;
2. that the driver was not lawfully arrested;
3. that the driver was not involved in an accident involving property damage or personal injury;
4. that the driver did not fail a preliminary breath test or refuse to take a preliminary breath test;
5. that the petitioner was not advised:
   a. that refusing the test would result in a six-month revocation of his license;
   b. that failing the test will subject the driver to criminal penalties and a license revocation of 90 days or more;
   c. that the driver has a right to a telephone call to an attorney to decide what to do about testing, but this call cannot delay the test unreasonably;
   d. that the driver has the right to an independent test by a person of his own choosing;
6. that the driver was not permitted a reasonable amount of time to contact and consult with an attorney;
7. that the driver did not refuse a blood-alcohol concentration test;
8. that any test taken did not accurately and reliably indicate a blood-alcohol content at or in excess of .10 percent;
9. that the pre-hearing license revocation procedures under *(state statute)* violate the petitioner's right to due process of law under the *(state)* and United States constitutions;
10. that the pre-hearing license revocation procedures under *(state statute)* violate the petitioner's privilege against self-incrimination under the *(state)* and United States constitutions.

The information above has been provided in accordance with and without waiving the driver's privilege against self-incrimination under the United States and *(state)* constitutions.

Dated this _____ day of ___________, 19____.

____

Attorney for Petitioner

§3.1.2 Collateral Estoppel

Counsel representing a client in a drunk driving case is likely to encounter a situation where an issue at a license suspension hearing, such as whether the client was driving, has already been adjudicated in court. And, of course, the reverse may be true: A motor vehicle department hearing officer may already have ruled on an issue before it has arisen in criminal court. In such cases, the doctrine of *collateral estoppel* should be considered.

Thus, for example, in *Gonzalez v. Municipal Court,* 242 Cal. Rptr. 60 (1987), the defendant was arraigned in court on a charge of drunk driving. Before the criminal matter was resolved, however, the Department of Motor Vehicles held a hearing to determine whether his driver's license should be suspended for having refused to submit to chemical testing at the time of his arrest. After considering the evidence, the hearing officer ruled that he had *not* refused to submit. Subsequently, the defendant made a motion in court to estop the prosecution from proving a refusal for the purpose of enhancing punishment. The motion was denied.

The appellate court reversed the trial court's ruling. In doing so, the court adopted the standards of the U.S. Supreme Court in *United States v. Utah Construction Co.,* 384 U.S. 394, 86 S. Ct. 1545, 16 L. Ed. 2d 642 (1966). In that case, the Supreme Court presented a three-prong test for determining whether a ruling by an administrative agency would be binding in subsequent court proceedings:

1. Was the civil proceeding a "judicial-like adversary proceeding"?
2. Did the administrative proceeding resolve the disputed fact?
3. Did the parties involved have an adequate opportunity to litigate their claim?

The California appellate court reviewed the procedures of a Department of Motor Vehicles hearing, noting that testimony was taken, a set of rules existed for procedures, the proceedings were recorded, and the hearing officer rendered a written decision. Finding that the proceeding *was* "judicial-like," the court then went on to find that the disputed fact was, in fact, resolved, and that there was adequate opportunity to litigate the issue.

The court specifically rejected the prosecution's argument that collateral estoppel could only apply if the former adjudication was in court: The issue is not whether the agency was a judicial body, but whether it had *functioned* in a judicial manner. Furthermore, the lower standard of proof in an administrative hearing did not preclude application of collateral estoppel: The less formal nature of a D.M.V. hearing does not prevent the issue from being "fully litigated." Finally, the court rejected the state's "floodgate" argument that permitting this doctrine would turn refusal license suspension hearings into full-blown trials. Accordingly, the court ruled that the state could not offer any evidence of the defendant's refusal at his criminal trial.

The California Supreme Court, however, subsequently adopted a contrary position. In *Gikas v. Zolin,* 25 Cal. Rptr. 2d 500 (Cal. 1993), that court ruled that a holding in a criminal case that a driver was not lawfully arrested did not prevent the DMV from suspending a license. First, a dismissal because of suppression of evidence was not an "acquittal." And, second, there was no privity: The DMV was free to relitigate the lawfulness of an arrest in its administrative hearing.

Similarly, a New Mexico appellate court held that a lack of privity between the state's motor vehicle department and the prosecuting attorney's office precluded application of the collateral estoppel doctrine.

In *State v. Bishop,* 832 P.2d 793 (N.M. App. 1992), a DUI defendant appealed a trial court denial of his motion to suppress the breath test results, arguing that the court was collaterally estopped from admitting those results after earlier license revocation proceedings had resulted in suppression. The district attorney's office was not represented at the revocation proceedings, the appellate court reasoned. "Moreover, because the more serious issues of criminal guilt or innocence are not at stake in an administrative hearing, the State may lack the incentive to fully litigate issues." Further, the court noted that to rule otherwise would require the state to intervene in every revocation hearing to avoid the risk of adverse rulings. Finally, the "integrity of the judicial system" required that adjudication of guilt or innocence be made in a judicial setting, not in an administrative one.

Oregon has held that civil proceedings do not provide a sufficient basis for application of the collateral estoppel doctrine. In *State v. Ratliff,* 744 P.2d 247 (Or. App. 1987), the court noted that Oregon's statutory collateral estoppel required the first proceeding to be before a court or judge; an implied consent hearing does not take place in a court, and a hearing officer is not a judge. Nor did the court find any constitutional basis for finding estoppel. Finally, the court reasoned that such hearings were simply too informal and expedited to justify the application of common-law collateral estoppel. See also *People v. Stice,* 523 N.E.2d 1054 (Ill. App. 1988), where an Illinois court worried that application of collateral estoppel after an implied consent hearing would "result in protracted proceedings with the rescission hearing being treated as a mini-trial."

On the other hand, Oregon also has recognized that a ruling in a *probation violation* hearing may constitute collateral estoppel. In *State v. Donovan,* 751 P.2d 1109 (Or. App. 1988), the court held that "it must appear, either upon the face of the record or be shown by extrinsic evidence, that the precise question was raised and determined in the former suit." 751 P.2d at 1112.

In *People v. Newman,* 516 N.E.2d 667 (Ill. App. 1987), the trial judge rescinded the defendant's statutory suspension because the test results were inadmissible due to foundational deficiencies. At trial, the defendant moved *in limine* to suppress the results of the test on the grounds of collateral estoppel; the motion was denied. On appeal, the ruling was affirmed on two grounds. First, foundational issues were questions of *law* — and collateral estoppel applied only to questions of *fact.* Second, the judge's ruling was "not a final judgment on the merits of an ultimate fact."

In *People v. Moore,* however, 539 N.E.2d 1380 (Ill. App. 1989), another Illinois judge had earlier rescinded a license suspension on the grounds that the arresting officer lacked probable cause to stop the defendant — and the defendant had then moved at trial to suppress the breath test results on the grounds that the issue of probable cause had already been decided. The trial judge granted the defendant's motion because of collateral estoppel. On appeal, the decision was affirmed, the court noting in passing that the doctrine would help render the administration of justice more efficient. "The evidence presented at the suspension hearing may be indicative of the strength or weakness of the State's case. The State might decide to dismiss a DUI criminal prosecution if the hearing indicates weakness or the defendant might decide to plead guilty if the hearing suggests a strong case for the State.'' 539 N.E.2d 1383.

Counsel in a DUI case may encounter a situation in which the prosecution takes one evidentiary position in the criminal case and the department of motor vehicles takes an inconsistent one in a license suspension hearing (or vice versa). In such a case, the doctrine of *collateral estoppel* may well apply to preclude a subsequent contradictory ruling.

Counsel should also consider, however, the possible application of a legal doctrine known as *judicial estoppel.* The doctrine is perhaps best illustrated by examination of a recent Illinois case. In *People v. Wisbrock,* 584 N.E.2d 513 (Ill. App. 1991), the defendant was arrested for DUI and tested on a breath machine; the result was a reading of ``.11% deficient sample'' — that is, the machine did not receive sufficient breath to provide a valid analysis, though the sample obtained was tested at .11 percent BAC.

The state DMV offered evidence of the reading at a license suspension hearing, claiming that Wisbrock had, in effect, refused to be tested by failing to provide a sufficient breath sample. Later, in a subsequent criminal proceeding for drunk driving, the prosecution prepared to offer evidence of the .11 percent test result. At the defendant's motion *in limine,* the trial court suppressed the test results. The state appealed.

The appellate court affirmed the suppression — on the ground of judicial estoppel. The court then set forth the requirements for application of the doctrine:

> The doctrine of judicial estoppel provides that when a party assumes a certain position in a legal proceeding, that party is estopped from assuming a contrary position in a subsequent legal proceeding [citation omitted]. For the doctrine to apply, five factors must be present: (1) the party must have taken two positions; (2) the positions must have been taken in separate judicial or quasi-judicial administrative proceedings; (3) the party must have intended for the trier of fact to accept the truth of the facts alleged; (4) the party must have succeeded in asserting the first position and received some benefit from it; and (5) the two positions must be inconsistent. [Id. at 515.]

Since the state had successfully taken the position at the quasi-judicial suspension hearing that the defendant had refused testing, it was estopped from later taking the position at trial that he *had* been tested and a .11 percent BAC reading resulted.

§3.2 The "Per Se" Suspension (.08 or .10 percent)

> Doubt is not a pleasant condition, but certainty is an absurd one.
>
> VOLTAIRE

The primary focus in most per se administrative hearings will be on the individual's blood-alcohol concentration. Other issues discussed elsewhere in this chapter should not be overlooked, of course: Was there sufficient evidence of driving? Was there probable cause to stop, detain, and arrest? Did the officer properly advise the individual of the implied consent provisions? But the central question will probably be the blood-alcohol concentration at the time of driving.

Counsel should take essentially the same position he would at trial, bearing in mind the differences in procedures, evidentiary standards, and burdens of proof. Thus, for example, attempts to "relate back" the BAC from the time of testing to the time of driving should be attacked (see the discussion of *retrograde extrapolation* in §5.2). And, certainly, any evidence of blood-alcohol tests should be objected to without a sufficient foundational showing. See, for example, *Cole v. Department of Public Safety,* 514 So. 2d 1205 (La. App. 1987), involving failure to prove maintenance of testing device by a properly certified technician; *Salter v. Hjelle,* 415 N.W.2d 801 (N.D. 1987), where the breath instrument operator's checklist was not offered.

In *Hjelle,* the North Dakota Supreme Court held that the state must show that the breath test was "fairly administered" before the license may be suspended. While recognizing that the foundational requirements for admissibility were not as stringent as in a courtroom, the court nevertheless required safeguards sufficient to ensure fair administration of chemical tests: The "legislature has struck a balance between procedural efficiency and substantive reality." 415 N.W.2d at 803. The offered evidence — the list of approved chemical tests, the list of certified chemical operators, and the officer's certified written report — were insufficient: In view of the fact that neither the officer nor the toxicologist testified, a showing of fair administration of the test required an offer of the operator's checklist.

And see *Owens v. Motor Vehicle Department,* 857 P.2d 144 (Or. App. 1993), where the motorist offered a microbiologist as an expert witness on the issue of the accuracy of a breath test. The hearing officer permitted the witness to testify very briefly, but then cut the motorist off from any further questions. The hearing officer ruled that the testimony was not relevant, since the reading had been obtained from a properly certified machine.

The appellate court vacated the resulting suspension, holding that a motorist has the right to produce evidence attacking the accuracy of the machine, whether certified or not.

If the client is acquitted of the drunk driving charge after having his license suspended, of course, the license should be reinstated by the state's motor vehicle department. In some cases, however, the department's view of what constitutes an "acquittal" may differ from the court's.

In *Claxton v. Zolin,* 10 Cal. Rptr. 2d 319 (Cal. App. 1992), for example, two consolidated cases involved that common issue. The two defendants were arrested for DUI, and each submitted to breath-alcohol analysis; when the results of the tests indicated blood-alcohol levels in excess of .08 percent, the DMV suspended the drivers' licenses. Subsequently, one defendant was found not guilty pursuant to a plea bargain; the other was found not guilty based on a stipulated set of facts. When the defendants applied for reinstatement of their licenses, the DMV refused, reasoning that reinstatement was required only when the acquittal resulted from a *contested proceeding.*

The two motorists filed writs of mandate. The appellate court granted the writs, ordering the DMV to set aside the license suspensions. The DMV could not look into the nature of the acquittals, the court said. As to what constituted an "acquittal," the court reasoned that the trial court's finding of not guilty was sufficient; this constituted a determination of the factual elements of the charge in the defendants' favor. Had the court simply *dismissed* the charges, the result presumably would have been different.

In *Mosier v. Department of Motor Vehicles,* 18 Cal. App. 4th 420 (1993), however, the defendant's license was taken under California's new "snatch" law (requiring immediate confiscation by the officer of the license) after a breath test indicated a BAC of over .08 percent; the DMV subsequently suspended his license for one year. Shortly thereafter, the prosecutor offered a plea bargain of a plea to reckless driving, citing "problems of proof" to the court; the defendant accepted. Nevertheless, the DMV refused to reverse its order of suspension.

The defendant sought a writ of mandate, citing a statute that requires reinstatement when the driver is "acquitted" of criminal charges. The writ was granted, and the DMV appealed.

The court of appeal reversed, holding that an acquittal is a disposition on the merits. "Problems of proof," according to the court, did not amount to "a factual finding by the trial court that Mosier was not guilty of driving with a blood alcohol level of .08 percent or more."

Counsel involved in plea bargaining drunk driving charges in the future should certainly keep this decision in mind. The appropriate procedure to follow for safeguarding a client's license appears to have been suggested in a comment by the court that there "need only be a stipulation between the parties as to the facts and a request that a not guilty finding be entered."

Accordingly, counsel accepting a reduction of charges should take steps to ensure that there is a stipulation on the record (presumably during the taking of the plea or in aa plea waiver form) that the defendant was not guilty on the facts.

§3.2.1 The Under-21 Driver: "Zero Tolerance"

As part of the continuing "get tough" policy nationwide, many states are enacting legislation directed at those drivers deemed least experienced and most susceptible to alcohol abuse: minors — that is, drivers under a given age, commonly 21.

These statutes are new, essentially experimental and subject to defects in their language. California's .01 percent per se statute, for example, applies a one-year suspension to any driver when he is "under the age of 21 years of age and had a blood-alcohol concentration of 0.01 percent or greater, as measured by a preliminary alcohol screening test."

This particular law is notable for three reasons. First, the measurement of BAC is *not* by weight, as with the "adult" per se statute. Second, the BAC must be measured by a P.B.T. — that is, a preliminary breath test administered in the field; if one is not "readily available" to the officer at the scene of detention, the test cannot be given. And third, the law is specific and appears clearly exclusive: A minor cannot have his license suspended under the usual laws. Thus if a P.B.T. is not "readily available" (and they often are not in most parts of California), for example, the individual simply cannot be tested — nor can his license be suspended for having .08 percent BAC from the later blood, breath, or urine test. And there is no provision for prior convictions in the "zero tolerance" statute: If the minor has priors, they simply have no effect.

These procedural flaws were probably unintentional, but they are likely to occur in other states as well since they are the direct result of pressure — and suggested statutory language — from the U.S. Department of Transportation. In other words, counsel should not automatically assume that the only difference between the adult and "zero tolerance" laws is the blood-alcohol level.

Questions of constitutionality will also emerge. Does a statute aimed only at younger drivers, for example, constitute a denial of equal protection? One court has held that a similar statute applicable only to drivers under 21 who refuse to take a chemical test was unconstitutional. See *Commonwealth v. Raines,* 847 S.W.2d 724 (Ky. 1993).

For a discussion of the criminal ramifications under "zero tolerance" statutes, see §1.4.1.

§3.2.2 Proof of Driving

Was the individual actually driving the vehicle? In *New Jersey v. Gately,* 498 A.2d 1271 (N.J. App. 1985), the defendant was acquitted of drunk driving when the state failed to prove that he was operating the vehicle in which he was found either asleep or passed out. However, the same judge also found that the defendant had violated the implied consent law. The appellate court reversed, holding that an element of a violation of the implied consent law was operation in fact.

On the other hand, the fact that the individual was not even driving also has been held to be irrelevant to the issues in a refusal hearing: Refusal to comply with an officer's lawful request to submit to blood-alcohol testing may be the sole issue. See, e.g., *Department of Transportation v. Cantanese,* 533 A.2d 512 (Pa. 1987). Of course, whether the individual was, in fact, driving may be relevant to the issue of whether the request *was* lawful — for example, whether the officer had probable cause to stop or arrest before asking for submission to a test.

Note that in many jurisdictions it is not necessary to prove that, in fact, the individual *was* driving — only that the officer had reasonable grounds for believing so. See, e.g., *Shaw v. Vermont District Court,* 563 A.2d 636 (Vt. 1989). But see *Furry v. Department of Transportation,* 464 N.W.2d 869 (Iowa 1991), in which the Iowa Supreme Court held that a reasonable belief by the police officer that the individual was driving is not in itself sufficient to trigger the provisions of the implied consent law: A person who is not *in fact* driving the vehicle is not an "operator" within the meaning of the law.

§3.2.3 Probable Cause and Arrest

The lack of probable cause to stop the client on the highway, detain him for investigation, and finally arrest him should never be overlooked when reviewing defenses to administrative suspensions. As in criminal cases, lack of probable cause to believe that a crime has been committed should be asserted as grounds for suppression of all ensuing observations and evidence.

The requirement of an arrest would seem to presume that the arrest is a *legal* one — for example, that it is not the result of a stop or detention without probable cause. See, e.g., *People v. Perlos,* 428 N.W.2d 685 (Mich. App. 1988). However, at least one state court has held to the contrary. In *Department of Transportation v. Wysocki,* 535 A.2d 77 (Pa. 1987), the defendant had been stopped at a roadblock and arrested for DUI; subsequently, he refused to submit to chemical testing. He appealed the suspension of his license on the grounds that the arrest was tainted by the illegal stop, and that therefore any evidence obtained as a result of the arrest — such as the refusal — should be excluded.

The Supreme Court of Pennsylvania rejected the defendant's argument, holding that "for purposes of a license suspension proceeding for refusal to submit to a breathalyzer test, *the legality of the arrest was immaterial.*" 535 A.2d at 79 (emphasis added). Incredibly, the court reasoned that the only requirement under the implied consent statute was the *physical act* of an arrest, not the legality of it. A strong dissenting opinion observed that "[t]he majority authorizes this abhorrent governmental intrusion upon us with the excuse that the proceedings arising out of this police state action involve nothing more than administrative agencies and, because of the admitted illegal stop, cannot result in a criminal prosecution." 535 A.2d at 80.

The Supreme Court of Alaska has taken a very different view. In *Whisenhunt v. Department of Public Safety,* 746 P.2d 1298 (Alaska 1987), that court reversed a license revocation where the suspect had been denied his right to counsel (under Alaskan case law, an individual has a right to consult counsel before deciding whether to submit to testing). The state argued that excluding evidence of blood alcohol from trial provided police with a sufficient deterrent and that extending the exclusionary rule to administrative hearings would have minimal effect on police conduct. In rejecting this position, the court said:

> Driving is such an important privilege in our society that license revocation alone can reasonably be regarded as a significant sanction. Because of this, the deterrent effect of the exclusionary rule . . . would be weakened significantly if the sanction of license revocation were excepted from the rule of exclusion. [746 P.2d at 1299.]

The court further refused to distinguish between criminal and civil proceedings in applying the exclusionary rule "where considerations of fundamental fairness are involved."

Aside from the question of probable cause to arrest, the issue also arises in administrative hearings of whether the driver was, in fact, under arrest. Thus, for example, in *Dawkins v. Department of Transportation,* 534 A.2d 573 (Pa. 1987), the driver was asked (while being treated at a hospital) to submit to testing; she was neither arrested nor in custody, although sufficient probable cause existed. The appellate court held that although a formal arrest was not necessary, a de facto arrest was. Since the defendant had not been placed in custody, the refusal was not sufficient for a license suspension. See also *Woods v. Department of Transportation,* 541 A.2d 846 (Pa. Commw. 1988); *Commonwealth v. Kohl,* 615 A.2d 308 (Pa. 1992).

The Supreme Court of Oregon, on the other hand, has held that "the existence of an arrest is not relevant to an analysis of the permissibility of the warrantless extraction of a blood sample under Oregon statutes or either the state or federal constitution." *State v. Milligan,* 748 P.2d 130, 133 (Or. 1988). In that case, the court upheld the legality of a blood extraction where probable cause existed, though no arrest — express or de facto — had been made. In another Oregon case, however, it was held that although a formal arrest was not necessary for a warrantless extraction of blood, there must be probable cause and the suspect must be under "constructive restraint." *State v. Langevin,* 748 P.2d 139 (Or. App. 1988).

Is the fact that the officer made the arrest enough to trigger the suspension provisions — or must the officer *advise* the individual that he is under arrest? In *Throlson v. Backes,* 466 N.W.2d 124, 127 (N.D. 1991), the North Dakota Supreme Court held that "where an officer does not inform a driver that he or she 'is or will be charged with' driving under the influence . . . there has been no legally effective request for testing and the driver's failure to submit to testing is not a 'refusal.' "

§3.2.4 Failure to Give a Choice of Tests

Generally, a driver has no right to choose which chemical test is to be given to him, absent statutory provisions to the contrary. See, e.g., *People v. Kiss,* 462 N.E.2d 546 (Ill. App. 1984). If, however, the implied consent statute provides for a choice of tests and the officer fails to give this choice, grounds may exist for contesting a license suspension. In *Connole v. Muzio,* 478 A.2d 274 (Conn. 1984), a Connecticut superior court reversed a commissioner's order suspending the defendant's license because he was only offered and only refused to take a blood or urine test (he was not offered a breath test):

> Among these jurisdictions which have considered similar arguments in matters of license suspension the position has been

taken that the burden rests with the police agency to demonstrate that the arrested person was fully apprised of his statutory rights at the time of arrest. *Adams v. Hardison,* 153 Ga. App. 152, 264 S.E.2d 693 (1980); *State v. Carranza,* 24 Wash. App. 311, 600 P.2d 701 (1979); *State v. Stewart,* 37 Ohio Misc. 112, 310 N.E.2d 271 (1973). The purpose of such warnings is to enable the arrestee to exercise an intelligent and informed judgment. In other words, "[t]he intent of the requirement for informing the driver of his statutory rights and obligations is to provide the opportunity for the driver to knowingly and intelligently make his decision." *Schoultz v. Department of Motor Vehicles,* 89 Wash. 2d 664, 668, 574 P.2d 1167 (1978).

It is the court's conclusion that the plaintiff was not afforded the option of a breath test. In the absence of notice to him, as required by statute, that such test was a choice available to him, it can hardly be said that the plaintiff was in a position to make an intelligent and informed judgment. Under the circumstances the plaintiff's refusal to submit to a blood or urine test does not present grounds for the suspension of his operator's license under the implied consent statute. See *Adams v. Hardison,* supra.

§3.3 The Refusal Suspension

> Policemen so cherish their status as keepers of the peace and protectors of the public that they have occasionally been known to beat to death those citizens or groups who question that status.
>
> David Mamet

If the defendant has been asked by the arresting officer to submit to a chemical test and advised properly by that officer of the nature of the implied consent law as required by the local jurisdiction, the court (and, later, the license suspension hearing officer) will find that the defendant, in fact, has refused to comply with the provisions of the law. The result will be that the prosecution can offer evidence of the refusal to the jury, and the jury probably will receive an instruction adverse to the defense on the significance of the refusal. Additionally, the defendant's driver's license will be suspended or revoked, usually regardless of innocence or guilt as to the drunk driving charge.

However, there are recurrent factual circumstances that can be argued successfully to have the client's action either not considered a refusal or to have the refusal mitigated to the extent of avoiding the normal sanctions. Thus, for example, if the defendant did not refuse specifically to take the test but merely failed to reply to the officer's request, the courts may well determine that no refusal took place. (See, e.g., *Commonwealth v. Hanson,* 484 S.W.2d 865 (Ky. 1972); *Commonwealth v. Guarino,* 339 A.2d 861 (Pa. 1975); *State v. Wilson,* 660 P.2d 528 (Hawaii 1983).)

Faced with a "refusal" case, defense counsel should immediately consider the following issues:

1. Do the facts constitute a true refusal? If so, were there legally excusable grounds?
2. Did the police follow proper procedures in demanding submission to a test?
3. Will the fact of refusal be admissible in a drunk driving trial? If so, is there an exculpatory explanation for the refusal?
4. What remedies are available to prevent a suspension or revocation of the client's driver's license?

The question of what type of conduct the courts have considered to constitute a refusal is dealt with in §3.3.1. Following this, §§3.3.2, 3.3.3 will cover the recurring question of client confusion as to the apparent conflict between implied consent on the one hand and the right to counsel and the privilege against self-incrimination on the other. Physical inability to complete chemical tests will be discussed in §3.3.4. Finally, §3.3.5 will address the common situation where the arrestee initially refuses to submit to chemical testing, then at some later point changes his mind and agrees to take a test.

For a discussion of refusal to submit to testing as evidence in trial, including a discussion of methods for suppressing such evidence, see §§11.4.1 and 11.4.2.

Counsel should also be aware that an increasing number of states are enacting legislation making a refusal to submit to chemical testing an independent offense. What is the *mens rea* of this new type of offense?

In *Brown v. State,* 739 P.2d 182 (Alaska App. 1987), an appellate court faced with this question first assessed the new law and analogized it to a statute making it an offense to tamper with evidence pertaining to a criminal investigation. The court then held:

> [I]n order to convict a person of refusing to submit to a chemical test of his or her breath, the state must first prove that the individual in question *knew or perhaps should have known* that the breath test was sought as evidence in connection with an investigation of his or her driving while intoxicated, and, second, that with that culpable mental state, he or she declined the test. [Id. at 186 (emphasis added).]

Noting that the defendant had acknowledged to the investigating officer that he was probably intoxicated, the court then commented that "it is fundamentally unfair to punish a defendant for concealing evidence where, *by virtue of his intoxication, he is ignorant of the purpose* for which the evidence is intended." Id. at 186 (emphasis added). Thus the court recognized that a drunk driving suspect's very condition of intoxication could preclude him from harboring the "culpable mental state" necessary to the corpus of the offense.

§3.3.1 What Constitutes a "Refusal"

What exactly constitutes a true refusal to take a blood-alcohol test is a matter for counsel to consider in reviewing the facts of an appropriate drunk driving case. This may be relevant to three issues: the suspension or revocation of the client's driver's license; the admissibility of the fact of refusal in trial; and the explanation of the refusal, if admitted, to the jury.

In most cases, refusal to submit to blood-alcohol testing is by express refusal: The defendant is asked by the police officer if he will take the test and the defendant signifies his consent or refusal. In many cases, however, a refusal is claimed to exist due to the defendant's conduct or other circumstances. One recurring situation, for example, involves the defendant demanding that the chemical test be administered by his own doctor or at least in his doctor's presence. Generally, however, an arrestee has no right to make such a demand a condition for cooperation. If under the law of the jurisdiction he has a right to have additional tests administered by his own physician, he cannot make this a condition for submitting to a test administered by the police. (See, e.g., *Beare v. Smith,* 82 S.D. 20, 140 N.W.2d 603 (1966).) Nevertheless, counsel should consider the same argument that can be made where the defendant has a mistaken belief that he has a right to counsel: The purpose of the implied consent statute is not served by punishing those who have an honest confusion about the law.

What if the client demands to see a blood technician's credentials before submitting to having a sample withdrawn: Does this amount to a refusal? In an interesting case, a California appellate court said no, reasoning that concern over AIDS and other communicable diseases made such precautions "not only reasonable but prudent." *Ross v. Department of Motor Vehicles,* 268 Cal. Rptr. 102 (1990).

Another issue is presented where a drunk driving suspect is taken to a hospital for withdrawal of blood, but refuses to sign a waiver of liability for the hospital. Does such a refusal legally constitute a refusal to submit to the blood-alcohol test? A Pennsylvania court has answered in the negative. In *Maffei v. Commonwealth,* 53 Pa. Commw. 182, 416 A.2d 1167 (1980), the court held that an arrestee did not have to sign a waiver of liability form in order to "consent" to a blood test:

> Although the law is clear that anything substantially short of an unqualified assent to an officer's request that the arrested motorist take the test constitutes a refusal to do so . . . nothing in the Vehicle Code requires a driver, as part of his consent to a blood test, to execute a document limiting or waiving the tester's liability. . . .
>
> [T]he motorist's duty to consent to a blood test cannot lawfully be burdened by adding (or upholding) the requirement that he also sign a form devised by a hospital. The statute provides that "[a]ny person who operates a motor vehicle . . . shall be deemed to have given consent to a chemical test of breath or blood." Further, the six month suspension provision applies when "any person placed under arrest for driving under the influence of alcohol is requested to submit to a chemical test and refuses to do so." 75 Pa. C.S. Sec. 1547(a), (b)(1), (i). A motorist is thus deemed to consent to a blood test, not a blood test accompanied by a signed waiver of liability. License suspension is a sanction for refusal to

> submit to a chemical test, not refusal of a test linked with execution of a release. [416 A.2d at 1169.]

What if an arrestee refuses to take a breath test, but the officer then proceeds to have a blood sample withdrawn and the arrestee does not resist? Is a refusal an *oral* act or a *physical* one? Does physical cooperation overcome an oral refusal? A California appellate court has held that "an oral refusal will support a suspension where the officer elects to honor it, but not where he chooses to proceed with a test notwithstanding, the arrestee is entirely cooperative, and no appreciable time is lost as a result of the initial lack of a positive verbal response." *Hart v. Department of Motor Vehicles,* 240 Cal. Rptr. 373, 376 (Cal. App. 1987). Commenting on the intent of the implied consent laws, the court noted that "Most any sound principle may [be] pushed to the point where it becomes ludicrous: that point was reached here."

Counsel may encounter a situation where the officer asked the client to take a *second test* after one test had been satisfactorily completed. This sometimes occurs where the officer wishes corroboration of a breath test. Does it constitute a refusal if the client declines to take part in the subsequent test?

The logical answer would seem to be that an arrestee is only required to submit to one test, assuming that it is satisfactorily completed: The officer should not be permitted to run the individual through as many tests as he wishes. And this was the holding of the Supreme Court of Pennsylvania in *Commonwealth Department of Transportation v. McFarren,* 525 A.2d 1185 (Pa. 1987), despite a statute to the contrary. In that case, the defendant completed a breath test, then refused the officer's request that he take a second breath test — in the face of warnings that his driver's license would be suspended if he refused. His license was suspended because the implied consent statute required the giving of "one *or more* chemical tests." The Supreme Court reversed, holding that to give the statute effect would be to grant the police "unbridled power":

> In order to justify a second intrusion, the police officer must establish circumstances which support the reasonableness of a second search. To hold otherwise would subject an individual to unreasonable searches and seizures in violation of Art. I. sec. 8 of our Constitution." [525 A.2d at 1188.]

The "reasonable circumstances" would involve, for example, an inconclusive first test due to equipment failure or inability of the arrestee to provide a satisfactory sample.

In *Department of Transportation Bureau of Licensing v. Fellmeth,* 528 A.2d 1090 (Pa. App. 1987), however, the appellate court held that minor defects in a first test may not constitute sufficient grounds to suspend an individual's license for failure to consent to a second test. In that case, the breath machine's printer malfunctioned during the first test, so that the printed record of the results reflected superimposed readings: The defendant refused the officer's request for a second breath test. The court reasoned that the printer malfunction was a minor one, and that three officers had seen the correct reading on a visual display and so could testify to it. Thus the court found that the first test was valid, and the defendant had fulfilled his statutory obligation:

> The desire of the police to have the evidence of Fellmeth's breath test recorded in the best possible form is understandable. However, that desire to enhance evidence, without more, does not undercut the fact that Fellmeth complied with his statutory duty by submitting to a valid test in the first instance. [Id. at 1090.]

It is common practice for officers to record a "refusal" where the machine fails to provide a reading or exhibits a "deficient sample" reading. The officer simply concludes that the suspect was purposely not blowing hard enough, or was obstructing the mouthpiece with his tongue. Rarely do officers ever consider the possibility that the breath machine itself may not be accepting a valid sample. Yet, this is a commonly encountered situation, but one difficult to prove — or disprove.

In *In re Budd,* 442 A.2d 404 (Pa. 1982), a Breathalyzer test was administered to the defendant several times, and each time the sound of air escaping from the mouthpiece of the device was heard. The Pennsylvania court held that the defendant's failure to tighten his lips around the instrument's mouthpiece, whereby no reading could be obtained, constituted a refusal. The court found that the motorist had not made an honest effort to take the test and, in effect, declined to take the test although he never verbally refused to submit, thus warranting suspension of his privilege to drive.

In *State v. Wilson,* 660 P.2d 528 (Hawaii 1983), however, the court took an opposite view. In that case a driver had agreed to take a breath test but the machine failed to register a reading. Believing he was purposely not blowing hard enough, the officer discountinued the test and indicated a refusal. The appellate court set aside the license revocation:

> The choice of taking a breathalyzer test cannot be deemed to be a refusal to take a blood test unless the driver, orally or in writing, expressly so indicates. When the breathalyzer failed to register, it was therefore incumbent upon the police to offer the appellant an opportunity to take a blood test. [660 P.2d 529.]

Dr. Michael Hlastala, a professor at the University of Washington's Department of Pulmonary and Critical Care Medicine, has stated in internet communications:

> There are several things that can limit a person from blowing the minimum required breath to satisfy any breath testing instrument. In the Intoxilyzer, a person must breathe for four seconds at a minimum pressure. This pressure occurs because of the resistance of the tubing. The greater the flow rate, the greater the pressure. The purpose of this limitation is to exclude the initial part of the breath, which comes from the airways and has a lower amount of alcohol. . . .
>
> There are a variety of conditions that can limit exhaled volume and effort. Lung volume decreases with increasing age (after 21 years), increases with increasing body height, is smaller in women than men, and decreases with lung disease (obstructive diseases such as asthma, chronic bronchitis, emphysema; restrictive diseases such as fibrosis, asbestos, cancer) . . . Basically, the breath alcohol test is designed for average folks, and it is quite inaccurate for them. But if someone has lung disease or a small lung volume for other reasons, the breath alcohol test is absolutely terrible. There are many "refusals" that are essentially caused by the limitations of the instrument itself.

Mary C. McMurray of Forensic Associates of Minneapolis has pointed out one of the "limitations." The original Intoxilyzer 5000 models have variable switches to activate the acceptance tone, which could be set for 2, 4, or 6 inches of water pressure.

The lower settings made it easier to activate the tone, but they also make it harder to meet the slope requirements since it is more difficult to maintain a constant pressure when blowing lightly. As a result, the officer interprets the "deficient sample" reading as a "refusal."

Another potential problem is the solenoid valve screen, designed to capture debris and prevent it from getting into the sample chamber. If they are not regularly cleaned or replaced they will become clogged — making it difficult or even impossible for an individual to provide an acceptable breath sample. Yet another possible defect that could prevent the capture of a breath sample is a leaking breath tube or mouthpiece.

Does an alcohol-screening device constitute a breath test for purposes of license suspension? In *Wall v. Commonwealth,* 539 A.2d 7 (Pa. Commw. 1988), the driver was tested in the field with an "alco-sensor." Subsequently, she was taken to the police station, where she submitted to one breath test but refused to take a second. The state's implied consent statute requires "two consecutive actual breath tests." The driver contended that the alco-sensor constituted the first test, and the first breath test at the police station the second — that is, she was not required to take a third, and so there was no refusal. The court disagreed, however, holding that the provisions for suspension did not apply to field tests.

§3.3.2 The Defective Implied Consent Advisement

Did the officer satisfactorily advise the client of the provisions of the state's implied consent law? Counsel should be aware of any possible noncompliance with the provisions of the jurisdiction's implied consent law by the arresting officer. If the statute provides, as many do, that the officer must explain to the arrestee the nature of the law and the consequences of his failure to submit to testing, any subsequent failure to do so probably will preclude any administrative suspension or revocation of the driver's license (*Kolb v. State,* 299 So. 2d 877 (La. 1974).) Further, noncompliance by the police may result in suppression of the chemical test results at trial. (*State v. Bellino,* 390 A.2d 1014 (Me. 1978).) If, on the other hand, the jurisdiction has no law requiring the police to explain the implied consent law, failure to advise the arrestee of the legal requirements for submitting to testing will have no effect. (*Hazlett v. Motor Vehicles Dept.,* 195 Kan. 439, 407 P.2d 551 (1965).)

In *Hudson v. Brown,* 612 N.E.2d 817 (Ohio App. 1993), a license suspension was reversed because of the arresting officer's failure to advise the driver of all consequences of a refusal. The state statute provided that "[a]ny person under arrest for operating a vehicle while under the influence . . . shall be advised . . . of the consequences of his refusal." The officer, however, failed to advise the driver that he would be required to pay a reinstatement fee and provide proof of insurance before his license would be reinstated.

Counsel should carefully consider the exact language used by the officer in his advisement of the state's implied consent provisions, particularly the language that warns the suspect what the ramifications will be for refusal to comply with testing. In *Commonwealth v. Landau,* 498 A.2d 47 (Pa. 1985), for example, the arresting officer told the driver that if she refused to submit to a test she would be "subject to" having her license suspended. The appellate court held that this advisement was not sufficient to meet the statutory requirement that the driver be informed that the license "*will* be" suspended:

> [I]t is clear that the use of "subject" serves to modify or qualify "suspension." . . . "[S]ubject" has a number of definitions suggesting a contingent, conditioned, or likely result. We believe, therefore, that the warning here issued to the appellee falls short of the standard of certainty required in these matters. [347 Pa. 633.]

For another example of an incomplete advisement, see *Buchanan v. Registrar,* 619 N.E.2d 523 (Ohio App. 1993). In that case, the motorist signed a written form advising him under the state's implied consent provisions that his license would be suspended if he refused to submit to blood-alcohol testing; he thereafter refused. On appeal from the resulting suspension, he contended that the form was not complete: It omitted the fact that, to obtain the return of the license after the suspension period was over, it was necessary to pay a license reinstatement fee and file proof of financial responsibility. The appellate court agreed and ordered the suspension reversed.

On the other hand, *adding* to the required implied consent advisement may also cause problems. In *Erdman v. State,* 861 S.W.2d 890 (Tex. App. 1993), the arresting officer properly advised the DUI suspect that a refusal would result in a 90-day suspension as well as admission of the fact of refusal in trial. However, he then went further, telling him that if he took the test and passed it, he would not be charged with drunk driving; if he refused, he would be charged and placed in jail. The appellate court reversed a denial of the defendant's motion to suppress, holding that the additional statements were "of the type that would normally result in considerable psychological pressure," thus rendering the consent involuntary.

What if the implied consent statute is phrased in "contingent" terms? In a case similar to *Landau* but involving different statutory language, the Supreme Court of Washington was confronted with the question of whether warnings stating that evidence of a refusal "shall" or "may" be used against them were so misleading that the suspects were deprived of an opportunity to make an intelligent choice. In *Washington v. Whitman County District Court,* 714 P.2d 1183 (1986), the state sought direct review of a number of trial court decisions in which DUI arrestees were advised either that refusals "shall" or "may" be used against them; all of these respondents had subsequently submitted to breath tests. The district court ordered all of the breath test results suppressed on the theory that since refusal evidence was not relevant and thus inadmissible, the warning was misleading and coercive. The superior court affirmed the ruling.

The Supreme Court of Washington noted that the state's implied consent statute was not phrased in the unconditional terms common in many states — that is, the Washington statute requires the officer to warn the advisee that evidence of refusal *may* be used against him. The court then reasoned:

> The word "may" merely expresses a contingency that may be possible, nothing more. . . . The word "shall" conveys to the accused absolute certainty that his refusal would be subsequently used against him. As a result, the warning actually read to the accused by the officer contains a more coercive impact than that required by statute. [Id. at 1187.]

The court then held that "the defendants in the 'shall' category were denied the opportunity of exercising an intelligent judgment concerning whether to exercise the statutory right of refusal" and that suppression of the breath test results was the appropriate remedy.

What if an officer fails to complete his admonition of implied consent because of belligerent and uncooperative conduct by the defendant? Does a subsequent failure to take a chemical test constitute a refusal? The Supreme Court of South Dakota has held that it does not.

In *Rans v. South Dakota Department of Commerce and Regulation*, 390 N.W.2d 64 (S.D. 1986), the arresting officer began to read the implied consent advisory to the defendant in the police car where he was being held. Before he could finish, however, the defendant exited the vehicle. The defendant was taken to the police station and, after several scuffles, was placed in a cell; he was hostile and very uncooperative while being transported. At no time was he ever read the entire implied consent warning.

A trial court reversed the administrative revocation of the defendant's license, ruling that the officer had not complied with the implied consent advisory requirements. On appeal to the state's supreme court, the prosecution argued that the defendant's conduct constituted a refusal. The court disagreed, reasoning that the officer had unilaterally decided that the defendant would not listen to the advisory and would refuse the test even if the advisory had been read. The court concluded that an officer's judgment cannot abrogate a statutory right.

Again, the officer's exact wording in advising the driver of the implied consent provisions should be considered carefully. Did the officer, for example, warn the driver that his license *could* be suspended if he refused to submit to testing — rather than that it *would* be suspended? A Pennsylvania court ordered a license reinstated in such a case, holding that using "could" was "inadequate to convey the standard of certainty of the suspension that is mandated by the statute." *Graves v. Commonwealth*, 535 A.2d 707, 708 (Pa. Commw. 1988). Similarly, an appellate court in Indiana reversed a license suspension where the arresting officer advised the driver that his license "may" be suspended if he refused a breath test. *State v. Huber,* 540 N.E.2d 140 (Ind. App. 1989).

In *State v. Coleman,* 517 So. 2d 1061 (La. App. 1987), the officer warned the defendant that the results of a chemical test could and would be used against him in court. Nevertheless, the appellate court reversed his conviction on the grounds that the breath test results should not have been admitted: The officer should have warned the defendant that the test results would be taken as "presumptive evidence of guilt."

For a brief discussion of the effects of dyslexia and/or attention deficit disorder (ADD) on a "refusal," see the new material in §3.3.4.

§3.3.3 Confusion: Implied Consent, *Miranda*, and the Right to Counsel

The DUI arrestee is often confused by the involved and apparently complex legal admonitions given him by the arresting officer. He is, for example, told that he has the right to refuse to incriminate himself (if he is not so advised, he is undoubtedly aware of this right from endless television shows). He is then told that he must take a chemical test — for the purpose of obtaining incriminating evidence against him. Understandably, the arrestee is confused and/or distrustful. The result is often a refusal to submit to blood-alcohol analysis.

A more common situation involves the defendant who believes that he has the right to consult with an attorney before he decides whether to submit to testing or not. In many jurisdictions, there is no right to see an attorney at this point. But the individual's good faith confusion in his legal rights, perhaps exacerbated by the officer's attempt to explain the apparent contradiction between implied consent and the right to counsel, often results in a refusal.

Thus, the first inquiry should be into whether the state provides the arrestee with the right to counsel before submission to chemical testing. If the right exists, the suspension should presumably be reversed; if it does not, counsel should review case authority for the effects of his client's good-faith belief in the existence of the right — possibly due to confusion induced by the *Miranda* advisement's reference to the right to counsel.

Right to counsel exists in jurisdiction. Some state decisions do recognize a constitutional right to counsel when a DUI suspect is requested to participate in chemical testing. In *Bunten v. Motor Vehicles Division,* 639 P.2d 135 (Or. App. 1982), an Oregon court held that a refusal by a motorist to take such a test did not constitute a "refusal" under that state's implied consent law where the refusal was based on a denied demand to see an attorney. And in *People v. Gusey,* 22 N.Y.2d 274, 239 N.E.2d 351 (1968), a New York court also held that there was no refusal under implied consent where the suspect was not given the opportunity to telephone his attorney.

In what could be a growing trend, an Arizona appellate court reversed a DUI conviction because the arresting officer warned the defendant that he had no right to consult with an attorney before submitting to a blood-alcohol test. In *Taylor v. Sherrill,* 802 P.2d 1058 (Ariz. App. 1990), the court held that this right to counsel before chemical testing was premised not only on the state's constitution, but on the Sixth Amendment to the U.S. Constitution as well. This remains, of course, the minority view, and the U.S. Supreme Court has yet to address the issue.

Another example of this trend can be found in *Delmore v. Commissioner of Public Safety,* 499 N.W.2d 839 (Minn. App. 1993), in which the court held that a driver has a right to obtain legal advice before submitting to a blood-alcohol test. This right, according to the court, included the right to consult with an attorney chosen by the driver. Accord, *Mulvaney v. Commissioner of Public Safety,* 509 N.W.2d 179 (Minn. App. 1993).

In the case of *Washington ex rel. Jucket v. Evergreen District Court,* 32 Wash. App. 49, 645 P.2d 734 (1982), the court held that a police officer has a duty to ensure that one arrested for a drunk driving offense has reasonable access to counsel if such access is timely requested, but he is not required to advise defendants of that right prior to administration of a Breathalyzer test when no request has been made. And see *Short v. Department of Transportation,* 447 N.W.2d 576 (Iowa App. 1989), where the court held that the driver had a limited right to consult with counsel before taking a breath test, and had invoked that right in good faith. In revoking the license suspension, the court concluded that the officer had erred in treating this exercise of his right as a refusal.

Other courts have held that a defendant's request to speak with an attorney does not constitute a refusal under the implied consent law. In *Moore v. State Motor Vehicle Division of Department of Transportation,* 638 P.2d 1171 (Or. 1982), the appellate court ruled that the driver's request to call his attorney after the police had asked him to take a Breathalyzer test did not amount to a refusal to take the test under Oregon law, where between 30 and 45 minutes passed from the time the defendant was taken to the police station to the time he was permitted to call his attorney, and where there was no evidence that any delay occasioned by a telephone call would have reduced the efficacy of the Breathalyzer test. The court relied on its earlier decision in *State v. Newton,* 291 Or. 788, 638 P.2d 398 (1981), for the proposition that the underlying justification for finding that a defendant's delay amounts to a constructive "refusal" is the efficacy of the test results; where the delay is significant, or the police themselves have illustrated by their own activities that delay is not important, the slight amount of time necessary to contact a lawyer cannot be considered the legal equivalent of a refusal.

The *Moore* decision makes it clear that suspension in Oregon of a driver's license cannot be predicated on a refusal arising simply from a driver's persistent request to speak to an attorney. See also *Bunten v. Motor Vehicles Division,* 639 P.2d 315 (Or. App. 1982).

A federal case has also held that state implied consent laws do not prohibit a defendant from requesting an attorney. According to *Heles v. South Dakota,* 530 F. Supp. 646 (1982), the police may not deny, without justification, the defendants request to contact an attorney prior to testing, if such request is made and if it does not unduly interfere with the administration of the test, since, as a matter of fairness, the government cannot compel people to make binding decisions about their legal rights without assistance of counsel when such assistance has been requested. The decision was subsequently vacated, however, on the grounds that the appellant had died during the appellate process and the case was thus rendered moot. *Heles v. South Dakota,* 682 F.2d 201 (8th Cir. 1982).

Does the right to consult with an attorney before deciding whether to submit to blood-alcohol testing also carry with it the attendant right to *privacy* during that consultation? In *Campbell v. Commissioner of Public Safety,* 489 N.W.2d 269 (Minn. App. 1992), for example, an appellate court reversed a license revocation for refusal where an officer sat six feet away from the suspect while he telephoned his attorney from the booking area. The officer's opportunity to eavesdrop was prejudicial, said the court, since the defendant "may not have been able to answer, or answer candidly, all pertinent questions his attorney asked."

On further appeal to the state's supreme court, however, the decision was reversed. In *Commissioner of Public Safety v. Campbell,* 494 N.W.2d 268, 270 (Minn. 1992), the court reasoned:

> We agree with the court of appeals' conclusion that the presence of a police officer in the room when the arrestee talks with the attorney may inhibit the arrestee. However, proper testing procedures generally require that the officer remain in the presence of an arrestee in order to impeach any later testimony by an arrestee who submits to testing that ingestion of something at the station might have affected the test results. Moreover, we believe experienced attorneys will understand the situation and ask "yes or no" questions that allow the attorneys to get the information they need to advise the arrestees properly.

What amount of time constitutes a reasonable opportunity to contact and consult with an attorney? In another Minnesota case, *Kuhn v. Commissioner of Public Safety,* 488 N.W.2d 838 (Minn. App. 1992), the defendant was arrested at 1:43 A.M. and advised of his rights and given access to a telephone and directory at 2:02 A.M. After three attempts and 24 minutes, he was unable to reach an attorney. The officer said, "Look, you got to take the test now," whereupon the defendant complied. His license was suspended when the results indicated a BAC of .24 percent.

On appeal, the prosecution argued that from a practical standpoint, the 20-minute waiting period for a breath test was a reasonable period of time to contact an attorney. The court disagreed, noting that there was no apparent attempt by the defendant to delay the test and that due to the difficulty of reaching an attorney at that time of morning, he should have been given more time.

There is no right to counsel in jurisdiction. Assuming that there is no right to counsel in the jurisdiction, however, counsel should argue in an appropriate case that an honest confusion about the law should not result in punitive sanctions. Whether the defendant had a mistaken but good faith belief in his immediate right to an attorney or whether he honestly misconstrued the officer's explanations of *Miranda* and/or the implied consent law, the purpose of the implied consent law is to punish those who *willfully* refuse to cooperate, not those who believe they are complying with the law. This argument has been repeatedly made with some success. (See, e.g., *State v. Lee,* 292 Minn. 473, 194 N.W.2d 766 (1972); *Swan v. Department of Public Safety,* 311 So. 2d 498 (La. 1975); *Rust v. Department of Motor Vehicles,* 267 Cal. App. 2d 545, 73 Cal. Rptr. 366 (1968).) At the very least, it should be argued that the police were obligated to explain to the defendant that he had no right to an attorney before taking the test. (See, e.g., *State v. Beckey,* 291 Minn. 483, 192 N.W.2d 441 (1971).)

In *Wright v. State,* 703 S.W.2d 859 (Ark. 1986), the Supreme Court of Arkansas also held that when the *Miranda* warning is given in connection with the implied consent law, the officer must explicitly inform the suspect that *Miranda* rights are not applicable to the decision of whether or not to take the test:

> It is easy to understand how confusion can result when the two sets of rights are read together. . . . Yet, the legislature intended that a suspect fully understand the consequences of refusing to take the test before making a decision. . . . [T]he suspect should not be held accountable for a refusal to take the test because of the inherent confusion caused by reading the two sets of rights together. [Id. at 852.]

The Supreme Court of Pennsylvania has required officers to specifically advise the DWI arrestee that the *Miranda* right to an attorney does not apply before blood-alcohol testing. In *Commonwealth Department of Transportation v. O'Connell,* 555 A.2d 873 (Pa. 1989), the defendant was arrested for drunk driving, advised pursuant to *Miranda,* and subsequently refused to take a breath test until after he spoke with his attorney. The trial court vacated the license suspension, finding his refusal to be "unknowing" since he had honestly believed he had a right to consult with counsel before submitting to testing. In upholding this view, the supreme court recognized the recurring problem:

> The problem in this case, and many similar cases that have arisen, is that these requests to take Breathalyzer tests take place as part of the investigation conducted by police in regards to a drunk driving charge which is criminal in nature. The police proceed with the *Miranda* warnings and at some point (usually when the driver asks to see his lawyer) stop questioning and abruptly change "hats" and ask the driver to submit to the Breathalyzer test. If the arrestee hesitates and attempts to exercise his *Miranda* right by asking to make a phone call, a refusal is recorded.
>
> This state of affairs is unacceptable because it is fraught with pitfalls for the arrestee who is not trained to recognize the difference between a civil or criminal investigation. . . .
>
> Accordingly, where an arrestee requests to speak to or call an attorney, or anyone else, when requested to take a Breathalyzer test, we insist that in addition to telling an arrestee that his license will be suspended for one year if he refuses to take a Breathalyzer test, the police instruct the arrestee that such rights are inapplicable to the Breathalyzer test and that the arrestee does not have the right to consult with an attorney or anyone else prior to taking the test. [555 A.2d 877–888.]

Since the officer had not so advised the defendant, the court upheld the trial court's action in vacating the license suspension. And see *Department of Transportation v. Martinez,* 582 A.2d 1160 (Pa. Commw. 1990), where the court found *Miranda* warnings in conjunction with a request to submit to chemical testing "per se confusing." Id. at 1162. Applying the holding in *O'Connell,* the court held that "the police have an affirmative duty, not contingent upon conditions of confusion, to warn defendants that *Miranda* does not apply to breath tests." See also *Department of Transportation v. Fiester,* 583 A.2d 31 (Pa. Commw. 1990), requiring the police to advise suspects of the distinction "even in situations where there is no overt demonstration of confusion." Id. at 35.

The Pennsylvania Supreme Court has since further clarified the requirements of the so-called "*O'Connell* warning." In *Commonwealth Department of Transportation v. Ingram,* 648 A.2d 285 (Pa. 1994), the court held that the police must inform the motorist that (1) his driving privileges will be suspended for one year if he refuses to submit to chemical testing, and (2) his right to counsel under *Miranda* does not apply to the testing procedure. The reason for the warnings, the court reiterated, is to prevent the "intrinsic inequity" of a suspect initially being told that he has a right to counsel, and later, when he asks to consult with counsel, having the request considered as a refusal. (See also *Department of Transportation v. Scott,* 684 A.2d 539 (1996); *Commonwealth v. Danforth,* 608 A.2d 1044 (1992).)

§3.3.4 Inability to Provide Sample or Understand Advisement

The physical inability of a defendant to take part in chemical testing probably will excuse him from suffering the sanctions of a refusal. See, for example, *Dorman v. Del Ponte,* 582 A.2d 473 (1990). Certainly, for example, if he has been involved in a traffic collision and has sustained a concussion or other serious injuries or is in some degree of shock, few courts would hold that a refusal to cooperate legally constitutes a refusal. This area may involve litigation on the issue of exactly how severe the injury was and how it affected the defendant's physical abilities and mental condition. A broken arm, for example, may be insufficient in itself to justify refusing to take a test, but a state of even mild shock may constitute a legal excuse.

In *Hughey v. Department of Motor Vehicles,* 1 Cal. Rptr. 2d 115 (Cal. App. 1991), an officer found a motorcycle driver at the scene of an accident. The driver had multiple abrasions but no apparent head injuries; he appeared, however, to be going "in and out" of a rational and responsive state. When the officer tried to arrest him after smelling alcohol, the driver became combative and was subdued with the help of several other officers and later placed in leg chains; at the station he refused to take a breath test.

The driver appealed his subsequent license suspension, citing a statute that provides that a person who is unconscious or in a condition rendering him incapable of refusal is deemed not to have refused. The court found for the driver, whereupon the DMV appealed further, arguing that an individual may not offer evidence at a suspension hearing of his previous incapacity: The only issue was whether the officer at the scene reasonably concluded that there was a refusal.

The appellate court affirmed, holding that the statute impliedly permits a driver to offer evidence "showing he or she should be deemed not to have refused to submit due to a medical condition unrelated to alcohol use." 1 Cal. Rptr. 2d at 120.

Similarly, in *Commonwealth Department of Transportation v. Groscost,* 596 A.2d 1217 (Pa. Commw. 1991), the defendant was involved in a car accident and, when repeatedly asked to submit to a breath-alcohol test, responded only by moaning. At a suspension trial, the defendant offered hospital records concerning his condition. The court eventually found for the defendant, and the DOT appealed, arguing that the hospital records were inadmissible.

The appellate court affirmed, holding that the lay testimony at trial alone was sufficient to sustain the defendant's burden of proving that he was physically unable to refuse. Medical evidence, the court held, is not necessary when the incapacitating injuries are obvious.

If the defendant is unable to exhale sufficient breath into a breath analysis machine due to emphysema, for example, failure to complete the test may be excused. (*Burson v. Collier,* 226 Ga. 427, 175 S.E.2d 660 (1970).) However, this may depend on the defendant's advising the police of his condition. (*McCoy v. State,* 595 P.2d 706 (Col. 1979).)

When confronted with a situation where the client was charged with a refusal when he was physically unable to complete a breath test because of pulmonary disability, counsel should consider a recent article by Briggs, et al., The Effects of Chronic Obstructive Airways Disease on the Ability to Drive and to Use a Roadside Alcometer, 84 Respiratory Medicine 43 (1990). In that article, researchers found that elderly individuals and those with poor pulmonary function were physically unable to activate a roadside breath testing device.

See also Gomm, Osselton, Broster, Johnson, and Upton, Study into the Ability of Patients with Impaired Lung Function to Use Breath Alcohol Devices, 31 (3) Medicine, Science and Law 221 (1991). The article discusses the availability and use of a device called a "spirometer" for testing the lung breath capacity of an individual who has been charged with refusal for failing to provide a sufficient breath sample. The article also discusses a study of 51 patients with such respiratory illnesses as asthma and emphysema, only two of whom were found to be capable of providing a breath sample sufficient to complete the test.

Counsel should not overlook the possibility that the "refusal" was due not to an inability of the client to provide a breath sample but rather to an inability of the machine to *accept* a sample. This can easily occur where the variable pressure switch has been set too high — i.e., the machine requires too much breath pressure to activate an acceptance. Even in machines with nonvariable pressure settings, that setting can be set too high or can be maladjusted.

On the other hand, the opposite may also be true: The machine may not accept a breath sample because *the suspect is blowing too hard.* If the individual's breath pressure sufficiently exceeds the machine's pressure setting, the machine may not accept a sample. This may be due to a triggering of the mouth alcohol detector because of its inability to "see" a gradual rise and plateau over a five- or six-second period, since the machine accepted the entire lung capacity in less than that period of time. Or it may be due to a final exertion by the suspect at the end of his exhalation, possibly in response to the officer's "Blow harder!" which may trigger the machine's slope detector.

One way to determine if such situations exist is to subpoena or obtain through discovery the usage logs of the particular machine for a period of time before and after the client's test. If there appears to be an unusually high incidence of "refusals," then a machine defect becomes the likely culprit.

Other physical conditions may legally affect the results of a refusal. In New York, for example, a drunk driving arrestee was even excused from his failure to complete the chemical testing procedure because his false teeth kept coming out while he was attempting to blow into the breath analysis machine. (*Application of Scott,* 171 N.Y.S.2d 210 (1958).)

Whether excessive intoxication amounting to an inability to understand the officer's request or to comply with it physically is a valid excuse is a subject of some disagreement among the jurisdictions. New York, for example, has held that intoxication did not justify a refusal, reasoning that to hold otherwise would lead to the result that the degree of an individual's accountability decreased as his intoxication became greater. (*Carey v. Melton,* 408 N.Y.S.2d 817 (1978).) On the other hand, Ohio has ruled that inability to understand the officer's request vitiates the refusal. (*Groff v. Rice,* 253 N.E.2d 318 (Ohio 1969).)

What if the driver's mental state was affected by a prescription drug? In *Commonwealth Department of Transportation v. Zetlins,* 614 A.2d 349 (Pa. Commw. 1992), the defendant refused to submit to chemical testing, and his license was ordered suspended — despite the fact that he offered evidence that he was suffering from the side effects of a prescription antibiotic and he was upset because his daughter was missing. On appeal, the court held that the effects of the drug and the stress combined to prevent a knowing or conscious refusal.

Counsel should also consider the possibility of inherent mental inability of the licensee — i.e., to understand the implied consent warnings. The author has been successful on two separate occasions in having license suspensions set aside where the clients were suffering from dyslexia and/or attention deficit disorder (ADD). In one case, the individual was asked to read and sign an impled consent advisement. He was unable to understand what he was trying to read, and the officer finally took his "lack of cooperation" as a refusal. In the other case, the client's attention became fixated on a revolving ceiling fan during the oral advisement by the officer; again, his inability to concentrate and confusion was interpreted by the officer as an attempt to avoid taking a chemical test. In both cases, documentation from physicians and testimony from the clients provided the evidence for the rulings.

Both conditions, incidentally, can be aggravated by stress — such as during arrest and investigation procedures.

§3.3.5 Attempts to "Cure" a Refusal

A recurring issue is whether a refusal can be *cured* — that is, can the driver change his mind after initially refusing? Although a driver's first impulse when asked to submit to a blood-alcohol test may be to refuse, many drivers subsequently reconsider and attempt to "cure" the refusal by agreeing to take a test. This is often attempted while the driver is still in police custody but after he has had an opportunity to telephone an attorney or a family member. The question of whether a driver can cure his refusal has troubled many courts. The question was raised in the case of *State v. Corrado,* 446 A.2d 1229 (N.J. 1982).

In the *Corrado* case, the following facts were related in the opinion of the Superior Court, Appellate Division:

> At the police station the officers questioned defendant before a videotape camera regarding his involvement in the accidents and his consumption of alcohol during that evening. The videotape was entered into evidence . . . and showed that at 9:25 P.M. defendant refused to take a breathalyzer test unless he could first consult with his attorney. This refusal was despite [the officer's] repeated warnings that he was required by law to submit to such an examination. See N.J.S.A. 39:4–50.2. During the interrogation defendant stated that he had had two or three beers with dinner between 8:45 and 9 P.M. that evening and that he had taken medically prescribed Valium at 2 P.M. that day in connection with treatment for an injury he had suffered earlier that month. Defendant claims that after consulting his attorney by telephone from the police station he requested the breathalyzer test but this request, made at 10:15 P.M., was refused by the police. [46 A.2d at 1231.]

Before beginning its analysis, the New Jersey court first cited the cases from other jurisdictions that had discussed the issue of the driver's right to "cure":

> We have been referred to various out-of-state decisions in the briefs of counsel. The majority rule in those cases which have an implied consent statute like ours, see N.J.S.A. 39:4–50.2, is that the initial refusal is final and hence that there is no right to "cure" an initial refusal. See *Zidell v. Bright,* 264 Cal. App. 2d 867, 71 Cal. Rptr. 111 (Ct. App. 1968); *Krueger v. Fulton,* 169 N.W.2d 875 (Iowa Sup. Ct. 1969); *Mills v. Bridges,* 93 Idaho 679, 471 P.2d 66 (Sup. Ct. 1970); *Commonwealth v. Schaefer,* 8 Pa. Cmwlth. 96, 300 A.2d 907 (1973); *Harlan v. State,* 113 N.H. 194, 308 A.2d 856 (Sup. Ct. 1973); *In re Brooks,* 27 Ohio St. 2d 66, 271 N.E.2d 810, 812 (Sup. Ct. 1971); *Petersen v. State,* 261 N.W.2d 405 (S.D. Sup. Ct. 1977), and *Seders v. Powell,* 298 N.C. 453, 259 S.E.2d 544 (Sup. Ct. 1979).
>
> Other jurisdictions have, however, refused to follow the line of cases represented by *Zidell* and *Krueger:* See *Lund v. Hjelle,* 224 N.W.2d 552 (N.D. Sup. Ct. 1974); *Zahtila v. Motor Vehicle Div.,* 560 P.2d 847 (Colo. App. 1977); *Sedlacek v. Pearson,* 204 Neb. 625, 284

> N.W.2d 556 (Sup. Ct. 1979), and *State v. Moore,* 614 P.2d 931 (Hawaii Sup. Ct. 1980). [Id. at 1232.]

After reviewing the cases cited above, the court presented the following summary:

> The cases expressing the majority view essentially turn on the question of the unreasonableness of having police officers turn aside from other duties to administer a test after the driver has initially refused.
>
> The cases allowing a "cure" generally do so on the basis that a change of mind after a relatively short delay does not prejudice the presentation of the state's evidence nor defeat the purpose of the implied consent statute. [Ibid.]

The court held that the driver did not have a right to cure his refusal. In reaching its decision the court emphasized that in New Jersey the driver did not have a right to consult with an attorney before deciding whether to submit to testing.

In *Larmer v. State,* 522 So. 2d 941 (Fla. App. 1988), however, the court held that a refusal can be changed — providing certain requirements are met. The Florida court quoted with approval from the Supreme Court of North Dakota in *Lund v. Hjelle,* 224 N.W.2d 552, 557 (N.D. 1974):

> [T]he subsequent consent to take the test cures the prior first refusal when the request to take the first test is made within a reasonable time after the prior first refusal; when such a test administered upon the subsequent consent would still be accurate; when testing equipment or facilities are still readily available; when honoring a request for a test, following a prior first refusal, will result in no substantial inconvenience or expense to the police; and when the individual requesting the test has been in police custody and observation for the whole time since his arrest. [522 So. 2d at 943.]

The court also cited *Zahtila v. Motor Vehicle Division,* 560 P.2d 847 (Colo. App. 1977), *State v. Moore,* 641 P.2d 935 (Haw. 1980), and *Gaunt v. Motor Vehicle Division,* 666 P.2d 524 (Ariz. App. 1983) with approval.

Quoting from *Moore,* the court reasoned that the better position is to reject any "rule of law which would rigidly and unreasonably bind an arrested person to his first words spoken, no matter how quickly and under what circumstances."

Finally, the Florida court discussed the policy favoring such a rule, quoting this time from *Gaunt:*

> By approving a flexible rule we believe that this important evidence will be more frequently available and therefore the prophylactic purpose of the implied consent law will be achieved. [*Gaunt,* 666 P.2d at 527; *Larmer,* 522 So. 2d at 944.]

The *Lund-Larmer* formula for curing a refusal has subsequently been followed by other courts. See, e.g., *Pickard v. Department of Public Safety,* 572 So. 2d 1098 (La. App. 1990). The opposing view of noncurability, however, was recently restated by a New Jersey appellate court. In *State v. Bernhardt,* 584 A.2d 854 (N.J. Super. 1991), the court held that "[p]rosecutions for drunk driving and for failure to give a breath sample are quasi-criminal proceedings and therefore notions of curing defects, as frequently occur in the commercial world . . . have no application absent a clear expression to the contrary by the Legislature." Id. at 859. And in *Baldwin v. State,* 849 P.2d 400 (Okla. 1993), the defendant initially refused to take the test after he was told he could not speak to an attorney, then later at the station tried to recant his refusal. The court found that there was no refusal, adopting the five prerequisites for a valid recantation set forth in *Lund.* Accord, *Rick v. State ex rel. Department of Public Safety,* 851 P.2d 1078 (Okla. 1993).

The New Mexico Supreme Court has adopted a more "specific" variation of the *Lund* formula. *State v. Suazao,* 877 P.2d 1088 (N.M. 1993). In rejecting the "bright line" approach and approving a flexible test for determining when a driver may cure an earlier refusal, the court set forth a five-part test. A defendant can "cure" an earlier refusal if:

1. he does so before the lapse of the time it would take to understand the consequences of his refusal;
2. the test would still be accurate;
3. the testing equipment is still available;
4. there is no substantial inconvenience to the police; and

5. the defendant has been in custody and under observation since his arrest.

An Idaho court applied similar reasoning in reversing a DUI conviction. Quoting from *Gaunt* in *Matter of Smith,* 770 P.2d 817 (Idaho App. 1989), the court observed that "If the test results would remain valid, and if no material inconvenience is caused to the police, we fail to see the harm in permitting the defendant to subsequently consent to take the test." *Gaunt,* 666 P.2d 524, 527; *Smith,* 770 P.2d 820. The Idaho court went on to observe that the United States Supreme Court in *South Dakota v. Neville* had noted that obtaining a test result is in the state's interest: "[T]he State wants [the motorist] to choose to take the test, for the inference of intoxication arising from a positive blood-alcohol test is far stronger than that arising from a refusal to take the test." 459 U.S. 553, 564 (1983). See also *State v. Ginnetti,* 556 A.2d 1339 (N.J. Super. 1989); *Schultz v. Commissioner of Public Safety,* 447 N.W.2d 17 (Minn. App. 1989).

Certainly, it would appear that adoption of a rule permitting reasonable "cure" of a refusal *would* result in fulfilling the purposes of the implied consent statutes — that is, blood-alcohol tests would be obtained more often. This alone would seem to constitute a strong policy argument for defense counsel in contesting a license suspension.

Checklist 1 The License Suspension Hearing

- ☐ Does the client have a right to appeal the suspension?
  - ☐ Has the department of motor vehicles complied with all statutory provisions for notice and hearing?
  - ☐ Has counsel complied with all relevant procedural requirements for appealing?
  - ☐ If permitted, has a request for a reporter been made?
  - ☐ If permitted, have interrogatories been sent prior to the hearing?
  - ☐ If only the officer's report is to be presented to substantiate the refusal, has counsel issued a subpoena so that the officer can be examined as an adverse witness?
- ☐ Did the officer have probable cause to stop and detain the client?
  - ☐ Did he have probable cause to arrest?

- ☐ Was a lawful arrest by an authorized officer made — prior to the refusal?
- ☐ Was the client informed of all material implied consent provisions?
  - ☐ Was he advised of the possible consequences of a refusal — including suspension of his license?
  - ☐ Was he advised that his refusal might be used against him at trial?
- ☐ Did the client's words and/or conduct legally constitute a refusal?
  - ☐ Did the client specifically refuse to take the test, or did he simply fail to respond to the officer's request?
- ☐ Was the client physically unable to comply with the request?
  - ☐ Had the client been involved in an automobile accident?
  - ☐ Did the client suffer from some physical disability, such as emphysema or other respiratory problem?
  - ☐ Was the client's bladder simply empty?
- ☐ Was the client's understanding of his obligation to submit to testing impaired?
  - ☐ Did the client suffer from shock or an emotional disability?
  - ☐ Was the client so intoxicated that he could not understand?
  - ☐ Did the client mistakenly believe that he had a right to counsel before submitting to a test?
  - ☐ Did the client mistakenly believe that he had a Fifth Amendment right to refuse?
  - ☐ Did the client mistakenly believe that his physician could administer the test or at least be present?
- ☐ After initially refusing, did the client later agree to submit to testing?
  - ☐ Would such a delay have materially affected the validity of the test?
- ☐ Was the client denied a right to counsel before deciding whether to submit to testing?
- ☐ Did the officer give the client a choice of blood-alcohol tests?
- ☐ Can an appeal or writ be taken from an adverse ruling by the hearing officer?
- ☐ Will any transcript of the hearing be available in time for use in cross-examination of the same officer at trial?

II

EVIDENCE

Love of peace, freedom, justice, truth — this is a myth that has been created by the folk mind, and if the artist does not look behind the myth to the reality he will indeed wander amid the phantoms which he creates.

VARDIS FISHER

4

FIELD EVIDENCE

§4.0 *Field Evidence and the Arresting Officer*

> Truths turn into dogmas the moment they are disputed.
>
> G. K. CHESTERTON

The evidence produced by the prosecution to establish that the defendant was driving a vehicle while under the influence will be of two very different kinds: observations of the officer and/or witnesses, usually at the scene of the driving, and chemical testing of the defendant's blood, breath, or urine. In some cases, such as where the defendant has refused to submit to the withdrawal of a chemical sample from his body, the evidence will be only of the former kind.

In all too many drunk driving cases, the trial evolves into a litigation of the reliability and accuracy of chemical examination. The testimony of police and lay witnesses, it is felt, is fallible, but evidence of a blood-alcohol reading rises above this to a level sanctified by "scientific method." As will be seen later, this notion is a fallacy; the various methods of blood-alcohol analysis are imperfect at best and easily susceptible to knowledgeable cross-examination. Nevertheless, most prosecutors will stress heavily their presentation of chemical evidence, often to the neglect of what may be very damning police testimony.

In a prosecution under a per se statute (driving with an excessive blood-alcohol level), of course, chemical evidence is critical. But even in such a case, neglecting field evidence is a mistake. First, the prosecution will invariably charge the defendant with both the per se statute *and* the traditional DUI statute. Second, field evidence will be used to *corroborate* the blood-alcohol reading. Handled correctly, however, it can also serve to *contradict* that reading.

It is to defense counsel's advantage to "lure" the prosecutor into neglecting his field evidence by vigorously challenging the chemical testing at pre-trial proceedings as well as at trial. Even experienced prosecutors will often react to these attacks by building up their presentation of chemical evidence and only curiosity presenting the testimony of lay witnesses or police officers who observed the defendant at the time of his intoxication. The result inevitably will be that the defendant is no longer on trial, but rather the method of chemical analysis is. The ultimate issue in the minds of the jurors becomes not whether the defendant was intoxicated, but whether the DataMaster is an accurate instrument and was functioning properly at the time of testing. Strange as it may seem, juries and prosecutors, when their minds are fixed on the question of whether a strange and complex scientific instrument was functioning correctly, are quite willing to ignore the eyewitness testimony of a police officer that the defendant reeked of alcohol and was staggering and falling down. If the defense counsel can succeed in creating such a shift of focus, he has taken a very large step toward obtaining an acquittal.

Regardless of other attitudes toward blood-alcohol test results, counsel must realize that the most relevant and critical evidence consists of the observations of witnesses, both police officers and citizens. Prosecutors may use the blood-alcohol reading to determine the limits of plea bargaining, courts may refer to it in deciding the severity of sentence, and juries may be led into focusing on it to the exclusion of more reliable evidence; but field observations constitute the most significant portion of a prosecution or defense case. And in a correctly handled trial, blood-alcohol readings will be treated as only one type of evidence, collateral to and supportive of the main evidence: eyewitness observations.

Field evidence may be broken down roughly into five categories:

1. observations of the defendant's erratic or otherwise unusual driving

2. observation of his physical appearance and conduct
3. the defendant's performance on a field sobriety test, including horizontal gaze nystagmus
4. incriminating statements, including refusal to submit to blood-alcohol testing
5. audiovisual evidence (tapes, film, and/or photographs)

In unusual circumstances, such as those involving a traffic accident where the defendant was injured or even unconscious, the types of evidence will be significantly altered.

§4.0.1 The Officer as DUI Witness

In most cases, the field evidence produced by the prosecution will be in the form of testimony from one or more police officers, usually the officer or officers who arrested the defendant. In some cases, such as where the initial police contact comes from a call to the scene of an accident, lay witness testimony — often of the occupants of the car involved in the collision with the defendant's vehicle — will be offered as an integral part of the prosecution case (and, in fact, will be necessary to establishing the "driving" element of the offense). Lay witness testimony is, of course, usually given less weight by the jury; it is the testimony of the trained, experienced, and "impartial" police officer that carries weight with the triers of fact. And it is this witness that a good drunk driving lawyer must learn to deal with.

Generally speaking, the testimony of a police officer can be approached in the following steps:

1. questioning the officer's qualifications and experience in the very limited area of drunk driving
2. establishing his predisposition to believe the defendant guilty at initial stages of the field detention
3. suggesting innocent explanations for incriminating observations
4. emphasizing the observations that tend to establish the defendant's sobriety
5. attacking the officer's observations, interrogations, and

testing procedures — including procedures the officer failed to follow

Counsel must deal with each officer on an individual basis, understanding at all times the jurors' attitudes toward his questioning. Where a knock-down cross-examination of an officer under one set of circumstances may be appropriate, a very tactful and respectful approach may be more productive under another.

Counsel also should be fully aware of who he is dealing with on the witness stand when he takes on a police officer: a professional witness. This is not a citizen who is shaken by his first appearance on the stand, but a person who has probably been there many times before. This is a witness who has lost his awe of the courtroom, who has sparred with skilled defense attorneys on many previous occasions, and who has learned to impress the jury with his calm and polite manners while taking every opportunity during cross-examination to ram the knife deeper into the defendant. He is, in short, usually a fairly skilled adversary who should be viewed as such; the days of the "dumb cop" are rapidly passing.

Perhaps above all, counsel should recognize that in confronting the police officer he is dealing with an individual, not a clone. Each officer is different; each has his own unique beliefs, attitudes, and prejudices; each varies in his degree of intelligence, honesty, and experience. In emphasizing the effect of these individual differences on an officer's conduct in the field, a study conducted by the National Highway Safety Administration (U.S. Department of Transportation Report #H5-801-230) found, among other things, that:

> The officer's age and experience play a role in his alcohol-related arrest decisions. Younger officers, and those with relatively few years of seniority, tend to have a more positive attitude toward alcohol-related enforcement and make more arrests on that charge than do their older officers. This result was found to hold true regardless of the type of department in which the officer serves or the specific type of duty to which he is assigned.
>
> The officer's personal use of alcohol is inversely related to his level of alcohol-related enforcement. Patrolmen who drink make significantly fewer arrests than those who do not, and those who drink frequently make significantly fewer arrests than those who use alcohol only occasionally.

Lack of knowledge concerning the relationship between alcohol and intoxication is widespread among police officers and imparts a negative influence on alcohol-related enforcement. Most officers underestimate — often by a wide margin — the amount of alcohol a suspect would have to consume in order to achieve the statutory limit of blood alcohol concentration. This seems to induce a tendency among officers to identify and sympathize with the suspects they encounter.

Specialized training has a strong positive influence on alcohol-related arrests. Patrolmen who have received instruction in the operation of breath testing devices and/or in alcohol-related enforcement — particularly in municipal departments — were found to lack this specialized training.

Specialization in duty assignment can also enhance alcohol-related enforcement. Patrolmen assigned to traffic divisions, in particular, produce higher arrest rates than those charged with general patrol duties. . . .

Near the end of the duty shift, alcohol-related investigations decrease substantially. This is particularly true in departments that have adopted relatively time-consuming procedures for processing alcohol-related arrests. . . .

Weather conditions also effect alcohol-related arrests. There is encouraging evidence that foul weather has a positive influence on the attitude of many officers: they are more appreciative of the risk posed by an alcohol-related suspect when driving conditions are hazardous, and are less likely to avoid the arrest when those conditions prevail. . . .

The suspect's attitude can have a strong influence on the arrest/no arrest decision. If the suspect proves uncooperative or argumentative, a positive influence for arrest results. Conversely, the likelihood of arrest decreases when the suspect seems cooperative. . . .

The suspect's race is a key distinguishing characteristic in alcohol-related cases. The officers surveyed — the overwhelming majority of whom were white — reported releasing significantly more non-white suspects than they arrested. The data do not suggest that this reflects a greater tendency to exercise discretion when dealing with non-white drivers. Rather, the officers seem more willing to initiate an investigation when the suspect is not of their own race.

Suspect's age is another distinguishing characteristic of these cases, and patrolmen reported releasing significantly more young suspects than they arrested. This appears to stem from two distinct

> causes. First, young officers exhibit more sympathy for young suspects, i.e., seem less disposed to arrest a driver of their own age group. Second, older officers seem more willing to stop young suspects, i.e., are more likely to conduct an investigation when the driver is young, even if the evidence of alcohol-related violation is not clear.
>
> Suspect's sex also plays a role in the arrest/no arrest decision. Patrolmen seem more reluctant to arrest a woman for alcohol-related violations, largely because processing of a female arrestee is generally more complex and time consuming. . . .

In a fascinating article entitled Psychology, Public Policy, and the Evidence for Alcohol Intoxication, American Psychologist 1070 (Oct. 1983), James W. Langenbrucher and Peter E. Nathan reported a series of experiments conducted at Rutgers University's Alcohol Behavior Research Laboratory to test the ability of social drinkers, bartenders, and police officers to estimate the sobriety of individuals. The results should be of considerable interest to any attorney representing a client charged with driving under the influence of alcohol — and may be admissible in evidence during direct or cross-examination of expert witnesses. The researchers addressed the specific issue of whether nonmedical observers can reliably judge an individual's level of intoxication.

The first experiment involved the testing of lay witnesses — 49 individuals who were themselves "social" drinkers. Two men and two women were employed as subjects; for some tests no alcohol was consumed, for others varying blood-alcohol levels of intoxication were reached. In each case the subject was brought into a room and was asked to sit down where the "witnesses" were sitting. The subject was then interviewed at length to elicit a range of verbal behavior and somatic and cognitive effects. When the interview was over, the subject rose from the chair and walked out of the room — again, in full view of the observers.

The witnesses' observations resulted in the conclusion:

> The assumption that social drinkers would prove to be accurate judges of the [blood-alcohol levels] of other persons was not confirmed. . . . On only 4 of 16 occasions did a significant number of subjects correctly classify a target on a three-stage categorical index of intoxication level. . . . If determining whether [a] man is sober or intoxicated is a matter of common observation, then our subjects apparently lacked this capacity. [Id. at 1072.]

The scientists next dealt with a type of witness with considerably more expertise in the area, 12 bartenders who were tested in the setting of a large cocktail lounge in a New Jersey hotel. The results again proved interesting:

> The bartenders correctly rated a target in only one of four instances. . . . Contrary to expectation, no relationship between years of experience as a bartender and [blood-alcohol level] estimation accuracy was found. These data suggest strongly that these bartenders did not possess and had not acquired special knowledge or skill in identifying intoxicated persons. [Id. at 1074.]

Finally, the psychologists proceeded to test 30 law enforcement officers from various New Jersey agencies. Of these, 15 were tested under conditions similar to those in the first experiment; another 15 were tested under conditions commonly encountered in a DUI traffic stop — at night, with the subject behind the wheel of a car, who is then asked to step out and conduct a series of field sobriety tests. The results: "When police observers in the laboratory condition were compared to social drinkers who had experienced an identical procedure, no difference in rating accuracy was found. . . . Officers in the arrest analogue condition were somewhat more accurate than their colleagues in the laboratory condition but not significantly so." Id. at 1076.

The scientists then concluded that "the results of the three experiments described here are not reassuring. All three of the subject groups studied — social drinkers, bartenders, and police officers — correctly judged targets' levels of intoxication only 25 percent of the time. . . ." Ibid.

In cross-examination of the police officer, as in all phases of trial, preparation represents the key to success. Besides learning the background and training of the officer, counsel should obtain all reports, statements, and transcripts relevant to the case, particularly if they involve the officer in question. Counsel should visit the scene of the arrest and determine the lighting conditions at the time, and he should note the distances involved, location of obstructions, etc. This not only permits more effective on-your-feet cross-examination but enhances counsel's own credibility in the eyes of the jury.

Counsel should try to interview the officer in advance of trial. If depositions are permitted, one should be taken; if not, informal questioning may be a possibility if handled tactfully. (But see §13.0.1).

Police officers usually have little independent recollection of the events in a given drunk driving investigation, relying heavily on memorization and periodic reference to their arrest report. This lack of memory should be clearly developed for the jury.

If counsel has the opportunity to examine the officer at an administrative license suspension hearing, he should ask if the report was reviewed prior to testimony and then make clear on the record every time the officer needs to "refresh his recollection" by reading the report. With sufficiently detailed cross-examination, the officer will repeatedly have to acknowledge that he cannot remember. He can then be confronted with this earlier inability to recall when he testifies later at trial with seemingly perfect recollection.

If the officer has to repeatedly refer to his report in his testimony in trial, counsel should move to have his entire testimony stricken on the grounds that he has no independent recollection. Using documents to refresh a witness's recollection is, of course, permitted under the rules of evidenced — *assuming that there is an existing memory.* If it becomes apparent that the witness is not testifying from refreshed memory, but is merely regurgitating the report, then the testimony is inadmissible.

Finally, counsel should attempt to have the trial court require police witnesses to testify in civilian clothing. The authoritarian or other effect of a police uniform on some jurors can be substantial.

§4.1 Driving Symptoms

> Opinions founded on prejudice are always sustained with the greatest violence.
>
> FRANCIS JEFFREY

In a typical case, the arresting officer will testify that his attention was first called to the defendant by his erratic or unusual driving:

He observed the defendant's vehicle to be traveling at a high rate of speed and weaving within his lane; the officer followed him for half a mile, during which time the defendant weaved across the lane lines four or five times and failed to stop at an intersection containing pedestrians; when the officer turned on his flashing red lights, the defendant failed to pull over for three city blocks; when he finally did pull over, he parked two feet from the curb, presenting a hazard to passing traffic.

How important are the driving symptoms in a DUI case? Most defense attorneys would probably consider the blood-alcohol evidence to be the most critical, followed perhaps by field sobriety tests. But the view of many experienced prosecutors is that the single most important area in obtaining a conviction is police testimony concerning the defendant's driving.

Prosecution manuals that the author has reviewed indicate that prosecutors recognize four major categories of evidence: driving, appearance and demeanor, FSTs, and blood-alcohol test or refusal. Of these, at least one manual states driving is the most important — and field sobriety tests, "which are not generally viewed by jurors as highly persuasive," the least.

While the author does not necessarily agree with this view, it may be helpful to understand what the approach of one's opponent may be.

Obviously, this testimony is damaging and must be dealt with by defense counsel on cross-examination. Fortunately, there are a number of recurring phenomena that help to "explain away" the officer's observations. Consider the salient points of his testimony that tend to establish intoxication:

1. speeding
2. weaving
3. failing to stop at occupied intersection
4. failure to pull over when flashed
5. hazardous parking

First, the officer's testimony as to the defendant's speeding should be turned in the defendant's favor. The officer should be led into admitting that control of a vehicle requires greater judgment and coordination as speed increases. If an area is posted for 45 miles per hour, for example, that is what is considered the maximum safe speed for a normal, sober driver. It follows, it should be pointed out through questioning (and later in argument), that driving in excess of that speed without mishap requires an even greater degree of judgment and coordination than that expected of a "normal, sober" person — and certainly much greater than that expected of an intoxicated driver. In other words, counsel should not attempt to disprove the officer's allegation of speeding but rather accept it and turn it to his advantage. The natural tendency of counsel to contest everything should be overcome; the client is, after all, on trial for drunk driving, not speeding.

"Weaving" is almost universally found in the arrest report of drunk driving cases. In fact, along with "bloodshot eyes," "odor of alcohol on breath," and "thick, slurred speech," it almost appears to be a prerequisite to any drunk driving arrest. Without question, there are many instances where disreputable police officers will add these elements to their reports to create the classic series of drunk driving symptoms. In even more cases, however, honest officers will be guilty of suggestive observation: Having decided that the suspect is or may be intoxicated, they fully expect to see the usual symptoms — and normal driving becomes weaving.

Through skillful questioning, and, again, through later argument, it should be pointed out that weaving within one's own lane is not nearly as unusual or symptomatic as it sounds. No driver actually steers his car in a geometrically straight line down the middle of his lane. Even the most sober of the jurors will find that he is constantly, almost subconsciously, correcting his course. Watch any attentive driver: his back-and-forth corrective motion of the steering wheel will be almost constant. And it would take a very skilled driver using all of his concentration to keep his car perfectly aligned with a straight line at 40 or 50 miles per hour.

One consideration that should not be overlooked in attempting to explain the defendant's "erratic" driving behavior is the condition of the vehicle. A number of mechanical conditions can contribute to weaving or to other erratic performance: faulty steering, faded brakes, defective suspension, incorrectly inflated tires, bent tie rods, sticking accelerator, etc. If the client confirms this, the mechanical condition should be authenticated prior to trial.

Very well, the officer replies, but the defendant was not just weaving within his lane; on four occasions he weaved all the way across the lane line. Again, this is not as terrible as it initially appears. The widths of the lane and of the car should be pointed out; commonly, a lane leaves about three feet on either side of the car. The average driver will periodically touch or cross a lane line through nothing more than inattentive driving. However, there is an added factor when a police officer follows a driver for any distance: *black-and-white fever.*

Black-and-white fever is simply the normal reaction of most motorists to being followed by a marked police vehicle. When the motorist becomes aware that a police car is following him, he becomes understandably nervous. As a result, anxious to see what the officer is doing, he begins watching the rearview mirror more and more. He becomes tense and his concentration on driving is broken. Most important, he keeps his eyes more on the mirror and less on the road ahead and must constantly correct his car's alignment with the road. The result: possible increase or decrease in speed (tension can cause the foot to depress the accelerator), erratic movements — and weaving. Any experienced and honest patrol officer will be thoroughly familiar with this phenomenon and will admit it on the witness stand.

Failing to stop at the occupied intersection may also be attributed to black-and-white fever: The driver was watching the patrol car in the rearview mirror and did not notice the pedestrian in the crosswalk. Whatever the reason, the officer should be asked if failing to stop at an intersection indicates drunk driving. Has he, for example, ever cited anyone for failing to stop at an intersection who was not under the influence? Of course he has. Again, the client is not contesting a citation for running an occupied intersection; counsel should concentrate not on disproving the fact but rather on showing that it has little or no bearing on the question of intoxication.

At this point, counsel may wish to question the officer as to why he never issued a citation for speeding, unsafe lane change, or failure to stop at an occupied crosswalk. Care should be taken, however, to use leading questions and maintain control of the examination. Never ask "why?" or the officer will give a long and compassionate explanation of how he did not want to add to the client's already serious criminal problems.

More important, counsel should consider asking the arresting officer why he did not pull the defendant over at an earlier point. Why, for example, was he not stopped after he had broken the law by speeding? If his weaving was so serious, why was he not cited immediately for making an unsafe lane change? And if he ran an occupied pedestrian zone, why was he not quickly pulled over? Again, the form of the questioning must be leading and control must be maintained by counsel. But the critical point here is not necessarily that the traffic infractions never occurred or the defendant would have been pulled over, but rather that the infractions were (1) not so serious as to indicate the driver was a threat to others on the road and (2) not enough in themselves to justify a detention for drunk driving. The questioning must be geared to establishing that the violations were simply not indicative of drunk driving. If the officer felt that the defendant was intoxicated, why did he permit him to continue on for almost a mile and endanger the lives of dozens of others on the highway?

The fourth observation of defendant's driving involved his failure to pull over when the officer turned on his flashing red lights and/or siren. There may be a number of explanations for this. The opposite of black-and-white fever may have taken place: The defendant was totally unaware of the red lights, particularly in daylight hours. Or if he saw them, he may have assumed they were intended for someone else, not an unreasonable assumption for someone who believes he has done nothing wrong. Or he may believe they are meant only to signal him to get out of the police car's way. As for the siren, it should be noted that lack of driver response to the sirens of ambulances has become an increasing problem as air conditioning and car stereo systems become more prevalent. With the windows rolled up, the air conditioner on, and the stereo blaring through large, door-mounted speakers, it is no surprise that a siren cannot be heard.

However, when the defendant finally pulled his vehicle over, he parked two feet away from the curb, presenting a hazard to passing traffic. This, it is suggested, is indicative of the poor judgment of an intoxicated driver. But it is also indicative of a very nervous and frightened driver. Few members of the jury would react coolly and dispassionately to being singled out of traffic by flashing red lights and sirens and pulled over to the side of the road. There is no question but that the blood pressure rises and the adrenalin begins pumping on such an occasion. Nervous, flustered, perhaps even near panic, a driver might be expected to act in somewhat less than a rational and calm manner; totally sober drivers have been known to cause traffic accidents under such circumstances. An honest police officer will admit this on the stand.

Finally, counsel who is experienced at drunk driving litigation may wish to ask the officer whether other driving conduct commonly associated with intoxication was present. Did the defendant, for example, continuously speed up and then slow down? Did he slam on the brakes in coming to a stop? Was he hugging the shoulder of the road? Was he holding up traffic by traveling too slowly? Obviously, counsel must be very sure of the answer before he asks such questions.

The prosecutor will attempt to show that the defendant's driving symptoms were indicative of a person under the influence of alcohol. It is up to defense counsel to turn the tables, to show that not only was there an innocent explanation for the driving observations but that those very observations may tend to establish the defendant's sobriety.

§4.1.1 The NHTSA Studies

The National Highway Traffic Safety Administration (NHTSA) has produced a pocket-size booklet intended primarily for law enforcement entitled Guide for Detecting Drunk Drivers at Night, DOT HS-805-711 (available free of charge from NHTSA, Administrative Operations Division, Room 4423, 400 Seventh Street, N.W., Washington, DC 20590). The booklet, based on NHTSA-sponsored research, contains a DUI Detection Guide, which identifies the nineteen most common and reliable initial indicators of drunk driving — along with the probability that the driver exhibiting the symptom is, in fact, under the influence.

The following is a list of the symptoms and their related indicia of intoxication. Thus, for example, the research indicates that "the chances are 65 out of 100" that a driver who is straddling a center or lane marker has a blood-alcohol concentration of .10 percent or higher.

Turning with wide radius	65
Straddling center or lane marker	65
Appearing to be drunk	60
Almost striking object or vehicle	60
Weaving	60
Driving on other than designated roadway	55
Swerving	55
Slow speed (more than 10 miles per hour below limit)	50
Stopping (without cause) in traffic lane	50
Drifting	50
Following too closely	45
Tires on center or lane marker	45
Braking erratically	45
Driving into opposing or crossing traffic	45
Signaling inconsistent with driving actions	40
Stopping inappropriately (other than in lane)	35
Turning abruptly or illegally	35
Accelerating or decelerating rapidly	30
Headlights off	30

It may come as a surprise to jurors that, for example, 40 out of 100 drivers "appearing to be drunk" to police officers are, in fact, not under the influence. Similarly, 40 out of 100 drivers who are weaving or who almost strike another vehicle are also legally sober.

The report notes that symptoms are rarely seen in isolation; officers usually see a number of driving symptoms before pulling the suspect over. The NHTSA research indicates that the chances of a driver being intoxicated when multiple symptoms are observed can also be calculated: "When two or more cues are seen, add 10 to the highest value among the cues observed." For example, if the subject is observed to be weaving (60) and following too closely (45), there are 70 chances out of 100 that he has a BAC of .10 percent or more.

Counsel can come to some rather striking results by using this approach in cases where the officer has testified to particularly bad driving symptoms. Consider, for example, where the officer testifies to having observed all of the following in the defendant before pulling him over: The suspect traveled at 25 miles per hour when the speed limit was 55 miles per hour, left his headlights off, weaved in traffic, crossed the center divider four times, straddled the lane marker for a quarter of a mile, appeared to be drunk, and, upon being pulled over, almost sideswiped a parked car.

On cross-examination, the NHTSA research figures can be used to show that 30 out of 100 individuals exhibiting these symptoms are *not* under the influence (i.e., add 10 percent to the highest figure of 60 percent, giving a figure of 70 percent).

§4.2 *Appearance and Behavior of Defendant*

> How seldom a fact is accurately stated; how almost invariably when a story has passed through the mind of a third person it becomes . . . little better than a falsehood; and this, too, though the narrator be the most truth-seeking person in existence.
>
> NATHANIEL HAWTHORNE

After counsel has tried a number of drunk driving cases, he will notice that the physical symptoms observed by the arresting officer tend to follow a set pattern, so much so, in fact, that many police departments print the symptoms in their report forms, with boxes next to them for the officer to check off. Faced with the commonness of these symptoms and with the officer's full expectation of encountering them, counsel should question whether they were ever seen at all. It is entirely possible that the officer "observed" the particular symptom because he has been conditioned to expect it. It is also possible that the officer is lying and has included the symptom because its absence weakens his case. Using discovery to obtain copies of other DUI reports written by the same officer can prove very helpful for cross-examination at trial.

Although the list is not comprehensive, the following represent the classic physical symptoms that will be found in a drunk driving police report with monotonous regularity:

1. staggered when stepped from car
2. fumbled with wallet

3. disheveled clothing
4. uncombed hair and/or unshaven face
5. bloodshot, bleary, or glassy eyes
6. odor of alcohol on the breath
7. thick and slurred speech
8. flushed face
9. slow pupil reaction to light

Consider, however, the following excerpts from a Joint Legislative Committee Report submitted to the governor of New York (N.Y. Leg. Doc. No. 25, pp. 11–12, 1953):

> The method of identification [of the drunken driver] presently used in most communities is totally inadequate. It usually takes the form of general observations by police officers and witnesses. These witnesses are asked to testify as to the presence or absence of the accepted signs of intoxication, the odor of the breath, slurred speech, hand tremors and clumsiness of movement. . . . [T]hese tests are not conclusive, since the common signs of intoxication have often been used to falsely accuse a sober person. A person's appearance and actions may be clearly abnormal yet the abnormality may not be due to alcohol. . . . It is obviously difficult for the arresting officer to know the accused's usual behavior. He often cannot tell, therefore, whether the accused's behavior at the time of apprehension is usual or unusual. . . . [T]hese signs, without further evidence, do not show positively whether the individual was under the influence of intoxicating liquors. . . .
>
> There are approximately 60 pathological conditions that have symptoms similar to those of alcoholism. An apparent alcohol condition might not be due to alcohol at all. It may be merely the result of injury or sickness. People taking medicines often act as if they had been imbibing too freely. The diabetic in need of, or with an overdose of, insulin may act as if he were intoxicated. Injuries to the nervous system or a concussion of the brain may create alcoholic symptoms. Hence it is evident that not even a physician — on observation alone — is able to accurately diagnose intoxication. How then can a law enforcement officer without any medical training be expected to make a determination as to intoxication? . . .

Despite the predisposition of officers to "see" DUI symptoms, similarity of symptoms of illness to those of intoxication, and the recognized unreliability of a medically untrained police officer's conclusions based on such symptoms, the great majority of jurisdictions continue to hold that the opinion testimony of an officer by itself constitutes sufficient grounds to support a conviction. (See, e.g., *Garrett v. State,* 146 Ga. App. 610, 247 S.E.2d 136 (1978); *People v. Coolidge,* 124 III. App. 2d 479, 259 N.E.2d 851 (1970).)

It must be recognized that a police officer's description of a defendant's physical appearance of inebriation can be devastating. And there is no way of avoiding the issue: Counsel must confront the officer on cross-examination and attempt to offer rational reasons for the seemingly damning symptoms. Fortunately, this is less difficult than it would appear initially.

§4.2.1 Initial Behavior

After testifying to the defendant's erratic driving, the officer will next point to his clumsy and uncoordinated behavior during the initial stages of their confrontation. Typically, the officer will recall that the defendant fumbled through his wallet after being asked to produce his driver's license and had considerable difficulty in finding it. Then, after being asked to step out of the vehicle, the defendant stumbled and almost fell down; it was repeatedly necessary, he may continue, for the defendant to brace himself by placing an arm against the car.

Once again, defense counsel will be faced with damning testimony. Yet once again there are avenues available for productive cross-examination. The course of questioning relative to the fumbling extraction of the driver's license should be apparent. As has been pointed out earlier, the vast majority of citizens who have been singled out from the flow of traffic by flashing red lights and sirens, pulled over by a marked police vehicle, and approached by a uniformed officer wearing a gun are going to be at least very nervous and probably emotionally upset. About the only types of individuals who will not react with a quickened pulse and a higher blood pressure are hardened criminals. It should be understandable, then, when the citizen nervously fumbles in trying to locate and extract his license from his wallet. Rather then being indicative of intoxication, such fumbling should be pointed out to the jury as being a perfectly normal reaction to a high-stress situation. It is the truly intoxicated individual who will feel a false calm, an alcohol-induced sense of ease.

There is, as is often the case in drunk driving situations, the other side of the coin: If no mention is made in the report or in testimony of fumbling for the license, counsel may wish to establish with careful questioning that his client had no trouble locating and removing the license when requested to do so, and then force the officer to admit that fumbling is a commonly observed phenomenon among drunk drivers.

Stumbling when alighting from the vehicle is another course of behavior widely observed by officers, often followed by apparent necessity for the defendant to brace himself against the car with an arm or by leaning. Counsel first should compare the severity of this conduct with the client's performance on the field sobriety tests. Although, in the officer's opinion, he will undoubtedly have flunked the tests, there will probably be little mention of stumbling or the need for lateral support from the car. The defendant may, for example, have touched his finger to his lip rather than to his nose in the finger-to-nose test, but he was apparently standing in an erect and unsupported position for an extended period of time when he performed the test. The apparent discrepancy should be brought out.

The distinct possibility of innocent explanations for the stumbling and need for support should be investigated with the client prior to cross-examination of the officer, and counsel should visit the scene of the arrest. Usually, the defendant's vehicle will be pulled over to the shoulder of the road or highway. As he steps out of his car, then, he may be stepping onto a soft or gravel surface, and one that may be at an angle or slope to the level road. This unexpected quality and angle of the surface could cause anyone to stumble initially; that the defendant did not continue to stumble is indicative of sobriety.

Another factor often present in such situations is that the defendant has been sitting behind the steering wheel for a half hour or more. Again, it is a common phenomenon, and one the jury can recognize, for an individual to stumble in his first steps after having been in a sitting position for an extended period of time and to be unsteady for a few moments thereafter (the first few moments after sitting through a motion picture can be used as an example). Counsel may even wish to point to the stiffness of witnesses after stepping down from testifying in the witness chair for an hour or more. This is true particularly of older persons, whose blood circulation, joint problems, and muscle tone may add to the problem.

There are many other considerations that may contribute to unsteadiness on the feet. Being nervous and/or emotionally upset can certainly be a factor. If enough adrenalin is pumping in the normal person's body, his muscles will actually begin to quiver and then even shake uncontrollably. If the defendant is wearing high heels like those found on a woman's dress shoes or on a man's western boots, it will be all the more difficult to maintain balance initially, particularly on an uneven road surface. If the stop is made at night, the darkness can make initial footing difficult, and this is complicated by the sounds, headlights, and air waves of passing cars.

If the officer's DUI report indicates that the defendant was "cooperative" in his attitude, counsel should ask him what a person's attitude has to do with whether or not they are under the influence. The officer will usually testify that intoxicated persons commonly become uncooperative and even aggressive. The obvious should then be spelled out — that is, ask the officer how he would describe the defendant's attitude. If cooperative, isn't this the *opposite* of the description of a person under the influence? If the defendant was *un*cooperative, on the other hand, the officer should be questioned concerning the existence of that "symptom" in arrests unrelated to intoxication and its nonexistence in many DUI arrests.

§4.2.2 Clothing and Grooming

Many police reports will indicate that the defendant's clothing was rumpled and/or soiled, that the shirt was not completely buttoned, and that his tie was loose and crooked.

The presumption, apparently, is that if an individual is not attired neatly then he must be intoxicated. This presumption, of course, will fall with even the slightest scrutiny. And, in fact, the presence of such "symptoms" in a police report probably does more harm to the prosecutor's cause than good. Certainly, such supposed symptoms of intoxication are easily explained, and this readiness of the officer to interpret anything as indicative of inebriation can be used by counsel to discredit other more valid symptoms.

Counsel should point out that the officer was not aware of the reasons for the defendant's disheveled clothing. Perhaps the defendant had been in those clothes for many hours and had even taken a nap in them. Possibly he had been involved in a particularly arduous or dirty physical task, or maybe he had simply loosened his clothing for reasons of comfort. In any event, counsel should stress the numerous reasonable explanations for the defendant's appearance, as well as the officer's predisposition immediately to assume the worst and his failure even to consider innocent explanations.

Similarly, police reports will carefully point out that the defendant's hair was unruly and he was unshaven. Again, just why uncombed hair or an unshaven face is evidence of intoxication is unclear, but they do appear with some frequency in the officers' observations. Presumably, sober people keep their hair neatly combed and their faces cleanly shaven, whereas inebriation somehow causes instant beard growth. Again, however, the officer will be leaving himself open to a myriad of innocent explanations for the defendant's appearance and to an inference in the jurors' minds of an unfair propensity to interpret everything in a light unfavorable to the defendant. And counsel should make every effort to reinforce this inference.

§4.2.3 Bloodshot Eyes

Rarely will there be a drunk driving case where the arresting officer does not record in his report that the defendant's eyes were bloodshot, glassy, and/or bleary. In addition, the really ambitious officer will shine a flashlight in the defendant's eyes and gleefully record that the pupil reaction was "slow," an indication of intoxication.

Granted that the truly inebriated individual will probably have reddened eyes due to the effect of alcohol on the capillaries in the eyes and that extensive intoxication can cause a glassy or bleary-eyed appearance, there are also any number of nonalcoholic reasons for such symptoms. In fact, it takes little imagination to come up with reasons for redness in the eyes. The success of commercial eye solutions such as Visine and Murine attests to this.

Fatigue is the most common cause for eyes being bloodshot, glassy, or bleary. It is quite possible that the defendant had been up for an extended period of time prior to the arrest, possibly for a day or two without sleep. As any juror will know from everyday experience, lack of sleep will cause the eyes to become reddened and glassy or bleary, and may cause other symptoms as well, such as disheveled clothing or erratic driving. Yet it is unlikely that the officer will have questioned the defendant as to innocent reasons for his inflamed or glassy eyes. Again, he will have just assumed that the condition was caused by alcohol.

Another recurring possibility is that the defendant's eyes are *normally* red or somewhat glassy. No one's eyes are perfectly white, and it is really a question of degree as to the normal redness in a given person's eyes. In some cases, a defendant may be suffering from an illness or a permanent eye defect that can cause a normally bloodshot appearance. The officer should be asked if he had seen the defendant on previous occasions, i.e., if he had compared the defendant's eyes with their everyday appearance. (The officer should, of course, be set up for this, and the client's eyes disguised with darkened glasses.) Counsel may even consider having the officer and the jury look at the defendant's eyes in court to see if they are reddened or bleary.

Most cities today suffer from air pollution, and a well-known effect of this is eye irritation. On a day of bad air quality, the average driver will suffer from eye inflammation. If this situation were applicable anytime during the 24 hours prior to the client's arrest, counsel should consider taking steps to introduce into evidence the statistics kept by the city's air pollution control agency, after, again, setting the officer up by having him deny that there was any significant pollution that day.

Counsel might consider asking the officer if, in the course of his investigations, he bothered to go back to the establishment the defendant was driving from to determine what the conditions were — that is, was the tavern, for example, filled with cigarette smoke? Did the officer even ask the defendant about this? Did the officer even *consider* this possibility when he wrote down that the defendant's eyes were red and watery? It can then be brought out that in the officer's own experience such places are often filled with smoke.

Still another cause of eye redness and glassiness is eye strain from extensive reading or other intense visual activity. Once again, the officer should be asked if he inquired into possible causes for the eye condition. He may be asked specifically if he was aware of what possible activities the defendant had been engaged in that may have been a contributing factor.

These are the most commonly recurring explanations for bloodshot, bleary, and/or glassy eyes. There are additional causes, but the point to be made by counsel is clear: There is a reasonable explanation for what the officer observed, an explanation that the officer was unwilling to explore in his haste to gather incriminating evidence.

§4.2.4 Flushed Face

Another automatic observation in a drunk driving investigation is the flushed face of the suspect. The rush of blood to the skin surface of the face is a well-known phenomenon, particularly of the individual who has been drinking heavily. Again, however, there are innumerable causes for the flushed appearance of a defendant's face that have nothing whatsoever to do with alcohol.

The first possibility is that the defendant's face is normally flushed, that is, the everyday condition of his complexion is ruddy. This is commonly found in older people as well as in individuals whose heavy drinking habits have caused burst blood vessels in the skin. Counsel should establish the fact that the officer had never seen the defendant prior to the arrest and thus draw the conclusion that the officer had nothing to compare the flushed appearance with. Of course, the officer probably will notice the defendant's appearance in court before he takes the stand and probably will testify his complexion was even redder at the time of the arrest. Nevertheless, his previous unfamiliarity should be established, and the jury should be permitted to view the defendant (whose face will probably grow even redder under all the attention) and come to their own conclusions as to what the officer had seen and thought.

In addition to the possibility of a permanently ruddy complexion, there are a number of temporary causes for a flushed appearance. Certainly, most individuals detained at the roadside by police officers for criminal investigation will tend to have one or more of a number of emotional reactions: fear, embarrassment, nervousness, anger. And it is common knowledge, which can be medically substantiated, that such emotional reactions can and usually do result in a rush of blood to the face. In the majority of drunk driving stops, then, it can be fully expected that the driver will have a flushed face at least for some period of time, regardless of his sobriety.

In questioning the officer concerning this observation, as well as his observations of other symptoms, counsel first should set him up. This is done here by establishing through a line of questioning that the officer was quite positive about the observation, that the symptom was taken into consideration in coming to the conclusion that the suspect was under the influence, and that, in fact, the flushed appearance was instrumental in formulating the officer's opinion of intoxication.

The officer's credibility often can be undermined by asking him whether he has ever seen individuals with flushed faces who were not inebriated or whether most persons who are stopped by him get flushed in the face from fear or anger. If he denies these obvious facts, the jury will tend to discount the rest of his testimony.

There is, of course, another possible explanation for the officer's observation of the defendant's flushed appearance. As with so many other physical symptoms the officer may "see" what is simply not there. Most police officers have already decided the suspect probably is intoxicated before they have even gotten out of their car. Conditioned to expect the classic symptoms — bloodshot eyes, flushed face — they then confirm their expectations. What may be a normally pink complexion becomes flushed.

Finally, as with all observations, counsel should consider the possibility that the officer is simply lying. While most police officers are basically truthful, many others will realize that the nonexistence of any of the classic symptoms will tend to throw doubt on the guilt of the defendant and thus on the quality of the officer's judgment.

§4.2.5 Odor of Alcohol on Breath

There is nothing so recurrent among police observations as the existence of an alcoholic odor to the drunk driving suspect's breath. Quite simply, counsel will probably never encounter a case involving driving under the influence of alcohol where his client was not observed to have had a strong or at least moderate odor of alcohol on his breath. If there was none smelled by the officer, the charge will almost assuredly be changed immediately to driving under the influence of drugs, regardless of the absence of any evidence of drug consumption.

While an odor of alcohol on the breath is the most dependably recurring symptom in an officer's report, it is also the most damaging. Unless the odor can be explained, the jury will reasonably conclude that the defendant had been drinking. Defense counsel's job then becomes one of establishing when and how much, and this will involve interrogation of the officer as to the nature and strength of the breath odor.

At the outset, it should be noted that alcohol has little or no odor, i.e., pure ethyl alcohol by itself will have no odor. What the officer is actually smelling is the flavoring of the liquor (brandy, scotch, beer, wine, etc.). And the odor of the flavoring can be deceptive as to the strength or amount drunk. Beer and wine, for example, are the least intoxicating of alcoholic beverages and yet they will cause the strongest odor on the breath; the officer will usually admit to an awareness of this. A single glass of wine or beer may well have a more powerful "odor of alcohol" on the breath than three or four shots of bourbon or scotch.

As illustrative of the point that ethanol has no odor — and thus that the strength of the odor of alcohol on the breath is irrelevant — counsel may wish to develop during cross-examination of the officer or expert that the drinking of so-called near beer will result in the ubiquitous language, "strong odor of alcohol on the breath." Yet there is no alcohol in near beer! Thus the odor — and strength of the odor — of alcohol on the breath has absolutely nothing to do with the amount, or even presence, of alcohol in the system. If permitted by the trial judge, this point can be made very effectively before a jury with a demonstration involving the defendant's consuming two bottles of near beer and then breathing into the face of the arresting officer and the jurors.

Counsel must therefore establish in the jury's mind that what the officer is smelling is not intoxicating; it is only associated indirectly with the intoxicant alcohol. There are two courses of attack: to question the source of the smell and/or to question the conclusion of intoxication.

The source of the odor of alcohol can easily be other than liquor. There are, for example, many products that are designed to stay in the throat area and that may smell somewhat like liquor on the breath. Mouthwash, deodorizing throat spray, and cough syrup are three of the more common of such items that may cause the officer to believe he has smelled liquor on the suspect's breath. Many illnesses can cause a type of breath that can be misinterpreted as alcoholic. A simple case of bad breath undoubtedly has been the true source of more than one officer's trigger-quick conclusion that he has smelled the odor of alcohol. And it is well known that belching causes the gaseous odors of the stomach to cling to the throat area for a period, often giving off a distinct odor of liquor or greatly magnifying the odorific effect of a single drink (if the officer denies this, he should be asked why the instructions for the operation of most breath analysis machines require that the test not be administered for at least ten minutes after any belching by the subject).

Having cast doubt on the source of the odor, counsel will next wish to question the validity of any conclusions about the amount or timing of consumption of alcohol. Again, alcohol has little or no odor: It is the beverage flavoring that the officer is smelling, and some of the weakest beverages have the strongest odors. It should follow, then, that it would be fallacious to conclude how much a subject has had to drink. It would be equally fallacious to attempt to determine when the drinking occurred and, in most cases, even what beverage was being consumed.

Rarely will counsel be confronted with a police officer who will claim to be able to tell you what, when, and how much the defendant had to drink, on the basis of smelling his breath. Such an officer is a boon to the defense, for he is shown up easily before the jury, and the remainder of his testimony will be cast into doubt. More commonly, the officer will admit that he could not tell what the defendant had been drinking but that it was a strong odor, and therefore he had been drinking a large amount recently.

The quantity of alcohol consumed cannot be determined by breath odor. As stated earlier, some of the weakest drinks leave the strongest odors on the breath. And some types of alcoholic beverages (liqueurs, notably, such as Kahlua or Grand Marnier) have a syrupy quality that will tend to stay in the mouth and throat area longer than others. The result is that the officer is smelling the fumes from the drink directly, and it will appear to be stronger.

Just as the amount of alcohol consumed cannot be estimated by breath odor, neither can the moment when the alcohol was drunk be determined accurately. If the officer insists, however, that he can tell how recent the drinking was by the strength of the breath odor, counsel may be able to place him on the horns of a dilemma: Strong odor of alcohol will mean, according to the officer, consumption of liquor within the previous 10 or 20 minutes, yet it is a physiological fact that alcohol does not have a maximum effect for nearly an hour after consumption. A very strong odor, then, can be interpreted to mean that at least much of the alcohol the officer is smelling will not yet have had an effect on the defendant — that is, he was not yet under the influence of the smelled liquor when he was stopped.

Counsel should bear in mind that the detection of alcohol on the drunk driving suspect's breath is the coup de graĉe in the minds of most police officers. In most cases, they suspect that a driver is under the influence when they first pull him over; smelling alcohol on his breath is confirmation. The rest of the observations, including the giving of the field sobriety tests, are pure window dressing. Accordingly, counsel should attempt in his cross-examination to relate this state of affairs to the jury. Prior to commencing the line of questioning concerning the odor of alcohol, for example, counsel may wish to establish the importance in the officer's mind of the smell of alcohol. Although officers will want to seem fair and appear to have withheld judgment until after further observations, most will feel fairly secure with the smell of alcohol as a symptom and will admit that this had a strong bearing on the "later" formulation of their opinion; if it did not, then the relative unimportance of breath odor will stand admitted. Once the importance to the officer of the odor of alcohol is established, counsel can then proceed to undermine the validity of such an observation. The officer's following observations will then be tainted by his earlier conclusions based on a faulty premise.

§4.2.6 Slurred Speech

Counsel will be confronted with few drunk driving police reports that do not indicate that the suspect's speech was slurred. Often the officer will have written a variation on a theme by describing the speech as "thick and slurred," "slurred and stuttering," or perhaps even "unintelligible."

Once again, counsel must deal with a critical aspect of the case: If the jury believes that the client was so intoxicated that his speech mannerisms were affected significantly, they will also conclude that he was so intoxicated that he could not safely operate a motor vehicle. But, again, there are a number of techniques that may be used in cross-examining the arresting officer on this issue.

First is the possibility that what the officer considered to be slurred, thick, or stuttering speech may, in fact, be the defendant's normal manner of speaking. As with other observations, counsel should establish in his questioning that the officer was unfamiliar with how the defendant sounded on other occasions. Of course, the jury will then be expecting to hear exactly how the defendant does talk, and counsel should expect to produce him for direct testimony or possibly lose credibility with the jury.

It should be noted that, as with police observations of flushed face, bloodshot eyes, etc., counsel should ask defense witnesses their opinion about the defendant's appearance and behavior. Although in the majority of cases the defendant will be alone at the time of his arrest, it will be a rare situation in which he cannot produce at least one friend or associate with whom he spent some time during the hour preceding the arrest. Even a spouse or friend who posts bail for him may help, if he or she was able to observe him within an hour or so after the arrest.

In preparing for cross-examination of the officer, counsel should examine carefully the arrest report for errors or inconsistencies. But it should also be studied for the possible effect its form may have on the officer's recorded observations. Many police reports will not permit the officer to report simply in the narrative what he observed. Rather, specific questions will be posed by the form, and answers will be given with boxes next to them to be checked. The suggestiveness and limitation of this common police approach should be brought out to the jury.

For example, one large police department has a drunk driving form that has a section designated "Speech," followed by boxes next to the terms "no impairment," "slurred," and "incoherent." There is no room in the form for any other possibilities; the officer must choose one. Consider the effect of such a form questionnaire. Obviously, the officer is not going to check off the box entitled "no impairment"; in effect, this would be to invite criticism of his decision to arrest and would certainly be used as evidence of sobriety in court. "Incoherent" will probably not be checked, for this would be overdoing it; how would an officer explain being able to understand the defendant's answers to his questions? And this leaves only one box remaining to check: "slurred."

Perhaps the most effective line of interrogation involves the situation in which the officer has testified that the defendant's speech was "incoherent," "confused," or so "slurred" as to be incomprehensible. Certainly, counsel should attempt to lead the officer into characterizing the speech as being so slurred as to be nearly impossible to understand. After this preparation, counsel should lay another foundation, preferably removed in time in order not to disclose the tactic, by asking the officer a long series of questions concerning the questions asked of the defendant in the field and at the police station. There will be no shortage of such questions; the client will probably have been asked dozens of questions concerning his drinking, his physical condition, who he is, where he lives and works, etc. After asking a few such questions committing the officer, the inquiries should be followed by a question to the effect of "And you *understood* that his telephone number was 482-5713?" Obviously, the officer will have to confirm this: He recorded the information accurately in the report. After a long, even exaggerated, series of such questions, counsel should ask the officer just what was confused or difficult to understand about his client's speech.

§4.2.7 Pupil Reaction

The pupil reaction test is a favorite of many traffic officers because of its simplicity and its aura of scientific objectivity and reliability. Although it is increasingly being replaced with the newer "horizontal gaze nystagmus" test (see text §4.3.5), it is still a commonly employed procedure; in some cases the arresting officer will administer both eye impairment tests.

The pupil reaction test is commonly given fairly early in the investigation, usually before the performance FSTs. It is accomplished by simply shining a flashlight in the suspect's eyes. The officer then observes the reaction of the pupil, noting the speed with which it contracts in reaction to the sudden increase in light. Generally speaking, the slower the contraction, the more intoxicated the individual. Thus the officer will usually testify that the defendant's eyes either contracted slowly when exposed to the light, or failed to respond to the light at all.

The well-trained officer will shine his light into the eyes of his partner (or some other presumably sober person) immediately after shining it into the suspect's eyes, again noting the reaction. This permits him to compare the relative speed of the pupil contraction between the two individuals — that is, it gives the officer a standard against which to judge the suspect's pupil reaction. If this was not done, the failure should be noted.

It is, of course, a scientific fact that alcohol will slow many responses of the human body, including the contraction of the pupil when confronted by light stimuli. However, the officer's testimony on this subject can be attacked in two ways. First, he is not qualified as an expert in this area. Second, the conclusion that the reaction was "slow" is meaningless without sufficient context.

Counsel should establish quickly the officer's complete lack of training in the physiology of the eye. He has no education in ophthalmology and is simply not qualified to administer eye tests or to evaluate their results. His informal field experiment should be revealed for what it is — a very crude attempt by a layman to conduct a medical examination.

The officer should then be interrogated with respect to what is meant by a "slow" pupil response: Slow in reaction to what? Was he timing the reaction? What size differential in millimeters was involved? Over what period of time? (The response is never timed.) If he did not measure the differential and time the response, how can the reaction be interpreted by a true expert at trial? If the officer used his partner for a comparison, he should be questioned with respect to the relative physiology of his partner's eyes — probably the eyes of a healthy, rested relatively young person — to those of the defendant.

The coffin can be nailed shut with a series of ophthalmological questions concerning the relative abilities of eyes to contract to light stimuli. The officer can be asked, for example, if he considered the possible effect of optic nerve ataxia? Oculomotor nerve weakness? Iritis? Does he even know what they mean? Is he aware that the common condition of farsightedness can affect pupil response time? These and similar questions should serve to firmly discredit the probative value of the pupil reaction test.

Independent of any pupil reaction test, some officers will testify that the defendant's pupils were simply dilated; it is a fact that consumption of alcohol raises the level of norepinephrine in the blood, which causes dilation. There are, of course, many reasons for dilation that have nothing to do with intoxication. It is interesting to note, for example, that such common over-the-counter remedies as Allerest and Sudafed contain compounds (phenylpropanolamine HCL and pseudoephedrine HCL, respectively) that also can cause dilation because of their similarity to norepinephrine. This, then, is another reason why counsel should carefully question his client concerning the hours of his pre-arrest activities — including the possibility that he ingested medication.

§4.2.8 False Symptoms from Abnormal Blood Sugar Level

As New York's Joint Legislative Committee noted in its reports on the unreliability of outward signs of intoxication (see §4.2), the similarity between the symptoms of alcohol intoxication and a diabetes attack is striking. The symptomatic reactions of a person in the early stages of a diabetes attack include shakiness, sweatiness, hunger, headaches, dizziness, mood changes, blurred vision, and paleness. Other moderate attack symptoms include nausea, irritability, crying, lightheadedness, numbness of lips or tongue, weakness, loss of coordination, and slurred speech or confusion. Especially in the early stages of a reaction, the symptoms are very similar to those usually displayed by a person under the influence of an alcoholic beverage.

Although the immediate effect of some alcohol may be to increase blood sugar, the effect over a period of hours may be to lower it, which can cause a diabetic reaction. The attack that may follow is of special concern to counsel for the diabetic driver, since even a small amount of alcohol on the breath combined with the symptoms of a diabetes attack may mislead some people into thinking that the driver is severely intoxicated.

Even when a blood-alcohol content test is taken, the acetone that is present in the breath of a person who is diabetic and suffering from an insulin reaction may cause an erroneously high reading. For a discussion of the effects of acetone on breath analysis, see §6.1.1.

Perfectly normal, healthy individuals can experience temporary conditions of hypoglycemia (low blood sugar) after consuming small amounts of alcohol — resulting in exaggerated but false symptoms of intoxication. According to Dr. Keith Ryan in his article entitled Alcohol and Blood Sugar Disorders, 8(2) Alcohol Health and Research World (1983–1984), consumption of even small amounts of alcohol can produce hypoglycemia — either "fasting glycemia" or "reactive glycemia."

Fasting glycemia can exist where the person drinking has not eaten for at least 24 hours or has been on a low carbohydrate diet. Production of glucose in the liver is stopped while the alcohol is broken down by the liver. Stored glucose would normally be used to maintain the blood-sugar level, but there will be little or no glucose stored in the liver if the individual has not eaten or has drastically reduced his carbohydrate intake. As a result, the blood sugar level will drop, and the central nervous system will be strongly affected — reflected in behavior similar to intoxication.

The second kind of low blood-sugar condition, reactive hypoglycemia, occurs because alcohol increases production of insulin by the pancreas. This rise in insulin causes a rapid fall in the blood-sugar level, with the same results as with fasting hypoglycemia — that is, false symptoms of intoxication. Hypoglycemia — and its attendant symptoms suggesting intoxication — is also commonly encountered in chronic alcoholics.

Unless counsel anticipates an outright dismissal as the result of revealing a defense based on a blood-sugar reaction, it may be wiser to preserve the defense for use at trial. If probable cause were based on a "reasonable man" test, an insulin reaction might undermine cause for arrest. As a general rule, however, probable cause exists subjectively within the mind of the officer and depends solely on his observations. The similarity between the symptoms of a diabetes attack and those displayed by a person under the influence of alcohol may serve to buttress rather than undermine the legal existence of probable cause. Diabetes therefore probably would not present a good defense to a valid arrest or a good objection to the admissibility of the blood-alcohol test that may follow. It may, however, create a reasonable doubt in the mind of the judge or jury sufficient to obtain an acquittal.

Checklist 2 Physical Appearance and Symptoms

Clothing and Grooming

- ☐ Is there an innocent explanation for the defendant's disheveled clothing?
- ☐ Why had the defendant not shaved or combed his hair?
- ☐ Are there any other witnesses to the defendant's appearance within an hour of the arrest?
- ☐ Can the officer's conclusions be used to discredit other testimony?

Eyes

- ☐ Does the defendant suffer from any eye disorder?
- ☐ Is the normal appearance of defendant's eyes red, glassy, bleary, or bloodshot?
- ☐ Was the defendant suffering from fatigue, lack of sleep, or eye strain?
- ☐ Was there significant air pollution on the day of the arrest?
- ☐ If a pupil reaction test was given:
    - ☐ Was the officer qualified to administer the test and render medical conclusions?
    - ☐ How were size of pupils and speed of their reaction measured?
    - ☐ Is the officer familiar with nonalcoholic causes of slow pupil reaction?

Flushed Face

- ☐ Is the defendant's facial complexion normally ruddy or red?
- ☐ Was the defendant nervous, angry, or otherwise emotionally upset at the time of the officer's observations?

- ☐ Are there causes for a flushed appearance other than alcohol?

Breath Odor

- ☐ As alcohol has little or no odor, was the officer smelling an unusually strong beverage flavoring such as that of beer or wine?
- ☐ Does the officer contend that he can tell what the defendant was drinking, when, and how much?
- ☐ Does or did the defendant simply have bad breath or acetone?
- ☐ Was the defendant belching prior to the officer smelling his breath?
- ☐ Had the defendant had a drink or two of a liqueur that clung to his mouth and throat?
- ☐ Did the presence of an odor of alcohol have an instrumental effect in the forming of the officer's opinion of intoxication?

Speech

- ☐ Was the officer familiar with the defendant's normal speech prior to the arrest?
- ☐ Does the defendant normally speak in a thick, slurred, stuttering, and/or confused manner?
- ☐ Did nervousness, anger, or embarrassment affect the defendant's speech?
- ☐ Are there any other witnesses to the defendant's speech characteristics within an hour of the arrest?
- ☐ Did the police report permit any alternatives but "normal," "slurred," or "incoherent"?
- ☐ Was the officer able to understand the defendant's answers to the numerous questions?
- ☐ Do any audio or video tapes exist?

§4.3 Field Sobriety Tests

> Opinion has caused more trouble on this little earth than plagues or earthquakes.
>
> VOLTAIRE

Assuming that the client did not refuse to cooperate and was not incapacitated by a traffic accident, counsel will be confronted with the arresting officer's analysis of the client's performance on one or more *field sobriety tests* (FSTs). These tests have a certain aura of objectivity and scientific reliability about them which impresses juries. It is defense counsel's task, of course, to expose these "tests" for the often unreliable and always very subjective procedures they are. In fact, the tests often present a "win-win" scenario for the officer. If the defendant performs poorly on the tests, the prosecution will point to them as scientific proof of alcohol-induced impairment. If the defendant does well, however, the clever prosecutor argues that this is "obvious" evidence of tolerance to alcohol — i.e, a thinly veiled accusation that the defendant is an alcoholic.

FSTs are generally administered in the field, that is, at the scene of the arrest. The theoretical purpose of the tests is one of screening — to determine if there is probable cause to arrest the individual for drunk driving. In fact, however, the officer has almost always already determined that the suspect is guilty and the field sobriety tests are administered solely to gather incriminating evidence.

Generally speaking, there are four different categories of field sobriety tests. The first three involve *performance* tests; two focus on physical performance, one on mental. A physical and a mental test may, however, be combined into one exercise as a *divided attention* test: in addition to testing physical and mental ability, the exercise tests the ability to coordinate physical *and* mental tasks at the same time. Commonly, for example, the suspect is asked to perform the one-leg stand while simultaneously counting backwards from 100 or estimating the passage of thirty seconds.

The fourth type of FSTs consist of *eye impairment* tests.

The first of the performance tests are designed to determine a subject's *balance.* The most commonly used balance tests are the walk-the-line, the leg raise (or one-leg stand), and the modified position of attention.

It is a common practice among officers administering balancing tests to "fail" a suspect because he raised his arms during performance. The officer will commonly explain that raising your arms during a walk-the-line or leg-lift test is a sign that the individual's balance is off due to intoxication. The officer may also testify that when he or she demonstrated the test for the suspect, *the officer* did *not* raise his or her arms.

Counsel should develop in cross-examination — and confirm during direct of the client if the client takes the stand — that using your arms for balance is a *natural,* instinctive, thing to do. This is such a common experience that if the officer denies that using your arms is a normal reaction to balancing, the officer's testimony can be developed in such a way that the officer will lose credibility with the jury.

As for the officer's demonstration in the field, it is an assumption on the officer's part that the defendant — or anyone in that situation — would notice that the officer was not using his or her arms. The focus of anyone taking the walk-the-line test, for example, will be on the line and the heel-to-toe steps, not on the arms.

Should the officer testify that he or she specifically instructed the defendant not to raise his or her arms during the tests, it should be developed that this is asking the defendant to do something that is awkward and unnatural. And a sober person asked to perform an awkward and unnatural act will usually do so in an awkward and unnatural way.

Walk-the-line test. The walk-the-line test, also referred to as the walk-and-turn test, is undoubtedly the most commonly encountered of the field sobriety tests. In it, the testing officer has the client walk along a line or crack in the pavement, heel-to-toe; usually, at the end of the line he is directed to pivot and return.

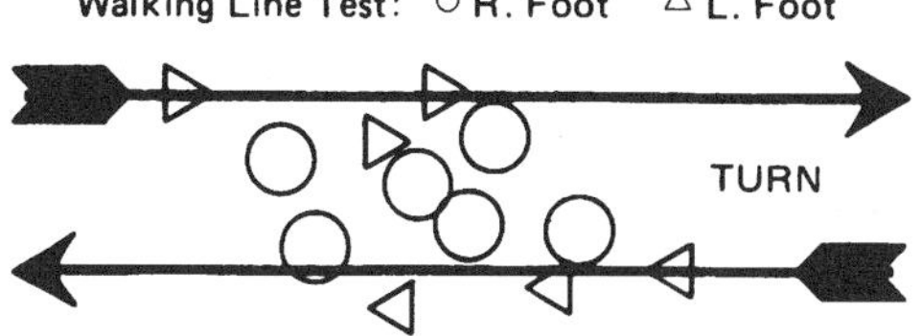

Walk-the-Line Test Result from Police Report

One problem that recurs with the walk-the-line test is that the line the suspect is being asked to walk is often imaginary. Rather than drawing a line in the dirt or pointing out an even crack in the pavement, the officer will tell the suspect to walk a line between two points or simply to walk a straight line. It should be clearly brought out in such a case that the line envisioned in the officer's mind was not the same line that the defendant had mentally drawn and followed.

The one-leg-stand. This test requires the suspect to stand on one leg for approximately 30 seconds, with the other leg held out at a 45-degree angle. Administered as a "divided attention" test, the individual is also told either to (1) put his leg back down after 30 seconds have passed, (2) count backwards from a number such as 1,000, or (3) recite the alphabet. A failure to maintain balance is an indication of intoxication, as is the inability to estimate time, count as directed, or recite the alphabet correctly. Again, however, it should be noted that it is difficult for many perfectly sober people to maintain their stance with a leg held rigidly outwards on the first attempt.

The one-leg-stand test, together with the walk-the-line (or walk-and-turn) and nystagmus tests, make up the National Highway Traffic Safety Administration's approved battery of "standardized" field sobriety tests (see §4.3.2). Due partly to the federal effort at uniformity in DUI enforcement, the three tests are finding increased acceptance among law enforcement agencies across the country.

The modified position of attention. In this test, the suspect is asked to assume a rigid position of attention with his head tilted back and eyes closed. Any swaying is considered evidence of intoxication. This test is suited particularly to experimentation with the jury or the officers. It is very difficult to hold steady without beginning to sway slightly for 15 or 30 seconds, although only close observers will be able to notice the swaying.

The modified position of attention test is designed to detect swaying in the suspect, presumably a symptom of intoxication. A scientific study, however, has concluded that even high doses of alcohol have little effect on body sway.

As reported in Fagen, Tiplady, and Scott, Effects of Ethanol on Psychomotor Performance, 59 British Journal of Anaesthesiology 961 (1987), researchers administered doses of alcohol to a number of subjects in proportion to their body weight and then tested them for body sway with a "Wright-Codoataxiameter." The results uniformly showed that body sway increased significantly only when 2.5 to 3 hours had passed after drinking had been concluded — in other words, during the so-called hangover period. Prior to that time, there was little, if any, noticeable sway in the subjects.

The second category of performance tests is designed to determine *coordination.* The most commonly used tests are the finger-to-nose, the finger-to-thumb, the hand-pat, and the coin pickup.

Finger-to-nose test. Almost as popular as the walk-the-line is the finger-to-nose test. In this FST, the defendant is asked to assume a position of attention, tilt his head back, and touch the tip of his right index finger to the tip of his nose; this is then repeated with the left index finger.

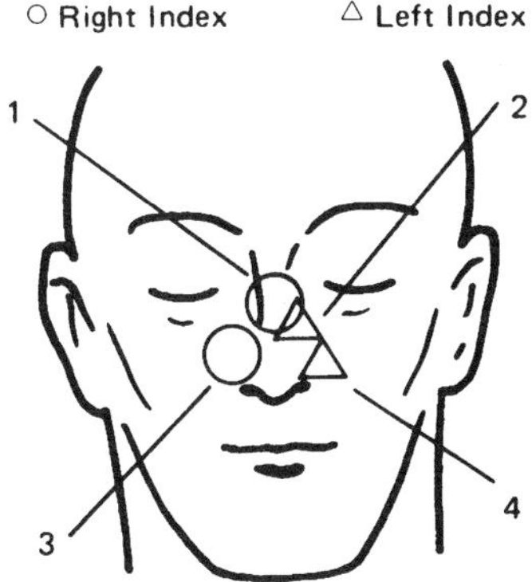

Finger-to-Nose Test Result from Police Report

A recurring problem with the finger-to-nose test is that the administering officer instructs the suspect to touch his nose with his finger — and then fails him because he did not touch the *tip* of his finger to the *tip* of his nose. In the officer's mind, of course, the test involves touching tip-to-tip, but it is not uncommon for the officer to fail to communicate this to the suspect. Thus when the suspect touches the flat of his finger to the bridge of his nose it is interpreted as a sign of intoxication — rather than the result of imprecise directions.

Counsel should listen carefully to the officer's testimony on direct examination concerning his test instructions. If he testifies that he told the defendant, for example, to "touch the tip of your nose" or "touch your nose with the tip of your finger," it should be pointed out on cross-examination that the defendant performed exactly as instructed.

Finger-to-thumb. Sometimes called the finger touch or finger count, this is a coordination test in which the suspect is told to touch the thumb of one hand to each of the four fingers in sequential order. Counsel will often find that if the client appeared to have performed satisfactorily, the officer will claim that he failed because he did it too slowly — although instructions as to speed are often not given.

The finger-to-thumb (or "finger count"). This is a coordination test in which the suspect is told to touch the thumb of one hand to the little finger of the same hand, then to each of the remaining fingers and back again to the little finger in quick succession. Counsel will find that if his client performed satisfactorily, the officer will often claim that he failed because he performed it "too slowly," although instructions as to speed are often not given.

The hand-pat. The suspect is instructed to hold one hand palm up, then pat the palm alternately with the back and palm of the other hand in a rapid but smooth motion. The officer fails the suspect for "chopping," "clapping," or going too slowly. As with other field sobriety tests, it is not uncommon for the officer to give incomplete or inaccurate instructions and/or a rushed demonstration.

Coin pickup. The arresting officer drops a coin or coins on the ground and instructs the suspect to pick them up. The suspect fails if he or she has any difficulty in collecting the coins.

Reverse counting. In this field sobriety test, the suspect is told to count from one to ten and then back down to one, a variation is to have him begin at 100 or 1000 and count down until told to stop.

Recited alphabet. This is a mental agility test asking the individual to recite the alphabet very quickly. It is a rare case in which the officer will not testify that the defendant skipped over some letters, or had to stop halfway through and start again.

Written alphabet. The suspect here is asked to write the alphabet on a piece of paper, and then to authenticate it with his or her signature. This is a test of both physical and mental ability: the focus can be on either the correctness of the alphabet or the handwriting itself. The prosecutor will view this as valuable physical evidence, independently corroborating the officer's testimony. As will be seen subsequently, however, if handled correctly by defense counsel it represents a very effective way to discredit the officer.

The fourth category of field sobriety tests does not involve performance of tasks by the suspect, but rather consists of determining whether there has been functional impairment of the suspect's eyes. These types of FSTs are particularly damaging because of their seemingly scientific nature. The two increasingly prevalent tests here are pupil reaction and gaze nystagmus.

Pupil reaction. In this test, the officer instructs the suspect to look straight ahead while the officer shines a flashlight or penlight into the suspect's eyes, noting the speed of pupil contraction. Often, the officer will testify that he compared this at the time with the pupil reaction of his or her partner (or some other presumably sober person) immediately after shining it into the suspect's eyes, again noting the reaction. This permits him to compare the relative speed of the pupil contraction between the two individuals — that is, it gives the officer a standard against which to judge the suspect's pupil reaction. If this was not done, the failure should be noted.

Nystagmus. The newest — and potentially most damaging — weapon in the officer's arsenal of field sobriety tests is nystagmus — more accurately, *horizontal gaze nystagmus.* This test involves the officer observing the movement of the suspect's eyeball on a lateral plane — when nystagmus (eye jerking) begins (referred to as "onset of nystagmus"), whether there is a uniform movement ("smooth pursuit"), and whether the eyeball jerks in a different fashion when back as far as it can go ("distinct nystagmus at extremes"). This test, part of the "standardized" battery of FSTs, is particularly subject to cross-examination due to the predictability of the officer's failure to understand, administer, and observe/

record the results. See §§13.0.5 and 13.1.11 concerning cross-examination of the officer.

Counsel may encounter other means of testing balance, coordination, and/or mental agility, but these have proven the most prevalent. In each case, the factors covered in the subsequent discussions should be considered as to their effect on the performance of the test in question.

Field sobriety tests are impressive on their face and, unchallenged, carry considerable weight with jurors. As will be seen in later sections, however, these physical exercises (a more accurate term than "tests") are very susceptible to attack on a wide variety of fronts. They are inherently unreliable, difficult for any sober person to perform — particularly considering the physical and emotional conditions under which they are given — and difficult for the already-predisposed officer to accurately assess, record, or recall.

§4.3.1 Validity of Field Sobriety Tests

How effective are these highly tauted field sobriety tests? Consider the research funded by the National Highway Traffic Safety Administration (NHTSA), which resulted in the later adoption of the so-called "standardized" field sobriety tests (see §4.3.2). In a 1977 study, researchers determined that the three most effective field sobriety tests (FSTs) were walk-and-turn, one-leg stand, and horizontal gaze nystagmus. Yet, even using just these supposedly more accurate tests, the researchers found that 47 percent of the subjects who would have been arrested based upon test performance actually had blood-alcohol concentrations of less than the legal limit of .10 percent. In other words, *almost half of all persons "failing" the tests were not legally under the influence of alcohol!* Burns and Moskowitz, Psychophysical Tests for DWI Arrest: Final Report, DOT-HS-802-424, NHTSA (1977).

In 1981, these same researchers conducted further tests in an attempt to improve the credibility of the proposed "standardized" battery of FSTs. The error rate improved somewhat: The false results dropped to 32 percent — i.e., "only" a third of all persons judged to be guilty by these tests were, in fact, innocent. Tharp, Burns, and Moskowitz, Development and Field Test of Psychophysical Tests for DWI Arrests: Final Report, DOT-HS-805-864, NHTSA (1981). Critics of this second "study," however, point out that the "reliability coefficients" for this self-serving research were far below accepted levels in the scientific community. See Cole and Nowaczyk, Field Sobriety Tests: Are They Designed for Failure?, 79 Perceptual and Motor Skills 99 (1994), where the authors noted, among other problems:

> The fact that these tests are largely unfamiliar to most people and not well practiced may make it more difficult for people to perform them. As few as two miscues in performance can result in an individual being classified as impaired because of alcohol consumption when the problem may actually be the result of the unfamiliarity with the test.

And, in fact, it appears the NHTSA-funded researchers used methods that ensured improved reliability figures. Apparently, to reduce the number of borderline subjects (those with blood-alcohol levels of, say, .09 or .11 percent), most of the subjects received either excessive amounts of alcohol so that their BACs were elevated to .15 percent, or very small amounts so that they were below .05 percent.

In 1983, NHTSA conducted a study to determine the efficacy of the various field sobriety tests. Anderson et al., Field Evaluation of a Behavioral Test Battery for DWI (DOT HS-806-475, September 1983). The study found that "at present, the tests and procedures used vary between local agencies and officers" and that "for many of these tests, the relationship between performance and specific BAC levels has not been well documented." As a result of this and other studies, NHTSA now recommends only three field sobriety tests: walk-and-turn (walk-the-line), one-leg-stand, and nystagmus (see §4.3.2).

In 1986, another group of researchers tested the efficacy of the proposed standardized FSTs. The study, reported in Halperin, Is the Driver Drunk? Oculomotor Sobriety Testing, 57 Journal of the American Optometer Association 654 (1986), involved testing the ability to determine whether a suspect's blood-alcohol level was above or below .10 percent — that is, whether he was "under the influence" in most states. The test, conducted under laboratory conditions, indicated that the walk-and-turn tests resulted in a correct assessment 75.1 percent of the time, the one-leg-stand 75.5 percent, and nystagmus 81.8 percent; when all three were given, a correct determination was arrived at in 83.4 percent of the cases. Put another way, these "improved" FSTs still identify roughly one-fourth of innocent DUI suspects as guilty — and this presumes honest and accurate administration of the tests by an experienced officer under ideal laboratory conditions.

In 1987, many of the original researchers at the Southern California Research Institute who had been federally funded to come up with a standardized battery published findings of their research. The study concluded that FSTs do not accurately measure driving impairment. In an article entitled Sobriety Tests for the Presence of Drugs, 3(1) Alcohol, Drugs and Driving 25 (1987), researchers recognized that such tests are designed to determine balance, steadiness, and reaction time but concluded that a connection between these factors and driving ability "is not apparent since neither a steady stance nor simple movement time is essential to the safe operation of a motor vehicle." While conceding that field sobriety tests may indicate the presence of alcohol, the researchers found that they do not necessarily measure driving ability.

In 1991, Dr. Spurgeon Cole of Clemson University conducted a study on the accuracy of FSTs. His staff videotaped 21 individuals performing six common field sobriety tests, then showed the tapes to 14 police officers and asked them to decide whether the suspects had "had too much to drink to drive." Unknown to the officers, the blood-alcohol concentration of each of the 21 subjects was .00 percent. The results: 46 percent of the time the officers gave their opinion that the subject was too inebriated to drive. In other words, the FSTs were hardly more accurate at predicting intoxication than flipping a coin. Cole & Nowaczyk, Field Sobriety Tests: Are They Designed for Failure?, 79 Perceptual and Motor Skills 99 (1994).

For an interesting summary of the defects inherent in field sobriety tests, see the same authors' excellent article, Separating Myth from Fact: A Review of Research on the Field Sobriety Tests, XIX(7) The Champion 40 (August 1995). (Note: Copies of either article can be obtained from Dr. Cole's office at 803-656-1480.)

One of the most preeminent blood-alcohol experts in the country, William Giguiere of Park Gilan Clinics (Burlingame, CA), has summarized some of the reasons that the field sobriety tests lack scientific validity in determining alcohol intoxication:

> FSTs were not designed by scientists as a result of investigations on alcohol's impairing effects of alcohol on driving, nor were they based on their ability to accurately predict BACs. Even the "standardized battery of FSTs" suggested by Burns and Moscowitz was based upon a review of what was being utilized in the field by police officers.
>
> Burns and Moscowitz made no attempt to develop a set of field tests that could be supported as reliable by scientific investigation. They simply considered the tests they observed and reduced them to a battery of three that could be expeditiously administered.
>
> Very little consideration was given to the issues of *specificity, sensitivity, and learning*. Each of these factors can profoundly affect the interpretation of tests results.
>
> Specificity refers to the ability of the test to measure the desired phenomenon which in this arena would be driving impairment caused by alcohol. Do FSTs, standardized or non-standardized, specifically determine driving impairment caused by alcohol? The answer is a resounding — NO! There are a host other reasons that could explain an individual's performance on FSTs, most of which are not remotely related to alcohol consumption.
>
> Sensitivity refers to the interpretation of the performance on the test to accurately assess a specific phenomenon such as driving impairment. For example, it is well established that the ingestion of a sufficient amount of alcohol will render a subject unconscious. However, if this criteria (comatose) was used to assess a subject for driving impairment caused by alcohol it would be of no value since the subject would be far beyond the point where he is alcohol impaired for purposes of driving. Thus, the test might be considered alcohol specific, but because it lacks the necessary sensitivity it is of little or no value.
>
> The largest component of systematic error is the error caused by the subject learning how to respond to the test stimuli, called the learning effect. While the subject is learning, his true score is masked by incorrect responses and slowed response time. As learning occurs, the number of errors caused by the learning effect dissipates, the number of incorrect responses diminish and the response time shortens. The test scores then become constant over successive trials and reach a state of stability. Only when an acceptable level of stability occurs can the performance be used to measure the individual's ability.

For a helpful survey of some of the issues in field sobriety tests, counsel may wish to read an article entitled "Proof and disproof of alcohol-induced driving impairment through evidence of observable intoxication and coordination testing," 9 Am. Jur. 3d Proof of Facts 459 (1990).

§4.3.2 "Standardized" Field Sobriety Tests

> Falsehood is never so successful as when she baits her hook with truth, and no opinions so falsely mislead us as those that are not wholly wrong, as no watches so effectively deceive the wearer as those that are sometimes right.
>
> CHARLES COLTON

The National Highway Traffic Safety Administration (NHTSA) has undertaken what is described as a program to develop "a behavioral test battery that is empirically related to blood alcohol concentration level." In other words, NHTSA set out to determine how well field sobriety tests predict blood-alcohol levels. See T. E. Anderson, R. M. Schweltz, and M. B. Snyder, Field Evaluation of a Behavioral Test Battery for DWI, DOT HS-806-475 (National Highway Traffic Safety Administration, September 1983).

The NHTSA study found that "[a]t present, the tests and procedures used vary between local agencies and officers." In addition, the study found that "[f]or many of these tests, the relationship between performance and specific BAC levels has not been well documented." After an initial study and further development, three different tests were recommended as a test battery that could be administered by police officers at roadside:

1. *One-Leg-Stand.* This test requires that the subject stand on one leg for approximately 30 seconds. The time requirement is important, because it makes the test sensitive to drivers with BACs in the .10 percent to .15 percent range, who may pass the test if they only have to balance for 10 to 20 seconds.
2. *Walk-and-Turn.* This is given in two parts. The first part requires that the subject balance heel-to-toe while listening to the instructions. In other words, the subject must

do two things at once — balance heel-to-toe and listen to the instructions. Doing two things at once is very difficult for an intoxicated person. The second part of the test requires that the subject take nine heel-to-toe steps along a line, turn around, and take nine heel-to-toe steps back.

3. *Gaze Nystagmus.* Nystagmus means a jerking of the eyes. Gaze nystagmus refers to a jerking of the eyes as they gaze to the side. Many people will exhibit some nystagmus, or jerking, as their eyes track to the extreme side. However, as people become more intoxicated, the onset of the nystagmus, or jerking, occurs after fewer degrees of lateral deviation, and the jerking at more extreme angles becomes more distinct. (For a discussion of the nystagmus test, see §4.3.5)

The first of the tests, the *one-leg-stand,* has four specific clues that the officer is supposed to look for:

1. sways while balancing
2. uses arms to balance
3. hops
4. puts foot down

The NHTSA-sponsored research indicates that when a suspect shows two or more of these clues or is unable to finish the test, there is a 65 percent reliability factor in predicting a .10 percent or higher BAC. Put another way, 35 out of 100 people who "fail" the test according to these criteria are *not* under the influence.

The second test, *walk-and-turn* or *walk-the-line,* involves eight clues:

1. can't balance during instructions
2. starts too soon
3. stops while walking
4. doesn't touch heel to toe
5. steps off the line
6. uses arms to balance
7. loses balance on turn or turns incorrectly
8. takes the wrong number of steps

Research with this test shows that if a suspect exhibits two or more clues or is unable to complete the test, there is a 68 percent reliability factor. Again, 32 percent of those failing the test will be legally sober.

The third test, *horizontal gaze nystagmus,* has three clues as to each eye:

1. As the eyeball is moved from side to side, does it move smoothly, or does it jerk noticeably? (As people become more under the influence of alcohol, their eyeballs exhibit a lack of smooth movement as they move from side to side.)
2. When the eyeball is moved as far to the side as possible and is kept at that position for several seconds, does it jerk distinctly? (Distinct jerkiness at maximum deviation of the eyeball is another clue of alcoholic influence.)
3. As the eyeball is drawn toward the side, does it start to jerk before it has moved through a 45-degree arc? (Onset of jerkiness prior to 45 degrees is another clue of alcoholic influence.)

Of the six possible clues (three clues per eye), the NHTSA-sponsored research indicates that the existence of four or more gives a 77 percent reliability factor.

These test results can be helpful to defense counsel where an officer places heavy reliance on these field sobriety tests. The impression he invariably gives the jury is that the tests are nearly foolproof in detecting drunk drivers — yet studies show that they fall far short of the "beyond a reasonable doubt" standard required for conviction.

The NHTSA manual on which state manuals are increasingly being based is entitled DWI Detection and Standardized Field Sobriety Testing, DOT-HS-808-112. It can be obtained from the National Technical Information Service in Springfield, Virginia (703-487-4640; fax 703-487-4815). The manual, which includes both a student and instructor version, and two videotapes are priced at $138.50 (specify order no. PB94780251).

The following NHTSA studies, which contain material critical of field sobriety tests used by law enforcement agencies across the country, can also be ordered:

- Psychological Tests for DWI Arrest, DOT-HS-802-424 (order no. PB269309; $27)
- Development and Field Test of Psychophysical Tests for DWI Arrest, DOT-HS-802-864 (order no. PB81203721; $19.50)
- Field Evaluation of a Behavioral Test Battery for DUI, DOT-HS-806-475 (order no. PB84121169; $12.50)
- Pilot Test of Selected DWI Detection Procedures for Use at Sobriety Checkpoints, DOT-HS-806-724 (order no. PB86170958; $19.50)

Certified copies for evidentiary purposes can be obtained for an additional $15.

The subsections following (§§4.3.3–4.3.5) set forth the correct procedures to be used by officers in administering the three standardized field sobriety tests, as described in the NHTSA pamphlet Improved Sobriety Testing (DOT HS-806-512). This material can be used by defense counsel in a drunk driving case in three ways. First, any tests other than these have been found to be ineffective by NHTSA's research and are not approved. Second, if any of these tests *are* administered (and counsel will increasingly encounter these tests as they become more widely accepted), the detailed procedures required by NHTSA can be contrasted with the methods actually used by the arresting officer. Third, the tests clearly establish that *objective scoring* is not only possible in field sobriety tests but required.

The following "scoring sheet," taken from the pamphlet, illustrates the scoring system and serves as an overview of the tests:

SCORING SHEET (CHECK AS MANY AS YOU OBSERVE)

GAZE NYSTAGMUS TEST

- [ ] Nystagmus in right eye is moderate or distinct when eye is moved as far as possible to the right.
- [ ] Right eye cannot follow moving object smoothly.
- [ ] Onset of gaze nystagmus in right eye occurs before 45 degrees (some white is visible).
- [ ] Nystagmus in left eye is moderate or distinct when eye is moved as far as possible to left.
- [ ] Left eye cannot follow moving object smoothly.

- [ ] Onset of gaze nystagmus in left eye occurs before 45 degrees (some white is visible).
- [ ] Total Score (Decision Point: 4)

WALK-AND-TURN TEST

- [ ] Cannot keep balance while listening to instructions.
- [ ] Starts before instructions are finished.
- [ ] Stops while walking to steady self.
- [ ] Does not touch heel to toe.
- [ ] Loses balance while walking (i.e., steps off line).
- [ ] Uses arms for balance.
- [ ] Loses balance while turning.
- [ ] Incorrect number of steps.
- [ ] Cannot do test (steps off line three or more times).
- [ ] Total Score (Decision Point: 2)

ONE-LEG-STAND TEST

- [ ] Sways while balancing.
- [ ] Uses arms to balance.
- [ ] Hopping.
- [ ] Puts foot down.
- [ ] Cannot do test (puts foot down three or more times).
- [ ] Total Score (Decision Point: 2)

Gaze Nystagmus Test Score

Walk & Turn Test Score	0	1	2	3	4	5	6
0							
1							
2							
3							
4							
5							
6							
7							
8							
9							

For a discussion of the admissibility of field sobriety tests, see §11.5.2; for material on cross-examination, see §13.0.5.

§4.3.3 Walk-and-Turn

The following material setting forth the proper procedures to follow in administering the walk-and-turn (also called the "heel-to-toe" or "walk-the-line") portion of the "standardized" field sobriety test is taken from the brochure distributed to law enforcement agencies by the National Highway Traffic Safety Administration (DOT HS-806-512). It can be used effectively in cross-examination to compare the arresting officer's methods with those recommended after extensive research by federal authorities. The material is also helpful for showing that the test can be scored objectively.

Instructions

Give each suspect the exact instructions listed below:

PLEASE PUT YOUR LEFT FOOT ON THE LINE AND THEN YOUR RIGHT FOOT IN FRONT OF IT LIKE THIS. *(Demonstrate heel-to-toe position.)*

(When the suspect assumes this position, continue with the instructions.) WHEN I TELL YOU TO BEGIN, TAKE NINE HEEL-TO-TOE STEPS DOWN THE LINE, TURN AROUND, AND TAKE NINE HEEL-TO-TOE STEPS BACK.

MAKE YOUR TURN BY KEEPING ONE FOOT ON THE LINE AND THEN USING YOUR OTHER FOOT TO TURN . . . LIKE THIS. *(Demonstrate as shown in the illustration by taking three or four heel-to-toe steps — then turning around by pivoting your left foot on the line and taking four steps with your right foot, as shown — then resuming the heel-to-toe position. Note that this is a very easy way to turn, but the suspect must follow your instructions.)*

KEEP YOUR HANDS AT YOUR SIDES, WATCH YOUR FEET AT ALL TIMES, AND COUNT YOUR STEPS OUT LOUD. DO YOU UNDERSTAND?

(Do not continue until the suspect indicates understanding, but at the same time do not repeat the whole set of instructions. You may repeat part of the instructions or answer the suspect's questions about how to perform the test. If the suspect does not watch his feet, remind him.)

(Once the suspect indicates understanding, say . . .) BEGIN AND COUNT YOUR FIRST STEP FROM THE HEEL-TO-TOE POSITION AS "ONE."

SCORING

You may observe a number of different behaviors when a suspect performs this test. Research, however, has demonstrated that the behaviors listed below are the most likely to be observed in someone with a BAC of 0.10 percent or more. In scoring this test, give only one point for each item observed (even if it is observed more than once) with a maximum score of nine points.

1) **Cannot keep balance while listening to the instructions.** Two tasks are required at the beginning of this test. The suspect must balance heel-to-toe on the line and, at the same time, listen carefully to the instructions. Typically, the person who is intoxicated can do only one of these things. He may listen to the instructions, but not keep his balance. Score this item if the **suspect does not maintain the heel-to-toe position throughout the instructions.** Do not score this item if the suspect sways or uses his arms to balance but maintains the heel-to-toe position.
2) **Starts before the instructions are finished.** The intoxicated person may also keep his balance, but not listen to the instructions. Since the first words you said in giving instructions for this test were: "When I tell you to begin," score

this item if the subject does not wait. Other aspects of not listening to the instructions are included in the other items.

3) **Stops while walking to steady self.** The suspect pauses for several seconds after one step. Do not score this item if the suspect is merely walking slowly.
4) **Does not touch heel-to-toe.** The suspect leaves a space of one half inch or more between the heel and toe on any step. Also score this item if the suspect does not walk straight along the line.
5) **Steps off the line.** The suspect steps so that one foot is entirely off the line. Only count this item once, even if the suspect steps off several times.
6) **Uses arms to balance.** The suspect raises one or both arms more than six inches from his sides in order to maintain his balance.
7) **Loses balance while turning.** The suspect removes the pivot foot from the line while turning. That is, score this item if both feet are removed from the line. Also score this item if the suspect clearly has not followed directions in turning; for example, he pivots in one movement instead of the four step movement that he was instructed to perform.
8) **Incorrect number of steps.** Score this item if the suspect takes more or less than nine steps in each direction.
9) **Cannot do the test.** Score this item if the suspect steps off the line three or more times, is in danger of falling, or otherwise demonstrates that he cannot do the test. If this item is scored, the suspect gets nine points for this test, the maximum score.

Should the suspect have difficulty with this test or (for example, if he steps off the line) have him repeat the test from the point of difficulty, not from the beginning. This test tends to lose its sensitivity if it is repeated several times.

Observe the suspect from three or four feet away and remain motionless while he performs the test. Being too close or excessive motion on your part will make it more difficult for the suspect to perform, even if he is sober.

If the suspect scores two or more points on this test classify his BAC as above 0.10 percent. Using this criterion, you will be able to correctly classify about 68 percent of your suspects with respect to whether they are drunk or sober. So your decision point on the Walk-and-Turn Test is *two.*

Test Conditions

This test should be given on level ground, on a hard, dry, nonslippery surface, and under conditions in which the suspect would be in no danger should he fall. Require him to perform the test elsewhere, or confine your decision to the results of the Gaze Nystagmus Test if these conditions cannot be met.

Some people have difficulty with balance even when sober. People more than 60 years of age, over 50 pounds overweight, or with physical impairments that affect their ability to balance should not be given this test. Individuals wearing heels more than two inches high should be given the opportunity to remove their shoes.

The Walk-and-Turn Test requires a line that the suspect can see. If a natural line is not present, draw one in the dirt with a stick or on the sidewalk with chalk. Walking parallel to a curb is also adequate.

The suspect must be able to see to perform this test. That is, his eyes must be open, and at night adequate lighting must be available. If you can see the suspect clearly, then the lighting is adequate; otherwise, use a flashlight to illuminate the line.

Requesting that the suspect watch his feet makes the test more difficult for the intoxicated person. Be sure that the suspect is doing so, or make an immediate correction. Individuals who cannot see out of one eye may also have trouble with this test because of poor depth perception.

Combined Scoring of Nystagmus Gaze and Walk-and-Turn Tests

The Decision Table below is designed to help you classify those suspects with a potential BAC of 0.10 percent or more. You will recall that the decision point on the Nystagmus Gaze Test was a score of *four,* while on the Walk-and-Turn Test it was a score of *two.* However, a suspect may score higher on one test and lower on the other. How do you make your decision? Find the box on the Decision Table where the two test scores intersect and see if it falls in the shaded area. (For example, suppose a suspect scored only three on the Nystagmus Gaze but got a *two* on the Walk-and-Turn. Is he intoxicated? The Decision Table says *yes.* But if he scored three on the Nystagmus Gaze and only one on the Walk-and-Turn, the Table says his BAC is probably below 0.10 percent.)

Using this method, your chances of correctly classifying your suspects as to whether they are intoxicated or sober are about 80 percent.

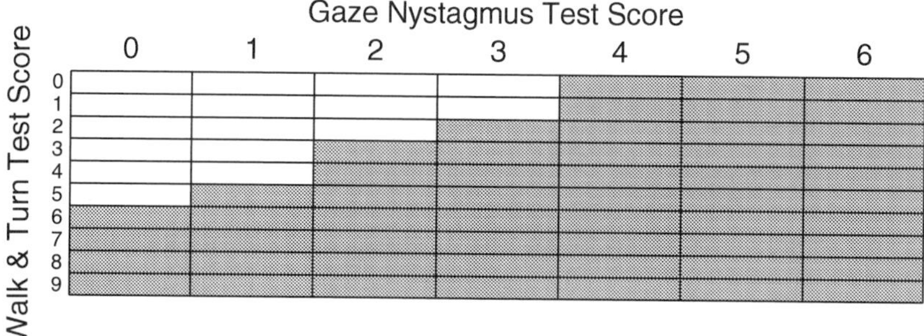

Decision Table

§4.3.4 One-Leg-Stand

The following material describes the proper procedures to follow in administering the one-leg-stand portion of the "standardized" field sobriety test. As with the preceding subsection, it is taken from the brochure distributed to law enforcement agencies by the National Highway Traffic Safety Administration (DOT HS-806-512) and can be used effectively in cross-examination to compare the arresting officer's methods with those recommended after extensive research by federal authorities. The material is also helpful for showing that the test can be scored objectively.

INSTRUCTIONS

Give the suspect the exact instructions listed below:

PLEASE STAND WITH YOUR HEELS TOGETHER AND YOUR ARMS DOWN AT YOUR SIDES, LIKE THIS. *(Demonstrate how you want the suspect to stand.)*

WHEN I TELL YOU TO, I WANT YOU TO RAISE ONE LEG ABOUT SIX INCHES OFF THE GROUND AND HOLD THAT POSITION. AT THE SAME TIME COUNT RAPIDLY FROM 1001 TO 1030, while watching your foot. Like this. *(You assume the position . . . and count aloud, "1001, 1002, 1003, etc.")*

DO YOU UNDERSTAND? *(Do not continue until the suspect indicates that he understands.)* BEGIN BY RAISING EITHER YOUR RIGHT OR YOUR LEFT FOOT.

(At the end of the count or after about 30 seconds, if the count is slow, tell the person to put his foot down — if necessary.)

Scoring

You may observe a number of different behaviors when a suspect performs this test. Researchers, however, have found that those behaviors listed below are the most likely to be observed in someone with a BAC of 0.10 percent or higher. In scoring this test, give only one point for each item observed, even if it is observed more than once. The maximum possible score on this test is five points.

1) **The suspect sways while balancing.** This refers to a side-to-side or back-and-forth motion while the suspect maintains the one-leg-stand position.
2) **Uses arms for balance.** He moves his arms six or more inches from the side of his body in order to keep this balance.
3) **Hopping.** He is able to keep one foot off the ground, but resorts to hopping on the anchor foot in order to maintain balance.
4) **Puts foot down.** The suspect is not able to maintain the one-leg-stand position, putting his foot down one or more times during the 30-second count.
5) **Cannot do test.** Score this item if the suspect puts his foot down three or more times during the 30-second count or otherwise demonstrates that he cannot do the test. If you score this item, give the suspect five points — the maximum for this test.

Remember that time is critical in this test. Research has shown that a person with a BAC of 0.10 percent can maintain his balance for up to 25 seconds, but seldom as long as 30.

If an individual scores two or more points on the One-Leg-Stand, there is a good chance his BAC is 0.10 percent or higher. So your decision point on this test is *two.* Using that criterion, you will correctly classify about 65 percent of the people you test as to whether they are sober or intoxicated.

Test Conditions

Like the Walk-and-Turn Test, the One-Leg-Stand should be given on level ground, on a hard, dry, non-slippery surface, and under conditions in which the suspect will be in no danger should he fall. If these guidelines can not be followed at the place where you stop the driver, you may be able to move to a better location. If not, base your decision on the Gaze Nystagmus Test alone.

Certain individuals are likely to have trouble with this test even when sober. People over 60 often have very poor balance. (Since very few elderly people are stopped at roadside, specific guidelines have not been established for them on this test.) This also applies to people who are 50 or more pounds overweight and to those with physical impairments that interfere with balance.

In administering this test, make certain the suspect's eyes are open and that there is adequate lighting for him to be able to have some frame of reference. If you can see the suspect fairly well, then the light is adequate. Otherwise, use a flashlight to illuminate the ground. In total darkness, the One-Leg-Stand is difficult even for sober people.

Observe the suspect from about three feet away and remain relatively motionless while he is performing the test. Being too close — just as in the Walk-and-Turn Test — makes the test more difficult. And, again, individuals with heels over two inches high should be given the opportunity to remove their shoes.

If the suspect puts his foot down, instruct him to continue the count from the point at which the foot touched the ground. And if the person counts very slowly, terminate the test after 30 seconds have elapsed.

§4.3.5 Horizontal Gaze Nystagmus

A new type of field sobriety test arose in the early 1980s in the western states. Used initially only on an experimental basis, the test quickly spread and is now being used by police agencies in almost all jurisdictions. This is the "horizontal gaze nystagmus" test. Although administered by the officer at the scene of the traffic stop as a field sobriety test, it should be recognized as, in reality, a superficial test to determine blood-alcohol content. It should also be recognized that evidence of the test can have devastating effects in a drunk driving trial. Properly handled by the defense, however, this test may never be admitted into evidence; if admitted, the test can be discredited.

Dr. L. F. Dell'Osso, Professor of Neurology at Case Western Reserve University School of Medicine, and Director of the Ocular Motor Neurophysiology Laboratory at the Veteran's Administration Medical Center in Cleveland, is a noted expert in the area of nystagmus. In an article entitled Nystagmus, Saccadic Intrusions/ Oscillations and Oscillopsia, 3 Current Neuro-Opthalmology 147 (1989), he has commented:

> Using nystagmus as an indicator of alcohol intoxication is an unfortunate choice, since many normal individuals have physiologic end-point nystagmus; small doses of tranquilizers that would not interfere with driving can produce nystagmus; nystagmus may be congenital or consequent to neurologic disease; and without a neuro-opthalmologist or someone knowledgeable about sophisticated methods of eye movement recordings, it is difficult to determine whether the nystagmus is pathologic. It is unreasonable that such difficult judgments have been placed in the hands of minimally trained officers.

Dr. Dell'Osso also lists 47 different kinds of nystagmus in the article.

The test is essentially a measurement of the movement of the eye. Simply stated, *nystagmus* means a jerking of the eyes. Although there are different types of nystagmus, the type involved in field sobriety testing is "horizontal gaze nystagmus," that is, the involuntary pendular (back and forth) movement of the eye. This type of nystagmus is commonly measured by the officer in one, two, or all of three different ways. *Vertical* nystagmus, it should be noted, is a different phenomenon with different causes than horizontal. Although often testified to by police officers on the issue of alcohol intoxication, the relevance of vertical nystagmus is primarily to indicate the presence of *drugs* in the body.

The first is to determine the *angle of onset* of the nystagmus. By measuring the angle at which the eye begins jerking, the officer can theoretically come to a rough approximation of the blood-alcohol concentration (see infra). The second method is to notice whether the jerking becomes more "*distinct*" when the eye is moved to the lateral extreme — that is, when there is no longer any white of the eye visible at the outside of the eye. The third technique is to notice the lack of "*smooth pursuit*": rather than following a moving object smoothly, the eye jumps or "tugs."

To administer the test, the officer instructs the suspect to "keep your head straight ahead and follow this object with your eyes." The officer then moves a finger or pencil, or a penlight at night, from the center of the device steadily toward one side. The object is held 12 to 15 inches directly in front, 2 to 3 inches above the eye being tested. The object is moved slowly (three to four seconds to complete the arc) in a level, even arc — maintaining the 12- to 15-inch distance. At the onset of nystagmus, the object is held for one to two seconds at the point and the officer notes the angle of onset. The jerking should continue as long as the individual stares at the object, even though it is no longer being moved. The officer then repeats the test with the other eye.

The eyes of a person under the influence of alcohol will begin to jerk sooner than those of a sober person, and the more intoxicated the individual the sooner the jerking. Thus, blood-alcohol content can be roughly estimated by the angle on the device; i.e., by that point at which jerking begins. In a study for the National Highway Traffic and Safety Administration, researchers concluded that the onset of nystagmus (jerking) at about 40 degrees would correlate with a blood-alcohol level of .10 percent; a level of .15 percent would be indicated where the involuntary movement began at about 35 degrees; onset at 30 degrees indicates a level of about .20 percent. Individuals with blood-alcohol levels above .20 percent often cannot even follow a moving object with their eyes. Thus, theoretically, a rough formula may be used to arrive at blood-alcohol content: Simply subtract the angle from 50 and convert to percent; for example, an angle of 37 degrees would convert to .13 percent blood alcohol. See V. Tharp, et al., Psychophysical Tests for DUI Arrest, DOT-HS-8-01970, 1981.

An alternative and increasingly common means of administering the test is to simply determine if jerking begins before the eye reaches a 45-degree angle. This is usually observed by the officer without the aid of any angle-measuring device, and obviously would be subject to question during cross-examination. If the jerking began at about 45 degrees, of course, this would indicate a blood-alcohol level of only .05 percent — and defense counsel may *want* the nystagmus evidence admitted.

As is discussed in §11.5.3, counsel should attack the nystagmus field sobriety test before trial. This motion *in limine* should present a two-prong approach:

1. suppression
2. limitation

For a discussion of cross-examination on nystagmus, see §13.2.1 and the sample cross-exam following that section.

The following material is taken from the pamphlet Improved Sobriety Testing (DOT HS-806-512) produced by NHTSA for the purpose of training officers in the correct procedures for administering the standardized field sobriety tests. Any deviation from these procedures (and counsel will encounter few if any officers who follow the protocol correctly) should provide material for cross-examination.

How the Test Works

As explained earlier, nystagmus means a jerking of the eyes. There are a number of different kinds of nystagmus, all of them influenced by alcohol. The test you will use at roadside is a test of "horizontal gaze nystagmus" — the nystagmus that occurs when the eyes gaze to the side. Many people will show some jerking if the eyes move far enough to the side. In intoxication, however, three signs will be observed:

1. The jerking of the eyes occurs much sooner. That is, the more intoxicated a person becomes, the less he has to move his eyes to the side in order for the jerking to occur.
2. If you have a suspect move his eyes as far to the side as possible, you can estimate in a general way the extent of intoxication. The greater the alcohol impairment, the more distinct the nystagmus will be in the extreme gaze position.
3. If the suspect is intoxicated, he cannot follow a slowly moving object smoothly with his eyes.

Estimating a 45-Degree Angle

Since the extent of impairment is indicated by the angle at which nystagmus begins, you will need to learn how to estimate this angle . . . particularly the angle of 45-degrees, since that is the crucial point for estimating BAC.

The page after the score sheets contains a square template you can use for practice. Cut this template out and attach it to a square of cardboard the same size for support.

To use this device, hold it up so that the person's nose is above the diagonal line. Be certain that one edge of the template is centered on the nose and perpendicular to (or, at right angles to) the face. Have the person you are examining follow a penlight or some other item until he is looking down the 45-degree diagonal. Note the position of his eye. With practice, you should be able to recognize this angle without using the template.

Examine the eyes of four or five people, so that you become familiar with what a 45-degree angle of gaze looks like. Next, practice without the device, but check your estimates periodically.

Practice until you can consistently estimate 45 degrees. Check yourself monthly with the device to be sure that your accuracy has been sustained.

Specific Procedures

Give the suspect the following instructions from a position of interrogation (that is, with your weapon away from the suspect):

I AM GOING TO CHECK YOUR EYES. (Request that the suspect remove glasses or hard contact lens at this time if they are being worn. Nystagmus is not influenced by how clearly the suspect can see the object he is to follow.) NOW KEEP YOUR HEAD STILL AND FOLLOW THIS (indicate what he is to follow) WITH YOUR EYES. DO NOT MOVE YOUR EYES BACK TO THE CENTER UNTIL I TELL YOU. (If the suspect moves his head, use a flashlight or your free hand as a chinrest.)

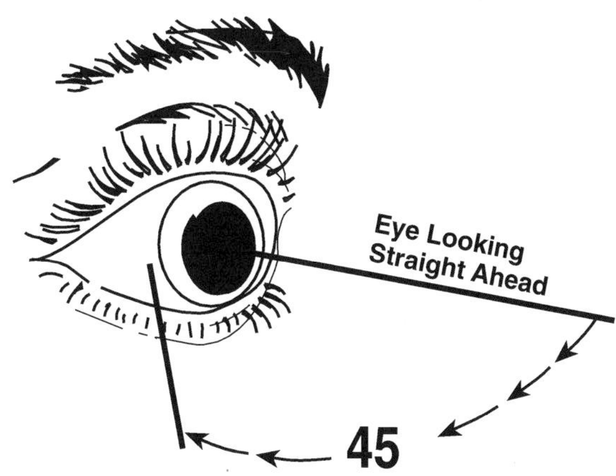

Check the suspect's right eye by moving the object to the suspect's right. Have the suspect follow the object until the eyes cannot move further to the side. Make this movement in about two seconds, and observe: 1) whether the suspect was able to follow the object smoothly or whether the motion was quite jerky; and 2) how distinct the nystagmus is at the maximum deviation.

Estimate where a 45-degree angle would be using the training procedure given [above].

Move the object a second time to the 45-degree angle of gaze, taking about four seconds. As the eye follows the object, watch for it to start jerking back and forth. If you think you see nystagmus, stop the movement to see if the jerking continues. If it does, this point is the angle of onset. If it does not, keep moving the object until the jerking does occur or until you reach the imaginary 45-degree line. Note whether or not the onset occurs *before* the 45-degree angle of gaze. (The onset point at a BAC of 0.10 percent is about 40 degrees.)

If the suspect's eyes start jerking before they reach 45 degrees, check to see that some white of the eye is still showing on the side closest to the ear, as in the photograph. If no white of the eye is showing, you either have taken the eye too far to the side (that is, more than 45 degrees) or the person has unusual eyes that will not deviate very far to the side. ***Use the criteria of onset before 45 degrees only if you can see some white at the outside of the eye.***

AN EYE DEVIATED TO 40 DEGREES — NOTE THE AMOUNT OF WHITE SHOWING ON THE OUTSIDE (CLOSEST TO THE EAR) OF THE EYE.

Repeat this entire procedure for the left eye. When observing the left eye at 45 degrees of gaze, some white of the eye again should be visible at the outside (closest to the ear) of the eye.

NOTE: Nystagmus may be due to causes other than alcohol in three or four percent of the population. These other causes include seizure medications, phencyclidine (PCP), barbiturates and other depressants. A large disparity between the performance of the right and left eye may indicate brain damage.

Scoring

You should look for three signs of intoxication in each eye. Give one point for each item checked for a maximum of six points.

1) **Onset of alcohol gaze nystagmus in the right eye occurs before 45 degrees.** Do not score this item unless some white is visible on the outside of the right eye (closest to the ear) at the point of onset.
2) **Nystagmus in the right eye when moved as far as possible to the right is moderate or distinct.** Do not score this item if you only see the faint jerking that occurs at the onset point.
3) **The right eye cannot follow a moving object smoothly.** If

you score this item, be sure that the jerkiness was not due to your moving the object in a jerky manner.

4) **Onset of alcohol gaze nystagmus in the left eye occurs before 45 degrees.** If you score this item, be certain that some white is visible on the outside of the left eye (closest to the ear) at the point of onset.
5) **Nystagmus in the left eye when it is moved as far as possible to the left is moderate or distinct.**
6) **The left eye cannot follow a moving object smoothly.**

If a suspect scores four or more points out of the six possible on this test, classify his BAC as above 0.10 percent. Using this criterion you will be able to correctly classify about 77 percent of your suspects with respect to whether they are drunk or sober. That probability was determined during limited laboratory and field testing and is given simply to help you weigh the various sobriety tests in this battery as you make your arrest decision.

TEST CONDITIONS

Very few test conditions will affect gaze nystagmus. Most of the test requirements given in this Manual are designed to make the observation of nystagmus as easy as possible for the officer doing the testing.

Nystagmus can be observed directly and requires no special equipment. You will need something for the suspect to follow with his eyes, but this can be as simple as the tip of your index finger. Officers who use this test frequently have the suspect follow a penlight. The object used should be held about eye level, so that the eyes are wide open when they look directly at it. It should be held about 12 to 15 inches in front of the eyes for ease of focus.

Glasses should be removed since they may block your view of the suspect's eyes. In addition, hard contact lens may restrict the boundaries of movement of the eyes. If this appears to happen, you may still conduct the tests. You should be aware that this factor may affect the reliability of this test and you should record this condition in your field notes.

In addition to the preceding material, counsel should also consider the research on which NHTSA relied in determining that nystagmus was a relatively reliable field sobriety test. One of those studies is found in a NHTSA brochure authored by V. Tharp entitled Psychophysical Tests For DUI Arrests (DOT HS-8-01970).

Although recommending the test, the author mentions the following additional procedures (emphasis is added by the author of this text to indicate potential sources for cross-examination):

> The person being tested should *remove all corrective lenses;* glasses may impede an officer's view of the eyes and hard contact lenses tend to limit the lateral movement of the eyes (which might prohibit the recognition of borderline cases). The occurrence of nystagmus is not affected by visual acuity. The stimulus should be positioned *above the eyes,* in order to elevate them and reduce squinting, and about 15 inches away from the eyes. At night if the street lighting is not adequate, *a penlight should be used* to illuminate the face and eyes. The officer should move the stimulus *at least twice in each direction,* looking at the eye on the side of the head to which he is moving the stimulus. The suspect must keep his/her head still. The officer's flashlight makes a good chinrest for suspects who persist with head movements. The first movement in each direction should be slow (i.e., at about *10 degrees per second*), while the second movement should be somewhat faster (i.e., at about *20 degrees per second*).
>
> During the first movement of the stimulus in each direction, the officer should look for the onset of nystagmus. When he first detects a slight jerking, he should *stop moving the stimulus* to make sure that the jerking continues. If the nystagmus stops, then the officer has not found the point of onset and he should continue his examination.
>
> When the officer finds the onset point, he should determine whether or not it occurs *before* 45 degrees with some of the conjunctiva (i.e., the white of the eye) showing. The 45 degree angle was chosen as a criterion because it is *close* to the expected onset point for a BAC of 0.10% and *because it is easy to estimate.* The 45 degree angle splits the right angle that runs from the tip of the nose to the center of the head to the middle of the ear. Since some individuals cannot deviate their eyes more than 45 degrees, *some white of the eye must show* to ascertain that nystagmus is not occurring at the most extreme deviation for that individual.
>
> Smooth pursuit eye movements should also be examined by a police officer at roadside, although this is *the least reliable of the three signs.* We recommend that the second movement of the stimulus in each direction be at about *20 degrees per second,* while the officer looks for impaired smooth pursuit. The officer must be careful to move the stimulus smoothly to be sure that impaired pursuit is not *due to his manner of moving the stimulus.* What a police officer will

> see as the BAC increases is: (1) at a BAC of 0.08%–0.10% impaired smooth movements interrupted by small jerks or saccades; (2) at a BAC in the range of 0.15% to 0.20% the eye movements will be characterized by much bigger saccades; (3) at high BACs (e.g., above 0.25%) most people cannot track at all.

Paranthetically, counsel should be aware that the technology now exists for videotaping nystagmus tests. This would, of course, provide an objective and verifiable record of the defendant's performance on the test. The EM/1 is an instrument developed by Eye Dynamics, Inc., of Torrance, California. Designed to be operated by a drug recognition expert (DRE), it has a separate video camera for each eye and records on videotape smooth pursuit, nystagmus, pupil reaction, and eyelid tremor. It has already been successfully used in court. See *State v. Rosasco,* no. TD 92-02-006 (County of Yavapai, Ariz. 1992). Another instrument, the EPS-100, is a computerized version of the EM/1; it evaluates the defendant's performance on a pass-fail basis. (In view of this technology, counsel may wish to ask the officer if his police agency has the instrument to corroborate his testimony — and why not.)

Checklist 3 Nystagmus

Admissibility

- ☐ Is evidence of the nystagmus test admissible in trial?
  - ☐ Is the officer qualified as an expert?
  - ☐ Does the test pass the state and/or *Frye* standards?
- ☐ Does the evidence consist of testimony as to the indicated blood-alcohol level — or as to whether the defendant passed or failed?
  - ☐ If nystagmus is being used as a test for blood-alcohol concentration, is it subject to the state's requirements for regulation of blood-alcohol analysis?
  - ☐ If the jury is told that "passed" or "failed" means above or below a given blood-alcohol level, does this constitute a blood-alcohol analysis in fact?
- ☐ If the evidence is limited to the issue of probable cause, has counsel already litigated the issue out of the presence of the jury?
- ☐ Has testimony concerning nystagmus been limited to excluding reference to specific blood-alcohol levels or "failing"?

Foundation

- ☐ Was the officer qualified to administer the horizontal gaze nystagmus test?
  - ☐ Has he had sufficient training and experience?
  - ☐ Is he familiar with the physiological theory behind the test?
  - ☐ Is the officer aware of the many sources for error inherent in the test?
  - ☐ Should the officer be examined on voir dire to determine his expertise?

Administration

- ☐ Was the test administered correctly?
  - ☐ Was the defendant wearing glasses or contact lenses at the time of testing?
  - ☐ Did the officer hold the object 15 inches away from the defendant's eyes — as recommended in the NHTSA standardized procedures?
  - ☐ If the test was administered under poor lighting conditions, was a penlight used (again, as recommended by NHTSA)?
  - ☐ Was the object moved at least twice in each direction (NHTSA)?
    - ☐ Was the first movement in each direction slow (10 degrees per second), with the second faster (20 degrees) — as per NHTSA?
  - ☐ Did the defendant keep his head still during the test?
    - ☐ Does this testimony conflict with the officer's earlier or later testimony that the defendant was staggering, weaving, or unstable on his feet?
  - ☐ Did the officer use the less accurate "smooth pursuit" method?
  - ☐ Did some white of the eye show at onset (NHTSA)?

Sources of Error

- ☐ Was the angle of onset measured accurately and honestly?
  - ☐ Was the angle of onset measured with a template — or by estimate?
    - ☐ Has the officer received training in estimating angles?
    - ☐ Has the officer undergone any checks (or re-checks) of his ability to estimate angles?
    - ☐ Did the officer simply use the defendant's shoulder to measure 45 degrees?
  - ☐ Was the jerking of the eye observed by the officer due to his moving the focal object in a jerking manner?

- ☐ Is there any evidence corroborative of the officer's testimony concerning the angle?
- ☐ Did the officer use the objective scoring system recommended by NHTSA?

☐ Are there any sources of possible error in the test?

- ☐ Is the officer aware of physiological grounds for error?
  - ☐ As an "expert," is he aware of specific studies indicating inaccuracies in the test?
- ☐ Did the officer consider the possible presence of drugs such as antihistamine or phencyclidine?
- ☐ Had the defendant consumed coffee, smoked a cigarette, or taken an aspirin?
- ☐ Did the defendant suffer from any physiological problems that would affect nystagmus — such as influenza, streptococcus, vertigo, or epilepsy?
- ☐ Is the defendant hypertensive or hypotensive?
- ☐ Was the defendant carsick?
- ☐ Were there any inner ear problems?
- ☐ Was the defendant suffering from eyestrain or eye muscle fatigue?
- ☐ Is the officer aware of the effects of circadian rhythm on the onset of nystagmus?

☐ Is the officer/expert aware of Umeda's and Sakata's study indicating that nystagmus is one of the least sensitive methods of measuring intoxication by eye measurement?

Checklist 4 Field Sobriety Tests

Initial Considerations

☐ Did the tests consist of the federally recommended "standardized" battery: walk-and-turn, one-leg stand, and nystagmus?

- ☐ If so, were they administered and scored as recommended?
- ☐ If not, why were tests that have been proven invalid used by the officer?

☐ Should a foundational motion *in limine* be made to exclude the tests?

- ☐ Should the officer and prosecutor be instructed to refrain from using such terms as "test" or "fail"?

Defendant's Condition

☐ Was the defendant suffering from any illness affecting his balance or coordination?

- ☐ Was the defendant taking any drugs or medication that might affect his balance?
- ☐ Did the defendant have any physical disabilities affecting his ability to take the tests?
- ☐ Was the defendant upset by or injured in a traffic collision?
- ☐ Was the defendant suffering from any emotional reactions to the procedure — fear, embarrassment, anger, nervousness?
- ☐ Was the defendant wearing shoes with high heels while performing the tests?

Administration of Field Sobriety Tests

- ☐ Were the tests given on a smooth and level area?
  - ☐ Was the area covered with gravel, loose dirt, or other possible obstructions?
  - ☐ Were the tests administered near passing vehicles, creating noise and wind waves?
  - ☐ What were the lighting conditions?
  - ☐ Did the weather conditions make the tests more difficult to perform?
  - ☐ Did the police vehicle have flashing lights creating a strobe effect?
- ☐ Could unclear instructions by the officer have contributed to test results?
  - ☐ Was the defendant given the opportunity to practice each of the tests once before attempting them? Why not?
  - ☐ What was the physical line used in the walk-the-line test?
  - ☐ Did he demonstrate to the defendant by first performing each test?
- ☐ Does "passing" involve a subjective opinion by the officer?
  - ☐ Had the officer already formed an opinion that the defendant was intoxicated?
  - ☐ Are there any objective criteria?
  - ☐ Did the officer use negative scoring?
  - ☐ Did the officer take into consideration the "impaired learning curve" (fear, nervousness) in assessing pass-fail?

Corroboration

- ☐ Were any videotapes or photographs taken of the defendant performing the tests?
  - ☐ Were any audio or video devices *available* to the officer — and why weren't they used?
- ☐ Are there any defense witnesses who observed the tests being given?

- ☐ Were any potential witnesses *prevented* by the police from viewing the tests?
- ☐ Did the officer diagram the walk-the-line and/or finger-to-nose tests as they were performed?
  - ☐ Was he capable of recalling all details when he later drafted his report?
- ☐ Can a comparison of the defendant's signature and/or handwriting be effectively made?

§4.4 Preliminary Breath Tests

> Truth does not do so much good in the world as the appearance of it does evil.
>
> FRANCOIS DE LA ROCHEFOUCAULD

The term "preliminary breath test" (PBT), sometimes called "alcohol screening device" (ASD) or "passive alcohol sensor" (PAS), covers a variety of different instruments increasingly being used by police officers in the field to obtain initial indications of blood-alcohol levels. Although their use has been relatively minimal as of this writing, the instruments are growing in popularity across the country, and it is almost certain that many if not most local law enforcement agencies will eventually join the national trend in enlisting this newest weapon in the DUI arsenal.

Some of these screening devices are used primarily to detect the *presence* of alcohol in the subject, or to roughly determine a "pass" or "fail" level (or, in some instances, an intermediary "warn" level). If the instrument indicates that alcohol is present in the subject, or if it reflects a possibly high blood-alcohol level by reading "fail," the officer can use this information in deciding whether to detain the individual for further field sobriety tests or even to arrest him for more accurate blood, breath, or urine testing. Other PBTs, however, indicate specific levels of blood-alcohol concentration.

There have basically been two types of PBTs, both designed to measure alcohol on the breath: *fuel cell* devices and *Taguchi gas sensor* devices.

The fuel cell device measures ethanol by electrochemically oxidizing it, or "burning it up," in a fuel cell. This oxidation generates a small amount of electrical current, which is then measured over a specific period of time. The more ethanol in the breath, the greater is the oxidation and the more current is generated, resulting in a higher blood-alcohol reading.

The primary problem with fuel cell devices is their lack of specificity: The devices will detect a large number of chemical compounds, indiscriminately "reading" them as ethanol (see the discussion on *specificity* in a later chapter). Although the manufacturers of the passive alcohol sensor claim in their advertisements that it "is unaffected by acetone, paint and glue fumes, foods, confectionary, methane, and practically any other substance likely to be found in the breath," the fact remains that "any" device using fuel cell oxidation is not specific for ethanol; the manufacturer's use of the term "practically" should certainly create suspicion.

A study has confirmed the nonspecificity of PBTs using electrochemical fuel cells. In Jones & Goldberg, Evaluation of Breath Alcohol Instruments I: In Vitro Experiments with Alcolmeter Pocket Model, 12 Forensic Science International 1 (1978), researchers found that an "Alcolmeter Pocket Model" reacted positively to ethanol — as well as to acetaldehyde, methanol, isopropanol, and n-propranolol.

In addition to their lack of specificity, fuel cell PBTs are subject to a number of infirmities. As with any breath-testing device, the possibility of "mouth alcohol" (see §6.2) always exists — and requires an observation period of 15 to 20 minutes to ensure that there has been no belching, burping, or regurgitation. This is usually a recognized procedure for evidentiary breath testing (i.e., using the DataMaster or Intoxilyzer 5000) and, depending upon the jurisdiction, may be prerequisite to admissibility. However, there is rarely any such requirement for a field preliminary breath test. And, in fact, the PBT test is commonly given shortly after the initial contact with the suspect — long before any 15–20 minute observation is possible. Thus, there is no way for the prosecution to exclude the possibility of mouth-alcohol contamination.

Fuel cell PBTs are also subject to a buildup of oxide film — or "poisoning" — on the electrode, causing false readings. See Rightmire, Rowland, Boos, and Beals, Ethyl Alcohol at Platinum

Electrodes, *Journal of the Electrochemical Society* 3 (1964). And they are very sensitive to operating temperature: Counsel should always determine whether the officer checked (and recorded) the device's operating temperature at the time of the test — or if the device even has a temperature gauge.

The usage logs (not to mention the calibration/maintenance records) of the PBT used on the client should be obtained in the course of discovery — and the time of any previous test determined. If the PBT was used with another suspect a few minutes before (such as may be common at a sobriety checkpoint), there is a very real possibility that the client's reading has been contaminated. The fuel cell device requires time for the reaction products from the earlier test to leave the surface of the cell. If reaction products are still present, they will be oxidized in the client's test, creating current flow that will increase the blood-alcohol reading.

The accuracy of one of the most popular non-passive PBTs, the Alco-Sensor III (see infra), has been tested in the laboratory. Researchers concluded that the device, utilizing an electrochemical fuel cell, was definitely not sufficiently accurate for use in evidentiary testing and, in fact, should be used with caution as a preliminary testing device. See Emerson, Hollyhead, and Isaacs, The Measurement of Breath Alcohol, 20 Journal of the Forensic Science Society 3 (1980). See also Gibb, et al., Accuracy and Usefulness of a Breath Alcohol Analyzer, 13 Annals of Emergency Medicine 516 (1984).

The second type of alcohol screening device includes those utilizing a "Taguchi gas sensor." These sensors are small porous stannic oxide semiconductor elements. Alcohol in the breath is attracted to the sensor, increasing its electrical conductivity; the more alcohol, the more electricity flows and the higher the reading.

There are two types of ASDs using Taguchi sensors: active and passive. The active devices involve capturing a breath sample from the suspect with the use of a mouthpiece; passive units do not. Both types have the same problem with specificity as the fuel cell devices. Specifically, Taguchi units will detect (and register as ethanol) methanol, acetic acid, ethylene glycol, paraldehyde, acetaldehyde, isopropanol, and other compounds. A second problem common to both active and passive Taguchi devices is that sensitivity varies according to the temperature in the environment and in the unit. In addition to these problems, passive devices will register alcohol in the air — such as from the breath of passengers in the suspect's car. The cumulative effect of all these problems in the passive device is reflected in a scientific study in which field trials showed that only *one-fourth* of all subjects who tested positive on the devices had, in fact, blood-alcohol concentrations of .10 percent or higher; another one-fourth had levels below .05 percent. Voas, Laboratory and Field Tests of a Passive Alcohol Sensing System, 4 Alcohol and Driving 3 (1983).

The Life-Loc PBA 3000 is, typical of the passive Taguchi sensor, built into the head of a modified police flashlight. The flashlight is held approximately five to seven-and-a-half inches from the subject's mouth, and an electronically controlled pump draws in a breath sample. Exposed to the sample, a fuel cell generates an electrical current proportional to the concentration of alcohol in the sample. An ultrasonic device then corrects the reading for the distance from the sensor to the subject.

A liquid crystal display registers either a numerical BAC or a message of "pass," "warning," or "fail." The sensors can be set so that the messages are triggered by given BACs — for example, "pass" can be set from .00 to .29, "warning" from .03 to .09, and "fail" for any reading higher than .10.

The flashlight sensor has inherent problems. First, it may be reading vapors from sources other than the subject's breath. There may be, for example, open containers of alcoholic beverages in the car, or someone may have spilled an alcoholic drink in the car or on the subject's clothing. Other individuals in the car may be contributing their breath. Second, the device is only sampling exhaled breath, and at a distance; any kind of accuracy requires that the breath consist of alveolar air — that is, deep lung air.

Which is the more accurate roadside PBT — the type using an electrochemical fuel cell sensor or the type utilizing the Taguchi gas sensor? A field study matched two of the most prominent types of flashlight sensors: (1) the passive alcohol sensor developed jointly under the sponsorship of the Insurance Institute for Highway Safety (IIHS) by Lion Laboratories of the United Kingdom and by Prototypes, Inc., of Maryland, and incorporating a fuel cell sensor; and (2) the Honda passive alcohol sensor developed by Nippon Seiki and using the Taguchi sensor.

The field study was conducted at actual sobriety checkpoints in Washington, D.C. The results: 20 percent of those detained after using the IIHS sensor subsequently proved to have levels below the legal limit (below .10 percent), while 41 percent of those detained with the Honda units proved to have unacceptably low levels. See Jones, Detection of Alcohol-Impaired Drivers Using a Passive Alcohol Sensor, 14 Journal of Police Science and Administration 2 (1986).

§4.4.1 The Alco-Sensor

The most commonly used preliminary breath test (PBT) instruments in use as of this writing appear to be Intoximeter's Alco-Sensor models II, III, and, increasingly, the newer model IV (Intoximeters, Inc., 8110 Lackland Road, St. Louis, MO 63114; (314) 429-4000). The Breathalyzer 7410, however, manufactured by National Draeger's Breathalyzer Division (makers of the new AlcoTest 7110 evidential machine), will undoubtedly see increasing use, as will CMI's Intoxilyzer 300 and 400.

The accuracy of the Alco-Sensor has been tested in the laboratory. Researchers using the model III concluded that the device, utilizing an electrochemical fuel cell, was definitely not sufficiently accurate for use in evidentiary testing and, in fact, should be used with caution as a preliminary testing device. See Emerson, Hollyhead, and Isaacs. The Measurement of Breath Alcohol, 20 Journal of the Forensic Science Society 3 (1980). See also Gibb, et al., Accuracy and Usefulness of a Breath Alcohol Analyzer, 13 Annals of Emergency Medicine 516 (1984).

It should perhaps also be noted that the Alco-Sensor, like many PBTs, can be manipulated by an officer to obtain the desired result. A simple paper clip can be used to increase the readings of the model II in increments of .01 percent, while a screwdriver will increase BAC levels on the models III and IV.

The Alco-Sensor III weighs about six ounces, is small enough to be carried in an officer's pocket, and runs on a nine-volt battery that normally lasts about 300 tests. It uses a fuel cell, consisting of five layers of material compressed into a wafer and soaked with an electrolyte, to analyze alcohol in the breath. An electrical piston pump within the device draws on cubic centimeter of breath into the fuel cell for analysis. The captured breath vapor is exposed to the active surface of the fuel cell and, through oxidation, any alcohol releases electrons that create an electronic flow along a conductor and out of the fuel cell. The current is amplified and then digitized and amplified by an internal computer. The resulting reading is automatically displayed initially as a two-digit approximation, then as a three-digit final reading. This reading remains in the computer's memory and can later be displayed by pressing a recall button as long as the machine has not been turned off or used to test another sample. The device can be used every 15 seconds if no alcohol is encountered; a two-minute wait is required if there is a positive reading.

The Alco-Sensor model IV is, apparently, seeing increasing acceptance in many states. The pocket-sized unit runs on a 22½-volt dry battery, theoretically capable of lasting for 1000 breath tests. There are four lights on the device: The "zero" light will illuminate if the result is .00–.01 percent; the "pass" indicator will light up if the result is .01–.08 percent; the "warn" light is activated by readings of .08–10 percent; and the "fail" indicator will light up the readings of .10 percent or more. These levels can be adjusted according to the legal BAC levels of the jurisdiction. The device can also be adjusted to report a specific blood-alcohol concentration, rather than a range, and can be connected to a printer to record results. Interestingly, the model IV is available in a memory configuration: It can electronically record all test results to memory for later recall (and discovery by defense counsel). The *absence* of such a readily available option in a given case, of course, should perhaps be the subject of some comment before a jury.

In administering the Alco-Sensor IV, the suspect is told to blow into the mouthpiece for as long as he can. While doing so, the officer presses the "read" button, activating a sampling valve and capturing a 1cc breath sample inside the fuel cell. The manual instructs the officer to push the button toward the end of the suspect's exhalation, in order to obtain the deepest alveolar air — i.e., the portion of the breath with the highest BAC. (Note: An optional system involves the use of a bag that fills up with 1100cc of breath before a sample is captured, ensuring a deep lung sample.) The PBT will give a maximum BAC reading within 15 to 60 seconds after the "read" button is pushed, utilyzing the 2100:1 partition ratio (see §6.0.1).

As the sample is drawn into the fuel cell, it is absorbed by a thin plastic membrane and is oxidized. An electric current is thereby generated, proportionate to the level of alcohol contained in the sample. The reading is determined by the amount of this current.

After the test is completed, the officer must push the "set" button to flush the sample from the device. However, the operating manual indicates that some alcohol may remain on the fuel cell surface despite this flushing. To prevent this from affecting the next test, the officer is instructed to push the "read" button after flushing to detect any residual alcohol; in fact, however, officers rarely perform this cautionary step — with predictable results. The manual also says that the officer should not give a test on the same device to another suspect until "sufficient time" (five minutes if the device is kept warm) has passed so that all traces of alcohol are eliminated from the device. If these cautionary steps are not followed, the manuals reads, "accumulative readings will result."

An additional problem with PBTs' using fuel cells is that an oxide film can accumulate on the electrode. This so-called "poisoning" of the electrode can cause false readings.

The Alco-Sensor (and all PBTs) is subject to the same problems of mouth alcohol contamination as are Intoxilyers, Intoximeters, etc. (see §6.2). Although it is rarely done by officers in the field, the manual clearly states that a 15-minute waiting period should be observed before testing to ensure the elimination of all mouth alcohol from burping, belching, recent ingestion, etc.

The manual also warns that "under no circumstances should raw cigarette smoke be blown into the instrument. It will permanently damage fuel cell." Counsel should consider the possible effects of a test on a cigarette smoker prior to the test on the client and before any calibration.

The unit is designed to operate at temperatures between 98 degrees (body temperature) and 68 degrees. Although the manual claims it will operate as low as 32 degrees (0 degrees centigrade — freezing), "some accuracy is sacrificed." The maximum efficiency range is 26 to 36 degrees centigrade. The temperature gauge on the back of the device will read between 20 to 36 degrees; if there is no reading, then the device is too hot or too cold to operate.

The following material relevant to the Alco-Sensor IV, reproduced from the California Highway Patrol's “Use and Calibration Protocol” (contained within the CHP's November 1994 “Statewide Preliminary Alcohol Screening Device Distribution Project”), contains the recommended procedures for:

1. Administration of the test;
2. Periodic accuracy checks;
3. Calibration procedures; and
4. Warranty.

Any deviation from such procedures in a given case should provide material for cross-examination. Additionally, the jury may find it of interest that the PAS device warranty is for only one year (labor), and may find it of even greater interest that the device is currently beyond its warranty period.

ALCO-SENSOR USE

A. The device's “SET” button should always be depressed prior to start of a test.

B. Insert the mouthpiece to activate the Alco-Sensor IV. The mouthpiece has a long end, which fits snugly and easily into the unit. When properly mounted, the mouthpiece turns the unit on. The display is capable of showing numerous items of information. Refer to Annex C for reference of display legends.

C. The internal temperature of the unit will be displayed. Note the temperature. If the temperature is below 10°C or above 40°C, the test is blocked. Remove the mouthpiece and place the unit in your pocket or other warm place to raise the temperature, or in a cool place to lower the temperature. The PAS device will come to an acceptable operating temperature in a short period of time.

D. The unit will then display “BLNK” (blank). This signifies that the unit is in the process of automatically running an air blank. During the first ten seconds a display consisting of alternating “<” and “>” characters appear. The unit should then display “.000.” If the unit displays “WAIT,” the unit is still clearing out the remnants of alcohol from a previous test. A test cannot be run unless the unit is free of alcohol. If "WAIT" persists more than three to four seconds, it is suggested, in order to preserve battery life, that the mouthpiece be removed and the process started again after 30 seconds. If a reading other than ".000" appears, further progress is blocked. The unit will then display "VOID" and after three seconds an intermittent beep will sound. The intermittent beep indicates that the mouthpiece should be removed (device deactivated). The process should be repeated after 30 seconds.

E. If the unit displays "SET," depress the set button. This would only occur if the "SET" button was not depressed prior to activation of the unit. The test cannot proceed unless the "SET" button is depressed.

F. When the display shows "TEST," instruct the subject to inhale deeply and exhale steadily through the mouthpiece. A "+" sign appears in the display window to indicate that the subject is exhaling with sufficient force to complete an automatic sample. If a "+" does not appear, instruct the subject to exhale harder. This "+" ensures that the subject is blowing into the unit and not feigning. When the subject has blown a minimum volume of approximately 1.2 liters, a second "+" sign appears. (Readout displays "+ +".) The sample will be taken only when this condition has been met and the flow diminishes, indicating the end of the exhalation is approaching. If both conditions are met the unit will automatically take a sample.

G. If the unit displays a "NOGO," there is not enough volume to provide a sample or the test has been interrupted. Begin the test again. This can be attempted three times before the sample is "VOID." If this occurs, remove the mouthpiece, reinsert the mouthpiece and begin the test again.

H. As soon as a successful breath sample has been obtained, the display will show alternating ">" and "<" characters. After a few seconds a two digit display will appear for three seconds (this is an approximation of the BAC). The display will then show alternating ">" and "<" characters for another 20–30 seconds. A final three digit reading will then be displayed.

I. After the test is complete the display will show "SET." Depress the set button. The unit will then begin to beep. Press the red button which will eject the mouthpiece. Mouthpieces should be disposed of properly at the completion of the test. Do not leave on ground.

J. At any time during the beeping period, and before the mouthpiece is ejected, depressing the "RECALL BUTTON" will display the three digit result of the test just completed.

ACCURACY CHECK

A. It is recommended that each unit be checked at least every 10 days or 150 tests. This will ensure that the unit is operating properly and to substantiate the accurate reading of the unit when testifying in court on the accuracy of the unit and the readings. The 10 day/150 test calibration is the same requirement (Title 17 California Code of Regulations) for the evidential breath testing machines used in California.

B. An accuracy check is the running of an air sample of known alcohol solution through the device's sampling system and checking to see that the unit reads the sample within an acceptable range. The check is performed when the temperature of the unit is between 10°C and 40°C.

C. The use of a wet alcohol simulator should be used to check and calibrate the PAS device. A Draeger Mark II, or similar, simulator is recommended. The simulator consists of a glass jar which holds 500cc of solution; a jar head which contains a heater thermostat, stirrer, and thermometer; and inlet and outlet ports for sampling headspace gas standing above the liquid solution.

D. The solution must be a known mixture of water/alcohol. PAS device users should check with their county forensics laboratory or local Department of Justice laboratory for information on acquiring or purchasing the required solution.

E. The operating temperature for the simulator is 34°C. Prior to testing the PAS device, plug the simulator into an electrical outlet and monitor the simulator's thermometer until the unit reaches operating temperature. If any other temperature is displayed, the testing should not be conducted. Additionally, prior to testing the PAS device, ensure that the jar head is secured to the jar. To check, cover the outlet port and blow into the intake port. Bubbles of air rising rapidly through the solution indicates that the jar head is not secured properly to the jar. If this occurs, examine the jar head and jar and ensure that a proper seal exists.

F. If the PAS device reading of the alcohol solution varies more than .005 percent from the known value of the solution, the PAS device shall be recalibrated by the following procedure.

CALIBRATION

A. Remove battery cover to expose calibration switch access holes.

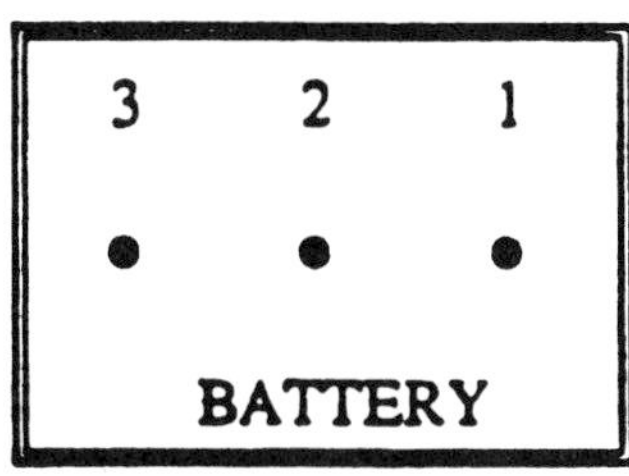

B. Insert a new mouthpiece and follow standard operation until the unit displays a blank reading of ".000."

C. While ".000" is still being displayed, press button #1 and hold down until a three-digit number is displayed (this will be the reading of the last calibration). When the three-digit number appears release the button. If the temperature is not in the range of 23°C to 27°C, the reading will show "TMP>" or "TMP<," in lieu of a three digit number, and the unit will void. If this occurs, remove the mouthpiece and correct the temperature before trying again. The internal temperature can be warmed by placing the unit in a pocket for a short time, or cooled by placing in a cool area for a short time.

D. If, after a few seconds, the display shows "SET," the set button should be depressed. The three-digit number will return to the display.

E. With the three-digit number in the display, adjust the number down (button #2) or number up (button #3) until the value of the calibration standard being used is displayed.

F. Press button #1 again and the display will read "CAL."

G. Attach the open end of the mouthpiece to the simulator outlet. Blow into the simulator inlet port for four seconds. After three seconds, press the "MANUAL BUTTON" on the unit to take the sample. The microprocessor will analyze the output from the fuel cell and will automatically make the necessary calibration adjustments. The numbers will be exactly as programmed in step E above.

H. Conclude the test by pressing the "SET BUTTON" when "SET" appears. Detach the simulator from the mouthpiece carefully so that the mouthpiece is not unseated from the unit.

I. Record the reading on the calibration log.

J. After a two minute wait, use a new mouthpiece to run an accuracy check. A reading no higher than .005 percent is allowed.

WARRANTY

A. All PAS devices will be repaired by the manufacturer free of charge if found to be inoperable or defective for a period of one (1) year for labor (until November 30, 1995) and two (2) years for parts (until November 30, 1996). All simulators will be repaired by the manufacturer free of charge, if found inoperable or defective for a period of one year (until September 15, 1995). All defective equipment will be repaired by the manufacturer and returned to the sending agency within thirty (30) days of the receipt by the manufacturer. Should an instrument require three (3) or more warranty repairs within the first year of operation, it will be considered a defective instrument and will be replaced free of charge with a new instrument upon request of the agency possessing the device.

B. The manufacturer, upon request, shall correct design flaws that are discovered with the equipment that prevent full compliance with the original specifications. The manufacturer shall notify the agencies that receive the devices of any design modifications that are made that may enhance the operation of the device, for a period of five years from the date of distribution.

SERVICE

Preliminary alcohol screening devices in need of repair shall be sent to:
Intoximeters, Inc.
1901 Locust St.
St. Louis, MO 63103
(314) 241-1158
(800) 451-8639

For a discussion of motions to suppress results of preliminary breath tests, see §11.5.5.

§4.4.2 Defense Use of Favorable PBT Evidence

In most jurisdictions, evidence of preliminary breath test results are not admissible in trial. As a result, defense counsel usually ignore them — even when the results may be favorable to the client. This is understandable, since the assumption is made that if the prosecution cannot introduce PBT evidence, then neither can the defense — i.e., the evidence is *per se* inadmissible.

Consider, however, the reasoning in an Arkansas case, *Patrick v. State,* 750 S.W.2d 391 (Ark. 1988). The appellate court accepted the defendant's reasoning that *since the PBT results were considered sufficiently reliable to establish probable cause to arrest him, they are sufficiently reliable to be admitted as exculpatory evidence.* See also, *Boyd v. City of Montgomery,* 472 So. 2d 694 (Ala. App. 1985).

Attorney John Tarantino of Providence, Rhode Island, points out that this is consistent with the decision in *Rock v. Arkansas,* 483 U.S. 44, 107 S. Ct. 2704 (1987), where the U.S. Supreme Court held that evidence of hypnosis offered by the defendant was admissible — even though not admissible if offered by the prosecution. The Court reasoned that prohibiting such evidence effectively precluded the defendant from presenting a defense. In other words, an accused's constitutional right to present evidence in his defense rises to a higher level than the prosecution's "right" to present evidence against him — and, thus, the standards for admissibility should reflect this.

Confronted with a situation where a preliminary breath test indicated low or no levels of alcohol (or, more realistically, where the client indicates he took such a test but police reports contain no mention of it), counsel should consider filing a motion *in limine* to obtain an advance ruling as to the admissibility of the intended evidence.

§4.5 Audiotapes and Videotapes

> The truth is not simply what you think it is; it is also the circumstances in which it is said, and to whom, why, and how it is said.
>
> VÁCLAV HAVEL

Police agencies throughout the country have made increasing use of audiovisual recording devices in drunk driving cases. Often financed by federal or state grants, these agencies are acquiring and making use of still cameras, motion picture cameras, sound tape recorders, and videotape machines, all in an effort to capture the intoxicated condition of a drunk driving arrestee for a jury.

Certainly, such evidence can be both dramatic and determinative in a given case. Hearing conflicting recollections and opinions is one thing, but being able to actually view and/or hear the defendant at the time of his alleged inebriation is quite another. The introduction of these modern devices was hailed by law enforcement agencies everywhere. Yet this enthusiasm has been somewhat dampened in recent years: The sword, it has been discovered, can cut both ways — the audiovisual evidence may well prove helpful to the defense.

In dealing with the presentation in court of motion pictures, videotapes, sound recordings, or still photographs, defense counsel should be familiar with the circumstances under which the filming, taping, or photographing took place. Understanding those circumstances, he must then establish the selective nature of the evidence.

Consider first the simplest and most common form of audiovisual evidence: the still photograph. Many officers will carry a still camera in their squad cars, while others will make use of one available at the police station or jail. Often, a Polaroid-type camera will be used. Four or five pictures of the defendant will be taken; usually they will show him stumbling while trying to walk the line, leaning during a balance test, or simply sitting in the booking cage with his hair and clothing disarranged. Obviously, the camera is being wielded by an individual whose primary interest is in obtaining incriminating, not exculpatory, evidence, and this must be stressed. Why were only *three* pictures taken? Why were no pictures taken of the defendant while he was *not* stumbling? Why were no pictures taken of the *other* tests? If there are no close-up photographs of the defendant, the officer should be questioned as to why none were taken, in view of his descriptions in the arrest report of bloodshot eyes, flushed face, disarranged hair, and wrinkled or soiled clothing. On the other hand, if the photographs available fail to show clearly bloodshot eyes, etc., this should be pointed out to the officer and the jury.

There is, of course, always the possibility that the officer is not showing all the photographs he took of the defendant, and this possibility should be brought out. Many officers simply will discard photographs that they feel are not helpful to the case. Even if an officer denies having done this, counsel should point out that there is probably no way anyone will ever know if other, presumably exculpatory, photographs exist. The police officer, interested in obtaining a conviction to justify his arrest, is the sole person who decides what to photograph and what resultant photographs to make available.

The use of sound tape recorders is also a fairly common practice. Such tapes can be used by law enforcement agencies to illustrate the ubiquitous "thick and slurred speech" of the suspect, to prove the incriminating statements made by him, and to show compliance with *Miranda* requirements. Again, however, the taping process is a selective one: The police determine what to tape, what not to tape, under what conditions, and how to edit or otherwise deal with the tape thereafter. And it is counsel's job to bring this out during cross-examination.

If the tape is used to present the defendant's admissions and compliance with *Miranda,* counsel should look for the possibility that it can be used against the prosecution in another respect. Presumably, the defendant's speech will be sufficiently clear on the tape to be understood, and it may well prove clear and normal enough to give the lie to the officer's testimony that the client's speech was thick, slurred, garbled, or unintelligible.

On the other hand, if the tape is offered to prove the slurred nature of the defendant's speech, counsel should be looking for another voice on the tape to compare it to. Given unprofessional taping equipment and procedures, the poor acoustics of the police station, and the normal activity going on in the background at the station, *any* voice may end up sounding slurred, garbled, or unintelligible. If another voice on the tape, presumably an officer's, appears, and it too appears fuzzy, this should be brought out. If there is no other voice, this simple yet important fact should be stressed; a lack of comparisons under such poor recording conditions should render the "evidence" irrelevant.

An added note: Juries do not like hidden tape recorders. It is a simple fact that most American citizens find the surreptitious use by police agencies of things like hidden tape recorders distasteful if not reminiscent of totalitarian regimes. If the taping was conducted without the defendant's knowledge, the details should be emphasized.

Motion picture films and videotape recordings can be the most effective form of audiovisual evidence — and the most damaging. Again, however, the camera is in the absolute control of an individual or individuals who are interested in seeing that the suspect is ultimately convicted, and this simple fact should be borne in mind constantly.

Rarely will the arresting officer in the field have the camera. Rather, the camera will probably be set up at the police station, commonly in a special room designated for that purpose. The room will probably be white, with bright lighting, and the camera or video recorder may be elevated above the suspect's view or hidden behind a one-way mirror; a clock may be on one wall to record the time on film, and a stripe may be painted on the floor for walk-the-line tests. Conducted under such conditions, cross-examination as to the filming or taping can prove difficult, particularly if the taping began with the defendant's entry into the room and continued without stopping until his exit. About the only thing counsel can do in such a situation is to question the test's conclusions or attack it on the grounds that only the test administered in the field at the time of the arrest an hour earlier is relevant.

Some law enforcement agencies use mobile video units dispatched by radio to the scene of an arrest. There is usually more room here for cross-examination, as the taping or filming will be more influenced by the subjective decisions of the police operator. Lighting conditions, angle of filming, distances, film speed, lack of continuous filming, selective filming, editing, etc., can all be factors in the final product. And, again, counsel should be looking at the film for evidence, such as a well-performed finger-to-nose test, a lack of leaning or stumbling, or an immaculately groomed and clothed appearance, that can be turned against the prosecution.

For a discussion of sanctions for destruction of videotape evidence, see §11.5.7. And refer to §11.5.6 for a discussion of suppression of videotapes.

5

INTRODUCTION TO BLOOD-ALCOHOL ANALYSIS

§5.0 *Forensic Alcohol Analysis*

> An error is the more dangerous in proportion to the degree of truth which it contains.
>
> HENRI FREDERIC AMIEL

In the past, the prosecutor's case in a drunk driving prosecution rested solely on the testimony of the arresting officer. The evidence against the defendant consisted entirely of the officer's observations of the defendant and of his opinion as to sobriety. But the pitfalls were many. The officer's word could be challenged, and there was nothing to corroborate his observations. The validity of his opinion could be questioned and his opinion often had little special education or training behind it. Perhaps most important, the prosecutor had to fit the defendant within a vague, ill-defined category entitled "under the influence." At no time could the prosecutor offer any evidence but outward symptoms and opinions, and at no time could he even spell out the offense beyond such amorphous phrases as "substantial impairment."

Two factors led to a drastic change in this situation. The first was the advent of advanced scientific techniques within criminalistics laboratories. Increasingly, law enforcement was turning to scientific methods of detection in proving criminal conduct. Then, in 1938, the American Medical Association set up a "Committee to Study Problems of Motor Vehicle Accidents"; at almost the same time, the National Safety Council established a "Committee on Tests for Intoxication." Studies by these committees resulted in a recommendation that legal standards be set for determining the intoxication of a driver by chemical testing. Although there was some disagreement among the prominent medical members of the committees, the consensus recognized that any individual who had a .15 percent of alcohol in his blood could be presumed to be under the influence of alcohol; anyone having less than .05 percent of alcohol could be presumed to be not under the influence; and those individuals falling in the .05–.15 percent midrange might or might not be under the influence — that is, the test would not be conclusive. The .15 level was lowered in 1960 by the recommendations of both committees to .10 percent (this vacillation of medical experts, incidentally, should give added ammunition to defense counsel for cross-examination). Since then, many states have lowered it even further — to .08 percent.

Armed with these findings and recommendations, prosecuting agencies throughout the country were able to obtain legislation requiring any driver to submit to chemical testing when requested by an officer. If the driver refused, these implied consent statutes automatically imposed sanctions, usually in the form of license suspension, regardless of the driver's guilt. When a blood-alcohol reading was obtained from the test, still other statutes determined what presumption, if any, was to be drawn legally from the reading, and the jury was to be instructed accordingly.

The prosecution now was armed with not merely the opinion of one officer, but with "science": He could now "prove" to the jury what the chemical state of the defendant's body was at the time of the arrest. Furthermore, he could now define for the jury exactly what "under the influence" consisted of: Quite simply, it meant having a blood-alcohol reading in excess of .08 or .10 percent. Prosecuting a drunk driving case became largely a matter of obtaining a blood-alcohol reading and comparing it to the statutory presumptive levels.

But even this was not enough. Backed by increasing public hysteria and the attendant political pressures, prosecutors have succeeded in obtaining the passage of so-called per se laws. These laws make it illegal simply to drive with a blood-alcohol level in excess of a certain amount — usually .10 or .08 percent. No longer is intoxication even relevant: The crime consists entirely of driving while having a given physiological condition. Under such statutes, chemical evidence has taken on even greater importance. The accused's right to jury trial has increasingly been supplanted by "trial by machine" — that is, innocence or guilt is largely determined by a breath analyzing device.

Yet blood-alcohol tests were designed only to corroborate the observations of witnesses, not to take their place. Many scientific studies have been completed and many statistics compiled concerning the validity of the recognized blood-alcohol testing methods and the presumptive levels. There is considerable disagreement within the medical and scientific communities as to any conclusions that can be drawn. There are still many unanswered questions regarding breath, blood, and urine tests and their correlation with impairment of driving ability. Individual tolerances to alcohol are completely ignored, as are the individual physiological differences in absorption and elimination. Testing devices vary in quality, and none of them is without numerous sources for error.

Nevertheless, the significance of chemical evidence in a drunk driving case is considerable. Many judges, for example, will not even permit a drunk driving defendant to enter a plea at his arraignment until the results of the blood or urine analysis are returned from the crime lab. Prosecutors in many, if not most, jurisdictions will use the blood-alcohol reading in a given case as a gauge in plea bargaining. If a reading is below .08 percent, for example, a traffic violation may be offered in lieu of a plea of guilty; if the reading is between .08 and .11 percent, a plea to the lesser-included offense of reckless driving may be offered; and if the figure is .12 percent or over, the prosecutor will probably insist on a straight plea as charged. Sentencing, too, is affected in many courts by the blood-alcohol level. As an example, one jurisdiction imposes one day in jail for each point over .10 percent in the defendant's blood-alcohol reading, resulting in an eight-day sentence for an individual with a level of .18 percent. And, of course, chemical evidence is all-important in a per se case.

Clearly, the pendulum has swung too far in the opposite direction: The results of all-too-fallible blood-alcohol tests are today accorded far more stature than they deserve. This is a reality that defense counsel must learn to deal with. He must constantly struggle to desanctify the testing procedures. Certainly, he must convince the jury that the procedure used in the case was not only generally unreliable but faulty as applied to the defendant.

Defense counsel will discover one benefit from this general feeling of reverence or mysticism toward the blood-alcohol reading. Many prosecutors, particularly inexperienced ones, will present the testimony of the police officer as almost an afterthought, relying instead on the blood-alcohol evidence to convict. Never mind that the officer can testify that the defendant was falling down and incoherent, the prosecutor will hurry on so that he can display the magic number to the jury. This is a common but serious tactical mistake, and one that defense counsel should take advantage of by shifting the focus of the trial from the defendant to the blood-alcohol test. The issue is changed subtly from the intoxication of the defendant to the accuracy of the testing procedure. Prosecutors can be protective of their chemical evidence and will concentrate their efforts on defending against the attacks of defense counsel on the breath machine, urinalysis, or blood analysis. The ultimate question in the jury's mind will subtly shift from one of whether the defendant was under the influence to one of whether the test was valid. If it was not valid, the defendant may well be acquitted, regardless of other damning evidence. In other words, defense counsel has succeeded in putting the blood-alcohol test on trial.

§5.1 Alcohol and the Human Body

Ethanol, or ethyl alcohol (grain alcohol), is one of the earliest and most widely used drugs in existence. It is a clear fluid whose low molecular weight and high solubility in water cause it to diffuse rapidly through body tissue membranes and reach equilibrium in tissues at levels proportional to water content. Blood, for example, will hold proportionately more alcohol than will muscle tissue.

The concentration of alcohol in an individual's body depends on the amount of water contained in that body. The more water present in the body, the more diluted the alcohol will become as it is absorbed into the system. And the simple fact is that individuals vary according to the percentage of water that exists in their bodies.

In a study entitled Pharmacokinetics of Ethanol in Plasma and Whole Blood: Estimation of Total Body Water by the Dilution Principle, Jones, Hahn, and Stalberg, 42 European Journal of Clinical Pharmacology 445 (1992), researchers confirmed that the body water content varies from person to person. The content in men, interestingly, decreases with age — that is, the blood-alcohol concentration will become higher. Further, where an individual has experienced trauma, as in an automobile accident, the body's percentage of water will decrease. The same can also happen due to pathological conditions, as in persons with diarrhea, heart failure, or impaired renal function.

For alcohol to produce its effect, it must reach the brain. To accomplish this, it first passes into the bloodstream after absorption through the walls of the stomach and small intestines. This is a simple biochemical process of diffusion, which will continue as long as the concentration of alcohol in the stomach and intestines is higher than that in the blood.

In contrast to ordinary foods and many drugs, alcohol is absorbed rapidly from the stomach and even more rapidly from the small intestine just beyond the stomach. In fact, the presence of alcohol is initially detectable about five minutes after consumption, and its maximum concentration within the body tissues is achieved in somewhere between ½ hour and 1½ hours. This rate of absorption can be accelerated if the subject has ingested significant amounts of water or materials containing water, and it can be slowed down if he has eaten food. The type of alcoholic beverage can also be a factor: beer will cause a slower increase in blood-alcohol concentration than distilled spirits, as well as a lower peak level and faster decline. Absorption is complete when the entire gastrointestinal tract reaches equilibrium with the remainder of the body; this can take as long as 2½ hours but commonly occurs within 30 to 90 minutes. In any event, the rate of absorption of alcohol — and, as a result, the effect on the nervous system — varies according to the individual.

Once absorbed through the stomach/intestine walls, the alcohol passes into the portal vein that carries it to the liver, then to the right side of the heart, and then to the lungs. From the lungs (where the exhaled alveolar air is measured by breath analysis machines), the alcohol is carried in arterial blood to the left side of the heart and from there into the body's general circulatory system, by which means it eventually reaches the brain.

Blood-alcohol analysis, then, is simply the attempt to measure the amount by weight of alcohol within the subject's blood at any given time. This amount, expressed as a percentage of the blood in which it is found, is then compared to a scale of percentages established by law for determining the presumptive levels of intoxication. The determination of the amount of alcohol in the blood can be accomplished directly by analyzing a sample of the subject's blood or indirectly by analyzing a sample of the subject's urine or breath.

The amount of alcohol found in the blood is the central issue in a per se charge. With a traditional DUI charge, however, it is only of secondary interest: It is the amount of alcohol actually absorbed into the brain that will affect an individual's ability to perceive, make judgments, and coordinate his movements — that is, his ability to operate a motor vehicle safely. But there is no practical means of measuring the alcohol absorbed by the body beyond that found in the bloodstream (or, even further removed, in the urine or the alveolar air). Because the bones, brain, fatty tissue, etc., contain a much lower percentage of water than does blood and because the alcohol level in blood is about 17 percent higher than that in the soft tissues, the concentration of alcohol in the entire body, including the brain, is always less than that in the blood. However, science has offered the "Widmark Factor R" — a designation of the ratio between the concentration of alcohol in the whole body divided by the concentration of alcohol in the blood. For men, this ratio averages about .67, with a range of .46 to .86; women usually have a somewhat lower ratio because of having a larger proportion of fatty tissue. Obviously, the fact that this ratio varies so widely according to the individual makes generalizations about a given individual very suspect.

In organs having a rich blood supply, such as the kidneys, brain, and liver, the tissues very quickly attain alcohol equilibrium with the arterial blood. Voluntary muscle tissue, however, has a much smaller blood flow per unit of weight and as a result requires longer to reach alcohol equilibrium after ingestion. Since the muscles make up about 40 percent of body weight, this delay in alcohol absorption by the muscles results in high concentrations of alcohol in arterial blood and in the brain during active absorption of alcohol. The result is the common phenomenon that an individual may appear greatly affected only a few minutes after taking two or three drinks, and then rapidly sober up within 15 to 30 minutes in apparent contradiction to normal expectations. This, of course, can raise serious doubts about the relevance of blood-alcohol tests.

Many factors can affect the rate of absorption and distribution of alcohol into the system and, ultimately, into the brain. The most common is that different individuals have different rates — and these rates can vary within a given individual. External factors also can cause variation. The effects of cold weather or extreme stress, for example, can cause less blood to be delivered to the muscles and more to the brain; with more blood being delivered to the brain, more alcohol is also delivered, thus raising the blood-alcohol level. Ritchie, The Aliphatic Alcohols, in Goodman and Gilman's The Pharmacological Basis of Therapeutics (7th ed. 1985). Therefore, it would appear that the stress caused by, say, field sobriety tests, arrest, and booking could themselves cause higher blood-alcohol levels when the individual is later tested at the police station.

Absorption and actual concentration are only two aspects of blood-alcohol theory. Elimination, or the rate of disappearance of alcohol from the body, is of equal importance. The body reduces the amount of alcohol by oxidation in the liver. The rate of this elimination is, once again, a matter that varies from one person's physiology to another's, but it appears probably to be independent of concentration. The rate of disappearance, called the "Widmark Factor B," is generally about .015 percent per hour — that is, the body will "burn off" about .015 percent alcohol in the blood in an hour. If an individual has a reading of .08, for example, he should have a reading an hour later (assuming, of course, no further consumption of alcohol) of about .065. Put another way, an individual will eliminate approximately ½ to ⅔ of an ounce of 100 proof whiskey in an hour. This rate of disappearance can vary from .010 percent to .020 percent per hour, although dissipation of as high as .06 percent has been scientifically observed. Again, the wide variation in individual rates of elimination gives the lie to attempts to test all drunk driving suspects on the theory of uniform burnoff rates (see §5.2 concerning retrograde extrapolation).

How does all this interpret into everyday experience? An *average* person of 150 to 170 pounds probably must consume, on an empty stomach, approximately 8 to 10 ounces of 100 proof whiskey (8 to 10 beers or 4 to 5 highballs) to reach a blood-alcohol level of .15 percent; this is equal to 15 parts of alcohol per 10,000 parts of blood in the subject's system by weight, or about 2 parts of alcohol by volume for every 1,000 parts of blood. But, again, the ever-present aspect of individuality can confound scientific premises. A heavy drinker, because of his altered physiology or biochemical reactions, may have to drink *12* ounces of 100 proof whiskey before that same level of .15 percent is reached. And a level of .15 percent can have wildly different effects on the nervous systems of different individuals and hence on their ability to operate motor vehicles safely.

All of this is, of course, theoretical. The one simple overriding fact that continues to frustrate attempts to measure blood-alcohol concentration is the incredible *variability* between one individual and another — and, within a single individual, from one moment to the next.

Dr. Kurt Dubowski, probably the most recognized expert in the field of blood-alcohol analysis, has succinctly summarized some of the problems with DUI blood-alcohol tests in an article entitled Absorption, Distribution and Elimination of Alcohol, 10 Journal of Studies on Alcohol Supp. 98 (1985):

> First, not all blood and breath alcohol curves follow the Widmark pattern, nor is the elimination phase linear. Second, alcohol absorption is not always complete within 60 to 90 minutes as often claimed. Third, the peak alcohol concentration cannot be validly predicted or established in an individual instance without frequent and timely measurement of alcohol concentrations. Fourth, it is not possible to establish whether an individual is in the absorption or elimination phase, or to establish the mean overall rate of alcohol elimination from the blood or breath, from the results of two consecutive blood or breath alcohol measurements, however timed. Fifth, significantly large short-term fluctuations occur in some subjects and result in marked positive and negative departures from the alcohol concentration trend line. Sixth, short-term

marked oscillation of the blood or breath alcohol concentration can occur at various points on the curve, resulting in repeated excursions of the alcohol concentration above and below a given concentration within a few minutes or for hours. Finally, no forensically valid forward or backward extrapolation of blood or breath alcohol concentrations is ordinarily possible in a given subject and occasion solely on the basis of time and individual analysis results.

As will be seen in subsequent sections, these are only a few of the sources of error in attempting to determine whether an individual is under the influence by chemically analyzing his blood, breath, or urine.

§5.1.1 Individual Tolerance

Most defendants in drunk driving cases are charged with two offenses: (1) driving under the influence of alcohol and (2) driving with a blood-alcohol level in excess of a given level (usually .10 percent or .08 percent, the so-called per se statute). As to the first offense, the prosecution usually offers the chemical test result not only on the per se count but also as evidence of intoxication; in most states, a presumption arises from the BAC (see §1.4.3). That evidence is, however, a rebuttable one — and one of the factors that should be used in rebuttal is the question of individual tolerance.

Scientific studies have repeatedly confirmed the existence of variability in individual tolerance. In a study reported in Sullivan, Hauptman, and Bronstein, Lack of Observable Intoxication in Humans with High Plasma Alcohol Concentrations, 32 Journal of Forensic Sciences 1160 (1987), for example, hospital patients with a history of alcohol abuse were clinically observed and tested after consuming significant amounts of alcohol. The researchers found essentially no correlation between the patients' BACs and their assessed levels of intoxication. This lack of correlation was attributed to the high tolerance developed from long-term alcohol abuse. See also Redmond, Alcohol Blood Levels, 16 Annals of Emergency Medicine 374 (1987), in which 20 patients studied in a detox unit of an English hospital showed no ill effects after being admitted with BACs above the *lethal* limit.

In another illuminating study, researchers investigated the

effect of intoxication on memory. The study found that increased blood-alcohol levels generally impaired the individual's ability to recall — but went on to find that the relationship between an individual's BAC and his *physical performance* was not significant. The scientists concluded that BAC as determined by breath analysis was a poor predictor of a person's ability to perform; in theory, this was due to individual differences in absorption and metabolism rates. Maylor and Rabbit, The Effect of Alcohol on Rate of Forgetting, 91 Psychopharmacology 230 (1987).

Research at the Alcohol Research Center at the University of Colorado confirms that the blood-alcohol level of an individual is a poor measure of intoxication due to individual tolerance. The following December 20, 1983, release from the University's Public Information Office summarizes the results of that research:

> Defining a "drunken driver" by measuring blood alcohol levels gives little indication of how impaired the individual's judgment or physical responses actually are, according to studies at the Alcohol Research Center at the University of Colorado, Boulder.
>
> Blood alcohol level, whether determined by "Breathalyzer" measurements, urine or blood samples, yields an objective-sounding number. But that figure tells little about one's ability to drive or function while "legally" drunk.
>
> "Individual differences in response and tolerance for alcohol vary so widely that one person may be incapacitated by a less-than-the-legal-limit alcohol dose, while others show almost no response to a fairly high blood alcohol reading," according to Gene Erwin, director of the Alcohol Research Center and professor of pharmacology.
>
> Both an acquired tolerance for alcohol and individual genetic differences account for the wide variations in response, he explained.
>
> Tolerance for alcohol can be built up both over the long term — through regular drinking — and in each individual encounter with alcohol, according to research Erwin has undertaken with colleagues Robert Plomin and Jim Wilson.
>
> In the laboratory, volunteers were given alcohol mixed with water or a sugar-free mixer (to eliminate body changes produced by sugar) until their blood alcohol level was 0.10 percent. At that level, most people performed poorly in terms of judgment, balance, muscle control and other physical tests.
>
> When kept at the same level of drunkenness for three hours,

> however, some gradually improved their performances. After building up their tolerance for alcohol in the laboratory situation, roughly analogous to social drinking, some people were able to perform as well while legally drunk as they had when sober.
>
> Others were not able to match their sober performance level. These individuals, the researchers believe, lack either the inherited or acquired ability to function with large alcohol doses.
>
> "In these tests, we're dealing with normal people, not alcoholics," Robert Plomin said. Much of the information on alcohol has involved alcoholics or individuals with what the scientists call "chronic acquired tolerance," not average folks. Generalizing from acutely tolerant people to the public at large does not allow for the wide variations of individual differences, they note.
>
> "The old 'pull over, buddy, and let's see you walk this straight line' approach to determining drunkenness is a much more accurate way to see how impaired an individual may be," Robert Plomin said. The roadside drunk-or-sober tests of performance are gradually being abandoned by law enforcement officers around the country, however, since the tests require subjective judgment — the officers' perceptions of the drivers' abilities.
>
> Most state laws now define drunken driving by blood alcohol level, a measure which does not eliminate this subjectivity.
>
> Dubbing such drunk driving laws "driving under the influence" or "driving while ability impaired," however, is a step in the wrong direction, Plomin cautioned. Some people are dangerously impaired below the legal blood-alcohol limit, while those with acute tolerance show almost no change at higher-than-legal levels.
>
> The research in individual responses to alcohol, undertaken over the past six years, incorporates findings from more than 100 individuals, including siblings and identical twins. One of the long-term goals of the research is to learn more about the genetic basis of alcoholism and alcohol response.

A number of studies have concluded that alcoholics and heavy drinkers tend to develop a tolerance to the effects of alcohol. Some studies have looked at the relationship between blood-alcohol concentrations and level of consciousness — that is, the level at which an individual will lose consciousness.

Generally, individuals with BACs of .30 percent or higher begin to lapse into a stupor or coma; levels above .40 percent are usually fatal. Yet, studies are commonly reporting that individuals with histories of chronic alcohol abuse survive levels of .73 percent, .78 percent, 1.12 percent, and even 1.5 percent. See, respectively, Chambers, et al., Blood Alcohol Levels, 4 Archives of Emergency Medicine 127 (1987); Hammond, et al., Blood Ethanol: A Report of Unusually High Levels in Living Patient, 226 Journal of the American Medical Association 63 (1973); Berild and Hasselbach, Survival After a Blood Alcohol Concentration of 1127 mg/dl, 2 Lancet 363 (1981); Johnson, et al., Survival After a Serum Ethanol Concentration of 1 ½%, 2 Lancet 1394 (1982).

The relevance of this information is, of course, that blood-alcohol concentration may not truly reflect an individual's degree of impairment in a non-per se drunk driving case — especially if the defendant has a history of alcohol abuse. Obviously, counsel must weigh the advantages and disadvantages of presenting evidence of a client's past alcohol abuse to a jury. Generic or hypothetical questions of an expert or officer concerning tolerance — including questions about the effects of alcohol abuse — would avoid the problem.

§5.2 *Retrograde Extrapolation: Projecting Test Levels Back to Time of Driving*

> Let a man get up and say, "Behold, this is the truth," and instantly I perceive a sandy cat filching a piece of fish in the background. Look, you have forgotten the cat, I say.
>
> VIRGINIA WOOLF

Whether in a per se or a traditional DUI case, the prosecutor will usually introduce chemical evidence of the defendant's blood-alcohol level. Of course, by itself this evidence is irrelevant: It reflects the blood-alcohol level of the defendant *at the time of testing* — not at the time of driving. And, of course, it is not a crime to be under the influence of alcohol in a police station or hospital.

Thus the prosecution will usually introduce evidence — usually through an expert witness — of *retrograde extrapolation.* Put simply, retrograde extrapolation is the computation back in time of the blood-alcohol level — that is, the estimation of the level at the time of driving.

In many states, this effort is made considerably easier by a statutory presumption that the blood-alcohol concentration at the time of driving was the same as at the time of testing. But counsel should be aware of two considerations. First, such statutes generally require that the test be administered within a given period of time after driving for the presumption to take effect; two hours is common. Second, this is a *rebuttable* presumption: Cross-examination of the expert and/or defense evidence (for example, testimony of the defendant) can "erase" the presumption.

In *McLean v. Moran,* 963 F.2d 1306 (9th Cir. 1992), the U.S. Court of Appeals addressed a Nevada law that provided as follows:

> In any criminal prosecution for a violation of [the DUI *per se* statute] in which it is alleged that the defendant was driving or in actual control of a vehicle while he had 0.10 percent or more by weight of alcohol in his blood, the amount of alcohol shown by a chemical analysis of his blood, urine, breath or other bodily substance is presumed to be no less than the amount present at the time of the alleged violation. [Id. at 1308.]

The Ninth Circuit granted the defendant's petition for habeas corpus, agreeing with her argument that the facts in the case operated to create a *conclusive* presumption and therefore unconstitutionally shifted the burden of proof to the accused. Although the court stopped short of finding that the statute was unconstitutional on its face, it noted that such presumptions are subject to a variety of interpretations and often raise serious constitutional questions.

In the continuing effort to facilitate convictions in drunk driving cases, some states have "solved" the evidentiary problem of retrograde extrapolation by defining the offense as simply having a given blood-alcohol concentration within a period of time after driving. The Pennsylvania Supreme Court, however, has held that such a statute (imposing criminal sanctions on drivers with .10 percent BAC within three hours of driving) violates the due process guarantees of the Fourteenth Amendment. In *Commonwealth v. Barud* (Pa. 1996) 681 A.2d 162, the court held that the statute unnecessarily encompasses both lawful and unlawful conduct, fails to provide a reasonable standard by which a person may gauge his conduct, and fails to require proof that a person's BAC exceeded .10 percent at the time of driving.

Absent a rebuttable presumption and/or evidence of retrograde extrapolation, it may be error to admit the results at all in a drunk driving trial. In *Vermont v. Dumont,* 499 A.2d 787 (Vt. 1985), the defendant was charged with violation of both the DUI and the per se (.10 percent BAC) statutes. He had been tested at .13 percent one hour and ten minutes after being stopped. At trial the results of the breath test were received into evidence; however, no evidence was presented of BAC at the time of operation of the car. The jury instructions indicated that the results were admitted only to corroborate the testimony of the officer that the defendant had had *something* to drink.

The Supreme Court of Vermont observed preliminarily:

> Proof of an offense under [the per se statute] requires the prosecution to produce evidence of the defendant's blood alcohol, and to relate that content back to the time of the operation of the automobile. . . .
>
> Proof of an offense under [the DUI statute] requires the prosecution to produce evidence of the defendant's condition at the time of operation. However, evidence of the results of a blood-alcohol test, even though not related back, is admissible to establish the fact that defendant had consumed some amount of intoxicating liquor before being stopped. [Id. at 789.]

The court then decided, however, that the actual *numerical* result of the test should not be introduced in a DUI case unless it is related back to the time of operation:

> A jury might erroneously use a numerical test result which has not been related back to the time of operation as evidence of actual intoxication at the time of the offense, particularly if the jury is familiar with the .10% blood alcohol content presumption. . . .
>
> In view of the marginal additional probative value of the numerical result, and the danger of its misuse by the jury, expert testimony concerning the blood-alcohol content test in a [DUI] prosecution should be strictly limited to whether the test demonstrates that the defendant did, in fact, consume any intoxicating liquor. The numerical result itself should be excluded unless it is related back to the time of operation and used pursuant to the permissive presumption. . . . [Id.]

Thus the actual reading cannot be used in either a per se or a DUI prosecution unless it is related back to the time of operation. Absent this, the prosecution can only offer evidence in a DUI case that a test was taken and that it did indicate that the defendant had consumed *some* alcohol.

Similarly, a Texas appellate court reversed a drunk driving conviction where the prosecution failed to relate the defendant's breath test results back to when she was driving. In *McCafferty v. State,* 748 S.W.2d 489 (Tex. App. 1988), the court noted that the state's expert witness made no attempt to "explain absorption and metabolization rates of intoxication, or in any way connect the breath test results at 4:45 A.M. to appellant's condition when driving at 2:30 A.M." See also *Desmond v. Superior Court,* 779 P.2d 1261 (Ariz. 1989); *State v. Ladwig,* 434 N.W.2d 594 (S.D. 1989); *Commonwealth v. Modaffare,* 601 A.2d 1233 (Pa. 1992).

The Supreme Court of New Jersey, however, has taken an opposite position. In *State v. Tischio,* 527 A.2d 388 (N.J. 1987), the defendant's motion at trial for a judgment of acquittal was denied despite the fact that the prosecution failed to offer any evidence relating a breath test taken one hour after the arrest back to the time of driving. The case involved a per se statute with an .11 percent reading.

In affirming the conviction, the court considered the legislative intent in passing the per se statute and determined that it was "to remove the obstacles impeding the efficient and successful prosecution of those who drink and drive. One such impediment has been the introduction of conflicting expert testimony. . . ." Id. at 393. Thus, the court decided, proving the offense "neither requires nor allows extrapolation evidence to demonstrate the defendant's blood-alcohol level while actually driving." Id. at 397.

An unusually strong dissent pointed out that the holding was not supported by prevailing law in the majority of other jurisdictions and was even contrary to an *amicus* brief filed by the Attorney General arguing that the offense relates to the time of driving and not of testing.

The *Tischio* case is representative of poorly reasoned decisions aimed solely at facilitating convictions in DUI prosecutions. The language of New Jersey's per se statute clearly referred to a driver who "*operates a motor vehicle* with a blood alcohol concentration of

0.10% or more'' — not one who has such a level one hour later. And it is certainly a source of some constitutional concern that the supreme court of this state has decided that ''conflicting expert testimony'' is an ''impediment'' to convicting those accused of drunk driving!

The Supreme Court of Ohio has apparently taken a rather strange ''compromise'' position. In *City of Newark v. Lucas,* 532 N.E.2d 130 (Ohio 1988), a blood sample was drawn after the expiration of the statutory two-hour time limit. The court reversed the per se conviction but affirmed the conviction for driving under the influence. Under the traditional DUI statute, the court reasoned, ''[t]he accuracy of the test is not the critical issue as it is in prosecutions for *per se* violations. . . . The test results, if probative, are merely considered in addition to all other evidence of impaired driving in a prosecution for [DUI].'' Id. at 134.

It would certainly seem that there should be some limits on *when* the test was administered. A Michigan appellate court faced this question in *People v. Schwab,* 433 N.W.2d 824 (Mich. App. 1988). In that case, a breath test was given to the defendant two and one-quarter hours after his arrest. The relevant statute provided that the BAC as determined by the test should be regarded as the BAC at the time of driving ''provided such test was administered within a reasonable time after the defendant's arrest.'' Without setting forth a ''bright line'' as to what constitutes a ''reasonable time,'' the court held that under the facts of the case a two and one-quarter-hour delay was not reasonable.

§5.2.1 The Fallacy of Retrograde Extrapolation

Counsel should be aware of serious flaws in retrograde extrapolation — flaws that must be made apparent to the jury. The extrapolation process depends on a number of premises, many of which are subject to criticism. Thus, for example, it is assumed that the absorption of alcohol was completed, that the elimination of alcohol in the particular individual follows a uniform and predictable rate, and that the individual's blood-alcohol ''curve'' may be accurately charted. Each of these assumptions, as will be seen, is fallacious.

The following comments from the noted blood-alcohol expert, Dr. Richard Jensen of Minneapolis, Minnesota, will give defense counsel a general introduction to the dangers of retrograde extrapolation:

> Retrograde extrapolation is the process whereby the result of a blood alcohol test taken sometime after an incident is used to determine the blood alcohol concentration at the time of the incident. In every case, there is insufficient information available to the expert to make this calculation. Assumptions are liable to be made which are not applicable to any specific individual. These assumptions would include that the alcohol was completely absorbed at the time of interest, the defendant eliminated alcohol at the average rate, and that the chemical test was proper and valid.
>
> It has been demonstrated by continuous flow analysis that blood alcohol levels do not rise and fall in a steady fashion, but do demonstrate spikes or steepling where a momentary blood alcohol elimination is 0.015 percent per hour; this can vary in the general population from 0.008 to 0.030 percent per hour, and may vary even more than that in certain individuals. Any extrapolation for more than several hours will make the range so broad as to be almost useless. In order for retrograde extrapolation to be made, it is important to know that the individual has essentially absorbed all the alcohol he consumed, and his blood alcohol is now decreasing.
>
> The rate of absorption is an unpredictable variable and will take anywhere from fifteen minutes to three hours after the last drink is consumed. There is some indication that this can be drawn out for up to six hours after the last drink is consumed under very extenuating circumstances. Any expert attempting a retrograde extrapolation should explain in detail the assumptions and the uncertainty involved. A specific individual could vary so greatly as to essentially make the extrapolation without value.

One variable in extrapolating blood-alcohol levels, the rate of *absorption* of alcohol, may be affected by a number of factors, such as the presence or absence of ingested food — and may vary further in relation to the amount and type of food consumed and when it was consumed. In an article entitled The Effect of Desmethylimipramine on the Absorption of Alcohol and Paracetamol, 52 Postgraduate Medical Journal 139 (Mar. 1976), a group of scientists acknowledged that alcohol absorption "varies from person to person and can be changed by food, posture, and disease. It can also be altered by a number of different drugs, particularly those which modify the actions of the autonomic nervous system.''

University of Oklahoma blood-alcohol expert Dr. Kurt Dubowski has conducted extensive experiments and has found that peak blood-alcohol concentration varied among his subjects from 14 minutes after ingestion of alcohol to 138 minutes after ingestion. In other words, there were some subjects who would absorb alcohol and reach peak concentration *ten times faster* than other subjects! Dubowski, Absorption, Distribution and Elimination of Alcohol: Highway Safety Aspects, Journal on Studies of Alcohol, Supp. No. 10 (July 1985); Mason and Dubowski, Breath Alcohol Analysis: Uses, Methods, and Some Forensic Problems — Review and Opinion, 21 Journal of Forensic Sciences 9 (1976).

Just as the absorption rate can vary from individual to individual, so can it fluctuate within a given individual. One scientist has concluded that assuming a continuous, uniform rate of absorption can lead to grossly inaccurate blood-alcohol concentration readings: BAC levels fluctuate in short-term oscillations within individuals. Simpson, Medicolegal Alcohol Determination: Implications and Consequences of Irregularities in Blood Alcohol Concentration vs. Time Curves, 16 Journal of Analytical Toxicology (1992).

Interestingly, Simpson went on to indicate that fear, pain, emotional disturbances, exercise, stimulants (such as coffee and nicotine), and shock can have the effect of decreasing absorption rates, thus throwing off any attempts to accurately extrapolate blood-alcohol levels to the time of driving. It would seem, then, that the circumstances of a drunk driving investigation and arrest, with the commonly associated fear and emotional disturbance in the suspect, would themselves trigger a physiological reaction directly affecting efforts to extrapolate.

For a discussion of the effects of food on absorption and attempts at retrograde extrapolation, see §5.2.

The *elimination* rate for alcohol in the human body has also been proven to vary widely from person to person. One of the variables determining the individual rate is the drinking habits or background of the individual. In Winek and Murphy's article, The Rate and Kinetic Order of Ethanol Elimination, 29 Forensic Science International, 159 (1984), scientists concluded that ''nondrinkers'' (defined as persons who consume less than 6 ounces of alcohol per month) eliminate ethyl alcohol at a rate of .012 gram percent/hour, while ''social drinkers'' (persons who consume between 6 and 30 ounces a month) have an average elimination rate of .015. Alcoholics, however, showed a .030 rate — *double* that of nonalcoholics! Certainly, such variations will drastically affect any attempts to use retrograde extrapolation to estimate blood-alcohol level at the time of driving based on blood-alcohol level at the time of testing.

In one study of ethanol elimination, the rate was observed to vary among individuals by a factor of four — that is, the individual observed to have the fastest rate eliminated alcohol four times faster than the one with the slowest rate. Jones, Disappearance Rate of Ethanol from the Blood of Human Subjects: Implications in Forensic Toxicology, 38(1) Journal of Forensics 103 (1993). Another study has shown that the elimination rate for alcohol in the human body can vary from .010 percent to as much as .064 percent, with an average rate of .022 percent. In other words, some individuals can eliminate alcohol at a rate six-and-one-half times faster than others. Such a wide variation would, of course, completely invalidate any attempts at retrograde extrapolation with any given individual. See Neuteboom and Jones; Disappearance Rate of Alcohol from the Blood of Drunk Drivers Calculated from Two Consecutive Samples: What Do the Results Really Mean?, 45 Forensic Science International 107 (1990).

Trauma resulting from an automobile accident has been clearly shown to have a significant impact on alcohol elimination — and thus on the accuracy of any retrograde extrapolation. Consequently, emergency ward physicians must often wait for serum ethanol levels to go down before an accurate neurological or psychiatric evaluation can be performed.

To verify this phenomenon, researchers studied 103 patients who had been admitted to a hospital's emergency unit in an intoxicated condition. They found that the *mean rate* of elimination of alcohol from the system was 20.43 mg/dl/hr; a standard deviation of 6.86 mg/dl/hr was expected, giving an anticipated range of 13.57 to 27.29 mg/dl/hr. The scientists, however, found a higher rate of deviation: Only 68 percent of the patients fell within the expected range of deviation. Their conclusion: For an accurate prediction of the rate of alcohol elimination in any given individual, it would be necessary to draw a *second* sample after several hours had passed.

An interesting article entitled Effects of Ethanol: 1. Acute Metabolic Tolerance and Ethnic Differences, 8 Alcoholism: Chemical and Experimental Research 226 (1984), written by Wilson, et al., describes studies in which elimination rates for alcohol varied depending on a number of factors. Individuals with Oriental ancestry, for example, eliminated alcohol considerably faster than Caucasians. Another variable is reflected in the fact that the elimination rate increased significantly after a second drink — a fact that should add to the increasing evidence that retrograde extrapolation is unrealistic.

An excellent review of extrapolation problems inherent in blood-alcohol analysis and of the unreliability of delayed testing can be found in Edward Fitzgerald and Dr. David Hume's article, The Single Chemical Test for Intoxication: A Challenge to Admissibility, The Champion 8 (June 1984). The authors discuss the difficulties in extrapolating the blood-alcohol level at the time of driving from the time of testing. Among other conclusions:

> The single chemical test for intoxication ought to be excluded as a proof of a defendant's "time of offense" BAC in any case where there is a delay between offense and obtaining a test sample which continues for more than thirty minutes. . . . As a general rule, a later single test cannot be supported as a reliable indicator of the earlier BAC. . . .
>
> A second chemical test for intoxication or even a series of such tests will not solve the essential problem, as long as there still remains a significant delay between the time of offense and the *first* sample collected. However, a second test, perhaps one-half hour after the first, ought to be required by statute when chemical tests are to be used in criminal cases. [pp. 17–18.]

Dr. Dubowski has also summarized the problem with retrograde extrapolation:

> It is unusual for enough reliable information to be available in a given case to permit a meaningful and fair value to be obtained by retrograde extrapolation. If attempted, it must be based on assumptions of uncertain validity, or the answer must be given in terms of a range of possible values so wide that it is rarely of any

> use. If retrograde extrapolation of a blood concentration is based on a breath analysis the difficulty is compounded. [21(1) Journal of Forensic Sciences 9 (January 1976).]

Counsel may also wish to consider a more recent study of the validity of retrograde extrapolation — one concluding that the process is a "dubious practice." Jones, et al., Peak Blood-Alcohol Concentration and the Time of Its Occurrence After Rapid Drinking on an Empty Stomach, 36(2) Journal of Forensic Sciences 376 (1991). In that study, researchers had a group of men aged 20 to 60 fast overnight and then consume either a shot of whiskey or a "screwdriver" cocktail. Subsequent blood analysis indicated that maximum blood-alcohol concentration among the cocktail drinkers was reached within 15 minutes of consumption. Among the whiskey drinkers, however, peak concentration was reached much later and varied considerably: 72 percent of the men reached peak BACs within 45 minutes, and 95 percent within 75 minutes.

The scientists noted that patterns of alcohol absorption vary widely among individuals and may depend on such factors as "the drinking pattern, the type of beverage consumed, the fed or fasted state, the nature (liquid or solid) and composition (fat, protein, or carbohydrate) of foodstuff in the stomach, the anatomy of the gastrointestinal canal, and the mental state of the subject."

See also a study entitled Physiological Variations in Blood Ethanol Measurements During the Post-Absorptive State, 30(5) Journal of the Forensic Science Society 273 (1990), where blood-alcohol concentrations varied erratically even when measured at three- to five-minute intervals.

Counsel may consider an expensive but very effective way of demonstrating for the jury the fallacies of retrograde extrapolation and uniform or "average" rates of absorption and elimination: Have the client tested by a recognized blood-alcohol expert. The expert can administer a known quantity of alcohol to the client, then test him every five minutes or so on a breath machine. The resulting data — illustrated perhaps on a graph — will reflect anything but the predictable and linear curve presumed by the prosecution.

Should counsel encounter the argument that such tests are not relevant to conditions at the time of the arrest, consider having the defense expert read and testify concerning an article that appeared in the British Journal of Clinical Pharmacology. Finch, Kendall and Mitchard, An Assessment of Gastric Emptying by Breathalyser, British Journal of Clinical Pharmacology 233 (1974). (See also O'Neil, Williams, and Dubowski, Variability in Blood Alcohol Concentrations: Implications for Estimating Individual Results, 44(2) Journal of Studies on Alcohol 222 (1983)). This article found that the ethanol concentration-time curve was very reproducible for any given individual — that is, the defense expert's tests will closely replicate conditions at the time of testing by the officer. In fact, testing an individual in a manner in which he serves as his own control is considerably more effective — and relevant — than comparing him to some fictional "average" person.

This method can also be effective in estimating the actual blood-alcohol concentration at the time of driving based on testimony of the client and/or witnesses as to actual consumption.

§5.2.2 Non-Linear Metabolism

Yet another problem in extrapolating an individual's blood-alcohol level is attempting to draft a line or curve based on a single test, or on two tests administered at nearly the same time. Quite simply, it is nearly impossible to determine whether the level was declining — as prosecutors always attempt to claim — or increasing. This requires at least two test results remote in time from one another, and preferably more. To put it geometrically, one can draw a line through two points and project that line, but one cannot do this with only one point. And even if two points (i.e., blood-alcohol levels) can be identified, the "line" is fictional: The increase/decrease in a person's blood-alcohol level is neither constant nor predictable.

An example of this fluctuating curve can be seen in Figure 5-1, obtained from studies reported in an Australian publication entitled Ethanol Ingestion Studies: Pilot Project (1979: Department of Transport, Office of Road Safety), and conducted at St. Vincent's Hospital in Fitzroy, Australia. The diagram represents the blood-alcohol content of a typical subject, as measured by a Breathalyzer and a Gas Chromatograph. Note not only the non-

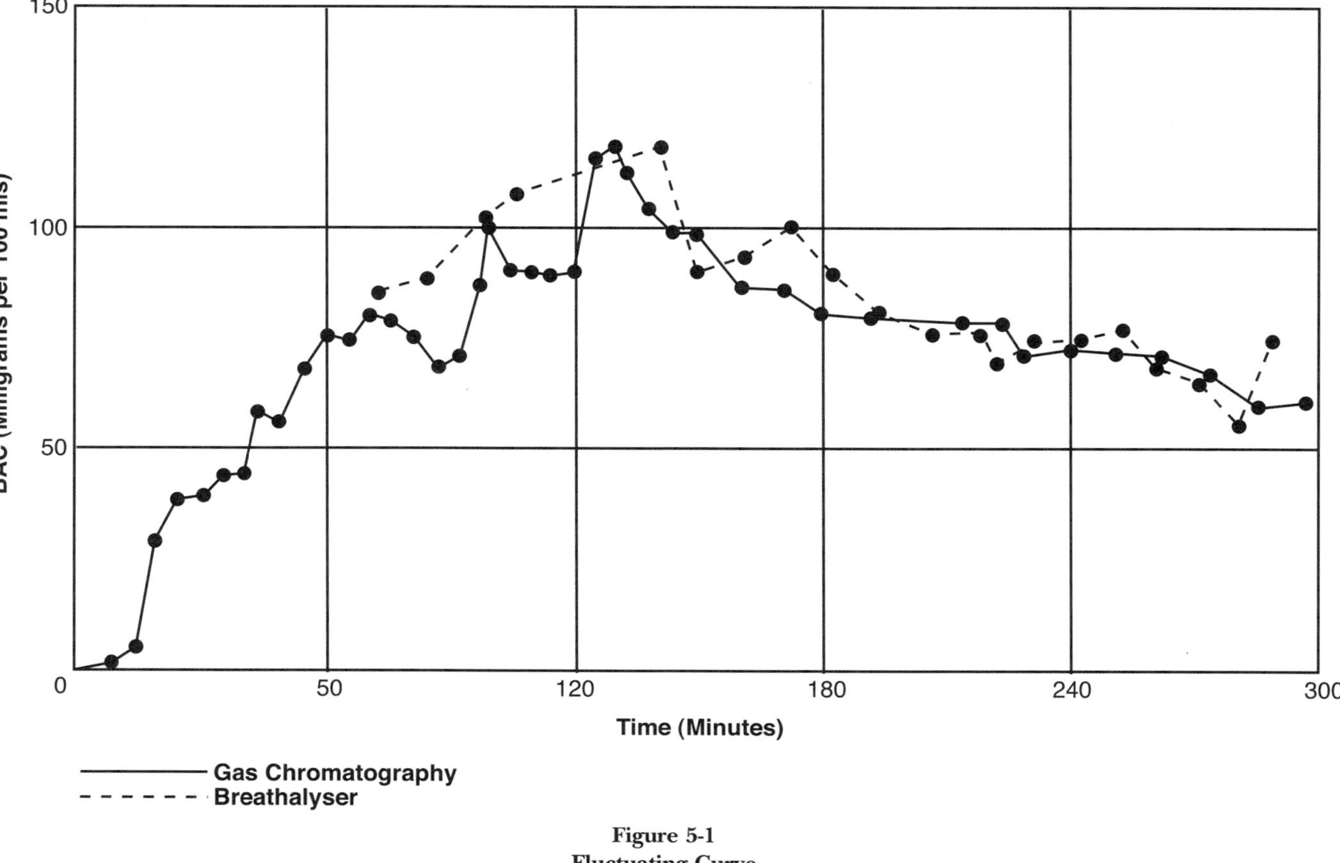

Figure 5-1
Fluctuating Curve

uniform peaks and valleys, but the lack of precise correlation between the two different instruments.

The problems inherent in attempting to extrapolate based on a single sample have caused many experts to strongly recommend that two samples isolated from one another in time be obtained. Thus, for example, with regard to urinalysis, criminalists at California's Department of Justice have recommended that "to determine if the BAC has increased or decreased during the time between voiding and the second urine sample, at least a 30-ml portion of the initial void sample should be collected, analyzed, and reported together with the second urine sample results." Biasatti and Valentine, Blood Alcohol Concentration Determined from Urine Samples as a Practical Equivalent or Alternative to Blood and Breath Alcohol Tests, 30 Journal of Forensic Sciences 194, 206 (1984). And the American Medical Association, in its pamphlet entitled Alcohol and the Impaired Driver: A Manual on the Medicolegal Aspects of Chemical Tests for Intoxication (1968), concludes that collection of "duplicate samples with a time lapse of at least 20 minutes . . . is recommended" (page 71).

§5.2.3 The Widmark Factors

The most significant theoretical problem with retrograde extrapolation is the use by the state's expert of Widmark's "r" and "beta" factors. These assumed values used in computing estimations of an individual's drinking pattern are impressive to a jury but very susceptible to cross-examination. The following materials, presented at the National College for DUI Defense's annual Summer Session at Harvard Law School, represents an excellent explanation of the problem — and the solution. They are reprinted with the kind permission of Michael Snure, of Kirkconnell, Lindsey, Snure & Henson in Winter Park, Florida.

> Retrograde extrapolation is often attempted by prosecution experts. Simply stated, an attempt to retrograde extrapolate a person's breath value is an attempt to determine or estimate what the person's breath test value would have been at an earlier time (presumably the time of the driving) based on a subsequent test. Because a person is rarely tested within a few minutes of driving, the subsequent breath test only gives a value for what the person's

breath test value was at the time they were tested. Retrograde extrapolation is a flawed method employed in an attempt to estimate what the person's breath test value would have been at the time of driving.

Many experts now agree that retrograde extrapolation is so imprecise or can be stated only with respect to such a broad range that it is virtually impossible or useless in the forensic setting. However, certain facts must be known before even a bastardized attempt to extrapolate can be made. The minimum factors which must be known are:

1. The time drinking began;
2. The amount and type of beverage consumed and at what rate;
3. The amount, type, and rate at which food was consumed;
4. The time drinking ceased;
5. The weight and gender of the person concerned;
6. Some indication of the subject's drinking experience and tolerance;
7. Indications of the physical observations of the person during the time in question; and
8. The person's general physical and emotional condition at the time.

Assuming that those variables are known an expert will then have to resort to the use of two very generalized assumptions which can be attacked.

The entire basis for retrograde extrapolation began following the research of Professor Widmark in the 1930s. The mechanisms for the absorption and elimination of alcohol from the body are fairly well understood. For a period of time after drinking, an individual's blood alcohol level may continue to rise, remain constant, or fall depending on whether the rate of absorption of the alcohol is greater than, equal to, or less than the elimination. This single factor seriously impairs the efforts to estimate from a single breath test measurement the breath test value at some prior time, or the amount of alcohol which must have been consumed to give a particular breath value.

Professor Widmark's research was originally published in German. Very few prosecution experts have ever read the entire text and are probably unfamiliar with the research. It should be remembered that Professor Widmark studied blood alcohol content as it changed with time after drinking. His subjects were required to consume a known amount of alcohol on an empty stomach after which blood samples were taken for analysis every fifteen minutes for three hours. The results were analyzed and plots were made of the blood alcohol content over the course of time. This was the genesis of the commonly referred to "blood alcohol curve."

The results indicated that the rate of decline in the blood alcohol curve was constant for an individual from day to day over time. The rate of decline among individuals though varied considerably from one to another. Widmark essentially calibrated his individual test subjects in order to estimate how much one would have to drink in order to reach the observed blood alcohol level. This method of calculation seemed reliable as long as the same approach was used which required the consumption of alcohol all at one time on an empty stomach. During the course of his research Widmark discovered what has been labeled as Widmark's r factor.

Widmark's r factor was the product of a test subject's calibration curve. Widmark would take a line and extend it straight back from the straight line portion of the alcohol curve until it intersected the time drinking began. This value would be an estimate of the theoretical blood alcohol level an individual could have if all the alcohol had been instantaneously absorbed and distributed throughout the body at the moment the drink was swallowed. This number would then be divided by the actual blood alcohol value and the result would be the r factor. While the r factor was quite constant and reproducible with regard to any given individual, it varied considerably from subject to subject. While this particular calculation seemed simple, its subsequent use in generalized approaches ignored the fundamental concept of its reliability which was that the true value of "r" for an individual must be known accurately to obtain a valid result. The only way to know the value accurately is to measure it.

Since it is rare for any individual defendant's r value to be known, experts have tended to use an assumed average value of 0.68 for Widmark's r value. This reportedly reflects the average value for the male subjects in Widmark's 1932 study. One should note that 0.68 is an arithmetic average that was obtained from a very small group of subjects. The entire subject base in Widmark's 1932 study was 20 men and 10 women.

Even though the arithmetic average for men in Widmark's study was 0.68, the range of values for the 20 subjects was from 0.52 to 0.86. The range for women was 0.47 to 0.64 with an average r value for women of 0.55.

Another researcher, Osterlind, has confirmed that the range of r values for men and women is substantial.

It is not scientifically sound nor is it borne out from the research for an expert to state that an "average person" would have an average r value. In the studies conducted there is not even a close grouping of observed results around the average r value associated for men and women. In Widmark's study, of the 30 subjects, only three had r values between 0.68 and 0.70. Nineteen were below 0.65 and eight were above 0.70.

Therefore, an arithmetic average r value cannot, with any reliability, be assigned to any individual. There was no correlation of r value by size, sex, age, or general physical condition.

Perhaps most fundamentally, there is no research to establish that the r values observed by Widmark under the conditions of simultaneous consumption on an empty stomach apply to the more complex drinking patterns of the real world. Finally, the danger of using the average r can be demonstrated by measuring values obtained with r at the extremes of its ranges. Calculating the amount of alcohol consumed based on a measured blood alcohol level using the average r of 0.68 could get results which are as much as 31% too high or 21% too low for a man and as much as 45% too high for a woman if calculated using the high and low ends of the r value ranges stated earlier.

The other insidious assumption in the retrograde extrapolation calculation is the beta factor which is commonly referred to as a rate of elimination. Widmark's research indicated that the arithmetic average for rate of elimination was 0.015% per hour. There is no basis on which to assume that everyone has essentially the same beta factor or elimination rate. Elimination rates have been studied and found to vary from values of .006% per hour to as high as .04% per hour. Moreover, the research does not find a tight grouping or bunching of elimination rates around any one average value.

An example of the amount of error which may be introduced to an extrapolation equation can be found by assigning an elimination rate of .015% for someone whose actual rate is .006%. This will result in a 150% overestimation of the person's blood alcohol level at an earlier time. Furthermore, any such calculation always involves the assumption that the person's blood alcohol level was declining throughout the entire period in question. This is often never known. The expert usually will perform retrograde extrapolation without any demonstrative knowledge of whether the time of the incident blood alcohol content was before or after the person's peak. It is almost universally assumed that the time in question occurred at or after a person reached the peak alcohol absorption. This assumption is baseless.

The outstanding consideration which must be established in cross-examining any expert who attempts to retrograde extrapolate is that the averaged values for r and beta are merely arithmetic averages. They are the result of adding values and dividing by the number of subjects. The range of values is wide and not tightly grouped or packed around any one value. Therefore while the results can be averaged for groups, no value can be predicted for any individual within that group.

Finally, the acknowledged authoritative prosecution expert, Kurt Dubowski, has essentially denounced the use of retrograde extrapolation because of the hazards inherent in the assumptions which must be made in the calculations.

Mr. Snure then offers the following checklist to be used in assessing prosecutorial evidence of retrograde extrapolation:

1. Does the expert know enough about the drinking pattern and the individual?
2. Does the expert recognize that the r factor is not a fixed number but varies across a broad range and is not applicable to any "average man"?
3. There is a wide range of r values with considerable distribution among the range even in small population samples and the values of r for men are higher than for women.
4. An r value cannot be arbitrarily assigned to someone, male or female, for purposes of making a reliable calculation.
5. The r values as originally obtained by Widmark were not obtained in any social drinking situation but were rather obtained in a clinical setting involving consumption of alcohol in one large dose on an empty stomach.
6. The beta factor is not a fixed number that could be applied to any individual person or average man.
7. The beta factors cover a wide range with substantial distribution across the range in both large and small populations.
8. The beta value cannot be assigned to any particular individual for the purpose of making any reliable calculations of the amount of alcohol consumed over time nor for the

purpose of reliably estimating someone's blood alcohol content at a prior time.

§5.2.4 The Rising Blood-Alcohol Level

The prosecution in drunk driving cases always assumes that the absorptive phase of alcohol ingestion is completed before the time of testing — that is, that the defendant was in the postabsorptive stage when he was tested on the breath machine. Thus the argument is made that the blood-alcohol concentration was falling at the time of testing — and, therefore, that the level was higher at the time of driving.

As the material in the text indicates, however, this assumption is fallacious for a number of reasons, such as food ingestion, pattern of drinking, and individual blood/breath partition ratio. The simple fact is that the suspect may still be absorbing alcohol into his system when he is tested. In other words, his BAC may be *rising* — and the reading, therefore, may be higher than the actual BAC at the time of driving.

In a recent study, researchers found that absorption continued for an average of 50 minutes after cessation of drinking. Tests taken with Intoxilyzer models 4011A, 4011AS, and 5000 consistently overestimated the blood-alcohol levels during this time period when compared to analyzed blood samples. Giguiere and Simpson, Medicolegal Alcohol Determination: In Vivo Blood/Breath Ratios as a Function of Time, Proceedings of the 27th Meeting of the International Association of Forensic Toxicologists 494 (October 1990).

Counsel should always determine from his client what the exact drinking pattern was on the night in question. In terms of a possible rising BAC defense, particular attention should be paid to what ingestion of alcohol took place in the one hour or so before the client began to drive (or, in an appropriate case, during the driving). Most DUI detentions occur within 15 minutes of the client entering the car; the blood-alcohol test commonly takes place an hour or so after this. Thus in most cases the arrestee who had "one for the road" is still absorbing alcohol at the time of the test — and even an accurate test result will be higher than the actual blood-alcohol concentration at the time of driving. Even if the suspect is not still absorbing alcohol into his system, his test BAC will almost certainly be higher than his driving BAC.

The mentioned 50-minute absorption period is, of course, an average; the actual period can vary from a half-hour to as long as three hours (see §5.1), and this can be extended by recent ingestion of food (see §5.3.5). Consequently, counsel should not discount the possibility of a rising BAC curve even when the test was administered two or three hours after the driving.

Is the defendant entitled to have the jury instructed as to his theory of a *rising* blood-alcohol level? This would certainly seem appropriate, and this was the holding in *State v. Drown,* 532 A.2d 575 (Vt. 1987). The defendant in that case established during cross-examination of the prosecution's expert that her level at the time of driving could have been as low as .085 percent, as opposed to the tested level of .147 percent. The trial judge refused the requested instruction, reasoning that it was only one of many possible theories. However, the appellate court reversed the conviction because "the court below failed to instruct on the defense theory, a substantial issue that was arguably supported by the evidence." Id. at 577.

The claim that the defendant's BAC was falling can, perhaps, be turned against the prosecution. One scientific study has concluded that impairment is greater during the rising phase of the BAC curve than during the falling. Nicholson, et al., Variability in Behavioral Impairment Involved in the Rising and Falling BAC Curve, Journal of Studies on Alcohol 349 (July 1992).

§5.3 General Sources of Error

> Men become civilized, not in proportion to their willingness to believe, but in proportion to their readiness to doubt.
>
> H. L. Mencken

The analysis of a drunk driving suspect's breath, blood, or urine is subject to a myriad of potential errors. Many of these are specific to the analytical method used. Non-specific analysis (§6.1.2) is specific to the analysis of breath samples, for example, and even more specific to breath machines using the infrared method of analysis. Fermentation, on the other hand, is a potential problem when dealing with the analysis of blood. These and other sources of error will be discussed in later sections dealing with the specific method of analysis.

There are many other "generic" sources of error, however, that are not specific and which can exist in the analysis of any of the three commonly obtained samples. Thus, for example, the effects of food on alcohol metabolism (§5.3.5) is relevant to blood, breath, and urine testing alike, and "inherent error" (§5.3.1) is recognized in any analytical procedure. And retrograde extrapolation, already discussed in the preceeding subsections, presents numerous problems regardless of the method of analysis used.

The material in the subsections that follow should be considered by counsel in dealing with a drunk driving case regardless of which method of analysis was employed. The sections relevant to the specific method should then also be studied.

§5.3.1 Inherent Error

Even if the proper procedures were correctly followed in a given blood, breath, or urine test, even if the instruments and/or computer systems used were functioning perfectly, and even if all chemicals, blanks, and standards were of the proper quantity and quality, blood-alcohol analysis is not a perfect process. Thus it is generally recognized by scientists that such analytical methods have an inherent, or "built-in," error factor. This, of course, should be brought out for the jury.

In *People v. Campos,* 138 Cal. App. 3d Supp. 1, 188 Cal. Rptr. 366 (1982), a California superior court held that a .10 percent per se case should be dismissed as a matter of law due to the inherent margin for inaccuracy in testing after a driver submitted to a blood test that resulted in a reading of .10 percent, and the "wet chemical" method used had an inaccuracy rate of plus or minus .005 percent. Accordingly, the court noted that it was "impossible to determine the alcohol content more precisely than that it was at some figure between .095 percent and .105 percent."

The court began its analysis by noting that the .10 issue was one of first impression in California. In reaching its result, the court reviewed cases from Delaware, Nebraska, and Hawaii:

In *State v. Rucker,* (1972 Del. Super. Ct.) 297 A.2d 400, a Delaware statute made it unlawful for a person to drive a motor vehicle "while such person's blood has reached a blood alcohol concentration of 1⁄10 of 1 percent or more, by weight, as shown by a chemical analysis of a blood, breath, or urine sample taken within 4 hours of the alleged offense, ..." Defendant had taken a breath test which showed a reading of .104 percent, but the test procedure had a margin of error of plus or minus .009 percent. . . . [T]he Delaware court observed that the statute did not purport to create a presumption. "It simply makes a blood alcohol concentration of 0.100 percent, or more as shown by specified types of tests, an element of the offense. If one has that concentration while driving, as determined by the test specified in the statute and if that test was administered within 4 hours after the alleged offense, 21 Del. C. Section 4176 directs that such person 'shall be guilty.' " (p. 402.) The court viewed the function of the trier of fact as limited to determining whether the test results showed the required percentage of alcohol in the blood, but "[t]he trier of fact is not free to disregard the mandate of the statute or to question the wisdom of the General Assembly in providing that test results constitute proof of that element of the crime." (p. 402.) It assumed that the Delaware General Assembly, in making the test result determinative, had taken into consideration the possibility of variations between the test results and the actual blood-alcohol content of the accused when it enacted the statute. . . .

In *State v. Bjornsen* (1978 Neb.) 271 N.W.2d 839, a majority of the Supreme Court of Nebraska reached a conclusion contrary to *Rucker* under a Nebraska statute worded similarly to the Delaware statute. It, too, made unlawful a person's operation of a motor vehicle "when that person has ten-hundredths of one percent or more by weight of alcohol in his body fluid as shown by chemical analysis of his blood, breath or urine." Defendant's chemical test resulted in a reading of .10 percent blood-alcohol content, but the state's criminalist testified that the reading could have been off as much as .005 percent, so that defendant's blood alcohol could have been as low as .095 percent. The prosecutor argued that, under the statute, so long as the chemical test result showed .10 percent or more any inaccuracies in the testing procedures were irrelevant. The court held: . . . "While the legislature has the acknowledged right to prescribe acceptable methods of testing for alcohol content in the body fluids and perhaps even the right to prescribe that such evidence is admissible in a court of law, it is a judicial determination as to whether this evidence is sufficient to sustain a con-

> viction. The Legislature has selected a particular percent of alcohol to be a criminal offense if present in a person operating a motor vehicle. It is not unreasonable to require that the test, designed to show that percent, do so outside of any error or tolerance inherent in the testing process, 271 N.W.2d at 840." [188 Cal. Rptr. at 368–369.]

The California court also considered the Hawaiian case of *State v. Boehmer,* 613 P.2d 916 (1980). In that case, the court of appeals of Hawaii recognized a .0165 percent error factor in the Breathalyzer test. The defendant had a blood-alcohol reading of .11 percent. The court, relying on the heavy burden of proof that the prosecutor has in a criminal case, reasoned further that the margin of error of the Breathalyzer test means that on any given test the defendant's actual blood-alcohol content could be .0165 percent more or less than the reading shown by the test. "Thus, the inherent margin of error could put defendant's actual blood-alcohol below the level necessary for the presumption to arise." Id. at 918. In its conclusion, the court cited with approval *State v. Bjornsen,* 201 Neb. 709, 271 N.W.2d 839 (1978), which held that in order for the statutory presumption to arise, "the results of such tests when taken together with its tolerance for error, must equal or exceed the statutory level." 271 N.W.2d at 840.

The *Campos* court reasoned that the difference between the *Rucker* and *Bjornsen* decisions was one of statutory interpretation. In *Rucker,* the Delaware court interpreted the statute as making the *test reading* the conclusive factor. In *Bjornsen,* the Nebraska court interpreted the statute as requiring a *blood-alcohol content* of .10 percent or more. In holding that the .10 reading should be dismissed, the California court sided with the Nebraska and Hawaii courts. In the words of the court:

> It is clear that the Legislature was not content with a test reading, no matter how inaccurate the testing procedure employed, as being sufficient to give rise to the presumption, but it required that there in fact be an alcohol content of .10% or more. Unless, however, the test reading exceeds 0.10% by the margin of error recognized in the testing process, there is no way that the trier of fact can be assured beyond any reasonable doubt that defendant's actual blood alcohol content was not below 0.10%. [Id. at 370.]

More recently, the Alaskan Supreme Court has held that chemical test results that would be below .10 percent after applying the inherent margin of error could not be used as the basis for a license revocation. *Haynes v. Department of Public Safety,* 865 P.2d 753 (Alaska 1993). In that case, the breath test result on an Intoximeter 3000 was .106 percent; the recognized inherent error was .01 percent per 210 liters of breath. Thus the actual BAC could have been anywhere from .096 percent to .116 percent. Holding that the margin of error must be applied in the driver's favor, the court concluded that there was insufficient evidence to find a BAC of .10 percent or higher.

But see *King v. Commonwealth,* 875 S.W.2d 903 (Ky. App. 1993), involving a reading of .100 percent on an Intoxilyzer 5000. The trial court found the margin of error to be only .005 percent, and the .100 percent reading was thus "accurate enough to be of probative value." The appellate court concluded that to exclude a reading with such a small margin of error would be requiring the prosecution to prove guilt beyond "any" doubt. Query: Would the Kentucky appellate court have come to a different conclusion if the recognized inherent error was .01 rather than .005?

Counsel should also consult the relevant statutes in his jurisdiction concerning the recognition of inherent error. Iowa's license revocation statute, for example, provides:

> The results of a chemical test may not be used as the basis for a license revocation of a person's motor vehicle license or nonresident driving privileges if the alcohol concentration indicated by the chemical test *minus the established margin of error inherent in the device* or method used to conduct the chemical test does not equal an alcohol concentration of .10 or more. [Iowa Code §321J.12]

§5.3.2 The Fallacy of the "Average Person"

One of the greatest sources of error in blood-alcohol testing is the consistently recurring fallacy that the individual tested is perfectly average in certain critical physiological traits. Put another way, obtaining an accurate blood-alcohol reading is completely dependent on the validity of a number of scientific assumptions. Unfortunately for the person being tested,these assumptions are usually incorrect: The person tested is rarely "average'' in even one of these critical characteristics, let alone in all of them.

Counsel in a DUI case will constantly be confronted by these almost-hidden assumptions. And it is very important that these false premises be brought out for the jury — along with the fact that the final readings fall with the presumptions.

Thus, for example, all breath testing devices depend on the assumption that the ratio between alcohol in the exhaled breath and alcohol in the blood is 1:2100. In fact, the machine is designed to produce a reading based on that assumption; the accuracy of the reading is directly tied to the accuracy of the presumption. Yet, as will be discussed more fully in §6.0.1, the actual ratio in any given individual can vary from 1:1300 to 1:3000, or even more widely. Thus a person with a true blood-alcohol level of .08 but a breath-to-blood ratio of 1:1700 would have a .10 reading on an ''accurate'' breath testing instrument.

Quite simply, these machines do not test individuals. Rather, they test the average person over and over again, but using the subject's breath.

Yet another example of the assumption of ''averageness'' can be found in urinalysis. When a subject's urine is analyzed for blood-alcohol, a presumption exists that there are 1.3 parts of alcohol in the bladder's urine for every 1 part of alcohol in the blood. This 1:1.3 ratio is as fallacious as the 1:2100 ratio — that is, it is based entirely on the ratio found in the *average* person. As is discussed more fully in §7.1.2, however, the actual ratio found in any given individual can vary greatly. And as the ratio is in error, so will be the final blood-alcohol reading.

Another example of this constant reliance on averages shows itself when the prosecutor offers evidence of retrograde extrapolation (see §5.2). The blood-alcohol level at the time of testing is not relevant to the charge, of course, and so the state will offer evidence to show what the level was when the defendant was driving. This is commonly done by extrapolating backward — that is, computing the earlier blood-alcohol level by estimating how much alcohol had been eliminated or ''burned off'' in the interim between driving and testing. But this requires two assumptions: The blood-alcohol level was declining, and the rate of elimination is known. This second assumption involves the further assumption that the ''burn-off'' rate was .015 percent per hour. How does the prosecution know that the defendant was eliminating (assuming he *was* eliminating) at that rate, and not at .005 percent or .3 percent? Quite simply, the prosecution does *not* know: It merely *assumes* that the defendant eliminates at the average rate. And, of course, error in such an assumption translates into error in the extrapolation.

The use of assumed averages by state experts when testifying in drunk driving cases is particularly egregious when estimating drinking activity based upon BAC test results. Stanley D. Dorrance, a forensic consultant with Forensic Science Services in Fresno, California, has made the following enlightening observations:

> Calculations of blood alcohol levels were first done in the 1930s by the Swedish psychologist Dr. E. M. P. Widmark (1889–1945). Widmark's Hypothesis is the formula on which experts base their blood alcohol calculation opinions. Most courts will generally accept these calculations with little or no scrutiny. Over the years experts have attempted to simplify the calculations by making generalizations. These generalizations can effectively make any calculation grossly inaccurate. By making the assumption that your client is an "average" person the expert maintains the calculations will be reasonably accurate. Nothing could be father from the truth. Only a very small percentage of the population is "average." However, because the calculations are being made by an "expert" the courts tend to give these calculations great weight. This, of course, can be your client's Waterloo.
>
> There are two variables in Widmark's Hypothesis that experts will simplify by using the value for the "average person." The first of these is the "burnoff rate," or the amount of alcohol that is eliminated by the body, generally in one hour. While the range of burnoff rates may vary from as low as 0.01% to 0.04% per hour, most state and local experts use an "average" burnoff rate of 0.02% per hour. This is of course a convenient number to use as it makes mental calculations of blood alcohol levels much easier. Generalization about your client can render calculations inaccurate by as much as 10–20%.
>
> The other variable, which is probably the least understood of all the variables in the Widmark Hypothesis, is the Widmark "r" factor. In basic terms the "r" factor is the ratio of the amount of alcohol found in the entire body versus the alcohol found only in the blood. Although the accepted "average" for a male is 0.68 the range is rather significant (0.51–0.85). The "average" Widmark

"r" factor for a female is 0.55 with a slightly smaller range (0.44–0.66). What most experts do not understand is the dramatic effect that weight can have on a person's "r" factor. As a person's weight (male or female) increases and they become more overweight for their size, their "r" factor can drop significantly. This lowering of the "r" factor stems partially from the fact that alcohol is not as soluble in "fat cells" as compared to other body cells. As the number of "fat cells" increase a larger percentage of the alcohol will stay in the blood and not be absorbed by these "fat cells." This accounts for the lower Widmark "r" factor for females, as they tend to have more body fat than males. As the percentage of fat increases the Widmark "r" factor decreases and causes a person's blood alcohol level to rise to higher levels with less alcohol. As a result of these variances, general calculations done by an "expert" can have an error factor of as much as 25%.

The "average" values used by the prosecution expert can have a very profound effect on your client's defense. Frequently one of the major issues in a DUI case is the number of drinks your client had to consume to reach the blood alcohol level they registered. Time and time again I have witnessed the state's expert very confidently and adamantly testify that the defendant had to consume 9 beers to reach the 0.10% blood alcohol level he registered one hour after being stopped. This calculation is erroneously based on the assumption the defendant is an "average" male of 175 lbs. This calculation assumes each beer will cause your client's blood alcohol to rise by 0.02% and each hour he "burns off" the equivalent of 0.02%. To register 0.10% four hours after the start of drinking requires 9 beers (0.10% ÷ 0.02 = 5 beers, plus 1 beer for each hour of burnoff, which in this example is 4).

The obvious dilemma for you is that your client maintains they consumed only 6 beers. The expert witness for the prosecution, however, will testify with great confidence that your client "*could not*" possibly have a blood alcohol level of 0.10% after consuming only 6 beers. This of course directly contradicts and scientifically refutes the testimony of your client! Although blatantly false, this impeaches your client's testimony and is devastating to their credibility, which in many cases is a major part of the defense.

This ubiquitous "average person" in the DUI arena is not limited to chemical analysis. We even find him with the arresting officer in the field. When the officer administers the increasingly common "horizontal gaze nystagmus" test as part of the battery of field sobriety tests, he operates on the assumption that the suspect is "Mr. Average." As has been discussed in §4.3.5, the officer has been trained to "read" at what angle the suspect's eyes begin jerking. A blood-alcohol reading can theoretically be obtained by subtracting the angle from 50; jerking at 35 degrees, for example, would mean the suspect has a blood-alcohol level of .15 percent. Where does the magic figure of 50 come from? The average person.

An alternative method of administering the nystagmus test is to "flunk" the person if jerking begins before 40 or 45 degrees. Why? Again, because the average person would theoretically have .10 or .05 percent alcohol in his blood at this point.

In either test, of course, we do not know what the individual's actual "baseline" is — that is, the angle at which his eyes would begin jerking if he were sober. In both cases, the individual is assumed to be physiologically identical to the theoretical "average person."

Don Nichols, one of the foremost DUI lawyers in the country today, points out to juries, in appropriate cases, that his client is female, Chinese, and deceased — despite obvious evidence to the contrary. He then explains that statistically there are more women than men in the world, more Chinese than any other nationality, and more dead human beings than living ones. Statistically, then, the *average* person is female, Chinese, and deceased — and so, according to the prosecution, must be his client. He usually also asks the jury how many of them have 2.3 children — the average in the United States.

Counsel must make clear to the jury in the course of the trial that the prosecution is making multiple erroneous assumptions about the defendant, and that these assumptions are critical to the validity of the blood-alcohol reading. As the computer technicians are fond of saying, "Garbage in — garbage out."

§5.3.3 Male vs. Female Metabolism of Alcohol

It has been known for some time that women are generally more susceptible to the effects of alcohol than men. This has generally been explained by pointing out that women are smaller and have relatively more fat and less water than men. But recent research seems to indicate that a more important reason may be that women have significantly lower amounts of an enzyme that provides a protective barrier in the stomach by breaking alcohol down before it circulates into the body.

An article appearing in the *Los Angeles Times,* Jan. 11, 1990, at A27, recounted how scientists at the University School of Medicine in Trieste, Italy, and the Veterans Affairs Medical Center, Bronx, New York, found that the stomach lining contains an enzyme called gastric alcohol dehydrogenase that breaks down alcohol. To determine the effects of the enzyme, they administered alcohol both orally and intravenously (i.e., bypassing the stomach) to a group of 14 nonalcoholic men, 6 alcoholic men, 17 nonalcoholic women, and 6 alcoholic women.

There were two interesting results. First, in both the nonalcoholic and alcoholic groups, women had higher blood-alcohol concentrations than men after ingesting an equivalent dose of ethanol; by contrast, there were no differences when the ethanol was taken intravenously. With weight differences taken into account, the researchers found that women became legally intoxicated after consuming 20 to 30 percent less alcohol than men; absent allowance for weight, an average-size woman reaches a given blood-alcohol level after consuming about 50 percent less alcohol than a man consumes to reach that level.

Second, the alcoholic men and women had significantly higher BAC levels after oral ingestion than the nonalcoholic men and women; the levels reached by alcoholic women indicated a nearly total absence of the protective enzyme in their stomachs.

The scientists concluded that legislatures may need to consider sex differences when defining safe levels of drinking for driving motor vehicles. Although they did not address the issue, the findings concerning alcoholics would also seem to pose some interesting legal and factual issues. For a further discussion of the study, see Frezza and Lieber, High Blood Alcohol Levels in Women: The Role of Decreased Gastric Alcohol Dehydrogenase Activity and First-Pass Metabolism, 322(2) New England Journal of Medicine 95 (1990).

An article in the Canadian Society of Forensic Science Journal has reported a finding that "[w]omen taking oral contraceptive steroids (O.C.S.) appeared to eliminate ethanol significantly faster than women not taking O.C.S." Papple, The Effect of Oral Contraceptive Steroids (O.C.S.) on the Rate of Post-Absorptive

Phase Decline of Blood Alcohol Concentration in the Adult Woman, 15:1 Canadian Society of Forensic Science Journal at 17 (1982).

The purpose of the study was to determine whether there was an interaction between O.C.S. and the metabolism of ethanol. The study compared females taking O.C.S. with males and with females not taking O.C.S. In addition, the study took into account the four phases of a woman's menstrual cycle for females taking O.C.S. and those not taking O.C.S.

The study found that O.C.S. stimulate the elimination of ethanol from the human bloodstream. The study also concludes that the position of the women in their menstrual cycle was not the determining factor in the difference in the ethanol elimination rate. More specifically, the study presented the following conclusions: No significant difference was seen in the rate of decline of BAC in women not taking O.C.S. compared to men, and a highly significant increase in the rate of decline was noted in women who were taking O.C.S.

Thus, if the expert attempts to estimate the alcohol concentration of the female at the time of driving, use of a standard elimination rate (e.g., 15 mg percent per hour) will result in a faulty extrapolation if the woman was taking oral contraceptive steroids.

Yet another example of sex difference in blood-alcohol analysis was uncovered in a study by Jeavons and Zeiner, Effects of Elevated Female Sex Steroids on Ethanol and Acetaldehyde Metabolism in Humans, 8(4) Alcoholism: Clinical and Experimental Research 352 (1984). This article revealed that women who were taking oral contraceptives and women who were pregnant had elevated acetaldehyde levels. Apparently, the ability to metabolize acetaldehyde decreases as the level of sex steroids increases. Put another way, women with a greater amount of sex steroids in their systems will also have a greater amount of acetaldehyde. Such women who take breath tests will also have inaccurately high blood-alcohol readings (see §6.1).

In an article entitled Determination of Liquid/Air Partition Coefficients for Dilute Solutions of Ethanol in Water, Whole Blood, and Plasma, published in Journal of Analytical Toxicology 193–197 (July/August 1983), Dr. A. W. Jones discusses an experiment comparing the blood/air ratio of men and women, concluding that the sexes have different ratios. Breath testing devices are calibrated based on an assumed blood/breath ratio of 2100 to 1 — an average for men (see §6.0.1). The Swedish experiments, however, would seem to indicate that a woman with a given blood-alcohol reading on a breath testing device may *actually* have a *lower* level than would a man with the same reading.

§5.3.4 Racial Differences

It is fairly well accepted in the scientific community that the rate of alcohol elimination is determined by genetic factors. And various studies have indicated that there are significant differences in the rate of alcohol metabolism between the races. Other studies, however, have contradicted these findings. One study, for example, found that American Indians metabolized alcohol more than twice as fast as Caucasians. Holzbecher, Elimination of Ethanol in Humans, 17 Canadian Society of Forensic Science Journal 182 (1984); Bennion and Li, Alcohol Metabolism in American Indians and Whites, 294 New England Journal of Medicine 9 (1976). Another concluded that whites have higher metabolic rates than Indians or Eskimos. Fenna, et al., Ethanol Metabolism in Various Racial Groups, 105 Canadian Medical Association Journal 472 (1971). Yet another scientist found little difference between Chinese, Japanese, and European subjects. Holzbecher, *supra.*

The body of scientific literature, however, seems to clearly indicate a racial — i.e., genetic — difference in the effects of alcohol. In one of this author's earlier books, research concerning the genetic origins of alcoholism was reviewed:

> This ethnic approach was first used in 1972 in a study of the comparative effects of alcohol on men and women in Japan, Taiwan, Korea and the United States.[24] Interested by the lower rate of alcoholism among Orientals, an American physician selected thirty-eight Japanese, twenty-four Taiwanese, twenty Koreans and thirty-four Americans as subjects (all between the ages of twenty-five and thirty-five). He fed each subject measured amounts of

[24] P. H. Wolff, Ethnic Differences in Alcohol Sensitivity, 175 *Science* 449 (1972).

beer, with Americans (that is, Caucasians) receiving more than twice as much per pound of body weight as the Orientals. He then measured the body's reaction to the alcohol by recording the flushing of the carlobe with an optical densitometer, as well as increases in pulse pressure. If there were no genetic differences in reactions to alcohol, the physician could expect to find that flushing (an indication of vessel dilation) and pulse pressure — both under the control of the autonomic nervous system — would be consistent among the various ethnic groups.

The results, however, clearly indicated a genetic factor in the reaction to alcohol. Fully 83 percent of the Oriental subjects responded to the measured amounts of alcohol with a marked flush, but only 6 percent of the Caucasians did, despite the latter having received larger doses. Similarly, increases in pulse pressures were observed in 74 percent of the Orientals, with only 3 percent (one adult) of the Caucasians demonstrating such a reaction.

To insure against any possible cultural effects on alcohol consumption, the physician next duplicated the experiment with Japanese, Taiwanese and American infants, giving them small amounts of port wine in a glucose solution. Again, the results showed that heredity rather than environment dictated the body's automatic reaction to alcohol: Of the oriental babies, 74 percent responded with flushing, but of the Caucasian babies, only 5 percent (one baby) so reacted. Clearly, the alcohol-induced changes in blood flow were not learned or conditioned responses.

The physician concluded that the often-observed fact that Orientals rarely became alcoholics may be attributable to the simple fact that their bodies are unable to accept even moderate amounts of alcohol without experiencing symptoms of intoxication. In any event, the first step was taken in the genetic explanation for alcoholism: The physiological reaction to alcohol itself appeared to be genetically determined.

These experiments were repeated by a team of scientists two years later, this time with twenty-four Chinese and twenty-four European subjects.[25] The results proved to be the same: Skin flushing, increased heart rate and decreased blood pressure in response to alcohol were much more noticeable in the Orientals. The scientists concluded that physiological rather than cultural factors determined the relatively low rate of alcoholism in Orientals.

In 1978 yet another ethnic comparison contrasted the relative

[25] J. A. Ewing et al., Alcohol Sensitivity and Ethnic Background, 131 *American Journal of Psychiatry* 206 (1974).

> abilities of forty-seven Japanese, thirty-nine Chinese and sixty-eight European subjects to metabolize alcohol in their bodies.[26] Again, the Japanese and Chinese were found to be similar in their ability to convert and eliminate alcohol, but the Europeans exhibited a distinctly slower metabolism.

Taylor, Born to Crime: The Genetic Causes of Criminal Behavior (Greenwood Press: London, 1984) at 113–114.

The apparent variables in play are the levels and types of the enzymes alcohol dehydrogenase (ADH) and aldehyde dehydrogenase (ALDH), both involved in the metabolism of alcohol. A number of studies have found that the characteristics of ADH vary not only among races but among geographically diverse populations. See, e.g., Eriksson, Genetic Aspects of the Relation Between Alcohol Metabolism and Consumption in Humans, 186 Mutation Research 241 (1987). And ALDH, thought to influence facial flushing through elimination of acetaldehyde, varies even more markedly. One study, for example, found that about 50 percent of Japanese subjects lacked one of the two types of ALDH (ALDH-1), while such a lack was not found among Caucasians. Yoshida, et al., Molecular Genetics of Alcohol-Metabolizing Enzymes, 16 Biochemical Society Transactions 230 (1988).

§5.3.5 Effects of Eating and Smoking

The delaying effects of food on alcohol absorption — and thus on any attempts to use retrograde extrapolation in guessing earlier blood-alcohol levels — have been documented. In A. W. Jones, Concentration-Time Profiles of Ethanol in Capillary Blood After Ingestion of Beer, 31 Journal of the Forensic Science Society 429 (1991), groups of subjects were given both light and regular beer on an empty stomach, during a normal lunch, and one to two hours after a meal.

The results of blood-alcohol testing showed lower peak BACs with light beer on an empty stomach than with regular beer; the same was true for beer consumed after a meal. Peak concentra-

[26] J. M. Hanna, Metabolic Responses of Chinese, Japanese and Europeans to Alcohol, 2 (1) *Alcoholism* 89 (1978).

tions for the two types of beer taken *during* a meal were similar, but the regular beer produced a slower rate of elimination.

Finally, peak BACs for both kinds of beer were lower with a full stomach, and those peaks were reached earlier. This confirmed earlier studies indicating that some of the ingested alcohol is trapped by food in the stomach, forming a so-called bound pool which is not absorbed immediately. The untrapped "free pool" of alcohol, on the other hand, is absorbed as if in an empty stomach, causing a peak BAC to be reached quickly. The bound pool of alcohol continues to be slowly absorbed, creating a slowly dropping level of blood-alcohol concentration.

See also Jones and Neri, Evaluation of Blood-Ethanol Profiles After Consumption of Alcohol Together with a Large Meal, 24(3) Canadian Society of Forensic Science Journal 165 (1991), for a study with similar results. After extensive experimentation involving ingestion of alcohol by 16 police officers, the researchers concluded that "[t]he results presented in this paper emphasize the need for caution when engaging in retrograde extrapolation."

Studies of the effects of ingesting food on blood-alcohol levels have also been conducted by scientists at the Southern California Research Institute. Conducted under a contract with the Highway Safety Research Institute, the results are contained in a final report entitled Methods for Estimating Expected Blood Alcohol Concentration, DOT HS-805-563 (U.S. Department of Transportation, National Highway Traffic Safety Administration, Wash., D.C. 20590). Among the findings:

> The limited literature on alcohol and food effects provides considerable evidence that food delays gastric emptying, and that it is the delay which slows the rate of alcohol absorption. In turn, it is the slower absorption process which underlies the lower BACs associated with food intake.
>
> If a drinker wishes to hold his or her BAC at a low to moderate level, what are the guidelines for food consumption? What is the best *time* to eat in relation to alcohol intake? What *type* of food is best? How *much* food is it necessary to eat to insure the desired effect? The data from this study indicate that the following are appropriate responses to these questions.
>
> In brief summary of the study findings, when food is eaten in close proximity to drinking alcohol, it can substantially reduce the BAC from the level that would be reached if the alcohol were con-

sumed on an empty stomach. Protein has the largest effect, and carbohydrates also are very effective.

Fatty foods are relatively ineffective in any quantity, and for the purposes of limiting BAC, it would be best to restrict the fat content of meals to a minimum, choosing instead foods which are largely protein and carbohydrates. Finally, a large amount of these latter types of food will be more effective than a small amount.

The findings regarding *time* of food intake show an inverse relationship; the greatest reduction in BAC was found at one-half hour, the shortest interval between eating and drinking which was examined. At an interval as long as two hours, the laboratory data show that the food exerted an effect. At four hours there was no effect of the food (as would be expected inasmuch as that period of time allows the food to pass through the stomach). Note that the findings regarding *time* of food intake are from pilot data only. This variable was not examined in the larger experiment in which the single interval of one-half hour between food intake and alcohol consumption was used.

The findings concerning the *amount of food* are fairly straightforward. A full meal will offer more protection than a snack, but even small amounts of food will have some effects on the BAC. In the laboratory 1000 calorie meals, which were either high in protein content or high in carbohydrate content, were followed by a 40% reduction in BAC. Certainly a change of that magnitude has practical significance to the individual.

Type of food is a more complex issue than the other variables of interest, but the data provide the basis for some recommendations. The person who expects to be drinking and would prefer to offset the alcohol to some extent by eating can be advised to consume a typical, full meal. For example, a meal which contains bread, meat, potatoes, and vegetables would be ideal. Such foods are largely protein and carbohydrates with a smaller proportion of the food being fats, and that kind of basic menu can be recommended. There is no evidence in these data to suggest that any specific, special foods should be eaten.

The pilot study and experiment findings have defined the food conditions which will make the maximum difference in BAC. It is important to emphasize, however, that these are not all-or-nothing variables. Rather, almost any food, eaten during the time interval of two hours or less prior to drinking, can be expected to produce some reduction in BAC compared to drinking in a fasted state. Although a small amount of food may have relatively minor effects, it would be unfortunate if the public believed that only a full meal would suffice. Snack foods, light meals, and typical party foods which accompany drinking all can be eaten with some benefit expected for the individual who wishes to minimize BAC.

There are some significant limits to these findings which should be noted. The alcohol beverage (80-proof vodka and orange juice mixed in a 1:1.5 ratio) was consumed over a half-hour period. No examination was made of other types of alcohol or of other alcohol concentrations, nor was it possible within the scope of this study to examine the condition in which alcohol is consumed as multiple drinks over a longer time period. The individual who may use the findings from this study as a basis for estimating BAC is likely not to duplicate the laboratory conditions and will need to be advised of the limits of the data.

Clearly a high calorie meal is more effective than a low calorie meal of equal weight. However, to determine whether weight of food is a critical variable, an additional test is needed. Specifically, the question requires comparisons of meals with equal calories but varying weight. The tests did not include this condition, and thus the issue is not resolved by these data.

Also, the findings are based on a study of male subjects only. It is expected that the effects of food on BAC will be closely similar for women, but no data have been obtained with female subjects.

Finally, the subjects were *young* men, ages 21–30 years, and "age" as a variable was not included in the study. It is possible that findings for older individuals will differ from those reported. Physiological changes, including changes in body composition, metabolic processes, and organ function which may occur with aging, presumably may affect the reported food-alcohol relationship.

It can reasonably be assumed that food will have some effect under these various conditions, but the extent of that effect has not been established. It is recommended that further study include a wider age range and include women as subjects. Additionally, if food is to find optimal use as an alcohol countermeasure, it will be necessary to examine the effects in circumstances more typical of social drinking. For example, it will be important to the alcohol user to know what may be expected if he/she has consumed an average-size, typical evening meal at 6 or 7 P.M. and then goes to a party or bar and drinks steadily for the rest of the evening without further food intake. Further study also will be needed to determine food effects on BAC when alcohol is consumed simultaneously with a meal. . . .

It is recommended that the following findings be incorporated into a pamphlet for drivers:

1. Eat a meal in close proximity to the time of drinking.
2. Eat a full meal, if possible, with a variety of foods which are largely protein and/or carbohydrates.
3. When it is not possible to have a meal before drinking, take advantage of whatever food is available. Almost any food will be better than no food at all.
4. Avoid drinking when no food has been eaten for more than two hours.

Food is not the only ingested substance that can affect the absorption of alcohol. A recent study indicates that *cigarette smoking* can also influence absorption — and thus the validity of attempts at retrograde extrapolation. In an article entitled Cigarette Smoking and Rate of Gastric Emptying: Effect on Alcohol Absorption, by Johnson, et al., 302 British Medical Journal 20 (1991), researchers tested blood samples of a group of smokers for blood-alcohol concentrations both after smoking and after prolonged abstinence. The result was that "areas under the venous blood alcohol concentration-time curves between zero and 30 minutes and 60 minutes and the peak blood alcohol concentrations were significantly less during the smoking period compared with the non-smoking period." Gastric emptying, as shown by scintillation cameras, was also found to be slower during the smoking evaluation. The scientists concluded that the effect of smoking on alcohol absorption has "considerable social and medicolegal relevance," and that the ingestion of nicotine should be taken into account in studies of alcohol absorption.

§5.3.6 Body Fat

As has been discussed earlier (§5.3.2), forensic alcohol analysis is based upon the premise that the subject is an "average person" — a premise that simply does not exist in the vast majority of cases. An example of this is the individual who has a higher percentage of body fat than normal.

Alcohol is distributed throughout the body according to the water content of blood and tissues. It is not, however, soluble in fat. Thus, if the tested subject has a higher percentage of fatty tissue in his body, there will be a lower "volume of distribution" — i.e., a smaller percentage of body mass absorbing the alcohol. See Hawkins and Kalant, The Metabolism of Ethanol and Its Metabolic Effects, 24 Pharmacological Review 67 (1972). Since the Widmark factor (see §5.2.3) varies inversely with the volume of distribution, the elimination rate of alcohol from the body will be quicker in a relatively fat person — thus further skewing any attempts at retrograde extrapolation (see §§5.2 *et seq.*).

Paranthetically, women, since they have a higher percentage of body fat than men, will also experience quicker elimination.

§5.3.7 Circadian Rhythm

Circadian rhythm is the term used to describe the cyclical phenomenon commonly known as "the body's internal clock." The human body experiences regular physiological changes over a period of roughly 24 hours (some researchers claim a 25-hour period): body temperature, sleep, hormonal and mineral levels, physical coordination, emotional state, mental acuity, etc. See, e.g., Bell, et al., Textbook of Physiology (Churchill Livingston, 10th ed. 1980).

Various studies have concluded that a part of this rhythmical change involves the capacity of the body to absorb alcohol. One study, for example, compared subjects consuming alcohol at 10:00 A.M. and at 10:00 P.M., and found that the morning consumption resulted in earlier and higher peak concentrations. Lakatua, et al., Observations on the Pharmacokinetics of Ethanol, Annual Review of Chronopharmacology 297 (1985). And Dubowski has confirmed that the time of day when an alcoholic drink is consumed may affect both the absorption rate and the peak concentration (time and quantity). Absorption, Distribution and Elimination of Alcohol, 10 Journal of Studies of Alcohol 98 (1985).

Obviously, the recognized effects of circadian rhythm add yet another variable to any attempts to estimate past blood-alcohol levels based upon chemical analysis.

§5.3.8 Zinc Deficiency

Scientific research appears to indicate that a high blood-alcohol level may not be indicative of alcohol consumption, but rather may be caused by a *deficiency of zinc* in the blood. In a study conducted at the University of North Dakota and reported in 46 American Journal of Clinical Nutrition 688 (1987), researchers experimented with the physiological effects of diets that had varied amounts of zinc. They discovered that the metabolism of alcohol was dramatically affected by zinc intake. For example, researchers found that for those subjects on a low zinc diet, blood-alcohol levels increased rapidly within 15 minutes of consumption of measured amounts of alcohol: roughly *twice* as much alcohol was present in their blood at this time as was present in those subjects on normal zinc diets. Furthermore, greater amounts of alcohol remained in the blood for a longer period of time when there was a zinc deficiency — that is, elimination rates were decreased.

Thus it appears that an individual with an insufficient amount of zinc in his diet will have higher peak blood-alcohol concentrations, and the alcohol will remain in his blood for a longer period of time.

Interestingly, it has been discovered that individuals who regularly consume large amounts of alcohol develop zinc deficiencies. This resulting zinc deficiency will in turn cause the phenomenon of higher initial concentrations and slower elimination. In other words, it is the problem drinker who is most likely to have abnormal absorption and elimination of alcohol — and it is therefore the problem drinker who becomes a very difficult subject for any attempts at retrograde extrapolation. To put it another way, the generally unreliable method of extrapolating blood alcohol levels becomes almost totally unreliable if the subject is an alcoholic or has a diet deficient in zinc.

§5.3.9 Internally Produced Alcohol

Is it possible to have an elevated blood-alcohol level without ever consuming any alcohol? There have been sporadic reports that certain people have alcohol in their blood or breath without ever actually having consumed any alcohol. Apparently, individuals' bodies *manufacture* alcohol internally — that is, "endogenous ethanol." Such a person could have alcohol on his breath and could show elevated blood-alcohol levels in breath, blood, or urine tests.

A recent article by three Swedish researchers confirms that ethanol may be found in samples of the blood or breath of healthy, abstaining individuals. Jones, Mardh, and Anggard, Determination of Endogenous Ethanol in Blood and Breath by Gas Chromatography — Mass Spectrometry, 18 Pharmacology, Biochemistry and Behavior 267–272 (Supp. 1 1983).

The article makes the following observations concerning the presence of alcohol in abstaining individuals:

> The occurrence of endogenous ethanol in biological fluids from healthy abstaining subjects was unequivocally established by the use of gas chromatography-mass spectrometry for analysis and with deuterium labelled analogues of ethanol as internal standards. . . .
>
> The occurrence of small amounts of ethanol in the blood and tissue from normal human subjects has interested scientists for more than a century. Most of the earlier experimental studies of this topic were hampered by technical difficulties and the methods of analysis used to quantitate ethanol lacked sufficient specificity.
>
> Nevertheless, in more recent work, employing gas chromatographic methods of analysis, increasing evidence has emerged to show that endogenous ethanol does exist, but the concentrations seen have large inter-individual variations. Our results, as yet on a relatively small material, show a markedly skewed distribution of values ranging from below detection limits (50 ng/ml (1.1 μM) to 1600 ng/ml (34.8 μM)) with a median value of 140 ng/ml (3.04 μM). The reason for the wide inter-individual variation in healthy abstaining subjects is hard to explain. . . .

6

BREATH ANALYSIS

§6.0 *The Reliability of Breath-Alcohol Analysis*

> No way of thinking, or doing, however ancient, can be trusted without proof. What everybody echoes or in silence passes by as true today may turn out to be falsehood tomorrow, mere smoke of opinion, which some had trusted for a cloud that would sprinkle fertilizing rain on their fields.
>
> HENRY DAVID THOREAU

Breath analysis is by far the most commonly used method of testing for blood-alcohol. While not as accurate or reliable as blood tests, it has generally been regarded in scientific circles as acceptably accurate if administered correctly. This regard is beginning to erode, however. An example of this is the comment of Dr. Michael Hlastala, Professor of Physiology, Biophysics and Medicine at the University of Washington:

> Breath testing, as currently used, is a very inaccurate method for measuring BAC. Even if the breath testing instrument is working perfectly, physiological variables prevent any reasonable accuracy. . . . Breath testing for alcohol using a single test method should not be used for scientific, medical or legal purposes where accuracy is important. [Hlastala, Physiological Errors Associated with Alcohol Breath Testing, 9(6) The Champion 19 (1985).]

A number of scientists who have conducted studies of breath-alcohol analysis have concurred with Dr. Hlastala in concluding that the method is inherently unreliable. Thus, for example, a recent study determined that breath readings vary at least 15 percent from actual blood-alcohol concentrations. Simpson, Accuracy and Precision of Breath-Alcohol Measurements for a Random Subject in the Postabsorptive State, 33(2) Clinical Chemistry 261 (1987). Furthermore, at least 23 percent of all individuals tested will have breath results in excess of true blood-alcohol levels. The author concluded that, "[g]iven the choice, it would seem that if a conclusion is to be made about the BAC of a random subject, especially when the conclusion can have serious consequences, it would be far preferable to make it on the basis of a direct [blood] measurement. . . ."

In another study, conducted by members of the toxicology section of the Wisconsin State Laboratory of Hygiene, only 33 percent of the breath test results correlated with corresponding blood tests. Reported in 32(4) Journal of Forensic Sciences 1235 (1987), the study involved a survey of 404 actual cases in Wisconsin in which defendants had been tested on a Breathalyzer (either the Model 900 or 900A) as well as by blood analysis. The two tests were considered to correlate when there was a difference of .01 percent or less.

One interesting aspect of the study was that in 11 of the cases, the defendant was shown to be intoxicated using one of the tests but not intoxicated when using the other.

At least one court has even reversed DUI convictions on the grounds that breath tests are inherently unreliable. In *State v. McGinley*, 550 A.2d 1305 (N.J. Super. 1988), the New Jersey Superior Court, Law Division, considered the consolidated appeals of four defendants whose convictions involved Breathalyzer tests. Although noting that the New Jersey Supreme Court had essentially taken judicial notice that the Breathalyzer models "900 and 900A are scientifically reliable," the court nevertheless felt free to consider new scientific evidence not previously available — evidence based in large part on the work of Dr. Kurt Dubowski:

> The scientific evidence upon which the defendants rely shows the following: (1) The breathalyzer is designed to test persons having a 2100/1 blood-breath ratio. Such ratios in fact vary from 1100/1 to 3200/1 and the variance can produce erroneous test results. High readings are produced in 14% of the population. (2) The temperature of the machine itself varies, affecting test results. (3)

> Body temperatures vary, affecting test results. (4) Hematocrit (the solid particles in whole blood) levels vary, particularly between males and females, affecting test results. These sources of error make breathalyzer test results suspect and, to insure reliability, require the substantial reduction of blood-alcohol percentages based on a translation of those results. The leading expert in the field, recognized as such by both State and defense, is of the opinion that the reduction should be .055. [550 A.2d at 1306.]

Dr. Dubowski has long advocated strict procedures for minimizing the many sources of error in breath testing. In a recent article entitled Quality Assurance in Breath-Alcohol Analysis, 18 Journal of Analytical Toxicology 270 (October 1994), he identified four "necessary safeguards" for breath testing:

1. A pre-test deprivation-observation period of at least 15 minutes (see the discussion of mouth alcohol in §6.2);
2. Blank tests immediately preceding each breath specimen collection step;
3. Analysis of at least two separate consecutive breath specimens, taken two to ten minutes apart (different results from duplicate analysis may indicate such problems as radio frequency interference; see §6.3.10);
4. An appropriate control test accompanying every subject test (see §6.3.6 for a discussion of calibration using a simulator).

Due largely to the inherent unreliability of breath analysis, the National Safety Council Committee on Alcohol and Other Drugs has recommended that at least *two* separate breath samples be collected and analyzed individually. As reported in a letter from Dr. Dubowski published in 9 American Journal of Forensic Medical Pathology 272 (1988), the Committee further recommended that the breath samples be collected at intervals of at least two and not more than ten minutes. This process of duplicate analysis has been widely advocated by experts in the past, most notably (and vociferously) by Dr. Richard Jensen. A 1995 Colorado Department of Health study indicates that, as of that time, 26 states provided for duplicate breath analysis, while 22 required only a single analysis. Of the 26 requiring two tests, 14 accept the lower of the two as the legal result and two states average the two results; most require that the two results be within .02 of one another. The material on duplicate breath testing referred to is the following:

> At least two separate breath samples should be collected and analyzed individually in performing any quantitative evidential breath-alcohol analysis. The breath samples should be collected at intervals of not less than 2 nor more than 10 minutes, after an initial deprivation period of at least 15 minutes. Reported breath-alcohol analysis results shall be truncated to two decimal places; and all results obtained shall be reported. Consecutive breath-alcohol analysis results within 0.02 g/210 L without regard to sign, shall be deemed to be in acceptable agreement.

National Safety Council, Committee on Alcohol and Other Drugs, "Recommendation of the Subcommittee on Technology," Appendix M, page 145 (1996 printing).

Whether acceptably accurate or not, breath analysis is the most convenient and economical method for the police, and the most convenient and least embarrassing or painful for the arrestee. As a result, counsel will probably encounter some sort of breath analyzing instrument in 70 to 80 percent of his drunk driving cases.

There are a number of different breath analyzing machines in use today. The most commonly encountered of these is the Intoxilyzer Model 5000, of which there are now a number of different versions (see §6.4.1). The second most popular of the machines is the Intoximeter 3000 (see §6.4.3), followed by the older version of the 5000, the Intoxilyzer 4011 (and its various permutations). The BAC DataMaster/Verifier (see §6.4.2) is now universally used in Washington, South Carolina, and Vermont, and is found sporadically in other states as well. Finally, the old 900/900A series of Breathalyzers are still found in a few jurisdictions.

Each of these machines utilizes its own mechanism for analyzing the alcoholic content of exhaled vapor. With the exception of the Breathalyzer, however, all use a common method: infrared spectroscopic analysis (the Breathalyzer employs the "wet chemical" technique). These machines operate on the principal that alcohol vapor captured in a chamber will absorb light waves of a certain frequency when beamed through it. The more alcohol present in the chamber (i.e., the higher the percentage of alcohol in the breath sample), the more light is absorbed. In theory, then, determining the alcohol concentration of the sample is simply a matter of measuring the amount of light that reaches a receptor at the other end of the chamber; the more light, the lower the alcohol content in the breath. A computer then translates the figure into blood-alcohol concentration, using the blood-breath partition ratio (see §6.0.1).

In approaching a case involving a breath analysis, counsel should be aware that there are a large number of potential problems, both theoretical and operational. As has already been seen in §§5.0–5.1, there exists a broad range of factors that can render any result of blood-alcohol analysis — breath, blood, or urine — unreliable. As seen in the following subsections, additional problems unique to breath analysis add to this unreliability.

§6.0.1 The Blood-Breath Partition Ratio

No matter what particular instrument is employed in a drunk driving case, the final determination of an individual's blood-alcohol level will be based on certain "scientific" presumptions. As will be seen, however, some of these presumptions simply do not always hold true. Thus defense counsel must consider not only the possibility of faulty operation of the instrument, but also the very real possibility that the final reading was computed on the basis of false presumptions in the underlying formula.

The most important of these presumptions begins with the principle that in concentrations below 20 percent, alcohol in water will always obey Henry's Law: For a fixed concentration of alcohol in water at a fixed temperature, the ratio of alcohol in air above water is fixed. Thus there will exist at least theoretically a constant ratio between the concentration of alcohol in the blood and the concentration of alcohol in the alveolar air of the lungs. The average ratio among human beings is generally accepted as being 1:2100 — that is, 2.1 liters of deep lung breath contain the same weight of alcohol as 1 cubic centimeter of pulmonary (lung) blood. This, of course, is only an *average:* The actual ratio operative in any given individual can vary from 1:1500 to 1:3000, with a resultant error in any breath analysis arising from the assumed

1:2100 ratio. This particular source of error in a breath analysis can mean a variation from the true reading of as much as .03. An individual with a ratio of 1:1500 with an actual blood-alcohol level of .07, for example, would have a reading on the breath instrument of .10, shifting him into a zone of presumed guilt.

A Japanese study of the validity of 1:2100 breath-to-blood ratio has concluded that the ratio in fact varies widely. See S. Tsukamoto, et al., An Experimental Study on the Ethanol Ratio of Breath to Blood, 37 Japan Journal of Legal Medicine 823 (1983). Further, the researchers found that breath-alcohol concentration tended to be higher during the absorption phase when compared to blood alcohol, and lower during the elimination phase. The conclusion of the Japanese scientists: It would be "difficult" to give a definite, constant breath/blood ratio, as it varies from individual to individual and changes according to the phase of absorption/elimination.

Dr. A. W. Jones, Assistant Professor in Experimental Alcohol Research at Sweden's Karolinska Institute, has confirmed the variation of blood-to-breath alcohol ratios in different individuals. In Viability of the Blood: Breath Alcohol Ratio in Vivo, 39(11) Journal of Studies on Alcohol 1931 (1978), Dr. Jones has summarized the results of extensive experiments he conducted to test the validity of the presumed ratio used in blood-alcohol analysis. He concluded, "It has been clearly demonstrated in this study that the blood:breath alcohol ratio varies from subject to subject and even within the same subject from time to time."

After extensive studies in the area, British physicians finally concluded that

> the blood/breath ratio should be regarded as nothing more than a statistical convenience suitable for defining the limits of a particular universe. Its use to derive individual blood alcohol levels from breath alcohol levels has little scientific justification and, more particularly, its use in this way for law enforcement can only be deplored. We reiterate our view that breath analysis is not an acceptable method for accurately determining blood alcohol concentrations. [Alobaidi, Hill and Payne, Significance of Variations in Blood/Breath Partition Coefficient of Alcohol, 2 British Medical Journal 1479, 1481 (December 18, 1976).]

The blood-breath partition coefficient can be affected by, among other things, an individual's age and the existence of lung disease. In an article appearing in 11(5) Alcoholism: Clinical and Experimental Research 440 (1987), Canadian scientists describe an experiment in which three control groups of subjects were given equal amounts of alcohol and subsequently tested on a Breathalyzer: ten individuals between the ages of 52 and 80 (median age, 70); ten individuals of roughly the same ages, but with chronic pulmonary disease; and ten healthy young men (median age, 33). Predictably, the researchers found that the healthy, younger men had an average partition ratio of 2283:1. The healthy but older subjects, however, had an average ratio of 3051:1. Finally, those older subjects with lung disease had an average coefficient ratio of 3760:1. The scientists concluded that both increasing age and lung disease can cause dramatically increased blood-breath partition ratios.

The Supreme Court of Nebraska has ruled that the results of breath tests conducted with an Intoxilyzer 4011AS are inadmissible because of their reliance on an assumed blood-breath ratio of 2100:1. In *State v. Burling*, 400 N.W.2d 872 (Neb. 1987), the defendant's expert witness testified that the machine uses a 2100:1 ratio in its computations but that an individual's actual ratio can vary from 1100:1 to 3400:1, and that forensic toxicologists no longer rely on the 2100:1 figure.

The supreme court expressed considerable concern with this expert's uncontroverted testimony. It estimated that if the defendant's true ratio had been 1100:1, for example, his true BAC reading would have been .08 percent rather than the .164 percent figure given the jury. In holding that use of the breath test results was error, the court dealt with the state's statute directing that chemical tests "shall be competent evidence in any prosecution under a state statute . . . involving operating a motor vehicle while under the influence":

> [T]he Legislature may not declare the weight to be given evidence or what evidence shall be conclusive proof of an issue of fact, . . . that is to say, determining whether evidence is of probative value is a legal question, and the Legislature cannot impair judicial analysis and resolution of such questions. [Id. at 876.]

The South Dakota Supreme Court has taken a different approach to the problem of variable partition ratios. In *State v. Hofer*, 512 N.W.2d 482 (S.D. 1994), the state's expert admitted that the

2100:1 ratio was a "committee compromise" and that scientific studies show that ratios vary over a wide range from 1142:1 to 3748:1. The supreme court, while acknowledging the "inaccuracy inherent in applying one ratio to all types of people," held that such factors go to the weight of the evidence rather than to its admissibility. The court did this by adopting the federal standard for new scientific evidence in *Daubert v. Merrel Dow,* 509 U.S. 529, 125 L.Ed.2d 469, 113 S. Ct. 2786 (1993), in place of the previous *Frye* standard.

An entirely different approach to "the partition problem" is simply to redefine the crime to avoid the question of variable ratios entirely. This "head-in-the-sand" approach was adopted in California and is quickly spreading to other states. The California legislature enacted a new version of their drunk driving statute, reading in relevant part: "For ypurposes of this article . . . percent, by weight, of alcohol in a person's blood is based upon grams of alcohol per 100 milliliters of blood *or grams of alcohol per 210 liters of breath*" (emphasis added).

In effect, the legislature simply ignored scientific fact and incorporated the conversion ratio into the statute itself (note the correlation between the partition ratio of 2100:1 and using 210 liters as the designated volume).

Do the provisions of the new DUI law make evidence concerning variations in the ratio irrelevant?

The California Supreme Court has replied in the affirmative. In *People v. Bransford,* 35 Cal. Rptr. 2d 613, 884 P.2d 70 (Cal. 1994), that court dealt a "death blow" to the argument that assumed partition ratios are not relevant to the defendant. The court ruled that the new statute prohibits "the act of driving with 0.08 percent or more of blood alcohol *as defined by* grams of alcohol in 210 liters of breath" (original emphasis). The court rejected the argument that the statute creates a conclusive presumption that the amount of alcohol in 210 liters of breath is the same as that in 100 milliliters of blood: the statute does not presume, the court said, it *defines* — that is, driving with a specified *breath*-alcohol level *is* the offense.

Thus the notoriously conservative California Supreme Court simply ignored science — in effect, judicially legislating scientific truth out of the picture much as was done in medieval days. Reflecting the well-known "double standard" in DUI cases, the court noted that allowing prosecutors to prove the offense by way of breath-alcohol rather than blood-alcohol "promotes the state's interest in reducing the danger to the public caused by those who drink and drive." The court went on to offer the following rather incredible justifications for its decision:

> It will increase the likelihood of convicting such a driver, because the prosecution need not prove actual impairment . . . Adjudication of such criminal charges will also require fewer legal resources, because fewer legal issues will arise. And individuals prosecuted under such a statute will be less likely to contest the charge.

The lone dissenting justice, however, offered a few of her own observations:

> [T]he majority has gone beyond the stringent prohibitions enacted by the Legislature and has on its own created the new crime of driving with alcohol in one's breath. This result is achieved only at a serious cost, for it not only tramples the long-standing rule that a court interpreting a criminal statute with two possible meanings must choose the one more favorable to the defendant, but it also invades the Legislature's exclusive power to create new crimes.

§6.0.2 The New Paradigm

Dr. Michael Hlastala (see §6.0) has formulated a rather revolutionary "new paradigm" for the breath test. After further extensive research at the University of Washington, he has discovered that the physiological processes involved in capturing a representative breath sample are significantly different from those previously assumed by scientists and forensic toxicologists. Any DUI attorney dealing with a breath machine should be aware of this new-view reality.

In conjunction with his lecture at the Third Annual Summer Session at Harvard Law School (National College for DUI Defense) in 1997, Dr. Hlastala presented the following material (which is reproduced here in its entirety with his kind permission):

> Over the years, breath testing has become a widely used method for quantitative determination of the level of intoxication of indi-

viduals suspected of driving while under the influence of alcohol. After recognition of the need for quantitative assessment of intoxication, blood alcohol concentration was considered as the single most important variable. However, concern about the invasive requirements of drawing a blood sample led to the development of the breath test as a non-invasive means of assessing level of intoxication. The breath test is an indirect test, but has been considered to be a good estimate of the blood alcohol concentration because of the assumption that an end-exhaled breath sample accurately reflects the alveolar (or deep-lung) air which is in equilibrium with the blood. In spite of the great deal of effort that has gone into the studies attempting to validate the breath test, forensic scientists and toxicologists still have a very limited understanding of the breath alcohol test and its limitations.

ANATOMY OF THE LUNGS

The lungs are located within the chest. This organ allows inspired air to come into close proximity with the blood so gases (such as oxygen and carbon dioxide) can exchange between the air and blood. The lung is made up of over 300 million small air sacs called alveoli. Outside air comes to the alveoli from the mouth or nose via the airways. The major airway leading to the lungs from the throat is the trachea. The trachea divides into the left and right "mainstem bronchi" (going to the left and right lungs), which divide further into the "lobar bronchi." This division goes on about 23 times until the alveoli are reached. Actually, some alveoli begin to appear at about the 17th generation airways. Surrounding each alveolus are small blood vessels. The thinness (less than 0.001 millimeter) of the membrane separating blood from the air in the lungs allows oxygen and carbon dioxide to exchange readily between the blood and air. Because of the large number of very small alveoli, there is a very large surface area (70 square meters) for this gas exchange process. For more details regarding the basics of lung physiology, see Hlastala and Berger (14).

SCIENTIFIC REVOLUTION

The evolution of scientific understanding depends on the continuous development of new ideas that form the bases of experimentation. This concept has been termed "scientific revolution" by Kuhn (23) who sees science as the movement from one paradigm to another (Figure 6-1). The term "paradigm" refers to a set of universally recognized scientific achievements that for a time pro-

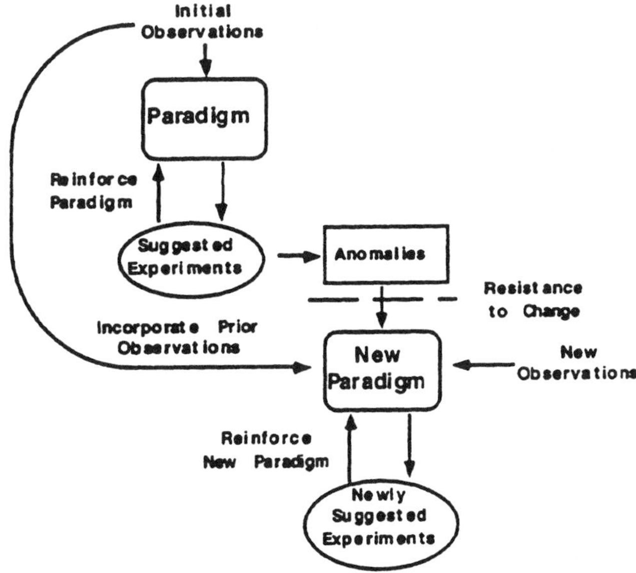

Figure 6-1
Kuhn's model of scientific revolution

vide a model or conceptual framework for a phenomenon. This paradigm represents the core principles that define the scientific understanding.

A paradigm is established after a number of initial observations are obtained. Experiments are then carried out to test hypotheses related to the paradigm. Usually, these experiments provide data which reinforce the paradigm. Occasionally, these experiments result in anomalies, or results which do not fit within the framework of the original paradigm, and are inconsistent with the predictions of the paradigm.

The accumulation of anomalies leads the scientist to develop a new paradigm, which provides a new framework for interpreting experimental results which accounts for the anomalies of the old paradigm as well as new observations. At that point, the new paradigm undergoes scrutiny through newly suggested experiments which provide data to reinforce the new paradigm. The new paradigm must account for the new observations as well as the prior observations. The transition from the old paradigm anomalies to the new paradigm always encounters enormous resistance to change. Resistance is crucial for this scientific progress to occur.

Eventually, it is likely that another set of anomalies with the new paradigm will lead to yet a third paradigm. This will occur as new technologies reveal new anomalies. Kuhn, a physicist turned philosopher, cites a number of paradigms that have evolved in his field in the form of scientific revolutions: Copernican astronomy, Newtonian physics, the wave theory of light, and quantum physics. These same ideas apply to different fields in very different scales. The concept of the paradigm can also be applied to the Alcohol Breath Test.

THE OLD PARADIGM

Development of the single breath test for alcohol (3, 10) took place in the early 1950s when the field of respiratory physiology was just beginning. At that time, it was generally understood that the first air exhaled from the lungs contained air from the airways and had little "alveolar air." It was thought that further exhalation would result in exhalation of air from the alveoli containing gas in equilibrium with pulmonary capillary blood (Figure 6-2). These concepts were held in the respiratory physiology community (7, 28)

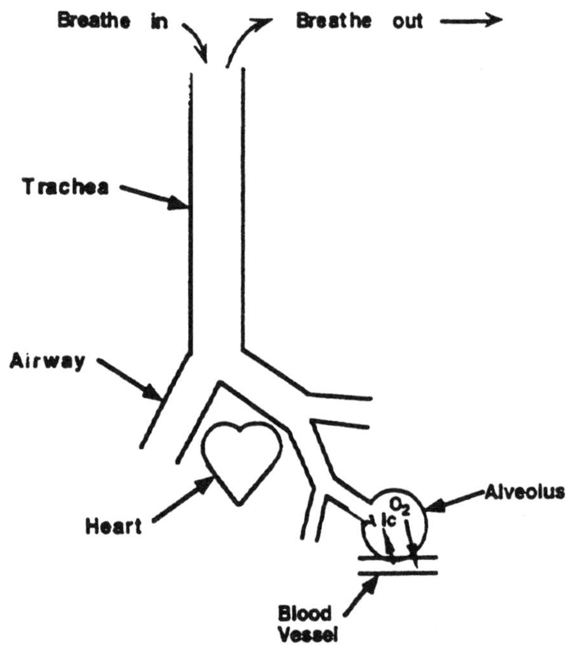

Figure 6-2
Old paradigm of alcohol exchange in the lung

and followed from data obtained with low solubility gases, such as nitrogen. Without the advantage of having present-day analytical equipment, the profile of exhaled alcohol could not be measured, but was expected to be identical to nitrogen (after a single breath of oxygen) and to appear as shown in Figure 6-3. The first part of the exhaled air was thought to come from the airways and was called the anatomic dead space and the later part of the exhaled air (with higher gas concentration) was thought to come from the alveolar regions. This later part of the exhaled gas profile was termed the alveolar plateau (7, 28). With a presumed flat exhaled alcohol profile, it was thought that end-exhaled alcohol concentration would be independent of exhaled volume after exhalation beyond anatomic dead space volume. It was further assumed that alveolar alcohol concentration was precisely related to the arterial blood alcohol concentration by virtue of the physical-chemical relationship known as the partition coefficient (11). The implicit assumption was that the alcohol concentration remained unchanged as alveolar air passed through the airways. Viewed through the limited perspective of respiratory physiology of the 1940's, the breath alcohol test seemed to be reasonable in principle

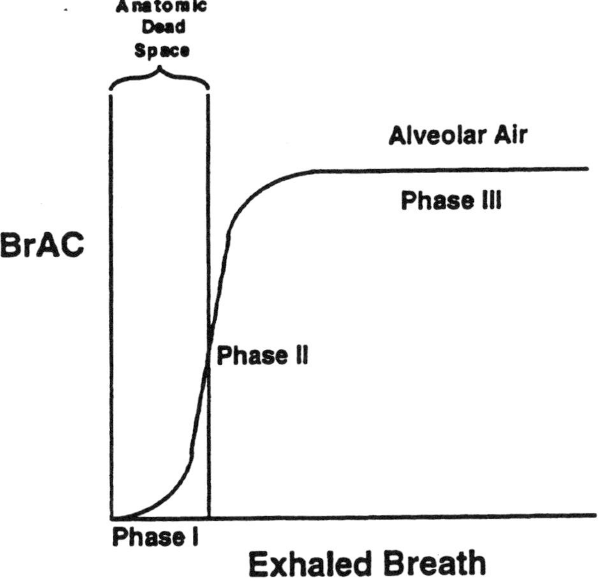

Figure 6-3
Assumed exhaled alcohol profile in the 1950s

and further development as a non-invasive measure of blood alcohol concentration was justifiable.

ANOMALIES

Since 1950, many studies have been performed to quantitate the relationship between breath alcohol concentration (BrAC) and blood alcohol concentration (BAC) with the goal of defining a precise relationship between the two for accurate non-invasive determination of BAC. These studies, undertaken to validate the use of breath tests by comparing BrAC and BAC in normal subjects, have shown a surprising amount of variability (cf. 6, 17, 24) which has not been improved (33, 34) in spite of advances in instrument technology. The physiology of lungs and of the body as a whole remains as the primary explanation for this variability (13, 22).

The alcohol breath test is a single exhalation maneuver. The subject is asked to inhale (preferably a full inhalation to total lung capacity, TLC) and then exhale (preferably a full exhalation to residual volume, RV) into the breath testing instrument. Very few restrictions (i.e., exhaled volume, exhaled flow rate, inhaled volume, pre-test breathing pattern, air temperature, etc.) are placed on the breathing maneuver. The constraints applied vary among the different breath testing instruments and among the operators administering the test, and the level of cooperation varies among subjects, resulting in substantial uncontrolled variation in the precise maneuver used for the breath test.

The lungs have a relatively simple, but non-uniform, anatomical structure. The airways are a branching, tree-like arrangement of tubes. Inspired air moves through progressively shorter, narrower and more numerous airways (39). These airways are lined with mucus at a temperature varying between approximately 34°C at the mouth and 37°C in the very smallest airways. However, this temperature range varies depending on the breathing pattern (25). The membranes separating the air in the alveoli and the blood in the capillaries are so thin that inert gases such as alcohol equilibrate between blood and air very rapidly (38). With exhalation, air within the alveoli is conducted along the airways to the mouth.

During inspiration, air is heated and humidified as it passes through the upper airways (25, 36). Some water within the mucous layer or watery sub-mucous layer will vaporize and heat stored in the airways will be picked up by the inspired gas and taken to the alveoli (16, 30, 36). During exhalation, the process reverses; fully humidified air at core body temperature is cooled by the cooler airway mucosa and water vapor condenses on the mucosa. This water and heat exchange process is vital because it conditions the inspired air to avoid damaging the delicate alveolar cells while conserving water and heat from major loss in the exhaled air. Under normal environmental conditions, exhaled gas has less heat and less water vapor than does alveolar air.

The dynamics of soluable gas exchange are similar to the dynamics of heat and water exchange. These processes are analyzed using analogous equations (2). The fact that respired air exchanges heat and water with the airways implies similar soluble gas exchange processes (15). This interaction of soluble gases with airway mucosa is well documented (1, 4, 5, 32). The degree of interaction is directly related to the solubility of the gas in the airway mucosa and mucous lining (1, 32). The very high solubility of alcohol in water guarantees its strong interaction with airway tissue. Because this interaction depends on temperature and airflow characteristics, variations in tidal volume and frequency can have a substantial effect on the alcohol concentration in the breath sample (20, 37). This variation is affected by the difference in temperature between the outside air and the alveolar air (18).

The exchanges of heat and of gas with the airways are complex and interactive processes. The relative significance of this exchange depends on the effective solubility of the gas in the mucosa. For the respiratory gases, oxygen and carbon dioxide, airway tissue solubility is small. For both water and alcohol airway solubility is quite large. Moreover, the exchange processes are interactive. During inspiration, heat, water, and alcohol are transported from the mucosa to the air. The exchange of heat cools the mucosa causing an increase in its alcohol solubility and, hence, a decrease in the partial pressure of alcohol in the mucosa and a reduction in alcohol flux into the airway lumen. These various processes have been integrated into a mathematical model developed by Tsu et al. (37) and further refined by George et al. (8), which shows that during normal breathing, the inspired air is equilibrated with alcohol, picking it up from the airways, before reaching the seventeenth generation airways (start of the alveolar region). Upon reaching the alveoli a small amount of additional alcohol is picked up because the solubility of alcohol in blood is lower than the solubility of alcohol in water (21). The equilibrium partial pressure of alcohol in vapor above blood is greater than in vapor above water at the same temperature. With exhalation, the excess alcohol picked up in the alveoli is rapidly lost to the airways within the sixteenth or fifteenth generation. Along the airway, more alcohol is lost to the airways. The alcohol that arrives at the mouth comes essentially from the airways and not from the alveoli. This is also the case for water vapor. The humidification of inspired air is performed by the airways.

The flux of alcohol from the mucus surface into the air (positive values) during inspiration and the flux of alcohol from the air to the mucus surface (negative values) during expiration is demonstrated in Figure 6-4. This figure was calculated using a mathematical model of the human airway structure (8). During inspiration, alcohol is taken up into the inspired air immediately at the mouth. The greatest alcohol uptake occurs in the trachea and generations 6 through 13. During expiration, the redeposition of alcohol occurs primarily at these same airway generations. The important conclusion from this work is that all of the alcohol that comes out of the mouth in the breath comes from the airway surfaces rather than from the alveolar regions.

The early basic assumption of the breath alcohol test was that the breath alcohol concentration was the same irrespective of the exhaled volume as long as the dead space volume is exhaled (as shown in Figure 6-3). However, Jones (20), and others (26,35) have shown that the breath alcohol concentration depends on exhaled volume. The breath testing instrument takes a sample of air from

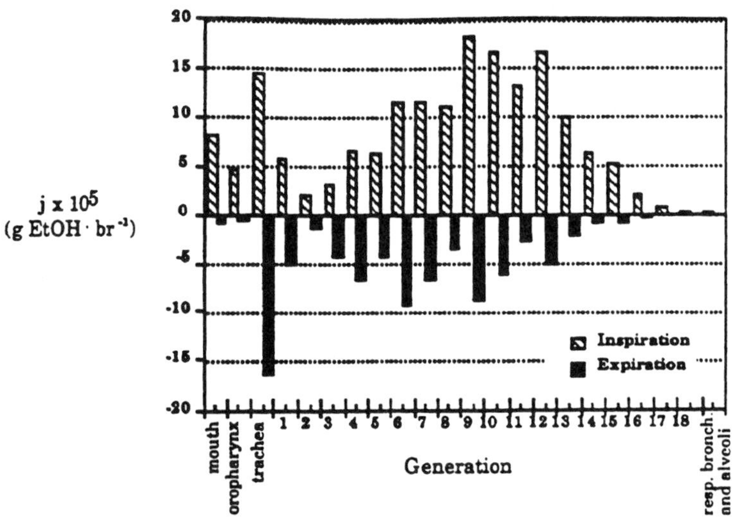

Figure 6-4
Flux of alcohol from mucus surface into air in airways for each airway generation

the end of the breath whenever the subject stops but the volume of breath exhaled is neither controlled nor measured. Therefore, the apparent breath alcohol concentration depends on the volume of air delivered to the breath testing instrument. The last part of the breath can be well above the average single breath alcohol level because the alveolar plateau has a positive slope that is dependent on air temperature (29).

A sloping alveolar plateau for various low solubility gases has been explained by several factors including stratified inhomogeneity (gas phase diffusion limitation) (31), convection-diffusion interaction (27), sequential exhalation from regions with differing $\dot{V}_A/\dot{Q}$ (31) and continuing gas exchange (9). None of these factors contribute substantially to the slope of the exhaled alcohol profile. Continuing gas exchange will contribute to the slope of the exhaled profile for respiratory gases (CO_2 and O_2), but not inert gases (9, 12, 31).

Further variation in BrAC will result from changing the breathing pattern immediately before delivering the sample breath. Hyperventilation for 20 seconds prior to delivering a sample breath to the breath tester causes an 11% reduction in BrAC (19). Three deep breaths prior to the sample breath reduces BrAC by 4% (26). After breath-holding for 15 seconds prior to exhalation, the BrAC increases by 12% (for a minimum exhalation) and 6% (for a maximum exhalation) (26). A 30 second breathhold prior to exhalation increases BrAC by 16% (19). These effects are caused by the respective cooling or warming of the airways and the data further support the airway surface interaction of alcohol as the mechanism causing the changing alcohol concentration during exhalation.

THE NEW PARADIGM

The conclusions of the above studies are that alcohol leaves the lungs by diffusing from the bronchial circulation through the airway tissue where it is picked up by the inspired air (Figure 6-5). By the time it reaches the alveoli, inspired air has taken up as much alcohol as is possible. Therefore, no additional alcohol can be picked up in the alveoli. On exhalation, some of the alcohol is redeposited on the airway surfaces. All of the alcohol exhaled at the mouth comes from the airway surface via the bronchial circulation. No alcohol originates from the pulmonary circulation in the alveoli. The fact that alcohol comes primarily from the airways is why the breath alcohol concentration can be so easily altered by changing the breathing pattern. This contributes to the very large

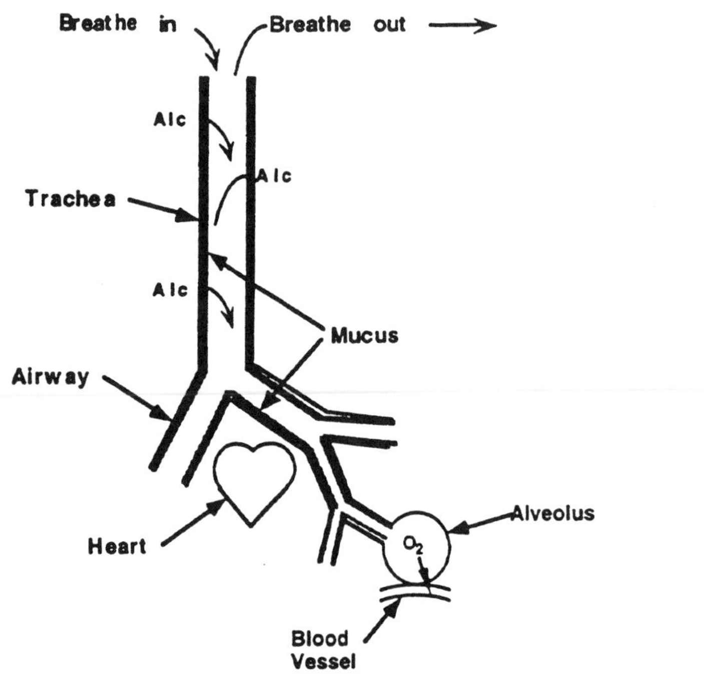

Figure 6-5
Schematic diagram of the human lung airways — Arrows show the exchange of alcohol during both inspiration and expiration

variation in the alcohol breath test readings obtained from actual subjects.

BREATH ALCOHOL CONCENTRATION

In most states, it is illegal to drive a motor vehicle with a breath alcohol concentration of 0.10 gm/210 liters or more. Have you ever considered what is meant by "breath"? What is the breath and to what part of the breath is the statute referring? Webster's New World Dictionary has several definitions of breath, but the most relevant is "air taken into the lungs and then let out." Air becomes breath when it goes into the lungs AND is exhaled from the lungs. The only air that fulfills that criteria is the air that is exhaled from the mouth or nose. Any air within the lungs is not breath. Only that which is exhaled can be considered as breath.

The exhaled alcohol profile is shown in Figure 6-6. At the beginning of exhalation, the breath has a zero or near-zero BrAC. As exhalation progresses, the BrAC increases, initially quite rapidly,

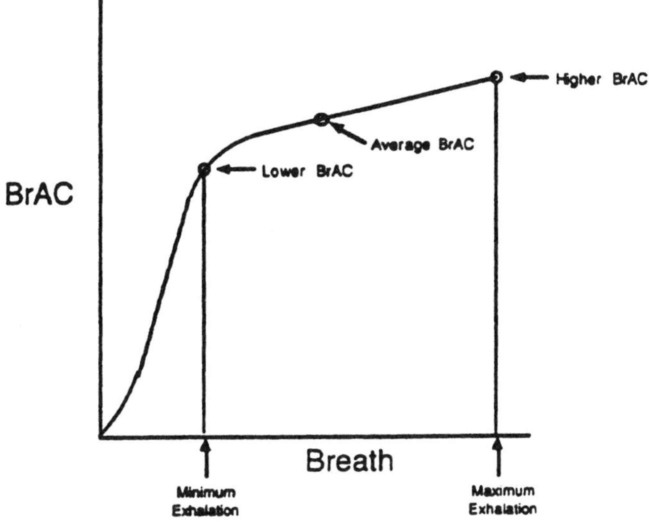

Figure 6-6
Exhaled breath alcohol profile

but eventually the rate of increase of BrAC slows down. It does not level off until the subject stops exhalation. All of this is "breath." Since the specific portion of the breath that is sought to determine alcohol concentration is not defined, we can only surmise that the average of the breath is meant. The average of the breath would include some initial breath with lower EtOH and some of the later breath with a higher concentration. The average of the breath alcohol will be a value that is near the five-second point of exhalation (Figure 6-7). If a subject exhales for five seconds and then stops, the BrAC will be close to the average of the entire breath. Any exhalation beyond this approximate time will result in a value that will be higher than the average BrAC. Therefore the average BrAC is ALWAYS less than the breath test machine reading.

Beware of the over-eager prosecution expert who may say that the part of the breath that the state wants is the "deep-lung air." This is incorrect and must be vigorously opposed. First of all the deep-lung air is not breath (by Webster's definition). The technician will say this because he/she believes (correctly so) that any sample of breath is usually lower than a deep-lung (alveolar) sample. When we had a blood standard (illegal to drive with a BAC of 0.10 mg/dl or more, as measured by the breath), this would be a reasonable argument. However, we now have a breath standard and, therefore, the deep-lung air is not relevant.

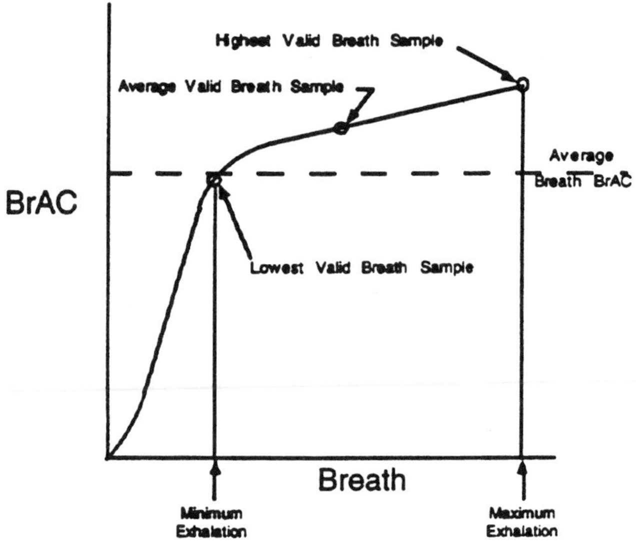

Figure 6-7
Exhaled breath alcohol profile showing average BrAC

The initial intent of the legislature was to provide a law that could make it much easier to prosecute by taking away the possibility of defense arguments concerning the variability between BrAC and BAC. In fact, the passage of the "breath per se" law has made it much more difficult for prosecution by virtue of a lack of definition of breath. In fact the average BrAC is actually much lower than any breath alcohol test machine reading. In effect, the legislature has dealt a blow to the prosecution because it is now impossible for the prosecution to prove that the average BrAC is greater than or equal to 0.10 gm/210L.

REFERENCES

1. Aharonson, E., H. Menkes, G. Gurtner, D. L. Swift and D. F. Proctor. Effect of respiratory airflow rate on removal of soluble vapors by the nose. J. Appl. Physiol. 37: 654–657, 1974.
2. Bird, R., W. Stewart and E. Lightfoot. Transport Phenomena. John Wiley & Sons, Inc. New York, 1960.
3. Borkenstein, R. and H. Smith. The Breathalyzer and its application. Med. Sci. Law. 2: 13, 1961.
4. Cander, L. and R. Forster. Determination of pulmonary parenchymal tissue volume and pulmonary capillary blood flow in man. J. Appl. Physiol. 14: 541–551, 1959.

5. Davies, C. D. Absorption of gases in the respiratory tract. Ann. Occup. Hyg. 29: 13–25, 1985.
6. Emerson, V., R. Holleyhead, M. Isaacs, N. Fuller and D. J. Hunt. The measurement of breath alcohol. J. Forens. Sci. 20: 3–70, 1980.
7. Fowler, W. Lung function studies. II. The respiratory dead space. Am. J. Physiol. 154: 405–416, 1948.
8. George, S., A. Babb and M. Hlastala. Dynamics of soluble gas exchange in the airways: III. Single exhalation breathing maneuver. J. Appl. Physiol. 75: 2439–2449, 1993.
9. Grønlund, J., E. Swenson, J. Ohlsson and M. Hlastala. Contribution of continuing gas exchange to phase III exhaled PCO_2 and PO_2 profiles. J. Appl. Physiol. 16: 547–571, 1987.
10. Harger, R., R. Forney and H. Barnes. Estimation of the level of blood alcohol from analysis of breath. J. Lab. Clin. Med. 36: 306–318, 1950.
11. Henry, W. Experiments on the quantity of gases absorbed by water at different temperature and under different pressures. Phil. Trans. Roy. Soc. 93: 29–42, 1803.
12. Hlastala, M. Model of fluctuating alveolar gas exchange during the respiratory cycle. Respirat. Physiol. 15: 214–232, 1972.
13. Hlastala, M. Physiological errors associated with alcohol breath testing. The Champion. July: 16–19, 1985.
14. Hlastala, M. and A. Berger. Physiology of Respiration. Oxford University Press. New York, 360 pp., 1996.
15. Hlastala, M. and E. Swenson. Airway gas exchange. In: The Bronchial Circulation. Ed.: J. Butler. Exec Ed.: C. Lenfant. Marcel Dekker, Inc. pp. 417–441, 1992.
16. Ingenito, E., J. Solway, E. McFadden Jr., B. Pichurko, E. Carvalho and J. Drazen. Finite difference analysis of respiratory heat transfer. J. Appl. Physiol. 61: 2252–2259, 1986.
17. Jones, A. Variability of the blood: breath alcohol ratio in vivo. J. Stud. Alc. 39: 1931–1939, 1978.
18. Jones, A. Effects of temperature and humidity of inhaled air on the concentration of ethanol in a man's exhaled breath. Clin. Sci. 63: 441–445, 1982.
19. Jones, A. How breathing technique can influence the results of breath-alcohol analysis. Med. Sci. Law. 22: 275–280, 1982.
20. Jones, A. Quantitative measurements of the alcohol concentration and the temperature of breath during a prolonged exhalation. Acta Physiol. Scand. 114: 407–412, 1982.
21. Jones, A. Determination of liquid/air partition coefficients for

dilute solutions of ethanol in water, whole blood, and plasma. J. Anal. Toxicol. 7: 193–197, 1983.
22. Jones, A. Physiological aspects of breath alcohol measurement. Alcohol, Drugs and Driving. 6: 1–25, 1990.
23. Kuhn, T. S. The Structure of Scientific Revolutions, International Encyclopedia of Unified Science. Neurath ed. The University of Chicago Press. Chicago. 1970.
24. Mason, M. and K. Dubowski. Breath-alcohol analysis: uses, methods, and some forensic problems — review and opinion. J. Forens. Sci. 9–41, 1976.
25. McFadden, E., Jr. Respiratory heat and water exchange: physiological and clinical implications. J. Appl. Physiol.: Respirat. Environ. Exercise Physiol. 54: 331–336, 1983.
26. Ohlsson, J., D. Ralph, M. Mandelkorn, A. Babb and M. Hlastala. Accurate measurement of blood alcohol concentration with isothermal rebreathing. J. Stud. Alc. 51: 6–13, 1990.
27. Paiva, M. and L. Engel. Pulmonary interdependence of gas transport. J. Appl. Physiol.: Respirat. Environ. Exercise Physiol. 47: 296–305, 1979.
28. Rahn, H., J. Mahoncy, A. Otis and W. Fenn. A method for the continuous analysis of alveolar air. J. Aviat. Med. 7: 173–178, 1946.
29. Ralph, D., M. Hlastala and A. Babb. Interaction of ethanol with airway mucosa during exhalation. Prog. Artific. Organs. 1119–1121, 1985.
30. Saidel, G., K. Kruse and F. Primiano Jr. Model simulation of heat and water transport dynamics in an airway. J. Biomech. Eng. 105: 189–193, 1983.
31. Scheid, P. and J. Piiper. Intrapulmonary gas mixing and stratification. In: Pulmonary Gas Exchange, Vol. I, J. B. West, Ed., Academic Press, pp. 87–130, 1981.
32. Schrikker, A., W. deVries, A. Zwart and S. Luijendijk. Uptake of highly soluble gases in the epithelium of the conducting airways. Pflügers Archiv. 405: 389–394, 1985.
33. Simpson, G. Accuracy and precision of breath-alcohol measurements for subjects in the absorptive state. Clin. Chem. 33: 753–756, 1987.
34. Simpson, G. Accuracy and precision of breath-alcohol measurements for a random subject in the postabsorptive state. Clin. Chem. 33: 261–268, 1987.
35. Slemeyer, A. An analytical model describing the exchange processes of alcohol in the respiratory system. In: Alcohol Drugs

and Traffic Safety, L. Goldberg, Edl, Almqvist and Wiksell International. pp. 456–468, 1981.

36. Tsu, M., A. Babb, D. Ralph and M. Hlastala. Dynamics of heat, water and soluble gas exchange in the human airways: I. A model study. Ann. Biomed. Eng. 16: 547–571, 1988.
37. Tsu, M., A. Babb, E. Sugiyama and M. Hlastala. Dynamics of soluble gas exchange in the airways: II. Effects of breathing conditions. Respirat. Physiol. 83: 261–276, 1991.
38. Wagner, P. Diffusion and chemical reaction in pulmonary gas exchange. Physiol. Rev. 57: 257–312, 1977.
39. Weibel, E. Morphometry of the human lung. Springer-Verlag, Heidelberg, 1963.

The preceding materials from Dr. Hlastala's presentation at the National College for DUI Defense's Third Summer Session at Harvard Law School have since been redrafted and published as an article, titled "The Alcohol Breath Test — a Review," in 84 Journal of the American Physiological Society 401 (February, 1998). Dr. Hlastala began and concluded that article as follows:

> The alcohol breath test (ABT) has been an enigma since it was developed in the 1950s. It has been used for more than 40 years without a clear understanding of the physiological mechanisms involved. A large degree of variability in the measured breath alcohol concentration has led to considerable consternation about the ABT. Substantial effort has gone into justifying the use of the test without regard to the physiological mechanisms involved. Over the past ten years, this understanding has advanced considerably with an infusion of physiological research related to soluble-gas exchange in the lungs. This review focuses primarily on these recent advances. . . .
>
> The theory of the ABT is old and outdated. In principle, the ABT, as currently used, is based on the respiratory physiology of the 1940s and 1950s. The physiological understanding of pulmonary alcohol exchange has gone through a tremendous evolution in the past 50 years, revealing that physiological variability has a great impact on the ABT: It is now clear that most of the variability is due to the physiological parameters that may change from one ABT to the next. Recognition that alcohol exchanges in the airways, rather than in the alveoli, opens up the ABT for a new wave of research to improve the accuracy of BrAC measurement.

§6.1 *Non-Specific Analysis*

> Doubt is not a pleasant condition, but certainty is an absurd one.
>
> VOLTAIRE

One of the major defects in many methods of blood-alcohol analysis is the failure to identify ethanol (also referred to as ethyl alcohol) to the exclusion of all other chemical compounds. To use the terminology of scientists, such methods are not *specific* for ethanol: They will detect other compounds as well, identifying any of them as "ethanol." Thus a client with other compounds in his blood or breath may have a high "blood-alcohol" reading with little or no ethanol in his body.

This problem of nonspecificity is most noticeable in the use of infrared breath analyzing instruments, such as the various Intoxilyzer models, the Intoximeter 3000, and the DataMaster CMI's so-called "state-of-the-art" Intoxilyzer Model 5000 (and its various permutations), the most widely used breath machine in service today, utilizes infrared spectroscopy. Yet infrared analysis is particularly susceptible to giving false readings due to nonspecificity. In fact, the single greatest flaw in the Intoxilyzer itself — and the most productive area for cross-examination — is the machine's inherent lack of specificity. The technical reason for this lack of specificity is that the Intoxilyzer is not designed to detect the molecule of ethyl alcohol (ethanol), but rather only a part of that molecule — the methyl group. In other words, it is the methyl group in the ethyl alcohol compound that is absorbing the infrared light, resulting in the eventual blood-alcohol reading. Thus the machine will "detect" *any* chemical compound and identify it as ethyl alcohol if it contains a methyl group compound within its molecular structure. The Intoxilyzer *assumes* that the methyl group is a part of an ethyl alcohol compound.

The simple fact is that there are numerous compounds that contain the methyl group. Among these are isopropyl alcohol, propane, butane, propylene, methane, ethane, ethyl chloride, acetic acid, butadiene, dimethylether, dimethylamine, and dimethylhydrazine. Acetone and acetaldehyde both contain the methyl group in the structure — and, interestingly, each can be found on the human breath. In fact, recent studies have found that over one hundred chemical compounds can be found on the breath at any given moment in time (see Table 1). More important, approximately 70 to 80 percent of these compounds contain methyl groups. And the infrared breath machine will detect each of these as "ethyl alcohol."

To make matters worse, the machine detects alcohol through "additive absorption." In other words, the more methyl groups the instrument detects by their absorbing the infrared energy, the higher will be the blood-alcohol reading. Thus all of the nonalcoholic compounds on the breath will have a *cumulative* effect — that is, the errors will be added one on top of another.

To approach this problem of specificity from another angle, ethanol has a peak absorption at approximately 3.39 microns, with the band of absorption declining rapidly on each side. However, ethanol has wide absorption bands and peaks at other wavelengths as well, such as bands in the 7.25, 9.5, and 11.0 micron range. Yet the Intoxilyzer screens out these wavelengths and attempts to identify the substance, ethanol, on the basis of only one, two, or three bands, depending on the model. This reduces the efficiency of the Intoxilyzer, since other elements besides ethanol absorb in these ranges, but few, if any, of them would also absorb in the 7.25, 9.5, and 11.0 micron ranges.

To make this point conceptually simpler, the analogy of fingerprint identification has been used. Ethanol has a "fingerprint" in that it will absorb energy wavelengths of roughly 3.39, 7.25, 9.5, and 11.0 microns. While many other substances have fingerprints that will include the 3.39 range or the 7.25 range or the 11.0 range, probably none of them will have all of them — that is, the full print of ethanol. By fingerprint analogy, then, absorption of light wavelengths at about 3.39 microns represents a single "point of identity"; absorption at several bands would represent more points of identity.

Certainly, fingerprint identification is considered more positive because there are many points of identity, and, conversely, availability of only one, two, or three points of identity in finger printing would preclude an expert's opinion as to similarity. Yet the Intoxilyzer attempts to identify a substance on the basis of one, two, or three points of identity, despite the availability of other points that would exclude all substances other than ethyl alcohol.

How prevalent are chemicals in the breath that can register on breath analyzing machines as ethanol? There have been a num-

TABLE 1
Normal Composite Compositional Profile of Human Expired Air

1. Acetone
2. Isoprene
3. Acetonitrile
4. p-Tolualdehyde
5. Toluene
6. 2,3-Dimethylhexane
7. Ethyl alcohol
8. Acetaldehyde
9. Dichloronitromethane
10. 2,2,4-Trimethyl-1-pentanol
11. n-Propyl acetate
12. 2,2-Dimethyl-1-pentanol
13. Cyclohexane
14. Hexane
15. Thiolacetic acid
16. 1-Heptanol
17. Cyclohexyl alcohol
18. Benzene
19. 2-Ethyl-1-hexanone
20. 2,3,5 Trimethylhexane
21. Ethyl 3-mercaptopropionate
22. Cycloheptatriene
23. p-Xylene
24. n-Butyl alcohol
25. 3,4 Dimethylhexane
26. Limonene
27. Isooctyl alcohol
28. Methyl-n-propyl sulfide
29. 2-Ethyl-4-methyl-1-pentanol
30. Neopentyl acetate
31. Trans-4-nonenal
32. n-Heptane
33. Ethylbenzene
34. 5-methyl-4-heptanone
35. Dimethyl sulfide
36. 2-Methyl-1-pentanol
37. p-Dichlorobenzene
38. Trans-3-hexen-1-ol
39. Capryl alcohol
40. Mesitylene
41. n-Hexylmercaptan
42. 3,4-Dimethylheptane
43. 2,3,3,4-Tetramethylpentane
44. 1-Chlorohexane
45. Dichloroacetylene
46. 2,2-Dimethyl-1-octanol
47. 2,2,3,3-Tetramethylhexane
48. o-Xylene
49. 2,3,3-Trimethylhexane
50. Isopropyl alcohol
51. 2,2-Dimethyl-1-hexanol
52. 2-Ethyl-1-butanol
53. 2,2-Dimethylheptane
54. Furan
55. Naphthalene
56. Thiocyclopentane
57. Cyclopentyl alcohol
58. n-Nonane
59. Ethyl phenyl acetate
60. n-Amyl alcohol
61. 2,4-Dimethylheptane
62. 2-Nitropropane
63. 2,6-Di-tert-butyl-4-methyl-phenol
64. Methyl-tert-butyl-ketone
65. Di-Tert-butyldisulfide
66. 2,2-Dimethyl-3-hexanone
67. 1,2-Diethylbenzene
68. 2,5-Dimethylheptane
69. 2-Methyl-3-heptanone
70. Isobutyl alcohol
71. m-Xylene
72. 2,2,5,5-Tetramethylhexane
73. n-Decanal
74. 3-Methyl-2-butanol
75. Propiophenone
76. Ethyl acetate
77. n-Decane
78. Isopropylbenzene
79. 3-Ethylpentane
80. Di-n-Butylamine
81. N-Dodecane
82. o-Dichlorobenzene
83. Allyl acetate
84. 3,3-Diethylpentane
85. n-Butyl acetoacetate
86. Benzylamine
87. Indene
88. Methylnaphthalene
89. 2-Methyl-3-pentanone
90. Coumarin
91. Phenylacetic acid
92. Ethyl valerate
93. 5-methyl-3-heptanone
94. n-Octane
95. Cumic alcohol
96. Methanol
97. 2,4-Dimethyl-3-hexanone
98. Octylacetate
99. Cycloheptadiene
100. 2-Methyl-1-octene
101. Ethyl-2-methylvalerate
102. o-Nitrotoluene

ber of recognized studies on the existence of chemical compounds on the breath — all concluding that a wide variety of compounds exists, including compounds containing the methyl group. The results of one such study are found in an article by Conkle, Camp, and Welch entitled Trace Composition of Human Respiratory Gas, 30 Archives of Environmental Health 290 (1975). The researchers analyzed the breath of eight test subjects, and found "the presence of 69 different compounds in the expired air of eight men." Id. at 292. Another article, by Krotoszynski, Gabriel and O'Neill, Characterization of Human Expired Air: A Promising Investigative and Diagnostic Technique, 15 Journal of Chromatographic Science 240 (1977), described analysis of air samples taken from 28 "average" human subjects. This study found that the "combined expired air comprises at least 102 various organic compounds of endogenous and exogenous origin." Id. at 244. The researchers further concluded that "40% of the constituents (70% of the mean organic contents) are common to 76% of the population studied." Id. at 244. Finally, Canadian scientists have reported that "approximately 200 compounds have been detected in the human breath." Manolis, The Diagnostic Potential of Breath Analysis, 29(1) Clinical Chemistry 5 (1983).

Potential sources of interference with breath-alcohol analysis seem almost limitless. Phil Price, a nationally prominent DUI attorney in Montgomery, Alabama, conducted a series of experiments in which subjects ingested various foods and were then tested on an Intoxilyzer 5000 (64-series). Interestingly, *bread* caused the highest readings! Using alcohol-free subjects, Price consistently obtained readings in the area of .05 percent after consumption of various types of bread products. Further, the slope detector failed to detect any interferent during the tests.

Price suggests that "bread testing may turn out to be an effective, inexpensive courtroom demonstration." The issue posed to the jury: "What weight do you give the test in this case done on a machine that tests positive on a mere bite of hot dog bun?"

Camphor, found in certain types of snuff and chewing tobacco, is yet another example of a common chemical compound that will be detected as ethyl alcohol by the nonspecific breath machines. In view of the widespread existence of interfering substances, counsel should certainly question the DUI client carefully concerning his environment, physical condition, and eating habits.

§6.1.1 Interferents on the Breath: Acetone and Acetaldehyde

Acetone is a primary example of an organic compound that is commonly found on the breath of perfectly normal, healthy individuals. Yet, acetone is one of the compounds that will be detected on many breath analyzing instruments as ethanol. In the Intoxilyzer, for example, it is detected because acetone absorbs infrared energy in the 3.38 to 3.40 micron range — the same range where ethanol is found. Therefore, if acetone were introduced into the Intoxilyzer, the machine would simply register the presence of alcohol despite its absence. If an individual had 525 micrograms per liter of acetone in the breath, he would register a blood-alcohol level of .02 to .03 percent. Thus, if an individual with a true blood-alcohol level of .08 percent had that amount of acetone, the Intoxilyzer would register in the area of .10 to .11 percent.

Counsel may encounter a prosecution expert witness who will testify that acetone is present in such small amounts that the impact on the blood-alcohol reading on a breath machine will be minimal. Another version of this testimony is that acetone present in the amounts required to reach unlawful BAC levels would be lethal. Usually, this "expert" is drawing his conclusion based upon a false presumption that the blood-air partition ratios are the same for both ethanol (ethyl alcohol) and acetone. In fact, however, the partition ratio for acetone is far less than for ethanol. The level for alcohol, used by the machine's computer, is 1:2100; the partition coefficient for acetone is only 1:275. Thus, an equivalent amount of acetone will have a far greater impact on the machine's reading than will ethanol.

The National Highway Traffic Safety Administration has published a report entitled The Likelihood of Acetone Interference in Breath Alcohol Measurement (DOT HS-806-922). The report basically summarizes scientific literature on the subject, concluding that normal individuals have insignificant levels of acetone on their breath. The data indicated, however, that *dieters* can have higher levels and that diabetics not in control of their blood-sugar had levels hundreds or even thousands of times higher than normal. Unfortunately, the authors did not determine what effect such levels would have on a breath testing device; they simply concluded that at levels rendering the individual "not too ill to drive," the breath reading would be raised by only .01 to .02 percent. The authors (and it must be recognized that this federal agency has been consistently law-enforcement-oriented, to the point of suppressing unfavorable results of radio frequency interference tests, for example) also conclude that the only instrument significantly affected by acetone interference is the Intoxilyzer 4011A.

By contrast, a more scientific article entitled Excretion of Low-Molecular Weight Volatile Substances in Human Breath: Focus on Endogenous Ethanol, 9 Journal of Analytical Toxicology 246 (1985), has concluded that acetone can exist in some normal individuals in quantities that can create falsely high results in a breath-alcohol test.

For a study confirming the effects of increased levels of acetone in dieters, see Frank and Flores, The Likelihood of Acetone Interference in Breath Alcohol Measurement, 3 Alcohol, Drugs and Driving 1 (1987). In that study, researchers found that fasting can increase acetone to levels sufficient to obtain readings of .06 percent on breath testing instruments.

Another major source of nonspecific detection in various methods of blood-alcohol analysis involves the presence in the body of *acetaldehyde.* Acetaldehyde is a chemical by-product in the body's metabolism of ethanol. As the ethanol is oxidized, or "burned off," acetaldehyde is produced; eventually, the acetaldehyde is converted to carbon dioxide and water.

This oxidation of alcohol with its attendant production of acetaldehyde takes place primarily in the liver. However, it can also occur in other tissues and fluids of the body — most notably in the lungs. And, since acetaldehyde, like acetone, will be "detected" as ethanol in many types of analysis, a falsely high blood-alcohol reading can result. This nonspecific detection of acetaldehyde in the breath is particularly noticeable in infrared spectroscopy, "wet chemical" analysis, and blood analysis using the oxidation technique.

In the past, this production of acetaldehyde has not been

seen to be a problem. When acetaldehyde is produced in the liver, it is sent into the blood and then into the lungs in small quantities. More recently, however, it has been discovered that alcohol is metabolized — and acetaldehyde produced — *in the lungs themselves.* The result can be a highly elevated amount of acetaldehyde in the lungs, with a subsequently large amount in the expired breath to register in a breath analyzing instrument as ethanol. The blood-air coefficient for acetaldehyde, incidentally, is even less than for acetone: 1:189.

This phenomenon of production of acetaldehyde in the lungs was commented on in a study by Jauhanen, Baraona, Hiyakawa, and Lieber entitled Origin of Breath Acetaldehyde During Ethanol Oxidation: Effect of Long-Term Cigarette Smoking, 100 Journal of Laboratory Clinical Medicine 908 (1982). The researchers discovered that the amount of acetaldehyde in the lungs was considerably greater than the amount that would be expected if passed from the liver by way of the blood into the lungs. Furthermore, the elevated amounts of acetaldehyde in the lungs were not predictable — they varied according to the individual. Thus, for example, it was found that acetaldehyde concentrations in the lungs were far greater for smokers than for nonsmokers. Translated into practical effect, smokers are more likely to have high blood-alcohol readings, regardless of their true blood-alcohol level.

In a subsequent study, it was found that breath acetaldehyde levels were found to indicate blood-alcohol levels 30 times higher than would be expected from direct blood analysis. Stowell, et al., A Reinvestigation of the Usefulness of Breath Analysis in the Determination of Blood Acetaldehyde Concentration, 8(5) Alcoholism: Clinical and Experimental Research 442 (1984). The conclusion of the researchers was, again, that the acetaldehyde in the lungs was not coming from the liver by way of the blood, but was being produced in the lungs themselves and exhaled in much larger quantities than would be expected. End result: falsely high breath test readings.

Another example of variances in acetaldehyde levels that can compound blood-alcohol analysis was reported by researchers studying alcoholics. In Lindros, et al., Elevated Blood Acetaldehyde in Alcoholics and Accelerated Ethanol Elimination, 13 (Supp. 1) Pharmacology, Biochemistry and Behavior 119 (1980), scientists discovered that acetaldehyde in the breath and blood of alcoholics was 5 to 55 times higher than that in nonalcoholics. Thus increased acetaldehyde — and consequent falsely high blood-alcohol readings — can be attributed to the makeup of the alcoholic's physiology. Of course, counsel should consider the risks in bringing this information out for the jury to ponder.

Thus it clearly appears that acetaldehyde is produced in the lungs themselves. With this elevated level of acetaldehyde in the lungs, there will be elevated levels in the breath. And apparently every breath analyzing device but those employing gas chromatography is fully capable of registering this compound as ethanol. Further, blood tests utilizing the process of oxidation reaction with potassium dichromate can be affected by acetaldehyde.

In their latest advertisements for the Intoxilyzer Model 5000, the manufacturer lists an acetaldehyde detector as a new option. In developing this option, the manufacturer has clearly acknowledged the often-denied problem of acetaldehyde interference. Whether the device is effective is, of course, another matter. Certainly, counsel confronted with a case involving the Model 5000 should determine whether the option was present; if not, that fact should be pointed out to the jury. In fact, the existence of such a device in this "state-of-the-art" instrument should be interesting to a jury in DUI cases involving *any* type of breath testing apparatus.

It is also interesting to note that the commonly observed symptoms of flushed face and bloodshot eyes are physiologically the result of the effects of acetaldehyde — not of alcohol itself. Thus such symptoms may actually tend to corroborate the falsity of a blood-alcohol test — that is, elevated acetaldehyde evidenced by a flushed face and bloodshot eyes may have caused the high breath test reading!

§6.1.2 Interferents on the Breath: Industrial Compounds

As has been discussed in previous sections, there are literally thousands of chemical compounds existing in the work and home environment that contain the methyl group — and, therefore, which can be inhaled or otherwise absorbed and later register as "ethyl alcohol" on breath machines. This pervasive problem of non-specific analysis was dramatically demonstrated in an interesting study involving an Intoxilyzer 4011-AS, a machine fairly typical of infrared breath-testing devices. In an article appearing in 7(4) Drinking/Driving Newsletter 3 (February 19, 1988), a test conducted by the Demers Laboratory in Springvale, Maine, is described wherein a subject was tested after exposure under realistic field conditions to *paint* and *glue*. The subject entered a test room and applied a pint of contact cement to a piece of plywood; he then applied a gallon of oil-base paint to a vertical surface. This activity lasted about one hour.

Twenty minutes after leaving the room, the subject was tested on the Intoxilyzer. Results? Despite the subject's having no alcohol in his body, the machine registered .12 percent — over the legal limit. The subject was tested again one-half hour later: Readings of .05 and .04 percent were obtained.

Another example of commonly encountered chemical compounds that can affect breath tests was described in a study reported in Giguiere, Lewis, Baselt, and Chang, Lacquer Fumes and the Intoxilyzer, 12 Journal of Analytical Toxicology 168 (1988). Scientists performed tests on a professional painter who was exposed to lacquer fumes under controlled conditions. In the first test, he sprayed paint in a room for 20 minutes, wearing a protective mask; his blood and breath were then tested. Although the blood test showed no presence of alcohol, an Intoxilyzer indicated a reading of .075 percent BAC.

Ten minutes later, the painter sprayed the same room for five minutes — but this time without the protective mask. The blood test again showed no BAC. The Intoxilyzer, however, registered a reading of .48 percent! Perhaps most interesting, the Intoxilyzer was equipped with an acetone detection light designed to detect the presence of any interfering compounds — yet at no time during the test did the light indicate the presence of any such compounds.

A scientific study has concluded that the Intoximeter 3000 and DataMaster are unreliable due to the fact that they only address acetone as a potential interferent. The study states:

> Two instruments using two modes of ethanol detection are the Intoximeter 3000 (3.4 micron infra-red plus Taguchi cell) and the BAC DataMaster (dual wavelength infra-red). These have proved

> unsuitable because acetone appears to be considered the only potential interfering substance. . . . In the selection of two modes of ethanol detection, each system must be chosen such that a comparison of the response from each mode would indicate a wide range of possible interfering substances, not just acetone.

Bell, Attaining Specificity in the Measurement of Ethanol in Breath, 40 Acta Medicinae Legalis et Socialis 107 (1990).

Toluene presents a particularly troublesome problem in breath-alcohol analysis for four reasons:

1. It is commonly encountered, as it is found in a wide range of industrial products (paints, thinner, cleaning solvents, petroleum products, etc.);
2. inhaled toluene can be retained in the membranes of the throat and lungs for up to three weeks;
3. toluene contains the methyl group in its molecular structure and therefore will be "detected" by any infrared breath machine (e.g., Intoxilyzers, Intoximeters, and Datamasters) as alcohol; and
4. toluene has a partition ratio of 7:1, rather than alcohol's 2100:1, and so a much greater volume of solvents, paint fumes, etc., will pass through the lungs and into the breath machine's sample chamber (roughly 300 times more will reach the machine than an equivalent amount of alcohol in the body). Counsel should confront the state's expert with this fact if he testifies that toxic amounts of toluene would be required to raise the BAC to significant levels.

In an article appearing on the front page of the August 24, 1988, edition of the Spokane Spokesman-Review, an individual in a Sandpoint, Idaho, jail awaiting trial for drunk driving claimed that he had been siphoning gasoline; when he sucked on the hose, he swallowed some of the gasoline, which later caused a high reading on a breath test. He managed to talk the sheriff into a demonstration to prove his story. Taken from his cell after one week of incarceration, he swallowed a cup of unleaded gasoline; after various periods of time, he blew into an Intoximeter.

The results? After 5 minutes, the reading was .00 percent; after 10 minutes, .04 percent; after 20 minutes, the machine registered .31 percent; and after one hour, the reading was .28 percent. Three hours after ingestion, the individual still blew a .24 percent on the Intoximeter! A quick call to a gasoline distributor confirmed that gasoline contains no alcohol.

This phenomenon has been scientifically verified in a study conducted by CMI, the manufacturer of the Intoxilyzer, and reported in 8(3) Drinking/Driving Law Letter 6 (1989). The CMI technicians mixed a simulator solution of 800 micrograms of gasoline with 500 milliliters of distilled water, then introduced it into an Intoxilyzer 5000. The solution produced readings of .619 percent, .631 percent, and .635 percent.

Diethyl ether is yet another substance that will be falsely detected as "alcohol" by breath testing instruments. The compound, which can be inhaled, is found in some automotive products and is used in the manufacture of plastics and smokeless gunpowder. See Bell, et al., Diethyl Ether Interference with Infrared Breath Analysis, 16 Journal of Analytical Toxicology (1992), for a study that concluded that "[t]he possibility of interference with an alcohol reading by ether or by other substances may therefore render prosecution more difficult, if not impossible."

In another study, researchers discovered that three other compounds found in common products falsely registered as ethyl alcohol on the machines. Cowan, et al., The Response of the Intoxilyzer 4011AS-A to a Number of Possible Interfering Substances, 35(4) Journal of Forensic Sciences 797 (1990). One of the substances, methyl ethyl ketone, is used in lacquers, paint removers, cements and adhesives, celluloid, and cleaning fluids. Another, toluene, is used in paints, lacquers, varnishes, and glues. The third is isopropanol, commonly known as rubbing alcohol.

The home environment is not without potential sources of interfering compounds. The burning of candles, incense, and oil lamps, for example, can create compounds in the air containing the methyl group — compounds that can be inhaled and even days later register on non-specific breath machines as "alcohol." According to an article in *Emagazine* (Nov./Dec. 1998), candles can emit acetone, benzene, lead, soot, and other pollutants. Testing conducted by the Bailey Engineering Corporation revealed that aromatic candles release "significant quantities of volatile organic compounds, and that the core wicks were made of lead," resulting in an increasingly serious problem called "black soot deposition.'' ''We've had at least two people who talked about waking up with a black ring around their nostrils,'' said a representative of Bailey. A spokesman for the National Association of Home Builders' Research Center reported that candles and other indoor combustible materials, including incense, potpourri, and oil lamps, are the prime suspects. An NAHB bulletin warned, ''Since seven out of ten homes burn candles on a regular basis, according to a study done by Smith and Kline, this issue is extremely far-reaching and has the potential for affecting millions of homes.''

As was discussed in the previous subsection, counsel may encounter a prosecution expert witness who will testify that commonly encountered interferents are present in such small amounts that the impact on the blood-alcohol reading on a breath machine will be minimal. Another version of this testimony is that such chemical compounds present in the amounts required to reach unlawful BAC levels would constitute lethal doses. Usually, this ''expert'' is drawing his conclusion based upon a false presumption that the blood-air partition ratios are the same for all compounds, including ethanol (ethyl alcohol). In fact, however, the partition ratio for industrial chemicals is usually far different than for ethanol. The ratio for alcohol, used by the machine's computer in analyzing any substance, is 1:2100. Consider, however, the following examples of partition coefficients for commonly inhaled industrial compounds:

Ethylene	0.14:1
Nitrous oxide	0.468:1
Toluene	5.5:1
Diethyl ether	15.2:1
Acetonitrile	578:1
Isopropanol	1671:1

Thus, an equivalent amount of an industrial chemical will have a far greater impact on the machine's reading than will ethanol.

§6.1.3 The Diabetic Client

Among the questions counsel should ask a new client is ''Are you a diabetic?'' As has been stated repeatedly in this text, the accuracy of blood-alcohol analysis — particularly analysis of breath samples — is entirely dependent upon the assumption that the subject is a normal, average, and healthy individual. In fact, very few such animals exist. But there are certain physiological conditions that are uniquely suited to creating false BAC readings. Diabetes is perhaps one of the more insidious — and common — of these.

Insulin is an enzyme inhibitor that is needed for the digestive system to break foods down into the basic nutrients for absorption into the body. In a normal person, the pancreas regulates the body's blood glucose (sugar) level by producing this insulin to keep it within the normal range of 90 to 120 mg/dl. Without sufficient insulin, the body would simply starve to death from lack of nutrients. And this is essentially what happens with diabetes (absent insulin therapy).

Diabetes is found in two versions. Type 1, known as "juvenile onset," is the more serious form and occurs when the pancreas does not produce insulin. Type 2, known as "adult onset," is triggered when the insulin produced by the pancreas is not produced or utilized correctly. Type 1 diabetes is always treated with insulin — either with injections or pump therapy. Type 2 is treated with diet, exercise, and, if necessary, insulin.

If the client is a diabetic, then there may be at least four separate consequences in terms of blood-alcohol analysis in a drunk driving investigation. First, the client may have been in a state of *ketoacidosis.* When the diabetic's blood sugar rises — usually about 250 mg/dl or higher — the body is unable to use carbohydrates as a source of fuel. Instead, the body tries to burn the stored fat as an alternative fuel source and, to do this, produces *ketones.* Perhaps gradually and over a period of days, the symptoms of diabetic ketoacidosis appear: drowsiness, flushed face, thirst, and loss of energy and appetite; more severe symptoms include rapid pulse and heavy breathing.

The first possible consequence of diabetes, then, is that the client's physiological condition may be emulating the outward signs of intoxication to a police officer: lethargy, flush face, drowsiness, impaired coordination, dulled mental alertness. Add to this the fact that ketones (and, as will be discussed, acetones) on the breath will cause a distinctive "bad breath," which can be confused with the ever-present "odor of alcohol on the breath."

Second, ketones on the breath will register as ethyl alcohol on most breath machines — at least, those that employ infrared analysis. The reason for this, as explained in §6.1, is that these machines are *non-specific:* They will register any of thousands of chemical compounds whose molecular structure is compatable with their infrared filters. Further, machines armed with so-called "interferent detectors" are usually ineffective in detecting ketones; most are designed to detect either acetone or acetaldehyde. Thus, a diabetic may produce a falsely high blood-alcohol reading.

Third, elevated levels of *acetone* on the breath can be found in diabetics (and in persons on diets associated with weight reduction of about one-half pound per week). Manolis, The Diagnostic Potential of Breath Analysis, 29(1) Clinical Chemistry 5 (1983). Again, acetone will both increase breath machine readings and possibly cause false symptoms of intoxication. A study confirming the effects of acetone in diabetics can be found in Mormann, Olsen, Sakshaug, and Morland, Measurement of Ethanol by Alkomat Breath Analyzer; Chemical Specificity and the Influence of Lung Function, Breath Technique and Environmental Temperature, 25 Blutalkohol 153 (1988). Diabetic subjects in that study also were found to have acetone levels sufficient to produce breath-alcohol readings of .06 percent.

Another study has confirmed that diabetics may give false indications of intoxication. In Brick, Diabetes, Breath Acetone and Breathalyzer Accuracy: A Case Study, 9(1) Alcohol, Drugs and Driving (1993), a researcher found that expired ketones in the breath of an untreated diabetic can contribute to erroneously high breath-alcohol readings. Further, the acetone on the breath from ketoacidosis will result in an odor of alcohol. Finally, behavioral patterns of a diabetic whose blood-sugar level has dropped will include slurred speech, slow gait, impaired motor control.

Fourth, any attempts at retrograde extrapolation — projecting BAC levels backwards to time of driving (see §5.2) — may be rendered even more unreliable in the case of a diabetic subject. This is simply because insulin increases the rate of oxidation (burnoff) of alcohol. Goodman and Goodman, The Pharmacological Basis of Therapeutics 535 (6th edition 1980).

§6.2 *Mouth Alcohol*

> Truth, like light, blinds. Falsehood, on the contrary, is a beautiful twilight that enhances every object.
>
> ALBERT CAMUS

One of the most prevalent causes of error in breath-alcohol analysis is the presence of alcohol in the mouth. This alcohol can contaminate the expired breath captured by the machine and elevate the test results radically. The machine's computer is assuming, of course, that the sample is 100 percent alveolar air from the lungs and is, in effect, multiplying it by 2100 (see discussion of partition ratio in §6.0.1) to obtain a blood-alcohol concentration. Thus the presence of even a tiny amount of undigested alcohol in the mouth can have a disproportionate impact on the reading.

One method of illustrating for a jury the effect of seemingly insignificant amounts of mouth alcohol is through the use of a 55-gallon drum and an eyedropper. A 55-gallon drum represents about the same capacity as 210 liters of breath — the volume used in determining breath-blood analysis. The eyedropper can contain, say, .10 grams of a dark (for visibility) liquid. During examination or argument, counsel can demonstrate for the jury how the tiny amount of alcohol can cause a "guilty" reading in the breath machine. Then the jury can be told (or possibly shown through another exhibit) how much smaller than a 55-gallon drum the defendant's breath sample was — and how infinitesimal an amount of mouth alcohol can be and still have a significant impact on the reading.

Mouth alcohol can exist in a number of ways. The most common situation occurs when the subject burps, belches, hiccups, or regurgitates within 15 or 20 minutes before being tested. This causes alcohol still in the stomach to rise up into the soft tissue of the esophagus and mouth, where it will stay until it has dissipated after that period of time. Any expired breath captured by a breath testing device will contain some of this undigested alcohol — and will cause the device to give a falsely high reading.

This phenomenon has been recognized by the American Medical Association's Committee on Medical Problems, in its Manual for Chemical Tests for Intoxication (1959): "True reactions with alcohol in expired breath from sources other than the alveolar air (eructation, regurgitation, vomiting) will, of course, vitiate the breath alcohol results. . . .'' And see Caddy, Sobell, and Sobell, Alcohol Breath Tests: Criterion Times for Avoiding Contamination by ''Mouth Alcohol,'' 10(6) Behavior Research Methods & Instrumentation 814–818 (1978), where the authors conclude that when a subject is given ethyl alcohol in concentrations ranging from 4 percent to over 95 percent, the time for total dissipation of the mouth alcohol ranged from 10 to 19 minutes.

To avoid this problem, police officers are usually instructed to watch the arrestee carefully for 15 or 20 minutes before testing him to ensure that he does not burp, belch, hiccup, or regurgitate; the machine's ''checklist'' will probably reflect this observation period as a required step. Failure to keep the arrestee under constant surveillance for the required time period can be grounds for suppression of the test results. Certainly, it opens the door during cross-examination for raising the issue of mouth alcohol.

As every experienced DUI lawyer knows, however, the officer rarely performs the required observation in the often-confused scene of arrest, booking, report writing, and setting up of the machine. And, as every experienced DUI lawyer knows, the officer will almost always testify that he *did* keep the individual under constant surveillance.

An effective approach in cross-examining the testing officer on this issue is to first establish what tasks he was performing during the 15 to 20 minute pre-test period. Usually, he is filling out arrest reports, reading and checking off the machine's checklist, and setting up the machine for the test (entering data into the machine's computer, noting the temperature, running the simulator solution test, recording the air blank, etc.). It is then a simple process of developing that he *could not* have watched the defendant continuously during the required period. Adding icing to the cake, it can often be brought out that this was done with the officer's head down while reading or writing, or with his back to the defendant. For a discussion of techniques for cross-examining the officer/operator concerning the 15- or 20-minute observation period preceding the breath test, see §13.1.

Mouth alcohol can also exist where substances containing alcohol have been ingested and still remain in the oral cavity or tissue of the esophagus. One reason may be that a recently consumed alcoholic beverage has not yet dissipated from the oral tissue, or because it has been captured in dentures. Or it may be caused by products such as cough syrup, mouthwash, or breath freshener, most of which contain alcohol (interestingly, breath fresheners are often used by apprehensive drivers being stopped by police).

The existence of dentures in a client's mouth at the time of breath-alcohol analysis can significantly elevate the results. The dentures can trap alcohol, causing vapors to be breathed directly into the instrument. This problem was recently investigated in a study conducted by the Colorado Department of Health and reported in 6(11) Drinking/Driving Law Letter 5 (May 29, 1987). In that study the state agency placed a wafer-style dental adhesive called Sea-Bond (Combe, Inc., White Plains, NY) into a subject's mouth and then had him drink approximately eight milliliters of a 50-percent ethyl alcohol and water solution. He was then tested on an infrared breath testing device and retested every five minutes for three-quarters of an hour. The results: He had an immediate reading of .480 percent — indicating a BAC level that would cause death in many individuals. The .480 percent reading was repeated at the five- and ten-minute tests; the BAC level dropped to .425 percent after 15 minutes, and .314 percent after 20. The subject was still registering .112 percent after 35 minutes — indicating a BAC level in excess of statutory limits, despite his having actually consumed an insignificant amount of alcohol.

As a result of the study, the department of health issued an advisory to the state's breath test operators to the effect that dental adhesives were to be considered a foreign object and that dentures were to be removed prior to any evidentiary testing.

An article entitled "Breath-Alcohol Concentration May Not Always Reflect the Concentration of Alcohol in Blood," 18 Journal of Analytical Toxicology 225 (July/Aug. 1994), focuses entirely on the case of a 37-year-old man who consistently recorded levels twice the legal limit on an Intoximeter 3000 — but who had an actual blood-alcohol concentration below the legal limit. The researchers conducted studies on the man in their laboratory and corroborated erroneous readings. Although they could not give an explanation, "it was noted that the subject had had extensive dental work carried out, involving three bridges . . . A forensic odontologist . . . expressed the view that a reservoir of alcohol might be retained within the spaces occupied by these bridges and that this might be a possible explanation for the excessively high breath-alcohol reading observed . . .''

Another possible source of alcohol trapped in the mouth is periodontal disease. This problem commonly creates cavities between the gums and the teeth. These pockets can easily collect and retain alcohol — which is later breathed into the breath machine.

If a client has used a cough syrup, mouthwash, or breath spray that may have still been present — even in minute quantities — when he took the breath test, the dramatic effects of this on the machine should, of course, be brought out for the jury.

It is often of considerable interest to jurors that such products *do* contain alcohol — and in amounts larger than would be assumed. Counsel should obtain a sample of the product consumed by the client and offer it — including the label with its contents — into evidence. If the label does not contain the actual percentage of alcohol in the listing of ingredients, counsel might wish to contact the manufacturer or have the product analyzed.

By way of illustration, the following is a list of some of the more popular products and their alcohol content:

Product	*Percentage of Alcohol*
Mouthwash	
Astring-O-Sol	76
Cepacol (regular)	14
Close-Up	14.5
Listerine	27
Listermint	6.5
Plax	7.5
Scope (original mint)	19
Signal	14.5
Throat spray	
Chloraseptic (original mint)	19
N'ICE (mint)	26
Sucrets (cherry)	12

Cough/cold remedies	
Comtrex Liquid	20
Contac Nighttime	25
Dimetapp DM	2.3
Nyquil	25
Robitussin	3.5
Triaminic Expectorant	5
Tylenol Multi-Symptom	7
Vicks Formula 44M	20
Vicks Formula 44	10

In order to determine the possible effects of mouthwash products on breath testing devices, an independent research company, Consumer Product Testing Service, Inc., evaluated the effect of Listerine mouthwash on a CMI Intoxilyzer (the study did not specify which model of Intoxilyzer was used). The results were reported in an article entitled Sobriety Testing: Intoxilyzers and Listerine Antiseptic, Feeney, et al., The Police Chief 70 (July 1985).

Seven individuals were tested on an Intoxilyzer at a police station, with readings of .00 percent. Each then rinsed his mouth with 20 milliliters of Listerine mouthwash for 30 seconds in accordance with directions on the label. All seven were then tested at intervals of one, three, five, and ten minutes.

The results indicated an average reading of .43 percent BAC at one minute — indicating a blood-alcohol level approaching lethal proportions. After three minutes, the average level was still .20 percent, despite the absence of any alcohol in the system. Even after five minutes, the average level was .11 percent — in excess of the amount designated by statutes. Although the average level fell to .01 percent after fully ten minutes, one of the seven subjects still registered a .03 percent.

In another interesting study, reported in 8(22) Drinking/Driving Law Letter 1 (October 27, 1989), a scientist tested the effects of Binaca breath spray on an Intoxilyzer 5000. A total of 23 tests were performed with varying amounts of Binaca (which contains alcohol) sprayed into the mouth and throat. In each case, an elevated blood-alcohol reading was obtained on the machine — varying from a low of .034 percent to as high as a "lethal'' level of .811 percent. The scientist also noted that the effects of the spray did not fall below detectable levels until after 18 minutes.

§6.2.1 Burping: The Pre-Test Observation Period

It is critical that the suspect be under constant observation for the 15 or 20 minutes immediately preceding his production of a breath sample. This is to ensure that there has been no burping, belching, regurgitation, or smoking, and that the residue from any pre-existing burping, for example, has had time to dissipate from the mouth and throat. This is such a critical prerequisite that foundational law may require it, the manufacturer's manuals stress its importance (regardless of the existence of any so-called mouth alcohol detectors), and law enforcement manuals and checklists always mandate it. Nevertheless, as mentioned in the text, it is common for operators to ignore this step — and swear that they complied with the requirement.

James Farragher Campbell of San Francisco, one of the premier DUI attorneys in California, offers the following insightful suggestions on cross-examining the officer and/or operator in this area. The author is grateful to Mr. Campbell for consenting to the reproduction of these materials.

> Under the best of conditions the collection of the breath sample by law enforcement in a DUI arrest can result in erroneous readings. Under the average situation erroneous readings are normal; and under the conditions that can occur in law enforcement breath collection encouraged by failure to correct poor performance, the collection process is a disaster.
>
> Under the best conditions the breath testing device will have been selected and checked for accuracy following the state's accepted scientific protocol. The machine will have to have been maintained in good working order and this ensured by repeated and regular calibration and maintenance checks. These inspections will have to have been performed by a licensed criminalist or toxicologist as called for under controlling state law.
>
> In collecting the breath sample the testing operator, who is usually the arresting officer, must strictly adhere to the manufacturer's instructions, and those received in the officer's ''certifica-

tion'' program. TO THE EXTENT THESE INSTRUCTIONS AND PROTOCOL ARE FOLLOWED DICTATES THE EXTENT THAT THE BREATH TEST CAN EVEN BEGIN TO BE CONSIDERED RELIABLE. Any failure to do so is an open door for attack by the defense. We will examine in the lecture, demonstrations and class discussion how these failures on the part of the testing operator can be turned into weapons for the defense. Be mindful that it is of course axiomatic that the extent to which the sample collection and testing standards are followed is the extent to which the limitation on the breath value can be relied upon. The operating officer's actual credentials, his/her training record, the equipment's maintenance records, repair records and regular calibration records should all be obtained, examined, and if viable, called into question by the defense.

Most states have developed minimum efficiency standards for technicians assigned to perform tests on human body fluids (blood and urine) to determine their alcohol content. These technicians are required to pass forensic laboratory standards; and, almost all of these individuals have at least a bachelor's of science degree. Yet when it comes to the breath test, the state is content to leave this testing up to the cop on the beat. An officer who probably had no more than a few hours of training. No real competence is required to operate the intoxilyzer. Any 12-year-old child who can read could administer the test. Also, keep in mind that the operator, who is usually the arresting officer, has a vested interest in the outcome of the test; which is very unlike the lab technician testing the blood or urine sample.

The sample collection is the very first step in the testing process and the only part of the testing process in which the arresting or operating officer will be involved. The very first part of that testing process, where the breath sample will be collected, is the required observation period by the operator of the test subject.

The logical place to examine your breath test results will begin therefore with the 15-minute, or in some states the 20-minute, observation period. This same observation period also provides the defense with its first opportunity to begin an attack on the breath results.

WHY IS THE 15-MINUTE OBSERVATION PERIOD SO IMPORTANT IN EVALUATING THE VALIDITY OF THE BREATH TEST?

Virtually all breath testing machines have recognized that no matter how accurate they claim to be, a false and misleading reading can occur if the machine receives a contaminated sample for testing. How can the sample become contaminated? The easiest way is mouth contamination. How is it detected? First and probably foremost by the test administrator by simply observing the test subject for the required time. In most cases this is prescribed by law to be 15 minutes prior to and continuously up to the time of the test. Why? So that the test subject does not put anything in their mouth, vomit, or regurgitate. Anything that was or is in the stomach can and will contain alcohol molecules which are not the alcohol molecules that the machine is designed to properly test.

The time frame for which the test subject is to be observed has changed over the years, and from state to state. Some require twenty (20) minutes, others require 15 minutes, of continuous observation time prior to the first test sample being blown into the machine. California's Title 17, which regulates the proper administration of breath testing, is illustrative of the normal pattern requirements on the observation period.

> Section 1219.3 BREATH COLLECTION.
>
> A breath sample shall be expired breath which is essentially alveolar in composition. The quantity of the breath sample shall be established by direct volumetric measurement. *The breath sample shall be collected only after the subject has been under continuous observation for at least fifteen minutes prior to collection of the breath sample,* during which time the subject must not have ingested alcoholic beverages or other fluids, regurgitated, vomited, eaten, or smoked [emphasis added].

Why is there a difference if this is a scientific principle? Why does the time frame change from year to year or state to state? Some states have even refused to enact any meaningful regulations to control this obvious scientific problem.

The whole purpose of the observation waiting period is to be sure that no residual alcohol or other contaminates are within the mouth cavity.

Indeed the study that has been conducted by Dr. Michael Hlastala, showing that mouth alcohol contamination may be, and probably is, caused by the alcohol molecules clinging to the trachea and mucous membranes and cilia that trap and sweep minute dust particles upward to the pharynx, is even stronger proof that the observation/waiting period must absolutely be followed; otherwise you have no basis in science to rely on the validity of the breath test result.

Remember, even if the testing officer did not see anything unusual in the time prior to the testing, the waiting period is vital for insuring the accuracy of the test itself.

In some states, unfortunately not the majority, the violation of the observation time period will function as rule of exclusion; while sadly in the majority of the states, a violation will go merely to the weight the jury will give the test result.

Also, remember that a reading of your state's intoxilyzer's operator's manual will require a continuous 15- or 20-minute observation period by the testing officer. If you look at the manual you will note that the operator is told that the mucous lining of the mouth cavity and nasal passages stores alcohol for a period of time even after the alcohol has been consumed. Normal body processes should eliminate the residual mouth alcohol within about 15 minutes. It is therefore required that the operator prior to the breath test observe that the test subject not smoke, eat, or introduce any substance into his or her mouth. If the test operator notices any of the foregoing, he or she is supposed to note the time and start the 15-minute observation period all over again.

Even if you have a valid and clearly defined 15-minute observation period, there still can be substances in the mouth that can trap the alcohol and completely throw off the possibility of eliminating the clearing of all mouth alcohol by simply following the 15-minute observation period. Some of these items are:

1. Tobacco, smoking and/or chewing (the latter is even a better conductor for the retention of the alcohol);
2. Chewing gum;
3. Mouth wash;
4. Dentures;
5. Denture adhesive;
6. Teeth braces and/or other orthodonture work;
7. Food particles, which can remain after a big meal, especially bread, meats, and any other matter that can easily lodge between the teeth;
8. Let your imagination go to work and think of all the thousands of possibilities.

The observation by the arresting officer who does not later perform the breath test does not count; it must be the testing officer. The observation in the back seat by the arresting officer who later administers the breath test also does not count. What kind of real observation is that?

For a discussion of cross-examination of the officer on the pre-test observation period, see §11.6.9.

§6.2.2 Heartburn, Reflux, and Hiatus Hernias

There are many potential sources for mouth-alcohol contamination. One of the more common of these is *acid reflux* — or as it is more commonly known, heartburn. This is usually caused by a medical condition called a *hiatus hernia,* and is often found among elderly, pregnant, and overweight clients. The symptoms can be a painful burning sensation in the chest, sudden regurgitation of acid fluid from the stomach, or belching. The result in a drunk driving case can be a false-high breath-machine reading.

The diaphragm is a sheet of muscle separating the chest from the abdomen. When food or drink goes down the throat (esophagus), it has to pass through an opening (hiatus) in the diaphragm to reach the stomach. There is muscular tissue around the hiatus that acts as a one-way valve to prevent the food/drink from flowing backward. Often, however, this muscle becomes weak and herniates, protruding upwards into the chest and esophagus. In many cases, the muscle is so weakened that the valve is unable to maintain a one-way flow from the esophagus to the stomach. When this happens, acidic fluid and/or gasses from the stomach well up into the esophagus. This process is called acid reflux (heartburn). Severe cases can result in esophageal ulcers.

If belching or acid reflux occurs, of course, any alcohol from the stomach will be reintroduced into the throat and mouth — and, consequently, into the breath machine. And, as has been discussed in §6.2, even a minuscule amount of alcohol introduced directly into the machine will have a hugely disproportionate effect on the blood-alcohol reading.

It should also be noted that alcohol itself (as well as cigarette smoke) can aggravate the symptoms. Acid reflux can also be triggered or exacerbated by stress — e.g., a drunk driving investigation and arrest.

Because of the prevalence of acid reflux, then, counsel should always inquire of his client as to the possibility of this condition. Many clients will not be aware that they suffer from it. They will, however, reply that they were taking Tums or Tagamet for an "upset stomach" or gas. If this has been a chronic problem, there is a good chance the client is suffering from a hiatus hernia.

One final comment: Antacids such as Tums or Tagamet are

designed to neutralize and/or absorb liquids. This can interfere with the normal metabolism of alcohol, thus throwing off the expected absorption rates of the individual — and, consequently, any attempts at retrograde extrapolation (see §5.2).

§6.2.3 The Saliva Effect

It would seem logical that *saliva* would contribute to the mouth-alcohol effect. Saliva is, of course, 98 percent water. And alcohol in the body is evenly distributed through the body's fluids. Thus, if there is alcohol in the blood, it will exist as well in the mouth's saliva: If a subject has a true blood-alcohol concentration of, say, .06 percent, the saliva in his mouth will contain at least .06 percent alcohol. Yet, this .06 percent alcohol solution in the mouth is being breathed directly into the machine — without being "attenuated" by passage through the alveolar sacs of the lungs. In other words, the alcohol in the saliva is being effectively "multiplied" by the computer in the breath machine inappropriately applying the 2100:1 partition ratio (see §6.0.1). Further, this alcohol in the saliva does not dissipate in 15 to 20 minutes, as does alcohol burped up into the mouth from the stomach: It stays in the saliva until eventually eliminated from the entire body.

If mouth alcohol is, in fact, a persistent problem in analyzing a breath sample, then it would seem to follow that rinsing the mouth out before breathing into the machine would reduce or even eliminate the problem. And that is exactly what researchers have discovered. Gaylard, Stambuk, and Morgan, Reductions in Breath Ethanol Readings in Normal Male Volunteers Following Mouth Rinsing with Water at Differing Temperatures, 22 Alcohol and Alcoholism 113 (1987).

In an experiment conducted by researchers at a hospital in London, subjects were kept free of alcohol for 48 hours and then given 0.5 gram of ethanol per kilogram of their body weight. They were then tested every six minutes on a breath testing device — sometimes after a mouth rinse with water and sometimes without a rinse. The scientists found that rinsing consistently reduced the blood-alcohol reading by a "significant" amount. Further, rinsing with cold water reduced the indicated BAC levels about twice as much as rinsing with warm water.

The researchers theorize that rinsing reduces the salivary ethanol concentration by diluting it: "As a result, the concentration of ethanol in the oral cavity is reduced resulting in a decrease in the concentration in the exhaled air, as it passes over the diluted aqueous (saliva) phase." The cooler water has a greater effect because it cools the mouth, thereby reducing the vapor pressure of alcohol in the exhaled breath and causing a reduced BAC reading.

The study would seem to confirm that the presence of mouth alcohol can be a problem in any given test. More disturbingly, it seems to suggest that mouth alcohol may be a problem in *every* breath test — that *all* breath tests are registering falsely high levels because of the presence of breath alcohol.

Finally, if the client arrested for drunk driving was involved in an accident, counsel should consider the possibility that there was *blood in his mouth* or nose at the time of the breath test. This blood may come from internal injuries or, more commonly, from dental injury or a cut in the lip or mouth tissue. But the effect is the same: The blood (and the alcohol in that blood) can enter the machine's mouthpiece, tube, and/or sample chamber. This may be accomplished by the expired breath absorbing some of the blood as it passes from the lungs into the machine, or by the client spraying blood into the tube as he blows. And, of course, the machine will greatly magnify the amount of alcohol in the oral blood since it is applying a 2100:1 partition ratio to convert the "breath" alcohol to blood.

§6.2.4 Food in the Teeth

Phil Price, a nationally known DUI attorney in Montgomery, Alabama, conducted an interesting series of tests with an Intoxilyzer 5000. Without consuming any alcoholic beverages, he submitted himself to repeated breath testing — after eating various types of food. His findings were startling. After eating almost any type of bread product — white loaf bread, donuts, pretzels, pastries, etc. — Mr. Price consistently registered low levels of blood-alcohol on the machine. These levels were commonly around .03 percent, but rose as high as .05 percent. Further, the Intoxilyzer's "slope detector" (mouth-alcohol detector; see §6.2.5) failed to indicate the presence of any alcohol in the mouth. P. Price, Intoxilyzer: A Bread Testing Device?, 15(4) Drinking/Driving Law Letter 52 (1996).

Reacting to the use of this article by defense attorneys in their state, employees at the Washington State Toxicology Laboratory conducted their own studies — this time with a DataMaster. Unfortunately, their research only confirmed Mr. Prices's findings. As reported in Logan and Distefano, Ethanol Content of Various Foods and Soft Drinks and their Potential for Interference with a Breath-Alcohol Test, 22 Journal of Analytical Toxicology 181 (May/June 1998), a variety of breads and soft drinks were tested at the lab and found to contain no alcohol. Alcohol-free subjects then ingested these products and provided breath samples into a DataMaster. The researchers' conclusions:

> We found that, particularly at low concentrations but as high as 0.046 g/210L, mouth alcohol, rather than expiratory breath alcohol, may be reported as apparent true breath alcohol . . .

Further:

> It is evident from these results that the slope detector feature was unable to distinguish mouth-alcohol concentrations at these very low levels.

The state police lab researchers added, however, that "When all three protections, slope detector, duplicate testing, and 15-minute deprivation period, are present, the potential for mouth-alcohol interference from bread or soft drinks is reduced to zero." This, of course, does not follow. First, as the researchers found (and as is discussed in §6.2.5), the slope detector is unreliable — and, as the studies revealed, simply did not work. Second, duplicate testing may result in roughly duplicate results if the source of the mouth alcohol has not changed in the intervening one or two minutes. Third, assuming that there is a pre-test observation period (a fiction in most actual DUI cases), of what value is it if the bread is wedged in the teeth? The researchers were using the 15-minute observation period, which has been found to be sufficient for the elimination of *liquids* from the oral cavity. But what if the source of the alcohol reading is not liquid? What if the source is a solid — one that is notorious for becoming wedged in teeth and stuck to gums?

What causes bread to register on breath machines as alcohol? The theory of the state lab's experts:

> Most baked products with listed contents indicating they contained yeast did in fact have some alcohol present. Alcohol is produced by the fermentation process in yeasts by their action on simple sugars used in preparing the dough. . . . Although most of the alcohol in the dough is lost during the baking process, some is evidently retained in the matrix of the bread. . . .

The researchers noted literature reporting intoxication in dogs eating pizza dough and sourdough. Suter, Presumed Ethanol Intoxication in Sheep Dogs Fed Uncooked Pizza Dough, 69(1) Australian Veterinary Journal 20 (1990); Thrall, et al., Ethanol Toxicosis Secondary to Sourdough Ingestion in a Dog, 184(12) Journal of American Veterinary Medical Association 1513 (1984).

It should be recalled that any levels of alcohol in the mouth will be "read" by the machine using a 1:2100 partition ratio: The machine's computer will assume the alcohol is in an alveolar sample. In other words, it will assume that the alcohol has been greatly attenuated by passage through the metabolic process and will, to put it simplistically, multiply the amount. Thus, even the tiniest amount of alcohol in the mouth will have a vastly disproportionate effect on the final reading.

Counsel should also bear in mind that bread is a very absorbant material. Bread stuck in the teeth or gums may absorb alcohol and hold it in the mouth. Thus, the machine may be getting a double dose of mouth alcohol — that already in the bread and that absorbed — long after any observation period.

§6.2.5 "Mouth-Alcohol Detectors"

Prosecution forensic experts will usually claim that mouth alcohol will be detected by the breath machine's *slope detector*. The truth, however, is that these devices are not reliable. For a discussion of the problems with slope detectors, see §6.4.1 (although the materials in §6.4.1 deal with the Intoxilyzer 5000, other machines utilize slope detectors as well.)

One of the foremost blood-alcohol experts in the country, Dr. Michael Hlastala of the University of Washington's Department of Medicine, has adroitly summarized the defect in the slope detector:

> The slope detector is problematic for all breath testing instruments and has been misrepresented by the manufacturers. When a subject with alcohol in the blood, with no extra alcohol in the breath, exhales, the breath alcohol continues to increase during exhalation. It does not reach a "plateau" until the end of airflow. It continues to rise giving a positive slope. If you swish a little alcohol in the mouth (and have no alcohol in the blood), wait awhile and exhale, the breath alcohol will rise until a peak is reached about ⅓ of the way into the exhalation, and then decline gradually. It is the declining breath alcohol (negative slope) that triggers the slope detector to register the breath as having mouth alcohol.
>
> If the subject has alcohol in the blood as well as the mouth, then the normal rising breath alcohol curve will add to the declining mouth alcohol curve to produce what is often a level curve. Thus, the slope detector is unable to detect the presence of mouth alcohol when some is present in the mouth, yet breath alcohol concentration will be higher than it should be. The slope detector cannot detect false mouth alcohol under this circumstance.
>
> Whenever the slope detector is checked, it is done with alcohol in the mouth, but not in the blood. Therefore, the slope detector serves no purpose and mouth alcohol frequently affects the breath alcohol reading.

Additionally, the *source* of the alcohol being breathed into the machine can also have an effect on the slope detector. As one forensic expert, Wayne Morris of Orlando, Florida, has observed:

> It should be noted that *mouth* alcohol is different from the contamination due to *trapped* alcohol or to other organics possibly arising from periodontal disease. The contribution from trapped alcohol (dentures, food particles, or possible cavities in the gum, etc.) or periodontis is a *constant* over the duration of the blow. The mouth alcohol detector requires that the contribution *decrease* over the duration of the blow: The normal increase in breath alcohol concentration from the blow is added to the decreasing mouth alcohol contribution and results in a decrease and rapid increase in the signal. If this is seen, then the Intoxilyzer 5000 prints out

> "Invalid Sample XXX" to represent the detection of mouth alcohol.
>
> With the effects of trapped alcohol or periodontia, the constant contribution of alcohol will cause a non-zero increase to the base-line value and then add the contribution of breath alcohol to the new base-line. The apparent breath alcohol concentration will represent the contribution of breath alcohol to the new base-line. The *apparent* breath alcohol concentration, then, will represent the contribution from the contaminant added to the *actual* breath alcohol concentration.
>
> The same situation exists with contributions from long-term exposures to organic solvents, such as those reported with painters, etc.

Of course, counsel can always ask the officer/operator or forensic expert, "If the slope detector detects mouth alcohol, why is it necessary to have a 15- or 20-minute observation period prior to administering the test?"

§6.3 Additional Sources of Error

> The most striking contradiction of our civilization is the fundamental reverence for truth which we possess and the thoroughgoing disregard for it which we practice.
>
> VILHJALMUR STEFANSSON

Consideration of possible sources of error in a breath test case should begin with the general and proceed to the specific. In other words, in developing a "theory of the case" to present to the jury (or to the prosecutor/judge in plea bargaining), look first to the underlying problems inherent in all blood-alcohol analysis and then narrow down to error increasingly characteristic of the specific case.

1. First, review the flaws underlying all forms of blood-alcohol analysis — blood, breath, and urine: inherent error, circadian rhythm, sexual/racial differences, effects of zinc, etc. See §§5.3 to 5.3.9.
2. Question the validity of any attempt to relate back the BAC

figure to the time of driving — and particularly the assumption that the BAC level is falling rather than rising. See §§5.2 to 5.2.4.

3. Proceed to the most common sources of error unique to *breath* analysis: breath-blood partition ratio, non-specificity, mouth alcohol. See §§6.0 to 6.2.2.
4. Narrow the inquiry down to less common but recurring errors in the use of a breath machine to determine blood-alcohol concentration: breathing pattern, radio frequency interference, hematocrit, defective simulator calibration, etc. See §§6.3.1 to 6.3.9.
5. Learn the theoretical and mechanical defects inherent in the specific machine that was used on the client — Intoxilyzer 5000, DataMaster, Draeger AlcoTest 7110, etc. See §6.4.
6. Finally, understand that the machine is testing a fictional "average person" and look to the physiological facts unique to the client (including, relevant to the non-BAC count, individual tolerance). See §§5.0, 5.1, 5.1.1, 5.3.2.

The material that follows will address step #5: factors that may cause error in a given breath test — some of them rather esoteric — and which recur in drunk driving cases with some frequency.

§6.3.1 Testing During the Absorptive State

Absorption of alcohol continues for anywhere from 45 minutes to two hours after drinking or even longer (see §5.1). Peak absorption normally occurs within an hour; this can range from as little as 15 minutes to as much as two-and-a-half hours. The presence of food in the stomach can delay this to as much as four hours, with two hours being common.

During this absorptive phase, the distribution of alcohol throughout the body is not uniform; uniformity of distribution — called "equilibrium" — will not occur until absorption is complete. In other words, some parts of the body will have a higher blood-alcohol concentration than others. One aspect of this non-uniformity is that the BAC in *arterial* blood will be higher than in *veinous* blood. During peak absorption, arterial BAC can be as much as 60 percent higher than veinous.

This becomes very relevant to breath-alcohol analysis because the alveolar air sacs in the lungs are bathed by arterial blood, not veinous: The diffusion of alcohol through the sacs and into the lung air will reflect the BAC of the body's arterial blood. Therefore, the breath sample obtained by the machine will be reflective of pulmonary BAC — which, during absorption, will be considerably higher than veinous BAC (and higher than the BAC in other parts of the body).

G. Simpson, one of the more noted experts in the field of blood-alcohol analysis, has written an interesting article in which he has concluded that

> . . . breath testing is not a reliable means of estimating a subject's BAC during absorption. . . . There is a significant likelihood that a given subject will be in the absorptive state when tested under field conditions. Because of large differences in arterial BAC and venous BAC during absorption, breath test results consistently overestimate the result that would be obtained from a blood test — by as much as 100% or more. In order to have some idea of the reliability of a given breath test result, it is essential to determine by some objective means whether the subject is in the absorptive or postabsorptive state. In the absence of such information, an appropriate value for the uncertainty associated with the absorptive state should be applied to all breath test results.

Simpson, Accuracy and Precision of Breath Alcohol Measurements for Subjects in the Absorptive State, 33(6) Clinical Chemistry 753 (1987).

Even in the postabsorptive phase, Simpson has found, breath tests are inherently unreliable. His research indicated uncertainty levels of 15 to 27 percent. In an earlier article, he noted:

> Over 90% of this uncertainty is due to biological variables of the subject, and at least 23% of subjects will have their actual blood-alcohol concentration overestimated. Manufacturers' specifications for the accuracy and precision of these instruments are inconsistent with the experimental values reported in the literature and I recommend that an appropriate amount of uncertainty be

> reflected in the results from these breath analyzers, especially when they are used for law-enforcement purposes.

Simpson, Accuracy and Precision of Breath Alcohol Measurements for Subjects in the Absorptive State, 33(2) Clinical Chemistry 261 (1987).

Which is the more relevant indicator of intoxication, arterial or veinous BAC? Veinous blood more accurately reflects the alcohol level in the brain tissue, and is thereby a more accurate indicator of intoxication than arterial blood would be.

Thus breath testing during the absorptive phase will result in an inaccurately high BAC reading. This inaccuracy is compounded by the fact that the 2100:1 alveolar air-to-blood ratio (see §6.0.1) was arrived at by researchers using veinous blood in their studies and assuming the absorptive state to be completed. In fact, during the absorptive phase an individual's ratio will be considerably lower than during the elimination phase.

The renowned blood-alcohol expert Dr. Kurt Dubowski of the University of Oklahoma has concluded: "When a blood test is allowed, an administered breath test is discriminatory, because in law enforcement practice the status of absorption is always uncertain."

In the results of a study presented before the International Association of Forensic Toxicologists (Perth, Australia), William Giguiere and G. Simpson (Park-Gilman Clinic, Cupertino, CA) found that "between 15–50 minutes after the cessation of drinking, Intoxilyzers consistently overestimated actual BAC by a large margin, the uncertainty in an Intoxilyzer result being +/−44% for 95% confidence limits in relation to BAC." The studies involved simultaneous measurements of blood and breath alcohol concentrations on 79 subjects under laboratory conditions, using Intoxilyzer 5000s to measure breath and gas chromatography to measure blood.

The scientists concluded that "[t]he error of uncertainty in breath test results, as determined by standard, accepted methods which are based upon a normal error curve, must be accounted for and reported whenever the results (of breath tests) are used for legal purposes."

For a discussion of the effects of obtaining a blood sample during the absorptive phase of *blood* analysis, see §7.0.5.

Widmark has pointed out many years ago in his landmark

book that a primary reason why a breath test given during the absorptive phase will be higher is that during this period alcohol vapors will be forced out of the stomach and into the breath by the contraction of the diaphragm muscles. Thus, the breath machine's reading will be a combination of both breath alcohol and stomach alcohol — and the machine will neither be able to differentiate nor detect the problem.

§6.3.2 Hematocrit

Yet another potential source of error in breath-alcohol analysis involves the variability in the composition of the blood.

Whole blood is made up of a mixture of solid particles suspended in a liquid. The solid particles consist of red blood cells, white blood cells, and clotting platelets; the liquid portion is called *plasma*. The percentage by volume of the solid particles is called the *hematocrit* of the blood. Thus, for example, a hematocrit of .47 would indicate that the individual's blood consists of 47 percent solid particles (cells and platelets) and 53 percent plasma.

Since plasma is a liquid and contains water, and alcohol is more soluble in water, it will contain a higher concentration of alcohol than will the solid particles in the blood. And the less plasma in the blood (i.e., the higher the hematocrit), the more concentrated the alcohol will be in the existing plasma. Thus the higher the hematocrit, the higher the alcohol concentration in the plasma. To put it another way, if two subjects have the same blood-alcohol concentration in their bodies but one has a higher hematocrit, that person's *plasma* will have a higher concentration of alcohol.

Applying this to breath analysis, the air in the lung is absorbing alcohol by diffusion from the blood washing the alveolar sacs in the lung tissue. This process follows Henry's Law, which applied to breath testing can be stated as: The concentration of alcohol in the deep lung air is directly proportional to the concentration of alcohol in the blood surrounding the alveolar sacs. However, Henry's Law applies to liquids, not solids, and so the breath is going to reflect the alcohol concentration in the plasma (a liquid) more than it will the alcohol concentration in the solid particles of the blood.

Since blood with a smaller percentage of plasma (higher hematocrit) will have a higher concentration of alcohol, the lung air will reflect this — that is, there will be a higher concentration of alcohol in the air above the alveolar sacs. In other words, the plasma in blood with a higher hematocrit (less plasma) will have a higher BAC and this will cause the breath to have a higher BAC.

Bottom line: Breath machines report falsely high blood-alcohol readings for persons who have blood with a high hematocrit.

What is a normal hematocrit? And what is the range of variation? The average hematocrit for men is 47 percent, with a range of 42 to 52; women's hematocrit averages 42 percent, and ranges from 37 to 47. But studies have shown that an individual's hematocrit can vary in time by as much as 15 percent.

The hematocrit of an individual can easily be determined by an appropriate blood test. And if it is high, counsel should consider introducing evidence of that figure — along with expert evidence of its significance (if necessary, during cross-examination of the state's expert).

The effect of an individual's hematocrit on breath analysis can be mathematically computed. The partition ratio of 2100:1 uniformly used in breath testing presumably uses a male-female average hematocrit of 45 percent. If the client's hematocrit is, say, 54 percent, the breath test result could be computed by multiplying it by 45/54. Assuming a breath test result of .11 percent, for example, the true BAC could be determined by the formula $.11 \times 45/54 = .09$. In other words, a person with a true BAC of .09 percent and a hematocrit of 54 percent would test on an otherwise accurate breath device as .11 percent.

Finally, counsel may wish to inquire of the client whether he is — or was at the time of the arrest — suffering from *anemia*. The percentage of plasma in an anemic subject's blood will be higher than normal. In other words, his blood will have a higher percentage of water. As alcohol is attracted to water, there will be a higher percentage of alcohol in the blood. Technically, this may not be a defense: The offense consists of blood-alcohol concentration and, as with sexual and racial variation in alcohol metabolism, there is no allowance for physiological differences. Nevertheless, juries are human, and evidence that the BAC reading does not accurately reflect the amount of alcohol consumed — that the defendant is being prosecuted largely because of his anemic condition — will go a long way toward an acquittal.

§6.3.3 Body Temperature

The effects of changes in body temperature from the norm of 98.6°F on breath-alcohol testing has been discussed in an article entitled Body Temperature and the Breathalyzer Boobytrap, 721 Michigan Bar Journal, September 1982. If because of illness, for example, the body temperature is elevated by 1°C (1.8°F), the 1:2100 blood-to-alveolar air ratio will be affected so as to produce a 7 percent higher test result. Higher body temperatures will, of course, result in greater errors.

Dr. Hlastala confirms this result. In the article mentioned earlier, he comments that even the average body temperature of a normal, healthy person "may vary by as much as 1°C above or below the normal mean value of 37°C or 1.8°F from the mean value of 98.6°F." (Physiological Errors Associated with Alcohol Breath Testing, 9(6) The Champion 18 (1985). Not only can the body temperature of any individual differ from the norm of 98.6°F, but the "temperature of any individual may vary from time to time during the day by as much as 1°C" (Id. at 18). Result? The partition ratio for alcohol in blood is altered. This interprets into a 6.5 percent error for every 1°C increase or decrease from the presumed normal body temperature.

In addition to affecting the partition ratio, an increase in body temperature can also cause a falsely high breath test reading by raising the *humidity* of the breath sample. It is an accepted fact that breath with a higher temperature contains a higher concentration of moisture than breath with a lower temperature. It is also an accepted fact that breath with a higher concentration of moisture will also contain a higher concentration of alcohol. Therefore, an individual with an elevated temperature is going to produce a breath sample with more moisture and thus more alcohol. And this deceptively higher BAC will be *in addition* to the error caused by the effect of temperature on the partition ratio.

§6.3.4 Breathing Pattern

The way a DUI suspect breathes immediately before breath testing may have an effect on the test results — often increasing the reading noticeably. A scientist in the Department of Alcohol and Drug Addiction Research at the Karolinska Institute in Stockholm, Sweden, has investigated the phenomenon at some length. In an article appearing in 22(4) Medical Science and the Law 275 (1982), entitled How Breathing Technique Can Influence the Results of Breath-Alcohol Analysis, Dr. A. W. Jones reports a series of experiments with a group of men who drank moderate doses of alcohol and whose blood-alcohol levels were then measured by gas chromatographic analysis of their breath. The breathing techniques of the subjects were then varied for the tests that immediately followed.

Dr. Jones found that holding one's breath for 30 seconds before expiration increased the concentration of alcohol by 15.7 percent. Hyperventilating for 20 seconds immediately before the analysis of breath, on the other hand, decreased the blood-alcohol level by 10.6 percent. Keeping the mouth closed for five minutes and using shallow nasal breathing resulted in increasing the ethanol concentration by 7.3 percent, and testing after a slow, 20-second exhalation increased levels by 2 percent.

These results were explained by Dr. Jones partly in terms of the rise or fall in the temperature of the breath. But an equally important factor is the amount of time the breath spends in contact with the mucous membranes of the upper respiratory tract. The scientist concluded:

> The influence of a person's breathing technique, before or during delivery of a breath sample, should be carefully considered when breath-alcohol instruments are used in medico-legal work for evidentiary testing. My experiments show that the duration of contact between the breath and the mucous membranes covering the respiratory tract is a key factor and that an increase in the time spent in contact increases the expired-ethanol concentration.

For another study coming to similar conclusions, see Ohlsson, et al., Accurate Measurement of Blood Alcohol Concentration with Isothermal Rebreathing, 51(1) Journal of Studies on Alcohol 6 (1990).

Dr. Michael Hlastala, Professor of Physiology, Biophysics, and Medicine at the University of Washington, has gone even further and concluded that "by changing breathing technique within normally required guidelines, a subject can change the equivalent BAC as measured by the breath from as little as 50% to over 150%

of the true BAC.'' (9(6) The Champion at 16 (1985)). Apparently, the heating and cooling of the breath in breathing causes changes in alcohol concentration during exhalation. As Dr. Hlastala has observed:

> By far, the most overlooked error in breath testing for alcohol is the pattern of breathing. . . .
>
> [A]ll breath testers attempt to take a sample from the end of the breath. . . . [But] the concentration of alcohol changes considerably during the breath. . . . The first part of the breath, after discarding the dead space, has an alcohol concentration much lower than the equivalent BAC. Whereas, the last part of the breath has an alcohol concentration that is much higher than the equivalent BAC. The last part of the breath can be over 50% above the blood alcohol level. . . . Thus, a breath tester reading of 0.14g% taken from the last part of the breath may indicate that the blood level is only 0.09g%. [Id. at 17–18.]

Dr. Hlastala explains that this takes place because as the subject breathes room air in, that air cools the airways. When he then breathes out, some of the alcohol in the expired breath coming from the warm lungs condenses on the surface of the airways. As he continues to breathe out, his airways are warmed by the breath, resulting in evaporation of some of the alcohol on the surface. Thus the latter portion of the subject's breath picks up additional alcohol from this evaporation. Result: a falsely high reading.

Subsequently, in a June 1997 Internet message, Dr. Hlastala elaborated on his explanation of the effects of breathing on BAC readings. He explained how breath machines give higher readings for individuals who exhale greater amounts of breath:

> No breath test instrument is able to obtain a sample of alveolar air without it changing. During exhalation, the alcohol level always changes as alcohol deposits on the airway mucous. In fact, the presumption of breath test instrument manufacturers that end-exhalation alcohol concentration is equal to alveolar concentration is absolutely incorrect from a scientific perspective. . . .
>
> . . . The machines do not control for the amount of breath exhaled and therefore discriminate against individuals who exhale greater amounts of breath before stopping their exhalation. It is the lack of control of breath that is the primary variable making the breath test very inaccurate.

In other words, the greater the amount of breath exhaled before a sample is captured, the more alcohol deposits on the mucous in the passage to be absorbed by the "end-exhalation" (captured sample at the end of the breath).

For a more complete understanding of this phenomenon and of Dr. Hlastala's research findings and important new "paradigm" of breath alcohol analysis, see §6.0.2.

There have been a number of other studies concerning the effects of breathing methods on breath-alcohol analysis since those reported by Jones and Hlastala. In one, for example, the blood-alcohol level of three subjects as tested on a breath instrument was decreased 24 percent after those subjects ran up and down stairs. In another, BACs of 39 subjects were raised between 5 percent and 15 percent by having them hold their breath for 20 seconds before breathing into the instrument. And in yet another, hyperventilation among 17 subjects resulted in elevating BAC readings by an average of 15 percent. For a discussion of these studies, see Mulder and Neuteboom, The Effects of Hypo- and Hyperventilation on Breath Alcohol Measurements, 24 Blutalkohol 341 (1987).

§6.3.5 Stress

Stress can also be a significant factor in any breath-alcohol analysis. Certainly, the average person stopped by a police officer, subjected to interrogation and field sobriety tests, arrested, taken to a police station in handcuffs, and there fingerprinted, photographed, and booked, is probably going to be suffering from stress. And with this stress — whether nervousness, anger, or fear — comes predictable physiological responses. The most important one is the secretion of adrenal hormones, notably epinephrin and norepinephrin. These hormones quickly burn sugar and fat as energy sources and dilate the body's capillary beds, including the lung's capillary beds, with a resultant increased blood flow and blood pressure.

Thus, because of the stress caused by the drunk driving arrest, the dynamic equilibrium between the blood and breath within the alveolar lung sacs is affected drastically: Blood is passing through the lung more quickly and under greater pressure, probably altering the presumptions on which the tests depend. While the effects of stress are impossible to measure quantitatively, they do take place, and the fact of the effects is known. In other words, although stress will probably affect the reading on a breath analysis machine, the exact amount of that effect can never be known.

§6.3.6 Simulator Calibration

The accuracy of a breath machine is dependent upon, among other things, the accuracy of its calibration. If a given machine is not accurately calibrated, its test results will be uniformly inaccurate.

Calibration is accomplished through the use of a *simulator* solution. This consists of a liquid solution of alcohol and water, with the percentage of alcohol being carefully prepared and controlled (commonly around .10 percent). The solution is placed inside a sealed glass jar, with an air space above the solution. The solution is heated to 34 degrees centigrade (the normal temperature of human breath) by a heating element; a thermostat connected to the heating element measures the temperature. The vapor in the air space is then transferred through a tube to the breath machine where it is analyzed. The reading is then compared to the known alcohol concentration of the simulator solution.

The problem of inaccurate calibration usually arises where the solution contains an alcohol concentration that is *less* than the specified concentration. If a breath machine is calibrated with such a solution, it will thereafter produce inflated BAC readings.

Basically, there are five main ways a breath-alcohol simulator can falsely calibrate a breath device. First, the alcohol and water in the solution may have been mixed at the laboratory in the wrong proportions. For a simulated BAC of .10 percent, the solution must consist of exactly 1.21 grams of 200 proof ethyl alcohol per liter of pure distilled water. Error here usually takes one of two forms: (1) The wrong amount of alcohol is added to the water, or (2) 190 proof alcohol (commonly stocked in laboratories) is used rather than 200 proof.

A second source of error occurs where there is a depletion of the alcohol in the solution during use. This often occurs where the glass container is not tightly sealed. Alcohol, being more volatile than water, will evaporate more quickly. The resulting solution will have a lower concentration of alcohol than specified — and the machine calibrated with this solution will give falsely high readings with DUI suspects.

Another way in which this depletion of alcohol in the calibration solution can occur is if the container is *permeable.* Mark E. Byrnes, a data quality/sampling specialist in Kennewick, Washington, recently discovered in the course of an audit of that state's toxicology laboratory that their simulator solution is routinely stored in *polypropylene* — not glass — bottles. Further, the lab does not cool these solutions to recommended temperatures. The result: a slow degradation of the calibration solutions over a period of time — and a false-high BAC reading on the miscalibrated breath machine. As Mr. Byrnes reported:

> According to the references cited, . . . volatile organic solutions (e.g., ethyl alcohol) should always be stored in glass as opposed to polypropylene containers, since some organic vapors can permeate through the polypropylene material, and some volatile organic compounds can chemically adhere to the walls of the polyproplylene bottle. In other words, storing volatile organic standard solutions in a polypropylene container may degrade (or otherwise negatively impact) the concentration of the solution over time . . .
>
> The cited references . . . also require volatile organic solutions (e.g., ethyl alcohol) to be refrigerated to 4 degrees Celsius when not in use to reduce the rate of chemical decomposition over time. This is particularly important when dealing with instrument calibration solutions since the degradation of calibration solutions will lead to the miscalibration of analytical instruments . . . Finally, the cited references also recommend that samples for volatile organic analysis (e.g., ethyl alcohol) be stored in containers with no head space (bottles completely full) in order to eliminate the transfer of volatile organics from the liquid to gas phase . . .
>
> The full impact of this finding is this: If a calibration solution degrades over time from a concentration of 0.080 to 0.060, the laboratory technician calibrating the instrument still treats the solution as if it has a concentration of 0.080. This results in the instrument being miscalibrated in favor of the prosecution. In other words, a defendant with an actual breath alcohol concentration of 0.060 may be charged with a breath alcohol concentration of 0.080. . . .

The references cited by Mr. Byrnes include: Standard Methods for the Examination of Water and Wastewater, 18th edition (American Public Health Association, 1992); 1997 Annual Book of ASTM Standards, Volume 11.02 (American Society for Testing Materials); Test Methods for Evaluating Solid Waste, Volume 1A (Environmental Protection Agency, 1996).

A third and related problem exists in some simulators that replace the vapor used up in calibrating with room (ambient) air. Since the vapor contained a higher concentration of alcohol than the solution, and the room air contains no alcohol, the resulting simulator solution will contain a steadily decreasing percentage of alcohol.

Fourth, the simulator may be operated at an incorrect temperature. In most states, the required operating temperature is 34 degrees centigrade, with a margin of plus or minus 0.2 degrees. If, however, the operating temperature is decreased by one degree — that is, 33 degrees — the concentration of alcohol in the simulator solution will be decreased by 6.8 percent. Using such a solution to calibrate a breath machine will also cause misleadingly high test results.

Finally, inaccurately high test readings can be obtained if there is *leakage* in the tube feeding the vapor from the simulator into the machine. If such leakage occurs, the vapor will be diluted with room air, resulting in a lower concentration of alcohol. This diluted test vapor will also cause the machine to give falsely high BAC readings when used with actual subjects. Certainly, counsel should check the maintenance records for the simulator; if a tube has been replaced since the client was tested, this may indicate a leak at the time of the test.

It should be noted that even an accurate calibration does not ensure accuracy beyond the blood-alcohol concentration tested for. In other words, a single-point calibration is not linear. A calibration using a solution of .10 percent with a reading on the machine of .10 percent only indicates that at that BAC the machine appears to be functioning accurately — it does not mean that the machine will correctly analyze, for example, a true BAC of .14 percent as .14 percent.

One illustrative means of relating this to a situation that the jury can understand and relate to is to liken the process to balancing the tires of an automobile: To balance a tire with weights effectively, the tire must be checked at various speeds — not just at one speed.

If the simulator solution is not relatively fresh, it can cause inaccurate calibration and significantly higher readings. A situation recently uncovered by defense attorneys in Ohio illustrates this problem. Guth Laboratories, which is the sole source of simulator solutions for about one-third of the states, warrants its solutions for only nine months — that is, the "shelf life" is only nine months after production. (The owner of the company, Richard Guth, recommends that the solution should be used no longer than 30 days or for 30 tests, whichever comes first.)

Each state, however, is free to tell Guth Laboratories what manufacture dates and expiration dates to place on the solution labels. In Ohio, the State Patrol has one-year expiration dates placed on the labels — clearly beyond the limits indicated by the manufacturer. Ohio DUI attorney Brad Koffel has reported that, in fact, state labs are using solutions that are *three years old.*

Garbage in, as the computer techs say, equals garbage out. Counsel in drunk driving cases should attempt to determine the source of the simulator solution used, the age of that batch, and the recommended shelf-life.

The usual procedure with law enforcement agencies is to replace the simulator solution after a period of time, for example, after 60 days in the field. The old solution is usually discarded. Counsel should confirm this in his cross-examination of the operator or expert witness — and then develop the fact that it would have been a very simple procedure to have tested the solution's integrity before discarding it. Without knowing if the solution's true concentration was, in fact, .10 percent as claimed, one can only say that it was possibly .10 percent when mixed by the laboratory weeks or months before the defendant was tested. The only accurate way to know what the solution concentration was at the time of the test is to analyze it *after* it has been replaced: If it was still .10 percent, then presumably it was .10 percent at the time of the test in question. But destruction of the solution made this check on the machine's accuracy impossible.

The following recommendations for quality control in simulator preparation and use are reproduced from "Recommendations for Preparation of Alcohol Reference Solutions for Control Tests of Breath Alcohol Testing Instruments by Means of Alcoholic Breath Simulators,'' National Safety Council, Committee on Alcohol and Other Drugs, ''Recommendation of the Subcommittee on Technology,'' Appendix K, pages 137–138 (1996 printing).

RECOMMENDATIONS:

The governmental agency responsible for the approval of breath alcohol testing instruments and methods of analysis should insure that alcohol reference solutions used to test breath alcohol instruments are properly prepared. Alcohol reference solutions should be prepared by or commercially prepared reference solutions or stock solutions should be analyzed by, the approving agency. Commercially prepared alcohol reference solutions or stock solutions should be analyzed by the agency or the agency's designee in addition to any analysis performed by the manufacturer or the manufacturer's designee. Preparation of alcohol reference solutions or the analysis of commercially prepared solutions or stock solutions should be conducted by qualified persons using generally recognized analytical procedures and equipment.

The alcohol concentration of the reference solutions should be known and traceable back to a standard reference material, such as National Institute of Standards and Technology (NIST, formerly National Bureau of Standards) Standard Reference Materials (SRMs).

PROCEDURES:

1. Alcohol reference solutions and alcohol stock solutions should be prepared from reagent grade ethanol. The hygroscopic properties and density of ethanol must be taken into account when determining the purity and quantity of ethanol to be used. Water used in the preparation of reference and stock solutions should be chemically pure and free of microorganisms.
2. The solutions should be so mixed that the final ethanol concentration is uniform and homogeneous. Homogeneity should be established by analytical measurement of the ethanol concentration of a sufficient number of the aliquots of the solution dispensed. It is recommended that the first and last aliquots dispensed and several of the intermediate aliquots, be analyzed. All aliquots should have ethanol concentrations within 2% of the target value.
3. The actual alcohol concentration of the final reference so-

lution should be established experimentally by a suitable method of analysis, such as titration against a primary standard of potassium dichromate traceable to NIST SRM 136e, or by gas chromatography against ethanol standards traceable to NIST SRM 1828. 1996 (EDITOR'S NOTE: NIST SRM 1828 has been discontinued and re-released as NIST SRM 1828a.)

4. The stability of reference solutions should be established by repeated analysis of the ethanol concentrations during typical storage conditions and actual use. The approving agency should establish the date beyond which the reference solutions should not be used ("Expiration Date"), and this should be reflected both on the label applied to each portion, and in the directions for use. Stability is enhanced if pure, microorganism-free reagents, equipment and conditions are used in the preparation of reference solutions, and if solutions are protected from temperature extremes and evaporation.
5. Many breath-alcohol testing programs purchase alcohol reference solutions. The quality assurance practices of the manufacturer do not replace the obligation of the approving agency (or qualified designee) independently to determine and verify the homogeneity, stability and accuracy of the ethanol concentration of reference solutions.
6. Some breath-alcohol testing programs provide or purchase measured portions of concentrated standard ethanol stock solutions (e.g., ampoules of stock solutions), to be diluted locally (or at point-of-use) to make reference solutions. Such solutions should be lot-checked to verify the concentration and volume and the ability reliably to produce a reference solution of the desired concentration when directions for dilution are followed. All prepared reference solutions should have ethanol concentrations within 2% of the target value. The processes of reference solution analysis and dilution and instrument calibration must be in the hands of qualified personnel who understand the importance of using the recommended equipment and following directions faithfully. The approving agency is responsible for verifying periodically the suitability of reference solutions and preparation procedures used in the field.

Counsel should consider using discovery procedures to obtain as much information as possible about the simulator solution used in the calibration of the instrument involved in the testing of his client. Should the trial judge balk at what may appear to be rather far-reaching inquiry, counsel may wish to mention a recent experience in Pennsylvania. In December 1987, that state's Auditor General held a news conference at which he demanded an immediate suspension of all breath testing because the manufacturer of the simulator solution used by many of Pennsylvania's law enforcement agencies, Systems Innovation, Inc., had been providing defective solutions. According to the Auditor General, the solutions had been "produced in the back room of a Radio Shack store" by unqualified individuals: This had been going on for five years and could have resulted in "thousands" of drunk driving convictions because of inaccurate test results. "The simple truth is that the machine has become the judge, and the judge is not reliable," the Auditor General was quoted as saying. "It has been letting guilty people go. It has been convicting the innocent."

The following represents a recognition by the manufacturer of the DataMaster of numerous problems that commonly occur in simulator calibrations. The comments and warnings are found in a mailing to law enforcement agencies titled "Reading This Can Save You Time and Aggravation," accompanied by instructions to "Please Forward to Breath Alcohol Testing Supervisor." Counsel should consider these sources of error in planning his or her cross-examination.

> READ THIS MEMO ON SIMULATORS AND SOLUTIONS!
>
> Periodically it seems that problems with solutions and simulators are more frequent than at other times. Many of the difficulties stem from (1) the mixing, and (2) the care of the solution after usage. Please review this memo and pass it along to other concerned operators and supervisors.
>
> SIMULATOR USAGE. The most critical link in the simulation process is the simulator, which is designed to operate with 500 ml of solution at an operating temperature of 34 degrees centigrade, +/−2 C. Most styles of simulators use a standard mercury thermostat to control a heating element, although several styles use solid-state temperature sensing. In this case there will be no thermostat.
>
> Some of the more common problems we see are:

MERCURY SEPARATION in the thermostat (usually white in color). Depending on exactly where it is separated, the simulator will run either too hot or too cold. Sometimes this can be corrected by putting the simulator in the freezer for a few hours (without solution, of course). If that doesn't work, you may be able to correct it by gently heating the bottom of the thermostat bulb, *and we do mean gently*. In any event, this problem must be corrected. If the temperature of the simulator is not hot enough, look for a separation in the main column of mercury. If the temperature is too cool, look for a bit of mercury that has separated at the top of the column, even possibly in the very top of the glass.

MERCURY SEPARATION in the thermometer (usually yellow in color). Although this problem does not affect the operation of the simulator, it does mean that you will not be able to verify the temperature. The corrective methods are the same as above. Remember, mercury is a hazardous substance. If you break the thermostat or thermometer, use proper disposal methods.

LEAKS around gaskets and seals make for low readings. Check the simulator jar lip for chips and cracks. A quick check procedure is to seal the OUTPUT side closed with a finger and blow into the INPUT side. Bubbles should be minimal and there should be a good deal of back pressure. If not, fix it! A leaking simulator will cause low readings.

INCORRECT HEADSPACE. Most simulators are designed to operate with approximately 500 ml of solution in the jar. Too little or too much can cause variations in condensation or vaporization rates, either of which can affect your reading, 500 ml will usually fill the jar to just below the baffle plate, and remember, the use of a jar other than the one suggested by the manufacturer can cause problems. Be sure any replacement jar is very close to the original size.

LOOSE OR LENGTHY connections from the simulator output to the breath tube of your instrument can cause leaks, condensation and the lowering of readings. Repeated tries will eventually let the condensate equilibrate and become a less significant factor. Keep the simulator tubes short and be certain the breath tube is warm. A cold breath tube will cause a low reading if you are simulating through it.

USE CAUTION that the simulator is always UNPLUGGED prior to immersion into solution, and never remove it from the solution without first unplugging or turning it off.

CLEANLINESS. Clean all parts of the simulator carefully after each use so that no algae or bacterial growth occurs on the operating parts. This growth will cause very rapid deterioration of the ethanol in the solution. And since the bugs will stay in the simulator, they will travel from simulator to bottle or flask and contaminate solutions well into the future.

DRY THE SIMULATOR. Failure to dry the insides, and the resultant moisture that remains also becomes a problem in that all the ethanol in the remaining water will have vaporized by the next time you simulate, leaving only pure water to dilute your solution.

USE A MOUTHPIECE between the simulator output and the breath tube of your instrument (if you are simulating through the breath tube) to prevent solution droplets from passing into the instrument.

STORAGE BETWEEN USES. Each time the solution is transferred from bottle to simulator and returned, it is weakened slightly, with some of the ethanol evaporating more quickly than the water. The simulator with the solution still in it should be allowed to cool to room temperature or preferably even refrigerated BEFORE returning it to the original container. *Always pour with the solution cold.*

CONTINUING USAGE. If it is necessary to leave the simulator out and either heated or unheated between uses, seal by connecting the input to the output with a piece of vinyl tubing. This will form a closed system and prevent undue loss of ethanol. It's a good idea to do this even while waiting for the simulator to warm up prior to use.

DON'T MICROWAVE. Don't even think of putting the solution or the water (if mixing) in a microwave to heat it. If you are mixing your own, start with the solution ampoule and water preferably both cold, but at least at the same room temperature.

BE PATIENT. Allow the simulator solution to warm up fully before using, not just until the operating temp is reached. Even though the temperature of the solution is correct, the metal base of the simulator may be cool and the vapor will tend to condense on it, lowering your reading. The headspace also requires more time to heat and to equilibrate. Allow an hour for the simulator to heat and stabilize. It's also a good idea to blow briefly through the simulator before using it on the instrument in order to fully equilibrate the headspace.

Remember, ethanol and water are the only contents of the solution and there is ABSOLUTELY NOTHING the manufacturer can do to it or add to it that will make it last longer or shorter than your care will allow. It is guaranteed correct when you crack the seal.

FOLLOW THIS CHECKLIST

1. Start with a clean dry simulator and cold solution or mix the ampoule and water. Use a clean flask and if not dry, rinsed with the same water you will be using to mix the solution.
2. Allow the simulator and solution to warm up for at least an hour with the input and the output connected to seal it off.
3. Make sure the tubes are as short as possible and that the instrument breath tube is warm if you are simulating through the breath tube.
4. Check simulator operating temperature and seal before using.
5. Do simulation.
6. If a Buckeye, allow simulator to cool or place in refrigerator for several hours before returning to the original container. Always do your pouring (either direction) with cold solutions.
7. Clean and dry the simulator and store with jar off to allow the tubing and internals of the simulator to dry.

§6.3.7 Used Mouthpieces

It is, of course, critical that the mouthpiece be changed with each new test. A used mouthpiece may contain particles or vapors from the previous user, thus falsely elevating the reading. In fact, the failure to replace the mouthpiece should be argued as grounds for suppression of the results. In *State v. Amant,* 504 So. 2d 1094 (La. App. 1987), a Louisiana appellate court ruled that the breath test results were inadmissible because the state had not been in strict compliance with regulatory procedures when it failed to show that a clean, new mouthpiece was used in administering an Intoxilyzer 5000 test to the defendant. In reversing the drunk driving conviction, the court said: "[T]his lack of evidence is a lapse in carrying the burden of proof, because it does not show strict compliance with the procedure. The re-use of a contaminated mouthpiece could have a strong bearing on the validity of the test results."

§6.3.8 Ambient Air

The approved procedure for administering a breath-alcohol test includes *purging* the sample chamber. The chamber which captures the subject's breath sample may still contain alcohol vapor from the previously tested DUI suspect. Before running a test, therefore, the chamber must be rinsed of any contaminants. This is done by flushing it out with ambient air — that is, air in the room where the test is being conducted. Theoretically, then, the breath sample is captured in a chamber containing no preexisting alcohol.

The problem is that ambient air is not necessarily "clean": it may well contain alcohol vapor. Certainly, in a room where DUI suspects are routinely tested on a breath machine, the air is likely to contain the exhaled breath of those suspects who have previously been tested. Each of these individuals has presumably sat in the room, breathing alcohol vapor into the air, while the officer or technician prepares the machine and fills out the paperwork. The result is that the chamber may be purged with alcohol-polluted air.

The only effective way to prevent this is to run a "*blank test*" after purging and before capturing the subject's sample. The test should, of course, read .00 percent; any other reading indicates the presence of contaminated ambient air. Nevertheless, many law enforcement agencies continue to administer breath tests without such blanks.

Even if a blank test *is* run and the "air blank" indicator reads .00 percent, that does not necessarily mean that there is no alcohol or interferent in the room air. Quite simply, the air blank will *always* read .00 percent, at least on the Intoxilyzer 5000. If there is alcohol or interferent in the ambiant air, the machine will adjust the base line — that is, the machine resets itself and the contaminated air becomes the new reference level.

§6.3.9 Incomplete Purging and the "Air Blank"

Disregarding ambient room air for the moment, as long as the breath machine's pump is efficiently expelling the breath-alcohol vapors from the sample chamber left from the preceding test, the subject's sample should be uncontaminated (i.e., its BAC reading will not be elevated from being mixed with ethanol remaining from previous tests). But how do we know that the pump is working correctly? The "air blank" is supposed to indicate the presence of any residual alcohol; if it reads .00 percent, the pump has done its job and the chamber is clean. Then how do we know if the "air blank" indicator is accurate?

Using his own state-certified Intoxilyzer 5000, noted DUI practitioner Richard Essen of Miami, Florida, ran tests to determine whether the "air blank" reading was reliable. He repeatedly forced ethanol into the tubes and sample chamber during the "air blank" mode, then tried to run tests. Interestingly, about 60 percent of the time the Intoxilyzer proceeded with the tests (i.e., with no indications of "invalid test," "ambient failed," or "check ambient conditions"). In each of those tests, the "air blank" read .000) despite the known presence of injected ethanol. In the other 40 percent of tests, the machine shut down.

Essen then proceeded to run tests after the machine had supposedly purged the sample chamber of the injected alcohol. The results were wildly erratic, with little or no correlation between the injected BAC level or the test sample level.

Finally, Essen reported his findings to state forensic experts. These experts replicated Essen's test — and produced similar results. They have since testified in trial that they cannot rely on the Intoxilyzer's "air blank" procedure. See Why the Intoxilyzer Isn't Worth a "Blank," 11(6) DWI Journal 1 (June 1996).

Essen's study was followed by further studies by toxicologist Wayne Morris. In an article scheduled to appear in DWI Journal's December 1996 issue, Morris and associate Robert Kopec repeatedly flushed the chambers of two Intoxilyzer 5000s (models 64 and 66) with ambient (room) air to purge it of contamination from preceding breath and simulator samples. The machines were calibrated. They then mixed simulator solutions of water mixed with either alcohol or toluene and cyclohexane and heated them to the correct 34°C temperature. They then "purged" the sample chambers while blowing the toluene-cyclohexane solution across the breath tube, thereby contaminating the chamber with hydrocarbons. Finally, tests were run with the alcohol solution.

The results as to both models were similar: "In all instances, the Air Blank readings were reported as zero, confirming the earlier results reported by Essen. Unlike the Essen study, the readings immediately following the contamination produced both higher and lower results . . . After the initial readings were obtained, additional testing of the simulator solutions always resulted in a series of readings which were higher than the expected result . . ."

Morris and Kopec concluded:

> The elevation of the readings after the initial readings following the contamination demonstrate the contribution of hydrocarbons to the apparent ethanol concentration reported by the Intoxilyzer. The successive decreases in the readings with time demonstrate that the purge is not efficient in cleansing the chamber of hydrocarbon contaminants. . . . Clearly the air blank zero cannot be relied upon to prove that the sample cell is free of interfering compounds.

As for the prosecution's argument that the machine's "fail safe" devices will detect the presence of interferents in such cases, the two men observed: "Since the interferent detector was never activated during these studies, the lack of an interferent flag is not a reliable indicator of contamination of the breath samples. Finally, the ambient air fail warning was not activated upon the contamination of the air purge in the majority of runs . . . Thus, the ambient air fail flag is not a reliable indicator of a clean or contaminated sample chamber."

Morris and Kopec also commented on another possible source of error:

> During the introduction of a breath sample, it is assumed that the upper lung air (dead space air) also forces out the contents of

> the sample chamber and in turn is forced out by the deep lung air sample which is then analyzed. It is further assumed that during this filling of the cell that minimal mixing occurs in the sample chamber between the different stages. However, there has been little, if any, reported testing of the Intoxilyzer 5000 to ensure that this purging is efficient or complete.

Dr. Dubowski, in his article Quality Assurance in Breath-Alcohol Analysis, 18 Journal of Analytical Toxicology 306 (October 1994), states that the following testing sequence is necessary to ensure an accurate result:

1. run air blank
2. run first breath test on subject
3. run second air blank
4. run second breath test on subject
5. run third air blank
6. run a control test (see §6.3.6 for discussion of simulator tests)
7. run fourth air blank

§6.3.10 Radio Frequency Interference (RFI)

In the first edition of this book (1981), the author advised readers that breath testing devices could give false readings due to interference from foreign radio waves. This warning was met with ridicule by prosecutors and law enforcement. Then, in February 1982, Smith & Wesson, a major manufacturer of breath testing devices, notified law enforcement agencies that its Breathalyzer Model 1000 had been found to experience interference from radio frequency transmissions under certain test conditions, resulting in false test results. Subsequent investigation suggested that the Breathalyzer Models 900 and 900A also were affected by various power levels.

The potential sources of RFI within the law enforcement environment are numerous — for example, AM and FM radios, police station dispatchers, hand-held police transmitters, teletypes, and police radar units. Each of these may emit the kind of interference that could cause specific breath testing apparatus to render false results. It was then learned that the federal government

(National Bureau of Standards) was testing for RFI sensitivity every type of breath testing device currently in use by law enforcement agencies.

On September 10, 1982, Smith & Wesson issued a customer advisory suggesting that *all* evidential breath testing instruments be tested as a matter of preparedness for possible courtroom testimony.

Late in 1984, Smith & Wesson announced the availability of a kit designed to improve the Model 900A's resistance to RFI. In a customer advisory letter from Smith & Wesson's production manager, users of the machine were told that a "Kit I," consisting of a combination of a filter box and amplifier board was available for $147, and a "Kit II," consisting of only the filter box, was priced at $72. Additionally, the Model 900A could be converted by the factory for $171.

At about the same time, CMI came out with its state-of-the-art breath testing instrument, the Intoxilyzer 5000 (see §6.4.1). This new machine has an "RFI Detector." Obviously, the marketing of a kit and an "RFI Detector" to inhibit radio frequency interference constitutes a clear recognition of the problem. In view of such steps by manufacturers, it is difficult to imagine any prosecutor or witness denying that the problem exists.

In May 1983, Don Nichols and Jim Kaster, Minneapolis attorneys and editors of the Drinking/Driving Law Letter, obtained a copy of the National Bureau of Standards (NBS) preliminary report of test results for electromagnetic interference (EMI). The report was dated March 25, 1983. NBS was under contract with the National Highway Traffic Safety Administration (NHTSA) to conduct testing on evidential breath testers (EBTs) currently in use by law enforcement officials nationwide.

The report contained the "bottom line" results of RFI testing. Each of 16 unidentified instruments (the contract for testing specifically required that individual machines be identified by secret code only) were subjected to four different frequencies typically present in the standard police environment. Of the 16 units tested, only six showed minimal interference at each frequency; 10 of the 16 showed substantial susceptibility on at least one frequency. The report characterizes the potential effect of EMI on the testing of alcohol vapors as "severe." This characterization is found on page two of the report, where the writer is describing the first in-house demonstration of EMI to NHTSA representatives in March 1982:

> Early in 1982, the Washington D.C. Metropolitan Police Department reported to NHTSA that EBTs were found to display erroneous BAC [blood-alcohol content] readings in the presence of electromagnetic fields from radio transmission. NHTSA contacted LESL [Law Enforcement Standards Laboratory] and TSC [Transportation Systems Center], and it was agreed that if EBTs were susceptible to electromagnetic interference, action must be taken to solve the problem, and that it might be necessary to modify the NHTSA standard to include electromagnetic interference (EMI) susceptibility requirements. On March 24, 1982, representatives of NHTSA, TSC, and NBS were given a demonstration by police officers who routinely conduct breath testing using an EBT in a mobile van. One police officer operated his handheld radio within 0.3 m (1 ft.) of the EBT and demonstrated that the electromagnetic field could severely affect the analysis of alcohol samples.

As a part of Nichols and Kaster's FOIA action, release was also sought of any preliminary drafts of the National Bureau of Standards (NBS) report on RFI and EMI, specifically, a preliminary report authored by Dr. John Adams of Boulder, Colorado. This report was rumored to be significantly different from the final report eventually released by the NHTSA. So different was the final edited version that it was reported that Dr. Adams asked to have his name removed from the list of those responsible, and, in fact, a review of contributors does not show the name of Dr. John Adams. The following are excerpts from the Adams report, which is entitled Effects for the Electromagnetic Fields on Evidential Breath Testers, written for the Electromagnetic Fields Division, National Bureau of Standards, Boulder, CO 80303:

> Eight of the 16 units tested showed potential EMI problems under the specific test conditions of nominal 10 volts per meter electric field strength.
>
> These results *cannot* be extrapolated to predict how individual EBTs would be affected at other levels of field strength or at other frequencies.
>
> These results show that EMI is a potential problem with many of the EBT units in current use. The additional measurement tech-

niques, standards, and test levels suggested in the section on "Future Efforts Needed" are needed to fully evaluate the effects of EMI on EBTs.

The states may have to take interim measures to determine the extent of their individual problems with EMI affecting EBTs.

Dr. Richard E. Jensen, of Forensic Associates in Minneapolis, offers the following comments concerning RFI:

Instrument failure because of radio frequency interference is a serious problem today. These problems can affect not only breath testing devices such as the Breathalyzer but also instruments in the forensic laboratories and clinical laboratories.

Radio frequency interference (RFI) is not a new or unique phenomenon. Communication systems employed by the armed forces in World War I experienced RFI, especially in areas where there was widespread use of radios in automobiles and airplanes. The complexity of radio communication has increased since that time, and the incidences of RFI have followed a similar pattern. A special-interest area of science, referred to as electromagnetic compatibility (EMC), has evolved out of this concern with RFI. In an effort to encompass the concerns of the entire electromagnetic spectrum, not just radio frequency, a broader designation has evolved: electromagnetic interference (EMI). (EMI and RFI will be used interchangeably in this discussion.) This discussion will deal specifically with radio frequency interference concerns: in evidential breath testing, in other forensic measurements, and in clinical laboratory measurements.

The preliminary research reported by the Electromagnetic Compatibility facility of the National Bureau of Standards has demonstrated that many evidential breath testing devices experience EMI. At least 10 of the 16 instruments tested demonstrated some susceptibility to RFI. What this means, of course, is that the problem is one of a generic nature and is not limited to any specific instrument or manufacturer.

There are a number of opinions as to how radio frequency interferes with the performance of evidential breath test devices. The diversity of opinion results from the application of various theories and because the methods of measurement from one manufacturer to another differ in technology. In order to accurately evaluate the potential effect of radio frequency on evidential breath testing, it is imperative that each device be examined in its permanent location. A variety of procedures have been devised to accomplish this evaluation. All of these procedures are designed with a holistic approach where one must consider not only the instrument being tested but also its immediate surroundings and the involvement of the operator. The results of these site evaluations provide for a variety of important conclusions.

At the present time it may be that the breath testing instrument is the best potential detector for radio frequency in its environment. In keeping with a systems approach, the instrument will provide the precise data required for a site evaluation, particularly when coupled with a well designed evaluation protocol. All instruments are not equally susceptible to EMI. Therefore, it is appropriate to survey any given site with the instrument normally employed in that location.

Even if operators are well-trained and measurements are well documented, RFI can occur. What then? There is absolutely no course of action except to decertify the affected instrument and immediately take it out of service. The instrument must remain out of service until the source of the interference is identified and eliminated or until the instrument can be modified to function in its environment. This course of action is dictated not only by the fact that these instruments are performing evidential analyses but also by the generally accepted practice of good analytical measurement. The concern should not be whether the results are high or low or whether they are to the benefit of the defendant but simply whether or not they are accurate.

It is not my intent to discuss the details of the modification of breath test instruments in order to make them less susceptible to RFI. However, the task of modification is not an overly difficult one and should be undertaken if there is any indication that the instrument may potentially be affected by radio frequency in a manner that would cause erroneous results. It is important to remember that the responsibility of electronic design is in the hands of the manufacturer and any subsequent modification must be coordinated by the manufacturer. Unfortunately, this is not often the case, Smith and Wesson has just recently offered a modification retrofit kit for the Model 900A.

The evidential testing of breath for alcohol concentration is not the only chemical test that may have the potential for interference of electromagnetic radiation. There are two additional areas that should cause intense concern. These are forensic analyses or examinations for the judicial system and clinical analyses for diagnostic purposes. The potential for interference is not only present in settings where these types of measurements are made, but there is the probability that the presence of an interference will cause a much larger deviation than those supposedly found in breath alcohol measurements. The Breathalyzer Model 900A, although capable of making accurate measurements, is not a sophisticated electronic instrument. Instruments such as gas chromatographs, mass spectrometers, and spectrophotometers are electronically more complex and therefore potentially more susceptible to the influence of electromagnetic radiation. In this great technological age there are literally an infinite number of instrumental measurements occurring on a regular basis. To attempt to discuss all of these measurements in detail would be impossible, but it is sufficient to state that there is the theoretical potential for radio frequency interference with each and every measurement. However, what should be of imminent concern are two specific areas of scientific measurement that could potentially affect each and every one of us directly at one time or another. As mentioned earlier, one area is forensic science and the other clinical chemistry. In the past decade both disciplines have enjoyed the benefits of great strides in technology. This is especially true in the complexity and number of instrumental measurements that are now being performed.

The responsibility of forensic science is to provide the judicial system with the results of the scientific examination of physical evidence. These results are most often interpretations based on an instrumental analytical measurement. In addition to the classical types of examinations accomplished by the use of both the stereo and compound microscopes, the instruments employed by forensic scientists have expanded to a wide variety of sophisticated electronic devices of which many are computer controlled. These instruments are most often in laboratories that are associated with law enforcement personnel. With the increased use of communications equipment by law enforcement agencies and the proliferation of radio frequencies employed by these agencies, scientific equipment in the forensic science laboratory is being exposed to more and varying electromagnetic radiation than ever before. Because of this potential for radio frequency interference, the analytical measurements and the interpretations based on those measurements may be incorrect. Does this mean that under these circumstances there is no chance for an accurate measurement? Absolutely not. All that needs be done is to employ the rules that govern good analytical measurements in any area of science. First, all measurements must be performed at least in duplicate, meaning two separate measurements are made on the same sample. The

> purpose of this procedure is to substantially reduce the effect of a systematic error, of which RFI is but one example. Systematic errors are those that can arise from identifiable sources that can occur in a sporadic manner and that generally are the cause of large, unpredictable deviations of the measured quantity. Second, these duplicate analyses must be accompanied by well designed and systematic programs of quality control and proficiency testing.
>
> The concerns outlined above can and should be expressed also for the clinical chemist and the measurements that are made on physiological samples for the purposes of diagnosing medical problems. The majority of clinical laboratories have sound programs of quality control and proficiency testing. However, there are very few clinical tests or procedures performed in duplicate, a practice that does not count for or ensure the absence of systematic error. Systematic errors can be from an infinite number of sources. The only way in which the presence or absence of a systematic error can be assured in an analytical measurement is by making that measurement in duplicate: two separate measurements on the same sample. Recently a sheriff's deputy in southern Minnesota related to me, "They don't like us to use our radios in the hospital; it louses up their tests." Need more be said?
>
> Finally, let it be said that this concern for radio frequency interference is not an overreaction. It is a scientific fact: One area of technology simply has not caught up with another. Radio frequency interference is a product of today's technological demands interacting with yesterday's design and manufacturing methods.

The prosecution may counter counsel's RFI attack by pointing out that the machine has an "RFI detector." The problem with such "detectors" is that they are simply not reliable. First, as repeated tests have demonstrated, there is a segment of the frequency band to which the detector is essentially blind. If there is a source of interference from a device emitting electromagnetic waves in this frequency range, it will not be detected.

Second, the detectors are rarely calibrated correctly. Most law enforcement agencies are unqualified to perform a complete maintenance and calibration. Commonly, the instrument will be sent back to the manufacturer for annual calibration of the various "fail-safe" devices (RFI detector, mouth alcohol detector, interferent detector, ambient air flag, etc.). In the meantime, the machine is often "calibrated" by police officers by simply using something like a hand-held police radio. The device may be activated three or four times from three or four different angles and distances from the breath machine; if the RFI detector is triggered, it is considered "calibrated."

Unfortunately, there are a couple of problems with this crude procedure. First, only the frequency used by the testing device is being tested; the procedure does not determine if frequencies used by any of dozens of other EMF-emitting devices in the area will be detected. Second, the "calibration" is usually done with the breath machine turned on but not during an actual capture and analysis — i.e., during actual operating conditions.

§6.3.11 Testing After an Auto Collision

Any breath test conducted after the subject has been involved in a traffic collision should be viewed with particular suspicion. Such an event can cause any of the following possible complications:

1. Oral blood. If the subject is bleeding in the mouth, has facial lacerations causing blood to drip into the mouth, has hemorrhaging in the throat area, or is coughing up blood, it is probable that this will affect any breath machine's reading (assuming that there is any measurable amount of alcohol in the blood). The alcohol in the blood will be breathed directly into the machine, rather than being measured as part of alcohol in the alveolar breath, and consequently will be increased by the computer's application of the partition ratio. In other words, the machine will "think" it is reading alcohol attenuated by processing through the lungs and will, in effect, greatly multiply the BAC reading to compensate. Thus, a minute amount of alcohol in the blood — less than .01 percent — could result in a very high reading. See discussion of "mouth alcohol," §§6.2 *et seq.*
2. Airbag propellants. An ever-increasing number of cars on the road have airbags designed to deploy in a collision. This can, of course, cause injuries to the driver/subject — including injuries causing blood in the mouth. Of more interest, however, is the probability that the driver will in-

hale some of the propellant used to launch the airbag. This chemical compound will then be both (1) absorbed into the throat tissue, and (2) metabolised and eventually exhaled with alveolar air. Depending upon the type of propellant used by the manufacturer, it may trigger false readings of alcohol. Most breath machines — particularly those based upon infrared technology (e.g., Intoxilyzer 5000, DataMaster) — are non-specific for alcohol and will "read" common industrial compounds. See §§6.1 *et seq.*

3. The *Tyndall effect.* To prevent sticking when deployed, airbags are packed in baking soda, talc, or both. These very fine particles are explosively disbursed into the air inside the vehicle — and breathed in by the driver/subject. Later, they are exhaled into the sample chamber of the breath machine. These microscopic particles can create the "Tyndall effect" — the scattering of light by the particles within the chamber. The machines, of course, are designed to measure the amount of projected infrared energy absorbed by ethanol (or more accurately, any chemical compound with the methyl group); the less energy making it through to the detector on the other end of the chamber, the higher the BAC reading. See §6.1. Because of the deflection of the light beam caused by the baking soda/talc particles, however, less light energy will reach the detector — causing a higher reading.
4. The physiological effects of stress. As was discussed at some length in §6.3.5, scientific studies have repeatedly shown that stress directly affects the body's metabolism of alcohol. The stress from an auto accident (or, for that matter, an investigation and arrest) can, for example, virtually stop the digestion process. Among other things, the pyloric valve may not release the contents of the stomach (including food saturated with alcohol) into the small intestine (where approximately 80 percent of alcohol is absorbed into the bloodstream). Given this, consider the following common scenario suggested by attorney William C. Head of Atlanta. Assume that a subject has consumed a couple of drinks at a bar and then has "one or two for the road" before leaving. He is in an auto accident twenty minutes later. An officer's preliminary breath test shows

(accurately) a .048 percent BAC. Due to injuries, he is taken to a hospital. Because of treatment, interrogation, field sobriety tests and paperwork, a blood sample is not drawn until 2 ½ hours after the accident. Because of the delay in absorption of the alcohol, the blood test comes back .102 percent BAC. Since the prosecutor reasons that the BAC had to have been falling — i.e., higher at the time of driving — he files DUI charges.

5. "Refusals." Any alleged refusal to submit to breath testing after a traffic collision should be subject to careful investigation. Chest injuries can prevent a person from being able to provide a full breath sample; lumbar strain or "whiplash" can cause pain sufficient to prevent breathing with enough pressure for the machine. Any failure, of course, is immediately interpreted by the officer as a "refusal."

Checklist 5 Breath Analysis

- ☐ Was the machine properly licensed and maintained?
- ☐ Was the operator properly trained and licensed?
- ☐ Was the machine accurately calibrated?
- ☐ Was the simulator solution mixed correctly?
- ☐ Could the alcohol in the solution have become depleted?
- ☐ What was the temperature of the solution?
- ☐ Could there have been leakage in the vapor tube?
- ☐ Could radio frequency interference (RFI) have affected the reading?
- ☐ What possible sources of RFI existed in the breath machine's environment?
- ☐ Does the machine use infrared spectroscopy?
- ☐ Is it specific for ethyl alcohol?
- ☐ What compounds found on the human breath will it detect as "alcohol"?
- ☐ Does the machine have an acetone detector? If yes, was it working properly? If no, why not?
- ☐ Does the machine have an acetaldehyde detector? If yes, was it working properly? If no, why not?
- ☐ Is the client a diabetic or has he been fasting?
- ☐ What compounds containing the methyl group has he ingested or been exposed to?

- ☐ Does the test result depend upon the assumption that the client's blood-breath partition ratio is 2100:1?
- ☐ Does this affect admissibility or weight?
- ☐ Is there a new "breath-alcohol" statute in the jurisdiction?
- ☐ Could the breath test have been conducted during the client's absorptive phase?
- ☐ Had the client recently eaten food before drinking?
- ☐ Was mouth alcohol present?
- ☐ Did the client burp, belch, hiccup, or regurgitate within 20 minutes of the breath test?
- ☐ Did he consume any alcohol within 20 minutes of the test?
- ☐ Does he wear dentures, use dental adhesive, or have dental caps that could trap alcohol?
- ☐ Did he use any mouthwash, cough syrup, throat spray, breath freshener, or other product containing alcohol?
- ☐ Was there any blood present in the client's mouth or nose at the time of the breath test?
- ☐ What is the client's hematocrit?
- ☐ What was the client's body temperature at the time of the test?
- ☐ Could the client's breathing pattern have affected the breath test?
- ☐ Could stress have had an effect on the test?
- ☐ Was a sterile new mouthpiece used?
- ☐ What is the "inherent error" recognized with the breath analyzing machine?
- ☐ Was the machine purged with room air containing alcohol vapor from the client or previously tested suspects?

§6.4 The Machines

> Truth, like light, blinds. Falsehood, on the contrary, is a beautiful twilight that enhances every object.
>
> ALBERT CAMUS

There are a wide variety of breath analyzing machines available on the market today. The National Highway Traffic Safety Administration (NHTSA) of the Department of Transportation periodically publishes an amended list of these machines that meet federal standards. A recent version of this list, entitled Model Specifications for Devices to Measure Breath Alcohol and Conforming Products List, sets forth 74 different federally approved machines. Many of these, however, are model variations, such as the Intoxilyzer 4011, 4011A, 4011AS, 4011AS-A, etc.

The majority of these different models are rarely used by law enforcement agencies. Counsel representing a client charged with drunk driving will usually encounter one of the following machines (or a modified version thereof):

1. The Intoxilyzer 5000
2. The DataMaster
3. The Intoximeter 3000
4. The Draeger Alco Test 7110
5. The Breathalyzer 900
6. The Intoxilyzer 4011
7. The Intoximeter EC/IR

The most commonly used machine in the United States at the time of this writing is the Intoxilyzer 5000. This device, manufactured by CMI, Inc., of Owensboro, Kentucky, is used in over 30 states. It is sold in a number of different permutations, or "series models"; some of these represent improvements in design, such as the addition of more filters (e.g., models 564 and 568), while others are simply state-specific versions to satisfy local requirements (e.g., Oregon's 568G and Georgia's 568GA). The Model 5000 is available with a number of options (acetone detector, radio frequency detector, etc.). As with most other breath testing machines, the 5000 utilizes the infrared spectrophotometric method of analysis (or infrared absorption as it is often called), and thus is particularly susceptible to problems of non-specificity (see §6.1). For a discussion of the Intoxilyzer 5000, see §6.4.1.

The second most commonly encountered breath device is the BAC DataMaster. This machine was originally developed and manufactured by Verax Systems in New York, but was sold in 1988 to National Patent Analytical Systems, Inc. (2541 Ashland Road, Mansfield, OH 44905). There are currently five different models: the BAC DataMaster, the BAC DataMaster-K, the portable BAC DataMaster cdm, and the DataMaster II. It is the first version, the BAC DataMaster that counsel can normally expect to encounter, possibly with some state-specific modifications. The recent popularity of the device is not due to any greater degree of sophistication or accuracy, but rather to its relatively low price. As with the Intoxilyzer 5000, the DataMaster uses infrared technology and is therefore particularly susceptible to the problems of non-specific analysis. For a discussion of the BAC DataMaster, see §6.4.2.

Third in current popularity (though rapidly losing ground) is the Intoximeter 3000, manufactured by Intoximeters, Inc. (1901 Locust Street, St. Louis, MO 63103). The device also uses infrared absorption and comes in a number of slightly different configurations. Recently, the 3000 has been discontinued by its manufacturer and replaced with the new Intoximeter EC-IR, a device which, like the Draeger, utilizes dual infrared and fuel cell technology. As of this writing, however, the EC-IR has received limited acceptance among law enforcement agencies. The Intoximeter 3000 is discussed in §6.4.3.

Fourth in prevalence is the "Model T" of breath-testing machines, the Breathalyzer 900 and its various permutations: the 900A, 1000, and 2000. These devices were developed by Smith and Wesson Electronics, but later sold to National Draeger, Inc (10 Technology Drive, Pittsburgh, PA 15275). Unlike the currently popular machines, the Breathalyzers utilized a *wet chemical* method of breath analysis rather than infrared spectrophotometry. The captured breath sample was passed through a potassium dichromate-sulfuric acid solution contained in a disposable ampoule. The machine then measured the amount of potassium dichromate required to oxidize the alcohol in the breath. At one time, the 900 and 900A were by far the most commonly used breath devices in the country. Today, they are long-discontinued antiques — yet antiques that are still found in a surprising number of jurisdictions, particular in rural areas. The Breathalyzer is discussed in §6.4.5.

Fifth in popularity, and the machine that this author feels to be current "state-of-the-art," is Draeger's new Alcotest 7110 Mark III. The relatively sophisticated device is unique in many respects. First, it is designed as a portable unit; although many evidential breath machines are transported by police agencies in vehicles, the 7110 is *designed* for this. Second, the 7110 uses *dual technology:* Its method of analysis utilizes both infrared spectrophotometry *and* fuel cell technology. Third, a more alcohol-specific 9.5-micron light filter is employed. The author expects this machine to spread rapidly, restrained only by its relatively high cost. For a discussion of the Alcotest 7110, see §6.4.6.

Finally, the Intoxilyzer 4011 and its variations, manufactured by CMI, was once widely used but is now only occasionally encountered. The 4011 uses infrared technology, but is no longer manufactured, having been superceded by the model 5000. For a discussion of the Intoxilyzer 4011, see §6.4.4.

Counsel dealing with a DataMaster, Intoxilyzer 5000, or Breathalyzer 900 might find the following comments from scientific researchers of interest:

> The accuracy, precision and specificity for ethanol of eight different evidential breath alcohol measuring devices were evaluated. Other factors of importance, such as susceptibility to radio frequency interference and variation in power supply voltage, were also examined. On the basis of the above criteria, three instruments were identified as more suitable than the remainder for evidential use . . . the Draeger Alcotest 7110, Siemens Alcomat V5.2F and Seres Ethylometre 679.

Bell and Gutowski, Evaluation of Breath Alcohol Measuring Device Intended for Evidential Use in Victoria, 40 Acta Medicinae Legalis et Socialis 95 (1990). To the author's knowledge, the Alcomat is little used in the United States, and the Ethylometre not at all. Among the five machines found less than suitable, however, were the Breathalyzer 900, the BAC DataMaster, and the Intoxilyzer 5000 — all in common use across the country. The Intoximeter 3000 was not included in the tests.

The chart on the following page, provided to the author by forensic toxicologist Anne ImObersteg of San Jose, California, compares the characteristics of the four evidentiary breath devices most likely to be encountered in the coming years. Note that the Alcotest 7410 Plus, developed by Draeger to satisfy California Department of Justice requirements, is a *hand-held* unit but one that may — unlike PBTs (see §4.4) — satisfy foundational requirements for admission into evidence for blood-alcohol concentration.

§6.4.1 Intoxilyzer 5000

For many years, the only means of testing blood alcohol through breath analysis was with instruments using the *wet chemical* technique, such as the Breathalyzer. In 1972, however, Omicron

FEATURE	DRAEGER ALCOTEST 7110	BAC DATAMASTER	INTOXILYZER 5000	ALCOTEST 7410 Plus
Technology	Fuel cell and IR	IR	IR	Fuel cell, heated
Wavelength	9.5 micron O-H bonds	3.37 micron and 3.44 micron	3.39 micron, 3.48 micron, 3.80 micron (reference) C-H stretch	NA
Number of filters	One. No chopper wheel or series of optical filters	Two	3 or 5	NA
Slope Detector	Yes	Yes	Yes	No
Ambient air check	Yes, by IR and Fuel cell	Yes	Yes	Yes
Breath temperature sensing	Optional	No	No	No
RFI Detector	Yes. Will abort test if RFI levels exceed preset limit	Yes. Antenna on back of instrument. If level is "excessive" the instrument will abort the test	Yes. Antenna in breath hose	Unknown
Sample requirements	Minimum flow rate of 2.5L/Min., Minimum breath volume of 1.5 Liter, Minimum blow duration of 4.5 seconds, level slope detection	Minimum flow rate of 1.5 L/min., Flow rate must drop below 1.5 L/min .001, Minimum breath volume of 1.5 Liter, Slow rise (≤0.001) in the IR reading	Minimum volume, Minimum time of 4 seconds, Pressure of 4″ H2O	Minimum time and pressure. Capable of storing 600+ evidential tests. Converts from screening to evidential mode by a press of the button.
Specificity	Ethanol specific; differentiates between isopropanol and methanol. Acetone does not affect it.	Acetone detect system	Acetone detect system only	Alcohol specific
Misc.	IR source has a pulsed output: no need for a filter wheel. Breath hose is 44 inches in length. Breath sample volume is measured and reported.	Developed in 1987	Other filters can be added for more specificity. Older instruments can be made Y2K acceptable.	Same as the Breathalyzer 7410, except has a real time clock, expanded memory capacity and a "one button read-out option" to recall test result.

Systems Corporation introduced a machine using a new method of analysis based on *infrared spectrophotometry* (also called infrared spectroscopy or, simply, infrared absorption). Their Model 4011 was faster, easier to use, and more economical and convenient than the Breathalyzer. There was no evidence, however, that the device was any more accurate; in fact, because of greater risk of nonspecific analysis (see §6.1), the machine may be *less* reliable.

A few years after introducing the Intoxilyzer, Omicron sold all rights to the instrument to CMI, Inc. Subsequently, CMI introduced a new, state-of-the-art breath testing device: the Model 5000. This machine also utilized infrared spectrophotometry in its analysis, but incorporated an internal computer and various supposedly "fail-safe" features. Further, CMI claimed to solve the non-specificity problem by using three separate wavelength band filters (subsequent versions employed five filters). In addition, the Model 5000 incorporated an "interference detector" that would theoretically advise the operator whenever foreign substances such as acetone are present in the breath. And acetaldehyde detectors and radio frequency detectors were available as options. Experience, however, has proven that each of these features is less than reliable in ensuring accurate results.

Before looking into the machine and addressing the proper procedures for administering a test, the theory behind its operation should be clearly understood.

Infrared spectrophotometric analysis is based upon the fact that different molecules absorb light energy at different frequencies. Water, for example, will absorb infrared light whose wavelength is 2.7 microns: when this 2.7-micron light passes through water vapor, its vibrations are absorbed by bonds between the oxygen and hydrogen atoms in the water molecule, causing the atoms to vibrate more strongly and the 2.7-micron energy to disappear.

A complex molecule has a number of different sets of bonds, and neighboring bonds will influence a basic vibration, changing it slightly. Ethyl alcohol has its hydrogen-oxygen bond vibrations shifted slightly by the nearby presence of carbon-hydrogen bonds. As a result, most of the absorption of light by ethyl alcohol will take place in the band range from 3.380 to 3.398 microns. The Intoxilyzer, then, simply shoots a beam of infrared light through the captured breath sample and measures how much of it is absorbed in that range; the more absorption, the higher the blood-alcohol concentration.

Mechanically, the heart of the Intoxilyzer 5000 is a nickel-plated sample chamber of 81cc capacity heated to 45 degrees centigrade. This chamber captures the breath sample from the subject being tested. A quartz iodide lamp at one end of the chamber then emits infrared light energy, which is directed through the breath in the chamber by a lens. At the opposite end of the chamber, a second lens focuses the energy leaving the chamber through three rotating filters and onto an energy detector.

The more recent versions of the 5000 have five of these light energy filters. The first filter is the internal reference standard, designed to produce light waves at ethyl alcohol's by being centered at 3.80 microns. Two filters, at 3.40 and 3.47 microns, are designed to distinguish between alcohol and the commonly encountered interferent acetone. Two more filters have been added to detect acetaldehyde (like acetone, produced in the body) and toluene (a common industrial compound). Properly calibrated, these filters are designed to detect and subtract out from the final reading any interfering substances.

When the non-absorbed infrared light reaches the energy detector, the amount is then measured and this information is transmitted to an internal Z-80 computer. This primitive computer compares the amount measured to a "zero reference point" — the amount of infrared energy reaching the detector when the sample chamber was earlier filled with ambient (room) air. The difference — theoretically the amount of light absorbed by the subject's breath sample — is then calculated. Based on the amount of alcohol in the breath thus measured, the computer then calculates the amount of alcohol in the subject's blood by applying an average blood-breath partition ratio of 2100:1 (see §6.0.1 for a discussion of the fallacies of this ratio).

As has already been seen in §§5.0 *et seq.* and §§6.1 *et seq.*, of course, this method of blood-alcohol analysis is subject to many variables and problems.

Additionally, the various "fail-safe" mechanisms available as standard or optional features have proven unreliable. As mentioned, the Intoxilyzer theoretically detects the presence of acetone (and in later models, acetaldehyde and toluene) on the breath, registers "interferent" on the visual display, and automatically subtracts the acetone from the final reading. Quite simply, extensive tests have shown that the detectors do not always work.

The Intoxilyzer 5000 also has circuitry that supposedly detects the presence of radio frequency interference (see §6.3.10) and aborts the test. Again, law enforcement agencies routinely deny that RFI exists as a problem. And again, tests in the field and in the laboratory have shown that these detectors (which can be desensitized by technicians to avoid constant aborted tests) are not reliable.

The machine also features a "slope detector," which theoretically determines whether there is alcohol or an interfering substance present in the mouth. When mouth alcohol (see §6.2) is present, the alcohol content curve reaches a maximum and then declines rapidly due to depletion of the mouth alcohol; this decline is recognized by the machine's computer, resulting in the message "invalid sample." Once again, however, the feature is defective. For a complete discussion see §6.2.5.

Of course, counsel can always ask the officer/operator or forensic expert, "If the slope detector detects mouth alcohol, why is it necessary to have a 15- or 20-minute observation period prior to administering the test?"

Relatively recently, CMI added an additional feature to the Model 5000 which analyzes the ambient (room) air that is used to purge the sample chamber (see §6.3.8). If the air is contaminated by alcohol vapor, the machine will theoretically display "ambient failed" and the printout will state "invalid test — check ambient conditions." As with other "fail-safe" devices on the machines, the efficacy of this new feature is open to question.

Counsel dealing with a Model 5000 can confront the state's expert with the manufacturer's own recognition of an inherent defect in the machine. CMI has recently developed and offered for sale a newer version of the Model 5000: the Intoxilyzer Model 5000/568G. The main difference between this and the previous model is that it has a nonreactive breath chamber. The chamber of the previous 5000s is nickel-coated and can develop oxide buildup. This oxide in the walls of the chamber can absorb ethanol and water vapor — which can then be released into captured breath samples, giving a falsely high reading.

It should be noted that the availability of detectors for acetone, acetaldehyde, mouth alcohol, contaminated ambient air, and RFI developed by the machine's manufacturers constitutes solid evidence of the existence and impact of these problems. Similarly, the production of a new model of the machine featuring a chamber that avoids oxide buildup is a clear recognition that previous models suffer from this defect.

The maintenance and calibration of the particular Intoxilyzer used in the client's case should also be investigated for possible malfunctions or erroneous results in the past or in the use of the machine since the test. Again, most states have statutory requirements for the regular maintenance of breath analyzing instruments, as well as for their calibration (see §11.6.8). Any deviation from these requirements should be noted, particularly any malfunctions of the instrument in the past, any erroneous readings, or any recent periods of time without maintenance or calibration. The Intoxilyzer should have a maintenance log and a calibration log that should indicate any abnormalities. Even if the machine has been maintained and calibrated properly for the past several months, the jury will be interested in knowing that it has had problems in the more distant past — that is, that it is fully *capable* of malfunctioning.

Again, most jurisdictions require proof that the instrument was in correct working order as a foundational requisite to the admissibility of the test results. Failure to show at least proper calibration at specified time intervals should preclude use of any test results at trial. See, e.g., *French v. State,* 484 S.W.2d 716 (Tex. 1972); *People v. Krulikowski,* 230 N.W.2d 290 (Mich. App. 1975). Certainly, any significant indications in the records that the machine was functioning improperly should be grounds for exclusion. (See *State v. Deimeke,* 500 S.W.2d 257 (Mo. 1973).) And in some states, the Intoxilyzer must have received a "certificate of inspection" within a specified period of time prior to the administration of the test in question.

Even assuming a perfectly maintained and calibrated machine, however, infrared spectroscopic testing devices have proven to produce results inconsistent with one another. In Alpert, Keiser, and Syzmanski, Theory and Practice of Infrared Spectroscopy 303 (2d ed. 1970), a study is reported in which laboratory spectroscopic tests — considered more reliable than spectroscopic tests conducted by law enforcement in the field — showed instrument-to-instrument variations of up to 20 percent of the measured results.

As with other breath testing devices, the Intoxilyzer depends on the presumption that the subject's blood to alveolar air ratio is exactly 1:2100, a false presumption in most cases and one that can result in an error of as much as .03 or more in the final reading. This source of error, as well as numerous other problems inherent in breath analysis, is covered in §§5.3 *et seq.*

The single greatest flaw in the Intoxilyzer itself — and the most productive area for cross-examination — is the machine's inherent lack of specificity. The technical reason for this lack of specificity is that the Intoxilyzer is not designed to detect the molecule of ethyl alcohol (ethanol), but rather only a part of that molecule — the methyl group. In other words, it is the methyl group in the ethyl alcohol compound that is absorbing the infrared light, resulting in the eventual blood-alcohol reading. Thus the machine will "detect" *any* chemical compound and identify it as ethyl alcohol if it contains a methyl group compound within its molecular structure. The Intoxilyzer only *assumes* that the methyl group is a part of an ethyl alcohol compound.

No matter what the manufacturer may claim, the prosecution's chemical expert will have to admit a simple fact: The absorption in the Intoxilyzer could be caused by substances other than ethanol. Thus one can never be sure that what the Intoxilyzer is measuring is alcohol.

A number of scientific studies have confirmed the practical reality of this problem. For example, in Caldwell and Kim, The Response of the Intoxilyzer 5000 to Five Potential Interfering Substances, 42(6) Journal of Forensic Science 1080 (1997), researchers found that commonly encountered industrial chemicals (which can easily be absorbed in the work environment and retained for hours afterwards) such as toluene, xylene, and isopropanol, will register as "alcohol" on the machine. The scientists further concluded that, for example, "home hobbyists using toluene-based glues or workers in the painting industry would contain toluene on their breaths at concentrations above (endogenous) background levels."

For a more complete discussion of nonspecificity, including a discussion of the effects of acetone and acetaldehyde on the Intoxilyzer, see §6.1.1.

The Intoxilyzer machine is fully capable of electrical or mechanical malfunctions, as is any machine. The accuracy of the Intoxilyzer depends, among other things, on the intensity of the light that is beamed through the breath sample; the final reading is determined by the amount of the light that is absorbed by the alcoholic vapor. Thus any reduction in the intensity of the light from the quartz-iodide lamp bulb in the Intoxilyzer will register as the presence of alcohol, and the greater the reduction, the higher the reading. A malfunction in the bulb, then, or a drop in the line voltage (the bulb is designed to perform at 105 to 130 volts) could result in a false reading. If the voltage falls below 95 volts, the machine is designed to abort the test. However, a lesser voltage drop or a drop at the end of the 10-second test interval would not necessarily trigger the "abort" circuit. Of course, the abort circuit is not free from malfunctions, either.

The effects of these fluctuations in the light source of Intoxilyzers has been discussed in Smith, Science, the Intoxilyzer, and Breath Alcohol Testing, The Champion 5 (June 1987): A dimming of the light would appear as a decrease in absorbance, resulting in a higher breath test result. As the author points out, this can be caused by, among other things, a decrease in the transparency of the bulb wall and alteration of filament characteristics — both natural results of use and age.

These and other problems are theoretically prevented by the regulation of current to the filaments by the instrument's "automatic gain control" (AGC). Normally, the AGC compensates for some problems by increasing current through the filament, raising its temperature and level of light. The AGC is, however, far from foolproof. For example, components can deteriorate to the point that the AGC cannot compensate for the decreased brightness.

Recognizing this problem, the manufacturers have incorporated a circuit whereby a minus sign on the display lights up to warn the operator that the AGC cannot sufficiently compensate — and that a falsely high reading could result. The trouble with this is that the operator's manual does not advise the testing officer as to what this minus sign indication *means:* Unless the officer has been independently advised of the significance of the minus sign, he will continue with the test ignorant of the problem.

Counsel should also consider the various potential sources of malfunction in the Intoxilyzer attributable to its sensitive but critically important system of optics. It is, of course, the measurement of nonabsorbed infrared light that determines the ultimate blood-alcohol level. The optics of the Intoxilyzer consist of a light source, fused quartz lenses for collimating and focusing the light beam, windows to seal the sample cell, a series of reflectors to lengthen the optical path of the sample cell, a narrow-band infrared filter, and a lead sulfide infrared detector. The light source is a quartz-iodide lamp, which produces light over a wide spectral range including both visible and infrared.

The possibility of a power surge should not be overlooked in cross-examination. An unpredictable fluctuation in line voltage can adversely affect the accuracy of the Intoxilyzer reading.

One of the problems that has developed during the use of the Intoxilyzer is electrical interference from nearby radio transmissions (see §6.3.10). Just as television sets sometimes pick up transmissions from amateur radio operators, so can the Intoxilyzer pick up and convert signals. In fact, it has been estimated by electrical engineers that the Intoxilyzer contains at least *100* components that are capable of picking up and converting extraneous signals. In one experiment conducted at a police station, a radio transmitter was turned on during the testing of an individual with a known blood-alcohol level of .07 percent. This individual was tested successfully twice at .07 percent, and then the nearby transmitter was turned on: The Intoxilyzer registered a reading of .14 percent — *twice* the true blood-alcohol level.

Counsel should also consider the effects of temperature, humidity, and age of the machine. The following comments by experts C. John Landry and Thomas Bleauvelt are reproduced courtesy of the California Public Defender's Association:

> Many of the electronic components in this machine are sensitive to variations in internal temperature. In other words, many of these components will have a certain output and linearity at one temperature but function differently at another temperature. While the temperature of the sample cell is thermostatically controlled, there is no precision temperature control with respect to any of the electronic components. None of these components is housed in a compartment in which the temperature is thermostatically controlled.
>
> While there is a fan, it simply causes air from the immediate

environment to enter an exit, and has little effect in cooling this air. Furthermore, the temperature of the electronic components depends primarily on what occurs within them.

While there are some heat sinks over some transistors, a heat sink is a little metal plate about 1¾ inches square and all it does in conjunction with the fan is to prevent a transistor from burning up. With respect to these transistors, the heat sinks do not prevent variation in temperature but only place an outside limit to it. There are no heat sinks on the linearizer board, and there are more than one hundred components in this machine which are sensitive to variations in temperature (and for which there are not heat sinks).

The Intoxilyzer is, electronically, a solid-state machine. All of its electronic components are solid-state in contrast to previous generation devices in which many gaseous state devices (vacuum tubes) were employed for detection and amplification.

It happens to be that the availability of free electrons and holes in a semiconductor's crystalline structure is highly dependent upon temperature. The higher the temperature the more charge carriers (electrons and holes) are available. The temperature can greatly change the electrical resistance of a diode or transistor. Solid-state devices are notoriously good detectors of temperature variation.

Variations in temperature cause changes in the effective resistance of diodes and transistors and also change the amplification factor of the latter. In both devices an increase in temperature also increases the number of available charge carriers (holes and electrons) within the semiconductor material. This effect lowers the resistance of the material and thus increases the current flowing through the device since the applied power supply voltage remain more or less constant. The increased current causes even more internal temperature rise which, in turn, releases more charge carriers lowering the resistance even further.

If the temperature is not maintained within allowable limits by some cooling device, typically a heat sink for transistors, the combination of increasing temperature, lowering resistance, increasing current and further increasing temperature will destroy the transistor.

The main point here is that every semiconductor device in the machine is temperature dependent and we have no test data to verify the accuracy of the machine over operating temperature range.

As far as we know the manufacturer of the Intoxilyzer has made no effort to test the machine for temperature sensitivity or

> to provide any such test data or verification of accuracy over a prescribed temperature range.
>
> Temperature, in particular could have a very significant effect on the linearizer because it uses a bunch of diodes and they are temperature sensitive, in addition to being radio wave detectors.
>
> The determination of accuracy checks which are performed by employees of the Regional Laboratory and various law enforcement agencies are almost always performed during the day. Since there are few driving under the influence arrests during the day, the Intoxilyzer is almost always turned off during the day and the determination of accuracy check almost always takes place immediately after the initial waiting period for the sample chamber to heat up. During the night, Intoxilyzers are frequently left on for considerable periods of time due to the number of arrests and tests. Electronic components tend to become hotter the longer a machine is left on.
>
> Age and atmospheric humidity can also affect the output and linearity of electronic components, and can combine with temperature in doing so. An electronic component may be more susceptible because of age to variation due to temperature. Such a component may also change in output and linearity due to temperature and humidity where it would not due to the same temperature alone.

It should be noted that the regulatory agencies of Colorado and New Hampshire have complained of defects in the Intoxilyzer 5000 — defects that should be of interest to any counsel confronted with a case involving this supposedly state-of-the-art breath machine. The letters were originally forwarded to the manufacturer of the 5000, CMI, Inc., and were subsequently discovered by and published in 10(2) Drinking/Driving Law Letter 1 (June 17, 1991). The contents of these letters should provide defense counsel with sufficient material to keep prosecution experts and/or officers busy on cross-examination for quite a while.

The first letter, dated December 31, 1990, is from J. Robert Zettl, Program Administrator, Toxicology, Colorado Department of Health (4210 East 11th Avenue, Denver, CO 80220-3716), and is addressed to Tom Myers, Vice President of CMI (note: emphasis has been added):

> Dear Mr. Myers:
>
> I am writing in response to several problems that have

occurred in connection with the Intoxilyzer Model 5000 and its use in the state of Colorado for DUI enforcement.

As you know, Colorado has had a long standing relationship with CMI and has used its breath alcohol testing devices since the early '70s. Within the last year, we have experienced a severe increase in the numbers of maintenance problems, manufacturing defects, and needs for repair with field unit Model 5000 Intoxilyzers. I have included a copy of repair histories on Colorado units for the past two years. For FY 89 we had a total of 188 repairs. For FY 90 we are projecting that to increase to over 290. This is an increase of some 56% in just one year.

When the unit is operating properly, it is accurate and precise in its determination of a breath alcohol concentration. The device is equal to, or superior in that regard to other units that are on the NHTSA/DOT approved products list. The problem is *the unit has a history of higher than average downtime when used in DUI enforcement and has lost credibility within our enforcement community.*

The problems which I am referring to are centered around the printer, instrument inconsistencies that are related to poor manufacturing quality control, and numerous electronic and voltage aberrations which cause the unit to shut down for no apparent reason.

The printer problems are very specific. *To continue to place this printer in production models is tantamount to malfeasance.* Your own service and sales force state that the printer is faulty and needs to be replaced. *If we were dealing with an automobile manufacturer the units would be recalled* and the repairs or service would be at the manufacturer's expense.

The numerous electronic problems are not specific. *The most distressing problem is the blank breath phantom or ghost readings of from .007 to over .025.* This situation has been known to you for over two years and has yet to be corrected. Another is the variant DVMs on new production units. IR source lamps have less than acceptable life expectancy, repair parts are hard to find or cross reference, changes are made without regard to customer notification, and replacement boards do not fit and have to be retrofitted before installation.

Manufacturing defects have been increasing over the past year. Most recently this was apparent in sample chambers that lost or are losing their plating. We have been experiencing an increasing number of poor quality parts and quality control on new units is not acceptable. This leads me to believe that CMI cares more for its profit than building a quality breath alcohol test device. To the best of my knowledge MPD/CMI has placed less emphasis on research and development and in redesigning the Model 5000 since the company was purchased over two years ago from Federal Signal. A competing company, Plus Four, has a retrofit which may or may not be of benefit to the increased precision, accuracy, and reliability of the Model 5000. What has CMI done to incorporate these changes into its production units?

We have surveyed other states that use the Model 5000 Intoxilyzer and have found that they too experience similar situations to the ones I have alluded. When asked if they were having any problems with the Model 5000 Intoxilyzers most stated no. These states, however, have seen fit to handle the increases in repairs and maintenance problems in a different manner. Namely by hiring more technicians to repair units, thus, on the surface, downtime is not an issue. Point of fact, we have an organization specifically oriented to the handling of problems with the Model 5000 Intoxilyzer, the Intoxilyzer 5000 Users Group.

In Colorado, we wish to put the blame where it belongs — on the manufacturer of *this inferior equipment.* With over 100 Model 5000 Intoxilyzers in the state it is common to have 5 to 10% down at any one time for various reasons. However, during the summer and fall of 1990 *that number has increased to over 25%* on many occasions. Even the units that are repaired at your parent factory or an authorized repair facility are returned to us in an inoperable condition thus further exacerbating the situation.

Colorado law enforcement agencies have lost faith in the Model 5000 Intoxilyzer. Many have had to lay out thousands of dollars for blood alcohol tests during times when their units are out of service. Many are in jeopardy of losing Law Enforcement Assistance Funding due to the lack of testing capabilities. I have attached four of the numerous letters that have been received in response to this problem.

The Colorado Division of Highway Safety, which supports many law enforcement agencies within Colorado, is seeking a return of its investment that was provided to my agency for training in an effort to decrease the downtime that we had been experiencing even before this year. See the attached letter from Mr. Helzer of the Colorado Division of Highway Safety.

The situation in Colorado is no longer tolerable and I am seeking relief either in the return of dollars spent by my agency in the handling of repairs, or in the form of replacement units for all devices that have more than 30 days of downtime in any one calendar year.

I have forwarded this letter and others that have been received in response to this situation to the Department of Transportation, NHTSA, the Attorney General's office in Colorado, the Model 5000 Users Group, State Highway Safety Coordinators, International Association of Chiefs of Police, and other law enforcement agencies who might find this information of interest.

I look forward to your response to this intolerable situation.

Sincerely,

The second letter, also addressed to Tom Myers, is from Susan Lefebre, Chemistry Program Manager, Public Health Laboratory, Division of Human Services, State of New Hampshire (again, emphasis has been added):

Dear Tom,

As a followup to our conference call on Thursday, along with Bill Schofield and Mark Gilmer, I am writing to document our concerns regarding the breath program in New Hampshire.

Since the program was instituted last January, we have tried to resolve the problem of poor correlation between the infrared results and sample capture analyses on field tests. Although covered in their initial training, many operators were not removing the mouthpiece from the breath tube prior to collection. In early May, it became clear that something other than the mouthpiece was also contributing to *captured sample values resulting in greater than 20% deviation from the infrared result.*

Public Health personnel have troubleshooted the cause and determined that *condensation builds up in the tygon hoses* associated with sample capture collection which is independent of the infrared analysis. Both software and hardware have been reviewed and tested. All of the work has been documented and will be reviewed with Bill Schofield when he arrives.

Over the period of nine months, we have discovered that *atmospheric conditions* do affect the correlation between the infrared results and sample capture analysis. Testing results from May show a high percentage of deviation. *Similar testing conducted as recently as a few weeks ago showed very slight deviation from infrared values, even when conditions were grossly exaggerated and should have produced a large discrepancy. It is for this reason that I believe that all hoses associated with sample capture collection must be heated to ensure accurate comparison to the State's sample.*

Other problems we have been encountering are:

MAILING — poor timeliness of shipping. For instance, material requested to be sent UPS 2nd day took 10 days to leave shipping.

PARTS — A. Breath tubes are not uniform. Although the lengths are close, they must be uniform to maintain the volume measurements given to calculate the correlation between sample capture and the infrared analysis.

B. The white connector to the breath tube does not stay adhered to the tube and the operator unknowingly tosses it, along with the mouthpiece, into the trash.

C. The grey wire has become crimped from usage resulting in *loss of heat to the tube, which will have an effect on the analysis.*

D. The cherry switch on the printer has failed on 9 of the units thus far.

E. Unstable DVM has occurred on 14 occasions.

F. Power supplies have been replaced on 7 units.

G. There have been 19 cases where chips were replaced affecting the ACA.

H. External standard out of tolerance has been documented at least 24 times.

SIMULATORS — I. We have lubricated 19 motors due to failure. Of these, 5 motors have had to be replaced along with 7 thermometers.

J. Screws on many of the simulators have begun to rust.

Unit failures resulting from other causes have been less numerous and we are monitoring their frequency of occurrence.

We have discussed many of the problems noted above with CMI personnel as requested. In some cases feedback was given or corrections were made to resolve the problems. On the other hand, we are still waiting to hear what will be done

> with the breath tubes, simulator motors, and the condensation problem continues to drain our resources and is taxing our ability to properly maintain the equipment.
>
> Ric Serve has been responsive and very helpful in repairing the major problems with the units. But regulations require that the units be further checked by Public Health personnel before they can be returned to the field.
>
> Time is running short where the courts will accept any breath result unless the consistency in correlation or results improves. At least one judge has said that he wants a new unit because he claims that his is the worst in the state. *A review of the instrument records shows the unit to be operating fine. The problem, though, can be traced to difficulties in obtaining a proper sample, which has a direct effect on the sample capture value when analyzed.*
>
> Again, as we discussed in our conversation on Thursday, I would like to have an acceptable resolution to the condensation problem by the end of the month. Timing for implementation of the unit changes can be determined afterwards.
>
> I am willing to discuss any questions you may have in order to raise our breath testing program to the level to which it is capable of achieving.
>
> Sincerely,

Counsel may wish to deliver copies of the contents of the letters to the expert/officer a week or two prior to his testimony so that he cannot avoid cross-examination by saying he is not familiar with them. The witness may then be asked if his opinion of the accuracy and dependability of the machine has been affected by the reports of defects in the letters — taking each of the many defects one at a time, possibly after first having the witness read the entire letter to the jury. If he claims not to have read the letters, counsel can inquire why he is not interested in possible defects in the machine and then ask him to read the letters and inquire as to each allegation whether this would affect his opinion.

As with all breath analysis instruments, defense counsel should consider the operator as the first possible source of error. Most jurisdictions have statutory regulations governing the training and/or experience required of officers before they are permitted to administer a breath test. Usually the requirements involve a requisite number of hours of instruction in the theory and operation of the particular instrument; in some states, formal certification or licensing is required. Certainly, counsel should determine whether the officer who administered the test to his client has received the required training. In more cases than would be expected, counsel will find that the officer simply has been told by fellow officers how to operate the machine (informal on-the-job training) or has received instruction at the local police academy, which may not qualify as a suitable place of instruction under the state's laws. Another possibility is that the operator has been trained on a breath analyzing model other than the one used on the client, or on an older version of the model actually used.

By establishing an operator's lack of experience or lack of training, counsel may well be able to challenge successfully the admissibility of the test results into evidence. In some jurisdictions, the unfamiliarity of the operator with the instrument's theory and operation can constitute sufficient grounds to deny the prosecutor the use of the evidence. (See, e.g., *State v. Mobley,* 160 S.E.2d 334 (N.C. 1968); *Pruitt v. State,* 184 S.E.2d 334 (W. Va. 1971).) And where the operator has not had the required training or has not obtained the necessary license, the test results generally will be held inadmissible. (See, e.g., *Klebs v. State,* 305 N.E.2d 781 (Ind. 1974).) Proof of licensing or training should be required by way of certified copies of official records rather than by submission of a copy of the license or course certificate given to the operator. (See *State v. Ghylin,* 222 N.W.2d 864 (N.D. 1974); *City of Monroe v. Robinson,* 316 So. 2d 119 (La. 1975).)

Even in those jurisdictions not having formal requirements for training the operator, defense counsel should interrogate the officer on the stand thoroughly as to his lack of experience, training, and/or specific knowledge of the instrument's theory and operation. Few officers, no matter how well trained, really understand how the Intoxilyzer works, and establishing this lack of knowledge or inexperience can be important in raising doubt in the jurors' minds about the results of the test.

Much of the following material has been adapted from the Operator's Manual supplied by the manufacturer. Thus counsel may find it helpful during cross-examination of the operator to determine whether he not only understands the theory of the machine but also whether the test was administered in accordance with the manufacturer's precise instructions.

According to CMI's manual, the following is the order of messages and commands given by the display. To conduct a breath test, the operator simply responds to the displayed messages and commands as indicated in the right-hand column:

Display Reads	*Meaning/Required Operator Action*
1. "READY TO START" or, scrolling across the display, "CMI . . . . . INTOXILYZER-ALCOHOL ANALYZER MODEL 5000 - - - PUSH BUTTON TO START TEST"; "PUSH BUTTON (flashing)"; "TIME ##HR ##MIN"	Insert a new mouthpiece in end of the breath tube. To start the test, push the Start Test button at any time.
2. "INSERT CARD (flashing)"	Insert an evidence card into the card slot located on the front panel of the instrument. Make sure to insert the card face up with the top edge "in" according to the instructions printed on the card. If S13 (Print Inhibit) is also in the "on" position, the instrument does not request an evidence card.
3. "AIR BLANK"	
4. "TIME ##HR ##MIN"	
5. "DATE MM/DD/YY" (European and Australian) "DATE DD/MM/YY"	
6. "AIR BLANK .000"	
7. ">> . . ."	
8. "PLEASE BLOW INTO MOUTHPIECE UNTIL TONE STOPS"; "PLEASE BLOW (flashing)"	Request subject to blow into the mouthpiece until the tone stops; the subject has three minutes to provide an adequate breath sample.

To insure delivery of a sufficient sample, the displayed command requests the subject to blow into the mouthpiece until the tone stops. The tone, however, does not actually stop until the subject stops blowing.

9. "PLEASE BLOW .###" followed by "PLEASE BLOW 0.###

In order to provide an adequate breath sample, a subject must blow for a minimum of four seconds. As the subject blows into the mouthpiece, the instrument sounds a continuous tone and displays the message to the left: "PLEASE BLOW .###". The three digit (optional two digit) number is the subject's rising (falling, constant) alcohol concentration. The continuous tone tells you that the subject is blowing with sufficient pressure. When the zero appears before the BAC value (0.###), the subject has delivered an adequate breath sample. Do not, however, instruct the subject to stop blowing when the zero appears.

If S5 (Display During Test) is "off," the instrument will not display the blood alcohol concentration value until the subject stops blowing and has delivered a sufficient breath sample. The instrument will also not display the zero indicating when the subject has delivered an adequate breath sample.

If the subject stops blowing before providing a sufficient sample, "PLEASE BLOW" flashes on the display and a beep sounds every five seconds. If this occurs, request the subject to blow into the mouthpiece until the tone stops.

In the event that the subject fails to provide an adequate breath sample within three minutes, "DEFICIENT SAMPLE" appears on the display accompanied by a low-high tone sounding intermittently for five seconds. Next the instrument displays "SUBJECT TEST .###" (the highest BAC value obtainable from the given breath samples), and completes the mode sequence. On the evidence card, the instrument indicates the highest obtainable BAC value by printing an asterisk (*) before "SUBJECT TEST ###". The asterisk (*) is a cross reference to the message printed at the bottom of the evidence card: "DEFICIENT SAMPLE-VALUE PRINTED WAS HIGHEST OBTAINED".

10. "SUBJECT TEST .###"

11. "AIR BLANK .###"

12. "TEST COMPLETE" — Remove evidence card after it is released by the instrument.

13. "READY TO START" or,
    scrolling across the display,
    "CMI . . . . .
    INTOXILYZER-ALCOHOL
    etc."

Regardless of which standard mode sequence the instrument is programmed to perform, your required actions will be the same as those shown in the typical ABA test. When S6 (Sample Capture Option) is "on," however, the instrument will insert new commands in the mode sequence chain requesting you to attach and detach a collector device. (See "The Sample Capture Option" page 30). Also, if the instrument is set to carry out the operations of a custom-programmed mode sequence, the displayed messages and commands and your required actions may vary.

The most common error messages that will be encountered in the newer Intoxilyzer 5000 models, along with the manufacturer's theoretical explanation, are:

USR Unstable reference. The computer was unable to establish a stable reference signal.
IVS Invalid Sample. Residual mouth alcohol was detected, belching occurred, the subject's breath sample did not meet the prescribed slope pattern for a normal individual.
RFI Radio Frequency Interference. High level of radio frequency interference was detected.
DEF Deficient Sample. The subject did not provided an adequate sample within the required time period.
REF Refusal. The start button was pressed again, the subject did not blow within three minutes after the "please blow" prompt.

The following is the manufacturer's summary of the various things that can go wrong during the administration of a test with the Intoxilyzer 5000, along with the recommended procedure for dealing with the problem. (Counsel should note that the extensive list of possible failures provides fertile ground for cross-examination of the operator or expert who feels the machine is "fail-safe.")

Intoxilyzer 5000 Operator's Guide

Message	*Explanation*	*Action Required*
"No Sample Given"	Person did not breathe hard enough to activate breath pressure switch during 3 minute period.	Restart test. Continue test until subject gives breath sample or refuses test.
"Insufficient sample"	Sample given did not meet requirements: a) adequate pressure, b) for a long enough time and c) reaching a level slope. "Insufficient Sample" is *not* the same as a refusal.	Test Complete. Note conditions of breath sample. (Length of blow, apparent effort, etc.) Do Not restart test.
"Refused"	"Start test" button was pushed during the "Please Blow" cycle	Test Complete. (If button pushed in error — restart test)
"Interferant Detected"	Acetone, toluene or other substance is present in the breath and could affect the test result.	1) Test complete — Do Not Restart. 2) Ask about diabetes, fasting, solvent exposure. 3) Ask for blood sample.
"Invalid sample-Residual Alcohol Present" "Inst. range exceeded"	— Mouth alcohol detected — Result higher than .60%	1) Check mouth 2) Wait/observe for 15 min. 3) Rerun test

Message	*Explanation*	*Action Required*
"Check Ambient Conditions"	Alcohol or other contaminant being introduced to breath chamber during "Air Blank"	1) Remove contaminants and subject's mouth from breath tube during Air Blank. 2) Rerun test
"Invalid Test"	Procedural error: button pushed at wrong time, sample given at wrong time, or card pulled from printer at wrong time.	Restart Test
"Inhibited RFI-Invalid Test"	Radio transmission near Intoxilyzer.	1) Remove radio source 2) Restart test
Evidence card jammed in printer	Improperly fed card or problem with printer.	1) Push "start test" button. The card should feed out. 2) If card remains, gently pull it out. 3) If portions of the card remain in printer, or problem repeats, call for service.
"Error" messages	— failed diagnostics	1) Push start test button. 2) If the problem persists push reset button at back of instrument. 3) If problem persists, turn instrument off, wait 30 seconds, turn back on.
"Invalid mode"	— mode switch set improperly	
"Stability Fail"-Unstable Reference	— electronic drift	
Display locked up	— electronic lock-up	

Message	*Explanation*	*Action Required*
General Instrument Failure	— component burn-out	4) If problem persists, place instrument "Out of Service" and report the problem. (See instructions on top of instrument)
Display locked up	— electronic lock-up	3) If problem persists, turn instrument off, wait 30 seconds, turn back on.
General Instrument Failure	— Component burn-out	4) If problem persists, place instrument "Out of Service" and report the problem. (See instructions on top of instrument)

ORANGE COUNTY SHERIFF-CORONER DEPARTMENT
INTOXILYZER 5000 PRECAUTIONARY CHECKLIST

(TO BE COMPLETED BY OFFICER, ALSO COMPLETE OFFICER'S BREATH TEST OBSERVATION BELOW)
DATE OF TEST 12-30-94 ARRESTING AGENCY CHP-WESTMINSTER CASE NUMBER ______
OFFICER'S NAME J. E. LANGAGER
SUBJECT'S NAME ______ SUB. DOB 12-18-65

NOTE: Subject must be under continuous observation from 15 minutes prior to the first breath sample until the final breath sample is collected. During this time, he/she must not eat, drink, or smoke anything and must not belch, burp, vomit, or regurgitate. If any of the above occurs, the test must be discontinued and the observation restarted or the subject must choose another chemical test.

OFFICER'S OBSERVATION OF SUBJECT FOR BREATH TEST STARTED AT: 1810 ; ENDED AT: 1825.
OFFICER'S INITIALS: [initialed]
OPERATOR'S OBSERVATION OF SUBJECT FOR BREATH TEST STARTED AT: 1825. OPR. INITIALS: [initialed]

TO BEGIN TEST: (OPERATOR MUST EITHER RESPOND TO OR COMPLETE EACH ITEM)

1. Ask subject "Do you have any breathing problems?" ☐ yes ☒ no OPR. Initials: [initialed]
If yes, describe: ______
2. Record the following: Instrument S/N 64-00 1 9 0 8 SIM. LOT# 113094 VALUE 0. 111 %
3. Press green start button and follow Intoxilyzer 5000 instructions. SIM. TEMP. 34.0 °C
(Use keyboard to enter information requested by display, press return after keyboard entries. After "N" is typed for "Review Data? Y/N", data is no longer entered with keyboard; write requested information in the appropriate spaces.)

WRITE CLOCK TIME: 1826 — of timepiece used for observation statement

RECORD RESULTS

AIR BLANK	CAL. CHECK	AIR BLANK	OPR. BREATH	AIR BLANK
0. 000	0. 109	0. 000	0. 00	0. 00

4. Demonstrate to the subject how to give a proper breath sample. Check that breath tube is warm. OPR. Initials: [initialed]
5. Discard operator's mouthpiece; place subject's mouthpiece into breath tube.
6. Ask the subject "Have you belched, burped, regurgitated, or vomited during the last 15 minutes?"
Response: ☐ yes ☒ no OPR. Initials: [initialed] (If yes, press the green start button to discontinue the test.)

RECORD RESULTS

SUB. BREATH	AIR BLANK	SUB. BREATH	AIR BLANK	* SUB. BREATH	AIR BLANK
0. 20	0. 00	0. 19	0. 00	0.	0.

* Complete only if 2 breath results do not agree within a 0.02%.

7. Ask the subject "Have you belched, burped, regurgitated, or vomited during the test?" ☐ yes ☒ no OPR. Initials: [initialed]
Comments: ______
8. Discard subject's mouthpiece. Insert test card when directed by the Intoxilyzer 5000.
9. I completed my continuous observation of the subject at 1831 (time), by which time the breath sampling on the subject had been completed. OPR. Initials: [initialed]
10. After card is printed, press green start button once to reprint card or twice to complete test. Obtain the subject's right thumbprint on test card. Sign test card, include date and time.
ATTACH TEST CARD TO INTOXILYZER 5000 PRECAUTIONARY CHECKLIST.

ADDITIONAL COMMENTS: ______
Operator's signature [signature] Agency CHP Date/Time 12-30-94 1832

***** COMPLETE OPERATOR'S LOG *****

F0680-350(R6/86)

Form 1
Intoxilyzer 5000 Checklist

THIS SIDE UP. THIS EDGE IN. FORM NUMBER F0680-356

```
LAGUNA BEACH POLICE DEPT. 2
INTOXILYZER - ALCOHOL ANALYZER
OCSD MODEL 5000    SN 64-001910
12/18/1994

SUB NAME =
SUB DOB  =06/09/68
OPER NAME=NUNEZ,M
CODE FOR AGENCY=LBPD
CASE NUMBER=94-6617
SIM LOT NUMBER=090994
OBS SIM TEMP=34.0

TEST               %BAC     TIME
AIR BLANK          .000    03:15PST
CAL. CHECK         .105    03:15PST
AIR BLANK          .000    03:16PST
OPER TEST          .00     03:17PST
AIR BLANK          .00     03:17PST
SUBJECT TEST       .09     03:18PST
AIR BLANK          .00     03:19PST
SUBJECT TEST       .09     03:20PST
AIR BLANK          .00     03:20PST
```

RIGHT THUMBPRINT

OPERATOR'S COMMENTS

OPERATOR'S SIGNATURE DATE 12/18/94 TIME

ORANGE COUNTY SHERIFF CORONER FORENSIC SCIENCE SERVICES

Form 2
Intoxilyzer 5000 Test Card for Recording Results

Counsel will find the following material offers valuable technical insight into the design, operation, and defects of the Intoxilyzer 5000. The author is grateful to forensic consultant Mary Catherine McMurray (Forensic Associates, Inc., of Minneapolis; tel. (612) 339-7903), who has extensive experience in the blood-alcohol field, for permission to reproduce this material.

DEMYSTIFYING THE INTOXILYZER 5000

GENERAL PRINCIPLES

INTRODUCTION

The proper function of any breath test instrument depends upon harmony and stability. The signals and voltages within the boards must be stable and work in harmony with each other. The boards must exist within a stable instrument.

Essential to tracking the processor signals, is an understanding of how these signals are generated. To facilitate this understanding a basic discussion of the *optical bench* and the *processor board* is necessary! The optical bench is the "heart" of the instrument (Figure 6-8). It is composed of a light source, the chamber lenses, the chamber, the filter wheel, the detector, and the processor. Even though the processor is an essential part of the optical bench it will be discussed separately.

THE IR LIGHT SOURCE

As the name indicates the IR light source is where the infrared light is generated. The IR[1] source must be able to provide adequate energy[2] of the required wavelengths and must provide a stable output of this infrared energy. The Intoxilyzer 5000 utilizes a (quartz iodide) tungsten filament halogen light bulb as an IR source. The bulb has been back-coated with a reflective material to optimize the IR energy directed into the sample chamber. Cloudy or opaque bulbs reduce signal output. Poor alignment of the IR source to the detector also reduces the strength of the signal. Weak signals require greater amplification than strong signals.

[1] IR is an abbreviation for Infrared Radiation. Infrared light is just below the red end of the visible light spectrum.

[2] Light is energy. When referring to light energy the term wavelengths is used. Each wavelength corresponds to a discrete amount of energy. Wavelengths are measured in microns (μ) 1 μ 0.000001 meter.

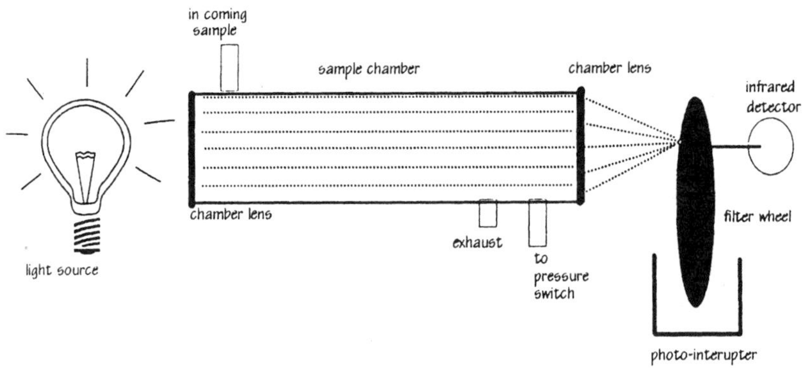

Figure 6-8
The Optical Bench

THE SAMPLE CHAMBER LENSES

The sample chamber lenses gather and focus the light energy entering and exiting the sample chamber. The lens mounted on the light source end of the chamber will gather the IR light and project it through the chamber.[3] The lens mounted at the exit side of the chamber will re-gather the light and focus it onto the filter wheel. The lenses should provide good gathering and focusing ability while blocking very little of the IR light. The Intoxilyzer 5000 uses Poly IR5 Fresnel 0.065″ thick lenses. Cloudy or opaque lenses will block light and reduce the signal output. Scratches on the lenses will scatter light reducing the signal output.

THE SAMPLE CHAMBER

The sample chamber is where the sample will be collected and held for the analysis. The sample chamber must be heated to avoid the development of condensation from the breath/air sample onto the surfaces of the lenses or the walls of the chamber itself. The temperature of the sample chamber must be relatively constant throughout the analysis. The operating temperature of the original sample chamber in the Intoxilyzer is 45° +/−5°C. It should be noted that sample chamber temperatures below 47°C have resulted

[3] The process of gathering the light and projecting it through the chamber is often called collimating. The reverse process, namely taking a column of light and focusing it is referred to as focusing.

in "ghost readings."[4] The newest version of the Intoxilyzer (the 500EN a.k.a. the 6801 series, the 1768 or the MN model) has a temperature range of 47° +/−5°C and is capable of reporting the actual temperature of the sample cell at the time of testing.

The sample chamber must be sealed so that the incoming sample will not leak out and outside air cannot enter, diluting the sample. The volume of the sample chamber is not a critical issue in the 6400 or 6600 series[5] instruments. In these older devices the analysis of the breath sample is not volume dependent, but rather time, pressure, and "slope"[6] dependent. In the 68 series[7] Intoxilyzers, the volume of the breath exhaled is much more critical. In these instruments the slope after a minimum volume of breath is exhaled[8] determines if a sample is adequate. The volume of the sample chamber is 81.4 cc for the older Intoxilyzer 5000s. The newest version of the Intoxilyzer[9] series, model 5000EN or 6801, is reported to have a sample chamber volume of 82.2 ml.

The 68 series Intoxilyzers have the ability to measure and report the volume of the breath sample that was delivered through the use of a pressure transducer.[10] As the breath moves past the

[4] Ghost readings, or blank breath phantom readings, ranging from 0.007 to 0.025 were reported in December 1990 by the State of Colorado Department of Public Health in a letter addressed to Tom Meyers at CMI. Other sources for ghost readings are unstable power supplies or DVM and debris in the sample chamber.

[5] The first four digits of the serial number indicate which series the device is. For example: if the serial number is 64-001122 the machine is a 6400 series.

[6] Slope detection in breath alcohol testing refers to the change in alcohol concentration over time during the analysis of a breath sample. A zero slope would indicate that the sample concentration is at a constant value. The leveling off of the sample concentration to an almost constant value is used as an indicator of having deep lung, or alveolar, air.

[7] The 68 series instruments have a cooled detector, three to five filters, and may have dry gas capabilities. The Federal Register identifies the three-filter device as a 5000 CD and the five-filter as a 5000 CD/FG5. The display and printing of the exhaled breath volume information can be controlled with a mode selection switch. Stat requested options on the 6800 instruments have included retrofitting the devices with pressure switches instead of pressure transducers. Such devices will not be capable of reporting sample volumes.

[8] The volume of breath is measured as a function of temperature change affecting a transducer.

[9] The 6801 series was created as a result of modifications requested by the Minnesota Bureau of Criminal Apprehension Laboratory after their evaluation of the five filter Intoxilyzer (the 5000 CD/FG5, a.k.a. the 768). Many of the modifications are esthetic in nature or intended to improve the maintenance accessibility of the device.

[10] A transducer is a semi-conductor that exhibits a relatively large change in resistance as a function of temperature.

transducer the temperature of the transducer changes causing a change in the flow of electric current through the transducer. The change in current flow during the course of the entire exhalation is then used to determine the volume of breath delivered. The duration of the exhalation (how many seconds did the person blow) is not measured or reported. The transducer is connected at the breath tube connector.

Of primary concern with all IR spectrophotometers is the *resolution* of the sample chamber. "Resolution" is a term used to describe how much light is able to pass through the chamber. The infrared light as it leaves the lens on the light source end will spread throughout the sample chamber so that the chamber is flooded with the IR light. It is then collected and focused onto the filter wheel as it exits the sample chamber. The resolution of the system should provide good contact between the IR light and the sample. Scratching, pitting, corroding, or condensation on the inner surfaces of the sample chamber[11] will reduce the resolution of the chamber and can cause poor precision in analysis.

THE FILTER WHEEL

The light exiting the chamber consists of IR, UV and visible light.[12] The light must be filtered so that only selected wavelengths of IR energy are allowed to pass onto the detector. Multiple wavelengths are utilized for analysis to increase the specificity of the analysis. The Intoxilyzer 5000 currently employs a filter wheel with *narrow band pass* filters[13] mounted in precise locations for the filtering of the IR light (Figure 6-9). Three-filter instruments[14] use the 3.80, 3.48 and 3.39 micron wavelengths. The five-filter instruments[15] use the 3.80, 3.52, 3.47, 3.40, and 3.36 micron wavelengths.

[11] The sample chambers of the 6400 and 6600 series Intoxilyzer 5000's have had problems associated with pitting and flaking of the sample chamber. See "Flaking or Flaky: CMI's Intoxilyzer Model, 5000" by Gil Sapir, J.D., M.Sc. Drinking Driving Law Letter Vol. 14, No. 23, Nov. 10, 1995.

[12] Infrared energy is lower in energy than the red end of the visible spectrum. Ultra-Violet (UV) light is just above the violet end of the visible spectrum. Visible light consists of red, orange, yellow, green, blue, indigo, and violet light.

[13] The narrow band pass filters allow only the IR light near the wavelengths desired to pass through and strike the detector.

[14] Three filter instruments can correct for acetone and water vapor.

[15] Five filter instruments are capable of identifying and correcting for acetone and water vapor and should stop testing if there is acetaldehyde, isopropanol, or toluene present.

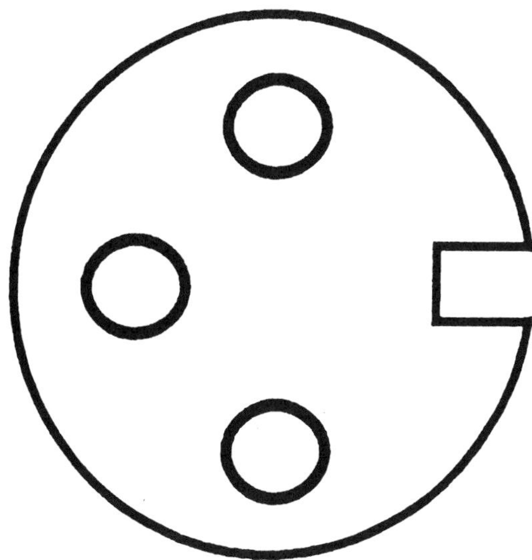

Figure 6-9
The Filter Wheel

The filters are also used to establish the *internal standards*[16] of the instrument. Dirty filters will reduce the output of the signal and can lead to processor instability.

The filter wheel rotates between the sample chamber and the detector at a constant speed between 1800 to 2400 rpm. The filter wheel has a notch out into it, which is placed so that it will align with a photo-interrupter. The photo-interrupter is a device, which has a light emitting diode (L.E.D.) on one face and a receptor on the other. As the filter wheel rotates between these two faces, the notch will line up with the photo-interrupter allowing a burst of energy from the L.E.D. to shoot through the notch and strike the receptor. If the filter wheel is turning at a constant speed this burst of energy should occur at the same time on each rotation and a timing base can be established for the separation of the three (or five) wavelengths and the sequencing of the analysis is created. Erratic motor speeds cause instability in the electronic signals, which can affect the timing of the device. One modification of the

[16] Internal Standards are not functionally equivalent to a calibration check using an alcohol standard. Internal standards are beam attenuators that may be used as voltage references but do nothing to check the analytical path or sample delivery system. Internal standards have never been approved by NHTSA as calibrating units for evidential or non-evidential breath alcohol testing devices.

6800 series is the use of two photo-interrupters with the filter wheel. One interrupter looks at the filters, while the other looks at the complete loop. The two interrupters synchronize the separation of the signals for each wavelength.

THE INTERNAL STANDARDS

The filters also act like lenses and will attenuate (focus) a portion of the IR light onto the detector resulting in the production of a unique amount of energy in the detector. In fact, whenever a particular filter is placed between the sample chamber and the detector the same amount of energy will be produced each and every time as long as the device is still in calibration. This energy production is unique for each and every filter giving each filter its own unique *internal standard factor.*[17] The internal standard factor can be directly linked to both the established channel voltages and the calibration of the instrument. The internal standards should reflect any changes or shifts in the channel voltages or the calibration but they are not a substitute for an external standard. Testing by this author has demonstrated that the calibration of the Intoxilyzer 5000 can drift out of tolerance on the analysis of vapor samples without the internal standard aborting the test.

THE IR DETECTOR

The endpoint for the light is the infrared detector. This is a very sophisticated device that does a rather simple job. The IR detector is responsible for converting the filtered IR light into electrical energy. When light of each of the filtered wavelengths strikes the detector a certain level of energy (signal) is produced for each wavelength. The amount of signal produced is directly proportional to the amount of light able to pass through the sample chamber and strike the detector. A noisy detector causes instability in the output signal (the DVM) of the detector.

THE 6800 AND 6801[18] SERIES INTOXILYZERS

The 68 series Intoxilyzers have cooled detectors.[19] The advantage of the cooled detector is the improved signal output from the detector requiring less amplification. This is significant because

[17] The internal standard factor is like a fingerprint for that filter.

[18] 6801 information is from seminar materials prepared by Eldon Ukestad of the MN BCA Lab for a seminar presented Nov. 7, 1997 in St. Paul, MN.

[19] The Intoxilyzer 1400 is also a cooled detect instrument.

whenever a signal is amplified, noise is also amplified. A stronger signal gives greater stability to the electronics of the instrument because there is less noise. The cooled detector has improved the low alcohol-concentration response. The cooled detectors are capable of accurately measuring alcohol concentrations down to 0.01 grams per 210 liters. The cooled detector is a single-stage, thermoelectrically cooled, lead-selenide detector with an integral thermistor for temperature regulation. Thermistor controlled electronic cooling maintains the internal temperature of the detector at approximately 0°C. The life expectancy for a cooled detector is at least seven years.

In the earlier section on sample chambers,it was discussed how the pressure transducer functions to determine if a sample is of sufficient volume and/or longevity. It must be noted at this time that some states have opted to purchase the 6800 series devices with a pressure switch instead of a transducer. This modification removes the ability to measure breath volume.

The calibration of the 6800 and 6801 series of devices are conducted through a programmed calibration mode. The three-digit assay values of the solutions used for the calibration (up to 5 solutions) are entered, through the keyboard, into the memory of the device. The various vapor samples are then introduced into the instrument — through the calibration port — and the instrument adjusts the signal responses appropriately and store the information digitally. Calibration of the analytical system is controlled by processor board hardware and software and is stored in memory there.

The specificity of the Intoxilyzers has been improved with the use of five filters. The additional wavelengths[20] for analysis have increased the likelihood of rejecting other chemical compounds. However, the failure to calibrate at these wavelengths removes the ability of the Intoxilyzer to make any corrections for these other compounds. In evaluation testing the five-filter instruments have flagged some chemical mixtures that displayed apparent alcohol concentrations.[21] If any type of interferant is flagged or subtracted

[20] The choice of the additional filters in the 3.5 μm range was unfortunate, in that the C-H bonds of the methyl group are still being sought. The 9.5 μm range is more specific for primary alcohols.

[21] An "apparent alcohol concentration" is a reading on a breath alcohol analyzer that is actually being caused by a chemical other than alcohol. The calibration for the Intoxilyzer assumes that the chemical being measured is ethanol. Not all chemicals will be measured in a 1:1 ratio with ethanol on the breath.

the test results must be verified through an alternate test other than breath.

The most significant change that occurred in the development of the 6801 series is the complete separation of the calibration path and the breath path. The breath path no longer passes through the solenoids, thus removing some of the uncomfortable back-pressure that is frequently complained about with the Intoxilyzer 5000. The two solenoid valves now isolate the simulator sample path from the sample chamber and pump exhaust except when a simulator sample is taken or an air blank is performed.[22] The complete separation of the calibration path and the breath path introduces the question of verifying the breath path calibration. The only way to assure that there is nothing in the breath path or software that would cause erroneous readings is by introducing a known sample through both paths.

SUMMARY OF THE OPTICAL BENCH

The IR source is projecting IR energy into and through the sample chamber where the light will spread, thereby flooding the chamber with IR energy. This IR energy is gathered and re-focused by the exit lens onto the filter wheel. The filter wheel is rotating at a constant speed between the chamber and the detector. When the notch of the filter wheel aligns with the photo-interrupter, a burst of light energy passes through and establishes the timing for the operation. As each filter aligns with the detector a specific wavelength of the IR light is allowed to pass and strike the detector. The strength of the signal created from the detector is based upon the amount of IR light of that wavelength that exits the sample chamber. A separate signal is established for each of the wavelengths utilized in the analysis. The signals are then sent to the processor for analysis.

THE PROCESSOR BOARD

When the filters in the filter wheel line up between the lens of the sample chamber and the detector, a burst of light strikes the detector causing a burst of energy to be produced. For each filter the detector will produce a corresponding burst of energy. The

[22] A cross connection between the simulator side of the pump exhaust and the simulator inlet equalizes pressure between the simulator inlet and outlet when the valves are not activated. The connection is closed by opening of the simulator inlet solenoid valve during simulator sampling through the calibration port.

bursts of energy, when amplified and rectified, are an electrical signal for that channel. The signals coming from each of the channels must then be massaged back into a single signal. After processing the signals from each channel the processor output is referred to as the DVM or differential voltage measurement. The change in the DVM during a test is directly related to the ethanol reading that is reported. Poor precision in ethanol readings can be caused by poor contact between the power board, processor board, and/or CPU board connectors.

The 68 series Intoxilyzers have a processor board that uses a slave microprocessor dedicated to the analytical tasks. All aspects of alcohol measurement and the discrimination of chemical interferants are managed by the slave microprocessor. This system updates the alcohol measurements every quarter of a second. Each alcohol concentration update is based on roughly 30 rotations of the filter wheel.

THE CHANNELS[23]

In the three-filter Intoxilyzer, two of the three wavelengths, the 3.48 and the 3.39 μm, are for measuring the alcohol and subtracting off acetone and water. The third wavelength, the 3.80 μm, demonstrates no reactivity with the alcohol molecule or other substances that are normally found in the breath of a normal individual. For this reason, the 3.80 μm wavelength is used as a reference channel[24] for the system. With the five-filter devices the 380 channel remains the reference channel, while the 347 channel is for quantifying alcohol and the remaining three channels — 352, 340, and 336 — are for detecting chemical interferants.

The signals generated by the detector are sent to the first stage amplifier. Here the signals from the detector begin the process of amplification. The signals are amplified so that any change in their strength is readily recognized. Amplification of a signal also includes amplification of any noise associated with that signal.

[23] The five-channel processor operates on the same principles as the three channel processor. The added filters improve the specificity of the analysis.

[24] At this point the term wavelength will be dropped and the term channel used instead. This change in terminology reflects the fact that we are no longer working with light energy, instead we are working with electrical energy. Therefore the 380 channel is the reference channel, the 348 channel is the alcohol analysis channel and the 339 is the acetone detection channel.

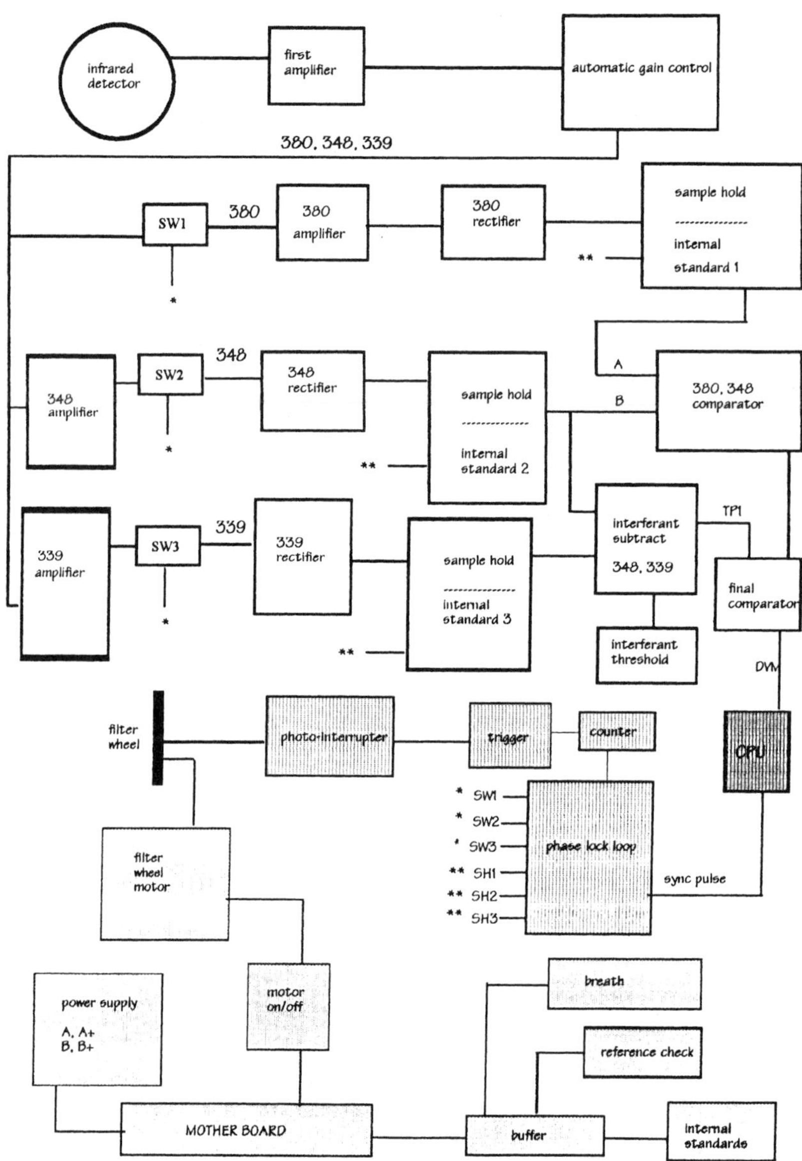

Figure 6-10
Tracking the Three-Channel Processor

THE AGC CIRCUIT

The next step in the process is for all three signals to pass through the Automatic Gain Control (AGC). The AGC circuit stabilizes and allows the system to compensate for variations in signal strength due to collection of dust or dirt on the light source, lenses, filters, or detector. It can also compensate for variations in signal strength resulting from the loss of signal due to aging of the light source. Once the signal has been stabilized by the AGC circuit it will branch out to the 380, 348, and 339 sections of the processor.

The AGC circuit is a very common system in devices where a constant output is required. A car radio is a common example of a device employing an AGC system. When you turn on a radio and adjust the volume to a comfortable volume, you do not have to continually readjust the volume depending on the distance you travel away from or towards the signal source. An AGC circuit does the adjusting for you, automatically increasing the volume as you move away from the tower and decreasing the volume as you move toward the tower. If there is not sufficient source signal to work with the radio station is lost.

ESTABLISHING THE TIMING AND BASE SEPARATION OF THE CHANNELS

Up to this point all three channels have been grouped together. Now each individual channel voltage must be isolated. Following the signal from the AGC it will come into contact with SW1, a high-speed switch. One could compare this high-speed switch to a gate. The gate is triggered to open at just the right moment in time to allow the passage of the 380 signal and then to close, blocking the passage of the other two signals. By this process the energy being conducted through the rest of the 380 circuitry is based on only the signal generated by the 3.80 μm light. The timing base for this event is established by the phase lock loop.

Earlier, the importance of the notch in the filter wheel and the photo-interrupter was discussed. It is that burst of energy which initiates the phase lock loop. The phase lock loop (PLL) consists of two primary components: the trigger and the counter. The burst of energy from the photo-interrupter is sent to the trigger and then to the counter. The counter will establish a time base of ten counts between each energy burst of the photo-interrupter. Each of the counts between these energy bursts can also be divided into units of ten, thereby establishing constant time base. The actual speed of the motor is not as critical as the requirement for a constant speed. The timing of all sequences is determined by the chopper revolutions.

The counter will send signals to other components at prescribed time counts. For example assume that there is a count of ten between the energy burst of the photo-interrupter and the 380 signal. By counting down from ten the counter can send a signal to SW1 opening the "gate" and then closing it again. This same process is used for SW2 and SW3 as well, so that a "burst" to "burst" event would be

BURST/9876543210/SW1open/380/SW1close/9876543210/SW2open/348/SW2close/9876543210/SW3open/339/SW3close/987654321/BURST

This is in essence the sequence that is used to isolate the three channels in the processor and occurs at a rate of 2200 +/− 200 times a minute.

AMPLIFICATION AND RECTIFICATION

After isolation the 380 signal it is once again amplified, this time in the 380 amplifier. The signal is then rectified. The signal prior to the 380 rectifier is the type of signal known as a sine wave. This type of signal cannot be measured using the voltmeter, nor is it a proper type of signal on which to base the analysis. By passing the 380 signal through the 380 rectifier the signal is now converted into a DC voltage level and is readily measurable. Careful examination of other channels will show that all of these sections undergo the same type of amplification and rectification as does the 380 channel.

THE ALCOHOL ANALYSIS

The 380 channel is the reference channel and the 348[25] channel is responsible for the alcohol analysis. The two signals are brought together in the 380, 348 comparitor. The voltage level of the reference channel and the alcohol channel are set to approximately the same voltage since the alcohol analysis is measured by determining the loss of 348 wavelength light. When these two voltages are fed into the 380, 348 comparitor a base line of the two channels is established. When an alcohol sample is measured the

[25] To avoid confusion here only the three channel processor will be discussed at this point. The five channel version should become self evident by the end of the discussion.

voltage level of the 348 channel will change due to a loss of the IR energy. This voltage change will also cause a change in the output of the 380, 348 comparitor. The comparitor output voltage change is directly proportional to the concentration of the alcohol in the sample chamber. This voltage is then sent to the final comparitor.

INTERFERANT SUBTRACT

The 339 channel is the channel used for monitoring the sample for substances other than alcohol. As discussed earlier, by selecting two wavelengths a ratio can be established between their reactivity to alcohol. This is accomplished by "tuning" the 339 channel to work in concert with the 348 channel. With the 348 channel set to 6.00 V_{DC},[26] the 339 channel is adjusted so when alcohol is placed into the sample chamber the voltage difference between the two channels remains constant. For example, if the 348 channel is set at 6.00 V_{DC} and the 339 channel is set at 4.00 V_{DC} there is a voltage difference of 2.00 V_{DC}. This voltage difference is now a constant. If the voltage of the 348 channel should drop 1.00 volt, making it 5.00 V_{DC}, the 339 should experience a parallel drop of 1.00 volt, making it 3.00 V_{DC}.

If an interfering substance is introduced along with the alcohol, this parallel balance may be upset. For example, if an alcohol and acetone vapor is introduced into the chamber and the 348 channel has an output of 5.00 V_{DC} while the 339 channel's output is 2.5 V_{DC}. The difference is now 2.5 V_{DC} instead of the 2.00 V_{DC} it was set at. This extra voltage difference (0.50 volt) is detected by the interferant subtract section of the processor. This difference of 0.50 V_{DC} is sent to the final comparitor where it will automatically be subtracted from the 380, 348 comparitor result. This system works to detect other substances, such as water, on the sample and continually adjusts for a "true" alcohol result, which contains no interfering substances. If the acetone subtract is not properly adjusted, the result will be "acetone" that is not there being added or subtracted. This can affect the detection and flagging of acetone. If the interferant detect is not set properly, then samples containing alcohol and any other interfering substance may not be accurately measured and reported.

INTERFERANT DETECT

All readings receive some type of adjustment, but only if there is a *significant* level of interferant is the operator notified of such.

[26] Volts DC current.

There is a threshold level for notifying the operator that a significant level of interferant is present. The interferant detect section of the processor is where this threshold level is established. The instrument can be adjusted so that when a particular level of interference is detected the instrument will, through tone and display, notify the operator that a significant level of interferant was detected and, depending on the software, may have been subtracted from the final analysis. The key here is that a significant level of interfering substance has been detected.[27,28] The threshold level is the lowest level that the operator will be notified at if there is an interferant detected. If the interferant detection flag is not properly adjusted the device may give false interferant flags or no flags at all when an interferant is present. Some state programs have recognized the unreliability of subtracting off an interferant by assuming that it is acetone and have instead chosen to only flag the interferant and not attempt to subtract it.

SAMPLE AND HOLD

After rectification, all three channels are fed into a "sample and hold" circuit. If you check the V_{DC} output at each of the channel test points it will appear to be one continuous voltage level even though it is not. Energy at each of the channel voltages is only being generated when the appropriate filter is in line with the detector. The signal being produced is in fact a series of energy bursts. Even though the signal production is quite rapid, 1800–2400 bursts per minute (optimum values) there are periods of zero energy production. Therefore the three channel processor incorporates what is called a "sample and hold" circuit.

The sample and hold circuit has the capability of capturing a burst of energy and holding onto it until the command is given to release that sample and capture another. What appears to be a constant V_{DC} output at the channel test points is in fact a number of samples of that channel's V_{DC} output. This allows the instrument to assess any variation in the voltage levels. Consequently, one

[27] Testing the system to determine if the interferant flag activates is not the same as testing to see if the system correctly subtracts the interferant. The accuracy of the subtraction mechanism is determined by testing an acetone and alcohol mixture of known concentrations. The flagging system is checked by testing an acetone solution of known concentration at or above the threshold level.

[28] The interferant flag can be adjusted to any level of sensitivity. States that do their own maintenance and calibration will set the flag at their own discretion. The manufacturer generally sets the flag at 0.2 mg/ml.

could state that the final analysis of a breath/air alcohol sample is in fact composed of 30 separate analyses per second of sample delivery time.

DIFFERENTIAL VOLTAGE MEASUREMENT (DVM)

The DVM is a representation of the combined output of all three channels. This system allows for visual observation of the stability of the entire processor board. A common misunderstanding of the DVM is that it is continually monitored and any drifts or fluctuations in the DVM will result in the device aborting the testing. This simply cannot be, because the change in the DVM during a sample analysis is directly related to the ethanol reading.

The DVM of the instrument can be displayed through settings on the mode function switches. During a diagnostic check or the "bird" section of an analysis (the Intoxilyzer screen displays >>>>>>...), the instrument is monitoring this voltage level and examining the stability of the signal. At this time it is determined whether or not the device is within its proper operational parameters of 0.020 to 0.600 and if there is any positive or negative drift. Only during a diagnostic check or the "bird" section immediately prior to a sample analysis is the DVM monitored for stability.

THE CENTRAL PROCESSING UNIT (CPU)

If the Optical Bench is the "heart" of the instrument, then the Central Processing Unit (CPU) is the "brain." It is here that all of the programmed features are stored and put into action. The final mathematical computations are performed here and all of the reporting and system control functions are established, maintained and monitored here. The major components of the CPU and their function are described below.

The Erasable Programmable Read Only Memory (EPROM) chips contain all of the preprogrammed functions for the instrument. The commands for sequencing, operation, and formatting of the test printouts, all of the data entry questions, the operational parameters and the mathematical formulas for the final analysis are stored here. The chips are customized to the specifications of each state program. Displayed and printed messages are part of the state customization. The EPROMs are occasionally "updated" to reflect changes in state statutes or changes desired by the agency that maintains the device. The proper operation of the new programming should be evaluated thoroughly to assure that the modifications requested function as desired and intended. Complete re-evaluation of all functions is necessary to assure that no other changes were made in the programming and that the device operates as intended. Newer Intoxilyzer models have EEPROMs (Electronically Erasable Programmable Read Only Memory) chips in addition to the EPROMs. EEPROMs have the potential of being reprogrammed using computer communications.

The Microprocessor is responsible for taking the information from the EPROMs and sorting it into logical sequences. It sends the proper commands to the selected chips, receives incoming data, and establishes the operational timing base for the other CPU components. The newer Intoxilyzers are using a faster microprocessor and EPROMs with more programmable memory are used.

The CPU Crystal establishes the speed of the "thinking" process of the microprocessor. The higher the frequency of the crystal the faster the microprocessor "thinks."

The Parallel Input Output Device (PIO) receives the sequencing command from the microprocessor and passes these commands on to the proper controllers for their specific functions. It receives incoming data as to the completion or current status of a task, which is returned back to the microprocessor.

The Real Time Clock (RTC) is the device by which the instrument maintains the time of day and the date for display and print. In the newer Intoxilyzers (68 series and some upgrades) the RTC is a Dallas clock/calendar/memory/back-up battery package. The battery maintained memory can store the date the simulator solution was last changed, the name of the operator who changed it, the number of simulator samples taken and the test results until they are polled (data is downloaded) by the host computer.

The Random Access Memory (RAM) stores data which is transient in nature. It is here that the time of an event, such as the time of a sample analysis, is held. The CPU RAM will hold this information until a printout is performed. After the instrument prints the results of an analysis the RAM will clear its memory and be ready to receive new information. If an instrument is set up with the telecommunication package, an additional RAM board is installed which will take the information from the CPU RAM and store data on all tests performed since the last time the unit was polled via external computer command. (Refer to the section on the ADAMS or COBRA Systems)

The Analog to Digital Converter (ADC) has the task of converting information which is sent in the form of analog signals, such as the voltage levels and changes from the three-channel processor, into digital information. It is in essence an interpreter for the different sections of the instrument permitting each to communicate with the CPU.

The Address and Data Buses. The address bus carries instructions and program commands from the EPROMs, microprocessor, etc. to selected chips, which perform the prescribed functions contained in the program. It is the communications line, which tells, or addresses, these selected chips. The data bus is the communications line, which collects and carries the data concerning the status of a particular task, result, or event. The information traveling along this bus is received by the properly selected chip and processed before the next set of instructions is released onto the address bus.

To put the complex operation of the CPU into sequence, keep in mind that there are a number of commands that must be issued, in sequence, while a constant flow of data is being input and processed. All of the operating instructions are contained in the long-term memory (EPROM). After accessing the EPROMs, the instructions pass along selected pathways (the address bus) to another section of the "brain" for processing into a logical order (the microprocessor). After the instructions have been processed into a logical order, the sequencing commands for the selected operations are passed onto the proper controllers for their specific functions and information on the status of the current operation is returned (the data bus) to the microprocessor.

At this point, information is being sent and received and logic "decisions" are being executed. For example, if there is an interferant present, the information on the amount of interferant to subtract is relayed on, and if above a set threshold level the interferant flag will need to be activated. All of these actions, if the analysis is to be completed correctly, depend on a rhythm being established (CPU crystal). The information being sent from the various components involved must be interpreted (ADC), so the incoming data can be properly received and assimilated. The flow of data, commands, processing, and interpretation continue until the test sequence is completed. To ensure that all of the procedures were followed correctly and to allow for the data to be printed on the test card, the data concerning the analysis is stored in the short-term memory (RAM). Data recall at a later point can be accomplished if there is a telecommunications package installed to store such data. (Refer to the section on ADAMS or COBRA Systems.)

ADAMS OR COBRA SYSTEMS

Both the ADAMS and COBRA systems are for data management, allowing the test results to be downloaded to a PC for record-keeping and management. COBRA is a Windows-based application and the data may be used with a number of data management programs. ADAMS is CMI's first attempt at creating a database management system. Any telecommunications require that there be an additional RAM board installed for storing the test information between pollings. When an instrument is polled, the accumulated data is downloaded to a personal computer for storage and the RAM is "cleared."

The importance of a data acquisition and management system is that *all* tests conducted can be documented. This complete documentation of testing can then be used for analysis of the field performance of the individual instruments. Database files that can be generated include subject test files, error message files, calibration files, diagnostic files, and maintenance files.

Checklist 6 Intoxilyzer 5000

- ☐ Was the machine properly licensed, calibrated, and maintained?
- ☐ Was the solution used to externally calibrate the Intoxilyzer accurately prepared?
- ☐ Was the room air used to flush the sample chamber contaminated with the alcoholic breath of test subjects?
- ☐ Do the machine's records indicate any failures or mechanical problems before or since the test?
- ☐ Has the machine been modified in any way affecting its status as a state-approved device?
- ☐ Does the machine incorporate all of the available features offered by CMI?
- ☐ Is there an acetone detector? (Was the client a diabetic or on a strict diet?)
- ☐ Is there an acetaldehyde detector?
- ☐ Is there a radio frequency interference detector?
- ☐ Is there a mouth alcohol detector?
- ☐ Was the operator/officer properly licensed and trained?
- ☐ Is he familiar with the theory and operation of the Intoxilyzer 5000?

- ☐ Did he follow the manufacturer's checklist? Can he recall each step?
- ☐ Did he observe the client constantly for 15 to 20 minutes before administering the test?
- ☐ Could the operator have manipulated the test results?
- ☐ Is the machine specific for alcohol?
- ☐ Does it use one, two, three, or five wavelengths?
- ☐ What other compounds found on the breath will be reported as alcohol by the machine?
- ☐ Could the client have had acetaldehyde in his system? Acetone? Ketones? Paint or glue fumes? Other compounds?
- ☐ Was there any source of radio frequency interference in the area of the Intoxilyzer when the client was tested?
- ☐ Any police transmitters? Walkie-talkies? Televisions? Electric door locks? Microwave ovens? Police car transmitters in the parking lot? Teletype machines? Computers? Radios? Fluorescent lighting?
- ☐ Could the 5000 have been affected by a mechanical or electrical problem, such as a drop in line voltage?
- ☐ Were there any possible problems with the machine's temperature, humidity, optics, or age?
- ☐ Are there any generic problems with breath testing?
- ☐ Can the prosecution establish that the client's partition ratio was 2100:1?
- ☐ Did the breath test take place during the client's absorptive state?
- ☐ Could mouth alcohol have been present? Does the client wear dentures or have dental caps? Was he bleeding in the mouth?
- ☐ What is the client's hematocrit and how could it have affected the breath test?
- ☐ Did the client have an elevated body temperature?
- ☐ Could stress or breathing pattern have elevated the Intoxilyzer's test results?
- ☐ Did room air used to flush the sample chamber contain alcoholic breath from test subjects?
- ☐ Are there any problems with blood-alcohol testing generally?
- ☐ Was the client a woman?
- ☐ Did the client have a rising BAC curve?
- ☐ Is any attempt to project BAC back to the time of driving based on evidence and scientifically accepted fact? (see retrograde extrapolation, §5.2)
- ☐ Could eating or smoking have affected alcohol metabolism?
- ☐ Could zinc in the client's body have been a factor?
- ☐ What is the inherent error in testing with an Intoxilyzer 5000?

§6.4.2 BAC DataMaster

The BAC (Breath Alcohol Computer) DataMaster was originally manufactured by Verax Systems in New York, but was sold in 1988 to National Patent Analytical Systems, Inc. (2541 Ashland Road, Mansfield, OH 44905). There are currently five different models: the BAC DataMaster, the BAC DataMaster-K, the portable BAC DataMaster cdm, and the DataMaster II. It is the first version, the BAC DataMaster, that counsel can normally expect to encounter, possibly with some state-specific modifications. The recent popularity of the device is not due to any greater degree of sophistication or accuracy, but rather to its relatively low price. As with the Intoxilyzer 5000 and 4011 and the Intoximeter 3000, the DataMaster uses the less expensive infrared technology and is therefore particularly susceptible to the problems of non-specific analysis. The machine uses two wavelength filters in an attempt to minimize this lack of specificity for ethanol but, as has been seen with the Intoxilyzer 5000's five-filter system, it has proven insufficient. A microcomputer is integrated into the machine to control sequencing, calibration, and self-checking, theoretically making it easier to use and less susceptible to operator error. Additionally, the software can be custom-designed to meet the requirements of a given jurisdiction or the specific needs of an agency.

The machine counsel will normally encounter, the BAC DataMaster, is usually enclosed in a white metallic case measuring approximately 8 inches tall by 23 inches wide by 15 inches deep, and weighs 45 pounds. A keyboard and printer are usually integrated into the device. The detachable breath tube contains a sealed wire-wrapped antenna for the purposes of detecting radio frequency interference (see §6.3.10). Further, the manufacturer offers two options, which if not purchased by the agency in question should be commented on by counsel in cross-examination. The first is an "external alcohol simulator standard pump outlet" for purposes of testing the accuracy of the machine. The second device is a sample preservation system — a mechanism for inserting a vial to capture and preserve a second breath sample for subsequent analysis, either for double-checking or for defense testing.

Operation. In terms of operation, the first step is to activate the machine and have it automatically purge its sample chamber with ambient (room) air and, in the process, "zeroing" itself. The subject is then visually prompted to blow into the Guth "Ultratrap" mouthpiece. This mouthpiece has three internal baffles, which help to prevent the introduction of saliva into the machine (in fact, however, the baffles may trap alcohol-laden saliva: This may then be breathed into the machine for a cumulative reading or, if the mouthpiece is not changed, sucked into the chamber during the next test purge phase, resulting in a false zero reference). The breath sample then passes across a thermistor, which theoretically detects the presence of mouth alcohol, through a valve and finally into the aluminum sample chamber. At one end of the chamber is the infrared light source; a lens focuses the light source and two mirrors are set up to extend the light path to an effective length of 1.1 meters. At the other end of the chamber is another lens, which focuses the beam of infrared light and passes it through a spinning wheel ("optical chopper"), which causes the light to pulsate. This pulsating light is then passed through the filters and finally reaches a detector. The detector translates the pulsing energy into an alternating electrical signal, which is then read by the computer as a blood-alcohol concentration.

The following represents the procedure for running a test, adapted from the Operator's Manual supplied by the manufacturer. As such, it should be useful to defense counsel in determining whether the officer followed proper procedures in administering the test.

> First, the operator pushes the start button. The instrument will start with "PUR" on the upper right display to show that the following steps are taking place:
>
> "PUR": Purges sample chamber with room air. Calculates alcohol zero. Calculates acetone zero.
>
> At the end of Purge stage, the computer runs a blank test:
>
> "BlN": Runs a sample test on room air in chamber. Displays result of blank measurement.

Next, the calibration to internal standard is performed:

> "CAL": The internal standard is flipped into the IR path, and the instrument is checked for proper calibration.

The machine is now ready for the subject test:

> "BLO": A long beep signal is given to indicate the instrument is ready for the subject sample. A valid sample must be collected within 2 minutes after the beep, or the test is aborted.

The display will show the measured absorption at the alcohol filter of the contents of the sample chamber during this 2-minute period, up until the time the computer determines a valid sample of deep lung breath has entered the machine. If acetone is present, this displayed value is not the true alcohol value. The instrument then calculates the true acetone and alcohol components of the sample by solving an equation that accounts for the two absorption readings.

The report is then printed, giving instrument number, date, time, results of blank test, results of internal calibration, and results of the subject test. Space for the officer's badge and subject name are provided at the bottom of the form.

If an acetone concentration greater than the acetone preset value has been measured, the instrument will first display the acetone equivalent, together with "ACE," and then calculate and display the alcohol content of the sample with "ALC" displayed. If acetone above the minimum is not detected, then only alcohol is calculated and displayed.

If no further test is initiated within 10 minutes, the instrument goes into "standby" mode. This is indicated by "the travelling dots" across the display.

The observer will notice a "supervisor panel control" on the BAC Verifier — an access panel on the right side that can only be opened with an appropriate key. Under this restricted access panel are a number of switches, which are used as follows:

> "SET": This switch together with "ADV" is used to reset the time — hours and minutes, and the date — day and month.
>
> "SUPR": This button initiates the supervisor mode, executes a special program to provide external standard sequencing, 3-digit display accuracy, and any other steps required.
>
> "TEST": This button initiates an internal self-diagnosis program that checks all parts of the instrument for proper operation and generates a report.

"NOVOL": The NOVOL button is used to override the internal requirements check for deep lung air. When pushed after the "BLO" signal, this switch will cause the instrument to complete the calculations and report. This switch can be used when running simulations if desired.

"COPY": This switch causes an extra copy of the last test run to be printed.

"YEAR": These two switches are used to set the year for the printed date.

"OPTION": Four option switches are available for selection of certain features. These switches can be individually programmed to fit a particular state's needs. Following are examples:

1. When in the on position the sequence is modified to include external storage of breath sample.
2. When in the on position, 3 copies of each test are printed. When in the off position, 1 copy is printed.
3. When in the on position, the sequence is modified to include an external standard on each subject test.
4. When in the on position, two digits are displayed. When in the off position, 3 digits are displayed.

As has has been mentioned, the BAC Verifier incorporates a microcomputer. The program can be individualized to suit a particular jurisdiction or law enforcement agency. Since the software is therefore critical to the accuracy of the machine, counsel should use discovery procedures to find out what has been programmed into the unit in question (as computer engineers are fond of saying, "garbage in equals garbage out").

A typical programmed sequence of operation follows:

POWER-ON	The program initializes all variables, does a preliminary self-check on internal components, then turns on the sample chamber heater control circuit and the lamp control circuit. The program remains in this loop until the sample chamber temperature has reached its operating point and stabilized, and until the lamp has been on and stabilized for a minimum period. While in this loop, the

instrument will accept paper feed and clock adjust commands, but will not accept a "start test" command. Three dashes (— — —) are displayed on the lower left display to indicate this phase.

AWAITING COMMAND — After the computer senses that the temperature is correct, it extinguishes the three dash display. The current time is displayed on the upper right display. The program will hold itself in this phase for 10 minutes, and then revert to standby if no start command has been received.

At this point, the operator may push the START button to initiate the test cycle.

PURGE — After sensing that the start button has been pushed, the computer shows "PUR" on the display, then turns on the purging pump to draw in fresh room air through the inlet tube, through the sample chamber, and out. The pump remains on for about 30 seconds. The computer then finds the alcohol and acetone, zero points, based on the room air in the sample chamber. First the alcohol zero is determined and the amplifiers automatically adjusted for this zero. This usually takes from 3 to 15 seconds. Next, the computer determines the acetone zero by pulling in the acetone filter (you'll hear a soft "thump" or, if you have the cover off, be able to see the rear solenoid on the detector go down). The acetone zero also takes from 3 to 15 seconds, and then the filter is released, with another soft "thump."

CALIBRATION

At this point the machine has zeroed itself to the ambient conditions of its environment. It now shows "CAL" on the display, and does a self-calibration. A quartz plate, of known infrared absorption, is inserted in the beam path. This may be observed by the front solenoid on the detector block being pulled in. The computer calculates the absorption of this plate, compresses it to the value originally calibrated for the machine at the factory, and calculates an adjustment factor, which is used in all calculations. Thus variations in beam intensity, reflectivity, or sensor sensitivity are automatically accommodated by the computer program. The end of the calibration phase is indicated by the letters "CAL" being extinguished, and by a soft thump as the calibration plate is released.

TEST

The machine is now ready for the subject sample. It presets a timer that will send the machine into standby mode if no valid sample is received within 2 minutes. The machine gives a long beep and shows the word "BLO" on the upper display to indicate it is ready. Flow of breath into the instrument is detected by the cooling of a negative temperature coefficient resistor. The rate of flow is inserted into a differential equation that is solved to give a corrected BAC reading. This technique is far superior to simplistic flow/time methods or a minimum volume test.

REPORT

When a valid sample has been determined by the sample control analysis logic, the computer determines the acetone component. This is observed as two soft thumps as the acetone filter is pulled in and released. Then the alcohol component is determined. If the acetone component is above the minimum present on the pre-test switches on the CPU board, then a separate alcohol and equivalent acetone calculation is undertaken and printed. If the acetone component is below the preset, only the alcohol component is printed. The printer will then produce the report reflecting data accumulated during the test. If the test has aborted for any reason, no report is printed.

Following is a DataMaster checklist and a DataMaster evidence card used in Orange County, California.

ORANGE COUNTY SHERIFF-CORONER DEPARTMENT
DATAMASTER PRECAUTIONARY CHECKLIST

TO BE COMPLETED BY OFFICER. ALSO BEGIN OBSERVATION PERIOD, IF APPLICABLE.

DATE OF TEST 013098 ARRESTING AGENCY CHP/SFS CASE NUMBER

SUBJECT'S NAME DL#/STATE C3874478

OFFICER'S NAME E. SUMNER 15V43 SUB.DOB 10 05 65

NOTE: Subject must be under continuous observation for at least 15 minutes prior to the starting of Step 1. The observation is continued during the test until the final breath sample is collected. During this entire time, he/she must not eat, drink, or smoke anything and must not belch, burp, vomit, or regurgitate. If any of the above occurs, the test must be discontinued and the observation period restarted or the subject must choose another chemical test.

To Begin Observation Period: TIME STAMP THE EVIDENCE TICKET

OBSERVATION PERIOD OF SUBJECT STARTED AT: 0410 INITIALS: [ES]

OPERATOR'S OBSERVATION OF SUBJECT STARTED AT: 0425 INITIALS: [GQ]

TO BEGIN TEST: *INITIAL THE BOX AFTER THE OBSERVATION PERIOD HAS BEEN COMPLETED.* INITIALS: [GQ]

1. Ask subject: "Do you have any breathing problems?" ☐ YES ☒ NO INITIALS: [GQ]
   Comments:

2. Record the following: INSTRUMENT S/N 950253 SIM. LOT# 120897 VALUE 0.108 %

3. Press the RUN key and follow the DataMaster's instructions. SIM. TEMP. 34.0 °C
   (Use keyboard to enter information requested by display. Press RETURN after keyboard entries. After "N" is typed for "REVIEW DATA? Y/N", data is no longer entered with keyboard. Write requested information in the appropriate spaces.)

RECORD RESULTS

AIR BLANK	CAL.CHECK	AIR BLANK
0.000	0.105	0.000

4. Check that the breath tube is warm. Demonstrate to the subject how to give a proper breath sample. INITIALS: [GQ]

OPR.BREATH	AIR BLANK
0.000	0.000

5. Discard operator's mouthpiece. Place subject's mouthpiece into breath tube.
6. Ask the subject: "Have you belched, burped, regurgitated, or vomited during the last 15 minutes?"
   ☐ YES ☒ NO (If yes, PRESS the ABT key to discontinue the test.) INITIALS: [GQ]

SUB.BREATH	AIR BLANK	SUB.BREATH	AIR BLANK	* SUB.BREATH	AIR BLANK
0.14	0.00	0.14	0.00	0.____	0.____

*COMPLETE ONLY IF 2 BREATH RESULTS DO NOT AGREE WITHIN A .02%

7. Ask the subject: "Have you belched, burped, regurgitated, or vomited during the test?"
   ☐ YES ☒ NO Comments: INITIALS: [GQ]
8. Discard the subject's mouthpiece. Insert the time stamped evidence ticket when directed by the DataMaster.
9. Obtain the subject's right thumbprint on the evidence ticket. Sign the evidence ticket. Include the date and time.
   ATTACH EVIDENCE TICKET TO DATAMASTER PRECAUTIONARY CHECKLIST.

ADDITIONAL COMMENTS:

"I COMPLETED MY CONTINUOUS OBSERVATION OF THE SUBJECT ABOVE, AT WHICH TIME THE BREATH SAMPLING HAD BEEN COMPLETED."

Operator's Signature [signature] Date 1/30/98 Time 0435 Agency CHP

dmchklst 6tm_tsm 2/4/97

Form 3
DataMaster Checklist

FACE THIS SIDE DOWN - THIS EDGE IN FIRST

ORANGE COUNTY SHERIFF-CORONER DEPARTMENT FORENSIC SCIENCE SERVICES

BAC DataMaster
Evidence Ticket

950249-0247-022198 initial: [handwritten initials]

SEAL BEACH JAIL
BAC DATAMASTER 950249

SUBJECT'S NAME:

DATE OF BIRTH: 05/31/48
STATE/LICENSE NUMBER:
CA/P0406735
OPERATOR'S NAME:
STALEY/S
AGENCY CODE: SBPD
CASE NUMBER: 98-0373
SIMULATOR LOT NUMBER: 120897

--- BREATH ANALYSIS ---

FEBRUARY 21, 1998		03:06
AIR BLANK	.000	03:07
INTERNAL STANDARD	VERIFIED	03:07
CALIBRATION CHECK	.103	03:08
AIR BLANK	.000	03:09
OPERATOR TEST	.000	03:10
AIR BLANK	.000	03:10
SUBJECT SAMPLE	.22	03:12
AIR BLANK	.00	03:13
SUBJECT SAMPLE	.21	03:14
AIR BLANK	.00	03:15

COMMENTS
GOOD TEST
PAC SET OFF [signature]
OPERATOR'S SIGNATURE

2-21-98 0315
DATE TIME

#60026

RIGHT THUMBPRINT

Form 4
DataMaster Evidence Ticket

Sources of error. As to the reliability of the DataMaster and possible sources of error, it should be noted that the device has encountered numerous problems. Washington State was one of the first to order the machine due primarily to its low cost. Eight of the first machines received, had to be returned because they failed to meet specifications; twenty-five have had to be repaired because of a variety of problems. Common problems included inaccurate readings because of meter valve instability, failure to detect the presence of acetaldehyde, and false readings caused by infrared lamp instability.

Initially, it should be clearly understood that although a relatively recent arrival on the breath-testing scene, the DataMaster is definitely not "state-of-the-art." Its main attraction is its low cost, and the more recently arrival, Draeger's Alcotest 7110 (see §6.4.6) is far more sophisticated, reliable — and expensive. That fact can, of course, be pointed out to a jury if the prosecution engages in its usual characterization of the DataMaster as the "newest, best" device available, along with a few of the following facts:

1. The DataMaster uses a 2400 band modem — considered ancient in today's computer technology where 56,000 baud is the norm.
2. The RFI detection system tests at only one frequency: What if there are interfering sources at other wavelengths?
3. The heart of the machine is the EPROM computer chip — yet law enforcement technicians do not know what the program is, so how can they determine if the computations are accurate?
4. The DataMaster's power supply consists of millivolts — and so is unusually sensitive to minor power fluctuations.
5. Like the modem, the machine's CPU is an old and primitive version.
6. The manufacturer of the DataMaster, National Patent, has become "Midwest Cable Co." and has discontinued making the machine, turning instead to production of cable cutters.
7. Since the manufacturer no longer makes any repairs or has any parts for replacement, all repairs and replace-

> ments must now be done by local laboratories — often with untrained personnel.

It should also be pointed out that the DataMaster has record-keeping capability as an option. If the model used does not have this, why not? Why does the law enforcement agency *not* want this "state of the art" feature that keeps a record of all tests, including any malfunctions?

The DataMaster has a number of components that are very sensitive to temperature change. Any variations in these temperatures — or the inability of the prosecution to verify the temperatures — should be brought out for the jury (and considered grounds for suppression).

1. The simulator solution, as with any breath machine, must be kept at 34 degrees centigrade, plus or minus .02; a decrease of one degree will cause a 6.8 percent decrease in the amount of alcohol, resulting in a falsely higher BAC reading for tested breath samples. A thermometer attached to the simulator is supposed to be checked by the operator.
2. The sample chamber must be heated to exactly 50 degrees; this is supposedly monitored by the machine's computer.
3. The detector must be cooled almost to freezing; this is also theoretically monitored by the computer.
4. The breath tube must be heated to 50 degrees. If not properly heated, condensation can form in the tube; this can capture alcohol during a test, which will be picked up by later breath samples. Despite the need for a 50-degree temperature, the Operator's Manual tells the operator only to "check that the mouthpiece is . . . warm to the touch."

It is also of interest that the DataMaster's Service Guide lists the following possible error messages on the DataMaster's LCD display — that is, things that can go wrong. Reviewing the list of possible malfunctions can go a long way toward correcting the jury's initial impression that the machine is nearly "fail-safe." Note, incidentally, that there is nothing to indicate that the *com-*

puter is malfunctioning, such as by not detecting and reporting the following malfunctions.

Temperature low
Temperature high
Printer error
CRC error
Pump error
System won't zero

This last entry is followed by the notation that "It is possible that there may be physical blockages of the IR (infrared) energy along the path from Source to Detector. . . . Possible causes of blockage":

a. Simulator solution in sample chamber. This can occur if the simulator is hooked up to the instrument incorrectly.
b. Cracked windows or mirrors.
c. Chopper wheel not turning.
d. Condensation or fog building up on windows or mirrors due to leakage in the system.
e. Any other foreign material in sample chamber.

The Service Guide then continues with a list of what it terms "functional errors" — that is, malfunctions for which there are no error messages to alert the operator:

No breath tube heat
Blinking stops, but no sample
Instrument samples early, by itself
Blinking does not stop when instrument is blown into
Supervisor buttons do not function
Difficult or impossible to blow into instrument
Improper operation of pump
No display
"Not calibrated"
Printer runs continuously
MTR button does not function

The Operator's Manual adds a few more ways the BAC Data-Master can malfunction:

Invalid sample (the manual reads "mouth alcohol is being detected, subject is not providing a proper sample, or the instrument is out of adjustment" — but does not indicate *which*)
RFI
Calibration error
Fatal systems error

These, the manuals stress, are only the more *common* sources of error possible with the DataMaster. The Service Guide adds the following interesting comment: "If your instrument exhibits a symptom that is not identified in this guide, please notify us so that we may update our *symptoms information library*" (emphasis added). This should be of interest to a jury for two reasons:

1. There is an entire *library* of things that can go wrong with this machine!
2. The manufacturers are not even aware of some things that can go wrong: They are soliciting information about newly discovered defects for their presumably ever-growing library. What malfunction will be discovered next?

It is also interesting to note that the DataMaster has an internal self-checking diagnostic system, run by its computer. Of course, garbage in equals garbage out, but in theory such a readily available diagnostic check might detect malfunctions in the machine. Yet these checks are only performed periodically — that is, not before each test. Despite the fact that such a check would detect, for example, whether the critical temperature of the sample chamber is 50 degrees, such a check is almost never done immediately before or after a DUI suspect is tested.

Of course, any machine using infrared absorption is susceptible to the problem of *nonspecific analysis;* such devices will interpret a wide range of compounds as ethyl alcohol. Thus, for example, the presence of *acetone* on a subject's breath (common among diabetics and dieters) can cause the BAC to give a falsely high BAC reading. In preparing for cross-examination concerning a BAC DataMaster, counsel should review the discussions of nonspecific analysis in §§6.1 and 6.4.1. For example, a scientific study has concluded that the DataMaster is unreliable due to the specificity problem:

> Two instruments using two modes of ethanol detection are the Intoximeter 3000 (3.4 micron infra-red plus Taguchi cell) and the BAC DataMaster (dual wavelength infra-red). These have proved unsuitable because acetone appears to be considered the only potential interfering substance. . . . In the selection of two modes of ethanol detection, each system must be chosen such that a comparison of the response from each mode would indicate a wide range of possible interfering substances, not just acetone.

Bell, Attaining Specificity in the Measurement of Ethanol in Breath, 40 Acta Medicinae Legalis et Socialis 107 (1990).

A variety of other problems inherent to varying degrees in any breath testing device can also exist with the DataMaster: varying partition ratios, mouth alcohol, radio frequency interference, testing during the absorptive state, varying hematocrit, elevated body temperature, breathing pattern, stress, contaminated ambient air, used mouthpieces, inaccurate simulator solutions, testing during the absorptive phase, rising BAC curves, gender-based differences in metabolism of alcohol, effects of zinc in the body, and so on. These materials, found in §§5.3 *et seq.* and 6.3 *et seq.* should also be reviewed before trial.

"The Lawyer's Guide to the DataMaster." The following explanations, observations and suggestions for fruitful cross-examination on the DataMaster are offered by premier DUI attorney Jon Scott Fox of Bellevue, Washington. The materials, which were presented in conjunction with Mr. Fox's demonstration-lecture, titled "Taming the Electronic Beast," at the National College for DUI Defense's Third Annual Summer Session at Harvard Law School in 1997, reflect his extensive experience with the machine in trials.

> The BAC Verifier/DataMaster II breath testing machine was first introduced in Washington state in 1985, but it remains an intimidating mystery to many defense attorneys in my state and probably is more intimidating in those states where it is considered "new technology." No doubt, more than a few otherwise capable

defense attorneys shy away from taking a DUI case to trial because they feel they lack the knowledge to effectively challenge the breath test results rendered on this infernal machine. That lack of knowledge also puts the attorney at an uncomfortable disadvantage when cross-examining the arresting officer and breath technician in matters relating to the breath test. Fear not. You don't need to be an expert in the intricate workings of the machine in order to deal with it (and the prosecution's "expert" witnesses) in court.

What follows is an update on the "new" software's database (the most recent version in use in Washington state) and some suggestions for cross examination, with a particular focus upon the officer who administers the breath test. This information will be discussed in detail at the seminar. Two descriptions of the workings of the "old software" DataMaster follow. Included are a simple explanation of the machine's workings — enough basic information for the defense attorney to confidently cross-examine regarding breath test issues and not look stupid and a detailed primer — information for those who want to know details of the innermost workings of the DataMaster.

I. NEW SOFTWARE — NEW DATABASE TO DECODE

You'll first know that you are dealing with a "new" DataMaster when you examine the breath test ticket. All breath test documents generated by the new machines in Washington state have a line at the top of the ticket indicating "software version," followed by a number and a date. Several different versions of software have been used in the field, and there are likely to be several more as the manufacturer and Washington state try to work out the bugs. In other states, the makeup of the database might vary somewhat. However, Washington's database can provide insight into the workings of DataMaster machines wherever located.

There are thirty-one codes in the new database, and a series of "subcodes" as well. Understanding these codes is crucial not only to reading the database but also to determining from the database potential areas of cross examination that may be useful in trial and administrative hearings at the Department of Licensing. Here are the codes as they appear in the database provided in cases litigated in Washington state.

1. DATE — Date of the text.
2. OBS TIME — Time the officer types in that observation began. The machine will not start unless the time entered is at least 15 minutes earlier than current DataMaster time.

3. OPERATOR — Name of person who administered the test.
4. CITATION — Citation number.
5. "T" (Test type)
   a. 1 = regular breath test.
   b. 2 = supervisory test run by a technician.
   c. 9 = error code happened. The code will be listed at the last field.
6. "S.T.M." Simulator Temperature "Y" = temp in limits; otherwise no record will be retained in the database.
7. AGENCY — Code for arresting agency.
8. DOB
9. SEX
10. RACE
11. LICENSE (state is first two letters, e.g., WAWHEELDM4459 = Wa.)
12. CO (County — a number, e.g., 03, etc.)
13. CR — Crime arrested for. 01 = DUI
14. ACC — (Y or N for accident; doesn't indicate fault but no doubt will be reported as "alcohol involved.")
15. DrinkLoc — Last drinking location by liquor control license number.
16. BATCH — Simulator solution batch number.
17. IS — Internal standard value as read by DataMaster on current test.
18. BA1 — "Breath Attempt One." This is the number of times that the person tried to blow into the machine, as defined by the voltage across the thermistor exceeding 1.5 volts on separate occasions throughout the attempt(s).
19. ET1 — "Exhalation Time One." How long the subject blew on the first attempt measured every quarter of a second. For example the number 36 in this column indicates a 9-second blow.
20. BrAC1 — "Breath alcohol, first sample." There are five possibilities:
   a. I = Incomplete test
   b. R = Refusal
   c. V = Invalid Sample
   d. X = Interference
   e. Test result, without the decimal point:
      i. 167 = .167, and if less than .10, the 0 is omitted, as in
      ii. 56 = .056 actual result, not .560.

21. INT.1 — Interference, if any, on first breath sample.
22. B1.TIME — This is the time printed opposite the first breath sample result on the printed out ticket. It indicates time of sample acceptance, not when the person began to blow.
23. SIM — Reading of the external standard. If not within .090 and .110, test is aborted.
24. INT.S — Interference, if any, on the simulator reading.
25. S.TIME — Time of acceptance of simulator sample
26. BA2 — Breath Attempt(s) Two. This is the number of "attempts" on second sample, measured as voltages over 1.5 across thermistor.
27. ET2 — "Exhalation Time Two"
28. BrAC2 — Second breath sample. Same five possibilities as on BrAC1.
29. INT.2 — Interference, if any, on second sample
30. B2.TIME — Time of acceptance of second subject sample
31. Err — This column will show the error codes.

ERROR CODES IN THE NEW SOFTWARE (COLUMN "ERR")

1. *SYSTEM WON'T ZERO — Unable to zero detector voltage.
2. TEMPERATURE LOW (Sample chamber below 45C)
3. TEMPERATURE HIGH (Sample chamber above 55C)
4. No code
5. *RADIO INTERFERENCE
6. FATAL SYSTEM ERROR (ADDRESS) — RAM, ROM, or PIA not responding properly
7. *CALIBRATION ERROR — Internal standard does not read within 10% of the value determined at time of calibration.
8. *PRINTER ERROR
9. RAM ERROR (ADDRESS) [previously called CRC Error] — RAM checksum does not match that calculated following last write.
10. PUMP ERROR — Flow detector does not detect pump operation.
11. BLANK ERROR — Instrument obtains reading greater than .003 during blank test.
12. DETECTOR OVERFLOW — Detector output exceeds that readable by the A/D converter.

13. FILTER ERROR — Filter solenoid not activating properly.
14. No code
15. SIMULATOR OUT OF RANGE — outside acceptable limits
16. No code
17. DATA MEMORY BATTERY LOW — RAM backup battery failing.
18. No code
19. AMBIENT FAIL — Ethanol or other substance detected in sample cell after purge.

The new DataMaster has a steeper learning curve than did the "old" machine still in use in most of western Washington, but in this writer's opinion, this only means that there are additional topics for cross examination, and more "reasons to doubt" to be established and argued in your summation to the jury.

II. FOUNDATIONAL ISSUES

The prosecution has a number of foundational issues to prove before the breath test may be admitted. A few of those issues can only be proved by testimony from the officer. Using the officer, the prosecution must prove:

1. That the officer who administered the breath test checked the subject's mouth at least fifteen minutes before the test, that no foreign substances were present, and that the subject did not vomit, eat, drink, or smoke 15 minutes before the test (WAC 448-13-040). *State v. Baker,* 56 Wn.2d 846 (1960);
2. That the simulator temperature was checked and found to be 34 degrees Centigrade plus or minus 0.2 degrees Centigrade (WAC 448-13-040);
3. The batch number of the simulator solution used in the test. *State v. Straka,* 116 Wn.2d 859 (1991);
4. That the officer was certified to operate the machine and was taught by a qualified instructor (WAC 448-13-150);
5. That the officer possessed a valid permit issued by the State Toxicologist for this purpose (RCW 46.61.506 (3));
6. That the officer completed "data entry" as part of the test (WAC 448-13-050(1)).

If the prosecution has not established a necessary foundational fact, defense counsel would be wise not to ask the officer about it and establish it for the prosecution. However, particularly regarding the "15 minute" rule, cross examination of the officer can reveal that the period of observation during the 15 minutes before the test was not uninterrupted or simply not performed.

1. Officer is Using Reference Manual and Typing during Observation.

   The machine requires the officer to answer a number of questions before a test can be run. This is the "data" part of the administration of a DataMaster breath test. Normally, the officer asks the client for this information, fills out a "Data Entry Form," and then types the answers into the machine when prompted. Particularly regarding questions 12 and 13, the officer will have to translate the answers given by the subject into "codes" to input into the machine by referring to a binder kept near the machine. He simply cannot write these answers down on the Data Entry Form, look up the codes and then type them into the machine all while keeping your client under continuous observation.
2. Officer Was Asking the "34 Questions" during the Observation Period.

   Many officers ask the questions included on the "alcohol influence report" just before giving the breath test. You can determine when the questions were asked by looking at question 28, where the subject is asked "What time is it?" and the officer's response, where he indicates the "correct" time. This form requires the officer to fill in thirty-four boxes, during which time it would be most difficult to keep the subject under observation.
3. Officer Was Out of the Room, Giving the Accused a "Private Conversation" with Counsel.

   In those cases where the accused requests counsel, the officer is required to provide access to counsel and a "private conversation." CrRLJ 3.1, *State v. Fitzsimmons,* 93 Wn.2d 436, 445, 610 P.2d 893 (1980). If the conversation was truly private and it occurred just before the breath test, the officer could not have had your client in continuous observation for the required period. Did he turn his back as he walked out the door to give your client privacy? Explore the privacy issue in a pretrial motion and determine whether this forms a basis to challenge the admission of the test results for lack of foundation.
4. Officer Used his Watch Instead of "DataMaster Time" to Measure the Fifteen-Minute Observation Period.

   The time "observation began" is listed on the breath

ticket because the officer typed in a response when prompted by the machine. This time does not necessarily coincide with the internal clock in the DataMaster, which is notoriously inaccurate. The DataMaster clock is to inaccurate and requires resetting so often, that technicians have been instructed *not* to fill out a maintenance sheet when they reset the time unless the time was more than one half-hour off! It is likely, then, that "DataMaster" time will not coincide with "officer time." The DataMaster indicates the time of the breath sample using its own clock. In cases where the observation period is close to 15 minutes, determine which clock the officer used to mark the commencement of observation. You might reveal that the officer's testimony regarding the 15-minute period is illusory.

5. Officer Should Have Restarted the Fifteen-Minute Period Because of an Invalid Sample.

   Many officers do not appreciate the difference between an incomplete sample and an invalid sample. If you know the difference, you might be able to show a violation of the 15-minute rule. An incomplete sample occurs when the individual blew earnestly but the machine did not accept the sample. An invalid sample occurs when the machine detects mouth alcohol. In the case of the incomplete sample, the officer can ask the individual to try again immediately. An invalid sample, on the other hand, requires *an additional 15-minute period of observation.* The DataMaster operator's manual directs the officer to "recheck the subject's mouth and have the subject under direct observation for an additional 15 minutes." (P. 3–8.)

   Do not assume that the officer appreciates the difference between an incomplete sample and an invalid sample. An incomplete sample will be recorded in the database, whereas an invalid sample is not recorded. If an officer writes that an "incomplete sample" occurred in his report, but the database shows no such entry it really was an invalid sample. If there was no additional 15-minute period of observation, the breath test results should be suppressed.

III. General Theory of Operation of the DataMaster

A. The Simple Explanation

In a nutshell, the DataMaster works as follows: After the cop types in the "demographic" data, the machine runs a room air ("blank") test and a check of its calibration using a quartz filter ("internal standard"). The defendant is then instructed to expel a long, steady breath sample into a baffled mouthpiece inserted into the "breath tube" (a new mouthpiece must be used for each sample). The breath travels down the tube (heated to minimize condensation) to the "thermistor." This device measures the air flow to insure that the defendant is blowing hard enough and with sufficient volume to give a "good" sample (i.e., alcohol saturated deep lung air).

The breath then travels through the "three-way valve" and into the "sample chamber," where the alcohol content is actually measured. The measurement takes place by passing a beam of "infrared light" through the sample chamber to the "detector." The light must bounce off mirrors at 45 degree angles (two 180 degree turns) in the sample chamber (necessary to lengthen the light path for greater resolution).

If alcohol is present in the breath sample, the detector will measure a loss of energy which is assumed to be caused by the presence of alcohol. In fact, the defendant's breath sample is tested four times per second as he or she blows into the machine, to make sure alcohol content is rising (as the breath comes from deeper and deeper in the lungs). The goal is to get the most alcohol saturated sample possible. Thus, the longer one blows the higher the result (the real reason for differences between your client's two breath samples).

The process of measuring the breath once every four seconds is commonly known as the "slope detector." This is designed to make sure that a "valid" sample is being introduced, since if mouth alcohol is present, the "slope" would be reversed, i.e., a higher concentration at the beginning rather than end of the breath. Should the machine detect an "invalid" sample, the test is aborted and the officer must start all over with a new 15 minute observation period. No record of the "invalid" test is retained in the database and an evidence ticket will not be printed.

When the detector sees alcohol due to a decrease in the amount of light striking the detector, it uses an extremely complicated (and secret) mathematical formula to compute the defendant's breath alcohol concentration in vapor. The test continues with another "blank" (room air) test and then a test of the "external standard" (simulator solution).

The simulator solution is a mixture of alcohol and water which approximates a .10 concentration in vapor. The mixture, kept in a jar attached to the back of the machine, must remain heated to 34 degrees Celsius (plus or minus .2 degrees). This causes the evaporation of alcohol at a predictable rate into the space in the jar above the solution (per Henry's Law). It is from this air space that the machine sucks a sample for testing between the defendant's two samples and the result must be between .090 and .110 (inclusive). It is this process (along with other factors) which the State Toxicologist claims "certifies" the machine's accuracy on each defendant's test.

Next is another room air/blank test, followed by the defendant's second sample, which must be within plus or minus 10 percent of the average of both tests in order to be "valid" (per WAC 448-13-060).

The test sequence ends with a final .00 blank test and the "evidence ticket" is printed out and ultimately used against the defendant at trial.

B. The Detailed Explanation

Conceptualize the infrared light source as a flashlight on one end of the sample chamber, and the molecules of ethanol as impediments to the light emanating from the flashlight reaching the end of the sample chamber. In essence, the DataMaster determines the difference between the amount of light emitted by the flashlight and that which is received by the detector at the end of the sample chamber. It assumes that any decrease in light is a result of ethanol molecules blocking (or absorbing) the light. There are numerous parts to the DataMaster worth discussing, as follows:

1. Breath Tube — The defendant's breath sample is introduced into the machine through a detachable breath tube that includes a heating wire. The heating wire is intended to heat the breath tube to approximately 50 degrees Centigrade. The purpose of this is to prevent condensation from developing in the breath tube, which could capture and retain alcohol and contaminate subsequent tests. There is no instrumental check of the temperature. The officer has been instructed to touch the breath tube to make sure that it is warm.

2. Thermistor — The thermistor monitors the breath flow rate. The defendant's breath cools the thermistor and as it cools electronic resistance increases. The machine's microprocessor monitors a voltage drop which must meet certain predetermined parameters for five seconds to be considered valid. The purpose of evaluating the breath flow rate is to ensure that a person is providing a sufficient sample of alveolar (deep lung) air. While the defendant cannot blow into the machine too strongly, if the person does not blow sufficiently, the machine will not accept the sample.

3. Three-Way Valve — The three-way valve has two inlet

parts and one outlet. Its purpose is to direct the flow of the air from either the simulator or from the breath tube and provide the sample into the sample chamber of the machine. When the vapor from the simulator solution is being introduced into the machine, the three-way valve shuts down the inlet from the breath tube. Conversely, when the breath sample is being provided, the vent from the simulator solution is theoretically shut. The valve is operated under the control of the microprocessor. There have been at least three different versions of this valve, and some DataMaster machines now come with a "five way" valve, which includes the capability to "recirculate" the simulator solution thus decreasing depletion of that solution.

4. Sample Chamber — The sample chamber holds 50 ml. of breath and is divided into three portions, essentially three tubes that are all next to each other. At the end of each tube are mirrors that reflect the infrared light into the next tube and eventually through the alcohol and interference filters to the infrared detector. The purpose of the mirrors is to increase the path length of the infrared light beam which improves resolution and allows for more precision of measurement. With the introduction of human breath or room air into the sample chamber, the potential exists for the accumulation of moisture and condensation to occur. Additionally, over the passage of time, dust and other debris can gather in the sample chamber, settling on the mirrors. The danger in the accumulation can be a partial deflection of the infrared light or the actual absorption of infrared energy by the water or debris, which can be misinterpreted by the infrared detector as ethanol.

5. Quartz Standard (Internal Standard) — During the testing sequence, a quartz crystal is inserted into the light beam. During calibration, the precise amount of infrared light that is allowed to pass through the quartz standard is determined. The quartz standard is a check on the internal calibration of the machine.

6. Infrared Source — The infrared source is a lamp that is controlled by a current regulation circuit and is activated by the machine's microprocessor as the breath sample is being introduced. The infrared beam generated by the lamp is passed through the sample chamber deflecting off each of the mirrors and eventually reaches the infrared detector. There have been at least two different versions of the lamp. The first type was self-contained and attached to the end of the sample chamber. The second (and newer) type mounts to a portion of the sample chamber. There have been six different manufacturers of the lamp.

7. Filters — There are two filters in the DataMaster: the alcohol filter and the interference filter (which is now called the acetone filter). Initially, the light passes through the alcohol filter, which is a narrow band pass filter designed to allow only a frequency with a wave length of 3.44 microns to pass through it. The alcohol filter is in place throughout the time that the individual is blowing into the machine. It is also in place when the quartz standard is lowered and when the simulator sample is being provided and also when the machine is zeroing.

The acetone filter is introduced into the path of the infrared light at other times during the measurement process. It too allows a narrow band pass of frequency with a wave length of 3.37 microns. The interference filter replaces the alcohol filter six times during the course of a test sequence. The switching back and forth of the alcohol and interference filters is controlled by the microprocessor. There have been at least two versions of filters used, with the more recent version having a smaller diameter.

8. Detector — The detector is another name for a transducer, which is a device that converts infrared energy into electrical energy. The electrical energy is forwarded to a digital converter and the microprocessor applies several mathematical formulae to interpret the result. The Breath Technicians say, "The detector receives the infrared energy inversely proportional to the concentration of alcohol in the sample chamber." In plain language, the detector determines the amount of light received from the infrared lamp, and the microprocessor compares that to the amount of infrared energy generated by the lamp. The detector is more "precise" when it operates at low temperatures. It is thus "cooled" nearly to freezing temperatures, by the detector cooler. There is no process by which the DataMaster monitors the cooling of the detector.

9. Detector Board — This is the circuit board that processes the signal received from the output of the detector. It is adjusted during calibration. There have been at least five versions of the detector board. The versions are claimed to be "functionally the same" but they do employ different circuitry to accomplish the same goal. The various versions look different in that the more recent versions have fewer potentiometers (called "pots" by technicians) — screw-like devices — to adjust the necessary voltages.

10. EPROMs and CPU — Most of the steps, functions, and calculations of the DataMaster are controlled by two very important parts of the computer, the Central Processing Unit (CPU) and the EPROMs. EPROM stands for Erasable, Programmable, Read-Only

Memory, and refers to small centipede-like "chips" that contain the DataMaster software. The EPROMs are literally the brains of the DataMaster which utilize the CPU to work for it. It instructs the CPU to make a certain calculations, and when the CPU has concluded that calculation, it asks the EPROM what to do next. Such a set of instructions is called, in computer geek-eze, an algorithm.

The EPROMs are identified by a number and each contains a portion of the operating computer code:

EPROM U-23:	"Service" routines. Math, printer, display characters, communications, modern instructions.
EPROMs U25 and U26:	Breath test sequence and machine interfaces.
EPROM U16:	Power-up vectors (alpha or numeric on keyboard) and data prompts.

11. CPU Board — This is the largest circuit board in the machine, and arguably the most critical. The CPU and EPROMs are on this board. There is also a clock chip (notoriously inaccurate) on this board, used to display the time. There is a battery-backed RAM memory section which stores the critical "calibration factors." There have been at least three versions of the board, and undoubtedly more to come.

12. Slope Detector — The slope detector is not a part of the DataMaster, it is a function of the software. Technically speaking, the "sample acceptance parameters" portion of the operating computer program also contains the slope detector. When the defendant blows into the machine, it commences taking readings of the sample every one-quarter of a second. This is accomplished by a chopper which interrupts the travel of the infrared light. In this way the DataMaster is able to plot a slope as the alcohol content of the breath rises.

The slope detector has two functions. The machine expects the initial breath to contain less alcohol than the latter portions of the sample. If, however, there is mouth alcohol present, the machine is designed to detect that fact since at some point in time the breath sample will contain less alcohol than the initial portion of the sample. In that event, the machine will assume mouth alcohol and abort the test with an "INVALID SAMPLE" reading. The slope detector is intended to insure that only deep-lung air is measured. It does this in the same manner as it detects the presence of mouth alcohol. It continues to monitor the alcohol content of the breath every one-quarter of a second. At some point in time, the slope that is being constantly calculated by the microprocessor begins to "level out." Once the machine determines that there is a "near zero slope" the test is concluded and the last alcohol reading is recorded.

13. Power Supply Board — A computer does not use straight 110 AC power which comes out of your wall. The many circuits in the DataMaster require at least seven separate power settings, such as seven and twelve volts DC. Some circuits require "millivolts." This circuit board is intended to supply reliable, smooth, "filtered" electricity which is essential to a properly operating computer. It is also designed to prevent the DataMaster from crashing when a power surge occurs. Judging from maintenance records we've seen, it is not very effective for this purpose.

14. Pump Driver Board — This provides circuitry to regulate the operation of the two pumps. Proper voltages must be maintained on this board for the pumps to run appropriately.

15. RFI Board — The "radio frequency interference" board provides the circuitry intended to detect unwanted radio energy that could influence a breath test reading. There is an antenna on the machine for this purpose. The operation of this board is suspect, since it is never tested in actual field conditions.

16. DataMaster Board — This circuit board contains the RAM memory chips which store breath test results for later downloading to a central computer. Up to 8K of data may be stored, but it is lost if the battery on this board expires. The Washington State Patrol intends to introduce a brand new version of the DataMaster into Eastern Washington in September 1995. The Patrol reports that while the outside of the machine looks a bit different (the keyboard is built into the cover) the only difference inside is that the DataMaster Board has been eliminated. The data retention function now exists on the CPU board. This means, of course, that the design of the CPU board has also changed.

17. Modem Board — This circuit board is plugged into the phone line and permits data transmission. It also allows the DataMaster to be called by another computer and operated by remote control. It transmits at 300 baud, the slowest rate possible for a modem. Most desktop computers with modems use 2,400, 9,600, 14,400, or 28,000 baud. This fact might be used with the more computer literate persons in a jury panel to demonstrate that the DataMaster is not at all "state of the art."

18. Simulator — This device attached to the top of a jar. Currently, peanut butter jars are the favored "jar of use." The

"external standard" is a water/alcohol solution in the jar, which is made in a batch by technicians at the State Toxicology Lab.

The DataMaster uses the simulator during each test between the two breath samples that are measured. The simulator holds the external standard in the jar and the solution is heated to 34 degrees Centigrade (plus or minus .2 degrees Centigrade). This should create a vapor of .100 alcohol content. The machine is programmed to suck the vapor into the machine at the appropriate time to determine that the machine is reading alcohol accurately.

DETAILED BREATH TEST SEQUENCE: A breath test sequence is commenced by the officer pushing the "RUN" button. This is done after the fifteen minute observation period has occurred and after the simulator solution temperature has been checked to be within the proper parameters. The instrument then displays "INSERT TICKET" and the operator inserts the evidence ticket in the appropriate slot marked "IN," face down. Thereafter, the machine sequentially displays 14 questions pertaining to the defendant and the circumstances of arrest. The officer uses a keyboard that is a part of the DataMaster to answer these questions. Once the questions have been answered, the machine asks the officer "REVIEW DATA?" allowing the officer to make sure that the information entered is correct. Once the officer is satisfied that the data is correct, he or she types "N" which stores the data into the memory of the machine and commences the breath test sequence. Once the process commences, the machine displays sequentially the following:

1. "PURGING" During the purging procedure, which occurs several times during the test, room air is being pumped into the sample chamber by means of a pump. The purpose of this purge is to clear the sample chamber of any alcohol remaining from previous tests, as well as to test the ambient room air for the presence of any alcohol or other interferant.

2. "AMBIENT ZEROING" This step is to set atmospheric ethyl alcohol to zero. What this means is that if the machine detects any alcohol during this phase it compensates for it by deducting that amount during the subsequent step's process. This is done all the way up to a .10! Later zeroing procedures only allow for a .003 reading. More than that will abort the test with an error code "SYSTEM WON'T ZERO."

3. Following these steps, the machine displays "BLANK TEST," which is the result of the zeroing process and is recorded on the evidence ticket.

4. "INTERNAL STANDARD CHECK" During this step the quartz filter is dropped into the infrared light source path. The quartz filter absorbs infrared energy in a known amount that is determined during the initial calibration of the machine. The infrared detector receives a reduced amount of infrared energy than was transmitted by the infrared source. The reduced intensity is evaluated mathematically by the microprocessor and a predetermined result must be achieved. This step is an evaluation of the machine's entire electronic system, signal analysis and processing system to determine that everything is working properly. It is recorded on the evidence ticket as "INTERNAL STANDARD VERIFIED."

The operator then removes a new mouth piece from its plastic bag and inserts it into the breath tube. The operator is instructed to avoid touching the mouth piece during this step. The machine now displays "SUBJECT REFUSE? (Y/N)." The officer has one minute to answer this question or the machine erases memory and the entire test procedure, including data entry, must be resequenced. If the defendant has refused a breath sample, the officer types "Y," the evidence ticket will document the refusal and the breath sampling sequence is automatically terminated. If the defendant has agreed to take the breath test, the officer types "N" and the display flashes "PLEASE BLOW." The officer is instructed to tell the defendant to "provide a slow, consistent, continuous breath sample through the mouth piece," and further to tell the defendant "blow until I tell you to stop." As the defendant blows into the machine, the words "PLEASE BLOW" no longer flash but remain on the display. The defendant must continue to blow until the machine displays "TEST RESULTS" and gives a two-digit alcohol content number.

If a sample has not been accepted by the machine after two minutes from the time "PLEASE BLOW" is displayed, the machine will again display "SUBJECT REFUSE? (Y/N)." At this point, the officer again answers that question according to his or her sometimes subjective evaluation of the defendant's intentions. As the defendant's breath sample is introduced into the machine through the breath tube, it passes the thermistor and enters the sample chamber. The infrared lamp is activated and the breath is evaluated at the rate of four times per second. It then passes through either the alcohol or interference filters depending on which has been sequenced to interrupt the light source. The detector calculates the amount of infrared energy that has reached it, forwards it to a digital converter and the microprocessor.

When the defendant blows into the machine, if the machine

detects mouth alcohol, it will display "INVALID SAMPLE." This should not be confused with an insufficient sample which results in an "INCOMPLETE" indication on the printout.

If an interfering substance is detected by the machine it will display "TEST RESULTS" with a two-digit interferant reading. The machine is designed to automatically subtract the interference value from the total reading and then display the actual breath alcohol as previously indicated. Whether it actually does so is hotly contested. The evidence ticket will show the presence of both the interfering substance and the adjusted alcohol level.

After the first result has been obtained, the machine will again sequentially display "PURGING," "AMBIENT ZEROING," "BLANK TEST" and "EXTERNAL STANDARD." The first of these displays indicate the machine is performing the functions previously described. On the evidence ticket, only the "BLANK TEST" and the "EXTERNAL STANDARD" are shown. After the first sample is tested, the microprocessor automatically activates the simulator. The result of the simulator solution test is printed on the evidence ticket in three digits. When the simulator is run, the machine displays "TEST RESULTS" with a three-digit alcohol number displayed. However, the evidence ticket reads "EXTERNAL STANDARD." The machine then again displays "PURGING," "AMBIENT ZEROING," and "BLANK TEST." The machine is again running those functions. Again, only the "BLANK TEST" is displayed on the evidence ticket. The officer again replaces the mouthpiece with one that is new and unused. After the machine shows "BLANK TEST," it again displays "SUBJECT REFUSED? (Y/N)" and a second breath sample is taken in the same manner as the first sample.

During a test "error codes" may appear. Error codes appear on the display panel when a malfunction occurs or a situation arises which either aborts the test or prevents an operator from proceeding. A description of various error codes follows:

Error Code 1: System Won't Zero Many situations cause this particular error code; however, they all relate to the circuitry detecting the presence of alcohol in the machine during the purging phase. This may or may not be a result of alcohol actually being present. What causes the "SYSTEM WON'T ZERO" error code is a decreased amount of infrared energy reaching the detector at a time when the microprocessor anticipates a greater amount. This can be caused by alcohol being present in the chamber, by an inadequate amount of light being sent from the infrared source, by a deflection of light by water or debris, or by complete or partial failure of the alcohol filter or interference filter to enter the infrared light beam at the appropriate time.

ERROR CODE 2: TEMPERATURE LOW This indicates that the sample chamber temperature is improper. If this message is displayed, the machine will not function.

ERROR CODE 3: TEMPERATURE HIGH This indicates that the sample chamber temperature is improper. If this message is displayed the machine will not function.

ERROR CODE 4: CYLINDER SEIZED This error code is designed to be used with DataMasters that have been configured with the optional (and not used in Washington) breath sample retention kit. This kit permits independent retesting of breath samples to check the accuracy of the DataMaster.

ERROR CODE 5: RADIO INTERFERENCE This error code is displayed when radio frequency interference is detected by the radio frequency antenna. This error code will be displayed only if the radio frequency antenna is operational. The microprocessor does not monitor the functioning of the antenna, nor is it regularly tested by maintenance technicians.

ERROR CODE 6: FATAL SYSTEMS ERROR **(address included)** This code occurs when there is a problem in the software programming located in the EPROMs, and results where some area of the software program shuts down.

ERROR CODE 7: CALIBRATION ERROR This code occurs if the quartz plate is pulled into the infrared path and the signal measured is not in accordance with the predetermined standard. This can also occur if in fact the machine is not calibrated. That can occur if for some reason the portion of the computer memory that retains the information for calibration is lost. In other words, the machine can "forget" its calibration. These calibration factors are all checked at the initiation of each test.

ERROR CODE 8: PRINTER ERROR This code is displayed if the evidence ticket jams or the printer malfunctions.

ERROR CODE 9: CRC ERROR **(address included)** CRC stands for Cyclic Redundancy Check. The error code is followed by a number which is giving a location in the memory where the error was found. The microprocessor goes through the information that is in the portion of the memory being checked and determines that it is all correct. If it is not, the error code is displayed.

The data entries that are made during the administration of a breath test are eventually stored in a central computer "database" at the State Crime Lab in Seattle. Also included in the database are the test results of all tests run on the machine and the recorded error codes. As to the individual tests, the database provides greater information regarding precision, since it records to three digits. It also records the time the test started (which is different from the first incident recorded on the evidence ticket — the blank test) as well as demographic information regarding the defendant and the incident. It can also disclose whether error codes occurred during the attempt to administer a test to the individual defendant.

As to the history of the machine, the database is invaluable. It can determine the frequency with which machines have experienced specific error codes, the proximity of such episodes to the client's test, the extent to which a machine yields imprecise results, whether such problems are episodic of chronic, and, when compared to repair records, whether the machine has been properly and timely repaired pursuant to State Patrol guidelines.

IV. CONCLUSION

Learn about the DataMaster to the extent that you are comfortable, generally, with the technology. You do not need to know every detail regarding the machine to be effective in court. Your attitude of disbelief of the machine's test results coupled with a few helpful answers gained during cross examination, should give you enough to nullify the test results by argument in your summation. You always have a chance to win. But only if you will try the case.

Checklist 7 BAC DataMaster

- ☐ Was the machine properly licensed, calibrated, and maintained?
- ☐ Was the solution used to externally calibrate the machine accurately prepared?
- ☐ Was the room air used to flush the sample chamber contaminated with the alcoholic breath of test subjects?
- ☐ Do the machine's records indicate any failures or mechanical problems before or since the test?
- ☐ Has the machine been modified in any way affecting its status as a state-approved device?
- ☐ Does the machine incorporate any "fail-safe" features?
- ☐ Is there an acetone detector? (Was the client a diabetic or on a strict diet?)
- ☐ Is there an acetaldehyde detector?
- ☐ Is there a radio frequency interference detector?

- ☐ Is there a mouth alcohol detector?
- ☐ Does the machine have the option for retaining a second breath sample? Why not?
- ☐ Was the operator/officer properly licensed and trained?
- ☐ Is he familiar with the theory and operation of the BAC DataMaster?
- ☐ Did he follow the manufacturer's checklist? Can he recall each step?
- ☐ Did he observe the client constantly for 15 to 20 minutes before administering the test?
- ☐ Could the operator have manipulated the test results?
- ☐ Is the machine specific for alcohol?
- ☐ What other compounds found on the breath will be reported as alcohol by the machine?
- ☐ Could the client have had acetaldehyde in his system? Acetone? Ketones? Paint or glue fumes? Other compounds?
- ☐ Was there any source of radio frequency interference in the area of the machine when the client was tested?
- ☐ Any police transmitters? Walkie-talkies? Televisions? Electric door locks? Microwave ovens? Police car transmitters in the parking lot? Teletype machines? Computers? Radios? Fluorescent lighting?
- ☐ Could the machine have been affected by a mechanical or electrical problem, such as a drop in line voltage?
- ☐ How many malfunctions are recognized as possible by the manufacturer?
- ☐ Are all of these detected by the machine's internal computer?
- ☐ Would a defect in the computer or its software be detectable?
- ☐ Were all operating temperatures as required by the manufacturer?
- ☐ Could condensation have formed in the breath tube as a result of being operated at an improper temperature?
- ☐ Were there any possible problems with the machine's temperature, humidity, optics, or age?
- ☐ Was a self-checking diagnostic system available in the DataMaster?
- ☐ Was it run immediately before or after the client's test? Why not?
- ☐ Are there any generic problems with breath testing?
- ☐ Can the prosecution establish that the client's partition ratio was 2100:1?
- ☐ Did the breath test take place during the client's absorptive state?
- ☐ Could mouth alcohol have been present? Does the client wear dentures or have dental caps? Was he bleeding in themouth?
- ☐ What is the client's hematocrit and how could it have affected the breath test?
- ☐ Did the client have an elevated body temperature?

- ☐ Could stress or breathing pattern have elevated the machine's test results?
- ☐ Did room air used to flush the sample chamber contain alcoholic breath from test subjects?
- ☐ Are there any problems with blood-alcohol testing generally?
- ☐ Was the client a woman?
- ☐ Did the client have a rising BAC curve?
- ☐ Is any attempt to project BAC back to the time of driving based on evidence and scientifically accepted fact? (see retrograde extrapolation, §5.2)
- ☐ Could eating or smoking have affected alcohol metabolism?
- ☐ Could zinc in the client's body have been a factor?
- ☐ What is the inherent error in testing with a BAC DataMaster?

§6.4.3 Intoximeter 3000

The original Intoximeter, manufactured by Intoximeter Associates, was at one time the most commonly used breath testing instrument in the world. The machine was used by the officer at the scene of the arrest. It came from the laboratory, and the officer simply broke the seal, collected the breath sample in a balloon, performed a quick preliminary field test, resealed the machine, and returned it to the laboratory for interpretation of the results. This proved very convenient, eliminated much of the "chain of custody" problem, and minimized the nonexpert officer's involvement. It also resulted in a reading at the scene of arrest, rather than later at the police station.

The same manufacturer (Intoximeter Associates) next brought out the Photo-Electric Intoximeter (P.E.I.), which operates very similarly to the Breathalyzer. By collecting only alveolar air rather than mixed expired air, the Photo-Electric Intoximeter avoided many of the problems inherent in the original Intoximeter.

The next versions of the Intoximeter were of the gas chromatography type. Perhaps the greatest advantage of the Gas Chromatograph Intoximeters was their specificity—that is, the machines will detect and register only alcohol, unlike such instruments as the Intoxilyzer, which may register other substances as alcohol. Manufactured by Intoximeters, Inc. (1901 Locust Street,

St. Louis, MO 63103), the models Mark II and Mark IV received relatively wide acceptance. The Mark II was originally developed by Cal Detect, a California corporation, and was later sold to Intoximeters, Inc. The Mark IV, similar in design and function although slightly different in appearance, also was developed originally by Cal Detect, Inc. This machine was capable of analyzing blood, urine, or breath, including preserved breath samples. Both machines require the periodic replacement of compressed carrier gas, purchased from local gas suppliers.

Finally, Intoximeters, Inc., brought out the Intoximeter Model 3000. This was to be their state-of-the-art breath-alcohol instrument and, like the Mark II and Mark IV, was developed by Don Hutson of Cal Detect, Inc., Richmond, California. Unlike the Mark II and Mark IV, however, the 3000 uses the principle of infrared spectroscopy rather than gas chromatography, thus incorporating the same principles used by the competing — and increasingly popular — Intoxilyzer 5000. And, like the Intoxilyzer 5000 and BAC Verifier, the 3000 utilizes a computer that has been incorporated directly into the instrument. In addition, the Model 3000 has an electrical conductivity cell, known as a "Taguchi cell," which theoretically will distinguish acetone and acetaldehyde from ethanol, thus avoiding some of the specificity problems of infrared analysis. In fact, however, the Taguchi cell is considered ineffective. As will be seen, it is the Taguchi cell (or its absence) that is the primary "Achilles heel" of the Intoximeter 3000.

Intoximeters, Inc. has recently discontinued manufacture of the Model 3000, although it is committed to providing parts and service in the future. Because of its wide acceptance across the country and its rugged design, however, the 3000 can be expected to be encountered for many years to come. In its place, the manufacturer has developed a new model, the Intoximeter EC-IR.

The EC-IR is a very different machine than the 3000. Although it retained the infrared detector to satisfy the states that wanted a machine utilizing infrared spectrophotometry, the actual measurement of alcohol is done by the machine's fuel cell. This cell uses small chemo-electrical cells to generate current from the catalytic oxidation of alcohol in the breath. The amount of electricity produced is theoretically proportional to the concentration of alcohol in the breath.

Although it has not been widely adopted as of this writing, the EC-IR has been approved by the Department of Transportation and counsel in some jurisdictions can expect to deal with it in the near future. It appears that the machine — the primary benefit of which appears to be its comparatively low cost — is being bypassed by many law enforcement agencies, largely in favor of the Datamaster and the new Draeger Alcotest 7110.

The Intoximeter Model 3000 functions much like the Intoxilyzer 5000 (see §6.4.1). The breath is captured through a mouthpiece into a tube, then into a two-chambered cell. A heated element then projects infrared light (3.45 microns) from one end of the cell through the two halves to the other end of the cell. One-half of the cell contains the breath sample from the tested subject; the other half is a reference cell, used to establish a zero point. A detector at the other end of the cell measures how much infrared energy passed through the sample cell — that is, how much was absorbed by the breath sample; the more light energy absorbed by the sample, the higher the concentration of alcohol in the breath. (For a more complete discussion of infrared analysis, see §§6.1 and 6.4.1).

The primary problem with the 3000 is, as has been mentioned, the Taguchi cell. The purpose of the Taguchi cell, or sensor, is to detect the presence of acetone in the breath sample. As has been discussed previously (see §6.1), infrared breath testing devices such as the Model 3000 are nonspecific for alcohol. The 3000 measures infrared light at a wavelength centered on 3.39 microns; the band width runs from 3.30 to 3.50 microns. Any compound on the breath that absorbs in those wavelengths will be detected by the machine as "alcohol." And, of course, there are a vast number of compounds that will absorb in this range — including acetone, commonly found on human breath.

A scientific study has concluded that the Intoximeter 3000 is unreliable due to the fact that it only addresses acetone as a potential interferant:

> Two instruments using two modes of ethanol detection are the Intoximeter 3000 (3.4 micron infra-red plus Taguchi cell) and the BAC DataMaster (dual wavelength infra-red). These have proved unsuitable because acetone appears to be considered the only potential interfering substance. . . . In the selection of two modes of

> ethanol detection, each system must be chosen such that a comparison of the response from each mode would indicate a wide range of possible interfering substances, not just acetone.

Bell, Attaining Specificity in the Measurement of Ethanol in Breath, 40 Acta Medicinae Legalis et Socialis 107 (1990).

The Taguchi sensor operates on the scientific principle that substances will oxidize at different and predictable temperatures. This oxidation causes a temperature change in a semiconductor in the sensor, thereby triggering a change in the semiconductor's electrical conductivity. The Model 3000's computer compares the alcohol measurement made by the infrared detectors with the electrical measurement made by the Taguchi sensor. If the Taguchi sensor indicates a lower breath-alcohol concentration than the infrared detectors, the computer registers the presence of a contaminant — and assumes that the contaminant is acetone. The computer then deducts the difference in the two measurements (i.e., the amount of acetone) from the infrared measurement of alcohol and reports the resulting figure as the tested subject's blood-alcohol concentration.

There are, however, a number of problems with the Taguchi sensor. To begin with, it is not sensitive enough to report a specific amount of acetone, instead giving readings of "high," "moderate," or "trace" acetone. More important, this sensitivity is not constant: The sensitivity of the Taguchi cell will change with time and use. The result, of course, will be inaccuracy in dealing with acetone interference.

An even more critical consequence of this varying sensitivity, however, is that the machine itself will be inaccurately calibrated. In running self-calibration, the Intoximeter 3000 compares the Taguchi and infrared measurements of known samples. If the sensitivity of the two devices is not constant, the calibration will be defective — and test results will be inaccurate. Thus counsel should always research when the Taguchi sensor was last calibrated with an external standard.

Counsel should also always determine whether the Taguchi sensor has been *removed.* Because of its instability, and the difficulty in maintaining constant sensitivity, many law enforcement officers across the country have simply *removed* the device from the machine. Of course, without the Taguchi cell, the Intoximeter

3000 is nothing more than a single wavelength breath testing machine. As such, it is *completely nonspecific for alcohol.* Even with the device, though, the 3000 can detect only the presence of acetone; any other compounds on the breath that will absorb light energy in the single wavelength band will still register as alcohol.

In addition to the Taguchi problem, the Intoximeter 3000 is subject to most of the infirmities of other forms of breath testing. Thus counsel should review the discussions in §§6.0, 6.2 *et seq.*, and §§6.3 *et seq.*, concerning such matters as blood-breath partition ratios, testing during the absorptive state, mouth alcohol, hematocrit, body temperature, breathing pattern, stress, simulator calibration, used mouthpieces, ambient air, radio frequency interference, retrograde extrapolation, inherent error, and the rising blood-alcohol curve.

As with any breath machine, the result is totally dependent on correct administration of the test by the officer/operator. For purposes of cross-examination, counsel may wish to consider the following material, adopted from the manufacturer's Supervisor's Manual for the Intoximeter 3000.

> USING THE INSTRUMENT — OPERATOR PROCEDURES
>
> The Test Operator's responsibility is to insure that a valid breath test is obtained from the subject. This involves a number of steps:
>
> Ensuring Proper Environmental Conditions
> Ensuring Proper Use of the Instrument
> Following Pretesting Procedures
> Providing Clear Test Instructions
> Giving the Actual Test
> Analyzing Problems in Running a Good Test
>
> A. PROPER ENVIRONMENTAL CONDITIONS
>
> The testing room should be free of radio transmitting equipment, including walkie-talkies, and of sources of organic fumes.
>
> B. PROPER USE OF THE INSTRUMENT
>
> Keep in mind that the operator should never tamper with anything inside the instrument. That job is the responsibility of a su-

pervisor or an authorized technician. Unauthorized access to components and settings will void the instrument warranty.

Do's and **Don'ts** spelled out at the beginning of this manual should be respected.

Proper use of the instrument requires familiarity with the special command keys highlighted in black:

START. The operator presses this key to start a test.

DEL. This stands for delete. If a typing error has been made, as seen on the display, the operator can use this key to erase the mistake before it is entered into the instrument's memory.

ENTER. Once the response to a question has been typed and verified as correct, the operator must press this key to continue the test sequence.

CLEAR. If a mistake is detected AFTER the ENTER key is pressed, the operator must use the CLEAR key, and begin the test all over again.

If the instrument is being used properly and good breath testing techniques are being employed, these are the only special keys the test operator should need to use. The remaining special command keys have more specialized functions, and are intended for use by a certified supervisor.

C. FOLLOWING PRETESTING PROCEDURES

The fifteen-twenty minute wait and observation is extremely important. During this time the subject should be observed for physical indications of drunkenness.

If the subject vomits, or burps, the waiting period should be started over to avoid any possibility that the breath sample could be affected by mouth or stomach alcohol.

During this period, the subject MUST NOT be allowed to smoke, drink, chew gum, use a mouth spray, or introduce anything into his mouth. This will prevent legal criticism of the sample taken.

Make sure the command, "PRESS START TO TEST," along with the day, date and time is moving across the display from right to left. Make sure this information is correct.

Insure there is enough printer paper, and that it is properly fed through the printer.

Insert a new, clean mouthpiece into the breath line.

D. PROVIDE CLEAR TEST INSTRUCTIONS TO THE SUBJECT

Upon request, the subject should take a slow, deep breath, and hold it momentarily.

Grasp the breath line, pull it. Then have the subject place the mouthpiece to his lips, and blow into it in a slow, even manner. The display will appear as follows:

XXX *- - - - -

An acceptable sample has been obtained when the instrument shows an asterisk (*) on the right side of the display.

XXX *- - - - -

YOU SHOULD ENCOURAGE THE SUBJECT TO BLOW UNTIL THE NUMBERS GO TO 000, even after the asterisk on the right has appeared.

A NOTE TO THE OPERATOR: The operator should encourage the subject to exhale as long as possible to permit sampling of air from the deepest alveolar recesses of the lungs. The instrument facilitates this process by displaying information on the subject's blowing pattern as well as on the breath alcohol level being monitored at any point in time. The trained operator can use this information to observe the test as it is actually being given and coach the subject to obtain the most accurate result.

1. Flow Monitoring. The subject must maintain his blowing rate above a certain minimum flow rate. An acceptable blowing rate is being obtained if the subject is able to produce an asterisk at left center of the display, together with a series of bars indicating the force of his blow (see above). Any attempt to fool the instrument with a series of rapid, shallow breath samples will cause the flow to drop below the minimum required, as indicated by the asterisk. If this occurs, the test will be aborted.
2. Slope Detection and Monitoring. If a subject is providing a valid sample, the alcohol content being detected will rise sharply when a subject first starts blowing, then level off as a deep lung sample is attained. This process is indicated by the 3 digit number on the left side of the display. It will go from a very large number, measured in hundreds and indicating a sharply rising BAC curve, to zero as deep lung air is being sampled and the curve flattens out. This process can be seen occurring as a subject with alcohol exhales into the instrument. The numbers give no indication of the ac-

tual BAC values being detected, only the extent to which a deep lung sample is being obtained.

E. THE ACTUAL TEST

Press the START KEY. In general, the instrument will pass through 2 stages:

The display will ask for subject test information. During this stage the operator must type and ENTER the answers to whatever questions the instrument asks. The particular questions asked will depend on how the IR is programmed. When names are typed in, up to 20 characters can be used. Within this limit the operator should enter a name in the following manner:

— complete last name, followed by:
— first name (legal, not nickname; may have to be abbreviated), followed by:
— middle initial.

Prepare itself for taking a breath test. The IR will now purge itself, test a sample of ambient air, typically check calibration with a standard, then purge and test a blank again. After this process is complete it will ask that the subject give a breath sample. Throughout this process the instrument will display other messages that represent:

— commands to the operator
— the operational status of the instrument
— test results

PRG. The IR is purging the sampling system with fresh air.
BLK. The IR is reading the air to insure no contaminants are present to affect the test results.
STD or XSTD. The IR is running an internal or external standard to insure that it is reading within specified accuracy requirements when an actual subject test is run. The result will be displayed and later printed.

Wait until the display shows the command, "SUBJECT BLOW," before asking the subject to take a breath and blow. The instrument will wait patiently for several minutes after this command is shown, so there is no need to rush the subject.
As the subject blows into the breath line, observe him closely

to make sure he is blowing evenly, and continues to blow until allowed to stop.

Watch the IR display. When an asterisk (*) appears on the right hand side of the display, an adequate sample has been obtained. As already discussed, the subject should be encouraged to keep blowing, for the best test results to be obtained. As the instrument analyzes a valid sample, it will display the status message, "ANALYZING." After the instrument finishes its analysis, the result will be displayed as "SUBJ. XX," and the results of the entire test sequence will be printed out.

F. A TYPICAL TEST SEQUENCE

An example of a typical test sequence follows. Such a sequence is programmed into the instrument to meet the specifications of the purchasing agency, and will therefore vary from state to state. The specific sequence for your agency is detailed in a separate supplement to this Manual.

1. "PRESS START TO TEST" — The circulating display also contains the current date, day and time. To begin a test press the "START" key.
2. "OPERATOR NAME" — Enter the name of the operator. Up to twenty characters can be entered. Press the "ENTER" key after entry is complete.
3. "SUBJECT NAME" — Enter the name of the subject. Up to twenty characters can be entered. Press the "ENTER" key after entry is complete. The instrument may go into a stand-by mode at this point.
4. "PRG" — The instrument is now purging the breath line, sample chamber and passages with fresh air.
5. "BLK" — During the blank cycle, the instrument takes a reading of the air to assure that the instrument is clean.

6(a). "XST" — The instrument is now running an external standard. If the display shows "STD," instrument is running internal standard [see 6(b) below]. After the external standard is obtained, the display will contain the message "ANALYZING." (Go to #7.)

6(b). "STD" — The instrument is now running an internal standard. If display shows "XST," instrument is running an external standard. [See 6(a) above.]

7. "STD .10" — Standard results are displayed. If the results of the standard are not within tolerances, the message

"HIGH ABORT" or "LOW ABORT" will appear in the display.

8. "PRG" — Instrument is now running a purge cycle.
9. "BLK" — The blank cycle is run to assure the instrument is clean.
10. "SUBJECT BLOW SUB" — The instrument is now ready for the subject's first test. When the subject blows, the minimum flow asterisk and a series of bars will appear in the display. The more bars in the display, the harder the subject is blowing. The subject should keep blowing until a star appears.
11. *** — The star indicates that a valid sample has been obtained. If the subject did not blow hard or long enough, the message "ABORTED" will appear in the display.
12. "ANALYZING" — The instrument is now analyzing the first sample. If the message "INTERFERING SUBSTANCE" appears, the interfering substance has been detected. If the message "MOUTH ALCOHOL" appears, mouth alcohol has been detected.
13. "SUBJ .13" — The instrument displays the first subject test results.
14. "PRG" — The instrument is now running a purge cycle.
15. "BLK" — The instrument is now running a blank cycle.
16. "SUBJECT BLOWS SUB" — The instrument is now ready to test the second subject test.
17. *** — The star indicates that a valid sample has been obtained.
18. "ANALYZING" — The instrument is now analyzing the second sample.
19. "SUBJ .13" — The instrument displays the second subject test results.
20. "PRG" — The instrument is now running a purge cycle.
21. "BLK" — The instrument is now running a blank cycle. At the end of this blank cycle, the printer will print the results. When the printer has finished, the display will return to the circulating mode. The instrument is now ready to start another test.

G. PROBLEMS IN RUNNING A GOOD TEST

The instrument will signal a problem with the instrument or an error in test procedure by displaying one of the following messages of an abnormal condition. As indicated below, the operator can deal easily with certain of these problems. Others require the attention of either a supervisor or a technician.

LOW TEMP. The instrument has just been plugged in, and the heaters have not brought the IR module up to operating temperature yet. Wait for up to an hour, depending on the ambient temperature. If this message remains the heaters may be malfunctioning and the assistance of a supervisor or technician is required.

STANDBY. The chopper motor has just turned on and the IR Source has just gone to full power. Wait 90 sec. for the IR System to stabilize, after which the "OPERATOR NAME" message will appear. If the "STANDBY" message persists AFTER 90 sec., press the RESET button and try START again.

REFERENCE CHANNEL HIGH or LOW. Sometimes comes up after pressing the start key. Wait one minute, or until "OPERATOR NAME" appears, allowing the test to proceed. If the message persists, it is an indication of a problem with the IR signal, possibly the source, detector, chopper, or one of the associated electronic components. In this case, the assistance of a supervisor or technician is required.

PRG-BLK cycling. If the Purge-Blank cycle keeps running, it may be that the sample chamber has been contaminated and that the instrument is trying to clean it out. With minor amounts of contamination, this cycle will end in a few minutes and the instrument may be used. If the cycle keeps repeating for an unduly long time however, it may mean that the instrument is in a false purge-blank loop. In this instance, the assistance of a supervisor or technician is required.

STD XXX HIGH ABORT or LOW ABORT. The results obtained from running a standard are out of tolerance. If an internal standard is being used, it may need maintenance. If it is operating properly some other component within the instrument may be causing this problem. The internal standard should not be adjusted without checking for other problems first. In this instance, the assistance of a supervisor or technician is required.

If an external simulator is being used, it should be checked for solution depletion or deviations from the programmed temperature of 34 degrees C. If these are known good, the instrument needs maintenance and recalibration.

MOUTH ALCOHOL. Wait 15 minutes and try to administer a test again. Be sure that the subject breathes evenly into the IR. Continuing MOUTH ALCOHOL messages may indicate a leak, or a noisy detector. In this instance, the assistance of a supervisor or technician is required.

INTERFERING SUBSTANCE. An organic compound has been detected in the sample in a concentration strong enough to abort the test.

ABORTED. The subject has given an insufficient breath sample, but the IR is about to let him try again (three time limit within the same test sequence).

INSUFFICIENT BREATH. The subject has been unable to provide a satisfactory breath sample in 3 opportunities.

TEST REFUSED. The subject has not blown into the breath line at all within the period allowed. The test may be restarted by pressing the START key and starting again.

SUMMARY FULL. The instrument memory has been filled with test data. The test data should be printed out and memory then purged using the "SU" Two Key command, with options 0, then X. In this instance, the assistance of a supervisor or technician is required.

There are a number of other problems for which no fault message is given, but which can be dealt with by the operator:

No display. Check to see if instrument is unplugged or if a fuse has blown. Otherwise try the CLEAR key. If that does not work, try pressing the RESET button.

Frozen display. The scrolling "PRESS START TO TEST" message is not moving. Try the CLEAR key. If that does not work, try pressing the RESET button.

Instrument Lockup. The IR will not progress to the next step in the test sequence. Try the CLEAR key; if this fails, then the RESET button.

Spelling Mistake. The DEL key may be used if the ENTER key has not been pressed yet. Otherwise the CLEAR key will have to be used and the test sequence restarted.

SHERIFF'S DEPARTMENT
COUNTY OF LOS ANGELES
IR-3000 Checklist

INSTR. #	BLOOD ALCOHOL RESULTS
4542	.11 % .12 % —
LOCATION	DATE TESTED
IDT. SO.	2-28-95

NAME OF SUBJECT		TIME TESTED
		01:33
WEIGHT	VIOLATION	FILE NUMBER
205	23152 (A) VC	—

Follow the directions on the instrument's digital display and check off each step as it is completed:

1. (X) Continuously observe subject for at least fifteen minutes before giving test, during which time the subject must not ingest alcohol or other fluids, regurgitate, vomit, eat, or smoke.
2. (X) Date and Time Check:

	Yours:	Instrument's: (from display)
Date:	2-28-95	2-28-95
Time:	01:32	01:28

3. (X) Press START Key.
4. (X) Type ARRESTING AGENCY (3 characters), press ENTER.
5. (X) Type OPERATOR'S NAME (Last, First), press ENTER.
6. (X) Type SUBJECT'S NAME (Last, First), press ENTER.
7. (X) Wait for the internal standard cycle to complete.
8. (X) Insert a new mouthpiece into the breath tube.
9. (X) When instrument displays flashing "SUB" obtain breath sample from subject.
10. (X) Wait for purge/blank cycle to complete.
11. (X) When instrument displays flashing "SUB", obtain second breath sample from subject.
12. ( ) If the two results differ by more than 0.02% the instrument will request a third breath sample; proceed as in steps 10 and 11 above.
13. (X) Remove the printed results, initial for identification, and attach to checklist in the space provided. Discard mouthpiece.
14. (✓) Transcribe the first two digits of each breath result into the Blood Alcohol Results box above. At least two results must differ by no more than 0.02%.

Operator (Name, I.D.#, Agency)
D.W. AVILA 13352 SFS/CHP

Witnessing Officer (If Any)

Remarks:

D.WA.
====================

TEST RECORD

INTOX 3000 SN:4542
INDUSTRY STATION
TUE FEB 28, 1995

<ARRESTING AGENCY>
CHP
<OPERATOR'S NAME>
DW AVILA
<SUBJECT'S NAME>

TEST	VALUE	TIME
BLK	.000	01:29
STD	.100	01:29
BLK	.000	01:30
SUBJ	.117	01:33
BLK	.000	01:34
SUBJ	.125	01:37

Form 5
Intoximeter 3000 Checklist and Test Record

Checklist 8 Intoximeter 3000

- ☐ Was the machine properly licensed, calibrated, and maintained?
- ☐ Was the Taguchi sensor recently calibrated with an external standard? command.
- ☐ Could fluctuating sensitivity of the Taguchi sensor have caused defective self-calibration of the machine?
- ☐ Was the solution used to externally calibrate the Intoximeter accurately prepared?
- ☐ Was the room air used to provide a reference contaminated with the alcoholic breath of test subjects?
- ☐ Do the machine's records indicate any failures or mechanical problems before or since the test?
- ☐ Has the Taguchi sensor been removed from the machine?
- ☐ Does this constitute a modification rendering the machine nonapproved by the relevant state agency?
- ☐ Were any steps taken to avoid the detection of acetone as alcohol by the machine?
- ☐ Was the client a diabetic or on a strict diet?
- ☐ Was the operator/officer properly licensed and trained?
- ☐ Is he familiar with the theory and operation of the Intoximeter 3000?
- ☐ Did he follow the manufacturer's checklist? Can he recall each step?
- ☐ Did he observe the client constantly for 15 to 20 minutes before administering the test?
- ☐ Could the operator have manipulated the test results?
- ☐ With or without a Taguchi sensor, what other compounds found on the breath will be reported as alcohol by the machine?
- ☐ Could the client have had acetaldehyde in his system? Ketones? Paint or glue fumes? Other compounds?
- ☐ Was there any source of radio frequency interference in the area of the Intoximeter when the client was tested?
- ☐ Any police transmitters? Walkie-talkies? Televisions? Electric door locks? Microwave ovens? Police car transmitters in the parking lot? Teletype machines? Computers?
- ☐ Could the Intoximeter have been affected by a mechanical or electrical problem, such as a drop in line voltage?
- ☐ Were there any possible problems with the machine's temperature, humidity, optics, or age?
- ☐ Are there any generic problems with breath testing?
- ☐ Can the prosecution establish that the client's partition ratio was 2100:1?
- ☐ Did the breath test take place during the client's absorptive state?

- ☐ Could mouth alcohol have been present? Does the client wear dentures or have dental caps? Was he bleeding in the mouth?
- ☐ What is the client's hematocrit and how could it have affected the breath test?
- ☐ Did the client have an elevated body temperature?
- ☐ Could stress or breathing pattern have elevated the Intoximeter's test results?
- ☐ Did room air used to flush the sample chamber contain alcoholic breath from test subjects?
- ☐ Are there any problems with blood-alcohol testing generally?
- ☐ Was the client a woman?
- ☐ Did the client have a rising BAC curve?
- ☐ Is any attempt to project BAC back to the time of driving based on evidence and scientifically accepted fact? (see retrograde extrapolation, §5.2)
- ☐ Could eating or smoking have affected alcohol metabolism?
- ☐ Could zinc in the client's body have been a factor?
- ☐ What is the inherent error in testing with an Intoximeter 3000?

§6.4.4 Intoxilyzer 4011

For many years, the only means of testing blood alcohol through breath analysis was with instruments using the wet chemical approach, such as the Breathalyzer. In 1972, however, two new instruments for breath-alcohol testing appeared on the criminology scene: the Intoxilyzer and the Intoximeter. The Intoxilyzer, originally known as the Omicron Intoxilyzer, was created and manufactured by the Omicron Systems Corporation of California and utilized a method of analysis based on infrared spectroscopy. It offered faster and easier operation than the Breathalyzer, as well as being more economical and convenient. There is no evidence, however, that it is any more accurate; in fact, due partly to inherent theoretical disadvantages, it may be less accurate.

A few years after introducing the Intoxilyzer, Omicron sold all rights to the instrument to C.M.I., Inc. (P.O. Drawer "D," Minturn, CO 81645), a subsidiary of Federal Signal Corporation. Then in 1988 Federal Signal sold C.M.I. to MPD, Inc., of Owensboro, Kentucky. The Model 4011 continued to be manufactured for a period. However, the early 4011s (serial numbers below 1200) had an absorption band of 3.39 microns — less specific for ethyl alcohol than the later models' 3.42-micron band. C.M.I. proceeded to make some changes in the original Model 4011, producing the Model 4011A. The primary change was the addition of a "slope detector," which would detect a rise in the computer printout, followed by a plateau that was interpreted as a sign that the deep alveolar air was available for analysis. Counsel may be confronted with a Model 4011AR; this is simply an old Model 4011 that has been modified to conform to the Model 4011A. However, in 1978 a Missouri judge issued a permanent injunction barring officials of that state from going through with a planned purchase of 226 Intoxilyzers from C.M.I., due to the lack of specificity of the machine — that is, detection of compounds other than ethyl alcohol. As a result, C.M.I. subsequently came out with the Model 4011AS, which operates on two wavelengths (3.39 and 3.48 microns); the theory is that detection of acetones is thereby reduced and specificity is increased. An "S" option was made available to modify the Model 4011A. An additional model, the 4011AW, has also been produced, as has a special modification designed to comply with California standards. Finally, the 4011ASA was brought out. This instrument has push-button controls rather than dials, and has a smaller sample chamber to accommodate individuals with less breath capacity. All of these 4011-series instruments are basically the same as the original 4011, the primary difference being modifications to conform to the 4011A specifications.

Subsequently, C.M.I. offered a newer, state-of-the-art breath testing device: the Intoxilyzer Model 5000. This instrument also utilizes infrared spectroscopy in its analysis, but incorporates a fairly sophisticated computer together with nonstandardized software. In addition, the machine purports to be able to solve the specificity problems by using three wavelength bands and by incorporating an "interference indicator" that will theoretically advise the operator whenever foreign compounds in the breath are introduced into the machine. This author expects that the Intoxilyzer 5000 will find increasing acceptance among law enforcement officials, and will eventually become the most widely used breath-alcohol device on the market.

The Intoxilyzer 4011 is designed to determine the level of alcohol in a breath sample by measuring the absorption of infrared energy by a gas. The infrared light source of the instrument produces a light at a wavelength that coincides with a major absorption band of ethyl alcohol (ethanol). As the concentration of ethanol vapor rises in the specially constructed sample cell, the amount of infrared energy reaching the detector circuit falls in a predictable manner. This decrease in energy is electronically processed, and the percent blood alcohol is displayed on a three-digit panel meter. This conversion is based on Henry's Law and the 1:2100 ratio of blood to alveolar air.

Infrared light is invisible, occupying the spectrum of light waves longer than .75 microns; the 4 to 15 micron region is called the mid-infrared and is commonly used in the identification of many substances. It is an interesting fact that every wavelength of light has associated with it certain vibrations. At the same time, chemical compounds are held together by an attraction between atoms that is called a bond and that vibrates at a constant rate for each type of molecule. An infrared color whose wavelength is 2.7 microns, for example, has the same vibration rate as the water molecule. When this 2.7 micron light passes through water vapor, its vibrations are picked up or absorbed by bonds between the oxygen and hydrogen atoms, causing the atoms to vibrate more strongly and the 2.7 micron energy to disappear.

A complex molecule has a number of different sets of bonds, and neighboring bonds will influence a basic vibration, changing it slightly. Ethyl alcohol, for example, has its hydrogen-oxygen bond vibration shifted slightly by the presence nearby of carbon-hydrogen bonds. Most of the ethyl alcohol absorption, therefore, will take place in the range from 3.380 to 3.398 microns. The Intoxilyzer, then, simply uses an optical filter serving as a color window that lets through only 3.380 to 3.400 micron energy to act with the gas from the breath vapor. Some absorption — that is, disappearance, of the energy would indicate the presence of a gaseous compound with identical wavelengths, presumably ethyl alcohol. Unfortunately, however, other compounds will also react within this narrow light energy range, including isopropyl and methyl alcohol.

The concentration of alcohol in the breath sample is determined by the amount of the light that passes through the breath sample containing ethyl alcohol. This is computed by the application of well-established laws of physics, notably the Lambert-Baer Law. Assuming that one knew the absorption coefficient, or "grabbing power," of the ethanol molecule for the light being sent through by the Intoxilyzer, as well as the length of the light path, one could measure the amount of light that was not absorbed at the other end and thereby compute the concentration of ethanol in the sample. Applying Henry's Law, the concentration of alcohol in the blood could then theoretically be computed.

The Intoxilyzer models 4011A and AS are housed in a cast aluminum console measuring approximately 21 inches by 9 inches by 19 inches and weighing 65 pounds. All controls face the operator, and a lockable security cover is sold as an option. The machine operates on 117 volt AC power and requires no ampoules or other chemicals for operation; the only external materials required are an evidence card and a disposable mouthpiece. Like the Breathalyzer, the Intoxilyzer is non-specific — that is, it will react to chemicals other than alcohol and record them as blood alcohol. In fact, the single greatest source of error for any Intoxilyzer is this lack of specificity (see §6.4.1).

The following materials, adapted from the manufacturer's manual for operators, should prove helpful to defense counsel in determining whether the administering officer correctly followed the proper procedures in giving the test.

The preliminary stages are as follows: (1) turn mode selector switch to "zero set" mode and power switch to "on"; (2) when the ready light turns on 10 seconds later, take the breath tube from the machine's base and hook it up to the pump tube; and (3) turn mode selector switch to "air blank" mode.

These operational stages follow the preliminary stages: (4) turn mode selector switch back to "zero set" mode; (5) push "zero adjust" knob down and turn until the digital reading is .000, .001, .002, or .003; if the number is flashing .000, turn the knob clockwise until flashing stops. If an improper zero setting occurs, the error light will activate when any test mode is selected and the printing until will shut down; (6) insert the bonded edge of the evidence card, hard copy facing the operator; (7) connect pump tube to breath tube; (8) turn mode selector switch to "air blank" mode; the pump will turn off after the 30-second purge, and the printer will print out "A" for "Air Blank" plus the two digits displayed; (9) turn mode selector switch to "zero set" and re-zero; (10) turn mode selector switch to "breath"; disconnect breath tube from pump tube; (11) instruct subject to blow into breath tube; the breath indicator lamp will activate if the subject is giving an adequate breath sample, and the numbers on the front panel will rise and then level off (indicating the sample cell is filled); after a proper sample is given, the printer will print "B" for "Breath," together with the first two digits of the display; (12) to purge the sample cell of breath, repeat steps (7) and (8); and (13) to obtain an additional breath test of the subject, repeat steps (9) (10), and (11).

The Model 4011AS is a standard model 4011A Intoxilyzer that has been manufactured with the "S" option. All operating controls and procedures are identical to those of the Model 4011A. The only outward indication of the "S" option is the addition of a red front panel indicator labeled "Interference." The "S" option is intended to detect the presence of acetone on the subject's breath. In the event that a subject with a substantial quantity of breath acetone is tested, a positive indication of this condition is displayed to the operator. If the subject delivers a breath sample that contains enough acetone to cause the display of the instrument to indicate a blood-alcohol level equal to or greater than .01 gm percent higher than the actual blood-alcohol level, the "Interference" light will be illuminated. In addition, the "Error" circuitry will be activated. This will have the effect of disabling the instrument printer, thus preventing the operator from obtaining a record of a test that could indicate a blood-alcohol level that is higher than the true value. In essence, the "S" option simply adds operation on a second wavelength. Thus the 4011AS operates on wavelengths of 3.39 and 3.48 microns. Although this reduces the possibility of acetone interference, it does not eliminate it. And the problem of detection of other compounds as ethyl alcohol remains.

The Intoxilyzer 4011A and 4011AS utilize a breath sampling system that allows individuals of varying lung capacities to complete a test. This system looks at the rate of rise of the digital readout as the person under test is blowing into the instrument to ascertain the "deep lung" nature of the breath sample. The person being tested must light the green breath lamp for a minimum of 3½ to 4 seconds and then continue blowing until a level readout has been reached in order for the instrument to print. Test time will vary from 4 to 5 seconds for a small-lunged individual, up to 10 to 15 seconds for a large-lunged individual. Average test time is on the order of 7 seconds.

A "Beam Attenuator Accessory" has been developed. This device allows a quick and simple method of performing a calibration verification with each breath test. The advantages of the accessory in this particular situation are that it requires less frequent mixing (and analysis) of solutions for the simulator, no significant change in the reference with regard to time or usage, and overall simplicity in operation of the instrument.

To use the accessory, the Intoxilyzer is switched to the "Calibrator" mode, the Beam Attenuator is inserted into the instrument, and the result is printed on the evidence card. An error condition will result and the printer will be deactivated if the instrument or accessory is used improperly. Each Beam Attenuator Accessory is matched to a particular Intoxilyzer, and a "Certificate of Calibration Verification" is supplied relating the Intoxilyzer, Beam Attenuator, and the reading that should be displayed when the accessory is used.

The steps for performing a calibration verification using the Beam Attenuator are as follows:

1. Turn the mode selector switch to "Zero Set" and properly zero instrument.
2. Turn mode selector to "Air Blank" and allow instrument to complete cycle.
3. Turn the mode selector to "Zero Set" to ensure that the instrument remains properly "zeroed."
4. Turn mode selector to "Calibrator."
5. Slide Beam Attenuator into the proper location on the lower right hand side of the instrument. It should be inserted such that the serial number tag can be read from the front of the instrument when the slide is fully inserted against the "Stops."
6. Allow instrument to complete cycle. If the reading on the front panel display is correct, the calibration verification is complete.
7. Remove Beam Attenuator. Instrument is ready for the next test.

NOTE: If Beam Attenuator is inserted in any mode other than "Calibrator," an error condition will result and no printout can be obtained.

Form 6 is an example of the Intoxilyzer 4011 test card. Form 7 is a checklist for calibration of the Intoxilyzer 4011.

INTOXILYZER TEST RECORD

% ALCOHOL IN BLOOD	INTOXILYZER PRINT CODE
•	A – AIR BLANK B – BREATH C – CALIBRATOR (Simulator)
•	
•	OBSERVED SUBJECT FOR REQUIRED OBSERVATION PERIOD AND FOLLOWED CHECK LIST
•	
•	OPERATOR'S INITIAL
•	INTOXILYZER LOCATION
•	INTOXILYZER SERIAL NUMBER
•	
•	DATE

SUBJECT'S NAME

TIME FIRST OBSERVED TIME TEST STARTED

OPERATOR

ADDITIONAL INFORMATION AND/OR REMARKS

Form 6
Intoxilyzer Test Card for Recording Test Results

LOS ANGELES COUNTY SHERIFF'S DEPARTMENT - CRIMINALISTICS LABORATORY - BREATH ALCOHOL SECTION ACCURACY DETERMINATION FORMAT - INTOXILYZER 4011

PREPARING FOR TEST

( )a. Add Simulator Solution to Simulator and plug it in to heat. NOTE: DO NOT PLUG IN SIMULATOR WITHOUT ADDING SOLUTION FIRST AS THIS WILL BURN OUT SIMULATOR HEATING ELEMENT.
( )b. Fill out the following items on the Accuracy Data Form: Print the Date, Operator name, Intoxilyzer Location and Instrument number, and Simulator Solution ID#. Do NOT write in any of the shaded portions (ie: Simulator Solution Value and Card values). These are for Laboratory use only.
( )c. Check that green READY light is on and that the pump tube is connected to the breath tube.
( )d. Turn Mode Selector switch to AIR BLANK.
( )e. Wait for yellow CYCLE COMPLETE light.
( )f. Turn Mode Selector switch to ZERO SET and adjust to .000 to .003.

BLANK - 1

( )a. Red ERROR light off.
( )b. Insert test card into the slot (card should be resting on the firm stop and the hard copy should be facing the operator).
( )c. Turn Mode Selector switch to AIR BLANK.
( )d. Wait for yellow CYCLE COMPLETE light; record BLANK result, to three digits, in box number "1" of the Accuracy Data Form.

TEST - 1 SIMULATOR SOLUTION

( )a. Turn Mode Selector switch to ZERO SET and re-zero to .000 to .003.
( )b. Check to see if Simulator is at 34°C. Wait for it if necessary.
( )c. Retractable breath tube connected to mouthpiece coming out side of Simulator.
( )d. Pump tube connected to mouthpiece on top of Simulator.
NOTE: If the Simulator is connected to the Intoxilyzer the wrong way the result will be the flooding of the instrument's sample chamber.
( )e. Turn Mode Selector switch to CALIBRATE.
( )f. Wait for yellow CYCLE COMPLETE light; record TEST result, to three digits, in box number "2".

BLANK - 2

( )a. Disconnect Simulator and re-connect pump tube to breath tube.
( )b. Turn Mode Selector switch to AIR BLANK.
( )c. Wait for yellow CYCLE COMPLETE light; record BLANK result, to three digits, in box number "3".

TEST - 2 SIMULATOR SOLUTION

( )a. Turn Mode Selector switch to ZERO SET and re-zero to .000 to .003.
( )b. Reconnect Simulator to breath tube and pump tube as before.
( )c. Turn Mode Selector switch to CALIBRATE.
( )d. Wait for yellow CYCLE COMPLETE light; record TEST result, to three digits, in box number "4".

BLANK - 3

( )a. Disconnect Simulator and re-connect pump tube to breath tube.
( )b. Turn Mode Selector switch to AIR BLANK.
( )c. Wait for yellow CYCLE COMPLETE light; record BLANK result, to three digits, in box number "5".

TEST - 3 SIMULATOR SOLUTION

( )a. Turn Mode Selector switch to ZERO SET and re-zero to .000 to .003.
( )b. Reconnect Simulator to breath tube and pump tube as before.
( )c. Turn Mode Selector switch to CALIBRATE.
( )d. Wait for yellow CYCLE COMPLETE light; record TEST result, to three digits, in box number "6".

Form 7
Intoxilyzer 4011 Calibration Checklist

LEAVING THE INSTRUMENT

( )a. Disconnect Simulator and re-connect pump tube to breath tube.
( )b. Turn Mode Selector switch to AIR BLANK.
( )c. Wait for yellow CYCLE COMPLETE light; record BLANK result, to three digits, in box number "7".
( )d. Turn Mode Selector switch to ZERO SET.
( )e. Re-insert the breath tube inside the case.
( )f. Remove the test card and mark it for identification.
( )g. Attach test card to check list.
( )h. Record any remarks (operator error, instrument malfunction, repeat analyses, etc.) under the "remarks" section of the Accuracy Data Form below. Include a description of what occurred and at which step on the check list.
( )i. Enter in the log book that an Accuracy Determination was conducted including: date, your name, your I.D. number, and the results of this determination.
( )j. Return the Accuracy Data Form, attached to the Simulator bottle, to the Los Angeles County Sheriff's Department Criminalistics Laboratory, Breath Section.

ACCURACY DATA FORM

Date	Operator				Location	
Intoxilyzer Number		BLANK		SIMULATOR		BLANK
		DCR	Card	DCR	Card	DCR / CARD
		1		2		7
Simulator Solution ID #	Value	3		4		
		5		6		
Remarks:						

ATTACH TEST CARD HERE

Form 7
(continued)

Checklist 9 The Intoxilyzer 4011

- ☐ Was the operator properly licensed or trained in the operation of the Intoxilyzer?
  - ☐ Is the operator familiar with the theory and operation of the instrument?
- ☐ Could the officer have manipulated the test result? Were there any witnesses to the testing?
- ☐ Did the operator follow the operator's checklist? Can he recall each step?
  - ☐ Did he warm the Intoxilyzer for the proper period before conducting the test?
- ☐ Do the specific machine's records indicate any failure to calibrate and/or maintain the machine adequately?
  - ☐ Has the machine suffered any malfunctions or erroneous readings before the client's test or since?
- ☐ Did the instrument use single, double, or triple absorption bands?
- ☐ What substances will the Intoxilyzer detect other than ethyl alcohol? Will these register as ethyl alcohol?
- ☐ Could acetone have been on the breath — i.e., was the client on a diet or is he diabetic?
- ☐ Could the client have had ketones in his system? Acetaldehyde? Other compounds?
- ☐ Is it possible the Intoxilyzer was affected by a mechanical or electrical problem, such as a drop in line voltage?
- ☐ Were there any sources of radio frequency interference in the area of the Intoxilyzer when the client was tested, such as police radio?
- ☐ Could the optics of the instrument have been defective?
- ☐ Are there any possible problems concerning the machine's temperature, humidity, or age?
- ☐ Is the Intoxilyzer model used approved by the state?
- ☐ Are any of the problems inherent in breath testing devices generally — such as use of the 1:2100 ratio in computing the results — present? (See Checklist 5 — Breath Analysis, §6.3 supra.)

§6.4.5 Breathalyzer 900/1000/2000

The Breathalyzer 900 — the "Model T" of breath testing — has long since been discontinued and is today considered an antique. Nevertheless, this primitive machine is still in use in a surprising number of jurisdictions, particularly in rural areas. Manufactured by Smith and Wesson, there have been five successive versions of the Breathalyzer: the Model 900 (and 900A), the Model 1000, the Model 1100, the Model 2000, and the Model 7010 (these should not be confused with the new Breathalyzer 7410 preliminary breath testing device, manufactured by National Draeger). The models 900 and 900A, however, were the only ones to find a broad market. With the exception of the model 7010, which uses infrared technology, all of the Breathalyzers are basically identical in function, the chief difference being that the later models incorporate computerized digital logic programming, which supposedly eliminates the possibility of the operator's manipulating the final reading or printout. An additional difference is that the 1000 and the 1100 require the presence of at least 452.5 milliliters of exhaled breath, thus presumably assuring that the final 52.5 cubic centimeters of breath that enter the machine for analysis are actually alveolar in nature; the Model 1000 differs from the 1100 only in that it prints the test results on multiple copy paper rather than simply displaying a result on its digital indicators.

In 1984, the German firm of National Draeger acquired the Breathalyzer Division of Smith and Wesson, which discontinued manufacturing breath testing devices; National Draeger continued for some time to produce the 900/900A and the 7010, discontinuing the 1000 and 2000. In the highly unlikely event that counsel encounters a Model 1000, however, he should consider the results of NHTSA reports concerning the accuracy of the Breathalyzer 1000. On March 7, 1985, the Attorney General of Pennsylvania held a news conference in which he stated:

> It [the Breathalyzer] was approved for use here based on the fact that it is rated as acceptable by the National Highway Traffic Safety Administration, but previously undisclosed NHTSA documents have now raised serious questions about whether these machines meet NHTSA's own standards. Specifically, the documents state that the Smith & Wesson 1000 failed NHTSA tests in 1980 and again in 1983. In the 1983 sampling, 60 percent of the machines tested failed to meet NHTSA accuracy standards.

A representative of NHTSA, however, subsequently claimed that the Attorney General was taking the test results "out of context."

The NHTSA report mentioned was the result of studies conducted in 1980 and 1983, recommending that the Breathalyzer 1000 be removed from the "Federal Qualified Products List." This confidential report was made public as a result of a Freedom of Information Act lawsuit brought by attorney Thomas J. Schuckert of Pittsburgh. The February 1980 report, entitled Results of an Investigation of the Performance of the Smith and Wesson Breathalyzer Model 1000 Breath Alcohol Tester, was written by A. L. Flores of the Traffic Systems Center in Cambridge, Massachusetts. Excerpts from that report:

> 88 Breathalyzers model 1000 were tested by the state of Maryland in 1978 for precision and accuracy according to the DOT standard. These tests were performed as part of a pre-procurement acceptance test; the units tested were new, obtained directly from the factory. 22 of the instruments failed to meet the requirements of the test. 7 of these 22 instruments had also malfunctioned. 11 other instruments met the requirements but were unacceptable due to malfunction. Thus, a total of 33 of the 88 instruments were unacceptable. 18 of the 22 instruments were re-tested and 11 of these were again found unsatisfactory, 4 due to the occurrence of malfunctions alone.
>
> During 1977–1978, 23 Breathalyzers model 1000 were in use in the District of Columbia. 95 malfunctions were recorded over a 21 month period. During the same period, in Schuylkill County, Pennsylvania, where 9 units were in use, 19 malfunctions were recorded. In North Carolina, the State Police had purchased 56 Breathalyzers model 1000 but the high initial malfunction rate encountered had caused the police to discontinue their use. . . .
>
> On-site tests were made of 30 instruments at police agencies in six states. 16 of these instruments were found not to meet precision/accuracy requirements and four malfunctions were encountered.
>
> The design of the 900 series Breathalyzer, on which the model 1000 is based, was straight-forward and utilized relatively few parts. On the other hand the model 1000 uses many more parts and is a far more complex instrument. The complexity of the instrument appears to present a problem in maintaining effective quality control of the manufacturing process.
>
> The above findings demonstrate that a substantial fraction of Breathalyzer model 1000 instruments fail to be in compliance with the Standard for evidential breath testers.

The state of Maryland has also conducted tests after many of the Model 1000 units it had purchased to replace the 900 and 900A units experienced a variety of malfunctions and had to be sent back to the manufacturer. The results are reported in an article entitled "An in-Vitro Study of the Accuracy and Precision of Breathalyzer Models 900, 900A and 1000," Captain et al., 30 Journal of Forensic Sciences 1058 (Oct. 1985).

During the study, 19 of the Model 1000 Breathalyzers exhibited mechanical malfunctions, and 15 of the units failed to meet accuracy standards. These 34 machines were returned to the manufacturer for repairs; on their return ten of them still failed to perform satisfactorily.

Ninety Model 1000s were tested by the state of Maryland. The ranges of measured BAC proved larger than acceptable and appeared to increase as actual blood-alcohol concentration increased. Thus, for example, the range of test results from a true .10 percent sample was from .092 percent to .148 percent; with a .15 percent sample, the results ranged from .125 percent to as high as *.246 percent* BAC.

The most common of the Breathalyzer models is the 900A. The instrument itself is a rather unimpressive-looking metal box, measuring 8½ inches by 9 inches by 10½ inches and weighing about 13 pounds. It is completely portable in design and operates as a 12-volt, DC unit; however, it contains a transformer adapting it to 110–120 volt, 60-cycle AC current.

There are three basic components to the Breathalyzer: the sample collection device, the expendable ampoule containing the alcohol-sensitive reagent, and the photometric device. All other parts of the instrument simply serve to supplement or control these components.

The instrument is basically self-contained, requiring only the addition of a sanitary mouthpiece, specially designed to prevent saliva from entering the sample tube, and an ampoule, containing 3 milliliters of 50 percent (by volume) sulfuric acid, 0.25 milligrams of potassium dichromate per milliliter, and a catalyst.

Analysis of blood alcohol by the Breathalyzer consists of three principal phases: collecting a sample of deep-lung breath, passing this sample through a potassium dichromate-sulfuric acid solution, and then measuring the amount of potassium dichromate required to oxidize the alcohol.

The first phase involves having the subject blow, with force, through a mouthpiece into a heated plastic tube. The breath raises a piston in a metal cylinder. When the piston reaches the top of its stroke, it is held in this position by a small magnet aligned with two fixed pole pieces. Two vent holes just below the piston permit the breath to escape so that, when blowing is stopped, the cylinder is full of the last breath. When blowing stops, the piston drops from its supporting iron plate sufficiently to cover the vent holes.

A special valve is incorporated in the top of the sample chamber. The valve and magnet operate on the same shaft, rotated by the control knob on the panel. When the valve is in the "take" position, the breath passes from the retractable sample tube to the sample chamber. The magnet is aligned with the fixed pole pieces and the piston is supported. When the valve is turned to "analyze," the magnet is disaligned with the pole pieces, and the piston, by its own weight, forces the measured amount of air through 3 milliliters of 50 percent (by volume) sulfuric acid in water, containing 0.25 milligrams of potassium dichromate per milliliter and a catalyst.

The sample chamber contains 56.5 milliliters. This is necessary because the breath is raised from mouth temperature (about 34° centigrade) to 50° ± 3° centigrade; the 52.5 milliliters of breath will occupy a larger volume at this higher temperature. Also, the delivery tube from the sample chamber to the test solution is full of room air before the test and full of breath after the test. This volume must be added to the cylinder volume. This adds up to approximately 56.5 milliliters. The breath bubbles through the test solution in about 30 seconds. One and a half minutes later the reaction is complete.

Before the test is started, the solution in the "test" ampoule is balanced photometrically against a reference ampoule. The reading light is moved back and forth between the two ampoules until the "null meter" centers. This indicates that each of the two photocells is receiving the same amount of light through the ampoules. At this point the blood-alcohol pointer is set on the baseline of the scale. During the analysis, the reading light is again turned on. If part of the potassium dichromate has been consumed by alcohol in the test ampoule, more light will reach the right hand cell and the "null meter" will no longer be centered.

The light is moved by the thumb wheel until the balance is again established as indicated by the centering of the "null meter." The distance the light was moved is directly proportional to the amount of potassium dichromate used, and this is related directly to the amount of alcohol in the breath. The scale is calibrated in percent blood-alcohol.

The actual operation of the Breathalyzer by the police officer should follow the steps recommended by the manufacturer. Any deviation from strict compliance with these steps should be considered by defense counsel as fertile ground for cross-examination and subsequent argument. The following materials, adapted from the manufacturer's manual for operators of the model 900A, should be helpful to defense counsel in determining whether the officer followed the recommended procedure in giving the test; the procedure for other models is substantially identical.

Step 1

Before turning instrument "on," verify center scale indication on NULL METER. Turn on the ON-OFF SWITCH and verify again the NULL on meter. Permit the instrument to warm up until the SAMPLE CHAMBER THERMOMETER reads 50° ± 3°C. Attaining this temperature should require about 20 minutes. This time has intentionally been kept long to ensure even heating of the sample chamber. DO NOT use the instrument until working temperature is reached for malfunction of the sample device will result due to condensation of moisture from the breath. (This condition may be corrected by flushing with air after working temperature has been reached. No damage results, but the test will be lost.)

Step 2

Gauge an ampul to see for yourself that it is within the limits of the gauge. The diameter of the small end of the gauge is 0.625″ and the large end is 0.650″. If it goes into the large end easily but will not go in the small end, it is correct. While inserted, the meniscus of the solution should be on or slightly above the edge of the gauge. Remove ampul from the gauge. Place the unopened ampul in the left-hand holder.

Step 3

Gauge a second ampul and after removing from the gauge break the top from the ampul. Remove the little rubber sleeve from the DELIVERY TUBE. Insert the upper end of a glass bubbler in this sleeve and insert the bubbler in the solution. It should extend to within about ⅛″ of the bottom of the ampul, however, it must not touch or the flow of air might be restricted. This can be checked by gently depressing the rubber sleeve after the ampul is placed in the holder and the sleeve reconnected to the delivery tube. There should be space around the bubbler at the neck of the ampul so that the air can vent freely.

Step 4

Turn the CONTROL KNOB to the TAKE position and, with the atomizer bulb, flush out the sample chamber for a few seconds. (5–10 bulbfulls of air.) Turn the CONTROL KNOB to ANALYZE and wait for the EMPTY SIGNAL LIGHT to come on.

Step 5

After 90 seconds, the READ light will illuminate allowing the operator to turn the LIGHT SWITCH on and adjust the LIGHT BALANCE KNOB until the NULL METER is centered. If the scale pointer moves off the scale, change the position of the pointer by pulling back and then turning the POINTER ADJUSTMENT KNOB.

Step 6

After the NULL METER is centered, pull back on the POINTER ADJUSTMENT KNOB and carefully set the pointer on the START line (just to the left of "0.00"). This position automatically subtracts the usual blank of about 0.003%.

Step 7

A new mouthpiece is inserted in the SAMPLE TUBE and the tube is pulled out immediately before the sample is to be taken. At all other times, it is kept inside the heated chamber to prevent condensation. Turn the CONTROL KNOB to TAKE. Show the subject what you want him to do by yourself blowing into a mouthpiece (not attached to the instrument). Tell him that he must blow as long as possible. Taking a deep breath will do no harm, but it will make the blowing period longer. He should blow vigorously, as long as possible, but he need not completely empty his lungs. If the sample is unsatisfactory, have him blow again. No matter how long he blows, only the predetermined amount of breath is retained in the sample chamber.

Turn the CONTROL KNOB to "Analyze."

Step 8

The FULL SIGNAL LIGHT will go out, and after 20–35 seconds the EMPTY SIGNAL LIGHT will come on. Wait for about a minute and a half. Fifteen seconds less or thirty seconds more will make no difference. Turn on the LIGHT SWITCH and again adjust the LIGHT BALANCE KNOB until the NULL METER is centered. The concentration of alcohol in the blood is now indicated on the BLOOD ALCOHOL SCALE.

This completes the analysis. Dispose of the test ampul, bubbler, and mouthpiece, remembering that the ampul contains acid. Turn the CONTROL KNOB to OFF and the ON-OFF SWITCH to OFF. The instrument can, however, be kept on indefinitely.

See also the Operator's Checklist in Form 8.

It should be noted that the manual specifically requires a longer warm-up period in cold weather. Also, the manual directs the operator to ensure that the ampoules, bubblers, and mouthpieces are kept inside the instrument so that they will be preheated when used. If the instrument is used in a police vehicle (it can operate off the vehicle's cigarette lighter outlet), "every precaution should be taken to avoid the instrument being subjected to vibration" (such as that normally experienced in a moving car).

Sources of error. The first source of error that defense counsel should consider involves the possibility of manipulation of the Breathalyzer by the operator to obtain a desired but inaccurate result. The integrity of the officer conducting the test should *always* be in issue. An all-too-common occurrence involves an officer who wants to have his judgment in the field to arrest the suspect justified by the test results. A reading indicating that the arrestee is, in fact, not under the influence of alcohol can be embarrassing to the officer and possibly even considered by him as an attack on his professional abilities. Quite simply, the dial that stamps the test results can be manipulated by the operator to achieve any blood-alcohol level he desires — totally independent of the instrument's analysis. Of course, the models 1000 and 1100 largely negated this problem through the use of digital indicators.

Related to this are the operator's qualifications to use the

Breathalyzer. Most jurisdictions have statutory provisions setting forth the requirements for an operator before he can use the instrument, usually involving a minimal number of hours of instruction in its theory and use; many states even require the operator to have a special license. Defense counsel will find that many officers simply have been told by fellow officers how to operate the machine or have been trained on another, perhaps older, model. Even in those states not having such requirements, defense counsel should question the operator for the jury's benefit as to his lack of experience, training, and/or specific knowledge of the instrument's theory and operation.

Another possible area for demonstrating error in the administration of the Breathalyzer test involves the use of the ampoules. The test ampoule must have a specific quantity and quality of chemicals, and any deviation will have a marked effect on the test results. To guarantee the integrity of the chemicals in the ampoules, the manufacturer will number the ampoules by batch, and these batches must be inspected and certified by the appropriate governmental agency. This inspection is usually accomplished by spot-checking one or two ampoules out of each numbered batch, breaking them open, and analyzing the contents. (The manufacturer of the ampoules for use in the Breathalyzer is not Smith & Wesson; the ampoules are produced by other companies and then usually tested by yet other private companies.) Should the prosecution be unable to prove through acceptable forms of evidence the integrity of the chemicals used in the batch from which the relevant ampoule was drawn, defense counsel should argue against the admission into evidence of the test results.

When the ampoule is manually broken by the Breathalyzer operator, it is not uncommon for a small amount of the solution contained inside to spill out. This could result in an erroneously high reading. Dust, smoke, or other contaminants that may fall into the opened ampoule can also cause false readings.

The chemicals in the ampoule, it should also be noted, are photosensitive. If stored in a sunlit area, therefore, the quality of those chemicals will deteriorate — again, resulting in erroneous blood-alcohol readings. Yet, strangely, the Breathalyzer manual fails to instruct law enforcement agencies to store these ampoules in dark areas.

On October 12, 1982, the United States Patent Office granted patent number 4,353,869 to Richard Guth of Harrisburg, Pennsylvania, for an ampoule assembly and holder. According to the patent description, the invention represents an improvement over existing ampoules in that it: (1) provides a cleaner break when removing the tip of the ampoule; (2) prevents accidental spilling of the chemicals within the ampoule; (3) prevents contaminants from entering the ampoule; (4) holds the bubbler tube firmly in place; and (5) provides a means to preserve the ampoule assembly.

In the specification of the patent, several criticisms are made of existing ampoules. For example, the patent discusses some of the problems that arise when the sulphuric acid and potassium dichromate solution are spilled, and there are obvious safety problems, including acid burns on the operator or suspect and damage to surrounding furniture, clothing, and the breath-testing apparatus itself. In addition, the breath-test results can be affected if some of the solution is spilled:

> The volume of solution in the ampoule determines the color change per unit of alcohol bubbled through the solution. Loss of the solution destroys breath test accuracy because less solution means greater color change for a given amount of alcohol. Thus, if solution is spilled from an ampoule, the ampoule must be discarded and a new ampoule broken open and used to conduct the test. [Patent #4,353,869, col. 1, lines 58–65.]

A more significant problem with the existing technology relates to the fact that the bubbler tube may not be properly positioned, thereby leading to erroneous results. The patent describes the problem as follows:

> The photo-optical test directs a light beam through the ampoule to determine the color change due to oxidized solution and, consequently, the amount of alcohol in the breath bubbled through the ampoule. During the photo-optical test, the bubbler tube is loose in the ampoule. The glass tube has an index of refraction different than the index of refraction of the solution in the ampoule. If the bubbler tube is off center or skewed with respect to the ampoule axis, the beam of light is refracted away from the photocell target, thereby unpredictably altering the output reading. Such an unpredictable output reading severely affects the

> reliability of the breath test in determining intoxication and any resultant criminality. [Patent #4,353,869, col. 1, lines 40–53.]

The new ampoule assembly, which is the subject of the patent, makes the following improvement:

> After bubbling, the ampoule is tested by the photo-optical apparatus and a light beam is passed through the ampoule to determine the color change due to oxidation of alcohol in the breath. The bubbler tube is left in place during this test. The stopper holds the bubbler tube on axis within the ampoule so that it does not refract the light beam passing through the ampoule away from the diametrically aligned photocell receptor. [Patent #4,353,869, col. 2, lines 63–68; col. 3, lines 1–2.]

Spills are prevented and the bubbler tube is held in position through the use of a Teflon stopper with a hole through the center for the bubbler tube. The invention includes an improved ampoule holder, which is used to verify both the ampoule's diameter and height of the acid solution. If the diameter and height are accurate, the operator leaves the ampoule in the holder and proceeds to break off the tip and insert the stopper and the bubbler tube. The ampoule, stopper, and bubbler tube, which have now become an integral assembly, are then removed from the holder and are inserted into the breath-testing apparatus. The patent describes the advantages as follows:

> The tight connection formed between the stopper and ampoule seals off the ampoule mouth so that, with the exception of the small vent passage which allows air to escape from the ampoule after it has been bubbled through the acid solution, the solution is confined within the ampoule. In practice, it is almost impossible to spill solution accidentally from the assembly. This represents a marked improvement over conventional practice where bubbler tubes are positioned freely in open ampoule mouths and accidental tipping or dropping of the ampoule nearly always spills solution. [Patent #4,353,869, col. 6, lines 52–61.]

In addition to preventing spills, the stopper protects the acid solution from contaminants that may affect the test results. The ampoule assembly, with stopper and bubbler tube in place, provides a safe and efficient method for preserving the ampoules and the acid solution. The bubbler tube is merely disconnected from the rubber tube connecting it to the outlet pipe on the Breathalyzer. The bubbler tube and vent are plugged and the ampoule may then be stored.

The information contained in Patent #4,353,869 will be useful to defense attorneys challenging the validity of existing breath-testing equipment. To prepare for trial, an attorney should obtain a certified copy of the patent from the Patent and Trademark Office by addressing the Commissioner of Patents and Trademarks, Washington, D.C. 20231. If time is a factor in a particular case, there are a number of patent search firms in Washington, D.C. that will obtain and forward a certified copy of the patent.

Counsel should be aware that the Breathalyzer should have been warmed up for at least 15 to 20 minutes before it was used by the operator on the suspect. This is necessary to prevent the piston from sticking and to heat the sample chamber to 45–50° centigrade. At 45 to 50° centigrade, 57 cubic centimeters of alveolar air are equal to 52.5 cubic centimeters at breath temperature (34° centigrade). Without an adequate warm-up period, however, 57 cubic centimeters would be collected and not 52.5 cubic centimeters at 34° centigrade. The result would be that more breath would be analyzed, containing a larger volume of alcohol, and a higher reading would be recorded.

There should also be a waiting period of 15 to 20 minutes during which the arrestee is constantly observed to ensure that he has not belched, regurgitated, or vomited. The residual effects of such biological functions can significantly raise the Breathalyzer test results. (See §§6.2 *et seq.*)

If the Breathalyzer was used in the field — that is, if it was transported in a vehicle prior to its use, defense counsel certainly should point out that the manufacturer of the instrument specifically indicates in its manual that any vibrations from the vehicle can have a harmful effect. In the vast majority of cases, however, the instrument is kept at a police station, usually in a designated room.

Another source of error in the Breathalyzer is the possibility that the valve assembly may malfunction. A leaking valve is a relatively common problem for the machine and will result in a portion of the breath sample going directly into the chemicals in the ampoule, rather than all of it going into the cylinder. An oxidation reduction will then take place, and an erroneously high blood-alcohol reading will be registered.

Yet another possible malfunction in the machine is a slippage in the clutch assembly. If this occurs, the pointer will not move the correct distance when the "null meter" is rezeroed after the breath has been received by the chemicals.

One of the chief problems with the Breathalyzer is that it is nonspecific as to alcohol. The potassium dichromate in the ampoule will react to certain chemicals other than alcohol, with the result that the machine can register a blood-alcohol reading based on reaction with nonalcohol compounds. Any volatile organic substance, and many nonvolatile substances as well, will react with the potassium dichromate in the same manner as will alcohol. These nonalcoholic substances can be on the breath, in the air, or introduced into the machine in other ways. As an example of this, a relatively common problem occurs when the operator inserts the test ampoule into the machine and in doing so touches that portion of the bubbler tube that is inserted into the ampoule. If the operator has any volatile organic substances (such as turpentine) on his hand, they may be transferred onto the bubbler tube; when the bubbler tube is then inserted into the ampoule, there could be a reaction that would register as blood alcohol.

All Breathalyzer models but the 900 are apparently susceptible to radio frequency interference. In fact, the problem first arose in 1982, when Smith & Wesson notified law enforcement agencies that its Breathalyzer Model 1000 experienced interference from radio frequency transmissions under certain test conditions, resulting in false test results. Subsequent investigation suggested that the Breathalyzer Models 900 and 900A would also be affected by various power levels. The potential sources of radio frequency interference within the law enforcement environment are numerous — for example, AM and FM radios, police station dispatchers, hand-held police transmitters, teletypes, and police radar units. Each of these may emit the kind of interference that could cause specific breath testing apparatus to render falsely high test results.

Checklist 10 The Breathalyzer 900

- ☐ Is the particular instrument that was used authorized and properly licensed?
- ☐ Do the records indicate that the machine was calibrated and maintained correctly?
  - ☐ Are there any malfunctions noted in the instrument's operator's log or calibration/maintenance records?
  - ☐ Have there been any malfunctions of the machine since the client's testing?
- ☐ Was the machine transported in a vehicle (and thus subject to vibration) prior to testing the arrestee?
- ☐ Did the operator warm the machine up for 15 to 20 minutes prior to taking a breath sample?
- ☐ Were the ampoules, bubblers, and mouthpiece also preheated as recommended by the manufacturer?
- ☐ Has the operator received the required training in use of the Breathalyzer?
  - ☐ Is the operator familiar with the theory and operation of the instrument?
  - ☐ Did he follow an approved operator's checklist in administering the test, checking off each step?
- ☐ Does the operator independently recall each step he took in preparing and administering the test?
- ☐ Did the operator keep the subject under constant surveillance for 15 to 20 minutes to ensure no belching, vomiting, or regurgitation before taking a breath sample?
- ☐ Is it possible for the operator to manipulate the machine to obtain a desired result? Were there any independent witnesses to the testing?
- ☐ Was a new, sterile mouthpiece used?
- ☐ Were the test ampoules properly numbered and examined by batch for chemical integrity?
  - ☐ Are they available for inspection and analysis, or were they destroyed?
- ☐ Is it possible the Breathalyzer suffered from valve leakage or clutch slippage?
- ☐ Were nonalcoholic volatile organic substances possibly introduced into the instrument?
- ☐ Were the ampoules kept in a sunlit location?
- ☐ Was spillage or contamination of the ampoule possible?
- ☐ Have radio frequency interference problems been considered?

☐ Are any of the problems inherent in breath testing devices generally — such as use of the 1:2100 ratio in computing the results — present? (See Checklist 6-5 — Breath Analysis Generally in §6.3 supra.)

§6.4.6 Alcotest 7110

As the Intoxilyzer 4011 and Intoximeter 3000 have increasingly been phased out in favor of the Intoxilyzer 5000 and DataMaster, a new breath testing device has been introduced into the market: the Alcotest 7110 Mark III. It is manufactured by National Draeger, Inc. (185 Suttle Street, Suite 105, Durango, CO; (970) 385-5555), the company that bought out Smith and Wesson's Breathalyzers some time ago. The machine should not, incidentally, be confused with Draeger's new hand-held PBT, the Breathalyzer 7410.

Although similar to existing machines such as the 5000 in a number of ways, the 7110 is unique in three significant respects. First, though an evidentiary machine, the 7110 is portable and so could be employed in the field. Counsel may be seeing them dispatched in mobile DUI units to the site of arrest.

Second, it employs two different technologies: infrared spectrophotometry and electrochemical fuel cell analysis. (The Intoxilyzer 5000 and 4011, Intoximeter 3000, and DataMaster use infrared only; PBT devices commonly use fuel cell/Taguchi cell.) This should result in a more alcohol-specific result — i.e., the ever-present non-specificity problem will be less an issue (but far from eradicated).

Third, the infrared section uses a 9.5-micron wavelength filter. Other machines use 3.4-micron filters. Significance: Virtually every chemical compound with the methyl group in its structure will show absorbance at this frequency. Interpretation: Thousands of chemicals will be "read" by the machines as ethanol, including, according to one study, at least 102 found on the human breath (i.e., again, the problem of non-specificity). At 9.5 microns, however, relatively few organic compounds — notably ethanol — will be absorbed, because there the frequency is directed at the more unique hydroxyl group rather than the far more common methyl group of the compound. It still leaves the machine subject to a few interfering compounds, however — notably esters and ethers (diethyl ether, for example, has caused significant readings on the 7110 — a fact with which counsel might want to confront the prosecution's "expert" witness when he testifies that it is absolutely specific).

It should be kept in mind that the 7110, though an improvement, is not without most of the other potential flaws in breath analysis — mouth alcohol, RFI, retrograde extrapolation, etc. And, of course, the device is only as good as maintenance, calibration, and operator administration permit.

Of course, such improvement may provide counsel with ammunition for cross-examination as to *other* breath machines: If the Draeger is "state of the art," what does that make the Intoxilyzer 5000? If this new machine operates on the principle that infrared in conjunction with fuel cell analysis is more reliable than infrared alone, then just how reliable is the DataMaster? If Draeger's engineers have determined that infrared analysis at the 9.5-micron range offers accuracy superior to that at 3.4 microns, then why do the Intoxilyzer/Intoximeter/DataMaster continue to use that frequency filters (answer: cost)?

The following materials produced by the manufacturer will provide some insight into the new Alcotest 7110. The first section relates to the technology and claimed improvements of the device. The second concerns the numerous sources of error — both machine error and operator error — that the manufacturer recognizes. These should prove helpful in cross-examination. Following Draeger's comments are some observations on the machine's characteristics, theory, and operation by an experienced forensic toxicologist.

TECHNOLOGY

Because of the limitations associated with infrared spectroscopy at the 3.4 wavelength, Draeger's engineering efforts were concentrated on designing an entirely new breath analyzer. The result is the Alcotest 7110 which utilizes both the 9.5 micron range of the IR spectrum and the Draeger electro-chemical fuel cell for analysis and measurement of breath alcohol. Although it has been realized for years that analyzing breath alcohol at the 9.5 micron range would provide answers to persistent legal and technical questions, only recently have advances in electronic SMD components and manufacturing methods made it possible to take advantage of the superior qualities of the 9.5 micron technology. Together with the new generation fuel cell, the Alcotest 7110 will provide test results of unsurpassed legal and forensic integrity, never before achievable by any breath alcohol instrumentation.

THE ALCOTEST® 7110 MKIII: A NEW ERA IN BREATH ALCOHOL ANALYSIS!

- The only EBT utilizing Dual Sensor Technology that measures a subject's breath alcohol concentration by two different and independent sensors.
  The only instrument available that measures alcohol at 9.5μm in the IR spectrum:
  — More specific for alcohol than 3.4μm IR instruments.
  — Acetone interference is not an issue.
  — The IR source and detector are completely enclosed in the small sample chamber, so no preventative maintenance or cleaning of the optics is required.
  Utilizes the Dräger Electrochemical Sensor (Fuel Cell) and sampling system:
  — Alcohol-specific
  — Analyzes the ambient air in the IR chamber to insure an alcohol-free zero set. Does not allow the IR system to assume an alcohol-free environment.
- The combination of IR and EC technologies makes the 7110 MKIII "*Ethanol*" specific.
- Measures the subject's breath volume and duration of the sample.
- On-Board diagnostics verify proper operation of internal systems 128 times per second.
- The smallest and lightest IR instrument available: 15.8″W × 5.1″H × 10.4″D, 16.5 lbs.
- Operates in AC and DC modes without additional accessories; ideal for mobile enforcement programs.
- Long, flexible, and electronically temperature-controlled breath hose.
- Accepts both Wet Bath and Dry Gas calibration checks.
- Simulator Temperature Probe constantly monitors the wet bath simulator solution to ensure proper operating temperature. No tests are possible if the operating temperature is not within NHTSA's specifications.
- The 7110 MKIII takes only minutes to calibrate.

- Accepts any standard PC-AT compatible keyboard.
- Windows™ based communications software program for 24-hour monitoring, and customized reporting.
- No preventative maintenance of analytical systems.

7110 BASIC ERROR CHECKING

This document describes the various errors that can occur while using the Alcotest 7110 MKIII. The 7110 divides errors into two main categories, named "Hardware Errors" and "Operating Errors."

HARDWARE ERRORS

Hardware errors are errors that cause the 7110 to become disabled, and are usually caused by an actual hardware problem. When a hardware error occurs, the 7110 will beep and display the message "ERROR [xxx]", and if applicable, a short message indicating the source of the problem (where xxx is the actual hardware error number). Once the unit has triggered a hardware error, user input from either the keyboard or the start button will not be recognized. Communications with the 7110 will not be possible.

Most conditions that can cause a hardware error are checked 128 times per second. This ensures that if a hardware problem occurs, it will immediately be detected, and the unit will be inoperable. For example, the 7110 checks the cuvette heater 128 times per second, making sure that the temperature is within range. If at any time the temperature drifts out of range, a Cuvette Heater Hardware Error will immediately be triggered, and the unit will not operate.

OPERATION ERRORS

The term "Operating Error" is used to describe an error that can be expected to occur, and that can be detected. For example, the errors "Blowing Not Allowed" and "Interference" are operating errors. Exactly how the 7110 handles operating errors depends on a number of things, such as how the unit is configured and when in the sequence of events the error occurs. When an operating error occurs during a subject test, the "default" error handling mechanism is for the unit to stop what it's doing, beep, display the error message, print out the current results, print out the error message, purge itself, and return to READY mode.

Hardware Errors

The following list describes all possible hardware errors that the 7110 may trigger.

EEPROM Defect (Error 2) — The 7110 checks for this error condition each time that a write operation on a EEPROM (Electrically Erasable Programmable Read Only Memory) cell is done.

RAM Defect (Error 4) — When the 7110 is switched ON, a series of self-tests are performed. One of the tests is to check for RAM (Random Access Memory) problems. A number of predetermined bytes are written to and read from each RAM location, ensuring that the value written is the same as the value read back.

Internal Battery (Error 8) — The internal batteries supply stand-by power (3 V) to the static RAM and the real time clock. The 7110 checks the battery voltage 128 times per second; if at any time the voltage dips below 2.1 Volts, an Internal Battery Supply hardware error is triggered. NOTE: THE INTERNAL BATTERIES MUST BE REPLACED WHILE THE UNIT IS POWERED ON.

Main Power Supply (Error 9) — The 7110 checks the main power supply 128 times per second, making sure that the input voltage is between 10.3 and 17 V (DC). If at any time the voltage goes outside of this range, a Main Power Supply hardware error is triggered.

Main System (Error 10) — If at any time the 7110 cannot control any of its data or address buses, a Main System error is triggered. The buses are used to carry signals between the controller and the various devices within the 7110 (such as the pump, the printer, etc.).

IR Sensor (Error 23) — The 7110 checks the signal from the IR detector 128 times per second, ensuring that the DC offset is in the correct range. An IR Sensor Hardware Error would indicate a problem with the IR source and/or detector.

EC Offset Error (Error 31) — The 7110 checks the signal from the EC sensor 128 times per second, ensuring that the DC offset is in the correct range (between 0.08 and 0.2 V). An EC Offset Hardware Error would indicate a problem with the EC Sensor.

EC Sensor System (Error 32) — A motor/pump is used to suck a 1 ccm sample out of the cuvette, into the EC sensor. This motor is repositioned for the next sample after the breath sample has been analyzed. The 7110 ensures that this motor is in the correct position, and that the motor has moved into the correct position within the appropriate amount of time. If this Hardware Error is triggered, there is most likely a problem with this motor.

EC Maximum (Error 35) — While analyzing a sample with the EC sensor, the 7110 expects to see a characteristic response. If the response of the EC Sensor does not match the expected characteristic response, an EC Maximum Hardware Error is triggered.

Flow Sensor Defect (Error 41) — The 7110 checks the signal from the flow sensor 128 times per second, ensuring that the value read by the flow sensor is in the correct range (between 1.22 and 3.75 V).

Pump Defect (Error 43) — When the 7110 does an air blank (or a purge), the flow of air is monitored. If the flow is too small (less than 1.5 Liters per minute), a Pump Defect Hardware Error is triggered. This error indicates either a problem with the pump, a problem with the internal plumbing in the unit, or a problem with the flow-related calibration values. See also Purge Error (an operating error).

Pressure Sensor Defect (Error 51) — The 7110 checks the signal from the pressure sensor 128 times per second, ensuring that the value read by the sensor is in the correct range (between 0.1 and 4.9 V).

Breath Hose Heater Defect (Error 71) — The 7110 checks the signal from the breath hose temperature regulator 128 times per second, ensuring that the value read by the sensor is in the correct range (between 0.5 and 4.5 V).

Cuvette Heater Defect (Error 72) — The 7110 checks the signal from the cuvette temperature regulator 128 times per second, ensuring that the value read by the sensor is in the correct range (between 0.5 and 4.5 V).

Mouthpiece Heater Defect (Error 73) — The 7110 checks the signal from the mouthpiece temperature regulator 128 times per second, ensuring that the value read by the sensor is in the correct range (between 0.5 and 4.5 V). This is applicable only to units equipped with breath temperature sensing capability.

Heater Regulation Error (Error 75) — Once the breath hose, cuvette, and mouthpiece (if equipped) have come to temperature, the 7110 checks to make sure that these components stay within operating temperature; this check is performed 128 times per second. The heaters are regulated by software, so this error checking is partly for hardware and partly for software.

Printer Defect (Error 81) — After every character sent to the printer, the 7110 waits for an acknowledgement from the printer. If this acknowledgement is not received, or is received incorrectly, a Printer Defect Hardware Error will be triggered.

Calibration Value Error (Error 101) — The 7110 expects all calibration values to be within a certain range; when a calibration value is entered or calculated, it is checked to make sure that it is within range, and if not, a Calibration Value Hardware Error is triggered.

EEPROM Data Loss (Error 112) — The 7110 keeps a running checksum of the values stored in EEPROM. When the unit is turned on, and each time just before a test is performed, the unit uses this checksum to ensure that the values stored in EEPROM have not been corrupted. If this error occurs, Draeger personnel must reset the 7110 checksum, operating parameters for the unit must be reset, and all components of the unit must be recalibrated.

Configuration Error (Error 113) — This error can only be triggered if the software in the unit does not match the hardware that the unit is equipped with. For example, if software instructs the unit to monitor the mouthpiece heater for breath temperature sensing, and no mouthpiece heater is equipped on the unit, the Configuration Hardware Error will be triggered.

Operating Errors

The following list describes all possible operating errors that the 7110 may trigger.

Standard Gas Supply — This error is triggered when the unit expects to receive an ethanol sample, and none is delivered (calibration and calibration checks). One common remedy to this problem is to make sure that there are no air leaks in the simulator, and to ensure that the simulator is connected properly to the unit. If using dry gas, ensure that there is gas in the canister, and that the flow is not obstructed.

Air Blank Check Failed — After purging, the unit analyzes the air sample, and expects the alcohol concentration to be zero. If the concentration is not zero, this error is triggered. This error indicates that there is alcohol present in the ambient air.

Mouth Alcohol — This error is triggered when the absorption slope, after reaching a peak, runs negative >50μg/L @ concentrations <200μg/L and when the slope runs negative <4% @ concentrations <200μg/L.

Interference — This error is triggered when an interfering substance is detected in a subject's breath sample. Note that the 7110 only tests for interfering substances when analyzing a subject's breath sample.

Measurement Out of Range, and Alcohol Concentra-

TION TOO HIGH — These errors are triggered when the unit analyzes a sample with a concentration greater than roughly 0.6% BAC (a very rare occurrence!).

DIFFERENCE IN MEASURED RESULTS — This error is only applicable when there is more than 1 subject breath test in the test sequence, and is triggered where the difference in subject breath test results is too great (0.01% BAC).

PLATEAU NOT REACHED — This error occurs when the subject's alcohol concentration does not become stable as the breath sample is delivered.

BLOWING NOT ALLOWED — This error occurs when air is delivered through the breath hose when it's not supposed to be. Depending on when this error occurs, the unit may either abort the test, or it may purge or continue where it left off.

BLOWING TIME EXPIRED — The unit will wait for the subject to deliver a breath sample for a pre-programmed amount of time (typically 2–3 minutes). If the sample is not delivered within this time frame, this error is triggered.

BLOW TIME TOO SHORT — If the amount of time that the subject blows is too small (typically less than 4.5 seconds), this error will be triggered.

BLOW TIME TOO LONG — The typical 7110 is not configured to check for this error; the longer the subject blows, the better.

BREATH VOLUME TOO SMALL — If the volume of breath delivered by the subject is too small (typically 1.5 liters), this error will be triggered.

BREATH VOLUME TOO LARGE — The typical 7110 is not configured to check for this error; the larger the volume delivered, the better.

BLOW VOLUME UNSTABLE — This error is only applicable when there is more than one subject breath test in the test sequence, and is triggered where the difference in the breath volumes of the subject breath tests is too large (10 liters).

BLOW TIME UNSTABLE — This error is only applicable when there is more than one subject breath test in the test sequence, and is triggered where the difference in the blow times of the subject breath tests is too large (30 seconds).

CALIBRATION CHECK OUT OF TOLERANCE — This error is triggered when the measured concentration of a calibration check done in the normal test sequence is out of tolerance.

FUNCTION NOT POSSIBLE — If the user attempts to execute a user function (also called an Escape Function) that cannot be implemented at that moment, this error condition is triggered. For example, the user function STND-CHECK can only be done when the unit is in READY mode. If the user tries to execute the STND-CHECK function when the unit is not in READY mode, the error condition will be triggered. The 7110 handles this error by displaying this message for a few seconds, and then returning control back to the user.

FUNCTION NOT AVAILABLE — If the user attempts to execute a user function that is not available, this error is triggered. The usual cause of this error is mistyping of the function name. For example, if the user wishes to perform the "SET-CLOCK" function, and accidentally types "SETT-CLOCK," this error will be triggered.

NO ADMITTANCE — This error is triggered when the operator attempts to perform a user function without using the appropriate function key. For example, if the unit is configured so that only operators with a black function key can use the "Calibrate" function, and an operator attempts to use the "Calibrate" function without using a black key, this error will be triggered.

KEYBOARD ERROR — This error is triggered when the parity of a character sent from the keyboard to the controller is incorrect.

QUICK RESET — At various times in the test sequence, the user may "abort" the current test by performing a quick-reset. This is accomplished by holding the start button pressed for approximately 2 seconds.

PARITY ERROR — This error is triggered when the parity of a byte read from the serial port is incorrect. In most cases, when a parity error occurs, the software will handle the error internally, without the user ever knowing that a parity error occurred. It is only when the software cannot overcome the problem that a parity error is triggered.

TIME FOR 2 TESTS EXPIRED — This error is only applicable when there is more than one subject breath test in the test sequence, and is triggered where the amount of time allotted for two valid breath samples has expired. Unless customer requirements dictate otherwise, the time allotted for 2 valid breath samples is so great that this error will never occur.

PURGE ERROR — When the 7110 does an error blank (or a purge), the flow of air is monitored, from which a volume is calculated. If the volume of air is too small after a fixed period of time, a purge error is triggered. This error indicates either a problem with the pump, a problem with the internal plumbing in the unit, or a problem with the flow-related calibration values. The difference between the hardware error "Pump Defect" and the operating error "Purge Error" is that when the problem is detected while the unit is in ready mode, the Purge Error is triggered. Otherwise, the Pump Defect hardware error is triggered.

BREATH TEMPERATURE INVALID — This error is only applicable when the unit is equipped with breath temperature sensing. There are two different sensors used to measure redundantly the breath temperature. If the two breath temperatures that these two sensors read are different by more than 0.5 degrees C, this error will be triggered. Also, if there is more than one subject breath test in the test sequence, this error will be triggered if any of the four measured breath temperatures differ by more than 0.5 degrees C. Also, if any measured breath temperature is less than 28 degrees C or greater than 40 degrees C, this error will be triggered. And finally, there is one more condition that can trigger this error. Just before the subject is expected to provide a breath sample, the two sensors measure the ambient temperature (the temperature of the heated mouthpiece). If the two measured temperatures differ by more than 0.5 degrees C, this error will be triggered. Unfortunately, at this point, many different conditions all trigger the same error.

SUBJECT REFUSAL — If the subject refuses to provide a breath sample, the Subject Refusal error is triggered. The operator can trigger this error by pressing the 'R' key while the unit is waiting for the subject to blow.

RFI — This error is only applicable when the unit is equipped with RFI detection. The unit measures RFI 128 times per second; if the measured value of RFI is above the preset threshold for ¼ seconds, the RFI error will be triggered. In READY mode, the RFI detector will be reset after 5 seconds.

DATA STORAGE ERROR — This error is only applicable when the unit is configured to store test results. After a test is complete, the unit attempts to store the results to memory. If there is not enough room in memory to store the results, this error will be triggered. At this point, memory should be cleared. However, if the memory is not cleared, the operation of the unit will not be affected; the measured test results will simply not be stored.

MODEM ERROR — This error is only applicable when the unit is equipped with an internal modem. The error is triggered when communications between the modem and the controller are not functioning. Usually, re-initializing the modem solves the problem. In some cases, it may be necessary to turn the power to the 7110 off, and then back on again. If this doesn't solve the problem, the internal modem likely needs to be replaced.

External Printer Error — This error is only applicable when the unit is equipped with an external printer. The error is triggered under a number of different conditions. If the external printer is off-line when the controller tries to communicate with it, the error will be triggered. If there is a paper jam, the error will be triggered. Basically, when communications between the external printer and the controller are not functioning, or if there is some sort of hardware problem with the printer, the error is triggered.

Memory Near Full — This error is only applicable when the unit is configured to store test results, and is actually more of a warning than an error. After a test is complete, results are stored to memory. When the memory is approximately 95% full, this error will be triggered. The purpose of this error is to warn the operator that it is time to clear the memory (probably should download the data first!).

Internal Battery Level Low — The internal batteries supply stand-by power (3 V) to the static RAM and the real time clock. The 7110 checks the battery voltage 128 times per second; if at any time the voltage dips below 2.3 Volts, an Internal Battery Level Low operating error is triggered (see also the hardware error Internal Battery).

Memory Corrupt — This error is only applicable when the unit is configured to store test results. Before performing any test which will cause data to be stored to memory, the unit checks to make sure that the structure of the memory is in a known state. If not, this error is triggered. This error is actually more of a warning than an error.

ALCOTEST 7110 MK III AND "INTERFERING" SUBSTANCES

SAFEGUARD 1

As previously mentioned, the 7110 MKIII's infrared sensor operates in the 9.5μm range of the infrared spectrum. Acetone, toluene, and acetaldehyde, the most common substances brought up by the defense, can have a slight influence in breath analyzers operating at the 3.4μm range of the infrared spectrum. By shifting the operating range to 9.5μm, the 7110 MKIII is free from the influence of these compounds as they relate to a living, breathing subject taking a breath test.

SAFEGUARD 2

The 7110 MKIII also employs an alcohol specific electrochemical (fuel cell) sensor that is not influenced by acetone, toluene, or acetaldehyde. This fuel cell was tested by NHTSA and found to be within its specifications for use in an evidential breath tester.

SAFEGUARD 3

During either calibration or a calibration check, the fuel cell sensor memorizes its response to ethanol in the form of a curvature analysis profile. From this analysis, the presence of methanol or isopropanol can be detected by comparing the time constant of the curve of ethanol compared to methanol or isopropanol. If the analysis of the subject's breath reveals different curvature characteristics, "Interference" will be displayed and the test invalidated.

SAFEGUARD 4

During a test, the subject's breath is analyzed by both the infrared and fuel cell sensors. There is a preset tolerance that both readings must fall within for a test to be valid. The results must be within a .008% up to a .08% and 10% thereafter. If the two results are within the preset tolerance, the results are displayed and printed. If, however, the two results exceed the preset tolerance, an interference message is displayed and the test invalidated.

Characteristics and Theory

(The author is grateful to Mary McMurray of Forensic Associates, Minneapolis, MN, for her assistance in providing the following information.)

The Draeger Alcotest 7110 MK III is a breath-alcohol analyzer intended for law enforcement and workplace testing. The testing sequences are automated and the alcohol results are displayed both on the LCD and the printout produced by the printer. The 7110 MK III uses two analytical methods — 9.5-micron infrared (IR) and electrochemical.

The Alcotest 7110 MK III is portable, fitted in a metal case measuring 15.8″W × 5.1″H × 10.4″D and weighing 16.5 lbs. The breath hose is flexible and the temperature is controlled with two temperature sensors. The display is a 40-character, illuminated, alphanumeric LC display, an internal printer, and can operate in either AC or DC modes. The keyboard is a standard PC-AT type. Peripheral connections may include the keyboard, communications port RS 232, RJ 11, a printer port, a receptacle for the simulator temperature probe, and a security key for protecting against unauthorized access to various operating functions.

The operating temperature of the 7110 MK III is 32° to 104°F (humidity 10 to 95 percent RH) allowing for testing under a wide range of ambient environmental conditions. The measurement range of the 7110 MK III is from 0.000 to 0.630 percent BAC with a resolution of 0.0001 percent BAC. The 7110 MK III has been by NHTSA and is on the conforming products list. Independent laboratory testing has also demonstrated that this device exceeds the OIML specifications.

The 512 kB RAM allows for the storage of up to 1,000 tests for total recall. If the communications package is utilized the built in "Smart-modem" can transfer data to a host PC. Remote testing and instrument emulation can be accomplished from the host PC. All testing data from every test conducted is capable of being stored as a part of the specific instrument's operational history. The database for each device can then become a part of the test instrument's quality assurance package. The operating program is stored on the flash EEPROM and changes or modifications can be loaded remotely via the host computer. This is an improvement over the EPROM chips used in other types of analyzers, which required opening the equipment and physically replacing the chips. The multiple-level password protection and the "Function Key" access protection is designed to protect the security of the operational program from unauthorized tampering and modification.

The 7110 is the first generation of breath alcohol analyzers that has the ability of measuring the temperature of the (breath) sample as it is being delivered. Just as the alcohol concentration of the simulator solution vapors depends on the temperature of the solution, the alcohol concentration of a breath sample is dependent on the temperature of the breath. The software programming of the 7110 can adjust the sample temperature to the same temperature as the alcohol standard that was utilized in the calibration process. The programming may include capturing the entire breath profile from the IR analysis for each subject test. This would then allow for independent evaluation of the breath profile if there were any question as to the quality of the individual breath sample.

An optional simulator temperature probe may be used to constantly monitor the wet bath simulator temperature to ensure proper operating temperature. No tests are possible if the operating temperature is not within the programmed specifications.

The 7110 MK III has two independent measuring systems — the 9.5 μm IR analysis of the end-portion of an exhaled breath and the electrochemical sensor analysis of a small portion of the breath taken from the optical chamber. The optical chamber (cuvette) is a 70 ml chamber with threaded end-caps that on the inside (cuvette side) are gold-plated mirrors. The IR source enters the cuvette from one end-cap opening and is reflected several times before exiting the opening in the opposite end-cap.

The Intoxilyzer® and the DataMaster® breath-alcohol analyzers employ the use of IR energy around the 3.4 μm range. This region of the IR spectrum corresponds to the C-H stretching motion of organic molecules. Virtually every organic compound will show some absorbance in this region of the IR spectra. Substances such as toluene, xylene, and diethyl ether have been shown to cause falsely elevated alcohol measurements on these types of alcohol analyzers without being identified as an interferent. The 9.5 μm region of the IR spectrum is in the "fingerprint" region for organic molecules. At this wavelength there is a strong C-O absorbance due to the C-OH stretching motion of primary alcohols. Ethanol is a primary alcohol. The concept of using this region of the IR spectra focuses on identifying the substance in the breath using the characteristics of what actually makes the molecule an alcohol, namely the hydroxyl (OH) group. But the question of specificity at this region is still not absolute. There is some overlap from the absorption bands of esters and ethers in this region. Diethyl ether was shown to cause significant alcohol readings on the Alcotest 7110.

The use of multiple wavelength analysis at the 9–10 μm range improves the specificity of the device. At this region of the IR spectrum the specific shape and position of the absorption lines makes the identification of interfering substances easier than at the 3.5 μm range. A second option to increased sensitivity is the addition of an electrochemical sensor. This latter option is what the 7110 MK III has done.

Electrochemical (a.k.a. EC or fuel cell) sensors can be used to measure the amount of alcohol in a breath sample by means of an electrochemical reaction. Electrochemical oxidation is a chemical process that uses a fuel (in this case ethyl alcohol) to generate an electrical current. The current generated by the oxidation of alcohol in a breath sample is proportional to the amount of ethanol oxidized. The current can be measured and translated into an alcohol concentration by means of the appropriate electronics.

Fuel cells are relatively specific for alcohol due to the fact that only small molecules will oxidize on the electrode surface without requiring an electrical current to initiate the process. However, many small molecule hydrocarbons other than ethanol (such as methane, carbon monoxide, acetaldehyde, and gasoline fumes) can be oxidized in a fuel cell.

The shape of the alcohol molecule is an important factor in the more sophisticated fuel cells. The reaction times for different types of alcohol (ethanol vs. methanol vs. isopropanol) are different. By carefully selecting the electrode material and the electrolyte to utilize this kinetic aspect it is possible to differentiate between ethanol and other alcohols.

Platinum The surface of the platinum plates is prepared in such a way as to enlarge the surface area. The molecular dispersion makes the plates turn black and are thus referred to as platinum-black.

Electrolyte Sulfuric acid (approximately 4 molar) is used as an electrolyte for the ionic transfer of electrons inside of the cell matrix.

Electrodes The transfer of electrons to the alcohol molecules (oxidation) occurs via the wires attached to the platinum-black plates. The platinum, when exposed to oxygen, will build a *potential* that is able to oxidize alcohol molecules. This positive potential means that there is essentially an electron-vacuum at that electrode. As soon as the alcohol molecules reach the electrodes, oxidation is initiated.

There are two types of oxidation:

> *Electrochemical oxidation* is the exchange of electron taking place via the wire-electrodes. The partial steps of the oxidation and reduction are physically separated.
>
> Movement of electrons = via electrodes (metallic)
> Movement of ions = via electrolyte (ionic)
>
> *Chemical oxidation* is the transfer of electrons as the result of direct contact of the molecules.

In a breath-alcohol test, the breath is directed to one of the electrodes where the oxidation process is triggered without applying any current to the electrodes. The electrons will travel via the wiring to the opposite electrode, which in turn triggers a reduction and consumption of the electrons. An electrolyte-filled matrix is entrapped between the two platinum plates and completes the electronic circuit. The electrolyte and the electrode material are selected such that the alcohol to be determined is electrochemically converted at the working electrode.

This balance of neutralizing the potential difference of electrons is important. Electrode 1 is the working electrode that is exposed to the gas and where the oxidation occurs. The reaction begins at that electrode. The alcohol molecules "dissolve" in the thin electrolyte-film on the surface of the catalyst. In this stage the dissolving process is what initiates the oxidizing on the platinum surface, which causes a small reduction on the platinum surface.

$$C_2H_5OH + 3\ H_2O \rightarrow 2\ CO_2 + 12\ H^+ + 12\ e^- \qquad \text{working electrode}$$

The presence of oxygen immediately refurbishes the platinum. The oxygen will eventually be reduced, but not in a direct relationship. The reduction of oxygen from the air takes place at electrode 2, the reference electrode.

$$3\ O_2 + 12\ H^+ + 12\ e^- \rightarrow 6\ H_2O \qquad \text{reference electrode}$$

The electrochemical sensors are not in a position to measure alcohol concentration directly, since the current produced is proportional to the number of molecules that come into contact with the working electrode inside of the sensor. A measurable amount of gas must be applied in a controlled manner to the working electrode in order to be able to determine or record concentrations. The sampling system accomplishes this task by drawing a fixed volume of the breath into the sensor.

The EC sensor of the 7110 MK III sampling system is designed to require the test subject to expel a minimum volume of breath before accepting a sample. Immediately subsequent to the IR analysis of the sample a piston is automatically activated and draws a 1cc sample of the breath (air) in the cuvette into the EC sensor. The total charge produced by the chemical reaction is then measured and quantified. Current microprocessor technology has made it feasible to record the sensor current by means of time integration. Initially there will be a sharp rise in the sensor signal due to the rapid absorption of the alcohol molecules. The subsequent exponential decrease reflects the tailing-off of the chemical reaction, which can take several minutes in the case of high concentrations. This results in a certain waiting period before the next test can begin.

For practical reasons, the current/time integration is not continued until the reaction has completely tailed off. Instead, integration is usually halted as soon as the sensor current has dropped to roughly 40 percent of the maximum value. The curve profile can then be used to extrapolate the total integral. This method has the advantage of not being dependent on the rate of chemical reaction. Should the rate of change vary due to ambient temperature or the effects of an aging fuel cell, the integration timer alters but the total integral neither decreases nor increases since the overall charge is only dependent on the absolute number of molecules converted.

Deviations from this ideal behavior are encountered at temperatures below 5°C. In order to maintain the measurement quality over the entire usage range, the back of the sensor may be provided with a ceramic heater, which raises the sensor temperature to a level 15°C above ambient temperature.

The printing of the EC analysis may be inhibited per an agency's request or program design.

Operation

The internal pump flushes the cuvette and breath hose with ambient air. After the purging cycle, an air sample from the cuvette is drawn into the EC sensor for analysis. This "ambient air check" procedure ensures that the air in the cuvette is free of any absorbing substances. The internal pump then purges the cuvette and breath hose with ambient air while the intensity of the IR energy is analyzed and stored as a reference. The dual sensors assure a true air blank analysis before setting the zero baseline of the IR.

The breath sample would then be introduced through a mouthpiece to the breath hose and into the cuvette. For a sample of breath to be accepted for analysis several criteria must first be satisfied. The sample must be delivered at a flow rate of 2.5 L/min or greater and be of at least 4.5 seconds in duration. Meeting these two criteria assures that a minimum volume of 1.5 L of breath is exhaled prior to analysis. A valid breath test is characterized by a nearly constant alcohol concentration in time (plateau) at the end of a subject's sample. The 7110 MK III defines the plateau requirement as the concentration cannot increase by more than 1 percent per ¼ second at concentrations above 0.04 percent BAC or by 0.001 percent BAC for lower concentrations.

Once the slope requirements have been met and the breath (air) flow has ceased, there is a short pause while the pressure of the cuvette reaches equilibrium with ambient pressure. Once this equilibrium is achieved, the intensity of the IR energy is analyzed. Immediately after the IR analysis, the EC sensor pulls a 1cc sample out of the cuvette for analysis.

The 7110 MK III continuously monitors the breath sample as it is being delivered. If after 4 seconds of blowing at the rate of 2.5

L/min or greater there is a negative slope the test will be aborted and flagged as "mouth alcohol." A negative slope is defined as three consecutive readings, each reading ¼ second apart, showing a drop in alcohol concentration of 0.0021 or greater. Mouth alcohol will also be flagged when the concentration drops more than a 0.010 or 5 percent, whichever is greater, from the IR peak value. An "interference" message is given and printed if the difference between the IR and the EC sensors exceed a preset tolerance. The factory set tolerance for the two analyses is 0.008 or 10 percent, whichever is greater. The software controls what the preset tolerance is and may be controlled by state or local regulations.

The 7110 MK III has the capability of collecting and storing data from all tests and operations performed on the test device. This data is retrievable via modem or computer connection and may be stored in a database. The database files are often customized by the purchasing agency and may include:

- all **subject tests** (tests conducted in a normal testing mode that is initiated with the start test button);
- all **calibration checks** (tests conducted in an ACA mode);
- all **diagnostics** or **systems tests** (at initial start-up and any diagnostic or system tests that are not a programmed part of a subject test); and
- **error messages** (instrumental and operational error log).

There may be additional database files, but these are the most basic files that would be used for quality control, diagnostic, and troubleshooting purposes. The computer databases provide a spreadsheet format for each file (i.e., all subject tests), with each test (each subject record), comprised of data fields representing each step of the test. The air blanks are generally not stored. The agency that purchases the alcohol analyzer with the data collection program will be able to specify what data is and isn't being collected as well as what the various files are called.

The usefulness of the database is that it is a complete record of all tests conducted. Every test, good or bad, should be there. The computer data is potentially the best source of quality assurance/quality control data available. The data should establish or discredit the functional stability, accuracy, and reliability of a specific test device. By cross-referencing the records in the various data files and message logs, an unbiased picture can be painted of the overall accuracy and reliability of the testing device. Trends and deviations from the normal should be monitored and investigated if persistent.

The 7110 MK III is capable of storing more than 1,000 tests.

Depending upon requested software options, the entire breath profile may be stored in the test memory.

CLAIMED NON-SPECIFICITY

The most notable characteristic of Draeger's Alcotest 7110 is the improved specificity for ethanol relative to existing breath testing machines on the market. As has been discussed, however, the Alcotest 7110 is still not specific for ethanol. The following chart lists the more common compounds that will be "read" as ethanol by the machine.

Selected Compounds with C-O Stretching Vibrations that Absorb in the 9–10 μm Region

	Compound	*B.P. (°C)*	*Selected Uses*
ALCOHOLS	n-Butyl Alcohol	117–118	Solvent for fats, waxes, resins, shellac, varnish, gums
	Menthol	212	Liqueurs, confectionary, perfumery, cigarettes, cough drops, nasal inhalers
	Methanol	64.7	Industrial solvent
	1-Pentanol	137.5	Industrial Solvent
ESTERS	Ethyl Acetate	77	Artificial fruit essences, solvent for varnishes, lacquers, aeroplane dopes, nitrocellulose
	Ethyl Butyrate	120–121	Manufacture of artificial rum, perfumery, pineapple flavor
	Isoamyl Acetate	142	Banana flavor, solvent for lacquers, celluloid, camphor
	Propyl Acetate	101.6	Flavoring agent, perfumes, solvent for resins, plastics, cellulose derivatives
ETHERS	Dioxane	101.1	Solvent for cellulose, acetate, resins, oils, waxes
	Ethyl Ether	34.6	Solvent for waxes, fats, oils, perfumes, alkaloids, gums

Tetrahydrofuran	66	Solvent for high polymers, especially polyvinyl chloride, solvent in histological techniques

NON-FACTORY MAINTENANCE

Finally, counsel should consider carefully the long-term maintenance records he has obtained for the Alcotest 7110 through pretrial discovery. In reviewing them, carefully look for any repairs or maintenance conducted by state or local laboratories or police agencies — as is the general practice in most jurisdictions. Then consider the following comments by the manufacturer, taken from the Operator's Manual (March 1998).

> The 7110 MK III must be inspected and serviced every 12 months. Repairs and general maintenance on 7110 MK III must be carried out only by Draeger Safety, Inc. representatives or certified service centers. Only genuine Draeger parts are to be used for maintenance replacement requirements.
>
> Electrical coupling with instruments not mentioned in the Operating or Service Manual are to be performed only after consulting Draeger Safety, Inc., Breathalyzer Division in Durango, CO.
>
> The liability for the proper function of the 7110 MK III is irrevocably transferred to the owner or operator if the 7110 MK III has been serviced or repaired by personnel not employed or authorized by Draeger Safety, Inc., or when the 7110 MK III is used in a manner not conforming to its intended use.
>
> Draeger Safety, Inc. cannot be held responsible for damage caused as a result of noncompliance with the recommendations given in the Operating Manual.

7

BLOOD AND URINE ANALYSIS

§7.0 Blood Analysis

> There are four chief obstacles in grasping truth, which hinder every man, however learned, and scarcely allow any one to win a clear title to learning, namely, submission to faulty and unworthy authority, influence of custom, popular prejudice, and concealment of our own ignorance accompanied by an ostentatious display of our knowledge.
>
> ROGER BACON

In the majority of drunk driving cases, defense counsel will be confronted with the use of a breath analyzing device in determining the client's blood-alcohol level. In a few cases, however, blood analysis will be the method used. This is the most accurate of the three common procedures, leaving the least room for cross-examination. While urinalysis and breath analysis are attempts to determine indirectly the amount of alcohol in the blood by measuring the alcohol in the urine or breath and then attempting to theorize what the corresponding amount of alcohol is in the blood, blood analysis takes the direct approach of analyzing the blood itself and measuring the amount of alcohol actually present in a given sample. No theories or inferences are used: The blood-alcohol level is analyzed directly. Nevertheless, there is room for cross-examination about the procedures employed in the blood analysis, if not about the underlying theory.

There are today three methods commonly used in the analysis of blood samples for blood-alcohol concentration: gas chromatography, enzymatic reaction, and dichromate.

Counsel is most likely to encounter the *gas chromatography* method of analysis, wherein a blood sample is analyzed by a gas chromatograph instrument. There are today two methods for utilizing this procedure. The most popular method currently in use is that of *head-space gas chromatography,* in which the ethanol is transferred from the liquid to the vapor above the liquid via the addition of a nonvolatile solution and heated; generally an internal standard is also added to the blood to aid in quantitation of results. So-called *direct injection* gas chromatography is also used commonly. In this procedure, whole blood or other substrate is injected directly into the instrument. The blood is flaked on a surface in the heated injection port and the volatiles, including alcohol, are carried into the column by carrier gas pressure. Glass inserts are used and then removed to prevent contamination or fouling of the instrument. Gas chromatography techniques measure a single parameter — the retention time — and are thus "specific" for ethanol under standard conditions.

It should be noted that any gas chromatograph instrument is subject to radio frequency interference (see §6.3.10) in its analysis from sources in or near the laboratory.

The second procedure for blood analysis is the *enzymatic* method. This procedure is highly technical and quite expensive and can be performed only in very sophisticated laboratories having specially trained personnel and the required special apparatus. Consequently, counsel will rarely encounter this method in drunk driving cases.

In very simplified terms, enzymatic analysis consists of measuring the reaction of the coenzyme nicotinamide adenine nucleotide, in the presence of the enzyme alcohol dehydrogenase, with ethyl alcohol. The result of this reaction is the production of NADH. The amount of NADH that results from the reaction of these enzymes with the alcohol in the blood is then measured on a spectrophotometer; the more NADH present, the higher the blood-alcohol level of the sample. Separation of the alcohol from the blood is not required: The enzymes react with the alcohol while still dispersed in the blood sample.

The third process for analyzing blood samples for alcohol content involves the *dichromate* method, also known as the *Kozelka-*

Hines method. Very briefly, the alcohol is first separated from the blood by diffusion or aeration. Potassium dichromate in a sulfuric solution reacts with the alcohol; the residual dichromate is then measured and the blood-alcohol level computed.

The main problem with the Kozelka-Hines method is that it is not *specific* for ethyl alcohol — that is, it can falsely report other compounds as alcohol. Thus, for example, such an analysis will react to acetone, acetaldehyde, methanol (wood alcohol), and isopropanol (rubbing alcohol). Acetone and acetaldehyde can be found in the blood, possibly causing increases in reported blood-alcohol concentrations of up to .05 percent; methanol and isopropanol can occur as contaminants in the laboratory.

As already mentioned, blood analysis is unquestionably the most *potentially* accurate method of determining a subject's blood-alcohol level. As with any testing process, however, there is always room for error and thus for cross-examination. Unfortunately, the intricacies of the blood-alcohol analyzing procedures and the theories behind them are often too complex for the average attorney to understand and handle intelligently in dealing with an expert on the stand. Faced with a drunk driving case involving the taking of a blood sample, counsel would be well advised to retain his own expert, assuming his client can afford the expense. The services of a laboratory chemist, a college professor, or a specialized physician can be invaluable not only in assisting counsel in cross-examining the prosecution's expert witness, but also in presenting defense testimony concerning the blood test and the physiological aspects of alcohol consumption generally and as applied to the client's case.

Should counsel have to confront the prosecutor's chemist without expert assistance, he should concentrate his attention on certain recurrent problem areas. Error in preparing the standard solutions in the laboratory is not uncommon; the dichromate solution must be prepared with precision and then standardized every day it is used. Counsel should also pay close attention to the procedures for reading the amount of titration solution used as well as the process for measuring the amount of blood.

There are, however, a few areas in which counsel easily can challenge the blood test without expertise. These involve the procedures used to withdraw and store the blood specimen.

First, counsel should investigate whether the individuals who withdrew the sample were properly licensed to do so by the state laws regulating blood-alcohol analysis. Usually, the individual has to be a licensed nurse, physician, or medical technician or at least has to have received specified training. If a blood sample kit was used to obtain the specimen, this too usually must be of an approved type. And, as with the individual who withdrew the blood, the laboratory technician or chemist who conducts the analysis normally must be appropriately certified. The laboratory itself also must have the required current license and/or current certification of inspection.

Counsel should always bear in mind the possible issue of chain of custody. The prosecution has the burden of establishing control of the blood sample from the time it left the client's arm to the time it was analyzed and, perhaps, if appropriate discovery motions are made, to the present. For a fuller discussion of the chain of custody issue, refer to §7.0.6.

The DUI attorney should be aware of the practice in many laboratories, particularly in the larger cities where the work load becomes very heavy, of conducting multiple analyses. Rather than analyze one blood sample at a time, the harried technician will line up a half-dozen samples or even more and run them through the analytic process. In some cases, the lab technician, much like a juggler trying to control five or six objects in the air, will even have two or three groups of samples at different stages of the analyzing procedure. It requires little imagination to picture the increased risk of error under such arrangements, error that never would be detected.

The Law Enforcement Standards Laboratory of the National Bureau of Standards' National Engineering Laboratory conducted a study to evaluate the proficiency of laboratories measuring the amount of alcohol in blood. The study involved "known sample" comparisons from 120 clinical laboratories from around the country on a voluntary basis. The results are contained in Report No. DOT-HS-806-193, U.S. Department of Transportation, National Highway Traffic Safety Administrator, and is available from the National Technical Information Service, Springfield, VA 22161. For those who believe that analysis of blood samples for alcohol content in a clinical laboratory setting is uniformly reliable, the following conclusion of the study will be of interest:

> A few labs did significantly poorer than the general run of labs, having (jointly) more than one-third of their measurements off by more than 20 percent.

Even among the "general run," laboratories showed a standard deviation of 3.8 percent.

See also Hodgson and Taylor, Evaluation of Fisher Toxichem Whole Blood Alcohol Controls (Humans), 20 Journal of Canadian Society of Forensic Science 87 (1987), where researchers compared the results of identical blood samples analyzed by various private laboratories. The results indicated that the resultant BACs routinely varied by 13 percent to 15.5 percent — despite involving identical samples.

§7.0.1 General Sources of Error

Some of the more common sources of error in blood analysis involve the contamination of the sample from bacteria or from using an alcohol swab, fermentation within the sample due to lack of preservative and/or refrigeration, withdrawal of the sample from an artery rather than a vein, analysis of plasma rather than whole blood, the possible effects of *Candida albicans,* and failure in chain of custody. These issues will be discussed in the subsections that follow.

A more comprehensive listing of possible errors in blood (and urine) analysis can be found in an article entitled Drunk Driving: Challenging the Blood or Urine Analysis. Samuels, 20(1) Medicine, Science and Law 14 (1980). Samuels offers the following possible causes of defective analysis:

1. The blood or urine sample was too small for accurate analysis.
2. The container leaked because of an improperly fitting lid.
3. The sample was old, stale, coagulated, dried up, or otherwise unfit for analysis.
4. The sample may have been contaminated by an officer or other person during the taking of the sample or the later opening of the container.

5. The analysis indicated was from another sample.
6. The blood specimen may have been drawn from a part of the body where there was a higher BAC.
7. Excessive plasma was squeezed into the sample (plasma tends to retain a higher proportion of alcohol).
8. If the defendant had given blood a few hours before the sample was drawn, the decreased volume of blood in the body would cause an elevated BAC.
9. The machine used to analyze the sample was inaccurate.
10. The individual performing the analysis was a trainee or otherwise unqualified.
11. The sample contained alcohol produced by the liver, rather than alcohol consumed by the defendant.

Another valuable checklist when dealing with blood analysis is suggested by the authors of an article entitled Blood Is Thicker Than Water: What You Need to Know to Challenge a Serum Blood Alcohol Result. The article, authored by law professor Carol A. Roehrenbeck and attorney Raymond W. Russell and appearing in the Fall 1993 issue of Criminal Justice, suggests the following as fruitful areas for cross-examination:

1. If gas chromatography was not used to analyze the blood sample, it should be pointed out that this is the favored method; the enzymatic procedure is considered less reliable for BAC testing.
2. The use of alcohol to cleanse the skin before withdrawing a blood sample will result in an elevated reading.
3. The blood sample must be properly sealed in the vial, or evaporation will result.
4. If the sample does not contain an anticoagulant and is not properly refrigerated, deterioration of the sample can result in the production of alcohol.
5. Was the instrument used for analysis specific for alcohol?
6. Was the equipment properly calibrated? (Note: The expiration date on the test package used to calibrate the equipment should be checked.)
7. The blood sample's chain of custody should be questioned, along with the possibility that the suspect's sample was mixed up with that of another individual.

Roehrenbeck and Russell also offer a checklist for dealing with analysis performed on blood serum rather than on whole blood. See §7.0.4.

The following is an excellent summary of procedures employed in the analysis of blood-alcohol concentration, combined with specific cross-examination issues. The material reproduced here with the kind permission of its author, Michael J. Snure of the law firm of Kirkconnell, Lindsey, Snure and Henson of Winter Park, Florida, was presented by Mr. Snure in conjunction with a lecture at the National College for DUI Defense's Third Annual Summer Session at Harvard Law School in 1997.

> Whether faced with a simple DUI with a legal blood draw or hospital blood draw, or a DUI Manslaughter or DUI With Serious Bodily Injuries with a legal blood test result, discrediting the blood-alcohol test results is critical to obtaining results in both pre-trial negotiated resolutions and at trial. The following describes in general the manufacturing process of blood-alcohol test kits, the collection, storage, and testing mechanisms for legal blood test results, and some collateral issues that must be explored in order to overcome legal blood test results. The scope of inquiry must include not only matters directly related to the manufacturer of the blood test kits, but also to the collection, storage, transportation, and testing of the blood test sample and, finally, to other matters that might call into question the accuracy of the blood test results such as witnesses' observations of an apparently sober defendant, or field sobriety tests where the defendant performs better than would be expected for a given blood-alcohol test result. In certain circumstances the mechanics of an accident can be reconstructed in a way that tends to discredit the blood-alcohol test results. Nevertheless, in attacking the blood-alcohol test result one must look beyond the testing of the sample itself.
>
> THE MANUFACTURING PROCESS
>
> Blood-alcohol kits are manufactured by commercial businesses in much the same way or with many of the attendant manufacturing processes of any other business. Most manufacturers make many types of blood-alcohol collection kits. However, only a few of those are designed for forensic or police use. Generally, the manufacturing plan will receive from chemical houses or manufacturers the chemicals that are intended to be introduced into the

kits for use as preservatives and anticoagulants. These chemicals are received in bulk from the chemical suppliers. The blood kit manufacturer will also receive in certain circumstances previously made collection tubes or test tubes or will manufacture its own test tubes from raw material to its specific size and volume dimensions. Even the rubber stoppers and labeling must be obtained or manufactured by the blood test kit manufacturer.

Once the bulk chemicals are obtained from the chemical distributors, the blood kit manufacturer will mix the chemicals in a ratio that is desired in the blood test kit. Asan example, if the ultimate goal of the manufacturer is to have 20 milligrams of sodium fluoride and 10 milligrams of disodium EDTA in a test tube, then the bulk powder chemicals will be mixed at a ratio of 2 to 1. The manufacturer claims to have a mixing formula that will ensure even distribution of the powdered chemicals such that any sample would be evenly distributed 2 to 1. Sampling is taken from the bulk mixture to ensure the 2 to 1 ratio from various places within the bulk product. The mixed chemicals are then stored in powder form until they are ready to be dispensed into the test tube vials. No further testing for accurate mixing is ever performed, at least with the major manufacturers of these kits.

The test tube vials after having been manufactured or purchased are placed on a conveyor belt and drawn along a manufacture line where the previously mixed bulk chemicals are dispensed *by weight only* into the test tubes. In other words, in the above example, 30 milligrams of a powdered substance will be dispensed into each vial as it moves along the production line. However, at no time are the vials ever checked to ensure that the proper amounts of each chemical — 20 milligrams and 10 milligrams — were dispensed into the vial. Complete reliance is placed on the earlier mixing procedure.

As the vials move along the production line quality control is conducted to ensure that the weight volume of 30 milligrams has been dispensed. There is some flexibility or tolerance allowed but the vials are never again checked for the 2 to 1 ratio of the chemicals. It would be easy to pull a few samples off the production line and test to see that the vial actually received the proper amounts of the chemicals intended.

Once all the particular vials in that manufacturing lot have had the stated amount of powder introduced they are collected onto a pallet-type device and placed in a small vacuum chamber. Stoppers are lightly set on top of the vials. The air is evacuated from the chamber, creating a vacuum. Stoppers previously lightly placed on the vial are then pressed into place, creating and maintaining the vacuum inside the vial. The chamber is then repressurized and the vacuum will theoretically remain inside the test tube vials. This is important because the vacuum pressure has been calculated to draw the required amount of blood into the tube without overfilling or underfilling. Obtaining the proper volume of blood in the tube is important because the type and amount of chemicals included as a preservative and anticoagulant are based on an assumed volume of blood. A different volume of blood could affect the usefulness of the chemicals for that volume.

The vials are then placed in a chamber where they are irradiated to create a sterile tube. Labels are then affixed, and the tubes are stored for assembly, with other components, of the ultimate blood alcohol collection kit.

The expiration dates on blood-alcohol collection kits generally refer to the date beyond which the vacuum will not be warranted by the manufacturer. The vacuum is important for two reasons. First, the vacuum is calculated by design to pull the proper volume of blood into the container when punctured by the vacutainer needle. Second, the vacuum, when properly sealed, maintains the sterile environment. If the vacuum has been compromised, then the proper volume of blood will not be drawn into the vial and the calculated amount of chemicals introduced into the vial as a preservative or anticoagulant will be out of specification with possible effect on the blood test results. Additionally, if the vacuum has been compromised, the tube is no longer sterile and bacteria may have entered the tube, which could cause spoiling or fermentation of the later collected blood alcohol sample.

This manufacturing process is similar to the blood-alcohol test tube collection vial manufacturing process in that bulk chemicals are obtained, a mixture is created, the gauze and the nonalcoholic solution are introduced and packaged. Along the way quality control is conducted to ensure the proper volume of chemical, its proper mixture, and proper packaging and labeling.

The other components of a blood-alcohol kit include a theoretically nonalcoholic site preparation wipe, usually obtained by contract from a separate manufacturer; a vacutainer device, which is simply a device designed to puncture the rubber stopper septum and a defendant's vein thereby allowing the vacuum to draw into the vial from the defendant's arm the required amount of blood; varying instruction sheets; and transportation components such as an internal box and an external mailer box. Also included within the kit are labeling materials and sealing materials that vary from manufacturer to manufacturer.

In certain instances the blood-alcohol collection kits are distributed from the manufacturer without the kit being sealed. In other words, when obtained by a law enforcement officer, the kit can be opened all the way to the vials without breaking any integrity seals. This of course gives rise to the possibility of tampering. It is possible to compromise the vacuum of a blood-alcohol test tube kit slightly by puncturing the rubber stopper septum and introducing bacteria, alcohol, or any other contaminant without destroying the entire vacuum, such that a person would not be readily able to detect that the vacuum had been compromised.

Importantly, when the kits are ultimately sealed after collection, the top of the stopper is not covered with integrity seal tape or labeling. In other words, the same puncture hole used to withdraw the blood from the defendant's arm could be used to introduce contaminants into the blood sample without detection after the defendant's blood had been drawn. This is a glaring integrity error that should be explored along with the fact that the kits are sent out from the manufacturer in an unsealed condition.

The purpose of the kits containing an anticoagulant and a preservative is to ensure that the blood test result reaches the analyst in a testable condition. A preservative, most commonly sodium fluoride, is designed to prevent bacterial contamination or spoilation of the blood. There are reported cases in the scientific literature of blood samples drawn from both living and deceased individuals where the blood concentration changed both up and down in value from the actual blood value based on bacterial contamination.

The purpose of an anticoagulant is to prevent the clotting of the blood. The reason that unclotted blood is desirable for testing is that whole blood has an equally distributed makeup of solid matter and serum or liquid. When blood is in an unclotted state, the blood-alcohol concentration is evenly distributed among the solid matter and the liquid. If the blood begins to clot (i.e., the solid matter joins together and expels its liquid) then the alcohol concentration in the serum or liquid portion of the blood will become artificially high relative to that volume of liquid. This is why alcohol concentrations in hospital blood tests, which only examine serum after the solid or fibrous matter has been removed, are artificially high — up to 30 percent higher than those obtained in tests of a true homogeneous whole blood sample. Clotting may appear to the naked eye as globs within the sample. Clotting that can be observed only under a microscope is known as microclotting. Blood that has been microclotted will not represent a true value because, even with a small degree of clotting, the blood-alcohol concentration in the remaining serum is artificially high. Most analysts only do a naked-eye visual inspection of the blood sample and either do not recognize the phenomenon of microclotting or claim that, if present, it would make such a small difference that it is insignificant, or that the pipettes or syringes they use are so small in diameter that if the blood sample was clotted to any significant degree it would not be testable.

CONSIDERATIONS FOR EVALUATING BLOOD (COLLECTION, STORAGE, AND TRANSPORTATION)

This section will discuss considerations surrounding the actual collection, storage, and transportation of the blood.

When a blood kit is needed for collection of a forensic blood sample, the kit is normally obtained from a paramedic or law enforcement officer. In conducting discovery, you should learn where the blood kit was kept prior to its being employed in the collection of the blood sample from your client. The most common response is that the kit has been in the trunk of a patrol car for many months. Although the chemicals contained within the vials are relatively inert and are probably not subject to decomposition or degradation as a result of high temperatures, most juries would view that as an unsatisfactory storage condition for the blood collection kit.

Most kits are shipped to law enforcement agencies in an unsealed condition. This means that the entire kit can be opened all the way to the vials without breaking any integrity seals. This gives rise to the possibility of tampering. Tampering could occur by inserting a fine-gauge needle into the rubber stopper and injecting into the tube a foreign substance that could alter the result. Such tampering would not necessarily impair the entire vacuum so that, even after being tampered with, the tube might well fill to the approximate level required, thereby not raising the concern of loss of vacuum or contamination. One of the questions to be asked in discovery is whether the vials appear to fill to the same level, which helps to determine whether the vacuum was relatively constant in each of the tubes. Another question to ask of the blood collector is whether he or she knows to what level the vials should fill and whether he or she made any conscious note in this case as to whether the vials did in fact fill to that level.

Once the blood has been collected, and the needle is pulled out, the needle puncture in the top of the rubber stopper self-seals. However, unless integrity tape is placed over the top of the rubber stopper, the original needle hole can be used to tamper with the sample after collection by simply inserting a smaller-gauge needle down through the same hole and injecting a foreign substance into the sample. There is no competent excuse for failing to seal the blood kit across the top of the stopper to avoid even the possibility of tampering.

The tubes should contain a powdered substance. Most forensic blood alcohol kits contain a powdered anticoagulant and preservative. If the kit contains a liquid, that should be noted and investigated immediately. Some blood collection kits, not generally used for forensic work, do contain a liquid. You must immediately discover what the contents were and how they would affect a legal blood analysis. There is no way to distinguish through visual inspection the types of chemicals in the tubes. The only way to determine whether both chemicals were present in the required amounts is to do a chemical analysis.

The purpose of a preservative is to prevent the blood from decomposing or to prevent bacteria from growing and changing the alcohol content in the sample. There are documented studies where the actual blood alcohol content in a sample changed both upwardly and downwardly through decomposition and fermentation. Therefore, determining the presence of a preservative is a very important part of an accurate scientific analysis. If the blood alcohol level in the sample has changed, the analyst will not be able to tell through any mechanism of analysis how much the alcohol level in the blood has increased or decreased since collection. Therefore, if the blood-alcohol level in your client's sample has increased since collection, there is no way to tell the difference between the alcohol that has fermented from the alcohol that was ingested, and your client would be subject to a false high result.

One way to know if an anticoagulant and a preservative are present in any given blood sample is to test that blood sample after collection, but before analysis, by the use of ion chromatography. There are published methodologies in the scientific literature to determine the presence of both preservatives and anticoagulants in blood samples through ion chromatography. However, these procedures are costly. Another way to have confidence that the blood sample does contain the proper amount of anticoagulant and the preservative is to enact a regulation that requires blood kits that are ordered for use in the state to be randomly sampled at a scientifically acceptable random number for the presence of the preservative and anticoagulant in the proper amounts. Once a large lot of blood kits passes this random inspection, one can then have a certain amount of confidence that the remaining kits contain the proper amounts of the proper chemicals.

The wipe contained within the kit should be alcohol-free. It is very rare for the used wipe to be included in the kit for analysis in the laboratory. Analysts claim that the used wipe is a biohazard. However, at some point it must be determined that the wipe was in fact nonalcoholic. This can be determined through random analysis, as described above, or through analysis of the used wipe, even though that has given rise to biohazard concerns. At a minimum, the packaging from the wipe should be preserved and returned in the kit so that the analyst knows that the wipe used was at least labeled and purported to be nonalcoholic. Otherwise, the analyst would have no way of knowing if the proper nonalcoholic antiseptic was used. There are documented studies in the scientific literature that establish that the use of an alcoholic swab could affect the outcome of a blood-alcohol test. Normally the alcohol contained in swabs is not ethyl alcohol, which is in alcohol we drink. However, there has been a documented discovery of a purported nonalcoholic wipe that did in fact contain ethyl alcohol. The simple lesson to be learned is that one is not safe relying on labeling but must rely instead on testing to make sure that the requirements of the regulations are met and that the integrity of the analysis is not compromised.

It is important that the puncture site for the collection of the blood sample be clean, because dirt or bacteria that may be collected into the blood sample could cause the blood to degrade or cause the alcohol in the blood to ferment and the alcohol level to increase. A proper amount of preservatives should prevent this. However, the concerns about the preservative referred to above are enhanced if the proper antiseptic is not employed.

Once the blood collection is completed and the kit properly labeled and sealed, its chain of custody through analysis must be firmly established. There are no guidelines for storage or transportation of collected blood kits. I once had a blood kit that was stored in the lunchroom refrigerator of a small agency for three days and then sent to the lab via United States mail; it did not reach its ultimate destination until five days later. This blood kit would have been exposed to extremely high temperatures, which are known to cause breakdowns in the blood and enhance the rate of fermentation. If the blood sample is to be sent to a laboratory, you should inquire about the storage conditions prior to analysis.

A word about hospital blood. If the blood is drawn in a hospital, not in a legal blood collection kit, a great deal of care should be used in discovery to determine exactly the chain of custody of the blood and the method of analysis used. Generally, blood drawn in hospitals is poorly labeled. Chain of custody is often difficult, if not impossible, to reconstruct, and the method of analysis used is not whole blood nor an approved method of analysis, either head-space or alcohol dehydrogenase. Most hospitals analyze serum and not whole blood. In a serum analysis, the blood-alcohol level is likely to be up to 30 percent higher than it would be in a whole blood analysis. This is because in a serum analysis all of the solid or particulate matter is spun out of the blood; therefore, the entire volume of alcohol that was formerly present in the greater volume of blood is now present in a lesser volume of serum only.

The DUI defense lawyer should also take care to discover all the necessary information if the client's blood is drawn at a hospital but sent to an outside laboratory for analysis. The problems with labeling and chain of custody are magnified under these circumstances. Also, most outside laboratories use serum analysis, with the same problems as those described above.

A LAWYER'S PRIMER ON BLOOD ANALYSIS AND GAS CHROMATOLOGY

Once the blood has been collected from the defendant and transported to the lab, it must be stored in the lab in a suitable environment. This usually means refrigeration. In deposing the laboratory analyst, one should determine whether the analyst knows the conditions under which the blood was stored, the temperature of the refrigerator, who had access to the refrigerator, and all other such custody and tampering related issues. One should then explore the exact circumstances under which the blood was taken from storage to the lab analyst's work area, and, if not analyzed immediately, the conditions under which it was stored in the work area, including who had access to the storage facility, whether it was refrigerated, etc. (One must know a great deal about the analyst before attempting to take his or her deposition. One way of securing information about the analyst is to request from the agency or laboratory the analyst's entire employment file, including the analyst's application for employment and licensure, his or her methodology on file, and his or her proficiency testing results.) The reason that the analyst's methodology must be on file is so that it can be examined and approved by the regulatory agency in an effort to ensure that the analyst is competent and that the methodology can produce accurate results.

Where a client has the money to retain a defense expert in the area of toxicology, the analyst's methodology should be obtained and critiqued by the defense expert for possible omissions or substandard methodology practices.

One should keep in mind that the gas chromatograph is a device containing a computer system. To ensure that the device is capable of measuring accurately, it is calibrated on a periodic basis. Calibration means that the instrument is tested at various known levels of an identifiable substance such as ethyl alcohol. It may be tested at levels such as .05, .10, .15, .20, .25, .30, .35, .40, and those results should graph out in a linear fashion to show that the machine is capable of measuring alcohol at those levels and all levels in between. One should inquire how the solutions are prepared at those various levels to be used in the calibration process. Are they aqueous (water) solutions containing levels of alcohol? If so, how did the alcohol get into the water? Who measured the alcohol? Was the volume of the alcohol in the aqueous solution measured by some other device before it was used to calibrate the gas chromatograph? How does one know that the mixture was done properly? Another possibility is that the gas chromatograph could be calibrated using whole blood standards, which are human whole blood samples obtained from a chemical supply house, purportedly containing known levels of alcohol concentration. If so, how were these samples obtained? Who measured the alcohol level in the sample before it was shipped? Has anyone measured the alcohol level in the samples since it was shipped to determine that it contains the level of alcohol that it is purported to contain by the manufacturer?

One should also inquire whether the lab has any internal operating manual or procedures that indicate on what basis and with what frequency the gas chromatograph should be calibrated. Are records kept of those calibrations? Are there regulations for the use of whole blood standards from chemical supply houses or for the creation of aqueous alcohol solutions? If so, what are they and how are they enforced?

One should also inquire whether the agency has an internal policy in writing regarding the periodic inspection and maintenance of the gas chromatograph and its various components. If so, where is it, what does it say, and how is compliance documented? One should inquire whether any outside agency conducts any inspection or maintenance procedures on the gas chromatographs. The maintenance and integrity of the machines, including their accuracy and reliability, may be left entirely to the internal operating procedures of the laboratory. We get more assurance of reliability when we buy fruit in a grocery store or gas at the gas pump because the measuring devices (i.e., the scales and the gas pump) are checked by an outside agency, the Department of Agriculture, to ensure that they are measuring correctly. At many laboratories we are required to simply take their word for their maintenance procedures, which ultimately establish the reliability and integrity of the machines they use.

One should also inquire whether the individual analyst knows what computer program is in the gas chromatograph, how that program was created, what the assumptions in the program are, and what the parameters of the program are. The computer program drives the operation of the instrument. The accuracy of the data in the program could greatly affect any results that the machine records. Therefore, the analyst must have an operating knowledge of the parameters of the computer software. One might inquire whether the software was purchased as a result of governmental bidding and whether the low bidder was accepted. One might also inquire whether there are competing companies that create the same type of computer software and, if so, find out what each says about the other's deficiencies.

Blood that is taken from the storage area and brought to the analyst's work area for analysis is laid out on a work table. Be aware that most analysts are going to analyze blood samples from as many as 20 subjects during any given testing run. Since each subject's blood must be tested in duplicate, this means that 40 separate vials could be in the work area at the time of any analysis run on the gas chromatograph. Control vials are also run between tests, driving the number of vials present up to over 50. This may raise the possibility of human error, such as mislabeling or confusion when results are presented to a jury, and may in fact account for a certain amount of error in the testing procedure.

The mechanics of the analysis are as follows. An individual's blood collection kit is opened and one of the two collection vials is extracted. That vial is opened and two samples of blood are drawn from that collection vial and deposited into two separate vials for analysis. The original collection tube is then restoppered and set aside with the rest of the kit, including the one unopened blood vial. One should inquire how much blood is extracted from the collection kit for sampling. How is it measured? What device is used to extract it from the blood collection vial and to deposit it into the sample vials? What is the diameter of this device or pipette? How does the analyst ensure that the blood extracted from the defendant's blood collection kit is deposited into a sample vial that bears the proper label? How is labeling accomplished? Does anyone assist the analyst? How are the labels created? How are they applied to the sample vials? How are the sample vials kept separate from other defendants' vials? When was the analysis done? Sometimes, with automated sampling, the gas chromatograph is left to run overnight with no analyst around to monitor the results as they come off.

As indicated, during the course of the testing of the two samples of the defendant's blood, a control sample is introduced into the machine to determine if it is measuring properly. The control standards should be set forth in the analyst's methodology. One should inquire whether this is whole blood or an aqueous ethanol solution, how it is prepared, how its concentration is determined, and inquire about all the other variables surrounding the creation of this control.

Consider the effect on a jury of the argument that your client's blood sample may very well have been the last two samples analyzed following 38 other blood samples and nine or ten control samples all containing alcohol through the same instrument within a short period of time. What about the effect of buildup or contamination in the instrument or column? What measures are taken to ensure that there is no buildup or contamination?

The two sample vials created by the analyst are then prepared to be mixed with certain other solutions and ready for creation of the headspace gas. The internal standard solution is a pre-mixed solution usually containing an alcohol, such as N-Propyl alcohol, mixed with a salting agent and an antioxidant. If an automatic sampler is used, a predetermined volume of this solution is drawn into the cavity of the syringe by a mechanically operated syringe. Syringe No. 2 has tubing inserted into the sample tube of the defendant's blood, and it mechanically draws into the cavity of the syringe a predetermined amount of blood from the defendant's sample. Who checks to see if the auto sampler works properly? If an automatic device is not used, this procedure must be done by hand, introducing the possibility of human error. Once these predetermined amounts of solution and blood have been drawn in, the tubing is removed from sample tube *A* and inserted into test tube *B*, which will become the headspace vial.

Syringe No. 2 is then activated to inject into the sample vial the predetermined volume of the defendant's blood. Syringe No. 1 is then activated to flush the tubing free of the defendant's blood and inject into test tube *B* the internal standard solution along with the chemicals contained therein. The contents of test tube *B* are now (1) a pre-measured portion of the defendant's blood, which is taken from the blood collection vial, and (2) an internal standard solution, which is selected and established by the analyst's methodology and injected into the tube either by this automatic process or by hand. Test tube *B* is then capped or crimped to form an airtight seal.

The liquid solution contains the subject's blood mixed with the internal standard solution and the salting agents. The air space between the top of the blood and the bottom of the crimp or stopper is called headspace. The theory of this method of analysis, called Henry's Law, is that if the defendant's blood contains a certain concentration of alcohol, then the gas created over the solution will contain a proportional amount of alcohol to the liquid blood. This concentration of alcohol is supposed to rise into the gas or headspace area between the liquid and the stopper in proportion to the defendant's blood. The process is helped along by chemicals, known as "salting agents," which are inserted in the standard solution that is mixed with the blood. One should inquire whether it is possible to add too much salting agent to the blood such that it could drive up into the headspace more alcohol than is actually proportionally present in the blood. This phenomenon, known as "salting out the blood," results in an artificially high alcohol value in the headspace gas. Keep in mind that the blood collection kit employed by the law enforcement officer generally contains two separate salt compounds; one acts as a preservative and the other as an anticoagulant. These salting agents are usually never measured and thus the analyst does not know how much of these chemicals were present before he added his own salting agents. One should inquire whether this could make a difference.

In some methodologies, the headspace vial is heated to facilitate the transfer of the alcohol vapor out of the blood into the gas or headspace. In other methodologies, it is either not heated or is heated to a different temperature. One should inquire about these variables and their general acceptability or acceptance in the scientific community.

Once a specified period of time has elapsed and, according to the analyst's methodology, enough time has elapsed to allow the proper proportional amount of alcohol gas to have escaped into the headspace, a needle is used to puncture the seal and extract a specified volume of that gas for injection onto the gas chromatograph. One should inquire exactly how this step is accomplished and what the possibilities are for contamination of the gas or its escape from the needle into the atmosphere, or other destruction of the integrity of the sample.

The gas that has been extracted from the headspace vial is injected into the gas chromatograph through a port. This gas meets with helium, a carrier gas that is injected into the gas chromatograph through another port. These combined gases are pushed through a column that is packed with a carbowax packing. At the end of the column is a flame ionization detector. The theory of the gas chromatograph, expressed in layman's terms, is that each different chemical substance will travel through the carbowax-packed column at different speeds. Therefore, you can identify the substance that is being pushed through the column by the amount of time it takes for that substance to clear the end of the column. Each chemical has a known time that it will take it to clear the column. Once the chemical comes off the end of the column it is detected by a flame ionization detector. This burns or ionizes the chemical. The ions then become electrical charges that can be measured by the gas chromatograph computer. The assumption is that the combination of the time it takes the chemical to come off the column combined with the measurement of the flame ionization detector will produce data that identify and quantify the substance. The computer in the gas chromatograph then creates a picture of the chemical. One should inquire how the computer has been programmed to recognize these various measurements and convert them into a diagram picture. One will also note in the picture that the internal standard solution is registered as N-propyl alcohol.

The matters we have discussed in connection with microclotting, fermentation, and the salting out of the blood can all affect the gas chromatographic analysis. If these issues are kept in mind during the discovery and deposition process, one can expect a greater insight into this process and the discovery of possible flaws or areas of concern that will give rise to reasonable doubt. Please do not underestimate the benefit that a defense expert toxicologist can be in assisting in the discovery and deposition process as well as in evaluating the results and preparing and giving trial testimony.

By understanding the use of blood in forensic situations, we will all become more comfortable and less intimidated, and we will achieve better results for our clients.

The following represents a detailed and exhaustive outline of potential sources of laboratory error in analyzing blood for alcoholic content, as seen by an acknowledged expert in the field of blood-alcohol analysis. The author is grateful to Dr. Herschel Frye, Professor of Chemistry at the University of the Pacific, and to the California Public Defender's Association for their assistance in providing this material.

General Sources of Error

1. sources of error in blood drawing equipment

a. Insufficient preservative or excess preservative. The former may allow bacterial action and the latter may tend to "salt out" the volatile solute.
b. Insufficient or excess anticoagulant. In the former case, ethanol may be unduly concentrated in the serum above the clot. "Salting out" may occur with excess solid.
c. Solution in blood of anti-oxidants in rubber stoppers used in blood tubes or vials. It has been demonstrated that the compound tributoxyethyl phosphate can dissolve in blood and fool even a Nitrogen phosphorus GC detector (not to mention FID).
d. Dirty or out-of-date evacuated containers often called "Vacutainers" after the brand marketed by Becton-Dickinson. I have found their quality control to be superior.
e. Dirty or plugged blood-drawing syringe. This is not a usual issue in this day of all-disposable blood drawing equipment.
f. Use of a swab containing alcohol. Most labs use Betadine or mercuric chloride. Even at worst, this error source is minor, leading to a maximum error of the order of 0.01% (my own data).
g. Any non-sterile equipment may introduce more microorganisms than the preservative can handle. This is likewise a rarity today.

2. sources of error in blood drawing

a. Source of blood: venous or capillary? This is an important point in the taking of post-mortem blood.
b. Operator contamination. However, remember that in most cases the person who does the analysis is not the person who drew the blood. Here's a chance to cross-examine two for the price of one!

Gas Chromatographic Methods

1. reagent error sources

a. Impure or incorrect (mislabelled) internal standard. The internal standard is something that should be both stable and pure; it should not be a usual substance in human blood, and it should have a retention time significantly different from that of the ethanol.
b. Impure or contaminated "salting out" chemical. This typical inorganic salt should be pure and should obviously be free of alcohol. This is an error which really applies only to "headspace" chromatography; no reagents are used in direct injection methods.

2. ancillary glassware errors

a. These are identical with 2. in Table 1. The volumes measured in chromatographic methods are small, and thus calibration of pipets is more important still.

3. errors involving injection method

a. Leaking syringe (manual methods) used for injection. Some material is forced back out past the plunger.
b. Defective auto-injector (automated methods) from misuse or lack of maintenance.
c. Leaking septum. This rubber-plastic insert should be changed every dozen or so injections to prevent loss of injectate.

4. instrument error source

a. Use of wrong carrier gas. The specific detector employed will require specific carrier gas such as helium, nitrogen, or argon.
b. Faulty regulators resulting in improper gas flow.
c. Improper column temperature control resulting in incorrect retention times for components.
d. Dirty or erratic detector. This important component needs special care. Be sure to ask the type used (i.e., TC, FID, EC, or NPD).
e. Malfunctioning amplifier circuit. Repair of such integrated ("breadboard") circuits is a job for an electronics expert.
f. Increased retention time or broad peaks due to stationary

phase "bleed" or to poisoning of column by foreign materials.

g. Improper instrument grounding leading to erratic amplifier output. Ask how grounding is accomplished.
h. Improper connection of chromatograph to recorder or printer. Are the connecting wires attached to the correct terminal and are they secure?
i. Improper settings on recorder or printer. Most current methods use the one millivolt setting; was this actually checked via observation? . . .

5. ERRORS CAUSED BY INTERFERING CHEMICAL SPECIES

a. Retention times for different chemical compounds — especially those with similar structures — may differ by only a small amount. Remember that GC is a technique which measures only a parameter; it is *not* unique for a chemical species. One reason for adding an internal standard is to keep a check on the retention time.
b. Similar retention times causing errors in interpretation such as the presence of "shoulders," etc. These errors may be enhanced by 4.f. above.
c. Chemical species from ambient air or operator.

6. OPERATOR ERRORS

a. As in 4.a. above.
b. Sloppy technique in sample introduction.
c. Incorrect recording of relevant data by operator.
d. Failure to note instrument malfunction and to act accordingly.
e. Selection of incorrect internal standard.
f. Presence of external radiofrequency signals due to operator.

ENZYMATIC METHODS

1. REAGENT ERROR SOURCES

a. Improperly prepared individual vials due to poor manufacturer quality control. How checked?
b. Contaminated deproteinizing solution. This is most often trichloroacetic acid; is it kept refrigerated and away from sources of contamination?
c. Contaminated or over-age buffer. Usual buffer is based on

glycine, although pyrophosphate is often used. In either case the buffer should be kept in the refrigerator and away from all sources of contamination.

d. Improper or over-age standard ethanol solution. This is best obtained in small sealed ampoules and should be used immediately. Typical concentrations are (in per cent w:v) 0.08, 0.10, 0.20, and 0.30.

2. ANCILLARY GLASSWARE ERRORS

a. . . . Properly calibrated pipets are an absolute necessity due to the small volumes handled.

3. INSTRUMENT ERRORS

a. Improper calibration of spectrophotometer. The wavelength 340 nm is critical; how was the instrument calibrated?
b. Dirty cuvets. These small sample containers must be kept scrupulously clean and in an environment free from alcohol.
c. Sluggish instrument response.
d. Excessive S/N ratio. . . .

4. OPERATOR ERRORS

a. Failure to wait requisite time before making measurements.
b. Improper techniques such as pipetting, sample agitation, etc.
c. Incorrect or inaccurate interpretation of readout.
d. Use of outdated vials to "save money."
e. Presence of interfering substances in the ambient air or on operator's person.

MICRODIFFUSION METHODS

1. REAGENT ERROR SOURCES

a. Impure or adulterated potassium dichromate (should be NBS grade or equivalent).
b. Impure or adulterated sulfuric acid (should be "reagent grade"). Excess acid should never be returned to the original container.
c. Impure or contaminated reducing agent (if any).

2. ANCILLARY GLASSWARE ERRORS

a. Improperly calibrated pipets, burets, volumetric flasks, etc. Recalibration should be done on a regular basis by skilled personnel.
b. Improper cleaning of glassware, including microdiffusion flasks. Incomplete cleaning or a residue of soap or detergent must be avoided! (Who oversees this important but unromantic step?)
c. Chipped tips on pipets and burets. Such glassware should be visually inspected before each use.

3. INSTRUMENT ERROR SOURCES

a. Improper maintenance. A regular program of preventive maintenance should be established and performed by trained and competent personnel. Logs should be maintained (and signed) for each instrument. Such items as sources and electronic components should be periodically replaced; internal optics should be *carefully* cleaned by an expert to prevent scratching.
b. Electronic and optical errors. Most of these may be eliminated or minimized by careful work and preventive maintenance as in 3.a.

4. OPERATOR ERRORS

a. Introduction of ethanol via the operator. Obviously the analyst should not return from a three Martini lunch and pipet blood sample by mouth! (Mouth pipetting should be avoided anyway.) Ethanol on the hands or body (as in shaving lotions or perfumes) may introduce error.
b. Sloppy technique in pipetting or titrating.
c. Erroneous procedure in the preparation of oxidant solutions such as weighing or volume errors.
d. Colorblind operators may consistently misread data.

§7.0.2 Sterilization of the Skin

Contamination of the blood sample is another ever-present possibility that can affect the accuracy of an analysis. Establishing the likelihood or even the possibility of contamination can cast doubt in the jury's mind on the reliability of the test results and may even be sufficient to undermine the foundational requirements for introduction of the results into evidence.

Forensic toxicologist Anne ImObersteg of Park-Gilman Clinics, Burlingame, California, has observed that "One of the greatest risks to the integrity of a forensic sample is the growth of microorganisms in an unrefrigerated sample which has not been adequately collected or preserved." Crucial to this is adequate sterilization of the skin:

> The human body naturally contains a variety of microbes on the skin and in the body. The amount and variety of microbes on the skin varies from individual to individual. For example, an average person per square centimeter has anywhere between 100 to 100,000 microbes depending on the time of day and whether they have been exercising. Thus, the prospective site must be properly cleaned with a non-alcoholic swab and with proper mechanical movement to minimize the drawing of microbes into the syringe.
>
> Despite the precautions of cleaning the arm before puncture, however, microorganisms living in skin pores or the skin layers may still survive. A needle puncture to draw the blood may pick up a plug of skin that will introduce microbes into the blood sample. Clinical inspection of the blood for these microbes may reveal survival even after cleansing.

One of the most common causes for contamination of the blood specimen is the failure to sterilize adequately the instruments involved. Many states have specific laws setting forth the requirements for sterilization of the hypodermic syringe, needle, and vial. (See, e.g., Va. Code Ann. §§18.1–55.1(d) (Code 1950, 1966 Supp. Ch. 636).) A few states go so far as to require that the blood sample must be taken with disposable syringes and needles that have been factory-wrapped and kept under "strictly sanitary and sterile conditions." (Iowa Code 321 B4 (Iowa Acts 1969, 63 G.A. Ch. 205, §14).) In most jurisdictions, defense counsel need not produce evidence of noncompliance; the prosecution has the burden of proving that the requirements were complied with. See, e.g., *Brush v. Commonwealth*, 136 S.E.2d 864 (Va. 1964).

In *State v. Setter*, 763 S.W.2d 228 (Mo. App. 1989), for example, the court reversed a DUI conviction where the state had failed to establish that the needle used to withdraw blood from the defendant had been sterilized. In so doing, the court noted that "other jurisdictions have consistently held that absolute and literal compliance with the technical requirements of [blood-alcohol testing] statutes and regulations is necessary."

Another occasionally fruitful area of inquiry involves the universal medical practice of sterilizing the subject's arm before inserting the hypodermic needle. The common practice, of course, is to swab with a strong solution of alcohol, usually a 70 percent solution. Yet this concentrated alcohol will be picked up in the needle as it enters the skin — and possibly as it leaves if a swab also is held against the skin as the needle is withdrawn — and will be drawn into the blood sample. The result is that the laboratory will be trying to isolate an infinitely tiny amount of alcohol in the blood to establish the blood-alcohol level, and there will be a concentrated dose of alcohol in the sample from the swabbing. The results are unpredictable, of course, depending on the amount of alcohol that was drawn into the sample, but in view of the microscopic amount of alcohol that the test is designed to detect, the effects could be dramatic. A perfectly sober individual, with not a drop of alcohol in his system, could end up with a reading of, say, .12 percent.

An Indiana appellate court considered the evidentiary effect of using alcohol to swab a suspect's arm before a blood sample is withdrawn. In *State v. Alderson,* 435 N.E.2d 614 (Ind. App. 1982), the court upheld a trial court exclusion of resulting blood-alcohol evidence:

> The State contends that the trial court erred in excluding evidence of the result of Alderson's blood-alcohol test. Although a portion of the State's argument is addressed to whether a proper chain of custody was established, the record reveals that the trial court excluded the test results on other grounds. Specifically, Alderson testified during an offer to prove that his arm was swabbed with a substance smelling of alcohol immediately before his blood was taken. There is some question as to whether using isopropyl as a sterilizing agent would distort the test results. The State was unable to produce the person who actually drew Alderson's blood or any other person who observed the procedures utilized in drawing the blood. The trial court ruled that the State failed to establish a sufficient foundation for the introduction of the test results.
>
> The State argues that the foundation was properly laid for two reasons. First, in the State's offer to prove, Doris Waters, the tech-

nician who ran the tests on Alderson's blood, testified that the customary hospital procedure was to not use isopropyl for sterilization when a blood-alcohol test was to be conducted. Second, the State asserts that Waters' testimony during the offer to prove established that the equipment used in the test could distinguish isopropyl from ethanol.

The State's offer to prove is far from conclusive. Cross-examination of Waters, with regard to the customary hospital practices, reveals the following:

Q. You have no way of knowing whether or not that was done in this instance?
A. I don't, to be fair and honest, I don't know.
Q. All right. You indicated on direct examination that there might be a possibility that alcohol swab was used in this particular possibility.
A. It's a possibility.
Q. Because you really don't know?
A. I don't know.
Q. You're not the watch-dog of everyone around there?
A. Right.
Q. And are people in the Emergency Room, do they have the same training as you do?
A. No.
Q. They don't; do they?
A. No.
Q. They are not involved in any analysis; are they?
A. No.
Q. Are they in the collection?
A. Yes.
Q. And no idea what goes on in the analysis?
A. No.
Q. You, for example, can appreciate the difference, because you are in an analyzing part of it. And you can appreciate the problems of alcohol. They have no reason to; right?
Q. Isn't that correct?
A. That's true. [Record at 317–318.]

The testimony regarding the equipment used is equally inconclusive.

Q. When you indicated on this, that this machine could test and tell a difference between blood-alcohol levels with ethanol ver-

> sus isopropyl; is that what you're relying on? This paragraph which, correct me if I'm wrong, that paragraph simply gives a formula for determining ethanol. It does not say anywhere on that that it distinguishes between; does it?
>
> *A.* No, it's not a distinction. [Record at 318–319.]
>
> Additionally, assuming that the equipment does have the capacity to distinguish between isopropyl and ethanol, there is nothing in the State's offer to prove which indicates that the appropriate tests were conducted. Under the circumstances of this case, the trial court did not err in ruling that the State failed to lay a proper foundation for the admission of the blood-alcohol test results. [435 N.E.2d at 615–616.]

Similarly, a New York court reversed a drunk driving conviction because alcohol was used to sterilize the defendant's arm prior to the blood withdrawal. See *People v. Ward,* 14 Misc. 2d 782, 178 N.Y.S.2d 708 (1958). An opposite result was achieved, however, in *Kaufman v. State,* 632 S.W.2d 685 (Tex. App. 1982), where the court held that swabbing the skin with a solution known as Zephiran (containing 2 percent ethyl alcohol) went to the weight — not the admissibility — of the results of the blood test.

It should be noted that Zephiran, which is the brand name for a benzalkonium chloride solution, is routinely used in many hospitals for withdrawing blood. Since it contains 2 percent ethanol, its use should be considered a violation of regulatory statutes prohibiting the use of ethyl alcohol. While the *Kaufman* court felt this to go to the weight of the evidence rather than to its admissibility, other jurisdictions have increasingly proven less flexible. Thus, for example, in affirming the suppression of blood test results because of swabbing with ethanol, a Missouri court noted that "other jurisdictions with similar (regulatory) statutes have determined that absolute and literal compliance is necessary." *State v. Hanners,* 774 S.W.2d 568 (Mo. App. 1989).

See also *State v. Mays,* 615 N.E.2d 641 (Ohio App. 1993), where the nurse sterilized the defendant's skin with Betadine before withdrawing a blood sample. The trial court suppressed the test results, ruling that though there was no evidence that Betadine contained alcohol, neither was there evidence that it did *not.* On appeal, the State pointed out that Betadine, in fact, contains no alcohol. Nevertheless, the appellate court affirmed the suppression: The burden was on the prosecution to establish a proper foundation for the blood test at the trial level.

It is not uncommon to find hospital personnel swabbing the skin with iodine before inserting the needle for a blood draw in the belief that it is a satisfactory substitute for an isopropyl alcohol swab. Tincture of iodine, as any tincture solution, is a mixture of powder in alcohol — and, thus, can have the same contaminating effect as an alcohol swab.

Of particular interest is the discovery that three brands of commercially prepared swabs used routinely throughout the United States contain benzalkonium chloride. An article appearing in 8(25) Drinking/Driving Law Letter 1 (Dec. 8, 1989), indicates that research conducted by a Colorado laboratory has revealed the following swabs to contain the compound — and measurable amounts of alcohol when analyzed: "Clinipad" antiseptic towelettes, "PDI" benzalkonium chloride antiseptic towelette, and "Triad" benzalkonium chloride antiseptic towelette. As a result, the Colorado Department of Health issued a memo "encouraging laboratories to evaluate the swabs they are currently using" and recommending the use of a fourth commercially prepared swab, "PDI" Povidone-Iodine Prep Pad, which does not contain benzalkonium chloride.

§7.0.3 Fermentation in the Vial

The care of the blood sample once taken from the subject should also be investigated. It is a common practice to let the blood specimen sit for days before analyzing it, due to delay in getting it to the laboratory, to a crowded schedule in the laboratory, or to simple neglect. But blood is an organic material and will decompose because of enzymes and bacterial action. One of the results of this decomposition is that alcohol is created in the blood. In a sample originally containing no alcohol, decomposition can cause a reading of .25 percent or even higher, depending on the stage of decay.

Usually the specimen will be refrigerated to prevent this. However, refrigeration will only slow down the decomposition process, not prevent it. To stop this decaying of the blood and the resultant formation of alcohol, a preservative such as a sodium fluoride solution should be added. Failure to do this — and it is not at all uncommon — should provide counsel with sufficient material at least to discredit the test results, if not prevent their admission into evidence.

Most blood-alcohol kits used to collect blood samples for alcohol testing use tubes containing 20 mg of sodium fluoride to preserve the blood sample. The noted Swedish expert on blood-alcohol analysis, A. W. Jones, however, claims that this is an insufficient amount to prevent fermentation: at least 100 mg should be used. Salting-Out Effect of Sodium Fluoride and its Influence on the Analysis of Ethanol by Headspace Gas Chromatography, 18 Journal of Analytical Toxicology 292 (September 1994). Dr. Jones also found that using sodium fluoride to preserve a blood sample actually *increased* the amount of alcohol in the sample when gas chromatography was used to analyze it. According to his research, even 10 mg of sodium fluoride "increased the concentration of ethanol in the equilibrated (34 degrees centigrade) headspace by 8.9% when compared with heparinized blood" (i.e., blood treated with an anticoagulant). This was due to a "salting-out" effect from the sodium fluoride.

Although many scientists believe that a preservative consisting of 1 percent of the sample is sufficient to stop the growth of microorganisms, many others feel that a 2 percent preservative such as sodium fluoride is required. See Dick and Stone, Alcohol Loss Arising from Microbial Contamination of Drivers' Blood Specimens, 34 Forensic Science International 17 (1987).

Clearly, the risk of fermentation will vary according to the amount of preservative used. However, it will also be directly affected by the length of time the sample is stored, and by the temperature at which it is stored. Sodium fluoride of 1 percent or less concentration is stable for only about two days. Kaye, The Collection and Handling of the Blood Alcohol Specimen, 74 American Journal of Clinical Pathology 743 (1980). And fluctuations from a storage temperature of 25 degrees centigrade will increase fermentation and production of alcohol. As toxicologist Anne ImObersteg of Park-Gilman Clinics in Burlingame, California, has observed:

> Even in a blood tube containing sodium fluoride, *Candida albicans,* the most common microbial culprit of ethanol production

in blood samples, can produce ethanol. Blume, Bacterial Contamination on BAC Stability, 60 American Journal of Clinical Pathology 700 (1973). Specimens stored at room temperature for more than five days showed significant alcohol formation (up to 0.08 percent maximum) in a study by Chang and Kollman, The Effect of Temperature on the Formation of Ethyl Alcohol by Candida Albacans in the Blood, 34(1) JFSCA 105 (Jan. 1989). Therefore, the third prong of sample integrity, storage temperature, is also crucial.

An anticoagulant such as potassium oxalate also should be added to the sample to prevent the blood from coagulating. However, counsel should insist that the prosecution establish exactly what chemicals were used as an anticoagulant as well as the possible side effects on the alcohol and blood. (For a case involving a reversal because an unidentified anticoagulant was added to a urine sample, read *State v. Smith,* 272 N.W.2d 859 (Iowa 1978).)

Once counsel has obtained the laboratory records through discovery, they should be reviewed for any notations concerning the condition of the blood sample when received. Quite often, the lab technician will enter an annotation such as "clotting" or "some coagulation." If so, this should be developed during cross-examination — and the inference made that if the anticoagulant was not working, then perhaps the preservative was similarly ineffective (resulting in fermentation and an elevated blood-alcohol concentration).

Assuming that preservatives and anticoagulants were in the vial when the blood sample was introduced, it should not be presumed that they were, in fact, mixed with the blood. In *State v. Schwalk,* 430 N.W.2d 319 (N.D. 1988), for example, the Supreme Court of North Dakota reversed a DUI conviction where a foundation had not been laid showing that the collecting officer mixed the blood and chemicals. The court refused to presume "compliance with step four, which requires that immediately upon placing the blood in the glass vial it must be inverted several times to dissolve the chemicals contained in the vial."

§7.0.4 Whole Blood Versus Serum/Plasma

Blood samples obtained in drunk driving cases are generally — but not always — analyzed as whole blood (sometimes called "legal blood"). If the sample is withdrawn for medical purposes, however, the test will probably be done with *serum* (often referred to as "medical blood"). Serum is the clear yellowish fluid obtained from separating whole blood into its solid and liquid components (usually by centrifuging the sample); the liquid portion of the blood is called *plasma,* which is similar to serum. A third method involves precipitating proteins from the blood sample and centrifuging it; the result is a clear liquid called "supernatant," which is then analyzed.

Will analysis of serum/plasma or supernatant result in the same blood-alcohol readings as analysis of the whole blood? In a study entitled Distribution of Ethanol: Plasma to Whole Blood Ratios, Hodgson and Shajani, 18 Forensic Science Journal 73 (1985), scientists attempted to determine the answer to this very question. The conclusion: Blood-alcohol concentrations in plasma were approximately *11 percent higher* than that of whole blood, and those in supernatant samples were about 5 percent higher.

Thus, for example, evidence of a client's blood-alcohol analysis indicating a .10 percent BAC may in fact reflect a true .09 percent if the plasma separation method of analysis was used. This has been confirmed in another study in which researchers concluded that a "person with an ethanol concentration of [.09 percent] in whole blood could have a reported concentration above [.10 percent] if either serum or plasma is analyzed." Winek & Carfagna, 11 Journal of Analytical Toxicology 267 (1987). Since many states permit the three types of "blood samples" to be used interchangeably in blood-alcohol analysis, counsel should certainly determine which type was actually used.

For a study that found that serum-alcohol concentration can be up to *20 percent higher* than blood-alcohol concentration, see Frajola, Blood Alcohol Testing in the Clinical Laboratories: Problems and Suggested Remedies, 39(3) Clinical Chemistry 377 (1993). And for a case in which an appellate court ruled that blood-alcohol tests using blood serum should be accompanied with an explanation to the jury that serum generally causes a higher result, see *Commonwealth v. Bartolacci,* 598 A.2d 287 (Pa. Super. 1991).

A simple technique for visually demonstrating the concept of testing blood that has aged and been subject to possible fermentation is to bring in a fresh vial of blood and compare it to the evidentiary sample withdrawn months earlier from the defendant. The fresh blood will be bright red, while the test sample will be nearly black.

See also *Commonwealth v. Wanner,* 605 A.2d 805 (Pa. Super. 1992), where the defendant appealed his DUI conviction on the grounds that the evidence of his blood-alcohol concentration was based on tests conducted on blood plasma rather than on whole blood, as required by statute. The appellate court agreed, citing the *Bartolacci* opinion; although that case addressed the use of blood serum rather than plasma, both involved tests on only portions of the blood. The court further found that tests on plasma resulted in BACs 15 to 20 percent higher than tests on whole blood.

See also *Melton v. State,* 597 N.E.2d 359 (Ind. App. 1992), where an appellate court reversed a DUI conviction where evidence of BAC was presented to the jury based on a test performed on blood plasma. Expert testimony from the state was required to convert the reading into a whole-blood figure, the court said; tests on blood plasma samples register 18 to 20 percent higher than tests on whole-blood samples.

The fact is that laboratories often report blood test results as blood-alcohol concentrations when they are, in fact, serum-alcohol concentrations. And, as Frajola points out in his article, even where the laboratory does so by using a conversion ratio, they apply an *average* serum-to-blood ratio.

Unfortunately, the ratio of serum alcohol to whole-blood alcohol varies from one individual to another, just as the blood-breath partition ratio varies. The actual conversion factor in translating serum results to whole-blood results ranges from 0.88 to 1.59, with a median of 1.15. See Relation Between Serum and Whole-Blood Ethanol Concentrations, 39 Clinical Chemistry 2288 (1993). Yet laboratories usually use a uniform ratio of 1.16:1 in converting a serum/plasma BAC figure — if the figure is converted at all.

Counsel confronted with a DUI case involving analysis performed on blood serum should definitely review an article entitled Blood Is Thicker Than Water: What You Need to Know to Challenge a Serum Blood Alcohol Result, appearing in the Fall 1993 issue of Criminal Justice. Its authors, law professor Carol A. Roehrenbeck and attorney Raymond W. Russell, suggest that the following points be developed in challenging the blood test's admissibility and attacking its credibility before the jury:

1. Serum blood contains more water than whole blood. As a result, the BAC in serum blood will be higher than in whole blood because alcohol has an affinity for water.
2. The higher the percentage of red blood cells in the tested individual's sample (note: see discussion of hematocrit in §8.1.5), the lower the percentage of water.
3. The percentage of red blood cells (and thus the amount of water) in a given individual's blood will vary from minute to minute.
4. The serum blood BAC reading must be converted to a whole-blood reading. However, the conversion factor used to obtain the whole-blood reading is not an absolute, but rather varies from one individual to another and even varies within a given individual from moment to moment.

Finally, counsel should be aware that although the general practice in nonmedical DUI cases is to analyze whole blood, the experts say that whole blood should never be used for blood-alcohol analysis: Plasma is the preferred method. The reason for this is that alcohol is not uniformly distributed among the cellular and noncellular components of blood. See, e.g., Dubowski, Absorption, Distribution and Elimination of Alcohol: Highway Safety Aspects, 10 Journal for Study of Alcohol Supplement 98 (1985).

Thus if plasma was analyzed, counsel should question the computation of blood-alcohol concentration. If, on the other hand, whole blood was analyzed, the reasons why this procedure is disfavored should be brought out.

§7.0.5 Arterial Versus Venous Blood

Blood samples from DUI suspects are commonly withdrawn from the vein rather than from the artery. Yet the blood-alcohol content of venous blood can be quite different from the content of arterial blood in a subject at a given time — and it is the blood in the arteries that is carrying alcohol into the brain, resulting in intoxication. Thus analysis of venous blood samples can be misleading.

In fact, researchers have concluded that using a single venous blood sample to determine an earlier blood-alcohol concentration produces a result that is equivalent to a wild guess. In an article entitled The Pharmacokinetics of Alcohol in Human Breath, Venous, and Arterial Blood After Oral Ingestion, Martin, et al., 26 European Journal of Clinical Pharmacology 619 (1984), scientists measured comparative BAC levels in the breath, arterial blood, and venous blood of subjects who had consumed known quantities of alcohol.

The researchers noticed that BAC of arterial blood was higher than that of venous blood during the absorptive phase — that is, while the alcohol was being absorbed by the body. Conversely, the venous samples had higher blood-alcohol levels than the arterial samples during the elimination phase of the blood-alcohol curve. Thus a venous blood sample taken during the elimination phase will be analyzed as having a higher BAC than is in fact being carried to the brain.

The conclusion of the scientists was that a venous blood sample does not accurately reflect the amount of alcohol entering the brain and so is not indicative of the true degree of intoxication.

Counsel should review his jurisdiction's statutory or administrative language concerning blood analysis and determine whether there is a requirement that the sample be arterial or venous blood. If one source is specified, the prosecution should be required to lay an evidentiary foundation as to the actual source for the sample. It is not uncommon for the technician or nurse withdrawing the sample to be unable to specify or recall whether an artery or a vein was tapped, other than to say what their usual practice is.

§7.0.6 Chain of Custody

As a part of the foundation for introduction into evidence of the results of any blood-alcohol test, the prosecution must establish a complete chain of evidence. In other words, the prosecutor must be able to trace, through competent evidence, exactly where the chemical sample was at all times, from when it was extracted from the defendant to the moment it was finally analyzed; in some instances, as, for example, with pre-trial discovery, the chain must be extended into the present. In addition to having to prove where the sample was, the prosecutor also will probably have to show in whose custody it was at all times and that it was properly labeled and stored. He must negate the possibilities that it was in an unidentifiable individual's control at any point in time and that the sample was misplaced or exchanged mistakenly for another sample. In short, the prosecution must clearly establish that the sample taken from the defendant was the one analyzed and could not have been tampered with.

Certainly counsel should always object to admission of the test results without a complete showing of chain of custody, if only to establish a record for appeal. Usually a number of individuals have handled the sample in question, among them the arresting officer, the medical technician or physician, the transporting officer, the individual in charge of evidence at the laboratory, and/or the laboratory technician or chemist. Counsel should insist on the testimony of each such individual or at least the testimony of a witness to the custody of the sample by the individual.

In addition to testimony of custody, the prosecution should be required to show that an accepted means of labeling the sample was used. Again, each jurisdiction varies in its requirements as to the labeling of evidence, and counsel should be familiar with them. Generally, however, the sample should have been labeled by the person who took the sample and at the time the sample was taken and placed in its container.

For a discussion of suppression of blood or urine evidence for failure to establish a chain of custody, see §11.6.12.

Assuming that the objection or motion to suppress is denied, however, the issue is far from dead. Counsel should emphasize in his cross-examination and argument the failure of the prosecution to establish that the blood analyzed was, in fact, the defendant's. All of the testimony and legal presumptions concerning blood-alcohol concentrations mean nothing if it cannot be proven *beyond a reasonable doubt* that the blood analyzed was not taken from someone else.

Checklist 11 Blood Analysis

- ☐ Was the laboratory conducting the analysis properly licensed?
- ☐ Was the individual drawing the blood sample qualified and/or licensed?
- ☐ Was the laboratory technician who analyzed the sample properly licensed?
- ☐ Was the equipment calibrated accurately?
- ☐ Was the syringe used to withdraw the sample sterilized?
- ☐ Was the arm swabbed with alcohol or any other substance that could contaminate the sample?
- ☐ Did the blood sample come from the client's artery or vein?
- ☐ Is there a regulation as to which must be used?
- ☐ Would an arterial sample give a falsely high BAC?
- ☐ Would a venous sample give a falsely high BAC?
- ☐ Was the blood sample refrigerated at all times?
- ☐ Was the proper preservative added and in the correct amount?
- ☐ Could sodium fluoride have caused a higher BAC because of a "salting out" effect?
- ☐ Was the proper anticoagulant added and in the correct amount?
- ☐ Was the vial properly sealed — or could evaporation have caused an increased BAC?
- ☐ Can the prosecution account for the chain of custody of the analyzed sample?
- ☐ What method of analysis was used?
- ☐ If gas chromatography, were there any sources of radio frequency interference in or near the laboratory?
- ☐ If the Kozelka-Hines (dichromate) method, could acetone, acetaldehyde, or other substances have caused a false BAC?
- ☐ Was the sample one of a larger batch of samples analyzed en masse?
- ☐ Did the analyzed sample consist of whole blood or of serum/plasma?
- ☐ If serum/plasma, has the laboratory adjusted the BAC downward to allow for the serum/plasma concentration being 15 to 20 percent higher?
- ☐ If so, did the laboratory use an average conversion ratio? Was that ratio demonstrably applicable to the client's sample?
- ☐ Is a portion of the blood sample available to counsel for independent analysis?

§7.1 Urinalysis

> There are no whole truths: all truths are half-truths. It is trying to treat them as whole truths that plays the devil.
>
> ALFRED NORTH WHITEHEAD

Urinalysis is the chemical analysis of a subject's urine. It has been used by police agencies as a means of determining a driver's blood-alcohol level since long before breath testing devices came on the scene. It is still used in a few jurisdictions, usually as an alternative to breath or blood analysis, but it is today probably the least commonly encountered of the analytic procedures. This is true for two reasons. First, taking a urine sample from an arrestee is time-consuming and, frankly, a distasteful job for the police officer. In jurisdictions requiring the sample to be taken at a hospital or laboratory rather than by the officer at the station, it involves considerably more time and trouble than a quick, on-the-spot breath test.

The second reason for the relative unpopularity of urinalysis is, quite simply, that it is the least accurate and reliable of the three methods of blood-alcohol analysis. As researchers at Duquesne University have concluded, "the unreliability of using a urine ethanol concentration to predict a blood ethanol concentration cannot be questioned." Winek, Murphy, and Winek, The Unreliability of Using a Urine Ethanol Concentration to Predict a Blood Ethanol Concentration, 25 Forensic Science International 277, 280 (1984).

Dr. Kurt Dubowski, probably the most recognized blood-alcohol expert in the country, prepared a document for the U.S. Department of Transportation entitled *Manual for Analysis of Ethanol and Biological Liquids.* That document concluded that:

> The only urine specimen which could, in theory, be confidently employed for alcohol analysis for purposes of estimating the co-existing BAC is ureteral [i.e., from the urethra] urine — clearly an impractical specimen for law enforcement purposes. . . .
>
> In summary, in the living human subject, only blood, saliva and urine are potentially usable specimens in law enforcement practice; of these only blood is sufficiently free of forensically-disabling disadvantages and contradictions to be a practical specimen material for routine applications.

Similarly, the National Safety Council's Committee on Alcohol and Drugs (Ad Hoc Committee on Testing and Training) has recommended that:

> Because of various problems in the interpretation of the results of the analysis of urine specimens for alcohol which cannot be readily overcome in law enforcement practice, urinalysis of urine for the purpose of determining blood alcohol is to be discouraged except under the strictly controlled conditions employed in determining renal [i.e., kidney] solute clearances.

Counsel will find that most forensic criminalists called by the prosecution will be familiar with the studies and recommendations of the Department of Transportation and the National Safety Council, as well as the works and expertise of Dr. Dubowski. They will also acknowledge that many states have now repealed legislation authorizing the use of urinalysis in drunk driving cases.

The theory underlying urinalysis is simple. Alcohol is secreted by the subject's kidney by diffusion into the urine. The concentration of alcohol in the urine at the time of secretion in the *average* person is about 1.33 times the concentration of alcohol in the blood at the same time. Therefore, measurement of the alcohol in the recently secreted urine, followed by a simple computation, should theoretically give the subject's blood-alcohol ratio.

The urine sample is obtained necessarily from urine voided by the arrestee. This represents urine that has been secreted by the kidney and passed into the bladder, where it sits until the subject urinates. Therefore, the urine that is being analyzed consists of a mixture of urine that has been secreted by the kidney over a period of time, at least since the last time the subject urinated. If the individual has not voided in 12 hours, for example, the specimen will contain a mixture of urine secreted by the kidney over that 12-hour period. In other words, the urine sample will not be indicative of the blood-alcohol level of the subject while he was driving within the past half hour or so, but rather probably will represent a chemical average of the level over the past 12 hours. Thus a man who had been drinking 8 or 10 hours earlier but who had "sobered" to a blood-alcohol level of zero by the time he was arrested while driving, will produce a sample that clearly indicates — falsely — the presence of alcohol in his blood.

To avoid or at least minimize this problem of urine accumulation, it is necessary to have the subject void his bladder prior to producing a sample. After a short wait, perhaps 15 or 20 minutes, he should then be able to produce additional urine for analysis.

Certainly, urinalysis is a completely undependable procedure where voiding has not taken place 15 or 20 minutes before the sample is obtained. In many jurisdictions today, this voiding is a legal prerequisite. (See, e.g., *State v. Donaldson,* 425 N.W.2d 531 (Neb. 1990), reversing a conviction where the sample was taken 33 minutes after voiding.) Where it is not, however, counsel should move to suppress the results of urinalysis where the defendant was not required to void his bladder and wait before giving a sample. The reason for this is set forth by the American Medical Association in its publication entitled Alcohol and the Impaired Driver: A Manual on the Aspects of Chemical Tests for Medicolegal Intoxication (1968: American Medical Association, 535 North Dearborn Street, Chicago, Illinois 60610):

> If a person starts drinking with the bladder full of urine, or has not voided for some hours, while the blood level of alcohol is decreasing, the level in the bladder may change more slowly than that of the blood as the latter rises or falls. This discrepancy can be overcome by having the subject empty his bladder and by taking the sample of urine after 20 minutes. [Id. at 19.]

In fact, obtaining only *one* sample of urine after a voiding is considerably less accurate than obtaining two samples isolated in time after a voiding. Although this is rarely done by law enforcement agencies, counsel should at least bring out for the jury the fact that the American Medical Association, in the same publication, states (at p.71) that collection of "duplicate samples with a time lapse of at least 20 minutes and complete voiding of the bladder so that no residual urine is retained is recommended."

The AMA's recommendation has been endorsed by criminalists employed by the largest state prosecuting agency in the country. In an article entitled Blood Alcohol Concentration Determined from Urine Samples as a Practical Equivalent or Alternative to Blood and Breath Alcohol Tests, 30 Journal of Forensic Sciences 194 (1984), Biasotti and Valentine, two criminalists with the Bureau of Forensic Sciences, California Department of Justice, concluded after considerable research and experimentation that "[a] second urine 'sample' taken at least 20 minutes to one hour after first voiding the bladder should be used to determine an equivalent % BAC." These criminalists went further, however:

> To validate further the accuracy of a BAC determined from the urine sample taken after first voiding the bladder, and to determine if the BAC has increased or decreased during the time between voiding and the second urine "sample," at least a 30-ml portion of the "void" urine sample should be collected, analyzed, and reported together with the second urine "sample" results. [Id. at 206.]

Even where the proper voiding procedures were followed, urinalysis is at best a relatively undependable method. Any honest prosecution expert witness, if pressed, will have to admit that of the three analytic procedures, urinalysis is generally considered third in reliable accuracy. If he refuses to, his attention — and that of the jury — should be directed to a booklet entitled Highway Safety Program Manual No. 8. Published by the National Highway Traffic and Safety Administration of the U.S. Department of Transportation, the manual sets forth proposed regulations for the development and operation of alcohol testing programs. This is in accordance with Chapter 4 of Title 23 of the U.S. Code, known as the Highway Safety Act of 1966, wherein uniform highway safety standards are to be established. The following recommendations from that manual will be of interest to the jury:

> Because of various problems in the interpretation of the results of analysis of urine for alcohol which cannot be readily overcome in law enforcement practice, urine analysis to determine equivalent alcohol concentration in blood is discouraged, except under strictly controlled conditions (e.g., hospitalized subject), or for the limited purpose of demonstrating recent ingestion of alcohol. Chemical tests of blood or breath are preferred.

The procedures used to analyze a subject's urine are basically the same as those used to analyze his blood: gas chromatography, enzymatic reaction, and the dichromate or Kazelka-Hines method. As discussed in §7.0, there are a number of potential problems with each of these procedures; the dichromate method is nonspecific for alcohol, for example, and gas chromatography is subject to radio frequency interference.

As with all methods of blood-alcohol analysis, counsel should consider first the training and qualifications of the individual obtaining the sample urine. In many jurisdictions, this person, whether a police officer or a laboratory technician, must have received specific instruction in the manner of collecting, preserving, storing, and transporting a urine sample. If the individual has not received the requisite training, the test results may be inadmissible. At the very least, the lack of training should be brought out for the jury's benefit to cast doubt on the accuracy of the test results.

The laboratory, too, usually must be properly licensed and/or possess a current certificate of inspection for the test results to be admissible. And the technician who conducted the analysis must have received the required licensing from the appropriate agency. Counsel should always bear in mind the ever-present possibility of gaps in the chain of custody of the urine sample. The prosecution has the burden of establishing the possession and control of the sample from the time it was taken to the time it was analyzed.

As with blood analysis, it is necessary to add some type of preservative to the urine specimen to prevent decomposition. If the specimen has been permitted to sit for a few days before it is analyzed, it will begin to decompose due to bacterial action. And decomposition can have an interesting side effect: the production of alcohol in the specimen from the decaying process. Refrigeration will serve only to slow down this decomposition, not to stop it altogether. To prevent this natural decay, a preservative such as sodium fluoride or mercuric chloride must be added to the urine sample.

Failure to add a preservative — and it is not at all uncommon — should provide counsel with sufficient material at least to discredit the test results and possibly to prevent their admission into evidence. Even if a preservative has been added to the sample, there is no guarantee that bacterial action will not have taken place. There are many different types of bacteria that can be found naturally in urine; if they are of the aerobic variety, they will produce reducing substances in the urine that can raise the alcohol level in the urine before the preservative can be added.

Where there has been a urine void, counsel should not overlook the discovery possibilities. Many law enforcement agencies require the suspect to place a sample from the void into a vial. This sample is then collected and stored along with the second test sample. A primary purpose of this practice is to prove that there was, in fact, a prior void. If such a void sample exists, it should be included in any discovery request and, along with the test sample, analyzed by an independent laboratory. Any significant variation in the two analytical results can prove extremely valuable as defense evidence:

1. A significant disparity between the two samples indicates unreliability of the analyses.
2. A lower void reading indicates a rising BAC.
3. A higher void reading indicates a lower true BAC (since the test sample theoretically consists of about 20cc of urine freshly secreted into the bladder mixed with 20cc of stale urine remaining after a void, the test result reflects a contaminated average of the two: a void sample of .12 percent and a test sample of .10 percent, for example, means that the BAC of an uncontaminated test sample would have been about .08 percent).

§7.1.1 The Incomplete Void

As discussed earlier (§7.1), any hope for accuracy in urinalysis depends entirely on obtaining a representative sample of the subject's urine. And this depends upon the subject emptying his bladder before a specimen is obtained. And, in fact, evidence of a void 20 minutes before obtaining the sample is a foundational requirement for the introduction into evidence of the resulting urinalysis. Absent a void, the sample represents nothing more than an average of what was in the person's system over the course of many earlier hours.

To illustrate: If an individual drinks a pint of bourbon in the evening, then goes to sleep, he will probably awaken the next morning with a blood-alcohol concentration of .00 percent. Yet his bladder will still contain all of the eliminated alcohol. In other words, a blood test will show a true BAC of .00 percent; a urinalysis, however, will indicate a false BAC of perhaps .15 percent or more.

Thus the bladder must be emptied and a sample taken of the urine being freshly secreted into the bladder. Roughly speaking, approximately 1cc of urine is secreted into the bladder per minute; in 20 minutes, roughly 20cc of new urine will be dripped into the bladder.

The problem with the voiding principle is that it is virtually *impossible* to empty one's bladder completely. Most experts will admit that there is usually about 10cc of urine left in the bladder after a supposedly "complete" void.

The mathematics are fairly simple. If about 20cc of new urine are added to about 10cc of old urine, the resulting mixture — and the resulting urine specimen — will consist of roughly ⅓ old urine. Therefore, the laboratory will be analyzing a sample which is heavily contaminated by alcohol that had been eliminated from the subject's blood before the void — probably many hours before.

To illustrate again: Assume an individual was drinking early in the day, reaching a BAC of .15 percent, then stopped drinking. A few hours later when he gets into his car his BAC has dropped to .06 percent — and he is stopped and arrested for drunk driving. He voids his bladder as requested by the officer; however, 10cc of the urine remains. Twenty minutes later he produces a test sample. The sample will probably consist of roughly ⅓ old urine and ⅔ new urine. Rather than a .06 percent BAC, then, the laboratory may determine the BAC to be in the area of .09 percent or more.

This scenario is often exacerbated in the case of a suspect who has been told by the officer that if he cannot produce a sample 20 minutes after the void, this inability will be considered a refusal — and grounds for suspension of his license. The worried suspect purposely does not void entirely, saving enough urine in his bladder to ensure that he will be able to produce a sample 20 minutes later. Result: The ensuing sample will have the 10cc of urine usually left as well as the additional urine that the suspect held back — and the BAC will be even more distorted by old urine.

§7.1.2 The Urine-to-Blood Ratio

A basic problem inherent in urinalysis is the underlying presumption that the concentration of alcohol in the urine at the time of secretion is 1.33 times greater than the concentration in the blood. As has been seen earlier, the presumed blood to alveolar air ratio of 1:2100 used in breath analysis actually varies anywhere from 1:1100 to 1:3000, according to the individual. Similarly, the presumed 1.33:1 ratio used in urinalysis is only a statistical average; any given individual's ratio can vary from as little as 0.8:1 to as much as 2.0:1 or even more. Translated into test results, an individual with a blood-urine ratio of 2.0:1 who has, for example, a true blood-alcohol level of .06 percent will have his urine sample analyzed as indicating a blood-alcohol level of .10 percent — that is, a presumably sober individual will be "scientifically proven" to be under the influence of alcohol. This ratio variance, it should be noted, occurs among normal, healthy people; illness or other physiological abnormalities can alter the presumed ratio even further.

The most respected expert in the field of blood-alcohol analysis has questioned urinalysis as a method for determining BAC because of this variability in ratios. Dr. Kurt Dubowski of the University of Oklahoma has written:

> There is massive documentation that the blood alcohol concentration cannot be established sufficiently reliably for forensic purposes from the alcohol concentration in a pooled bladder urine specimen because of the extensive variability of the blood:urine ratio of alcohol. [Dubowski, Absorption, Distribution and Elimination of Alcohol: Highway and Safety Aspects, Journal of Studies on Alcohol (July, 1985, supplement no. 10).]

British scientists at the Royal Air Force Hospital's Department of Pathology conducted a series of experiments to determine the accuracy of urinalysis in determining blood-alcohol levels and, specifically, the validity of the presumed conversion factor of 1.3 to 1. In an article entitled Further Observations on the Validity of Urine Alcohol Levels in Road Traffic Offenses, 17(4) Medical Science and the Law 269 (1977), scientists obtained both blood and urine samples from a number of men and women after the subjects consumed varying amounts of alcohol. In concluding that "urine alcohol estimation is unreliable," the scientists commented that "it is disturbing . . . to find that in this study the 1.33 conversion factor applied to only 2 of 59 cases."

In another article, Dr. James C. Garriott reviewed the problems involved in urinalysis. See J. C. Garriott, Forensic Aspects of Ethyl Alcohol, 3(2) Clinics in Laboratory Medicine 385–396 (June 1983). In a survey of the literature as it relates to urine testing, the author makes several interesting observations:

> Many studies have been performed to attempt to correlate urine alcohol with blood alcohol. . . . During the drinking period (pre-absorption period) the urine:blood ratio is less than 1.0, that is, the urine has a lower concentration of alcohol than the blood. In the post-absorption period, the urine concentration is higher. As the urine is formed, it has an alcohol concentration that is 1.33 times that of blood. Of course, the newly formed urine is diluted with the urine that resided in the bladder, so this ratio applies exactly only if all the urine is freshly formed. Then, as the blood concentrating declines due to metabolism, the urine concentration remains elevated, until the bladder empties and fresh urine is formed, again in the 1.33 ratio to blood. Studies have shown that 98 per cent of subjects tested by analyzing both blood and urine taken at the same time had a ratio of less than 1.45:1. Two cases had urinary ratios of 1.50 and 1.49:1 respectively.
>
> Therefore, it is apparent that the urine cannot be used reliably to extrapolate alcohol concentrations to corresponding blood values. [Footnotes omitted.]

The balance of the article is worth reading to obtain a general overview of the forensic aspects of ethyl alcohol.

In a 1984 study involving over 1,000 cases where blood and urine analysis were performed concurrently, scientists determined that the average urine- to blood-alcohol ratio was 1.57:1, with individual ratios ranging all the way from 0.7 to 21.0:1. This extremely wide range translates into quite large errors if the theoretical average of 1.3:1 is employed — as it uniformly is, of course.

The study, entitled The Unreliability of Using a Urine Ethanol Concentration to Predict a Blood Ethanol Concentration, 25

Forensic Science International 227 (1984), and coauthored by Charles L. Winek, Kathy L. Murphy, and Tracey A. Winek, used gas liquid chromatographic analysis of both blood and urine samples taken from the same individuals.

> . . . For the 714 cases where the BAC was greater than 0.10%, the mean urine to blood ratio was 1.18 with a range of 0.07–3.40. . . .
>
> The wide range . . . indicates the high probability of a large error being introduced into the calculation of a blood ethanol value from a urine ethanol concentration when using an average value from the ratio of urine to blood ethanol concentration.

Even Biasatti and Valentine, the two California state criminalists mentioned earlier, concluded in their article that "it should be conceded that a reasonable potential variation up to 1.5:1 could apply in some cases" (30 Journal of Forensic Sciences at 206). And the American Medical Association in their publication Alcohol and the Impaired Driver: A Manual on the Medico-legal Aspects of Chemical Tests for Intoxication, cited earlier, has found that "[t]he figures of the urine:blood-alcohol ratio range from 1.12 to 1.51, with an average alcohol ratio of 1.35" (Id. at 71).

For yet another scientific study questioning the validity of urinalysis in drunk driving cases, see Jones, Ethanol Distribution Ratios Between Urine and Capillary Blood in Controlled Experiments and in Apprehended Drinking Drivers, 37(1) Journal of Forensic Sciences 21 (1992). In that article Dr. Jones recommended that urine-alcohol concentration (UAC) not be translated with the 1.33-to-1 ratio into blood-alcohol concentration (BAC) because of "large inter-subject and intra-subject variations." The conversion cannot accurately be made when, among other things, "the previous drinking pattern, the frequency of urination, and the functioning of the kidneys and bladder are unknown." Dr. Jones noted further that actual UAC/BAC ratios observed were higher than ratios commonly set by statute — with the result that BACs based on urinalysis will be erroneously high.

§7.1.3 *Candida Albicans*

Even where preservatives have been added to the urine sample and in the proper amounts, the sample can be contaminated by a microbe commonly found in urine. This organism, called *Candida albicans,* has two interesting characteristics. First, its presence causes degeneration of the sample and a resultant increase in the level of alcohol. Second, *Candida albicans* is *immune* to sodium fluoride, the preservative most commonly used to kill such organisms. Thus alcohol can be created in the urine where none or very little existed before, even in the presence of preservatives.

The presence of "immaculately conceived" ethyl alcohol in the bladder has been confirmed by two physicians at Union Memorial Hospital in Baltimore. J. H. Mullholland and F. J. Townsend, Bladder Beer — A New Clinical Observation, 95 Transactions of the American Clinical Climatological Association 34 (1983). The physicians reported the odor of beer in three of their patients in an isolated hospital setting where there was no access to alcoholic beverages. When urine samples were taken and analyzed by gas chromatography, all three reflected ethyl alcohol content. Two of these were quantitatively tested, with results of .043 percent and .121 percent.

> The presence of alcohol in human specimens containing glucose and yeast should come as no surprise. Several have made this observation. Under normal circumstances trace amounts of alcohol may be found in the blood; the alcohol is then channeled into an energy pathway by hepatic alcohol dehydrogenase. . . . [T]he Japanese report the "auto-brewery syndrome" in which they have seen middle aged patients with bowel abnormalities, most often after surgery, who have yeast overgrowth, usually *Candida,* in the G.I. tract and who ferment ingested carbohydrates, producing enough alcohol to result in drunkenness.

In other words, the common presence of *Candida albicans* together with glucose will result in the production of ethyl alcohol — independently of any consumption of liquor. And as has been mentioned, *Candida* is apparently a tough brand of yeast — it resists the effects of the preservative most commonly added to urine samples, sodium fluoride, thus permitting continued autogeneration of ethyl alcohol in the sample itself.

Another possible problem can occur if the subject has certain kinds of chemicals containing reducing agents on his hands when he fills the sample jar or vial. These agents can be present in any of hundreds of compounds such as turpentine or paint.

As the subject handles the jar or vial, these chemicals can be transferred from his hands to the container and can subsequently cause a reduction of the potassium dichromate, thus giving an inaccurately high blood-alcohol reading. At the least, the police officer should have instructed the subject to thoroughly wash his hands with soap and water before producing a urine sample.

For further studies concerning the effects of *Candida albicans* and urinalysis, see: Blume & Lakatua, The Effect of Microbial Contamination, 60 American Journal of Clinical Pathology 700 (1973); Alexander, et al., Urinary Ethanol and Diabetes Mellitus, 5 Diabetic Medicine 463 (1983); Hayden, et al., The Stability of Alcohol Content in Samples of Blood and Urine, 146 Irish Journal of Medical Science 48 (1977); Bull & Lichtenwalner, Ethanol Levels in Infected Urine, 301 New England Journal of Medicine 614 (1979), Alexander, et al., Urinary Ethanol Levels and Diabetics, 1 Lancet 789 (1981); Neuteboom & Zweipfenning, The Stability of Alcohol Concentrations in Urine Specimens, 13 Journal of Analytical Toxicology 141 (1989).

Checklist 12 Urinalysis

- ☐ Is urinalysis an approved method of blood-alcohol analysis?
- ☐ Was a more accurate method available?
- ☐ Were duplicate samples obtained?
- ☐ Was the laboratory conducting the analysis properly licensed?
- ☐ Was the laboratory technician who analyzed the sample properly licensed?
- ☐ Was the equipment accurately calibrated?
- ☐ Was the sample one of a larger batch of samples analyzed en masse?
- ☐ How long after the arrest was the sample obtained?
- ☐ Was the client required to void his bladder 20 minutes before producing a sample?
- ☐ Did he void incompletely on purpose?
- ☐ Is it possible to void completely? Did old urine involuntarily left after a "complete" void contaminate the new urine?
- ☐ Did the urinalysis assume a urine:blood ratio of 1.33:1?
- ☐ What evidence exists of the client's actual ratio?
- ☐ What range of possible BACs would be obtained by applying the range of possible urine:blood ratios?

III

PRE-TRIAL

It is likewise to be observed that this society [of lawyers] hath a peculiar chant and jargon of their own, that no other mortal can understand, and wherein all their laws are written, which they take special care to multiply; whereby they have wholly confounded the very essence of truth and falsehood.

JONATHAN SWIFT,
GULLIVER'S TRAVELS

8

ANALYSIS AND ARRAIGNMENT

§8.0 Initial Client Contact

> The consequences of the infinitude of law is its uncertainty. Law was made that a plain man might know what he had to expect, and yet the most skillful practitioners differ about the event of my suit.
>
> WILLIAM GODWIN

If the initial meeting between counsel and his client takes place in jail, the first obligation will be to obtain the client's release as soon as possible. This may be accomplished by posting the bail in the form of cash (presumably from a friend or relative) or, if the jurisdiction permits, by pledging property. If cash or property is not readily available, a bail bondsman should be summoned; he will, of course, charge a fee for his services, often 10 percent of the bond.

If possible, counsel should attempt to speak with the desk sergeant, jailor, or watch commander and attempt to obtain the client's release on a written promise to appear without the necessity of bail. Many states call this an "own recognizance" release. Most police agencies will want the arrestee to "dry out" for three or four hours before his release, thus ensuring that he will not immediately drive under the influence again; however, a reasonable desk sergeant may be talked into releasing the client into the custody of his attorney with a promise to drive the client home.

Of course, counsel should not overlook the possibility of obtaining evidence if the contact is made within one or two hours of the arrest. For a discussion of this subject, see §10.1.

In most cases, though, the initial contact between client and counsel will take place in the law offices. And it is here that preparation for defense of the drunk driving charge begins with the gathering of information, the education of the client, and the initial preparation of the case. During this process, counsel should bear in mind one important fact concerning his client: The client is probably upset, worried, and confused. He may be an upstanding member of the community who has never been in trouble with the law before. Yet he has just been through the traumatic experience of being stopped by police in public, forced to perform degrading tests, handcuffed and taken to the police station, interrogated, tested on a breath analysis machine, fingerprinted, photographed, booked, and thrown in jail with hardened criminals. Now he is facing criminal prosecution and possibly more jail time. Counsel should exercise a certain amount of tact and compassion in dealing with his new client.

§8.0.1 The Interview

It is important to obtain a considerable amount of information relating both to the client's personal background and to the circumstances of the charge from the client during the initial interview. This process will, incidentally, probably have the beneficial side effect of calming the client and instilling confidence in his attorney.

Of course, the obvious personal information must be recorded: full name, address, phone number, marital status, place of business, etc. In addition, the client's educational and military background, as well as his professional and civic involvements, should be known. It is important for the attorney to know as much as he can about who his client is. This information may be needed, for example, to explain to the prosecutor during plea bargaining why your client should be treated differently from other defendants. It certainly will become relevant at the time of sentencing before a judge.

Counsel should also obtain the client's driver's license number and should check to make sure the license is current and not restricted. A social security number also will be required to obtain criminal and motor vehicle department records. Having the driver's license number and social security number will help to ensure that the client is not mistakenly charged with warrants out on another individual of the same name. If the client has ever used any other names, such as a maiden name in the case of a married female client, counsel should know these names.

Any prior criminal record should be noted. If the client appears reluctant to discuss this, he should be advised that the prosecutor will have the information and that counsel's mistakenly misrepresenting the client's record will only prove harmful. As a double check, counsel should order a copy of his new client's record, if one exists. This normally can be done by forwarding a written request together with the client's waiver and a nominal fee to the appropriate state law enforcement records organization.

Counsel also should take down the client's driving record and have a transcript of his driving history ordered from the motor vehicle department. As with the criminal record transcript, these serve a dual purpose: They ensure that the client is being truthful, thereby avoiding any embarrassing misrepresentations to the prosecutor or the court, and they guarantee that the prosecutor and the court will not be reviewing the case based on erroneous records. If the client has any previous convictions for drunk driving, counsel should record the details. Counsel especially must obtain information as to the legal procedures if a plea was taken. This will become relevant later in attacking the constitutionality of the prior conviction or convictions.

Counsel also should consult the statutes of his jurisdiction for the provisions relating to prior convictions, if relevant. The attorney should determine what the effect of a prior conviction will be on a conviction in the present case: Is there a mandatory jail sentence? Are there any sentence enhancements that apply? Will the license be suspended or revoked? Are there special educational/rehabilitational "diversion" programs available for repeat offenders that would obviate jail sentences and/or license suspensions?

It is a good idea for counsel to review the statutes concerning license suspensions. Is there an "administrative per se" suspension for an excessive blood-alcohol concentration? If the client refused to take a blood-alcohol test, is there an automatic license suspension — regardless of guilt — for his refusal? And any "point count" system should be thoroughly understood. Would a conviction on the drunk driving charge, when combined with two or three previous traffic offenses, result in a suspension of the client's license?

The client's medical history, particularly any physical handicaps or disabilities and any current illnesses, should also be covered. Did the client have a touch of influenza that would affect his balance and cause a flushed face and bloodshot eyes? Does he have a trick knee that made performance of the field sobriety tests awkward? Is the defendant plagued by an internal problem, such as diabetes, that might affect the chemical analysis of his blood-alcohol level? Was he on any drugs or medication?

Next, the client should be questioned in detail about the circumstances of his drinking, the driving, the arrest, and the chemical testing. Counsel should go over particularly the three or four hours before the arrest, recording the details so that counsel knows exactly what the defendant drank. What brands of liquor, in what amounts and with what mixers, at what intervals, and over what period of time did the defendant drink? Any foods eaten during that period should also be noted. The names, addresses, and phone numbers of any witnesses to the drinking also should be taken down. Particularly important are the identities of any witnesses who the client feels would be willing to testify that he had consumed only a total of one or two drinks or that, when he was last seen, the client did not appear to be under the influence.

The circumstances of the client's driving and his being stopped should then be examined. Were there any mechanical defects in the car's steering or suspension that would cause the car to behave erratically? Was the client merely exhausted and sleepy at the wheel? Was he watching the police car in the rearview mirror more than the road? Most important, were there any potential witnesses in the car who could testify to his condition and to the circumstances of the subsequent field sobriety test and arrest?

Counsel should question the client in great detail about the events following his being stopped. Did he have his driver's license and car registration with him? Did he fumble with his wallet in getting the driver's license out for the officer? Did the officer say why he was being stopped? Did the client stumble in stepping out of the car? Was he wearing high-heeled boots or shoes? Were his eyes bloodshot because of fatigue?

Presumably, the officer will ask some initial questions, such as whether the client had been drinking, how much, when, and where. To test orientation, he may also ask the client where he is and what time it is. It is critical that counsel know exactly what was said by his client; the police report will carry only a few — and these the most damning — of the client's statements.

The conduct and performance on the field sobriety tests must then be understood. How does the client think he did on the walk-the-line test (see §11.5.2)? Was the officer writing anything down as the test was administered, or was he merely committing the results to memory? Did the client feel he performed the finger-to-nose test satisfactorily? How about the position-of-attention balance test? Was his balance affected by a cold? Circumstances surrounding the giving of the test should also be noted: Was the test executed on a clean, level surface or on a sloping, gravel-strewn shoulder of the road? Did it take place while cars passed at high speed within a few feet? Was it done at night, with only a flashlight and rapidly passing headlights to assist the client? Was a nystagmus test given (see §4.3)?

The client then should be questioned concerning the events that took place after the arrest. Was the car impounded, released to a friend, or left where it stood? Was the client interrogated further? Was he advised of his constitutional *Miranda* rights? If so, when, where, and by whom? Counsel should not ignore the circumstances of the defendant's ride to the police station. On the way, did the police officer make any comments about the case?

Although the administration of a breath analysis test will be unfamiliar to the client and will have taken place under emotionally trying conditions, it should be covered. He should be asked who administered the test, if it was not the same officer who arrested him. Where was it conducted? The length of time that had passed from the time he was stopped to the time of testing should be known, as well as whether the client recalls seeing any other arrestees using the machine before him. If he had taken any cough syrups, breath sprays, mouthwash, or liqueurs within an hour of breathing into the machine, this should be known. If he had belched or regurgitated within the previous half-hour, this should also be recorded. If a urine sample was taken instead of a breath sample, was he asked to void his bladder first and then wait fifteen minutes before giving a sample? If a blood specimen was taken, did the sterilizing solution used on his skin smell like alcohol?

Finally, the attorney should not overlook the possibility of finding witnesses from the client's jail cell. If the client made friends with another arrestee in the cell, that person's name and location should be obtained for possible future use as a witness to prove the client's sobriety a few minutes after taking the chemical test.

The identity of the arresting agency should be known, as well as the bail status of the client. The date, time, and place of the arraignment should also be clearly understood.

Counsel may find Forms 9 and 10 useful in the interview of a drunk driving client. The second is a more compact version. The author is grateful to Don Nichols and Jim Kastner of Minneapolis, Minnesota, for permission to use these forms.

§8.0.2 Educating the Client

Counsel has an obligation to discuss with the client every important aspect of the case: the nature of the offense, the possible defenses, the legal procedures that will be involved, possible punishment, and the fee arrangement.

Initially counsel should explain to the client the exact nature of drunk driving. This entails going over the elements of the offense (see §§1.1, 1.2, and 1.3) and dispelling the client's misconceptions about the relationship of "drunk driving" to "driving under the influence." Counsel should make the client aware of the state's laws concerning burden of proof or presumptions arising from the blood-alcohol test, as well as of the meaning of the client's test results. Where applicable, the per se laws should be discussed. Explaining that he, of course, has not yet reviewed the police reports or any other prosecution evidence, counsel should try to go over the basic appearance of the case against his client. At the same time, counsel should explain possible defenses, particularly those that arise in light of the information initially supplied by the client. Witnesses must be located who saw the client just before the arrest, and perhaps a chemical expert should be

DWI INTAKE SHEET

NAME ______________ HOME PHONE ______________ SEX (M) __ (F) __

ADDRESS ______________ DOB ______________

DRIVER'S LICENSE NO. AND STATE ______________

PLACE OF EMPLOYMENT ______________

OFFICE PHONE ______________ LENGTH OF EMPLOYMENT ______________

SCHOOLING ______________

MAKE OF VEHICLE, YEAR AND OWNER ______________

VEHICLE LICENSE NO. ______________

PRIOR RECORD: OFFENSE(S) ______________
DATE(S) ______________

OFFENSE

Date ______________ Time ______________ Place (include county where incident occurred) ______________

Officer Making Arrest ______________

Governmental Agency ______________ Charges ______________

Describe briefly the facts leading up to your arrest, that is, why do you feel that you were stopped?

____

____

____

____

____

a. What did you say to the police officers and what did they say to you? What questions did the officers ask you? It is important that you answer this in detail. ______________

____

____

____

Form 9
Client Interview Questionaire

b. Were Miranda warnings (i.e., you have the right to remain silent, anything you say can and will be used against you . . .) given to you, and if so, when? What had you told the police prior to the warnings? After the warnings? ______________________________

____

____

____

If there was another vehicle involved in your arrest, what conversation did you have with the driver or passenger of the second or third vehicle? ______________________________

____

____

____

Were there any passengers in your vehicle when you were stopped? Before you were stopped? (Give all details) ______________________________

____

____

Did the officer making the arrest observe your behavior? ______________________________

____

Any statements made by you to others, when given and to whom? ______________________________

____

____

____

Were you involved in an accident? If so, give details. ______________________________

____

____

Was your vehicle searched? __________ Were you searched? ______________

State any property taken from your vehicle ______________________________

____

____

____

Form 9
(continued)

TESTS

Blood ________ Breath ____________ Urine __________

Given by ________________ At ________________________

Time _____ Which tests were offered to you? ________________

Result of tests ________________________________

What sobriety tests were given (such as touch your nose, walk a line, pick up coins or any other dexterity tests)? ____________________________

____

____

Did you consider yourself to be under the influence of an alcoholic beverage at the time of your arrest? ________________________

Did the drinks you had affect your driving? ________________

PHYSICAL CONDITION AT THE TIME OF ARREST

Alcohol and food consumed prior to arrest:

A. Last alcohol ________________________ Time __________

Quantity ________________________ Type __________

Next alcohol ________________________ Time __________
(If none, put none)

Quantity ________________________ Type __________

Next alcohol ________________________ Time __________

Quantity ________________________ Type __________

Next alcohol ________________________ Time __________

Quantity ________________________ Type __________

Next alcohol ________________________ Time __________

Quantity ________________________ Type __________

B. Last food ________________________ Time __________

Quantity ________________________ Type __________

Next food ________________________ Time __________

Quantity ________________________ Type __________

Next food ________________________ Time __________

Quantity ________________________ Type __________

Form 9
(continued)

What did you have to eat during the 12-hour period prior to your arrest?

____

____

____

When did you start drinking and in whose company were you at that time?

____

____

____

Describe the drinks you had prior to your arrest (what were you drinking, and the size of the drinks, etc.) ______________________

____

____

Name, address and telephone number of all persons with you during the time you were drinking ______________________

____

____

Would these persons be willing to testify that you were not under the influence of alcohol? Yes __________ No __________

MEDICAL

Were you under the care of a doctor at the time of your arrest? __________

Had you seen a dentist within the 24-hour period prior to your arrest?

____

Do you have any physical disability which would cause you to limp or have imperfect balance, or did you have any injuries at the time of the arrest that would cause you to look intoxicated? ______________________

____

Were you taking any medicine or drugs at that time such as cold pills, aspirin, antihistamines, tranquilizers, weight control pills, etc.? __________

____

Form 9
(continued)

Do you have a speech impairment caused by a medical problem? ______________

Do you wear false teeth? ____

Do you have diabetes? ____

Do you have heart disease? ____

Were you ill (high fever) at the time of offense? _____________________

Do you have any other medical problem that would influence your physical condition at the time of your arrest? _____________________________________

____

____

Was your stomach upset on the night in question? ______________________

Was it possible your stomach could have been upset, causing you to belch?

____

How were you dressed at the time of the alleged offense? _________________

____

a. What were the colors of your clothes? ________________________

____

b. What type of footwear were you wearing? ______________________

c. Were your clothes soiled or clean? ___________________________

d. Did you or do you wear glasses? If so, what is your corrective reading? ____

How many hours had you worked prior to the arrest? _____________________

CONDITION OF CAR

Steering mechanism: last date of repair or examination of vehicle by auto repair shop ____

Were there any mechanical defects in your car? _________________________

____

Weather and road conditions:

blacktop road __________ dirt road __________ pavement __________

dark __________ light __________ foggy __________ rainy __________

Form 9
(continued)

sleet ___________ hail __________ snow ___________ drizzle ___________

slippery ___________ normal __________ wet ___________ dry ___________

IMPLIED CONSENT

Were you advised of your right to take another test? ______________________

Were you advised of your right to have your physician take an additional blood test? ______________________

Were you advised you had the right to refuse the test? ______________________

Were you advised that you had a right to contact any attorney before deciding whether or not to take a test? ______________________

If you did not know of an attorney to contact, were you provided with access to a telephone book? ______________________

Were you provided with a private room to call your attorney? ______________________

____

Form 9
(continued)

DRINKING/DRIVER INTERVIEW CHECKLIST

Background
Date of Arrest: ______ Time: ______ Place of Arrest: ______
What did you say to the police? ______ What did they say to you? ______
Were Miranda Warnings given to you? ______ When? ______ Where? ______
What had you said prior to the Miranda Warnings? ______
Were there any passengers in your vehicle? ______ Please Identify: ______
Did you make any statements to others? ______ When and to whom? ______
Were you involved in an accident? ______ If so, give details. ______
Was your vehicle searched? ______ Were you searched? ______
Describe any property taken from you or your vehicle: ______

Testing
Tests Offered: Blood ______ Breath ______ Urine ______ Other ______
Tests Given: Blood ______ Breath ______ Urine ______ Other ______
Given by: ______ When Administered? ______ Time ______ Result ______
What field sobriety tests were given? ______ How did you do? ______
Did you consider yourself to be under the influence? ______
Describe how alcohol affected your driving? ______
When did you start drinking? ______ In whose company? ______
Describe each drink you had prior to your arrest: ______
What is your weight and body size? ______
Name, address, and phone number for all persons with whom you drank: ______
Would these persons be willing to testify? Yes ______ No ______
Did you consume any alcohol after your arrest? ______ What and when? ______

Medical History
Are you under the care of a doctor? ______ Please identify: ______
Had you seen a dentist within 24 hours of your arrest? ______ Identify ______
Do you have any physical disability? ______
Do you have any injuries that would cause you to look intoxicated? ______
Were you taking any medicine or drugs such as cold pills, antihistamines, tranquilizers, weight control pills, aspirin, etc.? ______
Do you wear false teeth? ______ Have diabetes? ______ Have heart disease? ______
Was your stomach upset at the time of arrest? ______
Do you wear glasses? ______ Contact lenses? ______ Corrective reading: ______
How many hours had you worked prior to the arrest? ______

Condition of Car and Roadway
Steering mechanism—last date of repair or examination: ______
Describe any mechanical defects in your car: ______
Weather and Road Conditions:
Blacktop ______ Dirt Road ______ Other ______
Dark ______ Light ______ Foggy ______ Rainy ______
Sleet ______ Hail ______ Snow ______ Drizzle ______
Slippery ______ Normal ______ Wet ______ Dry ______

Implied Consent (States vary as to rights given a defendant under Implied Consent Laws and a careful analysis of each state's laws should be incorporated into a practitioner's intake form.)
Were you advised that you could take another test? ______
Were you advised that you could contact an attorney? ______
Were you provided with a private room to call your attorney? ______
Name of attorney contacted: ______
Were you told that you were under arrest? ______

Form 10
Client Interview Form — Condensed Version

hired at the client's expense to counter the testimony of the prosecutor's chemist, criminologist, or other expert.

Invariably the question will be asked of counsel: What are my chances? Somehow, hearing a solid percentage figure makes the terrifying unknown more acceptable. Counsel should advise the client that further information must be obtained before an accurate assessment of the case can be made. Of course, if it is the relatively unusual case where certain known facts are almost dispositive — such as where no one actually saw the client driving — the attorney should explain this. If, on the other hand, the client has no witnesses, the arrest stemmed from a serious traffic accident that was his fault, empty bottles of liquor were found in his car, he threw up during the sobriety test, the chemical test result was sky-high, and he readily confessed to polishing off a bottle and a half of bourbon. . . . Well, he should certainly not be misled into thinking there is a substantial chance of an acquittal.

The attorney must also advise the client about the possible consequences of a conviction. The attorney should inform the client about the minimum and maximum penalties assigned by law for the charged offense — the possible jail sentences, fines, and probationary conditions. The client should also be made aware of the possible actions that could be taken against his driver's license, and for what reasons. The possibilities of an administrative hearing or appeal on the issue of license suspension or revocation should be covered. Additionally, the client should be told about the possibilities of educational or diversion programs as alternatives to normal sentencing, if they exist. Finally, counsel should probably let his client know that his insurance rates will rise with a drunk driving conviction — and possibly even with an acquittal.

The legal procedures that the client is about to embark on must also be gone over in detail. Exactly what an arraignment is, what a pre-trial hearing or conference consists of, how a trial date is set, the nature of a request for continuance — all of this should be explained. It is reassuring to the client to have a "road map" to the dark and mysterious legal ceremonies he is about to face. More important, however, it is critical that he know exactly when and where he is to make his court dates, so that ignorance or confusion does not result in a warrant being issued for his arrest for nonappearance.

Last, the fee arrangement must be clearly articulated. If the attorney charges an initial retainer that is to be applied against an hourly charge, he must explain to the client that the retainer must be paid before the arraignment. Counsel also should go over his hourly rate. If there is a per diem charge for trial work, counsel should also discuss that. And if the attorney's fees do not cover such costs as the hiring of an investigator or a chemical analyst, this should be brought to the client's attention. A clear and frank discussion of the financial aspects of the case at the outset will help prevent unpleasant disagreements later.

§8.0.3 The Retainer Agreement

In drafting a retainer agreement, counsel may wish to consider the model form beginning on page 584. The author is grateful to Douglas Cowan of Bellevue, Washington, for his permission to reproduce the agreement.

§8.1 Preliminary Investigation

> I'm trusting in the Lord and a good lawyer.
>
> Oliver North

There are a number of steps that counsel should take soon after the initial interview with the client.

As has already been pointed out, the client's criminal "rap sheet" and his driving record should be ordered from the appropriate agencies. Counsel should also obtain the client's medical records if they are relevant, and, if necessary, make an appointment to discuss the matter with the client's physician.

The next step is to contact the police agency or prosecutor's office and obtain copies, if they are completed and available, of any arrest reports, supplemental police reports, accident reports, or chemical analysis forms. In most cases, the prosecutor will relinquish these without requiring a discovery order.

Counsel should be sure to inquire of the police or prosecutor whether there are any tape recordings of his client, such as those

RETAINER & FEE AGREEMENT

The undersigned does hereby retain DOUGLAS L. COWAN, Inc., P.S., for representation on the following charge or charges:

____

occurring on or about the _____ day of ________, 199____, in ________ County, Washington.

The undersigned agrees to pay a retainer in the amount of $______, which is non-refundable, which sum is due immediately, and which shall be applied to the following fee schedule:

1. The sum of $______ if the matter is resolved without a trial;
2. The sum of $______ if the case is tried or is settled on the day of trial;
3. Other: ______________________________________

____

____

In addition thereto, the undersigned agrees to pay all costs associated with this action, including fees paid to expert witnesses, photographers, investigators, and for postage, copying and long distance calls.

I agree to pay an additional fee of $______ for additional representation regarding ______________________________

____

I understand that Mr. Cowan will begin work on my case when this amount has been paid and that no portion of this retainer fee is refundable to me. I further understand that if applicable, the additional fee for a trial must be paid no later than 10 days prior to the date set for trial. If I do not pay the fees or costs as agreed, I understand that Mr. Cowan will be relieved of any further obligation to represent me or to appear in court on my behalf and, in that event, I authorize him to withdraw from my case.

The fee schedule quoted herein does not include any revocation hearings, or appeals or writs to a higher court, whether pretrial or post-trial or whether initiated by me or by the prosecution, or retrials following a mistrial, successful appeal, or where a motion for a new trial is granted. I authorize Mr. Cowan to initiate any pre-trial appeal or writ if, in his opinion, my interests will best be served thereby, and if I am unavailable for consultation.

Form 11
Attorney's Retainer & Fee Agreement

I specifically authorize Mr. Cowan to take any action on my behalf, including the waiving of my right to a speedy trial or to a jury trial, if, in his opinion, my interests would best be served thereby.

I further understand that a 1.5% per month late charge will be imposed on any portion of the balance of the fees not paid on the due date established above, and that I will be responsible for any costs and reasonable attorneys fees incurred should collection procedures be necessary.

I have read and fully understand this contract and have discussed any questions I have with my attorney and I agree to its terms. I have received a copy of this contract.

DATED this ______ day of __________, 19____.

____

CLIENT

Form 11
(continued)

commonly taken during an interrogation session; any videotapes, used by some agencies to record field sobriety tests or the arrestee's general condition during booking; any photographs taken of the client or of any scenes relevant to the charge; or any transcripts of interrogation. Obtaining these items may take a longer time than obtaining arrest reports and so on, and may require a court order.

Assuming that a chemical sample was obtained, counsel should take steps immediately to have the sample preserved for possible analysis by the client's own chemist. Some states have statutes requiring that the blood, urine, or test ampoule from a Breathalyzer be preserved. In a state that does not, counsel should quickly make written demands on the police and prosecuting agencies for preservation and/or production of the samples. Even if the client cannot afford to hire a chemical analyst, nonproduction of the samples may well later supply grounds for a motion to suppress the results of the test.

Counsel should go over the calibration and maintenance records of the breath analysis machine. In most states there are statutes requiring the breath machine to be calibrated and maintained in a certain manner and at designated periods. Similarly, there may be laws concerning the training of personnel, handling of samples, and licensing of laboratories that analyze blood or urine. Failure to comply with these standards could result in suppression or, at least, a favorable jury instruction.

If counsel is with the client at the police station within an hour or two of his arrest, an effort should be made, if possible, to have some sort of chemical test administered to his client by nonpolice personnel. The most accurate method would be the drawing of a blood sample at a nearby hospital or doctor's office. This can then be analyzed by a chemist and introduced as defense evidence. By computing the "burn-off" rate, the chemist can estimate the blood-alcohol percentage at the time of the client's arrest and may be able at least to throw some doubt on the prosecutor's chemical test results.

The scene of the driving and the location of the arrest, including the area where the field sobriety test was given, should be visited personally by counsel. Having a picture of the place in his mind will be a great help to him in cross-examining the police officer at trial. Taking photographs of the scene may prove a valuable visual asset in counsel's presentation of the case to a jury; blowups can be particularly helpful.

§8.2 *Analysis of the Case*

> The standards of the law are standards of general application. The law takes no account of the infinite varieties of temperament, intellect, and education which make the internal character of a given act so different in different men.
>
> OLIVER WENDELL HOLMES, JR.

Once counsel has sufficient information relevant to the case — primarily through interviewing the client and obtaining reports from the police or prosecutor — he should sit down and consider the strengths and weak points of the case, possible defense strategies, necessary trial preparation, and the advisability of — and tactics for — plea bargaining. In other words, he should take stock of what he has to work with and make tentative plans based on his client's legal situation.

After an initial evaluation of the case, counsel will probably wish to consult with his client about certain options before proceeding with the case. Most important, the client will probably want to know *when* the jury trial will take place. Counsel must bear in mind, again, that he is dealing with a client who has probably never had a criminal problem before and who is probably convinced that he was not "drunk." Counsel must take pains to explain carefully the difference between "drunk" and "under the influence," the strengths and weaknesses of the case, and the possible merits of plea bargaining over going to trial.

§8.2.1 The Prosecution's Case

In analyzing the case against his client, counsel should consider a number of factors related to the prosecutor's case.

Initially, of course, the technical requirements for a *corpus delicti* must be present — and provable. In a per se case, can the state establish a blood-alcohol level in excess of the statutory amount? In a DUI case, can the prosecutor establish that the client was under the influence? Can he "put him behind the wheel"? And if he can, did the driving take place in a statutorily designated location — for example, a public highway?

In the majority of DUI cases the sole issue will be intoxication and/or blood-alcohol level. In considering prosecution evidence, counsel should review the police reports and discount much of what the client tells him. Counsel does this for two reasons. First, if the client was in fact under the influence — and this, it must be recognized, will be the situation in most cases — he will not have been in a condition to observe and recall as ably as the arresting officer. Second, in analyzing the prosecution case, it is best to consider it on its own merits, independent of defense evidence.

The initial factor to be considered is the client's driving symptoms. Was the initial police detention due to erratic driving or to a simple traffic violation? There is a difference, for example, between exceeding the speed limit by ten miles an hour and weaving wildly across a four-lane highway; in fact, an argument can be made that driving at excessive speeds requires greater judgment, reflexes, and coordination than a "drunk" driver is capable of — that is, speeding requires sobriety.

Counsel should study how the client reacted to attempts to stop him after the initial observations that attracted the police officer's attention. Did the client react quickly to a siren or flashing light and pull over to a safe location? Or did he continue for two miles, oblivious to the flashing red lights behind him, and finally swerve off onto the shoulder and slam on his brakes, coming to a stop with the rear end of his car jutting into traffic?

Next, counsel should consider the physical observations made by the arresting officer. The officer will almost always make detailed notes about the client's appearance during the detention: flushed face, bloodshot eyes, alcoholic breath, disarranged hair, rumpled clothing, etc. Similarly, he will study the defendant's conduct. Was the client antagonistic? Did he fumble with his wallet in trying to locate his license? Did he stumble when alighting from the car? Was he bracing himself with a hand against the car to stand?

Next, counsel should review the client's performance on the field sobriety test (see §4.3). Assuming the defendant was given two or three of the recognized tests, counsel should evaluate the performance with certain things in mind. First, the officer will be interpreting the performance subjectively and in a prejudicial way. He will probably have decided already that the client is guilty and will realize that a poor performance is both expected and required for conviction. Second, the client will be performing while in an emotionally upset state and under the most trying of conditions. Third, a perfect performance on most of the tests is difficult for most sober individuals to accomplish.

Then, what is undoubtedly the most critical part of the prosecutor's case will be examined: the chemical evidence. The test result must be obtained and then compared to the jurisdiction's per se law and standard for presumptions as to guilt. Probably the strongest prosecution readings are in the .14 percent to .24 percent blood-alcohol range. Lower than that, the conclusion becomes marginal; higher, any decent performance by the client draws the accuracy of the chemical analysis into question. Of course, the attorney must go into more than the results of the test. The testing process itself should be looked at. This requires questioning the training of the operator, the testing procedures, the maintenance and calibration records, laboratory qualifications, etc. And, of course, if no test was administered because of the client's refusal to cooperate, counsel must consider the legal effects of that refusal.

Certainly, counsel should study carefully any statements allegedly made by the client to police officers or other witnesses, both as to the statements' potential effect on a trier of fact and as to their admissibility on relevance or constitutional grounds.

After having reviewed the potential testimony that would be offered by police or chemical-expert testimony, counsel should review the possibility of lay witnesses that might be used as part of the prosecution case. In all probability, the names and addresses of any such witnesses will be listed in the police reports. Counsel will find that making an initial — and tactful — contact with these witnesses will contribute to his completely and accurately assessing the case. These witnesses may tend to corroborate the police version of the facts, but they may also point out discrepancies that will later cast doubt on police testimony. Many times the witnesses will have been involved in the case directly, perhaps as parties in a traffic accident with the client, and their bias must be kept in mind. Obviously, counsel must take care in interviewing any prosecution witnesses; subsequent accusations of witness tampering could be disastrous.

Finally, the existence and validity of any prior convictions of the client will have to be considered. The dates of the convictions are important if the jurisdiction's statutes have a cutoff date for increased punishment for repeat drunk drivers — for example, convictions within a five-year period. Counsel should give serious thought to the advisability of admitting the prior conviction if this will preclude the jury from hearing any mention of it.

§8.2.2 The Defense Case

The first consideration in assessing the strengths and weaknesses of the client's case is the availability of any witnesses. In the rare case, there will be a friend or two with the client in his car when the stop and arrest is made. This, of course, represents the ideal situation (assuming favorable testimony): The client's sobriety at the critical moment can be testified to, as well as his appearance, conduct, driving symptoms, performance on the field sobriety test, and the conditions under which the test was given. However, the situation often arises where the prosecutor questions testimony of friendly witnesses because they too were under the influence. Counsel should certainly consider the boomerang effects of such testimony. If the police turned the client's car over to a witness after the arrest, that would be clear evidence that the police thought he was sober. Although different legal standards are involved, the argument that none of the witnesses was arrested for "plain drunk" could be helpful, as could the fact that the witnesses' conditions were not mentioned in the police report.

Counsel should also consider the possible consequences of *not* calling readily available witnesses. Depending on the law in the jurisdiction, the prosecutor may be permitted to comment on the failure to call certain witnesses — and even obtain an instruction permitting the jury to draw an adverse inference.

In *State v. Bartholomew*, 829 S.W.2d 50 (Mo. App. 1992), three friends of the defendant were in the car with him when he was stopped by a police officer. After observing symptoms of intoxication and noting failures of various field sobriety tests, the officer escorted the defendant to his home, where his wife made breakfast for him before he was taken to jail. At trial, the prosecutor said in his summation: "Other people were there and I asked him, where are those people? Why aren't they here in the courtroom?" The defendant's objection was overruled and he was convicted.

On appeal, the court commented that no adverse inference may be drawn where an unproduced witness is equally available to both sides. Three factors were enumerated for determining whether a witness was "equally available":

> 1. Whether one party has superior ability to know or identify the witnesses;
> 2. The nature of the testimony the witness is expected to give; and
> 3. The relationship between the particular party and the witness which indicates that the witness would be likely to testify more favorably for one party than another. [Id. at 52.]

Turning to the facts, the court found that the defendant's wife and friends were clearly more available to the defense than to the prosecution. Thus the failure to call them legitimately gave rise to the inference that the testimony would have been unfavorable to the defense.

In most cases, though, the client will be alone when he is pulled over. Counsel must then consider the availability of testimony about earlier or later events. First, any significant contacts the client made in the hour or two before the arrest should be gone over. There are few cases where the client did not spend some time with a friend or business associate in the previous two hours. Even the testimony of a bartender could be helpful, if he can recall that the client was in his establishment for a significant period just prior to the arrest, consumed only two drinks, and appeared sober when he left. Counsel should not overlook the possibility of testimony as to the client's condition *after* his arrest. The client may have struck up a brief friendship with a fellow arrestee in his jail cell, an arrestee who could testify to the client's sober condition minutes after having been tested for blood-alcohol level. As in all cases, of course, counsel must contact such witnesses before assuming anything in analyzing the client's chances.

The client himself is a potential witness to almost everything that the prosecution witnesses will testify to. Whether he would be an effective witness is another issue, a critical issue that counsel must consider carefully. Counsel will have to evaluate the effect his client will have on a jury — his inherent credibility, his "empathy factor," his ability to deal with cross-examination — against the given fact that a jury will hold his failure to testify against him, regardless of the court's Fifth Amendment instructions.

The availability of character witnesses should not be considered as a substantial factor in most cases. In fact, there is a strong argument for not using character witnesses at all: An intelligent jury may feel that character testimony represents an admission of the weakness of the defense case on the issue of intoxication. In a rare, appropriate case, however, testimony from respected members of the community as to the client's usual sobriety, honesty, and responsibility can have a beneficial effect.

The defense strengthens its case considerably if the client can employ a chemical expert. Whether or not he has had the opportunity to chemically analyze the blood or the urine sample, the defense's expert will be helpful in countering the testimony of the prosecution's expert as to testing procedures, physiology of alcohol consumption, and the meaning of test results. This is certainly preferable to relying on cross-examination of the prosecutor's expert to establish flaws in the test. Of course, the services of a well-qualified expert in this field are not cheap; the decision to employ such a witness presumably will be the client's, after appropriate advice from counsel.

The last aspect of the defense case that must be reviewed is the possible presence of constitutional issues. Counsel must study the available facts carefully with an eye to the latest court decisions. If there were incriminating statements made at any point, counsel should immediately consider the *Miranda* possibilities. In such cases, the always debatable question of when the investigatory stage ended becomes critical. Counsel should never assume that an officer had probable cause to make the initial stop of the client's vehicle. In some cases, police routinely stop all vehicles leaving a certain bar or tavern after a certain hour on the assumption that most of them will contain drunk drivers. Nor should counsel take for granted probable cause to arrest. Often police arrest a defendant, despite his having done well on the field sobriety test, just so he can be made to take a chemical test. The attorney should keep in mind search and seizure as well, and he should examine closely the circumstances under which any drugs or bottles of liquor were found. Even the extraction of the blood-alcohol sample should be considered for the possibility that it was taken in a harsh and constitutionally impermissible manner. Finally, counsel must go over any prior convictions with a fine-tooth comb for any procedural defects rendering them unusable.

After having considered the strengths and weaknesses of the prosecution and defense cases, counsel should turn to the possibilities of punishment. Certainly, counsel must understand the statutory language and explain it to the client. More important than knowledge of the minimum and maximum possible sentences, however, is awareness of the common practice in the local courts. Most jurisdictions will tend to have a somewhat uniform approach to sentencing in certain situations, often through formal court policy. A first offender, for example, may be fined, forced to attend a DUI school, and placed on probation only; the existence of factors such as an accident, an unusually high blood-alcohol reading, or antagonism toward the police may increase the first-offender sentence. To "facilitate" the congested calendar, the court policy may favor lenient sentencing at the arraignment — and increasingly tougher treatment as time goes on. Whatever either the formal or unwritten policies of the court, counsel should be thoroughly familiar with them.

Counsel must understand the effect a prior conviction or multiple prior convictions will have on the sentence, both in terms of the statute and local court practice. If a mandatory minimum jail sentence and/or license suspension is required, counsel should make the client aware of this.

Certainly, in considering the possible punishments, counsel must consider the relative strengths and weaknesses of both the defense and prosecution cases. Plea bargaining is almost always a viable possibility, and the relative merits of the case will probably have a direct bearing on both the question of a plea to reduced charges — such as reckless driving — and the issue of sentencing. If the prosecution is convinced the defense is viable, and the court believes that the client is earnest about taking up court time for a lengthy trial, a lesser charge and/or sentence should result.

Alternatives to the normal types of criminal punishment also should be considered. Counsel will be doing his client a great service if he can convince the court that society is better served by rehabilitation than retribution, particularly in the case of the repeat offender. Counsel should argue for enrollment of the defendant in an educational or rehabilitative program as an alternative to jail or license suspension. If there is no such program available, counsel should be creative in suggesting possibilities such as Alcoholics Anonymous, psychiatric care, or electronic home arrest.

In analyzing the case, counsel should consider and advise his client about the possibilities both of license suspension or revocation and of the likelihood of increased automobile insurance premiums. If an administrative appeal from action against his license is possible, counsel should also consider this and bring it to the client's attention.

Finally, counsel should examine closely the procedural considerations of each drunk driving case. The possibilities of forum shopping within a given jurisdiction must be understood. Ideally, counsel will know the reputations of the available prosecutors and judges, as well as the procedures for challenging for cause or peremptorily. He will foresee any problems with calendar congestion within a court. He will be aware of speedy trial requirements. And he will understand something of the jury panel that will be available when the client's case comes up for trial — both its general reputation and the trend of its recent verdicts.

8.2.3 Evaluation

Once the strengths and weaknesses of both the prosecution and defense cases have been analyzed, the possible consequences foreseen, and the procedural possibilities understood, counsel can intelligently inform his client of "what the ballpark looks like" and advise him of the best way to proceed.

Counsel does no service to his client, however, if he paints a false picture of hope. It must be recognized that the majority of drunk driving arrests are not only justified but provable in court. In only a minority of cases does a defendant have a clear shot at an acquittal. If the client was drinking at a bar for two hours, then was stopped while driving alone and weaving across multiple lanes, performed poorly on the field sobriety test, and blew an .18 percent on the Intoxilyzer, he probably is best served by a quick disposition with the prosecutor that does the least damage to the client. Drawing the matter out — and, particularly, submitting the client to a trial — will, in such cases, usually result only in higher attorney's fees and a more severe sentence.

If, however, there is a viable defense — for example, the client has good witnesses or suffers from a medical condition affecting balance and/or his blood-alcohol level — then counsel should advise his client accordingly and proceed to map out his strategy in defending the case.

Whether or not the drunk driving case ever goes to trial, there will be certain pre-trial procedures that counsel will want to take advantage of. If, in his analysis, counsel determines that his client has a viable defense, then these procedures will serve to clarify the issues, expose the prosecution case, uncover defense evidence, suppress damaging testimony, and conceivably result in a dismissal of the charges. Even if a defense at trial would be untenable, such procedures will tend to strengthen counsel's position for plea bargaining.

Checklist 13 Evaluating the Case

Prosecutor's Case

- ☐ *Corpus delicti*
  - ☐ driving
  - ☐ vehicle
  - ☐ highway
  - ☐ under the influence or with an excessive blood-alcohol level
- ☐ Driving symptoms
- ☐ Client's appearance and conduct
- ☐ Field sobriety test
- ☐ Admissions by client
- ☐ Chemical test results
  - ☐ statutory effect
  - ☐ testing process
  - ☐ effect of refusal to take test
- ☐ Other witnesses
- ☐ Prior convictions

Defense's Case

- ☐ Witness available
  - ☐ with client at time of arrest
  - ☐ with client before or after arrest
- ☐ Client as witness
- ☐ Character witnesses
- ☐ Availability of chemical expert witness
- ☐ Constitutional considerations
  - ☐ probable cause to stop or arrest
  - ☐ *Miranda*
  - ☐ search and seizure
  - ☐ extraction of blood-alcohol sample
  - ☐ prior convictions
- ☐ Affirmative defenses
  - ☐ mistake of fact
  - ☐ necessity
  - ☐ duress
  - ☐ entrapment

Possible Punishment

- ☐ Statutory language
- ☐ Common practice in local courts
- ☐ Effect of prior convictions
- ☐ Applicability and effect of sentence enhancements
- ☐ Effect of relative prosecution/defense strengths
- ☐ Alternatives to punishment: programs
- ☐ License suspension/revocation
- ☐ Effect on automobile insurance

Procedural Considerations

- ☐ Forum shopping possibilities
- ☐ Available prosecutors
- ☐ Available judges
  - ☐ reputations
  - ☐ challenges
- ☐ Calendar congestion
- ☐ Speedy trial requirements
- ☐ Right to jury trial
- ☐ Jury panel
  - ☐ general reputation
  - ☐ recent verdicts

§8.3 The Arraignment

> Hogan's r-right whin he says: "Justice is blind." Blind she is, an' deef an' dumb an' has a wooden leg.
>
> MR. DOOLEY

At the arraignment, counsel will receive a copy of the complaint and, usually, a copy of the police report prepared by the arresting officer; if a blood or urine sample was taken, the laboratory report may not be available until some time after the arraignment. Counsel will identify himself and his client (if present) and, assuming no grounds for demurrer or a motion to quash (see infra) a plea will be entered. Depending on the practices of the court, either a pre-trial or trial date will then be set (in some courts both will be calendared in advance). If appropriate, the bail situation will be reviewed.

Counsel should consider a number of potential issues that may arise at the arraignment stage of a drunk driving case. First, has the *statute of limitations* run? This possibility should never be overlooked. Second, is the complaint itself technically defective? The subject of dealing with defective accusatory pleadings will be covered in §8.3.1. Third, is there a *double jeopardy* issue? For a discussion of double jeopardy as it applies to the drunk driving case see §8.3.2. And fourth, the question of *speedy trial* should be considered — particularly when the trial date is being set.

§8.3.1 The Defective Complaint

Counsel should review the accusatory pleading obtained at the arraignment. If the pleading appears defective on its face, the appropriate remedies within the jurisdiction should be considered — that is, a demurrer, a motion to quash the complaint, and/or a motion to dismiss. Depending on the jurisdiction, defects may be deemed waived if not made at the time of arraignment. Furthermore, if the demurrer is overruled or the motion denied, counsel must consider taking an immediate writ; failure to do so may, again, be considered a waiver of the error — or at least require a showing of actual prejudice.

A common practice among many prosecuting agencies is to use the arresting officer's citation or "notice to appear" as the criminal complaint. However, this procedure may not comply with the jurisdiction's formal requirements for accusatory pleadings, either for technical reasons of form, timeliness, or verification, or because of lack of specificity.

The single most common defect in accusatory pleadings is the failure of the prosecution to allege the defendant's conduct with sufficient *specificity*. Thus, for example, in *Garcia v. State,* 747 S.W.2d 379 (Tex. App. 1988), the defendant moved to quash the charging instrument (an information) where it alleged in general terms that he "did then and there drive and operate a motor vehicle in a public place . . . while intoxicated, when the Defendant did not have the normal use of his mental and physical facilities." The information did not specify whether the intoxication was caused by alcohol, a controlled substance, or a combination thereof. After a jury conviction, the defendant appealed.

The appellate court affirmed a lower appellate court's dismissal of the charges, reversing the trial court's denial of defendant's motion to quash:

> Generally, when a term is defined in the statutes, it need not be further alleged in the indictment.. . . However, when an act or omission by a defendant is statutorily defined, and that definition provides more than one way to commit the act or omission, then, upon timely request, the State must allege the manner and means it seeks to establish. [747 S.W.2d at 380.]

What if the complaint does not make clear whether the theory of intoxication is one of "loss of faculties" or one of blood alcohol concentration? In another Texas case, the appellate court reversed and remanded with instructions to the trial court to dismiss the information where the pleadings did not specify:

> [T]he appellant knew that the State had evidence as to his blood alcohol concentration, but could not have known if the State would attempt to prove it by relying on the scientific evidence or on the observations of the officer who arrested him while he was driving. Since the appellant did not know whether he had to attack the scientific or observation evidence, he could not have fully prepared his defense. [*Ray v. State,* 747 S.W.2d 437 (Tex. App. 1988).]

§8.3.2 Double Jeopardy

The Fifth Amendment specifically provides that no person shall "be subject for the same offense to be twice put in jeopardy of life or limb." This proscription against multiple prosecutions has been applied to the states through the Fourteenth Amendment (*Benton v. Maryland,* 395 U.S. 784, 89 S. Ct. 2056, 23 L. Ed. 2d 707 (1969)). And every state now has its own constitutional prohibition against double jeopardy.

For purposes of applying the defense of double jeopardy, it is important to determine exactly when jeopardy attached in the former trial. In court trials, jeopardy attaches when the first witness is sworn; in jury trials, when the jury is impaneled and sworn. 22 C.J.S. *Criminal Law* §241.

This protection against double jeopardy is, in fact, three-faceted: It prohibits a second prosecution on the same charges after either acquittal or conviction and prevents multiple punishments for the same offense. For a discussion of multiple punishments see §2.3.

Certainly, if the client has already been convicted or acquitted of the offense for which he now stands charged, a plea of "once in jeopardy" or a motion to dismiss clearly would be called for. A less clear problem presents itself, however, where the client has been convicted or acquitted of a lesser-included or related offense.

The most common example of a related offense would be "plain drunk" or "drunk in public." Quite often, a defendant is prosecuted for "plain drunk" and convicted or acquitted; it is then discovered by the prosecutor that he had been driving a car at the time, and charges of drunk driving are brought. The question of whether the defendant already has been placed once in jeopardy then arises.

Counsel should definitely assert this defense under such circumstances, both as a plea and, later, as a motion to dismiss. Few courts of the various states have ruled on the issue, and those that have seem to have held the defense inapplicable. (See, e.g., *State v. Eckert,* 186 Neb. 134, 181 N.W.2d 284 (1970).) Nevertheless, the defense of double jeopardy would seem at least arguably to apply in such case.

In those states having multiple statutes relating to misdemeanor drunk driving, double jeopardy more clearly applies. In such states, milder laws referring to "driving while *impaired*" are applied to drivers against whom the evidence is less than conclusive, and these laws carry milder punishments than their companion "driving while *intoxicated*" statutes. Under such statutory schemes, a conviction for impaired driving would definitely preclude subsequent prosecution for drunk driving. (See, e.g., *State v. Lanish,* 103 N.J. Super. 441, 247 A.2d 492 (1968).)

The most commonly recurring situation, however, involves a prosecution for drunk driving under a felony statute after an earlier prosecution for misdemeanor drunk driving (or the reverse). This situation is often encountered when a victim is involved; if the victim dies after the misdemeanor case has been resolved, the prosecution frequently files new charges of involuntary manslaughter or negligent homicide.

The U.S. Supreme Court has addressed this problem. In *Grady v. Corbin,* 495 U.S. 508, 110 S. Ct. 2084, 109 L. Ed. 2d 548 (1990), the defendant had been involved in an accident that resulted in injury to another. He was cited for drunk driving and for crossing a yellow line. Later, one of the persons injured died. Although the prosecution was aware of the death, the trial court was not notified, and the defendant pleaded guilty to the misdemeanor. Shortly thereafter, another prosecutor investigated the case and presented evidence to a grand jury; the grand jury indicted the defendant for reckless manslaughter, vehicular manslaughter, criminally negligent homicide, and misdemeanor drunk driving. At the arraignment, defense counsel moved to dismiss the indictment on the grounds of double jeopardy; the motion was denied, but the Court of Appeals of New York reversed the ruling.

The U.S. Supreme Court agreed with the Court of Appeals, rejecting the prosecution's theory that double jeopardy attached only when "the offenses have identical statutory elements or (when) one is a lesser included offense of the other." The inquiry is not what the statutory elements of the offenses are, the court held, but rather what the underlying *conduct* was that constituted each offense:

> We have long held, see *Blockberger v. United States,* 284 U.S. 299, 304, 76 L. Ed. 2d 306, 52 S. Ct. 180 (1932), that the Double Jeopardy Clause of the Fifth Amendment prohibits successive prose-

> cutions for the same criminal act or transaction under two criminal statutes whenever each statute does not "requir[e] proof of a fact which the other does not." In *Illinois v. Vitale,* 447 U.S. 410, 65 L. Ed. 2d 228, 100 S. Ct. 2260 (1980), we suggested that even if two successive prosecutions were not barred by the *Blockberger* test, the second prosecution would be barred if the prosecution sought to establish an essential element of the second crime by proving the conduct for which the defendant was convicted in the first prosecution. Today we adopt the suggestion set forth in *Vitale.* We hold that the Double Jeopardy Clause bars a subsequent prosecution if, to establish an essential element of an offense charged in that prosecution, the government will prove conduct that constitutes an offense for which the defendant has already been prosecuted. [109 L. Ed. 2d 557.]

Nor does the nature of the evidence the prosecution will produce determine whether double jeopardy attaches. "The critical inquiry is what conduct the State will prove," the Court noted, "not the evidence the State will use to prove that conduct."

Finally, the Court distinguished the issues of double jeopardy and multiple punishment:

> The *Blockberger* test is not the only standard for determining whether successive prosecutions impermissibly involve the same offense. Even if two offenses are sufficiently different to permit the imposition of consecutive sentences, successive prosecutions will be barred in some circumstances where the second prosecution requires the relitigation of factual issues already resolved by the first. [109 L. Ed. 2d 563.]

Prior to the standards announced in *Grady,* the state courts had come to consistently contradictory results when confronted with double jeopardy issues in a drunk driving case. How many of these decisions will be affected by *Grady,* however, remains to be seen.

Thus, for example, in *State v. Carter,* 353 S.E.2d 875 (S.C. 1987), the defendant was charged with both drunk driving and reckless homicide following his involvement in a fatal automobile accident. He was tried in South Carolina's lower (municipal) trial courts on the DUI charge and convicted. He was then tried in the higher (circuit) courts on the homicide charge and convicted despite a motion to dismiss for double jeopardy. On appeal, the Supreme Court of South Carolina relied on the U.S. Supreme Court decision in *Illinois v. Vitale,* 447 U.S. 410 (1980), in reversing the reckless homicide conviction: "[The] substantial claim of double jeopardy prohibits [the defendant's] subsequent prosecution for reckless homicide because the state relied on and proved the same facts of the adjudicated DUI offense to establish the reckless homicide."

In *People v. Jackson,* 514 N.E.2d 983 (Ill. 1987), however, the court reached an opposite conclusion on similar facts. In that case, a plea of guilty to drunk driving was held *not* to be a bar to subsequent prosecution for reckless homicide. The court held that the determinative factor was whether the elements of the offense were the same, not whether the same evidence was used. Applying the analysis of the Supreme Court in *Harris v. Oklahoma,* 433 U.S. 682, 97 S. Ct. 2912, 53 L. Ed. 2d 1054 (1977), the DUI charge was found not to be a "species of lesser-included offense."

In *Ex parte Petersen,* 738 S.W.2d 688 (Tex. Crim. App. 1987), the court held that a DUI conviction barred a prosecution for involuntary manslaughter: To prove the manslaughter case, the prosecutor would have to relitigate the DUI charge. In *State v. Escobar,* 30 Wash. App. 131, 633 P.2d 100 (1981), however, a defendant was convicted of driving under the influence. He was then charged with negligent homicide arising out of the same incident, on the theory that he had been driving the vehicle in a reckless manner (i.e., independent of the fact that he was intoxicated). He was convicted of the second charge. On appeal, the Washington Court of Appeals affirmed the conviction. The court recognized that driving under the influence and reckless driving are "constituent elements in the perpetration of the greater offense" (633 P.2d at 102), and that prosecution for a crime that is a constituent element violates the Double Jeopardy Clause. However, in this case the prosecution did not have available at the first trial an accident reconstruction expert's evidence to the effect that the defendant had been driving recklessly. Thus, said the court, there was no unconstitutional double jeopardy since the prosecution was "unable to proceed on the more serious charge at the outset because the additional facts necessary to sustain that charge had not been discovered despite the exercise of due diligence." Id. at 103.

A California court held that an acquittal of felony drunk driving bars subsequent prosecution for the lesser included offense of misdemeanor drunk driving. In *Sylvia v. People,* 180 Cal. Rptr. 251 (1982), the jury, in acquitting the defendant of felony drunk driving, was "hung" on the issue of whether he was guilty of the lesser-included offense of misdemeanor drunk driving. The prosecution then filed separate charges alleging that offense and obtained a conviction from another jury. The California Court of Appeals reversed, holding that a jury determination of not guilty of an offense includes by implication a finding that the defendant is also not guilty of any included offenses.

Counsel should be aware of two additional issues: "dual sovereignty" and the *Pearce* rule. Quite simply, the U.S. Supreme Court has held that a municipal court and a state court of the same state constitute courts of the same sovereignty, and conviction or acquittal on a charge in one is a bar to prosecution for the same offense in the other (*Waller v. Florida,* 297 U.S. 387, 90 S. Ct. 1184, 25 L. Ed. 2d 425 (1970)). And in *North Carolina v. Pearce,* 395 U.S. 711, 89 S. Ct. 2072, 25 L. Ed. 2d 656 (1969), the Supreme Court ruled that imposition of a more severe sentence, where a defendant's original conviction had been set aside and a new trial resulted in a second conviction, can take place only where affirmative reasons for doing so appear on the record, such as, for example, additional criminal conduct by the defendant since the first sentencing.

Finally, it should be kept in mind that the doctrine of collateral estoppel may well apply. The U.S. Supreme Court has held that when an issue of ultimate fact has been decided by a judgment of a court, it cannot be relitigated between the same parties. The Court has ruled that this was part of the Fifth Amendment's protection against double jeopardy (*Ashe v. Swenson,* 397 U.S. 436, 90 S. Ct. 1189 (1970)); this would seem to apply to the states by the *Benton* decision supra.

Thus where a defendant was acquitted of driving without a license on the grounds that he had not been shown to have been driving, the prosecution would be collaterally estopped from subsequently prosecuting him for drunk driving, the necessary element of driving having already been litigated adversely (*People v. Cornier,* 42 Misc. 2d 963, 249 N.Y.S.2d 521 (1964)).

For a fuller discussion of collateral estoppel, see §3.1.2.

For a discussion of the double jeopardy implications of administratively suspending an individual's driver's license because of driving with .08 or .10 percent blood alcohol and also criminally prosecuting him in court, see §3.0.1.

§8.4 *Plea Bargaining Considerations*

> The life of the law has not been logic; it has been experience. The felt necessities of the time, the prevalent moral and political theories, intuitions of public policy, avowed or unconscious, even the prejudices which judges share with their fellow men, have had a good deal to do with the syllogism in determining the rules by which men should be governed.
>
> OLIVER WENDELL HOLMES, JR.

The vast majority of drunk driving cases will end in some kind of guilty plea being entered by the defendant. Relatively few cases involving driving while intoxicated — perhaps ten percent at most — will actually go to jury trial. It does not follow, however, that counsel's job is done once he has evaluated the case thoroughly and come to the conclusion that the risks of trial outweigh the possibilities of obtaining an acquittal.

Certainly, it is an unofficial but well-understood policy in many courts that should a defendant choose a jury trial and lose, his punishment will be more severe than it would have been had he simply pleaded guilty. And in some courts there is an additional informal policy that sentencing will be more harsh as the case proceeds from arraignment to pre-trial proceedings and on to the date set for trial. There is little question that such unspoken but widely understood court policies constitute a denial of an accused's right to a jury trial and to due process of the law. A documented case involving such policies would make a fascinating appeal. Yet counsel must face and accept reality: These unofficial policies exist, they are widespread, and they serve to pressure defendants into pleading, thus unclogging the courts' congested calendars.

Prosecutorial coercion of pleas is not uncommon, either. One frequently encountered method is to threaten to amend the complaint with additional charges should the defendant refuse to plead guilty. Given the reluctance of judges to interfere with the prosecution's discretion in charging, the practice — particularly when it is unspoken — is often successful. For example, in *People v. Goeddeke,* 436 N.W.2d 407 (Mich. App. 1988), the defendant refused to plead guilty to drunk driving at the pre-trial conference. Thereafter, the prosecutor dismissed the charges and refiled a complaint charging drunk driving *and* second offense drunk driving. The defendant moved to dismiss on the grounds that the additional count amounted to prosecutorial vindictiveness for demanding a jury trial. The trial court granted the motion. On appeal, however, the court reversed, naively assuming that there was no reason to believe that the changes in the charging decision were vindictive.

There are, however, usually ways for competent counsel to deal with this game of judicial coercion. The first and most obvious is to play the game — attempt to accomplish effective plea bargaining at or before the arraignment, if the arraignment is the first unofficial "deadline." This will probably require informal discussions with the prosecutor, preferably in his office, before the demands of the courtroom are pressing on him. The prosecutor usually will appreciate an honest and fair evaluation of the strengths and weaknesses of both his case and that of the defense. Suggestions as to sentencing are appropriate, but counsel must bear in mind that the prosecutor will be much less concerned with the problems and/or rehabilitation of the defendant than he will be with plain old-fashioned punishment. Also, counsel must bear in mind that his recommendations as to sentence will have differing degrees of influence depending on the local court customs and policies. The judge may reserve all decisions as to punishment for himself, leaving only the question of what the charge is to the prosecutor, or he may happily act as a rubber stamp for whatever opposing counsel agree would be a mutually acceptable sentence.

This is not to say that counsel should "belly-up" for the prosecution. Far from it: Counsel must at all times attempt to deal from whatever position of strength he can. The weaknesses of the prosecution case should be emphasized; the strengths of the defense case stressed. Although this must be done in an honest manner — misrepresentation of facts or law is not only unethical but will prove counterproductive in dealing with this and other prosecutors in the future — it should be kept in mind that the prosecutor has probably had a chance to glance through the police report only superficially and is usually unaware of the strengths of the defense. The police rarely bother to include facts helpful to the defense in the reports they give to the prosecutor's office for filing of a complaint.

Nor are the facts of the case the only strength on which defense counsel can rely. Just as the courts apply pressure procedurally in most jurisdictions, so can the defense. There are a number of pre-trial motions that can and should be made in properly defending a drunk driving case. And, of course, there is the right to have a "full-blown" jury trial. Insisting on all of these procedural rights will prove a headache for the already overworked prosecutor and can tie the average court into knots, causing a calendar log jam that could result in other cases being dismissed for denial of speedy trial. Obviously, counsel must be tactful and extremely careful in wielding this procedural weapon. Just as the courts' policies on sentencing on a plea versus sentencing after a trial are unspoken, so should the power to tie up the court with motions and trials be only alluded to. And it is a gamble: Should the prosecutor and/or judge "hang tough," counsel may be faced with having to go through with his motions and trial and, for trying to "extort" the court, receiving an even tougher sentence for his client if he loses. Odd though it may seem, many courts resent such "extortion," yet feel perfectly ethical in extorting defendants into giving up their rights to trial.

In most cases, the prosecutor and defense counsel will be able only to present suggested sentencing to the judge as part of a proposed plea bargain; the judge will reserve the right either to approve or to assess independently his own sentence. Where at all possible, counsel should know what the intended sentence is to be. Pleading guilty "in the dark" is a risky business: Winning a reduced charge as part of a plea bargain with the prosecutor is a hollow victory if the judge then levies an even heavier sentence. Usually, however, judges are receptive to discussion of the case and of sentencing before the plea is taken. They realize that this facilitates plea bargaining, and most will agree to the sentencing arrived at by counsel if it is reasonable. There are a few, however, who will refuse to commit themselves until after the plea and/or probation report. If such a situation is unavoidable, counsel should attempt at least to set up an agreement whereby the client will be permitted to withdraw his plea should the sentence turn out to include, for example, incarceration in excess of two days.

Judges are individuals, as are prosecutors. And it is defense counsel's job to understand thoroughly each of the judges available in a particular drunk driving case — his attitudes, prejudices, unique characteristics, pet dislikes, and even political leanings. Most important, the judge's views toward drunk driving cases must be known: Does he, for example, have a particular enmity toward defendants charged with this offense, possibly because of an earlier automobile accident involving a drunk driver and a loved one?

Once the judges and prosecutors are known, counsel may be in a position to forum-shop — that is, maneuver the case into different court departments or divisions with different judges and possibly prosecutors. Make no mistake: Knowing the reputations of the judges and prosecutors, and being able to maneuver the case before the most receptive ones, constitutes perhaps the most valuable service counsel can perform for his client. Though it may sound like merely an administrative task, the selection of a judge — and, if assigned to courts, a prosecutor — will have more impact on the outcome of most cases than anything short of selection of defense counsel.

Obviously, counsel must understand the mechanics of forum-shopping. The local court procedures for assigning cases must be understood. If cases are assigned by docket number, every attempt should be made to obtain a number resulting in assignment to a particular court; if assigned by arraignment date, whatever steps necessary should be taken to have the client's arraignment set for a favorable date. The statutory procedures for challenging judges should, of course, be well known to counsel, both the challenge for cause and, if available, the peremptory challenge.

In going over the possibilities of plea bargaining, all lesser-included offenses must be understood. In some jurisdictions, "driving while impaired" is a charge separate from, and less serious than, "driving under the influence"; this certainly would constitute a lesser-included offense and may be an offense to which the prosecutor and judge would accept a plea. Reckless driving is another possibility; in many courts, prosecutors will accept a plea to the lesser offense of reckless driving in cases where the blood-alcohol level is below, for example, .13 percent. "Public drunk'' or ''plain drunk'' is another possibility. And perhaps the most obvious but least appreciated lesser-included offense — and the one probably doing the least damage to the client — is the traffic violation. If the prosecution case is weak, an offer of a plea to two or three traffic offenses (e.g., speeding, crossing a double line, and unsafe lane change) may be accepted; there is no criminal conviction, no jail, and the state motor vehicle agency may be required to consider the violations as but one offense on a ''point'' system, since they all arose from one course of conduct.

The handling of charged prior convictions can be determinative in plea bargaining. As mentioned earlier, the existence of such priors gives counsel more leeway for bargaining — offering a plea as charged, for example, in return for either a withdrawal of the prior allegation or a stipulation as to its unconstitutionality, at least for purposes of sentencing.

Sentencing possibilities should also be considered including the existence of any alleged factual enhancements. Amount of fine, time to pay the fine, formal versus informal probation, period of probation, license suspension or revocation, jail time —all of these are elements that may be played with in molding the sentence. Even the terms of one aspect — jail time — can be arranged favorably: Faced with the inevitability of incarceration, defense counsel may be able to work out terms whereby the client can serve the time on weekends, in the evenings as part of a ''work furlough'' program, under electronic ''house arrest,'' or at an honor camp rather than a jail.

Counsel should not overlook creative alternatives to normal sentencing provisions, and the drunk driving case provides a fertile field for these. Counsel may wish to consider the possibilities of psychiatric treatment, alcoholic rehabilitation centers, Alcoholics Anonymous, drunk driver programs, or public service work as conditions of probation, rather than jail, fine, and/or license suspension. These would probably prove more rehabilitative and helpful to the client, and the argument should be made to the court that a cured drunk driver presents less of a danger to the public than a punished one.

Finally, counsel should attempt to have the client plead *nolo contendere* (no contest) rather than guilty. Although the pleas are identical for criminal court purposes, a few states consider the *nolo* plea inadmissible as conclusive proof in civil cases or administrative proceedings such as a hearing to suspend the client's license.

In considering a plea of *nolo contendere,* counsel should be familiar with the legal ramifications of such a plea in his jurisdiction. It is a common conception that a *nolo* plea cannot be used in a civil proceeding. This is, quite simply, not true in most states, as was clearly pointed out in the recent case of *People v. Goodrum,* 279 Cal. Rptr. 120 (Cal. App. 1991). In *Goodrum,* the defendant was charged with felony drunk driving after causing an automobile accident while intoxicated; a civil wrongful death suit was also filed against him. He entered a plea of *nolo contendere* after the trial judge told him that such a plea was "identical to a plea of guilty except that it could not be used against him in a civil suit as an admission of liability." Id. at 121. Upon subsequently learning of the true nature of the plea, the defendant brought a writ of error *coram nobis,* seeking to withdraw his plea; the superior court denied the writ, and the defendant appealed.

The appellate court initially recognized that the writ was appropriate "whenever a defendant has been induced to enter the plea by misstatements made by a responsible public official." Id. And, the court stated, the writ should be granted "if the presentation at the hearing establishes that a reasonable person in the defendant's position, had he been correctly advised by the judge or other responsible official, would not have entered a guilty plea." Id. at 122.

However, the court went on to hold that the denial of the writ was not error. True, the *nolo contendere* plea *could* be used against the defendant in the wrongful death suit, but it did not amount to an admission of civil liability: The defendant, as the court explained, would not only "be entitled to explain his plea, he could also introduce the hearing transcript which establishes his understanding that his plea was *not* an admission of factual guilt. Such a plea would severely undercut the value of the plea as an admission." Id. at 123.

Query: Does the California court seriously believe that the effect of the plea on a civil jury would be "severely undercut"?

Checklist 14 The Arraignment

- ☐ Has the statute of limitations for any of the charged offenses expired?
- ☐ Has the client previously been charged, convicted, or acquitted of any offense arising out of the same course of conduct?
  - ☐ Is the appropriate remedy for double jeopardy a demurrer, motion to quash, or motion to dismiss?
- ☐ Does the complaint allege more than one offense arising from a single act?
  - ☐ Is there state authority precluding multiple prosecution and/or conviction?
  - ☐ Does the state have a mandatory joinder requirement?
  - ☐ Is the appropriate remedy demurrer, motion to quash, or motion to dismiss?
  - ☐ Must the prosecution elect which alternative offenses to pursue at a later time?
  - ☐ If convicted of multiple offenses arising from a single course of conduct, for which can the client be punished?
- ☐ Is the accusatory pleading defective?
  - ☐ Are there any technical defects (e.g., timeliness, form, verification)?
  - ☐ Does the pleading sufficiently state an offense?
  - ☐ Are the allegations factually sufficient to place the defendant on notice?
- ☐ Are there any bail issues to be resolved?

9

PRIOR CONVICTIONS

§9.0 *The Prior DUI Conviction*

> In no country perhaps in the world is law so general a study [as in America]. . . . This study renders men acute, inquisitive, dextrous, prompt in attack, ready in defense, full of resources. . . .
>
> EDMUND BURKE

In many cases, counsel will be confronted with a client charged with drunk driving who has had an earlier conviction for the same offense. In such situations, almost all states have statutes that provide for increased penalties — mandatory jail time, suspension of driver's license, higher fines, formal probation, etc. These statutory mandates for subsequent convictions significantly raise the stakes in defending a client against a charge of driving under the influence of alcohol: Loss of a license can result in the loss of a job, and a period of time in jail can be a traumatic experience for someone not hardened to the system.

At trial, counsel will have to make a difficult decision. Either he must admit the prior conviction charged in the complaint, thus ensuring a more severe sentence should his client be convicted of the pending charge, or he must deny the prior conviction and have the damaging evidence of earlier intoxication presented to the jury. For a discussion of the problem presented when a prosecutor refuses to accept an admission of the prior conviction so that he can present evidence of it to the jury, see §9.1.1. For a discussion of bifurcation of trial, see §9.2.

There is, however, a procedure available to defense counsel

whereby the risks at trial and the harsh mandatory sentencing provisions can be avoided: moving to strike the prior conviction as having been unconstitutionally obtained. This pre-trial motion to have the prior convictions declared unconstitutional has generally been used for convictions obtained as the result of a plea. If, however, the conviction was obtained as a result of a trial wherein significant constitutional rights of the client were violated, there is no reason why this may not be asserted as a ground for striking the prior conviction, independent of any appeals or lack of appeals from that conviction.

In reviewing the allegations of a prior conviction in the complaint, counsel should be familiar with the relevant statutes. Most states require, for example, that the prior conviction have taken place within a given period of time, commonly within five or seven years of the date of the subsequent offense or conviction.

Counsel should be aware not only of the *dates* of the priors and the time requirements of the applicable statutes, but also whether they refer to *commission* or *conviction.* Thus, for example, in *Hewitt v. Commonwealth,* 541 A.2d 1183 (Pa. Commw. 1988), a driver's license was revoked on "habitual offender" grounds — that is, he had three priors. On appeal, the driver claimed that the period of time between his first and third convictions exceeded the statutory five years. However, the appellate court held that "habitual offender status is attained when the *commission* of three specified offenses occurs within the statutory five-year period, even if the date of *conviction* for one of the offenses falls outside that period."

And in *Rogers v. State,* 738 S.W.2d 412 (Ark. 1987), the defendant was charged in a DUI case with having suffered three prior convictions within the previous three years. The Arkansas statute, however, referred to prior *offenses* — not prior *convictions.* The court held that while the incidents of drunk driving must, of course, have resulted in convictions, it is the date of the incident and not the date of the conviction that is relevant to the issue of sentence enhancement.

What effect does a judicial finding that a prior is unconstitutional have on the client's license? In some states, a finding that the prior conviction was unconstitutional is binding on that state's motor vehicle agency. In other words, the agency may not consider the prior conviction in deciding whether to suspend or revoke the client's driver's license. In other jurisdictions, however, the prior conviction will be considered regardless of subsequent legal pronouncements as to its constitutional validity. For a discussion of collateral estoppel, see §3.1.2.

Finally, counsel should never overlook the plea bargaining possibilities of moving to strike an alleged prior conviction. In many cases, the client would plead guilty willingly if it were not for the threat of a mandatory jail sentence and/or license suspension hanging over his head. On the other side, the prosecutor may realize the very real possibility that the record will not show a satisfaction of *Boykin*'s requirements, or he may simply not wish to go through the trouble of ordering records and contesting a hearing. In such circumstances, counsel may suggest that the prosecutor drop the allegations of a prior conviction in return for a plea. If the court must still, by law, consider the client's record, defense counsel and the prosecutor have the option of stipulating — at least for the purposes of the case before the court — that the prior conviction was obtained in violation of constitutional standards, thus relieving the court of its burden.

§9.0.1 Striking the Prior

The basis for attacking a prior plea is found in the landmark decision of the U.S. Supreme Court in *Boykin v. Alabama,* 395 U.S. 238, 89 S. Ct. 1709 (1969). In that case, the Court set forth certain constitutional requirements in the taking of a plea: The defendant must waive his right against self-incrimination, his right to confrontation, and his right to a jury trial, and he must be advised of the effect of a guilty plea. Taken together with *Gideon v. Wainwright,* 372 U.S. 335, 83 S. Ct. 792, 9 L. Ed. 2d 799 (1963), an additional requirement of advisement of the right to counsel and a waiver thereof is required where the defendant is not represented. All of this, the Court said, must be shown affirmatively in the court records; compliance will not be assumed from a silent record. (See, e.g., *Brady v. United States,* 397 U.S. 742 (1970); *Burgett v. Texas,* 389 U.S. 109 (1967); *State v. Troehler,* 546 So. 2d 109 (Fla. App. 1989); *State v. Hill,* 546 So. 2d 211 (La. App. 1989);

Axness v. Superior Court (DMV), 255 Cal. Rptr. 896 (Cal. App. 1988); *Monroe v. Coleman,* 304 So. 2d 332 (La. 1974); *In re Smiley,* 66 Cal. 2d 606, 58 Cal. Rptr. 579 (1967).)

Many jurisdictions have gone further and require that the record indicate that the defendant also was advised of the possible consequences of a guilty plea and of the nature of the charge against him. (See, e.g., *State v. Pfeifer,* 544 S.W.2d 317 (Mo. 1976); *Guthrie v. Commonwealth,* 212 Va. 602, 186 S.E.2d 68 (1972); *People v. Goodwin,* 50 Ill. 2d 99, 277 N.E.2d 131 (1971); *People v. Jones,* 36 Mich. App. 150, 193 N.W.2d 197 (1972); *People v. Brown,* 327 N.Y.S.2d 20 (1971); *In re Tahl,* 1 Cal. 3d 122, 81 Cal. Rptr. 577 (1969).) These additional requirements at least arguably mean that the defendant must have had the possible pleas, defenses, and punishment explained to him, all clearly on the record. (See, e.g., *In re Johnson,* 62 Cal. 2d 324, 42 Cal. Rptr. 228 (1965).) Usually, however, the defendant must show prejudice as to these other nonadvisements — that is, that the defendant would probably not have pleaded guilty had he been so advised.

Thus, for example, in *State v. Williams,* 720 P.2d 1010 (Haw. 1986), the Supreme Court of Hawaii held that the trial court erred in accepting the defendant's guilty plea without first informing him of the penalties or inquiring as to whether he knew or understood the penalties to which he was subject. The conviction was reversed and the case remanded.

The Supreme Court of Delaware has held that a defendant must be informed of the enhancement consequences of a plea for it to later be considered a valid prior:

> In our view, mandatory incarceration for a second offense is a direct, not a collateral, consequence of a plea of guilty. Therefore, in addition to any present punishment he faces, a defendant must also be advised of the range of possible penalties he will receive if convicted of a second offense. [*Krewson v. State,* 552 A.2d 840, 842 (Del. 1988).]

As another example of the increasingly demanding requirements for showing the validity of a prior conviction, Nebraska has now added the requirement that for a prior DUI conviction to be constitutionally valid for enhancement purposes, it must have been entered by the defendant *personally* — that is, not by counsel.

In *State v. Slezak,* 411 N.W.2d 632 (Neb. App. 1987), the prior conviction had been entered by the defendant's attorney on his behalf: The record did not indicate whether the defendant had been present at the time of the plea or whether he had ever been told of the plea. The court recognized that *in absentia* pleas through counsel were common, but now specifically added the requirement that the plea be personally entered before it could be used to enhance a DUI sentence. See also *Tipton v. Commonwealth,* 770 S.W.2d 239 (Ky. App. 1989), wherein the court held that a plea of guilty to drunk driving entered by counsel did not comply with *Boykin* — despite a state statute giving judges the discretion to accept such pleas.

For a DUI guilty plea to be constitutionally valid, the critical advisement of the right to counsel must include information that this right applies at *all* stages of criminal proceedings, not just at the arraignment or time of plea.

A California appellate court was faced with a situation in which an indigent defendant was arraigned with approximately 100 other persons. (For a discussion of group arraignments, see §9.0.3.) In *People v. Howell,* 223 Cal. Rptr. 818 (1986), the accused were advised by one attorney, provided by the court for the arraignment only, of various constitutional rights. In addition, the defendant filled out and signed a plea waiver form. The attorney also signed the form under printed language indicating he had advised the defendant of all constitutional rights enumerated. Neither the appointed attorney's advice nor the form, however, contained any representation that the defendant had been advised of the right to counsel at *all* — that is, subsequent — stages of the proceedings. The court's docket indicated that the attorney had been appointed "by the Court as attorney of record for this proceeding only."

> The constitutional right to appointed counsel does not exist solely at the arraignment. It applies to all stages of the proceedings. . . .
>
> The provision of an attorney for the arraignment only, who is delegated the responsibility to advise the defendants of their rights outside the presence of the judge, does not guarantee that defendants will be properly advised of the right to counsel at every stage of the proceeding. . . .
>
> If [Howell] had been made aware of his continuing right to

> an appointed attorney's services . . . he might have elected to proceed to trial. No record of counsel's chat with his multitudinous clientele was presented below, if any was made; and the magistrate did not even attempt to obtain a waiver of further legal assistance from Howell.

An Alaskan appellate court has gone even further. In *Petranovich v. Alaska,* 709 P.2d 867 (Alaska App. 1985), the defendant was arraigned as a part of a group and was informed of, among other things, the right to counsel. His guilty plea was alleged in a subsequent drunk driving charge. In the second case, he moved to set aside the conviction in the first case, arguing that he had not been informed "what an attorney could do for him" at the time of plea.

The appellate court agreed with the defendant's argument and reversed the trial court's denial of his motion: "To insure that all defendants enjoy the right to counsel, it must be clear from the record that the person has been informed of the role of a defense attorney and the advantages of being represented by one in a criminal proceeding."

Similarly, a Louisiana court reversed a conviction for a second offense DUI on the grounds that the prior conviction was unconstitutionally obtained because of an inadequate explanation of the disadvantages of self-representation and a failure to inquire into the defendant's literacy. In *State v. Bradley,* 535 So. 2d 1108 (La. App. 1988), the trial court had obtained an uncounseled plea of guilty after reading the usual litany of rights and getting waivers as to each.

> Before accepting the guilty plea, the trial court must inform defendant, on the record, of the consequences of proceeding without counsel. The court should assess, *with facts on the record,* defendant's literacy, competency, understanding and volition before accepting the waiver of counsel. . . .
>
> The trial court that accepted Bradley's 1983 guilty plea informed him of his right to counsel and to appointed counsel, but did not inquire about his literacy or competency. The court did not ask him if he understood, or inform him of, the disadvantages and consequences of self-representation. Under these circumstances, Bradley's statement that he did not wish to be represented

> by an attorney is not deemed to be a knowing and intelligent waiver of his right to counsel. [1d. at 1110.]

The possible *range* of punishment must arguably be clearly explained to a defendant for a conviction to pass constitutional scrutiny: It may not be sufficient that the defendant simply states that he is familiar with possible sentences. In *McMillan v. State,* 703 S.W.2d 341 (Tex. App. 1985), the trial court asked the defendant if he knew the range of punishment and the defendant replied that he did; he also signed a waiver form that stated that he "pleads guilty to the charge knowing the full possible range of punishment for the charge against him."

The appellate court held that a misdemeanor plea must satisfy the same requirements as for a felony plea, and this requires, among other things, that the defendant:

> is entitled to at least be informed of the maximum sentence which he may receive. Failure to so inform a defendant must render his plea of guilty non-voluntary because he cannot understand fully the consequences of that plea if he is uninformed as to the sentence that he may receive. (Citing *Boykin.*)

The court noted that the trial judge need not personally advise the defendant of the range of sentences: Advisement by way of printed form signed by the defendant, for example, or a finding that counsel has informed him, may be sufficient.

See also *Stamm v. State,* 556 N.E.2d 6 (Ind. App. 1990), for a case holding a prior conviction invalid where the defendant had not been advised of his right to confront witnesses.

Thus all or most of the following should be clearly reflected in the original court's docket sheet or reporter's transcript for the plea to have been valid:

1. if defendant is not represented, an advisement of the availability of counsel and a waiver thereof
2. waiver of the right against self-incrimination
3. waiver of the right to confront witnesses
4. waiver of the right to a jury trial
5. an explanation of the immediate effect of a guilty plea

6. an advisement of the possible later consequences of a guilty plea, including, arguably, the possible future use of the plea as a prior conviction in a subsequent drunk driving charge
7. an explanation of the nature of the charge, including, arguably, the possible available pleas and the possible defenses that may be available

Faced with such demanding requirements, there will be relatively few cases where the record will establish a constitutionally valid prior conviction for drunk driving. Nevertheless, counsel should be aware of one reality: Trial courts are generally reluctant to attack the procedures of a brother court and certainly reluctant to call into question the propriety of their own earlier procedures. In effect, the trial court is being asked to condemn another court, or itself, for having failed to follow constitutionally mandated procedures.

Although the burden of proving the fact of conviction is on the prosecution (see §9.1.6), once the prosecutor produces the appropriate records the burden shifts to the defendant to show that the prior is constitutionally defective. However, the records produced by the prosecutor to prove the conviction (usually the court docket) normally will serve to sustain the burden. As stated earlier, the appropriate advisements and waivers must be reflected in the records; a silent record is insufficient. If, therefore, the docket sheet does not reflect all of the appropriate advisements and waivers, defense counsel has sustained his burden of proof. It will then be incumbent on the prosecutor to produce evidence that the advisements and waivers were given, presumably through the reporter's transcript or witnesses, if either is available, or possibly by means of testimony from the judge taking the original plea.

Often there will be an entry in the docket showing that the defendant was advised generally of his rights and that he made the appropriate waivers. In some courts, there will be forms to be filled out by the defendant at the time of plea, acknowledging that he had been advised of his rights and was waiving them. But counsel should be aware that in many jurisdictions such general advisements and waivers are invalid: The docket or form must distinctly indicate the advisement of *each* separate right and the taking of *each* separate waiver. (See, e.g., *In re Johnson,* 62 Cal. 2d 324, 42 Cal. Rptr. 228 (1965).)

It is at least arguable that it is not sufficient for a court to ask for and receive a waiver of the key constitutional rights: The court must *explain* them. Thus, for example, in *United States v. Cochran,* 770 F.2d 850, 852 (9th Cir. 1985), the court noted that "[b]ecause a waiver is an 'intentional relinquishment or abandonment of a known right,' a trial court should make sure that a defendant knows what the right guarantees before waiving it." And in *United States v. Delgado,* 635 F.2d 889 (7th Cir. 1981), another federal court held that "before a judge accepts a waiver of the right to a jury trial, the court must interrogate the defendant 'to ensure that the defendant understands his right to a jury trial and the consequences of waiver.' " Id. at 890.

Addressing the question of the waiver of jury trial, the *Delgado* court held that courts

> should explain that a jury is composed of twelve members of the community, that defendant may participate in the selection of jurors, and that the verdict of the jury is unanimous. The court should inform the defendant that if he waives the jury, the judge will decide guilt or innocence. After informing the defendant of these factors, the trial court should then ascertain whether the defendant wishes to waive his right to a jury trial. Only after this type of inquiry will the court be able to determine that the defendant understands his right to a jury trial and the consequences of waiver. [Id.]

§9.0.2 The Uncounselled Prior: *Baldasar — Nichols*

Can a prior drunk driving conviction obtained from a defendant who was not represented by counsel be used later to enhance the punishment of a subsequent drunk driving offense?

The federal constitutional status of an uncounselled prior conviction has, until recently, been ambiguous. The United States Supreme Court in *Scott v. Illinois,* 440 U.S. 367, 59 L. Ed. 2d 383, 88 S. Ct. 1158 (1979), originally held that a defendant charged with a misdemeanor had no Sixth Amendment right to counsel if there was no sentence of imprisonment actually imposed — even if the offense was *punishable* by imprisonment. Then, one year later in *Baldasar v. Illinois,* 446 U.S. 222, 64 L. Ed. 2d 169, 100 S. Ct. 1585 (1980), the Court rendered a confusing *per curiam* opinion stating that a prior uncounselled misdemeanor conviction, valid under *Scott,* could *not* be collaterally used to convert a subsequent misdemeanor conviction into a felony. With three separate concurring opinions and a dissenting opinion, however, the exact holding was unclear.

Courts subsequently attempting to apply *Baldasar* took two different approaches. The narrow approach interpreted the decision as prohibiting only the use of uncounselled misdemeanor convictions to convert a misdemeanor into a felony; the broad approach prohibited the use of such convictions to impose an enhancement to imprisonment.

Fourteen years later, the Supreme Court clarified its position. In *Nichols v. United States,* 128 L. Ed. 2d 745 (1994), the Court expressly overruled *Baldasar* and held that an uncounselled prior conviction, constitutionally valid under *Scott* because no incarceration was actually imposed, could properly be used to enhance punishment in a prosecution for a subsequent offense — even though that enhanced punishment may entail imprisonment. The opinion, authored by Chief Justice Rehnquist, referred to federal sentencing guidelines, but specifically noted that such enhancements could also be imposed by "recidivist statutes which are commonplace in state criminal laws."

Thus the rules concerning an uncounselled prior in a drunk driving case (assuming it is a misdemeanor) are now clear. Under *Scott,* an uncounselled DUI conviction is constitutionally valid so long as no prison term was imposed; this is true even if the offense *could* have been punished with incarceration. And under *Nichols,* such an uncounselled DUI prior can validly be used to enhance punishment at a second or subsequent DUI conviction.

Of course, the *Nichols* decision does not preclude counsel from attacking a prior conviction under the provisions of his own *state* constitution — as is increasingly being done in other areas of the drunk driving field.

Despite the *Nichols* decision, whether the client was represented by an attorney remains a key factor to consider in judging the validity of a prior drunk driving conviction. In most jurisdictions, certainly, a conviction obtained from an individual acting *in propria persona* will be much more carefully scrutinized.

Of course, a conviction may have been unconstitutionally obtained even if the defendant was represented by counsel at the prior conviction. In some states, the presence of counsel has no effect; the court must still clearly advise the defendant and obtain the necessary waivers. In other states, however, presence of counsel will lead to a presumption that he properly advised his client of the rights and obtained waivers. But this presumption can be overcome by simply having the client testify, at the hearing to strike the prior conviction, that his attorney did not, in fact, advise him of one or more of the *Boykin* admonitions or that he did not waive certain rights.

§9.0.3 Priors from *en masse* Arraignments

Counsel may encounter the increasingly common situation of a prior conviction suffered after an "en masse" arraignment — that is, where the client was advised of his constitutional rights as one of a group of defendants in court. This procedure was examined in the case of *Louisiana v. Walpole,* 459 So. 2d 172 (La. App. 1984), where the defendant pleaded guilty to DUI following an en masse advisement of all defendants in the courtroom; she also signed two forms, one waiving her right to counsel and the other waiving her other constitutional rights and entering a guilty plea. The court held that the procedure was constitutionally insufficient.

> The Louisiana Supreme Court has repeatedly found disfavor in the use of "en masse" procedures in accepting guilty pleas. In *LeBlanc v. Watson,* 378 So. 2d 427 (La. 1979) the supreme court noted that the city court in Monroe continued to follow the procedure of collectively advising defendants of their right to counsel despite earlier disapproval of that procedure in *State v. Carlisle,* 315 So. 2d 675 (La. 1975). In *Carlisle* and *LeBlanc,* the supreme court concluded that the trial judge's en masse procedure could serve as a general introduction for defendants, but was not sufficient to assure that the accused in fact received instruction as to his rights, understood them, and intelligently and knowingly waived his right to counsel.
>
> The record in the present case is void of any colloquy between the trial court and the defendant concerning her right to counsel.

> The use of the waiver of the right to counsel form in the present case does not cure this deficiency. The form in no way reflects that the defendant understood her right to counsel. Further, the record is void of any attempt by the trial judge to personally assess the defendant's literacy, competency, understanding, and volition before he accepted the waiver of counsel.
>
> Therefore, we find the procedure used by the Bossier City Court to be inadequate in that there is no showing that the defendant knowing and intelligently waived her right to counsel. [Id. at 174–175.]

A similar situation presented itself to a Minnesota appellate court, with similar results. In *Minnesota v. Hanson,* 360 N.W.2d 460 (Minn. 1985), the defendant appealed a conviction for drunk driving within five years of a similar conviction, claiming that he was advised of his rights prior to the first conviction as a member of a group — but was never asked if he understood those rights. He was individually questioned by the trial judge, but only as to whether he wanted to see an attorney; after saying he did not wish to consult with counsel, the defendant entered a plea of guilty. Addressing his contention that the resulting prior conviction was unconstitutional and could not be used for purposes of sentence enhancement, the court said:

> When the group advisory as to constitutional rights is used, Rule 15.03 mandates that each defendant shall at *least* be individually questioned by the court as to whether he heard and understood the constitutional rights recited. The record from appellant's 1981 D.W.I. conviction does not display either that question or an answer by appellant that he understood the constitutional rights recited to the group and waived them. . . .
>
> Because of length, we will not reprint the entire group advisory given appellant except to note that it contained 383 words, 17 sentences, and approximately 25 different concepts in criminal law, including a mixture of rights depending on whether the charge was a petty misdemeanor or a misdemeanor. To assume that the average citizen, untrained in the law, would hold that recital in his mind and make a valid waiver of each and every right recited without at least being asked by the trial court whether he or she understood them all is to superficially gloss over the concept of fundamental fairness. [Id. at 461.]

For a case involving a conviction based on a guilty plea where the defendant was advised of her rights en masse by means of a *televised* message, see *Snowe v. State,* 533 N.E.2d 613 (Ind. App. 1989).

§9.0.4 Foreign, Juvenile, and *nolo* Priors

As states computerize their conviction records and become more cooperative with sister states in sharing information, counsel will increasingly encounter cases where a prior conviction suffered in another state is alleged in the DUI complaint. Generally, a foreign conviction may be used to enhance a sentence. However, counsel should take a close look not only at the procedures used in obtaining the plea but at the actual DUI statute itself. In *Shinault v. Virginia,* 321 S.E.2d 652 (Va. 1984), for example, the defendant appealed his sentencing as a third offender, claiming that one of the convictions had taken place in North Carolina and that the DUI offense there differed from that in Virginia. He pointed out that Virginia law permitted the use of foreign prior convictions for sentence enhancement only where the conviction was for violation of "the laws of any other state substantially similar to the provisions of" Virginia's DUI statutes. Va. Code §18.2-270. He then urged that although the DUI statutes of Virginia and North Carolina were on the surface similar, the Virginia statute created only a rebuttable presumption of intoxication where the blood-alcohol level was .10 percent or higher, whereas the North Carolina statute provided for a *conclusive* presumption at that level or above. The court concluded:

> [T]he differing effect of the two presumptions on one accused of driving while intoxicated is substantial. In Virginia, an accused may present evidence to rebut the presumption, and if such evidence creates a reasonable doubt as to his guilt, the fact finder must acquit. In North Carolina, however, mere proof that an accused's blood alcohol is 0.10 percent is conclusive to guilt. With such a fundamental difference, we cannot say that the North Carolina statute is "substantially similar" within the meaning of Code §18.2-270.
>
> We hold, therefore, that the trial court erred when it con-

sidered the North Carolina conviction as a prior offense. [Id. at 654.]

The fact that the prior conviction was suffered in a foreign jurisdiction should not preclude counsel from attacking its constitutionality in his own state's courts. In *Axness v. Superior Court (DMV),* 255 Cal. Rptr. 896 (Cal. App. 1988), for example, the appellant's California driver's license was suspended after he was convicted of drunk driving in California on the grounds that he had suffered a prior conviction within the statutory five years — in Minnesota. He appealed, challenging the constitutionality of the Minnesota conviction. The court of appeals initially pointed out that it had no jurisdiction to strike the foreign conviction per se, but that it *could* review the constitutional validity of that conviction as it related to its use in California:

> The fact that a prior conviction was sustained in another jurisdiction does not preclude such examination. "To the extent that any State makes its penal sanctions depend in part on the fact of prior convictions elsewhere, it must assume the burden of meeting attacks on the constitutionality of such convictions." [Id. at 898 (citation omitted).]

The court went on to find that the Minnesota record was silent as to whether the appellant had waived his right to counsel. Since a waiver will not be presumed from a silent record, the court found the conviction to be unconstitutional and rescinded the license suspension.

If the statute concerning enhancement is silent as to prior convictions suffered in a foreign state, counsel should argue that since it is not an offense in the native state to drive under the influence in another state, the incident cannot be used for increased punishment in the native state. This was essentially the position taken in *Suttle v. Commonwealth,* 774 S.W.2d 454 (Ky. App. 1989), where the Kentucky court held that a Tennessee conviction could not be used for enhancement:

> In our view, enhancement of DUI punishment can only be had by the use of prior DUI convictions obtained in this state. The prohibited activity is driving under the influence in Kentucky. Any-

> one who engages in this prohibited activity "anywhere in this state" is subject to punishment. [Statute cite.] Multiple violations of this prohibition can result in the enhancement of punishments upon subsequent convictions. In either case, however, the actor must have engaged in the prohibited activity while in this state.
>
> (The statute) is silent with respect to DUI convictions from a sister state and, as such, we believe our interpretation of the subject statute is a fair one. [774 S.W.2d 455.]

See also *People v. Shaw,* 545 N.E.2d 778 (Ill. App. 1989), where the Illinois court held an Iowa prior invalid, reasoning that the statute did not specifically permit the use of foreign convictions for enhancement.

Should counsel be confronted with a prior "conviction" suffered by the client in *juvenile court,* he should consider a two-prong attack: (1) First, *demur* to the allegation in the complaint; (2) if the demurrer is not sustained, file the usual motion to strike. The motion to strike will contain the usual grounds for attacking a prior conviction, and certainly it will be a rare juvenile court record that will show compliance with the requirements of *Boykin* et al. However, the demurrer initially attacks the allegation on its face, on the grounds that an alleged juvenile "conviction" does not legally constitute a conviction.

In fact, the general view is that there is no such thing as a "conviction" in a juvenile court: Juvenile proceedings are civil in nature and have been analogized to guardianship proceedings. Thus, for example, the Supreme Court of California has very clearly held that "adjudications of juvenile wrongdoings are not 'criminal convictions.' " *In re Joseph B.,* 196 Cal. Rptr. 348 (Cal. 1983). More specifically, it has been repeatedly held that juvenile proceedings cannot be used to enhance adult sentences. See, e.g., *In re Anthony R.,* 201 Cal. Rptr. 299 (Cal. App. 1984). As a Pennsylvania court has said in a drunk driving case, "The use of prior adjudications of delinquency to enhance sentencing for adult criminal convictions would defeat the purpose of the Juvenile Act." *Commonwealth v. Rudd,* 531 A.2d 515 (Pa. App. 1987). And see *State v. Blogna,* 573 N.E.2d 1223 (Ohio App. 1990), in which the court held that a juvenile judgment is not admissible against the individual in any subsequent criminal proceeding.

Finally, counsel may wish to consider the effects of a prior conviction based on a plea of *nolo contendere.* While this has generally been considered to be the equivalent of a "guilty" plea for all criminal purposes, an interesting ruling by an appellate court in North Carolina now calls this into question in the case of priors. In *Davis v. Hiatt,* 376 S.E.2d 44 (N.C. 1989), the Department of Motor Vehicles permanently revoked a motorist's license after his third DUI conviction; one prior conviction was the result of a "no contest" plea. The court held that such a plea to a *previous* charge did not constitute a prior for purposes of license suspension/revocation, distinguishing this from the same plea in a *present* case: "[T]he no contest plea does not establish the fact of guilt for any other purpose than that of the case to which it is entered." Query: Although the issue here was license suspension, could not the same argument be made where priors are alleged for enhancement? On the other hand, the court in *Commonwealth v. Kimmel,* 565 A.2d 426 (Pa. 1989), determined that the enhancement period runs from the date of the prior conviction to the date of the present offense.

§9.1 Prosecutorial Burden

> Justice *is* conscience, not a personal conscience but the conscience of the whole of humanity. Those who clearly recognize the voice of their own conscience usually recognize also the voice of justice.
>
> ALEXANDER SOLZHENITSYN

When attacking a prior conviction, counsel should bear in mind the important difference between the *burden of proof* and the *burden of producing evidence.* In the California case of *People v. Alvarez,* 182 Cal. Rptr. 118 (Calif. App. Dept. Super. Ct. 1982), the court specifically recognized that a defendant's initial *burden of producing evidence* that a prior conviction was constitutionally invalid did not shift the ultimate *burden of proof* from the prosecution:

> [T]he People have the burden of proof throughout the proceedings challenging the prior judgment to establish beyond a reasonable doubt that the prior conviction is constitutionally valid. . . . [I]t is the obligation of the People to establish by evidence beyond

a reasonable doubt that the challenged prior judgment of conviction is constitutionally valid. Initially, the People do this by producing evidence sufficient to justify a finding that defendant suffered the prior conviction. . . . This means that the People have the initial obligation of introducing evidence . . . which is sufficient to avoid a ruling against them on the issue of the constitutional validity of the challenged prior judgment of conviction. . . . The People ordinarily do this by introducing admissible evidence of the prior judgment of conviction and of the fact that the defendant challenging its validity is the same person who suffered the prior judgment.

Once the People establish that the defendant suffered the prior conviction; the burden of producing evidence shifts to the defendant, who must show that his constitutional rights were infringed in the prior proceedings. Imposing upon the defendant this burden of producing evidence on this issue means that he has the obligation to introduce evidence sufficient to avoid a ruling against him on his claim that the prior judgment of conviction is constitutionally invalid. . . . In our instant case, defendant met this burden when he introduced some evidence that his prior conviction is constitutionally invalid. . . . The docket entries in the prior proceeding provided sufficient factual evidence that the defendant's constitutional rights were infringed under *Buller,* supra. It was not necessary that the defendant produce all available evidence to satisfy this burden (of producing evidence). As the People have the continuing burden of proof throughout the proceedings to establish beyond a reasonable doubt that the prior conviction is valid, defendant need only produce evidence sufficient to raise a reasonable doubt as to the validity of the prior judgment in order to satisfy his burden. This certainly cannot be construed to mean that the defendant must produce all available evidence. The defendant successfully satisfies his burden by producing evidence showing a constitutional defect existed in the docket entries so as to avoid a ruling against him on the issue.

The oral evidence of the prior proceeding, which was available for review by a reporter's transcript, might have established beyond a reasonable doubt that the defendant Alvarez was actually and properly advised of his constitutional rights and that there was no constitutional infirmity. The People had the opportunity . . . to produce rebuttal evidence. This rebuttal evidence could have included the available reporter's transcript. After the People failed to produce any rebuttal evidence, the trial court correctly found

> the prior judgment of conviction constitutionally invalid. [Id. at 121–122.]

See also *State v. Fussy,* 467 N.W.2d 601 (Minn. 1991), holding that once the defendant raises the question of the constitutionality of a prior conviction, the prosecution has the burden of proving its validity.

Consider also the means used to prove the prior conviction. The Washington Appeals Court, in *State v. Scarpelli,* 31 Wash. App. 231, 639 P.2d 880 (1982), determined that the validity of a prior conviction for purposes of sentence enhancement requires that the record of the prior conviction show on its face that the defendant understood the maximum penalty to be imposed and knowingly waived counsel. In *Scarpelli,* the prosecution attempted to use a copy of the municipal court docket on the day of the first conviction as proof of its validity. The court ruled that such was not sufficient to show its validity and thus could not be used as the basis for sentence enhancement.

The usual procedure — and requirement — for proving a prior conviction is to offer a certified copy of the court docket. As part of the continuing trend to facilitate the prosecutor's job in DUI cases, however, some courts are now requiring considerably less. Thus, for example, computer printouts have been held sufficient by a New Jersey court, despite the obvious evidentiary problems. See *State v. Carey,* 557 A.2d 1036 (N.J. Super. 1989).

§9.1.1 Prosecutor's Refusal to Accept Admission of Prior

Counsel may well encounter the prosecutor who refuses to accept the admission of the prior conviction. Pointing out that he is free to present the evidence as he deems appropriate and is not required to accept stipulations or other offers, he insists on presenting evidence of the prior to the jury. The obvious purpose is, of course, to prejudice that jury.

The U.S. Supreme Court has recently condemned that practice. In *Old Chief v. United States,* 519 U.S. 172, 117 S. Ct. 644, 136 L.Ed.2d 574 (1997), the defendant was charged with possession of a firearm by a person with a prior felony conviction. He offered to stipulate to the prior, arguing under FRE section 403 that the probative value was "substantially outweighed by the danger of unfair prejudice." The federal prosecutor turned down the offer and the court permitted him to offer evidence of the prior conviction. Recognizing the tendency of such evidence to "lure the factfinder into declaring guilt on a ground different from proof specific to the offense charged," the Supreme Court reversed. The risk of prior conviction evidence, the Court said, is in "generalizing a defendant's earlier bad act into bad character and taking that as raising the odds that he did the later bad act now charged (or worse, as calling for preventive conviction even if he should happen to be innocent momentarily)."

> [T]here can be no question that evidence of the name or nature of the prior offense generally carries a risk of unfair prejudice to the defendant. That risk will vary from case to case, for the reasons already given, but will be substantial whenever the official record offered by the government would be arresting enough to lure a juror into a sequence of bad character reasoning. Where a prior conviction was for a gun crime or one similar to other charges in a pending case, the risk of unfair prejudice would be especially obvious. . . .

The government argued that the prosecution is not required to accept defense offers to stipulate, but is entitled to prove its case by evidence of its own choice. The Court agreed generally, but said that this rationale does not apply where evidence of a prior is relevant only to a defendant's legal status.

The factors enumerated by the Court fit the DUI situation well. First, the prior offense is identical to the charged offense (or, in some cases, very similar). Second, because of the seven-year limitation, the charged prior will always be recent to varying degrees. Third, in today's MADD- and media-inflamed environment, drunk driving is an inherently inflammatory subject evoking strong personal feelings (strong enough that a drunk driver was given the death penalty in 1997 in North Carolina). Finally, a prior in a DUI case is relevant only to the issue of the defendant's legal status.

For a discussion of bifurcation of trial as to offense and prior conviction, see §9.2.

§9.2 *Bifurcation of Trial*

> Trial. A formal inquiry designed to prove and put upon record the blameless characters of judges, advocates and jurors.
>
> AMBROSE BIERCE

If the client is being prosecuted under a sentence-enhancing statute — a statute changing the range of possible sentences where the defendant has prior drunk driving convictions — then the offense *may* acquire a fourth element of the *corpus delicti:* the prior conviction(s). In such a case, the prosecution must plead and prove beyond a reasonable doubt the existence of valid convictions for the statutorily designated crimes within the designated time period; insufficient evidence of this element at trial should be grounds for dismissal of the entire charge. If, however, the prior is considered as merely affecting the sentence, then existence of the conviction can be kept from the jury, at least, with an admission or stipulation as to the factual existence of the conviction. Thus whether a prior conviction constitutes an element of the offense becomes a critical matter.

The Supreme Court of Ohio, for example, has ruled that a prior conviction is an essential element of the offense when it is used to raise the *degree* of the offense, but it is not an element when it is used merely to enhance the penalty. In *State v. Allen,* 506 N.E.2d 199 (Ohio 1987), the defendant's amended complaint alleged two prior convictions. He agreed to stipulate to the priors provided they were not made known to the jury. The trial judge, however, decided that the prior convictions were essential elements of the offense because they increased the maximum sentence, and he therefore told the jury of the allegations over the objections of the defendant. The court of appeals reversed the conviction, holding that prior convictions are not an element of the offense. The supreme court agreed, saying that cited cases in which they were held to be an element did more than merely enhance the penalty: They "transformed the crime itself by increasing its degree." Id. at 201. In contrast, the present case involved priors that simply provided a "sentencing consideration of the court." Id. Finally, the court stated that the trial judge's instruction to the jury that the prior convictions were not material to the question of guilt on the current charge was insufficient to avoid reversible error.

Of course, the tactical aspects of this enhancing element should be carefully considered. Proof of the prior conviction should come in two forms: evidence of the fact of the conviction, and evidence of its constitutionality. The first is a question of fact, to be determined by the jury; the second is strictly a question of law, to be decided by the court and out of the presence of the jury. Thus counsel can safely attack the *constitutionality* of the conviction without the jury ever finding out about its possible existence; a pre-trial attack in the form of a motion to strike or suppress would be appropriate, together with affidavits, court documents, and/or testimony sufficient to raise the issue. On the other hand, if the defense is that the conviction does not factually *exist,* then it is a question of fact, and the jury will be told of the allegation of the prior conviction. In this case, counsel must make a very difficult tactical decision: Is he sure enough that the element cannot be proven that he is willing to risk prejudicing the jury with knowledge of prior instances of drunk driving? For despite any instructions to the contrary, a jury will be much more likely to convict the client in a DUI case if it even suspects that he has been guilty of drunk driving on earlier occasions.

One way to avoid this tactical "horns of a dilemma" is to *bifurcate* the trial. As in a murder case where the jury does not learn of insanity or death sentence matters until a second "trial" after a guilty verdict, so too with a DUI enhancement case: The jury first decides if the defendant committed the offense, and only if they find him guilty are they then told of the fourth element and instructed after receiving additional evidence to decide beyond a reasonable doubt if the prior conviction exists. This certainly seems the fairest way to proceed in such cases, and the only way the almost certain prejudicial effect of prior convictions can be avoided.

Thus, for example, the Supreme Court of Arkansas has reasserted the necessity for bifurcation in DUI cases involving allegations of prior convictions. In *Peters v. State,* 692 S.W.2d 243 (Ark. 1985), the defendant was charged with drunk driving and had been convicted of the offenses on three earlier occasions, triggering a statutory enhancement provision. The trial judge ordered a bifurcated trial. At the first stage the jury heard evidence of the current charge and returned with a guilty verdict. The judge then heard evidence in chambers to determine the number of prior convictions; he subsequently instructed the jury that the range of sentences should be based on three prior convictions.

On appeal, the defendant argued that the factual existence of the three prior convictions was a necessary element of the offense and that he was therefore denied his right to have the jury determine that element.

The Supreme Court of Arkansas concurred:

> [W]e agree the trial should be bifurcated. The jury must hear evidence of guilt or innocence. If the defendant is found guilty of the instance of DWI alleged, the jury will then hear evidence of previous convictions. The trial judge will still determine whether the accused was represented by, or entered a valid waiver of, counsel in the previous conviction alleged and will exclude evidence of any conviction not meeting the counsel requirement. This procedure protects the defendant from prejudice by preventing the jury from considering the three prior convictions during their initial determination of guilt or innocence. [Id. at 245.]

The American Bar Association and a growing number of states have adopted the position that a bifurcation is the appropriate procedure in a drunk driving trial where a prior conviction is alleged for purposes of sentence enhancement. As a California appellate court said in abandoning the so-called unitary approach to criminal cases involving prior allegations:

> [T]he defendant was entitled to a bifurcation of the trial which would have prevented the jury being advised of the alleged prior conviction unless it first found defendant guilty of the charged offense. The unitary procedure, though heretofore accepted in this state, needlessly exposed defendant to serious potential prejudice by revealing his prior criminality without advancing any legitimate state interest. [*People v. Bracamonte,* 174 Cal. Rptr. 191, 195 (1981).]

The California Supreme Court subsequently approved this view, holding that a defendant charged with a prior conviction has a right to have a bifurcated jury trial if undue prejudice would otherwise result. *People v. Calderon,* 9 Cal. 4th 69, 36 Cal. Rptr. 2d 333 (1994). The court set forth factors to be considered in determining whether prejudice would occur:

> Factors that affect the potential for prejudice include, but are not limited to, the degree to which the prior offense is similar to the charged offense [citations], how recently the prior conviction occurred, and the relative seriousness or inflammatory nature of the prior conviction as compared with the charged offense [citations].
>
> . . . The determination whether the risk of undue prejudice to the defendant requires that the trial be bifurcated rests within the sound discretion of the trial court, and that determination will be reversed on appeal only if the trial court abuses its discretion. We observe, however, that the risk of undue prejudice posed by the admission of evidence of a prior conviction, considered against the minimal inconvenience generally caused by bifurcating the trial, frequently will militate in favor of granting a defendant's timely request for bifurcation.
>
> We further observe that, in appropriate cases, the court may wish to grant conditionally a defendant's motion for bifurcation, and reconsider that ruling at the close of the prosecution's case in chief, and again at the close of the defense case, in light of subsequent developments in the proceedings.

Should the jurisdiction provide for a bifurcated trial, it would be reversible error for the trial judge to read the allegation during the "guilt phase" or for the prosecutor to mention the prior. However, a different situation may exist where the prior conviction does more than simply elevate the potential sentence: Is the prior a part of the *corpus* of the offense where it elevates it from a misdemeanor to a felony?

The logical answer would seem to be that the only difference of consequence between drunk driving as a misdemeanor and drunk driving as a felony is the *sentence*— that is, the offenses are identical, but the addition of the prior conviction elevates the potential sentence from, for example, county jail to state prison. Thus evidence of the prior should not be admitted during the guilt phase.

A Texas appellate court, however, has taken a different view. In *Addington v. State,* 730 S.W.2d 788 (Tex. App. 1987), an indictment was read to the jury that contained an allegation of two prior DUI convictions. The Texas Code of Criminal Procedure provided that "When prior convictions are alleged for purposes of enhancement only and are not jurisdictional, that portion of the indictment or information reciting such convictions shall not be read until the hearing on punishment is held. . . ." Nevertheless, the trial court held that the priors were *elements* of the felony offense and thus in issue in the guilt phase. The appellate court affirmed the subsequent conviction, characterizing the prior conviction in such cases as "a *special enhancement* because it elevates the offense from a misdemeanor to a felony."

This is, of course, "bootstrap" logic reminiscent of *Catch-22:* Evidence of a prior to enhance sentence is inadmissible unless the offense becomes punishable by an enhanced sentence.

A better approach to the problem of proving priors in DUI cases made felonies because of those priors was adopted by the Supreme Court of Florida. That court resolved a conflict among its lower courts by holding that where prior convictions are alleged as an element of the offense of felony drunk driving, the trial must be bifurcated:

> [T]he trial court must protect the defendant's presumption of innocence by withholding from the jury any allegations or facts about the alleged prior DUI offenses. If the jury takes a copy of the information or indictment into the jury room, the trial court must ensure that all portions stating the charge is a felony and detailing the alleged prior convictions have been excised from that copy. [*State v. Rodriguez,* 575 So. 2d 1262, 1266 (Fla. 1991).]

If the jury finds the defendant guilty of drunk driving, then what amounts to a court trial must follow to determine the validity of the priors:

> All evidence of the prior DUI convictions must be presented in open court and with full rights of confrontation, cross-examination, and representation by counsel. The trial court must be satisfied that the existence of three or more prior DUI convictions has been proved beyond a reasonable doubt before entering a conviction for felony DUI. [Id.]

Query, however: Is there not a constitutional right to a jury determination as to the factual *existence* of the priors, even if the constitutional *validity* of the priors is a strictly legal issue for determination by the court?

Checklist 15 Prior Convictions

- ☐ Has a prior conviction for drunk driving been, in fact, suffered by the defendant?
  - ☐ is the conviction for violation of a statute substantially identical?
- ☐ Has the prior conviction been formally alleged in the complaint?
- ☐ Did the conviction and/or date of the offense take place within the statutory time period?
- ☐ What are the sentencing and licensing ramifications of a conviction on a second (or subsequent) offense?
- ☐ Was the defendant represented by counsel at the time of the prior conviction?
- ☐ If conviction by plea, did the plea comply with the requirements of *Boykin*?
  - ☐ did the defendant waive his right against self-incrimination?
  - ☐ did he waive his right to confrontation?
  - ☐ did he waive his right to jury trial?
  - ☐ was he advised of the consequences of a guilty plea?
- ☐ Was defendant also advised of his right to counsel, if unrepresented, and did he waive this right?
- ☐ Was the client advised of his rights en masse?
- ☐ Can compliance with all of these requirements be shown by docket sheet, transcript, or at least by testimony?
  - ☐ is each waiver separately indicated?
- ☐ Are any further advisements required in the jurisdiction?
  - ☐ can prejudice be shown, if required?
- ☐ Does the prior involve a foreign, *nolo*, or juvenile conviction?
- ☐ Is defense counsel required to formally notify the court of record of the earlier conviction of any motions to strike the conviction?
- ☐ Can counsel move for bifurcation of the trial?

10

DISCOVERY

§10.0 *Discovery of DUI Evidence*

> No human being is constituted to know the truth, the whole truth, and nothing but the truth; and even the best of men must be content with fragments, with partial glimpses, never the full fruition. . . .
>
> WILLIAM OSLER

In the majority of states today, the defendant in a criminal case has certain fundamental rights concerning inspection before trial of relevant evidence that is under the prosecution's control. Even in those states without such clearly delineated procedures, however, counsel should make demand for pre-trial discovery on general principles of fair trial and due process, if for no other reason than to lay the groundwork for a possible appeal.

Discovery can be accomplished through informal means, or it may require the formal process of court motions. Certainly, the easiest procedure is for defense counsel and the prosecutor to come to an informal agreement as to what is discoverable and to have the appropriate materials voluntarily made available to the defense. In the more "enlightened" jurisdictions, the prosecutor will tend to follow this informal means of dealing with discovery for good reason: It saves time, makes the trial judge happy, satisfies the prosecutor's ethical obligation to produce possible defense evidence, and eliminates a possible ground for appeal. Most important, it results in a more truly "open" trial on the merits. Nevertheless, counsel will often be faced with the necessity of pursuing the formal path to discovery. In such a case, he must make the appropriate motions in the proper court.

Usually, it is unnecessary to serve the police agency or state blood-alcohol testing agency with copies of the discovery motion; service on the prosecutor will normally be considered service on the agency's counsel. If, however, evidence is being held by the agency rather than at the prosecutor's office, it would be good policy to serve a copy on the agency. A subpoena *duces tecum* (subpoena d.t.) ordering the agency to appear at the discovery hearing with the requested evidence would be proper. In fact, counsel should never overlook the possibilities of the subpoena d.t. when trying to obtain evidence from any source. See the example of a subpoena *duces tecum* for a breath test, together with a motion for an order directing a pre-trial inspection.

For a discussion of sanctions for prosecutorial noncompliance with discovery, see §10.0.3.

Counsel should not overlook the discovery possibilities of his jurisdiction's administrative license suspension proceedings. Most jurisdictions do not provide for deposition of the arresting officer — or, for that matter, of the individuals responsible for administering the breath test, taking and/or analyzing the blood or urine sample, or maintaining and calibrating the relevant instruments. The first opportunity to question these witnesses comes at the trial. But a suspension hearing can be used for that very purpose: detailed cross-examination of these witnesses, particularly the officer, and in many states without the interference of an opposing attorney.

Due process requires the availability of at least an administrative hearing for suspension or revocation of the license for either refusing to take a chemical test or, having taken one, for having an amount of alcohol in excess of the per se laws (see Chapter 3). In some states, the officer is called by the department of motor vehicles to testify to the facts necessary to sustain a suspension; in others, evidence is entirely in the form of hearsay police and laboratory reports. In either case, the hearing is a valuable opportunity to depose the prosecution's trial witnesses.

Where the department of motor vehicles normally proceeds with documentary evidence alone, counsel should demand that administrative or civil subpoenas be issued so that the client may be permitted his constitutional right to confront his accusers. If the proceedings are recorded, a copy of the transcript or the tape should be obtained for later use at trial. If they are not recorded, counsel should use his own stenotypist or tape recorder.

§10.0.1 Objects of Discovery

Before counsel pursues obtaining possible evidence from the prosecution, he should consider the evidence available to him from other sources. He should locate and interview any known witnesses. If percipient police officers will volunteer to be interviewed, this should be done to avoid surprise at trial (often, the prosecutor will be unaware of the contents of police testimony); if they will not, the right to conduct such interviews should be included in the motion for discovery. Of particular interest — and often overlooked — is the jailor; his observations of the client after the arresting officers have finished can be relevant. In addition to interviewing witnesses, counsel should view the scene of the arrest and administration of the field sobriety test.

Most of the relevant evidence in a drunk driving case will be in the control of the prosecution, and it is critical that defense counsel have an opportunity to review it. This review serves three purposes: It precludes surprise at trial, thereby permitting adjudication on the merits rather than on tactics. It makes available evidence of value to the defense. And, it offers information as to where evidence may be found. Such evidence in the prosecutor's control can be extensive in a drunk driving case, yet in the vast majority of such cases — even in those jurisdictions having liberal discovery policies — defense counsel is content simply to receive a copy of the arrest report and nothing more.

In any given case, counsel should attempt to review at least some of the following items that may be existent:

Police arrest and accident reports
Officer's rough field notes
Reports of arresting officer(s) from other DUI arrests
Booking slips and "mug shots"
Videotapes, motion pictures, or photographs
Sound tape recordings
Transcripts of interrogation

Radio dispatch logs/tapes
Identity and addresses of witnesses and officers
Results of chemical analysis
Information on chain of custody
Lab reports, and identity and location of laboratory
Calibration, maintenance and use logs
Periodic determinations of accuracy
Training manual for DUI investigations
Sources of radio frequency interference
Physicians' reports
Copy of breath printout
Client's driving and criminal record
Oral and written statements of client
Oral and written statements of witnesses
Training manual for breath analyzer operator
Licensing/certification of operator
Operator's checklist
Computer programs/software for breath machine
Ampoule lot number (if applicable)
Portion of blood or urine sample (if applicable)

In reviewing the primary arrest or crime report, counsel should bear in mind that there may be additional materials in supplemental reports, particularly where there has been an automobile accident involved or where a continuing or supplemental investigation is taking place. If a second police agency was briefly involved in stopping the client or in his arrest, any reports this agency holds may be relevant. These are often overlooked by the prosecution.

Booking slips, if filled out by the client, can be evidence of sobriety, demonstrating ability to read, comprehend, and respond. This goes for the existence of normal handwriting as well. A booking "mug shot" may indicate whether the client was, as reported by the police, dishevelled, bleary-eyed, etc.

With the increasing use of preliminary breath tests (PBTs) in the field, and the growing willingness of courts to allow results of the test into evidence, discovery concerning the device becomes important. As with any breath-testing apparatus, counsel should make the usual inquiries into operator training, experience, and certification; operator and technical manuals; computer memory records; and calibration, maintenance, and usage records.

Counsel must make himself aware of the existence of any videotape, audio tape recordings, or photographs. There is a twofold reason for this: first, to avoid a very unpleasant surprise during trial; and, second, to make use of possibly favorable evidence.

There is perhaps nothing so disconcerting as to prepare laboriously a case for trial, build it up for the jury through skillful cross-examination and presentation of defense witnesses, only to have the prosecutor smugly wheel in a projector or VCR and show the defendant falling-down drunk. A lot of time and effort can be saved by viewing or listening to the evidence beforehand; if sufficiently damaging, this may be determinative in the decision of whether to plead guilty or go to trial. With the chances of an acquittal reduced drastically by such graphic evidence, it is rarely worth the time, trauma, and expense to the client to litigate the matter. On the other hand, viewing the evidence may enable counsel to blunt the effect at trial. He may, for example, have sufficient time to investigate the circumstances of the filming, taping, or photographing and prepare for an effective cross-examination or foundational voir dire. Or he may attempt to block the introduction of the audiovisual evidence before it ever gets to the jury by making appropriate pre-trial suppression motions.

The second reason for determining the existence of any film or tape is simply that it may tend to exonerate the defendant. And this is the reason why law enforcement agencies are somewhat less enthusiastic about audiovisual devices now than they were originally: The police department's own videotape, for example, may directly contradict the arresting officer's descriptions of a defendant's condition or performance on a test. It is a well-known fact that habitual drinkers often do surprisingly well on field sobriety tests; having developed an individual tolerance to high levels of alcohol, they often can appear quite normal and are able to walk a line as well as a sober person. Even persons with less tolerance often do well in the lower levels of intoxication — those, for example, with readings in the .10 to .15 percent range. Although legally under the influence in this range, many such individuals will have objective symptoms often not discernible from those of a completely sober person, at least on film or tape. And there is nothing more damning to a prosecution case than to contradict directly the sworn testimony of the arresting officer with its own visual evidence.

It is critically important, therefore, for counsel to be aware of the existence of such potential evidence. And, once aware of it, he certainly should view the tapes or film and/or listen to the sound recordings. In considering the possible existence of such evidence, however, it should never be taken for granted that it will be mentioned in the police report or that the prosecutor will make it known before trial. If the evidence is damaging to the defense, the prosecutor may want to spring it as a surprise coup de grâce. If it is damaging to the prosecution, an unethical prosecutor may quietly sweep it under the rug; more commonly, the prosecutor will not even be aware of the existence of such evidence because the police simply have chosen not to tell him about it. Counsel, then, would be well advised to make appropriate discovery motions prior to trial, preferably including a requirement that the police produce all evidence not submitted to the prosecuting agency and specifically mentioning audiovisual evidence.

For a discussion of sanctions for destruction of videotape evidence, see §11.5.7.

Counsel should consider the ramifications of the *absence* of any audiovisual evidence where the equipment is available to the law enforcement agency. Because of the two-edged nature of audiovisual evidence, which police departments are discovering, the expensive equipment that initially was greeted with such enthusiasm is often stored away in a closet. If the equipment is available, and if it was not used, the obvious question should be posed to the officer and to the jury: Why not? Certainly, it should be pointed out, motion pictures or videotapes would be conclusive as to the defendant's innocence or guilt. Yet the police chose not to use the equipment and presented instead the officer's conclusions and opinions. Why?

A very fruitful area of inquiry that counsel should consider in discovery is the prevalence of *"xeroxed" symptoms* in DUI reports. Attorneys with substantial experience litigating drunk driving cases are all too familiar with the marked tendency of police officers to "see" identical symptoms in case after case. Of course, symptoms such as "alcoholic breath" or "thick and slurred speech'' are to be expected in most DUI cases. But some officers — either because of laziness, suggestibility, or outright dishonesty — carry this further: Each of their DUI reports is strikingly similar to the others. In each case, for example, the suspect will fumble with his wallet while looking for his driver's license, lean on the car's rear fender for support, sway exactly five inches in the one-leg-stand, and stop at ''M'' during the alphabet recital. Given the admitted existence of this tendency, how can counsel show this ''signature evidence'' to the jury?

The best way to accomplish this is through use of the discovery process. Included in the discovery motion should be a request for copies of — or access to — all DUI reports of the arresting officers for a given period of time. This writer has been successful by limiting the period to 15 days before and after the arrest, as well as the day of the arrest itself — a period of 31 days. This should not prove too burdensome to the prosecution, yet should give an indication of whether the arresting officer is reporting duplicate observations. If the prosecutor objects on the grounds of invasion of the rights of privacy of the suspects in those cases (it is amazing how concerned prosecutors can become at times for the rights of suspects), counsel can simply stipulate that the names and addresses of the suspects can be deleted before the DUI reports are turned over.

The arresting/investigating officers' rough notes, or ''field'' notes, should not be overlooked as an item for discovery. The officer's notes at the scene will often contradict the final formal report or contain additional information that may lead to exculpatory evidence: an angle of onset in a nystagmus test may be ''recalled'' differently after a contradictory breath test at the station. Also, the final version found in the formal report will inevitably be a distillation of the field notes — modified, interpreted, ''computerized,'' and otherwise changed from the original, sometimes to fit the prevailing needs of law enforcement rather than the truth. Such raw material as witnesses' or defendant's statements, their addresses and/or phone numbers, the officer's original observations and estimates of times and distances, field sobriety test performances, and impressions and opinions — all take different shape as they segue from notes to written report to database to computerized printout to supplemental revisions.

The problem, as any experienced criminal attorney knows, is

that officers usually destroy their notes after the formal arrest or accident report is completed. The reason, of course, is obvious — to prevent defense attorneys from getting them. Thus, we have the *Peace Officer's Sourcebook* specifically teaching California officers how to get rid of the notes (i.e., how to legally destroy evidence):

> Concerning retention of your field notes, case law has quite consistently held that it is proper for you to throw away your field investigation notes as long as (1) you destroy them in "good faith"; (2) you incorporate them into a formal report; (3) the formal report accurately reflects the contents of the notes; and (4) the prosecutor turns over a copy of your formal report to defense counsel before trial. . . . Now, in light of . . . the United States Supreme Court decisions in *Trombetta* (1984) and *Youngblood* (1988), there is essentially no risk involved if you met those criteria.

If the client was injured in an accident, certainly counsel should obtain the accident report and the name of the attending physician, together with any medical records that he made. A medical release form from the client may be necessary for this.

Any evidence or information concerning the chemical analysis should, of course, be included in the discovery request. In the case of urine or blood analysis, all materials concerning the withdrawal of the sample and its storage, analysis, and chain of custody should be covered. A portion of the blood or urine sample sufficient in amount for re-analysis must be obtained. If a breath machine is utilized, the form filled out by the operator, together with his training or other qualifications, should be reviewed, as well as all records relevant to the particular machine: daily usage log, calibration log, maintenance records, periodic determination of accuracy, etc. Counsel should also demand production of the mouthpiece used in the breath test. As these are usually disposable units, the prosecution will be unable to produce them. Yet they may constitute evidence of regurgitation — which can, of course, result in artificially high blood-alcohol readings. These and related matters will be covered in greater detail in other chapters.

Manuals of various types can be invaluable to the defense in establishing that proper procedures were not followed. These manuals may be issued by local or state law enforcement agencies, covering such subjects as field sobriety testing, urine sample collection, or administration of the horizontal gaze nystagmus test, or by manufacturers of breath analyzing instruments. Whether obtained through a discovery order or by subpoena *duces tecum,* counsel should carefully compare the procedures used by the officer(s) in the field and at the police station with those established in the manuals. As most criminal attorneys know, few police officers actually follow the detailed procedures set forth in these manuals — but jurors are quite interested to learn that the officer did not follow approved procedures and, perhaps, proves unable on cross-examination to even recite what the approved procedure *is.*

Counsel can usually expect resistance to attempts to obtain copies of such manuals. Clearly, they are relevant. A recent New York Supreme Court decision denied the prosecution relief from a subpoena *duces tecum* to the superintendent of the state police for a breath test operator's training manual.

> The manual in question is a specific set of instructions and procedures for the proper performance of chemical and psychophysical tests. It constitutes the most comprehensive evidence in regard to State Police procedure for the arrest and testing of DWI defendants. It is certainly direct evidence of both the procedures that should be followed as well as the consequences of not following those procedures. . . . The defendant is entitled to access to the manual by the subpoena *duces tecum* for the purpose of proving what the proper procedures in testing were and that his accusers failed to follow those procedures, if that be the case. [*Application of Constantine (People v. Leto),* 538 N.Y.S.2d 395, 396 (1989).]

The case was subsequently reversed, but only on the grounds that the defendant had failed to "put forth the requisite 'factual predicate' making it reasonably likely that this voluminous manual contains material exculpatory evidence unavailable from other sources." 557 N.Y.S.2d 611 (1991).

If counsel is successful in obtaining access to a breath instrument manufacturer's manual, he should carefully check it for any disclaimer of warranty — especially warranty of fitness for a particular purpose. Any such disclaimer, of course, can be used to considerable effect when cross-examining the State's blood-alcohol expert or instrument technician in front of a jury. The witness' claims concerning the machine's accuracy can be dramatically contrasted with the refusal of the manufacturer to back up such claims.

If counsel's jurisdiction does not require expert witnesses to introduce blood-alcohol evidence, the disclaimer can be introduced through a defense expert or simply by introduction of the warranty page itself.

For a very thorough approach to discovery in a breath-alcohol case, counsel may wish to obtain discovery of the program used to run the breath machine. As the saying goes in the Silicon Valley, "Garbage in — garbage out": the results of any breath test are only as good as the software running the analytical process. For a discussion of this interesting area, see §10.0.2.

As computers become more common in law enforcement, counsel should adjust his discovery targets as well. For example, an effective approach to attacking the officer's claim that he had the defendant under constant surveillance for the requisite 15 to 20 minutes before the breath test (see §6.2.1) is to subpoena the dispatch logs and/or tapes. These seem to have a habit of becoming "lost." An alternative and more effective method is to subpoena the records of the *on-board computer* in the officer's police car: These should automatically record all calls from the officer during and after the arrest — and will reliably establish the time framework necessary to undermine the credibility of any pre-test observation.

Another fruitful area of discovery inquiry involves the problem of radio frequency interface ("RFI"). This subject is discussed in detail in a later chapter. The crux of the problem is that radio waves from various electrical sources can interfere with the electronic components in most devices designed to analyze blood, breath, or urine — resulting in erroneous readings. Thus counsel will want to determine what possible sources of RFI existed at the time of analysis (radio transmitters, receivers, walkie-talkies, telephone switching equipment, door-locking devices, television, etc.) and where they were located. This will, of course, cause considerable work for the prosecution. Police officers and/or laboratory technicians will strongly resent this time-consuming job. Nevertheless, the potential of RFI for causing false blood-alcohol readings demands compliance with such discovery requests.

Anne ImObersteg, a forensic toxicologist with Park-Gilman Clinics in Cupertino, California, and former forensic alcohol supervisor at a major California crime lab (and, incidentally, an attorney), suggests the following minimum discovery in a breath case:

1. Calibration and maintenance records of the machine.
2. Periodic determinations of accuracy.
3. Test record summary ("usage logs") of all tests for three weeks before and after the client's test.
4. Radio dispatch logs of the officer (to compare the time of arrival at the station with the time the breath test was started for purposes of determining compliance with the 15-minute observation period).
5. Documentation of the operator's certification on the make and model of machine used by the law enforcement lab/agency (note: certification for the procedures used by one agency does not mean certification on a similar machine used by another agency).
6. Titration logs of the simulator solution used to check the machine's accuracy.

Forms 12 through 15 are representative of the materials counsel will seek to obtain from the arresting agency: booking report ("Jail Custody Record"), police report ("Sobriety Examination" and narrative), Intoximeter 3000 checklist and test record, and Intoxilyzer 5000 technician's calibration and maintenance log. A sample medical release form for obtaining any relevant medical information concerning the client, including withdrawal of blood samples, is also exhibited (Form 16).

FBI NO.

CII NO.

S.3.3. (REV. 4/79)

Santa Monica Police Department
ARREST & BOOKING REPORT

DR NO. 95-12345 CR#

BOOKING NO. 1234 | RPT. DIST. 22.01 | CR# | 1

ARRESTEE'S NAME (LAST, FIRST, MIDDLE) DRIVER, DAVID D. | TECH | 2

ADDRESS 123 ANY ST. | CITY ANYTOWN | SEX | 3

DESCENT WHT | HAIR BLK | EYES BRN | HEIGHT 5-9 | WEIGHT 160 | BIRTHDATE 8-1-51 | AGE | 4

BIRTHPLACE PHILADELPHIA PA | AKA/NICKNAME | 5

AG'Y. ARRESTING SMPD | DATE/TIME ARRESTED 8-21-95 | TIME BKD. 0220 | 6

DR. LIC. NO. L0743634 | VEH. LIC. NO. 123 ABC CA | LOC. BKG. SM JAIL | 7

LOCATION OF ARREST 2800 23RD | TOTAL BAIL $325.00 | 8

CHARGE 23102(A) CVC | 9

10

JAIL CUSTODY RECORD

LENGTH OF TIME RESIDED AT PRESENT RESIDENCE 7 YRS

LENGTH OF TIME RESIDED WITHIN STATE 25 YRS

LENGTH OF TIME EMPLOYED BY PRESENT EMPLOYER 5 YRS

MARITAL STATUS MARRIED

DEPENDENTS NUMBER 1 AGES 8 YRS

MISDEMEANOR DISPOSITION BY | HOLD | CITE

REASON

JAIL LOC. STM | ARRAIGN. DATE | TIME | COURT | HISTORY OF COMMUNICABLE DISEASES, IF YES, LIST NONE | 11

SOC. SEC. NO. 123-45-6789 | OBSERVABLE PHYSICAL ODDITIES BEARD | OCCUPATION SALESMAN | 12

EMPLOYER (FIRM OR PERSON'S NAME, CITY, & PHONE NO.) ANY CORP., ANYTOWN | SPECIAL MEDICAL PROBLEM NONE | 13

CLOTHING WORN RED/WHT SHT, BRN PTS, WHT SHOES | LOCATION AND DESCRIPTION OF VEHICLE AT SCENE / 80 CHEVY 2 DR BLUE | 14

IN CASE OF EMERGENCY NOTIFY (NAME, RELATIONSHIP, ADDRESS, CITY & PHONE NO.) NO ONE | 15

ARRESTING OFFICER BOLTON | BOOKING EMPLOYEE RICHARDS | SEARCHING OFFICER BOLTON | TRANSPORTING OFFICER BOLTON | 16

PROPERTY DEPOSITED IN PROPERTY ROOM ☐ EVIDENCE ☐ SAFE KEEPING

CASH NONE | PROPERTY NONE | 17

PROPERTY DEPOSITED IN JAIL SAFE

CASH $50.73 | PROPERTY WALLET, MISC. PAPERS, GLASSES, PHONE BOOK, KNIFE | 18

PRISONER'S SIG. FOR REC'T. OF PROPERTY FROM JAIL X | 19

SEE NARRATIVE OF OFFENSE REPORT

D.R.No. 91-12345

20. SUPERVISOR APPROVING | SERIAL NO. 2123 | 21. ARRESTING OFFICER(S) BOLTON | SERIAL NO. 1984B | DETAIL OPS

R & I

Form 12
Arrest and Booking Report

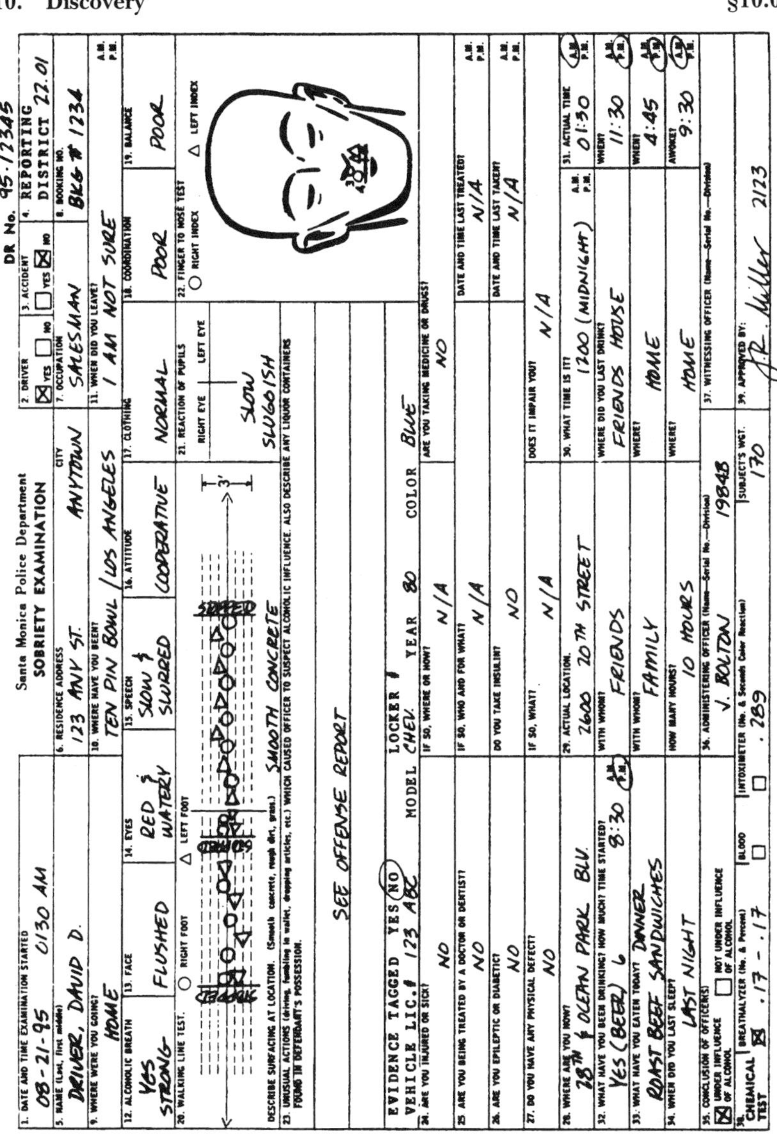

DR No. 95-12345

Santa Monica Police Department
SOBRIETY EXAMINATION

1. DATE AND TIME EXAMINATION STARTED: 08-21-95 0130 AM
2. DRIVER: [X] YES [ ] NO
3. ACCIDENT: [ ] YES [X] NO
4. REPORTING DISTRICT 22.01
5. NAME (Last, First middle): DRIVER, DAVID D.
6. RESIDENCE ADDRESS: 123 ANY ST. CITY: ANYTOWN
7. OCCUPATION: SALESMAN
8. BOOKING NO.: BKG # 1234
9. WHERE WERE YOU GOING? HOME
10. WHERE HAVE YOU BEEN? TEN PIN BOWL / LOS ANGELES
11. WHEN DID YOU LEAVE? I AM NOT SURE A.M. P.M.
12. ALCOHOLIC BREATH: YES STRONG
13. FACE: FLUSHED
14. EYES: RED & WATERY
15. SPEECH: SLOW & SLURRED
16. ATTITUDE: COOPERATIVE
17. CLOTHING: NORMAL
18. COORDINATION: POOR
19. BALANCE: POOR
20. WALKING LINE TEST. ○ RIGHT FOOT △ LEFT FOOT — 3'
21. REACTION OF PUPILS: RIGHT EYE | LEFT EYE — SLOW SLUGGISH
22. FINGER TO NOSE TEST: ○ RIGHT INDEX △ LEFT INDEX

DESCRIBE SURFACING AT LOCATION. (Smooth concrete, rough dirt, grass.) SMOOTH CONCRETE

23. UNUSUAL ACTIONS (driving, fumbling in wallet, dropping articles, etc.) WHICH CAUSED OFFICER TO SUSPECT ALCOHOLIC INFLUENCE. ALSO DESCRIBE ANY LIQUOR CONTAINERS FOUND IN DEFENDANT'S POSSESSION.

SEE OFFENSE REPORT

EVIDENCE TAGGED YES (NO) LOCKER #
VEHICLE LIC.# 123 ABC MODEL CHEV. YEAR 80 COLOR BLUE

24. ARE YOU INJURED OR SICK? NO — IF SO, WHERE OR HOW? N/A — ARE YOU TAKING MEDICINE OR DRUGS? NO
25. ARE YOU BEING TREATED BY A DOCTOR OR DENTIST? NO — IF SO, WHO AND FOR WHAT? N/A — DATE AND TIME LAST TREATED? N/A A.M. P.M.
26. ARE YOU EPILEPTIC OR DIABETIC? NO — DO YOU TAKE INSULIN? NO — DATE AND TIME LAST TAKEN? N/A A.M. P.M.
27. DO YOU HAVE ANY PHYSICAL DEFECT? NO — IF SO, WHAT? N/A — DOES IT IMPAIR YOU? N/A
28. WHERE ARE YOU NOW? 28TH & OCEAN PARK BLV.
29. ACTUAL LOCATION: 2600 20TH STREET
30. WHAT TIME IS IT? 1200 (MIDNIGHT) A.M. P.M.
31. ACTUAL TIME: 01:30 (A.M.) P.M.
32. WHAT HAVE YOU BEEN DRINKING? HOW MUCH? TIME STARTED? YES (BEER) 6 8:30 A.M. (P.M.) — WITH WHOM? FRIENDS — WHERE DID YOU LAST DRINK? FRIENDS HOUSE — WHEN? 11:30 A.M. (P.M.)
33. WHAT HAVE YOU EATEN TODAY? DINNER ROAST BEEF SANDWICHES — WITH WHOM? FAMILY — WHERE? HOME — WHEN? 4:45 A.M. (P.M.)
34. WHEN DID YOU LAST SLEEP? LAST NIGHT — HOW MANY HOURS? 10 HOURS — WHERE? HOME — AWOKE? 9:30 (A.M.) P.M.
35. CONCLUSION OF OFFICER(S): [X] UNDER INFLUENCE OF ALCOHOL [ ] NOT UNDER INFLUENCE OF ALCOHOL
36. ADMINISTERING OFFICER (Name—Serial No.—Division): J. BOLTON 19848
37. WITNESSING OFFICER (Name—Serial No.—Division):
38. CHEMICAL TEST: BREATHALYZER (No. & Percent) [X] .17 - .17 — BLOOD [ ] — INTOXIMETER (No. & Seconds Color Reaction) [ ] .289 — SUBJECT'S WGT. 170
39. APPROVED BY: J.R. Miller 2123

SMPD FORM #141 (Rev.9-77)

Form 13
Sobriety Examination (May Attach to Arrest and Booking Report)

INTOX. - DWI PAGE TWO
8-21-95 95-12345

On 8-21-95 at 0125 hours I, Officer Bolton, working Uniform Patrol in a clearly marked police vehicle, was assigned Radar Detail in the 2800 Block of 23rd St. My Police Vehicle was parked against the West curb facing Southbound. The speed limit in that area is 30 MPH. My radio unit, Ser. No. 744, was set at 45 miles, and calibrated, at which time I observed a blue Chevrolet traveling Northbound at a high rate of speed start to weave and enter the Southbound lane of traffic, passing my police vehicle, which the radar unit locked at the speed of the vehicle traveling at 45 MPH. I effected a U-Turn, traveling Northbound on 23rd, activating the emergency equipment of my police vehicle, observing the Chevrolet to effect a left turn, now traveling Westbound on Ocean Park Blvd. from 23rd St. Proceeding after the vehicle I observed it to continue to weave in the #1 lane of Westbound traffic to Ocean Park Blvd., then quickly change into the #2 lane, and I quickly closed the distance between our two vehicles, activating the spotlight of the police vehicle, illuminating the rear window of the Chevrolet, and effected a traffic stop in the 2600 Block of 20th St., facing Northbound.

I exited my police vehicle and approached the Chevrolet, observing the driver seated behind the wheel, detecting a strong odor of an alcoholic beverage emitting from the interior of the car on my initial contact. I asked the driver for his driver's license, observing that his eyes were red and watery, and that his movements were very slow and deliberate. The driver removed his wallet from his rear pants pocket, and after searching through it for approximately 1 minute, he recovered his license, handing it to me, noting the name of David Driver. I informed Driver the reason for the traffic stop, and also the erratic driving which I observed. He replied, "I am almost home. Can you give me a break?" I detected the strong odor of an alcoholic beverage emitting from his breath and person, observed his speech to be very slow and slurred, and believing that Driver had been drinking an alcoholic beverage, I requested that he step out from his vehicle. Driver complied with my request, and I noted, as he exited his vehicle, that he had to maintain both hands against the exterior portion of his car to maintain his balance as he staggered to the East sidewalk of 20th St., noting upon standing that he continued to sway from side to side.

I then administered a Field Sobriety Test from SMPD Form 14, which Driver failed. Refer to attached form.

Due to the manner of driving, physical symptoms of intoxication, and failure of the Field Sobriety Test, I felt that Driver was operating a motor vehicle while under the influence of an intoxicating beverage. I then placed him under arrest for 23102A CVC, Driving while under the Influence.

I then advised Driver of his obligation under 13353 CVC, and he selected the breath test. Driver was then handcuffed and placed in the rear

Form 13
(continued)

INTOX. - DWI PAGE THREE
8-21-95 95-12345

passenger seat of Police Unit 52 for transportation to the Santa Monica Jail Facilities. With the arrival of Assisting Officer Grant Driver's vehicle, a 1980 Chevy 2-D, blue in color, Calif. plate 123 ABC, was left legally parked and locked in the 2600 Block of 20th St. upon his request.

Driver was then transported to the Santa Monica Jail facilities for a breath test, which was conducted by ID Tech. Herman, Ser. No. 1477. This breath test was conducted on Instrument No. 289 at 0205 hours. The results of the breath test were .17% and .17% blood alcohol level.

Upon the completion of the breath test Driver was advised of his Constitutional Rights per Miranda, which I read from the SMPD Miranda Card. Upon completion, I asked Driver if he understood each and every one of his Rights, to which he replied yes. I continued, "Keeping these Rights in mind, do you wish to talk to me now without the presence of an attorney or any counsellor of your choice?" He said, yes. I then asked the remaining questions on SMPD Form 141, which Driver answered. Refer to attached form.

Driver was then booked, Bkg. No. 1234 for violation of 23102A CVC, Driving while under the Influence.

Report filed by Officer J. Bolton, 1984B

L. Nelson
APPROVED

(TAPE)

(RS)

Original - Record Bureau
2cc - City Prosecutor

Form 13
(continued)

SHERIFF'S DEPARTMENT
COUNTY OF LOS ANGELES
IR-3000 Checklist

INSTR. #	BLOOD ALCOHOL RESULTS
4542	.09 % .09 %
LOCATION	DATE TESTED
IND	4-29-95
NAME OF SUBJECT	TIME TESTED
	0214

WEIGHT	VIOLATION	FILE NUMBER
120	23152(A) V.C.	83-604

Follow the directions on the instrument's digital display and check off each step as it is completed:

1. (✓) Continuously observe subject for at least fifteen minutes before giving test, during which time the subject must not ingest alcohol or other fluids, regurgitate, vomit, eat, or smoke.
2. (✓) Date and Time Check: Yours: / Instrument's: (from display)
   Date: 04-29-95 / 04-29-95
   Time: 0205 / 0206
3. (✓) Press START Key.
4. (✓) Type ARRESTING AGENCY (3 characters), press ENTER.
5. (✓) Type OPERATOR'S NAME (Last, First), press ENTER.
6. (✓) Type SUBJECT'S NAME (Last, First), press ENTER.
7. (✓) Wait for the internal standard cycle to complete.
8. (✓) Insert a new mouthpiece into the breath tube.
9. (✓) When instrument displays flashing "SUB" obtain breath sample from subject.
10. (✓) Wait for purge/blank cycle to complete.
11. (✓) When instrument displays flashing "SUB", obtain second breath sample from subject.
12. ( ) If the two results differ by more than 0.02% the instrument will request a third breath sample; proceed as in steps 10 and 11 above.
13. (✓) Remove the printed results, initial for identification, and attach to checklist in the space provided. Discard mouthpiece.
14. (✓) Transcribe the first two digits of each breath result into the Blood Alcohol Results box above. At least two results must differ by no more than 0.02%.

Operator (Name, I.D.#, Agency)
FINN 13602 CHP/SFS

Witnessing Officer (If Any)

Remarks:

DAF

```
TEST RECORD

INTOX 3000    SN:4542
INDUSTRY STATION
SAT APR 29, 1995

<ARRESTING AGENCY>
CHP/SFS
<OPERATOR'S NAME>
FINN, D.
<SUBJECT'S NAME>
ESPINOSA

TEST    VALUE   TIME

BLK     .000    02:12
STD     .099    02:13

BLK     .000    02:13
SUBJ    .093    02:14

BLK     .000    02:15
SUBJ    .095    02:16
```

Form 14
Operator's Intoximeter 3000 Checklist

ORANGE COUNTY SHERIFF-CORONER
INTOXILYZER 5000
INSTRUMENT ACTIVITY LOG

1994 64-00 1906

DATE	TIME	CRIMINALIST	ACTIVITY
6-24-94	1035	K. W	Δ Sim soln 040194 .112% RFC → IOP @ OCSD# 1
6/28/94	1130	[illegible]	Δ SIM SOL'N (040194 .112%) RFC IOP
7/1/94	0800	[illegible]	Δ SIM SOL'N (040194 .112) RFC IOP
7/6/94	0930	[illegible]	Δ SIM SOL'N (040194 .112%) RFC IOP.
7/8/94	1300	[illegible]	Δ SIM SOL'N (040194 .112%) RFC IOP.
7-11-94	1620	K	Δ SIM Soln 040194 .112% RFC → IOP @ OCSD #1
7-15-94	1410	BM	Δ Sim Soln lot # 040194 .112% RFC → IOP
7-18-94	1410	K. W	Δ SIM Soln 061394 .110% RFC → IOP @ OCSD# 1
7/22/94	1400	[illegible]	Δ SIM SOL'N 061394 .110%. RFC IOP.
7/25/94	0825	[illegible]	Δ SIM SOL'N (061394 .110%) RFC IOP.
7-29-94	1625	K. W	Δ Sim Soln 061394 .110% RFC → IOP @ OCSD #1
8/1/94	1000	[illegible]	Δ SIM SOL'N (061394 .110%). RFC IOP.
8-4-94	1355	K. W	Δ Sim Soln 061394 .110% RFC → IOP @ OCSD# 1
8/9/94	1610	BM	Δ Sim Soln lot # 061394 .110% RFC → IOP
8/12/94	0850	BM	Δ Sim Soln lot # 061394 .110% RFC → IOP
8-15-94	1120	K. W	Δ Sim Soln 061394 .110% RFC → IOP @ OCSD# 1
8-19-94	1100	BM	Δ Sim Soln lot # 061394 .110% RFC → IOP

PAGE ___

Form 15
Intoxilyzer 5000 Calibration and Maintenance Log

To all physicians, hospitals, dispensaries, clinics, druggists, and veterans administration facilities:

You are hereby authorized to give my attorney, ________________ ________________, full particulars regarding my hospitalization, medical history, physical condition, diagnosis or treatment, all provisions of law to the contrary being hereby waived. A photostat of this authorization shall be as valid as the original.

Dated: ________________

Signature: ________________________________
(patient and client)

Form 16
Medical Release

The following represents a different version of a standardized drunk driving report, this one used statewide by the Kansas Highway Patrol. Notice that, unlike the Santa Monica Police Department form, this one utilizes standardized field sobriety tests and objective scoring methods approved by the National Highway Traffic Administration.

KANSAS HIGHWAY PATROL

Alcohol/Drug Influence Report

SUBJECT							
NAME: LAST JONES	FIRST ALICE		MIDDLE K.		SOCIAL SECURITY NUMBER 605-50-7737		
ADDRESS 2742 W. 13th			CITY Brown		STATE KS	ZIP CODE 67401	
SEX F	DATE OF BIRTH 2-4-64	HEIGHT 5-4	WEIGHT 105	HAIR Brown	EYES Hazel	SCARS/TATTOOS None	
ALIAS/NICKNAME(S) None			OCCUPATION Computer Operator				
DRIVER'S LICENSE NUMBER G2J4P6			STATE OF ISSUE KS	EXPIRATION 2-4-98	STATUS Valid		

VEHICLE							
YEAR 1989	MAKE Pontiac	MODEL Firebird	TYPE 2 dr.	COLOR Red	LICENSE NUMBER DFA 678	STATE KS	EXPIRATION 8-97
DISPOSITION (RELEASED, PARKED, TOWED, ETC.) Towed		RELEASED TO: Red Wagon Wrecker Service			COMMENTS: None		
CONTRABAND: ☒ YES ☐ NO ☐ FIREARMS ☐ DRUGS ☒ OTHER		DESCRIBE: Fifth of Jack Daniels					

REASON FOR STOP

On 5-5-95 (DATE), at approximately 0130 (TIME), on/at: 90th & Penn; (LOCATION) within the city limits of Wichita, Kansas, I observed the above vehicle doing the following:

____	Turning with a wide radius	X	Swerving	____	Driving into opposing traffic
____	Straddling center or lane marker	____	Slow speed (more than 10 below)	____	Signalling inconsistent with actions
____	Appearing to be drunk	____	Stopping without cause in a lane	____	Slow response to traffic signals
____	Almost striking an object	____	Following too closely	____	Stopping inappropriately
X	Weaving	____	Drifting	____	Turning abruptly or illegally
____	Driving on other than the roadway	____	Tires on center or lane marker	____	Accelerating or decelerating rapidly
		____	Braking erratically	____	Headlights off

OTHER: RS

SUBJECT OBSERVATIONS

Reaction time to emergency equipment? Slow RS	
Stopped vehicle properly? ☒ Yes ☐ No ☐ Other:	
Fumbled getting license? ☒ Yes ☐ No ☐ Other:	
Unsteady exiting vehicle? ☒ Yes ☐ No ☐ Other:	
Alcohol in vehicle? ☒ Yes ☐ No ☐ Other:	
BREATH:	Odor of alcoholic beverage ☐ None ☐ Faint ☐ Moderate ☒ Strong ☐ Other:
SPEECH:	☐ Good ☐ Fair ☐ Mumbled ☒ Slurred ☒ Profanity ☐ Soft ☐ Loud ☐ Other:
EYES:	☒ Bloodshot ☐ Watery ☐ Glazed ☐ Droopy ☐ Normal ☐ Other:
ATTITUDE:	☐ Polite ☐ Excited ☐ Talkative ☐ Carefree ☐ Sleepy ☒ Abusive ☐ Other: ☐ Cooperative ☒ Indifferent ☐ Antagonistic ☐ Cocky ☐ Combative ☐ Insulting
CLOTHING:	(Describe) Blue jeans, cowboy boots, green shirt, red jacket ☐ Stained ☐ Dirty ☐ Wet ☐ Unbuttoned ☐ Unzipped ☒ Other: Orderly
UNUSUAL ACTIONS:	☐ Laughing ☒ Crying ☐ Hiccoughing ☐ Belching ☐ Vomiting ☐ Other:
COMMENTS: Unable to complete Alphabet Test; Count Down Test: 68-53, had difficulty, missed 59 & 57; unable to understand and complete Finger Count Test.	

HP - 129 (Rev. 1 - 91)

Form 17
Police DUI Report

FIELD SOBRIETY TESTS

ONE LEG STAND

INSTRUCTIONS	TEST	0 to 10 SEC'S	11 to 20 SEC'S	21 to 30 SEC'S
STAND WITH YOUR HEELS TOGETHER AND YOUR ARMS DOWN AT YOUR SIDES, LIKE THIS. (Demonstrate how you want the subject to stand.)	1. **SWAYS WHILE BALANCING.** (Side-to-side or back-and-forth motion while maintaining the one leg stand position.)	0	1	1
WHEN I TELL YOU TO, I WANT YOU TO RAISE ONE LEG ABOUT SIX INCHES OFF THE GROUND AND HOLD THAT POSITION. AT THE SAME TIME, COUNT RAPIDLY FROM 1001 TO 1030 . . . LIKE THIS. (Assume the position and demonstrate.)	2. **USES ARMS TO BALANCE** (Moves arms 6 or more inches from side to maintain balance in the one leg stand position.)	0	2	1
	3. **HOPPING** (Able to keep one foot off the ground, but resorts to hopping to maintain balance.)	0	0	1
DO YOU UNDERSTAND? (Do not continue until the subject indicates that he understands.)	4. **PUTS FOOT DOWN** (Not able to maintain the one leg stand position. Putting foot down 1 or more times during 30 sec.)	1	0	1
BEGIN BY RAISING EITHER YOUR RIGHT OR LEFT FOOT. Indicate which foot the subject raised. (LEFT) RIGHT	5. **CANNOT DO THE TEST.** ☐ **(Score 5 points)**			TOTAL 4

COMMENTS: Counted slow - stopped her at 30 seconds

WALK AND TURN

INSTRUCTIONS	TEST	FIRST NINE STEPS	SECOND NINE STEPS
PUT YOUR LEFT FOOT ON THE LINE AND THEN YOUR RIGHT FOOT IN FRONT OF IT, LIKE THIS. (Demonstrate how you want the subject to stand.)	1. **LOSES BALANCE DURING INSTRUCTIONS.** (Does not maintain heel-to-toe position throughout the instructions.)		1
(When the subject assumes this position, continue with the instructions.) **WHEN I TELL YOU TO BEGIN, TAKE NINE HEEL TO TOE STEPS DOWN THE LINE, TURN AROUND, AND TAKE NINE HEEL TO TOE STEPS BACK.**	2. **STARTS BEFORE INSTRUCTIONS ARE FINISHED.** (Does not wait until you tell him to begin as per the instructions.)		0
	3. **STOPS WHILE WALKING.** (Pauses for several seconds after a step.)	0	0
MAKE YOUR TURN BY KEEPING YOUR LEFT FOOT ON THE LINE AND THEN USING YOUR OTHER FOOT TO TURN . . . LIKE THIS. (Demonstrate, make several small pivots, note that this is a very easy way to turn, but the subject must follow your instructions.)	4. **DOESN'T TOUCH HEEL-TO-TOE.** (Leaves 1/2 inch or more between heel and toe on any step.)	0	11
	5. **STEPS OFF THE LINE.** (Subject steps so that one foot is entirely off of the line.)	1	0
KEEP YOUR HANDS AT YOUR SIDES, WATCH YOUR FEET AT ALL TIMES AND COUNT YOUR STEPS OUT LOUD.	6. **USES ARMS TO BALANCE.** (Raises one or both arms 6 or more inches from sides in order to maintain balance.)	1	2
DO YOU UNDERSTAND? (Do not continue until the subject indicates that he understands.)	7. **IMPROPER TURN.** (Removes the pivot foot from the line while turning.)		0
BEGIN AND COUNT YOUR FIRST STEP FROM THE HEEL-TO-TOE POSITION AS ONE.	8. **INCORRECT NUMBER OF STEPS.** (Takes more or less than 9 steps in each direction. Don't count this item because he has trouble counting.)	9	11
	9. **CANNOT DO THE TEST.** ☐ **(Score 9 points)**		TOTAL 5

COMMENTS: Jones removed boots before the test

PAGE 2

Form 17
(continued)

ROADWAY SURFACE	SURFACE CONDITION	EDGE OF ROADWAY
X BLACKTOP	X DRY	X CURB
___ CONCRETE	___ WET	___ HARD/SOFT SHOULDER
___ GRAVEL	___ SNOW	___ DITCH
___ SAND/DIRT	___ ICE	___ GUARD RAIL
___ OTHER	___ OTHER	___ OTHER

FOOTWEAR	PHYSICAL PROBLEMS	WEATHER
X ~~SHOES~~/BOOTS	~~LEFT/RIGHT HIP~~	X CLEAR/~~CLOUDY~~
___ T-SHOES/SANDALS	~~LEFT/RIGHT KNEE~~	___ RAIN/FOG
___ HIGH/LOW HEELS	~~LEFT/RIGHT ANKLE~~	___ SNOW/SLEET
___ BAREFOOT	~~LEFT/RIGHT FOOT~~	X ~~WINDY~~/CALM
___ OTHER	___ OTHER	___ OTHER

COMMENTS: None

HORIZONTAL GAZE NYSTAGMUS

NOTE: Does subject wear contacts? ☐ YES ☒ NO

INSTRUCTIONS	TEST	LEFT	RIGHT
I AM GOING TO CHECK YOUR EYES. (Request subject to remove their glasses at this time.)	**1. EYE PURSUES SMOOTHLY.** (Be sure jerkiness was not due to your moving the object in a jerky manner.)	NO	NO
KEEPING YOUR HEAD STILL, FOLLOW THIS Pen **WITH YOUR EYES.** (Indicate what he is to follow.)	**2. DISTINCT NYSTAGMUS AT MAXIMUM DEVIATION.** (Do not mark unless some of the white is visible on both sides of iris.)	YES	YES
KEEP FOCUSING ON THIS UNTIL I TELL YOU TO STOP.	**3. NYSTAGMUS ONSET BEFORE 45 DEGREES.** (Do not mark if you only see faint jerking that occurs at the onset point.)	YES	YES

COMMENTS OR ADDITIONAL NOTES: Jones said she should have glasses and couldn't do this test because of poor eyesight

TOTAL: 6

SUSPECT ARRESTED: Date 5-5-95 Time 0145

DC - 27/IMPLIED CONSENT GIVEN? ☒ Yes ☐ No

DECISION CHART

Walk and Turn \ Nystagmus	0	1	2	3	4	5	6
0							
1							
2							
3							
4							
5							
6							
7							
8							
9							

Intersection: ☒ Shaded ☐ Unshaded

CHEMICAL TEST INFORMATION

Do you have anything in your mouth? ☐ Yes ☒ No Visually Inspected? ☒ Yes ☐ No

Type of test offered: ☐ Blood ☒ Breath ☐ Urine ☐ Refused **Observation Time Started:** 0210

Test sample taken by: Jim Dial Date 5-5-95 Time 0233

Location of test: Sedgwick County Jail Witnessed by: Trooper Smith

If breath was offered, indicate which test(s): ☐ 3000 ☐ 4011 ☒ 5000 ☐ MACS - 8 ☐ Other

TEST RESULTS: .14 grams of alcohol per 100 milliliters of blood or 210 liters of breath.

If test used was Blood, MACS - 8 or Urine, Test Analyzed by: NA Agency: NA

Date NA Time NA If the test was Urine, did test(s) indicate any drugs present? ☐ Yes ☐ No

PAGE 3

Form 17
(continued)

PERSONAL INTERVIEW

MIRANDA WARNING

1. You have the right to remain silent.
2. Anything you say can and will be used against you in a court of law.
3. You have the right to talk to a lawyer and have him present with you while you are being questioned.
4. If you cannot hire a lawyer, the court will appoint one for you.
5. You can decide at any time to exercise these rights and not answer any questions or make any statements.

WAIVER

After the warning and in order to secure a waiver, the following questions should be asked and an affirmative reply secured to each question:

1. Do you understand each of these rights I have explained to you?
☒ YES ☐ NO ☐ No Response ☐ Refer to Comments
2. Having these rights in mind, do you wish to talk to me now?
☒ YES ☐ NO ☐ No Response ☐ Refer to Comments

DATE 5-5-95 TIME 0210

NA = Not Applicable	NR = No Response	RC = Refer to Comments
RS = Refer to Supplemental Report		DA = Did Not Ask

1. Were you operating a vehicle? Up yours 2. Where were you going? Home, until you stopped me

3. Where were you coming from? JC's 4. What road were you on? Penn

5. What direction were you going? North 6. Without looking, what is the date and time now? Friday & midnight (actual) 5-5-95 0212 7. Have you been drinking or taking drugs? Hell, yes 8. What? Jack Daniels 9. How much? A fifth, I think 10. Where? I told you, JC's 11. What time did you start? 8 Thirty

12. What time did you stop? RC 13. Do you feel that you are under the influence now? Nope

14. Do you feel that you can operate a vehicle safely? Yesss! 15. Have you been involved in an accident today? Nope 16. Have you been drinking or taking drugs since the accident? DA 17. Are you injured or ill? No sir 18. What are your injuries or illness? DA 19. Have you been to see a doctor or dentist recently? No sir 20. When? DA 21. Why? DA

22. Do you take any prescription medicine? Ya 23. What? Aspirin

24. Are you a diabetic? No 25. Do you take insulin? No 26. Last dose? DA

27. Are you an epileptic? RS 28. Do you wear false teeth? No 29. When did you last sleep? NR 30. How many hours? NR 31. When did you last eat? Tonight

32. Do you want to see a doctor? What for? 33. Why? DA

COMMENTS OR ADDITIONAL NOTES: 12. When you stopped me, Stupid!

CHARGES

1. Operating a motor vehicle while under the influence of alcohol and/or drugs SECTION NO. 8-1567 NTA# 123456
2. Transporting an open container
3. Driving while suspended
4.
5.

Officer preparing report: Jim Dial (Printed) Jim Dial (Signature) 448 (Radio #) C (Troop)

PAGE 4

Form 17
(continued)

Kansas Highway Patrol
Supplemental Report Form

HP-129 X HP-133 ____ Acc. Report ____ Forfeiture ____

Offenders Name Last JONES	First ALICE	M.I. K.	605-50-7737 Social Security #

REASON FOR STOP:

Weaved 4-5 times in 10 blocks; nearly hit curb on two different occasions between 90th & 80th Streets.

PERSONAL INTERVIEW:

27. I don't know how you expect me to answer your stupid questions when I don't even know what the words that you're using mean!

SUBJECT OBSERVATIONS:

Reaction time to emergency equipment? I followed the car for 1/2 mile with my red light and siren on without any response from the driver. Suddenly the driver of the car turned right very abruptly and braked very hard when pulling to the side of the road.

Officer Preparing The Report Print Name Jim Dial	Radio Number 448

Troop Assigned C | Case # -- | Page 1 Of 1

HP-159

Form 17
(continued)

§10.0.2 Discovery of Computer Program in Breath Machine

If analyzing instruments such as the BAC DataMaster, Intoximeter 3000, or Intoxilyzer 5000 are involved in the case, counsel should consider a novel discovery tactic — one that, incidentally, will cause the prosecution unending headaches. These instruments use computer software — that is, analysis is done using a built-in program that incorporates such factors as the 2100:1 alveolar air-to-blood ratio in computing the final reading. Obviously, a defective program will adversely affect the accuracy of the reading — or, as computer buffs put it, "garbage in equals garbage out." Equally as obvious, counsel should be very interested in discovering the program used in the specific machine. Mechanically, this is not difficult: The machines are capable of producing a computer printout of their programming. The problem is that the manufacturers of these instruments will scream "trade secret" or "patent/copyright violation." The simple fact of the matter, however, is that all of the data in the programs are widely known scientific facts, and are not protectable — certainly not in the context of an accused's right to due process and fair trial.

The following memorandum from Wisconsin's Department of Transportation, reproduced in 5(6) Drinking/Driving Law Letter 1 (March 21, 1986), represents a reasonable approach to the problems presented by manufacturer's claims of "trade secret" when counsel seeks discovery of computer software used in breath analysis. Should counsel be confronted with the prosecutorial argument that discovery cannot be complied with, this approach should serve as an example of what can be done.

Date: December 9, 1985

To: All Concerned

From: Jerry Hancock
Assistant General Counsel
Department of Transportation

Subject: Intoxilyzer 5000 Discovery

This fall a defense motion was filed in Dane County Circuit Court seeking discovery of the internal computer program for the

Intoxilyzer 5000. As a result the Department of Transportation has made arrangements with the manufacturer of the Intoxilyzer 5000 to make a copy of the program available for inspection when discovery demands are made.

The company considers the information to be proprietary and a trade secret. The program is to be made available only if certain conditions are met:

1. The document will be kept under lock and key in the Department of Transportation office at 4802 Sheboygan Avenue, Madison, Wisconsin.

2. Access to the documents will be only by court order and only after the judge has reviewed and accepted the credentials of the defense expert who will examine the documents.

3. The expert offered by the defendant may not be associated in any way with a competitor of Federal Signal or its subsidiary CMI.

4. Under no circumstances will the documents be copied or removed from the Department of Transportation offices.

5. Access will be granted only for the purpose of allowing the defense expert to testify in a specific case.

Since the State Patrol administers the breath testing program on a statewide basis, we would like to develop a consistent approach to this issue. I am therefore enclosing a sample order and copies of the correspondence between the department and the manufacturer. After reviewing the correspondence this order was approved and signed by Judge Daniel R. Moeser in the case pending in Dane County. Hopefully the use of these documents on a statewide basis will provide the access to the information required by the defendant and adequate protection of the manufacturer's interest.

Thank you very much for your cooperation in this matter. If you have any questions, please feel free to contact me.

§10.0.3 Prosecutorial Resistance

Counsel should expect resistance to his attempts at discovery from the prosecution. This tends to be blanket resistance in all DUI cases, rather than in any particular case. The following approach, derived from a prosecutors' manual, might commonly be encountered in breath test cases — regardless of the facts:

Engineering drawings of the test instrument: The prosecutor should argue that he cannot be forced to gather evidence for the defense.

Written data supplied by the manufacturer: Same argument.

Written data collected by public agencies: Same argument.

Maintenance history of the breath machine used: The prosecutor should argue that this information is completely irrelevant.

Instructional manuals for the machine: Make the defense get this from the manufacturer.

Comparative tests by the Department of Health: The prosecutor should argue that this "may be totally irrelevant" and that, in any event, the defense should get it from the Department of Health.

Results of other breath tests: These are "totally irrelevant" and also protected by a right of privacy of those tested.

Calibrations: Again, these are "totally irrelevant."

Samples of calibration or control solutions: Prosecutors have claimed that there are no cases requiring these to be saved and produced.

Defense counsel will often encounter a prosecutorial argument that discovery materials cannot be produced because they are in the possession of other agencies, such as police departments, crime laboratories, state health agencies, etc., and thus it is up to the defense to obtain them with subpoenas, court orders, or whatever. Of course, this is usually nothing more than a tactic to make discovery difficult if not impossible to comply with: A simple phone call from the prosecuting agency will usually get cooperation from any law enforcement-related agency, whereas attempts by defense counsel through legal channels can become prohibitively time-consuming and expensive.

In *Hill v. Superior Court,* 10 Cal. 3d 812 (1974), the California Supreme Court held that if discoverable information is not actually in the possession of the prosecution, then the prosecution is required to make diligent and good faith efforts to *obtain and make available* to the defense pertinent information and materials *possessed by other agencies* within the criminal justice system. See also *Engstrom v. Superior Court,* 20 Cal. App. 3d 812 (1974). Similarly, a New York court rejected as "ludicrous" the prosecution's contention that documents relevant to calibration and certification of a breath machine and ampoules did not have to be produced because they were not within its control. *People v. Briggs,* 519 N.Y.S.2d 294 (1987).

For further authority for the proposition that the prosecution can be forced to obtain ordered discovery materials from a police agency — even though the agency is not a party — see *Robinson v. Superior Court,* 76 Cal. App. 3d 968, 977 (1978). If the prosecution refuses to comply and insists that the defendant use a subpoena to obtain the materials, an appropriate sanction is dismissal of the criminal charges. *People v. Bigelow,* 200 Cal. App. 3d 59, 245 Cal. Rptr. 771 (1988).

Checklist 16 Possible Items for Discovery

Field Evidence

☐ Police arrest or crime report
☐ Identity and addresses of officers and civilian witnesses
☐ Accident reports
☐ Photographs
☐ "Mug shots"
☐ Videotapes
☐ Sound tape recordings
☐ Transcripts of interrogation
☐ Booking slips
☐ Other DUI reports of arresting officers
☐ Nonrecorded statements of defendant
☐ Oral and written statements of all witnesses
☐ Client's driving and criminal records
☐ Manual for DUI investigation
☐ Officer's handwritten field notes
☐ Dispatch logs/tapes
☐ Records of police car's on-board computer

Scientific Evidence

☐ Portion of blood or urine sample for independent analysis
☐ Identity and address of examining physician
☐ Physicians' reports
☐ Identity and address of technician withdrawing blood
☐ Blood withdrawal and custody reports
☐ Identity and address of persons taking custody of urine sample
☐ Identity and address of laboratory
☐ Licensing and compliance records of laboratory
☐ Laboratory analysis reports
☐ Breath analysis machine's daily usage log

- ☐ Breath analysis machine's calibration log
- ☐ Breath analysis machine's maintenance and repair records
- ☐ Records of periodic determinations of accuracy for the machine
- ☐ All records relevant to chain of custody of chemical sample
- ☐ All records relevant to officer's training in use of breath analysis machine — including certification
- ☐ Training manual for breath analyzer operator
- ☐ All potential sources of radio frequency interference
- ☐ Existence of any "RFI-proofing" devices
- ☐ Breath analyzer mouthpiece used by client
- ☐ Computer program or software used in analyzing device (if applicable)
- ☐ Ampoule lot number (if applicable)
- ☐ Technical manual
- ☐ Operator's manual

§10.1 *Preservation and Production of Blood/Urine Sample*

> Knowledge consists in understanding the evidence that establishes the fact, not in the belief that it is a fact.
>
> CHARLES T. SPRADING

It is helpful to the successful defense of a drunk driving case for counsel to obtain independent analysis of the client's blood-alcohol level. This can be done through obtaining a blood, urine, or breath sample within an hour or two of the client's arrest or by gaining access to the sample taken by the police.

Inherent in a defendant's right to discovery in drunk driving cases is the right to have access to any chemical evidence that may or may not be used against him. Mere access to the chemical evidence is usually meaningless: There is little value in being given a vial of the defendant's blood, for example, for the purpose of merely looking at it. Courts granting such access, therefore, will go further and permit an analysis of the evidence by an independent chemist or laboratory.

Where the evidence is unavailable, either through police neglect or willful conduct, a motion to suppress the results of the test — and possibly a motion to dismiss — may lie. This will be treated in a subsequent chapter.

Finally, counsel should consider retaining the services of an expert in blood-alcohol analysis. Cost and availability are factors, of course, but such an expert can be helpful in analyzing the prosecution's breath, blood, or urine sample, analyzing any secondary sample, reviewing the propriety of prosecution analysis methods, and testifying in court as to blood-alcohol analysis generally and as to the specifics of the case.

Suggestions for locating blood-alcohol experts and retaining experts at court expense can be found in §§10.1.1 and 13.3.

Whatever the present state of law in the particular jurisdiction, counsel would be well-advised to make a demand for preservation and production of chemical evidence. Involving contradictory interpretations of constitutional law as it has, the ruling in any given jurisdiction is liable to change, and the absence of a demand that is both timely and properly served could preclude counsel from obtaining sanctions.

Accompanying the text is an illustrative motion to preserve and produce a blood sample. It is exhibited together with a declaration of the attorney, sample points and authorities, and a court order.

(Title of Court and Cause)

NOTICE OF MOTION TO PRESERVE AND PRODUCE BLOOD SAMPLE

TO: __________________________, District Attorney of the County of __________________, and his representative:

PLEASE TAKE NOTICE that on _____________, at ______M or as soon thereafter as the matter can be heard in the above-entitled Court, Defendant __________________________ will move the Court for an order to preserve the blood sample taken from Defendant on or about ______________________ and to produce a portion of that sample sufficient to permit subsequent independent blood-alcohol analysis.

The motion will be based upon this Notice of Motion, the attached Memorandum of Points and Authorities and the Declaration of __________________________, all papers and documents presently on file herein, and any evidence or argument that may be produced at the time of the hearing.

DATED: ____________

Respectfully submitted,

____

(signature)

POINTS AND
AUTHORITIES

It is the duty of the prosecution to preserve evidence which may be useful to the Defendant. *Eleazer v. Superior Court,* 1 Cal. 3d 847 (1970), *Brady v. Maryland,* 373 U.S. 83 (1963). See also *People v. Hitch,* 12 Cal. 3d 641 (1974). This constitutionally mandated duty to preserve existing material evidence in a drunk driving case has recently been reaffirmed by the United States Supreme Court. *California v. Trombetta,* 104 S. Ct. 2528, 81 L. Ed. 2d 413 (1984).

Respectfully submitted,

____
(signature)

DECLARATION OF

____

I, ________________________, say that:

I am the attorney of record for the Defendant herein, ________________________. Mr. ____________ is charged with violation of Vehicle Code Sections 23153(a) and (b) — i.e. "felony drunk driving."

This case is currently set for preliminary hearing on __________________ in the Municipal Court of the ____________ Judicial District.

A blood sample was extracted from Defendant on or about __________________, while he was in the custody of members of the __________________ County Sheriff's Department. This sample was subsequently analyzed by members of the Sheriff's Criminalistics Laboratory, resulting in a reading of 0.18% alcohol.

An independent analysis of this sample is necessary to determine the accuracy of the analysis by the Sheriff's Department. I believe such an analysis is necessary for me to adequately prepare for trial, as Defendant has no other means for determining his blood-alcohol level at the time of testing and/or driving.

In order to obtain a portion of the blood sample, it is first necessary to place the People's counsel on notice that the sample is needed and must be preserved.

I declare under penalty of perjury under the laws of the State of __________________ that the foregoing is true and correct to the best of my knowledge.

DATED: ____________

____

(signature)

(Title of Court and Cause)

ORDER TO PRESERVE AND PRODUCE BLOOD SAMPLE

The Motion of Defendant for an order to preserve and produce a blood sample came on regularly for hearing before this Court on ______________. ______________________ appeared for Defendant, and a representative of the District Attorney of __________________ County appeared for the People. Good cause appearing,

IT IS HEREBY ORDERED that the District Attorney of ______________ County or his designated representative preserve the blood sample extracted from Defendant on or about ______________.

IT IS FURTHER ORDERED that a portion of the sample sufficient in quantity to be analyzed for blood-alcohol content be produced and given to counsel for Defendant for purposes of analysis.

DATED: __________

____

Judge of the Municipal Court

§10.1.1 Obtaining an Independent Blood/Urine Sample

An increasing number of states require that the law enforcement agency administering the chemical test (particularly a breath test) in a drunk driving case comply with an arrestee's request for additional chemical testing at the arrestee's own expense. Some of these states further require that the agency must advise the subject that he has a right to independent testing, or even that he has a right to have a breath sample taken and preserved by law enforcement officials. Police authorities should be reminded of such statutes where they apply.

Counsel may be called by his client directly from the police station. Usually this will occur during the booking procedures and within an hour of the actual arrest. In such circumstances, counsel should do more than just attempt to arrange for bail or an "own recognizance" release: He should immediately attempt to arrange for a drawing of a blood or urine sample for later analysis.

Obviously time is of the essence here. A blood sample withdrawn four or five hours after the arrest will have relatively little probative value. One drawn an hour or two after the arrest, however, will be quite relevant, as the "burn-off" or elimination rate of alcohol can be computed and the probable blood-alcohol level at the time the client was driving subsequently estimated.

Upon hearing from his client at the jail, counsel should make an immediate demand by telephone of the desk sergeant, watch commander, or jailor that a blood or urine sample be taken or that the client be made available for the taking of such samples. If the prosecutor's office is open, it should also be contacted immediately, if for no other reason than to make a record of the demand.

The next step is to arrange for the taking and preservation of the sample. Rarely will there be a breath machine available to counsel from an independent source; urine and blood analysis are the only possibilities. But, as will be seen in subsequent chapters, merely obtaining a vial of blood or a jar of urine and taking it to a laboratory is insufficient and will undoubtedly render the test results inadmissible. Rather, counsel must be familiar with certain foundational requirements for the collecting of samples — voiding the bladder and avoiding alcohol swabs, for example — and should have access to specialists who can proceed quickly to the jail and collect the blood or urine sample from the client. Obviously, knowledge of the location and around-the-clock availability of such a qualified individual, whether a physician or a laboratory technician, is a valuable asset to any lawyer who handles drunk driving cases.

At the very least, counsel should attempt either to visit the jail and obtain a urine sample or to request by telephone that the police take such a sample. Again, counsel should be aware of the foundational requirements of such evidence: Care must be taken that the jar is sterile, that the client voided his bladder and waited for fifteen minutes before urinating the sample, and that the sample is rushed to a laboratory for proper refrigeration and introduction of preservatives, if necessary.

Should the police be uncooperative in permitting a chemical sample to be taken from the client, counsel may well have subsequent legal remedies. In all likelihood, there will be insufficient time within which to obtain a court order. But refusing to make such defense evidence available may constitute grounds for suppression of the state's blood-alcohol evidence. See §11.6.10.

As with the refusal of police to permit independent testing, denial of an arrestee's access to an attorney may result in an infringement of his due process right to obtain independent blood-alcohol evidence. The Supreme Court of Arizona, for example, has recognized that the right to obtain independent testing can be denied by refusing an arrestee access to an attorney. In *McNutt v. Superior Court,* 648 P.2d 122 (Ariz. 1982), the defendant was arrested for drunk driving and at the jail asked to telephone his attorney so that an independent chemical test could be taken. The law enforcement officials denied this request. In affirming an order to the trial court to dismiss the charge, the court stated:

> This action by the state clearly violated petitioner's "right to counsel in private with an attorney . . . as soon as feasible after a defendant is taken into custody" guaranteed by Ariz. R. Crim. P.6-1(a). We agree with the Court of Appeals of New York, which said, "[L]aw enforcement officials may not, without justification, prevent access between the criminal accused and his lawyer, available in person or by immediate telephone communication, if such access does not interfere unduly with the matter at hand." [Cites.]. . . . The state's action resulted in petitioner not being able to attempt to gather evidence exculpating him on the issue of intoxication. [Id. at 124.]

For a further discussion of moving to dismiss or suppress on the grounds of denial of access to counsel, see §11.6.3.

The highest court of Maryland has gone even further, holding that not only does a DUI suspect have a due process right to an in-person meeting with his attorney before deciding whether to submit to chemical testing, but he also has a right to *have an independent breath test administered before deciding whether to submit to the testing or not. Brosan v. Cochran,* 516 A.2d 970 (Md. 1986). (See discussion in §11.6.3.)

Of course, counsel should be aware that obtaining an independent sample is a two-edged sword: The prosecution may be entitled to discover the results of this second test and possibly even produce it as corroborating evidence of the first test. Furthermore, the prosecution may be permitted to comment on the failure of the defense to produce evidence of the results of any second test or even on the failure to have a second sample analyzed.

In *State ex rel. McDougall v. Corcoran,* 735 P.2d 767 (Ariz. 1987), the prosecutor (over objection) established during examination of the officer that the defendant had obtained a second breath sample after submitting to the required breath test. Later, during his closing argument, he commented on the defendant's failure to offer any evidence of a second test:

> We don't know in this case what happened with the second sample. You can wonder to yourself what did happen. If it was to his benefit, a reasonable inference would be that he would have brought that evidence forward to you, but he didn't in this case.

The Supreme Court of Arizona affirmed the conviction, holding that "Even where the defendant does not take the stand, the prosecutor may properly comment on the failure to present exculpatory evidence which would substantiate defendant's story, as long as it does not constitute a comment on defendant's silence." 735 P.2d at 770. The court dismissed defense arguments that the questions and comment violated the defendant's Fifth Amendment rights, resulted in an impermissible shift of the burden of proof, and violated the attorney-client privilege. See also *Cunningham v. State,* 768 P.2d 634 (Alaska App. 1989).

This case involved a breath sample captured and preserved by the police officer and without counsel present: There was no confidential communication. Should counsel have a blood or urine sample obtained under different circumstances, however, there could be a very strong argument that the attorney-client privilege *does* protect both the results and fact of the second sample and/or test. An Alaskan appellate court, for example, has held that the attorney-client privilege is triggered when the defense attorney contacts an expert to analyze the independent sample. In *Oines v. State,* 803 P.2d 884 (Alaska App. 1990), the defendant obtained an independent blood sample after producing a .109 percent result on a police breath test; the second test also resulted in .109 percent. The prosecution then called the defense expert and had him testify over objection to the independent test result. The court held that communications to defense counsel by the expert cannot be disclosed, reasoning that "[i]f the state were allowed to subpoena [defense expert witnesses], the defense counsel's initial efforts to become fully informed as to the possibility or likelihood of . . . valid . . . defense(s) may be inhibited because of the potential that an adverse opinion will be used by the state." Id. at 886.

What if the arresting officer appropriates the independent test sample and tells the suspect to get another one? In *State v. Pipkin,* 364 S.E.2d 464 (S.C. 1988), the defendant had requested an independent test after having submitted to a Breathalyzer test. He was taken to the hospital and a blood sample was drawn. However, the officer took the sample for the prosecution's use, telling the defendant to give an additional sample if he wanted one for his own use; the defendant refused. Over objection, both the breath and blood tests were admitted into evidence.

The Supreme Court of South Carolina reversed and remanded, with instructions that both tests be suppressed. This was done on two grounds. First, the implied consent statute did not permit the officer to obtain a second test sample. Second, the taking "compromised" the defendant's right to an independent test.

What if the individual cannot afford an independent test? Does he have a right to such a test at state expense? A West Virginia court has replied in the affirmative, holding that to rule otherwise would constitute a denial of equal protection. *Moczek v. Bechtold,* 363 S.E.2d 238 (W. Va. 1987).

The right to an independent test may not rely on the arrestee consenting to a primary test, depending on the language of the applicable statute. In other words, even if the arrestee *refuses* to submit to blood-alcohol testing, counsel may be able to argue that he still has a right to an independent blood or urine sample for later defense analysis. The issue was presented to the trial court in *Commonwealth v. Sharpe,* 565 A.2d 496 (Pa. Super. 1989), where the defendant had refused to be tested, then had obtained a blood sample on his own immediately after his release one hour after arrest. The trial judge refused to permit evidence of the .07 percent test result because of his refusal. On appeal, the trial court's refusal was deemed error and the conviction was vacated.

What if the officer does not *request* the suspect to submit to blood-alcohol testing? Does the individual still have a right to an independent test? No, says the Supreme Court of Washington. In *State v. Entzel,* 805 P.2d 228 (Wash. 1991), the arresting officer did not ask the suspect to submit to a breath test after he had already refused to take field sobriety tests. The defendant appealed his conviction, claiming that he had been denied possibly exculpatory evidence by not being advised of, and offered, an independent test as required under the implied consent law. The supreme court held that since the officer did not invoke the implied consent law, he had no affirmative duty to advise the defendant of his right to an independent test. Further, although the state had an obligation to preserve material evidence, it did "not have to seek out exculpatory evidence or conduct tests to exonerate a defendant." Id. at 230.

An important evidentiary issue concerning independent testing for blood alcohol involves the question of compliance with state statutes on blood-alcohol procedures and standards: Must the *defendant* show compliance with such statutes as a foundation for admission of the results — as is required of the prosecution? Commonly, such statutes require a showing, for example, that the breath-testing device has been properly calibrated and maintained, that the operator is qualified, and that approved procedures have been followed.

The issue was squarely presented in an Oregon case, *State v. Milstead,* 57 Or. App. 658, 646 P.2d 63 (1982), involving the frustrated attempts of a defendant to place in evidence a .01 percent Breathalyzer reading over the prosecutor's successful objection that the defendant had not shown compliance with the provisions of the state statutory foundation requirements. In holding that a defendant *can* introduce blood-alcohol evidence without complying with such requirements, the Oregon court reasoned:

> In deciding whether O.R.S. 748.815 (the foundational requirements statute) should apply to a favorable breath-test result that defendant seeks to introduce, we must first determine the purpose of the Implied Consent Law. Generally, breathalyzer results are offered by the state to prove a violation of O.R.S. 487.540(1), and their admissibility is restricted only in DUII prosecutions. O.R.S. 487.815 does not apply in any other criminal or civil actions. O.R.S. 487.815(3)(c) places the burden on the state to test and certify the equipment before its regular use and periodically thereafter. Therefore, the statute will generally act to prevent conviction of persons for DUII as a result of faulty equipment or procedures. This is the principal purpose of the statute. See *State v. Fogel,* 254 Or. 268, 274, 459 P.2d 873 (1969). Clearly, the purpose of preventing conviction on unreliable evidence does not justify excluding the results of tests performed by the state sought to be introduced by a defendant when the test result has an exculpatory tendency. If the state, in fact, believes the test was unreliable, it may offer evidence to that effect in rebuttal. The trier of fact may or may not believe that evidence. Moreover, it does not necessarily follow that a test result is not accurate merely because the machine on which the test was made has not been tested for accuracy within the time specified. The certification requirement is a condition to the test's use by the state to convict, not to its use by defendant to cast doubt upon the state's other proof of intoxication. [646 P.2d at 65–66.]

The court then applied this reasoning to a situation where the defendant obtained an independent test (as opposed to where he seeks to introduce the results of the test administered by the police):

> Also, a person arrested for DUI may obtain an independent chemical or blood test by a qualified person under O.R.S.-487.810, which is admissible without certification or approval of the test administrators or their methods and machinery. Defects in such tests presumably go to the weight accorded the evidence, not to its admissibility. It would appear logical that the same should be true for state-administered test results offered by a defendant. Because defendant could introduce uncertified private test results, we perceive no purpose to be served by refusing to permit her to intro-

> duce uncertified state test results. Similarly, a defendant who has taken a breath test at the request of an officer and obtained a favorable reading would be unlikely to request another test pursuant to O.R.S. 487.810. O.R.S. 487.815 imposes the duty on the state to conduct state-requested tests in compliance with methods approved, and by persons possessing valid permits, issued by the Health Division or the Department of State Police and with equipment tested in accordance with O.R.S. 487.815(3)(c). However, the Implied Consent Law does not require that a defendant prove that a breathalyzer test was administered in compliance with O.R.S. 487.815 before the result can be admitted. [646 P.2d at 66.]

In a footnote, the court added:

> It should also be noted that the breathalyzer is the state's test. The state alone has control of the equipment, methods and operators. It is therefore reasonable to require state compliance with the Implied Consent Law and to exclude breathalyzer evidence in the absence of such compliance. It is not reasonable to impose the same restriction on a defendant who has no such control. [646 P.2d at 66.]

§10.1.2 Independent Analysis and the Defense Expert

The services of an independent expert in blood-alcohol analysis can be invaluable in the defense of a drunk driving case. Such an individual can:

1. Perform an independent analysis of the breath, blood, or urine sample obtained from the prosecution;
2. Perform an analysis of the secondary breath, blood, or urine sample requested by the client after the primary test;
3. Advise counsel as to defects in the prosecution's analysis methods and productive areas for cross-examination;
4. Testify concerning deficiencies and sources of error in blood-alcohol analysis generally; and
5. Testify concerning errors and improper procedures in the analysis of the client's breath, blood, or urine.

Availability of such witnesses and the expense in retaining their services can, of course, be a problem.

Expert blood-alcohol witnesses for the defense can often be found on the faculties of local colleges, commonly in the medical and science departments — particularly in the fields of analytical chemistry, toxicology, biochemistry, pharmacology, and forensic science. Individuals who have retired from careers in crime laboratories of law enforcement agencies represent another possible source. Medical doctors may also be competent to testify about blood-alcohol analysis.

The Forensic Services Directory may be useful in locating an expert. This is produced by the National Forensic Center, which also provides an automated list of expert witnesses through WESTLAW and LEXIS. While a majority of the experts listed in the Directory would have no application to a drinking/driving case, several categories have direct application, including chemistry, biological sciences, pharmacology, toxicology, medicine, and electrical engineering. The Directory does not purport to be a complete listing of all experts, but rather contains only the names of those who have submitted materials to the Center.

The Directory may be obtained from Forensic Services Directory, Inc., P.O. Box 3161, Princeton, NJ 08540 (800-526-5177). The price for the 1994 edition is $112.50, plus $5 shipping.

Another valuable source for locating expert witnesses nationwide is the Directory of Alcohol Related Forensic Experts. Revised annually and priced at $49, the 1994–1995 edition is available from Whitaker Newsletters, 313 South Avenue, P.O. Box 192, Fanwood, NJ 07023 (800-359-6049).

Yet another sourcebook is the Published Directory of Alcohol-Related Forensic Experts, available from Intercom Group, 2115 Fourth Street, Suite B, Berkeley, CA 94710. The telephone number is (800) 327-9893, and the price is $95.00 (as of 1991).

(Note: Some of the telephone numbers and prices of the directories have been changed. Please see the new "Resources" section following the Table of Cases for updated information, as well as for a more extensive listing of sources for finding blood-alcohol experts.)

§10.1.3 Getting a Court-Appointed Blood-Alcohol Expert

Should counsel be representing a client *pro bono* or as a member of a public defender's office, he should research the laws of the jurisdiction for authority to have the chemical evidence analyzed at the state's expense. In fact, even privately retained counsel may be able to argue successfully that the small legal fee charged his client exhausted the client's funds to the point where he now qualifies financially under the terms of the applicable statute for court-appointed assistance.

In most cases, this authority will be discretionary with the court and will include not only the ability to appoint an independent laboratory or chemist to analyze the blood, urine, or breath at state expense but also the power to direct that the analyst appear at the proper time in court to testify on behalf of the defendant, also at state expense. As a part of this authority, of course, the court can order the police or prosecuting agency to produce the evidence or deliver it to the appointed chemist.

In some jurisdictions, this power does not seem to be tied up with the question of financial ability; the court is free to appoint experts in any case it deems appropriate.

In a growing number of states, this right to have chemical experts appointed has been deemed to fall within the constitutional rights to counsel, due process, and equal protection. (See, e.g., *State v. Powers,* 96 Idaho 833, 537 P.2d 136 (1975); *State v. Ryan,* 133 N.J. Super. 1, 334 A.2d 402 (1975); *Torres v. Municipal Court,* 50 Cal. App. 3d 778, 123 Cal. Rptr. 553 (1975).) And if a state does not grant such assistance in an appropriate case, a defendant may be able to apply to the federal courts for relief (*United States v. Hartfield,* 513 F.2d 254 (9th Cir. 1975)).

Certainly, in view of the critical importance of introducing defense evidence to counter the extremely damaging chemical evidence offered by the prosecution, counsel should consider moving for appointment of an independent expert to analyze the chemical sample and testify in court as to the results.

In most cases, it should be noted, the defendant will have the *burden of proof* in his request for court-appointed analysis or expert testimony. Thus, for example, in *State v. Underwood,* 756 P.2d 72 (Or. App. 1988), the defendant moved for a grant of investigative expenses for the purpose of hiring an expert to determine whether his use of DMSO could have affected the Intoxilyzer reading. The appellate court found no abuse of the trial court's discretion in denying the motion, since the defendant had failed to show that the expert was necessary for the adequate defense of his case.

In his argument and/or written points and authorities, counsel should stress the relative disparity in the parties' access to scientific evidence and witnesses (and in the application of statutory presumptions). This is particularly true where the state will be calling an expert witness to testify against the defendant: If the prosecution feels an expert witness is a necessary part of the case, why is it less so for the defense? To limit the defense to explaining the theoretical and specific problems in the chemical test through cross-examination of an adverse witness is inherently unfair and a denial of due process. This inequality concerning the very heart of the case — the blood-alcohol evidence — demands that, at the very least, the defense should have access to the services of an independent blood-alcohol expert.

For a federal case in which the court rejected the state's argument that defense counsel could use the library to gather information with which to attack the state's chemical evidence, see *Little v. Armontrout,* 835 F.2d 1240 (8th Cir. 1987). For a discussion of sources for blood-alcohol experts, see §14.1.

Accompanying the text are examples of an order appointing an independent laboratory, together with an order to produce the chemical sample, and an order appointing a chemical expert to testify on behalf of the defendant.

(Title of Court and Cause)

ORDER APPOINTING
INDEPENDENT LABORATORY
AND ORDER TO PRODUCE

Good cause having been shown,

THE _____________ POLICE DEPARTMENT is ordered to produce a ____________ sample taken from the defendant on or about ____________ at ____________ Police Station and make it available to *(name of attorney or chemist)*, for analysis;

IT IS FURTHER ORDERED that ______________________ obtain from the ____________ POLICE DEPARTMENT, located at __________________________, the above-described __________ sample and analyze it for alcohol content, preservative, and anticoagulant, and otherwise inspect the integrity of the sample, utilizing whatever tests are necessary in order to accomplish that end; and that the laboratory submit a report of its findings to *(name of attorney)* at *(address of attorney)*, upon completion of the analysis.

This appointment is made pursuant to Section ____ of the ____ Code. All costs incurred are to be paid by ________ County.

____

Judge of the
Municipal Court

(Title of Court and Cause)

ORDER FOR APPOINTMENT OF CHEMICAL EXPERT TO TESTIFY AT PRE-TRIAL MOTIONS AND/OR TRIAL

Based upon the representations and oral declaration of ____ ________________________, attorney for defendant herein, and GOOD CAUSE APPEARING THEREFORE, it is ordered that:

Pursuant to the provisions of section ______________ of the __________ Code, ________________________ is appointed to assist the defense and testify on behalf of the defense at any pre-trial motions and/or the trial of this matter.

Due to this Court's finding that the defendant is indigent, the services of said chemical expert are to be paid for at public expense.

The above-mentioned matter is set for trial on __________ ____________________, and will be assigned to a trial court from Division ___________ of the above-entitled court, the Honorable ________________________, Judge Presiding.

DATED this ______ day of ____________, 19____.

____

Judge of the Municipal Court

§10.2 *Preservation and Production of the Breath Sample:* **Trombetta**

> I have never seen a situation so dismal that a policeman couldn't make it worse.
>
> BRENDAN BEHAN

In many cases, the client's chemical sample will be unavailable.

Most breath machines are not equipped to save a breath sample. Once analysis has been completed, the defendant's blood or urine sample similarly may be discarded.

The battle over the consequences of destruction of chemical evidence was first resolved in a California case (*Van Halen v. Municipal Court,* 3 Cal. App. 3d 233, 83 Cal. Rptr. 140 (1969)), where the court reversed a conviction for drunk driving on the grounds that the police had failed to produce the test ampoule in response to a defense subpoena *duces tecum;* police policy had been to routinely destroy each ampoule after use. The appellate court reasoned that the ampoule could have been defective due to optically defective glass, improper quantity of solution within, or improper chemical composition of the liquid, all these factors affecting the Breathalyzer reading. The court went on to say that in each case where a motion to dismiss is made the trial court must determine whether a denial of due process had occurred by the nonproduction of the ampoule. This would involve in each case a finding of whether it was "technically possible to determine, by post-test examination and analysis, whether the test result was or was not accurate."

The California Supreme Court subsequently affirmed the *Van Halen* position, stating that

> . . . the test ampoule, its contents and the reference ampoule customarily used in the test constitute material evidence on the issue of the driver's guilt or innocence of the charge of driving under the influence of intoxicating liquor. We conclude that the investigative agency involved in the test has a duty to preserve and disclose such evidence. [*People v. Hitch,* 12 Cal. 3d 641, 527 P.2d 361 (1974).]

The U.S. Supreme Court finally addressed the issue of whether the state has an obligation to provide a defendant with a breath sample. The Court reviewed the holding of a California appellate court, which had reviewed its earlier holdings in *Van Halen* and *Hitch,* in *People v. Trombetta,* 142 Cal. App. 3d 138, 190 Cal. Rptr. 319 (1983). In that case, it had been conceded that no effort had been made to capture actual breath specimens in an Intoxilyzer test for later testing, even though a "field crimper-indium tube encapsulation kit" was approved for use by the California Department of Health Services. The California court discussed the nature of this kit:

> This "kit" can be used in the field to collect a breath sample which is separate from the sample collected by the Intoxilyzer. The device is independent from the breath testing devices and is in effect only a breath collection as opposed to a breath testing device. The subject blows into an indium tube which captures the breath sample. The indium tube is a soft metal device used to capture and preserve a breath specimen for late analysis. The tube originally is in a single piece but when the sample is blown into the tube, it can be crimped to hold the breath sample in three separate compartments. These containers can then be placed in a gas chromatograph (intoximeter) device which will test the sample for blood alcohol content. The gas chromatograph is an approved device for blood alcohol determination; the indium tube is approved for use with the gas chromatograph if the sample is tested within 14 days of collection. (Instruments Approved for Breath Alcohol Analysis, Dept. of Health, Dec. 20, 1979.) [142 Cal. App. 3d 143.]

The California court then concluded:

> Due process demands simply that where evidence is collected by the state, as it is with the Intoxilyzer, or any other breath testing device, law enforcement agencies must establish and follow rigorous and systematic procedures to preserve the captured evidence or its equivalent for the use of the defendant. [142 Cal. App. 3d 145.]

The California Supreme Court subsequently denied a hearing in *People v. Trombetta.*

In 1984, however, the U.S. Supreme Court reversed the California decision. In *California v. Trombetta,* 467 U.S. 479, 104 S. Ct. 2528, 81 L. Ed. 2d 413 (1984), the court rendered a unanimous decision that essentially stated that the state is *not* required to preserve a breath sample for subsequent defense testing:

> Given our precedents in this area, we cannot agree with the California Court of Appeal that the State's failure to retain breath samples for respondents constitutes a violation of the Federal Constitution. To begin with, California authorities in this case did not destroy respondents' breath samples in a calculated effort to cir-

> cumvent the disclosure requirements established by *Brady v. Maryland* and its progeny. In failing to preserve breath samples for respondents, the officers here were acting "in good faith and in accord with their normal practices." *Killian v. United States,* [368 U.S. 231 (1961)]. The record contains no allegation of official animus towards respondents or of a conscious effort to suppress exculpatory evidence.
>
> More importantly, California's policy of not preserving breath samples is without constitutional defect. Whatever duty the Constitution imposes on the States to preserve evidence, that duty must be limited to evidence that might be expected to play a significant role in the suspect's defense. To meet this standard of constitutional materiality, see *United States v. Agurs,* 427 U.S., at 109–110, evidence must both possess an exculpatory value that was apparent before the evidence was destroyed, and also be of such a nature that the defendant would be unable to obtain comparable evidence by other reasonably available means. Neither of these conditions is met on the facts of this case. [467 U.S. 479, 104 S. Ct. at 2534.]

The Supreme Court discussed at some length what it felt to be the basic reliability of the Intoxilyzer testing procedures used in *Trombetta.* The Court then continued:

> Even if one were to assume that the Intoxilyzer results in this case were inaccurate and that breath samples might therefore have been exculpatory, it does not follow that respondents were without alternative means of demonstrating their innocence. Respondents and *amici* have identified only a limited number of ways in which an Intoxilyzer might malfunction: faulty calibration, extraneous interference with machine measurements, and operator error. See Brief for Respondents 32–34; Brief for California Public Defender's Association, et al., as *Amici Curiae* 25–40. Respondents were perfectly capable of raising these issues without resort to preserved breath samples. To protect against faulty calibration, California gives drunk driving defendants the opportunity to inspect the machine used to test their breath as well as that machine's weekly calibration results and the breath samples used in the calibrations. Respondents could have utilized this data to impeach the machine's reliability. As to improper measurements, the parties have identified only two sources capable of interfering with test results: radio waves and chemicals that appear in the blood of those who are dieting. For defendants whose test results might have been

> affected by either of these factors, it remains possible to introduce at trial evidence demonstrating that the defendant was dieting at the time of the test or that the test was conducted near a source of radio waves. Finally, as to operator error, the defendant retains the right to cross-examine the law enforcement officer who administered the Intoxilyzer test, and to attempt to raise doubts in the mind of the fact-finder whether the test was properly administered. [Id. at 2535.]

The holding of *California v. Trombetta* is, however, somewhat unclear. The court reaffirmed the *Brady* principle that the state may not — even inadvertently — *destroy* possibly exculpatory evidence. The court found factually, however, that no evidence was destroyed in Trombetta's case: The sample taken was simply used up in testing, and the police, said the court, were under no obligation to gather *additional* breath samples for defense use. What the court apparently did not recognize was that many breath analyzing machines use up only a small portion of the breath actually captured from the suspect. Whether the remaining portion of the sample is simply purged from the machine or otherwise discarded, it *is* (if only for a moment) in the possession of the agency — and by purging or discarding *is* destroyed.

In any event, defense counsel should not abandon the *Trombetta* issue. The U.S. Supreme Court has held that there is no right under the U.S. Constitution to production of breath samples — but the argument may still be made that there is a right under the *state's* constitution. Thus, for example, the Supreme Court of New Hampshire has rendered an opinion that its own constitution's due process clause requires that a second breath sample be retained by the police for later defense analysis. *Opinion of the Justices*, 557 A.2d 1355 (N.H. 1989). Unimpressed by *Trombetta*, the court reasoned that not even the right to obtain a later test at his own expense protected a suspect's right to due process:

> A suspect would face numerous practical difficulties in obtaining a second sample on his or her own. While in police custody, the suspect would have to locate an available, licensed technician capable of promptly performing a second test, no matter what time of day or night. Even if a defendant successfully obtained an independent second test, the results would not have the same evi-

> dentiary force as would a second test performed on the same machine at approximately the same time. [557 A.2d at 1357.]

The court went on to note that "the technology existed for taking such a sample and the cost of it was reasonable."

§10.3 The Discovery Motion

> There is danger that, if the Court does not temper its doctrinaire logic with a little practical wisdom, it will convert the constitutional Bill of Rights into a suicide pact.
>
> ROBERT HOUGHWOUT JACKSON

In making motions to compel discovery, counsel should, of course, ensure that the latest applicable law has been researched on the subject. The motion must be properly noticed and accompanied by concise declarations or affidavits and thorough points and authorities. Proof of service on the prosecuting agency must be attached.

Timeliness of the motion should always be kept in mind. A late demand for production of a blood sample, for example, will be futile if it has been routinely destroyed after a period of time by the police. Certainly, the court will consider last-minute attempts at discovery just before trial without sympathy.

Finally, the order requested should be a *continuing* one, requiring the prosecution to turn over evidence that subsequently comes to their attention.

The following is a particularly extensive example of a discovery motion where a blood sample was obtained and tested. The author is grateful to J. Gary Trichter of Houston, Texas, for providing the materials. Although defense counsel should find these documents helpful, he should be aware that these are examples only and should not be used without reference to local laws, procedures, and form.

For an example of a subpoena *duces tecum* served on a state blood-alcohol regulatory agency in a breath-testing case, see §10.4.

(Title of Court and Cause)

ACCUSED'S MOTION FOR DISCOVERY IN DWI PROSECUTION (BLOOD TEST)

TO THE HONORABLE JUDGE OF SAID COURT:

COMES NOW, ____________________, the Accused in the above styled and numbered cause, under the authority of Article 6701(1)-5 §3(e), Tex. High. Code Ann. (Vernon) and Article 39.14, Tex. Code Crim. Pro., and requests this Honorable Court to instruct the prosecutor in this case to produce the following items for inspection, copying or photographing:

GRANTED/DENIED/ AGREED	1. All statements, written or oral, and any evidence of acts amounting to statements alleged to have been made by the Defendant, including res gestae statements.
GRANTED/DENIED/ AGREED	2. All audio and video electronic recordings which contain purported conduct and conversations of the Accused. Production and duplication will occur at: Time: ____________________ Date: ____________________ Location: ____________________
GRANTED/DENIED/ AGREED	3. A list of all State's witnesses. 4. The specific names of the State's witness who:
GRANTED/DENIED/ AGREED	(A) Extracted the blood specimen from the Defendant. (B) Analyzed the blood specimen of the Defendant.

(C) Will interpret the blood alcohol concentration analysis by testifying for the prosecution.

5. All physical evidence, photographs, or diagrams intended for use by the State at trial. Said request to include:

GRANTED/DENIED/ AGREED	(A) The booking photographs taken of the Defendant.
GRANTED/DENIED/ AGREED	(B) Diagrams, charts, or photographs intended for use by either prosecution witnesses or the prosecutor.
GRANTED/DENIED/ AGREED	(C) Any signatures or writing samples taken of the Accused during the booking process.
GRANTED/DENIED/ AGREED	(D) Any written materials prepared by the State that were used in interrogation of the Defendant.

6. Any written waiver or any evidence of waiver alleged by the Government to have been made by the Accused concerning the Accused's Constitutional or statutory rights. Specifically, request is made with regard to:

GRANTED/DENIED/ AGREED	(A) *Miranda v. Arizona,* 384 U.S. 436 (1966) (custodial interrogation procedural safeguards).
GRANTED/DENIED/ AGREED	(B) Article 38.22, Tex. Code Crim. Proc. (custodial interrogation procedural safeguards).
GRANTED/DENIED/ AGREED	(C) *Edwards v. Arizona,* 451 U.S. 477 (1981) (right to counsel).

GRANTED/DENIED/AGREED (D) Consent to any investigative detention, search, or seizure.

GRANTED/DENIED/AGREED (E) The Defendant's right to a second, independent chemical test under authority of Article 67011-5 §3(d).

GRANTED/DENIED/AGREED 7. Evidence of any extraneous offenses.

GRANTED/DENIED/AGREED 8. All evidence which would be exculpatory or mitigatory at the guilt/innocence or punishment stage of the trial, such production to include any and all statements of all persons who the Government does not plan to call as witnesses, but who have provided statements about the Defendant, intoxilyzer, or simulator, whether written or oral, in this case.

GRANTED/DENIED/AGREED 9. A list bearing the names of all persons who participated in any prearrest investigation of the Accused for the offense now before the Court and all officers who participated in the arrest and subsequent investigation of this cause.

GRANTED/DENIED/AGREED 10. (A) The handwritten and typed notes of the law enforcement officers who investigated and participated in any manner in this case.

(B) Further, that all said notes be ordered to be present at any and all contested hearings from purposes of cross-examination after the witness has testified.

GRANTED/DENIED/AGREED 11. The criminal arrest and conviction records, if any, of all witnesses who will testify for the State of Texas in this cause, whether they be agents of the State of Texas or otherwise. Such production to include evidence of bad character for being truthful or peaceful and law abiding and evidence of specific acts of misconduct of all informants and other persons who may have aided the prosecution in investigation of this case.

GRANTED/DENIED/ AGREED

12. All laboratory, fingerprint, or scientific reports in any way connected with the prosecution of this cause. In particular, a copy of the blood-alcohol analysis test records, notes, and memoranda of the Defendant analysis is requested.

GRANTED/DENIED/ AGREED

13. All photographic prints that were made and also all negative prints not developed for any reason that were made by the investigating law enforcement agencies in this investigation which have not been produced for inspection by the Defendant.

GRANTED/DENIED/ AGREED

14. The exact job description and duties of the person who extracted the blood specimen from the Defendant.

GRANTED/DENIED/ AGREED

15. The names of all professional licenses held by the person who extracted the blood specimen from the Defendant, along with the names and addresses of the licensing agencies.

GRANTED/DENIED/ AGREED

16. The number of blood specimens taken from the Defendant.

GRANTED/DENIED/AGREED

17. The amount of blood taken from the Defendant.

GRANTED/DENIED/AGREED

18. A detailed description of the procedure utilized to extract the blood specimen from the Defendant. Said description to be specific enough to allow another person to exactly repeat the same procedure.

GRANTED/DENIED/AGREED

19. The location where the blood specimen was drawn from the Defendant's body (arterial or venous).

GRANTED/DENIED/AGREED

20. A detailed description as to how the location on the Defendant's body was prepped for the drawing of the blood specimen.

GRANTED/DENIED/AGREED

21. The name and description of the product which was used to prep the location where the blood specimen was drawn from the Defendant.

GRANTED/DENIED/AGREED

22. A detailed description of the sterilization procedures utilized on the instruments used to draw the blood specimen from the Defendant.

GRANTED/DENIED/AGREED

23. A detailed description of the method used to preserve the blood specimen taken from the Defendant. Said production to include the name and composition of any preservative used as well as the amount of the preservative used.

GRANTED/DENIED/AGREED

24. A detailed description as to how the blood specimen of the Defendant was stored and at what temperature it was stored.

GRANTED/DENIED/AGREED 25. The exact time the blood specimen was taken from the Defendant.

GRANTED/DENIED/AGREED 26. A detailed description of any procedures, guidelines, or instructions (whether written or oral) given to the person who withdrew the blood specimen from the Defendant by his supervisors as to how blood specimens are to be taken.

GRANTED/DENIED/AGREED 27. The names of any articles, books, or treatises relied upon or considered authority by the person who extracted the blood specimen from Defendant on the topic of taking blood specimens.

GRANTED/DENIED/AGREED 28. The name of the supervisor of the person who extracted the blood specimen from the Defendant.

GRANTED/DENIED/AGREED 29. All supervision records for the six-month period preceding the date the blood specimen was taken of the individual who extracted the blood specimen from the Defendant.

GRANTED/DENIED/AGREED 30. A copy of any health department license, hospital license, clinical license, etc., of the place where the blood specimen was taken from the Defendant.

GRANTED/DENIED/AGREED 31. An opportunity for the defense to view, inspect, and photographically record the physical location where the blood specimen was taken from the Defendant.

Time: ____________________

Date: ____________________

Location: ____________________

GRANTED/DENIED/ AGREED

32. Any written orders, instructions, or memoranda to the person who extracted the blood sample from the Defendant from his supervisors indicating that he should not speak to defendants, defense counsel, or generally to members of the public concerning any opinion he might have formed with regard to the intoxication of a defendant or events witnessed.

GRANTED/DENIED/ AGREED

33. The title, job description, and duties of the person who performed the blood alcohol concentration analysis on the blood specimen drawn from the Defendant.

GRANTED/DENIED/ AGREED

34. The names of any professional licenses held by the person who performed the blood alcohol concentration analysis as well as the names and addresses of any licensing agency.

GRANTED/DENIED/ AGREED

35. The names of all journal articles, textbooks, treatises, manuals, or dictionaries which the person who performed the blood alcohol concentration analysis deems authoritative in the field of blood alcohol concentration testing.

GRANTED/DENIED/ AGREED

36. The names of individuals whom the person who performed the blood alcohol concentration analysis deems authorities in the field of blood-alcohol concentration analysis testing.

GRANTED/DENIED/ AGREED

37. The date the State performed the alcohol concentration analysis on the blood specimen drawn from the Defendant.

GRANTED/DENIED/ AGREED	38. The number of analyses performed on the blood specimen taken from the Defendant.
GRANTED/DENIED/ AGREED	39. The number of other blood specimens of other Defendants tested at the same time as the Defendant's blood sample was tested.
GRANTED/DENIED/ AGREED	40. Any written procedures, instructions, or guidelines (whether written or oral) by the Texas Department of Public Safety or Houston Police Department as to how blood-alcohol concentration analyses are to be performed.
GRANTED/DENIED/ AGREED	41. Any procedure utilized by the Houston Police Department Forensic Laboratory to double-check their blood-alcohol analyses, i.e., any verification by other laboratories.
GRANTED/DENIED/ AGREED	42. A detailed description of the manner, method, and procedures used to perform the alcohol concentration analysis of the Defendant's blood specimen. Said description to include the instruments utilized, their size and model number; identification of all fluids, chemicals, reagents, and compounds by measurement and temperature; the make and model of any spectrophometer used and the light wavelength it was calibrated for; a record of the specific times each portion of the analysis was performed. Said description be specific enough to allow another person to exactly repeat the same procedure.

GRANTED/DENIED/AGREED

43. (A) The brand and model of spectrophometer used and a designation of whether the same was a single- or double-beam instrument.

GRANTED/DENIED/AGREED

(B) A detailed description of any repairs, modifications, or changes performed on the spectrophometer utilized in the blood-alcohol concentration analysis of the Defendant's blood specimen. Said description to include the last time the spectrophometer was calibrated and the name of the person who and/or entity which performed the calibration and any repair.

GRANTED/DENIED/AGREED

44. The result or results of the blood-alcohol concentration analysis performed on the specimen of blood taken from the Defendant.

GRANTED/DENIED/AGREED

45. The tolerances of the results of the analyses, i.e., the ranges of potential error.

GRANTED/DENIED/AGREED

46. The amount of the blood specimen tested.

GRANTED/DENIED/AGREED

47. An opportunity for the Defense to view, inspect, and photographically record the location where the blood-alcohol analysis was performed.

GRANTED/DENIED/AGREED

48. The names of all other fluids, chemicals, reagents, and compounds which were also stored in the same location as was the Defendant's blood specimen prior to and after the time it was tested. Said production to designate "prior" and "after" test.

GRANTED/DENIED/AGREED 49. The name of the person who prepared the potassium dichromate solution and the date that said solution was prepared.

GRANTED/DENIED/AGREED 50. A detailed description of any separate tests which were performed to determine the presence of acetone in the blood specimen taken from the Defendant.

GRANTED/DENIED/AGREED 51. All information the individual who performed the alcohol concentration analysis had in regard to the Defendant at the time he rendered his opinion on the degree of the Defendant's intoxication.

GRANTED/DENIED/AGREED 52. The name of the specific blood-alcohol concentration analysis performed, i.e., Dubowski.

GRANTED/DENIED/AGREED 53. The name of the person who prepared the calibration curve utilized in the alcohol concentration analysis.

GRANTED/DENIED/AGREED 54. A detailed description of the type of water used in preparation of the alcohol standard, i.e., distilled, deionized, or tap. Said description to contain any analysis performed on the water and what minerals were checked for in the water.

GRANTED/DENIED/AGREED 55. The type of pipette utilized in the alcohol concentration analysis, i.e., was it to deliver or to contain.

GRANTED/DENIED/AGREED 56. A detailed description of the manner, method, and procedures used to clean the alcohol concentration analysis' instruments and apparatus prior to their use in testing the Defendant's blood specimen.

GRANTED/DENIED/AGREED — 57. A detailed description of any automatic dispenser utilized for the dichromate solution.

GRANTED/DENIED/AGREED — (A) Said description to state when the dispenser was last calibrated and by whom.

GRANTED/DENIED/AGREED — (B) Said description to state when the dispenser was last repaired, the reason for the repair, the nature of the repair, and by whom it was repaired.

GRANTED/DENIED/AGREED — 58. A detailed description as to how ethanol was specifically identified in the blood-alcohol concentration analysis.

GRANTED/DENIED/AGREED — 59. A detailed description of all other testing done to determine the presence of interfering substances, i.e., the Schiff test.

GRANTED/DENIED/AGREED — 60. An opportunity to view and inspect the container or test tube, and any writing or memoranda thereof, which was used to store the blood specimen taken of the Defendant.

Time: ____________________

Date: ____________________

Location: ________________

GRANTED/DENIED/AGREED — 61. The written automobile inventory procedures of the law enforcement agency which impounded and inventoried the Defendant's vehicle and any written inventory of that vehicle.

GRANTED/DENIED/ AGREED

62. All character evidence sought to be admitted by the State during the guilt/innocence and/or punishment phases of this case under Tex. R. Crim. Evid. 404(a), (b), and (c).

And in support of this Motion, the Accused would show the Court as follows:

I

The items requested are in the exclusive possession, custody, and control of the Government, and the Accused has no other means of ascertaining the disclosures requested.

II

The items requested are not privileged.

III

The items and information are material to this cause and to the issues of guilt or innocence and punishment to be determined in this cause.

IV

The Accused will not be properly prepared to go to trial without such information and inspection, nor can the Accused adequately prepare a defense to the charges against him.

V

That absent such discovery the Accused's rights under Article 6701(1)-5, §3(e), Tex. High. Code Ann. (Vernon), Article 39.14, Tex. Code of Crim. Proc., Article 1, §10 of the Constitution of the State of Texas, and the Fourth, Fifth, Sixth, and Fourteenth Amendments to the Constitution of the United States will be violated, to his irreparable injury, and thus deprive the Accused of a fair trial herein.

VI

Evidence of a prior criminal record, including convictions for felony offenses and misdemeanor offenses, particularly those misdemeanor offenses involving moral turpitude and acts of misconduct, are relevant and material for impeachment purposes and to shed light on the bias, prejudice, motive, and ill feelings on the part of any witness testifying in this cause.

WHEREFORE, PREMISES CONSIDERED, the Accused prays this Court to grant this Motion in all respects and to:

GRANTED/DENIED 1. Order all law enforcement agents to retain any notes made in the course of their investigation and to turn them over to the prosecutor in this cause;

GRANTED/DENIED 2. Order the prosecutor to be under a continuing duty to disclose any information which the Court orders but which the Government at present does not possess;

GRANTED/DENIED 3. Prohibit the Government from introducing evidence at trial which the Court orders the Government to reveal but it fails to do so;

GRANTED/DENIED 4. Inspect the files of the State and all law enforcement agencies and question the Government's law enforcement agents assigned to this case so that a judicial determination of the existence of exculpatory or mitigatory evidence can be made; and,

GRANTED/DENIED 5. Order further relief that this Court deems equitable and necessary.

GRANTED/DENIED 6. All said production to be made by the State on the ______________ day of ______________, 1987, at the law office of defense counsel at 10:00 A.M.

DATED: ______________

Respectfully submitted,

____
(signature)

§10.4 The Subpoena Duces Tecum

> Crime is common. Logic is rare. Therefore it is upon the logic rather than upon the crime that you should dwell.
>
> SIR ARTHUR CONAN DOYLE

Where material not in the possession of the prosecution cannot be obtained by means of informal discovery or through a motion to compel discovery, counsel should consider the direct approach: the issuance of a subpoena *duces tecum.* The most commonly encountered situation calling for this method in drunk driving cases involves information and materials relating to the blood-alcohol analysis.

The following represents a very thorough subpoena d.t. successfully used on numerous occasions by Phillip B. Price, Sr., of Huntsville, Alabama.

**IN THE CIRCUIT COURT
OF MADISON COUNTY, ALABAMA**

STATE OF ALABAMA,	)	
	)	
PLAINTIFF,	)	
	)	
VS.	)	CASE NO. ____________
	)	
(NAME)	)	
	)	
DEFENDANT.	)	

*MOTION FOR ORDER
DIRECTING PRE-TRIAL
INSPECTION*

COMES NOW the defendant through counsel, and would show unto the Court as follows:

1. The Defendant is charged with driving under the influence of alcohol; said case being set for trial on ______________, 1991.

2. That defense counsel has prepared a Subpoena Duces Tecum to the Technical Director of the Department of Forensic Science for the State of Alabama, a copy of which is attached hereto as Exhibit "A" for reference.

3. That to enable counsel to prepare a defense for the accused, as a right protected by the Sixth Amendment to the United States Constitution as well as Article 1, Section 6 of the Constitution of the State of Alabama, counsel needs an order pursuant to Rule 17.3(b) of the Alabama Rules of Criminal Procedure directing that the books, papers, documents and other objects designated in said Subpoena Duces Tecum be produced before the Court at a time prior to trial, and upon production that the Court will permit the defendant and counsel for the defendant to inspect and copy said items. *Brady v. Maryland,* 373 U.S. 83 (83 S.

Ct. 1194, 10 L. Ed. 2d 215). See also comments to Rule 16.1, Alabama Rules of Criminal Procedure.

Respectfully submitted this _____ day of ____________, 1991.

____

PHILLIP B. PRICE, SR.
ATTORNEY FOR DEFENDANT
113 North Side Square
Huntsville, Alabama 35801
(205) 536-6000

CERTIFICATE OF SERVICE

I hereby certify that a copy of the foregoing Motion has been forwarded to (NAME), via U.S. Mail, this the ___________ day of _________, 1991.

____

Phillip B. Price, Sr.

IN THE CIRCUIT COURT
OF MADISON COUNTY, ALABAMA

STATE OF ALABAMA,	)	
	)	
PLAINTIFF,	)	
	)	
VS.	)	CASE NO. ______________
	)	
(NAME)	)	
	)	
DEFENDANT.	)	

SUBPOENA DUCES TECUM

TO: *Technical Director of the Alabama Department of*
Forensic Science
231 Montgomery Street
Montgomery, Alabama 36104

You are ordered to appear in the above-named court on the following date, time and place and bring the following documents, books or papers or other things to be produced on behalf of the *defendant.*

Date: *February 15, 1991*

Time: *9:00* A.M.

Place: *Courtroom #6, Madison County Courthouse,*
Huntsville, Alabama 35801.

Things to be Produced:

1. Any and all criteria used for the approval of the Intoxilyzer Model 5000 in the State of Alabama.

2. Any and all experiments and scientific performance criteria that were used for the Intoxilyzer Model 5000 in the State of Alabama.

3. Any and all written scientific performance criteria used for the approval of the Intoxilyzer Model 5000 in the State of Alabama.

4. Any and all documents under your supervision and control regarding the scientific performance criteria used for the approval of the Intoxilyzer Model 5000 in the State of Alabama.

5. Any and all data collected to establish that the linearity of the Intoxilyzer Model 5000 was acceptable over the range of 0.00 to 0.40 percent ethyl alcohol.

6. Any and all documents under your supervision and control which deal, in any way whatsoever, with the experiments done prior to or subsequent to the approval of the Intoxilyzer Model 5000 by the State of Alabama, regarding whether or not it is directly related to the blood alcohol concentration of individuals tested.

7. Any and all data and the source of data collected that shows whether or not the Intoxilyzer Model 5000, as used in the State of Alabama, was capable of providing test results of no greater than 0.003 percent ethyl alcohol when alcohol-free subjects were tested.

8. Any and all data collected by the State of Alabama in showing whether or not the Intoxilyzer Model 5000, as used in Alabama, was capable of detecting residual mouth alcohol in human subjects.

9. Any and all data and the source of data collected by the State of Alabama regarding the Intoxilyzer Model 5000, as used in Alabama, to show whether or not it could detect the presence of acetone or other detones in alcohol-free subjects.

10. Describe in specific detail what documents or other tangible evidence are within the custody and control of the Department of Forensic Sciences or other administrative agencies under the control of the State of Alabama as it relates to the Intoxilyzer Model 5000 and whether or not it can detect the presence of acetone or other ketone bodies in alcohol-free subjects.

11. Provide any and all data and the source of data collected by the State of Alabama in showing the Intoxilyzer Model 5000,

as used in Alabama, could detect acetone or other ketones in human subjects demonstrating a positive ethyl alcohol concentration in their blood.

12. Describe in specific detail all data and the source of data collected by the State of Alabama in showing that the Intoxilyzer Model 5000 as used in Alabama can or cannot detect acetone or other detones in human subjects demonstrating a positive ethyl alcohol concentration in their blood.

13. Provide any and all data collected by the State of Alabama in showing that the Intoxilyzer Model 5000, as used in Alabama, could detect acetone or other ketones in human subjects demonstrating a positive ethyl alcohol concentration in their blood.

14. Any and all data and the source of data collected by the State of Alabama in showing whether or not the Intoxilyzer Model 5000, as used in Alabama, can or cannot detect acetone or other ketones in human subjects demonstrating a positive ethyl alcohol concentration in their blood.

15. Any and all data collected by the State of Alabama in testing the Intoxilyzer Model 5000, as used in Alabama, to show that the radio frequency interference detector operates properly and functions when testing human subjects for positive ethyl alcohol content of their breath.

16. Any and all data and the source of data collected by the State of Alabama in testing the Intoxilyzer Model 5000, that shows whether or not the radio frequency interference detector operates properly and functions when testing human subjects for positive alcohol content of their breath.

17. Any and all data showing the test conducted by the State of Alabama to show that all individuals, when tested in the field, would provide an adequate sample for testing to the Intoxilyzer Model 5000 in the State of Alabama.

18. Any and all data and the source of data collected by the State of Alabama used in the Intoxilyzer Model 5000 that shows that all individuals when tested in the field would provide an adequate sample for testing to the Intoxilyzer Model 5000 in the State of Alabama.

19. Any and all data collected by the State of Alabama in studying the potential interference of substances other than acetone in human subjects when tested in the Intoxilyzer Model 5000.

20. Any and all data and the source of data on which the slope

detector was designed for use with human subjects using the Intoxilyzer Model 5000 in the State of Alabama.

21. Provide the purchase order, design specifications, and other notes and memoranda submitted to the manufacture of the Intoxilyzer Model 5000 by the State of Alabama when the purchase was made.

22. Any and all data and the source of data regarding control regarding the purchase order, design specifications, and other notes and memoranda submitted to the manufacturer of the Intoxilyzer Model 5000 by the State of Alabama when the purchase was made.

23. Provide any and all notes, correspondence, and memoranda collected by the State of Alabama in its evaluation and determination of the performance criteria, characteristics, and justification for purchasing the Intoxilyzer Model 5000 for the State of Alabama.

24. Any and all data and the source of data collected by the State of Alabama in its evaluation and determination of the performance criteria, characteristics and justification for purchasing the Intoxilyzer 5000 for the State of Alabama.

25. A copy of the most current record of the breath-testing device's maintenance and certification records, including repairs, replacement of parts, unscheduled maintenance and records or station logs by any person whomsoever in the history of the instrument's use, including but not limited to, the following:

(i) Inventory record(s);
(ii) Preliminary evaluation(s);
(iii) Certification(s);
(iv) Evaluation/Certification procedure(s);
(v) Repair form(s);
(vi) Telephone complaint forms;
(vii) Calibration checks and printouts;
(viii) Supervisory control tests and printouts;
(ix) Disparity tests.

26. Copies of all administrative staff manuals or instruction to staff of the State Toxicologist, Alabama Department of Public Safety, State Department of Forensic Sciences, Madison County Sheriff's Department, City of Huntsville Police Department and/

or prosecuting authority in this case relating to the testing of blood, breath, or urine for the determination of the alcohol content thereof;

27. Copies of all technical manuals, training manuals, operator manuals, and maintenance manuals and any other written materials relating to the Intoxilyzer 5000;

28. Copies of all planning policies and goals and interim and final planning decisions of the State Board of Health, Department of Forensic Science, Alabama State Department of Public Safety, Madison County Sheriff's Department and City of Huntsville Police Department, and/or prosecuting authority in this case in relation to the approval and use of the Intoxilyzer 5000 in criminal prosecutions in this state;

29. Copies of all factual staff reports and studies, factual consultants' reports and studies, scientific reports and studies, and any other factual information derived from tests, studies, reports, or surveys, whether conducted by public employees or others, in the possession of or considered by the Alabama Department of Public Health, State Department of Forensic Science, Alabama State Department of Public Safety, Madison County Sheriff's Department, City of Huntsville Police Department, and/or prosecuting authority in this case relating to the testing of blood, breath, or urine for the determination of the alcohol content thereof and/or the approval and/or use of the Intoxilyzer 5000 in criminal prosecutions in this State;

30. Copies of correspondence and materials referred to therein by and with the agency relating to any regulatory, supervisory, or enforcement responsibilities of the agency, whereby the agency determines or opines upon, or is asked to determine or opine upon, the rights of the State, the public, a subdivision of state government, or any private party in the possession of or considered by the Alabama Board of Health, Department of Forensic Science, Alabama Department of Public Safety, Madison County Sheriff's Department, City of Huntsville Police Department, and/or the prosecuting authority relating to the testing of blood, breath, or urine for the determination of the alcoholic content thereof, and/or the approval and/or use of the Intoxilyzer 5000 in criminal prosecutions in this State;

31. Copies of all other facts, data, studies, research, or other information made available to the Alabama State Board of Health,

Alabama Department of Forensic Science, Alabama State Department of Public Safety, Madison County Sheriff's Department, City of Huntsville Police Department, the prosecuting authority herein, or any other state or private agency involved in the process of evaluation and/or approval of the Intoxilyzer 5000 for use in criminal prosecutions in the STATE OF ALABAMA, including but not limited to any such materials gathered by the manufacturer, private research laboratory, or other source whatsoever which was considered in the process of testing and approving the use of the BAC Verifier DataMaster by the State Board of Health;

32. Copies of all correspondence, documents, contract proposals, bid specifications, memoranda, and any other materials within the State's or City's possession relevant to the bidding, purchase, and approval process involving the Intoxilyzer 5000 by the Department of Forensic Science, Alabama State Department of Public Health, Madison County Sheriff's Department and the City of Huntsville Police Department and/or any other police or prosecuting authority or other governmental authority or private person or agency involved in the approval or purchasing process;

33. A current copy of the data base and necessary interpretive information concerning the Intoxilyzer 5000 in the possession of the State Department of Safety, Alabama State Department of Public Health, Alabama Department of Forensic Science, City of Huntsville Police Department, Madison County Sheriff's Department or Alabama State Patrol, said information to be produced in the form of a 5¼-inch floppy disk and in ASCII text. The following definitions apply to this demand:

(a) "Data base" is defined as all those bits of information currently or previously polled from any Intoxilyzer 5000 in use in the STATE OF ALABAMA during any period of time, which information was stored in the electronic memory, whether hard disk or floppy disk, or otherwise, of a computer in the possession of the Alabama State Department of Health, the Alabama State Patrol, or any other police, prosecuting, or governmental authority keeping such information;

(b) "Polled" refers to the transfer of information by telephone modem or otherwise, from an individual Intoxilyzer 5000 to the memory of a computer under the control of those persons referred to in (a) above.

(c) "Necessary interpretive information" refers to that information necessary:

(i) to interpret the bits of information, such as the format of coding of information and that information necessary to interpret the various codes therein; and

(ii) to run (analyze) the information on an IBM PC computer, such as supplying the identity of the operating system and level of operating system, and type of data base management program utilized by the computer retaining the data base.

34. A copy of the mathematical formula or formulae utilized in the Intoxilyzer 5000 in determining the acetone measurement in the breath sample;

35. A copy of the mathematical formula or formulae utilized in the Intoxilyzer 5000 in determining the existence of any other interferent in the subject's breath sample.

36. A copy of the formula or formulae utilized in the Intoxilyzer 5000 for determination of the alcohol content in a breath sample.

37. Copies of any other formula or formulae utilized in the Intoxilyzer 5000 at any state of the process involved in the administration of a breath test pursuant to the *Code of Alabama,* 1975, Sec. 32-5a-195, *et seq.*

38. Copies of all mathematical formulae utilized in the Intoxilyzer 5000 used by the Huntsville Police Department, Alabama Department of Public Safety, or Alabama Highway Patrol, Madison County Sheriff's Department and the City of Huntsville Police Department in the evaluation, testing and certification process which was in any way related to the decision to purchase breath testing devices from the Federal Signal Corporation in carrying out any of the processes listed above which differ from those utilized by the Intoxilyzer 5000 in performing the same function.

39. A copy of the internal computer program for the Intoxilyzer 5000 including the source code, schematic diagrams (both electronic and mechanical) and flow diagrams.

40. Copies of the internal computer program for the Intoxilyzer 5000 used by the Alabama State Patrol in the evaluation testing and certification process which was in any way related to the decision to purchase breath testing devices from the Federal Signal Corporation, including the source code, schematic diagrams (both electronic and mechanical) and flow diagrams.

41. A copy of the manufacturer's specifications and instructions for the initial calibration of the Intoxilyzer 5000 along with a copy of any manual or instructions issued by the State Department of Forensic Science, Alabama State Department of Public Safety or City of Huntsville Police Department, Madison County Sheriff's Department or Alabama Highway Patrol, modifying, amending, correcting, or otherwise changing the manufacturer's recommendations regarding calibration of said instruments.

YOU ARE FURTHER NOTIFIED that the failure to comply with these requests will result in defendant moving for appropriate relief at time of hearing or trial.

This Subpoena Duces Tecum is based upon application of the *defendant.*

________________________ ________________________

Date Clerk's Signature

11

SUPPRESSION OF EVIDENCE

§11.0 *Probable Cause to Stop, Detain, and Arrest*

> [A] lawyer is an artist whether he likes it or not. The question is not whether he is an artist, for in this he has no choice, but rather how good an artist he is going to be.
>
> SOKOL
> LANGUAGE AND LITIGATION

As with any criminal matter, the drunk driving case affords defense counsel the opportunity to suppress prosecution evidence. Probable cause to stop, search, and seizure, probable cause to arrest, obtaining incriminating statements without a prior advisement of rights, denial of right to counsel — all these potentially are present in defending a client against a charge of driving under the influence of alcohol.

Probable cause to stop the driver of a motor vehicle may be an issue in any DUI case. Wide latitude generally is granted traffic officers, and anything even close to a traffic offense or driving symptoms indicative of intoxication probably will justify the initial stop in the court's eyes. If, however, it can be proven that the officers merely are engaged in a dragnet, or a DUI ''stakeout'' (e.g., stopping all drivers leaving a particular bar or tavern), then probable cause is likely to be found lacking. (If the arresting officer denies such a practice, counsel should attempt to determine how many other DUI arrests involving the bar or tavern took place within a few days of the client's arrest.) All subsequent evidence would then, of course, be suppressed and the charges dismissed.

As with any police stop, the officer in a drunk driving case must be able to point to "specific and articulable facts" that provide him with reasonable grounds for believing the driver is intoxicated; a mere hunch is not sufficient.

Similarly, the officer must have both *authority* and probable cause to justify an arrest for driving under the influence. Generally, police officers may make an arrest when they reasonably believe a felony (e.g., felony drunk driving, vehicular manslaughter) has been committed, or where a misdemeanor (e.g., drunk driving) is committed in their presence. Obviously, counsel should familiarize himself in appropriate cases with the applicable law in his jurisdiction relating to arrest in drunk driving cases. Should an arrest be invalid, then the "fruit of the poisonous tree" doctrine of *Wong Sun v. United States,* 371 U.S. 471 (1963), would apply, and all evidence resulting therefrom — field sobriety test, confession, chemical evidence, etc. — would be thrown out.

The nature of the arrest should not be overlooked. If the individual is arrested for a traffic infraction — for example, speeding — and then is given an investigative breath test before being released, counsel should consider grounds for moving to suppress. In *McDaniel v. State,* 526 So. 2d 642 (Ala. App. 1988), a DUI conviction was reversed because a person arrested for speeding was entitled to release forthwith on giving bond. In order to be subject to the continuing custody necessary for a breath test, the person actually must be charged with drunk driving.

Counsel should consider pre-trial suppression of evidence concerning field sobriety tests where the police officer did not yet have probable cause to arrest the suspect for drunk driving. Such situations are common, as the primary purpose of such tests is to determine whether the suspect may be intoxicated or not.

In *People v. Carlson,* 677 P.2d 310 (Colo. 1984), the Colorado Supreme Court addressed the issue of whether a police officer could order a driver to perform field sobriety tests if he did not have probable cause to arrest:

> Roadside sobriety testing constitutes a full "search" in the constitutional sense of that term and therefore must be supported by probable cause. The sole purpose of roadside sobriety testing is to acquire evidence of criminal conduct on the part of the suspect.

> Intrusions into privacy for the exclusive purpose of gathering evidence of criminal activity have traditionally required, at the outset of the intrusion, probable cause to believe that a crime has been committed. See *Michigan v. Clifford,* — U.S. — (1984) (52 U.S.L.W. 4056, decided January 11, 1984); *Sibron v. New York,* 392 U.S. 40 (1968); *Warden v. Hayden,* 387 U.S. 294 (1967). Moreover, the scope of the intrusion involved in the testing process cannot be characterized as anything less than substantial. When considered in terms of its intrusive potential, a roadside sobriety test is not far removed from chemical testing, pursuant to the implied consent law. . . . Indeed, in some respects, roadside sobriety testing might be considered more invasive of privacy interests than chemical testing. The latter is usually performed in the relatively obscure setting of a station house or hospital, while roadside sobriety testing will often take place on or near a public street with the suspect exposed to the full view of motorists, pedestrians, or anyone else who happens to be in the area. Were this type of intrusive search to be permitted on less than probable cause, the "exception" created by *Terry* [*v. Ohio,* 392 U.S. 1 (1968),] and its progeny would swallow the general rule that searches and seizures are reasonable if based on probable cause. . . .
>
> To satisfy constitutional guarantees against unlawful searches and seizures, therefore, a roadside sobriety test can be administered only when there is probable cause to arrest the driver for driving under the influence of, or while his ability is impaired by intoxicating liquor or other chemical substance, or when the driver voluntarily consents to perform the test. [667 P.2d at 317.]

The obtaining of blood, breath, or urine samples from a suspect clearly constitutes a search of his body and a seizure of the sample. As in all cases, then, once the defense establishes that there was no search warrant, the prosecution bears the burden of proving that the search was made incident to a lawful arrest.

If the trial court is inclined to rule against a motion to suppress for lack of probable cause, counsel should consider arguing that the issue is one of fact and, therefore, an appropriate jury instruction should be given. In *Stone v. State,* 685 S.W.2d 791 (Tex. App. 1985), the defendant argued that the car was not weaving as claimed by the arresting officer and that therefore there was insufficient probable cause to pull her over. Her request for the following jury instruction was denied by the court:

> You are instructed that before an officer is entitled to stop a moving vehicle, he must have probable cause to do so. In this case it is conceded that the only probable cause to stop the Defendant's vehicle was the fact that the defendant supposedly was weaving in the highway. On the other hand, the Defendant and her witness testified that the Defendant was able to properly operate her motor vehicle on the occasion in question.
>
> It is for you to determine at the outset of your deliberation whether or not Defendant's driving of her vehicle was such as the officer has described, and it is the burden of proof on the State in this regard that you must find the Defendant was driving as the officer indicates, beyond a reasonable doubt. In the event you are not satisfied beyond a reasonable doubt that the Defendant drove as the officer testified, then you will have no further evidence to consider, and you should bring in a verdict of acquittal. [Id. at 793.]

The appellate court reversed the ensuing conviction, holding that the evidence, "although contradictory, was sufficient to raise the issue of lack of probable cause. Having objected to the charge, called the omission to the court's attention, and requested a charge, Stone was entitled to have the jury charged on the question of probable cause" (Id. at 793).

This position was reaffirmed in *Johnson v. State,* 743 S.W.2d 307 (Tex. App. 1987):

> Texas courts have uniformly held that the question of whether probable cause exists for a warrantless search is solely a question of law for determination by the court. . . . However, when the facts alleged to constitute probable cause are controverted, the defendant has the statutory right to have the jury charged on this issue. [Id. at 310, 311.]

The accompanying pleading represents an example of a notice of motion to suppress evidence.

(Title of Cause and Court)

NOTICE OF MOTION TO SUPPRESS EVIDENCE

TO: ______________________, COUNTY ATTORNEY OF ______________ COUNTY, AND TO THE CLERK OF THE MUNICIPAL COURT:

Notice is hereby given that on ____________, 19___, at __________, or as soon thereafter as counsel can be heard in Division _________ of the above-entitled court, the defendant will move the Court for an order to suppress as evidence all tangible or intangible things obtained as a result of searches of defendant's person and vehicle by members of the __________ Sheriff's Department on _________, 19___.

Specifically, defendant will move to suppress the following evidence:

1. All evidence of any nature obtained as a result of the taking of a blood sample from defendant on _________;
2. All statements allegedly made by defendant to any officer on said date;
3. All observations allegedly made by any officer of defendant while driving or thereafter;
4. All other items, tangible or intangible, obtained as a result of any search.

This motion will be based upon this notice, the pleadings, records and files in this action, and upon oral and documentary evidence to be produced at the hearing of this motion.

DATED: __________

____

Attorney for Defendant

§11.0.1 The Citizen Informant

What about "tips" received by police officers from citizens? This is an increasingly common occurrence in DUI cases. As part of the recent nationwide crackdown on drunk driving, for example, a number of states have initiated programs whereby members of the public can call a toll-free telephone number and report individuals who they feel are driving a vehicle under the influence of alcohol and/or drugs. A police unit will then be dispatched to investigate.

Such procedures should raise questions of probable cause. Can, for example, a police officer assert the existence of such a phone call as sufficient basis for an arrest? The average citizen does not have sufficient expertise to determine whether an individual is under the influence; lay opinion evidence of drunkenness may be admissible in court, but is lay opinion evidence as to the less intoxicated state of "under the influence"?

Counsel should consider such phone reporting cases — or *any* case involving a citizen tip — for what they are: informant cases. As an informant situation, the usual issues — reliability, tested or untested, etc. — should be reviewed.

The question of whether a police officer can stop a vehicle on the basis of information received from an unidentified informant that the driver is under the influence has been addressed by a number of state courts, with varying conclusions. The Court of Appeals of Washington, in *Campbell v. State of Washington Department of Licensing,* 644 P.2d 1219 (Wash. App. 1982), held:

> In the absence of any corroborative information or observation, a police officer is not authorized to stop a vehicle on the sole basis that a passing motorist points to a vehicle and announces that it is being driven by a drunk driver. . . .
>
> [W]here . . . an informant's uncorroborated tip constitutes the sole justification for the officer's initial detention of the suspect the tip must possess an "indicia of reliability." [Cites.] An uncorroborated tip possesses sufficient "indicia of reliability" where (1) the source of information is reliable *and* (2) the report contains enough objective facts to justify the pursuit and detention of the suspect. [Cites.] [Id. at 1220.]

The Minnesota Supreme Court, however, came to a different conclusion, although assessing the validity of a traffic stop with the same standards. In *Marben v. State, Department of Public Safety,* 294 N.W.2d 697 (Minn. 1980), the court found a stop based on an informant's tip valid:

> It should be emphasized that the factual basis required to support a stop for a "routine traffic check" is minimal. An actual violation of the Vehicle and Traffic Law need not be detectable. . . . All that is required is that the stop be not the product of mere whim, caprice or idle curiosity. It is enough if the stop is based upon "specific and articulable facts which, taken together with rational inferences from those facts, reasonably warrant [the] intrusion." [Cite.]
>
> Also, the factual basis for stopping a vehicle need not arise from the officer's personal observation, but may be supplied by information required from another person. [Cites.] [Id. at 699.]

The Minnesota Supreme Court seems to have subsequently qualified this position. In *Olson v. Commissioner of Public Safety,* 371 N.W.2d 552 (Minn. 1985), that court dealt with a situation where a deputy sheriff relied solely on a radio dispatch that "a citizen had called in reporting that he observed a — possibly a drunken driver." The anonymous caller described the vehicle, including license number and location. After locating and following the car, the deputy pulled the defendant over, determined that he was in fact under the influence, and arrested him. The trial court ruled that the deputy's reliance on the dispatcher's message justified a stop and investigation. The state supreme court disagreed:

> Whether, however, the evidence uncovered in the course of the stop is admissible depends on whether the dispatcher, who issued the message to the deputies, was in possession of specific and articulable facts supporting a reasonable suspicion that there was a drunk driver on the road. . . .
>
> On this record, there is a complete lack of even the most minimal indicia of reliability for the anonymous tip. If police cannot stop a car on the highway on the basis of mere whim, neither can they stop on the basis, for all they know, of the mere whim of an anonymous caller. [Id. at 555, 556.]

Even "specific and articulable facts" from an anonymous informant may not be sufficient. In *Oregon v. Black,* 721 P.2d 842 (Or. 1986), the police received a phone call from an unidentified woman stating that a Ford Escort, traveling north on Highway 199, was speeding and weaving. The information was relayed to a patrolman, who subsequently spotted the car. Although he did not observe any erratic driving or speeding, he stopped the car and later arrested the defendant for drunk driving. The Oregon appellate court sustained the trial court's granting of the defendant's motion to suppress all evidence obtained after the stop:

> The anonymous tip had no indicia of reliability. First, the caller did not identify herself. That a person providing information to the police identifies herself is not independently significant; what is significant is that, by doing so, she exposes herself to possible criminal and civil prosecution if her report is false and perhaps a charge of perjury if she later changes her story while testifying in the case. Second, it is not clear how the caller received her information. It cannot be inferred from the meager record that she personally observed what she reported. Third, the trooper's personal observations did not corroborate the tip. He did not observe any erratic driving or speeding. . . . That the anonymous informant had accurately described defendant's car is not a sufficient indication of reliability. [Id. at 846.]

A California appellate court, on the other hand, affirmed a DUI conviction where a defendant was initially detained based on an anonymous tip. In *People v. Willard,* 228 Cal. Rptr. 895 (1986), a patrolman was stopped by a motorist who told him that the car behind him was being driven by "a drunk." The motorist drove off, and the officer stopped the indicated car. The officer noticed erratic driving, but he was afraid to let the driver go further, as they were near a freeway on-ramp.

On appeal, the defendant first argued that there existed no presumption that the anonymous tip was reliable. The court disagreed, reasoning that all the indicia of a reliable citizen were present, and the officer could reasonably rely on what the informant told him. The court rejected language in *People v. Ramey,* 545 P.2d 1333 (Cal. 1976), which required the furnishing of a name and address of an informant to show his reliability, holding that the "exigency of the circumstances" due to the possibility of the defendant getting away and endangering lives while the officer got the information excused the requirement. Furthermore, the informant acted openly and without apparent motive.

The defendant's second argument was that the information given was insufficient to justify a stop and detention: The bald statement that the defendant was drunk was conclusory and without underlying facts to justify an opinion by the officer. The court replied by saying that: "The information of a reliable citizen witness may be taken at face value, [cites], and we believe the statement that defendant's vehicle was being driven by what the motorist believed was a 'drunk' is, and would be commonly understood to be, a statement of fact by the motorist."

In the opinion of this writer, the *Willard* case is one of the most strained and poorly reasoned opinions to be published in the DUI field in some time. Ignoring clear constitutional requirements, it is typical of those cases that adopt a double standard in dealing with drunk driving offenses.

Counsel should be aware of two danger areas involving the citizen informant. First, the information supplied by the informant must be limited to the issue of probable cause. So that the jury will not hear the damning evidence, counsel should ensure that the probable cause issue is heard by the court before trial or otherwise out of the jury's presence. Certainly, it would seem clear that the evidence constitutes classic *hearsay* and, with no opportunity to cross-examine, a denial of the right of *confrontation.*

Second, the information offered by the prosecution to establish probable cause may constitute *double* hearsay — if, for example, the arresting officer is testifying as to what a police radio dispatcher hold him that a citizen told the dispatcher. Certainly defense counsel should argue that at the very least the radio dispatcher (or other person receiving the telephone call) should be produced in court. The prosecution will often have difficulty in doing so; if the receiver of the call is produced, he may well have difficulty recalling exactly what was said, particularly where he is receiving a large number of such calls over a period of time.

Checklist 17 Probable Cause

The Stop

- ☐ Did the officer have probable cause to stop the client's car?
- ☐ Are there "specific and articulable facts" present?
- ☐ Did probable cause depend at least in part on a "tip"?

- ☐ Is the informant known and reliable?
- ☐ Was the information forwarded by a dispatcher or other source constituting "double hearsay"?
- ☐ Is there any risk of a jury hearing evidence of the informant's information?

Detention

- ☐ Did the officer have probable cause to detain the client for further investigation?
- ☐ Was the detention unreasonably long in time?

Arrest

- ☐ Did the officer have probable cause to arrest the client?
- ☐ Did the officer have legal authority to make an arrest?
- ☐ Did a lawful arrest precede any blood-alcohol test or interrogation?

Procedure

- ☐ Should counsel litigate issues of probable cause in pre-trial motions?
- ☐ Are there factual issues appropriate to jury determination?
- ☐ Does counsel want a jury to hear evidence of probable cause?

§11.1 Sobriety Checkpoints: Sitz

> Public opinion's always in advance of the law.
>
> John Galsworthy

An increasingly prevalent practice used to detect the drunk driver involves the use of roadblocks or checkpoints. Commonly, law enforcement agencies will set up a roadblock on a selected road or highway, much as is done with equipment safety checks or license/registration inspection. If the driver's speech sounds slurred or his breath has an odor of alcohol, he will be asked to leave the car and perform field sobriety tests at the scene.

On June 14, 1990, the U.S. Supreme Court finally handed down its long-awaited decision on the constitutionality of DUI roadblocks. In *Michigan Department of State Police v. Sitz,* 496 U.S. 444 (1990), the Court reversed the state appellate court and held that the checkpoint operation in question did not violate the

Fourth Amendment's prohibition against unreasonable searches and seizures.

In a predictable 6-3 decision authored by Chief Justice Rehnquist, the Court acknowledged that roadblocks do constitute a "seizure" within the meaning of the Fourth Amendment. However, the Chief Justice wrote, this must be viewed in the context of weighing the need and effectiveness of the roadblock against minimal intrusion on individual liberties. With demonstrated need and effectiveness, and minimal intrusion, sobriety checkpoints are constitutionally acceptable.

Respondents in *Sitz* had argued that any balancing tests were inappropriate: The sole question was whether the police had *probable cause* to stop any individual drivers. There must be a special governmental need "beyond the normal need," respondents argued, before a balancing test is appropriate. Oddly, however, Rehnquist quickly dismissed this rather obvious point with almost no comment.

Justice Brennan, with Marshall joining, dissented:

> Presumably, the Court purports to draw support from *Martinez-Fuentez,* supra, which is the only case in which the Court has upheld a program that subjects the public to suspicionless seizures. . . . In *Martinez-Fuentez,* the Court explained that suspicionless stops were justified because "a requirement that stops . . . be based on reasonable suspicion would be impractical because the flow of traffic tends to be too heavy to allow the particularized study of a given car that would enable it to be identified as a possible carrier of illegal aliens." [Cite omitted.] There has been no showing in this case that there is a similar difficulty in detecting individuals who are driving under the influence of alcohol, nor is it intuitively obvious that such a difficulty exists. [Cite omitted.] That stopping every car might make it easier to prevent drunken driving . . . is an insufficient justification for abandoning the requirement of individualized suspicion. . . . Without proof that the police cannot develop individualized suspicion that a person is driving while impaired by alcohol, I believe the constitutional balance must be struck in favor of protecting the public against even the "minimally intrusive" seizures involved in this case. . . .
>
> Moved by whatever momentary evil has aroused their fears, officials — perhaps even supported by a majority of citizens — may be tempted to conduct searches that sacrifice the liberty of each citizen to assuage the perceived evil. But the Fourth Amendment

> rests on the principle that a true balance between the individual and society depends on the recognition of "the right to be let alone — the most comprehensive of rights and the right most valued by civilized men. [Cite omitted.]" [496 U.S. at 458–459.]

Justice Stevens, joined by Brennan and Marshall, wrote a separate dissenting opinion. Addressing the question of effectiveness, he observed that the checkpoint that netted only two arrests involved 19 police officers — officers who could have been on patrol searching for drunk drivers. In reviewing the testimony and very revealing statistical data, he noted that "the findings of the trial court, based on an extensive record and affirmed by the Michigan Court of Appeals, indicate that the net effect of sobriety checkpoints on traffic safety is infinitesimal and possibly negative."

As to subjective intrusion, Stevens distinguished the facts in *Martinez-Fuentes,* so heavily relied on by Rehnquist:

> A motorist with advance notice of the location of a permanent checkpoint [as in *Martinez-Fuentes*] has an opportunity to avoid the search entirely, or at least to prepare for, and limit, the intrusion on her privacy.
>
> No such opportunity is available in the case of a random stop or a temporary checkpoint, which both depend for their effectiveness on the element of surprise. A driver who discovers an unexpected checkpoint on a familiar local road will be startled and distressed. . . .
>
> This element of surprise is the most obvious distinction between the sobriety checkpoints permitted by today's majority and the interior border checkpoints approved by this Court in *Martinez-Fuentes.* [Id. at 463.]

Finally, Stevens noted that part of the balancing equation was being ignored: "The most disturbing aspect of the Court's decision today is that it appears to give no weight to the citizen's interest in freedom from suspicionless unannounced investigatory seizures."

Confronted with a DUI case involving a roadblock/checkpoint, counsel must consider the adequacy of the procedures employed: Was the roadblock conducted in a constitutionally permissible manner? Even Chief Justice Rehnquist implicitly acknowledged that there must exist "guidelines" concerning such matters as location, publicity, and roadblock operation. Note that in *Sitz* the roadblock was set up only after a "Sobriety Checkpoint Advisory Committee" had been appointed to establish guidelines; this committee consisted of representatives of the state police, local police, prosecutors, and the University of Michigan Transportation Research Institute.

But what *are* the "guidelines"? Rehnquist's opinion in *Sitz* leaves the question of minimal adequacy of such standards unanswered, presumably to be determined on a case-by-case basis. Counsel may find some guidance in the decisions of sister states. In one of the most influential of these pre-*Sitz* cases, the California Supreme Court set forth what it felt to be the procedural safeguards required for a DUI roadblock to comply with Fourth Amendment requirements. *Ingersoll v. Palmer,* 743 P.2d 1299 (Cal. 1987).

In the absence of guidelines from the U.S. Supreme Court in *Sitz,* counsel may wish to look to an alternative federal source in arguing the constitutional invalidity of a given checkpoint or roadblock. The National Highway Traffic Safety Administration (NHTSA) has published a report that reviews recommended procedures for drinking/driving roadblocks. See The Use of Safety Checkpoints for DWI Enforcement, DOT HS-806-476 (National Highway Traffic Safety Administration, September 1983). The report reviews legal issues relating to roadblocks ("safety checkpoints") and suggests guidelines for their use in drunk driving law enforcement. Ten suggestions are made "to help ensure that safety checkpoints are used legally, effectively and safely":

1. *Ongoing DWI Program* — Any agency considering safety checkpoints should integrate them with an ongoing, systematic and aggressive enforcement program. The use of checkpoints alone will not sustain the perception of risk so essential to an effective general deterrence program. In fact, if drinking drivers believe that their chances of being caught are only at safety checkpoints, their perception of risk of arrest may be quite low.
2. *Judicial Support* — When officials decide that they intend to use this technique, they should involve their prosecuting authority . . . in the planning process to determine

legally acceptable procedures. This person can detail the types of evidential information that will be needed to prosecute cases emanating from checkpoint apprehension.

The jurisdiction's presiding judge should be informed of the proposed checkpoints and procedures, an essential step if the judiciary is to accept their use. The judge can provide insight on what activities would be required to successfully adjudicate such cases. If a judge cannot be persuaded that this technique is acceptable, its implementation will be futile.

3. *Existing Policy Guidelines* — Any jurisdiction considering safety checkpoints should prepare written policy/guidelines which outline how roadblocks are to be conducted prior to starting to use them. The courts have been very clear in directing that safety checkpoints be planned in advance. [See *State v. Hillesheim,* 291 N.W.2d 314, 318 (Iowa 1980).] Failure to do so has been used as evidence that roadblock techniques were discretionary.
4. *Site Selection* — Planners should take into consideration the safety and visibility to oncoming motorists: Safety checkpoints cannot be of less public benefit than the behavior they are trying to displace, nor can they create more of a traffic hazard than the results of the driving behavior they are trying to modify.

   Planners should remember to select a site that allows officers to pull vehicles out of the traffic stream without causing significant subjective intrusion (fright to the drivers and/or creating a traffic backup). Furthermore, officers' safety must be taken into account when deciding where to locate the checkpoint.

   Checkpoint locations should be selected in advance by officers other than those manning the checkpoint according to objective criteria that will maximize contact with DWIs, for example, locations with a high incidence of DWI-related fatalities, nighttime injuries or nighttime single vehicle crashes.

   If every vehicle is not to be stopped, the method used to determine which ones will be stopped must appear in the administrative order authorizing the use of the safety checkpoints.

5. *Warning Devices*—Special care should be taken to provide adequate warning to approaching motorists that a roadblock-type checkpoint has been established. Such notice can be accomplished with warning signs, flares and police cars with warning lights flashing. If possible, warning signs should be placed along the roadway well in advance of the checkpoint to alert motorists that they will be required to stop. . . . Signs should be placed to provide advance warning as to why motorists are being stopped, but at the same time should not give impaired motorists the opportunity to avoid the checkpoint.
6. *Visibility of Police Authority*—The visibility of uniformed officers and their marked police vehicles makes the power of the police presence obvious and serves to reassure motorists of the legitimate nature of the activity. This is an important aspect of any safety checkpoint. This is also part of the effort to reduce the intrusion to the passing motorists who will be affected by the checkpoint surveillance.
7. *Chemical Test Logistics*—Since DWI arrests are to be anticipated at the selected location, the logistics of chemical testing must also be included. A system for expeditiously transporting suspected violators to chemical test sites must be established.
8. *Contingency Planning*—If intermittent traffic conditions cause the officers to stray from the predetermined order of selecting motorists to stop (e.g., if a traffic backup occurs), the reasons for the departure must be thoroughly documented. Courts have allowed this deviation as long as records are kept documenting the necessity to deviate from the interview sequence. *United States v. Prichard,* 645 F.2d 854. If such an event occurs, jurisdictions must have prepared alternative plans in advance to handle the checkpoint.

If too much traffic develops at a checkpoint, causing a backup that cannot be easily alleviated, the officer in charge of the checkpoint may consider discontinuing operation at that site and moving to an alternative site. The alternative site should have been identified in advance in the administrative order that first established the checkpoint surveillance, and should be prepared for operation.

9. *Detection and Investigation Techniques* — An agency considering safety checkpoints should ensure that the officers who staff it are properly trained in detecting alcohol-impaired drivers. The implementation of safety checkpoints that allow legally intoxicated drivers to pass through undetected will not be able to achieve a general deterrence effect. Examples of the kind of actions officers are taking during initial contact with a driver at a checkpoint are:
   - Request his or her license and registration.
   - Use a divided attention task (e.g., after requesting the driver's license, while the driver is looking for it, the officer engages him in conversation).
   - Question the driver regarding his origination/destination, whether he had been drinking, etc.

   Police are using these approaches to try to quickly detect whether a driver has been drinking. Once an officer's suspicion has been raised, further investigation can take place out of the traffic lane without impeding the flow of traffic. These and other approaches are currently being studied. If an officer feels it is necessary to move a suspect's car after he suspects the driver is impaired, it will be necessary for someone *other* than the suspect to drive the car. . . .
10. *Public Information* — To obtain maximum benefit in terms of its general deterrence effect, a safety checkpoint program should be aggressively publicized. The majority of drivers will most likely never encounter a checkpoint, but will only learn of it through media reports (and perhaps by word of mouth). These two valuable forms of public communication will greatly enhance any such program, however, and should be consistently employed.

As the Supreme Court becomes increasingly conservative in its efforts to achieve public order at the expense of individual rights, many lawyers and state courts are turning for the first time to their own state *constitutions* to protect their citizens.

After holding that DUI checkpoints were constitutional, the U.S. Supreme Court remanded the case of *Michigan Department of State Police v. Sitz* to the Michigan Court of Appeals for proceedings not inconsistent with its opinion. Thus that state court was confronted with the same task that faced the South Dakota court in *South Dakota v. Neville* when the Supreme Court reversed its finding that evidence of refusal violated the Fifth Amendment (see §11.4.1). And the results were similar: On remand, both state courts sidestepped the federal ruling and upheld their previous results by looking instead to their *state* constitutions. *Sitz v. Department of State Police,* 485 N.W.2d 135 (Mich. App. 1992).

The Michigan appellate court began by noting that the state constitution generally offered the same protections as the federal Constitution. However, when the U.S. Supreme Court suddenly adopted a standard permitting suspicionless stops by roving roadblocks, it altered the course of federal rights and created an "enormous departure" from earlier Michigan decisions. "This is especially true where, as here, the effectiveness of the roadblocks in question in preventing drunk driving is negligible, only one arrest after 126 stops." 485 N.W.2d at 139. The appellate court decided that any such "radical" new standard should be adopted, if at all, only by the Michigan Supreme Court.

Certainly, counsel confronted with a roadblock issue — or, for that matter, any constitutional issue — should consider the possibilities present in his own state's constitution, whether *stare decisis* exists yet or not. This trend toward state protection in the increasing absence of federal protection is a new one, and counsel's case may well be the landmark case for his state. In any event, the record should be protected in the event of a subsequent favorable ruling in another case.

An example of this approach in the DUI field can be found in the 1986 case of *Nelson v. Lane County,* 720 P.2d 1291 (Or. App. 1986). In *Nelson* a driver was stopped and detained at a police DUI roadblock. Subsequently, she sued for damages and injunctive and declaratory relief, claiming that her statutory, state constitutional, and federal constitutional rights had been infringed. On appeal from a trial court granting of the state's motion for summary judgment, the case was reversed and remanded. The Oregon appellate court held that although the roadblock may not have violated the plaintiff's rights under the Fourth Amendment, it may well have violated her rights under Article I, section 9 of the Oregon Constitution prohibiting unreasonable search and seizure.

Similarly, the Supreme Court of Washington recently has held that sobriety checkpoints violate the right to privacy guaranteed by the state's constitution. In *City of Seattle v. Mesiani,* 755 P.2d 775 (Wash. 1988), the court based its holding on an article in the constitution reading, "No person shall be disturbed in his private affairs, or his home invaded, without authority of law." Although concluding that this provided greater protection than the Fourth Amendment, the court relied on federal cases. Thus the court found that DUI roadblocks failed to meet the three-prong balancing test as required by *Brown v. Texas,* 443 U.S. 47 (1979).

The Minnesota Supreme Court has joined the ranks of states turning to their own constitutions to protect their citizens against sobriety checkpoints. In two companion cases, that court disagreed with the *Sitz'* balancing test, holding that even "minimally intrusive" stops at checkpoints are impermissible: the stopping of vehicles "must be based on individualized suspicion." *Ascher v. Commissioner of Public Safety,* 519 N.W.2d 183 (Minn. 1994); *Gray v. Commissioner of Public Safety,* 519 N.W.2d 187 (Minn. 1994).

In a continuing trend evidencing growing displeasure with a federal retreat from constitutional protection, the Idaho Supreme Court held DUI roadblocks to be in violation of the state's constitution. In *State v. Henderson,* 756 P.2d 1057 (Idaho 1988), that court found that the evidence indicated roadblocks generally were considered to be a less effective means of enforcing drunk driving laws than roving police patrols and normal vehicular stops, while at the same time being more obtrusive. Accordingly, the court held the practice unlawful, noting that each state has the "sovereign right to adopt in its own Constitution individual liberties more expansive than those conferred by the Federal Constitution." See also *State v. Church,* 538 So. 2d 993 (La. 1989).

In *King v. State,* 816 S.W.2d 447 (Tex. App. 1991), a defendant had been stopped at a roadblock supposedly set up to check driver's licenses; when alcohol was detected on the defendant's breath, he was arrested for drunk driving. On appeal from his conviction, the defendant argued that the roadblock was a violation of his rights under both the Texas and federal constitutions.

The appellate court reversed and remanded for a new trial, ordering the suppression of evidence obtained as a result of the roadblock. The court held that the arrest was unlawful since police intent at the roadblock was unclear (translation: the police lied) as to whether the roadblock had been set up to check licenses as claimed by the state (and authorized by statute) or was merely a subterfuge to catch drunk drivers:

> If police stop all traffic traveling in both directions in broad daylight along a street used by a variety of citizens, we would have little trouble in determining their intent. However, when police conduct a roadblock at a "target site," a site specifically chosen because of its high probability of DWI violations, in the middle of the night, only stopping traffic traveling away from bars along a street where bars are closing, their intent is not clear. [Id. at 450.]

See also *Garcia v. State,* 853 S.W.2d 157 (Tex. App. 1993), in which a roadblock was found invalid because of the lack of an administrative scheme authorized by the state legislature. As in *King,* the court found that the checkpoint was a "subterfuge for a more general investigation."

The court went on to find the roadblock invalid under *both* the Texas and federal constitutions. Addressing *Michigan Department of State Police v. Sitz,* the court pointed out that, unlike Michigan, Texas did not have a legislatively developed procedure for establishing roadblocks, as required by *Sitz.*

In *Commonwealth v. Trivitt,* 650 A.2d 104 (Pa. Super. 1994), an appellate court similarly held that a DUI roadblock was invalid under the state constitution. The director of the county Center for Highway Safety and the supervising officer at the roadblock both testified that the site of the sobriety checkpoint was chosen because of its high incidence of DUI accidents and arrests. On cross-examination, however, they could not give specific data concerning the number of arrests or accidents in the preceding year. The court rejected the "bald-faced" testimony and held that "at the very least" there must be available "information sufficient to specify the number of DUI-related arrests and/or accidents within the relevant time period."

See also *State v. Wagner,* 821 S.W.2d 188 (Tex. App. 1991), wherein a Texas court suppressed evidence obtained as the result of a roadblock on the grounds that there was no evidence that a legislative scheme had been adopted. The only evidence offered by the prosecution was that the acting police chief had promulgated a general policy concerning sobriety checkpoints.

See also *Holt v. State,* 887 S.W.2d 16 (Tex. Crim. App. 1994), similarly requiring a statewide legislative authorization for roadblocks and a case-by-case consideration of individual roadblocks. Rejecting authorization from a city council and guidelines written by a committee of police supervisors, the court noted that it would not "blindly defer" to law enforcement techniques chosen by politically accountable officials.

In *State v. Fedak,* 825 P.2d 1068 (Haw. App. 1992), an appellate court reversed a DUI conviction when it found that the sobriety checkpoint involved was unconstitutional. In that case, a roadblock had lawfully been set up by the Honolulu Police Department in accordance with the terms of a regulatory statute. However, the officer in charge at the scene moved the roadblock to avoid traffic congestion. The statute authorized only "division level commanders" to select checkpoint sites; officers in charge were authorized only to *terminate* the roadblock when congestion became a problem.

In *People v. Banks,* 13 Cal. Rptr. 2d 920 (Cal. App. 1992), a California appellate court found a sobriety checkpoint constitutionally invalid because it had been administered without advance publicity. Furthermore, the fact that the defendant had personal knowledge of the checkpoint did not alleviate the infirmity.

The California Supreme Court reversed, 5-2, holding in a somewhat confusing opinion that advance publicity was a *factor* in determining the constitutional validity of a checkpoint — but not a *prerequisite. People v. Banks,* 6 Cal. 4th 926 (1993). Perhaps the most accurate explanation of the ruling comes from the dissent:

> In my view the majority wants it both ways. Clearly it does not wish to encourage law enforcement officials to announce sobriety checkpoints in advance, but it also does not want to hold that advance publicity is irrelevant. . . . In summary, the majority view invites law enforcement officials to dispense with advance publicity while reassuring those who fear for the vitality of the Fourth Amendment that all of the *Ingersoll* factors, including advance publicity, are still in effect. In view of this ambiguous message, the only prudent course of action is for law enforcement officials and courts to continue to determine in each case whether the lack of advance

> publicity has made each particular checkpoint too intrusive to satisfy the Fourth Amendment. Only then can we be confident that the Fourth Amendment is still alive and well.

The dissent then suggested in the following analysis that advance publicity is still an important factor:

> Perhaps the majority means to say only this: While the presence or absence of advance publicity is still relevant in assessing the intrusiveness, and thus the constitutionality, of sobriety checkpoints, an unpublicized checkpoint can still pass constitutional muster if it obtains a high score on the other seven *Ingersoll* factors. In a footnote the majority invites this interpretation with the statement that "nothing in our decision should be construed to suggest that any of the eight guidelines set forth in *Ingersoll,* including advance publicity, are not relevant to a consideration of the intrusiveness of a sobriety checkpoint stop."
>
> If this is the correct interpretation of the majority opinion, then it is still possible as a matter of logic that the lack of advance publicity in a particular case will be decisive in holding unconstitutional a checkpoint that does not score high on the other seven *Ingersoll* factors.

In *Commonwealth v. Donnelly,* 614 N.E.2d 1018 (Mass. App. 1993), the defendant was stopped at a DWI roadblock and arrested for drunk driving. He moved to suppress all evidence as having been obtained without probable cause, arguing that the roadblock did not meet standard, neutral guidelines. Specifically, he pointed out that there were no demonstrable grounds for believing that the site of the roadblock was a "problem area." The motion was denied and the defendant was convicted.

The appellate court agreed with the defense, noting that the only evidence the state produced concerning prior alcohol-related incidents in the area was a 1989 police letter describing arrests two years before the roadblock in question was established. Further, the state offered no evidence of the results of two recent roadblocks in the same area. This reliance on old information, together with the failure to produce recent information, resulted in a site selected, in effect, at the discretion of the police. See also *Commonwealth v. Amaral,* 495 N.E.2d 276 (Mass. 1986).

Faced with a drunk driving case involving a checkpoint stop, counsel should move for pre-trial *discovery* of all the facts relevant to the establishment and operation of the roadblock, in order to properly challenge whether any legal guidelines have been complied with. Such a motion might include, for example, a request for the identities of the individuals who authorized the roadblock; copies of all memoranda authorizing them and outlining the procedures to be followed; diagrams of the physical setups; publicity releases; the identities of each person arrested at the roadblock (for defense questioning as to procedures they encountered); the identities of all officers present; and so on. Armed with this information and material, counsel will be prepared to present a pretrial motion to suppress and/or dismiss.

Checklist 18 Sobriety Checkpoints

- ☐ Did the client's DUI stop result from a roadblock or checkpoint?
- ☐ Is there a legislatively developed procedure for roadblocks?
- ☐ Do guidelines exist by statute or case precedent?
- ☐ Did the roadblock or checkpoint comply with acceptable standards?
- ☐ Was the decision-making process accomplished at the *supervisorial* level?
- ☐ Were effective limits placed on the *discretion* of officers at the checkpoint?
- ☐ Was the checkpoint administered in a *safe* manner?
- ☐ Was the *location* chosen a reasonable one?
- ☐ How intrusive were the *time* and *duration* of the checkpoint?
- ☐ Were sufficient *indicia of authority* clearly visible to the public?
- ☐ Was the *length of detention* minimal?
- ☐ Was there sufficient advance *publicity* as to the time, location, and nature of the checkpoint?
- ☐ What reports, memoranda, notes, etc., are available through discovery?
- ☐ Was the roadblock valid under the relevant provisions of the *state* constitution?

§11.1.1 Evasion of Sobriety Checkpoints

What if a driver attempts to evade a valid DUI roadblock? Does this constitute probable cause to stop the vehicle and investigate? No, according to the Supreme Court of Oregon. In *Pooler v. Motor Vehicles Department,* 755 P.2d 701 (Or. 1988), the driver was stopped after he made a U-turn before reaching a roadblock.

This was held to constitute an insufficient basis for a reasonable suspicion that a crime had been committed. See also *State v. Talbot,* 792 P.2d 489 (Utah 1990).

In *People v. Rocket,* 594 N.Y.S.2d 568 (Just. Ct. 1992), a New York court agreed with the Oregon decision, holding that a legal turn into an intersecting roadway immediately before a DWI roadblock did not constitute probable cause to justify an investigatory stop. The court said that it

> was compelled to find that extension of sobriety checkpoints which include the stopping of every vehicle which lawfully turns off onto a public right of way prior to entering the checkpoint would be unduly invasive of the individual rights and freedoms protected by the U.S. Constitution and the Constitution of the State of New York. [Id. at 570.]

An Arkansas court, however, has come to an opposite conclusion. In *Coffman v. State,* 759 S.W.2d 573 (Ark. App. 1988), the court held that "[t]o a trained police officer, the fact that a motorist attempted to avoid the roadblock in this case would surely excite a reasonable suspicion that, at the very least, the motorist was drunk, driving a stolen vehicle, did not have a valid driver's license, or had some car light defect." Id. at 575. See also *Snyder v. State,* 538 N.E.2d 961 (Ind. App. 1989). And in *State v. Hester,* 584 A.2d 256 (N.J. Super. 1990), the defendant made a U-turn to avoid a DUI checkpoint approximately 300 feet ahead of him; based on this apparent avoidance, he was then pulled over by police. The appellate court chose to view the issue in terms of whether a reasonable driver would think that he could avoid the checkpoint or that he must proceed on to it. Adopting the latter view, the court then concluded that the stop was a minimal intrusion when balanced against the state's interests.

§11.1.2 "Electronic Roadblocks"

Counsel may encounter the increasingly prevalent police practice of randomly conducting radio checks on the license plates of passing cars to "see what comes up." The ACLU recently challenged this practice in a New Jersey case where two motorists were separately stopped by officers using "mobile data terminals"

(MDTs). In both cases, the citizens were cited for driving without insurance and driving with suspended licenses. At the trial of one, the officer testified that he ran an electronic check for no reason other than he was behind the defendant's car and routinely conducted random checks of license plates if he was "not doing anything else." In the trial of the other motorist, that officer testified he routinely conducted 200 or more random computer searches of license plates per day while on patrol.

The ACLU argued that this practice of indiscriminately searching personal information of innocent motorists, when there was no evidence of wrongdoing, constituted an unconstitutional "electronic roadblock." Further, the ACLU argued, the disclosure by the Department of Motor Vehicles of this information through the use of these MDTs violated the federal Driver's Privacy Protection Act of 1994 (an act that has been duplicated in the legislation of most states).

The state's Supreme Court agreed in part. In *State v. Donis,* 157 N.J. 44 (1998), that court held that the practice was a violation of the state's statutory right to privacy: Access to personal information is not authorized unless there is some reasonable and individual suspicion of wrongdoing. The court refused to reverse the convictions, but ordered the DMV to modify the MDT displays so that an initial search would display only the registration status of the vehicle, the license status of the driver, and whether the vehicle had been reported stolen. If the initial search indicated a stolen vehicle or suspended license, then a more detailed electronic search for information would be justified. The court further directed the Attorney General to "promulgate guidelines that establish disciplinary measures that will be imposed on any law enforcement officer for improperly using the MDT" to access the database for personal or impermissible reasons, such as targeting minority drivers.

Unfortunately, however, the New Jersey Supreme Court declined to address the constitutional question of whether "electronic roadblocks" constituted an invalid search under the Fourth and Fourteenth Amendments.

Counsel confronted with a case in which a DUI client has been initially stopped through this practice should move for suppression/dismissal on the grounds that it constitutes an unlawful search under both the federal and state constitutions — and on the further grounds that it is a violation of the state and federal driver protection provisions. The Driver's Privacy Protection Act of 1994, 18 USC 2721 *et seq.*, reads in part as follows:

> (a) In general. Except as provided in subsection (b), a State department of motor vehicles, and any officer, employee, or contractor thereof, shall not knowingly disclose or otherwise make available to any person or entity personal information about any individual obtained by the department in connection with a motor vehicle record.
>
> (b) Permissible uses. Personal information referred to in subsection (a) shall be disclosed for use in connection with matters of motor vehicle or driver safety and theft, motor vehicle emissions . . . and may be disclosed as follows:
>
> (1) For use by any government agency, including any court or law enforcement agency, in carrying out its functions. . . .

Note that this does not permit a DMV to release information to an officer where that officer is conducting random searches of information without "individual suspicion of wrongdoing," as that would not be "carrying out" the police agency's "functions."

§11.2 Unlawful Arrest

> It is my belief that there are "absolutes" in our Bill of Rights, and that they were put there on purpose by men who knew what words meant, and meant their prohibitions to be "absolute."
>
> HUGO BLACK

Related to, yet distinct from, the issue of probable cause to arrest is the question of the existence of a *lawful* arrest. There may be probable cause to believe the offense of driving under the influence of alcohol has been committed, but the arrest itself is without lawful authority: The officer may be out of his jurisdiction, for example, or the offense may not have been committed in his presence. Or there may simply have been no arrest made at all prior to a blood-alcohol test being administered.

It is not uncommon for officers to arrest suspects for drunk driving after, for example, arriving at the scene of an accident. If the arrest is for *misdemeanor* drunk driving, counsel should certainly consider suppression of all evidence obtained thereafter on the grounds that the arrest was without lawful authority: The offense — at least the driving element — was not committed in the officer's *presence.* Thus, for example, in *Durant v. City of Suffolk,* 358 S.E.2d 732 (Va. App. 1987), the court reversed a conviction where the arresting officer did not actually see the defendant driving: He must have "direct personal knowledge, through his sight, hearing, or other senses that [the offense] is then and there being committed." 358 S.E.2d at 733.

Of course, counsel must be familiar with the applicable statutes involved. California's statutory requirement of presence, for example, has five exceptions in DUI cases. The two most commonly encountered of these permit the officer to make an arrest where the offense was committed outside of his presence if either (1) the suspect was involved in a traffic accident or (2) that person was "observed by the peace officer in or about a vehicle which is obstructing a roadway." Calif. Vehicle Code §40300.5.

Where an officer has not been present during the driving and thus has no probable cause to detain or arrest, he may attempt to satisfy the presence requirement by claiming that he *did* observe the suspect to be "drunk in public." Thus, for example, in *People v. Lively,* 13 Cal. Rptr. 2d 368 (Cal. App. 1992), the officer found the defendant sitting in the driver's seat of his car, legally parked and with the engine off. Noting an alcoholic odor on his breath and other signs of intoxication, the officer asked him to get out of the car and administered a field sobriety test. The defendant was then arrested for drunk driving.

On appeal, the defendant argued that the officer had no probable cause to arrest him for DUI, since the offense was not committed in his presence. The prosecution argued that the defendant *did* commit the offense of public intoxication in the officer's presence, and thus there was probable cause to arrest for that offense — and the subsequent breath tests were therefore admissible.

The appellate court recognized that, like most states, California's "public drunk" offense required a considerably stronger showing of intoxication than did the DUI statute: The suspect must have been "unable to exercise care for his own safety or the safety of others." Incredibly, the court then used the kind of twisted logic that has become typical of the double standard in DUI cases. To justify the arrest, the court reasoned that "whenever a person so intoxicated that his motor skills are impaired is found as a potential driver behind the steering wheel of a car, this constitutes evidence the person is unable to exercise due care for his safety or the safety of others."

Proximity to a vehicle apparently drastically reduces the quantum of proof necessary to arrest (or presumably to convict) under the "public drunk" statute. Further, this apparently implies a legal presumption that the suspect *will* drive the vehicle; merely sitting in a car certainly poses no threat to anyone's safety.

If the officer conducting the investigation did not observe the suspect actually driving, he may request a witnessing civilian to make a "citizen's arrest." Counsel should research the law concerning the requirements for a valid citizen's arrest in his state. Generally, there must be some formalities followed, and the citizen must independently have sufficient probable cause for an arrest. See, e.g., *Keene v. Commissioner of Public Safety*, 360 N.W.2d 357 (Minn. App. 1984).

Questions of jurisdiction may arise in a drunk driving case where the arrest took place outside of the officer's city or county. There are, however, exceptions to the jurisdictional requirements for a lawful arrest — most obviously, in DUI cases particularly, where there is "hot pursuit." Less obviously, the law in many parts of the country permits local governments or law enforcement agencies to grant advance consent to another government or agency to make arrests within its borders; this consent is sometimes required to be in official written form.

In a few states and counties/cities, laws prohibit any law enforcement officer from making an arrest unless he meets certain uniform criteria — such as being in uniform and/or making the stop in a marked police vehicle.

For a discussion of the requirement that there be a formal arrest before an evidentiary chemical test is conducted, see §11.6.1.

§11.3 Incriminating Statements

> It is wise to be silent when occasion requires, and better than to speak, though never so well.
>
> PLUTARCH

As in any criminal case, the most damaging evidence may come from the defendant himself in the form of admissions or even formal confessions. Usually, these incriminating statements come in answer to a series of questions posed by the police officer as a part of his preliminary investigation. These questions tend to follow a rather routine format, and are generally geared to determining:

1. how much the suspect has had to drink
2. when and where he was drinking
3. whether his memory or mental awareness has been impaired ("Where are you? What time is it?")
4. the absence of any fatigue, illness, or medical condition (to preclude later claims affecting symptoms or chemical analysis)
5. the possible presence of drugs or medication

These questions are, in fact, so predictable that many police agencies have formalized the interrogation of drunk driving suspects by setting forth in the police report form a series of questions to be asked routinely.

Regardless of how routine the questioning in a drunk driving case may be, all of the constitutional safeguards should still apply, at least theoretically. Counsel should be thoroughly familiar with the *Miranda* line of cases up to the latest decisions; interpretations of what procedural requirements are necessary and under what conditions change constantly.

Counsel should not overlook the opportunities for suppressing what can be very damning evidence: the client's refusal to submit to blood-alcohol testing. (The relevance and admissibility of refusal evidence should be distinguished from the administrative consequences to the client's driver's license for refusing to submit. See §3.3.) Nor should he necessarily limit his inquiry to the blood-alcohol issue: *Any* refusal, most notably a refusal to take field sobriety tests, should be considered as potential suppression material.

Depending on the jurisdiction, the prosecution may allege a refusal as a sentencing enhancement in the complaint. The complaint would be read to the jury and the prosecution permitted to offer evidence of the fact of refusal. Clearly, evidence of the refusal would be relevant and legally authorized. And the jury may be given an instruction on consciousness of guilt.

But what if the defendant *stipulates* or *admits* the fact of refusal? Can the enhancement be deleted from the reading and evidence barred as not relevant to a contested issue — or can the prosecution insist that it is not required to accept defense offers to stipulate, but is entitled to prove its case by evidence of its own choice? Counsel may consider an argument by analogy to pleading and proof of prior convictions: See the discussion of the U.S. Supreme Court's recent decision in *Old Chief v. United States,* 519 U.S. 172, 136 L.Ed.2d 574, 117 S. Ct. 644 (1997), supra §9.1.1, where the Court held that a prosecutor could not refuse to accept a stipulation of the existence of a prior conviction.

Assuming that evidence of the client's refusal to submit to chemical testing is ruled admissible, counsel must, of course, provide the jury with an acceptable reason for the refusal (i.e., other than "consciousness of guilt"). There are many reasons commonly encountered, such as confusion concerning the right not to incriminate oneself, the belief that one has a right to speak with an attorney first, and so forth.

Finally, the existence of a refusal may be turned against the prosecution in trial (see §13.1.13).

As in all criminal prosecutions, of course, evidence of a defendant's incriminating statements in a drunk driving case may not be introduced until there has been sufficient prima facie evidence presented to independently establish the *corpus delicti.*

Thus, for example, in *North Carolina v. Trexler,* 334 S.E.2d 414 (N.C. App. 1985), the state offered the testimony of a civilian witness that he heard a loud noise and saw a car lying upside down on the highway; someone was leaving the car. About 30 minutes later, an officer arrived and questioned the defendant, who in his opinion was intoxicated. He was permitted to testify that the defendant said he had been driving the car at the time of the accident and that he had not drunk any alcoholic beverage since the accident. The appellate court reversed: "We do not believe . . . that proof that there was an accident and an intoxicated person later came to the scene proves in this case the crime that someone had been driving while impaired. Without proof of the *corpus delicti* the statement of the defendant . . . should not have been admitted."

It is not uncommon for drunk driving suspects to provide perhaps the most damaging evidence of all: a statement — spontaneous or in response to questioning — in which the suspect indicates a previous arrest or conviction for drunk driving. In such cases, of course, counsel should make every effort to suppress the statements. The primary grounds should be that the statements are irrelevant: They are extremely prejudicial (i.e., *legal* prejudice) while offering little, if any, probative value.

The recent decision of a Missouri appellate court illustrates this position. In *State v. Kessler,* 745 S.W.2d 846 (Mo. App. 1988), the arresting officers overheard the defendant in a post-arrest telephone conversation say that "he did not have to take a second test, and he had [the trooper] over a barrel and there was no way anyone was going to convict him of a third offense DWI." At trial, statement was permitted into evidence. The appellate court reversed and remanded, holding that "Evidence of other crimes is admissible [only] when it tends to establish a defendant's guilt for the crime with which he is charged." 745 S.W.2d at 847.

The admissibility of refusal evidence is another critical area for counsel's pre-trial consideration. Evidence that the client refused to submit to blood-alcohol analysis will, of course, be offered by the prosecution as evidence of his guilt. Such evidence can have a very prejudicial impact on the jury, at least in the absence of the defendant taking the stand and giving a credible explanation for refusing.

One avenue of attack is constitutional in nature: The refusal is an exercise in the defendant's right not to incriminate himself. As the material in §11.4.1 reflects, this argument must rely on *state* constitutional provisions and case law rather than federal.

Another approach to pre-trial suppression is that the refusal is not *relevant.* The only relevance of refusal evidence is that it shows consciousness of guilt. But there are many reasons for refusing — most commonly, for example, confusion on the part of the defendant after hearing apparently conflicting rights in a *Miranda* advisement (see §11.4.2).

The Pennsylvania Supreme Court, for example, has held that police officers must explain to DUI suspects that the right to counsel mentioned in the *Miranda* warning does not apply to their decision on whether to submit to blood-alcohol testing.

In *Commonwealth v. Danforth,* 608 A.2d 1044 (Pa. 1992), the court commented on the overwhelming unfairness of informing the motorist that he has a right to speak with a lawyer when, in fact, he does not:

> [W]e hold that when *Miranda* warnings are followed by a police request for chemical testing, the police have an affirmative duty not only to inform the arrestee that refusal to submit to chemical testing will result in suspension of his driving privileges, but also that the arrestee does not have a right to speak with an attorney or anyone else in connection with his decision as to whether he will submit to chemical testing. [Id. at 1046.]

The failure of the officer to advise the suspect adequately under the state's implied consent law may constitute grounds for suppression of evidence of refusal. Thus, for example, in *State v. Denny,* 536 A.2d 1242 (N.H. 1987), the Supreme Court of New Hampshire reversed a drunk driving conviction in which the arresting officer failed to advise the defendant that his refusal to submit to chemical testing could be used against him. However, the court reached this conclusion on the basis of the *state* — not the federal — constitution. See also *Vandiver v. State,* 429 S.E.2d 318 (Ga. App. 1993), where the court held that evidence of a defendant's refusal to take a blood-alcohol test was inadmissible if the arresting officer failed to read the implied consent warning at the time of arrest.

Yet another avenue for attacking the admissibility of refusal evidence lies in the argument that its admission undermines the statutory right of refusal. Several states have now held that such evidence is inadmissible for this reason. Thus a Missouri court in *City of St. Joseph v. Johnson,* 539 S.W.2d 784 (1976), held that "by statute, the motorist had an absolute right to refuse the test and the exercise of that right could not be used to create an unfavorable inference against him.'' And in *People v. Hayes,* 235 N.W.2d 182 (Mich. App. 1975), a Michigan court reasoned thus:

> The admission of a defendant's refusal to submit to an intoxication test would render nugatory the choice which the statute provides him. . . . If the fact that a defendant has chosen not to submit to a test can be placed before the jury as an inference of his guilt, then he will be put in the position of having to risk providing evidence for the prosecution by submitting to the test or of certainly providing it by refusing to submit. It would be fundamentally unfair to put a defendant in such a ''damned if he does, damned if he doesn't'' position. The Legislature provided a definite choice, and we cannot render a decision which would make that choice an illusory one. [235 N.W.2d at 184–185.]

Michigan subsequently provided by statute (M.S.A. §9.2325(1)(8)) for the following jury instruction to be given in DUI cases involving a refusal to provide a blood-alcohol sample.

> If a jury instruction regarding a defendant's refusal to submit to a chemical test under this section is requested by the prosecution or the defendant, the jury instruction shall be given as follows:
>
> Evidence was admitted in this case which, if believed by the jury, could prove that the defendant had exercised his or her right to refuse a chemical test. You are instructed that such a refusal is within the statutory rights of the defendant and is not evidence of his guilt. You are not to consider such a refusal in determining the guilt or innocence of the defendant.

Relying on this statute, a Michigan court of appeals ruled that refusal evidence is inadmissible in all except certain limited situations. In *People v. Duke,* 357 N.W.2d 775 (Mich. App. 1984), the court reasoned as follows:

> Michigan has no such bright-line legislative mandate as to when evidence of refusal may be admitted. It has only an injunction against admission for the purpose of proof of guilt or innocence. Logically then, evidence of the refusal may not be admitted to prove the elements of the crime.
>
> The most obvious examples of circumstances where such evidence could be admitted are:

> a. Where the defendant denies being given an opportunity to take a Breathalyzer test,
> b. Where the defendant claims that he took the test and the results were exculpatory,
> c. Where the defendant challenges the competency of any of the testing done by the officer, or
> d. Where the defendant challenges the credibility of the officer.
>
> Evidence of refusal to take the test is proper in situations such as the above where the defendant opens the controversy by a showing of lack of credibility or competence of the police officer and it is necessary to rebut defendant's evidence.
>
> We then decide that, until such time as the Legislature or Supreme Court clarifies the purpose of M.C.L. §257.625a(8); M.S.A. §9.2325(1)(8), evidence of refusal to take the tests provided by statute should not be admitted in the case in chief as it is not evidence of guilt or innocence or an essential element of the prosecutor's case.

Thus defense counsel has various potential methods of attacking the prosecution's offer of refusal evidence:

1. state constitutional grounds (self-incrimination);
2. failure of police to adequately inform defendant under implied consent law;
3. if a traffic accident is involved, defendant's emotional/mental condition precludes his understanding the officer's instructions;
4. relevance;
5. probative value is outweighed by prejudicial effect;
6. statutory right of refusal would be negated; or
7. the conduct did not legally constitute a refusal.

It should be noted that, failing in attempts to suppress refusal evidence, counsel certainly should be permitted to offer evidence of the reason *why* he refused to take the test. Thus, for example, a DUI conviction was reversed and remanded where the trial court refused to permit the defense to elicit testimony from the arresting officer that the defendant had offered to take a blood or urine test rather than the offered breath test, as well as expert testimony that a blood test is more reliable than breath analysis. *State v. Williams,* 367 N.W.2d 310 (Iowa App. 1985). As the appellate court stated:

> Defendant was not permitted to present evidence that he was willing to take other tests which he considered to be more accurate and was not allowed to show that his opinion about the accuracy of the tests was shared by an expert witness. He was foreclosed, therefore, from rebutting the natural inference from the State's evidence that his refusal was an attempt to conceal his level of intoxication. [Id. at 313.]

§11.3.1 *Miranda* and the DUI Case

The essence of the *Miranda* holding should perhaps be repeated here:

> [T]he prosecution may not use statements, whether exculpatory or inculpatory, stemming from custodial interrogation of the defendant unless it demonstrates the use of procedural safeguards effective to secure the privilege against self-incrimination. By custodial interrogation, we mean questioning initiated by law enforcement officers after a person has been taken into custody *or otherwise deprived of his freedom of action in any significant way.* As for the procedural safeguards to be employed, unless other fully effective means are devised to inform accused persons of their right of silence and to assure a continuous opportunity to exercise it, the following measures are required. Prior to any questioning, the person must be warned that he has a right to remain silent, that any statement he does make may be used as evidence against him, and that he has a right to the presence of an attorney, either retained or appointed. The defendant may waive effectuation of these rights, provided the waiver is made voluntarily, *knowingly and intelligently.* . . . [*Miranda v. Arizona,* 384 U.S. 436, 444 (1966) (Emphasis added).]

There is, of course, a never-ending body of law interpreting these basic requirements, and counsel will presumably be familiar with it, particularly as it applies to drunk driving detentions and arrests. This text does not propose to attempt to cover this extensive area of law. It should be recognized, however, that a special set of constitutional standards seems to exist within the judicial community when it deals with drunk driving cases. The issue of when the *Miranda* warnings are required is an example: Most courts will find that point to exist long past when probable cause to arrest actually arises, permitting a thorough interrogation of a suspect without proper advisement. And the U.S. Supreme Court in *Berkemer v. McCarty* has apparently endorsed this (see discussion infra).

While it would seem obvious that the requirements of *Miranda* apply to DUI situations — nothing in that decision indicates that misdemeanors are excluded from its coverage — there has been some question in a few jurisdictions as to whether a DUI suspect must be advised of his rights before questioning. Most notably, the Fourth Circuit decided in *Clay v. Riddle,* 541 F.2d 456 (4th Cir. 1983), that *Miranda* warnings were not required for misdemeanor traffic offenses. The decision was based on two factors: the court's awareness of the language in *Miranda* that the *Miranda* decision was "not intended to hamper" the traditional investigative functions of the police, and the *Clay* court's emphasis that "the unlawful incident [in *Clay*] was a commonplace event — a traffic offense. . . ." 541 F.2d at 457. Apparently very few states have adopted this reasoning.

Later that year, however, the Sixth Circuit held directly to the contrary. In *McCarty v. Herdman,* 716 F.2d 361 (6th Cir. 1983), the court held that "the language of the fifth amendment does not limit the privilege against self-incrimination to those charged with felonies. . . . We hold that *Miranda* warnings must be given to *all* individuals prior to custodial interrogation, whether the offense investigated be a felony or a misdemeanor traffic offense." Id. at 363. The court then considered the two factors relied on in *Clay.* "First, the traditional investigative police functions will not be hampered by requiring *Miranda* warnings prior to custodial interrogations in misdemeanor traffic offenses," the court wrote. "Second, we attach no significance to the fact that traffic offenses are 'commonplace' events. The privilege against self-incrimination is an enduring right, undiminished by the number of people who enjoy it or the frequency of its exercise." Id. at 364.

The issue was accepted by the U.S. Supreme Court for a resolution of the conflict between the two circuits. The Court rendered its decision in *Berkemer v. McCarty,* 468 U.S. 420 (1984), affirming the application of *Miranda* to drunk driving cases but qualifying the circumstances under which warnings must be given:

> We hold therefore that a person subjected to custodial interrogation is entitled to the benefit of the procedural safeguards enunciated in *Miranda,* regardless of the nature or severity of the offense of which he is suspected or for which he was arrested. . . .
>
> If a motorist who has been detained pursuant to a traffic stop thereafter is subjected to treatment that renders him "in custody" for practical purposes, he will be entitled to the full panoply of protections prescribed by *Miranda.* . . .
>
> Admittedly, our adherence to the doctrine just recounted will mean that the police and lower courts will continue occasionally to have difficulty deciding exactly when a suspect has been taken into custody. Either a rule that *Miranda* applies to all traffic stops or a rule that a suspect need not be advised of his rights until he is formally placed under arrest would provide a clearer, more easily administered line. However, each of these two alternatives has drawbacks that make it unacceptable. . . . [468 U.S. at 434–436.]

Thus, though recognizing the application of *Miranda,* the Supreme Court of the United States endorsed the existing tendency of courts across the country to create "special" rules for the application of constitutional safeguards to DUI cases — in this instance, delaying the point at which *Miranda* warnings must be given. Nevertheless, counsel should always be aware of the possible presence of the following issues particularly relevant to drunk driving cases:

1. was the questioning a part of a preliminary investigation, or subsequent to that point in time when probable cause to arrest existed or when the defendant was, in effect, "in custody"?
2. was the defendant too intoxicated to understand these constitutional rights?
3. if the defendant waived any rights, was he too intoxicated to do so *intelligently?*

The first issue was defined somewhat ambiguously in *Berkemer: Miranda* advisements need not be given until that point in time when the DUI suspect is treated as if he were in custody. But counsel should consider basing his arguments on *state* constitutional protections as well, independently of the U.S. Supreme Court's "double standard" application of the Fifth Amendment. Thus under the defendant's state's self-incrimination provisions, counsel should make the traditional arguments: Exactly when did the finger of suspicion center on the suspect so as to require a giving of the rights? In other words, when did the detention stop being a preliminary investigation and become a gathering of incriminating evidence? To put it still another way, when did the police officer have sufficient reasonable grounds to justify an arrest of the suspect for driving under the influence?

These and other standards are commonly applied to isolate that point in time when the suspect must be advised of his constitutional rights. Again, this text will not deal with the vast body of precedent relevant to this issue, but will only point out the obvious: Counsel should make every effort to establish the existence of cause to arrest at a time prior to when the defendant made the incriminating statements.

Whether or not a moment at which the defendant could have been arrested was reached and whether or not the questioning was part of a preliminary investigation may not be the only standards. Counsel should be prepared to argue strongly that the *Miranda* warnings were required at an even earlier point in time — when the defendant was pulled over and initially observed inside his car. The Supreme Court in *Miranda* specifically stated that the rights must be given after a person has been taken into custody "or otherwise deprived of his freedom of action in any significant way." *Berkemer* restated this in terms of being treated "as if" in custody. Certainly, the officer should be asked at the suppression hearing if the defendant had been free to leave at any time after he had been pulled over; no judge or jury will believe the officer if he answers in the affirmative. Since the defendant was not free to leave (i.e., his freedom of action had been deprived in a significant way), the admonitions were required. If they were not given — and they almost certainly were not at that point — then all subsequent statements given in reply to police questioning must be suppressed.

If counsel is successful in arguing for greater safeguards under his state constitution, establishing an early probable cause point may not be that difficult. The officer will have already seen the defendant's erratic driving, rumpled clothing, flushed face, and bloodshot eyes, and will have observed the defendant's thick and slurred speech. It will be difficult for him to testify honestly at a suppression hearing that he did *not* feel that the suspect was "probably" under the influence. In most cases, the officer also will have observed the defendant fumble through his wallet and stumble and/or lean against the car, all before any questioning. This, of course, adds to the strength of counsel's argument that enough evidence existed to justify an admonition of rights. Where the questioning is after one or more field sobriety tests, it is almost inconceivable that probable cause to arrest did not exist. Certainly, if the officer testifies that he still did not believe he had sufficient evidence to justify an arrest, that opinion should be aggressively used against him in trial to minimize the importance of the preceding observations.

In each case defense counsel should argue that the proximity of the admissions and the arrest, the presence of sufficient incriminating evidence (the officer's observations and opinion), and the true purpose of the questioning (to gather evidence, rather than to investigate), taken together, require a suppression of the statements. In fact, the following argument should be made where appropriate: Either the officer had probable cause to stop the suspect, observe his symptoms, and immediately arrest him, in which case any interrogative statements are inadmissible unless warnings were immediately given, or there was no probable cause to stop and hold him, in which case the detention was a violation of the Fourth Amendment and any subsequent statements of any kind are inadmissible.

An examination of many police reports will indicate that the officer made the initial stop based on little more than a hunch. He will be unable to articulate later — if he is honest — any specific violation of law that he observed. Under such circumstances, the stop and initial detention can be argued as having deprived the defendant of his freedom of movement to a degree that, in effect, placed him in custody, regardless of how the police characterize it. If the detention/arrest is without probable cause, subsequent statements (and other evidence, such as chemical tests) are inadmissible.

The second and third issues commonly found in drunk driving cases present relatively unique opportunities to defense counsel. The charge of driving under the influence, by its very nature, involves the consumption of alcohol to the extent that it impairs the individual's judgment and coordination. The language differs from jurisdiction to jurisdiction, but essentially the prosecutor is trying to prove that the defendant was so intoxicated that his mental and physical abilities were dangerously impaired. Yet *Miranda* and attendant cases infer that the suspect must be capable of understanding his rights and specifically require that any waiver of any such rights be made "knowingly and intelligently."

Quite simply, the prosecution should not have it both ways: If the defendant was too intoxicated to drive safely, then he was probably too intoxicated to understand his rights and to waive them intelligently. The burden of establishing compliance with the mandated constitutional safeguards is on the prosecution. It is the prosecutor, therefore, who must prove that any waiver of rights was made knowingly and intelligently. It is he, in other words, who must attempt to establish in court that the defendant was not, in fact, *too* intoxicated. This places the prosecutor on the horns of a dilemma and should provide defense counsel with interesting possibilities: If the defendant was too intoxicated to operate a vehicle safely, he was at least arguably too intoxicated to understand and intelligently waive his rights before interrogation. The requirements of *Miranda* are clear: The waiver must be made voluntarily, *intelligently,* and *knowingly.* Yet, the same arresting officer who testifies at a suppression hearing that the defendant exhibited the clearness of mind necessary to intelligently waive his constitutional rights will later testify at trial that the defendant was so under the influence of alcohol that his judgment was seriously impaired.

In *State v. Bramlett,* 609 P.2d 345 (N.M. 1980), a New Mexico appellate court held that such contradictory evidence from a police officer "offends the standards of fundamental fairness under the due process clause" and was unworthy of belief. As the court reasoned:

> The officers testified that they believed Bramlett knew and understood what he had been advised when the second and third state-

> ments were given by him. In view, however, of their detailed description of his condition at 5:00 P.M. — staggering, slurred speech, difficulty in walking, strong alcoholic smell — and the intoxication test level of .23, it is difficult to reconcile their conclusion of his extreme intoxication with their opinion of his judgmental awareness of his rights and an intelligent waiver of them.
>
> . . . If defendant was so intoxicated that in the judgment of these witnesses he could not function safely, it is a contradiction of their own testimony and actions to believe that their opposing assessment of his ability to understand constitutes sufficient evidence that the statements and the waivers were given knowingly and voluntarily. [609 P.2d at 350.]

Subsequent to its decision in *Berkemer,* the Supreme Court has addressed an interesting issue within the *Miranda* context: Does requiring a drunk driving suspect to *recite the alphabet* violate his Fifth Amendment right? The question was presented to the Court after a Pennsylvania court held that asking a DUI suspect to recite the alphabet as part of a field sobriety test constitutes interrogation under *Miranda* because it is "essentially communicative in nature." Because the court found that the defendant was "in custody" at the time of the request and had not been advised of his rights, it held that evidence of the test had been improperly admitted and reversed the conviction. *Commonwealth v. Bruder,* 528 A.2d 1385 (Pa. App. 1987). This position was upheld in an identical factual situation one year later in *Commonwealth v. Peth,* 542 A.2d 1015 (Pa. Super. 1988). Subsequently, the U.S. Supreme Court reversed *Bruder.* In *Pennsylvania v. Bruder,* 488 U.S. 9 (1988), the Court held that the defendant was not yet put "in custody" at the time of the alphabet recitation, citing *Berkemer.* However, the Court did *not* address the question of whether recitation of the alphabet was "testimonial" or not.

For a subsequent state appellate court decision holding that an alphabet recitation is not testimonial in nature and thus does not violate the privilege against self-incrimination, see *People v. Bugbee,* 559 N.E.2d 554 (Ill. App. 1990). For a discussion of the Supreme Court ruling in *Pennsylvania v. Muniz* concerning the constitutional validity of asking and videotaping questions designed to test mental dexterity, see §11.5.1.

§11.3.2 The *Corpus* Rule

The prosecution in drunk driving cases occasionally attempts to introduce a defendant's statements to prove its case. The issue invariably arises (particularly in accident or hit-and-run cases) when the state attempts to prove the necessary driving element of the *corpus delecti* by offering the admission that he was, in fact, driving The evidence codes of most states, however, require there to be independent evidence of driving before a defendant's admissions may be used.

As in all criminal prosecutions, evidence of a defendant's incriminating statements in a drunk driving case may not be introduced until there has been sufficient independent evidence presented to establish a prima facie case. [See *People v. Kelley* (1937) 27 Cal. App. 2d Supp. 771, 70 P2d 276; *People v. Nelson* (1983) 140 Cal. App. 3d Supp. 1, 189 Cal. Rptr. 845] The issue invariably arises when the prosecution attempts to prove the driving element of the corpus delicti.

Proof that the defendant was, at some time, driving the vehicle is usually accomplished through testimony of the arresting officers, commonly from their observations of a traffic violation or erratic driving. Sometimes, particularly after an accident, testimony of civilian witnesses is used to "put the defendant behind the wheel." Occasionally, there is no direct eyewitness available, and the prosecution must attempt to establish driving with either circumstantial evidence or the defendant's admission or both. The most common situation involves an automobile parked in an erratic manner or wrapped around a telephone pole, with the defendant found unconscious in the car or sitting down nearby.

In such cases, the first thing counsel must remember is that admissions to driving by the defendant will not supply a missing element of the corpus: the prosecution must establish at least a prima facie case as to all elements of the offense before statements by the defendant will be admitted into evidence. Of course, the corpus need not be established beyond a reasonable doubt; the prosecution only has to produce enough evidence to corroborate the admissions. Nevertheless, it is a common practice of prosecutors — whether by design or out of ignorance — to attempt to establish the fact that the defendant was driving solely through the introduction of the defendant's statements to the police or witnesses.

The prosecution may not have to prove that the *defendant* committed the offense, however. The identity of the perpetrator is not an element of the offense. See, e.g., *Ernst v. Municipal Court,* 163 Cal. Rptr. 861 (1980). It need only be shown that *a crime* was committed — by *someone.* In other words, before the defendant's statements may be offered the prosecution must prove *prima facie* that someone was driving a vehicle and that the driver was under the influence at the time. The statements may then be admitted to show that it was the defendant. The prosecution must then, of course, prove the elements beyond a reasonable doubt — as well as prove that the defendant was the driver.

A number of appellate cases exist where DUI convictions were reversed because of admissions admitted to prove driving. Thus, for example, in *People v. Nelson* (1983) 140 Cal. App. 3d Supp. 1, 189 Cal. Rptr. 845, civilian witnesses saw a car hit a freeway guardrail and two men — including the defendant — thrown from the car; however, they could not tell which one had been the driver. The defendant later admitted to the investigating officer that he had been driving. On appeal, the court held:

> [W]here the offense is driving under the influence . . . the corpus delicti is established by a prima facie showing that: (1) an individual, (2) while under the influence of intoxicating liquor and any drug, (3) drove a vehicle on a highway. . . .
>
> In the instant case . . . other than defendant's own statements, there was no proof whatsoever that defendant was the driver of the vehicle. . . . Under these circumstances, it was error for the trial court to allow testimony regarding defendant's admission that he was the driver of the vehicle. [*People v. Nelson* (1983) 140 Cal. App. 3d Supp. 1, 3, 189 Cal. Rptr. 845, 846–847]

This situation is to be distinguished with that presented in *People v. Ellena* (1924) 67 Cal. App. 683, 228 P 389. In that case, there were three individuals in a car involved in an accident. Although the defendant confessed to being the driver, no witnesses could put the defendant behind the wheel. The admission was held to be admissible, however, since the prosecution was able to prove that *all three* of the car's occupants were under the influence:

since one of them had to have been driving, then the car had been driven by an intoxicated person. So, the corpus existed since *someone* had been driving drunk. The admission then served to identify the actual driver.

Checklist 19 Incriminating Statements

- ☐ Did the client make any incriminating statements?
- ☐ Has counsel reviewed all police reports, audio/video tapes, transcripts, etc.?
- ☐ Will the officer testify about any statements not appearing in discovery materials?
- ☐ Did the officer have probable cause to stop, detain, and arrest?
- ☐ Was the statement given as a result of custodial interrogation?
- ☐ Was *Miranda* given?
- ☐ Do the facts comply with *Berkemer?*
- ☐ Was the waiver given intelligently (and therefore soberly)?
- ☐ Is there any physical record of the waiver?
- ☐ Is the statement relevant to the issue of intoxication?
- ☐ Does any probative value outweigh the prejudicial effect?
- ☐ Has the prosecution established a prima facie *corpus* before attempting to introduce the statement?
- ☐ Is the appropriate procedure for suppression a pre-trial motion, an objection, or a motion out of hearing of the jury?
- ☐ Can the *corpus* of the offense be independently proven?

§11.4 Refusal Evidence

> In case of dissension, never dare to judge till you have heard the other side.
>
> EURIPIDES

The most damaging result of a refusal to submit to a chemical test is usually not the suspension or revocation of the client's driver's license but rather the effect that the fact of refusal will have on a trial, for certainly any jury will draw from a refusal the adverse inference of consciousness of guilt — that is, that the defendant refused to submit to a chemical test because he knew the results would reflect the many drinks he had taken. And any exculpatory explanation by the defendant of why he failed to take the test may be dampened by an instruction from the court to the effect that the refusal may be viewed as evidencing a consciousness of guilt.

Counsel, then, must attempt vigorously to suppress evidence of the refusal, preferably during pre-trial procedures but, in any event, outside of the hearing of the jury and before any mention concerning the refusal is made by the prosecutor. Generally, there are three possible avenues of attack in attempting a suppression: statutory provisions, constitutional considerations, and foundational defects (relevance). Counsel may also wish to argue that the words or conduct of the client did not legally amount to a refusal and therefore is irrelevant. See §3.3.1 for a discussion of what constitutes a refusal for purposes of license suspension.

In a few states, legislation specifically directed toward the issue authorizes the introduction into evidence of the fact of refusal. (See, e.g., Iowa Code §321 B11 (Acts 1969, 63 G.A. Ch. 205, §10, eff. July 1969).) In others, the relevant statute establishes the opposite position: The failure of the defendant to submit to chemical testing can neither be offered as evidence nor be commented upon. (See, e.g., Maryland Ann. Code, Art. 35, §100 cc (1969 Ch. 157).) And in a very few jurisdictions, the law provides that evidence of the refusal is admissible only in the event the defendant takes the stand in his own defense. (See, e.g., N.D. Cent. Code §39-20-08.)

In those states without such legislation — and even, in appropriate circumstances, in states having such legislation — counsel should consider arguing that the introduction of evidence of refusal constitutes a denial of the defendant's constitutional rights. Specifically, admission of the fact of refusal amounts to a violation of the privilege against self-incrimination.

§11.4.1 Self-Incrimination: *Neville*

The courts have been fairly uniform in ruling that communicative or testimonial evidence is protected by the Fifth Amendment, while physical evidence is not. The issue of whether the testing of body chemistry falls within the communicative or physical category was resolved in *Schmerber v. California,* 384 U.S. 757 (1966), wherein the Supreme Court held that the results of a blood test taken over the suspect's objections were admissible, "[s]ince the blood test evidence, although an incriminating product of compulsion, was neither petitioner's testimony nor evidence relating to some communicative act or writing by the petitioner. . . ." The question remains, however, of whether the *refusal* to submit to chemical testing is admissible. It would seem that a refusal, unlike the chemical test result itself, is communicative rather than physical in nature.

Although the trend in law had been to hold that introduction of a defendant's refusal to take a blood-alcohol test does not violate his Fifth Amendment privilege, one state supreme court case deviated from that trend. The South Dakota Supreme Court, in *State v. Neville,* 312 N.W.2d 723 (S.D. 1981), held that the defendant's statement of refusal is communicative in nature: A defendant's silence or refusal to submit to a requested blood test is a tacit or overt expression and communication of defendant's thoughts. The court also determined that this testimonial evidence was compelled for Fifth Amendment purposes — the suspect was compelled to choose between submitting to a perhaps unpleasant examination and producing testimonial evidence against himself, "thereby casting doubt upon the 'voluntariness' of the testimonial evidence thereby obtained." 312 N.W.2d at 726.

Two years later, however, the United States Supreme Court reversed the *Neville* decision (*South Dakota v. Neville,* 459 U.S. 553 (1983)). In a 7-2 decision written by Justice O'Connor, the Court ruled that the state court had misapplied the self-incrimination doctrine because a refusal is a matter of free choice, not compulsion. The dissenting justices felt that the Court should not have decided the case, since the state court's decision rested on state as well as federal grounds.

Although this decision now precludes any federal Fifth Amendment argument as to the admissibility of the fact of refusal, there would appear to be nothing to prevent using this approach on a *state* constitutional theory. In fact, on remand of *Neville,* the South Dakota Supreme Court again suppressed evidence of the defendant's refusal and asserted independent *state* constitutional grounds for determining the admissibility of refusal evidence. In *State v. Neville,* 346 N.W.2d 425, 427–428 (S.D. 1984), that court stated:

> While the Supreme Court determined that evidence of an accused's refusal to take a blood test does not infringe upon Fifth

> Amendment rights, their decision is not controlling of our decision herein. We alone determine the extent of protection afforded under our state constitution, but also, as stated by the Supreme Court, "[i]t is elementary that states are free to provide greater protections in their criminal justice system than the Federal Constitution requires." *California v. Ramos,* — U.S. — , 103 S. Ct. 3446, 74 L. Ed. 2d 19 (1982) [other citations omitted].

See also *Farmer v. Commonwealth,* 390 S.E.2d 775 (Va. App. 1990), holding that admitting evidence of a defendant's refusal constituted a violation of his right against self-incrimination under Virginia's state constitution.

A case decided by a Texas court adopts the view that a state may not introduce evidence that the accused was offered and refused a Breathalyzer test after his arrest for driving while intoxicated. *Castleberry v. State,* 631 S.W.2d 542 (Tex. App. 1982). And in *People v. Nasself,* 468 N.E.2d 466 (Ill. App. 1984), an Illinois appellate court ruled that a defendant's initial refusal was not admissible where he later agreed to — and did — take the test.

In *Deering v. Brown,* 839 F.2d 539 (9th Cir. 1988), however, the U.S. Court of Appeals for the Ninth Circuit affirmed the Alaskan U.S. District Court's denial of a writ of habeus corpus where evidence that the defendant remained *silent* when asked to take a breath test had been admitted into evidence. Rejecting the defendant's argument that this constituted impermissible comment on his Fifth Amendment right to remain silent, the court held that the silence was "nontestimonial" and therefore not protected, citing *Neville v. South Dakota.*

However, a strong dissent pointed out that the majority was evading the issue by phrasing it in terms of the defendant's "silent refusal" — rather than focusing on the essential issue of whether evidence of the defendant's silence was used or not. The dissent also distinguished *Neville,* since that case involved an *affirmative statement* that constituted a refusal; in *Deering,* however, the question was whether the defendant's silence could be used against him to *show* a criminally punishable refusal.

11.4.2 Relevance

Perhaps the most productive avenue for attacking the admissibility of refusal evidence is the foundational one: testimony concerning a refusal to submit to blood-alcohol testing is simply not *relevant.* Put a different way, the minimal probative value of the fact of refusal is heavily outweighed by the highly prejudicial inference that will inevitably be drawn by the jury. Of course, this inference is the sole reason the prosecutor has for offering the evidence of refusal, that is, to show consciousness of guilt in the mind of the defendant. The argument should be made that this "evidence" has little or no probative value, because it certainly does not tend to prove that the defendant was in fact under the influence of alcohol. Further, it does not even tend to establish that he was aware of his intoxication or was trying to hide anything; there are, after all, any number of reasons why an arrestee might refuse to comply with the officer's request. For example, the defendant may have mistakenly believed that he had a Fifth Amendment right not to take the test — not an unusual conclusion after a *Miranda* warning. Though he is legally wrong, the point is that the *reason* for the refusal was not consciousness of guilt. The fact that a defendant refused to submit to a test neither establishes nor necessarily tends to establish any fact, and the jury can only speculate about why the defendant refused.

Although some courts have rejected this argument, others have expressly held that the failure to administer or the refusal to take such a test is of no probative value unless there are circumstances present, such as admissions by conduct, that would otherwise be admissible.

This view was adopted by the appellate court in *State v. Chavez,* 629 P.2d 1242 (N.M. App. 1981):

> [T]he fact of the defendant's refusal would be no more a relevant circumstance to establish consciousness of guilt than the fact of the arresting officer's refraining from obtaining a warrant indicates that he believed that the defendant was not intoxicated. . . . [Evidence of refusal] was simply not relevant evidence. [629 P.2d at 1243.]

See also *State v. Parker,* 558 P.2d 1361 (Wash. App. 1976); *State v. Monroe,* 171 A.2d 419 (Conn. 1961). Accord *City of St. Joseph v. Johnson,* 539 S.W.2d 784 (Mo. 1976); *Crawley v. State,* 413 S.W.2d 370 (Tenn. 1967); *State v. Severson,* 75 N.W.2d 316 (N.D. 1956); *City of Columbus v. Mullins,* 123 N.E.2d 422 (Ohio 1954); *People v. Knutson,* 149 N.E.2d 461 (Ill. App. 1958).)

Subsequent to the *Neville* decision, discussed supra, a Washington appellate court reiterated that state's position that refusal evidence was not relevant. In *City of Seattle v. Boulinger,* 680 P.2d 67 (Wash. App. 1984), that court held:

> The evidence is not relevant. The City has no affirmative duty to establish that the defendant was afforded an opportunity to prove his sobriety. See *People v. Reeder,* 370 Mich. 378, 121 N.W.2d 840, 842 (1963). Moreover, any arguable probative value is substantially outweighed by the danger of unfair prejudice to the defendant. ER 403. A defendant may have valid reasons for refusing a test, reasons which do not reflect consciousness of guilt; it is probable that the jury will ascribe undue weight to the refusal. The City also contends that the error, if any, was harmless because the evidence of guilt was overwhelming, and the error was nonconstitutional. "[E]rror is not prejudicial unless, within reasonable probabilities, had the error not occurred, the outcome of the trial would have been materially affected." *State v. Cunningham,* 93 Wash. 2d 823, 831, 613 P.2d 1139 (1980). [680 P.2d at 68.]

The Supreme Court of Washington subsequently affirmed the position of the appellate court in *Boulinger.* In *State v. Zwicker,* 713 P.2d 1101 (Wash. 1986), the state sought review of two lower court rulings holding that evidence of a refusal was irrelevant and prejudicial. Washington's applicable evidentiary statute reads that:

> The refusal of a person to submit to a test of his blood . . . is admissible into evidence at a subsequent criminal trial without any comment and with a jury instruction, where applicable, that there shall be no speculation as to the reason for the refusal and that no inference is to be drawn from the refusal. [Wash. Rev. Code §46.20.308; Id. at 1103.]

The supreme court noted that the language prevented the prosecution from arguing that guilt could be inferred from the defendant's refusal. Since refusal evidence could not be used to infer guilt, the court concluded, then it was not relevant: "Not being probative of the existence of any fact that is of consequence to the determination of guilt, refusal evidence is not properly a part of the State's case in chief." The court did note, however, that a defendant could "open the door" by attacking the credibility or competence of police breath analyzing procedures. The refusal evidence being prejudicial, the court found it reversible error to have admitted the evidence even with cautionary jury instructions at trial.

A Kansas court rejected the admission of refusal testimony into evidence after weighing the prejudicial effect of admitting evidence of a refusal against its limited probative value (*State v. Wilson,* 613 P.2d 384 (Kan. App. 1980)):

> Several cases have held that the evidentiary value of this type of evidence does not have sufficient probative value to justify its admission. [Cites.] As we view the matter, it is unquestionable that such evidence has probative value; however, we are concerned that the prejudicial effect on the jury would outweigh its probative value. We likewise hold the view that admission of such evidence would be too high a price to pay for the privilege of driving on the highway. [613 P.2d at 387.]

A Maryland appellate court has also recently ruled that evidence of refusal to submit to blood-alcohol testing is not relevant to the issue of guilt. In *Krauss v. State,* 587 A.2d 1102 (Md. App. 1991), the court reversed a drunk driving conviction after finding that introduction of evidence of a refusal was prejudicial error:

> In short . . . there appeared no sound reason for the State to introduce evidence of the refusal except to influence the jury toward a verdict of guilty. In the circumstances, evidence of the refusal had no proper relation to the only proposition for which it may reasonably be said to have been offered, namely the guilt of the accused. Thus, it was not material. The refusal had no proper probative value to establish the guilt of the accused. Thus, it was irrelevant. [Id. at 1107.]

At the very least, counsel should demand an evidentiary hearing and force the prosecution to establish a satisfactory foundation concerning the reason for the refusal. In *City of Columbus v. Maxey,* 530 N.E.2d 958 (Ohio App. 1988), for example, the defendant refused to take a chemical test until he could speak with an attorney. His motion for an evidentiary hearing to suppress evidence of the refusal on the grounds it was not relevant to consciousness of guilt was denied. On appeal, the court took note of

Neville, then held that the question of whether a refusal was in "good faith" or not — that is, showed consciousness of guilt — must be determined by an evidentiary hearing:

> Ohio courts have recognized that not all refusals to take chemical tests to determine alcohol content are based on "consciousness of guilt." They have held that, in some circumstances, people in good faith refuse to take such a test because they first wish to consult with counsel. In such a case, such a request to consult with an attorney before deciding to take the test does not constitute a refusal to take the test and therefore cannot be offered as evidence of guilt. [530 N.E.2d at 960 (citations omitted).]

The court also held that the trial judge erred not only in denying an evidentiary hearing on the reasons for the refusal, but in ignoring the possibility of good faith in instructing the jury as to the significance of the refusal.

Note: Subsequent to the decisions of the Washington courts in *State v. Parker, City of Seattle v. Boulinger,* and *State v. Zwicker,* a statute was enacted which allowed evidence of a refusal into evidence. Wash. Rev. Code 46.61.517. The state Supreme Court affirmed the new law in *State v. Long,* 112 Wash. 2d 266 (1989), although in doing so it reserved to the trial court the responsibility of determining on a case-by-case basis whether the evidence would tend to distract or confuse the jury or whether the prejudice of such evidence would outweigh its probative value.

§11.4.3 Refusal to Take Field Sobriety Tests

Closely related to the issue of the admissibility of evidence that a defendant refused to take a blood-alcohol test is the question of refusal to submit to field sobriety tests.

In *State v. Green,* 684 P.2d 575 (Or. 1984), an Oregon appellate court upheld a trial court suppression of evidence that the defendant had refused to perform any FST, finding such evidence violative of the state constitution's provision against self-incrimination:

> The state argues that the specie of evidence it seeks to use in this case is analogous to evidence of flight or a breath test refusal

> and is, therefore, admissible. We disagree. Evidence of refusal to take a field sobriety test is also communicative, but it is in a different category from evidence of flight or evidence of refusal to provide *required* non-communicative evidence. There is no statutory or other legal requirement that a driver take the field sobriety tests, either before or after arrest. While an officer may properly request a driver to do so, the officer may go no further. Because defendant had no obligation to take the test, there could also be no conditions placed on his refusal. Use of the fact that he refused enables the state to obtain communicative evidence to which it would otherwise have no right, as a result of defendant's refusal to provide non-communicative evidence to which it also had no right.

Oregon's Supreme Court subsequently affirmed this position. In *State v. Fish,* 893 P.2d 1023 (1995), that court held that a defendant's refusal to submit to field sobriety testing is inadmissible at trial under the self-incrimination clause of the state constitution. Such evidence is "testimonial," the court reasoned, because it is the same as offering a defendant's statement, "I refuse to perform field sobriety tests because I believe I will fail them." Yet, he is "compelled" to make such a statement because he is given the choice of either incriminating himself by taking the tests or refusing and having that refusal used against him in court.

A Massachusetts court has followed suit, holding evidence of a refusal to take field sobriety tests violated the state constitution. The court reasoned that permitting refusal evidence would be "unsound" because a driver, who is not required to submit to the field sobriety tests, would be placed in a *Catch-22* situation: take the test and possibly incriminate himself, or refuse and have that refusal used to help prove his guilt. *Commonwealth v. McGrail,* 647 N.E.2d 712 (Mass. 1995).

Whether such a result could be obtained today under the U.S. Constitution is doubtful. The Supreme Court has consistently viewed evidence such as field sobriety tests to be physical in nature, rather than testimonial, and thus not protected by the Fifth Amendment. See, e.g., *Pennsylvania v. Muniz,* 491 U.S. 582, 110 S. Ct. 2638, 110 L. Ed. 2d 528 (1990).

Nevertheless, there appears to be a growing number of courts holding that a refusal to submit to field sobriety testing is inadmissible, at least if there is no statutory obligation to submit. Thus, for example, in *Taylor v. State,* 625 So. 2d 911 (Fla. App. 1993), the appellate court ruled that the refusal was inadmissible for three reasons. First, since the tests are not compulsory, it would be unfair to hold a defendant's refusal against him. Second, it would be equally unfair to comment upon the refusal where he was not warned that it would be admitted into evidence. And third, the court reasoned, evidence of a refusal was simply not probative of guilt: It "may have been occasioned by nothing more than his desire to exercise his choice not to submit." See also *Farmer v. Commonwealth,* 390 S.E.2d 775 (Va. App. 1990).

Where there are legal consequences to refusing to take field sobriety tests, counsel should consider moving to suppress any *statements* made by the defendant in reply to questioning during performance of the tests.

In *State v. Harrison,* 851 P.2d 611 (Or. App. 1993), the defendant was asked to take a field sobriety test and advised of the consequences of refusing. During the ensuing tests, he was asked how he thought he performed on them, what his intoxication level was, and whether he thought he was driving under the influence.

On appeal, the defendant argued that because the questions were interspersed with the FSTs, he could have believed that a refusal to answer them constituted a refusal to take the tests — that is, his replies were involuntary. The trial court agreed, suppressing all statements made after the defendant was advised of the consequences of refusing to perform. The state appealed.

The appellate court agreed in part but held that the answers to questions asked after the defendant was arrested should not have been suppressed. The defendant could not have been confused since a clear break in time separated the tests and these later questions.

Can a refusal to submit to field sobriety tests be considered in determining whether there is probable cause to arrest? Yes, according to at least one appellate court. In *State v. Babbit,* 525 N.W.2d 102 (Wis. App. 1994), the court reasoned that a refusal was relevant to "consciousness of guilt," which was in turn relevant to the question of whether probable cause existed. The court justified this attenuated reasoning by noting that it was contrary to "public policy and the state's interest in combatting the problem of intoxicated drivers" to permit a driver "who refuses to cooperate with the police" from gaining a "significant benefit" from the refusal.

In other words, a refusal to take FSTs may not actually be relevant to probable cause — but it will be considered relevant in order to stop DUI suspects from refusing.

Oregon, on the other hand, takes the opposite view: "[R]efusal to consent to field sobriety tests cannot be used to establish probable cause to believe that a defendant is intoxicated." *State v. Gilmour* (Or. App. 1995) 901 P.2d 894. See also, *State v. Niles* (Or. App. 1985) 703 P.2d 1030; *State v. Fish* (Or. 1995) 893 P.2d 1023.

Counsel should usually be able to challenge the admissibility of a refusal to take an officer's field sobriety tests — on the grounds that such evidence is not *relevant.* In theory, the relevance of such a refusal is that it tends to show *consciousness of guilt.* If, however, there is another reason why the defendant refused — for example, the officer was hostile or the defendant thought he had a Fifth Amendment right to refuse — then the relevance disappears. And, of course, the prosecutor as the proponent of the evidence has the foundational burden of showing relevance.

For a closely related discussion of the relevance of a refusal to submit to blood-alcohol testing, see §11.4.2.

Checklist 20 Refusal to Submit to Chemical Testing

- ☐ Was there probable cause to stop, detain, and arrest the client?
- ☐ Was the client properly advised under *Miranda* and the implied consent law?
- ☐ Do the client's words and/or conduct constitute a refusal?
- ☐ If they arguably do not, does any probative value outweigh the prejudicial effect?
- ☐ Does state authority affect the admissibility of refusal evidence?
- ☐ Are there any statutes governing the admissibility of refusal evidence?
- ☐ Does such evidence violate a statutory right to refuse?
- ☐ Does such evidence violate the state constitution's prohibition against self-incrimination?
- ☐ Is the evidence of refusal relevant?
- ☐ Was the refusal due to consciousness of guilt?
- ☐ Can the prosecution lay a foundation showing the reason for the refusal?
- ☐ Did the client refuse to take field sobriety tests?

§11.5 Field Evidence

> It is a piece of idle sentimentality that truth, merely as truth, has any inherent power denied to error of prevailing against the dungeon and the stake.
>
> JOHN STUART MILL

The usual focus of the attorney in a drunk driving case is, understandably, on the blood-alcohol evidence. Such evidence seems particularly damaging in view of its apparent scientific and objective nature, and quickly becomes the target of attack. Too, the avenues of attack are clear: Blood-alcohol tests are subject to extensive regulatory requirements; the theories and applications of the tests are defective in numerous regards; and test results are the product of possibly invalid stops, detentions, arrests, and implied-consent advisements.

But counsel should never overlook or underestimate the influence on a jury of the arresting officer's testimony. In this writer's opinion, such evidence is more influential in affecting the verdict than evidence of blood-alcohol content — assuming, of course, effective cross-examination of the blood-alcohol expert.

Thus the key to victory or defeat in the DUI case still lies with the old-fashioned cop. Defense counsel *must* be able to deal effectively with this experienced and professional witness. One way is through skillful cross-examination. Another, however, is to simply keep him from testifying in the first place — through pre-trial motions to suppress.

The most common type of field evidence is the "field sobriety test," usually conducted by the officer at the scene of the investigative detention. These tests are designed to test the physical and mental abilities of the driver. Performance tests, such as the walk-the-line (or heel-to-toe) and the one-leg stand, are aimed at coordination and balance. Verbal tests, such as alphabet recitation and reverse counting, are intended to determine mental acuity. Some of these tests are designed to accomplish both purposes, as well as test "divided attention" — that is, the ability of the suspect to perform physical and mental tasks at the same time. An example of this would be a one-leg-stand test during which the suspect is required to count backwards from 30.

In what appears to be the beginning of a trend, the admissibility of field sobriety tests is finally being challenged in isolated cases across the country. Two grounds have been used for challenging the long-accepted tests. First, some of the FSTs violate the individual's Fifth Amendment rights. Second, the tests are presented as scientific in nature but fail to satisfy the foundational requirements for scientific evidence.

Oregon has taken an even more radical view toward field sobriety tests, characterizing them as "searches" of the person requiring a warrant or probable cause with exigent circumstances. See, e.g., *State v. Gilmour* (Or. App. 1995) 901 P.2d 894; *State v. Fish* (Or. 1995) 893 P.2d 1023. Further, the prosecution cannot comment on the defendant's refusal to submit to the tests.

§11.5.1 Verbal Field Sobriety Tests: *Muniz*

Until relatively recently, the admissibility of field sobriety tests was simply assumed; defense lawyers did not even consider challenging them. The first major crack in the wall appeared with the U.S. Supreme Court decision in *Pennsylvania v. Muniz,* 496 U.S. 582 (1990). In that case, Muniz was arrested for drunk driving and, on videotape at the police station, given a series of field sobriety tests. During the procedure, and without any *Miranda* advisement, the arresting officer asked Muniz seven questions concerning his name, address, physical characteristics, and age. The suspect stumbled over two answers. In a question designed to test his mental acuity, he was then asked, "Do you know what the date was of your sixth birthday?" Muniz's reply was inaudible. The officer again asked, "When you turned six years old, do you remember what the date was?" Muniz replied, "No, I don't."

The Supreme Court held that the answer to the birthday question was inadmissible. The reply constituted a testimonial response to custodial interrogation and therefore required a *Miranda* advisement and waiver.

The Court noted that questioning for purposes of observing a defendant's *slurred speech* would be permissible without *Miranda;* requiring a suspect to exhibit his speech ability related to the gathering of *physical* rather than testimonial evidence. But asking him a question designed to test his mental dexterity related to the *content* of the reply rather than its physical — that is, slurred —

nature. In other words, the birthday question was aimed at *what* was said rather than *how* it was said.

Thus, the *Muniz* decision would seem to stand for the proposition that a drunk driving suspect cannot — after being placed "in custody" and without a *Miranda* advisement and waiver — be asked any questions designed to test his mental state. This would extend to such commonly asked questions as, "Where are you right now?" "What time is it?" or "What day of the week was yesterday?"

Relying on the *Muniz* case, the Florida Supreme Court has extended the U.S. Supreme Court's reasoning to encompass the commonly used *alphabet* recitation test. In *Allred v. State,* 622 S.E.2d 984 (Fla. 1993), the court held that the Fifth Amendment barred officers from asking a DWI suspect to recite the alphabet without first advising him of his *Miranda* rights. The alphabet test was aimed at the content (incorrect recitation) of a person's replies, said the court, not at the manner (slurring) of his speech. Like the birthday question in *Muniz,* the test was self-incriminating because it forced the suspect to disclose information that would reveal whether his mental processes were confused.

The *Muniz* reasoning would appear to apply as well to field sobriety tests involving *counting.* Thus, for example, evidence of commonly used tests in which the defendant is told to rapidly count forward from 1001 to 1030, or backward from 10 or 100, should be suppressed in the absence of *Miranda* warnings.

It should, perhaps, be noted that one of the three "standardized" FSTs approved by the NHTSA requires the individual to count while standing on one leg. It should also be noted that another of the three approved NHTSA tests is the walk-the-line: The suspect is instructed to walk nine heel-to-toe steps in one direction, then turn, and walk nine back — counting each step as he takes it. If the suspect takes an incorrect number of steps — that is, his counting is incorrect — then this is a factor in whether he passes or fails.

§11.5.2 Field Sobriety Tests

The *Muniz* decision challenging the admissibility of mental acuity tests on *Miranda* grounds (see §11.5.1) caused some defense lawyers to reconsider the admissibility of the tests on other grounds as well. This, together with the development of "standardized" tests by the NHTSA, resulted in the beginnings of challenges to the tests on *foundational* grounds — specifically, on the grounds that the officer administering the tests was not qualified and/or that the tests themselves are not acceptably reliable.

Satisfactory evidence of the skill and knowledge of the officer is, of course, required for admissibility of the tests when challenged. Trial judges, however, tend to readily find "expertise" anytime the officer has gone through standard training and has even minimal experience. But does "expertise" equal *reliability?* While a witness may be considered an expert because of training and experience, is his testimony reliable — an issue that can perhaps only be determined by inquiry into his actual knowledge rather than reliance upon the fact of training and experience? Put another way: Is the testimony of all experts necessarily reliable? Unfortunately, the argument that *Daubert v. Merrell Dow Pharmaceuticals,* 509 U.S. 579 (1993), required scientific expert testimony to be shown reliable has been thought not to apply to field sobriety tests (other than horizontal gaze nystagmus) because the holding addressed only *scientific* evidence. This view has been changed by a Supreme Court ruling that may have interesting application to DUI cases.

In *Kumho Tire v. Carmichael, — U.S. —* (March 23, 1999), the Court ruled that their decision in *Daubert* applied to non-scientific expert testimony as well:

> We conclude that *Daubert's* general holding — setting forth the trial judge's general "gatekeeping" obligation — applies not only to testimony based on "scientific" knowledge, but also to testimony based on "technical" and "other specialized" knowledge.

The judge must determine whether the expert in a technical or "other specialized" field (for example, field sobriety testing) had "sufficient specialized knowledge" to assist the jurors in deciding the case.

Thus, even if the officer administering the FSTs is found to qualify as an "expert," it would seem that counsel should be free to question the officer as to the foundational question of his reliability as an expert witness — i.e., to *test* his knowledge and skills.

In those jurisdictions that have rejected the federal standard set forth in *Daubert* (retaining the old *Frye* standard), the argument should nevertheless be made that the reasoning applies. In those states not requiring expertise, reliability of the testimony should still be a foundational issue — on relevance grounds alone. In any event, counsel might consider a can't-have-your-cake-and-eat-it-too approach. Simply, the officer is either a (non-scientific) expert on FSTs or he is not:

1. If the officer *is* an expert on field sobriety tests . . .
   a. Then there should be a foundation — both as to the validity of the tests and to his training, experience, and actual administration; and
   b. He can then be confronted with studies (e.g., So. Cal. Research Institute), federal standards (NHTSA standardized TSTs), journal articles (e.g., published studies by Dr. Spurgeon Cole), etc. — i.e., counsel now has a conduit for introducing literature undermining the FSTs themselves.
2. If the officer is *not* an expert, clearly expertise is not required . . .
   a. Then cross-exam and argument: Field sobriety tests are nothing more than exercises that any lay person can administer and interpret.
   b. The officer should be instructed to refrain from using expert/scientific terminology such as "test," "failed," "points," etc.
   c. The defense is entitled to an instruction to the jury that:
      (1) The officer is not an expert in giving or interpreting the tests; and
      (2) The tests are neither scientific nor anything that any juror could not give and interpret him- or herself.

A second foundational attack can be made on the FSTs themselves. Whether considered "quasi-scientific" in nature or not, there is increasing evidence that the tests are clearly lacking in reliability. An example of this approach can be found in a Florida trial court decision. In a pre-trial hearing involving three consolidated cases in Collier County (*State v. Carriere,* Case No. 92-8538; *State v. Haag,* Case No. 92-6223; *State v. Zeppiero*), Dr. Marcelline Burns testified that the three standardized NHTSA field sobriety tests were based on recognized scientific principles; if administered as recommended by NHTSA's manual, there was a direct correlation between performance and impairment caused by alcohol. Dr. Burns added, however, that the scientific reliability of the tests is questionable if they are *not* administered properly.

Based on this and other expert testimony, the trial judge suppressed evidence of the field sobriety tests in the three cases on the grounds that the prosecution had failed to establish that the tests were administered in a scientifically acceptable manner.

Dr. Burns, it should be noted, was one of two members of the Southern California Research Institute hired by NHTSA in 1977, and again in 1981, to test the reliability of various field sobriety tests. Dr. Burns found the nystagmus, walk-the-line, and one-leg-stand tests the most reliable indicators of intoxication. Her studies with police officers also led her to conclude that the officers were more effective in estimating blood-alcohol levels in drivers when the officers gave the tests after receiving training in administration and scoring procedures. It was her report (DOT HS-8-01970) that led to the NHTSA's adoption of the three tests as the "standardized" FSTs.

Meanwhile, the federal government was contracting with other research organizations. In 1981 the Department of Transportation received a report from the Decision Science Consortium, Inc., of Falls Church, Virginia. Based on this report and the report from the Southern California Research Institute, the DOT concluded that many of the field sobriety tests being used by law enforcement across the country were unreliable.

Then, in 1992, Dr. Spurgeon Cole, of Clemson University, conducted a study on the accuracy of FSTs. His staff videotaped suspects performing the tests, then showed the tapes to police officers and asked them to decide whether the suspects were impaired or whether their blood-alcohol levels were over or under .10 percent.

Dr. Cole found that *the officers were wrong approximately 50 percent of the time.*

The relevance of all of this should be clear. Extensive scientific research has been conducted on the reliability of field sobriety tests. That research has concluded that certain tests, if administered and scored in an approved manner, have a scientific basis for correlating performance with intoxication. The corollaries, specifically expressed in some of the research, are that:

1. *other field sobriety tests are not scientifically valid;* and
2. even the three approved FSTs are not scientifically valid *if administered and/or scored in an unapproved manner.*

Accordingly, counsel representing a client in a drunk driving case should no longer limit his or her attacks of field sobriety tests to cross-examination of the officer. Counsel also should make pre-trial motions to suppress the results of the test on constitutional and foundational grounds.

A trial court order from Florida suggests an interesting pre-trial approach to limiting the damage of field sobriety tests. In *State v. Becker,* Case No. 91-9543WA (Pinellas County Court, Crim. Div., September 10, 1992), defense counsel challenged the admissibility of the FSTs in a pre-trial motion on the grounds that they constituted *scientific* evidence — and that the state had failed to satisfy the foundational requirements of the *Frye* test of wide acceptance within the scientific community. As part of the motion, he presented expert testimony on the design of the tests.

The trial court concluded that this testimony "left no doubt that the field sobriety tests are not a valid scientific testing instrument for a variety of reasons." Consequently, the tests were inadmissible *as scientific evidence.* The court went on to say, however, that the tests were admissible as *nonscientific* evidence. In other words, jurors were capable of listening to the observations of the officer during the FST and concluding for themselves whether the defendant's driving abilities were impaired.

The important point is that the court noted that the tests could still be excluded if their probative value was outweighed by their prejudicial impact. This could occur if the tests were presented in a way that gave them a *scientific aura.* Therefore, the court issued a pre-trial order, which it summed up as follows.

> All reference to the tasks referred to as the "field sobriety tests" in any way which infers that the tasks or results have any scientific validity will be excluded. This includes the use of such terms as "tests," "results," "pass," "fail," "points," and any other word or phrase which attaches significance to the procedures more than simple physical and mental tasks that produce certain observations that can be related to the jury by video or a witness.

Six months after the *Becker* decision, another Florida trial court rendered an expanded ruling. In *State v. Webb,* Case No. 92-4-3654-TT (Bay County Court, March 2, 1993), the court ordered evidence of all field sobriety tests suppressed without a *Frye* foundation — regardless of whether testimony inferred a scientific validity to them. The reason given was that officers tended to use language that created the *impression* that FSTs constituted a scientific testing process that generated empirical results.

Interestingly, defense counsel's pre-trial motion to suppress was based on two grounds. First, of course, the FSTs were to be presented to the jury as scientific in nature without a foundational showing of scientific acceptance. Second, FSTs are used to determine the extent of an individual's intoxication — and, as such, are subject to the stringent requirements of the state's administrative laws regarding blood-alcohol analysis.

Counsel may wish to consider the benefits of obtaining such an order to minimize the significance of FSTs during jury voir dire, opening statement, cross-examination of the officer, summation, and jury instructions.

§11.5.3 Nystagmus

The results of horizontal gaze nystagmus (HGN) tests are not, of course, intended as a substitute for actual blood-alcohol testing; the purpose of the procedure is strictly a field screening one, like other field sobriety tests. Certainly the results in terms of blood-alcohol level should not be legally admissible — and defense counsel should strenuously argue against their admission if the results are so offered. Counsel should argue inadmissibility due to failure of the procedure to comply with *Frye*-type requirements for scientific evidence — that is, horizontal gaze nystagmus is not yet widely accepted within the scientific community as a blood-alcohol testing procedure. In addition, the test does not comply with state blood-alcohol testing regulations: In effect, this field sobriety test is a test for blood-alcohol, and as such it must comply with the appropriate legal standards — that is, maintenance, calibration, licensing, etc. Finally, the officer is not qualified as an expert: In testifying to the defendant's blood-alcohol level based on the nystagmus test, the officer is actually giving his "medical" opinion.

Thus counsel has three fruitful areas of attacking the admissibility of horizontal gaze nystagmus test results:

1. *Frye* foundational standards
2. lack of expertise of the officer
3. blood-alcohol testing regulations

Note that if the officer merely testifies that the defendant "flunked" the nystagmus test, this changes nothing: One "flunks" by having a reading in excess of a certain blood-alcohol level — and so the test remains one designed to determine the blood-alcohol content of an individual.

Initially, it should be argued that evidence of the HGN test is inadmissible because it does not comply with the state's *foundational* requirements for new scientific technology. To the extent that admissibility of nystagmus depends upon it being "widely accepted within the scientific community," it should be noted that the continued validity of the *Frye* standard may be in some doubt. The U.S. Supreme Court has rejected the "general acceptance" standard after 70 years of use and has opted for a more liberal approach giving broader discretion to the trial court. *Daubert v. Merrell Dow,* 507 U.S. 904 (1993).

Frye, according to the Court, was superceded by new Rule 702 of the Federal Rules of Evidence. That rule states that "if scientific, technical, or other specialized knowledge will assist the trier of fact to understand the evidence or to determine a fact in issue," then an expert "may testify thereto." Thus general acceptance in the scientific community is no longer the relevant inquiry. Rule 702 gives the trial judge discretion in ensuring that an expert's testimony is relevant and rests on a reliable foundation.

Of course, *Daubert* and Rule 702 apply only to the federal courts. But since the *Frye* decision in 1923, most of the states have chosen to follow the general acceptance standard. It is likely that some of those states will, over the coming years, continue to follow the federal lead. If so, the impact on drunk driving cases will obviously be considerable. The prosecution will certainly find it easier to get in new forms of evidence such as nystagmus. The defense will also benefit with fewer restrictions to introducing evidence concerning such subjects as varying partition ratios, radio frequency interference, rising blood-alcohol levels, and nonspecific analysis.

The initial indications are, however, that many states will resist the abandonment of the *Frye* standard. In *People v. Leahy,* 882 P.2d 321 (Cal. 1994), for example, the California Supreme Court rejected the new federal guidelines on scientific evidence. In a 6 to 1 vote, the court reasserted the continuing validity of *Frye,* holding that nystagmus must be "generally accepted by a typical cross-section of the relevant scientific community":

> Although the *Frye* test may be difficult to apply and at times exclude relevant evidence, it has proven its value over 60 years. It has prevented justice from becoming a matter of amateur guesswork based on unreliable techniques and has helped to assure that determinations of guilt or innocence are not influenced by the vagaries of pseudo-science.

See also *State v. Cissne,* 865 P.2d 564 (Wash. App. 1994), where a Washington appellate court similarly rejected *Daubert,* reversing a DUI conviction where nystagmus evidence had been admitted without a foundational showing of compliance with *Frye.*

Assuming that nystagmus evidence overcomes the *Frye* hurdle, the prosecution must still establish that the officer administering the test is properly qualified to do so. Exactly what degree of training, knowledge, and experience will satisfy this requirement will vary from one jurisdiction to another. Certainly, however, the overwhelming majority of states require some degree of *expertise.* In *People v. Williams,* 5 Cal. Rptr. 2d 130 (Cal. App. 1992), for example, the arresting officer was permitted at trial to testify that in his opinion — based partly on the nystagmus test — the defendant was under the influence of alcohol. This was permitted by the trial court after the officer testified that he had received 10 hours of classroom instruction on nystagmus at the CHP Academy, 8 hours of laboratory time, and had given the test in the field about 250 times. The trial court ruled that this was insufficient evidence to qualify the officer as an expert, but then permitted his testimony as a *lay* witness.

The court of appeals reversed, holding that the testimony had, in fact, been offered as that of an expert: Administration of a nystagmus test was "beyond common experience" and thus required expertise. The court then ruled that the officer was not qualified to give expert testimony concerning nystagmus:

> [The officer's] testimony concerning how he gave the HGN test to appellant and what he observed during the test may be admissible if it is linked to testimony of a qualified expert who can give a meaningful explanation of the test results to the jury. Without some connection to qualified expert testimony, however, [the officer's] description of the test and his observations of nystagmus are irrelevant. [Id. at 135.]

See also the discussion in §11.5.2 of *Kumho Tire v. Carmichael,* — U.S. — (March 23, 1999), holding that all expert testimony must be shown to be reliable under Federal Rules of Evidence 702, regardless of whether it is scientific per *Daubert.*

It should also be argued that the test is inadmissible because it was *administered* improperly. In cross-examining on this issue, counsel should make extensive use of NHTSA's recommended — and very detailed — procedures for giving the test (see §4.3.5).

Finally, counsel should argue a third ground for attacking the admissibility of nystagmus: It does not comply with the state's blood-alcohol regulations. Nystagmus must be recognized as being essentially an attempt to test for an individual's blood-alcohol concentration — either for the specific level or to determine whether it is over or under .08 percent (or .10 percent). As such, the test must meet the standards for blood-alcohol analyses (calibration, maintenance, accuracy, licensing, etc.) set forth by statute or administrative regulations.

The Arizona Supreme Court in *State v. Superior Court (Blake),* 718 P.2d 171 (Ariz. 1986) recognized this issue:

> When referring to the tests to be administered to determine BAC, the (regulatory) statute speaks in terms of *taking* blood, urine or breath samples from the defendant for *analyses.* [Cites.] Clearly, BAC under (the statute) is to be determined deductively from analysis of bodily fluids, not inductively from observation of involuntary bodily movements. [Original emphasis]

Since the appearance and rapid spread of the horizontal gaze nystagmus test, state courts have taken contradictory approaches to its admissibility.

In the first appellate decision to address the issue of the admissibility of nystagmus, a California court rejected the test. In reversing a drunk driving conviction because of error in admitting the officer's testimony concerning the nystagmus test, the court in *People v. Loomis,* 156 Cal. App. 3d Supp. 1 (1984), held that the test was inadmissible for two independent reasons. First, the officer's testimony concerning the defendant's blood-alcohol level based on the nystagmus test constituted an expert opinion, and the officer was not qualified as a medical expert:

> [T]he trial court erred when it ruled the officer was not testifying as an expert but could give an opinion of blood-alcohol level based on his training, experience and the number of times he had given the nystagmus test. [Id. at 6.]

The court continued, however:

> Even if the officer's testimony had been offered as an expert opinion, it would have been error to allow it. . . . The test for determining the underlying reliability of a new scientific technique was described in the germinal case of *Frye v. U.S.* (D.C. Cir. 1923) 293 F.2d 1013, 1014. . . . [T]he thing from which the deduction is made must be *sufficiently established to have gained general acceptance in the particular field in which it belongs.* Applying this rule to the present case makes it clear the testimony regarding Loomis' blood alcohol level based on the lateral gaze nystagmus test was inadmissible. [156 Cal. App. 3d Supp. at 6 (original emphasis).]

Since the pioneer *Loomis* decision, California appellate courts have failed to reach a uniform view. In *People v. Joehnk,* 35 Cal. App. 4th 1488 (1995), the court found that "no reason exists why police officers would be deemed unqualified to administer and report the results of those tests." In *People v. Ojeda,* 225 Cal. App. 3d 404 (1990), however, the court held that "without a showing of expertise a police officer is not qualified to make a numerical correlation between HGN and blood alcohol level." Of course, there is a vast difference between testimony as to "passing" or "failing" the HGN test, and testimony as to what the actual BAC indication was.

Since *Loomis,* courts across the country have also differed in their foundational requirements for nystagmus. In *State v. Witte,*

836 P.2d 1110 (Kan. 1992), for example, the Kansas Supreme Court was confronted with the issue when the trial judge admitted HGN evidence on the grounds that "if the other types of [field sobriety] tests are admissible, then the eye test is admissible as an observation by a layperson who has been a police officer who has had some training in it."

The supreme court first reviewed the decisions in other jurisdictions, then rejected the state's argument that nystagmus tests were not different from any other field sobriety test and that since they were not scientific in nature they did not have to comply with the *Frye* standard. The problem with that reasoning, the court said, was that the nystagmus test relied for its legitimacy on that very scientific nature rather than on common knowledge; a balance test, on the other hand, rested on matters known to the general public.

The court stated that nystagmus evidence could become admissible only when the foundational requirements of *Frye* are met. This would require that "a trial court first should have an opportunity to examine, weigh, and decide disputed facts to determine whether the test is sufficiently reliable." 836 P.2d at 1121. In applying the *Frye* test, the court noted the disagreement within the scientific community concerning the accuracy of the HGN test — and further noted the many causes of nystagmus besides intoxication (see §4.3.5). Finding that the state had failed to show the reliability of the test at trial, the court held its admissibility to have been error.

Similarly, in *People v. Dakuras,* 527 N.E.2d 163 (Ill. App. 1988), the trial court had suppressed the test on the grounds that it did not comply with *Frye.* The appellate court upheld the suppression — but on different grounds:

> [t]he only method by which evidence of a defendant's blood-alcohol concentration may be determined in Illinois is by analysis of the person's blood, urine, breath or other bodily substance. . . . Thus, a horizontal gaze nystagmus test, which does not analyze any bodily substance, would not be admissible to prove blood-alcohol concentration in any prosecution for . . . driving under the influence of alcohol. . . . [Id. at 166.]

See also *State v. Barker,* 366 S.E.2d 642 (W. Va. 1988).

The majority of jurisdictions that have addressed the issue

have similarly held that some showing of scientific acceptance must be made as foundational to admission of nystagmus evidence. See, e.g., *People v. Vega,* 496 N.E.2d 501 (Ill. App. 1986); *State v. Barker,* 366 S.E.2d 642 (W. Va. 1988); *Commonwealth v. Miller,* 532 A.2d 1186 (Pa. App. 1987); *Dressel v. State,* 596 So. 2d 602 (Ala. App. 1991).

A growing number of states, however, have taken the position that a *Frye*-type foundation need not be laid (or that, in the alternative, the scientific validity of nystagmus has already been widely established). In *City of Fargo v. McLaughlin,* 512 N.W.2d 700 (N.D. 1994), for example, the North Dakota Supreme Court held it was unnecessary to require expert testimony that nystagmus was "widely accepted" within the scientific community. The only foundational requirement, according to the court, was a showing that the officer was properly trained and experienced and that the test was properly administered. The court noted, however, that the test results were admissible only as circumstantial evidence of intoxication — that is, the officer could not testify to any specific blood-alcohol level based on the test. See also *Howard v. State,* 744 S.W.2d 640 (Tex. App. 1987); *State v. Nagel,* 506 N.E.2d 285 (Ohio App. 1986); *State v. Clark,* 762 P.2d 853 (Mont. 1988).

The *City of Fargo* court relied heavily in its decision upon what it termed the "seminal" case on nystagmus: *State v. Superior Court (Blake),* (*supra*). In that case, the Arizona Supreme Court dealt with a situation where the arresting officer testified at an evidentiary hearing that a nystagmus test he administered to the defendant resulted in his estimation of a blood-alcohol content of at least .10 percent. The court held that if properly administered by a trained officer, the test satisfies the *Frye* standard for reliability and is admissible both to help establish probable cause to arrest and to corroborate subsequent blood-alcohol analysis. As to probable cause:

> Information sufficient to raise a suspicion of criminal behavior by definition need not pass tests of admissibility under our rules of evidence. [Id. at 181.]

As to admissibility in trial:

> The "general acceptance" requirement does not necessitate a showing of universal acceptance of the reliability of the scientific

> principle and procedure. . . . Neither must the principle and procedure be absolutely accurate or certain. . . . We therefore hold that, with proper foundation as to the techniques used and the officer's ability to use it [cites], testimony of defendant's nystagmus is admissible on the issue of a defendant's blood-alcohol level as would other field sobriety test results on the question of the accuracy of the chemical analysis. [Id.]

The court went on, however, to severely limit its ruling:

> Our holding *does not mean* that evidence of nystagmus is admissible to prove BAC of .10 percent or more in the absence of a laboratory chemical analysis of blood, breath or urine. Such a use of HGN test results would raise a number of due process problems different from those associated with the chemical testing of bodily fluids. The arresting officer's "reading" of the HGN test cannot be verified or duplicated by an independent party. [Cites.] The test's recognized margin of error provides problems as to criminal convictions which require proof of guilt beyond a reasonable doubt. The circumstances under which the test is administered at roadside may affect the reliability of the test results. Nystagmus may be caused by conditions other than alcohol intoxication. And finally, the far more accurate chemical testing devices are readily available (original emphasis). [Id.]

The Arizona Supreme Court subsequently clarified its holding in *Blake.* In *State ex rel. Hamilton v. Lopresti,* 799 P.2d 855 (Ariz. 1990), the court said:

> We clarify and reemphasize here that HGN test results, although satisfying [the] *Frye* [test] for limited purposes, are inadmissible to estimate BAC in any manner, including estimates of BAC over .10%, in the absence of a chemical analysis of blood, breath, or urine. In the absence of a chemical analysis, the use of HGN test results, as with observations from other field sobriety tests, is to be limited to showing a symptom or clue of impairment. . . . The officer may not testify regarding accuracy in estimating BAC from the test, nor may the officer estimate whether BAC was above or below .10%. The officer's testimony is limited to describing the results of the test and explaining that, based on the officer's experience, the results indicated a neurological im-

> pairment, one cause of which could be alcohol intoxication. [*Lopresti,* 799 P.2d 855, 857–858.]

The high court warned of "the scientific aura that the State would give to the HGN test" over and above other field sobriety tests, and emphasized that gaze nystagmus test results were simply inadequate to establish a blood-alcohol content over .10 percent in the absence of chemical test results.

In what appears to be developing as the consensus approach to nystagmus evidence, the Arkansas Supreme Court has also limited the officer to testifying in qualitative rather than quantitative terms. In *Whitson v. State,* 863 S.W.2d 794 (Ark. 1993), the court held that nystagmus was "relevant for the limited purpose of generally indicating the presence of alcohol." HGN was considered simply another field sobriety test, to be used along with such tests as "walk-the-line" and "finger-to-nose" in determining the *presence* of alcohol — not the blood-alcohol level.

If the judge admits evidence of nystagmus into trial, counsel must next move to *limit* the form of the testimony. In other words, the officer must be precluded from testifying, for example, that "the results of the nystagmus test indicated that the defendant's blood-alcohol concentration was .16 percent." Clearly, case law across the country is uniform in prohibiting the officer from testifying that the nystagmus test indicated a specific blood-alcohol level. Among other objections, such evidence violates state regulations concerning blood-alcohol analysis (calibration, maintenance, standards, and so on).

What often happens, however, is that the officer tells the jury that test results showed the defendant's blood-alcohol level as being "high," "above the legal limit," "over .10 percent," or that he "failed." Counsel should argue that this is simply another means for introducing evidence of actual BAC since it infers a specific blood-alcohol level. Rather, the officer should be limited to testifying as to nystagmus in the same way in which he or she testifies as to other field sobriety tests. Thus, for example, the officer can testify that "based upon this and other observations, I formed the opinion that the defendant was under the influence and placed him under arrest."

In summary, then, there appears to be a gradually emerging

view as to the admissibility of HGN evidence. This view can be roughly summarized as follows:

1. The officer must be properly qualified to administer the nystagmus test.
2. If the nystagmus evidence satisfies the *Frye* test (or if the test is not applicable), it is admissible:
   a. to establish probable cause to arrest; and
   b. along with other field sobriety tests as circumstantial evidence of intoxication or to indicate the presence of alcohol in the defendant.
3. Nystagmus evidence is never admissible to prove the specific blood-alcohol concentration of the defendant.

Counsel should consider a motion *in limine* to restrict the language used by the officer in his testimony concerning nystagmus. It is common, for example, for the officer to say that the test indicated the defendant's BAC was over .08 percent, or that he "failed" the test. Testimony that the level was over the statutory limit is, of course, an indirect way of offering evidence of the specific blood-alcohol concentration — that is, that nystagmus indicated a BAC of .08 percent or higher. And testifying that he "failed" is simply another way of saying that it was over the limit. The officer should be limited to testifying that the nystagmus test indicated the presence of alcohol or, in the alternative, that his opinion of intoxication was based on all of his observations, among which were the field sobriety tests (including nystagmus).

Assuming that nystagmus evidence was wrongly admitted, does this constitute reversible error? It is difficult to imagine more prejudicial evidence than a test that is presented as an objective and scientific analysis of an accused's blood-alcohol concentration. And the Supreme Court of Alabama has agreed, reversing an appellate court that had held that the admission of nystagmus evidence was not reversible error in light of the existence of other evidence sufficient to sustain a finding of guilt. In *Ex parte Malone,* 575 So. 2d 106 (Ala. 1990), the appellate court found that the nystagmus evidence had been erroneously admitted because the prosecution had failed to offer evidence of the reliability of the test or of the principle on which it was based. However, the court affirmed the conviction because of overwhelming evidence of guilt independent of the nystagmus test. The supreme court reversed, reasoning that "[o]verwhelming evidence of guilt does not render prejudicial error harmless." Id. at 107. The court also noted that the lower court had admitted that a jury "might give undue weight to [nystagmus] evidence since it may appear to lend the certainty of an exact discipline to problematic factfinding." Id.

And in *State v. Witte* (supra) the prosecution argued that the erroneous admission of nystagmus evidence was harmless — that other evidence presented was sufficient to support a conviction, including a .103 percent breath test. In rejecting this argument as well, the court noted that the machine used to test the defendant had been shown at trial to have registered an incorrect calibration percentage just prior to the defendant's test. "Here, the admission of the HGN test results . . . may have influenced the jury by leading the jury to believe one scientific test supported and gave credibility to the other." 836 P.2d at 1121. The court reversed the conviction and remanded the case. The Kansas Supreme Court elaborated on the reasons for the unreliability of the nystagmus test:

> Nystagmus can be caused by problems in an individual's inner ear . . . Physiological problems such as certain kinds of diseases may also result in gaze nystagmus. Influenza, streptococcus infections, vertigo, measles, syphilis, arteriosclerosis, muscular dystrophy, multiple sclerosis, Korsakoff's Syndrome, brain hemorrhage, epilepsy, and other physiological disorders all have been shown to cause nystagmus. Furthermore, conditions such as hypertension, motion sickness, sunstroke, eyestrain, eye muscle fatigue, glaucoma, and changes in atmospheric pressure may result in nystagmus. The consumption of common substances such as caffeine, nicotine, or aspirin also lead to nystagmus almost identical to that caused by alcohol consumption. [*State v. Witte* (Kan. 1992) 836 P.2d 1110.]

For a further discussion of the case law on the issue, see Ludington, "Horizontal Gaze Nystagmus Test: Use in Impaired Driving Prosecution," 60 A.L.R.4th 1129 (1988). For a discussion of the nystagmus test itself, including areas for cross-examination, see §§4.3.5 and 13.0.5.

§11.5.4 Pupil Reaction Test

The pupil reaction test is a favorite of many traffic officers because of its simplicity and its aura of scientific objectivity and reliability. Although it is increasingly being replaced with the newer "horizontal gaze nystagmus" test (see text §4.3.5), it is still a commonly employed procedure; in some cases the arresting officer will administer both eye impairment tests.

The pupil reaction test is commonly given fairly early in the investigation, usually before the performance FSTs. It is accomplished by simply shining a flashlight in the suspect's eyes. The officer then observes the reaction of the pupil, noting the speed with which it contracts in reaction to the sudden increase in light. Generally speaking, the slower the contraction, the more intoxicated the individual. Thus the officer will usually testify that the defendant's eyes either contracted slowly when exposed to the light, or failed to respond to the light at all.

The well-trained officer will shine his light into the eyes of his partner (or some other presumably sober person) immediately after shining it into the suspect's eyes, again noting the reaction. This permits him to compare the relative speed of the pupil contraction between the two individuals — that is, it gives the officer a standard against which to judge the suspect's pupil reaction. If this was not done, the failure should be noted.

It is, of course, a scientific fact that alcohol will slow many responses of the human body, including the contraction of the pupil when confronted by light stimuli. However, the officer's testimony on this subject can be attacked in two ways. First, he is not qualified as an expert in this area. Second, the conclusion that the reaction was "slow" is meaningless without sufficient context.

Counsel should establish quickly the officer's complete lack of training in the physiology of the eye. He has no education in ophthalmology and is simply not qualified to administer eye tests or to evaluate their results. His informal field experiment should be revealed for what it is — a very crude attempt by a layman to conduct a medical examination.

The officer should then be interrogated with respect to what is meant by a "slow" pupil response: Slow in reaction to what? Was he timing the reaction? What size differential in millimeters was involved? Over what period of time? (The response is never timed.) If he did not measure the differential and time the response, how can the reaction be interpreted by a true expert at trial? If the officer used his partner for a comparison, he should be questioned with respect to the relative physiology of his partner's eyes — probably the eyes of a healthy, rested, relatively young person — to those of the defendant.

The coffin can be nailed shut with a series of ophthalmological questions concerning the relative abilities of eyes to contract to light stimuli. The officer can be asked, for example, if he considered the possible effect of optic nerve ataxia? Oculomotor nerve weakness? Iritis? Does he even know what they mean? Is he aware that the common condition of farsightedness can affect pupil response time? These and similar questions should serve to firmly discredit the probative value of the pupil reaction test.

Independent of any pupil reaction test, some officers will testify that the defendant's pupils were simply dilated; it is a fact that consumption of alcohol raises the level of norepinephrine in the blood, which causes dilation. There are, of course, many reasons for dilation that have nothing to do with intoxication. It is interesting to note, for example, that such common over-the-counter remedies as Allerest and Sudafed contain compounds (phenylpropanolamine HCL and pseudoephedrine HCL, respectively) that also can cause dilation because of their similarity to norepinephrine. This, then, is another reason why counsel should carefully question his client concerning the hours of his pre-arrest activities — including the possibility that he ingested medication.

§11.5.5 Preliminary Breath Tests

If a preliminary breath test (PBT), sometimes referred to as an alcohol screening device (ASD) or preliminary alcohol screen (PAS), was used during the investigation, counsel should certainly make a pretrial motion to suppress the results.

Initially, three separate issues must be recognized and distinguished — each of them involving foundational issues:

1. Are the test results admissible to establish probable cause to arrest for drunk driving?
2. Even if admissible to show the arresting officer's reasonable suspicion, are the results admissible at trial?

3. If admissible at trial, are the *numerical* results (including evidence of "pass-fail," which is simply an indirect means of indicating a BAC over or under the legal limit) admissible — or only the fact that the PBT indicated:
   a. the *presence* of alcohol; or
   b. that the results were a factor in the officer's opinion of intoxication.

As discussed in §4.4, the PBT is a relatively primitive device for measuring blood-alcohol concentration. As such, the device rarely meets the foundational requirements and regulatory requirements for the admission of blood-alcohol evidence at trial (it should be recognized, however, that some states are beginning to accept numerical results from certain PBT devices, particularly the more advanced unit manufactured by Draeger). The majority view is that the PBT test is designed solely for the officer's use in helping to determine whether there are sufficient grounds to make an arrest and administer an evidentiary test at the police station. Thus, the test result — assuming sufficient foundational evidence — is generally considered admissible on the issue of probable cause; this issue should, of course, be litigated before trial — or, at least, out of the presence of the jury. Thereafter, the PBT results are inadmissible at trial, since the only relevance is as to an issue already litigated. As the New York Court of Appeals held:

> We agree with the Appellate Division that the trial court erred in admitting evidence, over defendant's objection, that he was arrested "based on the results" of an Alco-Sensor test. The state purpose of this proof was to permit the prosecution to establish that the arresting officer had "reasonable grounds" to give defendant a Breathalyzer test. The evidence should have been excluded as irrelevant since reasonable cause is not an element of the crime charged and defendant, at no time, raised an issue with regard to the existence of reasonable cause to give the Breathalyzer test. [*People v. Thomas,* 70 NY2d 823, 523 NYS2d 437 (1987).]

Obviously, then, a pre-trial hearing should be conducted to determine if the procedure must comply with any statutory blood-alcohol analysis regulations, whether the instrument requires state approval, whether the test is generally recognized as reliable, whether the instrument was properly maintained and calibrated by licensed individuals, whether the administering officer was sufficiently trained, and whether the specific test was properly conducted.

The Supreme Court of Iowa was confronted with the question of the admissibility of ASD/PBT evidence in the case of *State v. Deshaw,* 404 N.W.2d 156 (Iowa 1987). The trial court had denied a pre-trial motion *in limine* to bar the evidence despite a statute that provided that the results of such tests could not be used in court but were to be used only to assist in the decision of whether to make an arrest or not. The trial court had reasoned that the phrase "the results" referred to the actual numerical reading from the test: Testimony that the test indicated the *presence* of alcohol was admissible.

In reversing the conviction, the supreme court noted that the legislature had made the results inadmissible because "The problem with this quick, convenient test is unreliability." 404 N.W.2d at 158. The court then concluded that the test is as unreliable in detecting the presence of alcohol as it is in determining the actual blood-alcohol concentration.

In *People v. Keskinen,* 441 N.W.2d 79 (Mich. App. 1989), the same issue was presented to a Michigan court — with similar results. In reversing a drunk driving conviction for error in permitting evidence of an alcohol screening/preliminary breath test, the court held that the results were relevant only to the issue of probable cause for the arrest. Further, a cautionary instruction given to the jury did not render the error harmless.

And in *People v. Rose,* 643 N.E.2d 865 (Ill. App. 1994), a state statute permitted PBTs to be used to determine whether further chemical testing was justified, but said nothing about whether the results could be used in trial on the issue of intoxication. The appellate court reviewed the legislative history of the statute, then concluded that the primary purpose of the statue was to aid law enforcement in determining whether probable cause to arrest existed. Accordingly, the results of PBT tests were held inadmissible for any other purpose.

In *State v. Ifill,* 560 A.2d 1075 (Me. 1989), evidence of the results of an ALERT test were admitted in a jury trial on the issue of probable cause and state of mind as a field sobriety test. In vacating the conviction, the Supreme Court of Maine noted that probable cause was not an issue for the jury, then rejected the test as a field sobriety test:

> Tests of physical dexterity, coordination, speech or memory provide observations from which jurors may draw their own conclusions about a defendant's sobriety. The ALERT test, on the other hand, is meaningless to a jury unless the pass-fail result is perceived as scientifically reliable. It is precisely that false sense of reliability that renders unavailing a trial court instruction that the jury need not accept the test results. [560 A.2d at 1077.]

In *People v. Bury,* 41 Cal. App. 4th 1194, 58 Cal. Rptr. 2d 682 (Cal. App. 1996), a lower appellate court held that the *numerical results* of a "preliminary alcohol screening" (PAS) device (an Alco-Sensor) were admissible on the issue of blood-alcohol concentration in a jury trial. The case is distinguishable, however, in that the defendant's attorney objected to the admissibility of the test results on *Frye* grounds alone — that is, the PBT was not broadly accepted within the scientific community as a test for blood-alcohol concentration. He did *not* object to its admissibility on foundational grounds — that is, the test was reliable, accurate, and in compliance with state requirements for breath testing.

The court noted that "to properly contest the foundational requirements for the admissibility of the PAS evidence, appellant should have questioned whether the testing apparatus was in proper working order, whether the test was properly administered, and whether the operator was competent and qualified. He also did not challenge Ventura County's compliance with State law. . . . Appellant's failure to object to any of these foundational requirements for establishing the reliability of the PAS evidence is a waiver of his entitlement to a review of the evidence on this ground."

The California case serves as a lesson, of course: counsel must exercise care in his objections at the trial level and in specifying his grounds for appeal. Unfortunately, the *Bury* case will now undoubtedly be misapplied by other courts that have not read the specific reasons for the ruling, and the BAC results of PBTs will be admitted in many trials.

The court also quoted from *State v. Schimmel,* 409 N.W.2d 335, 337 n.1 (N.D. 1987), as to the ALERT test's lack of accuracy.

For other decisions agreeing with *Deshaw* and *Keskinen* that preliminary breath test results are admissible only on the limited issue of probable cause to arrest, see *City of Fargo v. Ruether,* 490 N.W.2d 481 (N.D. 1992), and *State v. Bresson,* 554 N.E.2d 1330 (Ohio 1990). For cases concluding along with the court in *Ifill* that this is a question of law and therefore PBT evidence should never go to a jury, see *State v. Zell,* 491 N.W.2d 196 (Iowa App. 1992), and *People v. Keskinen.*

Counsel may also consider more creative ways to argue that PAS evidence should be excluded from trial — i.e., issues beyond the expected foundational ones. For example:

1. The diminished probative value of the relatively primitive PBT is outweighed by the prejudicial effect.
2. The evidentiary test provided for by the implied consent law is the exclusive means for proving BAC levels.
3. The client was not advised that he was under no obligation to submit to the PBT test.
4. The officer did not advise the client that the PBT results could be used against him in court.
5. The PBT results should be excluded because its probative value will be outweighed by the undue consumption of time in litigating foundational compliance.

What if the ASD/PBT indicates no presence of alcohol? In *Patrick v. State,* 750 S.W.2d 391 (Ark. 1988), the defendant was precluded at trial from offering evidence that an Alco-Analyzer II administered to him at the police station did not provide a reading; the prosecutor had argued successfully in his pre-trial motion to exclude that since he could not offer evidence of a positive reading to prove guilt because the ASD was not approved, the defense should not be allowed to offer evidence of a negative reading to prove innocence. The Supreme Court of Arkansas reversed, holding that evidence of a negative test was "not so inherently unreliable that a jury cannot rationally evaluate it."

For a discussion of the preliminary breath test itself, see §4.4.

§11.5.6 Videotapes, Audiotapes, and Photographs

The possibility of suppressing any audiovisual evidence should be considered carefully. If, in fact, the evidence is damaging to the defendant, cross-examination will be of minimal value, and argument of almost none; the film or tape speaks eloquently for itself. The best course lies in trying to prevent the introduction of the evidence through the use of both pre-trial motions to suppress and foundational voir dire.

A foundational challenge to the evidence may well prove fruitful. The filming or taping in question will probably have been done by police officers, not by professional cameramen or sound technicians, and it may have been done under unreliable conditions. It may be argued successfully that an officer filmed only the most incriminating aspects of a test and ignored the rest, thus giving an unreliable and unfair picture of what actually occurred. Perhaps the angle of the camera resulted in a deceptive picture, or improper developing procedures affected the results. Or maybe the tape or film is technically flawed, being out of focus, for example, or having been edited or spliced by the police. For whatever reasons, counsel should consider arguing that the foundational requirements for evidence have not been met — that is, that the audiovisual evidence is unreliable and/or inaccurate and that any relevance or probative value is vastly outweighed by its highly prejudicial effect.

Such foundational attacks should, of course, be made out of the presence of the jury. Preferably, the attack will come in the form of a motion prior to trial. At the very least, counsel should insist on a voir dire examination while the jury is excused, pointing out that awareness by the jury of the existence of film or tape suppressed by the defense is extremely prejudicial regardless of subsequent instructions from the court.

When a videotape is made of a suspect at the time of his arrest, what foundation must be laid to permit the introduction of the tape into evidence? That was the question presented in the case of *People v. Strozier,* 116 Misc. 2d 103, 455 N.Y.S.2d 217 (1982).

The court began its analysis by noting that "[t]he video tape is merely a mechanical reproduction of the observations made by the individual(s) who witnessed the actions of the defendant." The question of admissibility was, therefore, directed toward a determination "that the video tape fairly and accurately portrays what was observed." To make that determination the court said it would require foundation through the testimony of either the operator of the video camera or another suitable individual.

Specifically, the court required that the following foundation be laid prior to admissibility of the videotape:

> 1. the identity of the subject matter, i.e., the defendant;
> 2. properly promulgated rules and regulations of the police agency utilizing the videotape program;
> 3. the competency of the operator of the video tape machine including his training, certification if required by the police department rules and regulations and actual experience if applicable (If the operator is unavailable, an individual who was a participant in the video recording might suffice.);
> 4. the type of video equipment used, including the operation method, the type of lens and lens adjustment, the lighting of both the equipment and the area in which the suspect is video taped, the velocity of the video tape camera and the type and quality of the film;
> 5. evidence as to the playback of the video tape before the trier of fact, which should include the speed in which the playback is run as it specifically relates to the speed at which the video tape is made;
> 6. testimony of an individual(s) specifically stating that the video tape fairly, truly and accurately represents the subject matter of the video tape;
> 7. the officer testifying should also affirmatively state that the video tape has not been altered and suffers no distortions. But if it has been altered or is distorted, to state the basis of the alteration and/or distortion and the explanation for the alteration and/or distortion;
> 8. continuity of possession of the video tape after the tape had been completed, i.e., chain of custody. [455 N.Y.S.2d at 219.]

A second question raised by the *Strozier* case related to possible incriminating statements made by the driver during the videotaping. In response to this question, the court imposed the following requirements:

> [S]hould any question arise as to the possible incriminating statements made by the defendant during the course of the video tap-

> ing, the court, out of the presence of the jury, should review the video tape and make a determination as to the incriminating nature of the statements. Should the court determine that the statements were in fact incriminating, a further decision must be rendered as to whether the defendant's statements were obtained in violation of his or her constitutional rights under *Miranda v. Arizona* (384 U.S. 436). Should the court determine that the defendant's constitutional rights were violated, the incriminating statements must be excised from the video tape prior to its viewing by the jury. [Id. at 220.]

In imposing the foregoing requirement, however, the court was careful to state that "this requirement should not be construed as a prerequisite application of *Miranda* warnings to obtaining physical evidence or requesting performance tests." Ibid.

Does a drunk driving suspect have a constitutional right not to be *secretly* taped? Some states have adopted statutory rules that govern the taking of taped confessions or the conduct for making videotapes. Texas, for example, has a statute that requires that an accused be told, among other things, that a recording is being made. See Vernon's Ann. Texas C.C.P. Art. 38.22, Sec. 3. Failure to comply with that statutory provision prevents the evidence from being used directly as substantive evidence, or indirectly for impeachment. See *Ragan v. State,* 642 S.W.2d 489 (Tex. Crim. App. 1982).

Likewise, Minnesota has a statutory rule requiring that a defendant be given a contemporaneous copy of any confession. Failure of compliance can result in suppression of the evidence. See Minn. Stat. §611.033; see also *State v. Shaw,* 204 N.W.2d 397 (Minn. 1978).

Counsel should review applicable local statutes or ordinances for similar pertinent provisions. The requirements imposed by statute or rules of procedure are in addition to those imposed by applicable constitutional provisions.

What if the arresting officer had the equipment to tape record the defendant but fails to use it? Can defense counsel comment upon this failure?

The probative value of a videotape (or audiotape or photograph) is obvious: It captures the statements or actions of a driver at an earlier point in time, presumably close to the alleged criminal activity. If the state has videotape equipment and fails to use it, counsel for the driver may want to argue that the state has missed an opportunity to obtain crucial evidence. Taking that a step further, counsel may argue that the evidence, if obtained, *would* have been exculpatory.

In *Jacobson v. State,* 551 P.2d 935 (Alaska 1976), the court considered whether the defense attorney could argue in summation about the importance of the state's failure to produce a videotape. The trial court prevented counsel from arguing that the state had the opportunity to make a videotape but failed. The trial testimony in question was as follows:

Q: Trooper Lown, was there a videotape of the defendant, to verify the statements you're talking about?
A: No.
Q: You didn't have — you know, when you took him to the station, there is a videotape camera there, isn't there?
A: Yes.
Q: And you could have had him perform the tests that you're talking about before a videotape, couldn't you?
A: Obviously, if there wasn't one made, there was some reason why there wasn't. Probably there was no tape available or the machine was broken, because it is a practice that is observed by state troopers that whenever a person is arrested under this charge, a videotape is made, unless there is no tape or the machine is broken.
Q: So there really is no evidence to substantiate your oral statement that he swayed?
A: Other than my statement, no. [Id. at 940.]

Appellant's counsel attempted to argue the absence of the tape in closing argument. The state objected and the trial court sustained the objection.

On appeal, the supreme court reversed, reasoning, in part:

> We are of the view that the trial court's ruling was erroneous in light of the officer's testimony on cross-examination. Officer Lown never asserted that he knew the machine to be broken or lacking tape. At most, he tried to explain the lack of tape by speculating that probably there was no tape or the machine was broken because if the machine were operative and had a tape, a tape would have been made. Since by the officer's own testimony it was normal practice to make such tapes, counsel's argument concerning the

> reasons for the departure from normal practice was within the range of permissible final argument. Further study of the record has convinced us that, given the quality of the state's evidence, the error of refusing to allow appellant's counsel to argue the lack of videotape to the jury was prejudicial error under the standard of *Love v. State,* 457 P.2d 622, 630 (Alaska 1969). [Id. at 941.]

Similarly, in *Logan v. State,* 757 S.W.2d 160 (Tex. App. 1988), it was held to be reversible error to preclude defense counsel from either offering evidence that videotaping was not conducted or commenting on the absence of such evidence:

> A defendant may argue to the jury that the State failed to make a visual recording. . . . A defendant may use the absence of a videotape in an attempt to create a reasonable doubt in the juror's minds. . . .
>
> Appellant should have been permitted to elicit testimony concerning the facts surrounding the failure to videotape; e.g., visual recording equipment was available, operational, and in close proximity; or the county was required to provide such equipment. Only then could appellant effectively make a jury argument about the absence of a visual recording. [Id. at 162 (citations omitted).]

Gary Trichter, the noted DUI practitioner from Houston, refers in trial to videotapes as "truth-ensuring devices":

Q. Officer, after you arrested Mr. Jones, you brought him back to the station?
A. Yes, I did.
Q. And when you got there, you turned on the truth-ensuring device you have there?
A. What do you mean?
Q. Officer, you have a truth-ensuring device at the station, don't you?
A. I don't know what you're talking about.
Q. Officer, it's called a videocamera. It's a device that records everything. You have one of those at the station?
A. Oh, yes.
Q. And I assume you made sure that in this case it was turned on?
A. Well, no.
Q. You had a videocamera right there, something that would show us the truth, and you kept it off?

Finally, counsel might consider the possibility of arguing that a *right to counsel* exists before videotapes may be taken, at least where the tapes depict conduct after the arrest. In *Granberry v. State,* 745 S.W.2d 34 (Tex. App. 1987), the court rejected the argument that the defendant's rights were violated when he was videotaped at the police station after asking to see a lawyer. However, a dissenting justice commented as follows:

> I submit that there is no more critical time in the processing of a D.W.I. suspect than when the State uses video and audio tapes to prove the elements alleged in the indictment. Once a person has been arrested for D.W.I., *the filing of a formal complaint will inevitably follow.* How then can we allow the State to delay the filing of a formal complaint in order to audio and videotape the accused performing acts which prove the elements of the offense with which he is charged? It is clear that we would not allow the State to engage in a procedure that would require a person accused of any other felony to perform acts in a videotape room when those very acts would prove the elements of the offense with which he is charged. . . . This would not be allowed whether it occurred prior to or subsequent to the formal filing of the complaint. [745 S.W.2d at 38–39 (original emphasis).]

For a discussion of sanctions for destruction of videotape evidence, see §11.5.7.

§11.5.7 "Spoliation": Lost and Erased Tapes

Videotapes are a recent development in drunk driving cases. For years, many police agencies experimented with motion pictures, capturing the defendant while he attempted to perform the field sobriety tests in the field or at the police station. There were two drawbacks, however: high cost and delay in obtaining the developed film. Now videotape machines have reduced the cost and permitted instant playback. As a result, the use of videotapes has spread throughout the country, assisted in the past by federal grants under the Omnibus Crime Control and Safe Streets Act. In some situations, filming is done in the field with cameras carried in the patrol car; in most, though, the camera is mounted, often in a manner not visible to the arrestee, in a special room set up for giving field sobriety tests.

What appeared to be the definitive evidence of intoxication, however, has not worked out; increasingly, many police agencies are abandoning the practice of videotaping. The simple reason is that while young and relatively inexperienced drinkers would show blatant signs of intoxication on the tape, the older and more experienced "hard" drinkers were able to pull themselves together and behave in a manner that did not disclose their true condition, particularly if they became aware that they were being filmed. The result was that despite very high readings from blood-alcohol analysis, defense counsel was able to obtain acquittals by showing the contradictory videotape.

It is not uncommon, therefore, to encounter police officers who will simply erase a videotape if the client does not appear intoxicated on it. The more usual situation, however, involves an accidental erasure. Faced with either type of destruction of clearly material evidence, counsel should move for a dismissal. At the very least, a motion to suppress the officer's testimony as to the field sobriety test — or whatever appeared on the tape — should be made.

The pivotal U.S. Supreme Court cases on destruction of evidence are *Brady v. Maryland,* 373 U.S. 83 (1963); *California v. Trombetta,* 467 U.S. 479 (1984); and *Arizona v. Youngblood,* 488 U.S. 51 (1988). *Brady* is, of course, the landmark case, standing for the proposition that the prosecution must produce on request any evidence that is material to the issue of guilt. The Court in *Trombetta* held that if evidence had an exculpatory value (i.e., it could have played a significant role for the defense) that was apparent at the time it was destroyed, then that destruction constitutes a violation of due process. And in *Youngblood* the Court dealt with evidence that was potentially useful — but not clearly exculpatory; it held that due process was violated in such a situation only if the evidence was destroyed in bad faith.

To summarize the law of "spoliation," then, a four-step process for determining whether sanctions should be imposed has gradually developed in the course of the *Brady-Trombetta-Youngblood* series of cases (along with *U.S. v. Agurs,* 427 U.S. 97, 96 S. Ct. 2392, 49 L. Ed.2d 342 (1976):

1. If the lost/destroyed evidence could not possibly have had any exculpatory value, the police are under no duty to preserve it.
2. If the evidence is material and in the possession of the police, it must be turned over if it is requested (*Brady*) or if it is exculpatory; that is, it could have played a significant defense role (*Agurs*).
3. If exculpatory and the evidence has been lost or destroyed, destruction constitutes a denial of due process (*Trombetta*).
4. If the evidence was only "potentially useful" and was destroyed by the police, it is a denial of due process if done in "bad faith" (*Youngblood*).

For a further discussion of sanctions for police destruction or erasure of audiotapes and videotapes, see Tarentino, Videotape Evidence in Drunk Driving Cases (Part I), 7(2) DWI Journal 1; Tarentino, Videotape Evidence in Drunk Driving Cases (Part II), 7(3) DWI Journal 1, Trichter, Getting Back to Nuts and Bolts: Dismissals for Destruction of Exculpatory Evidence, 16(2) The Champion 33.

Of course, exactly what constitutes "bad faith" in a given situation is open to endless argument. Does destruction, loss, or erasure of a videotape through *negligence* constitute bad faith? Gross negligence? Reckless disregard for the rights of the accused? As to whether the videotape had an exculpatory value, there is no way to determine what an erased or destroyed videotape contained — other than, perhaps, the client's and officer's dubious testimony as to how the client would have appeared. Certainly, the videotape is *material.*

The very fact that the government authorities have taken the time and undergone the expense of taping would seem to be an admission that the evidence is material. In a drunk driving case, the closeness in time between the taping and the alleged criminal conduct dictates that the evidence is material.

The Supreme Court of South Carolina was called upon to interpret the requirements of the U.S. Constitution in a case involving a defendant whose field sobriety test had been videotaped — and then erased. In *State v. Jackson,* 396 S.E.2d 101 (S.C. 1990), that court reviewed *Brady* and *Youngblood* and then reversed the conviction:

> In the case at bar, the videotape was clearly "material." The exculpatory value was apparent before its destruction because one assistant solicitor was willing to drop the charges because of it. In addition, Jackson had no other evidence and could not obtain evidence of comparable value. Although the destruction of the tape was explained to the jury, the value of the tape could not be replaced. [Id. at 102.]

In *Thorne v. Department of Public Safety,* 774 P.2d 1326 (Alaska 1989), the Supreme Court of Alaska held that the destruction of a videotape of the arrestee's field sobriety test deprived him of "a meaningful and fundamentally fair (license suspension) hearing." The court observed that "where the burden of preservation is so minimal, and the evidence is of even slight potential relevance, the state bears a heavy burden in justifying its destruction." But see *Gamboa v. State,* 774 S.W.2d 111 (Tex. App. 1989), where the court required a showing of bad faith destruction.

For another example of sanctions where a potentially exculpatory videotape was lost by the prosecution, see *Commonwealth v. Cameron,* 520 N.E.2d 1326 (Mass. App. 1988). In that case, the appellate court reversed a DUI conviction, finding that "If there is no evidence of bad faith on the part of the Commonwealth as the [trial] judge so found, there is nonetheless ample evidence of the Commonwealth's culpability by reason of negligence or inadvertence." 520 N.E.2d at 1332.

And in *City of Seattle v. Fettig,* 519 P.2d 1002 (Wash. App. 1974), the police negligently destroyed the videotape prior to trial but after a municipal court judge had viewed the tape. The defendant requested dismissal on the ground of suppression of material, exculpatory evidence. In the alternative, the defendant requested an instruction from the court that the jury could infer that the destroyed evidence was favorable to the defendant. The trial court denied both requests. The defendant was convicted, and he appealed.

The Washington Court of Appeals reversed, reasoning in part:

> Although the police destroyed the videotape, their acts are chargeable to the prosecutor; the suppression therefore was "by the prosecution." *Barbee v. Warden,* 331 F.2d 842 (4th Cir. 1964); *Impler v. Craven,* 298 F. Supp. 795, 806 (C.D. Cal. 1969); *Evans v.*

> *Kropp,* 254 F. Supp. 218, 222 (E.D. Mich. 1966). Moreover, that the suppression was negligent rather than deliberate is not material here; the defendant's due process rights are affected in either case. See *Giglio v. United States,* 405 U.S. 150, 31 L. Ed. 2d 104, 92 S. Ct. 763 (1972); *Thomas v. United States,* 343 F.2d 49 (9th Cir. 1965); *Hanson v. Cupp,* 5 Ore. App. 312, 484 P.2d 847 (1971). [519 P.2d at 1004.]

The crucial question, according to the court, was whether the missing evidence was "material evidence favorable to the defendant." The defendant, as part of his offer of proof, presented testimony from a municipal court judge who had reviewed the tape before its destruction. The court stated that the tape illustrated "a want of intoxication." From that, the appellate court found that the defendant had shown that the evidence was material. The court held:

> The requirement of *Brady* that the suppressed evidence be material and favorable to the defendant is satisfied. The negligent destruction of the videotape therefore violated the due process clause of the Fourteenth Amendment. [Id. at 1005.]

The defendant's conviction was therefore reversed, without remand to the trial court for a new trial. In dictum, the Washington Court of Appeals added that the trial court properly refused to give the proposed defense jury instruction, reasoning that there "is no rule of law or statute that requires a jury to presume that suppressed evidence is favorable to the accused."

§11.5.8 Police Obstruction of Witnesses

Suppression of the officer's testimony concerning the field sobriety test may possibly be obtained under another theory as well: refusal of the officer to permit a potential defense witness to view the FST. The situation commonly occurs where the suspect is stopped and asked to perform the FST and passengers in the car are removed from the immediate scene or otherwise prevented from watching the test.

This happened in a California case, where the officer ordered the passenger to sit in the front seat of the suspect's car and not turn around to watch the FST being administered. At a suppression hearing, the officer testified that this was "common practice" because friends of suspects sometimes try to interfere with the investigation or arrest.

The trial judge granted the defendant's motion to suppress the officer's testimony concerning the field sobriety test. In an unreported memorandum decision on April 28, 1983, Judge Runston G. Marino of the North County Municipal Court in San Diego concluded:

> Our law gives to every person, including those charged with a crime, the right to summon witnesses in his own defense. The purpose of this right is to assure that a criminal defendant is not deprived of liberty or property without first having an opportunity to be heard. Although police officers have a duty to arrest those suspected of violating the law they must be fair and cannot suppress evidence. *In re Newberry,* 175 C.A.2d 862 (1969). The People are not authorized to control criminal proceedings by deciding which material witness will or will not be called. . . . [T]he defense has been prevented, by the unjustified actions of law enforcement, from presenting a material witness as to the guilt or innocence of the defendant. *People v. Mejia,* 57 C.A.3d 574 (1976).
>
> In fashioning a sanction for the unjustified suppression of evidence the Court has the wide discretion to fashion an appropriate remedy. *People v. Hitch,* 12 C.3d 641 (1974); *People v. Zamora,* 20 Cal. 3d 88 (1980). In the instant case the driving error of the defendant was minimal and there was no chemical test. Thus the critical evidence will be the defendant's performance on the F.S.T. and the reason(s) for the refusal. Under these circumstances the actions of the police have prevented a fair trial for the defendant. *People v. Mejia,* supra. The appropriate sanction is dismissal. . . .

§11.6 Blood-Alcohol Evidence

> Science is nothing but trained and organized common sense.
>
> T. H. Huxley

The single most potentially devastating piece of evidence in the prosecution's arsenal in a drunk driving case is, of course, the result of a blood-alcohol test. In the traditional DUI case, the reading of blood-alcohol concentration (BAC) will give rise to legal presumptions (see §1.3.1). If the client is charged with a per se offense (see §3.2) — that is, driving with an excessive BAC — then the evidence will constitute nearly the entire case. And, in any event, the jury will tend to give great weight to blood-alcohol evidence because of its scientific aura and its impartial nature.

Defense counsel's task is to show the jury that the highly vaunted blood-alcohol test is, in fact, subject to unending flaws and errors. The materials contained in Chapter 8 of the text will assist counsel in pointing out the unreliability of such evidence. Obviously, though, the most effective way of dealing with blood-alcohol evidence is to keep it from ever reaching the jury in the first place — by making pre-trial motions to suppress.

§11.6.1 Test Given Prior to Formal Arrest

Any arrest must, of course, be a lawful one. This may involve the question of whether the officer had probable cause to stop, detain, or arrest the suspect. See §11.0. Or it may concern the lawfulness of the arrest in other ways, involving such issues as jurisdiction, the "presence" requirement, "citizen's arrest," or the need for the officer to be in uniform and/or in a marked car. See §11.2.

Independent of the questions of the legality of the arrest, however, is the question of whether there has been *any* arrest made prior to administration of the evidentiary chemical test. This is a recurrent situation when the suspect is involved in an automobile accident and is in the hospital; when the police arrive, as part of their initial investigation they have a blood sample drawn. Some courts will grant motions to suppress, at least where the suspect did not consent. (See, e.g., *State v. Baker,* 171 N.W.2d 798 (Neb. 1969).) Others, however, permit the taking of a chemical sample prior to arrest. (See, e.g., *State v. Deshner,* 489 P.2d 1290 (Mont. 1971).) The conflict in decisions seems to hinge on whether the suspect had consented and on the interpretation given to the forceful-blood-extraction case of *Schmerber v. California,* 384 U.S. 757 (1966). Those courts upholding the extraction of a chemical sample prior to arrest tend to involve consenting suspects and/or a reading of *Schmerber* excusing the absence of a lawful arrest (in fact, *Schmerber* relates to the question of whether a search warrant is needed where there is the threat of destruction of evidence).

Some states have statutes requiring the drunk driving suspect to formally be placed under arrest before he may be subjected to a blood, breath, or urine test that may be used in court. That is, there must be an arrest *in fact;* the suspect cannot simply be brought to the police station for "further investigation" — including chemical testing. If the suspect is not arrested until after an evidentiary test, then the results of that test are probably without legal authority and subject to suppression.

California's provision, found in its "implied consent" statute, is fairly typical of those found in many states:

> Any person who drives a motor vehicle is deemed to have given his or her consent to chemical testing of his or her blood or breath for the purpose of determining the alcoholic content of his or her blood, *if lawfully arrested* for any offense allegedly committed in violation of [DUI statutes]. [Vehicle Code §23157(a)(1)(A).]

Evidentiary testing should, of course, be distinguished from breath testing with a PBT (preliminary breath test device) in the field for purposes of assisting the officer to determine probable cause to make an arrest.

§11.6.2 Defective Implied Consent Advisement

Almost all states today have laws that require drivers to submit to a chemical test when requested as a condition of being granted the privilege of driving. These *implied consent laws* have been upheld against constitutional attack.

Included within the language of most of these statutes are the specific rights of the arrestee and directions as to how the chemical test is to be administered. Counsel should be thoroughly familiar with this language, as it is not uncommon for police officers to neglect their obligations under the statute, by failing to advise the suspect of his right to a choice of tests, for example, or by failing to administer the test correctly. The statute may even require that the terms of the implied consent law be explained to the arrestee before a test is administered.

In May 1998, the U.S. Court of Appeals (9th Circuit) addressed a class action against a municipality and its police officers for systematically denying DUI arrestees the choice of blood, breath, or urine testing. In *Nelson et al. v. City of Irvine,* 143 F.2d 1196 (9th Cir. 1998) — F.3d — (9th Cir. 1998, #96-56813), the court was confronted with a familiar pattern of conduct among many officers:

> Officer Gielish . . . asked Nelson if he "had a problem" with taking a blood test. Nelson was not advised that he had a choice of a blood, urine or breath test and, as he interpreted the officer's question as rhetorical, he felt he had no choice in the matter. Nelson submitted to the blood test without offering any verbal or physical resistance, but had he been given a choice, he now alleges he would have selected a breath or urine test. . . . The claims of other plaintiffs provide variations on the same theme.

The court unanimously held that the Fourth Amendment requires the police to use the least intrusive method of obtaining evidence reasonably available. When a suspect is willing and able to provide a breath or urine sample, no exigency (e.g., destruction of alcohol by the liver) exists to require withdrawal of a blood sample:

> When an arrestee has agreed to submit to a breath or urine test which is available and of similar evidentiary value, the government's need for a blood test disappears. Under such circumstances, it is unreasonable to require a blood test and the Fourth Amendment is violated. Further, when a DUI suspect agrees to take an available alternative test of equal evidentiary value, the risk that evidence will be lost disappears and the exigent circumstances that excused police from obtaining a warrant likewise disappears, rendering a warrantless nonconsensual blood test in such circumstances unconstitutional.

The court further held that, as a matter of law, a valid claim for assault and battery against the officers and blood technicians had been stated.

The court did not address the question of whether a failure

of the officer to advise the arrestee of his right to a choice of tests constituted a violation of due process, as the argument was not raised below. However, counsel for plaintiffs have reported to this author that during oral argument the justices seemed very interested in the issue. Until the issue is addressed, the *Nelson* decision would appear limited to those cases where the arrestee agrees to submit to breath or urine testing (even after an initial refusal) but is nevertheless given a blood test; existing law provides no sanction for non-advisement of the right to a choice.

A Washington appellate court reversed a DUI conviction where the defendant was not fully advised of the consequence of refusing to submit to blood-alcohol testing. In *City of Spokane v. Holmberg,* 745 P.2d 49 (Wash. App. 1987), the court held that failure to give the full warning under the implied consent statute required suppression of subsequently obtained blood-alcohol evidence. The court focused on the mandatory language of the implied consent statute, which requires that the officer "*shall* warn the driver . . . (b) that his or her refusal to take the test may be used against him or her in a subsequent criminal trial," and concluded that requiring strict compliance with the advisory requirement was the "better rule."

Additionally, the statute may provide for the right to an additional sample for defense analysis — and for the advisement as to this right. Thus, for example, a Georgia appellate court has held that failure of the police to advise a suspect of his right to an independent analysis of his blood must result in suppression of evidence of chemical test results. *Georgia v. McCard,* 326 S.E.2d 856 (Ga. App. 1985). The court further rejected the prosecution's theory that merely denying the state the benefits of a legal presumption arising from the test was sufficient.

An Arkansas appellate court reversed and remanded where the advisement of the availability of a second test was not complete. In *Mitchel v. City of North Little Rock,* 692 S.W.2d 624 (Ark. Ct. App. 1985), the defendant submitted to a breath test with a resultant reading of .20 percent. He was subsequently advised of his right to an additional blood or urine test — but was not advised that the additional test could also be of his *breath.* The court held that the trial judge committed error in admitting the results of the breath test, since the defendant "was not advised of the full range of tests available to him."

What if a suspect is coerced into consenting to blood-alcohol testing? In *Vermont v. Kozel*, 505 A.2d 1221 (Vt. 1986), the defendant was told by the arresting officer that he would be "lodged" overnight for a court appearance the next day if he refused to take a breath test. At a motion to suppress the results of the test, the trial court found that "[t]he advice was proper and sensible under the circumstances and not a threat." The supreme court disagreed, reversing the conviction:

> To sanction the evidentiary use of a test obtained under these conditions was error. . . .
>
> The statute . . . does not state that a defendant may be lodged for refusing to submit to a breath test. . . . [C]oercion of this sort is improper, and the results of the breath test should have been suppressed. [Id. at 1223–1224.]

See also *Erdman v. State*, 861 S.W.2d 890 (Tex. App. 1993), where the arresting officer properly advised the DUI suspect that a refusal would result in a 90-day suspension as well as admission of the fact of refusal in trial. However, he then went further, telling him that if he took the test and passed it, he would not be charged with drunk driving; if he refused, he would be charged and placed in jail. The appellate court reversed a denial of the defendant's motion to suppress, holding that the additional statements were "of the type that would normally result in considerable psychological pressure," thus rendering the consent involuntary.

If, after a review of the applicable law and the facts of the case, counsel feels that the arresting officer failed to comply with the directives of the statute, he should certainly consider filing a motion to suppress. The argument should be made that the language of the statute was intended to protect his client's rights and that a refusal to suppress resultant evidence would leave him without a remedy and leave the police free to continue to disregard the statute.

§11.6.3 Denial of Access to Counsel

A commonly recurring situation in drunk driving cases involves the refusal of police to permit the arrestee to make a phone call to his attorney or, the defendant having made the call, fail to permit counsel to see his client. This is more common than might be suspected, as the prevalent attitude among many police officers is that intoxicated arrestees should be "dried out," that is, sobered up, for three or four hours before being returned to society; the arrestee is considered too inebriated to use a phone, and visits from lawyers are considered a source of interference.

Yet, isolation of the client at this critical time can have devastating effects on his subsequent ability to conduct a defense. It is during this very post-booking period that his counsel may be able to obtain direct evidence as to intoxication. He may, for example, be able to obtain a urine sample within an hour or two of the arrest; even a sample taken three hours later is of more evidentiary help than none at all. He may be able to enforce statutes requiring the police to make available at the suspect's expense a blood test at a nearby doctor's office. Or he may simply have a witness with him to observe the client's appearance, conduct, and coordination for later testimony. As can readily be seen, access to an attorney during this period when the client is supposedly still under the influence can be the difference between conviction and acquittal. And just as readily, it can be seen that the police would not be particularly enthusiastic about permitting such gathering of evidence.

Confronted with a willful or inadvertent denial of access to an attorney, counsel is presented with two questions:

1. Is there a right to consult with an attorney prior to submitting to blood-alcohol testing?
2. If such a right exists, what is the remedy for a violation of this right?

The existence of a right to counsel prior to testing will depend upon state statute and precedent: There appears to be no federal authority on point. And, predictably, recognition of such a right varies from jurisdiction to jurisdiction.

In *McNutt v. Superior Court,* 648 P.2d 122 (Ariz. 1982), for example, the defendant was arrested for drunk driving and at the jail asked to telephone his attorney so that an independent chemical test could be taken. The law enforcement officials refused this request. In affirming an order to the trial court to dismiss the charge, the Supreme Court of Arizona stated:

> This action by the state clearly violated petitioner's "right to counsel in private with an attorney . . . as soon as feasible after a defendant is taken into custody" guaranteed by Ariz. R. Crim. P.6.1(a). We agree with the Court of Appeals of New York, which said, "[L]aw enforcement officials may not, without justification, prevent access between the criminal accused and his lawyer, available in person or by immediate telephone communication, if such access does not interfere unduly with the matter at hand." [Cites.] [Id. at 124.]

The Arizona Supreme Court subsequently distinguished between criminal and civil cases in ruling on the existence of a right to counsel before deciding whether to submit to chemical testing. In *Kunzler v. Pima County Superior Court,* 744 P.2d 669 (Ariz. 1987), the court held that in a criminal proceeding the defendant has a right to consult with counsel provided that the consultation did not "hinder the investigative process." Thus the court reversed the conviction and remanded the case to the trial court with instructions to suppress the breath test if it found that the defendant could have contacted his lawyer without interfering with the test process.

In the companion case of *Kunzler v. Miller,* 744 P.2d 671 (Ariz. 1987), however, the same court ruled that there is no such right to counsel before testing in the context of a proceeding that is civil in nature — such as in a license suspension hearing.

The Supreme Court of Arizona has subsequently reiterated its position that an arrestee has a constitutional right to contact counsel before submitting to a breath test, suggesting in doing so that a convenient time for advisement of this right would be at the beginning of the 20-minute pre-test observation period:

> We cannot imagine many cases where this would be a disruption of the procedures followed by the police in preparing to administer a breath test to a driver. Informing the driver that he may not call his attorney before taking the test misstates the law and violates the driver's right to counsel under the Sixth Amendment of the United States Constitution. Because this is a basic constitutional right, the burden is upon the state to show that a phone call would in fact be disruptive of an ongoing investigation. Evidence obtained in violation of this procedure should be suppressed. [*State v. Juarez,* 775 P.2d 1140 (Ariz. 1989).]

In *State v. Bristor,* 682 P.2d 122 (Kan. 1984), the Kansas Court of Appeals upheld the trial court's suppression of blood-alcohol test results because the defendant had been given no opportunity to consult with counsel before making a decision whether to submit or not:

> The Kansas appellate courts have consistently held that there is no duty upon the arresting officer to explain to the accused his rights under the foregoing statutes. . . .
>
> The question obviously is how can an accused make an intelligent decision regarding submission to a BAT if he is ignorant of his various rights, and how can he in his ignorance protect those rights, if the officer is under no duty to enlighten him. The answer, clearly, is that only through the advice and counsel of an attorney can the accused be expected to make his decisions in an intelligent and knowledgeable manner. [Id. at 127.]

The Supreme Court of Vermont has taken a similar position. In *State v. Carmody,* 442 A.2d 1292 (Vt. 1982), the defendant was detained for chemical testing on suspicion of drunk driving; she demanded to see her fiancé but never asked to see her attorney. The police denied her access to her fiancé and read her the implied consent law of that state; she refused to submit to a chemical test. The court reversed the subsequent administrative revocation of her license for refusing, and reversed as well the subsequent conviction for drunk driving, remanding for a new trial without evidence of the refusal. Emphasizing that no arrest had been formally made at the time of requesting a chemical test of the defendant, the court reasoned:

> Under these circumstances, where the State has forgone any claim of an arrest or entitlement to benefits which would flow from our finding of one, we cannot say that de facto arrest occurred, and the refusal to allow the defendant to make the requested phone call must be considered an unauthorized restraint on her. [442 A.2d at 1293.]

The Supreme Court of Oregon similarly has found a right to consult with counsel before deciding whether to submit to chemical testing. In *State v. Spencer,* 750 P.2d 147 (Or. 1988), the court based its holding on the state constitution's guarantee of the right to counsel "in all criminal prosecutions." Does the administration of a breath test before deciding whether to file any charges constitute a "criminal proceeding"?

> A person taken into formal custody by the police on a potentially criminal charge is confronted with the full legal power of the state, regardless of whether a formal charge has been filed. Where such custody is complete, neither the lack of a selected charge nor the possibility that the police may think better of the entire matter changes the fact that the arrested person is, at that moment, ensnared in a "criminal prosecution." [750 P.2d at 155–156.]

The court reversed and remanded for a suppression of the breath test, finding it unnecessary to address the question of whether there is a similar right under the U.S. Constitution.

The Supreme Court of North Dakota has held that there is a qualified right to consult with counsel before deciding whether to submit to blood-alcohol tests. In *Kuntz v. State Highway Commissioner,* 405 N.W.2d 285 (N.D. 1987), videotapes showed that the defendant repeatedly asked to speak with an attorney and that the officer repeatedly told him he could call his lawyer after the breath test. He refused to take the test, and his driver's license was accordingly revoked. On appeal, the defendant argued that he had a statutory right to counsel before taking the test, citing a statute that read that "[t]he accused in all cases must be taken before a magistrate without unnecessary delay and any attorney at law entitled to practice in the courts of record of this state, at his request, may visit such person after his arrest."

In reversing the license revocation, the North Dakota Supreme Court agreed that there was a right to consult with counsel before deciding whether to take a breath test, so long as the request for consultation does not materially interfere with the administration of the test.

The right to consult with an attorney impliedly carries with it the right to consult with him *privately*. It is not sufficient that the law enforcement agency provide access to the lawyer — it must provide an environment in which confidential communications can take place, at least where this would not unduly delay the investigation or arrest.

This issue was directly presented to the Supreme Court of

Arizona in *Arizona v. Holland,* 711 P.2d 592 (Ariz. 1985). In that case a DUI arrestee was taken to the police station and permitted to call his attorney. However, a police officer refused to leave the room during the telephone conversation. Because the officer was close enough to hear the conversation, the attorney felt unable to ask certain questions that may have elicited incriminating information concerning his client's conduct that evening. Without this information, the attorney could not advise the client whether to take a breath test or not. The client took the test and failed.

On appeal, the supreme court recognized that: "[T]he right to counsel includes the right to consult in private with an attorney. [Cites.] Further, it is universally accepted that effective representation is not possible without the right of a defendant to confer in private with his counsel. [Cites.]"

The court then considered the state's argument that since the defendant had no right to consult with his attorney concerning whether to submit to a breath test to begin with, the lack of privacy was irrelevant:

> Defendant is not arguing he was improperly denied the opportunity to consult with counsel prior to taking the breathalyzer test. Instead, defendant maintains that where, as in this case, a person is allowed to consult with counsel he has a right to do so in private. We agree. . . .
>
> Admittedly, under *Campbell* [*Campbell v. Superior Court,* 479 P.2d 685 (1971)], a person is not entitled to consult with counsel prior to deciding whether or not to take a breathalyzer. . . . *Campbell* does not negate the right to counsel. All *Campbell* says is that the police need not wait for the defendant to consult with counsel before the sobriety tests are conducted. We believe the law is clear — if the defendant talks to his counsel, he must be allowed to do so in a meaningful way. [Id. at 595.]

Under *Holland,* then, the police need not provide access to counsel before a chemical test is administered. However, when access *is* given, privacy must be provided. For a contrary result, see *City of Grand Forks v. Soli,* 479 N.W.2d 872 (N.D. 1992), where the court refused to find that an officer's presence during the defendant's telephone conversation with his attorney interfered with his right to consult with an attorney.

What amount of time constitutes a reasonable opportunity to

contact and consult with an attorney? In *Kuhn v. Commissioner of Public Safety,* 488 N.W.2d 838 (Minn. App. 1992), the defendant was arrested at 1:43 A.M. and advised of his rights and given access to a telephone and directory at 2:02 A.M. After three attempts and 24 minutes, he was unable to reach an attorney. The officer said, "Look, you got to take the test now," whereupon the defendant complied. His license was suspended when the results indicated a BAC of .24 percent.

On appeal, the prosecution argued that from a practical standpoint, the 20-minute waiting period for a breath test was a reasonable period of time to contact an attorney. The court disagreed, noting that there was no apparent attempt by the defendant to delay the test and that due to the difficulty of reaching an attorney at that time of morning, he should have been given more time.

A similar situation was presented in *Village of Lexington v. Reddington,* 621 N.E.2d 758 (Ohio App. 1993), where the police gave the defendant only 20 minutes to use the telephone in order to contact an attorney. In reversing the DUI conviction and remanding for suppression of the breath test results, the court noted that it had been 3:00 A.M. on New Year's Day and there was still another hour left within which to administer a valid breath test.

In *State v. Garvey,* 595 A.2d 267 (Vt. 1991), the defendant was arrested and, pursuant to Vermont law, attempted to contact an attorney before deciding whether to submit to a chemical test. After 14 phone calls, however, he was unable to reach an attorney. After 43 minutes, the officer again asked the defendant to submit to testing (state law imposed a time limit of 30 minutes). The defendant refused to do so without first speaking with a lawyer. The officer thereupon entered a refusal.

On appeal from a court's affirmation of a license suspension, the state supreme court held that no time limit could be imposed. Further, and more important, the court held that the state must provide the suspect with a public defender before the suspect decides whether to submit to testing — regardless of his financial condition. Recognizing that this would impose a burden on the state, the court nevertheless observed, "We have little doubt that statewide twenty-four-hour coverage of DUI calls is not an insurmountable management task." Id. at 268.

See also *State v. Rodenheffer,* 580 N.E.2d 864 (Ohio Mun.

1991), in which an Ohio court held that giving a DUI suspect only 15 minutes to contact an attorney before submitting to a breath test was unreasonable and a violation of the right to counsel.

The highest court of Maryland has held that not only does a DUI suspect have a due process right to an in-person meeting with his attorney before deciding whether to submit to chemical testing, but he also has a right to *have an independent breath test administered before deciding whether to submit to the testing or not.* In *Brosan v. Cochran,* 516 A.2d 970 (Md. 1986), the defendant was arrested for drunk driving and permitted to call his attorney. When the attorney arrived at the police station, however, he was not permitted to meet with his client. In the absence of advice from his attorney, the defendant refused to take a breath test. Subsequently, the attorney successfully obtained a preliminary injunction from the circuit court requiring the Maryland State Police Department to allow suspects face-to-face meetings with their attorneys before deciding whether to take or refuse a breath test. As a result, the superintendent of the department issued an order allowing the face-to-face meetings, but prohibiting the attorney from administering an independent breath test prior to the suspect deciding whether to take the police-administered breath test. At the hearing on the permanent injunction, the circuit court also considered this new department order. The court issued a permanent injunction, requiring not only that suspects be afforded in-person access to their attorney but also that the police permit the attorney to administer a breath test to his client "as long as the device does not impair or impede the department's own testing." 516 A.2d 973.

> It is not the duty of the police, in the interest of high conviction rates, to withhold from the accused information which he may find relevant in deciding whether to exercise his right of refusal. Police may bar the use of breathalyzers, but only for legitimate reasons — where their use may impair accurate police testing. [Id. at 973.]

On appeal by the Superintendent, the Maryland Court of Appeals (Maryland's equivalent of the supreme court) affirmed the judgment of the circuit court:

> It is axiomatic that the right to counsel carries with it the right to the *effective assistance* of counsel. . . . Simply because the attorney-

> administered test involves an instrument and requires a subsequent reading of the test results does not mean that the information thereby conveyed between attorney and client is not a communication within the contemplation of *Sites* [*Sites v. State,* 481 A.2d 192 (1984)]. On the contrary, we think the exchange of such information, although not exclusively verbal, is nevertheless a communication between attorney and client. As such, it is in the circumstances, where requested, part of the process constitutionally due a drunk driving suspect under the rationale of *Sykes.* (Emphasis by the court.) [516 A.2d 976.]

The court went on to say that the only real issue was whether the communication — including testing — would "unreasonably impede" police procedures. The court emphasized the importance of a driver's license in today's world and the critical nature of the decision whether to submit to state testing: "[T]he decision whether to submit to the State test is of the most fundamental importance in determining the ultimate resolution of the suspect's case."

Assuming that the existence of a right to counsel prior to chemical testing is recognized and that the right has been denied, the question becomes one of remedy. Two possible remedies exist: suppression of evidence and dismissal of charges.

The first approach involves a motion to suppress blood-alcohol evidence (or evidence of refusal to submit to chemical testing) on the grounds that the evidence was obtained as a result of the police failure to permit the accused to consult with an attorney before deciding whether to submit to testing and, if submitting, which test to take. This would seem a natural and logical remedy and one which many courts have taken.

A convincing argument can be made, however, that the denial of access to counsel at a critical stage directly affects the accused's right to a fair trial. And, as a number of the previously discussed cases indicate, the deprivation of such a fundamental right should result in the dismissal of charges (or, in the case of an administrative license suspension, a reinstatement of the license).

While motions to suppress tend to be definable and tangible (i.e., a given denial of a right can be seen to lead directly or indirectly to a given quantum of evidence), the motion to dismiss based on due process often involves vaguer and more arguable grounds. Among other reasons, the law is less concise as to just what constitutes a denial of fair trial and what does not. And because of this, perhaps, defense counsel will have a greater opportunity to exercise "creative legal analysis," to analyze the facts and the law, and to formulate a plausible theory for dismissal.

§11.6.4 Denial of Choice of Tests

What is the remedy — if any — where the police refuse to honor a suspect's choice of blood-alcohol tests, but instead requires him to submit to one of their own choosing?

In *Nelson v. City of Irvine,* 143 F.2d 1196 (9th Cir. 1998), a civil rights action was brought by a number of individuals who had been arrested for DUI by officers of a city police department and forced to provide blood samples. The case involved the following fact patterns:

- After his arrest, Nelson was asked if he "had a problem" with taking a blood test. Nelson agreed to the test, but was never told that he had a statutory right to his choice of blood, breath, or urine test.
- Fernandez was told he was "going to get a blood sample"; he did not resist, believing he had no choice.
- Tyler was not advised of his right to choose, and was told he would be held in jail over the weekend if he did not cooperate by giving a blood sample.
- Caruso was not told of any right to choose, but rather that she had to submit to blood testing.
- Capler agreed to a blood test, then changed his mind and requested a breath test. He was told that he could not alter his decision.
- Giordano was halfway through a breath test when she was told she was doing it wrong and was then required to give a blood sample.
- Chancellor was offered only a blood or urine test, but was also told if he chose urine he would remain in jail for seventeen hours; a breath test was never offered.
- Heil was not advised of any choice: He was simply told that

> if he did not cooperate in giving a blood sample, he would be strapped into a chair and the sample taken by force — and that he would be jailed for an additional 48 hours.

California law provided that a person arrested for drunk driving "has the choice of whether the test shall be of his or her blood, breath, or urine, and the officer shall advise the person that he or she has that choice." Cal. Vehicle Code §23157.

The U.S. Court of Appeals initially noted the U.S. Supreme Court holding in *Schmerber v. California,* 384 U.S. 757 (1966), that blood may be drawn from an arrestee who has refused a breath test. See §11.6.6. That decision did not, however, consider the question of whether police could draw blood when other tests were available or requested.

The court in *Nelson* noted the underlying rationale in *Schmerber:* exigent circumstances. Because of the dissipating nature of blood-alcohol in the body, obtaining a warrant was unreasonable and immediate testing to avoid loss of evidence was justified. In the facts before the court, however, the exigency existed only because the police failed to perform the requested test:

> Neither side disputes that it is the rapid dissipation of alcohol from the blood of the arrestee that creates the initial exigency. When an arrestee requests but is denied the choice of an available breath or urine test, the exigency used to justify the warrantless blood test continues only because of the City's failure to perform the requested alternative test. Whenever a DUI arrestee consents to a breath or urine tests, and such tests are available, the administration of whether the breath or urine test would preserve the evidence and end the exigency. In such cases, because the sole justification advanced to excuse the officers from obtaining a warrant disappeared when the exigency ended, the blood tests were not only unnecessary and unreasonable, but violated the Fourth Amendment's warrant requirements.

The court remanded the separate cases, stating that facts developed at trial "may affect the ultimate determination whether the plaintiffs' requests for alternative forms of testing, which the police refused to respect, were in fact reasonable under the circumstances."

§11.6.5 Delayed Testing: Sample Obtained Too Remote in Time

The longer the period that passes between the time the suspect is observed driving and the time he is given an evidentiary chemical test, the less reliable is the projected estimate of his blood-alcohol concentration when driving. See the discussion of retrograde extrapolation, §5.2. An extensive delay, however, may be sufficient to render the test results inadmissible altogether.

Many states have statutory or administrative rules governing the time limitations for chemical testing and setting forth consequences for noncompliance. In some jurisdictions, delayed testing does not affect admissibility but, rather, "goes to the weight of the evidence." In others, testing beyond a certain period of time — commonly two or three hours — bars the results from evidence. And in yet other states, a compromise position is taken whereby the test results are admitted but the legal (rebuttable) presumption of the same BAC at the time of driving disappears. California's statute is representative of this last approach:

> In any prosecution under this subdivision, it is a rebuttable presumption that the person had 0.08 percent or more, by weight, of alcohol in his or her blood at the time of driving the vehicle if the person has a 0.08 percent or more, by weight, of alcohol in his or her blood at the time of the performance of a chemical test *within three hours after the driving.* [Vehicle Code §23152(b).]

If no such statute or administrative regulation governs the issue, counsel should consider making an argument that a chemical test performed too long after the driving should be inadmissible on the grounds that it is not *relevant.* The longer the period of time that has intervened, of course, the less connection between the results of the test and the blood-alcohol level when driving. Couched in the terms of a different concept of evidence law, the *probative value* of the test results has greatly diminished while the *prejudicial effect* is high. At the very least, a cautionary jury instruction should be requested — and discussed at length in argument.

§11.6.6 Forceful Seizure of Blood Sample: *Rochin — Schmerber*

The Fourth Amendment protects citizens from unreasonable searches of their persons and seizures therefrom. Certainly the withdrawal of blood constitutes a search and seizure of the person; accordingly, to be permissible the withdrawal must be "reasonable." What constitutes a reasonable taking of blood is an area of some legal dispute.

If a suspect voluntarily consents to having a blood sample withdrawn, he is deemed to have waived his constitutional rights. The waiver, of course, must be free and voluntary and not a product of police coercion, express or implied. And in those states having implied consent statutes — that is, laws requiring submission to chemical tests as a condition of driving, there is a waiver by law. These statutes have withstood constitutional attack.

The litigable issue arises where force is used by the police in drawing a blood sample from an unwilling or unconscious drunk driving suspect: Does this constitute civilized conduct within the meaning of due process as required by the Fourteenth Amendment?

Rochin v. California, 342 U.S. 165 (1952), was the first case to address this problem, although indirectly. The Supreme Court in that case found that forcing a defendant's mouth open and pumping his stomach to obtain narcotics constituted "conduct that shocks the conscience" and a violation of the Fourth and Fourteenth Amendments. Then, in *Breithaupt v. Abram,* 352 U.S. 432 (1966), the Court directly addressed the question of blood withdrawal from an unconscious drunk driving suspect, holding that the taking of a sample by a physician under regulated conditions was not offensive. However, the Court specifically ruled that the taking of chemical samples under less civilized conditions may not be sanctioned. Finally, the situation where the suspect was conscious and refused to consent came up in *Schmerber v. California,* 384 U.S. 757 (1966). There, the Court relied on *Breithaupt,* holding again that if the blood was taken under humane and medically accepted circumstances, due process requirements are not violated.

Breithaupt and *Schmerber* both involved the withdrawal of blood under nonviolent conditions with the use of proper medical procedures. The question remains whether a sample taken by police through the use of force — implied or actual — would be admissible in court. Certainly, in view of *Rochin,* there are limitations on the force that police may use under such circumstances.

Since these decisions, some states have passed legislation providing that no chemical sample may be taken from a suspect if he refuses to cooperate. See, e.g., *Thrower v. State,* 539 So. 2d 1127 (Ala. App. 1988). This provision is usually tacked on to the implied consent law and provides further for the suspension of the suspect's driver's license for refusing. Where the state courts have addressed the issue of force, the general consensus seems to be that force may be used providing it is not the oppressive force used in *Rochin.* Consent obtained through deceit or coercion is probably invalid. (See, e.g., *People v. Wheatly,* 284 N.E.2d 353 (Ill. App. 1972).)

In *Carleton v. Superior Court,* 216 Cal. Rptr. 890 (Cal. App. 1985), a California Court of Appeal was confronted with a situation where a defendant had to be restrained by six individuals for a blood sample to be withdrawn. The court held that this was not an excessive use of force:

> The degree of force necessary to overcome a defendant's resistance to the taking of a blood sample turns on the size and strength of the individual defendant. Less force will be necessary to restrain the proverbial 98 pound weakling. Considerably more force will be required to subdue the 280 pound weight-lifting champion. At the outer extremes it may be impossible to control such physical behemoths without the use of tranquilizers propelled from dart guns similar to those used by veterinarians to pacify large animals. Such intrusions would, of course, be constitutionally objectionable.
>
> Here scientific assistance was unnecessary. Carlton was controlled by six persons all of whom were necessary to permit the withdrawal of his blood in a medically approved fashion. . . .
>
> Although this degree of force may approach the brink of excessiveness, it was not excessive. Carlton's self-induced brief physical restraint before and during the withdrawal of a blood sample is not conscience shocking. [Id. at 896.]

What if the suspect has already given the police a sample? May the police nevertheless use force to obtain another sample? In *People v. Fiscalini,* 279 Cal. Rptr. 682 (Cal. App. 1991), the defendant was arrested for drunk driving and, when given a choice of tests at the police station, gave the officers a urine sample. In order to test for both alcohol *and* drugs, the officers then asked him to give them a blood sample as well. The defendant refused, whereupon the officers obtained the sample by force.

The subsequent conviction was reversed on appeal:

> Enactment of the implied consent law is tantamount to governmental acknowledgment a urine test is functionally equivalent to a blood test for evidentiary purposes with respect to blood alcohol level. . . . Thus, having already obtained one sample from Fiscalini with his consent, the government did not demonstrate any need to force him to undergo a second intrusion. [Id. at 685.]

Whether the nonconsensual withdrawal of blood constitutes compulsory self-incrimination is yet another issue. The Supreme Court has interpreted the Fifth Amendment as protecting only speech and thought and does not require an "exclusion of his body as evidence" *Holt v. United States,* 218 U.S. 245 (1910). And *Schmerber* concluded that a blood sample constituted physical evidence, rather than testimonial. As a result, the Fifth Amendment does not provide grounds for objection to the introduction of any blood-alcohol evidence — blood, breath, or urine.

§11.6.7 The Physician-Patient Privilege (Blood)

In relatively rare situations, the drunk driving suspect will be taken either to the offices of a medical doctor or to a doctor at or near the police station. The primary purpose may be to extract a blood or urine sample, but an equally, if not more, important reason is to obtain a medical opinion based on symptoms as to intoxication. In the more commonly encountered situation, a suspect injured in an automobile collision will be taken to a hospital for treatment. The doctor then will be available to testify at the trial that in his expert opinion the defendant was under the influence of alcohol and/or drugs to the extent that he was incapable of safely operating a motor vehicle. Presumably, the doctor's medical observations will be much more resistant to defense counsel's attack than will be the observations and conclusions of the medically untrained police officer.

Defense counsel may have available a means of preventing the doctor from testifying: the physician-patient privilege. Assuming the existence of this privilege in the jurisdiction, and assuming its recognized application to criminal cases, counsel should argue that the doctor's observations were a direct result of his treatment of the defendant, that is, that the primary purpose of bringing the doctor and suspect together was to render medical aid, and thus a physician-patient relationship came into existence. As the doctor's observations and resultant opinion arose from that relationship, the defendant should be able to assert the privilege and prevent the doctor from testifying. It should be recognized, however, that the court may well find that the primary purpose of the doctor's presence was to aid in the gathering of evidence, rather than to administer medical care. Certainly, the defense has a stronger position when the defendant was seriously injured or where he was taken to the medical facilities at his own request.

The specific privilege statute applicable in the jurisdiction should be examined on this issue. Well over half of the states have such statutes, but some of them apply the privilege to civil cases only. In some, the issue may revolve around whether the doctor's presence was strictly for the purpose of obtaining a chemical sample or whether medical treatment was also given. In yet others, observations, statements, or evidence will be found privileged only if they were necessary to the doctor's treatment or prescription of care. Finally, the jurisdiction's statute may void the privilege in the event of the presence of nonmedical third parties — for example, police officers.

In *People v. Walljasper*, 422 N.E.2d 251 (Ill. App. 1981), the defendant had been involved in an automobile accident and was subsequently taken to a hospital for treatment. He was later arrested and tried for drunk driving and reckless homicide. At the trial, the attending physician testified that in his opinion the defendant was under the influence of alcohol at the time the doctor rendered medical treatment. The Illinois appellate court reversed the convictions on both charges, holding that the physician's opinion fell within the scope of the physician-patient privilege.

The doctor's observations and medical opinion may not be all that can be suppressed successfully. Where a blood or urine sample has been taken by the doctor, counsel should argue that the results of the laboratory analysis should be suppressed as being protected by the physician-patient privilege, at least when the sample was taken for diagnostic purposes. The privilege issue was considered by the Missouri Court of Appeals in *Gozenbach v. Ruddy*, 645 S.W.2d 27 (Mo. 1982), which involved a driver who was admitted to the hospital for treatment of injuries, during which time a test was conducted to determine his blood-alcohol content. This was at the direction of a physician for treatment purposes, not at the request of the police, and no police officers were present at the hospital.

The court analyzed the physician-patient privilege as follows:

> We must look to the physician-patient privilege statute for guidance. For the most part, courts in other jurisdictions have followed the dictates of their particular statutes. Where the statute of a state was broad, it usually found the physician-patient privilege applicable in criminal cases. [Annot., 7 A.L.R.3rd 1458, 1460.]
>
> Our statute, §491.060(5), is couched in broad language:
>
>> The following persons shall be incompetent to testify: . . .
>>
>> (5) A physician or surgeon, concerning any information which he may have acquired from any patient while attending him in a professional character, and which information was necessary to enable him to prescribe for such patient as a physician, or do any act for him as a surgeon.
>
> There is nothing in the language in this statute suggesting the privilege it affords applies only in civil cases. See *Ragsdale v. State*, 432 S.W.2d 11, 13 (Ark. 1968). If the legislature had intended an exception for criminal cases, it should have so provided. Absent such direction from the legislature, we will not infer an exception to §491.060(5). [645 S.W.2d at 28.]

This situation was again presented in *Kansas v. Pitchford*, 697 P.2d 896 (Kan. 1985). In that case, the defendant left the scene of an accident but was subsequently arrested and taken to the hospital due to bleeding. At the hospital, the defendant resisted treatment; suspecting the existence of alcohol or drugs, the treating physician ordered a blood sample taken. The results indicated a blood-alcohol level of .22 percent. A copy of the blood test results were given to the arresting officer on his request. The defendant later moved to suppress the results of that test, citing the physician-patient privilege. The trial court granted the motion. In support of an interlocutory appeal, the prosecution argued that the results were not privileged information because the defendant had not been a patient and because the emergency room physician was not his personal doctor. The court first reviewed the three requirements necessary for the existence of a privilege:

> (1) There must be a "patient" (who in this case would be the "holder of the privilege") and a "physician"; (2) there must be a "confidential communication between physician and patient"; and (3) either the physician or the patient must have "reasonably believed the communication necessary or helpful to enable the physician" to treat or diagnose the patient's condition. *State v. George,* 223 Kan. at 510, 575 P.2d 511. [Id. at 899.]

The court then addressed the prosecution's arguments:

> Here, Dr. McGovern ordered the blood test for purposes of treatment. Though not the defendant's personal physician, McGovern was an "interested" physician. Cf. 61 Am. Jur. 2d, Physicians, Surgeons, Etc. §160 (a doctor in a hospital enters into a physician-patient relationship with every patient brought into the hospital). [Ibid.]

Finally, the Kansas appellate court concluded that the privilege did, in fact, apply:

> Determining whether the defendant was a "patient" does not turn on whether he voluntarily consulted a physician. The controlling fact is that the defendant was taken to the hospital for purposes of treatment. See McCormick on Evidence §99, p. 247, n.4 (3rd ed. 1984). Here, the officer's testimony indicated they believed the defendant needed medical aid; acting on this belief, they transported him to the hospital. Once at the hospital, Dr. McGovern treated the defendant. For purposes of K.S.A. 60-427, the defendant was a "patient." . . .
>
> We conclude that defendant was a patient, the blood test was a communication and the test was secured for the purpose of diagnosis and treatment. The test results were therefore privileged, and the trial court did not err in suppressing them. [Id. at 900.]

In *New York v. Petro,* 504 N.Y.S.2d 67 (N.Y. 1986), the defendant was involved in an automobile collision and was taken in an ambulance to a hospital. En route to the hospital, and while he was in a semiconscious state, a blood sample was taken for the purpose of diagnosis. He was subsequently charged with vehicular manslaughter, drunk driving, and negligent homicide. Based on the physician-patient privilege, the trial court granted defendant's motion to suppress the test results and dismiss all charges. The appellate court affirmed.

And in *State v. Schreiber,* 573 A.2d 942 (N.J. 199), a New Jersey court was confronted with a situation where a physician called police and informed them of the results of a blood test taken on the defendant after he had been brought in for treatment of injuries from a car accident. The court reversed the conviction, holding that the physician's "tip" violated the physician-patient privilege.

It must be recognized, however, that if there is a trend in the physician-patient appellate decisions, it is in the direction of limiting its application in DUI cases. Thus, for example, in *State v. Berluchaux,* 522 So. 2d 600 (La. App. 1988), the defendant was involved in a collision; as part of treatment at a hospital, the attending physician ordered a blood sample drawn. The prosecution issued a subpoena *duces tecum* for the medical records — including the results of blood tests. The trial court's denial of defendant's motion to suppress was sustained on appeal. In doing so, the court emphasized that there was a difference between *testimonial communications* — protected by the physician-patient privilege — and *medical records* — which were admissible as an exception to the hearsay rule.

In another decision applying a restrictive interpretation of the privilege, an Ohio appellate court was confronted with a situation in which the defendant had been taken to a hospital and blood tests ordered by the attending physician for purposes of treatment. Incredibly, the court held that the test results were not within the privilege, since the test had been conducted by the witness technician:

> Assuming the blood-alcohol test administered in connection with [appellant's] physical examination constitutes a communication, it was the medical technologist who conducted the test who testified here as to the results, not the attending physician. The relationship of medical technologist and patient not being named

> in the [privilege] statute, the medical technologist is not prohibited by the statute from testifying. [*State v. McKinnon*, 525 N.E.2d 821, 823 (Ohio App. 1987).]

According to this reasoning, of course, a legal secretary could be subpoenaed and permitted to testify to confidential communications he recorded between an attorney and his client. Decisions such as that in *McKinnon* are perhaps best explained as examples of what has become known as the "drunk driving exception to the Constitution."

Similarly, a Pennsylvania court had held that the statutory requirement that hospitals obtain and report blood tests to officers having probable cause to obtain the information takes precedence over the patient's expectations of confidentiality. Despite the fact that the tests were taken by attending physicians for the purpose of treating the injured defendant, and that the defendant refused the officer's request that he submit to implied consent testing, the court ruled that both the blood test results and the refusal were admissible. *Commonwealth v. Hipp*, 551 A.2d 1086 (Pa. Super. 1988).

See also *Commonwealth v. Ellis*, 608 A.2d 1090 (Pa. Super. 1992), where hospital personnel drew blood from the defendant and tested it for alcohol concentration — without a request from the police. The appellate court held, first, that there was no Fourth Amendment violation, even without probable cause, since there was no state action. Turning next to the hospital's breach of confidentiality, the court ruled that suppression of the evidence was not the appropriate remedy; the exclusionary rule was designed to deter only police misconduct. And see *State v. Boysaw*, 532 N.E.2d 154 (Ohio App. 1987), in which an Ohio appellate court ruled such evidence admissible, noting that the physician-patient privilege must be strictly construed against the person asserting it both because it was unknown at common law and in light of competing interests of public policy.

In *Schultz v. State*, 417 N.E.2d 1127 (Ind. App. 1981), the Indiana Court of Appeals held that a blood sample drawn at the request of the defendant's attending physician was evidence that fell within the privilege. However, the court ruled, the resulting blood-alcohol test results could be admitted into evidence against the defendant because he had put his physical condition in issue by voluntarily taking the stand and testifying that he had not been intoxicated. "It is well settled," the court reasoned, "that the physician-patient privilege is waived by a party's voluntary testimony."

In *State v. Schreiber,* 585 A.2d 945 (N.J. 1991), a New Jersey appellate court finally abandoned the tortured pretexts used by other courts in finding that the physician-patient privilege does not apply in specific DUI cases. Rather, this court simply held that the privilege did not apply to DUI cases for reasons of public policy: The public's right to be free of the scourge of drunken driving far outweighed the right of an individual to present a complete defense using the privilege. Applying the privilege to DUI cases, the court reasoned, would clearly weaken the broader policy goals of curbing "the senseless havoc and destruction caused by intoxicated drivers." Id. at 949.

The reasoning of the court, while refreshingly direct, is fairly typical of the "double standard" increasingly encountered in drunk driving cases. And the logic is, as usual, frightening in its implications: The right of the public to be free of crime is being used increasingly as a justification for abandoning the rights of the accused.

If the jurisdiction has no physician-patient privilege, counsel may wish to consider blocking police/prosecutorial access to a hospital's blood sample and/or analysis through extra-judicial means.

Federal authority exists that prohibits the release of patient information without that patient's consent from any hospital having any federal connections (which indirectly covers most hospitals). 42 U.S.C. §299(dd)(3). Subdivision (a) of that statute makes it a federal offense to disclose without the patient's consent

> records of the identity, diagnosis, prognosis, or treatment of any patient which are maintained in connection with the performance of any program or activity relating to . . . alcohol abuse . . . treatment . . . which is conducted, regulated, or directly or indirectly assisted by any department or agency of the United States. . . .

It would appear that the statute applies to the typical DUI scenario where the defendant is taken to the hospital after an accident and blood is drawn during or in conjunction with examination, diagnosis, or treatment. Blood withdrawal and analysis relating to injuries from an accident allegedly caused by excessive consumption of alcohol would qualify as "records of the identity, diagnosis, prognosis, or treatment of any patient which are maintained in connection with the performance of any . . . activity relating to . . . alcohol abuse . . . treatment. . . ."

Subsection (c) further applies the provisions to criminal prosecutions:

> . . . no record referred to in subsection (a) of this section may be used to initiate or substantiate any criminal charges against a patient or to conduct any investigation of a patient.

Thus, a timely letter to the hospital warning of civil — if not criminal — liability should they release the sample or analysis without the client's permission may well prove to be effective with a legally and fiscally cautious hospital administrator.

Does a DUI suspect have a reasonable expectation of *privacy* as to blood test results obtained by an attending physician? According to the Supreme Court of Michigan, he does not. In *People v. Perlos,* 462 N.W.2d 310 (1990), the court held that the provisions of the state's implied consent statute requiring test results to be turned over to the police on request resulted in a "diminished expectation of privacy" for those who drive. The court also addressed a challenge to the statute on the grounds of equal protection, finding a rational basis for treating hospitalized drivers differently from arrested drivers who were not hospitalized.

Distinct but closely related to the issue of physician-patient privilege as to the blood test results is the question of whether a patient/suspect has a right of privacy as to the physical premises where he is a patient. If, for example, a police officer enters an emergency room where the individual is being treated, does that individual have a reasonable expectation of privacy? Does third party consent by a nurse or physician waive this? Are they without authority absent the patient's delegation?

§11.6.8 Noncompliance with Testing Regulations

The majority of states now have statutory schemes for regulating the chemical testing of drunk driving suspects. Often the applicable regulations will be found in the state's administrative codes or health codes and will be directed to ensuring the following:

1. the police operators of breath analysis instruments have the proper training and certification
2. the laboratories conducting the analysis of blood or urine samples and the regulation of breath machines and reference chemicals are properly staffed, operated, and licensed
3. the samples are correctly preserved and stored
4. standards for analytic procedures are met
5. proper laboratory and breath machine records are kept
6. breath instruments are properly calibrated and maintained

These administrative laws can be quite complex, involving detailed technical and scientific requirements. Yet, counsel should master them; his opponent in court — and, very possibly, the judge — has probably not. Often, the only other person in the courtroom who understands the statutory scheme will be the prosecutor's chemical expert. Of course, it will be the prosecutor, not the expert, who must argue the matter. As a result, the judge may rely on defense counsel's expertise, at least as to matters of law.

Because of the demanding and complex nature of these requirements, counsel will often find that the testing of his client did, in fact, fail in some respect to comply with the law. What, then, is the remedy? Certainly, counsel should move to suppress the evidence if there has been statutory noncompliance. The argument should be made that satisfaction of the regulations is a legal prerequisite for admission into evidence. In the alternative, counsel should argue that all evidence must have a foundational showing of relevance and dependability and that statutory noncompliance is at least presumptive of irrelevance and undependability.

The trend of authority appears to stand for the proposition that substantial failure to comply with statutory regulation of blood-alcohol testing precludes admissibility of the results, rather than simply affecting the weight to be accorded them. Thus, for example, in *State v. Setter,* 763 S.W.2d 228 (Mo. App. 1989), a drunk driving conviction was reversed where the state failed to establish that the needle used to withdraw blood from the defendant had been sterilized. The court noted that "other jurisdictions have consistently held that absolute and literal compliance with the technical requirements of (blood alcohol testing) statutes and regulations is necessary." A few months later, the Missouri court affirmed a suppression of blood test results because the nurse withdrawing the sample had swabbed the defendant's skin with isopropyl alcohol and there had been no showing that the needle was sterile. *State v. Hanners,* 774 S.W.2d 568 (Mo. App. 1989). Referring to its earlier decision in *Setter,* the court again noted that "other jurisdictions with similar statutes have determined that absolute and literal compliance is necessary." For a further discussion of the effects of swabs on blood samples, see §7.0.2.

A growing majority of jurisdictions are adopting the view of the *Setter* court. An excellent example of this can be found in *People v. Keith,* 564 N.E.2d 901 (Ill. App. 1990), where the court held that the results of a breath test were inadmissible because the operator's license had expired the day before the test was administered to the defendant. And in *State v. Ofa,* 828 P.2d 813 (Haw. App. 1992), an appellate court reversed a DUI conviction where the results of a breath test were admitted without showing that the solutions used in calibrating the machine had a known temperature. In remanding with instructions to enter a judgment of acquittal, the court said that the failure of the calibration logs to indicate the temperature of the solutions called the accuracy of the test results into question.

Similarly, an Oklahoma court reversed a DUI conviction on the grounds that the results of a breath test were introduced at trial despite a lack of any records indicating compliance with state maintenance requirements. In *McManus v. Oklahoma,* 695 P.2d 884 (Okla. 1985), that court reasoned:

> The admission of the test results was objected to repeatedly. While the test appears, from the troopers' testimony, to have been administered in accordance with the rules, the record reveals no mention of maintenance procedures by the state. Having failed to meet their burden of proving complete compliance with the

> Board's rules, the results of the breathalyzer should not have been admitted and the appellant's Motion to Suppress should have been granted. [Id. at 886.]

And in *Donaldson v. State,* 561 So. 2d 648 (Fla. App. 1990), the court reversed a DUI conviction for failure to establish a sufficient foundation of maintenance of the breath machine. Faced with a silent record, the court refused to presume due performance of official duty, reasoning that to hold otherwise would shift the burden of proof to the defendant. See also *State v. Wolfe,* 369 N.W.2d 458 (Iowa App. 1985), where the appellate court held that the failure of the prosecution to comply with state law requiring evidence of the accuracy and reliability of a breath machine rendered its admission into evidence error and a resulting conviction was reversed. The Supreme Court of Florida subsequently affirmed the decision in *Donaldson* and in so doing set forth the requirements for admissibility of blood-alcohol test results. In *State v. Donaldson,* 579 So. 2d 728 (Fla. 1991), the court held that the state must prove that "1) a breathalyzer test was performed substantially in accordance with the methods approved by the HRS, by a person trained and qualified to conduct it, and 2) the machine itself has been calibrated, tested, and inspected in accordance with HRS regulations to assure its accuracy before the results of a breathalyzer test may be introduced." Id. at 729.

Despite this trend, however, the U.S.C.A. has held that the partial results of an incomplete breath test are admissible. In *U.S. v. Brannon,* 146 F.3d 1194 (9th Cir. 1998), the defendant had been arrested on a military base in California and subjected to an Intoxilyzer 5000 test. He blew for only two seconds, during which the machine registered a reading of .15 percent, then stopped. As the Intoxilyzer required at least three seconds to reach a final reading, it printed a test card reading "Deficient Sample." The defendant, told to blow again, merely feigned blowing by puffing out his cheeks. He was charged with DUI, the BAC test result was admitted over objection at trial, and he was convicted. On appeal, the defendant raised non-compliance with *Daubert v. Merrel Dow Pharmaceuticals* due to the lack of a complete test.

In a 2-1 majority opinion exhibiting little if any understanding of the technology underlying the Intoxilyzer, the court held:

> A single uncompleted test is not what the scientific literature recommends [cites]. But as the method by which a breathalyzer works is unchallenged, the objection to an incomplete test goes not to forbid scientific employed but to the reliability of the test result reported . . .
>
> Every scientific method known to humanity is subject to error, both mechanical and human. The best way of running a breathalyzer is to have a period of observation of the subject fifteen minutes before the tests preceding each of the two actual tests, and to run a control test following the actual test. [Cite]. Omission of these safeguards lowers the reliability of the tests, it does not eliminate them as scientific aids to a factfinder investigating drunkeness.

The court dismissed the defendant's argument that California law required two complete tests for admissibility, amazingly concluding that "any error was likely to favor the defendant." The dissenting justice wrote that the procedure was a "hurried observation of a flashing LED readout," not a reliable scientific result. For a thoughtful legal critique of *Brannon,* see Tarantino, Why Half a Load Isn't Better than None: Incomplete Breath Tests Should Be Inadmissible, 13(10) DWI Journal 1 (Oct. 1998).

A New York court has held that the procedures used to prepare the solution for the ampoules used in the Breathalyzer 900A rendered the test results inadmissible. In *People v. Serrano,* 539 N.Y.S.2d 845 (N.Y. Crim. Ct. 1989), the court conducted a pretrial investigatory hearing into the practices of the laboratory preparing the ampoules, Systems Innovations, Inc. (SII); the defense motion and hearing was prompted by a critical report from the Pennsylvania Auditor General. Among other evidence produced at the hearing was the testimony of a former SII worker, who related that the ampoule solutions were mixed in five-gallon jugs, while the simulator solutions were mixed in the same 55-gallon drum "used to make coffee and kool-aid."

The court concluded that the certificates of analysis for the ampoule lots were defective: The lots contained solution from a number of five-gallon batches, and "only those ampoules filled from a single vessel of the chemical solution can properly be included in and labelled as part of the *same* lot for sampling and certification purposes."

An Illinois appellate court affirmed a trial court's granting of a defense motion *in limine* to suppress evidence of a breath test where the administering officer did not observe the defendant for the necessary 20 minutes. *People v. Haney,* 507 N.E.2d 230 (Ill. App. 1987). At the pretrial hearing, the prosecution argued that there was no evidence of anything that occurred during the 20-minute period that would affect the test results. The court held that this was irrelevant, as the reason for the observation period is to "prevent an accused from being subjected to nonconsensual or inaccurate testing procedures by law enforcement officers." 507 N.E.2d at 231. Thus the only issue was whether the officer had or had not kept the defendant under constant surveillance for 20 minutes immediately prior to the breath test, not whether something could have happened during that period to affect the results. See also *State v. Kirn,* 767 P.2d 1238 (Haw. 1989), involving a reversal where no evidence was offered to prove that the officer observed the defendant continuously for 15 minutes prior to the test. And see *People v. Bertsch,* 538 N.E.2d 1306 (Ill. App. 1989), where the officer was unable to observe the defendant consistently for the requisite 20 minutes because he was writing traffic citations.

A Louisiana court reversed a DUI conviction where blood-alcohol evidence was admitted without a proper foundation showing compliance with statutory testing regulations. In *State v. Farleigh,* 490 So. 2d 490 (La. App. 1986), the defendant established during his motion to suppress that the state had failed to follow such required procedures as identifying the person who took the sample, and showing that a replicate sample was taken. The evidence offered by the prosecution only showed that a "Dr. Muller" withdrew the sample; no evidence was offered that he was in fact a doctor or other qualified person. The appellate court held that failure to follow statutory regulations made introduction of the test result error and so prejudicial that the conviction could not stand even in the presence of other evidence of intoxication.

See also *State v. Lindsey,* 524 So. 2d 253 (La. App. 1988), where another Louisiana appellate court reversed and remanded a DUI conviction for failure of the prosecution to lay a sufficient foundation for a blood test. In doing so, the court referred to the recent Louisiana Supreme Court decision in *State v. Rowell,* 517 So. 2d 799 (La. 1988):

> [I]n order for the prosecution to utilize the statutory presumption of intoxication arising from the chemical analysis of a defendant's blood pursuant to (statute), it must show that the State has promulgated detailed procedures which will ensure the integrity and reliability of the chemical test and also that the State has *strictly complied* with the promulgated procedures. [524 So. 2d at 254 (emphasis added).]

The Supreme Court of Pennsylvania has reversed a drunk driving conviction and discharged the defendant where evidence of his blood-alcohol level was obtained through the use of a Breathalyzer Model 1000. *Commonwealth v. McGinnis,* 515 A.2d 847 (Pa. 1986). Although the Model 1000 was specifically approved for use under the regulatory statute, the actual machine used on the defendant had been modified — and neither the modification nor the modified version had been approved. See also *State v. Polak,* 598 So. 2d 150 (Fla. App. 1992), where an appellate court affirmed the suppression of a defendant's Intoximeter 3000 test results on the grounds that bypassing the machine's acetone detector constituted a "substantial modification" — and thus required recertification before test results would be admissible.

A Texas court reversed a DUI conviction where a blood sample had been withdrawn from the defendant by a nurse in a first aid room at a "justice center": The relevant statute required that the "sample must be taken by a physician or in a physician's office or a hospital licensed by the Texas Department of Health." *Turner v. State,* 734 S.W.2d 186 (Tex. App. 1987). And in *Greaves v. North Dakota State Highway Commissioner,* 432 N.W.2d 879 (N.D. 1988), a license revocation was vacated where a police officer withdrew a blood sample from the suspect; although the officer was an "emergency medical technician," the court held that the arrest was not a "medical emergency" and so he was not qualified to take a sample.

In *Gulley v. State,* 501 So. 2d 1388 (Fla. App. 1987), a defendant was charged with manslaughter and vehicular homicide after a blood sample, taken with his consent at a hospital, was analyzed at .117 percent. He moved to suppress the results before trial, claiming that the state had failed to comply with Florida's blood-alcohol regulatory statutes in that (1) the blood had not been drawn by authorized persons, and (2) the vial had not contained an acceptable anticoagulant. He renewed his attack during trial, adding a third grounds to his objection: The analysis was conducted by an individual who was not properly licensed. On appeal, the convictions were reversed on the grounds that such violations render the test results inadmissible; error in admitting the results along with expert testimony was prejudicial and required a new trial.

The fact that the laboratory where a blood sample was analyzed was duly licensed does not necessarily satisfy the foundational requirements for admissibility. In *People v. Campbell,* 539 N.E.2d 584 (N.Y. App. 1989), the court affirmed reversals of convictions where the prosecution had failed to establish that the *method* of analysis (the laboratory used the DuPont Automatic Clinical Analyzer) was reliable.

In *State v. Franks,* 360 S.E.2d 473 (N.C. App. 1987), the prosecution offered nothing more than the testimony of the officer who administered a breath test to the defendant that he was certified to operate the machine: No independent evidence of his certification was presented. The court reversed the conviction, holding that evidence of the test was inadmissible absent compliance with the regulatory statute, which included a requirement that operators be certified.

In *State v. Lambert,* 594 N.E.2d 1112 (Ohio App. 1991), an appellate court reversed a DUI conviction on the grounds that the breath-machine operator had not been checked periodically for proficiency.

In that case, the defendant was arrested and given a breath test on a BAC Verifier by a local police officer. As in many states, Ohio law required quasi-expert supervision — that is, that the test be "performed by a senior operator or an operator who is under the general direction of a senior operator." A lieutenant with the Ohio State Highway Patrol testified that he had performed a calibration test on the machine at the police station four days before it was used on the defendant; he had not, however, controlled or directed the activities of the local police in the administration of tests. At trial, the defendant's motion to suppress the test results for lack of foundation was denied.

The appellate court reversed, holding that the role of senior operators in assuring accuracy required their periodic presence at the police station to test the machine *and to check the performance of the operators.*

Finally, the court rejected the usual argument that there had been "substantial compliance" with foundational requirements, noting that there appeared to be no realistic or human impediments to full compliance with the senior operator regulation.

What is the prosecution's *burden of proof* for establishing a sufficient foundation for admissibility of chemical test results? In the case of *People v. Sesman,* 521 N.Y.S.2d 626 (1987), the applicable statute required the breath test to be administered within two hours after arrest. The records showed the arrest at 8:20 P.M. and the test at 10:19 P.M.; accordingly, the trial court denied defendant's motion to suppress. On appeal, however, the appellate court reviewed the factual basis for the two times and concluded that they were merely approximations. Thus the issue arose: What is the burden of proof?

After considerable analysis, the court concluded that the standard was proof *beyond a reasonable doubt.* Finding that the approximations of time did not meet such a standard, the court granted the defendant's motion. See also *Atkinson v. State,* 871 S.W.2d 252 (Tex. Ct. App. 1994), holding that it was reversible error to refuse a defense instruction that the breath test result could be considered only if the jury found that the officer complied with testing regulation *beyond a reasonable doubt.*

Many courts today, however, will hold that the failure of the prosecution to satisfy all the demands of the chemical testing laws goes only to the weight of the evidence, not to its admissibility. In other words, the defense is free to produce evidence for the jury that all statutory requirements were not met. In such cases, the exclusion argument should still be made, for appellate reasons if for no other. More important, counsel should ask the court for specific instructions to be given to the jury setting forth the applicable law and advising them of their right to reject the chemical test results should they find them to be unreliable due to procedural noncompliance.

Additionally, counsel should argue that a jury instruction concerning the legal presumption of intoxication should *not* be given. In *Briscoe v. State,* 479 A.2d 1385 (Md. App. 1984), a Maryland appellate court reversed convictions for DUI and manslaughter:

In the case before us, there was evidence that Briscoe's blood, tested as a result of standard medical procedures and not pursuant to §§10-302–10-306, had an alcohol content of .27. A doctor testified that a person with that much alcohol in his blood would be "pretty drunk." There was other evidence tending to show Briscoe's intoxication. Had this evidence and other evidence presented gone to the jury under normal instructions, Briscoe would have little to argue on appeal. That, however, did not occur. In the face of a timely objection, the trial judge read to the jury §10-307, including subsection (e) which provides

> If at the time of testing there was in the person's blood 0.13 percent or more of weight of alcohol, as determined by an analysis of the person's blood or breath, it shall be prima facie evidence that the defendant was intoxicated.

This instruction, which the State concedes should not have been given, plainly told the jury that they could indulge in a prima facie inference that Briscoe was intoxicated. The statutory "prima facie evidence" language is, of course, addressed to the trial judge. It tells him, in effect, that if certain evidence has been introduced (after compliance with the statutory preconditions) there is a case sufficient to go to the jury — a case in which the jury may but is not required to find intoxication. In the case before us, we cannot hold the "prima facie evidence" instruction was not prejudicial so far as the driving while intoxicated charge is concerned. Use of the "prima facie evidence" wording of §10-307(e) might have incorrectly persuaded the jury that this was a statutory presumption, thus requiring Briscoe to rebut it. Further, use of the statutory language might well have bolstered the doctor's credibility in the jury's eyes and could have provided that degree of certainty needed to produce a verdict beyond a reasonable doubt. [Id. at 1386–1387.]

§11.6.9 Lack of Pre-Test Observation Period (Breath)

The following comments are presented with the consent of James Farragher Campbell of San Francisco. For a preliminary discussion of the pre-test observation period in using breath machines, see §6.2.1.

The 15-minute observation period, which is mandated under most states' laws, is an often overlooked, but a critical point of attack on the breath test results.

As in all matters of criminal defense, you have to start with a detailed analysis of the arrest report, as well as any other reports that will provide any information or documentation on the event. Never overlook the obvious. Was the 15-minute period of observation followed? In many situations the observation period just isn't followed by the arresting/testing officer. And in many more situations than you would think, it is possible to show the jury that the 15-minute observation period was not followed.

It is also noteworthy to mention that the attack on the credibility of the arresting/testing officer will also go hand-in-hand with other areas of attack, such as the roadside field tests, the driving observations, and/or the officer's personal observations of those ever-present "objective signs of intoxication." Defense counsel should be aware however that it is your author's opinion that it is not often wise to attack every and any area of the arresting officer's testimony, you should select only those that are essential to your defense. And as a result, failure if any for the 15-minute observation period should be assessed just as any other part of the overall tactic in the defense case. Where warranted however, it is hoped that the following materials, as supplemented and expanded through the oral class presentation, will be of assistance to you in defending your clients when the 15-minute observation period is in issue.

The following may be illustrative of the cross of the arresting/operating officer on the importance of the 15-minute waiting period:

Q. Officer you have received extensive training in the actual theory and proper administration of the intoxilyzer?

A. Yes I have.

Q. How many hours do you think you have spent in training as well as actual hands on application for the proper administration of the intoxilyzer text?

A. Oh, I would say probably about 12 hours in both classroom training and actual use of the instrument before I was certified to operate it.

Q. I see that you refer to the intoxilyzer as an "instrument." I guess this means that it is something more than just another electrical machine that all of us use and operate in our daily lives?

A. Yes, it's not just another machine. It's not like your VCR or something like that. It really is a scientific instrument.

Q. Well, I also suspect that is why you had to receive such extensive training before you could test anyone on this instrument?
A. I am most certain of that.
Q. Tell me, when you were instructed on the use and administration of this instrument, did you receive instruction on the importance of following the checklist in properly administering the test?
A. Yes.
Q. Were you instructed that if the checklist was not followed it would call into question the validity or accuracy of the test itself?
A. Well you have to, you are supposed to follow the checklist. But I don't know if the failure to follow it will make the test bad. I never heard of that.
Q. Officer were you instructed that this checklist was established by the state to ensure that all of the established scientific steps would be met so that the test could be admitted into evidence in a court of law?
A. Yes.
Q. And the State, as well as you in law enforcement, has no interest in introducing evidence which is not reliable?
A. No.
Q. When the State sets out in a statute or your department or the State Department of Health sets out in regulations how these tests should be administered, you would want to follow those regulations wouldn't you?
A. Yes.
Q. These testing procedures that you are to follow are not there just to make the test look legitimate are they?
A. You have to follow the test procedures, yes.
Q. No, officer, I mean these testing rules that you are asked to follow, they are there for a good scientific reason, aren't they? They are not there just so it looks to a jury that you are doing the test very carefully?
A. No, they are not there to impress a jury. We have to follow these procedures to ensure the test is accurate.
Q. Precisely. If you did not observe this defendant for the required 15 minutes that the State, and the entire body of scientists who have studied and prepared the testing procedure, then don't you think that your test result might not be valid?
A. I don't think that is going to matter all that much, because I did not see anything prior to the test that could or would cause a problem with the test.

Q. Even though the great body of scientific wisdom in this field is to the contrary?
A. That's right, counsel.

And, of course, in your summation you could point out to the jury that the state's primary goal is not to just go through the motions and try to make the testing process look good, but to actually ensure a reliable and accurate test result. Whether the effective checks are implemented calls into serious question the reliability of the test results themselves.

DISCOVERY

Remember, you cannot go to war without weapons. You will locate and collect these weapons through the discovery process, your own investigation, and hard work.

The first point of the discovery process is to review, review, and review the arresting officer's report. Do not just read it and think you know what is said. Often things hide and will only be discovered after careful reading and thinking through the report.

One of the most important facts in the report for purposes of the breath test administration is the time frame in which all of this took place. Often the police officer is involved in other activities during the testing process. He or she may be writing the arrest report, covering other business at the jail, or simply not paying attention to the actual time during which the breath test is being completed. This information can be a welcome seed-bed of hope for cross-examination material. Think of the obvious things that can or should take place at the station and which follow the "routine of human nature" as opposed to the stilted routine that the cop would like the jury to think they follow.

SLOPE DETECTOR

The so called "slope detector" should be addressed and debunked. The concept of the slope detector sounds good in theory, but like a lot of other things in the DUI world, things are not what they always appear to be.

As we all have learned, the application of Henry's Law to breath testing is critically dependent upon the sampling of deep lung or medically proper alveolar air. (The air from the lung coming from the alveolar region of the lungs where the tiny alveolar air sacks come into contact with the blood.) This air then allows the mandated average breath/blood ratio of 2100 to 1 to kick in and, in turn, lets the preprogrammed formula in the intoxilyzer compute blood-alcohol levels. Remember, the intoxliyzer assumes that the sample delivered to its sample chamber is alveolar in nature, but the machine does not ensure deep lung air sampling. Therein lies the problem.

The Intoxilyzer Model 5000 (and even the older models 4011A and 4011AW) has a slope detector. This slope detector — or slope "detective" as I sometimes call it — is supposed to tell the operator if mouth alcohol has entered the sample chamber and is being tested instead of the deep lung/alveolar air mentioned above. There are, however, a couple of problems.

When an arrestee, the suspected drunk driver, blows into the intoxilyzer and that driver does in fact have alcohol in his or her blood, and no extra alcohol in his or her mouth, and exhales, the breath-alcohol concentration continues to increase during the exhalation. The alcohol content reading does not reach a "plateau" until the end of the airflow, it will continue to rise and show a positive upward slope. If the testee has no alcohol in the blood, but does have mouth alcohol, which can come from any number of sources, the breath alcohol concentration will rise until a peak is reached, which is usually about ⅓ of the way into the breath exhalation, and then the slope will decline gradually. It is this declining breath-alcohol concentration that triggers the "slope detector" to indicate that the subject is blowing mouth alcohol instead of alveolar air.

However, the problem is that when the testee blowing into the intoxilyzer has alcohol in the blood as well as the mouth, then the normal rising breath-alcohol curve will add to the declining mouth-alcohol curve to produce what is quite often a level curve; therefore, the "slope detective" is unable to detect the presence of the mouth alcohol, and the blood alcohol will register much higher than it should.

Also of special note is the simple fact that when the "slope detector" is checked in those places where the state wants to at least pretend it is trying to be fair, it is never done with alcohol in the blood. It is always checked with a simulation of mouth alcohol. Not mouth and blood alcohol.

Also to be mentioned is that in California, as may be the case in other jurisdictions as well, the Intoxilyzer Model 5000 does not note a deficient sample and record the highest BAC score as called for in the operator's manual. Instead, machines purchased in California by the Department of Justice have been modified so that the allowable parameters have been increased before a printout is aborted. The subject's BAC is allowed to climb as much as 0.04 percent for each 0.6 of a second, or to decrease by 0.002 percent. Furthermore, and most importantly, these machines will not usually provide a printout of the highest BAC obtained, unless there is a 0.02 percent agreement between two consecutive tests. In my opinion this can result in two mouth-alcohol test readings viewed as acceptable under California law.

§11.6.10 Denial of Independent Sample

Where the client has been denied an opportunity to obtain a sample of blood or urine for independent analysis, counsel should consider appropriate remedies. This assumes, of course, that the jurisdiction recognizes the right to an independent test, either by statute or case law. Remedies may include suppression of the prosecution's own blood-alcohol evidence — if it exists — or, in appropriate cases, dismissal of charges.

Thus, for example, in *State v. George,* 754 P.2d 460 (Kan.App. 1988), the defendant moved to suppress the state's breath test on the grounds that the officer refused his request for an independent blood test. Asked one hour after the breath test had been administered, the officer had replied that the defendant would have to be taken to a hospital, a lab technician or doctor would have to be found, and the test would end up being taken over two hours after the driving. A state statute provided that an arrestee "shall have a reasonable opportunity to have an additional test by a physician of the person's own choosing." Was the defendant's request here "reasonable"? In reversing the conviction and remanding, the appellate court held that inconvenience to the officer is no excuse, that the defendant's delayed request was nevertheless "reasonable," and the officer's refusal "impaired George's ability to procure probative evidence and to prepare a defense."

A Michigan appellate court reversed a drunk driving conviction and dismissed the charge where the arresting officers talked the defendant out of his request for a second chemical test. In *People v. Underwood,* 396 N.W.2d 443 (Mich. App. 1986), the defendant asserted his statutory right to have a second chemical test administered. He eventually withdrew his request when the arresting officers told him that "the test was silly and stupid, that the test would show a higher blood alcohol level, and that the defendant was going to jail anyway.'' On appeal, the court reasoned that ''respect for the statutory right should be given willingly, and not reluctantly. Although defendant was eventually persuaded by the officers' remarks, he was deprived of an opportunity to obtain exculpatory evidence by an independent test.'' 396 N.W.2d 444.

See also *State v. Durkee,* 584 So. 2d 1080 (Fla. App. 1991), where the court considered two consolidated cases in which DUI suspects were denied the opportunity to obtain independent blood samples. In one case, the defendant refused to take a breath test unless he was also permitted to obtain a blood test; in the other, he demanded an independent blood test both before and after submitting to breath testing. The appellate court concluded that there was a right to an independent test and that the proper sanction for denial of this right was suppression of the breath test evidence.

Even if a drunk driving suspect refuses to submit to a chemical test, he may still have a due process right to an independent test. See, e.g., *Snyder v. State* (Alaska 1996) 930 P.2d 1274.

Where the suspect has a right to an independent test, this right assumes that the police will assist him to the extent necessary to facilitate the testing. In *New York v. Batista,* 491 N.Y.S.2d 966 (N.Y. 1985), for example, the defendant asked soon after her arrest, ''Well, can I take my blood test?'' The officer replied, ''No, we don't do the blood test for you.'' No further discussions took place concerning an independent test. On appeal, the state argued, first, that this question did not sufficiently constitute a demand for independent testing. The appellate court rejected this position. The state's second argument was that the police were not obligated to make the arrangements for testing for her: She could have used her right to make a telephone call to arrange for such a test. The court rejected this as well, saying that ''[i]t seems most unlikely that a defendant, no matter how sophisticated, could arrange for the appropriate medical personnel to appear where she was being held to administer the test within two hours of her arrest.'' See also *State v. Karmen,* 554 A.2d 670 (Vt. 1988). See also *Lockard v. Town of Killen,* 565 So. 2d 679 (Ala. 1990), holding that police have a duty to transport an arrestee to a place where an independent test can be administered.

In *State v. McNichols,* 884 P.2d 620 (Wash. App. 1994), the defendant requested a blood test 15 minutes after taking the required breath test. The jailors did not administer such a test, nor did they advise him that he could use the phone and arrange for someone to come to the jail to administer one. By the time the defendant was finally booked and released, it had been three hours since the breath test. The appellate court reversed the conviction: the jailors had a duty to inform the defendant that "[t]hey were not required to help him obtain the test, but [that] he could have someone come to the jail to administer a test and he could use the telephones to make necessary arrangements if that is what he wanted." Further, the court said, suppression of the breath test was an insufficient remedy. Reversal and dismissal of charges was required: Merely suppressing the evidence would not eliminate the prejudice because a favorable independent blood test result could help the defendant prove his innocence.

A Georgia appellate court has held that the police must assist a defendant in contacting his family doctor for an independent test. In *State v. White,* 373 S.E.2d 840 (Ga. App. 1988), the defendant requested an independent blood test and gave the arresting officer the name of his physician; he could not, however, recall the doctor's address or telephone number. He was then taken to jail where he submitted to a breath test; no independent test was ever given. At trial, the breath test was suppressed after the officer admitted that the defendant was not given a chance to find the doctor's address or phone number. The appellate court sustained this ruling, noting that "the officers did not even permit him to make the necessary arrangements to take the desired test by denying him access to information which would have provided the telephone number and/or address of his personal physician." Id. at 841–842.

Another Georgia appellate court has upheld the exclusion of a .27 percent breath test given the defendant on the grounds that he was denied an independent blood sample. In *State v. Buffington,* 377 S.E.2d 548 (Ga. App. 1989), the arresting officer administered a breath test to the defendant, then took him to a hospital for withdrawal of the requested sample. Unfortunately, the defendant did not have enough cash to pay for the test. Rather than permit him to negotiate with the hospital or call nearby relatives for money, however, the officer simply returned him to the police station.

For a similar Georgia case involving an officer's refusal to permit a defendant to obtain correct change to pay for a test, see *Gordon v. State,* 378 S.E.2d 362 (Ga. App. 1989). See also *Brady v. City of Lawrenceville,* 425 S.E.2d 404 (Ga. App. 1992), in which the court reversed a DWI conviction after the trial judge failed to suppress the state's blood-alcohol evidence. The defense had asked for the suppression as a sanction for the arresting officer's failure to wait half an hour for the defendant to make financial arrangements for an independent blood test.

In *State v. Hicks,* 550 A.2d 512 (N.J. Super. 1988), the arresting officer refused to permit the defendant to make a phone call from the scene of his accident. On appeal, the court held:

> If defendant did, in fact, request an opportunity to make a telephone call so that he could, through his wife or directly, seek legal or medical advice concerning the conduct of an independent examination, or to arrange for same, defendant should be able to challenge the admission of the breathalyzer examinations. [Id. at 515.]

In *Ward v. State,* 758 P.2d 87 (Alaska 1988), the arrested defendant asked for an independent blood test to be taken at the Alaska Native Medical Center. The officer refused, explaining that the state had no contract for blood testing with that facility. He offered to take the defendant to another facility, but the defendant refused.

At trial, the defendant moved to suppress the state's Intoximeter test on the grounds that he was denied his statutory right to an independent test. The motion was denied. On appeal, the Supreme Court of Alaska reversed, noting that the statutory language gave every arrestee the right to an independent test by qualified personnel "of a person's own choosing" — and that the existence of a state contract was irrelevant.

What if the police permit an independent blood sample to be taken but then fail to refrigerate it so that the sample becomes invalid for analysis? In *Montana v. Swanson,* 722 P.2d 155 (Mont. 1986), the defendant refused to take a breath test after being properly advised under the state's implied consent law. However, he said he would submit to a blood test. The officer explained that this would be done at his expense and took him to a hospital, where a sample was withdrawn. The defendant was then taken back to the police station with the sample and booked. Despite a label on the sample reading "Keep refrigerated," the sample was taken from the defendant during booking and placed on a counter in the booking room; it remained there for two days before it was finally placed in a refrigerator. At trial, the defendant's motion for dismissal for denial of his due process right to gather exculpatory evidence was denied.

On appeal to the Supreme Court of Montana, the prosecution argued that the statutory right to an independent test arose only after the defendant had taken the test offered by the officer; since he refused, there was no right. The court rejected this argument, holding that the right was not conditional.

The prosecution next argued that it was the defendant's obligation to see that the sample was properly cared for. Again, the court disagreed: "Once the sample was taken from Swanson, the police had a duty to see to its safekeeping. The sample should have been refrigerated. . . . This careless handling of the sample deprived Swanson of his due process right to gather possibly exculpating evidence."

The Supreme Court of Montana subsequently reaffirmed its holding that a refusal to submit to testing does not eliminate the right of the arrestee to an independent test. In *State & City of Bozeman v. Peterson,* 739 P.2d 958 (Mont. 1986), the defendant refused to take a breath test and was subsequently denied his request for a blood sample. The court reasoned that the right to an independent test did not depend on compliance with the implied consent law: "[T]he purpose of the rule is to assure a defendant's due process right to obtain exculpatory evidence." 739 P.2d at 961.

For a further discussion of the right to an independent test and related issues, see §10.1.2.

§11.6.11 Noncompliance with Discovery

After a study of the relevant law in his jurisdiction, counsel should argue that due process considerations dictate that all evidence possibly affecting the validity of the blood, urine, or breath test must be produced for the defendant's examination. Prosecutorial failure to comply with an order granting such discovery should constitute grounds for a suppression of the blood-alcohol evidence.

In the case of *People v. Corley,* 507 N.Y.S.2d 491 (N.Y. 1986), for example, the Supreme Court of New York; Appellate Division, reversed convictions for both driving under the influence and driving with a BAC level of .10 percent, because of failure to comply with discovery. The defendant had demanded production of any written "reports or documents" associated with the tests; the prosecution responded by supplying only the test results. Five minutes before trial, defense counsel was handed additional information relevant to evidence required for laying a proper foundation for admission of evidence of the Breathalyzer results. Defense counsel moved to suppress the test results or, in the alternative, for a continuance; both motions were denied. On appeal, the court held that the defendant's request was not too broadly worded and that the prosecution had failed to comply. This failure was not deemed harmless: The documents would have been useful to the defense on the issues of both admissibility and credibility of the test results. Since the per se count (driving with a BAC level of .10 percent) depended entirely on this evidence, this was reversed; and, as it was impossible to determine the impact of the test results on the second (DUI) verdict, this count was also reversed and remanded for new trial.

Counsel is often confronted with a prosecutor or court that requires the defense to assume the almost impossible task of tracking down which bureaucratic governmental agency has which discovery materials or information. On this issue, a Missouri appellate court has made it clear that the burden is on the state, not on the defendant. In *State v. McNeary,* 721 S.W.2d 168 (Mo. App. 1986), defense counsel sent a letter to the arresting officer requesting information concerning the type of testing device used, the testing and accuracy of the machine, the qualifications of the operator, and the procedures used in testing. The officer called the attorney and answered questions "to the best of his knowledge"; he sent him a copy of the ticket and a "Breathalyzer Operational Checklist." On appeal, the court found that although the officer did not have sufficient knowledge, the requested information had been sent to the Department of Health and to the prosecutor's office. In ruling that the state's discovery statute had not been complied with and thus admission of test evidence was error, the court reversed and remanded: "[I]n this case the relevant and necessary information had been requested but not supplied. It is not the duty of the driver to figure out which agency has the information — the duty is upon the state, when properly requested, to supply the information."

In a similar vein, a New Jersey court held that the State could not "atomize itself into hundreds of totally independent agencies" and thus claim that discovery material was not available to it. In *State v. Tull,* 560 A.2d 1331 (N.J. Super. 1989), the court held that any relevant material held by another agency of the state was in the "constructive possession" of the prosecuting agency: "(A) prosecutor may not refuse a discovery demand simply because the information or materials are not in the municipal offices or within easy reach."

Counsel has a stronger argument for suppression, of course, where the case involves the loss or destruction of a blood or urine sample. Nevertheless, the trend of recent appellate decisions appears to be to impose on the defendant the almost impossible burden of proving "bad faith" in the destruction or loss. Thus, for example, the Nevada Supreme Court has refused to affirm a trial court's dismissal of drunk driving charges where the police stored the defendant's blood sample for about a year and finally destroyed it to make room for new samples before he could have an independent test conducted. *State v. Hall,* 768 P.2d 349 (Nev. 1989). In its decision, the court referred to *Trombetta,* then quoted from *Arizona v. Youngblood,* 488 U.S. 51, 109 S. Ct. 333, 337, 102 L. Ed. 2d 281 (1988), to the effect that "unless a criminal defendant can show bad faith on the part of the police, failure to preserve potentially useful evidence does not constitute a denial of due process of law."

Where the blood sample still exists, of course, the defendant clearly has the right to access — even if the sample is an old one. Thus, for example, in *People v. Karpeles,* 549 N.Y.S.2d 903 (1989), the prosecution's argument that the passage of seven months since withdrawal of the sample rendered it useless for testing was rejected: The defendant's right to discovery of the sample is absolute.

Certainly, the United States Supreme Court's development of the law on preservation of evidence has proved confusing and contradictory. At the risk of oversimplification, however, the following analytical approach may prove helpful to the DUI practitioner:

1. The evidence (reports, tapes, blood-alcohol sample, etc.) is *in the possession* of the police:
   a. If it is *material to the issue of guilt,* it must be produced on request. *Brady v. Maryland,* 373 U.S. 83, S. Ct. 1194, 10 L. Ed. 2d 215 (1963).
   b. If the evidence is *exculpatory,* it must be produced even *without* any request. *United States v. Agurs,* 427 U.S. 97, 96 S. Ct. 2392, 49 L. Ed. 2d 342 (1976).
2. The evidence is *not* in the possession of the police, but *was* at one time:
   a. If it had an *exculpatory value*— that is, it could have played a significant role for the defense — that was apparent at the time of its destruction, then that destruction constitutes a violation of due process. *California v. Trombetta,* 467 U.S. 479, 104 S. Ct. 2528, 81 L. Ed. 2d 413.
   b. If it was "*potentially useful*" evidence, but short of the exculpatory potential discussed in *Trombetta,* then due process is violated only if it was destroyed in *bad faith. Arizona v. Youngblood,* 488 U.S. 51, 109 S. Ct. 333, 102 L. Ed. 2d 281 (1988).

§11.6.12 Chain of Custody

As a part of the foundation for introduction into evidence of the results of any blood-alcohol test, the prosecution must establish a complete chain of evidence. In other words, the prosecutor must be able to trace, through competent evidence, exactly where the chemical sample was at all times, from when it was extracted from the defendant to the moment it was finally analyzed; in some instances, as, for example, with pre-trial discovery, the chain must be extended into the present. In addition to having to prove where the sample was, the prosecutor also will probably have to show in whose custody it was at all times and that it was properly labeled and stored. He must negate the possibilities that it was in an unidentifiable individual's control at any point in time and that the sample was misplaced or exchanged mistakenly for another sample. In short, the prosecution must clearly establish that the sample taken from the defendant was the one analyzed and could not have been tampered with.

This is the law that applies to all physical evidence in a criminal case. And, as with many such laws, the attitude of many courts has been to require only "substantial compliance" when dealing with a drunk driving case. Thus in *People v. Pack,* 199 Cal. App. 2d 857, 19 Cal. Rptr. 186 (1962), where there was no showing of custody from the time the laboratory received a vial of blood to the time it was placed in a refrigerator, the court simply inferred it was placed there by a laboratory technician. And in *State v. Fornier,* 167 A.2d 56 (N.H. 1961), neither the police officer nor the physician who withdrew the blood could identify the vial, and there was no evidence of how the vial of blood got from the police station to the laboratory; the court simply held that it was "not necessary that each evidentiary fact relied upon by the State be established beyond a reasonable doubt."

A regulatory approach to the effect of a gap in the chain of custody was shown in *Montana v. McDonald,* 697 P.2d 1328 (Mont. 1985), where the Montana Supreme Court addressed the question of whether a "missing link" in the chain of custody rendered the test results inadmissible or simply affected the weight to be given that evidence. After reviewing the state's administrative requirements for blood-alcohol testing, the Court concluded that test results obtained without compliance with such requirements relating to chain of custody were inadmissible, and remanded the case for new trial.

Certainly counsel should always object to admission of the test results without a complete showing of chain of custody, if only to establish a record for appeal. Usually a number of individuals have handled the sample in question, among them the arresting officer, the medical technician or physician, the transporting officer, the individual in charge of evidence at the laboratory, and/or the laboratory technician or chemist. Counsel should insist on the testimony of each such individual or at least the testimony of a witness to the custody of the sample by the individual.

In addition to testimony of custody, the prosecution should be required to show that an accepted means of labeling the sample was used. Again, each jurisdiction varies in its requirements as to the labeling of evidence, and counsel should be familiar with them. Generally, however, the sample should have been labeled by the person who took the sample and at the time the sample was taken and placed in its container.

In *State v. Nygaard,* 426 N.W.2d 547 (N.D. 1988), the defendant objected to the introduction of a blood test on the grounds that the officer did not "seal the vial with one layer of tape and label the vial with the name of the subject and the arresting officer" as required on the prescribed form. The objection was overruled. On appeal, the Supreme Court of North Dakota reversed and remanded for this failure to establish a satisfactory chain of custody.

Similarly, the Supreme Court of South Carolina reversed a DUI conviction on the grounds that the chain of custody of the defendant's blood sample was defective:

> Here, no one present in the emergency room (E/R) could identify the person who sealed and labeled the blood with Williams' patient number. Additionally, although the blood sample was received in the laboratory, neither the E/R nor laboratory personnel could recall by whom it was transported. Moreover, Williams' E/R record was initially mislabeled as that of (another patient). [*State v. Williams,* 392 S.E.2d 181, 182 (S.C. 1990).]

Technically, a break in the chain of custody can occur any time the sample is stored in a location that is accessible to individuals who are not custodians of the sample. Thus, for example, a court has held that blood-alcohol evidence was inadmissible where the vial of blood was taken home by an officer, kept in his refrigerator overnight, and then mailed to the laboratory for analysis. *People v. Sansalone,* 208 Misc. 491, 146 N.Y.S.2d 359 (1955). And where a blood sample was kept in an unlocked refrigerator for 12 days in the hospital where the blood was withdrawn, the court held the results inadmissible. *People v. Pfendler,* 29 Misc. 2d 991, 212 N.Y.S.2d 927 (1961); but see *Patterson v. State,* 160 S.E.2d 815 (Ga. 1968).

Whether placing a sample in the mails is an acceptable part

of the chain of custody is another subject of considerable disagreement. Certainly, the practice of mailing blood or urine samples from the police station to a distant laboratory is a common one. Generally, the results will be admitted if the individuals who mailed and received the sample in the mail can testify to their control and the details of the mailing. See, e.g., *Abrego v. State,* 248 S.W.2d 490 (Tex. Crim. App. 1952).) Some courts have required a showing that the sample was sent by certified or registered mail, while others have invoked a presumption that articles entering the United States Postal Service will be delivered in the same condition.

The following argument for suppression of blood-alcohol evidence for failure to establish a satisfactory chain of custody of a blood sample has been used successfully by Don Nichols and Jim Kaster of Minneapolis:

THE STATE FAILED TO ESTABLISH A COMPLETE CHAIN OF CUSTODY

Before the evidence such as the results of the blood sample taken in this case may be admitted into evidence, the party seeking to have the evidence admitted must establish a complete chain of custody. It is hornbook law that to establish a "chain of custody" there must be a "testimonial tracing . . . of the item with sufficient completeness to render it improbable that the original item has been either exchanged with another or been contaminated or tampered with." McCormick on Evidence at 528 (2d ed. 1972).

This issue has been discussed numerous times in many courts and has been repeatedly upheld. In the case of *Bauer v. Veith,* 130 N.W.2d 897 (Mich. 1967), the Michigan Supreme Court stated that:

> Where it "appears that the various steps in keeping and transportation" of the specimen, part, or object from the time it was taken from the body until the time of the analysis "were not traced or shown by the evidence" the identification of the thing analyzed is insufficient and the presumptions that the official duty is properly performed and that public records are correct will not supply missing links in the chain. [130 N.W.2d at 899 (quoting Annot., 21 A.L.R.2d 1216, 1220).]

Likewise, in *Williams v. District Court,* 195 N.W. 594 (Iowa 1923), the court stated:

> We have held that, in order that proof may be admitted of the contents of a bottle or package, claimed to have been taken from a defendant, it is necessary to establish a complete chain of evidence tracing the possession of the exhibit from the defendant to the final custodian, and if one link in the chain is entirely missing, the exhibit can not be introduced into evidence. [195 N.W. at 595.]

In the present case, there is no evidence to account for the blood sample between the time Officer Beltrand placed it in the refrigerator at the St. Louis Park Police Department on 25 September 1978 and the time when it was received by Mr. Engman, the chemist at the BCA. The testimony also indicated that the refrigerator was unlocked and that any number of people had access to it. Clearly, the chain of custody in the present case is not complete. During the above-mentioned period, any number of persons may have handled the blood sample and tampered with its contents.

In *State v. Foster,* 422 P.2d 964 (Kansas 1967), the Supreme Court of Kansas held that if a blood sample is placed in the mail, the chain of evidence is broken and it may not be introduced into evidence:

> In this case the chain of evidence connecting the defendant with the blood sample breaks with the posting of the sample by Trooper Wiltse. However likely the facts are as claimed by the State, the abstract is void of evidence to prove it. [422 P.2d at 969.]

Similarly, in this case, the state offered no evidence other than the fact that the arresting officer placed the blood sample in a refrigerator in the St. Louis Park Police Station.

Because the state failed to establish a chain of custody as required by the law of evidence, the respondent has objected to admission of any evidence relating to the blood sample.

Checklist 21 Suppressing Blood-Alcohol Evidence

- ☐ Did the officer have probable cause to stop, detain, and arrest the client?
- ☐ Was the client in fact under arrest at the time of the chemical test?
  - ☐ Did the officer have legal authority to make an arrest under the circumstances?
- ☐ Did the client consent to testing?
  - ☐ Was he given the correct implied consent admonishment?
  - ☐ Was the consent obtained through coercion?
  - ☐ Is there any independent evidence of the consent?

- ☐ Did the client have a right to a choice of tests?
  - ☐ Was he advised of this right?
- ☐ Was the client denied access to counsel before submitting to a test?
- ☐ Was a blood sample obtained through excessive force?
- ☐ Was the client denied an opportunity to have an independent blood-alcohol test?
  - ☐ Did the officer advise him of this right?
  - ☐ Did the officer assist or offer to assist in obtaining the independent sample?
- ☐ Can the prosecution establish a sufficient foundation for the introduction of the blood-alcohol evidence?
  - ☐ Have the statutory regulations for blood-alcohol analysis been complied with?
  - ☐ Is the laboratory properly licensed?
  - ☐ Was the officer conducting the breath test adequately trained and certified?
  - ☐ Was the client under constant observation for 15 to 20 minutes prior to the breath test?
  - ☐ Was the sample obtained and analyzed within the required time limits?
- ☐ Is there a sufficient chain of custody for the blood or urine sample?
- ☐ Is there a physician-patient privilege or other legal block to disclosure?
- ☐ Has the prosecution complied with discovery?
  - ☐ Is the blood or urine sample available for re-analysis?

IV

TRIAL

Furthermore they utterlie exclude and banishe all attorneies, proctours and sergeants at the lawe; whiche craftelly dispute of the lawes. . . . So shall there be lesse circumstance of wordes, and the trueth shal soner come to light. . . .

SIR THOMAS MORE
UTOPIA

12

SETTING THE STAGE

§12.0 *Jury Selection*

> I'm no idealist to believe firmly in the integrity of our courts and in the jury system — that is no ideal to me, it is a living, working reality. Gentlemen, a court is no better than each man of you sitting before me on this jury. A court is only as sound as its jury, and a jury is only as sound as the men who make it up.
>
> HARPER LEE
> *To Kill a Mockingbird*

Perhaps the most critical phase of a drunk driving jury trial — or, for that matter, of any jury trial — is the selection of the men and women who will serve on the jury. It is all too common for attorneys to minimize the importance of this stage of the trial, to ask simply a few cursory questions of the veniremen, and to accept any juror who does not belong to a temperance organization. This is a crucial mistake, for no matter what evidence will be produced and what brilliant arguments made, much of the outcome is predetermined by the character of the 12 individuals who have been selected to decide the case.

Ideally, voir dire examination of prospective jurors should serve four basic purposes: detection of any blatant prejudices that would serve to disqualify a juror for cause; determination of less obvious attitudes that, while not legally sufficient to justify a challenge for cause, will give reason to exercise a peremptory challenge; pre-instruction of the jury as to key facts and law in a light favorable to the defense; and establishing a general rapport between defense counsel and the jurors. Of course, the technical purpose for voir dire is simply to isolate prejudices that would justify a challenge; in some jurisdictions, questioning may be limited to exercising challenges for cause only. Nevertheless, a competent trial attorney will conduct his examination in a way to accomplish all four goals. Obviously, in those few jurisdictions in which the trial judge reserves voir dire exclusively to himself, counsel will be unable to accomplish his purposes. Even in such a situation, however, the judge may be receptive to written questions submitted by counsel to be posed to potential jurors by the judge.

Voir dire examination is, of course, a subject about which an entire volume could be written. For the purposes of this discussion, only the most important aspects, as they apply to a drunk driving case, will be covered.

The first area gone into during voir dire is the general background of the potential juror or jurors. This phase of the questioning will often be conducted by the judge or perhaps will be elicited by the juror replying aloud to a series of form questions written on a blackboard next to the jury box. Each lawyer has his own personal theories and prejudices about the general type of juror he wants or does not want. Many good criminal defense lawyers will prefer younger jurors, members of minority racial and ethnic groups, and city dwellers. Prosecutors, on the other hand, tend to select older citizens, ex-military men, Anglo-Nordics and Asians, and small-town or country dwellers.

A survey reported in an article entitled Driving Under the Influence; California Public Opinion, 1981, 3 Abstracts & Reviews in Alcohol and Driving 3 (July 1982), may provide some answers to the question of what type of person would make the best juror in a drinking/driving case. The article was written by Sally Davis, who is the director of the California Department of Alcohol and Drug Programs.

One important question addressed by the survey is what type of person is most likely to consume too much alcohol and then drive a vehicle. If one accepts the premise that such a person is more likely to be favorable to the defense, then both sides in a drinking/driving case could benefit from examining the results of the survey. From the defense lawyer's perspective, the best juror is male, 18 to 24 years of age, white, a heavy drinker, drives 15,000 or more miles a year, is a high school graduate, and has had three or more accidents in the past five years. From the prosecutor's viewpoint, the best juror is female, over 60 years of age, Asian, an abstainer, and a college graduate who does not drive or who drives but has had no accidents in the past five years.

Doug Cowan of Bellevue, Washington, offers his own insights into what types of individuals generally make the best — and worst — jurors in a drunk driving case:

> Typically, the qualities of sympathetic defense jurors in DWI cases are:
>
> 1. Drinkers who admit to having more than two drinks at one sitting
> 2. Middle to lower class
> 3. Those who appear "underdressed" for a courtroom
> 4. Blue collar workers
> 5. Country music fans
> 6. Rugby, softball, dart, or pool team members (especially with tavern sponsors)
> 7. Smokers
> 8. Overweight persons who drink
> 9. Social, easygoing, happy people
> 10. Individualists
> 11. Those who have contested traffic tickets
> 12. Those who root for the underdog
> 13. Retired noncommissioned military personnel
> 14. Persons distrustful of government
> 15. Beer and bourbon drinkers
> 16. Optimists
> 17. Anyone you instinctively like
>
> Typical qualities of poor defense jurors in DWI cases are:
>
> 1. Nondrinkers and recovering alcoholics
> 2. MADD members and sympathizers
> 3. Up-tight, judgmental, unhappy people
> 4. Physical fitness buffs (non-team sports)
> 5. Those with connections to police or prosecution
> 6. Those with close friends or family members with drinking problems
> 7. Those with experience with accidents involving a drinking driver

8. Computer lovers
9. Engineers and technical types
10. Pessimists
11. Persons in the medical professions
12. Persons employed in the insurance industry
13. Retired military officers
14. Supervisors
15. White wine drinkers
16. Those who never drive after drinking
17. Anyone who you instinctively dislike

Following the general background questioning, the first substantive area for in-depth questioning during voir dire involves the attitude of the prospective juror toward law enforcement officers. A drunk driving trial represents that relatively rare type of case where the guilt or innocence of the defendant depends in large part on the *opinion* of a police officer. The defense will spend most of its time disputing the officer's opinion and trying to offer evidence that he was mistaken or even lying. Therefore it is essential to eliminate any juror who would be biased in favor of the officer. While such an attitude may sometimes be discovered during skillful questioning, it is more common to encounter the juror who will never admit in any way that he would favor one side. This means that the chief means of ferreting out such individuals is to determine which jurors have any kind of connection with law enforcement, either through having been directly employed or otherwise involved with a law enforcement agency or, more commonly, through being related to or close friends with a police officer, probation officer, prosecutor, judge, etc.

Generally speaking, it has been the experience of criminal defense lawyers that a juror with any significant relationship to someone involved in the criminal justice system is going to be prosecution-minded more often than not. This is probably even more true in drunk driving trials than in other criminal cases because of the necessity of directly challenging the opinion or veracity of the arresting officer, and possibly that of the police chemist or criminologist.

The potential jurors should be advised that the officer will be vigorously cross-examined on the stand and that his actions and opinions will be challenged. They should then be asked if they would hold it against the defendant for so attacking the officer; if nothing else, this psychologically prepares the jury for watching an officer being "raked over the coals."

Along the same lines, the jurors should be asked whether they would find it difficult to disagree with the officer's opinion or even to disbelieve his testimony. One delicate way to pose this is to ask the juror if he believes that a police officer could make a mistake in his job like any other person. Pushing harder, counsel can then ask, in the rarely appropriate case, if the juror thought it possible for a police officer to lie. (It should be noted, however, that greater success is usually achieved by attempting to establish that an officer made a *mistake* rather than trying to call him a liar; many jurors will at least subconsciously leap to the defense of the officer, taking the attack on the officer as an attack on "law and order.")

Another related question that can be asked profitably is whether the juror feels that he can give the testimony of the defense witnesses the same weight as he would give the testimony of the officer. This serves to bring to the surface the normal tendency of individuals to grant greater credibility to figures of authority.

Many defense lawyers make the mistake of believing that, once a pro-law-enforcement attitude has surfaced or a close relationship with a law enforcement official has been disclosed, the juror will bend over backwards to be impartial, to the point of even becoming defense-oriented. Believing this can be a very critical error.

It is often helpful to determine which jurors have ever received and/or contested traffic citations. Further tactful questioning into their attitude toward these experiences may reflect a willingness to disbelieve police officers — or even a suppressed anger at police for a minor injustice in the juror's past. Bringing this out may result in the prosecutor's exercising a challenge against that juror, but the value of remaining veniremen hearing such experiences should not be discounted.

The next important area of inquiry involves the potential juror's use of alcohol. The trial judge may ask a question here himself, often relating to whether any of the jurors abstain from the use of alcoholic beverages. This, however, is not enough. Defense counsel must not only determine whether anyone is a teetotaler, but also just what the attitudes of the various jurors are toward drinking. Although difficult to determine tactfully, counsel should attempt to find out the frequency with which the various jurors consume alcoholic beverages. In other words, it is important not only to identify those who do not drink at all but to find jurors who limit their drinking in any way.

Quite simply, jurors who abstain or drink very infrequently are going to tend to be prosecution-oriented. No matter how adamantly a juror says that he can be fair-minded and impartial, even if he means it, his life-style is so different from that of the defendant that he will have difficulty being objective. It is a simple fact that most people who do not drink, or who limit their drinking, disapprove of those who drink more freely. A good rule in drunk driving cases is always to challenge any venireman who restricts his drinking for any reason.

Counsel should attempt next to isolate anyone in the prospective jury who has had an experience with a drunk driver in the past or whose friend or close relative has had such an experience. Again this will require tactful questioning, but it is important to find out if there are any potential jurors who have suffered property damage or worse because of a drunken driver. The last thing the client needs is to have a frustrated juror with a vendetta against drunk drivers.

Attorneys in drunk driving cases are increasingly encountering members of Mothers Against Drunk Driving in the panel during jury selection. Does membership in MADD constitute grounds for a challenge for cause? For a discussion of the affirmative position, see *City of Cheney v. Grunewald,* 780 P.2d 1332 (Wash. 1989). But see *Lord v. State,* 392 S.E.2d 17 (Ga. 1990), for the contrary argument.

Jury experience is yet another important area of inquiry. Counsel should determine the criminal jury experience of each potential juror — that is, the number of criminal jury trials he has served in, how many of them were drunk driving cases, how many involved the same kind of chemical test used on the client, and how many resulted in a verdict.

Generally speaking, experienced jurors tend to be more favorably disposed to the prosecution. They have heard the defenses before, and they grow skeptical. If counsel can, he should ask the juror whether he spoke with the prosecutor after the trial in any of the cases. This is, of course, a common enough practice, but it indicates two things about the juror. First, the juror was probably exposed to propaganda or to the knowledge that incriminating facts such as the existence of prior arrests or convictions are routinely withheld from the jury. Second, the fact that the juror took the trouble to converse with the prosecutor after trial indicates that he may well be prosecution-oriented.

Relevant to this, defense counsel should always keep in mind the fact that many prosecuting agencies routinely keep a master jury list — a record of how current members of the jury panel have fared in past criminal verdicts. If a prosecutor does not challenge a potential juror who has had significant criminal jury trial experience, it may well be because that juror has a "good" record (i.e., convictions) in previous cases.

In addition, counsel should question potential jurors in a drunk driving case about their attitudes toward the legal theories applicable to the client's case. A certain amount of pre-instruction can be very helpful here. The juror should be asked if he realizes that it is not per se unlawful to drive a vehicle after drinking alcoholic beverages. A surprising number of people do not realize this simple truth, and it should be clearly elicited from potential jurors that they would not be prejudiced by the fact that the defendant admittedly had a drink or two before taking the wheel.

The defense theory of the case should, of course, be explained to the jury panel in the course of voir dire. It is usually not enough to simply punch holes in the prosecutor's version of what happened — the jury must be given an alternate version to believe in. If any veniremen seem hostile or even less than receptive to this theory of the case, they should probably be challenged.

Counsel also should investigate attitudes toward the presumption of innocence and the prosecution's burden of proof beyond a reasonable doubt, at the same time indoctrinating the jurors on these important concepts.

It is, of course, critical to both inquire and pre-instruct as to blood-alcohol evidence, particularly where the defendant is charged with a per se offense (i.e., driving with an excessive blood-alcohol level). Counsel should ask questions designed to determine if jurors harbor a blind faith in anything smacking of science. Questions should also be designed to pre-instruct — to focus the trial on the blood-alcohol test rather than on the defendant, and to eliminate existing belief in the accuracy of the test. In discussing breath-alcohol evidence with a juror, for example, counsel may wish to liken the Intoxilyzer to other machines more familiar to jurors. Ask a juror if he or she has a dishwasher in the kitchen — or a garbage disposal, a blender, a stereo system, a vacuum cleaner, an automobile. Have any of these machines ever malfunctioned? (The breath-alcohol device incidentally, should never be referred to as an "instrument," a word that carries with it a certain aura of precision; rather, it should always be called a machine or "the box.") Thus jurors are brought to consider the blood-alcohol testing device as just another mechanical contraption, much like the machines commonly encountered around the house — and, like those machines, frustratingly subject to problems.

If possible, counsel should attempt to obtain the actual breath analyzing device used by his client, or one similar to it, and have it visible to the jury throughout the trial — including during the jury selection process. This deflates the prosecutor's blood-alcohol evidence. The reading did not come from on high, but rather from that ordinary little metal box over there. Jurors are often surprised to discover how small and unimpressive these devices are. Second, the constant presence of the machine helps to focus the primary issue in the trial on the question of the reliability of the machine rather than on whether the defendant was intoxicated or not.

The difference between fact and opinion should be gone into with the jury panel, with an explanation that drunk driving is an "opinion crime." In other words, they should be pre-instructed that there will be no direct evidence of intoxication, but rather only opinions of police officers and possibly of chemical analysts. Even chemical testing in a per se case constitutes, in essence, opinion evidence of what the blood-alcohol level was at the time of driving. The jurors should then be reminded that they must reach a verdict based on their analysis of the *facts*.

During the course of questioning potential jurors, counsel should consistently attempt to "humanize" the client and "dehumanize" the prosecutor. Jurors are human, and they feel empathy toward humans. So, for example, counsel should refer to his client as "Bill Jones" and to the prosecutor as "the state's attorney"; the contest becomes one between a human being (like each juror) and an impersonal bureaucracy.

Beyond the substantive areas of inquiry during voir dire, defense counsel should be aware of certain elementary tactical considerations. Above all, counsel should always bear in mind that to a large degree a trial is a "contest of impressions," and voir dire is the first chance for the jurors to form their impressions. It is helpful and quite impressive if counsel can quickly memorize the names of the jurors he is questioning, so that he can call them by name without referring to a sheet of paper; everyone likes to feel noticed and important enough to be remembered. Also, counsel should be careful not to *interrogate* a juror during the voir dire process. It is easy for an attorney to slip into his witness examination technique, but counsel will establish a much more friendly rapport and mutual respect if he *talks with* the juror, rather than interrogating him.

As with all trials, counsel should keep track of his peremptory challenges to avoid being caught with none left. If one or two peremptories are not saved, inevitably the next juror turns out to be a retired Army colonel who never touches alcohol.

Finally, consideration should be given to requesting individual voir dire — that is, questioning each juror in isolation from the others. This should certainly be requested where the inquiry is into juror's attitudes toward drinking, experiences of the juror or friends/relatives with drunk driving in the past, or instances of harm suffered at the hands of drunk drivers.

§12.0.1 Illustrative Jury Voir Dire

The following, composed by the National Jury Project (310 4th Avenue South, Suite 700, Minneapolis, MN 55415), represents an example of a brief but effective DUI voir dire.

> This is my client *John Jones* (touch client) and he is a citizen accused of DUI (say full charge). Being honest, if you pay attention at all to any news source — TV, radio, paper, big news in our state on the National news (*60 Minutes, 20-20*) — drunk driving is a major concern of people in this country and (pause) especially, our state. News sources have led the way in helping us all realize drinking and driving is not good.
>
> So, under our law, anyone (pass open hand in front of jury) who has a drink and drives is potentially driving under the influence. The real test of the law, the standard, is whether this affects a driver's ability to control and operate his vehicle.

I suppose you all know that I have to know a little about you. It is my job and responsibility to find out enough about you to help you and me decide whether this is the right case for you to sit on. All (your client's name), the Judge and the prosecutor ask is for you to be honest. If I ask you anything you do not, for any reason, want to answer here, please just say so or raise your hand or in some way let us know and I'm sure the judge will be supportive of your answering the question at the bench or in some other personal and private way. We only want the truth.

Drinking alcohol is a part of our society. Most American citizens either presently drink or have in the past.

(Raise your hand)

1. Who has ever had a drink or a beer or a glass of wine?
2. Who still every now and then has a drink?
3. Who drank at one time and now does not drink anymore?

(If yes,)

4. Please, if you don't mind, tell me what made you decide not to drink anymore?
5. What is your religion?
   Who feels for religious, moral, or personal reasons drinking is wrong or not a good thing to do?

Please tell me your feelings about that.

NOTE: Have jurors (with hands raised) react to each other's comments.

6. Who feels it is o.k. to drink alcohol?
7. Does anyone belong to a church, club or any organization that disapproves of alcohol (please be honest)?
8. Who drives a car or truck or any moving vehicle?
9. The standard, as a judge will instruct you, as to whether a person should be convicted of D.U.I. is whether a driver is impaired in operating his or her vehicle. Who would agree that there is a difference between having a drink or so and being able to drive a car and being impaired in doing so?

(For raised hands) Tell me why.

10. Who thinks after one drink *no one* should drive? Tell me about that.

REQUEST TO BE DONE AT THE BENCH

11. This is personal and I feel uncomfortable asking it but has anyone or anyone close to you ever had an unfortunate or painful (touch diaphragm) experience with alcohol that might color or in any way affect your perception or

feelings about someone that drinks or is accused of a crime that involves alcohol?

12. Has anyone here or anyone you know ever been injured by a person who had been drinking?

ASK A COUPLE OF JURORS:

13. What do you feel about gas stations that sell beer? (Get other jurors to react to their statements)
14. Who has given a contribution to or has in any way been involved in any anti-alcohol or drinking and driving advertisements or public information about these issues?
15. Has anyone ever worked for any alcohol or other drug rehabilitation center or counseling program? Which one? Job responsibilities?
16. Who has ever worked in any hospital or medical facility? Who will admit that you have heard of mistakes happening with lab tests?

    (Find receptive juror) Tell me about some of the possibilities of mix-ups or improper results when a medical facility deals with thousands of lab tests.
17. Everyone works with some machine or appliance every day that measures something, maybe that is an oven, tire gauge, a fuel gauge or temperature gauge on your car, even the radar detectors for speed could be inaccurate. Who has recently had a machine or appliance that measures something be inaccurate or malfunction? Tell me about that.
18. Who works with machines in their jobs? What kind? What do they measure? Who repairs them? How often are they checked? Who is responsible for quality or accuracy control?

    Have you ever been responsible for their accuracy?
19. If your ability or competency is questioned, what do you feel at that moment?

    How do you feel if that was done in public?
20. Who has ever supervised anyone?

    How have you seen people behave when someone is asked to explain their job performance?
21. Who has ever taken a course or worked in chemistry, biology, engineering, mechanics, etc.?
22. What does scientific mean? Who thinks a so-called scientist or his or her machine or analysis can be wrong?

    Tell me about that.
23. The real issue here is not whether (client's name) drank

and drove but whether his (her) drinking impaired his ability to operate his vehicle. Who feels they can closely look at the distinction, difference between these 2 standards?

What should be looked at?

24. What is the difference between suspicion and proof? This will be what you must as individual jurors (persons) determine.

    Who feels they can look at the difference between these two views of life?

25. Every life situation is different.

    Who has sat on another case with the same charge?

    What effect might that have on you here?

For a more involved voir dire, the following comments and illustrations may prove instructive. The author is grateful to Flem Whited III of Daytona Beach, Florida, for his kind permission to use these materials.

> The process of jury selection is, as in any criminal trial, a critical one in drunk driving litigation. The following represents an excellent approach to the voir dire of potential jurors.
>
> After you have obtained thorough background information on all the jurors, it is advisable to start your discussions with them relative to the work at hand. I have listed what I believe to be the areas that should be specifically covered in each and every case. It is not an all inclusive list, but the only thing that I can think of that should be added are specific bad facts that have to do with your particular case. As an example, if you have a client that has used excessive profanity or that was overly abusive to a police officer, then these types of things should be covered. The order that I have them listed, I believe, gives you an easy transition from one specific topic to another and would help the flow of the conversation. They are in order, not necessarily of importance, but again the heavy topics are saved for the very end and hopefully by the time you get to the topics of presumption of innocence, burden of proof and the concept of reasonable doubt you will have a talkative group that is comfortable with you.
>
> 1. Approach to Jury Service
>
> Try to ask each and every juror what their feelings were when they received their jury summons. If service on the jury is going to cost

them time and money on the job and their thoughts are going to be somewhere else during your trial then you don't want them there. You may also be able to make points with other jurors by showing your concern for these people. This is another reason for a challenge for cause. You are looking for people with a happy, pleasant attitude. If they receive their jury summons and it immediately put a bad taste in their mouth for one reason or another, then you want to know about that. The first step in obtaining a group of people who can be fair and impartial to your client and apply the principles of law is to find a group of people who are not preoccupied with being somewhere else and approach jury service with a very civic minded attitude.

EXAMPLE:

Mrs. Smith, when you got your Jury Summons, what went on in your mind?

2. Sitting in Judgment

Find out from each and every juror if they have any hesitation with sitting in judgment of a fellow citizen.

EXAMPLE:

Mrs. Jones, Mr. Johnson and Mrs. Willis have had the opportunity to sit on juries in the past. They have had the opportunity to listen to the Judge's instructions in previous cases and deliberate and make tough decisions. In our country when a person is accused of a crime and they deny that they committed a crime, they have a right to a trial and at that time to have jurors listen to what happened. You will be the judges of the facts. There is only one judge of the law and that's His Honor, but there will be six judges of the facts. Further, at that trial the people who have accused him of the crime have to prove that crime, each and every element of that crime, beyond and to the exclusion of every reasonable doubt. Do you have any hesitation in sitting in judgment to listen to the facts and at the end ask yourself if the state has eliminated all reasonable doubt?

3. Sympathy or Emotion

This should be covered in accident and death cases. The jury will be instructed sympathy for the Defendant should play no role in their verdict and by the same token you should make them understand and be aware that sympathy for the person injured or killed should play no role in their verdict either.

EXAMPLE:

Mrs. Jones, in this case there will be evidence that a person died in a car accident. The prosecutor and the judge have talked to you and you have all agreed that whatever sympathy you have toward the defendant should play no role in your verdict and by the same token while we all agree that sympathy is a natural emotion for all of us, that sympathy (for the person injured or killed and the family) should play no part in your verdict either.

Mrs. Jones if you are selected as one of the jurors to hear this case, can you assure me and Mr. Cooper that sympathy will play no part in your verdict?

4. Unique Nature of the Charge

Review with the jurors the difference between facts and opinions. Let them know that the charge of DUI necessarily requires that someone give an opinion on whether or not your client is guilty of the crime and this is different than most other crimes. Various examples can be used. Be creative when you use these and analogize the charge of DUI with other crimes where people are not allowed to give an opinion on the ultimate fact. Obtain commitments from them that they will base their verdict on the facts and they will not necessarily accept an opinion for face value. Commit them to looking beyond the opinion and requiring facts for their verdict.

EXAMPLE:

All of us have opinions on any number of subjects and if I were to tell you that in my opinion that the Tampa Bay Buccaneers were the best football team in the National Football League you might look at me rather strange. You might even say, while I can respect your opinion Mr. Whited, what are the facts upon which you base your opinion?

EXAMPLE:

Ladies and Gentlemen, as you know Mr. . . . is charged with driving under the influence of an alcoholic beverage. There will be testimony from the police officer, and probably others that on August the 4th, 1987, Mr. Cooper, in their opinion, was impaired by alcohol. My question to each and every one of you is: Will you agree to not accept the opinion of the police officers at face value and will you look beyond their opinions for facts upon which to base your verdict?

5. Concept of Elements

Let the jury know that the crime of DUI is made up of elements and that the state must prove each and every element beyond and to the exclusion of every reasonable doubt and that if they have a reasonable doubt as to any one of those elements, then the verdict is not guilty.

EXAMPLE:

Miss Jones, as you know Mr. Cooper is charged with driving under the influence. I believe the judge will tell you, at some point in time, that in order for the state to prove their case to you beyond and to the exclusion of every reasonable doubt that they have to prove to you that: 1) he was driving, 2) he was under the influence of an alcoholic beverage, and 3) he was impaired by that alcohol. The judge is also going to tell you that each of these elements must be proved to you beyond and to the exclusion of every reasonable doubt and that if you have a reasonable doubt as to any one of the elements, that the verdict is not guilty. Will you agree that if you have a reasonable doubt as to any one of the elements that your verdict will be not guilty? As an example, if the state proves to your satisfaction and beyond a reasonable doubt that Mr. Cooper was driving and that he was under the influence of an alcoholic beverage but they have not proved to you that he was impaired by alcohol, will you agree that the proper verdict under those circumstances, would be a verdict of not guilty? Mr. Jones, same question to you.

6. Role of the Jury

The most important part of voir dire, in my opinion, is to make sure that each and every juror knows what their function in the process is. Their sole job when the door is shut and the deliberations start is to ask themselves if they have a reasonable doubt as to any one of the elements. If they have a reasonable doubt, then the verdict is not guilty. They must understand that, if after hearing the evidence and deliberating there is a doubt in their mind and it is a doubt upon which a reason can be placed, that the proper verdict is not guilty. They must understand that if they don't like your client, don't like his behavior on that evening, think he might be guilty or believe that he probably is guilty, but if they have a reasonable doubt, then the verdict is not guilty. They must understand that this is not a police decision and their function is different from that of the police. Policemen do not apply the concept of reasonable doubt, they generally don't get the entire story. The police haven't had the opportunity to hear the witnesses. Their function is entirely different. Let them know that a verdict of not guilty does not necessarily mean that the policeman was wrong in the decision that he made and that the concept of probable cause to arrest somebody is clearly different and has a different role in our country than proof beyond and to the exclusion of every reasonable doubt.

7. Police Officer Testimony

Obtain commitments from them that they will give no greater weight to the testimony of the police officer than they would any other witness. Ask them if they believe that police officers are infallible or are they subject to making mistakes like all the rest of us.

EXAMPLE:

Mr. Sims, there will be testimony in this trial from a police officer. My question to you sir, is will you give any greater weight to his testimony than to that of a lay person or someone who is not a police officer?

I guess what I am trying to ask you Mr. Sims, is that do you think someone is special just because they are a police officer and you should give them preferential treatment or give their testimony preferential treatment just because they are a police officer, or do you feel that they are subject to making mistakes and errors in judgment just like all the rest of us?

8. Field Sobriety Testing

When discussing the topic of field sobriety testing it is important to question each and every juror regarding their knowledge of these types of tests. More specifically, inquiries should be made whether they have seen anything on television, read anything in the newspapers, talked to any other persons about them or have any knowledge whatsoever regarding the accuracy and reliability of these types of tests. Your theme of the case should be that even if someone has failed these tests, it does not necessarily mean that they were impaired by alcohol. All it may mean is that they don't have the ability to do these tests, and not that they were impaired by alcohol.

EXAMPLE:

> Mrs. Williams, there is going to be some testimony in this trial regarding something called roadside sobriety or agility tests. What I would like to know is if you have heard anything, read anything or received any information whatsoever from any source regarding the accuracy or reliability of these types of tests.
>
> Now if testimony comes into this trial regarding these types of tests and that in someone's opinion, Mr. Cooper failed these tests, will you keep an open mind regarding the results of these tests and not conclude that Mr. Cooper may be impaired by alcohol just because he failed them?

9. Breath Test Machines

a. Your handling of this subject will depend upon what you anticipate your trial testimony to be. If you do not anticipate any testimony at your trial regarding various breakdowns and malfunctions of the machine, then I would not advise asking all those questions relating to the fallibility of various types of other products. Of course, if you anticipate that there will be testimony regarding certain periods of malfunctions and various breakdowns on the part of the machine that is coming into evidence, then it would be advisable to do that.

b. Most of the time this type of evidence doesn't come into trial and the purpose of your voir dire questions should be very similar to that of field sobriety testing. Your inquiries should be focused on whether or not any of the potential jurors have heard of these machines, either through the news media or conversations with other persons, and, more importantly, whether or not they have formed an opinion regarding the degree of accuracy or fallibility of these machines.

c. If you intend to either present expert testimony regarding the assumptions that these machines are based upon or you will have the ability to extract that information out of the breath test maintenance operator or some state witness then you should obtain commitments from each and every juror that they will keep an open mind regarding the information from these machines and give it the weight that they feel it deserves during the course of their deliberations.

d. You may end up in a trial where you have a machine that has not malfunctioned, or you will have no testimony regarding the assumptions upon which it is based or any information beyond just the number that it reported. If you have this type of situation, the commitments that I just stated above are most important.

EXAMPLE:

Mrs. Williams, there may come into evidence in this trial the results of some type of breath test machine or breath analyzer. My question to you is have you heard anything or read anything from any source regarding these types of machines.

Have you formed any opinions regarding the accuracy or reliability or fallibility of these types of machines?

Mrs. Williams the testimony in this case may show that the machine in question was authorized for use in the state by some governmental agency. My question to you is, if I am able to present to you evidence relating the fallibility of this machine, or let's say some evidence that may tend to show you that it does not do exactly what it is supposed to do, can you keep an open mind and will you evaluate all the evidence or will you give it some sort of preferential treatment just because the government said it was okay to use?

I guess the point that I am trying to make is that will each and every one of you keep an open mind and listen to all the evidence that comes into this trial regarding these types of machines and give it the weight that you feel that it deserves?

10. Expert Witness Testimony

If you plan on using an expert witness to testify regarding any aspect to your case, either regarding the machine used or the field sobriety testing, the subject of expert witness testimony should be covered in your voir dire. The purpose of your question should be to insure that each and every juror will keep a fair and open mind regarding the subject of this testimony and will not discredit the testimony because your client has had to hire and pay for someone to testify.

EXAMPLE:

Mrs. Jones, let's say that you had some plumbing problems around your house or a car won't run just quite right. What would be the first thing that you would do in order to solve those problems?

If you did not know anything about plumbing or car repair you would probably call someone who knows something about those particular areas.

I think that we can all agree that finding someone to work on either our homes or our cars would be a very important decision to make. Mrs. Jones, if you did not know anything about plumbing or car repair how would you go about finding someone to help?

I believe that we all can agree that if we did not know anyone that could do these things and was proficient at what they do, then we would ask questions and make sure that whoever we hire knew what they were doing and would be honest with us regarding their work.

Mrs. Williams if you had hired someone to repair your plumbing or your car, or give you advice in a certain area, would you think bad of that advice or help if the person had to charge you money and you had to pay them for their work?

The point that I am trying to make is there may be testimony in this case from someone the law calls an expert witness. Now an expert witness is nothing more than someone who has special knowledge about certain topics. The evidence is going to show in this case that Mr. Cooper did not know anything about these breath test machines and he had to go somewhere and find out something about them and there may be testimony from someone in this case regarding these types of machines and who has special knowledge of these machines that Mr. Cooper had to hire and pay in order to come in and give this information to you. Now this is not much different than the police officers who are getting paid to come to court and testify for the state, but the evidence might be that Mr. Cooper had to pay this person to testify and that this person may have testified in similar cases in the past.

My question to you is that when evaluating this type of testimony and the testimony of this person, will you discredit it in any way because the person has been paid or testified in similar cases, or will you give it the weight that you feel it deserves based upon the credentials of the person who is testifying? Will you agree that you will listen and keep an open mind and give the testimony the weight that you feel it deserves based upon what you hear of the person's credentials and his ability to know what he says he knows?

11. Personal Alcohol Consumption

a. Here you want to make sure that all the jurors understand that consuming alcohol and then driving a car is not illegal. They must understand that if a person has consumed alcohol and then drives a car that they have not committed a crime and that the charge in this case is not consuming alcohol and driving a car.

b. Some of the jurors have probably consumed alcohol in the past and you should make sure that each and every juror knows that how alcohol affects their normal faculties and, more specifically, whatever amount they have consumed and its effect on their normal faculties has no application in this case. The testimony in this trial may be that your client consumed twelve beers over the course of nine hours. We all know that sounds like an enormous amount of alcohol for someone to consume. You may have a juror who drank at some point and time in their life and consumed two glasses of wine and became impaired. What you are trying to do in voir dire is to make sure that they do not apply or even consider the effects of alcohol that they have consumed and its effect on them and impose that standard on your client.

c. You have to make them agree that everybody is different and that how alcohol affects them may not be the same as how alcohol affects your client.

EXAMPLE:

Mrs. Jones, the charge in this case is that Mr. Cooper operated a motor vehicle while he was under the influence of an alcoholic beverage to the extent that he was impaired by that alcohol or that his blood alcohol level exceeded a certain limit. The charge in this case is not that he consumed alcohol and then drove an automobile. Do you understand that drinking alcohol and driving a car is not a crime and will you agree to not hold it against Mr. Cooper just because he drank alcohol and drove a car?

The point of it all is the state has to prove to you all beyond and to the exclusion of every reasonable doubt all the elements of the crime and that he was impaired by alcohol or that his blood alcohol level was over a certain level, will you hold them to that level of proof and not hold it against Mr. Cooper just because he consumed alcohol and drove a car?

Now the matters to be determined in this trial necessarily relate to Mr. Cooper and not to anybody else in the world. Can we all agree that we all are different and that alcohol affects everybody in different ways?

Will all of you agree that during the course of your deliberations your attention will be directed to whether alcohol has affected Mr. Cooper's normal faculties and agree that how it affects your own normal faculties makes no difference?

12. Defendant Not Testifying

a. If your client is not going to testify for one reason or another you need to obtain commitments from each juror that they will not in any way hold it against him for not telling his side of the story. The jury has to understand that the burden is on the state to prove this crime and not the Defendant to prove anything.

b. It is important to go over all the questions regarding Defendant's right not to testify even if your client is going to testify. When this is done the jury will have an understanding of the rights that he had and that he is waiving all those rights in order to tell his side of the story. Of course if your client is not going to testify then you have committed the jury to the proposition that the burden is on the state and not on the accused.

c. Commitments should be obtained from the jurors that they will not hold it against your client for not testifying; that they will not in any way feel uncomfortable or think that your client is trying to hide something from them by not testifying.

d. You must make them understand that your client's entry of a not guilty plea is tantamount to saying to the state and to the jury and to everyone concerned that I am not guilty and I did not do what they have me charged with.

EXAMPLE:

Mrs. Williams you have heard that if a person is accused of a crime that they have the right to remain silent, haven't you?

I think we can all agree that it is fundamental to our system of justice that a person has a right not to say anything.

Mr. Sims, if Mr. Cooper does not testify in this trial, will you in any way hold that against him, or will you follow the law on that particular subject as the judge will instruct you later on in the trial?

If the choice is made by me for Mr. Cooper not to testify, will any of you hold it against him or think that he is hiding something from you or in anyway feel uncomfortable with the fact that he did not come forward and tell you his side of the story?

You see, ladies and gentlemen, the ball is in the prosecutor's court in this trial and not in Mr. Cooper's. Will you in any way hold it against him if the decision is made for him not to testify?

13. Presumption of Innocence

a. When discussing the presumption of innocence you have to make the jurors understand that the prosecutor and Defendant do not start out on equal ground. The presumption of innocence tips the scales heavily in the favor of the Defendant. The state has to overcome the presumption by coming forward with evidence that convinces them to the exclusion of every reasonable doubt that he in fact committed the crime with which he is charged.

b. An easy way to lead into the presumption of innocence is the distinction between civil and criminal trials. There will no doubt be someone in the jury panel who has served on a civil jury in the past. You should make sure that the jury understands and knows that in a criminal proceeding more cherished rights are at stake than in civil cases. When a person's life, liberty and property are at stake, certain legal concepts such as due process and presumption of innocence apply. Acknowledge to them that in civil cases the only issue is whether one person wants money from someone else for some reason or that there may be some equitable action, such as contractual rights or something of that nature. They must know that the proceeding they are now in is far more important than that and that far greater and more important rights are involved. Explain to them that is why we have something called the presumption of innocence.

c. Use the scales of justice to your benefit here and if you are not allowed to use the black board or any other type of marker, then use your arms to display to them how the scales are tipped in favor of the Defendant when the case starts.

d. Once they have acknowledged all these principles then each and every juror should be questioned as to what their verdict would be if at this very moment they had to vote either guilty or not guilty. This is a very good example of the presumption in the sense of how it applies.

e. This is an excellent way to show the judge that the jurors do not really know what the presumption means regardless of the fact that at this point in time they have all agreed that they know what the presumption of innocence is and that they will apply it in this case. You may start getting objections from the prosecutor and it is an excellent way to show to the judge that you have the right to make these inquiries because, notwithstanding what the jurors have said to the judge or the prosecutor that they really do not know what these concepts mean and that it is important that they understand them and agree to apply them in this case in order for them to be fair and impartial.

EXAMPLE:

Mrs. Jones, you have heard the judge tell you that in this case Mr. Cooper is presumed innocent. What does that concept mean to you?

Ladies and gentlemen the judge has told you that Mr. Cooper is presumed innocent as he sits before you today. This is one of our fundamental principles of justice and it is one reason this proceeding is different from civil trials. In a civil trial, all that is generally wanted from one side or the other is money. When a person's life, liberty and property are at stake, higher and more important and more cherished rights are involved. What the presumption of innocence does is tip the scales of justice in the favor of the Defendant when the trial starts.

Mr. Jones, do you have any problem with applying the presumption of innocence in this case?

Recognizing that we do not start out equal and that Mr. Cooper is presumed innocent and the state has the burden to prove their charges beyond every reasonable doubt, and that you have not heard any evidence at this point in time, if you had to choose between guilty and not guilty, right now, Mrs. Smith, what verdict would you have to reach recognizing that Mr. Cooper is presumed innocent?

Mrs. Jones, do you agree that the proper verdict right now would have to be not guilty?

Mrs. Sims, how would you have to vote under these circumstances?

14. Burden of Proof

a. Your goal when discussing this topic is to ensure that the jurors understand who has to prove what.

b. An easy way to explain that is to engage them in a discussion of what trials are all about, both civil and criminal. The fact that the state has chosen to charge your client with a crime necessarily means that they have the burden of coming forward with proof during the course of the trial and that if they do not come forward with the necessary degree of proof then the verdict would have to be not guilty.

EXAMPLE:

Ladies and gentlemen, in addition to Mr. Cooper being presumed innocent as he sits before you today, it is also the law in our land that when a person is charged with a crime, the state has what we call the burden of proof. What this means essentially is that the state, having charged Mr. Cooper with a crime, has the obligation to come forward with evidence to prove to you what they have alleged he has done. Ladies and gentlemen, you will not hear from the judge's mouth at any point in time that Mr. Cooper has the burden to prove to you anything. In fact, the only burden in this case is on the state to prove what they say he did. My question to you, Mrs. Sims, is that if the judge tells you that the burden is on the state to prove the charges against Mr. Cooper, will you keep the burden in this case where it belongs, which is on the state?

Mr. Williams, essentially the same question to you sir, do you understand that the burden is on the state to prove their case against Mr. Cooper and that he does not have the obligation to prove anything to you sir?

Do you think that it is unfair for the state to have the burden in this case and it is the law in this country that the Defendant does not have to prove his innocence?

Can we all agree that, if that's the law of our land that we will apply it in this case and not impose any burden on Mr. Cooper at all and keep the burden on the state where it started and where it rightly should be?

15. Proof Beyond the Exclusion of Every Reasonable Doubt

Once you have gone through the presumption of innocence and the burden of proof with the jurors, you now have to get them to understand that not only is the Defendant presumed innocent and the burden of proving something in the case is on the state, that the degree to which they have to prove their allegations is beyond and to the exclusion of every reasonable doubt. They have to understand that if after hearing all the evidence in the case they have one single solitary doubt regarding the proof of any elements of the crime charged, that the proper and just verdict is a verdict of not guilty. They must understand that justice is done and everyone wins when all the rules of law that the judge reads them have been applied during their deliberations.

EXAMPLE:

Ladies and gentlemen, one of the other rules of law that applies in this case is that the state has the burden to prove these charges against Mr. Cooper beyond and to the exclusion of every reasonable doubt. That essentially means, ladies and gentlemen, that if after hearing all the evidence in this case you have a doubt and there is a reason upon which that doubt is founded, then the verdict is not guilty. This is not a civil case. In civil cases when one party sues another and all they want is money they start out equal and the only degree to which they have to prove their case is by a preponderance of the evidence or the greater weight of the evidence. If you tip the scales of justice ever so slightly, you have won. It is not like other types of cases that we have in the law where one party wants something from somebody else that they have to prove their case, so to speak, by clear and convincing evidence. Here, the state has the burden to prove to you each and every element of the offense beyond and to the exclusion of reasonable doubt. This is the highest burden of proof that the law recognizes and it is an awesome burden.

Mrs. Jones, do you feel that it is unfair to hold the state to such a high burden of proof?

Mrs. Jones, if the judge tells you that the state has to prove the case beyond and to the exclusion of every reasonable doubt, will you agree to apply that standard in your deliberation?

If after having heard all the evidence and deliberating with your fellow jurors, you have a doubt in your mind, what would be your verdict, guilty or not guilty?

Mr. Williams, do you agree that if Mr. Cooper might be guilty or that he probably is guilty and you really do not like what happened on the night of June the 4th, 1987, but you have a doubt, and

> it is a doubt upon which a reason can be attached then the proper verdict is not guilty?

This is absolutely the most important part of your voir dire. Each and every juror should be questioned individually, looked right in the eye, making sure that they understand the concept of reasonable doubt, and that their entire role and the question that they have to ask themselves during their deliberations is, "Do I have doubt and is there reason upon which I can find that doubt?" You will lose your case if you do not cover this area very thoroughly, very methodically and very sincerely.

16. Objections to Evidence

Make sure that the jurors understand that during the course of the trial there will be various objections to certain pieces of evidence in the trial and that the reasons for those objects deal with technical points of law that both the prosecutor and yourself have been trained in and commit them to agree that they will not hold that against the prosecutor or you if certain objects are made during the course of the trial.

EXAMPLE:

> Ladies and gentlemen of the jury, there will no doubt be various objections to certain questions in this trial. Will you all agree not to hold it against the prosecutor or myself if we make these objections? They're all a lot of technical rules of law that deal with the way questions have to be phrased and asked, and both prosecutor and myself are acting in good faith if we genuinely believe that something should not come into the trial.

Doug Cowan of Bellevue, Washington, uses a broader, less issue-oriented method of voire dire. Rather than direct his queries to attitudes about specific legal and factual issues, he prefers questions aimed at finding out what kind of a person the juror is and what his attitudes and values are generally. The answers to these questions, of course, will tell him much about what the potential juror's attitudes will be toward the drunk driving case.

If limited to a relatively brief voire dire, Mr. Cowan would suggest a few of his favorite questions:

What do you enjoy doing in your spare time?
Given a choice, what occupation would you choose to pursue other than your present one? Why?

What's your favorite television program?
What's your favorite cop show?
What's your favorite movie?
What book have you most recently read?
What magazines do you subscribe to or read regularly?
Who would you say is the greatest living American?
Which historical figure do you particularly admire?
Do you have a favorite tavern or cocktail lounge?
To which organizations do you belong?
To which organizations have you belonged in the past?
Do you ever visit sports bars?
Do you have any bumper stickers on your vehicles?
What activities are you involved in at school or church?
Who's your favorite radio talk show host?
Have you ever been called on to lead a group or supervise a project?
Does your job involve supervising other persons?
Have you ever been called on to mediate a dispute? How did you handle it?
Where do you usually socialize with people from work?
Do you ever stop off at a tavern or lounge to visit with friends or coworkers after work?
What is your beverage of choice?
What kind of music do you enjoy?

If limited to only a single question, incidentally, Doug Cowan would ask the potential juror, "What is your beverage of choice?"

§12.0.2 Sample Proposed Written Questions

An increasing number of jurisdictions are limiting voire dire by counsel, or eliminating it altogether in favor of voire dire by the court. In such cases, it is common practice to permit counsel either to submit written questionnaires for jurors to read and complete, or to submit proposed questions in writing for the judge to pose to the jury panel.

Doug Cowan of Bellevue, Washington, generally regarded as the most knowledgeable DUI attorney in that state, often submits the following "General Questions to the Jury" for use in a judge's voire dire:

IN THE KING COUNTY DISTRICT COURT, __________ DIVISION STATE OF WASHINGTON

THE PEOPLE OF THE STATE OF WASHINGTON, Plaintiff,	)	NO. ______
vs.	)	DEFENDANT'S GENERAL QUESTIONS TO THE JURY
JOHN DOE, Defendant,	)	

(1) Has anyone been involved in law enforcement, probation or counseling of persons in the criminal justice system?
(2) Does anyone have any friends or family members involved with law enforcement in any capacity?
(3) Does anyone not drink alcohol?
(4) Does anyone not drive?
(5) Has anyone ever contested a traffic ticket of any kind?
(6) Has anyone ever had a particularly pleasant or unpleasant experience with a police officer?
(7) Has anyone, any family member or close friend ever been involved in a traffic accident involving alcohol?
(8) Has anyone or any family member ever been involved in the insurance business in any way?
(9) Does anyone have a bumper sticker on any of their vehicles?
(10) Is anyone against mandatory seat belt laws?

(11) Is anyone against mandatory helmet laws?
(12) Has anyone ever testified in court?
(13) Has anyone ever contributed money to any organization advocating stricter laws regarding drinking and driving; i.e. MADD, SADD, etc.?
(14) Has anyone or any family member or close friend had problems with alcohol?
(15) Does anyone favor tougher laws regarding drinking and driving?
(16) Does anyone believe it should be against the law to drive after drinking any alcohol at all?
(17) Has anyone or any family member ever worked in the medical profession?
(18) Does anyone use a computer either in their work or at home?
(19) Does anyone have any particular feelings about drinking and driving of which the court should be aware?
(20) Of those who have already sat on juries during this term, has anyone discussed the case with either of the attorneys involved at the conclusion of that case?

____

Douglas L. Cowan
Attorney for Defendant

When the court requests written questionnaires from counsel to be completed by members of the jury panel prior to jury selection, Mr. Cowan has been satisfied with the results of using the following list:

JUROR QUESTIONNAIRE Juror #______

Please carefully consider and answer the following questions. All answers shall remain strictly confidential.

(1) Have you been involved in law enforcement, probation or counseling of persons in the criminal justice system?
No ____ Yes: (explain) ____________________________

(2) Do you have any friends or family members involved with law enforcement in any capacity?
No ____ Yes: (explain) ______________________________
(3) Do you drink alcoholic beverages?
No ____ Yes ____
(4) If you drink, what is your usual drink of choice?
____
(5) Do you drive a car?
No ____ Yes ____
(6) Have you ever contested a traffic ticket of any kind?
No ____ Yes: (explain) ______________________________
(7) Have you ever had a particularly pleasant or unpleasant experience with a police officer?
No ____ Yes: (explain) ______________________________
(8) Do you have any bumper stickers on any of your vehicles?
No ____ Yes: (explain) ______________________________
(9) Have you ever testified in court?
No ____ Yes: (explain) ______________________________
(10) Have you ever been involved in a traffic accident involving alcohol?
No ____ Yes: (explain) ______________________________
(11) Have you ever performed "field sobriety tests"?
No ____ Yes ____
(12) Do you favor mandatory seatbelt laws?
No ____ Yes ____
(13) Do you favor mandatory motorcycle helmet laws?
No ____ Yes ____
(14) Have you ever contributed money to or belonged to any organization advocating stricter laws regarding drinking and driving (MADD, SADD, etc)?
No ____ Yes: (explain) ______________________________
(15) Do you favor tougher laws regarding drinking and driving?
No ____ Yes: (explain) ______________________________
(16) Do you believe that, on the whole, the Criminal Justice System is:
a) too lenient ____ b) too harsh ____ c) about right ____
(explain) ______________________________
(17) Have you ever participated in any function, seminar, class or program involving the subject of drug or alcohol abuse?
No ____ Yes: (explain) ______________________________
(18) Do you believe it should be against the law to drive after drinking any alcohol at all?
No ____ Yes: (explain) ______________________________

(19) Have you ever read any articles or books, or viewed television programs or movies concerning the subject of drinking and driving?
No ____ Yes: (explain) ______________________________

(20) Have you ever worked or volunteered in a medical, social or other program or clinic which involved alcohol or drug counseling?
No ____ Yes: (explain) ______________________________

(21) Have you or any close friends or relatives ever had problems related to alcohol use?
No ____ Yes: (explain) ______________________________

(22) Have you or any family member ever been employed in the medical profession?
No ____ Yes: (explain) ______________________________

(23) Have you or any family member ever been employed in the auto insurance industry?
No ____ Yes: (explain) ______________________________

(24) Have you ever been accused of something you didn't do?
No ____ Yes: (explain) ______________________________

(25) Have you ever accused someone of something they didn't do?
No ____ Yes: (explain) ______________________________

(26) Do you own a gun for personal protection?
No ____ Yes: (explain) ______________________________

(27) Do you now or have you ever used a computer in work or at home?
No ____ Yes: (explain) ______________________________

(28) Have you ever taken any instruction or classes in how to use a computer?
No ____ Yes: (explain) ______________________________

(29) Please describe your proficiency level in using a computer:
a) Not proficient at all ____ b) Slightly proficient ____
c) Of average proficiency ____ d) Very proficient ____

(30) Please describe your "comfort level" in using computers:
a) Very uncomfortable ____ b) Somewhat uncomfortable ____
c) Comfortable ____ d) Very comfortable ____

(31) Please consider the following statement: Persons who have nothing to hide should allow their homes or offices to be searched without a warrant.
Disagree ____ Agree: (comment) ______________________________

(32) Have you ever worked with scientific or laboratory testing or measuring equipment?
No ____ Yes: (explain) ______________________________

(33) Do you smoke?
No ____ Yes ____

(34) Do you favor stricter laws limiting sale or use of cigarettes?
No ____ Yes ____

(35) Do you favor stricter laws limiting sale or use of alcohol products?
No ____ Yes ____

(36) Would you like to serve on the jury in this case (a DWI)?
No ____ Yes ____ Why: ________________

§12.0.3 Discovery of Prosecution Records on Jurors

The prosecution often has a considerable edge in the selection of a jury, an edge that places the defense at a distinct disadvantage. In many jurisdictions, the prosecuting agency will keep a record of all jurors who have served in a criminal trial over a given period of years — along with information concerning the charges involved and the verdict. More importantly, these files often indicate how the juror voted, if known, and any comments by the prosecutor in the case about the jury or individual juror.

Clearly, the defense has no ability to gather this kind of data. Just as clearly, such information would seem to constitute more than just an "edge" for the state. The disparity of access to critical information concerning the jury selection process amounts to fundamental unfairness — and a denial of due process.

The following discovery motion, aimed at forcing the State to disclose this information, was provided by Howard J. Weintraub (900 Peachtree Center Tower, 230 Peachtree Street, N.W., Atlanta, GA 30303; (404) 522-5200).

(Title of Court and Cause)

MOTION FOR DISCLOSURE OF PRIOR PETIT JURY AND GRAND JURY SERVICE AND FOR DISCOVERY OF INFORMATION ON PROSPECTIVE JURORS AND BRIEF IN SUPPORT THEREOF

Comes now the Defendant, by and through her undersigned counsel, and respectfully files this motion. In support thereof, Defendant shows as follows:

1

The City of Atlanta Solicitor's Office has certain written or recorded information that reflects the past petit and grand jury service of prospective jurors. This information identifies the petit juries and grand juries on which the prospective jurors have served, the types of cases on which said persons have served, the verdicts rendered in such cases, and the sentences imposed when a guilty verdict was reached. Such information may be available to the Solicitor's Office for its examination and utilization in screening the individual jurors who would be present on the panel in this case.

2

This past petit jury and grand jury service information is necessary in order for Defendant to make a determination as to whether the provisions of OCGA §§15-12-3 and 15-12-4 have been properly complied with in this case.

3

The past petit jury and grand jury service information requested is also material to the matters involved in this case, and furthermore, said information is material to the preparation of an adequate defense. More specifically, Defendant shows the Court as follows:

(a) Such information concerning past jury service that may be available to and referred to by the Solicitor's Office is not automatically available to Defendant and her counsel. This information is necessary and material in order for Defendant to preserve the just administration of criminal laws and to ensure Defendant a fair trial.
(b) This information does not constitute the work product of any attorney representing the State in this case or of his/her investigators.
(c) Denial of this information would deprive Defendant of a fair and impartial trial as guaranteed to her by the Due Process Clause of the Fifth and Fourteenth Amendments to the United States Constitution, and Article I, Section I, Paragraph I of the Constitution of Georgia (1983).
(d) Defendant further contends that this information, available to the prosecution during the selection of a jury and unavailable to the defense, constitutes a material advantage to the State of Georgia, that cannot be overcome by Defendant other than by order of this Court. Said unfair advantage of the State is repugnant to the concept of basic individual rights and to Defendant's right to a fair trial.

4

Further, Defendant respectfully moves this Court to order the prosecution to make available to defense counsel, well in advance of trial, all other information presently available to the prosecution about each prospective juror and all other information that may, through the exercise of due diligence, become available to the prosecution. Denial of said information would deprive Defendant of a fair and impartial trial as guaranteed to her by the Due Process Clause of the Fifth and Fourteenth Amendments to the United States Constitution and Article I, Section I, Paragraph I of the Constitution of Georgia (1983).

Wherefore, for all of the foregoing reasons, Defendant respectfully prays as follows:

(a) That a hearing be held on this matter;
(b) That the Court grant this motion and order the disclosure requested herein;
(c) That Defendant be allowed to amend this Motion if disclosure to her of the requested evidence may provide further bases for relief;
(d) That Defendant be allowed to file any additional motions challenging the indictment against her if any violation of Georgia law is discovered from the information; and
(e) For such other and further relief as the Court deems just and proper.

This, the ______ day of ____________, 1999

Respectfully submitted,

____

(*signature*)

§12.0.4 The Right to a Jury Trial in DUI Cases

Counsel in a drunk driving case may initially be confronted with the prosecutorial position that his client has no right to a jury trial due to the nature of the statute. In *State v. Whirley*, 421 So. 2d 555 (Fla. 1982), a Florida court of appeals reviewed the issue of whether or not the drinking driver is entitled to a jury trial when charged with violation of a municipal ordinance. The court held:

> When one is charged with a violation of both a city ordinance and a state statute, one is entitled to a trial by jury only if the penalty imposed removes the offense from the category of petty offenses defined in *Baldwin v. New York*, 399 U.S. 66, 90 S. Ct. 1866, 26 L. Ed. 2d 437 (1970). Because the maximum sentence that could be imposed on Whirley for violating section 316.193(3) does not exceed six months in jail and a $500 fine, she is not entitled to a trial by jury. [421 So. 2d at 556.]

The case raises an interesting problem of whether the drinking/driving offense is distinguishable from the petty offense outlined in *Baldwin v. New York*. In the DUI offense the defendant is frequently subject to a very severe punishment above and beyond the actual fine and jail sentence imposed; namely, suspension or revocation of a desperately needed driver's license.

In 1989, the U.S. Supreme Court clarified the right to jury trial in DUI cases. In *Blanton v. City of North Las Vegas*, 489 U.S. 538 (1989), the Court established a *presumed* "bright line" standard between a "serious offense" and a "petty offense."

> In using the word "penalty," we do not refer solely to the maximum prison term authorized for a particular offense. A legislature's view of the seriousness of an offense also is reflected in the other penalties that it attaches to the offense. . . . Primary emphasis, however, must be placed on the maximum authorized period of incarceration. Penalties such as probation or a fine may engender "a significant infringement of personal freedom . . . but they cannot approximate in severity the loss of liberty that a prison term entails. Indeed, because incarceration is an 'intrinsically different' form of punishment . . . it is the most powerful indication of whether an offense is 'serious.' " [489 U.S. at 542.]

The Court continued:

> Although we did not hold in *Baldwin* . . . that an offense carrying a maximum prison term of six months or less automatically qualifies as a "petty" offense, and decline to do so today, we do find it appropriate to presume for purposes of the Sixth Amendment that society views such offenses as "petty." A defendant is entitled to jury trial in such circumstances only if he can demonstrate that any additional statutory penalties, viewed in conjunction with the maximum authorized period of incarceration, are so severe that they clearly reflect a legislative determination that the offense in question is a "serious" one. This standard albeit somewhat imprecise, should ensure the availability of a jury trial in the rare situation where a legislature packs an offense it deems "serious" with onerous penalties that nonetheless "do not puncture the 6-month incarceration line." [489 U.S. at 543 (citations omitted).]

Since the ruling in *Blanton,* the Eighth Circuit has ruled that a license revocation of fifteen years as a "collateral consequence" to a drunk driving conviction triggered a right to a jury trial as a matter of law. *Richter v. Fairbanks,* 903 F.2d 1202 (8th Cir. 1990). On the other hand, the Supreme Court of New Jersey has held that a *ten*-year suspension did *not* render the offense sufficiently "serious" that a jury trial was required. *State v. Hamm,* 577 A.2d 1259 (N.J. 1990).

Subsequent to the *Blanton* decision, the U.S. Supreme Court has had an opportunity to apply its own standards for the right to jury trial in a drunk driving case. In *United States v. Nachtigal,* 113 S. Ct. 1072 (1993), the defendant was arrested for driving under the influence in Yosemite National Park. He demanded a jury trial, but the federal magistrate decided that the offense, which was punishable by six months' incarceration and a $5,000 fine, was "petty" under *Blanton* and refused the demand.

On appeal from the ensuing conviction, the federal district court reversed, holding that the combination of six months' incarceration and a large fine indicated a legislative intent that the offense was serious. The Ninth Circuit Court of Appeals affirmed, noting that seven of the nine states within the circuit afforded the right to jury trial in DUI cases.

The Supreme Court reversed the district and circuit courts,

noting the presumption that the offense was petty in nature if punishment was limited to six months or less in jail. The addition of a $5,000 fine failed to overcome this presumption.

Of course, a state is free to adopt a more liberal standard than the minimum federal requirements by granting its citizens a right to jury trial under its own constitution. Thus, for example, in *City of Pasco v. Mace,* 653 P.2d 618 (Wash. 1982), the Washington Supreme Court refused to draw a line between crimes and petty crimes, but instead guaranteed the right to a jury trial for all "crimes." And in *State v. Jordan,* 825 P.2d 1065 (Haw. 1992), the court was confronted with the question of whether a defendant accused of drunk driving continued to have a right to a jury trial after the maximum sentence had been legislatively reduced to 30 days' incarceration for first offenders and 60 days for second offenders. The court responded in the affirmative. Noting that "the penalty that may be imposed is only of minor importance," the court said the critical inquiry is whether the offense was "of a serious nature." Here, it was clear that despite the reduction in possible punishment, the legislature continued to view DUI as a serious crime.

Counsel should not overlook the *aggregate* sentence his client is facing in arguing that a right to jury trial exists. If, for example, the client is charged with drunk driving and a license violation, the *total* potential period of incarceration should be viewed in terms of a consecutive sentence. Thus, for example, a Louisiana appellate court reversed convictions for DUI and "improper lane change" where the maximum possible term for the first was six months and for the second 30 days, holding that the potential maximum sentence of seven months gave the defendant the right to a jury trial. *State v. Thorpe,* 521 So. 2d 682 (La. App. 1988). Similarly, if the defendant is charged with drunk driving with a *prior conviction* and the potential enhanced sentence exceeds six months, a jury trial should be required.

Rebuffed in *State v. Thorpe,* Louisiana prosecutors developed an even more devious method for denying those accused of their right to jury trial. In *State v. Wallace,* 539 So. 2d 123 (La. App. 1989), the defendant was charged with drunk driving and three other offenses — all arising out of the same incident. Rather than charge him in one bill of information, however, the prosecution broke up the charges and charged him in separate bills — thus avoiding the six-month limit on nonjury trials. The defendant's motion to consolidate was denied and he was convicted by a judge. The convictions were reversed on appeal, the court holding that the denial of the motion was an abuse of discretion.

What if the client is charged with both the traditional DUI offense and the newer per se offense — as is common practice? Since the client could be *convicted* of both offenses in most jurisdictions but not *sentenced* as to both, the sentences could probably not be added up for purposes of determining whether a right to jury trial exists.

As of this writing, there are only five states that do not permit jury trials for drunk driving cases which involve maximum sentences of six months' incarceration: Nevada, Louisiana, Mississippi, New Jersey, and New Mexico.

§12.1 The Opening Statement

> A lawyer without history or literature is a mechanic, a mere working mason; if he possesses some knowledge of these, he may venture to call himself an architect.
>
> Sir Walter Scott

Whether or not to make an opening statement and whether to make it before the prosecution case or before the defense case are subjects of heated debate among trial lawyers. This is largely a matter of personal preference, but it is considered by many to be wiser to reserve any intended opening statement until the completion of the prosecution's case, if for no other reason than to deny the prosecutor the chance to adjust his presentation of evidence to the preview of the defense case that has been presented. The element of surprise is, after all, one of the few weapons available to the defense. Another good reason for reserving opening statement is to prevent the prosecution evidence from backfiring against you; it is safer to wait and see exactly what the prosecutor has to offer before telling the jury what the defense will present.

There is, in fact, an argument for giving no opening statement at all. If the jurors are told exactly what evidence will be presented, they may grow bored when the testimony is actually elicited. Too, the impact of evidence can be greater when the jury is not expecting it.

It is the author's view that the opening statement is of critical importance in a drunk driving case — potentially the single most critical element of the trial within counsel's control or influence — and should never be waived. This becomes even more true as courts across the country increasingly restrict the attorney's role in voir dire during the jury selection process.

Certainly, there is a benefit to orienting the jury, to providing them with a "road map" of where they will be going so that evidence will make sense as it is presented. And there is value in "taking the wind out of the sails" of the prosecutor's case — that is, lessening the impact of his evidence by preparing the jury. But the main benefit to an opening statement is providing an alternative "picture" so that the one presented by the prosecution is not accepted as unchallenged by the highly impressionable juror.

It is a simple psychological truth that a juror is most malleable at the beginning of a trial. Nature abhors a vacuum: The human mind deals with the unknown by grasping whatever facts are available to fill that void. Thus whatever set of facts are presented to the juror during this initial formative period will tend to be accepted — and will resist later change. The wet cement dries, and any contradictory facts presented later in the trial will be dealing with a version by then set in hard concrete.

If an opening statement is to be given, counsel should consider the objectives he wishes to achieve and review the contents of the statement with those objectives in mind. The prosecutor's opening statement must be neutralized, for example, in effect cancelling any de facto "presumption of guilt" jurors may have acquired. Weaknesses in the state's case should be disclosed during the opening statement; jurors will thereafter be attentive to evidence concerning these flaws.

It is not enough to attack the state's case, of course: The defense must present an alternative view of what happened. A believable defense theory of the case must be clearly formulated and presented to the jury. Then defense evidence should be effectively summarized in a logical and easily digested way. Legal defenses on which the client will rely should be gone over in layman's language. If there are weaknesses in the defense case, it is better to present them now so that subsequent dramatic impact is lessened and the flaws can be explained or presented in a softer light.

If the defendant is going to testify (and Fifth Amendment jury instructions notwithstanding, it is difficult to win without the defendant's taking the stand), this fact should be strongly emphasized to the jury. It should be explained that he has the right not to testify, but that he is anxious for the chance to tell the jurors why he is innocent. An alternative theory, however, is that whether or not he will testify should not be mentioned in an opening statement. This serves two purposes. First, it keeps the prosecutor guessing: How extensively should be prepare for cross-examination of the defendant — if at all? Second, it maximizes the dramatic effect when the defendant does take the stand — climaxing a building curiosity in the minds of the jury.

The opening statement should, of course, be consistent with questions asked and statements made during jury selection. And, as in voir dire, the client should be humanized ("John Jones") and the prosecutor dehumanized ("counsel for the state" or "the state's attorney").

Finally, counsel should remember to move for exclusion of all witnesses during his making of the opening statement. Obviously, it damages effective cross-examination if the witness gets a previous of what the defense position is and what the defense expects to prove during cross-examination.

John Tarantino, a former regent of the National College for DUI Defense and editor of DWI Journal, offers the following insights and examples for presenting winning opening statements in drunk driving cases. (The material from 3(1) DWI Journal 1 is reproduced with the kind permission of Mr. Tarantino.)

Attorneys Neglect Power of Opening Statements

In civil cases, the message is clear: the opening statement is a critical part of the civil case. Many jurors make up their minds on the basis of the opening statement; the evidence that is presented later only serves to reinforce jurors' conclusions formed during the opening statement. Unfortunately, in criminal cases, both prosecutors and defense attorneys often are ignorant of the opportunities provided by opening statements. As a result, the effects of this important and evanescent litigation tool in persuading jurors remain unrealized.

The greatest offenders in this regard are attorneys who defend accused drunk drivers. For a variety of reasons, these attorneys fail to make an opening statement or [to] make an effective statement. For example, they may be afraid of laying out their "surprise defense," and thereby alerting the prosecutor. Instead, they merely recite a series of facts that they intend to present, attack the prosecutor's facts, or try in some way to disguise and reiterate their closing argument by changing a few words around for the opening statement.

This article demonstrates the shortfalls and inadequacies of these approaches and advocates the civil theory of opening statement. It will explain how to use the opening statement in a drunk driving case in a strong and non-defensive way to win cases. Because the suggestions made are adaptable to any kind of drunk driving case — even the "sure losers," there is no longer "an excuse" for failing to give a non-defensive opening statement.

Waiver of Opening Statement Is Rarely Advisable

Rarely should the drunk driving defense attorney waive an opening statement. Under extremely limited circumstances, however, the attorney might waive an opening statement in a drunk driving case. If the defense is one based solely on a statutory technicality, an opening may be waived. The failure of the arresting police officer to inform the defendant of a certain right, or to afford the opportunity to an independent test are examples when waiver may be appropriate.

Cases in which the client possesses a severe physical disability that you do not want to bring to the jury's attention immediately also present a situation in which waiver of the opening statement may be appropriate. You may want the jurors to learn of the disability only when the defendant is asked to make the difficult trip to the stand. Such cases are extremely rare, however, and generally it is better not to gamble that your waiver of the opening statement will produce a dramatic effect, unless you have total confidence in your ability as an advocate and are one of the few extremely skilled trial attorneys. Consider instead whether the opening statement should be made immediately after the prosecutor's statement or should be reserved until the conclusion of the State's case.

Reserving Opening Statement Is Tactical Decision

If an opening statement is waived altogether, the jury will hear all of the prosecutor's evidence in the light most favorable to the State. Even if opening is made, but reserved, the jury will listen, observe and assimilate facts consistent with the prosecutor's opening. As a result, there is a real advantage in opening immediately after the prosecutor opens. The opening statement permits you to communicate directly with the jury and to educate both the jury and the judge on the reasons why your client should not be found guilty. The opening statement also provides a vehicle for lessening the impact of the prosecutor's statement.

Under specific circumstances, it may be advisable to reserve (as opposed to waive) the opening statement until the conclusion of the State's case. These circumstances are limited and usually occur only when your defense is an extremely technical one or where you anticipate a motion for acquittal at the close of the State's case. Examples of when an opening statement might be reserved are as follows:

1. If you are as yet uncertain as to whether the client will testify.
2. If evidence or witnesses exist of which the State is unaware, but which the State may be able to rebut if the prosecutor has sufficient time and advance notice.
3. If the defense case depends entirely upon the State's case, and you need to formulate your defense as the State presents its case.
4. If you have had a particularly strong voir dire in which a good relationship with the jury has developed, and the trial is expected to be a long and involved one.

In the last instance, the immediate impression of the defense's opening statement may be lost after a strong voir dire. In such situations it may be best to reserve the opening statement until the close of the State's case.

Limit Opening Statement to Single Theme

Remember that the opening statement sets the tone for the entire defense theory of the case. There must be a theme to the opening statement. You must not merely ramble on about the facts or try to address each of the assertions made in the prosecutor's opening statement. To the extent possible try to limit the opening to a single theme and try the case as if it were based on that single theme. Obviously, in cases in which there is little or no defense you must attack each point of the State's case when you are given an opportunity to do so. In such cases you should still, however, have one central theme to the opening even though you must employ a shotgun approach to the actual defense of the case.

For example, you may want to focus your theme on the presumption of innocence. The opening in such a case may begin as follows:

> Ladies and gentlemen, I represent the defendant, Dan Johnson, who has been accused by the State of driving under the influence of alcohol. Dan will not testify in this trial nor will he present any witnesses. Dan's lifestyle, his drinking history, his likes, dislikes and views are irrelevant and are not proper subject matters for you to judge. The only issue before you today is, did Dan Johnson on October 21, 1987 commit the crime of driving under the influence of alcohol.
>
> The prosecutor will not present a single witness who will testify that he or she ever saw Dan Johnson drive the car. All we know is that a police officer arrived at the scene of a single vehicle accident, where Dan Johnson was present. As a result of his observations of Dan Johnson, the police officer *inferred* that Dan must have been driving under the influence of alcohol. No one will tell you what actually took place; no one will place Dan Johnson behind the wheel; no one will tell you whether Dan Johnson actually consumed a drink containing alcohol that night.
>
> Rather, the State will rely on a machine, a non-living, nonbreathing nonhuman witness. The State will ask you to place your trust in that machine and the State will ask you to convict a man, a human being, someone who stands before you presumed to be innocent, based upon what a machine says.
>
> Under our system of justice, which is the best system in the world, it is the prosecution's job to present evidence that will persuade beyond a reasonable doubt that you, as jurors, and not the police, the prosecutor or the machine, know with certainty that Dan Johnson was driving under the influence of alcohol. It is only if you conclude with such certainty that Dan Johnson was driving under the influence of alcohol that you will be able to return a guilty verdict.

Opening Statement Undercuts "Bad Facts"

Most drunk driving cases involve "bad facts," or facts that do not place the defendant in a favorable light. There are, however, ways to deal with bad facts in the opening statement. Assume, for example, that your client has three prior drunk driving arrests and convictions. Even though you know these facts are legally irrelevant to show the defendant's guilt as to the current charge, you fear that the facts will undoubtedly influence the jury in concluding that the defendant was actually driving under the influence for purposes of the present charge. The following is an example of how to create a positive image from these negative facts:

The State has not charged, nor could it charge Dan Johnson with being a drunk. Thank goodness for that because Dan Johnson has on three previous occasions admitted that he was driving under the influence of alcohol. As a result he was convicted, based upon his admission of guilt. He has admitted the crime of driving under the influence in the past, and if that kind of history were a crime in and of itself then he would be guilty again, no question about it. But that's not the way our system works. The prosecutor has charged Dan Johnson with driving under the influence on a particular occasion and that is the issue that you must resolve as the triers of fact today. In our society we will not convict someone of being a bad person because of prior bad acts. As a society, we have concluded that this is not fair. That conclusion will be tested today and the fairness of our system will be tested today based upon this very case.

As I said before, Dan Johnson has been convicted three times of driving under the influence of alcohol. He didn't have a trial in those cases; he admitted what he had done. He was charged and he took his punishment. To this charge, however, Dan Johnson has said for the first time, "No, I am not guilty!" He not only said this when he pleaded just prior to this trial, but he will tell you again himself, in the flesh, when he takes the witness stand to testify in his own defense. He will tell you that he was not drunk. He will tell you that he was not driving erratically. He will tell you a variety of things about that night from which we hope you will conclude that he was not driving under the influence. And finally, he will tell you, as I have just said, that he has been convicted of drunk driving in the past.

Ladies and gentlemen, that is a fact you would never have known but for Dan Johnson's testimony today. But it is also a fact that should have no influence in your determination of whether Dan Johnson is guilty of the crime for which he is charged.

Deliver Opening Statement Promises

One of the major pitfalls in any defense is to make a promise that cannot be delivered. To win a drunk driving case, you must be perceived as credible by the jury. If you make a promise in the opening statement and that promise is not fulfilled, your credibility will be severely weakened if not totally shattered. If the jurors believe that you intentionally sought to deceive them, you can be sure that they will return a guilty verdict.

It is important to explain to the jurors the facts upon which you will rely so that they will focus on them when those facts develop during the trial. But it is equally important to be conservative in your evaluation of what kind of evidence you will have available to you either on your own direct examination or through the cross-examination of the State's witnesses. Many times a fact or admission that you thought would come out on cross-examination is not successfully elicited.

Err on the side of caution. You can always bring home the points made on cross-examination during your closing argument, but you can never take back a promise once made during the opening statement.

Avoid Defense Admissions in Opening Statement

Another danger defense attorneys face is the possibility of making judicial admissions during the opening statement that can then be used to bind your client or that can be used by the State in meeting its burden of proof. This can happen when the State has difficulty proving one of the elements of the offense, but you supply that missing element through an admission made during the opening statement. In one case, for example, defense counsel's admission that the defendant was "behind the wheel" was held to have established the requisite driving element necessary to prove the crime charged. In such cases, if you supply the necessary admission, then the client may be convicted even if the State has no other proof of driving [*State v. Cassada,* 58 Or.App. 84 (1982); *see also,* Tarantino, *Defending Drinking Drivers 2d §620, 6-5 (Santa Ana: James, 1986)* (1987 Supp.)].

Scrutinize Prosecutor's Opening Statement

You can learn a great deal by watching the jury during the prosecutor's opening statement. You will be able to determine what points the jury seems most interested in and you will be able to focus on any potential rebuttal you have for those points during your defense opening.

Be careful to note any prejudicial remarks made by the prosecutor during the opening. If this occurs, you should immediately move for a mistrial or at least request a curative instruction.

Focus on Defense Strengths

If you have a case in which a favorable defense applies, focus on that evidence during your opening statement. For example, in a case in which there is a high breath test result but a favorable videotape, the following opening might be used:

> Ladies and gentlemen, this case presents a unique opportunity for you. In most cases you have to reach your conclusions based upon what some witness told you that he or she saw the defendant do. For

example, a police officer might tell you how the defendant performed and failed several field sobriety tests, or the State might offer evidence of what the defendant's blood alcohol content was based upon some machine's test result. From that evidence you would be asked to judge credibility and then determine whether the defendant should be convicted of the crime charged.

But in this case, things are different because you can actually see, hear and decide for yourself what happened to the defendant that night in the police station because what happened is on videotape. The videotape acts as a silent witness, a witness that shows you what actually happened. In this case you need not merely rely upon what someone else said happened; you can look at the videotape and relive those events. You can see how the defendant performed those tests on the videotape; you can listen to his speech; you can judge his coordination; and you can draw conclusions from that tape about his attitude, his demeanor and his coordination. From the videotape you will be able to determine from your own observations whether the defendant was intoxicated. That tape will be played for you, and you will have an opportunity to look at it, to study, to examine it and to conclude from that tape how you will vote.

Humanize the Client/Dehumanize the Prosecutor

One of the most important things you can do during the opening statement is to have the jurors realize that they are judging a particular individual who is an actual person — not just a named defendant. You must do everything possible to humanize your client. If the court allows, call your client by his or her first name when appropriate. Approach your client while you are examining him or her. Try to look comfortable with your client at counsel table. Make the jury understand that they are judging and will have to convict a human being. It is more difficult for jurors to convict someone they know, as opposed to a removed "defendant."

On the other hand, do everything possible to dehumanize the prosecutor. Continually refer to him or her as "the prosecutor." Do not call him or her by name. Try to make the prosecutor as unreal and inhuman as possible. It is harder for a jury to warm up and accept "the prosecutor" than it is to accept John Smith, the district attorney.

Maintain Professional Relationship with Court and Prosecutor

You must always strive to foster and maintain a professional relationship with the court and the prosecutor. Your professionalism will enhance your credibility with the judge and the jury. This professionalism should come across during all aspects of the trial, but especially during the opening statement.

Remember that the opening statement is not an appropriate time to argue, but it is a time to be persuasive. Present a logical and believable narrative to the jury, focus on your strengths, and when appropriate, apprise the jury of the weaknesses in your case. Above all, establish a central theme from which, consistent with the evidence that will be presented, the jury will return a verdict of not guilty.

DWI Checklist
Opening Statements

1. Consider the following alternatives in determining whether, and when, the opening statement should be made:
   a. Extremely limited circumstances for waiver.
   b. Immediate opening.
   c. Reservation of opening until close of the State's case.
2. Set a theme for the opening, remembering to:
   a. Apprise the jury of the presumption of innocence.
   b. Present evidence in light most favorable to the defense.
   c. Inform the jury of any weaknesses in the defense case and any defenses upon which you plan to rely.
   d. Be consistent with a verdict of not guilty.
3. Focus on the strengths of the defense.
   a. Create a positive image from negative facts.
   b. If defendant is going to testify, maximize the event by explaining that the defendant need not testify but he or she wants to explain why he or she is not guilty.
   c. Personalize the defendant; dehumanize the prosecutor.
4. Avoid making promises that cannot be fulfilled.
5. Be careful not to make judicial admissions that can be used against the client.
6. Determine and address those points of prosecutor's opening statements that most interest the jurors, and note any prejudicial remarks.

§12.1.1 Illustrative Opening Statement

The reader may benefit from the following comments and excellent sample opening statement graciously provided by DUI specialist Flem Whited III of Daytona Beach, Florida.

An opening statement should always be made. In my opinion, reserving your right to make an opening statement until after the close of the state's evidence is a fatal mistake. Studies have shown that most jurors believe that most persons charged with crimes are guilty of something when the trial starts. That belief is enhanced after the state makes its opening statement. The defense attorney should absolutely, positively make an opening statement in each and every case to neutralize the damaging effects of the state's opening statement and to let the jury know that there is another side of the story.

Whether or not you have the absolute right to make an opening statement may be subject to state statute, rules of criminal procedure, or a local rule. There does not seem to be any Constitutional right to make an opening statement. I would suggest that you review the following cases: *United States v. Stanfield,* 521 F.2d 1122 (9th Cir. 1975); *United States v. Dinitz,* 424 U.S. 600 (1976); *United States v. Hershenow,* 680 F.2d 847 (1st Cir. 1982); *United States v. Salovitz,* 701 F.2d 17 (2d Cir. 1983).

The single most important function the opening statement provides in trial is to neutralize the state's opening. In describing to the jurors what the evidence will show, you will be educating them regarding your theory of defense. Your purpose should be to review the facts that will come out in evidence that are favorable to your client. Review the rules of law that the jury members have agreed to apply in the case, and at the close of your opening statement relate to the jury that at the end of the trial you are going to be asking them to return a verdict of not guilty. Express to them the confidence you have that the evidence will show that there is truly reasonable doubt.

Your opening statement should follow a definite path. The following is a suggested structure or outline of where you should start and where you should stop in your opening statement.

1. Introduction

At this point you should thank the jury for their open and candid answers to all your questions. Introduce them to the stage of the proceedings you are in. You should reiterate that your client was arrested, taken to jail, and when given his first opportunity to either accept or deny his guilt, that he denied it and that that is what led us to where we are today. Your introduction should also include a brief review of the rules of law that apply. When they listen to the evidence that comes into trial they must be mindful of the fact that the evidence that the prosecution shows must eliminate all reasonable doubt that Mr. Cooper was, in fact, impaired while he was driving his automobile.

2. Review of the Evidence

When making the opening statement, you should review the evidence that will be presented in descriptive terms, but not so descriptive as to tip specific facts. If you are going to argue the field sobriety test was given in an unsuitable location, then in your opening statement explain to the jury that the evidence is going to show exactly where this roadside sobriety test took place and under what circumstances, using those terms. If your client has some health problem or physical disability that the trooper or police officer did not address during the course of his investigation, then in your opening statement you should tell the jury that your client, if he is going to testify, is going to come forward and tell you exactly how he did on the roadside sobriety test, and he is going to tell you in no uncertain terms his physical condition at the time and the circumstances under which he was given these tests. This way you are acknowledging to them what the evidence is going to show without telling them exactly what the evidence is, so you do not tip the prosecutor off prior to the direct examination of their witnesses.

3. Closing Your Opening

Let the jurors know that you are sure that the evidence is going to show, in this case, that there will be a reasonable doubt in their minds as to whether or not your client is guilty of driving under the influence to the extent that his normal faculties were impaired. Let them know that at the closing of the case you are going to be asking them to return a verdict of not guilty based upon the evidence as it comes in during the trial.

The following is an example of a good opening statement.

> Good morning, ladies and gentlemen of the jury. We have reached that point in the trial that the judge has just described to you as the opening statement. It is now that the lawyers for both sides have the opportunity to tell you what the evidence is going to show in the case. It serves a valuable function in this trial, in that it allows you to get an overview of what the evidence is going to show

in the trial so that when that evidence comes out you will not be surprised by it and will understand the importance of it when it does come out in the trial. The evidence is going to show us, ladies and gentlemen, that on September 4th, 1987, Mr. Cooper was arrested by a police officer and taken to jail. At his first opportunity to admit that he committed the crime or deny that he committed a crime, he denied it and said that he wanted his day in court. We have been through the first part of the trial, voir dire. There, all of us acknowledged that this trial would be conducted according to the rules of law that we discussed in voir dire. We acknowledged that the rules of law relating the presumption of innocence and the burden of proof and the law that the State must prove its case beyond and to the exclusion of every reasonable doubt would apply in this case. As you review the evidence in this case and listen to it as it comes into this trial, be mindful of these most important rules of law.

Ladies and gentlemen, you have just heard what the prosecutor has said the evidence will show as far as the state is concerned. They have indicated to you that a highway patrol trooper responded to the scene of an accident and after conducting an accident investigation, thought Mr. Cooper was impaired by alcohol. The trooper dutifully administered a roadside sobriety test and after that roadside sobriety test placed Mr. Cooper under arrest for driving under the influence. The evidence will show you a lot more than just that. You are going to be given the benefit, through the evidence, of the entire evening that Mr. Cooper spent. Fortunately for all of us, there will be evidence at this trial of Mr. Cooper's movement throughout the evening. You have just heard from the prosecution that a trooper arrived at the scene of a crime and placed Mr. Cooper under arrest. The evidence will show you that his total time on the scene and involvement with Mr. Cooper was probably no more than five to ten minutes. The evidence will further show you that the police officer involved did not know Mr. Cooper before this day and has not seen or observed him in circumstances that did not involve an automobile accident. You will have the benefit of evidence showing you exactly what Mr. Cooper did when he got home from work, exactly what he had to drink, and where he went. You will be given facts relating to his ability to walk, talk, judge distances, act in emergencies, drive a car, and generally do the things that he does in his normal daily life before the accident.

Ladies and gentlemen, the evidence is going to show you that on September 4th, 1987, Mr. Cooper got off work, came home, and met with his friends. He consumed one beer after work, and he and his friends decided to spend an evening out mingling with other people their age. The evidence is going to show you, ladies and gentlemen, that a conscious decision was made on behalf of all these people that one person would be the designated driver this evening.

Gary Cooper was that designated driver and it was the decision of all parties that he would restrict his consumption of alcohol so that his friends could consume more if they so desired. Ladies and gentlemen, the evidence is going to show you that they did exactly what they planned to do. That they left their home and went to one location where other young folks were and from there went to another location where other people about the same age were likely to be. The evidence will show you, ladies and gentlemen, that during the course of the entire evening, from approximately eight o'clock in the evening until when the accident occurred, Mr. Cooper only consumed two twelve-ounce cans of beer. The evidence is going to show you why he did this and the evidence will show you, based upon the witnesses' observations of his ability to walk, talk, and judge distances, that in no way was he impaired prior to the time that this accident occurred. The evidence is going to show you that there was an accident and that who caused the accident is a matter of dispute. The evidence will show you that when the trooper arrived on the scene, he immediately went to the driver and the occupants of the other car and talked to them. The evidence is going to show you that he did not ask any questions of the passengers of Mr. Cooper's vehicle other than their names and addresses. The evidence will show you that he did not ask them their version of the accident or what color the light was as they observed it and when they went through it. The evidence will show you that he did not ask any questions of the passengers of Mr. Cooper's vehicle relating to his state of sobriety prior to this action. The evidence is going to show you that the accident virtually totalled both automobiles and that Mr. Cooper's vehicle had to be towed from the scene because it was undrivable. The passengers in Mr. Cooper's vehicle will give you the benefit of their observations of him both before and after the accident occurred. They will also give you the benefit of their observations of him as he took the roadside sobriety test.

Ladies and gentlemen, you will try to determine Mr. Cooper's state of emotional well-being after the accident and will no doubt decide that he was not the same person after the accident as he was before the accident. The evidence will show you that within ten to fifteen minutes of being involved in an accident that left two vehicles virtually undrivable, he was subjected to this roadside sobriety test, and the evidence, including both Mr. Cooper's testimony and that of observers, will show you how he performed on that test and why.

Ladies and gentlemen, there is one thing I am sure the evidence will show you in this case and that is that there is a reasonable doubt as to whether or not Gary Cooper was impaired by alcohol before this accident occurred. At the close of this trial, I am going to come before you and ask that you return a verdict of not guilty based on the evidence that comes into this trial. Thank you.

§12.2 Using Demonstrative Evidence

> Whatsoever is almost true is quite false, and among the most dangerous of errors, because being so near truth, it is more likely to lead astray.
>
> HENRY WARD BEEGHER

"A picture is worth a thousand words" — and a visual demonstration is worth twice that. It is an accepted psychological fact, of course, that audiovisual evidence has a significantly greater impact on jurors than mere testimony. In this age of constant and rapid-fire visual stimulation, such forms of evidence will hold the juror's attention for a greater period of time and will remain in the memory longer and more vividly.

The drunk driving case presents unique opportunities for using demonstrative evidence in trial. Driving symptoms and traffic conditions, roadside field sobriety tests, the theory and administration of blood-alcohol testing — these and other areas lend themselves well to visual explanation and reconstruction. In fact, counsel in a DUI trial is limited by little more than imagination and budget in illustrating for the jury what are often very complex considerations.

Photographs of the scene where the defendant took the field sobriety tests are the simplest and most obvious examples of the use of audiovisual evidence. However, the imaginative use of demonstrative evidence can be considerably more effective.

As an example, Phillip Price of Montgomery, Alabama, is fond of using children's toys in reconstructing the events surrounding his client's arrest. To help the jury understand the difficult circumstances under which field sobriety tests are conducted, he sets up a small toy figure representing his client. Then he closely surrounds the figure with the appropriate number of officers — represented by large, muscular police figures (Price prefers "He-Men, Masters of the Universe"). Then he adds a large toy police car or two, again depending upon the facts, with emergency lights brightly flashing. Finally, he may have trucks and cars passing nearby with headlights. If permitted by the court, he then turns out the lights in the courtroom to simulate the nighttime conditions under which the tests were administered.

Another attorney, confronted with a case with a high blood-alcohol reading, obtains an estimate from the officer or expert witness as to how many beers would have to have been consumed by the defendant to reach that level. The witness may estimate, for example, that the defendant probably drank 14 12-ounce cans of beer over three hours. The attorney then has the witness pour 14 cans of beer into a five-gallon clear plastic water jug. The result is visually impressive: It is difficult for the jury to believe that anyone could have consumed the huge quantity of foaming beer in the jug.

Again, the possible uses for graphic means of presenting evidence in drunk driving trials are almost endless. The following comments, however, present a few of the more traditional uses. The author is grateful to Douglas Cowan of Bellevue, Washington, for his permission to use this material:

> The kinds of demonstrative evidence that can be utilized in a drunk driving trial, and the uses to which they can be put, are limited only by the defense lawyer's imagination. Keep in mind that demonstrative evidence that will be effective in trial can be equally effective during plea negotiations.
>
> Photographs are the most frequently used demonstrative evidence. In our firm, we have an investigator who visits the scene of the arrest for any case that appears likely to go to trial. The investigator is trained to note lighting, traffic, and topographical conditions, and to photograph the same when appropriate. There is nothing more effective than a large photograph showing the scene where a client was required to perform various feats of balance and coordination, while a large semi bears down on the scene at an obviously high speed. The visual impact graphically portrays the difficulty that a client would have not only in performing the tasks required, but in maintaining concentration.
>
> Also effective is the use of photographs to show that the scene of the field tests was not level, as claimed, or to show the extent of debris and pebbles strewn upon the location of the tests.
>
> We have also, on occasion, utilized the services of a videographer to videotape the same locations. Videotape is even more effective for recreating the route that was followed by the client with the officer in hot pursuit. Effectively done, a videotape can show the difficulty a driver would experience in seeing lane dividers or fog lines, and can expose potholes or other defects in the road that could explain why the client was not driving a perfectly straight line. Furthermore, on occasion, the use of a videotape, or

a photograph, can demonstrate that the officer could not possibly have seen what he or she claims to have seen.

We consider our demonstrative evidence library to be most effective in attacking breath tests, the resources of which should be readily available to all DUI defense practitioners throughout the country.

We start with an enlarged schematic diagram of our breath testing machine, the BAC Verifier DataMaster. While the use of schematics often carries the risk of lending credibility to a machine, we find the use of the schematic to be particularly helpful during opening statements, when we can show the various important components and highlight those that may have significance in the specific case being tried.

We also have a blown-up, full-color photograph of the inside of the machine, as well as of the simulator, with solution attached. The combination graphically demonstrates the complexities of the machine, and lends credibility to the assertion that all of the components must be working in concert for the machine to work.

The operator's manual can be a gold mine of demonstrative evidence. There are often diagrams, graphs, or charts that can be blown up to emphasize a point; and the point is even more graphically demonstrated when the source comes from a state resource rather than from the defense. The operator's manual for the DataMaster, for example, contains two alcohol curves, one of which shows the impact of eating on absorption. These are particularly helpful when a state's expert attempts to engage in speculative retrograde extrapolation.

Most operator manuals contain a section that instructs an officer what to do when problems are encountered. A blow-up of the appropriate page, or pages, can be used when an officer has failed to follow those instructions.

The effectiveness of this technique is enhanced when the operator's manual is used in conjunction with a service manual or troubleshooting guide that explains in lengthy detail what the manufacturer requires to be done in the event of a problem.

In the State of Washington, each DataMaster creates a database. The database is a computer-generated compilation of every test ever run on the machine, not only those administered to actual defendants, but those run by the crime lab during testing, during routine maintenance, or for certification. It also records "error codes," i.e., indications that a malfunction occurred.

It is amazing how many times an operator has attempted to deal with a malfunction by simply turning the machine off and turning it back on again, rather than following the manufacturer's recommendations for repair and maintenance.

Accordingly, when we identify such an occurrence we use a blow-up of the operator's manual page that instructs an officer what to do when problems are encountered, as well as a blow-up of those pages of the service manual that instruct the crime lab on how to respond to a given problem.

By reviewing the database and the blow-ups, and by showing that the state's expert has no repair records indicating that the manufacturer's recommendations were followed on a given occasion, we can show the number of occasions in which complex maintenance procedures were not followed on a particular machine — generally both before and after our client was subjected to testing on this machine.

Parenthetically, if our client's breath test appears on a page of the database on which a number of error codes appear, a blow-up of that page is extremely effective in creating doubt as to the proper working condition of the machine on the date of the client's test.

Another effective use of demonstrative evidence is to blow up pages of scientific journals that contain information helpful to the defense. We prefer to focus on articles by state's experts, such as Dr. Kurt Dubowski. For example, on occasion we have summarized the conclusions that appear on page 106 of his article in Volume 10 of the Journal of Studies on Alcohol (July 1985), which conclude that there is no validity to the concept of retrograde extrapolation. Additionally, we have enlarged some of the actual blood-alcohol curves upon which his conclusions are based.

13

CROSS-EXAMINATION

§13.0 The Arresting Officer

> Our civilization has decided . . . that determining the guilt or innocence of men is a thing too important to be trusted to trained men. . . . When it wants a library catalogued, or the solar system discovered, or any trifle of that kind, it uses up its specialists. But when it wishes anything done which is really serious, it collects twelve of the ordinary men standing round. The same thing was done, if I remember right, by the Founder of Christianity.
>
> G. K. Chesterton

In most cases, the field evidence produced by the prosecution will be in the form of testimony from one or more police officers, usually the officer or officers who arrested the defendant. In some cases, such as where the initial police contact comes from a call to the scene of an accident, lay witness testimony — often of the occupants of the car involved in the collision with the defendant's vehicle — will be offered as an integral part of the prosecution case (and, in fact, will be necessary to establishing the "driving" element of the offense). Lay witness testimony is, of course, usually given less weight by the jury; it is the testimony of the trained, experienced, and "impartial" police officer that carries weight with the triers of fact. And it is this witness that a good drunk driving lawyer must learn to deal with.

Generally speaking, the testimony of a police officer can be approached in the following steps:

1. questioning the officer's qualifications and experience in the very limited area of drunk driving
2. establishing his predisposition to believe the defendant guilty at initial stages of the field detention
3. suggesting innocent explanations for incriminating observations
4. emphasizing the observations that tend to establish the defendant's sobriety
5. attacking the officer's observations, interrogations, and testing procedures — including procedures the officer failed to follow

Counsel must deal with each officer on an individual basis, understanding at all times the jurors' attitudes toward his questioning. Where a knock-down cross-examination of an officer under one set of circumstances may be appropriate, a very tactful and respectful approach may be more productive under another.

Counsel also should be fully aware of who he is dealing with on the witness stand when he takes on a police officer: a professional witness. This is not a citizen who is shaken by his first appearance on the stand, but a person who has probably been there many times before. This is a witness who has lost his awe of the courtroom, who has sparred with skilled defense attorneys on many previous occasions, and who has learned to impress the jury with his calm and polite manners while taking every opportunity during cross-examination to ram the knife deeper into the defendant. He is, in short, usually a fairly skilled adversary who should be viewed as such; the days of the "dumb cop" are rapidly passing.

Perhaps above all, counsel should recognize that in confronting the police officer he is dealing with an individual, not a clone. Each officer is different; each has his own unique beliefs, attitudes, and prejudices; each varies in his degree of intelligence, honesty, and experience. In emphasizing the effect of these individual differences on an officer's conduct in the field, a relatively recent study conducted by the National Highway Safety Administration (U.S. Department of Transportation Report #H5-801-230) found, among other things, that:

> The officer's age and experience play a role in his alcohol-related arrest decisions. Younger officers, and those with relatively

few years of seniority, tend to have a more positive attitude toward alcohol-related enforcement and make more arrests on that charge than do their older officers. This result was found to hold true regardless of the type of department in which the officer serves or the specific type of duty to which he is assigned.

The officer's personal use of alcohol is inversely related to his level of alcohol-related enforcement. Patrolmen who drink make significantly fewer arrests than those who do not, and those who drink frequently make significantly fewer arrests than those who use alcohol only occasionally.

Lack of knowledge concerning the relationship between alcohol and intoxication is widespread among police officers and imparts a negative influence on alcohol-related enforcement. Most officers underestimate — often by a wide margin — the amount of alcohol a suspect would have to consume in order to achieve the statutory limit of blood alcohol concentration. This seems to induce a tendency among officers to identify and sympathize with the suspects they encounter.

Specialized training has a strong positive influence on alcohol-related arrests. Patrolmen who have received instruction in the operation of breath testing devices and/or in alcohol-related enforcement — particularly in municipal departments — were found to lack this specialized training.

Specialization in duty assignment can also enhance alcohol-related enforcement. Patrolmen assigned to traffic divisions, in particular, produce higher arrest rates than those charged with general patrol duties. . . .

Near the end of the duty shift, alcohol-related investigations decrease substantially. This is particularly true in departments that have adopted relatively time-consuming procedures for processing alcohol-related arrests. . . .

Weather conditions also effect alcohol-related arrests. There is encouraging evidence that foul weather has a positive influence on the attitude of many officers: they are more appreciative of the risk posed by an alcohol-related suspect when driving conditions are hazardous, and are less likely to avoid the arrest when those conditions prevail. . . .

The suspect's attitude can have a strong influence on the arrest/no arrest decision. If the suspect proves uncooperative or argumentative, a positive influence for arrest results. Conversely, the likelihood of arrest decreases when the suspect seems cooperative. . . .

The suspect's race is a key distinguishing characteristic in

> alcohol-related cases. The officers surveyed — the overwhelming majority of whom were white — reported releasing significantly more non-white suspects than they arrested. The data do not suggest that this reflects a greater tendency to exercise discretion when dealing with non-white drivers. Rather, the officers seem more willing to initiate an investigation when the suspect is not of their own race.
>
> Suspect's age is another distinguishing characteristic of these cases, and patrolmen reported releasing significantly more young suspects than they arrested. This appears to stem from two distinct causes. First, young officers exhibit more sympathy for young suspects, i.e., seem less disposed to arrest a driver of their own age group. Second, older officers seem more willing to stop young suspects, i.e., are more likely to conduct an investigation when the driver is young, even if the evidence of alcohol-related violation is not clear.
>
> Suspect's sex also plays a role in the arrest/no arrest decision. Patrolmen seem more reluctant to arrest a woman for alcohol-related violations, largely because processing of a female arrestee is generally more complex and time consuming. . . .

In a fascinating article entitled Psychology, Public Policy, and the Evidence for Alcohol Intoxication, American Psychologist 1070 (Oct. 1983), James W. Langenbrucher and Peter E. Nathan reported a series of experiments conducted at Rutgers University's Alcohol Behavior Research Laboratory to test the ability of social drinkers, bartenders, and police officers to estimate the sobriety of individuals. The results should be of considerable interest to any attorney representing a client charged with driving under the influence of alcohol — and may be admissible in evidence during direct or cross-examination of expert witnesses. The researchers addressed the specific issue of whether nonmedical observers can reliably judge an individual's level of intoxication.

The first experiment involved the testing of lay witnesses — 49 individuals who were themselves "social" drinkers. Two men and two women were employed as subjects; for some tests no alcohol was consumed, for others varying blood-alcohol levels of intoxication were reached. In each case the subject was brought into a room and was asked to sit down where the "witnesses" were sitting. The subject was then interviewed at length to elicit a range of verbal behavior and somatic and cognitive effects. When the interview was over, the subject rose from the chair and walked out of the room — again, in full view of the observers.

The witnesses' observations resulted in the conclusion:

> The assumption that social drinkers would prove to be accurate judges of the [blood-alcohol levels] of other persons was not confirmed. . . . On only 4 of 16 occasions did a significant number of subjects correctly classify a target on a three-stage categorical index of intoxication level. . . . If determining whether [a] man is sober or intoxicated is a matter of common observation, then our subjects apparently lacked this capacity. [Id. at 1072.]

The scientists next dealt with a type of witness with considerably more expertise in the area, 12 bartenders who were tested in the setting of a large cocktail lounge in a New Jersey hotel. The results again proved interesting:

> The bartenders correctly rated a target in only one of four instances. . . . Contrary to expectation, no relationship between years of experience as a bartender and [blood-alcohol level] estimation accuracy was found. These data suggest strongly that these bartenders did not possess and had not acquired special knowledge or skill in identifying intoxicated persons. [Id. at 1074.]

Finally, the psychologists proceeded to test 30 law enforcement officers from various New Jersey agencies. Of these, 15 were tested under conditions similar to those in the first experiment; another 15 were tested under conditions commonly encountered in a DUI traffic stop — at night, with the subject behind the wheel of a car, who is then asked to step out and conduct a series of field sobriety tests. The results: ''When police observers in the laboratory condition were compared to social drinkers who had experienced an identical procedure, no difference in rating accuracy was found. . . . Officers in the arrest analogue condition were somewhat more accurate than their colleagues in the laboratory condition but not significantly so.'' Id. at 1076.

The scientists then concluded that ''the results of the three experiments described here are not reassuring. All three of the subject groups studied — social drinkers, bartenders, and police officers — correctly judged targets' levels of intoxication only 25 percent of the time. . . .'' Ibid.

In cross-examination of the police officer, as in all phases of trial, preparation represents the key to success. Besides learning the background and training of the officer; counsel should obtain all reports, statements, and transcripts relevant to the case, particularly if they involve the officer in question. Counsel should visit the scene of the arrest and determine the lighting conditions at the time, and he should note the distances involved, location of obstructions, etc. This not only permits more effective on-your-feet cross-examination but enhances counsel's own credibility in the eyes of the jury.

Counsel should try to interview the officer in advance of trial. If depositions are permitted, one should be taken; if not, informal questioning may be a possibility if handled tactfully. (But see §13.0.1.)

Police officers usually have little independent recollection of the events in a given drunk driving investigation, relying heavily on memorization and periodic reference to their arrest report. This lack of memory should be clearly developed for the jury.

If counsel has the opportunity to examine the officer at an administrative license suspension hearing, he should ask if the report was reviewed prior to testimony and then make clear on the record every time the officer needs to "refresh his recollection" by reading the report. With sufficiently detailed cross-examination, the officer will repeatedly have to acknowledge that he cannot remember. He can then be confronted with this earlier inability to recall when he testifies later at trial with seemingly perfect recollection.

If the officer has to repeatedly refer to his report in his testimony in trial, counsel should move to have his entire testimony stricken on the grounds that he has no independent recollection. Using documents to refresh a witness's recollection is, of course, permitted under the rules of evidence — *assuming that there is an existing memory.* If it becomes apparent that the witness is not testifying from refreshed memory, but is merely regurgitating the report, then the testimony is inadmissible.

Finally, counsel should attempt to have the trial court require police witnesses to testify in civilian clothing. The authoritarian or other effect of a police uniform on some jurors can be substantial.

§13.0.1 Preparation

Most defense attorneys in drunk driving cases do little more to prepare for cross-examination of the arresting officer than review the arrest report. This is tantamount to playing on the officer's field and accepting his version of the rules.

Counsel should *prepare* well in advance for cross-examination of this all-important witness. Appropriate motions to exclude portions of the officer's testimony should, of course, be made prior to trial (see Chapter 11). And discovery of such items as videotapes, "mug shots," and nonrecorded oral statements should be obtained. But other, less obvious, avenues of preparation are available as well.

The author has been successful in the recent past with filing discovery motions containing a request for arrest reports executed by the arresting officer *in other cases.* The motion asks for all reports completed by the officer in any other drunk driving cases that occurred within 15 of his working days of the arrest in question — that is, reports of all DUI arrests for a period of 31 of the officer's working days. Attached to the motion is a declaration setting forth the reasons for the request:

> Copies of reports made by the arresting officer herein in other cases involving driving under the influence of alcohol or drugs are necessary to determine whether this officer was engaged in the common practice of merely reproducing standard or so-called "xeroxed" symptoms and observations in his arrests.

It is a simple fact of life, as any experienced drunk driving lawyer knows, that many officers tend to "see" the same symptoms in case after case. Whether out of laziness, preconception, or dishonesty, the officer will begin reproducing symptoms in his report. This is particularly true of experienced officers who handle many DUI cases, as the repetition becomes tedious and the officer soon realizes that defense attorneys will not have access to his other reports. Thus, for example, many or all of the officer's reports will reflect that the suspect fumbled with his wallet getting out his driver's license, missed "Q" in the alphabet, stumbled on the third step of the walk-the-line test, and swayed exactly three inches on the modified-position-of-attention test.

The prosecutor will usually oppose this motion on three grounds. First, the request is merely a "fishing expedition": There is no evidence that the officer in fact uses "xeroxed symptoms." The reply, of course, is that this is a *Catch-22:* How can anyone *know* if the officer is doing this without copies of other reports to review?

The second prosecution argument is that obtaining such reports is "unduly burdensome" and expensive. This oft-used reply can be countered with an explanation that, in most cases, there may be typically only four or five reports involved in a 31-day period. And, of course, the defense is perfectly willing to reimburse the prosecution for the costs of reproducing the reports.

Finally, the prosecutor will counter the request for discovery with a sudden and touching concern for the privacy of the individuals arrested in the other cases. Again, the reply is simple: obliterate the names, addresses, and other identifying information from the reports before turning them over to the defense. Such information is unimportant to the purposes for which the reports will be used.

A collateral request should also be made for the daily work logs of the officer for the same period of time. This acts as a check on full compliance with the discovery order: Any log entry showing an arrest by the officer for drunk driving should be matched with a corresponding arrest report.

Another technique useful in preparing for cross-examination of the officer is to *mail* relevant written material to him a few weeks before trial. An example of such material would be a copy of the National Highway Traffic Safety Administration's *Improved Sobriety Testing* brochure, in which standardized field sobriety tests and objective scoring are explained (see §4.3.2). He can then be questioned on his own techniques as opposed to those recommended by NHTSA; if the officer is considered an expert witness and reads the material, its contents may be admissible in evidence. If the officer replies that he has not read the material, he can be questioned as to why he is not interested in relevant literature in his field of expertise.

Since the author first suggested this tactic of fowarding material to officers before trial, the practice has apparently become widespread. Counsel should be aware that there may be an internal policy within the police agency to refuse to respond to such requests. The following is an excerpt from an entry in the February 27, 1998, Operations Digest of the City of Phoenix Police Department:

> DRIVING UNDER THE INFLUENCE (DUI) MATERIALS FROM THE NATIONAL HIGHWAY TRAFFIC SAFETY ADMINISTRATION (NHTSA): Recently, defense attorneys have requested that officers read DUI materials from NHTSA or other alcohol-related items prior to trial. Officers are under no obligation to read these or any other materials. The Legal Unit strongly advises that officers DO NOT do this and that they tell the prosecutor about the request. Having officers read this material is an attempt by the defense attorney to enter the material during testimony in court through a hearsay exception dealing with learned treatises . . . [Arizona Rules of Evidence 803 (18).]

Yet a third effective method for preparing for the officer's testimony is to *depose* him. Only a few states currently make provision for depositions of officers in criminal cases. However, every state provides for an administrative hearing (at least if requested) when an individual's driver's license is suspended. And most of these states either require the testimony of the arresting officer or permit the licensee to confront him by serving a civil subpoena to compel his testimony.

The value of this procedure in defending the criminal charges should not be overlooked. The suspension hearing usually occurs before the trial and, in effect, provides defense counsel with an opportunity for a free deposition. Further, officers often do not take these hearings very seriously and only peremptorily review their reports before testifying. The result is that a thorough examination will often produce errors and lack of recollection that would not normally occur in a trial setting.

If the department of motor vehicles does not record the proceedings, of course, counsel should bring his own tape recorder to the hearing. The tapes can thereafter be used to impeach or intimidate the officer in trial, either by playing the tapes or by offering a transcription.

The author has found that such a tape also has considerable value in plea bargaining discussions.

§13.0.2 Strategy: The *Judo* Approach

The natural instinct of the defense lawyer in a drunk driving trial is to *attack* the arresting officer on cross-examination. And this is an understandable attitude: The officer is, in most cases, the only witness against the defendant, and it is his observations and opinions that will convict.

It is the author's experience, however, that a more effective strategy in dealing with most officers is to avoid frontal confrontation. As in the sport of *judo,* the force of the officer's testimony should be *deflected* rather than directly opposed. In other words, the position should be taken in most trials that the officer is not *lying,* but instead is simply — and understandably — *mistaken.* This mistake may be due to predisposition (see §13.1.3), selective recollection (see, e.g., §13.1.3), observing symptoms for which there are innocent explanations, lack of experience, or other reasons of human frailty. To put it another way, the officer is not a liar, he is simply *human* — and, thus, subject to error. (In fact, the author sometimes opens his cross-examination with the question, "Officer, is it possible that you could be wrong in your opinion?" A positive answer can be used pursuasively in urging reasonable doubt during argument; a negative answer reveals a rigid personality.)

First, it is a simple fact that most jurors are reluctant to believe that any police officer is lying. Despite all of the news stories, movies, and television shows depicting lying cops, the average citizen still prefers to see this authority figure as essentially honest. Attacking that figure will often accomplish only resentment among some jurors, particularly those who see an attack on an officer as an attack on authority generally. Jurors would generally much prefer to believe that an officer has a demonstrably mistaken but good-faith belief in the defendant's intoxication.

Second, it is also a fact that most officers will deal with being attacked by counterattacking. This will not usually be obvious, of course. The officer will simply mention little or nothing helpful to the defendant, while taking every opportunity to volunteer damning recollections. Approached in a less combative mode, however, the officer is often willing to admit exonerating facts and possibilities. In other words, it is easier to draw flies with honey than with vinegar.

Third, it is difficult to convince the jury that the breath machine was wrong *and* the officer is lying. This is expecting them to swallow a lot. It is considerably easier to take the position that the machine and the officer were in error for understandable and explainable reasons. This is particularly true where, as is usually the case, the officer drafts his arrest report (on which he later relies for recollection in testifying) *after* he knows what the breath test result is; the report is likely to reflect the apparent — but erroneous — corroboration from the machine.

Of course, there will be situations where a frontal attack is necessary. This commonly occurs in refusal cases, where because of confrontation with the officer, the defendant refuses to cooperate in submitting to blood-alcohol analysis. In this scenario, of course, the confrontation not only provides a reason why the officer may not be testifying truthfully, but also serves to provide a nonincriminatory explanation for the refusal.

§13.0.3 Attacking the Foundation: Training and Experience

To establish the impressive credentials of his witness, the prosecutor initially will ask the officer questions relating to his police training and experience relative to observing, recognizing, and arresting drunk drivers. If no such questioning takes place, defense counsel should immediately see a red flag. It is entirely possible that the prosecutor is avoiding the area of training and experience because the officer is relatively inexperienced in drunk driving cases or is even a "rookie"; it is also possible that a very clever prosecutor is setting defense counsel up for embarrassing cross-examination as to the qualifications of an exceptionally experienced officer.

Counsel should, of course, make every attempt before trial to investigate the police officer who will be testifying. He should have at least a general idea of the officer's background and experience, if for no other reason than to avoid examination in that area. Any lack of experience or training in the area of drunk driving should, on the other hand, be explored: For example, if this is only the officer's third arrest for drunk driving or if he has never received any specialized training on the breath analysis machine, this should be brought out. As always, however, violation of the cardinal rule against asking a question to which counsel does not *already know* the answer invariably will lead to trouble.

The officer should be examined on his specific qualifications as to two separate areas: (1) the basis for his opinion as to intoxication and (2) the basis for his opinion that the client was unable to safely operate a motor vehicle. In most jurisdictions, the applicable statute defines drunk driving in terms of intoxication to the degree that the defendant was not able to operate a vehicle as safely as a reasonable person. Yet defense counsel commonly ignore the officer's qualifications as to this latter aspect, despite the fact that it is inseparable from the concept of intoxication in a drunk driving trial.

In many cases, the prosecutor will not even attempt to lay a foundation of the police officer's expertise in the area of intoxication, unless the officer's experience is especially noteworthy. The reason for this is that lay opinion on the issue of intoxication is generally held to be admissible. However, the standard for a drunk driving offense is "under the influence" as opposed to "drunk," and the laws of the particular jurisdiction may or may not be clear as to whether lay opinion is admissible as to this condition. Certainly, in appropriate cases — that is, where the officer is known to be relatively inexperienced, the argument should be made that *under the influence* is a more refined concept than are the general terms of *drunk* or *intoxicated* and therefore requires more expertise to recognize. The officer should then be examined, preferably on voir dire and before his opinion is given to the jury.

Even if an officer is qualified, whether as an expert or lay witness, to give an opinion on the issue of whether the defendant was under the influence, he may not be qualified to render an opinion as to whether the defendant was able to safely operate a motor vehicle. Again, the concepts of *under the influence* and *safe operation of a motor vehicle* may be intertwined, and so the prosecutor may not attempt to lay a foundation of expertise. And again, counsel should seriously consider challenging the witness where appropriate. While a lay witness may be able to recognize intoxication, he is less likely to be able to recognize relative abilities of safe vehicle operation: The concepts should be considered as separate and distinct.

In most jurisdictions, the rendering of an opinion by the officer concerning intoxication does not violate the "ultimate issue" rule. However, the *form* in which the opinion is given may violate the rule. Thus, for example, in *State v. Maurer,* 409 N.W.2d 196 (Iowa App. 1987), the following direct examination of the arresting officer took place:

Q. Do you have an opinion, sitting there today, based upon what you had observed at the point of the arrest, as to whether or not [the defendant] had been operating a motor vehicle while under the influence of an alcoholic beverage?

A. Yes, sir. Based on the sum total of my observations with speed, [the defendant's] attitude, his physical characteristics, including his eyes and balance, his inability to do field sobriety testing and the horizontal gaze nystagmus test, it is my opinion *beyond any reasonable doubt* that the defendant was operating a motor vehicle upon a public highway while he was under the influence of an alcoholic beverage. [Id. at 197 (emphasis added).]

Defense counsel immediately objected, on the grounds that the opinion concerned an ultimate issue since it was framed in terms of reasonable doubt, but was overruled.

On appeal, the court held that the opinion did, in fact, violate the "ultimate fact" rule:

> When a standard . . . has been fixed by law, no witness whether expert or non-expert, nor however qualified, is permitted to express an opinion as to whether or not the person or the conduct in question measures up to that standard. On that question the court must instruct the jury as to the law, and the jury must draw its own conclusion from the evidence. [Id. at 198.]

The court held that by giving an opinion that the defendant was driving while intoxicated "beyond a reasonable doubt," he was in effect giving an opinion that the defendant was guilty.

Counsel should also consider arguing that opinion testimony as to safe vehicle operation addresses the ultimate issue in the trial and effectively takes the case out of the jury's hands. At the very least, such critical opinion evidence should be susceptible to the usual rules requiring specialized training, experience, etc.

Relative to his expertise in safe vehicle operation, the officer can be asked any of a long list of questions regarding highway safety statistics, vehicle operation tests, alcohol-coordination experiments, etc. He can be asked whether he has read specific texts or articles recognized in the field, what courses in biochemistry he has taken, what experiments in human reaction under various levels of intoxication he has performed, what articles in the area he has written, how many times he has qualified in court as an expert on the biochemical effects of alcohol, and so on *ad infinitum.* Rarely will any police officer shine under such questioning; on the other hand, of course, counsel must not take this to ludicrous extremes.

§13.0.4 Undermining the Field Sobriety Tests

Commonly, counsel will find that his client has been given two or three field sobriety tests, probably the same set of tests that he will encounter in defending other drunk driving cases, as most police agencies favor a given set of FSTs.

These "tests" are presented to the jury as quasi-scientific and objective methods of examining a defendant's degree of intoxication. And counsel must recognize that there is, in the jurors' eyes, a certain scientific and objective quality to the tests and that they therefore constitute a real danger. On the surface, at least, the tests seem simple enough and easy for any sober person to perform. However, it becomes defense counsel's job to illustrate through effective cross-examination that:

1. the defendant's emotional and/or physical condition (independent of alcohol) affected his ability to perform
2. the tests were administered under difficult conditions
3. the officer was biased in his analysis, and/or recorded the results inaccurately
4. the tests are not as easily performed to the officer's standards by a sober person as it would initially appear

Counsel must always keep in mind that the FSTs are usually given merely as a formality: The officer has almost always already made up his mind that the suspect is under the influence, and he is now simply gathering evidence to support his opinion. The test results will invariably reflect this. Every effort should be made to inculcate this reality in the jurors' minds.

The first consideration should be the physical conditions under which the client performed the test. Counsel should have visited the scene of the arrest and seen the quality of road surface. It is one thing to perform the test on the smooth, level floor of a courtroom under even lighting conditions; it is quite another to walk over gravel or broken dirt along the sloping shoulder of a highway at night.

Counsel may wish to consider the feasibility of requesting the trial judge to permit a *jury view,* so that the jurors can view for themselves some of the conditions under which the field sobriety tests were administered. Counsel should request that the view be taken at night, if this was when the tests were given. In an appropriate case, this can be considerably more effective than simply submitting photographs.

Many states have statutory provisions or court rules governing jury views. Even without such authority, however, the trial court has inherent discretion to permit such procedures. See, e.g., *State v. O'Day,* 175 So. 838 (La. 1937). In deciding whether to grant such a request, the court should consider the importance "of the information to be gained by the view, the extent to which this information has or could have been secured from maps, photographs, or diagrams, and the extent to which the place or object to be viewed has changed in appearance since the controversy arose. . . ." McCormick on Evidence §216 (3d ed. 1984).

The officer should be asked if he considered giving the field sobriety test to the defendant in the dry, warm, level, and well-lit conditions of the police station. The answer will almost always be "no." If he replies that this would have required arresting the defendant first, ask whether the officer considered giving a *second* test under the fairer conditions at the police station after arresting him — either to corroborate the earlier questionable test or to determine that it was not valid.

The officer can also be asked to describe in detail the conditions at the scene of the field sobriety tests. Due perhaps to the volume of arrests the officer has made, together with the passage of time, in over half of all cases he will be unable to do this accurately. And inaccuracy in this respect calls into question accuracy in other parts of his testimony. Of course, counsel should have photographs of the scene to use in cross-examination.

Counsel should find out what type of shoes his client was wearing when he performed the test. If his client is a woman, was she wearing high heels? If a man, did he have on cowboy boots or elevator soles? Obviously, performing a test on high heels places the defendant at a considerable disadvantage.

Consider also the weather at the time of the test. Rain, snow, and wind all can adversely affect a sober individual's ability to, for example, walk a line steadily heel-to-toe.

Was the client suffering from illnesses or physiological disabilities? Even a common cold can cause the defendant to perform poorly; sinus and ear congestion can have a decided effect on an individual's balance. And if the client is suffering from a trick knee or arthritis, for example, his ability to perform will be impaired. In such cases, particularly those involving an older client, counsel should always make repeated reference to the difference in physical ability between the defendant and the young, healthy, physically fit police officer.

Even if the defendant was not suffering from illness or physical impairment, counsel should ask the officer if he bothered to find out if any illness or impairment were present, assuming, of course, that counsel knows the answer will be negative.

Counsel should consider the effects of his client's emotional condition at the time. There is no question but that an understandably nervous, angry, or frightened suspect will be unable to perform a FST as well as a police officer in the calm of a courthouse.

Gary Trichter of Houston, Texas, emphasizes the officer's lack of a "standard" against which to measure the defendant's performance on the field sobriety test. He develops during cross-examination that all individuals vary in their mental and physical facilities — weight, strength, speed, coordination, balance, memory, ability to learn new motor skills, ability to comprehend instructions, etc. Then he gets the officer to admit that he has no knowledge of what the "normal range" of mental or physical facilities is for the prosecutor, the judge, juror number two — or the defendant as he sits in court.

Finally, Trichter develops the specifics. What would the defendant's *normal* (i.e., sober) balance be in a heel-to-toe test? What would his normal range be in a touch-the-nose test? A one-leg-lift test? How much would he *normally* sway in a modified-position-of-attention test? What would his speech be like under normal conditions? And so on.

Another technique is to have the officer describe for the jury what is meant by a "learning curve." Usually, the officer will not understand what this means. Counsel can then ask the officer if he isn't familiar with the obvious fact that a person who has never been arrested before (assuming the client fits this description) will be very nervous and embarrassed, particularly when he knows that he will probably be arrested if he fails the tests. Knowing that, isn't the officer aware of the well-known fact that nervousness and/or embarrassment adversely affect the learning curve? In other words, the officer's hasty instructions and cursory demonstration (if any at all) would not be sufficient — and so the defective performance by the defendant was due not to intoxication but rather to *misunderstanding the directions.* Ask the officer if he considered this factor in making his final decision to arrest the defendant; it will be difficult for him to say "yes" if he has admitted he is unfamiliar with the "learning curve."

If, as is commonly done, the client had a cup of coffee or two to "sober up" before hitting the road, counsel should be aware of the possibly synergistic effect of caffeine and alcohol. This effect can be brought out in cross-examination either of the officer or of the state's blood-alcohol expert — although it is doubtful that either will be aware of the recent research in this area. The definitive studies were done in Great Britain and were reported in an article entitled Interactions of Alcohol and Caffeine on Human Reaction Time, authored by Osborne and Rogers, in Aviation, Space and Environmental Medicine 528 (June 1983). In that article, the researchers concluded:

> [A]lcohol has always been categorized as a central depressant and caffeine as a central stimulant. Therefore it should follow that an antagonistic interaction should occur when these two drugs are ingested simultaneously. But as these results illustrate, this is not necessarily the case. . . .

> [C]affeine has the effect of potentiating the detrimental effects already induced by alcohol. . . .
>
> Caffeine has a synergistic interaction with alcohol. . . .
>
> [M]otor skills which involve delicate muscular coordination and accurate timing have been found to be adversely affected by caffeine. . . .

Thus, coffee taken before driving can combine with even small amounts of alcohol to impair coordination to a degree beyond what would be expected from the alcohol alone. And it is this coordination, of course, that is theoretically being measured by field sobriety tests. In other words, a poor performance on such a test may be more attributable to coffee than to alcohol. Certainly, the officer should be asked if he is aware of such a phenomenon, and if he took it into consideration in subjectively assessing the defendant's performance.

Yet another factor that may adversely affect a client's performance on the FSTs but has nothing to do with the consumption of alcohol is his *circadian rhythm.* The circadian rhythm is that 24-hour biological alarm clock in each of our bodies, most noticeable when we experience jet lag. Researchers have found that individuals will perform more poorly in tests during the low point of the circadian rhythm — that is, during the hours after midnight and into the early morning. In Herbert and Jeffcoate, Circadian Variation in Effects of Ethanol in Man, 18 (Suppl. 1) Pharmacology, Biochemistry and Behavior 555 (1983), British physicians and psychiatrists reported that "the same blood alcohol level is associated with a significantly greater impairment of different aspects of psychological functioning when achieved in the morning" (Id. at 556). The researchers concluded that "the differences we have found . . . must be attributable to circadian change in susceptibility of the body to its effect" (Id.).

It is a common practice among officers administering balancing tests to "fail" a suspect because he raised his arms during performance. The officer will commonly explain that raising your arms during a walk-the-line or leg-lift test is a sign that the individual's balance is off due to intoxication. He may also testify that when he demonstrated the test for the suspect, *he* did *not* raise his arms.

Counsel should develop in cross-examination — and confirm

during direct examination of the client if he takes the stand — that using your arms for balance is a *natural,* even instinctive, thing to do. This is such a common experience that if the officer denies that using your arms is a normal method of balancing, his testimony can be developed in such a way that he will lose credibility with the jury.

As for the officer's demonstration in the field, it is an assumption on his part that the defendant — or anyone in that situation — would notice that the officer was not using his arms. The focus of anyone taking the walk-the-line test, for example, will be on the line and the heel-to-toe movement, not on the arms.

Should the officer testify that he specifically instructed the defendant not to raise his arms during the tests, it should be developed that this is asking him to do something that is awkward and unnatural. And a sober person asked to perform an awkward and unnatural act will usually do so in an awkward and unnatural way — which the officer will see as symptomatic of intoxication.

Les Hulnick of Wichita, Kansas, notes that during the officer's instructions concerning the one-leg-stand test, he commonly tells the suspect, "If you put your foot down, lift it back up." Of course, the reasonable inference from this, Hulnick develops during cross-examination and/or summation, is that it is perfectly *permissible* to put your foot down!

The written alphabet test is often viewed by the prosecution as particularly valuable evidence, second perhaps only to the blood-alcohol test results. This is because it is *physical* evidence, obtained directly from the defendant himself — and thus independently corroborating the officer's entire testimony. If handled correctly by the defense, however, this "showcase" evidence can be turned into a cornerstone of the defense case, discrediting that same officer's testimony.

The focus of the prosecutor will be on the alphabet — that is, on the fact that two or three letters are missing or out of order. The focus of the defense, however, should be upon the *writing* itself, and, even more important, on the *signature* that the officer demanded to authenticate this piece of evidence. (If there is no signature, find one in a booking slip or bail receipt.) Counsel should have his client write out the alphabet again and affix his signature as before. Take a look as well at the client's signature on his driver's license. Now compare all of these. In most cases, the handwriting or printing of the alphabet will be similar. In others, the alphabet will appear slightly more "shaky"; this, of course, can be easily attributed to the understandable nervousness of a person asked to write under such trying circumstances.

The key is the signature. In most cases, even an intoxicated person can perform the nearly automatic task of signing his name without noticeable impairment. And this similarity in signatures can be impressive to a jury.

For a discussion of signatures as evidence in DUI cases, see Woodford, Forensic Comparison of Signatures in Alcohol Related Cases, 3(12) DWI Journal, Dec. 1988; Galbraith, Alcohol: Its Effects on Handwriting, 31 J. Forensic Science 2580 (1986). In the first article, Dr. James Woodford presents research on the issue, concluding that:

> Deviated signatures are weak prosecutorial evidence because they can be explained by non-alcohol-related circumstances. . . . This limitation makes the test unsuitable for the prosecution to rely on. However, as a test for the defense, the *absence* of "drunk writing" virtually proves sobriety. If insignificant changes occur in one's personal signature after consuming a quantity of alcohol, there is likewise insignificant change in one's ability to operate a vehicle and act properly in an emergency situation.

Counsel should begin by asking the officer on cross-examination if during his investigation he compared the defendant's signature on the alphabet test to his signature on his driver's license. Quite simply, the police never do. Yet this can be used to show the jury that the officer was not interested in giving a fair test to the defendant: What could be easier and more telling than such a simple comparison?

Counsel should then give the officer the defendant's driver's license or, in the alternative, an exemplar given by the defendant while the jury watched. He should then be asked something to the effect, "Before the jury compares these, officer, would you care to point out to them how they show Mr. Jones to have been intoxicated?" This is a violation of the cardinal "yes-no" rule of cross-examination, of course, but the circumstances justify it: Either he will admit that they don't show intoxication, or he will struggle to find a miniscule difference — thereby validating the defense theory that he was bending over backwards to interpret *anything* the defendant did in an incriminating light.

The prosecution is then "hoisted by its own petard": The test can thereafter be presented to the jury as the only truly objective evidence produced by the officer. The written alphabet and signature represent the only test or observation that can be independently reviewed by the jury — that is, the only one that does not involve a subjective interpretation of a biased officer. And that evidence clearly shows that the motor coordination and mental acuity reflected in the defendant's handwriting were not significantly impaired.

Mention should be made here of the advisability of having the officer demonstrate the test or tests in the courtroom. This is, of course, a gamble: The officer may very well perform the tests perfectly. In fact, the prosecutor may take the decision away from defense counsel by having the officer perform the tests during direct examination. If a mistake is made by the officer — for example, one finger touches the lip — it should be magnified as illustrating how even a perfectly fit man under controlled conditions can "fail" the test. If no mistake is made, losses should be minimized by emphasizing the contrasts between the physical conditions of the officer and the defendant, their emotional states, their relative familiarity with the tests, and the environmental conditions under which the tests were performed. In the final analysis, it is probably preferable to avoid taking the risk of having the officer perform the tests.

The ability of the jurors to perform the tests is another matter. Assuming no objections from trial judge, counsel in argument should consider inviting the jurors to attempt to perform each of the field sobriety tests in the privacy of the jury room. Counsel can almost be assured that most of the jurors will be unable to perform the tests perfectly, and some, particularly older jurors and women wearing heels, will have considerable difficulty. In asking jurors to try the tests, it should be pointed out that they will be taking the FSTs under much less strenuous conditions than those encountered by the defendant.

There are other factors affecting an individual's ability to perform on a field sobriety test. The effect of car headlights passing at high speed at night can be disconcerting, and the air waves set up by these cars can have an effect on the attempts of the defendant to maintain his balance on the side of the road. If there has been an accident in which medical treatment was not required, the defendant may still have been suffering from shock or an undiagnosed concussion or leg injury, any of which can affect balance and coordination.

The officer will usually admit that no field sobriety test can by itself be considered as conclusive evidence that the defendant was under the influence. In fact, even the totality of all tests given should be viewed in the entire context of all observations — erratic driving, flushed face, etc. In other words, an overview of all conduct and symptoms would be considered by even a biased police officer before concluding that a suspect is intoxicated. Having established this, counsel can then develop for the jury that this officer *was* biased in taking that subjective overview.

Finally, counsel must demonstrate for the jury the completely subjective nature of the officer's "decision" as to whether the defendant "passed" or "failed" any or all of the field sobriety tests. One very effective method for accomplishing this is to confront the officer with the availability of objectively scored NHTSA tests.

§13.0.5 Using Nystagmus to Expose the Officer

The prosecution in a drunk driving case typically relies heavily upon its "scientific" evidence in trial, since this appears reliable, objective, and is impressive to the jury. Obviously, the blood, breath, or urine test will be the cornerstone. To corroborate this evidence, however, and to verify the condition of the defendant at the time of driving rather than at the time of the chemical test, the prosecution will present the officer's field sobriety tests — including the second cornerstone: the seemingly objective and "scientific" horizontal gaze nystagmus (HGN) test. Thus, the emphasis in the officer's testimony will usually be upon this apparently quasi-medical "examination." And, absent effective cross-examination by the defense, nystagmus evidence can be devastating. Unfortunately, most defense attorneys have little scientific background and are usually lacking in sufficient familiarity with the test to properly challenge the officer.

In fact, however, nystagmus represents a unique opportunity for the defense.

A very effective strategy is to turn the prosecution's strength against it by exploiting a very simple truth: The officer rarely understands anything but the bare mechanics of the nystagmus test (and he usually gets even that wrong). Most officers receive only an hour or two of training on HGN, often received on the job — and usually from another officer (who learned it from yet another officer). In other words, the arresting officer is basically ignorant about all but the most superficial aspects of administering the test. He develops his "expertise" by administering the same test over and over again — always incorrectly. And although there may be a foundational requirement that he be trained and knowledgable — even possess expertise — about the theory and administration of the test, the reality is that behind a few technical terms, he knows almost nothing. (The author often begins cross-examination on nystagmus by asking the officer what the word nystagmus *means;* few of these "experts" are able to respond.)

Thus, the defense attorney is presented with a rare opportunity. The prosecution has relied heavily upon the HGN test to convince the jury of the scientific and objective nature of the field sobriety tests, and further, to convince them of the officer's skill and knowledge in administering and interpreting them. With effective cross-examination, the defense can expose the officer's ignorance about the nystagmus test — and, thus, cast into doubt the validity of the other field sobriety tests as well (not to mention his credibility about observed driving, symptoms of intoxication, administration of the breath-alcohol test, etc.). In other words, exposure of the HGN test will taint the entire case.

There are many ways to accomplish this.

The measurement of the angle of onset of nystagmus, for example, is critical: If the officer estimates the angle incorrectly, the results will be correspondingly invalid. There are a number of ways of dealing with this complete lack of precision: pointing out that the officer was trained with a protractor, but used none during the defendant's test; asking the officer if he has practiced estimating 45-degree angle measurements monthly, as recommended by NHTSA; etc.

A particularly effective tactic of exposing this involves the practice common among police officers of estimating the angle by using the suspect's shoulder to estimate 45 degrees. The test begins with the suspect staring at the officer's pencil, finger, or other object, then following it as the officer moves it laterally. If nystagmus first occurs prior to the officer's finger or pencil reaching the end of the suspect's shoulder, the officer assumes this corresponds with approximately 45 degrees. This is not a secret: Most officers who use this method, when pressed for a basis for their guess of the angle, explain the method. It should be readily apparent to anyone — including jurors — that this is hardly a model of precision, and nowhere near the relative accuracy of the protractor used in training. More importantly, however, there are at least two variables in the method that can significantly affect the results. First, the geometry underlying this crude measurement depends upon the finger or pencil being 12 to 15 inches from the eyes and remaining uniform. Secondly, and the greatest flaw, any accuracy depends upon the assumption that *all people's shoulder widths are identical.* Pressed, the officer will have to admit that his measurements do not vary with the individual: The end of the shoulder represents 45 degrees — whether a burly linebacker or a diminutive housewife.

There are many other ways of discrediting the nystagmus test — once counsel is familiar with the theory and proper procedures. Detailed questioning as to each of the three elements of the test will quickly expose the officer's ignorance: "How could you tell the eyeball was at its extreme?" "Please describe *distinct* nystagmus, as opposed to regular nystagmus," etc. Many officers do not administer all three elements of the nystagmus test ("angle of onset," "lack of smooth pursuit," and "distinct nystagmus at extremes") — although all three must be given for a valid test. Commonly, they may give only one — typically, onset of nystagmus before 45 degrees. Or they may simply testify vaguely that "nystagmus was detected," "suspect had early onset," or simply, "suspect failed"; such language is usually a sure sign that the officer did not know what he was doing.

The simple fact is that few officers understand or give the HGN test correctly. None gives the tests exactly as recommended by the NHTSA manual — the contents of which are incorporated into many law enforcement training manuals (counsel should, of course, obtain a copy of the manual through the discovery process).

There are many tactics to use in cross-examination on nystagmus. But the strategy is clear: The prosecution has staked its credibility on the scientific precision of the nystagmus test; cross-examination has exposed it as a crude and unreliable charade, administered by an ignorant and unqualified layman. If the state's most "scientific" evidence is so seriously flawed, what of the rest?

In preparing for the cross-examination of the police officer who administered the nystagmus test, counsel should consider sending the officer copies of scientific articles and government reports on the subject (for example, the NHTSA manual on the very detailed procedures recommended for administering the test), along with a letter explaining that you will question him concerning their contents. As the officer is usually claimed by the prosecution to be an "expert" on nystagmus, the officer may be cross-examined concerning any literature on the subject that he or she has read and considered.

If the officer does read the material, of course, it presents a wonderful opportunity for the defense to get the contents of these articles and studies admitted over a hearsay objection. The jury can then be shown, for example, that nystagmus is not completely reliable or that the officer failed to follow the NHTSA procedures or objective scoring system.

If the officer does *not* read the material, counsel can easily develop on cross-examination that this "expert" is not interested in keeping abreast of the literature in the area. The officer can then be asked if he or she agrees with certain procedures recommended by NHTSA, for example, or with certain studies indicating dozens of innocent, nonalcoholic causes of nystagmus.

Obviously, careful pre-trial discovery can prove very helpful to the attorney preparing to cross-examine an officer on the issue of nystagmus. Counsel should find out about the officer's training on the subject, both at the police academy and in the field. Was this knowledge gained from expert ophthalmologists or merely from other police officers? How many hours was the officer trained? Is there a continuing training process, such as that recommended by NHTSA for monthly estimation of angle of onset with a protractor? Has the officer received any certification?

Counsel also should try to obtain any training manuals used by the police agency involved. The procedures in these for administering the nystagmus test should then be compared with those used by the officer in the field, as well as with those recommended by NHTSA. The NHTSA manual on which state manuals are increasingly being based is entitled DWI Detection and Standardized Field Sobriety Testing, DOT-HS-808-112. It can be obtained from the National Technical Information Service in Springfield, Virginia (703-487-4640; fax 703-487-4815). The manual, which includes both a student and instructor version, and two videotapes are priced at $138.50 (specify order no. PB94780251).

The following NHTSA studies, which contain material critical of field sobriety tests used by law enforcement agencies across the country, can also be ordered:

- Psychological Tests for DWI Arrest, DOT-HS-802-424 (order no. PB269309; $27)
- Development and Field Test of Psychophysical Tests for DWI Arrest, DOT-HS-805-864 (order no. PB81203721; $19.50)
- Field Evaluation of a Behavioral Test Battery for DUI, DOT-HS-806-475 (order no. PB84121169; $12.50)
- Pilot Test of Selected DWI Detection Procedures for Use at Sobriety Checkpoints, DOT-HS-806-724 (order no. PB86170958; $19.50)

Certified copies for evidentiary purposes can be obtained for an additional $15.

Also useful are copies of the officer's previous reports of drunk driving arrests: Do they reflect *signature* evidence? That is, do the suspects always appear to have the same or similar nystagus reactions? Indications that the suspects arrested by the officer nearly *always* exhibit eye jerking at 38 degrees, for example, or that they always move their heads during the test, cast doubt on that officer's credibility.

Nystagmus is a relatively new procedure and there has been little research done yet on its flaws. However, a number of possibly fruitful areas may be mentioned at this point. First, of course, there is absolutely no record of the results of the test. Although cloaked in scientific garb, the simple fact remains that the police officer decides at what point eye jerking began. He may have been mistaken about exactly when jerking began, may have positioned the device incorrectly, or may have administered the test in some other faulty way. And, of course, he may be lying; unlike with most breath testing devices, there is no record of the results in the nystagmus procedure.

According to federal standards set forth in a pamphlet entitled Improved Sobriety Testing (1984: DOT HS-806-512, National Highway and Traffic Safety Administration), the officer is simply instructed as follows:

> [Y]ou will need to learn how to estimate this angle. . . .
>
> Cut [an angle-measuring] template out and attach it to a square of cardboard. . . .
>
> Examine the eyes of four or five people, so that you become familiar with what a 45-degree angle of gaze looks like. Next, practice without the device, but check your estimates periodically.
>
> Practice until you can consistently estimate 45 degrees. Check yourself monthly with the device to be sure that your accuracy has been sustained.

This training procedure of developing the ability of the officer to estimate angles should create suspicions by itself. In any event, these suggested procedures can probably be contrasted favorably with the training procedures — if any — that the officer underwent, particularly the suggestion that the officer undergo a monthly re-check of his ability to estimate angles.

Laboratory of Criminalistics attempted to determine the reliability of nystagmus in predicting actual blood-alcohol levels. As reported in 25 Journal of the Forensic Society 476 (1985), 12 police officers measured the angle of onset of nystagmus in 129 actual cases where individuals had been arrested for drunk driving but had not yet been tested by blood, breath, or urine analysis. The officers used a special protractor to help them accurately measure the angle of onset. Result? The officers consistently overestimated the angle at low blood-alcohol concentrations and underestimated it at high BAC levels. The researchers from the police crime lab concluded that nystagmus cannot be used to accurately predict the blood-alcohol concentration.

A number of drugs may result in horizontal gaze nystagmus

readings that falsely indicate alcohol intoxication. Horizontal gaze nystagmus is well documented as occurring with ingestion of barbiturates, antihistamines, and phencyclidine. A number of other drugs may also produce horizontal gaze nystagmus, especially other depressants and anticonvulsants. Apparently, the consumption of toxic substances such as caffeine, nicotine, or aspirin can also cause nystagmus.

Physiological problems such as brain damage or certain kinds of diseases may also result in gaze nystagmus problems. The following conditions, for example, have been shown to cause nystagmus: influenza, streptococcus infections, vertigo, measles, hypertension, hypotension, arteriosclerosis, muscular dystrophy, multiple sclerosis, brain hemorrhage, epilepsy, psychogenic disorders, syphilis, and Korsakoff's syndrome. Motion sickness and sunstroke can also affect the results of a nystagmus test, as can changes in atmospheric pressure.

Problems in the defendant's inner ear labyrinth are another source of error, as are eye problems such as congenitally poor vision due to bilateral amblyopia, eyestrain, eye muscle fatigue, and glaucoma.

If the defendant was wearing hard contact lenses at the time of the test, they may well prevent extreme lateral eye movement, resulting in early jerking of the eye. The NHTSA-recommended procedures mentioned above specifically advise the officer to have the suspect remove all corrective lenses, especially hard contact lenses.

Perhaps most interestingly, a tired driver may have a falsely high blood-alcohol reading. Prolonged use of the eyes with insufficient lighting or in strained positions can cause temporary nystagmus. Furthermore, Tharp reports that the angle of onset of nystagmus at a blood-alcohol level of 0.19 percent decreases by about five degrees when the circadian rhythm of an individual reaches its nadir. Therefore Tharp concludes that officers should adjust their criteria by about five degrees between midnight and 5:00 A.M. The Kansas Supreme Court has apparently relied on this volume, in fact, in elaborating on the reasons for the unreliability of the nystagmus test:

> Nystagmus can be caused by problems in an individual's inner ear . . . Physiological problems such as certain kinds of diseases may

> also result in gaze nystagmus. Influenza, streptococcus infections, vertigo, measles, syphilis, arteriosclerosis, muscular dystrophy, multiple sclerosis, Korsakoff's Syndrome, brain hemorrhage, epilepsy, and other physiological disorders all have been shown to cause nystagmus. Furthermore, conditions such as hypertension, motion sickness, sunstroke, eyestrain, eye muscle fatigue, glaucoma, and changes in atmospheric pressure may result in nystagmus. The consumption of common substances such as caffeine, nicotine, or aspirin also lead to nystagmus almost identical to that caused by alcohol consumption. [*State v. Witte* (Kan. 1992) 836 P.2d 1110.]

Finally, counsel should inquire on cross-examination as to what objective criteria the officer used in deciding whether the defendant "passed" or "failed." Usually, the criteria are subjective — with the possible exception of the "45 degree" test. This lack of objective standards should be contrasted with the very precise scoring system recommended by the National Highway Traffic and Safety Administration in their widely used pamphlet, Improved Sobriety Testing (see §4.3.5).

For an illustrative cross-examination of the officer on the subject of nystagmus, see §13.2.1.

For a discussion of the proper method for administration of the three nystagmus tests, see the discussion of the federal standards established by the National Highway Traffic Safety Administration in §4.3.5. This material, setting forth very precise procedures for administering the nystagmus test, can be used with particular effect in cross-examination.

If the prosecution calls an expert to testify concerning nystagmus (the officer should be considered *not* qualified), counsel should, of course, inquire as to his qualifications, where he received his training on gaze nystagmus, and whether he has ever qualified as an expert in nystagmus before. Cross-examination should then proceed to question the ability of the expert to correlate the defendant's nystagmus to a particular blood-alcohol concentration, emphasizing his failure to rule out the possibility of other causes of nystagmus mentioned earlier. Has the expert actually examined the defendant himself for any physiological problems? Has he examined him for nystagmus?

Counsel may consider asking the expert if he agrees with an interesting article by Y. Umeda and E. Sakata entitled Alcohol and the Oculomotor System, 87 Annals of Otology Rhinology 69

(1978), wherein scientists concluded that gaze nystagmus was one of the least sensitive eye measures of alcohol intoxication.

§13.0.6 Confronting the Officer with His Training Manual

One of the most valuable tools for the DUI defense practitioner that has come about as a result of the NHTSA studies mentioned in earlier chapters is the NHTSA Student Manual entitled *DWI Detection and Standardized Field Sobriety Testing.* This manual can be obtained from the Transportation Safety Institute in Oklahoma City, Oklahoma, by calling (405) 954-3112 or by contacting the National Technical Information Service in Springfield, Virginia, or through Professional Reference Services at (612) 349-6777. Every police officer who was trained by NHTSA guidelines will have been issued a student manual — possibly disguised as or converted into a local training manual. The manual discusses the three-test battery of the Walk-and-Turn, the One-Leg-Stand, and the HGN tests. There are valuable gems to be found in section VIII of the student manual. Included in this section of the manual are the standardized elements of the Walk-and-Turn and the One-Leg-Stand. One could use this portion of the manual in the cross-examination of the NHTSA-trained officer. For example, suppose the police officer fails to ask the defendant to look at his foot on the One-Leg-Stand Test. "If any one of the standardized test elements is changed, the validity of the test is compromised." The officer could then be asked if this is a true statement.

Also included in section VIII of the student manual are the test conditions necessary for proper administration. This is the section of the student manual used most often in the cross-examination of the arresting officer. In discussing the proper conditions for the One-Leg-Stand Test, the NHTSA manual states:

> [S]ome people have difficulty with the one leg stand even when sober. The test criteria for the one leg stand is not necessarily valid for suspects 60 years of age and older, or 50 pounds or more overweight. Persons with injuries to their legs or inner ear disorders may have difficulty with the test. Individuals wearing heels more than two inches high should be given the opportunity to remove shoes. The one leg stand requires a "reasonably level and smooth

surface. There should be adequate lighting for the suspect to have some visual frame of reference."

It is interesting to note that the test conditions necessary, presumably without any further research by NHTSA, mysteriously changed between 1987 and 1991. For example, on the One-Leg-Stand, the requirement of a "hard, dry, level non-slipping surface" was changed from the 1987 NHTSA student manual to the 1991 NHTSA student manual. The 1991 student manual changed to a "reasonably level and smooth surface." In contrast, it is extremely strange that NHTSA not only did not change the test conditions for the Walk-and-Turn Test from the 1987 manual to the 1991 version, but they kept the typographical error in as well! In both the 1987 version and the 1991 version, the requirement for the Walk-and-Turn is that it must be performed on a high, dry, level, non-slipping surface. The wording was kept the same for both the 1987 and the 1991 NHTSA student manuals. Obviously the intent was for the word "high" to read "hard"; however, the typo still exists in the 1991 manual.

The manual can also be used in the cross-examination of the arresting officer as it relates to the One-Leg-Stand and the Walk-and-Turn Test insofar as the percentage of reliability given to the particular test by NHTSA. For example, on page VIII-21, one could ask the officer if one were to use solely the One-Leg-Stand Test, we, in determining whether or not to convict the accused, would misclassify about 35 percent of the people. That would mean that if we were to use that one test, we would convict 35 innocent people out of every 100 that were on trial. Certainly this would be more than tantamount to a reasonable doubt. For the Walk-and-Turn, we would convict 32 innocent people out of 100.

The NHTSA Instructor's Manual

The next "level" of NHTSA manual for use by the DUI defense practitioner is the NHTSA F.S.T. instructors manual. Any law enforcement officer who "boasts" from the witness stand that he or she has been certified by NHTSA to teach the NHTSA field sobriety tests will possess the instructor's manual and is subject to be cross-examined therefrom. It is entitled *DWI Detection and Standardized Field Sobriety Testing . . . Instructors Manual.* The cost is about $52.00 and can be ordered from the National Technical Information Service in Springfield, Virginia, or one may call (420) 954-3112, or contact Professional Reference Services in Minneapolis, Minnesota, at (612) 349-6777. One can use this manual in cross-examination of the officer in various ways. For example, suppose you are defending an individual with breath alcohol readings of 0.17 percent. Suppose further that same individual looks and sounds very sober on videotape taken on the evening of the arrest. One could ask the following questions of the officer:

Q. Mr. Smith's state of inebriation was *not* evident to you prior to giving the field sobriety tests, was it?
A. No.
Q. And isn't it true that a person's state of inebriation would be evident without testing if his true blood alcohol is over a .15 percent?
A. Not necessarily.
Q. Refer to page 17 of your NHTSA instructor's manual. Is it not true that your manual states that if the blood alcohol content is above a .15 percent, the subject's state of inebriation usually will be evident without standardized sobriety testing?
A. That's what it says.
Q. So the fact that inebriation was not evident to you prior to giving your roadside maneuvers could be an indication that Mr. Smith's true BAC was not over .15 percent, isn't that correct?
A. I don't know.

Suppose the client cannot afford an expert and no other witness will be available to testify to predict BAC using the Widmark formula. Suppose further the accused will testify that he had consumed five-and-one-half drinks in a two-hour period and further, the evidence was that he weighed 200 pounds. To some jurors, five-and-one-half drinks might seem like a lot of alcoholic beverage. One can refer the NHTSA-instructor-trained officer to page 18 of his or her manual, go to the chart that appears there, and ask the officer if the chart shows that if an individual weighing 200 pounds, and who consumed five-and-one-half drinks over a two-hour period, their "true" blood alcohol content would be between a 0.04 percent and a 0.06 percent, below the level of 0.08 percent!

The DUI defense practitioner is often faced with the situation wherein the accused has made several very minor mistakes on their performance of the roadside maneuvers. The manual discusses what it takes for the *student* of the NHTSA field sobriety course to pass a successful completion of the classroom training. The following paragraph is of interest:

> Experience suggests that the vast majority of students who have applied themselves diligently during the training will "pass" the proficiency examination on their first attempt. However, a few require additional practice before they can "pass." It is also recommended that students be given additional coaching to correct their errors of omission or commission, and be re-examined at a later date.

One may then use a comparison of the standard used in grading the officer in his NHTSA training class versus the standard used by that same officer on the accused. Establish the fact that during his training to become certified in the standardized field sobriety testing course, the officer had to study over and over how to administer the maneuvers properly. Even then, the officer/student would have practiced the proper administration over and over and made mistakes from time to time. When they make mistakes, they are given the opportunity to be re-examined at a later date. This is totally different from the opportunities given to the accused in the field. Number one, he has never been able to practice the maneuvers, and number two, he was not given an opportunity to be re-examined, either later at the station or at any subsequent time or place. The manual states that students,in order to pass the course in proper administration of the tests, must make at least an 80 percent for successful completion of the classroom training. Certainly one could then analogize that the performance (correct) of the accused on his test he took at roadside done correctly was certainly a lot greater than 80 percent! Suppose, for example, the accused was asked to perform the Walk-and-Turn Test and the officer testified he stepped off the line twice, did the turn improperly and was not heel to toe three times. That is a total of six mistakes. If one compares that six with the total amount of mistakes possible, one gets a percentage correct of greater than 80 percent. For example, 18 steps on the line, 18 counts out loud, 18 steps with arms side to side, 18 times to count sequentially correct, 18 times to walk heel to toe, four things to do right on turn (pivot on one foot and take three pivot steps), and 18 times to look at your feet. That's a total of 112 things to do. With six mistakes that makes a percentage correct on that maneuver of 95 percent, certainly a passing score.

The manual includes the procedure used for testing each student's ability to administer the three instructor's standardized field sobriety tests. According to the manual:

> "Passing" that test requires that the students administer the complete test battery at least once, in an instructor's presence *without deleting or erroneously performing any of the critical administrative elements of the tests.*

The manual then sets out the criteria of the necessary elements of the tests that must be given in the proper administration of each of the tests. Suppose, in administering the Walk-and-Turn Test, the officer failed to instruct the accused to look at his feet and to not raise his arms from his sides:

Q. Isn't it true, Officer Jones, according to your instructor's manual, that if you leave out one of the critical administrative elements of the test, then you have failed in the proper administration of the tests?
A. Yes.
Q. Isn't it true, according to your manual, two of the critical elements of the Walk-and-Turn Test, are to instruct the subject to look at the feet while walking, and also, to instruct the subject not to raise the arms from the sides?
A. Correct.
Q. You did not instruct Mr. Accused in either one of the elements, did you?
A. No sir.
Q. So, you yourself failed in the administration of the tests. Isn't that true?
A. Uh . . .
Q. Officer Jones, what does the phrase "garbage in, garbage out" mean?

Certainly then, this would give defense counsel fuel to argue in closing argument. How can one say the accused "failed a test" wherein the person giving the test "failed" in the proper administration of that same test?

The instructor's manual could also be used to establish the fact that six tests were used initially in the studies by NHTSA, however, the research concluded that only three tests came out as indicators of distinguishing BACs above 0.10 percent. In other words, the Finger-to-Nose and the Alphabet Test can be de-emphasized due to their being dropped by NHTSA as indicators of intoxication.

§13.0.7 Revealing Negative Scoring

An effective tactic in cross-examining the officer concerning his grading of the field sobriety test is to point out that he uses a negative scoring system. In effect, the suspect starts out with a perfect score: 0. Conceptually, then, the officer subtracts a "point" for every mistake the suspect makes. However, he never *adds* a point when the suspect does something *right*. This approach, of course, suggests a highly unfair ratchet effect — and a "no win" scenario for the suspect.

The following comments on the art of cross-examining the arresting officer on the subject of field sobriety tests are from a noted practitioner in the field and should be of interest to the reader. The author wishes to thank James Farragher Campbell of San Francisco for his kind permission to use these materials.

> Factors that are always present, in some form or another, which point to defendant's favor, have to be integrated into the cross-examination of the arresting officer. Evidence tending to suggest that the defendant had complete control of his senses, and as a result, his physical and mental abilities were not impaired to the extent that he could not safely operate a vehicle on the roadway. Almost every officer has generated documents or memoranda that can be used in questioning that officer and that may go to support the defendant's position, or negate that of the officer's, by suggesting that the defendant was not intoxicated. Such documentary evidence would show that the defendant was oriented as to time and place, that he was conversant and alert in conversation, that his question-and-answer orientation was logical, that his writing was not any different than what would be expected under less extraneous situations, that he was sensitized to the circumstances, that is, he was cooperative and respectful to the police or in the alter-

native he was aware of the "railroading position" that the arresting officers were placing him in or any other set of circumstances that goes to document what occurred. What actually occurred however, must be broken down in questioning step-by-step. As an example, if the arresting officer says the defendant "failed the F.S.T.s," ask him to illustrate, to explain in detail how the defendant failed. Force him to show before the jury that the defendant's performance was actually very good or acceptable rather than "failed."

To illustrate the above consider the following:

Q. Now you asked Mr. Brown to perform what you called a modified position of attention test, is that correct?
A. Yes.

Here you may wish to use a visual demonstration of the cross-examination to illustrate the total lack of weight the jury should attach to this test. The author suggests the following graph:

Modified Position of Attention

1	_____	_____	Feet together
2	_____	_____	Hands at sides
3	_____	_____	Head back
4	_____	_____	Eyes closed

Go to the chart and, with a red marking pen, conduct the cross-examination as follows:

Q. Officer, it is a fact, is it not, that these sobriety tests are designed to not only test muscle coordination but also what's known as divided attention and the ability to follow directions. These are skills and traits that are needed in order to safely operate a motor vehicle, isn't that true?
A. Yes.
Q. And it is true, is it not, that you are required to explain and demonstrate the test which you have asked the defendant to perform at the roadside?
A. Yes.
Q. And isn't it true that you in fact did that for Mr. Brown?
A. Yes.
Q. So, if you direct your attention to the chart the first thing you asked him to do was to put his feet together? [Counsel dem-

onstrates how the test is done by putting his feet together in front of the jury.]

A. Yes.

Q. And you in fact did demonstrate that and the defendant did understand that instruction, did he not?

A. Yes.

Q. So let's check here to show that the defendant did understand the instruction on putting his feet together. And it's true, is it not, that the defendant did in fact follow and put his feet together?

A. Yes.

Q. So let's put another check here to show that the defendant not only followed the instruction but also performed as instructed. And you also then explained to him to put his hands at his side, did you not?

A. Yes.

Q. Did the defendant appear to understand the instruction?

A. Yes.

Q. Then let's put a check to show that he understood the second instruction. [You should now have three checks on the chart — two under number one for following the instruction and performing it and one under number two for following the instruction, another soon to follow for actually performing the test.]

Q. And in fact the defendant did as demonstrated and requested and put his hands at his sides?

A. Yes. [The second check under number two is now added to the chart.]

Q. And you asked him then to put his head back and you demonstrated that request, did you not?

A. Yes.

Q. Let's put a check now to show that. Did you tell the defendant to close his eyes?

A. Yes I did.

Q. Did you demonstrate that?

A. No, I did not because it is our policy not to do that for our own personal protection and safety.

Q. So you explained this one to him but instead of demonstrating it as the other three steps of the test, you asked him simply to follow your oral instructions?

A. That's correct.

Q. The defendant did in fact follow the instructions because he performed that portion of the test by closing his eyes, did he not?

A. Yes, he did.
Q. So he understood the instructions. Let's put another check, and he did in fact do as requested, so we'll put another check. [You should now have two checks under each of the four steps of the modified position of attention test.]
Officer, you asked him to perform this test which is comprised of four parts, you demonstrated each and he did each; that is a total of eight points as I view this. What did he do wrong to fail the test?
A. As I said before, he swayed from side to side approximately two to three inches from the center.
Q. Officer, in fairness to the defendant, did you tell him not to sway?
A. No.
Q. Oh! He was graded on something he was not told was on the test?!

By using the above method, you have convincingly demonstrated to the jury through the officer's own testimony that Defendant did everything he was asked to do. The officer's assessment that he failed the test is a hollow one indeed. This cross-examination demonstrated the total subjectivity of the officer's assessment of the observation as well as demonstrating an affirmative response to a heavy factor in the defendant's favor. He passed the test. (You are encouraged to be creative and devise similar checklists and procedures for other sobriety tests.)

Checklist 22 General Cross-Examination Rules

The following general rules, many applicable to cross-examination of most witnesses, apply with particular force to dealing with police officers.

☐ Memorize all dates, times, places, and persons' names prior to examination.
☐ Pay close attention to direct examination, taking concise notes.
☐ Have reports and transcripts of prior testimony logically organized for quick access.
☐ Be thoroughly familiar with the rules and procedures for impeachment.
☐ Avoid asking a question to which you do not know the answer.

- ☐ Use leading questions, calling for a yes or no answer.
- ☐ Never ask "why," "what did you do next," or any question permitting the officer to assume control with a narrative answer.
- ☐ Avoid asking argumentative questions.
- ☐ Establish that the officer does not have an independent recollection of the events, but must rely on a report reflecting primarily incriminating facts.
- ☐ Never allow the officer to retell his earlier story.
- ☐ Establish what the officer did *not* do as well as what he did.
- ☐ Emphasize the officer's observations of the defendant that tend to establish sobriety.
- ☐ Never permit an officer simply to conclude that the defendant "failed" a particular test.
- ☐ Pierce the officer's use of "legalese," police jargon, or scientific terms.
- ☐ Maintain control of the examination at all times.
- ☐ Keep the officer to the facts — avoid letting him translate them into opinion.
- ☐ Show the jury how unfair the officer was in his evaluations of the defendant's appearance and performance.
- ☐ Establish the officer's predisposition.
- ☐ Avoid confrontation with the officer if possible, offering instead reasonable explanations.
- ☐ Establish symptom elimination.

§13.1 Techniques for Cross-Examination of the Officer

> The dictum that truth always triumphs over persecution is one of those pleasant falsehoods which men repeat after one another till they pass into commonplaces, but which all experience refutes.
>
> John Stuart Mill

Trial is an art. The key to the art, as in all art, is *creativity* — the ability to perceive "facts" in new ways, to approach the task unfettered by rigid adherence to tradition. Often this is simply a matter of stepping back and looking at a problem from a new perspective.

The complexities and unique characteristics of drunk driving litigation offer abundant opportunity to the defense attorney for the practice of his art. This is particularly true of the soul of that art: cross-examination of the officer.

The following represent a few of the more successful tactics created by the author for past DUI trials. Some are of recent origin; others have been around for a while (from the December 1988 issue of the National Association of Criminal Defense Lawyers' *The Champion:* "Taylor's patented approach to crossing the cop in a drunk driving case has been termed creating 'the Wedge' and can be regarded as so fundamental that newer drunk driving practitioners may not be aware that Taylor was its originator"). They by no means constitute a comprehensive list of possible approaches to cross-examination of the officer, nor are they even appropriate for every case or for every attorney. They have worked well for the author; some may work well for the reader.

§13.1.1 The Infallible Cop

The first — and simplest — of the suggested tactics in cross-examination of the arresting officer in a drunk driving case consists of nothing more than a single question. It is a question that can be asked to maximum effect at the onset of examination or at its conclusion. And it is a question that has the potential to impair the officer's credibility, no matter how he answers it. The question:

> "Officer, you testified that you believe Mr. Johnson was under the influence of alcohol. Is it possible that you are *wrong?*"

The officer has, of course, two possible answers. If he replies in the negative, counsel can then develop the rigid nature of his character — that is, that he does not make mistakes, that error is not possible, that he is perfect and above human frailty. Developed correctly, this rigidity will color the rest of his testimony in the eyes of the jury.

What if the officer admits that he *could* be wrong? Counsel can then point out in his argument to the jury that even the officer has doubts about the client's guilt. And if the officer is not absolutely certain, how can the jury be convinced *beyond a reasonable doubt?*

The author is fond of asking the question slowly and in a nonconfrontational manner at the outset of cross-examination. The opening question always holds the jury's attention the most and has the potential for the greatest impact. Perhaps more importantly, the question-and-answer can set the tone for the remainder of the officer's testimony: The jury will thereafter tend to view him as either rigid or unsure of his own opinion.

§13.1.2 Selective Recall

It should be established at the outset of cross-examination that the officer does not, in fact, have an independent recollection of all of the events to which he is testifying so smoothly. This can be done by asking questions concerning details, which will require him to refer to his DUI report, or by simply asking him if he felt it necessary to "review" his report before testifying for the prosecution. Another method — which can be used in conjunction with those mentioned — is to ask the officer how many arrests he has made since that of the defendant and how many in the preceding six months. He should then be asked if he claims to have an independent recollection of the facts in each of these cases. If he replies that he does, the jury will tend to disbelieve him.

After establishing that the officer does not have an independent recollection, his credibility is, of course, impaired somewhat. To damage it further, it should be developed in cross-examination that the report contains only *incriminating* facts. In other words, the officer wrote down only "relevant" observations — that is, observations that indicated intoxication. Quite simply, facts that indicated sobriety are not entered in the report. Counsel can ask the officer, for example, why he did not write down that the defendant's clothing was *not* disarranged, or that he did *not* fumble with his wallet in retrieving his driver's license. Counsel should then make it again clear that the officer is testifying based primarily on what his DUI report says — a report that has omitted all exculpatory facts. In other words, the officer is *incapable* of testifying to any but incriminating observations — a fact the jury will find interesting.

§13.1.3 The Wedge

A primary tactic in cross-examination of the arresting officer is to commit him to isolating the moment during his observations when he formed the opinion that the client was under the influence of alcohol. This is a simple tactic, and one fairly easy to accomplish. Yet the dual results can be devastating to the prosecution's case.

Quite simply, counsel accomplishes this limitation of the officer by going down the list of each of the officer's observations and tests chronologically. After each, the officer is asked if the particular observation or field sobriety test caused him to believe the defendant was definitely under the influence. This can be done most subtly by asking the officer if he then formed the opinion of intoxication or if he then arrested the defendant. At some point along the line of questioning, the officer must finally state that the last observation caused him to form the belief that the defendant was under the influence; he will often add, suspiciously, that the opinion was based on the cumulative effect of all observations up to that point.

The officer is now committed — and limited. And there is little he can do to prevent counsel from proceeding to minimize the effect of every one of his observations because of it.

The first effect of establishing exactly when the police officer decided the defendant was intoxicated is *symptom elimination* — that is, the minimizing of each earlier observation as a grounds for believing the client was intoxicated. Certainly, no officer will testify that he immediately formed the opinion that a suspect was under the influence after seeing red eyes and hearing slurred speech, even though most, in fact, do just that. Rather, the officer will try to show how open-minded and fair he is by refraining from forming any opinion until sufficient evidence has accumulated. The result, however, is to dampen the impact of each observation on the jury and, more important, the impact of the totality of these observations.

A very brief example:

Q. Now, Officer Smith, you testified that you observed my client to "stagger" as he stepped out of his car. Did you arrest him for driving under the influence at that time?

A. No.
Q. Then I presume you had not yet formed the definite opinion he was under the influence?
A. That's correct.
Q. And did you arrest him after observing his face to be "flushed"?
A. No.
Q. Then apparently these observations were not sufficient to justify a conclusion that he was under the influence?
A. I wanted to investigate further, in all fairness to your client.
Q. I see. And did you arrest him after hearing his "thick and slurred" speech?
A. No.
Q. After smelling a "strong odor of alcohol" on his breath?
A. I felt he was probably drunk.
Q. You mean, I assume, "under the influence"?
A. I mean under the influence.
Q. But you didn't arrest him?
A. No.
Q. Then you apparently were not yet convinced?
A. I felt it would be better to conduct a complete investigation.
Q. But you felt there was insufficient evidence *at this point* to arrest him?
A. I just felt I needed more.
Q. At what point did you form the opinion he was definitely under the influence of alcohol?
A. About the time he failed the first of the field sobriety tests.
Q. Then all the symptoms you observed prior to that did not constitute sufficient grounds, in your opinion, to arrest my client for driving under the influence?
A. I felt I wanted to see more.

The second effect of this limiting procedure automatically follows the first: If the observations prior to the officer's forming his opinion were insufficient to justify an arrest, then all of those *subsequent* were tainted. In other words, after the opinion was formed, any observations were colored by preconception: The officer was observing and interpreting after having already decided the suspect was intoxicated. In effect, he is gathering evidence for the sole purpose of supporting his recently formed opinion. This *predisposition* to interpret everything in a guilty light would have, of course, a significant bearing on the notoriously subjective "grading" of a suspect's performance on the field sobriety tests.

Again, a brief example of questioning:

Q. Officer Smith, you had already formed the opinion my client was under the influence when you administered the second field sobriety test, hadn't you?
A. Well. . . .
Q. Didn't you testify earlier that you definitely felt he was intoxicated after he failed the first test?
A. Yes.
Q. But you then gave him two more such tests?
A. Standard procedure.
Q. But you *knew* he was intoxicated when you gave him the second test?
A. I was pretty sure, yes.
Q. And you *knew* he was intoxicated when you gave him the third test?
A. Yes, that's right.
Q. And you fully expected him to fail those two tests as well?
A. Yes, I suppose so.
Q. You would have been surprised if he had passed?
A. Yes, I would have been.
Q. Who decides whether he passed those last two tests?
A. Well, I suppose. . . .
Q. *You* do, don't you, Officer Smith?
A. I indicate my opinion.
Q. You indicate in the report your interpretation of what the suspect did in the test, and you report whether he passed or failed, in your opinion?
A. Yes.

§13.1.4 The Magic Memory

The attorney who finds himself in a drunk driving case will quickly become aware of a rather incredible natural phenomenon: The superhuman memory of the arresting officer. He will discover that this witness possesses mental powers far beyond those of mere mortals — the ability to recall the facts of a DUI investigation in finite detail many months after the fact. And this despite the fact that the event was undistinguishable from dozens of other arrests made by the officer during the period.

Nowhere is this awesome talent more apparent than when the officer calmly walks to the chalkboard during direct examination and carefully draws a diagram of the defendant's performance on the ''walk-and-turn'' field sobriety test. The diagram, probably reproduced from the arrest report, will feature two straight lines or arrows and a series of steps. Commonly, there will be nine steps in each direction, with a circle representing the right steps and a triangle the left. The effect is, of course, impressive: The jury is able to see a clear and accurate record of the defendant's pathetic performance at the scene.

The officer will then, perhaps, go on to diagram in similar fashion the finger-to-nose test (circle for left finger, triangle for right, two touches each on various parts of the cartoon face) and the alphabet recitation (''The defendant missed b, r, w, and repeated x''). He will, of course, already have diagrammed in impressive detail the entire course of the defendant's car while following him — every weaving, swerving, and drifting motion for over a half-mile.

All of this the officer can recall now from the stand quite clearly and with considerable confidence.

The ''magic memory'' is a tactic designed to point out the obvious: No one can recall an event with this kind of detail. It must, however, be preceded by a series of apparently innocuous questions designed to establish two simple facts.

First, early in the cross-examination counsel should have developed the officer's reliance upon the arrest report to ''refresh'' his recollection. In doing this, it should be clearly brought out that the report was written at some time after the arrest; commonly, this is done an hour or two later at the police station.

Second, counsel must discreetly establish what the officer had in his hands while the client was performing the field sobriety tests. Again, the usual reply is that he had a flashlight in his left hand and nothing in his right (it is the policy of many law enforcement agencies to require officers to keep their gun hand free during such detentions), or that he had nothing in either hand.

Counsel can now proceed to the payoff: How was the officer able to remember the walk-and-turn test in such incredible detail *two hours later* when he drafted the report in the police station?

How could he recall where each of eighteen steps landed — and each as to angle and relative distance? And the four locations where the fingers missed the nose? And the alphabet? And every maneuver of the defendant's car? And every statement he made?

A common reply by many officers at this point is to claim that he was taking notes on a "field pad" as the defendant performed the tests. And this, of course, is why the seemingly innocent second series of questions were asked. The back door has been shut: The officer could not have been taking notes if he had a flashlight in his left hand during the tests.

§13.1.5 Xeroxed Symptoms

Yet another phenomenon that counsel in the drunk driving field will encounter is the amazing similarity of symptoms observed by individual officers. Suspects arrested by one officer always seem to lean against the car for support as they exit, then stumble on the third step of the walk-and-turn test, and finally miss "W" in the alphabet recitation. Another officer will invariably encounter individuals who fumble with their wallet, sway exactly three inches on the modified-position-of-attention test, and touch down at 21 seconds on the one-leg-stand.

The "phenomenon" is, of course, due to laziness, poor memory, and/or dishonesty. Unless counsel is familiar with a particular officer, however, the existence of these "xeroxed symptoms" is likely to go undiscovered. And it is the author's experience that the practice is becoming increasingly widespread. (During a recess in a recent trial, the author was told by a bailiff about an afternoon spent watching football on television with a friend, a California Highway Patrolman. During the commercials, the officer busied himself filling out DUI arrest reports — physical appearance, field sobriety tests, etc. The bailiff asked him how he could remember all of the facts from these past arrests. The officer casually replied that they were not for *past* arrests!)

The provable existence of xeroxed symptoms can be devastating to the state's case. To determine whether they exist, counsel should include in his discovery motion a request for all reports made out by the officer in other DUI cases during a given period of time (see §13.0.1) — for example, for 15 of the officer's working days before and after the arrest. Included should be a request for the officer's daily activity logs, reflecting any DUI arrests made; this serves as a means for checking that all reports have been produced. The motion should be accompanied by counsel's declaration setting forth the reasons for the purpose of the request.

Predictably, the prosecutor will oppose this request vehemently, usually on three grounds. First, the request is a "fishing expedition": The defense has not shown that the officer is reproducing similar symptoms in other cases. The reply to this, of course, is that of *Catch-22:* How can the defense *know* whether this is being done without reviewing his other reports? Second, the prosecution will claim that the request is "burdensome." The answer is that the request has been limited to a short period of time, representing relatively few DUI arrests; the defense will be willing to pay for costs and even conduct the search, if necessary.

Finally, the prosecuting attorney will develop a sudden and touching concern for the rights of privacy of the arrested individuals in the other reports. The counter to this is that the defense has no objection to the names, addresses, or any other identifying information being excised from the report; the only relevance of the reports is the reported symptoms of intoxication.

Armed with four or five DUI reports reflecting a number of identical symptoms, counsel can easily proceed to destroy the officer on the stand (the use of a chart can be particularly effective in revealing this practice to a jury).

§13.1.6 The Disappearing Sway

As with most effective tactics, the "disappearing sway" is quite simple. It consists of nothing more than contrasting two apparently contradictory observations by the officer. As with any tactic, of course, its effectiveness depends upon how it is done.

The horizontal gaze nystagmus test (see §4.3.5) is a potential subject of examination in a number of different contexts. Defense counsel may raise a question of probable cause to arrest and, at a pre-trial hearing on the issue, the officer will testify to his administration of the test in the field; the question may also arise during an administrative hearing on the client's driver's license suspension. Nystagmus may be the subject of a pre-trial challenge on *Frye* or other foundational grounds; again, the officer will probably testify about giving the test to the defendant. Or the issue may be raised during trial in a foundational voir dire of the officer (out of the jury's presence).

In whatever context, the officer will describe how he administered the test — including giving directions to the defendant to *keep his head absolutely still* during the test. And he will explain that the defendant did, in fact, remain perfectly still during the officer's examination for nystagmus. He will say this because he will also have to admit that the test results are completely invalid if the subject moves his head.

Armed with this testimony (and, preferably, a copy of the transcript), counsel can now address one of the more damning observations the officer has recounted to the jury: The defendant was staggering while he walked and constantly swaying when standing still. In fact, the officer will often even give the jury exact measurements of the sway — for example, that he swayed in a three-inch radius circle while attempting to perform the one-leg-stand test.

How is it possible to have such a pronounced and constant sway — and yet suddenly become perfectly still and rock stable for a nystagmus test?

§13.1.7 The Negative Pregnant

The criminal defense attorney has a natural instinct in trial to *attack,* to confront the witness and try to disprove the validity of his testimony. In drunk driving trials this usually consists of attacking the various symptoms of intoxication to which the officer has testified: weaving in traffic, bloodshot eyes, thick-and-slurred speech, stepping off the line in the walk-and-turn test, and so on. The efforts of counsel in cross-examination are directed to disproving the existence or implication of each of the symptoms.

The focus, in other words, is upon what *is* — rather than upon what is *not.*

Defense counsel should not limit his perceptions in constructing cross-examination to what the officer has testified to. He should also consider what the officer has *not* testified to. And the simple fact is that there are dozens — perhaps hundreds — of *pos-*

sible symptoms which could exist in any given drunk driving investigation. The key to "the negative pregnant" is simply to identify these for the jury — and then point out their absence in the client's case.

In most DUI trials, for example, the officer will begin his testimony with a description of what attracted his attention initially: the defendant's driving. Let us assume a particularly bad case where the officer testifies that he was weaving and his headlights were off. Applying "the negative pregnant," the officer should be asked if any of the *other* common driving symptoms were observed. And he should be asked about specific symptoms.

One approach here is to use the 20 driving symptoms recognized by the National Highway Traffic Safety Administration as "visual clues" of drunk driving (see §4.1.1 and the NHTSA pamphlet Guide for Detecting Drunk Drivers at Night, DOT HS-805-711). The officer can be taken down the list one-by-one: Did Mr. Johnson straddle a lane line? Was he drifting? Braking erratically? Accelerating or decelerating rapidly? And so on.

An effective technique is to graphically list the 20 symptoms on a chart or chalkboard. As the officer finally identifies the one or two symptoms he *did* see, counsel can check them off. The end result: only 2 of 20 symptoms checked. Put another way, a "score" of 80 percent!

This technique should be repeated with other observations as well. Consider all of the possible symptoms encountered in other cases: flushed face, bloodshot eyes, strong/moderate/weak odor of alcohol on breath, dilated eyes, slow pupil reaction, thick speech, slurred speech, messy clothing, fumbling with wallet for license, cannot locate registration, staggering, combative attitude, inappropriately happy attitude, leaning against the car for support, falling down, vomiting, inability to understand questions and/or directions, interrupting with distracting questions, and so on. Then contrast what the officer observed with what he did *not* observe. Again, this can be accomplished by asking about one nonexistent symptom at a time, with a chart or blackboard to illustrate all of the symptoms of intoxication that the defendant did not exhibit.

Continue to use this tactic with the field sobriety tests. Consider all of the different ways the client *could* have erred in attempting to perform each test but did not. As with the driving symptoms, use can be made of federal research in this area, NHTSA's "standardized" battery of field sobriety tests sets forth specific criteria for grading what are fast becoming the most commonly encountered tests: the walk-and-turn and the one-leg-stand. The walk-and-turn test lists nine separate mistakes the suspect can make. Yet, in most DUI cases the officer simply states that, for example, the defendant stepped off the line and lost his balance during the turn. This reflects only two of nine *possible* errors. And, again, a graphic listing of the nine possible symptoms, with only two being checked, can be effective (a score of nearly 80 percent).

The key to "the negative pregnant" is to go beyond the officer's arrest report, to think outside of his testimony. Do not be limited by what is in the report. Consider what is *not* in it.

§13.1.8 Reverse Impairment

This tactic rests upon a simple scientifically proven fact: Alcohol impairs an individual's mental facilities before it impairs his physical abilities. Put another way, by the time a drunk driving suspect exhibits impaired balance, coordination, and reflexes, his comprehension and communicative skills will already have been damaged.

In his cross-examination, counsel should have the officer acknowledge that he asked dozens of questions of the defendant. Some of these were investigatory in nature: What have you had to drink? How much? When? Where are you now? What time is it? Have you had anything to eat? Where were you drinking? Many of the questions, however, simply concern "bookkeeping" matters, but they are also critical to the "reverse impairment" tactic. These consist of such questions as: Name? Address? Telephone number? How old are you? Do you wear glasses? Where do you work? Are you sick or injured? Do you have any physical impairments? Are you taking any medication? Are you a diabetic? And so on. The arrest report will usually reflect this information, and it should be brought out on cross-examination that the officer obtained most or all of it from questioning the defendant.

From all of this it can be developed that the client was asked a rather impressive list of questions during the course of the investigation and afterwards at the police station — *and he understood them!* He not only understood the officer's myriad of questions, *he gave intelligent answers!* In other words, his mental facilities were apparently *not* impaired: He was able to understand dozens of questions, process them and recollect extensive information, and finally formulate articulate responses.

After the officer admits that the defendent did apparently understand his questions and gave seemingly accurate answers, he should be asked to *again* acknowledge that alcohol affects mental facilities first, then physical. He can then be confronted with the contradiction: How could the defendant have exhibited the physical impairment described at length by the officer — without apparent mental impairment?

§13.1.9 The Rigged Scoreboard

An effective tactic in cross-examining the arresting officer in a drunk driving case is to point out the unfairness of his method of *grading* the defendant's performance on the field sobriety tests. This not only tends to discredit the tests, it casts doubt upon the officer's objectivity and fairness generally.

There are two techniques for developing this biased scoring system: the *negative* and the *subjective.* Both can be used.

The first method in cross-examining the officer is to point out that he uses a negative scoring system. In effect, the suspect starts out with a score of zero. Conceptually, then, the officer subtracts a point for every mistake the suspect makes. However, he never *adds* a point when the suspect does something *right.* This approach, of course, suggests a highly unfair ratchet effect — and a "no win" scenario for the suspect.

The second technique involves establishing the completely subjective criteria for determining whether a suspect has "passed" or "failed" a field sobriety test. This is, of course, the opinion of an officer who has almost certainly already formed an opinion that the individual is intoxicated — and this *predisposition* should be clearly developed (see §13.1.3).

Having emphasized the subjective nature of the scoring, counsel should then develop the availability of *objective* scoring. The following approach, taken from a recent case tried by the author, will illustrate:

Q. Officer, you say Mr. Johnson failed the walk-and-turn test.
A. That's right.
Q. What was his *score?*
A. His score?
Q. Yes. What was his score on the test? 60 percent? 70 percent?
A. There's no score, counselor.
Q. You didn't give him any score?
A. Of course not.
Q. You just decided he didn't do as well as you'd like?
A. He failed. He didn't perform satisfactorily.
Q. Satisfactorily. So rather than use an *impartial* scoring system, *you* just decided it was unsatisfactory?
A. You can't score the test, counselor.
Q. I beg your pardon?
A. There is no scoring system. You can't score a walk-and-turn test.
Q. It can't be done?
A. No.
Q. Officer, isn't it a fact that police in almost every state are now using objective scoring for this test?
A. I'm not aware of that.
Q. You're not aware? You're not aware that the federal government has developed standardized field sobriety tests with objective scoring?
A. No.
Q. Officer, did you receive the pamphlet I mailed you three weeks ago? The one describing how this test is supposed to be given — and scored?
A. I may have. I don't recall.
Q. You don't recall.
A. No. I may have.
Q. Would it surprise you to learn that there are nine possible points in scoring the walk-and-turn test?
A. Like I said, I don't know about any of those tests.
Q. Is it still your testimony that it is not *possible* to use a fair and objective method for scoring the test? That it can't be done?
A. Mr. Johnson failed the test, counselor. It was a fair test and he failed.
Q. Officer, did you ever take tests in school?
A. Of course.
Q. Ever fail any of them?
A. Failed my share.

Q. Get a score?
(Witness nods)
A. What if you took a test with nine true-false questions?
Q. Yeah?
A. And when you got it back, there was nothing to show if you missed any of them. It just says, "Not satisfactory." Think that would be fair?
(Objection by prosecutor)

If the officer denies that an objective scoring system is used by other law enforcement agencies, counsel might consider showing him the following form distributed by the Kansas Highway Patrol and uniformly used by patrol officers, throughout the state. Note that there are 17 possible points on the one-leg-stand and 22 on the walk-and-turn.

FIELD SOBRIETY TESTS

ONE LEG STAND

INSTRUCTIONS

STAND WITH YOUR HEELS TOGETHER AND YOUR ARMS DOWN AT YOUR SIDES, LIKE THIS. (Demonstrate how you want the subject to stand.)

WHEN I TELL YOU TO, I WANT YOU TO RAISE ONE LEG ABOUT SIX INCHES OFF THE GROUND AND HOLD THAT POSITION. AT THE SAME TIME, COUNT RAPIDLY FROM 1001 TO 1030 . . . LIKE THIS. (Assume the position and demonstrate.)

DO YOU UNDERSTAND? (Do not continue until the subject indicates that he understands.)

BEGIN BY RAISING EITHER YOUR RIGHT OR LEFT FOOT.
Indicate which foot the subject raised. LEFT RIGHT

TEST

	0 to 10 SEC'S	11 to 20 SEC'S	21 to 30 SEC'S
1. **SWAYS WHILE BALANCING.** (Side-to-side or back-and-forth motion while maintaining the one leg stand position.)			
2. **USES ARMS TO BALANCE** (Moves arms 6 or more inches from side to maintain balance in the one leg stand position.)			
3. **HOPPING** (Able to keep one foot off the ground, but resorts to hopping to maintain balance.)			
4. **PUTS FOOT DOWN** (Not able to maintain the one leg stand position. Putting foot down 1 or more times during 30 sec.)			

5. **CANNOT DO THE TEST.** ☐ **(Score 5 points)**

TOTAL ☐

COMMENTS: ____________________

WALK AND TURN

INSTRUCTIONS

PUT YOUR LEFT FOOT ON THE LINE AND THEN YOUR RIGHT FOOT IN FRONT OF IT, LIKE THIS. (Demonstrate how you want the subject to stand.)

(When the subject assumes this position, continue with the instructions.) **WHEN I TELL YOU TO BEGIN, TAKE NINE HEEL TO TOE STEPS DOWN THE LINE, TURN AROUND, AND TAKE NINE HEEL TO TOE STEPS BACK.**

MAKE YOUR TURN BY KEEPING YOUR LEFT FOOT ON THE LINE AND THEN USING YOUR OTHER FOOT TO TURN . . . LIKE THIS. (Demonstrate, make several small pivots, note that this is a very easy way to turn, but the subject must follow your instructions.)

KEEP YOUR HANDS AT YOUR SIDES, WATCH YOUR FEET AT ALL TIMES AND COUNT YOUR STEPS OUT LOUD.

DO YOU UNDERSTAND? (Do not continue until the subject indicates that he understands.)

BEGIN AND COUNT YOUR FIRST STEP FROM THE HEEL-TO-TOE POSITION AS ONE.

TEST

1. **LOSES BALANCE DURING INSTRUCTIONS.** (Does not maintain heel-to-toe position throughout the instructions.) ☐
2. **STARTS BEFORE INSTRUCTIONS ARE FINISHED.** (Does not wait until you tell him to begin as per the instructions.)

	FIRST NINE STEPS	SECOND NINE STEPS
3. **STOPS WHILE WALKING.** (Pauses for several seconds after a step.)		
4. **DOESN'T TOUCH HEEL-TO-TOE.** (Leaves 1/2 inch or more between heel and toe on any step.)		
5. **STEPS OFF THE LINE.** (Subject steps so that one foot is entirely off of the line.)		
6. **USES ARMS TO BALANCE.** (Raises one or both arms 6 or more inches from sides in order to maintain balance.)		

7. **IMPROPER TURN.** (Removes the pivot foot from the line while turning.) ☐

	FIRST NINE STEPS	SECOND NINE STEPS
8. **INCORRECT NUMBER OF STEPS.** (Takes more or less than 9 steps in each direction. Don't count this item because he has trouble counting.)		

9. **CANNOT DO THE TEST.** ☐ **(Score 9 points)**

TOTAL ☐

COMMENTS: ____________________

PAGE 2

Form 18
Field Sobriety Tests

§13.1.10 The Memory Chart

Gary Trichter of Houston, Texas, uses a technique designed to take advantage of a common practice of many officers. To avoid contradiction or impeachment, these officers will simply answer the defense lawyer's questions with an evasive "I don't recall," "I don't know," or "I'm not sure." And, of course, in many cases the answers are truthful: confronted with effective cross-examination, officers will often be forced to admit a lack of recollection or knowledge.

To summarize Trichter's tactic, he simply keeps a running score on such answers. He maintains a large chart on an easel for the jury to view, with three columns: "Don't know," "Not sure," and "Don't recall." Each time the officer gives one of these answers, Trichter walks over to the chart and places a mark in the appropriate column.

By the end of the trial, the chart usually has a large number of marks on it (Trichter asks the officer to place his signature on the chart, indicating he agrees with the number of deficiencies indicated). And, of course, unreliability of the officer's testimony is graphically embedded in the jurors' minds.

§13.1.11 Geometry for Cops

A cornerstone of the prosecution's case is the supposedly objective and "scientific" *horizontal gaze nystagmus* test. This evidence can be devastating if not properly exposed on cross-examination. As was discussed in §13.0.7, however, defense counsel can turn the HGN test against the prosecution, using it to discredit the entire case. One way to accomplish this is to challenge the method used by the officer for estimating the *angle of onset* of nystagmus.

The measurement of the angle of onset is, of course, critical: If the officer estimates the 45-degree angle incorrectly, the results will be correspondingly invalid. There are a number of ways of dealing with this complete lack of precision: pointing out that the officer was trained with a protractor, but used none during the defendant's test; asking the officer if he has practiced estimating

45-degree angle measurements with a protractor on a monthly basis, as recommended by the NHTSA manual; etc.

A particularly effective tactic of exposing this complete lack of precision in what is presented as a scientifically precise test involves the practice common among police officers of estimating the angle by using the suspect's *shoulder* to estimate 45 degrees. The test begins with the suspect staring at the officer's pencil, finger, or other object held directly in front of him, then following it as the officer moves it laterally. If nystagmus first occurs prior to the officer's finger or pencil reaching an imaginary line from the suspect's shoulder, the officer assumes this corresponds with approximately 45 degrees. This is not a secret: Most officers who use this method, when pressed for a basis for their estimate of the angle, explain the method.

It should be readily apparent to anyone — including jurors — that this is hardly a model of precision, and nowhere near the relative accuracy of the protractor used in training. More importantly, however, there are at least two variables in the method that can significantly affect the results. First, the geometry underlying this crude measurement depends upon the finger or pencil being 12 to 15 inches from the eyes and remaining uniform. Secondly, and the greatest flaw, any accuracy depends upon the assumption that *all people's shoulder widths are identical.* Pressed, the officer will have to admit that his measurements do not vary with the individual: The end of the shoulder represents 45 degrees — whether a burly lumberjack or a diminutive housewife. The result: Since the theoretical 45-degree angle will be reached later by the broad-shouldered lumberjack, the onset is more likely to occur before then. Put another way, the broader the suspect's shoulders, the earlier in degrees the onset of nystagmus — and the more likely a false indication of intoxication.

This can be effectively demonstrated for the jury by picking out two individuals in the courtroom with visibly different shoulder widths — one of them possibly the defendant — and having the officer explain as he conducts the tests. A simple alternative is to diagram the basic geometry involved for the jury on a blackboard or chart during cross-examination (or, ideally, have one prepared by a graphics firm).

§13.1.12 How to Make Big Money in Drunk Driving

Once again, Houston's Gary Trichter offers the following interesting strategy in cross-examining the arresting officer in a DUI case:

> In many metropolitan areas, law enforcement agencies have established special drunken driving task forces. These are the officers that appear in court most often, and therefore are the ones that make the most overtime pay. Indeed, some patrol officers have been known to make a pay equivalent to that of a lieutenant. Experience and common sense demonstrate that drunken driving defendants who contest the charges are generally those that do not appear to be intoxicated. Accordingly, a persuasive jury argument can be made that these task force officers purposely make arrests of drinking drivers, even if they are not intoxicated, because it is this type of defendant that will cause them to come to court where the officer can make extra money.
>
> Through discovery or through state freedom of information/open records statutes, defense counsel can often secure payroll records indicating both base pay and overtime pay. For example, during a jury voir dire, panel members are not usually disturbed to learn that an officer has a regular salary of $26,000. Similarly, jurors are not disturbed that the officer makes $1,000, $3,000, $5,000 or even $7,000 a year in overtime. Jurors, however, appear to be somewhat disturbed that an officer can make $9,000, $11,000, $13,000 and $15,000 a year in overtime. It is at this level of overtime that the jury begins to sense the officers may be arresting innocent drinkers for drunken driving. At figures of $16,000 through $22,000 jurors have often been heard to say that they would not trust anything the officer had to say. It is here that the officer's credibility and motive are clearly in question. Payroll records in these metropolitan areas often show that these task force officers do indeed make overtime at amounts that are above $10,000 a year.

§13.1.13 The Two-Edged Sword of Refusal

Assuming that evidence of the client's refusal to submit to chemical testing is ruled admissible, counsel must, of course, provide the jury with an acceptable reason for the refusal (i.e., other than "consciousness of guilt"). Among the many reasons commonly encountered are confusion concerning the right not to incriminate oneself, the belief that one has a right to speak with an attorney first, and so forth.

An effective argument can be developed through questioning of the officer and/or defendant that the client's refusal is an indication of "consciousness of *innocence.*" Assuming that an arrested driver honestly believes himself to be sober, how would he feel toward the officer who is falsely arresting him? A sober, reasonable person would probably feel distrust toward that officer. If that person feels he was arrested after performing well on the field sobriety tests given by the officer, how would he view a breath test administered by that same officer? Would he trust such a test?

Of course, "the best defense is a good offense" — and evidence of a refusal can easily be turned against the prosecution. In cross-examination of the officer, it can be readily established (in most states) that he had the power — the legal authority — to obtain a blood sample over the defendant's objections (see, e.g., *Schmerber v. California*). In other words, the officer did not have to simply accept the refusal, but could have *forcibly* had a blood sample drawn (assuming the procedure was not "shocking to the conscience," per *Schmerber*). Yet the officer chose not to. Objective, scientific corroboration of the officer's opinion was readily available — and he declined. Why? Why would the officer *prefer* circumstantial evidence over direct evidence? Why would he *rather not* have clear and definitive chemical proof? Why would this officer prefer to rely entirely on his own testimony instead? A possible answer: the officer realized that the blood-alcohol analysis might prove the defendant innocent.

This line of questioning can be effectively used as well in the situation where the client insists that he did *not* refuse (i.e., that the officer is lying). If counsel is to convince the jury that the officer is misrepresenting the facts, he must provide the jurors with a *reason:* Why would an officer falsely claim that a DUI suspect refused to submit to chemical testing? Again, the answer is: With a simple deception, the officer both (1) eliminates scientific evidence that might contradict his observations and opinion, and (2) creates a "consciousness of guilt" inference.

§13.1.14 The Bomb

The final technique for the DUI defense lawyer involves nothing more than asking a single question. But the effect can be considerable: The answer can, in fact, cast doubt on the cumulative effect of the officer's entire testimony.

The question: "Officer, would you have booked my client for drunk driving if the breath test had turned out to be .05 percent?"

In almost every case, the officer will reply reluctantly that the defendant would have been released and charges never brought if the blood-alcohol test indicated a level below the statutory minimum. This simply reflects fairly universal policy. And this is true despite the fact that suspects can be charged under either the DUI or per se statute, or both.

In his argument (or during continued cross-examination), counsel can then point out that despite all of the seemingly damning testimony from the officer concerning the client's symptoms, he would not have arrested him for drunk driving if a breath machine disagreed with his opinion. This would seem to cast doubt upon the validity of that opinion as well as on the significance of all of the symptoms of intoxication.

The author often asks "the bomb" as the final question in cross-examination, leaving the jury with what is frequently a surprising revelation. The following excerpt from one of his recent trials may serve as an example:

Q. By the way, Sergeant, what if Mr. Johnson had blown a .06 on the breath test?
A. What?
Q. Well, what would you have done?
A. I guess I would have released him.
Q. You wouldn't have booked him for DUI?
A. Not if he blew a .06.
Q. The weaving, the slurred speech, bloodshot eyes, field sobriety tests. . . . you still would have let him go?
A. Yeah.
Q. Insufficient evidence of intoxication?
A. I guess.

§13.2 Illustrative Cross-Examination of Arresting Officer

Truth has a way of shifting under pressure.
CURTIS BOK

The following represents a fairly brief example of a cross-examination of an investigating officer in a drunk driving case. The dialogue is illustrative only and purely fictional in origin; it should be viewed as merely suggestive and not considered as necessarily consistent with the laws and procedures applicable to counsel's particular case.

The illustration is also far from comprehensive in scope, touching on only some of the more commonly recurring issues. Most notably, the nystagmus test is not covered; a lengthy illustrative cross-examination on this subject is found in §13.2.1. Operation of a breath machine is only superficially treated, primarily in the area of mouth alcohol from belching; counsel should review the materials in Chapter 6. Finally, many of the tactics previously discussed in §13.1 are also not included here to avoid repetition.

Recollection of Events

Q. Officer Smith, you prepared a police report in this matter?
A. Yes, I did.
Q. When was this?
A. About an hour later, after the arrest. It was in the station — the police station.
Q. I see. And in this report you set down the facts of this case?
A. That's right.
Q. Now, you reviewed this report before testifying here, didn't you?
A. What do you mean?
Q. I mean, before taking the stand to testify here this morning, you read that report, didn't you?
A. Sure, I looked it over.
Q. You read the report before testifying because you cannot recall on your own what happened in this case, right?
A. No. Well, I can recall that night mostly, but maybe not everything.
Q. The fact is, you read the report this morning to help you remember the events surrounding Mr. Kelly's arrest?
A. It helps, yes sir.

Q. Can you recall the facts of this case without reading the report?
A. I think so.
Q. Would you please tell the jury what year, model, and color of the car Mr. Kelly was driving?
A. Uh, I think it was . . . a Chevy? I'm not sure.
Q. Would you care to refer to your report?
A. Yes, sir. (Reads.) A Honda, 1994, red in color.
Q. I see. Now, what did Mr. Kelly tell you when you asked him what if any medications he had been taking?
A. I'm not sure.
Q. Would you care to read your report?
A. (Reads.) I don't see anything about that.
Q. But until you read your report, you did not know if you asked him that question or not?
A. (Nods.)
Q. The simple fact is, Officer Smith, you cannot testify here today about this case without reading your police report, isn't that true?
A. I can testify all right. But the report helps, sure.
Q. How many arrests of any kind have you made in the four months since you arrested Mr. Kelly?
A. Oh, I don't know, maybe 50 or so.
Q. And how many arrests in the four months before?
A. I suppose another 50, give or take.
Q. About 100 arrests in the period four months before and since Mr. Kelly's arrest?
A. About, yes sir.
Q. Mr. Kelly's, then, is only one of 100?
A. If you want to put it that way.
Q. Can you recall the details of each of these 100 arrests here today — without reading from the police reports?
A. Uh, I think so.
Q. Now, Officer Smith, did Mr. Kelly lean against his car for support when he stepped out of the car?
A. I don't think so.
Q. Would you like to read your report again?
A. No. He didn't lean, no.
Q. That is a common symptom of an intoxicated driver, isn't it?
A. Yes sir, sometimes.
Q. I assume you wrote in the arrest report that he did *not* lean against the car for support?
A. (Reads report.) No, sir.
Q. You did not?
A. No, sir.

Q. The fact of the matter is, Officer Smith, you only wrote down *incriminating* facts in that report, isn't that so?
A. Evidence, yes sir.
Q. You did not write down any exculpatory facts — that is, things you observed that tended to show Mr. Kelly was *not* under the influence?
A. Uh, I wrote down what I thought was important.
Q. In fact, your report contains *nothing* that tends to show Mr. Kelly was not intoxicated?
A. That may be.
Q. Officer Smith, you have difficulty testifying here today without first reading your report.
A. It helps, yes sir.
Q. But your report contains only possibly *incriminating* observations — you have left out facts that show Mr. Kelly was innocent, isn't that true?
A. I can't put everything in the report, sir.
Q. But the simple fact is, isn't it, that you are only *capable* of testifying to observations that point to intoxication?
A. I don't understand.
Q. You are not capable of testifying to observations showing Mr. Kelly was *not* under the influence for the simple reason that you never wrote them down — and you can only testify to what is in the report?
A. I can recall. The report helps, but I can recall.

Driving Symptoms

Q. Now, Officer Smith, you say your attention was first drawn to Mr. Kelly by the fact that his car was weaving?
A. That's correct, counsel.
Q. Have you ever issued a citation for crossing a lane line?
A. Of course — dozens of times.
Q. Did you arrest any of these drivers for driving under the influence?
A. No.
Q. Then is it safe to assume that, in your opinion, weaving across lane lines does not necessarily mean the driver is under the influence?
A. Well, sure.
Q. I assume that if the weaving is pronounced, you would issue a citation.
A. Usually.
Q. Did you issue a citation to Mr. Kelly for weaving or crossing the lane lines?
A. No.
Q. Should you observe a driver who is driving recklessly, or presenting

a danger to other drivers, you would remove him from traffic as quickly as possible, would you not?
A. I suppose so, yes.
Q. How far did you follow my client?
A. Oh, about four or five blocks, I would say.
Q. You did not choose to remove him from traffic immediately?
A. Well, no.
Q. Were you able to see Mr. Kelly's car clearly in the traffic?
A. Definitely. I had a clear field of vision.
Q. Weren't you quite a distance back?
A. No, I was just four or five car lengths behind him.
Q. Officer, have you ever heard of the expression "black and white fever"?
A. Sure.
Q. Would you please explain the term to the members of the jury?
A. It's kind of a reaction people have when they're driving and there's a "black and white" — a marked police car — following them.
Q. And what kind of a reaction is that?
A. They tend to watch the rearview mirror more than they do the road.
Q. Result?
A. Sometimes their car starts weaving.
Q. And even fails to stop for traffic lights?
A. Sometimes.
Q. You testified you were only four or five car lengths behind Mr. Kelly?
A. Yes.
Q. Were you in a marked car?
A. Yes.
Q. And you watched him weaving?
A. Yes.
Q. By the way, was the vehicle impounded by you?
A. Our normal procedure is to turn the vehicle over to a responsible relative or friend of the suspect's.
Q. To whom did you turn my client's car over?
A. I gave the keys to his wife, who was sitting in the passenger seat.
Q. You would not entrust the car to another person who was under the influence, would you, Officer Smith?
A. Of course not.
Q. Then Mr. Kelly's wife was sober?
A. I believe s[illegible]
Q. Did you [illegible]n when he first saw the flashing red lights?
A. No.
Q. Then yo[illegible]'t know when he first saw them?
A. No.

Q. It's possible he pulled over as soon as he saw them?
A. It's possible.
Q. It is also possible that he thought it was an ambulance or fire truck?
A. I doubt it; we stayed right behind him.
Q. Then is it possible some of his driving symptoms were nervousness or an attempt to get out of your way?
A. I doubt it.
Q. Is it impossible?
A. Oh, I suppose it's a possibility.
Q. Officer, do you ever have trouble working your way through traffic on a Code 3 — that is, answering an emergency call with the siren going?
A. Sure, many times.
Q. Some of the drivers don't hear it?
A. That's right.
Q. They've got their windows rolled up and their radios on, right?
A. Yes.
Q. Were Mr. Kelly's windows rolled up while he was driving?
A. I don't know.
Q. And was there a radio in the car?
A. I guess there probably was.
Q. Would you say the average person you pull over is somewhat apprehensive, nervous?
A. Some of them are.
Q. And being pulled over, their attention is directed to you?
A. Some of them.
Q. Does it seem so odd, then, that they end up parking a couple of feet from the curb?
A. I don't know.
Q. Is Mr. Kelly the first to react to flashing lights and sirens by making a less-than-perfect parking attempt?
A. It happens.

Initial Observations

Q. Officer, I presume you've sat through a movie before, then suddenly tried to get up and walk out of the theatre?
A. Sure.
Q. From sitting for so long, the circulation is cut down, so that the effect is to stagger stiffly somewhat, is that not so?
A. I believe that's the reason.
Q. And the older the individual, the more pronounced this effect will be?

A. I suppose so.
Q. Do you know for how long Mr. Kelly had been sitting in the driver's seat before he was required to step out of the car?
A. No.
Q. I noticed in your testimony that you observed Mr. Kelly to stagger as he stepped out of his car.
A. That's correct.
Q. And you interpreted this as a sign of intoxication?
A. A sign — one of many.
Q. This staggering, as you've called it, was a significant factor in your eventual opinion that he was under the influence?
A. One of the factors.
Q. In fact, it was the first thing you observed — the first thing that struck you in beginning to form your opinion?
A. It was one of the first things, I suppose.
Q. Would you characterize Mr. Kelly at the scene as being calm, cool, and collected?
A. Hardly.
Q. He was nervous, flustered?
A. I guess that would be pretty accurate.
Q. I noticed you testified he had some difficulty fumbling with his wallet, trying to find his driver's license?
A. Yes.
Q. As if he were very nervous, flustered?
A. Or drunk.
Q. Or nervous or flustered?
A. I suppose that's possible, too.
Q. By the way, Officer Smith, did you question Mr. Kelly as to his recent illness?
A. Illness?
Q. Yes. I assume you knew he was suffering from a cold at the time of his arrest?
A. No.
Q. You know, of course, that a cold can have a pronounced effect on the inner ear, thus throwing an individual's equilibrium off?
A. Uh, sure.
Q. Looking at my client today, Officer, would you characterize his face as pale?
A. No.
Q. More like a normal, ruddy complexion?
A. I suppose — normal, yes.
Q. You had never seen him prior to characterizing his face as "flushed"?

A. No.
Q. So you did not know at the time whether a ruddy — or flushed — complexion was abnormal for him?
A. Not at the time, no. But he seemed redder then than he does now.
Q. What are the normal biological symptoms of nervousness or fear?
A. Huh?
Q. Specifically, what happens to the face when a person is afraid, embarrassed, or nervous?
A. It turns red, I guess.
Q. Becomes flushed?
A. Yes.
Q. Alright. You said that Mr. Kelly's eyes were bloodshot and glassy.
A. Yes.
Q. What do his eyes usually look like?
A. I don't know.
Q. Why did you write that down?
A. Because it's a symptom of having drunk too much.
Q. But a person's eyes may be normally bloodshot?
A. I suppose.
Q. Do you know how long Mr. Kelly had been without sleep when he was arrested?
A. No.
Q. Do you know how much reading or strenuous visual work he had been involved in during the previous 24 hours?
A. No.
Q. Bloodshot and glassy eyes can be symptomatic of fatigue, lack of sleep, or eyestrain, can they not?
A. Yes, I guess so.
Q. How was the smog on the day of the arrest, Officer?
A. I don't recall.
Q. But can't air pollution cause these eye symptoms as well?
A. I guess so.
Q. Now, I presume you had never spoken with Mr. Kelly prior to this incident?
A. No, never.
Q. So you don't know what his normal speech patterns are?
A. No.
Q. Then, it's entirely possible that his normal speech is "thick and slurred," isn't it?
A. I doubt it.
Q. That's impossible?
A. Well, no. I suppose it's possible.
Q. You asked him what his name was?

A. Yes.
Q. And his address?
A. Yes.
Q. And where he had been drinking?
A. Yes.
Q. And how much he had been drinking?
A. Yes.
Q. And who the woman with him was?
A. Yes.
Q. And a number of other questions?
A. Yes.
Q. And he answered these questions satisfactorily?
A. Yes.
Q. Then apparently you had no difficulty in understanding what he was saying?
A. I could understand.
Q. And apparently he had no difficulty in understanding your questions and in responding intelligently to them?
A. I suppose not.
Q. I see, in your report, under "Speech" you have checked the box next to "slurred."
A. Yes.
Q. The only other boxes are "incoherent" and "no impairment."
A. That's right.
Q. Well, since you were questioning Mr. Kelly, I assume "incoherent" didn't apply.
A. Right.
Q. So you only had a choice of two: "slurred" or "no impairment"?
A. Yes.
Q. No other choices?
A. I guess not.
Q. And "no impairment" wouldn't be corroborative of a drunk driving arrest, would it?
A. No.
Q. Officer Smith, could you tell how many drinks Mr. Kelly had consumed by smelling his breath?
A. I could tell he had had a lot.
Q. Oh? And could you tell what kind of drink he had consumed?
A. Well, no — not really.
Q. Could you tell by his breath when he consumed the drinks?
A. No.
Q. It could have been hours earlier?
A. Maybe.

Q. Then I assume a person could be stone sober and have a smell of alcohol on his breath?
A. He wasn't stone sober.
Q. Just speaking hypothetically, a person could be stone sober and still have a smell of alcohol on his breath?
A. I guess so.
Q. You could tell Mr. Kelly had had a lot to drink by smelling his breath?
A. Yes.
Q. How?
A. The smell. It was mighty strong.
Q. Officer, suppose I were to tell you that pure alcohol has absolutely no smell.
A. Huh?
Q. The alcohol in the drink — the alcohol itself has no smell to it. The smell comes from the beverage flavoring: scotch, gin, bourbon.
A. Well. . . .
Q. If alcohol has no smell, then what you are smelling is simply the drink's flavoring, isn't that right?
A. I don't know.
Q. You didn't realize that alcohol is odorless?
A. Well, alcohol all by itself, I guess so.
Q. Since it doesn't have any odor, how can you tell how much alcohol was consumed by smelling?
A. Well, I don't know.
Q. Now, I notice you testified that Mr. Kelly's clothing appeared rumpled and disarranged.
A. That's right.
Q. What time of day was this?
A. About 10 o'clock at night.
Q. Do you know how long he had been in those clothes without being able to change?
A. No.
Q. For all you know, then, he could have spent 24 hours in them and just finished changing a flat tire in the rain?
A. I don't know what he did.

Symptom Elimination

Q. Now, Officer Smith, you testified that you observed Mr. Kelly "stagger" as he stepped out of his car. Did you arrest him for driving under the influence at that time?
A. No.

Q. Then I presume you had not yet formed the definite opinion he was under the influence?
A. That's correct.
Q. And did you arrest him after observing his face to be "flushed"?
A. No.
Q. Then apparently these symptoms were not sufficient to justify a conclusion that he was under the influence?
A. I wanted to investigate further.
Q. And did you arrest him after hearing his "thick and slurred" speech?
A. No.
Q. After smelling a "strong odor of alcohol" on his breath?
A. I felt he was probably drunk.
Q. You mean under the influence?
A. I mean under the influence.
Q. But you didn't arrest him?
A. No.
Q. Then you apparently were not yet convinced?
A. I felt it would be better to conduct a complete investigation.
Q. But you felt there was insufficient evidence at this point to arrest him?
A. I just felt I wanted more.
Q. At what point did you form the opinion he was definitely under the influence of alcohol?
A. About the time he failed the first of the "field sobriety tests," the "walk-the-line."
Q. Then all the symptoms you observed prior to that did not constitute sufficient grounds, in your opinion, to arrest Mr. Kelly?
A. I felt I needed more.

Field Sobriety Tests

Q. Now, Officer Smith, where was this field sobriety test administered?
A. At the scene.
Q. You mean on the highway, next to the car?
A. That's right.
Q. At what time of day or night?
A. About 10 P.M.
Q. And was there any traffic on that highway at that time?
A. Oh, yes, quite a bit of traffic.
Q. What was the surface like where Mr. Kelly walked this line?
A. It was on the shoulder of the highway. Dirt or gravel, I think.
Q. And I presume it slopes off of the paved highway?

A. A little, yes.
Q. So Mr. Kelly was asked to perform this test of balance on a sloped surface covered with gravel?
A. Well, yes.
Q. And with cars whizzing by, with air pressure waves hitting him?
A. There were some cars.
Q. And their headlights flashing on and off of him?
A. That couldn't be helped.
Q. What was the source of light for the test?
A. Well, I guess the headlights from my police car.
Q. Headlights directly in his face?
A. They weren't in his face most of the time.
Q. Were the flashing red lights on top of the car on?
A. Yes, I believe so.
Q. Setting up a strobe effect?
A. I don't know.
Q. And on top of this, as you've already testified, Mr. Kelly was somewhat rattled — nervous and embarrassed?
A. Well, he seemed a little nervous, yes.
Q. Did you ask him if he had any physical disabilities before he performed this test?
A. No.
Q. Then you were not aware that he has a weak ankle from an old injury and suffers from arthritis?
A. He didn't say anything about that.
Q. By the way, Officer Smith, you weren't wearing high-heeled shoes or boots when you demonstrated the walk-the-line test, were you?
A. High heels? Of course not.
Q. Then why did you make Mr. Kelly perform the test wearing his Western boots?
A. I wasn't aware he was wearing them.
Q. Wouldn't it have been considerably more fair if he had been permitted to take them off?
A. Well, I guess so, but I didn't know.
Q. What did you have in your hands while he was walking the line, Officer?
A. In my hands? Well, let's see — a flashlight.
Q. That's all?
A. Yes.
Q. Then I presume you wrote your report back at the station?
A. That's right.
Q. An hour later?
A. Oh, maybe 45 minutes.

Q. It was 45 minutes later, then, that you recorded the results of the tests?
A. Yes.
Q. And you could recall in your mind exactly where each of my client's footsteps were?
A. Well, yes.
Q. By this diagram in your report, there were 18 footsteps, each of them different in relation to the line, and each of them taking but a fraction of a second.
A. Yes.
Q. And you recalled 45 minutes later where each of them had landed?
A. I believe so.
Q. Do you have a photographic memory?
A. No.
Q. And you also were able to instantly memorize each finger touch to the nose area?
A. I had a general idea, I guess.
Q. A general idea? Then this report is not accurate?
A. Well, generally.
Q. Did you draw the line that Mr. Kelly was asked to walk?
A. No. I pointed to an object on the shoulder, and told him to walk an imaginary line between it and where he was standing.
Q. Then there was no line?
A. There was — in his head.
Q. But you don't know what was in his head?
A. No, but I could draw the same line in my head while he was walking.
Q. Is it possible that the line in his head was not the line in yours?
A. It's possible, I guess.
Q. Now, on the finger-to-nose test, what constitutes passing?
A. Touching the tip of the nose four times, twice with each index finger, eyes closed.
Q. If you touch the side of the nose, or the upper lip once, it's a fail?
A. Yes.
Q. Isn't it a fact that perfectly sober people often have difficulty performing this test?
A. I don't know.
Q. And this finger-to-nose test, you testified Mr. Kelly failed it?
A. Yes, sir.
Q. What was his score?
A. His score?
Q. Yes, what was his score?
A. I don't understand, sir. There is no score.
Q. No score? But how does someone pass?

A. Well, they perform satisfactorily.
Q. And who decides if they performed satisfactorily?
A. Well, I do.
Q. It is your subjective *opinion* that decides pass or fail?
A. My opinion.
Q. There are no objective standards?
A. My opinion, sir, and I've had training.
Q. But you have testified that you had *already* formed the opinion that Mr. Kelly was intoxicated?
A. That's correct.
Q. And you *then* gave him the finger-to-nose test — after you decided he was guilty?
A. Yes, sir.
Q. And after having already decided he was guilty, you then decided he failed the next test you gave him?
A. If you want to put it that way, sir.
Q. By the way, Officer Smith, I assume you took the "learning curve" effect into consideration when deciding whether Mr. Kelly passed or failed.
A. Learning curve?
Q. You *are* aware of the effects of nervousness and embarrassment on a person's learning curve?
A. I . . . I'm not sure.
Q. Aren't you aware, Officer, that the ability of a person to learn or follow directions is impaired when he is nervous, scared, or embarrassed?
A. Yes, I guess so.
Q. In other words, a frightened or nervous person would have more difficulty in understanding and following your directions on how to perform the various field sobriety tests?
A. I explain very clearly, and I even demonstrate them.
Q. Of course, but you *are* aware of the phenomenon?
A. Yes.
Q. And so it is possible that performing unsatisfactorily on a test could simply mean that the subject did not understand how you wanted him to perform it?
A. That's possible, I suppose.
Q. And, of course, you took this impaired learning curve into consideration in deciding whether Mr. Kelly passed these field sobriety tests or not?
A. Uh, I suppose . . . yes.
Q. I see, in your report, you checked the box next to "cooperative," rather than the one next to "argumentative" or "antagonistic."

A. Yes, sir.
Q. What is the relevance of that?
A. Well, it's common to encounter bad attitudes in DUI cases.
Q. So this uncooperative attitude is a common symptom of an intoxicated person?
A. Common, yes.
Q. But Mr. Kelly exhibited the *opposite* of this symptom of intoxication?
A. He was cooperative.
Q. Now, Officer Smith, you asked Mr. Kelly to write down the alphabet, right?
A. Yes, sir.
Q. And you have already identified as Exhibit 6 that piece of paper?
A. Yes, sir.
Q. And you had Mr. Kelly sign that piece of paper?
A. Yes, sir.
Q. This was to see how well he could write?
A. That, and the ability to recite the alphabet.
Q. When was the last time since grammar school *you* were asked to recite the alphabet on paper, Officer?
A. I don't know.
Q. In any event, impaired handwriting is a sign of intoxication?
A. Yes, sir.
Q. If a person is nervous or frightened, wouldn't adrenaline be pumping through his system?
A. I'm not a scientist.
Q. But you *are* aware that shaking hands is a symptom of fear or nervousness?
A. I suppose so.
Q. Couldn't this affect handwriting?
A. Maybe.
Q. Well, be that as it may, it is fortunate that you were able to compare Mr. Kelly's handwriting on the test with an exemplar in the field.
A. What?
Q. You *did* compare Mr. Kelly's signature on the alphabet with the signature on his driver's license, didn't you?
A. I don't . . . no.
Q. But you did ask to see his license?
A. Yes.
Q. And you inspected it?
A. Yes, sir, I did, but only to see if he had a valid license.
Q. And his signature appeared on that license?
A. I assume it did.

Q. So you had a perfect example of his normal signature — there, at the scene of the arrest?
A. I suppose so.
Q. But you never bothered to compare the signature on the test with that on the license?
A. No, sir.
Q. Weren't you interested in finding out if the handwriting was impaired by drinking?
A. I didn't think of it, quite frankly.
Q. You just *assumed* that the handwriting was impaired.
A. It looked pretty sloppy.
Q. I have here Mr. Kelly's driver's license, ask that it be marked Exhibit F, and show it to you. Please compare it to Exhibit 6, the alphabet test. Now please explain to the jury how the two signatures differ — that is, how the signature on Exhibit 6 shows Mr. Kelly to have been impaired by alcohol.
A. I . . . I'm not an expert.
Q. Officer Smith, this Exhibit 6 represents the only *tangible* piece of evidence you have produced, the single physical item which the jury can look at and decide for itself. Now I ask you, do you see any significant difference between the two signatures?
A. I can't say.

Establishing Predisposition

Q. Officer Smith, you had already formed the opinion Mr. Kelly was under the influence when you administered the second field sobriety test, hadn't you?
A. Well . . .
Q. Didn't you testify earlier that you definitely felt he was intoxicated after he failed the first test?
A. Yes.
Q. Then why give him two more?
A. Standard procedure.
Q. But you knew he was intoxicated when you gave him the second test?
A. I was pretty sure, yes.
Q. And you knew he was intoxicated when you gave him the third test?
A. Yes.
Q. And you fully expected him to fail those two tests as well?
A. Yes.
Q. You would have been surprised if he had passed?
A. Yes, I would have been.

Q. Who decides whether he passed those last two tests?
A. Well, I guess. . . .
Q. You do, don't you, Officer Smith?
A. I indicate my opinion.
Q. You indicate in the report your interpretation of what the suspect did in the test, and you report whether he passed or failed, in your opinion?
A. Yes, I guess so.

Motive or Bias

Q. Officer Smith, do you know what a quota system is?
A. We don't have that.
Q. Do you know what it is?
A. Sure I do; I've heard of it.
Q. Would you please tell the jury what a quota system is?
A. Well, that's where a police department — some police departments — have a sort of quota of arrests that their officers have to make.
Q. You mean, like requiring a traffic officer to produce 10 drunk driving arrests per week?
A. Yes, something like that.
Q. And what happens if the officer can't produce 10 drunk drivers?
A. Well, I don't know. I mean, we don't have a quota system.
Q. In those agencies that do have the system, isn't it a fact that the officer could be disciplined? Or have his efficiency or promotion records adversely affected?
A. I suppose that happens.
Q. These quotas are not made public, are they?
A. Not to my knowledge.
Q. Because they are rather unfair, isn't that right?
A. I wouldn't know.
Q. I mean, such a system would tend to force officers into arresting innocent drivers, or borderline cases, wouldn't it?
A. Possibly, but I wouldn't know.
Q. Why are these quota systems kept quite from the public?
A. I really wouldn't know, counsel.
Q. I assume — hypothetically speaking, of course — that if your department had such a quota system, you wouldn't be permitted to admit it here in court?
A. Counsel, we have no such system.
Q. No, of course not. By the way, Officer Smith, what would have happened if Mr. Kelly had blown a low figure on the Breathalyzer?

A. What do you mean?
Q. Well, suppose after you had arrested him, the Breathalyzer had shown a reading of .04 percent — that is, that he was sober?
A. Well, I suppose we would have released him.
Q. Just let him go? No charges brought?
A. Sure. The machine says he's not intoxicated.
Q. But what about your arrest report — what about all of your observations and your opinions?
A. That didn't happen in this case, counsel.
Q. I realize that. But hypothetically, now: Would you have released him despite everything you've testified you observed and concluded?
A. I suppose so.
Q. But wouldn't that have reflected on your professional judgment?
A. I don't understand the question.
Q. Well, in your professional judgment, Mr. Kelly was under the influence. Yet, the machine said you were wrong — you made a mistake. Wouldn't that make you look bad?
A. In your hypothetical, I suppose so.
Q. And if that happened a number of times — arrests where the person had to be released because you were proven wrong — your professional reputation would begin to suffer, wouldn't it?
A. Hypothetically, counsel. But my reputation happens to be quite good.
Q. Of course, Officer. Nevertheless, that Breathalyzer represents judgment time on you doesn't it?
A. It's only one additional piece of evidence.
Q. Isn't the truth, Officer Smith, that you *hope* that a machine will corroborate your judgment?
A. Well, sure.
Q. And that if it does not, you will look bad?
A. Everyone makes mistakes, counsel.
Q. Incidentally, it is possible to produce whatever results you want on this machine?
A. Pardon me?
Q. The Breathalyzer — the operator can simply stamp whatever test result on the card he wants?
A. If you're suggesting —
Q. I'm not suggesting anything, Officer Smith. I'm merely asking a simple question: Is it, or is it not, possible for you to produce whatever test result you want by stamping the card at whatever blood-alcohol level you desire?
A. Hypothetically, yes — I suppose it's possible. *I* sure wouldn't.

Operation of the Breath Machine

Q. Officer Smith, I presume you've received training in the use of the Intoxilyzer?
A. At the police academy, yes.
Q. This was a course on the Intoxilyzer 5000?
A. Well, it was on criminalistics — laboratory stuff.
Q. This "stuff" included the Intoxilyzer?
A. It included breath testing, yes.
Q. Specifically, the Intoxilyzer 5000?
A. I believe it was the Breathalyzer.
Q. And what model of the Breathalyzer was used in your training?
A. Model?
Q. Yes — what specific model were you working with the academy?
A. I don't recall.
Q. You mean, you've never been trained on the Intoxilyzer 5000 itself?
A. Sure, at the station.
Q. Then, you were trained by other police officers in the field — sort of "on-the-job" training?
A. That's correct.
Q. And these officers — how did they train you?
A. Well, they sort of showed me how to operate it, and showed me the checklist, and told me to follow it.
Q. They just ran it through once or twice, and told you to follow the checklist?
A. More or less.
Q. And I presume these officers received *their* training on this instrument in the same way?
A. I wouldn't know.
Q. Do you know what alveolar air is, Officer Smith?
A. No.
Q. Does the ratio of 1 to 2100 mean anything to you?
A. Not really.
Q. When was the last malfunction of the Intoxilyzer you used on Mr. Kelly?
A. The last time it didn't work right?
Q. Yes.
A. I don't really know.
Q. Don't you check the calibration and maintenance records before using the machine?
A. That's not my job.
Q. So you didn't even know if the machine was functioning correctly when you administered it to Mr. Kelly?

A. It seemed to be working okay.
Q. All right. I understand that Mr. Kelly was booked — that is, fingerprinted and so on — and then taken to the room where the machine is kept, is that correct?
A. That's right.
Q. How soon after the booking?
A. Immediately. The jailor brought him into me, in the room where the machine was, and I gave him the test right away so the test results would be as close to the time of driving as possible.
Q. Of course. And you were not present during booking?
A. No. Like I said, the jailor handled that. I was writing down my report, and getting the machine ready.
Q. Did Mr. Kelly belch or regurgitate within 15 minutes before taking the test?
A. Regurgitate? No, not to my knowledge.
Q. But you weren't watching him during those 15 minutes — he was being booked.
A. Well, I didn't hear that he did.
Q. You don't know, isn't that true?
A. I suppose not.
Q. It's quite possible that Mr. Kelly belched or regurgitated within 15 minutes of breathing into the machine?
A. It's possible, I suppose.
Q. Don't the instructions — the operator's checklist — specifically tell you to observe the subject for 15 minutes before giving him the test, to make sure he doesn't belch or regurgitate?
A. I think so, yes.
Q. But you didn't follow these instructions.
A. I guess not.
Q. What other instructions for operating the Breathalyzer did you chose to ignore?
A. None, counsel. I followed the checklist.
Q. Do you know why belching or regurgitation is of concern in a breath test?
A. I've heard it can affect the test.
Q. In fact, belching or regurgitation brings alcohol into the throat and mouth, where it can then be breathed directly into the machine, isn't that right?
A. I believe that's right.
Q. And the result of that belching or regurgitation would be an inaccurately high reading, wouldn't it?
A. That could happen.
Q. Did it happen with Mr. Kelly?

A. I doubt it.
Q. But you simply don't know.
A. No.

For a discussion of techniques for cross-examining the operator and/or officer concerning the 15- or 20-minute observation period, see §11.6.9.

§13.2.1 Illustrative Cross-Examination on Nystagmus

The following represents a rough outline of an illustrative cross-examination conducted by the author at a drunk driving seminar presented by Washburn University Law School in Topeka, Kansas. The "witness" for the demonstration was the chief training officer for the Kansas Highway Patrol.

Qualifications

Q. Sergeant, do you hold a degree in ophthalmology?
A. No, I do not.
Q. In optometry?
A. Of course not.
Q. In physiology?
A. No.
Q. I see. How many medical courses *have* you taken on the physiology of the eye?
A. I haven't taken any, counselor.
Q. Well, how many independent studies have you conducted on the physiological causes of nystagmus?
A. Independent studies?
Q. Yes.
A. None.
Q. None. Are you familiar with the effects of *bilateral amblyopia* on nystagmus?
A. No, I am not.
Q. The effects of *Korsakoff's syndrome?*
A. No.
Q. Tell me, sergeant, are you *licensed* anywhere in this country to diagnose eye disfunction?
A. Of course not.
Q. To determine physiological causes of nystagmus?

A. No.
Q. Well, how many times have you *qualified as an expert* in court on the physiology of the eye?
A. On the physiology of the eye, I have not.
Q. How many times on the physiological effects of alcohol on eye musculature?
A. Never.
Q. Sergeant, did you receive training in nystagmus at the highway patrol academy?
A. I did.
Q. How many hours?
A. As I recall, it was six hours of demonstration and instruction.
Q. How many hours do *all* recruits or officers get?
A. Six hours.
Q. So, you got the same training as any other police officer?
A. Correct.
Q. Then you did not receive any *special* training in nystagmus, other than what everyone routinely gets?
A. No.
Q. Who were your teachers?
A. My teachers?
Q. Yes. Who instructed you on nystagmus?
A. The training officer. I don't recall his name.
Q. Another highway patrolman, like yourself?
A. Yes.
Q. Then, the only training you received on nystagmus was from another police officer?
A. That's correct.
Q. You received no training from qualified physicians?
A. No.
Q. Sergeant, what *does* cause nystagmus?
A. What do you mean?
Q. Nystagmus — jerking of the eyes. . . . What causes it?
A. What causes it?
Q. Yes. Could you please explain the *physiology of normal* nystagmus.
A. I'm not sure I can.
Q. Well, can you explain the chemical effects of alcohol on that physiological process?
A. Alcohol makes the jerking start earlier.
Q. Yes, but why?
A. I don't know.
Q. Are you familiar with *other causes* for early nystagmus — that is, other than alcohol?

A. I've read something about it.
Q. Are you familiar with the effects of a streptococcus infection on nystagmus?
A. No, I'm not.
Q. The effects of hypertension on nystagmus?
A. No.
Q. The effects of motion sickness, such as in a car?
A. No.
Q. The effects of caffeine?
A. No.
Q. Nicotine?
A. No.
Q. Aspirin?
A. No, counselor, I'm not.
Q. Antihistamines? Depressants? Anticonvulsants?
A. As I said, no.
Q. Flu? Epilepsy? Inner ear problems?
A. No.
Q. Isn't it true, Sergeant, that these and dozens of other conditions can cause early onset of nystagmus?
A. I couldn't say.
Q. You only know about *one* possible cause, right? Alcohol?
A. Alcohol causes nystagmus, yes.
Q. By the way, Sergeant, was my client suffering from any of these conditions — flu, epilepsy, car sickness?
A. I really couldn't say.
Q. Had he taken any aspirin in the hours before you gave him your version of the nystagmus test?
A. I couldn't say.
Q. Had he smoked a cigarette?
A. As I've said, I don't really know.
Q. Drunk any coffee?
A. Counselor, I have no way of knowing.
Q. Sergeant, did you even bother to ask him?
A. Obviously not.
Q. Are you familiar with "circadian rhythm"?
A. Circadian rhythm?
Q. Yes.
A. No, I'm not.
Q. You are not familiar with the fact that our bodies have a "biological clock" that governs our physiological functions? A subconscious 24-hour clock that tells our bodies what to do, when it's time to sleep, that sort of thing?

A. Oh, yes, I've heard of that.
Q. Then you're aware that from midnight to 5:00 A.M., this circadian rhythm decreases the angle of nystagmus onset by one degree?
A. I was not aware of that, no.
Q. This would *increase* your reading of a person's level of intoxication, wouldn't it?
A. By a small amount, I suppose.
Q. You would think his blood-alcohol level was higher than it actually was, right?
A. By a small amount.
Q. Yet, you were not *aware* of this phenomenon?
A. Not as it related to nystagmus.
Q. Sergeant, do you consider yourself an expert on nystagmus?
A. I believe I am.
Q. Do you understand how it works?
A. You mean the physiology?
Q. Yes.
A. I can't say I do.
Q. Do you understand the dozens of potential causes of early nystagmus — besides alcohol?
A. I've already said I was not familiar with these.
Q. What *is* nystagmus, Sergeant?
A. What is it?
Q. Yes. Why does the eye react the way it does? What conditions or substances can cause it?
A. I couldn't say.
Q. Nevertheless, you consider yourself an expert?
A. I am qualified, yes.

Theory

Q. Sergeant, assume in a given case that you've got an angle of onset before 45 degrees.
A. Okay.
Q. What does that tell you?
A. The subject is probably under the influence of alcohol.
Q. Where does the 45-degrees figure come from?
A. I don't know.
Q. Isn't it true that this figure is based on the physiological reaction of the *average* person?
A. I believe so, yes.
Q. Was my client average?
A. What?

Q. Well, you *assumed* that his reactions would be identical to an average person's, right?
A. I suppose so, yes.
Q. The validity of this nystagmus test depends on this assumption, doesn't it?
A. I . . . I really can't say.
Q. What percentage of the population in this country *is* average in their nystagmus reactions, Sergeant?
A. I'm sure I couldn't tell you.
Q. What is the range of deviation?
A. I couldn't tell you.
Q. If my client was *not* average, what was his "baseline"?
A. Baseline?
Q. Yes. At what angle would onset of nystagmus truly indicate the effects of alcohol? 42 degrees? 51 degrees?
A. I can't give you these answers, counselor.
Q. Well, anyway, is it correct to say: *If* he were average, the angle of onset you observed that night would have indicated failure of the test?
A. Yes.
Q. But we don't *know* if he's average?
A. I suppose not.
Q. So we don't *know* if he failed or not, do we?
A. Based upon my training and experience, your client failed the test.
Q. Sergeant, you're familiar with the 1984 report, entitled "Improved Sobriety Testing"?
A. You mailed me a copy, yes.
Q. It's published by the federal government, the National Highway Traffic Safety Administration, to create reliable standards for field sobriety tests?
A. I believe that's correct.
Q. It is the NHTSA report that established 45 degrees as the baseline for the nystagmus test?
A. I don't know if they set the figure, but it's in the report, yes.
Q. As I requested, you brought that report with you today?
A. I did.
Q. What are the reasons given in the report for the 45-degrees figure?
A. I don't recall.
Q. Please feel free to refer to the report at any time, Sergeant, but aren't there two reasons?
A. That sounds familiar.
Q. Isn't the first reason that 45 degrees is *close* to the angle of onset for a person with a .10 percent blood-alcohol concentration?

A. Again, that sounds familiar.
Q. And what is the second reason for using the nystagmus field sobriety test to determine intoxication?
A. I don't recall.
Q. (Reading from report) ". . . and because it is easy to estimate." Is that correct, Sergeant?
A. That's what it says.
Q. You mean, nystagmus is used to test for intoxication because it's only close — to how an average person's eyes will react?
A. Apparently.
Q. And because it's easy for the police?
A. Apparently.
Q. Sergeant, does the report indicate a third reason for using nystagmus?
A. A third reason?
Q. Does it say the test should be used because it's accurate?
A. Apparently not.
Q. Sergeant, do *you* consider nystagmus an accurate test of intoxication?
A. I think it's fairly accurate, yes.
Q. But the state of Kansas has not approved it as a blood-alcohol test, have they?
A. A blood-alcohol test? No.
Q. You've read an article concerning a study of the accuracy of nystagmus, reported in 25 Journal of the Forensic Society 476 (1985)?
A. I believe that's one of the things you mailed me.
Q. The study was conducted by a law enforcement agency — the Santa Clara County Criminalistics Laboratory, in California?
A. I believe so.
Q. They analyzed 129 actual cases where nystagmus was given — and compared them with actual BACs, right?
A. I believe so.
Q. What were the results of that study?
A. I believe there was some discrepancy.
Q. The officers consistently erred in estimating BAC, correct?
A. There was some error.
Q. What was the conclusion reached by these researchers, Sergeant?
A. They felt there were potential problems with nystagmus.
Q. In fact, didn't they conclude that nystagmus cannot be used to predict accurately the blood-alcohol level of a suspect?
A. Something like that, yes.
Q. You've read "Psychophysical Tests for DUI Arrest" by Tharp, a study commissioned by NHTSA?

A. Again, counselor, I believe you mailed it to me.
Q. Well, didn't that study conclude that some individuals with *no* alcohol in their systems demonstrated early onset of nystagmus?
A. I believe so.
Q. In other words, the nystagmus test showed perfectly sober people to be intoxicated?
A. Apparently it can happen in isolated instances.

Administration of Test

(Note: Have the officer demonstrate exactly how he administered the nystagmus test to the client in field.)

Q. In the demonstration you just gave, I notice that you didn't ask my client if he was wearing contact lenses?
A. It must have slipped my mind.
Q. In the NHTSA report, didn't it say that contacts can limit lateral eye movement, causing nystagmus?
A. That's correct.
Q. What type of template did you use in measuring the angle of onset?
A. I didn't use a template. No one in the highway patrol uses one.
Q. You did not use a template? Well, what kind of device did you use to measure the angle of onset?
A. None.
Q. None? You simply guessed what the angle was?
A. I didn't guess, counselor, I estimated. It was an estimate based upon extensive training and practice.
Q. You used protractors to check your accuracy during this training, didn't you?
A. Yes.
Q. But you didn't use one that night with my client?
A. As I said, I don't ever use one, nor does anyone else on the patrol.
Q. Sergeant, if we performed a little test right here in the courtroom, do you think you could detect the difference between 38 and 39 degrees?
A. I . . . maybe not.
Q. 42 and 44 degrees?
A. Maybe, I'm not sure.
Q. The accuracy of this test depends entirely on your ability to . . . estimate?
A. Of course.
Q. Well, when was the last time you had your accuracy checked?

A. Checked?
Q. Yes. How often do you get your ability to estimate angles checked for accuracy?
A. I'm not aware of any such procedure.
Q. Directing your attention to the NHTSA manual again, Sergeant . . .
A. Yes?
Q. Don't these federal reliability standards recommend monthly checks with a template to maintain accuracy in estimating the angle of onset?
A. I don't recall reading that.
Q. Would you like a moment to review the report?
A. No, I'm sure it's in there.
Q. Do you agree with the recommendation of monthly checks for accuracy?
A. I really don't think it's necessary.
Q. Are you saying you disagree with the national experts? Or are you saying that your accuracy doesn't need periodic checks?
A. I . . . just don't think it's necessary.
Q. You would agree that the accuracy of guessing the angle is critical to the validity of the test results?
A. Estimating, counselor, not guessing. And, yes, I would agree. The results depend on the estimate of the angle.
Q. As the computer people say, "Garbage in, garbage out," right?
A. Yes.
Q. Incidentally, Sergeant, do we have any evidence of the angle in this case?
A. Evidence?
Q. Yes. Besides your testimony: Do we have any corroboration of what the angle was?
A. Corroboration . . .
Q. Is there a videotape? Another witness?
A. No, of course not.
Q. I see. Then this nystagmus test depends entirely on your accuracy . . .
A. Yes.
Q. . . . and, of course, on your honesty?

(Have him *demonstrate* again.)

Q. I notice that you're holding the pen level with the eyes? And about six inches away?
A. Yes, that's about right.
Q. Doesn't the NHTSA manual direct officers to hold the object *above* the eyes?

A. I don't recall that.
Q. (Reading) "The stimulus should be positioned above the eyes."
A. This is the way we were trained.
Q. (Reading) "about 15 inches away from the eyes."
A. I'm doing it the way we were taught, counselor.
Q. Sergeant, the NHTSA manual indicates that the validity of the test depends, among other things, on the subject keeping his head perfectly still, right?
A. Yes, and that's how we are trained.
Q. Fine, then for once, you agree with the national experts: The validity of the nystagmus test you gave my client depended upon him keeping his head perfectly still?
A. I agree.
Q. But, Sergeant, don't you recall your testimony on direct examination?
A. What testimony?
Q. Didn't you testify earlier today that my client swayed during the position-of-attention test?
A. He . . . during that test, yes, there was some swaying.
Q. Eight to ten inches, as I recall.
A. Yes.
Q. In fact, didn't you testify, under oath, that he staggered when he stepped out of the car?
A. That's correct.
Q. And was it not your sworn testimony that he appeared unsteady on his feet during your investigatory detention?
A. That's what happened, yes.
Q. Well, Sergeant, which is it: Was he swaying, staggering, and unsteady — or was he "perfectly still"?
A. As I recall, he managed to remain steady during the nystagmus test.
Q. He just suddenly stopped swaying?
A. Apparently.
Q. In your demonstration, I noticed that you conducted four movements during the test?
A. That's correct. Two on each eye, just like the NHTSA manual suggests.
Q. How would you characterize the movements: fast or slow?
A. I don't know. Just the way you saw.
Q. All four movements appeared to be at the same speed.
A. I suppose so, yes.
Q. That's contrary to the procedure recommended by NHTSA, isn't it?

A. It's how I was trained.
Q. (Reading) "The first movement in each direction should be slow. . . . The second movement should be somewhat faster."
A. Uh-huh.
Q. How many degrees per second do you move the pen during the test, Sergeant?
A. Degrees per second? I don't do it that way.
Q. Isn't it a fact that the federal guidelines recommend 10 degrees per second on the first movement, and 20 degrees per second on the second one?
A. Well, that's not how we do it.
Q. You disagree with these national standards?
A. I do it the way everyone else on the patrol does it.
Q. So you believe your own system is more accurate?
A. It's accurate, sure.
Q. Sergeant, at what angle did you first detect jerking in my client's eyes?
A. It was before 45 degrees. 41 degrees, as I recall.
Q. What did you do then?
A. What did I do? I estimated the angle, and determined that he failed the test.
Q. (Reading) "When he first detects a slight jerking, he should stop moving the stimulus to make sure that the jerking continues . . ." That's from the NHTSA manual, Sergeant. I didn't notice you do that in your demonstration.
A. When the jerking starts, that's the end of the test.
Q. (Reading) "If the nystagmus stops, then the officer has not found the point of onset and he should continue his examination. . . ." Do you recall these instructions from the NHTSA manual?
A. Not really.
Q. According to the manual, initial jerking of the eyes may be a false sign of nystagmus, right?
A. Maybe.
Q. According to the manual, you're supposed to stop movement when jerking starts and watch to see if the jerking continues.
A. If that's what it says.
Q. If you don't stop and wait, if you just end the test, you may get a false point of onset, right?
A. Maybe.
Q. And a false result — maybe showing a sober person to be intoxicated?
A. If you get a false result.

Q. You're trained to look for three signs of intoxication in the nystagmus test — angle of onset, smooth pursuit, and distinctive jerking at maximum deviation?
A. Correct.
Q. And, in fact, the NHTSA manual recommends using all three criteria in the test, right?
A. Correct.
Q. So when you conducted the test, you moved the pen to the lateral extremes of my client's eye range?
A. I did.
Q. Did you note how much white of his eyes was showing at the extremes?
A. Whites of his eyes? That has nothing to do with distinctive jerking at the extremes.
Q. So you did not take note of the whites of his eyes in this test of yours?
A. Of course not.
Q. (Reading) "Since some individuals cannot deviate their eyes more than 45 degrees, some white of the eye must show to ascertain that nystagmus is not occurring at the most extreme deviation for that individual."
A. That's not how we were trained.
Q. In other words, the jerking you saw in my client's eyes could have been because he was at his extreme deviation at 45 degrees — not because he was intoxicated?
A. I doubt that, counselor.
Q. Well, we don't know, do we? Because you did not check. What was the amplitude of nystagmus at the maximum lateral deviation?
A. The what?
Q. The degree of eye jerking at the furthest movement of the eye, Sergeant.
A. Maximum deviation, yes, there was distinctive jerking at the maximum deviation.
Q. But what was the amplitude?
A. I didn't really notice.
Q. Did you consider "smooth pursuit" as a factor in the nystagmus test?
A. I did.
Q. And did you consider this an accurate indication of intoxication?
A. I did.
Q. As accurate as onset?
A. Yes.

Q. You place a lot of weight on it?
A. I suppose so, yes.
Q. Then, again, you disagree with NHTSA? (Reading) "Smooth pursuit eye movement . . . is the *least* reliable of the three signs."
A. My understanding was that all three were equally reliable.
Q. Sergeant, what was my client's score on your nystagmus test?
A. Score?
Q. Yes, what was his total score on the test?
A. There's no score, counselor. You either pass or fail. He failed.
Q. (Feigning surprise) Then your test is entirely subjective?
A. It is based upon my observations.
Q. *You* decide whether he passed or failed?
A. Of course.
Q. Why do you chose not to use an impartial, objective scoring system?
A. You can't score a nystagmus test, counselor. Either the jerking indicates intoxication or it doesn't.
Q. Are you aware that NHTSA recommends an objective scoring system?
A. I am not.

(Have him review the report.)

Q. Have you now reviewed NHTSA's scoring sheet?
A. I have.
Q. Apparently, using the objective system, four of six possible points indicates failure, right?
A. Apparently.
Q. Do you still think it's not possible to use an objective method for deciding whether a person passes or fails the test?
A. I suppose it's possible, but it's not how we were trained.
Q. Sergeant, you've read the NHTSA law enforcement booklet, Guide for Detecting Drunk Drivers at Night?
A. I think that was in the stuff you mailed me.
Q. Isn't it true that NHTSA studies indicate that even if nystagmus is administered exactly as recommended, the test has only a 77 percent reliability factor?
A. That's what it says.
Q. So, even if the test is done as recommended, you will be right only three out of four times?
A. Apparently.
Q. Even *if* you gave the test as recommended, one-fourth of those who "fail" will be . . . innocent?
A. Apparently.
Q. And you admit that you did *not* give the test as recommended?
A. I gave it the way I was taught.

§13.3 *The Breath Operator and/or Blood-Alcohol Expert: Strategy and Techniques*

> In battle, one engages with the orthodox . . . and gains victory through the unorthodox.
>
> SUN TZU

General Sun Tzu wrote this over 2,000 years ago. He also made a few other observations that are relevant to counsel's critical battle with the state's blood-alcohol expert.

> Warfare is the Tao of deception . . . When committed to employing your forces, feign inactivity. When your objective is nearby, make it appear as if distant.

In a traditional DUI case, the focus of the jury will be upon the arresting officer's testimony: the defendant's driving, his physical symptoms, the field sobriety tests, incriminating statements, and the officer's opinion of sobriety. Even in a per se case (.08 or .10 percent), the jury will look for blood-alcohol evidence to corroborate the officer's observations. The key to winning drunk driving trials has not changed with the proliferation of per se laws and new methods of blood-alcohol analysis: It is still the cop.

This suggests a basic *strategy* in DUI cases — a strategy with which the author has been repeatedly successful. The strategy is simple: Attack the machine. Attack it constantly. Attack it in pretrial motions, during jury selection, in opening statement, certainly during cross-examination, in closing argument, and in requested jury instructions. Invariably, this unrelenting attack on the machine will have two consequences.

First, the prosecutor confronted with an endless barrage of attacks on his prized scientific evidence will go on the defense.

> If I dare ask: if the enemy is numerous, disciplined and about to advance, how should we respond to them? I would say: first, seize something that they love. . . .

And prosecutors invariably love the scientific nature of breath machines. As a result, the prosecutor will concentrate his efforts on rebutting the attacks and convincing the jury that the machine really was maintained, calibrated, and operated correctly and is based on sound scientific principles. In doing so, of course, he is shifting his attention away from the damning testimony of the officer and onto the questioned machine. As Sun Tzu wrote:

> One who can be victorious attacks; one who cannot be victorious assumes a defensive posture.

The second result of attacking the machine will be that the jury's focus will be subtly shifted. At the beginning of the trial, the issue will be whether the client was under the influence (or over .08 percent) beyond a reasonable doubt. By the time the jury begins deliberation, the issue in their minds will be whether the machine was accurate and reliable — beyond a reasonable doubt. And doubt about the machine will translate into acquittals as to both the DUI and the per se charges; the testimony of the officer will be overlooked in the focus on the machine.

In the following pages, the author presents what he has found to be some of the most effective techniques for cross-examination of the state's breath machine operator, technician, and/or forensic blood-alcohol expert. It should be understood that this expert is rarely an objective, impartial witness: He is a law enforcement employee whose job is to convince juries that the machine is infallible. It should also be understood, of course, that his knowledge and experience make him a dangerous adversary. As with any expert witness, then, defense counsel must prepare for cross-examination by educating himself about the very complex field of blood-alcohol analysis and, if possible, about the specific witness.

> In general, he who occupies the battleground first and awaits the enemy will be at ease.

The following questions have been drafted by forensic toxicologist Anne ImObersteg of San Jose, California. They represent what an experienced expert blood-alcohol expert would ask a prosecution's blood-alcohol expert on cross-examination — and so should be seriously considered by counsel facing such a task.

Qualifications

Q. What degree do you hold?

Q. Have you taken any formal University classes in toxicology or pharmacology?

Q. How many alcohol and driving correlation studies have you attended?

Field sobriety tests

Q. What is a correlation or impairment study?

Q. Have you ever attended such a study?

Q. Did all the subjects show impairment in, for example, reaction time at a same BAC?

Q. Isn't it true that two people at the same BAC can perform differently on an FST?

Q. What are the factors that can influence how someone performs on an FST?

Q. Isn't it true that the environment in which the test is given can impact a person's performance?

Q. Isn't it true that a person's physical characteristics, such as age, weight, medical problems, can impact a person's performance?

Q. If Mr. X had a medical problem that affected his performance on the test, the test would be meaningless in the determination of impairment, correct?

Q. Isn't it true that the Federal Government has studied FSTs extensively since 1981 and has published guidelines for law enforcement to use in administering the FSTs?

Q. Isn't it true that the error rate of the police officers in determining physical impairment due to alcohol was as high as 46 percent?

Q. Isn't it true that these tests were conducted in a laboratory?

Q. What three tests have they recommended the police to use as their FST battery?

Q. Have you read Professor Cole's publication on FSTs in a field setting?

Q. Are you aware of Professor Cole's study where the error rate was over 50 percent?

Maintenance records

Q. When was the last time this instrument was brought in for maintenance?

Q. What functions did you test on the instrument?

Q. Isn't it true that you did not check the RFI detection system/slope detection system to determine it is working reliably?

Q. Although you checked XYZ, there is no guarantee that it was operating correctly on the date of the test, is there?

Q. Did you calibrate the instrument by changing the response of the instrument to solutions of known alcohol concentrations?

Q. Did you follow your laboratory's procedure which is on file at the DHS?

Q. Do you have a Maintenance Certificate from the manufacturer of the instrument which certifies you to fix their instrument?

Q. If you make an error in the calibration of the instrument, this error can affect the reliability of subsequent subject breath tests, isn't that so?

Q. Are the records you see before you the only maintenance records kept by the laboratory for this instrument?

Q. Is the calibrating unit used to calibrate this instrument on the DOT list of acceptable calibrating units? (Federal Register Aug. 13, 1997, Vol., 62, No. 156 or later)

Instrument accuracy

Q. Isn't it true that the determination of accuracy performed by the DOT were accomplished using a simulator?

Q. Human breath is different than a simulator, isn't it?

Q. In fact, human breath can be quite variable, isn't that so?

Q. Don't administrative regulations allow two subsequent breath samples from the same person to differ as much as 0.02 percent?

Q. In fact, since the third digit is eliminated from the test, the difference between the two breath samples can be as much as 0.029 percent, isn't that so?

Q. How many breath test record cards have you seen?

Q. Isn't it true that it is not unusual to see differences of 0.02 percent between two breaths from the same individual? Have you ever heard the term "95 percent confidence level?"

Q. Isn't it common to use statistical methods in science?

Q. If you were to perform a scientific test, analyzing a series of breaths on the instrument, you could get an average reading of the breaths, couldn't you?

Q. But around this average there would be a variation, isn't that so?

Q. Some breaths could be quite a bit lower than the average and some could be higher, isn't that so?

Q. For example, if I were to give a test, and one person got 100 percent and another got 0 percent on the test, the average would be 50 percent, isn't that so?

Q. But neither person taking the test is anywhere close to 50 percent, are they?

Q. What is the 95 percent confidence level, using the manufacturer's 0.01 percent as the variation, and two breath samples?

Q. Have you heard of Dr. A. W. Jones?

Q. Isn't it true that Dr. Jones stated in "The Physiological Aspects of Breath Testing" that the 95 percent confidence level is 0.015 percent?

Q. What is the 95 percent confidence level, using Title 17 and your observed variation of 0.02 percent, and two breath samples? (.028 percent)

Non-specificity

Q. How does the instrument determine BAC through infrared energy absorption?

Q. Please draw the ethanol molecule and show me what part of the molecule absorbs the light at the wavelength measured by the instrument.

Q. Don't all organic molecules have carbon and hydrogen?

Q. Isn't it true that there are many other molecules that absorb at the same wavelengths set in the instrument?

Q. Does the instrument specifically identify the type of alcohol found in alcoholic beverages?

Q. Does the instrument specifically identify a compound?

Q. For an identification of a compound, wouldn't you need to look at the full infrared spectrum rather than a small piece?

Q. Doesn't an infrared spectrophotometer perform a scan of a compound with the entire spectrum of wavelengths to make an identification?

Q. If a compound absorbs energy at 3.48 microns and 3.39 microns, wouldn't the instrument report it as ethanol even if it is not?

Q. Isn't it true that the latest generation of instruments have added two more wavelengths for the instrument to look for in an effort to circumvent this obvious problem of misidentification?

Rising blood-alcohol level

Q. In fact, if the person had drinks close to the time of the stop, there is more evidence that the person is likely on the rising or absorption side of the curve, isn't that so?

Q. And if a person is on the rising side of the curve, you cannot accurately determine their blood alcohol at the time of the stop, isn't that so?

Q. And you definitely cannot forensically back-extrapolate to a higher blood alcohol level, can you?

Breath pressure and temperature

Q. Is there any way that a person's method of blowing can affect the result?

Q. What is normal body temperature?

Q. If a subject had a higher body temperature, would this affect the result?

Q. Why is the temperature of the simulator that is introduced from the simulator 34 degrees?

Q. What would happen if the true temperature were 36 degrees?

Q. Does the instrument measure breath temperature?

Q. Is the breath temperature the same for all people who blow into the instrument?

Q. What is the temperature of pure alveolar air?

Q. Does the instrument's Operating Manual state that the subject should take a deep breath and blow into the machine?

Mouth alcohol and the pre-test observation period

Q. What does IVS mean?

Q. Doesn't IVS mean that the instrument received a breath sample that was characteristic of mouth alcohol?

Q. Doesn't the instrument's Operating Manual state that this is a flag for mouth alcohol?

Q. Isn't it true that the Operator's Manual says to wait 15 minutes when the operator gets this error message before beginning another breath analysis?

Q. Isn't it true that when alcohol is brought up into the mouth from a burp or regurgitation that it takes 15 to 20 minutes to rid the mouth of the alcohol?

Q. And if the subject burped, bringing alcohol into the mouth prior to the test, the resulting reading on the instrument could be inaccurate and much higher than what the subject's BAC really is. Isn't that true?

Q. When training police officers on the method used in this County, does the instructor teach the officer that Title 17 requires a 15 minute continuous observation?

Q. In your opinion, if the subject is in the back seat of the patrol car, and Officer X is driving the vehicle, with his eyes on the road like any prudent driver, is he "continuously" observing the subject?

Radio frequency interference

Q. What is RFI?
Q. Isn't RFI also known as electromagnetic interference?
Q. How does electromagnetic interference affect the instrument?
Q. How do you know if the antenna/detector on the instrument is working?
Q. If the interference reaches the instrument at a direction not picked up by the detection antenna, isn't it possible that the instrument will be subject to changes in currents and voltages?
Q. Isn't the ultimate calculation BrAC by the instrument a function of voltage changes?
Q. When was the last time this instrument was checked to determine if the instrument always detects RFI when it is present?
Q. Isn't it true that the Intoxilyzer 5000 Manual states that when the instrument detects RFI, that the Operator must locate the source of RFI and either remove the source from the instrument's operational environment or move the instrument to a new environment free from RFI?
Q. And this action was not done in this instance, was it?
Q. What is USR?
Q. Doesn't it mean "unstable reference?"
Q. What is a reference?
Q. Doesn't it mean that the microprocessor was unable to obtain a stable reference signal?
Q. If there is an indication the the instrument is having difficulty obtaining a stable reference signal, the reliability of a valid test result is called into question, isn't it?

Periodic accuracy checks

Q. Are the records you see before you the only calibration check records kept by the laboratory for this instrument?
Q. Is the calibrating unit used to check the calibration of this instrument on the DOT list of acceptable calibrating units?
Q. How often does Title 17 mandate that the accuracy of the instrument is to be checked?
Q. Even if the instrument appears to be operating correctly every 10

days or 150 subjects, there is no proof that it is operating correctly on the day of my client's test, is there?

Q. How often is the calibration solution supposed to be changed?
Q. Doesn't the true value of the solution decreases with each use?
Q. If the true value of the solution has decreased, this test result would indicate that the instrument is reading falsely high, wouldn't it?
Q. Isn't it true that all accuracy determinations are done with a simulator rather than human breath?
Q. What is the allowable deviation from the average that the simulator solution is allowed to read on the instrument?

§13.3.1 The Smart Machine

In testifying about breath analyzing machines like the Intoxilyzer 5000, Intoximeter 3000, and BAC Verifier/Datamaster, the state's expert will usually emphasize their sophistication and computerized operation. Many experts will even call the device a "smart" machine, referring to the fact that it is self-analyzing, self-calibrating, and self-correcting; human error is largely avoided. The new model, the jury is told, is a tremendous improvement over previous breath testing devices. The breath machine is presented as a "fail-safe," state-of-the-art product of laboratory science and the computer age.

In cross-examination, counsel should challenge this view of the machine immediately. The jury must see that the machine is exactly that: a machine (*not,* incidentally, an "instrument"). And, like any machine, it is capable of malfunction and error. The breath analyzing device should be compared to machines with which the jury is familiar. This detracts from the scientific aura and awe in which it is initially held by most jurors. It also brings it into the everyday world of dishwashers and vacuum cleaners with which they are familiar — that is, machines that malfunction and break down.

Q. This machine is mass-produced, isn't it?
A. I don't know what you mean.
Q. Well, there are hundreds, maybe thousands of them out there, right?
A. I don't know how many.
Q. And, like any mass-produced machine, it can malfunction? Break down?

A. It can, yes, of course.
Q. Like a vacuum cleaner? Or a car?
A. As I said, occasional problems are not common, but certainly a possibility.
Q. Like any kitchen appliance, then, it can develop problems?
A. It is a possibility.

Having put the machine into some perspective, the expert witness' view of the device as a "smart" machine or state-of-the-art should be investigated.

Q. You've referred to this as a "smart" machine.
A. Yes, it is capable of self-diagnosis. It's internal computer can correct for specific problems.
Q. And that it is "state-of-the-art"?
A. Yes.
Q. And before your department got this "smart" machine, you had the Breathalyzer 900A, right?
A. That's correct.
Q. The Breathalyzer was a relatively primitive device, was it not?
A. I think that's fair to say.
Q. I assume you've testified in court many times in cases involving the Breathalyzer?
A. I have.
Q. Did you testify in those cases that it was a "dumb" machine?
A. Of course not.
Q. Did you testify that it was an antique — that it was *not* state-of-the-art?
A. No.
Q. You testified that it was an accurate, reliable machine, right?
A. Basically, yes.
Q. And then you junked it and got the next year's model. (Objection)

The expert witness should be asked if the machine is *infallible:* Is it capable of making mistakes? Of course, no witness confronted with this question will claim that error is impossible; such a claim would in itself discredit him. Counsel may then wish to lead the witness through a number of possible errors of which the machine is capable (see §§6.0, 7.0, and 6.4).

The witness' inference of infallibility can also be challenged by asking him about *inherent error* (see §5.3.1). He must acknowledge the existence of inherent error, of course, but the concept is universally accepted in the scientific community.

Q. So, as I understand it, even if this machine was calibrated perfectly, even if it was working perfectly, it could still be off by .01?
A. It's possible.

(For an effective extension of this technique, see §13.3.3: "Close enough for government work.")

Counsel may then wish to ask the witness which is the more reliable and accurate method of analysis: breath or blood? There are very few forensic experts who would deny that blood is the more accurate procedure — and, therefore, that breath analysis is *less* accurate.

Q. To find out the concentration of alcohol in a person's blood, what is the most accurate method of analysis?
A. What do you mean?
Q. I mean, which is more accurate: blood analysis or breath analysis?
A. Well, of course, blood analysis is quite accurate.
Q. More accurate than this machine?
A. Analysis of the blood would be the most accurate, yes.
Q. Was blood analysis an available method of analysis in this case?
A. I assume it was available.
Q. And it would have been more accurate than this machine?
A. It is potentially more accurate.
Q. But it was not used?
A. Apparently not.

Counsel should be aware of what "fail-safe" devices the breath machine features: acetone detectors, acetaldehyde detectors, mouth alcohol "slope detectors," RFI detectors, ambient air contaminant detectors. If any of these are not available with the breath machine used, or if available and not purchased as an option, this should be clearly brought out.

Q. Now, there is a way of avoiding the problem of acetone on the breath, is there not?
A. What do you mean?

Q. Well, there is such a thing as an acetone detector, isn't there?
A. Yes.
Q. And this device will detect the presence of acetone?
A. I believe so.
Q. So, with this device installed in the machine, there will be no false readings because of acetone?
A. Probably not.
Q. I assume the machine used to test my client had such a device?
A. No.
Q. It did not?
A. No.
Q. It is available from the manufacturer, isn't it?
A. I believe so.
Q. But it was not ordered by your department?
A. No.

Finally, the witness's pride in the computerized nature of the breath machine can be turned against him.

Q. You've said that this machine is run by an internal computer?
A. That's correct.
Q. A Z-80 computer?
A. I believe so.
Q. That's a fairly early, primitive computer?
A. It's been around for a little while, but it's perfectly reliable.
Q. And I assume it runs the machine by using software?
A. Of course.
Q. The computer is only as accurate and reliable as the software, right?
A. That's right.
Q. No matter how good the machine is, it only works as well as the software lets it?
A. I suppose you could say that.
Q. "Garbage in, garbage out," right?
A. Yes.
Q. So . . . what's in the software?
A. What do you mean?
Q. Well, how does the software program work? What does it do? Who programmed it?
A. I don't know. That's a trade secret of the manufacturer.
Q. A secret.
A. Yes.
Q. So no one knows what's in it? Or how it works?

A. Only the manufacturer.
Q. So, if something was wrong in the programming, why, you would never know, would you?
A. I suppose not.
Q. And this jury would never know.

§13.3.2 The Spiked Aspirin

John Tarantino of Providence, Rhode Island, a recognized expert in the DUI field and the editor of the *DWI Journal,* uses a technique to illustrate for jurors the significance of the breath testing machine's fallibility.

In the course of cross-examination of the state's expert, Tarantino commits him to a mathematical degree of accuracy. Given that no expert will claim that the machines never malfunction, the expert commonly (and grudgingly) concedes that the device is accurate 99 percent of the time. (This is, of course, a ridiculously inflated view of the machine's reliability, but counsel must remember that the witness is not an impartial scientist.)

Q. The Intoxilyzer 5000 does make mistakes, doesn't it?
A. Not very often.
Q. But it's not dead accurate 100 percent of the time?
A. Maybe not 100 percent.
Q. Well, what figure would you say? Is it 95 percent accurate?
A. Higher than that.
Q. 98 percent?
A. If I had to give a mathematical figure, I would say the 5000 is accurate 99 percent of the time.
Q. 99?
A. Yes.

During closing argument, then, Tarantino brings this figure home to the jurors in a way they can understand. He brings a clear bottle of aspirin to court with him. Emphasizing the critical importance of the breath machine to his client's life, he holds the bottle up for them to see and points out that there are 100 tablets inside, each identical in appearance:

> Ladies and gentlemen, 99 of these tablets are aspirin. One, however, is strychnine. If you had a headache, would you take one?

§13.3.3 Close Enough for Government Work

An effective tactic in cross-examining the expert witness is to emphasize the various margins of error recognized in blood-alcohol analysis. This can be done by taking the range of error and dealing with it as a percentage of the measured BAC, then relating it to an everyday experience the jurors can appreciate.

One area involves *inherent error,* a fact any expert will acknowledge and one recognized by judicial precedent (see §5.3.1). Counsel should be familiar with what error is, in fact, recognized in his jurisdiction; in some, for example, it is plus or minus .01 percent BAC, while in others it is plus or minus 1 percent (or less) of the BAC figure.

Q. In this case, the reading was .11 percent, right?
A. That's correct.
Q. And recognized inherent error is .01 either way?
A. That's correct.
Q. So, the range of inherent error would be, roughly, from .10 percent to .12 percent?
A. Roughly.
Q. That's about a 20 percent margin, isn't it?
A. At that reading, about that, yes.
Q. Let's see. . . . You're saying that even if this "smart" machine is working *perfectly* . . . even if there are no errors, no mistakes . . . even then, the best it can do in this case is be 80 percent accurate?
A. I wouldn't put it that way.
Q. And it *does* make mistakes?
A. Malfunctions are possible.
Q. 80 percent accuracy, not including malfunctions.
A. Well. . . .

Counsel can then go on to the range of error in calibration, emphasizing the permissible variance using simulator solutions. Breath-alcohol testing regulations usually require that the simulator test reading be within a range of 10 percent of the true simulator concentration. For example, if the simulator solution contains .10 percent alcohol in a water base, the calibration reading of the machine before the defendant is tested should be within 10 percent of that .10 percent reading — that is, between .09 percent and .11 percent BAC.

Again, this acceptable range of accuracy should be made clear for the jury. The range from .09 percent to .11 percent represents a spread of .02 percent — or a *20 percent range of error!* How reliable can such a machine be if it is considered "accurate" when its readings can fluctuate by ⅕th? Is this just "close enough for government work"?

The "acceptable error" can be dramatized by comparing it to something the jurors understand: money. Assume that a juror takes his car to a mechanic for repairs. The actual cost for parts and labor is $100, but the mechanic submits a bill to the juror for $110. Would this $10 overcharge be "acceptable accuracy" to the juror?

What if the mechanic tells the juror that he has a $20 margin to play with — that any charge from $90 to $110 is "close enough"?

Of course, these two "acceptable" ranges of error can be *added* by counsel for the jury. The resulting range of error can then assume completely ridiculous proportions: With the breath machine working perfectly, the BAC can still vary 20 percent either way — or a margin of error of *40 percent!*

§13.3.4 How Infrared Works — And Why It Doesn't

The vast majority of breath machines in use today utilize the infrared spectrophotometric method of analysis. And the primary weakness of this method is that it is *nonspecific* for alcohol — that is, it will falsely register other chemical compounds as ethyl alcohol (see §6.1.2). This is not always an easy concept for jurors to grasp, yet it is of critical importance to the defense.

Dr. Richard Jensen of Minneapolis, Minnesota, one of the foremost authorities on blood-alcohol analysis in the country, uses a simple demonstration during his testimony to illustrate the idea. (In the event counsel does not have the luxury of a defense expert toxicologist, he may wish to use it in his cross-examination of the state's expert.)

Dr. Jensen brings large, colorful plastic models of the molecular structure of three compounds — ethyl alcohol, acetone, and some other interferent such as toluene (glue) or isopropyl alcohol. If the judge permits, he leaves the witness chair and has someone stand at one point in the courtroom with a flashlight, representing the source of infrared light; another individual will stand at the other end of the room with a small dish or face mirror, representing the light detector at the other end of the imaginary "sample chamber." A third person stands in the middle, holding the molecule of ethyl alcohol. Dr. Jensen then explains the theory of infrared absorption — how the beam of infrared light passes through the chamber containing a sample of the defendant's breath and is partially absorbed by the alcohol molecule before reaching the detector. The amount getting through to the detector, of course, determines the blood-alcohol concentration.

Dr. Jensen then takes the alcohol model and approaches the jury, showing them the portion of the molecule representing the "methyl group." The infrared light, he explains, is absorbed by this portion of the alcohol model. Then he shows them the model of the acetone molecule, pointing out that it has the same methyl group in its structure.

Dr. Jensen then has a fourth person take the model of the acetone molecule. Explaining that acetone is commonly found on the human breath, he has the individual stand with it in the "chamber" along with the person again holding the alcohol molecule. He then demonstrates how the light from the flashlight is now absorbed by *both* molecules, resulting in less light energy getting through. The methyl group in each molecule is absorbing the infrared energy.

Finally, Dr. Jensen shows the jury the model of the toluene or isopropyl molecule, again pointing out the methyl portion. He has a fifth person enter the "chamber" holding the model, then demonstrates how *all three* molecules are now absorbing light from the beam — and the detector registers an even higher concentration of "alcohol."

Juries invariably appreciate this nontechnical demonstration of how the breath machine works. And, invariably, the problem of nonspecific analysis is deeply etched into their minds.

§13.3.5 The Defective Warranty

An effective technique is to compare the breath testing machine to kitchen appliances and other everyday machines with which the jurors are familiar — machines that malfunction and break down. This can be developed even further by bringing out in cross-examination of the state's expert that the breath machine — like other machines — carries a *warranty*. Unlike some kitchen appliances, however, this machine's warranty is *not* unconditional.

Consider, for example, the following language taken from the Statement of Warranty in the manual for the state-of-the-art Intoxilyzer 5000:

> CMI Inc. . . . warrants that each new product will be free from defects in material and workmanship, under normal use and service, for a period of *one year* from the date of delivery to the first user-purchaser. . . .
>
> Repaired components are warranted for a period of 90 days from the date of repair. . . .
>
> *There are no other warranties express or implied, including but not limited to any implied warranties of merchantability or fitness for a particular purpose. In no event shall CMI be liable for . . . any indirect or consequential damages arising out of any such defect in material or workmanship.* [Emphasis in the original.]

The terms of this warranty (or the warranty of any other breath machine, obtainable through discovery) should be clearly brought home to the jury. The limited period of the warranty can be emphasized:

Q. You have read this warranty, marked defense exhibit A?
A. I have.
Q. As I understand it, this machine carries a warranty of only *one year?*
A. Apparently.
Q. That's less than the warranty for most *toasters,* isn't it?
(Objection sustained)
Q. Well, how long has this Intoxilyzer 5000 that was used on my client been in service?
A. I believe it's been in service for slightly less than three years.
Q. Three years.
A. Yes.
Q. So it's no longer under warranty?
A. Apparently not.

Q. In other words, the machine's manufacturer can no longer guarantee that it will work right?
A. You'd have to discuss that with them, counselor.

The time limitations on the warranted repairs can also be pointed out:

Q. According to the maintenance records on this machine, there have been a number of repairs?
A. That's normal.
Q. So, I guess some things went wrong with the machine, and it had to be sent back to be fixed, huh?
A. Yes. Of course, the instrument is accurately calibrated after any repairs are made.
Q. Uh-huh. And how long do these repairs last?
A. I don't understand.
Q. Well, how long is the warranty on these repairs?
A. The manufacturer's warranty?
Q. Yes.
A. I believe it's 90 days.
Q. Only 90 days.
A. Yes.
Q. The manufacturer says that after 90 days, he can't guarantee the machine's going to work right?
A. That's not . . . It's a warranty, that's all.
Q. Do *you* guys ever make any repairs on the machine?
A. The crime lab?
Q. Yes.
A. Yes, occasionally. Minor ones.
Q. Is there any warranty if you guys do the repairs, rather than the manufacturer?
A. No.

The specific nature of the warranty is usually of considerable interest to most jurors unfamiliar with legal subtleties:

Q. I see it says there are no warranties of "fitness for a particular purpose."
A. That's what it says.
Q. You mean, the manufacturer says he can't guarantee this machine

is any good for any particular purpose — *such as testing for blood-alcohol?*
A. I'm not a lawyer.
Q. Do you understand "fit for a particular purpose"?
A. I understand the language, yes.
Q. And the guys who make this machine, they can't say it's fit for any particular purpose?

Finally, the manufacturer's attempt in the warranty at limiting liability can be developed:

Q. "In no event shall CMI be liable for any . . . indirect or consequential damages arising out of any such defect in material or workmanship."
A. Is that a question?
Q. That's what it says, right?
A. Yes.
Q. So, the people who make this machine, they won't be responsible for any malfunctions?
A. I couldn't say.
Q. That's what it says, doesn't it? Once they sell it, *they won't be responsible for any harm it causes?*

In summation, counsel can point out that the machine should not be given any credibility: If its manufacturer has so little confidence in it, why should the jury?

(According to the Supervisor's Manual for the Intoximeter 3000, incidentally, the warranty period for that machine "shall be pursuant to stipulation." Counsel must determine through discovery the terms of the warranty as negotiated with his state or local law enforcement agency. As with the Intoxilyzer 5000, however, repairs performed by Intoximeters, Inc., are warranted for only 90 days.)

The warranty issued by National Patent Analytical Systems for their DataMaster breath machine is reproduced in Form 20. The last paragraph contains the words "no . . . implied warranties of . . . fitness for a particular purpose" like the warranties of other breath testing machines. Note that the National Patent Analytical Systems warranty is a two-year warranty instead of the one-year warranty offered by CMI for the Intoxilyzer 5000. (This superior

Statement of Warranty

CMI Inc., a subsidiary of MPD, Inc. warrants that each new product will be free from defects in material and workmanship, under normal use and service, for a period of **one year** from the date of delivery to the first user-purchaser. CMI's obligation is limited to repairing or replacing, as CMI may elect, any part or parts of such product which CMI's examination discloses to be defective in material or workmanship. Warranty repairs will be performed only at authorized factory service centers; however, CMI reserves the right to authorize other repair centers to perform warranty repairs/exchanges. Such authorization must be granted in advance and in writing.

Any part or parts considered to be covered by the conditions of this warranty shall be returned, freight prepaid, to an authorized warranty service facility.

During the warranty period, CMI will pay the shipping charges to return a repaired product to the customer if the product was covered by this warranty. Repaired components are warranted for a period of 90 days from the date of repair, and that warranty is subject to the same limitations as this warranty. Components not repaired **do not receive** an extended 90 day warranty.

Warranty coverage extends only to the original purchaser and does not cover replacement of parts that are, by their nature, expendable. This warranty is voided if the product is adversely affected by attaching any feature or device to it, or is in any way tampered with or modified without express written permission from CMI management.

There are no other warranties expressed or implied, including but not limited to, any implied warranties of merchantability or fitness for a particular purpose. In no event shall CMI be liable for any loss of profits or any indirect or consequential damages arising out of any such defect in material or workmanship.

a subsidiary of
MPD, Inc.

CMI Inc., a subsidiary of MPD, Inc.
316 East Ninth Street
Owensboro, Kentucky 42301
(502) 685-6200 or 1-800-942-4011

 F-WNTY11/88

Form 19
Manufacturer's Warranty for Intoxilyzer 5000

BAC DataMaster
2 Year Warranty

National Patent Analytical Systems, Inc. warrants that all new products will be free from defects in workmanship and materials, under normal and intended service for a period of one year from date of shipment. National Patent Analytical Systems further warrants that the BAC DataMaster will be free from defects in workmanship and materials under normal and intended usage for a period of one year after the end of the first year from date of shipment with the exception of the Breath Tube and Keyboard Cable Assembly, when applicable. National Patent Analytical Systems will provide all warranty repairs at the plant facility in Mansfield, Ohio and reserves the right to authorize other repair centers to perform such repairs. Such authorization must be granted in writing prior to performance of such.

Requests for warranty repairs should be made by calling the Plant at 419-526-6727 prior to shipping. A Return Authorization Number will be issued. Items or instruments for repair must be returned to the Plant at 2260 N Main Street Mansfield, Ohio 44903 freight paid. Collect shipments will not be accepted. Repairs are warranted through the end of the Warranty Period.

The Warranty coverage extends only to the original purchaser and does not cover replacement of parts that are, by their nature, expendable. This warranty is voided in the event of any modifications to the instrument that are made without the written consent of National Patent Analytical Systems, Inc. The warranty does not cover negligence, abuse by the customer or subject, fire, theft or acts of God. The equipment must be used in accordance with the Manufacturers published operation procedures, or operating procedures published or instructed by an appropriate and authorized state or governmental controlling agency.

There are no other warranties expressed or implied including, but not limited to, any implied warranties of merchantability or fitness for a particular purpose. In no event shall National Patent Analytical Systems be liable for any loss of profit or any indirect or consequential damages arising out of any such defect in material or workmanship.

Serial Number______________ Date of Shipment______________

National Patent Analytical Systems, Inc.
2260 N. Main St., PO Box 1435, Mansfield, Ohio 44901 (Ph) 419-526-NPAS (Fax) 526-9446

Form 20
Manufacturer's Warranty for DataMaster

warranty can, of course, be brought out in cross-examination on the Intoxilyzer 5000.)

§13.3.6 RFI Magic

The problem of radio frequency interference is often ridiculed by prosecutors as an imaginary concept dreamed up by clever defense attorneys, derisively referring to it as "smoke" or "magic." Of course, RFI can be verified by any expert familiar with the problem. And the availability of "RFI detectors" from the various machines' manufacturers is further evidence of the phenomenon.

One simple means for bringing the concept of radio frequency interference home to the jury is to relate it to everyday experience. If a defense expert is not available, this can be accomplished during cross-examination of the state's expert (or later in closing argument):

Q. So it's basically radio waves in the air, entering an electronic device and causing it to malfunction?
A. I suppose you could say that.
Q. Well, the other day, I saw this sign at a restaurant. It said, "Warning: Microwave in Use."
A. Yes.
Q. Is that what we're talking about?
A. That would be an example of RFI, yes.
Q. The radio waves given off by the microwave oven in the restaurant, they might interfere with electronic gizmos the customers have?
A. Yes.
Q. Like a pacemaker in a customer's heart?
A. I believe that's why they post the signs.
Q. The microwave could cause the pacemaker to malfunction?
A. It could happen.
Q. And the guy could die?

To bring it home to breath testing, Reese Joye, an eminent DUI specialist in Charleston, South Carolina, eliminates all doubt about the existence of RFI with a simple demonstration.

Joye obtained a gauge from an older breath machine and had it mounted on a small box; the gauge has a needle and a BAC scale. Inside the box is some of the circuitry from the machine, connected to the gauge. He then purchased a walkie-talkie, such as is commonly found in police stations.

Joye has the expert witness explain what the two devices are, acknowledging that walkie-talkies are used by the police agency administering the breath test to the defendant. He then instructs the witness to activate the power to the breath machine gauge, positioning it so that the jury can see it clearly; the needle rests at zero. Finally, he has him turn the walkie-talkie to "transmit" and move it around the gauge.

As the walkie-talkie is turned on and passed over the gauge, the needle will begin moving up and down the blood-alcohol scale, sometimes jerking wildly.

Joye has shown the jurors that RFI clearly exists — while at the same time visually relating it to a breath test.

§13.3.7 A Ton of Beer

Where the evidence indicates a client was drinking beer and his blood-alcohol concentration is particularly high, say .20 percent or more, counsel may wish to use a visual technique employed with success by Phillip Price of Montgomery, Alabama.

During the cross-examination of the prosecution's forensic expert, Price obtains an estimate of the amount of beer an individual of the client's weight would have to have consumed to reach the indicated BAC over the relevant period of time, say two hours. Usually, this involves a rather large number of 12-ounce cans of beer — perhaps a dozen or more.

Price then brings a five-gallon jug into the courtroom and sets it on a table where it is clearly visible to the jury; the jug is clear plastic or glass, of the type used to contain drinking water. He then produces the number of cans of beer indicated by the witness — and asks him to pour them one at a time into the jug. In pouring the cans into the jug, the beer invariably foams, creating a large head (note: lite beer foams more than regular).

The result is an impressive amount of beer and foam — far too large a quantity for any stomach to contain, and seemingly too much for any human being to consume.

Price then confirms with the expert witness that this represents the amount of beer consumed by one person over the two or three hours indicated. He may then ask him, "Do you think *you* could drink this much in two hours?" If a time period is not available, the witness can be asked, "Do you think *you* could drink this much in an evening?" or "Do you think *you* could hold this much beer?"

§13.3.8 The Invisible Breath Sample

In a breath test, the amount of alcohol actually tested is amazingly tiny — so minuscule, in fact, that counsel should illustrate how little the machine has to work with.

It is worth pointing out to the jury during cross-examination of the state's expert that a reading of .10 percent on a machine means that the subject's blood contained .10 grams of alcohol in 100 milliliters (cubic centimeters) of blood, or .001 grams per cubic centimeter of blood. When a normal sample of 50 cubic centimeters of the subject's breath is captured by the Intoxilyzer 5000, for example, Henry's Law tells us that the equivalent of 1/40 of a cubic centimeter of blood is represented by this sample. Since a cubic centimeter contains 20 drops, 1/40 of a cubic centimeter contains half a drop. Assuming a .10 percent reading of blood-alcohol content, *five one-hundredths of one percent* of a drop of alcohol is being measured — an amount invisible to the naked eye.

While the Intoxilyzer captures a larger sample than the Intoximeter (400cc), the amount of alcohol analyzed is still infinitesimal. Since 2100 times as much alcohol is present in the blood as in the breath, a .10 percent reading will be based on an alcoholic concentration in the breath sample of .000048 gm/dl by weight or forty-eight millionths of a gram of alcohol per decaliter of breath. Since we are analyzing 400ml of breath, there are .00019 grams of pure alcohol being measured, or *nineteen hundred-thousandths* of a gram of alcohol. Yet another way of looking at it, the Intoxilyzer is attempting to measure the volume of alcohol found in *five ten-thousandths* of a milliliter of 100 proof liquor — again, an amount invisible to the naked eye. When confronted with possible sources for error, and with the rather unimpressive appearance of the small, portable instrument, many jurors are reluctant to believe that the device could accurately measure such a tiny amount of alcohol in the blood.

One possibly effective method for illustrating this graphically for a jury is through the use of a 55-gallon drum and an eyedropper. A 55-gallon drum represents about the same capacity as 210 liters of breath — the volume used in determining breath-blood analysis; the eyedropper can contain .10 grams (or whatever amount the machine indicated in the case) of dark (for visibility) liquid. During examination or argument, counsel can demonstrate for the jury how the tiny amount of alcohol can cause a significant reading in the breath machine. Then the jury can be told (or possibly shown through another demonstration) how much smaller than a 55-gallon drum the defendant's breath sample was — and how infinitesimal the amount of alcohol measured.

§13.3.9 Wonder Blood

If counsel is dealing with a DUI case in which the analysis was conducted on a sample of the client's blood, one of the primary avenues of attack concerns the possibility of *fermentation,* a naturally degenerative process that produces alcohol (see §7.0.3). The expert will counter, of course, with the claim that fermentation could not have occurred since a *preservative* such as sodium fluoride was added to the sample. As the discussion in §7.0.3 indicated, the correct amount of preservative required to prevent fermentation is a subject of debate. And most experts feel that preservatives are not enough: The sample must be constantly refrigerated as well.

An effective way to illustrate this in a manner that can be immediately appreciated by the nontechnical jury is to bring in a wrapped loaf of white bread that has been sitting in counsel's kitchen for a week or so.

Q. So, you're saying as long as there was sodium fluoride in the blood sample, it couldn't have gone bad?
A. There would be no fermentation, that is correct.
Q. And just so we understand each other, fermentation is just another way of saying rotting, right? Spoiling?
A. I suppose you could say that.

Q. As long as there's a preservative present, then no spoiling, huh?
A. That is correct.
Q. (Producing the loaf of bread) Are you familiar with Wonder Bread?
A. I am.
Q. Do you know if it has any preservatives in it?
A. I . . . I don't really know. I suppose it does. Most processed food does.
Q. Would you care to read the ingredients on the label?
A. I'm sure it has preservatives, counsel.
Q. So, then, I guess this bread won't spoil, right?
A. I assume it will, eventually.
Q. Even though it's loaded with preservatives?
A. Yes.
Q. In fact, it'll start getting moldy in just a few days, right?
A. Maybe.
Q. Well, *you've* bought bread before, haven't you?
A. Of course.
Q. With preservatives in it?
A. I assume so.
Q. And how long did it last before it went bad?

§13.3.10 Purple Urine

In many states, a suspect's blood-alcohol concentration is determined with urinalysis. As the discussion in § 7.1 indicated, this is by far the least accurate of the three available methods of analysis. The primary reason for this is the fact that it is completely dependent on the subject *voiding* his bladder and then waiting 20 minutes for fresh urine to be secreted into the bladder for a more representative sample. And it is virtually impossible for an individual to *completely* void his bladder: There will usually be about 10cc of old urine left (see §7.1.1). This urine will combine with approximately 20cc of fresh urine produced during the wait, resulting in a sample that is one-third old urine — urine that may contain alcohol from many hours before the subject was driving.

James Farragher Campbell, a noted DUI practitioner from San Francisco, illustrates this for the jury during his cross-examination of the state's forensic expert. He brings a glass beaker into court, along with a partially filled bottle of apple juice and a partially filled bottle of grape juice. He has the witness fill one beaker halfway with grape juice; the beaker represents the defendant's bladder, the grape juice the old urine already there before the void.

Campbell then has the witness pour all but a small amount of the dark purple grape juice out of the bladder/beaker; this is the "void," with 10cc left. Then he has him pour the light yellow apple juice into the beaker — very slowly, emphasizing that this is the new urine dripping into the bladder over a period of 20 minutes. When all of the apple juice has been poured out, Campbell asks the witness to hold up the beaker/bladder with the "new" urine that will constitute the sample to be tested.

The sample to be analyzed is still purple, clearly contaminated by the old urine.

§13.3.11 A Lot of Hot Air

Gary Trichter of Houston, Texas, uses a technique designed to contrast the amount of breath tested with the amount used as a reference in the drunk driving per se statute:

> Breath test devices generally do not test the amount of air from the body which is required by statute. For example, the Intoxilyzer 5000 sample chamber volume is approximately 82.5 centimeters while most breath test alcohol concentration statutes require that 210 liters of air be tested. Defense counsel can demonstrate the insufficiency of the prosecution's test process by showing these differences to the jury. Using a large inflatable device such as those found in liquor stores, i.e. a blow up of a beer can, the legal requirement can be contrasted to the volume actually tested (5 cubic inches). Here, the point of the demonstration is to show that the breath test took approximately 5–7 seconds of breath whereas to blow up a device the size of a 55-gallon drum (210 liters) takes a much longer period of time. This is a particularly fun demonstration when counsel has the state's expert attempt the inflation within the 5–7 second period. As a point of information, an error in measurement of substance in one pint will be increased 2545 times if the analysis of 82.5 centimeter volume was then computed on the basis of 210 liters.

§13.3.12 The Virgin Vial

As any seasoned defense attorney knows, most police officers are more than willing to "bend the truth" to achieve what they consider a desired objective. This is all the more so when the issue may involve the officer's own competence or compliance with the law. The same can probably be said of medical technicians when called to the witness stand to explain their performance of an official duty: Defensiveness supercedes accuracy. A perfect example of this is the testimony of the officer (or nurse/medical technician) when asked to describe his gathering of the blood or urine sample, particularly in the usual situation where a prepackaged blood- or urine-gathering kit is used.

The tactic is a simple one. During cross-examination, focus on the issue of sterilization of the vial used to contain the blood or urine, with the attendant implications of possible fermentation of the sample:

Q. "And this vial had been sterilized?"
A. "Yes."
Q. "You did not actually see it sterilized?"
A. "No, of course not."
Q. "Well, did you visually inspect it?"
A. "Yes, I did."
Q. "And it appeared to you to be clean?"
A. "It did."
Q. "No prints or smudges?"
A. "No."
Q. "No dust or dirt?"
A. "No."
Q. "Did you inspect the bottom of the vial to see if there was anything lying down there?"
A. "I did."
Q. "See anything there?"
A. "Nothing."
Q. "Completely bare?"
A. "Completely bare."
Q. "So, before you handed the vial to the defendant to urinate into, officer [or, before you injected the withdrawn blood into the vial, Ms. Jones], you were confident the vial was absolutely clean?"
A. "I was."
Q. "And you are absolutely sure there was nothing in that vial before the urine [blood] was placed in there?"
A. "I am."

The hook has now been set. No blood test is valid without both *preservative* (commonly, sodium fluoride) and *anticoagulent* in the sample; for a valid urinalysis, only preservative must be present (see §7.0.3). In some cases, this may be added after the sample is gathered. Most law enforcement agencies, however, use prepackaged kits for blood or urine samples; many medical facilities also use such kits for blood draws. These kits usually have a small amount of powder in the bottom of the vials: preservative (and, if blood, anticoagulent). In such cases, the officer/technician is now completely exposed to an attack on the credibility of the blood-alcohol analysis. Cross-examination now shifts to the issue of fermentation and compliance with state regulations concerning the withdrawal and storage of blood/urine samples.

Q. "Now, Officer, you have testified that for an accurate result, it is critical there be no fermentation in the vial?"
A. "That's correct."
Q. "And the method used to prevent this fermentation is to use a preservative, correct?"
A. "Yes."
Q. "What does this preservative look like?"
A. "Well . . . It's just a powder. Sort of white, but off-color."
Q. "Uh-huh. And do you use a lot of it?"
A. "Not really. Just a small amount."
Q. "But certainly enough for you to see?"
A. "Sure."
Q. "And where does this preservative come from?"
A. "Come from?"
Q. "Yes: Do you add it to the sample?"
A. "No, no. It's already in the vial. It comes from the factory with the kit, already in the vial."
Q. "It's a powder at the bottom, easily visible?"
A. "Yes."
Q. "So fermentation could have caused a false reading in this case?"
A. "What?"
Q. "Well, since no preservative was used here, fermentation could be a serious problem, correct?"
A. "I don't understand."
Q. "Didn't you testify earlier that before you placed the sample into the vial, you inspected it and there was nothing in it? That it was completely bare?"
A. "Well, I . . ."
Q. "Did you want to change that testimony?"

§13.4 Illustrative Cross-Examination of Operator/Expert

> Whoever undertakes to set himself up as a judge in the field of Truth and Knowledge is shipwrecked by the laughter of the gods.
>
> ALBERT EINSTEIN

In cross-examining the prosecution's breath machine operator, technician, or forensic expert, counsel will want to confront him with the opinions and conclusions of experts who have done research in the area of blood-alcohol analysis. A recurring problem, however, is the expert who will either cleverly pretend ignorance of the article to preclude its use for impeachment or simply be honestly unaware of the material. Counsel may consider avoiding this problem in advance by simply mailing copies of the articles to the expert two or three weeks before trial, together with a cover letter explaining the basic subject matter of the articles and advising the expert that he will be asked about them on cross-examination. Usually the expert will then read them. If he does not, it should be clearly brought out on cross-examination that he was aware of the relevance of the material but chose to ignore it despite its availability.

Counsel might also wish to find out exactly what scientific journals the expert's agency or laboratory subscribes to. Very likely, some of the articles counsel will wish to ask the expert about will be in these journals. Thus, for example, the Journal of Studies on Alcohol, Forensic Science International, Journal of Chromatographic Science, and Journal of Analytical Toxicology, among others, are commonly found in laboratory libraries. If the expert has ready access to the articles but nevertheless has not read them, it should be brought out that this is an expert who simply does not care to keep up on developments in his field.

Finally, in preparing his cross-examination, defense counsel may be interested to learn prosecution methods for direct examination. The following sample strategy lists some of the techniques found in the manual of a major prosecution agency.

1. If there are two or more different readings from a breath instrument, have the expert explain the discrepancy by the *manner* in which the defendant breathed during the sample capture.

2. If there are two readings within .02 percent of each other, when you ask the expert what the defendant's reading was have him give a single reading that is an *average* of the two readings.
3. If the defendant performs well on the field sobriety test, have the expert explain *tolerance* as the ability to mask or hide physical symptoms of impairment through acquired experience.
4. Again, if there is a good FST, the expert can testify that a poor performance is a good indication of intoxication — but a good performance does *not* mean the person is *not* under the influence.
5. Have the expert give his opinion that, based on his review of the maintenance and calibration records, the breath instrument was giving correct readings at the time the defendant was tested.
6. Ask the expert what his opinion is of the defendant's degree of intoxication at the time of the breath test, based upon the results of the test. Then, ask for his opinion as to the degree of intoxication at the time of arrest — "*only if it is favorable to the People's case*" to do so.
7. Have the expert testify how many drinks were in the defendant, based upon the "modified Smith-Widmark formula": (body weight) × (breath instrument reading) × (.26 for men; .21 or .23 for women) = number of ounces of 100 proof alcohol. If relevant, explain this also in terms of 10 proof beer and/or 25 proof wine and/or 80/86 proof spirits. If there is retrograde extrapolation, give the estimate as of the time of arrest.
8. If the defendant claims to have consumed only, say, two beers, ask the expert if it would be possible to have the breath test result obtained after having only two beers.

The illustrative cross-examination that follows, covering breath, blood, and urine, is necessarily brief. Certainly, it should not be considered as exhaustive, nor should it even be relied on as entirely appropriate in any given case. And, to avoid duplication, none of the methods discussed in §§13.3.1–13.1.12 (*Cross-Examination Techniques*) are repeated here; these should, however, be considered carefully in planning the attack on the state's expert.

Bias

Q. Mr Johnson, by whom are you employed?
A. The County Sheriff's Department, the criminalistics laboratory.
Q. You are paid, then, by a police agency to testify in court?
A. That is one of the things I'm paid to do.
Q. You testify only for the people who pay you, isn't that true?
A. I'm not sure I understand the question.
Q. Well, you testify only for the Sheriff's Department — in cases where a deputy sheriff makes an arrest that leads to a trial?
A. That's true.
Q. How many times have you testified for the defense?
A. That's not my job.
Q. You have *never* testified on behalf of a defendant?
A. That's not my job, counselor.
Q. Then, in every drunk driving case, you always testify on behalf of the prosecution, regardless of the facts?
A. That's correct.
Q. And no matter what the results of the chemical tests, you will always testify against the defendant?
A. If you want to put it that way.
Q. Incidentally, when you applied for this job, do you recall the job description?
A. Job description?
Q. Yes, the description of the duties of the job.
A. I recall vaguely.
Q. Isn't it true that the primary purpose of the job was advertised to be to "aid the prosecution"?
A. I believe that's accurate.
Q. *Not* to *seek the truth?*
A. Well, those are not inconsistent, counselor.
Q. Your primary job is to help the prosecution convict my client, correct?
A. My job is to testify concerning blood-alcohol analysis.
Q. The fact is, nothing in your job description — nothing in your announced duties — refers to simply testifying to the truth in any given case . . . no matter what the result?

Qualifications

Q. Now, you mentioned on direct examination that you had received a degree in chemistry.
A. Yes.
Q. That is a doctorate we are speaking of, I presume.

A. No, it is not.
Q. A master's degree, then?
A. Counselor, you are well aware that I have a bachelor's degree.
Q. A bachelor's degree. Then you have done no postgraduate work in the field?
A. That's correct.
Q. And when did you receive the undergraduate degree?
A. Eight years ago.
Q. I see. Then you have received no formal education in your field for eight years?
A. I keep up on developments in the field through reading journals, books, and so on — the same as a physician would.
Q. Then you have, of course, read Dr. Glenn Forrester's *The Use of Chemical Tests for Alcohol in Traffic Law Enforcement?*
A. I'm familiar with it.
Q. Have you *read* it?
A. I haven't actually read it, no.
Q. You have read the Foreny and Hughes text, *Combined Effects of Alcohol and Other Drugs?*
A. Not. . . . No.
Q. Well, have you read the American Medical Association's *Alcohol and the Impaired Driver: A Manual on the Medicological Aspects of Chemical Tests for Intoxication?*
A. I'm familiar with it. But, no — I haven't actually read it.
Q. What about Donigan's text, *Chemical Tests and the Law?*
A. No.
Q. Roach's *Biological Aspects of Alcohol?*
A. Counselor, I'm rather busy with my duties at the laboratory.
Q. I see.

Physiology of Alcohol Consumption

Q. Now, you've testified that my client had a reading of .13.
A. That's correct.
Q. And this means that at the time the sample was taken, there was .13 of 1 percent of alcohol in his blood?
A. Yes.
Q. What about the percentage at the time he was driving?
A. Well, it would be close to that.
Q. If the sample was taken one hour after he was stopped on the road, wouldn't there be a difference?
A. Of course. From the time the alcohol is consumed, it is gradually

absorbed into the bloodstream. The intoxication effect continues to rise until it reaches a peak value, then declines.

Q. Then we really don't know what the reading was an hour before the test?

A. Absorption rates can be estimated. The peak value will be reached one hour after ingestion.

Q. You mentioned that you are familiar with Dr. Glenn Forrester's *Chemical Tests for Alcohol in Traffic Law Enforcement?*

A. Yes, I believe so.

Q. Doesn't he say that on an empty stomach, over half of the alcohol will be absorbed in 15 minutes, and all of it in 1 to 2 hours?

A. I believe he does.

Q. Don't most experts agree that under ordinary circumstances a peak value will be reached between 45 and 75 minutes after consumption?

A. That's approximately right.

Q. You have read Dr. Clarence Muehilberger's article entitled "The Physiological Action of Alcohol"?

A. That sounds familiar.

Q. Doesn't he write that the rate of absorption of alcohol depends on the amount swallowed, the type of food and liquid already in the stomach, and the time it is in the stomach?

A. That's correct.

Q. Isn't it a fact that absorption time is radically affected by the presence of food and/or liquid in the stomach?

A. It is affected.

Q. Why is that?

A. The presence of liquid can have an effect on the absorption time. Food retards the absorption time for various reasons.

Q. Then it is quite possible that alcohol consumed shortly before my client's arrest was not affecting him, but registered at its peak value when the sample was taken one hour later?

A. That's possible.

Q. Now, the alcohol metabolizes in the body?

A. Yes.

Q. And I believe you testified that the alcohol is eliminated from the system at a rate of approximately .015 percent per hour, is that correct?

A. That's right. Estimating in this case, with a reading of .13 one hour after the arrest, I would estimate that your client had a reading of .145 at the time of his arrest.

Q. You are familiar with Dr. Kurt Dubowski's book, *Alcohol and Traffic Safety?*
A. Yes, I am.
Q. Did he not conduct a study of the alcohol clearance rate of 922 men and find the rate to vary from .006 and .04 percent per hour?
A. I believe he did.
Q. Applying this, is it entirely possible — assuming the correctness of the .13 reading — my client's level at the time of his arrest was .09 rather than .145?
A. Not probable — but yes, possible.
Q. Now, under Dubowski's study, one individual can have an elimination rate seven times faster than another?
A. From his study, yes.
Q. And according to Dr. Forrester and other experts, some people can absorb alcohol twice as fast as others?
A. That's true
Q. Then your testimony as to my client's level of blood-alcohol at the time he was actually driving is based on guesswork?
A. It is based on scientific analysis, corrected by applying proven averages.
Q. Do not a person's age and weight also affect the rate that alcohol is absorbed?
A. Weight and size, yes. Not age, except insofar as it affects tolerance.
Q. And the type of drinks consumed?
A. Mixes, water — yes.
Q. Well, isn't it true that if you don't know the subject's weight, what he had to eat and drink, the time of the last drink, and what amount and type of mix was involved, you can't accurately estimate the blood-alcohol level one hour earlier?
A. Those factors would be helpful for accuracy.
Q. Can you determine whether the amount of alcohol in my client's system was increasing or decreasing at the time of his arrest?
A. I would need a second sample, removed in time from the first sample.
Q. Then, it is entirely possible that my client was more intoxicated when he was tested than when he was driving?
A. And it is equally possible he was less intoxicated.
Q. Mr. Johnson, would you please define tolerance as it relates to this case?
A. Tolerance is the individual's ability to withstand the effects of alcohol.
Q. Do you mean that different persons have different reactions to alcohol?

A. That's true.
Q. If two individuals both have a reading of, say, .12, one may be able to safely operate a motor vehicle and one may not?
A. That's possible
Q. Is there a method you have of determining a person's individual tolerance?
A. No.
Q. Then my client may have a very high tolerance level?
A. That's possible.
Q. And a blood-alcohol level that for one person may mean he was under the influence may not mean my client was under the influence?
A. We do not know your client's tolerance.

Retrograde Extrapolation

Q. This process of estimating what the blood-alcohol level was at the time of driving, based on the level at the time of testing — assuming the test was valid — is called "retrograde extrapolation," isn't it?
A. That's correct.
Q. It is guesswork, nothing more, correct?
A. It is an estimate based on known data.
Q. But we do not *know* the level at time of driving — we are guessing?
A. An informed estimate.
Q. And this guess, or estimate, is based on a number of factors — what you call "known data"?
A. Yes, that's correct.
Q. And if this data is wrong, then the guess will be wrong? As the computer boys say, "garbage in — garbage out"?
A. The accuracy of the estimate will be adversely affected, correct.
Q. Well, these variables or factors include the elimination rate?
A. Yes.
Q. But we do not *know* what Mr. Kelly's absorption rate was, do we?
A. We know the average.
Q. Then you are only estimating the blood-alcohol level of this fictitious average driver — not of Mr. Kelly?
A. Obviously, I do not know Mr. Kelly's individual physiology.
Q. Exactly. And you do not know his absorption rate either?
A. I said that
Q. So, again we are only guessing the blood-alcohol level of a man or woman who happens to have an exactly average absorption rate?
A. If you choose to phrase it in that way.
Q. Now, this retrograde extrapolation, as I understand it, basically in-

volves projecting a straight line from the blood-alcohol level of the test to the blood-alcohol level at the time of driving, correct?
A. Yes, at a rate of loss of .02 or possibly .015 percent per hour.
Q. Right. Now, how many breath samples were taken from Mr. Kelly for testing?
A. I am aware of only one.
Q. One. Now, sir, would you please go over to that blackboard?
A. Very well.
Q. Thank you. Now, please draw a point.
A. Like this?
Q. Yes, thank you. Now, applying the laws of geometry, would you please extend a line through the point?
A. Extend a line?
Q. Yes. Using those rules of geometry from high school days, please project a line through the point.
A. I'm afraid I don't understand. In what direction do you want the line?
Q. Don't you know, sir?
A. Of course not, counselor.
Q. Why not?
A. Let's not play games, counselor. It requires two or more points before I can project a line.
Q. Then you can't project a line without at least two points?
A. You know that.
Q. Yet, you *have* done exactly that in your retrograde extrapolation of Mr. Kelly's blood-alcohol test?
A. I beg your pardon?
Q. In your direct testimony, you said you took a single point — Mr. Kelly's .13 test result — and on a graph of time and blood-alcohol you projected the level at time of driving to be .145.
A. All right.
Q. So you projected a line backward and upward based on one single point?
A. Well, that's different, counselor. I knew the rate of elimination — .015 percent.
Q. This is the *average* rate of elimination — not Mr. Kelly's?
A. The average rate. And so I could extrapolate to .145 one hour earlier.
Q. But why did you project *upward* — rather than *downward?* In other words, why did you assume his blood-alcohol level was going down rather than going up?
A. I assumed he was not drinking while he was driving, or after the arrest, counselor.

Q. But if he had been drinking before he drove, it would take time for the alcohol to be absorbed?
A. Yes.
Q. And we have already established that the absorption rate varies with each individual?
A. To some degree, yes.
Q. And so Mr. Kelly's body could still be absorbing alcohol at the time of the test one hour after he stopped drinking?
A. I suppose so.
Q. And we don't know at what rate he was eliminating?
A. We know the average rate.
Q. Then it is entirely possible that his blood-alcohol level was *rising* after he was stopped by Officer Smith?
A. That's possible.
Q. And that his level at the time of the breath test was *higher* than at the time of driving?
A. It's possible.
Q. It's not only possible, sir, in fact it's just as likely as guessing that it was lower, isn't that so?
A. In my experience, it's more likely it was falling.
Q. So this retrograde extrapolation is nothing more than double guessing; guessing that the level is rising, and guessing that the rate of increase is .015 percent.
A. I would not characterize it as guessing.
Q. You prefer "estimating."
A. Yes.
Q. We could have determined that the level was rising or falling if we had a *second* test an hour or so after the first, couldn't we?
A. Yes.
Q. We could then project a line through *two* points, right?
A. That's correct.
Q. But that wasn't done by Officer Smith in this case, was it?
A. Apparently not.
Q. In fact, sir, this process involves *three* guesses: You are also guessing that the extrapolation backward is in the form of a straight line, aren't you?
A. I am assuming an elimination rate of .015 percent per hour.
Q. A constant, uniform loss of .015 percent?
A. Yes.
Q. But the loss is not uniform, is it?
A. I really don't know.
Q. And the blood-alcohol level is also affected by absorption at the same time?

A. It can be.
Q. In fact, then, a person's blood-alcohol level, if plotted on your graph, would resemble a *curve* more than a straight line?
A. That's true.
Q. But you have given your opinion of Mr. Kelly's blood-alcohol level at the time of driving based on a straight-line extrapolation, haven't you?
A. Unless one knows the shape of the curve, one cannot extrapolate at all.
Q. Exactly. And we do *not* know the shape of the blood-alcohol curve in Mr. Kelly's case, do we?
A. Obviously not.
Q. And, in fact, this curve is not even or uniform in its curvature, is it?
A. That's true.
Q. It has hills and spikes and valleys and sharp dips?
A. There is usually some. . . . Yes, that's correct.
Q. So, it's even possible Mr. Kelly was tested during one of these hills or spikes — that is, when his blood-alcohol level shot up temporarily?
A. It's not probable.
Q. But entirely possible?
A. Possible.
Q. As possible as his having a straight-line blood-alcohol level that is falling at a known, constant, and uniform rate?
A. I really couldn't say.

Radio Frequency Interference

Q. Now, this blood-alcohol reading was obtained by using an Intoxilyzer?
A. That's correct.
Q. You are familiar with the problem of radio frequency interference, or RFI?
A. I have heard of it.
Q. What is RFI, sir?
A. The electronic circuitry in most instruments may be susceptible to interference from radio waves from other sources.
Q. In fact, we are surrounded at this very moment with thousands of different sources of radio waves, hitting us as we speak?
A. That's correct.
Q. Have you ever seen a sign in a restaurant reading "Warning: Microwave in Use"?
A. Yes, of course.

Q. What is the meaning or purpose of the sign?
A. To warn heart pacemaker users to stay away because electromagnetic waves can interfere with the pacemaker.
Q. You are aware that Smith and Wesson, the manufacturer of the Breathalyzer, discovered in 1982 that its machines were giving false readings because of RFI?
A. I had heard that.
Q. And are you familiar with the studies after that by the federal government's National Highway and Traffic Safety Administration on RFI?
A. I am since you sent me copies of the report last week, counselor.
Q. And you considered this report before testifying to your opinion this morning?
A. Yes.
Q. This federal agency tested all 16 known brands and models of breath testing devices, did it not?
A. Apparently.
Q. And isn't it a fact that 10 of these models failed?
A. That's what the report says.
Q. In other words, most models used in the United States today can give false readings because of RFI?
A. Apparently.
Q. In fact, sir, this report specifically found the Intoxilyzer — the machine used to test Mr. Kelly — to be unacceptably affected by RFI, didn't it?
A. That's what the report says.
Q. In view of this report, sir, has the machine used in this case been tested for radio frequency interference?
A. I don't know. Not to my knowledge.

Partition Ratio

Q. Now, Mr. Johnson, the reading obtained from a subject's breath sample on a breath analyzing device is based on the premise that there is an alcohol concentration ratio of 1:2100 between breath and blood, correct?
A. Yes. In other words, if we multiply breath-alcohol concentration by 2100, we will arrive at a blood-alcohol equivalent.
Q. This 1:2100 ratio is merely an average, is it not?
A. That's correct.
Q. Then doesn't the final reading rest on the assumption that the subject falls within this "normal" ratio?
A. Yes.

Q. In fact, though, don't individuals vary from 1:1500 to 1:3000?
A. There is some variance.
Q. Well, suppose we have an individual with a ratio of 1:1500 and an actual breath concentration of .0000476 gm/dl. What would be his true blood concentration?
A. Let's see. I believe it would be .07.
Q. And what would be the reading on this same person if the "normal" ratio were to be used?
A. It would be .10.
Q. Then a person who is, in fact, not under the influence — he would falsely be presumed by law to be under the influence?
A. In your hypothetical, yes.

Inherent Error

Q. Are you familiar with the concept of "acceptable analytical error"?
A. Yes. That is the composite of error which is inherent to the technique, together with error contributed by the analyst.
Q. What is acceptable analytical error in blood-alcohol analysis?
A. Plus or minus .01 percent.
Q. This means that my client's reading may be .12 rather than .13, and still be acceptable?
A. That's correct.
Q. It is simply *assumed* that this method of testing is *inherently* inaccurate?
A. Not inaccurate. There is simply a range of error inherent in the testing.

Stress

Q. Mr. Johnson, the accuracy of the reading is affected by the individual's pulmonary function, is it not?
A. It can be.
Q. Well, the accuracy depends on obtaining a sample of breath uncontaminated and undiluted from the lung's alveolar air sacs, doesn't it?
A. That's true.
Q. Supposing there was an accumulation of smog or other toxic substance in the lungs, wouldn't this affect pulmonary function and thus the sample's purity?
A. It could.
Q. Are you saying, then, that different readings could be obtained on

two individuals with equal amounts of alcohol in their system, but one living in the smog of Los Angeles, the other in the clean air of the desert?
A. That is a remote possibility.
Q. Now, assume that my client was rather shaken up by being arrested. What effect can this have on the human system?
A. Adrenal hormones will be secreted, particularly epinephrin and norepinephrin.
Q. This increases strength and energy?
A. Yes.
Q. And what effect, if any, on the capillary beds in the lungs?
A. The blood pressure and rate of blood flow would be increased.
Q. Wouldn't this radically alter the dynamic equilibrium between blood and breath within the alveolar air sacs?
A. Well, blood would pass through the lungs more quickly than normal.
Q. And couldn't this drastically alter the blood equivalent alcohol normally to be expected?
A. It could.
Q. Then, stress or excitement can result in an inaccurate blood-alcohol reading?
A. It's possible, I suppose.
Q. By the way, how much alveolar air is being analyzed by the machine?
A. One-fourth of a cubic centimeter.
Q. In terms we can understand — ounces or drops?
A. About five liquid drops.
Q. If there were .15 of one percent of alcohol in those five drops, how much alcohol would that represent — in ounces?
A. A few billionths of an ounce.
Q. Invisible to the eye?
A. Invisible.
Q. And that's what you are trying to measure here?
A. Yes.

Mouth Alcohol

Q. Mr. Johnson, what would be the effect of a subject belching or regurgitating just before breathing into the instrument?
A. I suppose alcoholic substances in his stomach could be lodged in, or coat the surface of, his throat and mouth area.
Q. Result on test?
A. He would be breathing alcohol vapors directly into the machine; it would cause an inaccurately high reading. But that is why we advise

the officers to keep the subject under observation for 15 minutes before testing him.

Q. But you do not personally know if this was done in my client's case?

A. No, I don't.

Q. One other matter, Mr. Johnson. What would be the effect of a subject having recently gargled with Listerine or sprayed his throat with a spray?

A. Well, most of them have alcohol in them, 25 percent or so. I suppose if it clung to the throat or mouth area long enough, it could result in the alcohol being exhaled into the instrument.

Q. And the reading?

A. It would be quite high, I would expect.

Q. These mouthwashes and sprays are designed to stay in the throat area for as long as possible, aren't they?

A. I wouldn't know.

Q. What about someone who had recently swallowed cough syrup for a sore throat?

A. Most of them have alcohol in them.

Q. And wouldn't their syrupy quality, designed as they are to cling to the throat lining, cause the liquid to stay in the throat area for a considerable period of time, even hours?

A. I wouldn't know how long.

Q. Again, this could cause a high reading on the breath instrument?

A. Yes, it could.

Q. Wouldn't this also be true of certain thick liqueurs, such as Kahlua?

A. To some extent, I suppose so.

Q. Then a person having only one drink of Kahlua may have a reading indicating he was under the influence?

A. It's possible, perhaps.

Nonspecific Analysis

Q. Now, sir, this machine, the Intoxilyzer. . . .

A. Yes?

Q. It is not specific for ethyl alcohol, is it? By that, I mean, it will detect substances other than alcohol?

A. It is acceptably specific.

Q. Acceptably? Does it, or does it not, detect chemical compounds other than ethyl alcohol?

A. It will detect a few other compounds.

Q. And these compounds will be registered as if they were ethyl alcohol?

A. It is possible, but it's highly unlikely they would be found in the breath.
Q. Sir, isn't it a fact that studies have shown that the average person may have over 100 different chemical compounds on his breath at any given time?
A. I really don't know.
Q. You *are* aware that 70 to 80 percent of all compounds on the human breath contain the methyl group in their molecular structures?
A. I am not aware of that, no.
Q. I see. Well, you know what the methyl group is?
A. Yes, that's a molecular unit, commonly found in chemical compounds.
Q. Quite common.
A. Yes.
Q. In fact, it is a part of such compounds as propane, butane, isopropyl alcohol, methane, ethane, ethyl chloride, acetic acid, butadiene, dimethylether, dimethylamine, dimethylhydrazine — to name but a very few of the many.
A. True.
Q. And ethyl alcohol as well — the compound found in liquor.
A. Correct.
Q. Now, you testified on direct exam that the Intoxilyzer detects ethyl alcohol by shooting infrared light through the breath sample.
A. Yes.
Q. And the more ethyl alcohol in the sample, the more infrared light or energy is absorbed, resulting in higher readings?
A. That's correct.
Q. The fact is, it is the methyl group in the ethyl alcohol compound that absorbs the energy — not the ethyl alcohol compound itself, isn't that so?
A. That's correct.
Q. So if there are any of these commonly encountered compounds that contain methyl groups, this Intoxilyzer will read them as ethyl alcohol?
A. If they were in the sample, yes.
Q. And the detection is cumulative, isn't it? That is, if there are ten or fifteen such compounds in the sample, the machine will, in effect, add them all up and then show them as ethyl alcohol?
A. In theory, yes.
Q. Is it just *theory,* sir, or does this machine actually detect *any* compound containing the methyl group as ethyl alcohol — even if it is not?
A. It will, yes, counselor.

Q. And you are not aware that 70 to 80 percent of all compounds on the human breath contain the methyl group?
A. I am not familiar with those studies, as I have already indicated.
Q. Do you know what acetone is?
A. Yes.
Q. That is a compound containing the methyl group, isn't it?
A. That's correct.
Q. And the machine will read this acetone and register it as ethyl alcohol?
A. If it were in the breath sample.
Q. The fact is, sir, acetone is commonly found on the breath, is it not?
A. I don't know if I would say "commonly."
Q. Diabetics usually have acetone on their breath, don't they?
A. I believe so.
Q. And anyone who is on a diet may have acetone on his or her breath?
A. I've heard that.
Q. And even ordinary people under ordinary circumstances can have acetone on their breath?
A. I'm not a physician.
Q. But you are apparently an expert in the area of blood-alcohol analysis.
A. Correct.
Q. So, please tell us, if Mr. Kelly had 525 micrograms per liter of acetone in his breath, how would this affect the reading on the Intoxilyzer?
A. I really don't know.
Q. In fact, it would raise it by approximately .03 percent, wouldn't it? So that a true .08, for example, would read .11?
A. I said I don't know.
Q. You *are* an expert in blood-alcohol analysis?
A. That's correct.
Q. Sir, you are aware that the manufacturer of the Intoxilyzer Model 5000 subsequently came out with a newer, improved version?
A. Newer, yes.
Q. And this newer model has an acetone detector, does it not?
A. I believe so.
Q. Does the old one?
A. No.
Q. And the new 5000 also uses three bands of infrared light, does it not?
A. That's my understanding.
Q. This makes it more specific for ethyl alcohol than the old model used in this case, doesn't it?

A. More specific, yes.
Q. By the way, this newer Model 5000 also has a radio frequency interference detector, too, doesn't it?
A. I think so.
Q. Does the machine used in this case have one?
A. You know it does not, counselor.

Absorptive State

Q. Mr. Johnson, was the breath test administered to my client during his *absorptive phase?*
A. Absorptive phase?
Q. The body continues to absorb alcohol for 45 minutes to 2 or 3 hours after drinking, right?
A. Oh, yes. Well, I could not tell you if he was in his absorptive phase.
Q. You do not know.
A. No.
Q. Yet you will agree that a breath test given during this absorptive phase may be inaccurately high?
A. I'm not aware of that.
Q. You *are* aware that while alcohol is still absorbing into the body — before it reaches equilibrium — the distribution throughout the body will not be uniform?
A. Yes.
Q. In other words, the alcohol level will be higher in some parts of the body than in others.
A. That could be true.
Q. In particular, there will be a higher concentration of alcohol in the arteries than in the veins, right?
A. I believe that's correct.
Q. And it's the arteries that feed the lung with blood, right?
A. Yes.
Q. And the alcohol from this arterial blood diffuses across the air sacs in the lungs into the breath?
A. That's correct.
Q. So, during this 45 minutes to 2 or 3 hours, the alcohol in the breath will be more concentrated than in the rest of the body?
A. I suppose that's possible.
Q. And the breath sample would give an inaccurately high result?
A. I suppose it could happen.
Q. You recognize Dr. Kurt Dubowski as the leading expert in the U.S. today on blood-alcohol analysis?
A. I think that's fair to say.

Q. Do you agree with his statement, that "When a blood test is allowed, an administered breath test is discriminatory, because in law enforcement practice the status of absorption is always uncertain." Do you agree?
A. Breath testing is an acceptable, reliable method of blood-alcohol testing.
Q. Do you agree with Dr. Dubowski that breath testing should never be used if blood tests are available?
A. No.

Blood Analysis

Q. Mr. Johnson, was the blood sample drawn from my client during his *absorptive phase?*
A. I could not tell you.
Q. You do not know.
A. No.
Q. Yet you will agree that a breath test given during this absorptive phase may be inaccurately high?
A. I'm not aware of that.
Q. You *are* aware that while alcohol is still absorbing into the body — before it reaches equilibrium — the distribution throughout the body will not be uniform?
A. Yes.
Q. In other words, the alcohol level will be higher in some parts of the body than in others.
A. That could be true.
Q. In particular, there will be a higher concentration of alcohol in the arteries than in the veins, right?
A. I believe that's correct.
Q. Incidentally, was this sample taken from the artery or the vein?
A. I couldn't say. I wasn't there.
Q. Well, it was drawn from the artery rather than the vein, it could have a higher blood-alcohol concentration, couldn't it?
A. Possibly.
Q. Mr. Johnson, was there acetone in my client's blood?
A. I don't know. Some people have it, some don't.
Q. If there is acetone in the blood, is it removed before testing?
A. It is usually filtered out.
Q. If the acetone is not filtered successfully, how will the acetone show up in the final test?

A. It will appear as additional alcohol.
Q. Now, you've mentioned the dichromate and the titrating solutions; were the amounts used measured and standardized each day before use?
A. Not each day, but they were measured and standardized accurately.
Q. But isn't daily standardization the most accurate method?
A. Yes.
Q. And if the amount or standardization were inaccurate, wouldn't the blood-alcohol reading also be inaccurate?
A. That's true.
Q. How many tests of my client's blood sample were run?
A. One.
Q. Only one? Doesn't your laboratory make a practice of running two tests in *felony* cases?
A. That's true.
Q. Why?
A. To detect any possible error.
Q. Then if there was an error in the testing of my client's sample, we would not know about it?
A. If there was an error.
Q. Now, Mr. Johnson, I presume you were the technician who analyzed my client's blood sample?
A. I was, according to the records.
Q. You don't recall analyzing the specimen?
A. Counselor, I analyze hundreds of such specimens every week.
Q. Then you don't remember actually analyzing his particular blood specimen?
A. It was one of probably two or three dozen I did that day. We're rather busy at the lab. I have to analyze them in batches.
Q. Batches?
A. Yes, I run a half-dozen specimens through at a time.
Q. But doesn't this increase the risk of error in analysis or recordkeeping?
A. Slightly, perhaps. But it's necessary due to the volume of work.
Q. Who withdrew the blood sample from my client?
A. I believe Nurse Fleming did.
Q. And in withdrawing it, what type of antiseptic was used in the swab?
A. I don't know.
Q. Well, normally, nurses use an alcohol swab before inserting a hypodermic needle, do they not?

A. Normally, but not where a blood sample is being taken for alcohol analysis.
Q. If my client's arm was swabbed with alcohol, wouldn't it affect the analysis?
A. Yes.
Q. In fact, if even an infinitesimal amount of alcohol on the skin from the swab were to contaminate the sample, the reading could jump from .00 to .20 or .30, could it not?
A. If alcohol were used.
Q. And we do not know that it wasn't?
A. I do not know.
Q. Mr. Johnson, had the needle and syringe been sterilized and kept under sterile conditions before use on my client?
A. I presume so.
Q. But you don't know?
A. No, I don't know.
Q. And the blood sample — when did your laboratory receive the sample?
A. I believe it was July seventh.
Q. Three days after the sample was extracted.
A. Apparently.
Q. Do you know where the sample lay for those three days?
A. No, I don't. A refrigerator at the hospital, I would guess.
Q. But, again, you don't know?
A. That's right.
Q. Blood can decompose like any other organic matter, can it not?
A. Of course.
Q. And isn't it a fact that as blood decomposes, alcohol is chemically created?
A. That can be an effect of decomposition.
Q. If the sample were refrigerated — and, of course, we don't know that it ever was — wouldn't that simply slow down decomposition?
A. Yes.
Q. It wouldn't *stop* it — merely slow it down?
A. That's correct, but it would be slowed down to almost nil.
Q. Isn't it standard practice to add a preservative to the blood specimen?
A. Yes. Something like sodium fluoride.
Q. Do you know if this was done in the present case?
A. I don't recall. I'll have to check the records.
Q. Was an anticoagulant added?
A. I believe it was. Potassium oxalate.
Q. Can't all of these chemicals — sodium fluoride, potassium oxalate,

the swabbing solution — can't they all have a side effect on the blood?
A. Negligible.
Q. Do you know what *amounts* of preservative and anticoagulant, if any, were used?
A. I said I don't recall. I assume some were added, as that's the standard procedure, but I don't know and I wouldn't know the amounts either.
Q. You said potassium oxalate was added — how much?
A. I would have to check.
Q. The amount is critical, is it not?
A. You need enough, yes.
Q. If there is not enough anticoagulant, ethyl alcohol may be concentrated in the serum above the clot?
A. Possibly.
Q. And if there is not enough preservative, bacteria could grow — creating ethyl alcohol?
A. Possibly.
Q. Yet too much preservative or anticoagulant can also cause erroneous readings?
A. Possibly.
Q. Now, you testified you used the microdiffusion method of blood analysis?
A. That's correct.
Q. Did you calibrate the pipets, burets, and volumetric flasks?
A. That is done by lab personnel.
Q. Do you know for a fact that it was done with the equipment used in testing Mr. Kelly's blood sample?
A. Not personally, of course not.
Q. Improperly calibrated equipment could cause false results, isn't that so?
A. If improperly calibrated, yes.
Q. And did you clean all the glassware, including the microdiffusion flasks?
A. Counselor, that's not my job.
Q. You did not?
A. I did not — but I'm sure it was done.
Q. But you cannot testify that it was done — or done correctly?
A. No.
Q. Incomplete cleaning, or leaving a residue of soap or detergent, could affect accuracy, right?
A. It could, if it happened.
Q. Now, did you check the purity of the reagent?

A. Again, that's not my job.
Q. Impure or adulterated potassium dichromate or sulfuric acid could affect the accuracy of the analysis?
A. It could.
Q. And an impure or contaminated reducing agent?
A. That could also have an effect, if the agent were impure or contaminated — which I very much doubt.
Q. But you simply don't know.
A. I cannot testify. . . . No, I don't know for a fact.
Q. Now, sir, are you familiar with a study of the accuracy of blood-alcohol laboratories around the country?
A. Yes, you sent it to me last week, counselor.
Q. That is report number DOT-JS-806-193, Department of Transportation?
A. All right.
Q. And did not that study report that a significant number of laboratories analyzing blood and urine samples were unacceptably unreliable in their analysis?
A. I believe that was a finding.
Q. In fact, these laboratories produced test results in which fully one-third were off by more than 20 percent?
A. I believe that's right.

Urinalysis

Q. Mr. Johnson, have you read the U.S. Department of Transportation's Highway Safety Program Manual No. 8, issued by the National Highway Traffic and Safety Administration?
A. I have heard of it.
Q. Do you recall this statement in that manual? "Because of various problems in the interpretation of the results of analysis of urine for alcohol which cannot be readily overcome in law enforcement practice, urine analysis to determine equivalent alcohol concentration in blood is discouraged. . . ."
A. No, I do not recall reading it.
Q. In your opinion, which is the more accurate, blood analysis or urinalysis?
A. Blood analysis is the most accurate.
Q. Now, the blood-alcohol ratio of .15 that you've arrived at is based on the premise that the concentration of alcohol in the urine at the time it is secreted in the kidneys is approximately 1.3 times that in the circulating blood, is that correct?

A. Yes, that is correct.
Q. The ratio of 1:1.3 represents the *average* blood-urine ratio, does it not?
A. Yes.
Q. But isn't it true that normal, healthy individuals may vary from 1:0.8 to 1:2 or even more?
A. There is some individual variance.
Q. Well, now, let's assume that my client's tested urine alcohol was .20. What would be the blood-alcohol reading applying the average blood-urine ratio of 1:1.3?
A. About .15, as is the case here.
Q. And what would be the reading if my client had an individual blood-urine ratio of 1:2?
A. It would be about .09.
Q. Do you mean that the urine sample you analyzed in this case may contain only .09 percent alcohol?
A. It's possible, but not likely.
Q. Now, alcohol acts as a diuretic when consumed, altering body fluid salt concentration, does it not?
A. That's true.
Q. And fluctuation of salt content can cause hydration or dehydration to some degree?
A. Yes.
Q. And if there is hydration or dehydration, is not the urine-alcohol ratio invalidated?
A. Hydration or dehydration can have an effect.
Q. I see. Urine secreted in the kidneys is continuously draining into the urinary bladder, is it not?
A. That's correct.
Q. Then the pool of urine found in the bladder at any given time represents the accumulation of urine secreted since the last emptying of the bladder, does it not?
A. Yes.
Q. Then isn't the alcoholic content of a specimen taken from the bladder urine really a composite of the different blood-alcohol levels over that period of time?
A. Yes. But the subject is normally asked to void his bladder, then wait 20 minutes before giving a true sample.
Q. Isn't it a fact that it is *impossible* to completely void the bladder?
A. I don't know if it's impossible.
Q. Most individuals can't do it though, can they?
A. Not entirely.

Q. In fact, there's usually about 10 cc of urine left after a so-called "complete" void, right?
A. I believe that's correct.
Q. And there is usually about 1 cc of fresh urine dripping into the bladder per minute?
A. I believe so.
Q. So, over the next 20 minutes, the individual will produce about 20 cc of new urine in the bladder?
A. Yes.
Q. Well, then, the sample that you analyze will *not* be fresh urine, will it?
A. Not entirely.
Q. In fact, it will be about 10 cc old urine and 20 cc new urine — or about one-third old urine, right?
A. Roughly.
Q. So the test would be contaminated by alcohol that may have been consumed hours before driving — alcohol that had long since burned off?
A. That could be.
Q. In fact, if my client had stopped drinking three or four hours before he was tested and was not under the influence at the time of testing, the analysis could indicate he was under the influence at the time of testing?
A. That's possible.
Q. Now, suppose a subject did not wash his hands before handling the vial to urinate in it. Could this cause any contamination?
A. It could.
Q. If he had some form of reducing agent on his hands, from paint, turpentine, or some other compound, this could cause a reduction of the potassium dichromate, couldn't it?
A. It could.
Q. How would this affect the reading?
A. It would elevate the blood-alcohol reading.
Q. Sir, isn't it true that bacteria may be present in the vial into which the subject urinates?
A. Yes, that's why we add an antibacterial agent, such as sodium fluoride or mercuric chloride. This kills the bacteria.
Q. And there may also be bacteria in the urine itself, as it is introduced into the vial?
A. The additive will kill this bacteria as well.
Q. If the bacteria is *not* all killed, a process of fermentation will take place, will it not?

A. If bacteria are present, yes.
Q. And the result of this fermentation of organic matter is the production of ethyl alcohol?
A. Yes.
Q. This is the same process of fermentation that we use to create wine, beer, or liquor?
A. Basically, yes. But of course any bacteria in the urine is killed.
Q. What of aerobic bacteria in the urine? Won't they utilize oxidizing substances and then leave the urine with a preponderance of reducing substances — before the antibacterial agent is added?
A. That's possible.
Q. What would the result be on the blood-alcohol reading?
A. It may elevate the reading.
Q. Have you heard of the organism called *Candida albicans?*
A. I have heard of it. A yeast, I believe.
Q. It is found in the urine, is it not?
A. It can be, yes.
Q. And its presence can cause fermentation, resulting in the production of ethyl alcohol?
A. Yes.
Q. And this can occur in both the bladder and in the vial?
A. I suppose so.
Q. In fact, sir, isn't it true that *Candida albicans* is resistant to such antibacterial compounds as sodium fluoride?
A. I've heard that. You sent me some material last week concerning a Dr. Richard Jensen.
Q. Are you familiar with an article entitled "Bladder Beer — A New Clinical Observation," in volume 95 of the Transactions of the American Clinical Association?
A. You sent it to me last week, yes.
Q. And didn't physicians in that study discuss subjects who had urine samples containing substantial amounts of alcohol — but who had not actually consumed any alcohol?
A. That's what the article says,
Q. And this was believed due to fermentation?
A. Apparently.
Q. So it's possible Mr. Kelly's urine sample, by the time you analyzed it, contained alcohol produced by fermentation in the bladder or in the vial?
A. It's possible, I suppose.
Q. You have no way of knowing, do you?
A. I cannot say for sure one way or the other, no.

Q. Now, as I understand your testimony, Mr. Kelly's urine sample was analyzed by you using gas chromatography, correct?
A. Yes, headspace chromatography.
Q. An impure or incorrect internal standard could give a false result, couldn't it?
A. If it were impure or incorrect.
Q. You did not personally check the quality or quantity, did you?
A. Not personally, no.
Q. And impure or contaminated "salting out" chemicals can also cause errors?
A. Again, if they existed.
Q. And again, you cannot testify they did *not* exist?
A. I cannot.
Q. And if any of the glassware used were not properly cleaned, or had detergent residue?
A. This could cause problems, I suppose.
Q. You do not clean the glassware you use?
A. This is done by lab personnel.
Q. What if the wrong type or amount of carrier gas was used?
A. Again, it could adversely affect the results.
Q. And a faulty regulator controlling gas flow?
A. Yes. Error.
Q. Improper column temperature control?
A. Again, if it existed, and there is no evidence here that it did, it could affect the reading.
Q. There is also no evidence it did *not* exist, is there?
A. I cannot say, counselor.
Q. What if there were a dirty or erratic detector?
A. It could cause problems.
Q. A malfunctioning circuit board?
A. All of these things could cause erroneous readings, yes.
Q. Improper grounding?
A. Yes.
Q. Faulty connection between the chromatograph and the recorder or printer?
A. Yes.
Q. Improper settings on the recorder or printer?
A. Again, yes.
Q. Well, sir, actually there appear to be any number of things that could cause erroneous blood-alcohol readings in Mr. Kelly's urine sample, don't there?
A. In theory.

§13.5 The Percipient Witness

> It is more from carelessness about the truth, than from intention of lying, that there is so much falsehood in the world.
>
> SAMUEL JOHNSON

In a relatively few drunk driving cases, the observations of the police officer will be supplemented by the testimony of percipient private citizens. In the vast majority of such situations, the case will involve a traffic accident of some type: Either the defendant struck another vehicle, or he collided with a stationary object such as a traffic light or telephone pole. In these cases, the testimony of such witnesses is not only supplemental to the arresting officer's testimony but will be necessary to establishing the driving element of the *corpus delicti,* assuming that the officer arrived on the scene after the accident.

In almost all jurisdictions, the opinion of a lay witness is admissible on the issue of intoxication. The reason for this is that it is felt that the average person has sufficient personal experience with drinking and/or with observing drinkers to offer an opinion. Counsel, however, should initially take a two-pronged attack relevant to this opinion: first, attempt to keep the opinion out on foundational grounds; and, failing in this, attempt to establish on cross-examination the witness's lack of ability to recognize an individual under the influence.

Counsel should make a motion, either before the trial or during a foundational challenge at the inception of the testimony, to preclude the giving of an opinion by the witness. The witness should, it must be argued, be limited to testifying as to what he observed — that is, flushed face, staggering gait, or whatever, and prohibited from rendering an opinion or conclusion as to the defendant's legal condition. That condition is, after all, the ultimate issue in the trial: It is for the jury to determine after hearing all of the evidence. Most important, however, the witness is simply not qualified to give such an opinion; he may be incapable of judging whether an individual is "under the influence." This can be pointed out very easily by conducting voir dire of the witness and asking him to explain the difference between "drunk" and "under the influence"; very few private citizens will be able to. If the judge insists on instructing the witness as to the legal definition of "under the influence," the witness still will be hard pressed to explain the difference between "inability to care for one's self and for the safety of others" (a common definition of "public drunk") and "inability to safely operate a motor vehicle" (a common definition of "under the influence"). Certainly, a careful cross-examination as to the comparative symptoms of the two states of inebriation should illustrate clearly the witness's understandable confusion.

If the court rules that the witness nevertheless may give his opinion to the jury, counsel must then establish the expertise of that opinion. Again, the witness's inability to discern legally or symptomatically the difference between a person who is drunk and one who is under the influence must be pointed out graphically. Much of what has already been discussed in earlier chapters relevant to cross-examination of the arresting officer will apply to the lay witness as well. Counsel's best tactics involve bringing out possible innocent explanations for symptoms of intoxication. Here, however, counsel will have a considerably easier time of it: The witness is a novice, inexperienced both at recognizing a drunk driver and at testifying in court. In addition, psychological considerations, including issues of motive, bias, or prejudice, will enter the picture.

The physical condition of both the eyewitness and the scene of the observation may serve to be a limiting factor in the witness's ability to view accurately and to recollect rationally. It is a rare situation where the witness, even with perfect physiological faculties, calmly observes under perfect conditions an exciting incident, one probably involving the witness directly, and has the presence of mind to note details for purposes of future testimony. Therefore, the visual capabilities of the witness and the physical limitations of the scene of the incident should be explored thoroughly in preparing cross-examination.

The information supplied by the witness to the police should be carefully considered as sources for impeachment: The more detail the witness will commit himself to, the more opportunity for error. And it is the rare witness who can supply accurate, detailed information to the police. Descriptions of the defendant's clothing and condition, of the car's make, model, and year, etc., should not be overlooked. If a witness is inaccurate in one area, the jury will be more receptive to the idea that he is inaccurate in another. In reviewing a police report for such information given by a witness, however, it should be kept in mind that officers sometimes leave out details that prove erroneous.

The emotional condition of the witness is a relatively safe ground for inquiry. In most drunk driving cases involving a citizen witness, the witness will have been involved in a traffic accident of some sort with the defendant; if not directly involved, he will probably have witnessed such an accident. As a result, he will probably have made his observations of the defendant and formed any opinions as to sobriety while under the influence of an emotional reaction to the accident. Anger, fear, or simple excitement, all normal reactions, can affect an individual's ability to observe, conclude, and later recollect rationally. If the individual was injured in the accident, even slightly, there is the possible presence of trauma or shock, rendering any observations almost meaningless. Every attempt should be made to establish that the witness was excited, nervous, angry, or frightened. Should the witness defensively deny any emotional reaction during the incident, the jury may disbelieve the absence of such a normal reaction, and his credibility will suffer accordingly.

The very nature of the crime observed may have an effect on the witness's testimony. Having helplessly watched previous drunk drivers or criminal offenders generally, the witness may feel anger and a resultant hatred toward the suspected offender in the instant case. A sense of frustration from living in a world of seemingly unpunished crime and violence may cause a witness to want to testify against someone; his impotence in the face of years of crime is salved by finally punishing one of "them."

Counsel should never overlook the possibility that the witness has had a bad past experience with a drunk driver. It is an all-too-common occurrence to encounter a witness who has lost a friend, relative, or loved one at some time to a drunken driver. This should, of course, be brought out sympathetically. If counsel is to make the suggestion that this experience may have colored the witness's observations and testimony, he should do so with considerable tact.

The implanting of suggestion is yet another ever-present consideration. In subtle, perhaps not even conscious, ways the police can indicate to a witness their own personal beliefs as to intoxication, symptoms, etc. The simple phrasing of a question, for example, can subconsciously direct the witness toward a desired answer.

The wish to help is a factor that can influence a witness's testimony. Feeling an urge to render assistance to authority figures, the witness is again predisposed to offer damning evidence. After giving information tentatively at the time of the incident, he becomes more convinced of the defendant's intoxication as he is questioned by police officers and, later, the prosecutor. Related to this is the witness who craves attention, who wants to be liked, and needs to feel important. An inability to affirm a suspect's intoxicated condition will mean to the witness that he will not receive the attention he craves; by pointing to the defendant, he becomes the star witness.

Finally, counsel must not overlook the possibility of outright perjury. There can be a number of reasons why a witness will lie willfully on the stand, but the most common motive in a drunk driving case involves a traffic collision. If the witness and the defendant were involved in an accident that gave rise to the criminal charges, two possible motives clearly stand out. First, the witness may expect to gain financially; in most jurisdictions, a criminal conviction is admissible on the issue of fault and would be determinative in a legal action filed by the witness against the defendant. Second, the witness simply may wish to cause injury to the defendant; injured physically or financially himself by the defendant in the accident, he now wants retribution. These obvious motives for lying should, of course, be brought out very clearly for the jury.

§13.5.1 Illustrative Cross-Examination: The Percipient Witness

Q. Mr. Jensen, you are the only person to have seen my client, Mr. Kelly, driving his automobile on the evening of his arrest, are you not?

A. Yes, I suppose so.

Q. And you are the only person, besides Mr. Kelly, to have witnessed the accident between his car and yours, at least the only one to have come forward to testify?

A. That's right.

Q. And it is your testimony that Mr. Kelly ran through a red light and

struck you while you were proceeding on a green light through the intersection?
A. Yes, that is my testimony, sir.

Perception

Q. Mr. Jensen, I see you are carrying glasses today?
A. Yes.
Q. I presume you were wearing them at the time of the accident?
A. Well, no. But I don't really need them; I only use them for reading.
Q. They are bifocals, are they not?
A. Yes.
Q. And what are the upper halves of the lenses for?
A. My doctor seemed to think I needed them for astigmatism, but I don't.
Q. Astigmatism? You mean, to assist you in seeing people and objects like cars and traffic lights?
A. I suppose so. But I don't need them, except for reading.
Q. What is your vision today, uncorrected?
A. Uh, well, I don't know.
Q. What was it when your optometrist last examined you?
A. I don't recall.
Q. Was it 20/20?
A. No, it wasn't 20/20.
Q. It was less than that?
A. I guess so.
Q. According to your optometrist, then, your vision is impaired?
A. That's what he says. But I can see fine.
Q. When was the last time you saw your optometrist?
A. Well, about two years ago, I think.
Q. Two years. And you've had no corrective treatment since then?
A. No.
Q. Astigmatism is often degenerative, that is, it tends to get worse if not corrected, does it not?
A. I wouldn't know. Like I said, I can see just fine.
Q. Do you have a current driver's license?
A. Sure.
Q. Does the license specify that you are required to wear corrective lenses when you drive?
A. It says that, but it's not true.
Q. Mr. Jensen, isn't it possible that *you* were the one who had entered the intersection against the traffic light because you didn't see it?
A. No, it is not.

Opinion as to Intoxication

Q. You've testified that, in your opinion, Mr. Kelly was drunk at the time he collided with your vehicle.
A. I have, and it's true.
Q. Mr. Kelly was drunk at the time of the accident?
A. He most certainly was.
Q. Then I presume he was also under the influence?
A. I beg your pardon?
Q. You *do* understand the difference between "drunk" and "under the influence"?
A. Well . . .
Q. Mr. Jensen, what *is* the difference?
A. I . . . I thought it was the same thing.
Q. No one from the police department or prosecutor's office has advised you exactly what constitutes "under the influence"?
A. Well, no.
Q. Then you are not familiar with the meaning of "under the influence" as opposed to "drunk"?
A. Uh, I guess not.
Q. Then you cannot really say whether Mr. Kelly was under the influence or not, can you?
A. I could tell he'd been drinking something.
Q. But you couldn't tell whether he was "under the influence" of alcohol?
A. Well, maybe not. I'm not sure what you mean.
Q. Have *you* ever felt, well, "tipsy" from drinking alcoholic beverages, Mr. Jensen?
A. Sure. I guess everybody has.
Q. And have you ever driven a vehicle while you were tipsy?
A. Of course not. It's against the law.
Q. Never?
A. Never.
Q. Then how can you testify that you felt my client was too intoxicated to drive safely?
A. What do you mean?
Q. Well, if you have never experienced what it's like to drive while intoxicated, how do you know at what point drinking will make driving a vehicle unsafe?
A. Well, you don't have to be a drunk to recognize one.
Q. Mr. Jensen, do you frequent bars, taverns, or cocktail lounges?
A. No, I do not.
Q. Do you engage in heavy drinking with friends or associates?

A. No, I do not.
Q. Do you often find yourself in places where heavy drinking is going on?
A. I stay away from places like that.
Q. I see. But you consider yourself an expert at recognizing symptoms of intoxication?
A. I can recognize a drunk when I see one.
Q. Yes, but can you recognize someone who is "under the influence"?
A. Sure.

Emotional Condition at the Scene

Q. Mr. Jensen, I presume you were a little shaken up after the accident.
A. You bet I was. I had to go to the hospital later for a checkup.
Q. You were upset, nervous?
A. Wouldn't you be?
Q. Frightened?
A. You bet. I was still shaking after the officer finished questioning me. You don't have someone smashing into you every day.
Q. Is it possible that you were suffering from shock?
A. Maybe. The doctor said I could have had some mild shock.
Q. Were you angry at being involved in a collision?
A. Of course I was.
Q. You were frightened, nervous, angry — and possibly suffering from shock.
A. Yes.
Q. Yet you were able to carefully observe Mr. Kelly, analyze his symptoms, and conclude that he was intoxicated?
A. Yes.
Q. The officer questioned you at the scene of the accident?
A. Yes, he did.
Q. This was before he questioned Mr. Kelly, wasn't it?
A. After.
Q. After he questioned Mr. Kelly. Then I presume the officer told you that he thought Mr. Kelly was intoxicated.
A. Yes, as a matter of fact, he did. He agreed with my opinion.
Q. And, of course, the officer is an expert on these matters, is he not?
A. He sure is.
Q. So the officer — the expert — told you at the scene that Mr. Kelly was under the influence of alcohol?
A. That's right.
Q. And you didn't disagree with him?
A. No, I didn't.

Q. And you don't disagree with his expert opinion today?
A. No, I don't.
Q. Hypothetically, Mr. Jensen, if you had felt Mr. Kelly was not intoxicated, and this officer had said he was — which of you do you think would most probably be right?
A. Well, the officer, I guess. He's the expert.
Q. But he told you he thought Mr. Kelly was under the influence, and you agreed with him?
A. Yes, that's right.
Q. And you're sticking to that, right?
A. I sure am.

Motive and Bias

Q. Have you ever had a close friend or relative injured in an accident with a drunk driver?
A. Thank God, no.
Q. You've read about such cases, of course?
A. Of course.
Q. Have you ever wished you could get your hands on one of those drunk drivers that cause so much harm to others?
A. Sure, I guess everyone has.
Q. How do you feel toward Mr. Kelly today?
A. Toward him? Nothing, really.
Q. What did you feel toward him after the accident? Anger?
A. Anger? Sure, I was angry.
Q. Did you feel any desire to seek revenge against him — to get back at him for what he'd done to you?
A. Well, maybe so. Anyone would, I guess.
Q. Would you want to cause damage to him by testifying against him in court?
A. I'm testifying because I was subpoenaed. I'm not trying to get any revenge.
Q. Then you're no longer angry at Mr. Kelly for causing the accident?
A. Well, no, not really.
Q. It's forgive and forget?
A. Yes, I suppose so.
Q. I see. By the way, Mr. Jensen, don't you have a lawsuit pending against Mr. Kelly?
A. Well, yes.
Q. You are suing him as a result of this automobile collision?
A. That's right.
Q. And how much are you suing him for?

A. Ten thousand dollars.
Q. Ten thousand dollars?
A. Ten thousand dollars.
Q. One of the reasons you're asking for damages, according to the complaint, is because you continue to suffer emotional damage. Is that true?
A. Well, yes. That's true.
Q. But you're no longer angry at Mr. Kelly?
A. No.
Q. Forgive and forget?
A. I suppose.
Q. This lawsuit you've filed — it's based on an allegation that Mr. Kelly was driving under the influence of alcohol, is it not?
A. That's right.
Q. Then the success of your lawsuit pretty much depends on being able to prove that he was intoxicated?
A. I suppose so.
Q. If you can prove Mr. Kelly was intoxicated, you can win ten thousand dollars.
A. Well, I don't know if I would put it that way.
Q. How would you put it?
A. Well, the lawsuit — I mean, that's up to a jury, isn't it? I just want what I deserve.

14

THE DEFENSE

§14.0 The Sobriety Witness

> Truth is forever absolute, but opinion is truth filtered through the moods, the blood, the disposition of the spectator.
>
> WENDELL PHILLIPS

The ideal witness is one who was in the car when the defendant was pulled over and subsequently arrested. That witness will be able to testify as to the defendant's driving, his objective symptoms (clear speech, nonalcoholic breath, etc.), and general sobriety. (Lay opinion on the issue of intoxication, it should be remembered, is generally admissible.) Additionally, the witness will be able to testify as to the circumstances under which the field sobriety tests were given and how the defendant actually performed. If the officer takes the defendant some distance away or orders the witness to stay away, the obvious conclusion for the jury will be that the officer did not want any witnesses.

One common reaction to such a witness by the police officer at trial is to claim that the witness was as inebriated as the defendant. Counsel should be prepared for this and should determine whether the officer had followed the common procedure of turning the keys to the defendant's car over to the witness in order to avoid the problem of impounding the vehicle. If he did, point out that it is obvious that no officer would turn a vehicle over to an intoxicated person to drive home. Even if this procedure was not followed, it should be noted that nothing in the police report indicates the witness was under the influence. In any event, the witness was not arrested for being drunk.

If the witness had been with the defendant during the hours prior to the arrest, he becomes the rare "perfect" witness. He can testify to how many drinks, if any, the defendant consumed in the relevant hours before the arrest. There is a very real danger here, however. The perfect witness can become a disaster if it develops that he and/or the defendant had consumed "a few." The prosecutor will undoubtedly attempt to establish that the witness is a drinking buddy of the defendant's, a "bar fly" who had downed a number of drinks with the defendant prior to the arrest. Certainly, if the witness had been drinking more than socially in the company of the defendant, counsel should be aware of this and probably decline to call him to the stand.

Beyond the ideal witness who is percipient to the arrest, there are witnesses who are percipient to circumstantial facts. Included within this category would be a friend with whom the defendant had had dinner an hour before the arrest, a fellow arrestee in the defendant's cell, or a relative or bail bondsman who observed him within an hour or so after the arrest.

A word about *character witnesses*. The first suggestion the client is likely to make to his lawyer in a drunk driving case is to put on the stand a series of witnesses to testify to what a great guy he is. The client assumes that once it is firmly established that he is a sterling and respected member of the community and has not touched alcohol in years, no jury in the world will convict him of drunk driving.

Of course, this simply is not true. Not only is the value of character witnesses overrated, but there is an inherent danger in their use at all. By concentrating on the general character of the defendant, the jury may very well conclude that the defense is impliedly admitting his guilt. The typical juror may be thinking to himself that the defense would not spend so much time on the collateral issue of character if it had a strong case on the direct issue of whether he was intoxicated at the time of his arrest. A variation on an old legal saying may be subconsciously in the jury's mind: If the facts are on your side, argue facts; if the law is on your side, argue law; if neither the law nor the facts are on your side, argue character.

§14.0.1 Illustrative Direct Examination of Sobriety Witness

Observed Drinking

Q. Now, Mr. Adams, on the evening of January seventh of this year, were you at any time with my client, Mr. Kelly?
A. I was.
Q. Where was this?
A. At the Hofbrau Restaurant.
Q. For what purpose were you with Mr. Kelly?
A. We had a business meeting, and we ended up having dinner there.
Q. I see. And when did you first meet Mr. Kelly that evening at the Hofbrau?
A. Oh, it was about seven o'clock, something like that. The appointment was for six-thirty, but I was late.
Q. And when did you finally leave his company later that same evening?
A. Around nine-thirty.
Q. Now, during that period of two or two-and-a-half hours, you were alone with Mr. Kelly?
A. We had one other business associate with us, but yes, the three of us were alone.
Q. And you observed Mr. Kelly to eat a meal during that two to two-and-a-half-hour period?
A. That's correct.
Q. Now, before the dinner, were any of the three of you drinking alcoholic beverages?
A. Yes. I believe I had a martini, and Mr. Kelly had a martini also, as I recall. Our mutual friend had a glass of wine.
Q. And this was about what time?
A. Oh, it must have been about seven-thirty or so — just before dinner.
Q. Now, as you know, Mr. Kelly was arrested later that evening at nine-thirty. So this drink was taken by Mr. Kelly about two hours before his arrest?
A. Yes.
Q. Incidentally, was this a double martini we're talking about?
A. Oh, no. In fact, the drinks were all rather small.
Q. All right. Were you aware, by the way, if Mr. Kelly had consumed any other drinks before meeting you that night?
A. I can't say for sure, but I doubt it. I'd called him at his office at six-thirty, and he was still there. To my knowledge, they don't permit drinking where he works, that is, at the bank.

Q. In any event, did Mr. Kelly appear to you to be under the influence of alcohol when you met him at seven?
A. Absolutely not.
Q. No alcoholic odor on his breath?
A. No.
Q. Fine. Now, were any more alcoholic beverages consumed after that first round?
A. Let's see. No more cocktails. As I recall, we went into the dining room and had dinner. Yes, with dinner we shared a bottle of wine, a cabernet sauvignon, in fact. We each had a glass.
Q. So Mr. Kelly consumed a glass of wine with his meal?
A. That's right. One full glass.
Q. And were there any further drinks taken by any of the three of you that evening?
A. I believe our mutual friend had an after-dinner Grand Marnier. But Mr. Kelly, no.
Q. And you and Mr. Kelly parted company at about nine-thirty?
A. That's right.
Q. At about the time he was arrested?
A. Yes. Of course, I didn't see that. It took place a few blocks from the Hofbrau.
Q. But apparently Mr. Kelly had no time to have another drink elsewhere before being arrested.
A. I wouldn't think so.
Q. Your testimony, then, Mr. Adams, is that between about seven and nine-thirty on the evening of the arrest, you witnessed Mr. Kelly consume a single martini — small in size — and a glass of wine with his dinner. Is that correct?
A. That's correct.
Q. And he consumed no other alcoholic drinks during that time?
A. None.

Intoxication

Q. Very well. Now, have you ever seen a person who is under the influence of alcohol, Mr. Adams?
A. Of course. Many times.
Q. Have you, in fact, been under the influence at some time yourself?
A. Most of us have, but yes, I have.
Q. What is it about a person's appearance or manner that indicates he's under the influence?
A. Well, his speech changes, gets slurred slightly. And he begins to have

trouble with his balance and, well, his eyes and face get a little red. And his eyelids get heavy. The coordination will be a little off, too.

Q. Do you understand the legal distinction between "drunk" and "under the influence"?

A. Yes. You explained it to me. "Drunk" is a more severe stage of intoxication, as I understand it, where the person has trouble even caring for himself. Falling down, that kind of thing. "Under the influence" involves an impaired ability to operate a car.

Q. Fine. Now, Mr. Adams, I ask you this: When you left Mr. Kelly at nine-thirty that evening, was he under the influence of alcohol?

A. No, of course not.

Q. Are you absolutely sure?

A. Absolutely. Mr. Kelly was as sober as you or I.

Q. And did he appear to be able to operate his vehicle safely?

A. Certainly.

Q. With no impairment whatsoever due to alcohol?

A. None.

Q. Would you have had any reservations in driving home as a passenger in his car that night, Mr. Adams?

A. No reservations at all.

Neutralizing Anticipated Cross-Examination

Q. Now, I'm sure this thought has occurred to one or two of the jurors: Did you yourself feel the effects of any alcohol that evening?

A. No, I did not. As I explained, I have felt the effects on previous occasions, and I would be able to recognize them in myself. And no, I felt no effects. Certainly not with two drinks over a two-and-a-half-hour period.

Q. Fine, thank you. Now, you've testified that this was a business meeting. I presume you and Mr. Kelly are business associates?

A. That's correct. I work at another bank, and we do business on occasion.

Q. Does this business depend in any way on your testimony here today?

A. Of course not.

Q. Regardless of the nature of your testimony, this business relationship will continue?

A. Naturally. Mr. Kelly is a respected member of the financial community. A false arrest on erroneous charges will not change that.

Q. Your testimony, then, is the absolute truth?

A. Sir, I would not commit perjury for any individual.

Q. Thank you, Mr. Adams. One last question: You are testifying here today because you were compelled by subpoena to appear, isn't that right?

A. That's correct.

§14.0.2 Preparing the Sobriety Witness for Cross-Examination

If counsel intends to call a sobriety witness — that is, one who can testify to the defendant's condition just before or after the arrest — he should have some idea of what cross-examination to expect. The following suggestions culled from those found by the author in manuals for prosecutors who are cross-examining such a witness may prove helpful to the defense in preparing the witness for that cross-exam and in structuring direct examination.

1. Begin by establishing the witness' relationship to the defendant — that he is helping a friend in trouble.
2. Pin the witness down to places and times he was with the defendant, the nature of the activities, and the number of drinks consumed by each of them. Try to establish that he was not watching the defendant closely enough to know whether he was sober.
3. Contrast the witness' apparent "total recall" with former occasions where he drank with the defendant, asking for details of what and how many drinks were consumed on those occasions, what clothing was worn, etc.
4. Establish in the jurors' minds that the witness had enough alcohol himself on the date in question to discredit his recollection.
5. Commonly, the witness will say that the defendant was not "drunk" or "intoxicated." Ask him if he was "under the influence," and to explain the difference between "drunk" and "under the influence."
6. Ask the witness to give a description of a person who is drunk (slurred speech, staggering, etc.). Once a list of symptoms is established, work down the scale of intoxication. The witness will often concede that the defendant was "loose," "relaxed," or "having a good time."
7. A witness will often say that the defendant was not too

intoxicated to drive. Ask the witness to describe the symptoms of a person he feels *is* too intoxicated to drive, then establish that less extreme symptoms can indicate impairment of judgment, coordination, etc.

8. Ask if the witness has ever seen the defendant drunk/under the influence before. If he has not, establish that he would not know what the defendant would look or act like under the influence of alcohol; if he has, run down the list of symptoms reported by the officer and ask the witness if those were observed by him at the time.
9. Ask the witness if he observed the defendant as closely as the officer did, or if he gave the defendant any balance or coordination tests.
10. Toward the end of cross-examination, ask the witness if he knew what the defendant's condition was *at the time of arrest.*
11. Ask the witness a series of questions that will permit you to argue that his opinion leads to only one conclusion: the officer grabbed the defendant off the street for no reason whatsoever. (Was he perfectly sober — as sober as in court today? There was no impairment of his speech? The car was driven absolutely straight down the road? There was nothing in his driving that would attract the attention of the police? There was nothing in his appearance to create suspicion? Etc.)
12. If the defense calls a *bartender* as a witness to the defendant's sobriety shortly before the arrest, he will usually testify that he served him only two drinks and that he appeared perfectly unaffected when he left. Test his recall by asking such details as what clothing the defendant was wearing and who was with him — and what clothing other customers in the bar were wearing, etc. Establish that there were other customers in the bar taking his attention. Ask him about symptoms of a person who is "drunk" versus "under the influence." Make him relate the substance of his conversations with the defendant and/or his attorney after the arrest, and how many times they have talked. Establish motive — that he could lose his job and/or liquor license if it was shown that he served alcohol to a drunk.

There are three points to establish with the bartender: (1) his recollection is questionable due to lack of focus on the defendant; (2) if he can recall, he is looking for symptoms of a person who is *too drunk* to serve — not for more subtle symptoms; and (3) admitting he served an intoxicated customer would be admitting to a violation of law.

§14.1 *The Defense Blood-Alcohol Expert*

Doubt is not a pleasant condition, but certainty is an absurd one.
VOLTAIRE

In most drunk driving cases, it is a distinct luxury to have the services of a defense expert. Such witnesses, if they can be found, usually charge a healthy fee for their time spent waiting and testifying in court, a fee well worth the service, but one that will be added to the attorney's fee for the client to shoulder. As a result, defense counsel will often find that he must rely on cross-examination of the prosecution expert witness, who is typically a chemist employed by the city or county criminalistics laboratory or police agency. By cross-examination of such an expert, counsel must seek to establish favorable facts concerning intoxication and alcohol analysis. This is a poor second choice, since counsel probably will be dealing with an adverse witness interested less in scientific truth than in justifying his employment by facilitating a conviction.

Counsel should be aware of the ever-present double standard that applies in drunk driving cases when offering a defense expert's testimony. It is not uncommon for some judges to find the defense expert unqualified or his testimony irrelevant, while the state's expert is routinely permitted to testify. In *Fultz v. State,* 770 S.W.2d 595 (Tex. App. 1989), exclusion of a defense expert who would have testified to sources of error in the Intoxilyzer 4011AS-A was deemed to constitute a clear abuse of discretion and the conviction was reversed.

As the U.S. Supreme Court said in *Washington v. Texas,* 388 U.S. 14, 19 (1967), "the right to offer the testimony of witnesses, if necessary, is in plain terms the right to present a defense. Just as an accused has the right to confront the prosecution's witnesses to challenge their testimony, he has the right to present his witnesses to challenge their testimony. This right is a fundamental element of due process."

The grounds most commonly stated by trial judges for excluding evidence attacking blood-alcohol tests is that the accuracy and reliability of the tests have been acknowledged by the legislature or are a matter of judicial notice. See, e.g., *People v. Capporelli,* 502 N.E.2d 11 (Ill. App. 1988); *State v. Downie,* 550 A.2d 1313 (N.J. Super. 1988); *City of Columbus v. Taylor,* 529 N.E.2d 1382 (Ohio 1988). On appeal, a number of courts have recognized that restricting the defense in this manner is error — but is only "harmless error." See, e.g., *Luoma v. City of Minneapolis,* 398 N.W.2d 650 (Minn. App. 1987).

Fortunately, the majority of courts continue to recognize the U.S. Constitution and permit an accused the basic right of a defendant to attack the evidence against him. See, e.g., *People v. Thompson,* 215 Cal. App. 3d 7, 265 Cal. Rptr. 105 (1989), recognizing the right to present evidence that the breath partition ratio used in the breath machine varies among individuals. As one court recognized, it is "imperative that a defendant, in order to receive a fair trial, must be permitted to attack the reliability of the test results." *Commonwealth v. Shiffler,* 541 A.2d 780, 783 (Pa. 1988). Nor does a violation of this constitutional right constitute harmless error. See, e.g., *State v. Lowther,* 740 P.2d 1017 (Haw. 1987).

Even the general reliability of a breath machine or other method of blood-alcohol analysis should be subject to attack. In the *Lowther* case cited, for example, a defense expert witness gave his opinion that the Intoxilyzer 4011AS "doesn't accurately measure the amount of alcohol in a person's blood." Id. at 1019. The trial court struck the testimony and instructed the jury to disregard it because the state supreme court had already ruled that the machine was a reliable instrument. On appeal, the conviction was reversed. The appellate court said that the supreme court had simply relieved the prosecution of having to present foundational evidence of the machine's general reliability; it had not conclusively established its reliability, and so the defendant was free to challenge it.

Counsel certainly should take advantage of the expert's services prior to trial by discussing with him the facts of the case as well as the nature of the biological processes involved in alcohol consumption and the flaws in the various methods of blood-alcohol analysis. A knowledgeable expert can be a gold mine of information. Besides suggesting possible cross-examination on the particular case, he can be the source of a valuable general education for the drunk driving lawyer.

Counsel may wish to consider calling a different type of expert: a *pharmacologist.* Rather than (or in addition to) using a forensic toxicologist to attack the testing process itself, an effective approach is to *contrast the symptomology.* In other words, attack the problem from the "other end": The symptoms the pharmacologist would expect of a person with a blood-alcohol concentration of, e.g., .16 percent do not correspond with the symptoms described by the officer or with the performance on the field sobriety tests. Put another way, the expert can testify to what the symptoms and expected performance of a person with .16 percent would be — and compare that with the testimony of the officer. Rather than (or in addition to) using the expert witness to attack the validity of the BAC evidence by addressing the chemical test, he attacks its validity by addressing the contradiction of results: The symptoms and FST performance contradict the chemical test results.

Ideally, of course, the chemical test can be attacked in both ways with a single, well-qualified expert witness.

There are a number of ways to locate a competent expert in the area of blood-alcohol analysis. Expert blood-alcohol witnesses for the defense can often be found on the faculties of local colleges, commonly in the medical and science departments — particularly in the fields of analytical chemistry, toxicology, biochemistry, pharmacology, and forensic science. Individuals who have retired from careers in crime laboratories of law enforcement agencies represent another possible source. Medical doctors may also be competent to testify about blood-alcohol analysis. Fellow members of the defense bar may have had good and bad dealings with drunk driving expert witnesses before. Both prosecutors and prosecution expert witnesses also can be helpful if approached correctly. These individuals probably have encountered a wide range of defense experts in their time and are in a good position to judge the best of them.

The Forensic Services Directory may be useful in locating an expert. This is produced by the National Forensic Center, which also provides an automated list of expert witnesses through WESTLAW and LEXIS. While a majority of the experts listed in the Directory would have no application to a drinking/driving case, several categories have direct application, including chemistry, biological sciences, pharmacology, toxicology, medicine, and electrical engineering. The Directory does not purport to be a complete listing of all experts, but rather contains only the names of those who have submitted materials to the Center.

The Directory may be obtained from Forensic Services Directory, Inc., P.O. Box 3161, Princeton, NJ 08540 (800-526-5177). The price for the 1994 edition is $112.50, plus $5 shipping.

Another valuable source for locating expert witnesses nationwide is the Directory of Alcohol Related Forensic Experts. Revised annually and priced at $49, the 1994–1995 edition is available from Whitaker Newsletters, 313 South Avenue, P.O. Box 192, Fanwood, NJ 07023 (800-359-6049).

(Note: Some of the telephone numbers and prices of the directories may have been changed. Please see the "Resources" section herein for additional sources for forensic experts.)

§14.1.1 Illustrative Direct Examination of Defense Expert

The following direct examination of a defense expert is taken from an actual DUI trial transcript. The questioning is by one of the premier drunk driving defense lawyers in the country, Howard Price of Atlanta. The witness is Dr. Richard Jensen of Minneapolis, in the author's opinion the best blood-alcohol expert available to the defense today. The instrument involved is the Intoxilyzer Model 5000.

Price's strategy is to focus on a few selected issues, rather than "shotgunning" by conducting a broad attack on the machine. Here, he addresses mouth alcohol, duplicate analysis, lack of a standard (simulator solution), continued alcohol absorption, and the rising BAC curve. Notice, incidentally, how Price also uses Dr. Jensen to attack the significance of the field sobriety test results.

Q. Mr. Jensen, what is your occupation?
A. I am an analytical chemist and toxicologist.

Q. Would you tell the jury what an analytical — what did you say?
A. Chemist.
Q. Chemist and toxicology, tell the jury what that is.
A. Analytical chemistry is that branch of chemistry that deals with analysis of chemical components usually found in very small concentrations. We develop the method of analysis and evaluate the accuracy of the reliability of those methods of analysis.

That, incidentally, for a chemist relates to toxicology. Toxicology is that branch of medical science that deals with concentration and the effect of toxic materials on human and animal systems. In order to evaluate the effect of toxic materials, we have to be able to measure the concentration. That's where the chemistry comes in. You measure the concentration in very small quantities to evaluate what is there, how much is there, and then to interpret the effect on the concentrations of those materials on the human system. It's an interrelationship there having to do with analysis and the interpretation.
Q. Where are you employed presently?
A. I am employed with Forensic Associates, Incorporated, in Minneapolis, Minnesota.
Q. Is that why you talk so funny?
A. I'm afraid that's probably true.
Q. Would you tell the Court, as well as the ladies and gentlemen of the jury, what your academic background is?
A. I attended Iowa State University in Ames, Iowa, where I graduated in 1960 with a Bachelor of Science degree with a major in chemistry. I left there and continued my education at the University of Iowa, in Iowa City, where I obtained a Master of Science degree, where I conducted research and did a thesis in analytical chemistry, and in 1964 received a Master's degree. In 1965 I received a Ph.D. degree from the University of Iowa in the same area of analytical chemistry.
Q. Are you a member presently of any professional and learned societies?
A. Yes, I am.
Q. Would you tell the jury what those are?
A. I am a member of the American Academy of Forensic Sciences, Midwest Association of Forensic Sciences, American Chemical Society, and two learned societies. One is Phi Lambda Epsilon, which recognizes excellence in academics, chemistry, and Sigma Xi, excellence in research in chemistry.
Q. I presume after you got all this education you got a job?
A. Fortunately, yes.
Q. Tell the jury what your job history has been.

A. Upon receiving my doctoral degree, I taught for one year at a Minnesota state university, Mankato State University. There I taught undergraduate chemistry, graduate chemistry, and directed the graduate research.

I then went to a private liberal arts college in St. Peter, Minnesota, Gustavus Adolphus College, and there I taught for 13 and a half years. During that time I taught a variety of courses in instrumental analysis, analytical chemistry, clinical chemistry. I was Chairman of the Chemistry Department there from 1976 until 1979.

I left on a sabbatical leave of absence in 1979 and joined the crime laboratory for the State of Minnesota. There for six months I participated in every section of that laboratory. I conducted analyses, conducted research, evaluated physical evidence. After six months there I was asked to remain as temporary supervisor of the alcohol testing section. I remained in that position for six months.

In August of 1980, I applied for and was given one of the positions of assistant director of the laboratory for the State of Minnesota and coordinated the chemical testing program. My responsibilities and duties in that position were to oversee all of the analyses done in the chemical parts of the crime laboratory, that is, the sections of toxicology, chemistry, breath testing, and blood testing. I conducted research. I did human subject studies. I evaluated physical evidence. I did all that besides the normal management day-to-day operational management things that had to be done.

I left that position in April of 1984, continuing my work in toxicology, by joining a private laboratory in Boulder, Colorado, there working under a contract with the Colorado Highway Patrol and 120 of the law enforcement agencies, continuing to analyze breath and blood and tissue samples for alcohol and other drugs. I was there from August of 1984.

I then returned to Minneapolis and started my own organization, Forensic Associates. I have been in that position since. I also have the appointment of Director of Forensic Toxicology for Medox Laboratories in St. Paul, Minnesota, which is a large nationally oriented laboratory, conducting toxicological analyses.

Q. Thank you. You have a Ph.D. So it's Dr. Jensen, is it not?

A. That is correct.

Q. Do you have any professional publications, Dr. Jensen?

A. Yes, I do.

Q. What do they deal with?

A. My 19 publications deal with methods of analyses, that is, they are specific publications on how to conduct analyses for small concentrations of material, how to evaluate those methods as to accuracy and reliability. Some of them are newly designed methods of analyses.

Q. In relation to the effects of alcohol on individuals, have you yourself done any studies?

A. Yes, I have.

Q. Would you tell the jury about those.

A. Primarily, in my work at the crime laboratory for the State of Minnesota, one of the things that we did was to evaluate the effects of alcohol on human subjects as part of our breath testing program for officers. In this particular circumstance I was involved in the testing of approximately four- to five-hundred human subjects as to the effects of alcohol, methods of testing alcohol, and the accuracy and reliability of those methods. And what we would do, of course, is with the consent of the individual being tested we would give them accurately measured doses of alcohol over periods of time, measured periods of time, note the effects on those individuals, and then measure their alcohol concentration by a variety of means to determine the concentration versus the effects of alcohol.

I continued doing that in my work in Colorado, and on an occasional basis continue to do that now, but not nearly with the volume of subjects as I did when I was with the crime laboratory.

Q. All right. By that are you saying that you actually did perform studies yourself on four- to five-hundred human beings?

A. Absolutely. I wasn't the only one involved, nor was I the one doing all of the work on all of the subjects, but was involved in many phases and in some cases all of the phases of the studies.

Q. That's what you call a human subject study?

A. That is correct.

Q. And in that you studied the various effects of certain alcohol concentrations on various individuals.

A. That is correct, plus evaluated certain methods of analyses for alcohol on an individual.

Q. Such as?

A. Breath testing, various breath testing devices. One of my charges and responsibilities was to evaluate evidential breath testing devices and make recommendations to the director of the laboratory as to which one we were going to use in the State of Minnesota.

Q. And when you say evidential breath testing devices, you are talking about —

A. I'm talking about those devices which are used as a final analysis to determine breath alcohol concentration, not the devices — when I say evidential, not the devices that are used as preliminary screening devices at roadside, although we did evaluate those. But that's the differentiation between the two.

Q. Are you familiar with scientific literature that exists on the effects of alcohol on us as human beings?

A. Yes, I am.

Q. How did you become familiar with those?

A. Well, as part of my training and experience from the time I became associated with the area of forensic sciences, teaching courses in forensic sciences in college, and then in my work in the crime lab continuing my work I made a practice to keep very close watch on all scientific literature as it related to the effects of alcohol and in determining concentrations of alcohol. I subscribe to a computer data search system that searches more than 200 libraries throughout the world for articles on alcohol.

Q. You are familiar, are you not, with various breath testing devices?

A. Yes, I am.

Q. How many breath testing devices have you used or actually run tests on?

A. That's hard to tell. I guess I couldn't give you a number. I can name a few.

Q. All right.

A. In the Breathalyzer line — these are makes and models of breath testing devices. I have personally operated the Breathalyzer 900, 900-A, the 1000 and 2000. In the Intoxilyzer line, I have operated the Intoxilyzer Model 4011-A. I have conducted studies on all of these also, 4011-A, 4011-AS, 4011-ASA, 5000. On the Intoximeter line, the Intoximeter Model 3000 and the Intoximeter GCI. I have also conducted studies on the BAC Verifier and the BAC Verifier Datamaster II. I didn't keep track of those. I can't tell you how many that was.

Q. All of those are different types of devices, breath testing devices?

A. All different types of devices. Some are based on different physical chemical principles of making the measurement, but all designed, if operated properly, to measure concentration of breath alcohol.

Q. And that is the amount of alcohol in the breath?

A. Yes.

Q. Are you familiar specifically, Dr. Jensen, with an instrument called the Intoxilyzer 5000?

A. Yes, I am.

Q. Is that one of the breath testing machines that you are familiar with?

A. Absolutely. It's probably the one I have done the most work with.

Q. Tell the jury how you became familiar and how you are familiar with such a machine.

A. One of the jobs that I had as assistant director of the laboratory was to evaluate a large variety of evidential breath testing devices, because we were selecting a new one in the State of Minnesota. The one that we chose and the one that I supported strongly in the evaluation was the Intoxilyzer Model 5000. I was impressed enough with that that I continued to use it in my work after I left the State of Minnesota. I ordered an Intoxilyzer 5000 and I still use it to this day in my work in corporate toxicology.

Q. Dr. Jensen, are you familiar with the methods by which one can estimate an individual's alcoholic concentration, the amount of alcohol in his blood, based upon certain facts?

A. Yes, I am.

Q. What facts would you need, Dr. Jensen, to make such an estimate?

A. In a situation where we make an estimate of an individual's alcohol concentration one has to know — this is based on the work of Widmark in 1932. One has to know what time the drinking started, what time the drinking stopped, the amount of alcohol beverage consumed, the type of alcohol beverage that was consumed, and the height and weight of the individual that consumed the alcohol beverage, and also we would need to know the sex of the individual, and we would want to know at what time he wished to have such a prediction made, at what time after the drinking ceases.

Q. If you would assume, Dr. Jensen, that we are talking about [the defendant] here in the courtroom and assume that he is five foot, six inches tall, weighs between 130 and 135 pounds, that at approximately 9 o'clock P.M. he consumed dinner consisting of fried chicken, french fries, salad and coffee. Assume further that approximately between the hours of 9:45 and just after 12:30 he consumed four 12-ounce beers, specifically Chihuahua beer. Based upon that, can you estimate what his blood alcohol concentration would be at 1:58 A.M., which would be the time he allegedly blew into the Intoxilyzer 5000 machine?

A. What time did he quit drinking?

Q. Just after 12:30.

A. Yes, sir, I can.

Q. Would you do that for the ladies and gentlemen of the jury, please?

A. You had asked me that same question prior to this particular point in time and I have made that estimation based upon the facts you have given me. They haven't changed from the time that we initially spoke. It is my estimation that an individual of that height and weight and sex, drinking that amount of alcohol over that period of time, provided all of the alcohol is absorbed at 1:58 A.M., he would have an alcoholic concentration of approximately .05 to .07 percent blood alcohol.

Q. .05 to .07 percent?

A. That is correct.

Q. Using that same data or that same assumption, the same hypothetical situation, can you also make an estimate of this same individual's blood-alcohol content at 1:08, which, according to the testimony, is the time he was driving the automobile?

A. Based upon the facts that you have given me, I don't believe that I could give you a specific number at that time.

Q. All right, sir. Would it be consistent with one having a blood-alcohol content between .05 and .07 percent that he would not be staggering?

A. That would be consistent.

Q. Assume that he was asked to stand on one leg, keeping his arms down to his side, looking down at his foot while standing on one leg, look at his other foot held 6 to 8 inches off the ground, and count from 1 to 30, and assume further that that person put his foot down one time somewhere in the early 20's, and he may have swayed a bit, would that be consistent with one having a blood-alcohol content of between .05 and .07 percent?

A. Yes, that would be consistent.

Q. Assume, Dr. Jensen, that an individual was asked to stand with his left foot in front of his right foot on a marked line on a roadway. Assume further he was asked to keep his arms down to his side while the officer gave him the following instructions: To walk heel-to-toe nine paces on a marked line and then turn around and walk nine paces back, counting out loud each time he made a step, and assume that that individual stepped off that line on two occasions while not even looking at the line, Dr. Jensen, is that consistent with an individual that has a blood-alcohol content of .05 to .07 percent?

A. Yes, it is very consistent with that.

Q. Assume further, Dr. Jensen, that an individual was asked to recite his ABCs without singing them and at the same time while doing so was asked to keep his feet together, his arms down at his side, and his head held back and his eyes closed. Assume further that that individual left out the letter "U" in the alphabet. Is that consistent with one having a blood-alcohol content of between .05 and .07?

A. Yes, it is.

Q. I am going to show you what has been marked as City's Exhibit No. 2 which shows a test value from an Intoxilyzer 5000 breath testing machine, and it shows a test value taken at 1:58 of .14 —

Before I get to that let me ask you one other question. The test value of .14 percent. The things that I have talked about so far, standing on one leg, walking on a line, leaving out the letter "U," based on your studies and knowledge, Dr. Jensen, is it consistent with a .14 blood-alcohol content that an individual would do that well on those tests?

A. Oh, very much so, yes.

Q. How can you explain the difference between your opinion of .05 and .07 percent based on the data that you have and a test value of a .14 percent blood-alcohol content on an Intoxilyzer 5000?

Mr. Joffrion: Your honor, I object to that question.

The Court: Overruled.

Q. You may answer.

A. There are a variety of reasons why there may be a wide discrepancy, and certainly there could be any number of reasons from a scientific point of view in making those measurements, but there are three general areas that I can think of where there might be a problem in a measurement such as this. One area, which is readily acknowledgeable in the area of evidential breath testing, where a single measurement is made such as we have in this particular case, that is, a single exhalation, if the individual is still absorbing alcohol into the bloodstream, that is, they still have alcohol in their stomach, there is the opportunity for that alcohol to contaminate the oral cavity, providing a higher alcohol concentration in the oral cavity than you have in the deep lung or alveolar portion, and it adds to it and you have an elevated alcohol concentration. That's a consequence of having a single measurement made.

Along the same line, in terms of conducting the proper scientific measurement for an unknown quantity, which is what we are doing here — we don't know the concentration of alcohol on the breath. There are certain things that we have to do to assure ourselves that that's an accurate and reliable measurement. One — that's a minimum — we must take two measurements. We must do a duplicate analysis, two exhalations, in case something occurs with one or both of those, and if there is a wide difference between the two, we can tell that there is something wrong. That guarantees the reliability, and it must be reliable.

The second is that it has to be accurate. That's the standard of all measurements, chemical measurements. A standard is measured to the same time you measure the unknown, to prove that your measuring device is operating properly at the time you use it, and prove that the calibration is proper, that is, that it has been adjusted to do what you want it to do.

Q. Excuse me. Let me interrupt. By a standard you are talking about some sort of solution injected into the machine with a known alcoholic content?

A. A vapor. What we normally used with evidential breath testing — we use something that is called a simulator. It simulates a sample of vapor of known alcoholic concentration which is introduced into the breath testing device, and you must obtain a proper reading, that is, it must be within certain close tolerances or limits. If you do that every time you measure an unknown to make sure that it is operating at that time period that's the important time, when you are measuring the unknown.

If I can continue.

Q. Yes, sir. Excuse me.

A. The third area that has a potential explanation — and I have to let you know that there is no way for anybody to say precisely there is this large difference. But the third area is the fact that if the individual is still absorbing alcohol, that is, still from the stomach into the bloodstream, that individual's blood-breath ratio, the amount of alcohol in their blood versus the amount of alcohol on their breath when the exchange takes place in the deep lung portion, the alveolar portion, that ratio will be considerably different than when the machine of the instrument is calibrated at, at that point in time, when active absorption is going on, you can receive a falsely high reading in comparison with a venous blood level.

Q. So that I can just recap one, two, and three, one would be the presence of mouth alcohol in the oral cavity?

A. Yes.

Q. Secondly, a short-term version of what you just told us would be what?

A. The short-term version in terms of the accuracy and reliability would be that certainly you must get a minimum put into any scientific test. You need two tests and measure your standard. So accuracy and reliability.

Q. Now, accuracy and reliability, in short, what you are saying is that there is no known standard injected into the machine at the time the test was given.

A. That is correct, there was only a single determination made, which is the worst kind of measurement to make.

Q. One test —

A. And no standard.

Q. Would two tests, Dr. Jensen, given in short terms apart, do away with the presence of mouth alcohol?

A. It wouldn't do away with the presence of mouth alcohol because if it's there that's there, but what it would do, which is precisely why you do this sort of thing in chemical testing, is if you have a contaminated sample provided to an evidential breath testing device, that is, by alcohol in the mouth, your first reading will be quite high. If you have 45 minutes between the two readings, which is common in most of the states in doing the testing, the second breath test will be considerably lower. You will have two numbers that are separated by quite a large amount and that tells you that you know something is wrong, because the two numbers should agree very closely, the two values that you get. If they don't agree, then there is something that we call a systematic error present, the systematic error being the presence of mouth alcohol, and then that either one or both of those numbers is then wrong. A single measurement won't tell you that.

Q. And what would a known standard, the solution that we know what the alcoholic content is, what would that tell us at the time it is injected into the machine at the time of testing?

A. It would tell you two important things, the two things that are critical, as it has to do with the accuracy. Is the device operating properly at the time the unknown is measured, and is it operating at its proper calibration level. We calibrate all devices at 2100:1. Is it operating at that level.

Q. And the third explanation of why this could be a .14, you told the jury, is you said something about absorption, that the alcohol would still be absorbing into the system?

A. If the individual being tested is actively absorbing alcohol, that is, going from the stomach into the bloodstream, your breath-alcohol concentration will be considerably higher than your venous blood-alcohol concentration, and it would be disproportionately higher until your physiological — your human system — reaches an equilibrium. Everything got in, everything got distributed and settled down is really what it boils down to. While you are actively absorbing the system is out of whack. It's essentially displaced. It's out of balance. So your breath alcohol will be higher in comparison with venous blood.

Q. Dr. Jensen, if you would, assume the same facts that we talked about just a while ago, and that is that this person had eaten a chicken dinner at approximately 9 o'clock and that he had consumed between 9:45 and just after 12:30 four beverages, and that he was at the breath test at 1:58. Do you have any judgment as to whether or not he would still be absorbing?

A. I would say there is a good opportunity, a good chance, that he is still absorbing alcohol. There is truly no way of knowing, but the absorption process is a variable one, the amount of time it takes. It generally takes much more time when it's absorbed after eating. That is not an unusual time. We are certainly looking at an area of 30 to 90 minutes and perhaps even longer, the time that it takes for complete absorption to occur. It can take as long as two hours or more.

Q. Then it would take longer to absorb alcohol if it had been ingested after a fried chicken dinner?

A. After any meal it would take longer. It depends upon the content. In this case the content is not important. Whenever you consume alcohol on top of a meal it delays the absorption of that alcohol because it tends to retain the alcohol and the meal in your stomach longer. If it stays in the stomach, then it doesn't get into the bloodstream as rapidly.

Q. Dr. Jensen, just for the sake of this one question, I want you to just assume that this test result of .14 is accurate to show the breath-alcohol test at 1:58. Does that indicate or can it indicate what the blood alcohol was at 1:08, which is the time he was driving the automobile?

A. No, it can't in particular in this circumstance.

Q. Would it be likely that it would be lower than a .10 at that time?

A. Yes, the likelihood would be very good that it would be a great deal lower than .10 just because of the delayed absorption of the alcohol, and then at 1:08, some half hour after consuming the last beverage, then the individual is still absorbing the alcohol and the alcohol concentration is rising through the time he is operating the motor vehicle and it would be high at some time later.

Q. Your witness.

§14.1.2 Preparing the Defense Expert for Cross-Examination

In the event a defense expert is retained, counsel should carefully prepare him for direct and cross-examination. He probably will have testified on previous occasions and will know what to expect generally. Nevertheless, each case is different, and preparation will avoid embarrassment to the expert and an unpleasant surprise to counsel.

Besides questions concerning the frailties inherent in the specific method of blood-alcohol analysis involved in the case, the expert should be examined concerning such subjects as the validity of the .08 or .10 percent presumptive levels, the existence and effect of individual tolerance to alcohol, application of the Widmark formula, the innocent causes for various physical symptoms of intoxication, and the effects of any injuries or disorders suffered by the defendant on his symptoms or performance.

Counsel should explain to the expert witness that the prosecutor will probably attack his motives, bias, and credentials. The witness may be asked, for example, whether he is being paid by the defendant to testify and how much? Will his fee be affected by the verdict of the jury? Has he ever qualified in court as an expert before? Has he ever testified for the prosecution or only for the defense? How much money a year does he make by testifying for defendants in drunk driving cases? Has he ever conducted any controlled experiments concerning driving under the influence of alcohol? This line of questioning will often end with a query to the effect that the expert did not see the defendant on the day of his arrest and so cannot say whether he was under the influence or not.

So long as the expert witness is prepared for such questioning — and the types of questions vary markedly little from one experienced prosecutor to another — he should not be rattled when it comes and should be able to offer reasonable answers. Of course, the sword cuts both ways: A nearly identical line of questioning can and should be asked of the prosecutor's expert witness.

In preparing the defense blood-alcohol expert for cross-examination, counsel might want to keep the following sample strategy for prosecutors in mind. This material is derived from suggestions made in an actual prosecutor's manual.

1. The most effective method of discrediting the defense expert witness is to obtain copies of transcripts of his testimony in other trials; locate inconsistencies with his testimony in the instant case.
2. If possible, have the prosecution expert observe the defense expert's testimony and make suggestions for fruitful areas of cross-examination.
3. If the expert testifies that not all people are under the influence with BACs of .10 percent, ask him at what level he *does* believe all people are under the influence. Then have him admit that this is a distinctly minority view.

4. Make the expert admit that the National Safety Council has established .08 percent as the level, and that the American Medical Association has stated that individuals with .10 percent "suffer a severe, significant, and dangerous deterioration in driving abilities."
5. Force him to admit that:
   a. alcohol slows down a person's ability to process and act upon information.
   b. the body experiences an effect from the first alcoholic drink.
   c. it is possible for a given individual to be impaired after two drinks.
6. Ask the witness what symptoms a person under the influence would exhibit. Then present him with a hypothetical officer (based upon the arresting officer) and ask him if such a person would be qualified to observe such symptoms.
7. Enumerate each of the symptoms observed by the officer, one at a time, and ask the defense expert if such an observation was, in fact, symptomatic of being under the influence.
8. Then ask the expert: If you had observed all of these symptoms in one person, would it be your opinion that the person was under the influence?
9. Establish that if a person shows the outward physical symptoms, then he is already mentally impaired.
10. The defense attorney will give the expert a hypothetical set of facts based on which the expert will estimate the defendant's BAC at below .10 percent. Discredit this opinion by attacking the factual assumptions underlying the opinion:
    a. The truthfulness of the defendant's story of how many drinks he had: Ask the expert if it is not common for persons arrested for DUI to lie about the amount they have had to drink.
    b. The partition ratio: Establish that the expert is using a favorable extreme of the range partition ratios in estimating BAC — for example, 1500 to 1 in breath tests and 2.4 to 1 in urinalysis. Ask him how many people he has observed with such an extreme ratio, and what

percentage of the population has it. Ask him if he *knows* what the defendant's partition ratio actually is.

c. Establish that he is also assuming that the test given the defendant was erroneous — and that he has no evidence or personal knowledge to warrant this.

11. Have the defense expert admit that the test administered is one approved by the State of California. Ask him if he is claiming that it is not possible to obtain an accurate reading with the test used.
12. Have the expert confirm the numerous methods of calibration, testing with standards, purging, replacing mouthpieces, multiple tests, etc., to ensure accurate test results.
13. Toward the end of cross-examination, point out the obvious — that, unlike the officer, the expert never had a chance to observe the defendant at the time in question.
14. Ask the expert when he was retained by the defense, how much he is being paid, and how much of the fee is yet to be collected.
15. Establish how many times he has testified in DUI cases, what percentage of those were for the defense — and that he hopes to continue to be retained by the defense in the future.

§14.2 The Defense Police Expert

> A witness cannot give evidence of his age unless he can remember being born.
>
> JUDGE BLAGDEN

In most drunk driving cases, the defense has been limited to attacking the state's witnesses by way of cross-examination. The arresting officer testifies to his observations in the field and defense counsel then attempts to impeach him. In most jurisdictions the prosecution then calls a blood-alcohol expert (toxicologist, criminalist, or technician) and, again, the defense is largely limited to attacking him on cross-examination. In other words, the traditional defense approach has been limited to attack: The state threw up a structure and the defense threw rocks at it.

This limited approach is changing. With greatly increased penalties, individuals accused of DUI are increasingly willing to pay higher legal fees and this has translated into more time and resources available for the defense of a case. This, together with widespread CLE programs in the field and an increasingly sophisticated DUI bar, is beginning to change the traditional approaches to drunk driving defense. Among other things, counsel are now beginning to produce their own witnesses. As discussed in §13.3, many attorneys are now calling blood-alcohol experts of their own to both discredit the state's version of the defendant's physiological condition and to offer an alternative version.

The author has recently been successful with carrying this process one step further: retaining expert witnesses in the field of drunk driving investigations.

Assuming that there is financial ability and that such witnesses are available, there is no reason counsel should be limited to accepting what the arresting officer says on the stand. Cross-examination can certainly be effective, but an alternate — and possibly more qualified and objective — view from another law enforcement source can be devastating to the state's case.

The author has called retired police officers who are experienced and highly qualified to testify to:

1. flaws in the arresting officer's investigative methods;
2. the *correct* procedures that should have been used in the investigation;
3. the expert's opinion as to
   a. the credibility of the officer's opinion, and
   b. whether the defendant was intoxicated or should have been arrested.

Such a witness can, for example, testify that the field sobriety tests were conducted under circumstances which rendered them unreliable, or that they did not comply with the National Highway Traffic Safety Administration's "standardized" FSTs (see §7.5). He can testify that the driving symptoms were not indicative of intoxication, or that the breath test was administered improperly. If the witness ever served in a supervisory capacity, he can be asked if the arresting officer's report would have survived the usual supervisory review before being forwarded to the prosecuting agency.

Qualified law enforcement witnesses are available if counsel is willing to look. Many retired officers are highly qualified and are willing — even flattered — to earn extra money by offering their expertise on the witness stand. Of course, officers should probably be sought who are retired from a law enforcement agency other than that involved in the pending trial; if a city police officer is involved, a retired state trooper or county sheriff would be appropriate.

A particularly excellent source for highly qualified witnesses in this field might be the police academies. If counsel can obtain a certified instructor — active or retired — then he has the best possible expert witness.

By way of example, Rick Swope of Davie, Florida, is a DUI expert with the Broward County Sheriff's Department. Swope teaches criminology, is a certified instructor on the Intoxilyzer 5000, and is NHTSA-certified as an instructor on standardized field sobriety tests. He is only one example of the kinds of witnesses that are available should defense counsel choose to make the effort to find them in his own jurisdiction. Armed with such a witness, counsel is no longer limited to accepting what the arresting officer is willing to admit on cross-examination.

§14.3 Should the Defendant Testify?

> All I mean by truth is what I can't help thinking.
>
> Oliver Wendell Holmes, Jr.

The defendant himself represents, at least potentially, the most critical witness in the trial. He was a witness to almost everything that the arresting officer observed, but only he knows what alcohol, if any, he had consumed on the day in question. He, then, is in a unique position to testify about the ultimate issues in the case. At the same time, his character will be under the closest scrutiny while he is on the witness stand. The jurors will be studying every inflection of the voice, every hand movement, every look in his eyes. They want to understand just who this man is: Is he the *type* of person who would get drunk? Would he go out and drive in a car while under the influence? Is he lying to them?

The defendant represents a potentially valuable, perhaps the most valuable, witness available to the defense. He may also be the *only* witness available to the defense. Yet defense counsel is going to have to make the most important decision in the trial: whether to put the defendant on the stand at all. For as valuable as he may be to the defense, he represents a far greater liability should his testimony not go well. At least in this respect, the defendant can be the best witness available to the prosecution. The jury *expects* the defendant to say he was not under the influence. If his testimony comes off without a hitch, it is no surprise. If, however, he makes any little slip during direct or cross-examination — and the opportunities are countless — then the trial may well be lost. Yet the effects of not permitting the defendant to testify must also be weighed.

There are basically two schools of thought on the critical issue of whether to permit the defendant to take the witness stand.

On the one hand, advocates of permitting him to testify point to a simple reality: If he does not testify, the jury will automatically assume that he is hiding something, that he is afraid to submit to the light of truth. If he is truly innocent, the juror's thinking goes, what does he risk by taking the witness stand? Why would he *not* want to tell what happened? Of course, the court will later instruct the jury that the fact that the defendant chose to exercise his Fifth Amendment right not to testify cannot be used against him; and, of course, consciously or otherwise, the jury will completely disregard the instruction.

On the other hand, many experienced drunk driving attorneys point out that most defense verdicts result because of deficiencies in the prosecution case, not because the defendant took the stand and testified, predictably, that he was not under the influence. Even where the defendant honestly believes that he was stone sober, he represents a greater potential asset to the prosecution than to the defense. Despite not making a serious blunder, few defendants can walk away from cross-examination by a competent prosecutor without looking somewhat foolish. In all too many cases, it is pointed out, the scales are tipped adversely with the defendant's appearance on the stand. Without his testimony, the prosecution case had simply been insufficient.

Counsel also should consider the possibility that the prosecutor may use the defendant to provide demonstrative evidence for comparison purposes. He may, for example, ask the defendant to perform the field sobriety tests — and then compare the resulting performance with videotapes or the officer's testimony.

Does such a procedure violate a defendant's constitutional right against self-incrimination? That depends on how the performance is characterized. In *Macia v. State,* 515 So. 2d 206 (Fla. 1987), the court ordered the defendant to comply with the prosecutor's request that she state her name and perform the same FSTs as at the scene of the arrest. On appeal, it was held that neither the FSTs nor the voice exemplar were communicative or testimonial in nature, and thus were not protected.

Aside from tactical considerations, counsel may also have to deal with an ethical problem. What happens when a client frankly advises his attorney that he was in fact under the influence of alcohol? This will happen on many occasions, and it immediately places the defense attorney in a quandary. If counsel is convinced that the client is correct in his conclusion that he was under the influence, the decision should already have been made: The client will not testify. To present dishonest testimony to the court amounts to subornation of perjury and is a violation of the canon of ethics and of an attorney's duties as an officer of the court. At the same time, it should be recognized that a defendant who does not believe himself innocent will be all the less convincing to a jury and will represent an even greater threat to the defense under cross-examination. In such a case, counsel should advise his client at the outset that he will undertake representation only on the condition that the defendant not testify. Surprisingly, very few defendants will seem to object to this: They are usually relieved to learn that they will not have to testify and have a greater respect for the ethics of the attorney.

If, however, counsel believes that the defendant may be incorrect in his conclusion that he was under the influence, he should not feel precluded from considering the defendant's testimony. Exactly what constitutes "under the influence" is a vague and difficult issue. Experts differ, so a lay defendant could not be expected to know whether he had achieved that indefinable state. Too many individuals charged with criminal offenses seem to suffer from a psychological reaction that manifests itself in the desire to be punished. Perhaps the police or court system represents an authoritarian figure to some, but experienced criminal lawyers are familiar with the phenomenon of innocent individuals who come to believe that they *must* be guilty.

There is no easy answer to the question of whether to place the defendant on the witness stand. The decision will rest on the facts of each individual case. Initially, counsel should assess his client: What type of a person is he? Does he *look* like a habitual drinker? Or does he look like a respectable businessperson? The defendant's appearance alone may be enough to tip the scales in favor of putting him on the stand or not. What will his testimony be? If he is going to take the stand and tell the jury that he was bar-hopping from one tavern to another with friends but only had one or two drinks, then he is probably better off staying in his seat behind the counsel table. Does he appear to be straightforward and sincere when he tells counsel what happened? If not, he probably will not appear credible to the jury either.

Counsel may wish to consider the possible tactical ramifications of calling a client if the client is an alcoholic. More specifically, he should very carefully consider the possibility that defense evidence may enable the prosecution to question him concerning his alcoholism.

In *Gokey v. State,* 510 N.E.2d 703 (Ind. App. 1987), the defense in a vehicular homicide trial offered testimony that no one who saw him at the time of the accident thought he had been drinking: This was offered to challenge the validity of the breath test. The prosecution then cross-examined the defendant concerning his alcoholism. In its rebuttal case, the prosecution produced an expert who testified that "an alcoholic would not show the effects of a high blood alcohol content as much as a nonalcoholic." On appeal, the defendant claimed that questions concerning his alcoholism were intended solely to prejudice him before the jury. The appellate court disagreed, holding that any prejudice was outweighed by the probative value of showing how the defendant's alcoholic condition could influence his response to alcohol consumption.

Counsel also should consider what alternative evidence is available. If he has one eyewitness to the police stop and arrest and another to the fact that the defendant had only one drink during the previous three hours, then why take the risk of placing the defendant in jeopardy? On the other hand, if the defense has no other witnesses, putting the defendant on the stand may be preferable to resting without putting on any case at all, in essence, a "belly-up" in the eyes of the jury.

What is the status of the prosecutor's case when he has rested? If the case is strong enough, perhaps nothing is lost by having the defendant take the stand. If the prosecution case is generally weak, however, or even lacking in some important respect, why supply the missing ingredient by making the defendant available for cross-examination? In accident cases, for example, it will probably never be known how many defense attorneys have placed their clients on the stand only to supply promptly the missing proof that the defendant had in fact been behind the wheel of the car.

The quality of the prosecutor himself may be a factor in the decision. A very skilled one can make hamburger out of even an articulate and intelligent defendant. On the other hand, a fumbling prosecutor presents that much less a risk to a defendant placed on the stand. If the prosecutor is particularly vicious or obnoxious, letting him badger the defendant can often result in a sympathy vote from the jurors.

Whatever the final decision, counsel never should advise the prosecuting attorney whether the defendant will testify. The prosecutor should not know this until the defendant is walking toward the witness chair. Let him spend valuable time preparing cross-examination for a nonexistent witness; let him skimp on his preparation because of doubt that the defendant will testify. In most cases, the prosecutor will expect the defendant to testify. When he does not, the prosecutor may be denied a part of his case that he was relying on the defendant to supply.

§14.3.1 Illustrative Direct Examination of the Defendant

Alcohol Consumption

Q. Mr. Kelly, you are the defendant in this case, are you not?
A. I am.
Q. As the defendant, are you aware that you have a constitutional right under the Fifth Amendment to refuse to testify?
A. You explained that to me.
Q. And no one can force you to testify?
A. I understand that.

Q. Do you, nevertheless, choose to take this witness stand and testify — and subject yourself to cross-examination by the prosecutor?
A. I most certainly do.
Q. Very well. Now, you have heard the testimony of Mr. Adams earlier today.
A. I have.
Q. Is the content of that testimony essentially correct?
A. Yes, it is. We met for dinner at the Hofbrau at about seven, and we parted company at about nine-thirty. Another fellow had dinner with us. I had a martini — a single — and a glass of red wine of some type, I forget the name.
Q. All right. Had you had any alcoholic beverages before meeting Mr. Adams that evening?
A. No, none.
Q. The only alcoholic drinks you had at any time that day before the arrest were the martini and the glass of wine?
A. That's right. And, as Mr. Adams pointed out, the martini was somewhat small.
Q. The martini was consumed approximately two hours before the arrest?
A. I believe so.
Q. And the wine about an hour before the arrest?
A. Well, it took me a half-hour or an hour to drink it. I sipped it through dinner, you see. But yes, about an hour or so before the arrest.
Q. Now, you are familiar with the difference between "drunk" and "under the influence," Mr. Kelly?
A. I am now.
Q. And you have seen persons "under the influence" of alcohol?
A. Yes.
Q. Have you yourself ever been "under the influence"?
A. Yes, I have. Although I have never attempted to drive a vehicle in that condition.
Q. What does it feel like — being "under the influence" of alcohol?
A. Well, as I recall, a warm, rosy feeling. A little bit of dizziness, or lightness. A little trouble forming words. Some sleepiness.
Q. Very well. Now I ask you the critical question: Were you "under the influence" of alcohol at the time you were arrested?
A. I most definitely was not.
Q. You are quite sure?
A. I am quite sure.
Q. You are aware that driving "under the influence" is a misdemeanor?

A. Yes.
Q. And that committing perjury — lying here under oath — is a much more serious offense, a felony?
A. Yes, I am.

Driving Symptoms and Officer's Initial Observations

Q. Now, Mr. Kelly, the officer apparently pulled you over for weaving.
A. That's right.
Q. When did you first become aware of the officer's presence on the road?
A. As soon as I pulled out of the Hofbrau parking lot.
Q. You mean he immediately began following you as soon as you pulled out of the parking lot?
A. That's right. He stayed three or four car lengths behind me from the time we left the Hofbrau to the time he pulled me over — about a mile later.
Q. How do you know he was three or four car lengths the whole time?
A. I could see him in the rearview mirror.
Q. The entire time?
A. No, of course not. I had to watch the road ahead of me.
Q. But you were constantly glancing up at the rearview mirror?
A. Yes.
Q. Why?
A. Well, I was concerned. I mean, wouldn't anyone be worried if a police car immediately began following him?
Q. Were you able to keep your eyes on the road ahead enough to operate safely?
A. Yes, I think so.
Q. But not as much as you normally would?
A. No, I suppose not.
Q. Did it occur to you as you kept looking in the rearview mirror that your driving would be affected, that is, that the car would begin swerving slightly?
A. No, it did not occur to me.
Q. All right: Now, you are also aware, are you not, that the officer observed your eyes to be bloodshot, your face flushed, and your speech thick and slurred.
A. I am aware of those things, yes.
Q. Were your eyes bloodshot that night?
A. They may well have been. You see, I'm a senior teller at a bank here in town. And I had to work late that day balancing out figures. I didn't get away until about seven o'clock that evening. In other

words, I'd been working on figures — book after book of figures — for about 11 hours. I had a headache, and my eyes had been strained pretty severely. It is quite possible they were reddened.

Q. I see. And could your face have been red or flushed, as the officer testified?

A. Again, he may well have been correct. I was quite nervous and excited when I was pulled over. You see, I've never been stopped by the police before. And, well, I was quite upset. When I get nervous like that, upset, I'm afraid the blood rushes to my face. I know I feel very hot in the face.

Q. Fine. And the thick and slurred speech?

A. I'm not sure what the officer means by "thick and slurred." I normally talk very, very slowly, as you can see. And when I get nervous or excited, I tend to stutter or have trouble speaking clearly.

Q. All right. Do you recall the officer testifying that you fumbled with your wallet when you tried to get out your driver's license?

A. Yes, that took place as he said. But it was not because of alcohol. As I said, I get very nervous and excited. I've never dealt with the police before, and I was shaking — my fingers were shaking — and I guess I was fumbling. And, like he said, I even dropped the wallet once.

Q. And, apparently, you stumbled as you stepped out of the car?

A. I probably did. I honestly can't recall, but I do have an arthritis problem — particularly in the knees. It's worse when it's cold outside, like it was the night of the arrest.

Field Sobriety Tests

Q. Now, Mr. Kelly, you were asked to perform some exercises — what are called "field sobriety tests"?

A. I was. Three of them.

Q. And where were these tests administered?

A. Next to my car. On the shoulder of the highway, next to where I pulled over.

Q. Was the car between you and the traffic?

A. No. I performed the tests on the traffic side of my car.

Q. Then cars were continually passing near you as you did the tests?

A. They certainly were, just a few feet away. And it was rather difficult, not to mention embarrassing. The cars were passing just 5 or 10 feet from me.

Q. What type of surface was this shoulder, by the way?

A. Gravel.

Q. Gravel. And was it level or sloped?

A. The shoulder sloped off from the paved road.
Q. Then, apparently you were trying to perform the tests on a graveled surface that was not level?
A. That's correct.
Q. Now, this was at night. What type of lighting was used?
A. Uh, the flashlight held by the officer. And the passing cars — their headlights.
Q. Then your lighting was all from mobile sources, that is, moving lights?
A. Yes.
Q. All right. Now, did you have any trouble with the walk-the-line test?
A. I didn't think so, but apparently the officer does.
Q. You had no trouble walking straight, heel-to-toe?
A. Well, as I said, I have an arthritic condition. And this made it a little troublesome.
Q. By the way, how old are you, Mr. Kelly?
A. Forty-six.
Q. And do you receive treatment for this painful condition?
A. Yes. Dr. Eskin gives me therapeutic treatment if it gets particularly bad.
Q. I see. Now, getting back to the walk-the-line test, did you observe what the officer had in his hands while you were performing the test?
A. Well, he had the flashlight in one hand. I don't recall anything in the other.
Q. Then he was not writing anything down while you performed the test?
A. No, I don't believe he was.
Q. Presumably, then, the diagram of your test results was later written down from memory?
A. Apparently. I know he didn't write anything on any paper until we were back in the police station.
Q. All right. What about the finger-to-nose test?
A. Well, again, I thought it was done well.
Q. Do you recall touching your nose once with each index finger?
A. Yes, I do.
Q. The officer testified you touched at the first joint of each index finger, rather than the tip.
A. That's true. But that's what I thought he wanted. I mean, he only said to touch my nose with the end of my index finger. By "end," I thought he meant the last digit, the last segment. I didn't realize he meant the tip of it.

Q. And the alphabet test, Mr. Kelly? The officer testified that you stumbled on the letters at one point and had to start over.
A. He's right again. I was just nervous, very nervous and upset. I mean, I was standing on a highway in the middle of the night, with a police officer with a gun shining a flashlight on me. And people driving by and staring. I was upset. And I guess I stumbled over the alphabet.

The Breathalyzer

Q. Now, Mr. Kelly, you were asked to breathe into a breath machine, were you not?
A. Yes, I was.
Q. And you did so?
A. Yes, I did.
Q. Were you given a choice as to what type of blood-alcohol test to take?
A. Yes. I chose the breath machine because the officer said it would be the quickest and the easiest. He said if it showed I was sober, I could be released right away.
Q. You realized you could refuse to take a test?
A. I suppose so, yes.
Q. But you chose instead to cooperate — to give a breath sample for chemical analysis?
A. That's correct. I assumed it would show I was sober.
Q. All right. Now, where were you during the 15 minutes before you breathed into the machine?
A. Well, they took my picture and then my fingerprints. . . .
Q. "They"?
A. The man in charge of the jail.
Q. I see. Was the arresting officer present during these procedures?
A. No. I think he was getting the breath machine ready in another room.
Q. And where did you go after the fingerprinting and photographing?
A. They took me into a small, empty room. And I sat there for about five minutes before the officer — the one who had arrested me — came to get me to take the breath test.
Q. You were alone in this room?
A. Yes.
Q. Then, the arresting officer was not with you for most of the 15 minutes preceding the administration of the test?
A. That's correct.
Q. And he could not have observed you to see if you belched or regurgitated?

A. No.
Q. Mr. Kelly, *did* you belch or regurgitate during this period?
A. I can't honestly recall whether I did or not.
Q. You realize that if you *had* belched or regurgitated, this could possibly account for a high breath-alcohol reading?
A. I realize that. But I can't honestly say. Belching just isn't something that stays in your memory. I may have — it's certainly possible. But I can't really recall.
Q. All right. Now, had you gargled or sprayed your mouth with anything before you were arrested?
A. Well, yes. I keep some throat spray in the glove compartment. You see, I smoke cigars occasionally. In any event, I pulled it out and sprayed my throat just before the officer pulled me over.
Q. Why?
A. Well, quite honestly, I was afraid he was going to stop me and then smell the wine or martini on my breath and then jump to conclusions. So I sprayed my breath to kill the smell. I guess it didn't work.
Q. What type of spray was this?
A. Listerine Mint.
Q. Do you realize that contains a significant amount of alcohol?
A. No, I didn't.
Q. That you were spraying alcohol directly into your throat?
A. No.
Q. And this was how long before you breathed into the machine?
A. Oh, about a half-hour, I guess.
Q. Now, Mr. Kelly, let me ask you once again: Under penalty of perjury, were you under the influence of alcohol at the time you were arrested?
A. No, I was not.

§14.3.2 Preparing the Defendant for Cross-Examination

The decision has been made to have the defendant testify. The next step is to prepare him for both direct examination and cross-examination.

Initially, the law relevant to the case should be explained to the defendant. He should be told exactly what is meant by the term "under the influence," what the significance of the field sobriety and blood-alcohol tests are, what effect injuries or illnesses can have on those tests, etc. This is *not* done to suggest to the defendant that he manufacture facts to support a defense to the charges. Rather, it is to acquaint him with some of the very complicated aspects of a drunk driving case, aspects that he will be unfamiliar with. How can a defendant testify under oath that he was not under the influence if he does not understand what that term means? How can he deal with cross-examination concerning a walk-the-line test if he does not understand the procedure correctly? How will he know that his diabetic condition is relevant to his blood-alcohol analysis? It is perfectly proper and ethical for counsel to educate his client on the law and facts of a drunk driving case. In fact, it would border on incompetence to place a client on the stand with no knowledge of the relevant law or procedures.

The defendant then should be prepared generally for taking the witness stand. It should go without saying that the client be well-groomed and tastefully attired in relatively conservative clothing. A trial has been described as a "contest of impressions," and there is much to this. The jury is primarily interested in the defendant's testimony as a means of determining what *kind* of man he is. The defendant should be instructed to look his questioner directly in the eyes and to answer questions courteously, regardless of the tone of the inquisitor. A calm, polite reply to a sarcastic or accusatory question can be quite effective. He also should be made aware of the negative conclusions often drawn by jurors from such absent-minded mannerisms on the stand as shifting in the chair, looking down or away from the questioner, fidgeting with his fingers, looking to his lawyer for help, and so on.

Counsel should go over the general tenor of direct examination as well as some of the more important questions. Certainly, no question should be asked that the defendant is not expecting or at least to which counsel is not confident of the answer.

The real preparation, of course, will involve cross-examination. The defendant's testimony and very possibly the entire case will succeed or fail depending on how well he conducts himself under questioning by the prosecuting attorney. Before getting into specific questions to anticipate, counsel should prepare his client for the general nature of cross-examination. Defense counsel will be able to object where this is called for, it should be explained, but the client will essentially be on his own. The jury resents constant objections from an attorney and feels that the attorney is trying to hide something if he objects frequently. Knowledge of the prosecutor is invaluable in advising the client of what the general quality of the questioning will be like. Perhaps the prosecutor has a very polite, ingratiating, deceptively gentle style: Then the client should be careful, avoid the psychological urge to embrace him as a friend, and should think before he answers. Perhaps the prosecuting attorney is a "hard charger," lashing out at the witness: The client should remain calm, polite, controlling the natural emotional reactions the prosecutor is trying to incite.

An invaluable method of preparing the defendant is simply for defense counsel himself to conduct a "dry run" cross-examination in the privacy of his own office. A half-hour of vigorous questioning, pressing hard on the weak points of the case, will do much toward steeling the client for his "baptism of fire."

Counsel should explore with the defendant, both in discussion and simulated cross-examination, subject areas expected to be covered by the prosecutor in his cross-examination. The client should, for example, be made aware that he will probably be asked a long series of questions concerning the times and places where he was during the hours preceding the arrest. The prosecutor is trying simply to pin him down to a web of details. Defense counsel should do the same in his preparation of the defendant, questioning him in rapid-fire order as to exactly where, when, and with whom he did what.

The defendant may be asked if he is familiar with the symptoms of a person under the influence of alcohol. This is a loaded question, of course. A negative answer would seem to preclude the defendant from testifying whether he himself was under the influence, while an affirmative reply would infer that he is all too well acquainted with the effects of excessive drinking. He can testify that he has observed the symptoms of persons whom he and others felt to be under the influence as he understands that term. A clever prosecutor may then go down the list of symptoms noted by the arresting officer in the case, asking if each was symptomatic of intoxication in the defendant's experience.

The defendant may be asked questions concerning the amount of time he spent drinking on the day in question. Perhaps he had two beers at a tavern after work. The prosecutor will first establish that he drank each beer in about 15 minutes and then confirm that he spent three hours in the tavern. The jury will find it hard to believe that the defendant spent 2½ hours in a tavern without drinking. Again, simple awareness by the defendant of the prosecutor's tactic is half the solution.

The opportunity for drinking during the hours before the arrest is another common area of prosecutorial inquiry. The prosecutor will attempt to establish the constant and ready access the defendant had two alcoholic beverages. If he was at home for three or four hours before the arrest, the prosecutor will elicit the fact that there was beer in the refrigerator, wine in the cellar, and dozens of bottles of liquor in the home bar. Of course, those beverages are there every day, but the inference is clear. If the defendant was on the way home from work, the prosecutor will ask what cocktail lounges or taverns are on the route, thereby establishing both their availability and the defendant's knowledge of them.

Another recurrent subject for cross-examination involves attempting to get the defendant to admit having felt *some* effect from the drink or two he said he had. This may be couched in such terms as "relaxed," "more sociable," or "less tense," but once the door is open, the legal requirement of "affected" or "impaired" is not far away. The defendant may be asked if he can honestly say he was in the same condition after having the two drinks as he is in court now.

The defendant may be asked on the stand to produce his driver's license. He should be made aware that the purpose for this will be to show how quickly and efficiently he pulls it from his wallet, in contrast to the fumbling testified to by the arresting officer. He may be asked to draw a diagram of his driving path or of his performance on a field sobriety test. Prosecutors know that inexperienced witnesses are notoriously poor at diagramming on a board in front of a jury. During pre-trial preparation, counsel should have his client try some board diagramming. Or he may be asked why he did not tell the officer of an injury or illness that affected his test performance. Perhaps the defendant did not think it relevant — he is not acquainted with drunk driving procedures — and the officer did not bother to ask if there were any medical problems.

Inevitably, the prosecutor will go into the question of why available witnesses were not called. He will begin by establishing through cross-examination the existence of numerous individuals who had seen or talked with the defendant during the four or five hours prior to the arrest. He then will ask why they were not called to testify to the defendant's sobriety during that period. Are the witnesses available? What are their names? Have you made any efforts to locate them? Have you asked any of them to testify for you? Why not? This can be a damaging line of questioning, but awareness can at least take the sting out. The defendant should be able to identify the individuals, if possible, and explain why they were not testifying, either because they refused or were unavailable or the defendant did not want to embarrass them or perhaps did not want anyone to know he had been arrested.

The prosecutor will attempt to make it look as though the defendant, particularly if he has done well in the witness chair, merely was mouthing what his lawyer told him to say. Therefore he will ask a line of questions such as: Have you discussed your testimony with your attorney? Did the two of you talk over what you would testify to? Did he tell you what some of my questions might be? Did he tell you what to say? At this point, of course, defense counsel can counter the classic question with the classic answer. Anticipating the question, "Did he tell you what to say?" counsel should always advise his client to tell the truth and then remind him of this advice just before he takes the stand. The answer, "Yes, he told me to just tell the truth," can be very effective. The attorney-client privilege should, of course, be kept in mind.

Finally, counsel preparing his client for taking the stand in a drunk driving case may wish to consider some of the following prosecution tactics, taken from prosecution manuals.

1. Pin the defendant down as to everything he did during the 24 hours prior to his arrest — food and drink consumed, places visited, work activities, etc.
2. Have him mention every person who saw him during the period between drinking and arrest, then find out if any effort was made to find them — and if not called as witnesses, comment on this in argument.
3. If the defendant gives medical reasons for his appearance or performance, ask him if he told the officer of the problems — and comment in argument on the failure of the defense to corroborate this with medical witnesses.
4. If the defendant admits to some weaving, have him diagram the driving pattern on the same chart used by the

officer but with a different color marker. If he tries to give a reason for the driving, ask him if he explained this to the officer.

5. If the officer testified that the defendant had trouble getting his license out, ask the defendant to get it out and then have the court take notice that it was done quickly and without fumbling.
6. Request that the defendant walk past the jurors in the same way as he did when stopped by the officer; later, ask the officer on rebuttal to compare this with what he saw at the scene of the arrest.
7. Ask the defendant to evaluate his own field sobriety test, step by step. If he admits to any problems with the test but offers an excuse, ask if he gave the excuse to the officer.
8. *Never* ask the defendant to perform the FST in front of the jury as he did for the officer: He will perform the tests poorly. Object if the defense attorney asks his client to demonstrate his performance.
9. Pin the defendant down as to his opinion of his own sobriety and whether he felt any effects from any admitted drinks; most defendants will claim some minimal drinking at a bar with friends, and this should be exploited fully (denial of any effects will usually be disbelieved).
10. Ask the defendant if his present condition is exactly the same as it was at the arrest scene. Usually the defendant will deny this but claim the difference was due to something other than alcohol — in which case, go into every detail in which the situation was different and, finally, ask if these differences might be partly due to his drinking.
11. Get the defendant to admit that he has enough experience with alcohol to be familiar with the symptoms it produces. Then go through each of the symptoms to which the officer testified, asking the defendant if, in his experience, the symptom is a sign that too much alcohol has been consumed.

Kimberly de la Garza, of Houston, Texas, has lectured extensively on the subject of preparing witnesses and defendants for cross-examination in a drunk driving case. The following comments and suggestions by Ms. de la Garza concerning preparation of the defendant for cross, taken with her permission from seminar materials prepared by her, should be very helpful to the attorney planning to put his client on the stand:

> If you have not properly prepared your client these questions will not come as a surprise. Going over these and other possible questions that the prosecutor may ask will insure that the witness will not be confused or tricked but will be prepared with a well-thought-out and truthful answer.
>
> **1. Q. You have discussed your testimony with your attorney, haven't you?**
>
> *Bad Answer:* No [or Sure].
>
> *Truthful and Well-Reasoned Answer:* Of course, this whole thing has been a very frightening and confusing experience for me and my attorney has talked to me on several occasions to help me with my fears and to explain this court process to me so that I can better understand it.
>
> **Q. Isn't it a fact that your attorney told you what your answers to my questions should be?**
>
> *Bad Answer:* Yes.
>
> *Truthful and Well-Reasoned Answer:* He told me to answer all questions truthfully. He also told me not to let you trick me or put words in my mouth and to listen carefully to your questions because they might be confusing.
>
> *Rationale:* Obviously the well-prepared client will have visited with his attorney about what to expect at trial, particularly since unlike the officer, your client has no experience testifying. A prepared client has discovered implicitly how not to undermine the defense of his case, but he has been told to answer truthfully, albeit carefully.
>
> **2. Q. In preparing for trial, you discussed the facts with your attorney, didn't you?**
>
> *Bad Answer:* No.
>
> *Truthful and Well-Reasoned Answer:* We did agree that it was important to get as many facts as possible to the jury today so they would see that the officer is simply mistaken about my being intoxicated. But we didn't all remember the same things.
>
> *Rationale:* Be honest. Of course you discussed the facts with

your attorney and your witnesses. However, let the jury know that the witnesses did not get together and nail down a "perfect story." It also implies that the Defendant wants the "whole truth" out.

Note: This type of question can also be defused on direct examination by asking general questions of your client such as, "You've never testified before, have you? Did we talk about what you could expect at trial? Did I give you any instructions about how to answer questions?" Your instruction to your client, of course, was to tell the truth.

3. Q. Mr. Defendant, how do you define intoxication?

Bad Answers: Drunk; falling down; under the influence; or I think you described it best when you were talking to the jury panel earlier — slurring, swaying, unable to balance.

Truthful and Well-Reasoned Answer: Having lost the normal use of one's mental and physical faculties.

Rationale: Let the jury know we are all on the same page. An opinion on intoxication will lose its strength if it is not based on the legal definition, which is the one used by the prosecutor, the officers, and ultimately, the jury.

4. Q. And that's the definition you've always used for intoxication?

Bad Answer: Yes. (unless, of course, it is)

Truthful and Well-Reasoned Answer: No, that's the legal definition of intoxication as it was explained to me by my attorney.

Rationale: Of course that is not the definition he has always used. Be up front with the jury. Let them know that this attorney prepares his clients for battle. If the client does not know the definition, he will probably define drunk and set himself up for a fall.

5. Q. How would you describe an intoxicated person generally? For what characteristics do you look?

Bad Answer: Bloodshot eyes, loss of balance, slurring.

Truthful and Well-Reasoned Answer: I think it varies from person to person. You have to really know someone to be able to say for sure whether certain characteristics that look like signs of intoxication aren't caused by something else. Some people slur their words when tired or excited. Some have bloodshot eyes naturally or as a result of smoke or lack of sleep. Some people are klutzy in general or have injuries.

Rationale: Do not commit yourself to agreeing with the prosecutor or the police. Also be aware that a prosecutor may ask specific leading questions that seem to require an agreement if the witness wants to appear reasonable. Beware. The following example illustrates how general, seemingly unarguable points can get a client in trouble.

Q. Would you agree with me, sir, that alcohol impairs your ability to react?
A. Yes.
Q. That it impairs — slows the time for you to maybe apply the brakes. True?
A. Yes.
Q. It can impair your mental faculties and your memory?
A. Yes.
Q. You may forget the alphabet, say, or lose your judgment. Would you agree with all that?
A. Yes.
Q. Would you also agree that it affects your physical faculties?
A. Yes.
Q. You might not be able to walk a straight line.
A. Right.
Q. You may sway.
A. Yes.
Q. You may have slurred speech or loss of balance.
A. Yes.

Truthful and Well-Reasoned Answer: Alcohol will affect certain skills depending on whether a person is intoxicated and to what degree. On the night I was arrested, though, I was not intoxicated, and I can only speculate about how it might affect me on another occasion.

[*or*]

It's possible depending on the person, the amount of alcohol, and other things like tiredness or hunger.

6. Q. How do you act when you are intoxicated?

Bad Answer: I lose my balance, have bloodshot eyes.

Truthful and Well-Reasoned Answer: The best answer will include those signs of intoxication that are specific to the client. Any characteristics that are normal for the client when not intoxicated should *not* be included in his description, even though they might indicate intoxication in others — i.e., bloodshot eyes, loss of balance.

Rationale: Do not track the offense report. If the client describes to the jury the same characteristics that the officer says formed the basis for the arrest, he will have admitted his guilt. Generally, any characteristics for which your client has an explanation should not be included in his description.

7. Q. How do you explain the strong odor of alcohol on your breath?

Bad Answer: I don't know; the officer is lying.

Truthful and Well-Reasoned Answer: I'm sure there was an odor of alcohol as I did have alcohol to drink, but as to whether it was strong or weak, I would think that depends on who is describing it.

8. Q. How do you explain that you had bloodshot eyes?

Bad Answer: I don't know.

Truthful and Well-Reasoned Answer: I was tired; I had been subjected to cigarette smoke most of the day and evening; I am a welder (obviously not applicable to all clients).

Rationale: Almost any explanation will do as there are *many* reasons for bloodshot eyes. It gets a little more difficult to explain slurred speech or some of the other "symptoms," but look realistically at the possible explanations. Decide if there is a reasonable explanation or even if there is a real need to explain in the first place. (The prosecutor may be exaggerating a misstep or an occasional misstatement.)

9. Q. In your video (or according to the officer) you failed to keep your arms by your side when asked to raise one leg and hold it 6″ off the ground. Didn't you understand the officer's directions to keep your hands by your side?

Bad Answer: I guess I didn't understand; I couldn't keep my balance.

Truthful and Well-Reasoned Answer: You're right, I didn't keep my hands by my side because that is unnatural for a person to do when trying to balance. I have always used my arms for balance because that is a normal thing to do — just like you see acrobats do in the circus. If they don't want you to move your arms they should say so or have you hold your arms behind your back.

Rationale: It is not fair to ask someone to do something that is not normal or that contributes to loss of balance if balance is what the test is about.

10. Q. In your video (or according to the officer) you swayed a lot when you were asked to close your eyes, tilt your head back for 30 seconds while keeping your feet together. You did sway, didn't you?

Bad Answer: No.

Truthful and Well-Reasoned Answer: I probably did because I always do. I have done that exercise several times since my arrest to check what is normal for me and I do sway normally.

[*or*]

I wasn't trying to remain perfectly still or at attention because the officer didn't say he was testing me on my ability to remain still. I thought he was testing me on whether I could estimate 30 seconds with my eyes closed, my head tilted back and my feet together — it just doesn't seem fair to me that he was testing me on something he didn't tell me about so I could actually try to do what the test was all about.

Rationale: Again, it is not fair to ask someone to do something that is not normal or to test on something other than what you are asked to do.

11. Q. Do you think your memory is better than the officer's?

Bad Answer: Yes. [or No]

Truthful and Well-Reasoned Answer: I do not know whether it would be about all things, but this was my only arrest (if it is). Being interrogated by the officers and put in jail made an impression on me I will never forget, and no one remembers that night better than I do.

Rationale: How could your client possibly know whose memory is better generally? However, this was a nightmare he will never forget. This type response reinforces the fact that the officer has made numerous arrests since then, but this was the client's first.

12. Q. Ms. Defendant, isn't it more likely that you were so intoxicated *you* don't remember that evening?

Bad Answer: Yes. [or No]

Truthful and Well-Reasoned Answer: I was not intoxicated. I found out that if one has any alcohol on her breath and is not extremely coordinated she will be arrested for DWI no matter whether she is or not.

Rationale: What is or is not "more likely" has no bearing on what actually occurred. Don't let your client get tricked into answering hypothetically when he can answer based on the facts he knows. Additionally, let the jury know what a nightmare this has been and how easily the same thing could happen to anyone who has an alcoholic drink and drives. The Defendant should have already testified on direct that he was not intoxicated. This reaffirms that.

13. Q. Mr. Defendant, what do you normally drink when you go out?

Bad Answer: Scotch. [or Bud] [or Zombies].

Truthful and Well-Reasoned Answer: I do not *normally* drink. Occasionally, I will have wine with my dinner or a mixed drink at a cocktail party.

Rationale: The prosecutor is trying to establish a habit or pattern of drinking. Most people do have a favorite drink and if not prepared with a well thought-out answer will appear to drink all the time.

14. Q. How many drinks did you have on December 31, 1989?

Bad Answer: I told the officer I had four (4) drinks, but I really had three (3).

Truthful and Well-Reasoned Answer: I told the officer I had four (4) drinks, but I was so nervous I didn't stop to think. When I later went over the events of the evening, I realized it was actually three (3) [or I ordered four (4), but only had one sip of the last one].

[*or*]

Bad Answer: I don't remember.

Truthful and Well-Reasoned Answer: I had three (3) drinks. I told the officer that night that I had three drinks and I am telling this jury that I only had three drinks.

Rationale: The facts do not change. The attorney knew this question was coming so the defendant should be prepared for it. Show consistent answers or be prepared to explain the discrepancy. The time period over which he had the admitted number of drinks should have already been discussed/explained on direct examination.

15. Q. What time was your first drink, second . . . ?

Bad Answer: 7:00, then 9:30 . . .

Truthful and Well-Reasoned Answer: I had my first drink about seven when I got to the restaurant. My second was sometime before we left the restaurant, which was at 9:30.

Rationale: No one would be expected to remember exact times, but references to other things that occurred help make the timetable more credible. This also lets the jury know the Defendant was not just out to drink.

16. Q. What did you have to eat that night?

Bad Answer: I had no dinner.

Truthful and Well-Reasoned Answer: [List *everything* you had to eat for the day. Think.]

Rationale: Food in the stomach affects the absorption of alcohol into the blood stream. People tend to forget snacks between meals, but it all adds up. It also takes longer to digest some foods than one might think.

17. Q. Sir, you would agree with me, wouldn't you, that we only have your word for the number of drinks you had?

Bad Answer: True; I guess so.

Truthful and Well-Reasoned Answer: If you are insinuating that I would lie to this jury just because no one can contradict me, you are wrong. Not only do people have drinks alone, but even in public, it is rare for someone to count the number of drinks another person has. The proof that I only had two (2) drinks is in the videotape [or in the testimony of those who know me that I appeared normal].

Rationale: People do not count each other's drinks and it makes no sense to imply that one might be lying because others did not count his drinks.

18. Q. Mr. Defendant, have you been intoxicated before?

Bad Answer: Yes (with no explanation); No (unless it's true).

Truthful and Well-Reasoned Answer: (First DWI) Yes, when I was in college; When I was much younger; Before I had the responsibility of a family; I had someone drive me home; I took a taxi. (Subsequent DWI's: Defense counsel should already be on his feet).

Rationale: This shows you have either outgrown those "wild oat'' days or that you have enough sense not to drive when intoxicated. Had the client been intoxicated he would have let someone else drive.

19. Q. How many drinks does it take to get you drunk?

Bad Answer: Six [or any specific number or amount].

Truthful and Well-Reasoned Answer: If you mean ''intoxicated,'' it depends on what I'm drinking, how much I have had to drink, how much I have had to eat and a number of other factors.

Rationale: Try to avoid a set number of drinks. If the client admits on the stand it takes six drinks to get him drunk and he told officers he had three drinks he must have been half-drunk.

20. Q. Mr. Defendant, you told the officer you had three beers [or two martinis]. How many beers [martinis] does it take to make you intoxicated?

Bad Answer: Four [or any specific number].

Truthful and Well-Reasoned Answer: Depending on how much I had to eat, what I was drinking, and over what period of time, I could probably drink from three to five beers (martinis, etc.) without losing my normal mental and physical faculties. However, if you're asking if the number of drinks I had the night I was arrested would get me intoxicated, the answer is No!

Rationale: Do not set an unbelievably high number; the jury will not be fooled by this or they will think they are dealing with an alcoholic. Use a range. Don't be evasive.

21. Q. Would you attend an important business meeting after having that many drinks?

Bad Answer: No. [or Yes.]

Truthful and Well-Reasoned Answer: I would certainly be able to, but I probably would not simply because alcohol is a social thing and has no place in a professional or work setting.

Rationale: Reaffirm that you were not impaired. The prosecutor would like to lead you into saying that you would not because your judgment might be impaired.

22. Q. Would you allow a surgeon who had that many drinks to operate on your child?

Bad Answer: No.

Truthful and Well-Reasoned Answer: Although he might be able to, without knowing him, knowing what he had eaten, how little sleep he had the night before, or when he had the drinks, I would not take the risk.

Rationale: Be realistic, but reaffirm the numerous factors involved in determining how much alcohol will cause intoxication. It also gives the jury the idea that an observer may not be able to judge.

23. Q. Who is the better judge of a person's intoxication — the person who has been drinking or someone who has not been drinking?

Bad Answer: One who has not been drinking.

Truthful and Well-Reasoned Answer: While I cannot answer for everyone, in my case I am the best judge of how I feel. Someone who has never met me before could not possibly know what is normal for me. I know what is normal for me while the other person would just be guessing.

Rationale: Implicit in the prosecutor's question is the fact that a trained, sober officer would not be mistaken and that the drinking defendant is mistaken. This thought-out answer should make sense to the jury.

24. Q. Sir, are you telling this jury that you felt no effect whatsoever from the alcohol you had to drink — not even a warm feeling or a little lightheadedness?

Bad Answer: Sure, I got a little buzz.

Truthful and Well-Reasoned Answer: I may have felt some sensation, sometimes I do even after one drink, but it did not affect my mental or physical skills.

Rationale: Most people do feel "something" after a first drink, and a jury would probably think it unreasonable to deny it. However, the definition of intoxication is specific for loss of normal use. This distinction is best taken care of during voir dire.

25. Q. Mr. Defendant, are you saying that the officer is lying?

Bad Answer: Yes. He is lying.

Truthful and Well-Reasoned Answer: I would not like to think he is lying. So much time has passed and he has made so many stops since he stopped me, I just believe he has forgotten some of the details or possibly has me confused with someone else.

[*or*]

Truthful and Well-Reasoned Answer: He has misinterpreted what he saw of me that night and concluded I was intoxicated probably because he is specifically looking for intoxicated drivers.

Rationale: The jury wants to believe our officers tell the truth. If we cannot believe law enforcement officers, who can we believe? Do not set yourself up by suggesting the officer is lying unless you have a lay-down hand. Remember, DWI is an opinion crime and everyone has an opinion whether it is right or not.

26. Q. You consider yourself a safe driver, don't you? You generally don't break the law, do you?

A. I am a safe driver and usually obey traffic laws.

Q. Yet you were speeding, weren't you?

Bad Answer: No, I wasn't. [Unless, it's true.]

Truthful and Well-Reasoned Answer: Yes, but I did have full control of the car and could have stopped, if necessary.

Rationale: It generally does not hurt to admit a traffic offense. Most people do break some traffic laws, at least occasionally. However, if the traffic infraction is in question for probable cause purposes, the client or his fact witness can testify that the radar machine must not have been working properly or the operator made a mistake about which car was speeding. Remember not to call the officer a liar unless you can prove it.

27. Q. In spite of your assertedly normal appearance, the officer arrested you and now you are being prosecuted. You believe, don't you, that there must be a conspiracy between the police and the District Attorney's office to harass and persecute you?

Bad Answer: Yes.

Truthful and Well-Reasoned Answer: I believe their job is not to give the benefit of the doubt to someone who might be intoxicated. That's why we have juries — to decide if someone is really guilty.

Rationale: A jury will not believe a paranoid defendant. Most juries want the officers to err on the side of caution. This answer lets them know that you don't disagree in general with law enforcement, but the officers just happen to be wrong in this instance.

28. Q. You refused to take the intoxilyzer test because you knew it would have showed you were intoxicated, isn't that true? You knew it would be all over, didn't you?

Bad Answer: I knew it might be over .10.

Truthful and Well-Reasoned Answer: I know that the intoxilyzer is just a machine and machines break down. Maybe if I had been intoxicated I would have let the officer talk me into taking the intoxilyzer, but I was not going to let a machine decide my fate when I knew I was *not* intoxicated. I preferred to trust a jury of my fellow citizens.

Rationale: The jury has probably heard or read something about the intoxilyzer. This answer would seem to be consistent with someone who is in control of his normal mental faculties.

29. Q. In the videotape (or on the roadside with the officer), you had the opportunity to perform exercises and show us your mental and physical faculties but you chose not to, didn't you? Wasn't it because you knew you would fail those tests because you were intoxicated?

Bad Answer: I didn't know how I would do on them; I guess I did keep information from this jury.

Truthful and Well-Reasoned Answer: I have always heard that an arrested person should *always* talk to a lawyer before doing or saying anything. I chose not to do the tests, but not because I was intoxicated. I felt the officer had already made up his mind to arrest me and there was nothing I could do to change that.

Rationale: This reminds the jury that your client was concerned about his legal rights and was not sure what to do.

30. Q. So what you're saying is you had the opportunity to show a later jury that you were not intoxicated, and you didn't take it?

Bad Answer: Yes.

Truthful and Well-Reasoned Answer: I wanted to ask a lawyer what I should do. Besides, I thought in this country you don't have to prove your innocence or has that law changed?

Rationale: The jury should be made to realize how unfair it is for a person to be arrested and required to make decisions without a lawyer.

31. Q. You'd do anything to keep from going to jail wouldn't you?

Bad Answer: Yes. [No.]

Truthful and Well-Reasoned Answer: I would not lie. If I thought I was guilty I would have just paid the fine and not insisted on a trial or I would have taken the probation you offered me.

Rationale: This answer shows the jury that the client was offered some fine and no jail time which he turned down because he was innocent.

32. Q. Mr. Defendant, you don't want to be convicted of DWI, do you?

Bad Answer: No.

Truthful and Well-Reasoned Answer: Of course not, no innocent person would want to be convicted. However, if your question really is ''would I lie to avoid being convicted?'' then absolutely not, my integrity as a person means too much to me to give up my honesty when I could have already taken the probation you offered me.

Note: This is a great opportunity for the client to get a little indignant with the prosecutor for calling him a liar. Indeed, his indignation will enhance his credibility.

15

CLOSING

§15.0 Summation: Strategy and Illustration

> It ain't what a man don't know that makes him a fool, but what he does know that ain't so.
>
> JOSH BILLINGS

The following material presents an excellent approach to closing argument in a drunk driving case. The author is indebted to Flem Whited III, of Daytona Beach, Florida, for his kindness in granting permission to reproduce these materials.

Initial approach. You should begin your closing arguments by an acknowledgement to the jury that you understand it has been a long day and that you appreciate their attention throughout the trial. Ask them to pay an equal amount of attention to your closing argument as it is just as important as all other aspects of the trial.

It is important, at this point, to inform the jury that during your closing argument you will be making reference to various facts that have been testified to at trial. You are not going to attempt to mislead them in any way and any reference to certain testimony during the trial is based on your best recollection. If theirs is different, they should rely on their own memories.

Purpose of closing argument. It is important to inform the jury of the exact purpose of the closing argument. You should inform them that it is at this point in the trial that you will be reviewing the evidence that has been presented and relating it to the law that applies to the case so that it will help them in their deliberations to come to the proper verdict.

Role of the jury. You must make it perfectly clear what role the jury plays in the criminal justice system.

Review all that has happened up until this point in time. Specifically, inform the jurors that your client

1. was arrested and taken to jail;
2. was given an opportunity to enter a plea to this case;
3. entered his not guilty plea, which necessarily led to the trial; and
4. could have given up and pleaded guilty at any time, but hasn't.

Let them know how your client was treated by the police.

Make sure that they are told that the arresting officer has made up his mind as to the guilt or innocence of your client. He made up his mind when he placed your client under arrest and took him to jail on the day in question.

If your client had an opportunity to deny that he was impaired by alcohol during the day in question, then make sure you inform the jury that he denied his guilt and that he has maintained that position throughout the proceedings. The jury should also know that when your client denied he was impaired, he knew nothing about the rules of law that apply to jury trials, but denied guilt because of his sincere belief that alcohol did not affect his normal faculties at that time.

Finally, make sure the jury understands that it is their role to review the police conduct and apply the appropriate rules of law in order to determine guilt or innocence. It is only the jury — not the police officers — who can find the defendant guilty or not guilty. Make sure they understand the difference between the role of the jury and the role of the police officers. The officer does not apply the reasonable doubt standard. Probable cause is different from reasonable doubt. He may have had enough probable cause for the arrest, but he did not have the whole story. A verdict of not guilty is not a slap in the face of the police officer.

Reminder of commitments. In your voir dire examination you should have obtained certain commitments from each juror personally regarding various aspects of your case. These commitments should have been obtained in two categories: the facts that may be presented at trial and the law that applies. Some commitments should be:

1. A police officer should not be treated differently or his testimony given any greater weight simply because he is a police officer.
2. They would keep an open mind regarding any evidence presented as a result of a breath test machine and the field sobriety test.
3. They would not hold it against your client just because he is young, likes to ride motorcycles, has tattoos, and uses an excessive amount of profanity toward police officers. Obviously, any other negative aspects of your case would apply here.
4. They understood the presumption of innocence and will apply it in this case.
5. The burden of proof is on the State to prove your client's guilt beyond and to the exclusion of every reasonable doubt; and if there was a reasonable doubt, they would find your client not guilty.

Make sure that after reviewing each and every commitment with the jury that you let them know that you believed them when they made the commitments and that you believe them now when it is time to apply those commitments. For example:

> You will recall during voir dire Gary Cooper and I asked each and every one of you personally if you understood the presumption of innocence and if you could apply it in this case. You told me at that time that you would apply it in this case and I believed you when you told me so.
>
> We discussed the burden of proof being beyond and to the exclusion of every reasonable doubt and you all agreed that that was not an unreasonable burden and that you would hold the State to that high degree of proof; I believed you when you made that commitment to me then, and I believe you will apply it during your deliberations now.

> Each and every one of you agreed with me that a police officer's testimony should be given no greater weight just because he is a police officer and that you would give the same weight to lay testimony that you could to that of a police officer.

Each and every commitment that the jury made, although being cautious not to nauseate, should be reviewed with them.

Review of the law. After reviewing the commitments, make sure you move into a closer look at the law that you have just reminded them they are committed to follow. Here you should use the actual jury instructions. Make sure not to read directly from them; the judge instructs on matters of law.

Presumption of innocence and burden of proof. Make sure the jury understands that this is not a civil trial where all someone wants is money and where both sides start out even. Let them know that the presumption of innocence tips the scales of justice down in favor of your client.

Be descriptive when explaining the presumption of innocence either by way of arm gestures or a chalkboard. Your example is an excellent way to describe to the jury the presumption of innocence and the degree of proof that is necessary in order to eliminate all reasonable doubt.

What is reasonable doubt and how do you know it when you see it? Reasonable doubt is not a possible speculative, imaginary, or forced doubt. In other words, if you have to strain to find reasonable doubt, then it is not there.

Reasonable doubt is present when there is a doubt as to the guilt of your client, and there is a reason for that doubt. There must be an abiding conviction of guilty for the State to have met its burden of proof. If the State does not have an abiding conviction of guilt, then the charge is not proven beyond a reasonable doubt and the verdict is not guilty.

Be very careful not to read from the jury instructions. When referring to jury instructions and the law, always be mindful to qualify your statements.

Reasonable doubt can be found from the evidence, the conflict in the evidence, or the lack of evidence.

The jury must be reminded to constantly question themselves, asking Has the State eliminated all reasonable doubt? Is the doubt that I have reasonable?

The verdict must be based on the evidence that is presented, and one cannot speculate on what could or might have been the proof. What is the proof?

An example of the above is:

> What is the proof, ladies and gentlemen, that Gary Cooper's blood-alcohol level was over .10? Where's the beef? It's not there. What is the prosecution asking you to do? The answer is: He is giving you no proof, but we are to assume what he says is correct anyway. Can we say *just because* he was a .23 one hour after the arrest that that automatically makes him over .10 at the time of driving? Where's the evidence for us to come to that conclusion? Well, ladies and gentlemen, there is none. I would submit to you that we don't convict people in this country with *just because.* Just because he is a .23, he had to be over .10? Just because he slipped off the line once, he can't walk normally?

You should close the review of the law by summing it up in a very concise statement. For example:

> Ladies and gentlemen, the law that applies to this case is very simple. Gary Cooper has been charged with the offense of driving under the influence of alcohol to the extent that his normal faculties were impaired or driving with a blood-alcohol level that exceeded the legal limit. He is presumed innocent and his guilt must be proved beyond and to the exclusion of all reasonable doubt. If all doubt has been eliminated from your minds after reviewing the evidence, then your verdict should be guilty. But, if after reviewing the evidence, you have a doubt and there is a reason for that doubt and there is not an abiding conviction of guilt, then the verdict is not guilty. Let us now review the evidence that has been presented, being mindful of the law that applies.

Weighing the evidence. There are various rules that apply to weighing the evidence. Touch on all the rules of weighing the evidence during your review of the facts rather than devoting a special place to them as you have the presumption of innocence, burden of proof, and concepts of reasonable doubt.

The judge will give you certain rules or guidelines when considering the testimony of witnesses. They are:

1. *The ability of the witness to see what he has testified to.* When reviewing the testimony of one witness or the other, use this rule if it helps.
2. *Did the witness have an accurate memory?* Police officers almost always remember the bad things and either forget or overlook the good ones. An example would be the ability of your client to quickly and easily find his wallet and produce his driver's license and registration. If the police officer does not recall these facts, then it should have been brought out on cross-examination that had the defendant had trouble with these facts the officer would surely have written them down. The fact that they are not present in the officer's offense report or in his testimony is indicative of the fact that they did not occur. If the police officer or any witness has waivered or vacillated on any point, then make sure that point, or the quality of that testimony, is related to the jury instruction regarding the waivering and vacillating conviction of guilt and the jury instruction relating to the accuracy of their memory.
3. *Was the witness straightforward and honest in answering the questions?* If you have a police officer who simply will not answer a question in a straightforward manner, then combine that flaw with the jury instruction on how to evaluate that testimony. Simple questions can be answered with simple responses, and if the police officer constantly avoids the question, relate that fact to this jury instruction.

It is insulting when the words *weighing the evidence* are used. We have scales of justice. There must be some meaning to their constant reference to poundage and scales. One technique you can follow when discussing the facts is to use the scales and put certain facts on one side or the other, and see if the weight of the State's case is such that it tips the scales completely down.

Interest in the case. You can be guaranteed that your client has interest in the case. It is unavoidable and should be addressed in your closing argument at some point because you can be certain that in the prosecutor's rebuttal he will bring it out. In reviewing your client's testimony to the jury, let them know that the judge will instruct them regarding this particular aspect of weighing testimony. Also remind them that your client took an oath to tell the truth, took the witness stand, and — in the face of the rule of law that allowed him to remain silent — waived those rights and subjected himself to the cross-examination of an experienced prosecutor in order to tell his side.

Prior inconsistent statement. Did the witness make a statement that is inconsistent with his court testimony? This can be used effectively in the final argument when related to the final instruction on weighing the evidence. The jury may believe or disbelieve all or any part of the evidence or testimony of any witness.

If the police officer made a prior inconsistent statement and you brought this out in your cross-examination, then hammer home the inherent unreliability of the rest of his testimony. Do not let the prosecutor get away with the "Nobody's perfect" and "He can't remember everything" arguments. Police officers are professional witnesses, and every time they arrest someone there is the potential for trial. It is their job to document the facts of each and every case. They are supposed to be trained professionals, and to do a lousy job at trial is indicative of their overall quality of work.

When you have a case where there is a prior inconsistency in the statement and you want to call into question the ability to believe other portions of a witness's testimony, the following interesting analogy can be used:

> Ladies and gentlemen of the jury, the testimony of the arresting officer and the inconsistent statements he has made are much like the time, and I'm sure you all have been in this situation, where you have ordered a big bowl of Irish stew. You dig in with your soup spoon and the first piece of meat that you bite into is spoiled. Do you then just lay that spoiled piece of meat aside and continue to eat the rest of that soup? Or do you push the rest of the bowl aside?

Review of the facts. When reviewing the facts, be sure to do so with an eye toward jury instruction on how you can have a reasonable doubt. In Florida our instruction says that a reasonable doubt can be found from the evidence, lack of evidence, or a conflict of evidence. It goes on to say that for the State to convict, there must be an abiding conviction of guilt. The jury is told that if they have an abiding conviction of guilt — but it is one that waivers and vacillates — then the charge is not proven and the verdict is not guilty. If your jurisdiction has words similar to these, then be sure to use them over and over again in your closing argument so the jury understands exactly the extent to which the charge has to be proven in order for there to be a guilty verdict. What is an abiding conviction of guilt? When can there be no doubt on which a good reason cannot be found? These are very heavy burdens that the State has to meet and must be emphasized in your closing argument. For example:

> Ladies and gentlemen of the jury, it is the law of this land that before a person accused of a crime can be branded with a criminal conviction, guilt must be proven to the point in your mind that you have no reasonable doubt. If you have a reasonable doubt, then the proper verdict is not guilty. But that is only common sense. Whenever in our daily lives we have important decisions to make, we want to make sure that we do the right thing. The law is no different. It is not a stranger to common sense. It has evolved over hundreds of years, and it is the law of this land and of this country that if you have a reasonable doubt, then the verdict is not guilty. Gary Cooper alone does not win when these principles of law are applied. We all do, because the law has been followed. The judge has told us that it has been the law in this land for two hundred years and no other law applies, and to not follow the law as instructed would be a miscarriage of justice.

When reviewing the facts, be sure to let the jury know how certain evidence got in without the officer's help. Typical examples are:

1. All the good things that your client did.
2. All that the police officer does not recall. "Don't recalls" are the same as an admission that the client performed properly. Any police officer will have to admit that if he did not write something in his report, that is tantamount to its not happening. It is a rare occasion when a police

officer does not note each and every sign of impairment that he observes when coming to the conclusion that your client was driving under the influence. Force the police officer to admit the fact that if he does not remember, it is tantamount to your client's performing that task favorably.

3. Problems with the breath test machines.
4. Inherent weaknesses in breath testing machines, such as 2100:1; nonspecificity; and time of stop vs. time of test.

For example:

> Why was it that it was not until cross-examination that we heard Gary Cooper got out of his car without any problems, produced his driver's license with no problems, and found his registration without any difficulty?
>
> Is the urge for conviction so great that the police officer did not want to tell you these things until it was dragged out of him? Why did he hold these things back?
>
> Do you think that the prosecutor and the police officer just took a chance and hoped that I would not ask all these questions?
>
> Do you think that they wanted you to look at Gary Cooper with one eye closed?
>
> Why did I ask these questions? One reason is so that you could have the whole story and could make an informed decision. Another reason we wanted you to have these facts is that when you make an important decision — and believe me this is an important decision in Gary Cooper's life — you should have all the information necessary before you can make that decision. The question that you have to ask in this case is: Is a reasonable doubt in my mind? Don't you think it would be nice to be able to have all the facts in order to make that decision? Did the prosecutor paint half the picture for you and want you to make the decision with only half of what occurred that evening? It appears so. How would you have felt if you were forced to make that decision and I had not asked those questions on cross-examination of the police officer regarding all the things that Gary Cooper did properly and all the things that the police officer forgot to tell you?
>
> Ladies and gentlemen, would you buy a house without checking to see if it had termites, or crawling underneath it to see if the wood was sound, or looking up in the attic to see if it was properly insulated? Would you buy a used car without taking it to a me-

chanic to have it checked out to make sure that it was perfectly sound?

I think we all know the answers to these questions. The mission that you have today is even more important than those examples that I just gave you. You must use the same care, caution, and concern in deciding the question before you today as you would in any situation that comes from your daily lives. The question that you have to ask is: Is there a reasonable doubt in my mind and, by the same token, has the prosecutor eliminated all doubt from my mind?

Ladies and gentlemen, think about what the evidence was when the State finished their questioning of Officer Brown regarding the maintenance and operation of the machine in this case. You would have been left with the idea that the number was absolutely perfect. But we found out that that was not the case. Everybody is subjected to the same standard. The officer admitted that he did not know what Gary Cooper's blood/breath conversion ratio was. We are just taking a chance at Gary Cooper's being the same as what the machine is programmed to be. Can we take that chance? When we do not really know, can we say beyond and to the exclusion of reasonable doubt that we will depend on it?

Who is trying to hide these things from you, ladies and gentlemen? Why was it not until cross-examination that we did hear about any of these things? That evidence stands before you as unrebutted. There is no doubt that the machine is based on averages and is not specific for ethyl alcohol, but notwithstanding any of that, we were not told that on direct examination. It's as if the State wants you to believe that the machine can do something that it cannot. There is absolutely no evidence in this case, ladies and gentlemen, of what Gary Cooper's blood-alcohol level was at the time that he was operating his motor vehicle. The machine cannot tell you that. The machine cannot talk; all that it can do is give you a number at the time that the test was taken. I submit to you that that number is absolutely worthless. The judge will tell you that a reasonable doubt can be found for the lack of evidence. It can be found from the evidence or from a conflict in the evidence. If we then say that it is against the law to drive with a blood-alcohol level greater than .10 percent, then let's look at the evidence that has been presented in this case regarding what Gary Cooper's blood-alcohol level was at the time that he was operating his motor vehicle. The arresting officer did not tell us what it was, the person who performed the test on Gary Cooper did not tell us what it was, and the maintenance operator did not tell us what it was. All we

> have is a number at some remote period in time; the machine did not tell us. There has been absolutely no evidence whatsoever that has been presented to you to prove what Gary Cooper's blood-alcohol level was at the time he was driving his car. Where does that leave us? It leaves us with absolutely nothing, not one single solitary piece of evidence that we can look at to conclude what a blood-alcohol level was. You agreed in voir dire that you would not speculate and that you would hold the State to the burden of proving to each and every one of you each and every element of the offense beyond and to the exclusion of every reasonable doubt. Ladies and gentlemen, they simply have not done it in this case. The judge will tell you that a reasonable doubt is not a possible, speculative, imaginary, or forced doubt. Ladies and gentlemen, we are not asking you to do any of those things. I would suggest to you that the prosecution is asking you to speculate and imagine and is trying to force upon you the proof in this case. Ladies and gentlemen, the answer to the question, "Is there a reasonable doubt in my mind as to Gary Cooper's blood-alcohol level at the time that he was stopped?" in this case is an easy one to answer. There is no evidence of a blood-alcohol level at the time that he was arrested, and, ladies and gentlemen, I would submit to you that if there is no evidence on this point, then there has to be a doubt in your mind, and there is no other kind of doubt that it can be other than a reasonable one.

Field sobriety testing. Always remember when dealing with field sobriety tests that they are just that — tests. During my life most, if not all, of the tests that I have taken I have had the ability to study and prepare for, so that the tests have been fair ones. There also have been times that I have not been perfect, or have only done marginally well, but I still passed. These same rules do not apply to field sobriety tests. Field sobriety testing has become more and more complex over the years and easier and easier to fail. The arguments outlined here that should be made to the jury must be developed through your cross-examination of the police officer and, from time to time, the direct examination of your client.

Does failure to successfully complete the tasks offered by the officer mean that you are impaired by alcohol, or does it mean that you just cannot successfully do the exercises that he has asked you to do? Remember: All the police officer has at this point is the probability that your client has been consuming an alcoholic beverage at the time, unless he has gone into custodial interrogation, and your client has admitted what he had to drink.

Emphasize the subjective grading of the test by the police officer. If a point system is used, then emphasize how easy it is to fail. Also, the point should be made that, while there is a point system that is being used, various aspects of the grading remain subjective.

The defendant is generally expected to perceive the instructions that the police officer has given him the first time that they are given. If the police officer has to repeat the instructions, why is it that that is a sign of your client's inability to understand them rather than the officer's inability to communicate them effectively? The fact that your client asked questions during the instruction phase of the field sobriety testing should not be counted against him. Rather, it should be argued that that is a sign of his understanding of how important the tests are and of his desire to perform the tests in the manner that he has been instructed to.

Remember that people are on trial for having their normal faculties impaired — that is, their ability to walk, talk, judge distances, act in emergencies, drive a car, and generally carry out normal daily activities. Ask yourself — and have the jury ask themselves — what people are being asked to do and whether the tasks they are being asked to perform are not more difficult than what a person normally does. The bottom line is that there is absolutely nothing normal a person is being asked to do when asked to perform a field sobriety test; that should not have any relation whatsoever to whether the person is impaired by alcohol.

If you have a video involved and your client does not perform well on the field sobriety test, make sure to emphasize those section of the video that show him walking to and from various points in a normal manner or standing in a normal manner. If he has the ability to walk normally and does so without much difficulty, then emphasize this as the only objective evidence that the jurors have of whether of not his ability to walk normally has been impaired at all. They should remember and view those parts of the video that display your client's true normal faculties, not his ability to stand on one leg and touch his finger to his nose with his eyes closed.

Each field sobriety test should be viewed closely to determine exactly what the instructions are. Once you have obtained all the instructions from the police officer on cross-examination, you should find out from that police officer what complaints he had with your client's performance and all the things that your client did on that particular test. As an example, we will assume that your client was given the heel-to-toe test and that he used his arms for balance while standing heel-to-toe listening to the instructions, stepped off the line twice (going forward), turned improperly, and stepped off the line once on his return trip. The total number of tasks that your client had to perform on this test would be approximately 56. To arrive at that figure, we have counted nine steps forward, nine steps counted out loud, and nine steps hitting his heel to his toe. That amounts to 27 total tasks, which anyone could fail at. Add those 27 with the 27 coming back along, with the turn and the ability to stand without using your arms for balance while listening to instructions, and you have 56 tasks on this one test alone. Now, if we apply the number of deficiencies to the number of total tasks, we have essentially someone who has properly done 90 percent of what was asked of him, but who still failed. Make these types of percentage arguments to the jury in closing arguments rather than during cross-examination of the police officer. Doing so is more effective because the police officers and prosecutors will always find a way to get around this type of argument if you raise it in cross-examination. If you give it in your closing argument, you will not have the problem of the police officer to deal with. What you have essentially done is turned failure into success. Here is a police officer who has failed someone for doing approximately five things wrong out of a total of 56 things he could have done. That is absurd and that absurdity should be driven home with no uncertain terms to the members of the jury. During voir dire, you always leave on the jury someone who has some physical defect, is overweight or advanced in years, and you must make sure that they understand that all it could take is the odor of alcohol on their breath and the inability to do these ridiculous tests to get a trip to the jail.

Closing your closing. It has to happen. At some point, you have to stop talking. After following the above format, you have thoroughly reviewed the facts and explained to the jury how those facts apply to the law as it relates to their search for reasonable doubt. You have been logical, methodical, and fair throughout the entire closing argument, but now you simply must stop.

Don't let your closing just fade out. By the time you have finished reviewing all the facts, you should be emotionally charged. Don't just say, "Well, I guess I've said all I can. Please find Gary Cooper not guilty." One suggested closing might be:

> Ladies and gentlemen of the jury, it has come to that point when you will go your way and I'll go mine. Since we probably won't be seeing each other again, I want to take this opportunity on behalf of Gary Cooper and myself to thank you for your attention here today, and I hope that this trial has been a meaningful experience for you.
>
> Today you have had bestowed on you the greatest power a group of people can have: the power to decide the guilt or innocence of a fellow citizen — the power to decide the fate of Gary Cooper. I know you will exercise that power with wisdom and compassion.
>
> I have tried to show you, within the limits of my ability, that there is reasonable doubt and that there is but one verdict, and that is the verdict of not guilty. But I can't give you the courage to return it. For that you'll have to look within yourselves.
>
> But I do know one thing and that is that the State of Florida does not deserve a conviction based on the pitiful proof that has been given you today. If that's all it takes to convict someone, then no one is safe.
>
> I ask you to return a verdict of not guilty and, if you do, I can assure you that you can then walk out of this courtroom with your heads held high.

§15.1 Jury Instructions

> "Let the jury consider their verdict," the King said, for about the twentieth time that day.
> "No, no!" said the Queen. "Sentence first — verdict afterwards."
>
> LEWIS CARROLL

There is considerable disagreement among trial lawyers about the relative importance of jury instructions in a drunk driving case.

One view suggests that most jurors will disregard almost completely the tedious language that is read at great length by the judge at the end of the trial. They tend to become bored with the overly long monologue, cannot understand most of the technical words, and usually rely in the final analysis on rather simple, commonsense considerations. The other view, however, stresses that the jurors look to the instructions as their legal guide. The language not only sets forth the shape and size of the "playing field" within which the jurors can operate (i.e., defines the offense, interprets the evidence, and limits the jurors' functions) but supplies the single most common source for appellate issues. Too, the instructions will have a significant effect on the content of counsel's argument to the jury.

There should be no question that the formulation and giving of jury instructions constitutes an important phase of the drunk driving jury trial, perhaps more so than in most other criminal cases. The jury is instructed specifically as to what the offense consists of — that is, the meaning of such nebulous phrases as "under the influence" and "impaired ability to operate a motor vehicle," and what presumptions of guilt apply as well as many other critical areas. Because of their confusion concerning many of the drunk driving definitions and the complexities of chemical evidence, juries may tend to pay closer attention to instructions in drunk driving trials.

Yet perhaps the most recurrent oversight of defense counsel in such trials is the failure both to review adequately the proposed instructions and to submit requested defense instructions. This tendency simply to accept whatever jury instructions the court intends to give is bad enough in the usual criminal case; it can be especially damaging in a drunk driving trial.

Most states have given the trial judge the responsibility for properly instructing the jury, and as a result many judges tend to draft and give instructions without considering the desires of the defense attorney. At the same time, an unfortunate tendency has developed in which tired or lazy judges have relied increasingly on the prosecuting attorney to supply an "appropriate" set of instructions. In many cases, this set will constitute all the instructions that the jury will hear. Presumably, the prosecutor will submit instructions that are used widely and approved legally, but it is still likely that they will reflect a prosecution bias. It is certainly unlikely they will contain any directions or definitions reflecting a defense theory of the case.

It is defense counsel's legal right and duty to examine every instruction that the trial judge intends to give. Counsel will occasionally encounter a judge who will refuse to permit him to review the instructions. In such a case, he should carefully place this on the record for appellate purposes; faced with this, most judges will reluctantly permit counsel to examine the proposed instructions. It should also be remembered that neglecting to object to the giving of an instruction or to the failure of the judge to give a proposed instruction will prevent counsel from raising the issue on appeal.

In addition to the right to review, defense counsel should have the right to propose deletions or additions to the intended instructions as well as the right to offer suggested defense instructions. (See, e.g., *Banner v. Commonwealth,* 204 Va. 640, 133 S.E.2d 305 (1963); *People v. Modesto,* 59 Cal. 2d 722, 382 P.2d 33 (1963).) This is a right that should be exercised strenuously; every conceivable issue should be considered for the possibility that an acceptable instruction could be given that would cast a favorable light on the defense.

Counsel should never lose sight of the fact that in dealing with the trial judge he is dealing with a human being. Confronted with a complete, neatly wrapped package of approved instructions by the prosecution, the judge after a long and hard trial may be less than enthusiastic toward defense counsel's picking away at each of the instructions and offering new ones slanted to the defense. A suggested procedure here is for counsel to submit his *own* neatly wrapped, complete set of instructions, many of which reflect strong defense views. At the same time, counsel should have available a second set of instructions (again, complete so that the judge need add nothing) that incorporates both defense and prosecution theories on the issues. After initial argument between opposing counsel, the trial judge may well be receptive to the sudden presentation of this compromise set of instructions. Thus many of the defense positions will be presented by the judge where none would have been before.

Counsel should be aware that he does not have to prove that his theory concerning a particular instruction is correct and applicable beyond a reasonable doubt. Rather he need only show that a prima facie case on the issue was presented in the course of the trial. (See, e.g., *State v. Rio,* 20 Wash. 2d 446, 230 P.2d 308, *cert. denied,* 342 U.S. 867 (1951).) If, for example, the defendant testified that he was suffering from some illness or disability at the time of his arrest, counsel should be able to have an instruction read to the effect that the jury could discount the results of the field sobriety tests and/or the chemical tests if it felt these tests were affected significantly by the disability or illness.

In the discussion to follow, the subject of specific instructions will be general in nature due to the wide variety of applicable statutes, precedent, and forms in local use. Instructions should be obtained from forms approved for use by the jurisdiction or more commonly in the case of defense instructions, composed by counsel on the basis of relevant statutes and case law.

The first area that defense counsel should consider for possible instructions involves defining the term "under the influence" for the jury. This is critical because it defines the crime for a group of 12 laypeople who are unsure just what the offense consists of. Counsel should try to prevent the giving of any instruction that attempts to distinguish "drunk" from "under the influence," as this tends to minimize the degree of intoxication required to justify a conviction. Rather, a definition should be sought that emphasizes the required "significant" or "substantial" impairment of an accused's physical *and* mental abilities.

This leads to the next area requiring an instruction: the definition of the degree of impairment required. Again, this is important, as it continues to define the crime itself. As mentioned earlier, each jurisdiction has its own standards as to what degree of impairment is required to support a conviction for drunk driving; these vary from the "slightest degree" of impairment to the more common "substantial" or "appreciable" impairment. If there is any room for interpretation of existing law, obviously defense counsel should propose instructions that require proof of the greatest degree of impairment. If nothing else, counsel should insist that the precise meaning of "impaired" be left up to the jury to decide; he can then argue to the jury that the dictionary's definition of the term indicates a *significant* disability.

In *Commonwealth v. Brochu,* 501 N.E.2d 532 (Mass. App. 1986), a trial court gave a common instruction that only required a finding that alcohol influenced the defendant to some degree, rather than requiring a finding that the alcohol diminished her ability to operate the motor vehicle. In part, that instruction read:

> Being under the influence means . . . that the defendant at the time was influenced in some perceptible degree by intoxicating liquor that he or she has taken, influenced in some perceptible degree. . . . It does not mean that a person could not drive a car or drive it safely. . . . The focus is not upon the manner in which the vehicle is operated; . . . the focus is on the individual in question. . . . [Id. at 532–533.]

The appellate court cited *Commonwealth v. Connolly,* 474 N.E.2d 1106 (Mass. App. 1985), for the rule that the state must prove that alcohol diminished the defendant's ability to operate a motor vehicle safely. It need not be shown that he or she actually drove unsafely, of course, but the prosecution must "prove a diminished *capacity* to operate safely." Thus the *Brochu* court ruled that the instruction given created a substantial risk of a miscarriage of justice and reversed the conviction, remanding the case for a new trial.

The ability to drive is related directly to the definition of "impairment," and any instruction that attempts to define the offense of drunk driving should make this clear. The fact that a defendant could not stand on one foot for an extended period of time for the arresting officer or walk a straight line heel-to-toe is not the issue; the sole question is whether his ability to operate a motor vehicle was affected. Just *how* affected is, again, an area for dispute between defense counsel and the prosecuting attorney. Backed with case law and/or similar instructions given in other courts, counsel should argue for the use of words such as *significant, substantial,* and *appreciable.* Thus instructed, the jury is more likely to excuse a slight impairment in the defendant's ability to drive.

Concerning the per se offense, counsel should request of the court two important instructions. First, assuming the client has taken the stand and has testified to what he thought his blood-alcohol level was, counsel should ask for an instruction advising the jury that the defendant is *qualified* to give an opinion of what his blood-alcohol level was at the time he was driving. This is based on the reasoning of courts across the country that are upholding the constitutionality of per se statutes against vagueness attacks, saying an individual does know if he is violating a per se statute or not because he *knows* what his blood-alcohol level is. See §1.4.

The second per se instruction should recite the law of *mistake of fact* — that is, that a mistake of fact is a complete defense to any crime. This should, of course, be tailored to the per se offense: If the defendant honestly believed that his blood-alcohol level was less than .10 percent, then he is not guilty of the crime of driving with higher than .10 percent alcohol in his blood. For a fuller discussion, see §1.9.4.

The full *corpus* of the offense must, of course, be proven by the prosecution. Aside from the question of intoxication, or blood-alcohol level, the prosecution must establish beyond a reasonable doubt that the defendant was actually driving and that he was driving within the defined area — for example, a "road" or "highway" (see §1.2.3). This will require suitable instructions as to what constitutes proof of driving and what the definition of "road" or "highway" is. If the defendant was not actually witnessed to be driving the vehicle, counsel should request an instruction to the effect that the defendant should be acquitted unless the prosecution is able to prove beyond a reasonable doubt that the defendant actually was driving the car. If the vehicle was not running or was not capable of running, an instruction should be requested that advises the jury that "driving a motor vehicle" requires proof that the vehicle could in fact be driven. Finally, if the location of the driving is an issue, a favorable definition of "road," "highway," or whatever the applicable statutory language is, should be requested.

Turning next to the chemical tests, defense counsel must attempt to minimize the effect of the prosecution's expert chemist. He must ask the court to advise the jury that the testimony of an expert witness can be disregarded if it so chooses. Furthermore, expertise is not required to render an opinion on the issue of intoxication: Any lay witness can testify whether he felt the defendant was under the influence of alcohol.

The statutory presumptions deriving from the blood-alcohol levels will, of course, be given. But in many courts, only that presumption applicable to the actual test result will be supplied. If the test given the defendant indicated a .13 percent level, for example, the jury would be instructed simply that a reading in excess of .10 percent would result in a presumption that he was under the influence. It is very important for defense counsel to have the jury instructed on the full range of presumptions — that is, on the presumptions resulting from readings of .00 to over .10 percent. Without such an instruction, the jury may well conclude that the court feels that the test results were accurate and that the giving of instructions in the event the test result was really below .10 percent was unnecessary. Counsel should argue that his examination of defense witnesses and cross-examination of prosecution witnesses established at least arguably that the actual blood-alcohol level *may* have been below .10 percent and that therefore the jury should be instructed that if it believes the level were between .10 and .05, no presumption attaches. If he can go a step further, the instruction should include the presumption of sobriety at levels below .05.

There should be an instruction that establishes in clear language the fact that the presumption is only that: a *presumption.* It is not an absolute fact but is only a presumed fact that is completely *rebuttable.* (See, e.g., *Jones v. Forrest City,* 239 Ark. 211, 388 S.W.2d 386 (1965).) Any instruction given that infers that the presumption *requires* rather than *permits* a finding of intoxication would probably constitute reversible error. (See, e.g., *State v. Hansen,* 203 N.W.2d 216 (Iowa 1972).) Therefore, counsel should consider requesting an instruction that clearly states the rebuttable nature of the presumption and that advises the jury that it is free to acquit the defendant despite the presumption. (See, e.g., *State v. Royall,* 14 N.C. App. 214, 188 S.E.2d 50 (1972).)

In *Commonwealth v. Williams,* 471 N.E.2d 394 (Mass. App. 1984), the defendant was convicted under a traditional DUI statute after the trial judge instructed the jury that as a result of a .12 percent Breathalyzer reading "there shall be an inference that the defendant was under the influence of intoxicating liquor." In reversing the conviction, the Massachusetts appellate court stated:

> There was no other ameliorating instruction which put the matter of the test score in the proper context of a permissive, as distinguished from a mandatory, inference. A reasonable juror could only have understood the instruction as mandating the inference that the defendant was under the influence of intoxicating liquor and as shifting the burden of persuasion on that element of the crime. [Id. at 395.]

A further attempt to minimize the damaging effect of the chemical test should be made by requesting an instruction concerning the applicable statutory regulation of blood-alcohol analysis (see §11.6.8). Assuming that the prosecution has failed to provide evidence that the tests complied with the statutory requirements or, alternatively, that defense counsel has produced prima facie evidence (probably during cross-examination of the officer or expert) that the testing procedures did not comply, an instruction should be given that advises the jury that it is free to disregard the test results if it believes the requirements were not fully met. Even where there is a conflict in the evidence as to whether the statutory requirements had been complied with, the defense should be entitled to an instruction advising the jury that it is free to ignore the test results. (See, e.g., *People v. Rawlings,* 42 Cal. App. 3d 952, 117 Cal. Rptr. 651 (1974).) In fact, counsel might consider the even stronger instruction that the test results cannot be considered unless the jury finds beyond a reasonable doubt that the statutory requirements were complied with. (*State v. Winters,* 34 Or. App. 157, 578 P.2d 439 (1978).) In most jurisdictions, however, noncompliance has been held to affect only the weight to be given the test results.

If the case involves a refusal by the client to submit to a chemical test, counsel should refer to the law of the jurisdiction relating to the implications of a refusal. If the arrestee has a right to refuse, of course, any instruction that advises the jury of the fact that he did refuse should be objected to strenuously. Where comment is permitted, counsel should attempt to ensure that the instruction includes language to the effect that a refusal is not sufficient in itself to establish guilt but is only one of many factors to be considered. (See, e.g., *People v. Sudduth,* 55 Cal. Rptr. 393, 421 P.2d 401 (1966).)

Counsel should also request an instruction concerning the *relevance* of refusal evidence. The language of the instruction should make it clear that there are many reasons for refusing or failing to submit to chemical testing, and that consciousness of guilt is only one of these. If there has been testimony that the defendant believed he had a Fifth Amendment right to refuse, or a right to consult with counsel before deciding whether to submit, the jury should be told that such a refusal, if believed, is not to be considered in deciding whether he is guilty.

Where the defendant made damaging admissions during the course of his initial detention or later arrest, every attempt should be made to minimize their effect. The jury must be instructed that an admission of consumption of alcohol, for example, is not enough to establish intoxication beyond a reasonable doubt. The prosecution must establish the defendant's intoxication through independent means.

If probable cause to stop, detain, or arrest the defendant is a factual issue, appropriate instructions should be requested and given. If possible, a special finding as to this issue should be requested, as jurors are often incapable of disregarding evidence obtained as a result of a stop, detention, or arrest without sufficient probable cause. Thus, for example, a Texas appellate court reversed a DUI conviction where the trial court had refused to give an instruction on "the officer's right to stop the vehicle." (*Jacobs v. State,* 734 S.W.2d 704 (Tex. App. 1987).) The court held that an instruction must be given any time the defendant challenges the validity of the traffic stop. For a more complete discussion of probable cause in a DUI case, see §11.0.

Where there has been evidence that drugs as well as alcohol had been consumed, an instruction concerning the combined effect would be appropriate. However, counsel should object to any such instruction where there is no evidence of drug usage. In many jurisdictions the "combined influence" instruction is routinely inserted in the standard set of jury instructions, but a forceful objection should be made that the giving of such an instruction would result very possibly in an inference in the jurors' minds that the defendant had, in fact, used drugs.

Counsel should always consider the tactical advantages and disadvantages of an instruction as to *lesser included offenses.* As any experienced criminal lawyer knows, the average jury is less likely to convict a defendant of the charged offense if there is a "compromise" instruction given: The reluctance of a jury to acquit altogether in a close case is overcome by offering jurors the opportunity to convict on a less serious crime. For the same reasons, such an instruction in a strong defense case may lead to a conviction on the lesser offense rather than an outright acquittal.

Thus counsel may wish to request a misdemeanor drunk driving instruction where the charge is vehicular manslaughter, for example, or a reckless driving instruction where the charge is drunk driving. In *Comeau v. State,* 758 P.2d 108 (Alaska App. 1988), for example, the court reversed a DUI conviction because the defendant had been refused an instruction that reckless driving and negligent driving were lesser included offenses. For discussions of what constitutes a "lesser included" or "necessarily included" offense, see §8.3.2.

The Supreme Court of California is but one of many that have held that a defendant has an absolute *right* to have the jury instructed on a lesser related offense. See *People v. Geiger,* 199 Cal. Rptr. 45 (1984). In fact, the offense need not be one "necessarily included," but can be "one closely related to that charged and shown by the evidence": The offense must have an "inherent relationship" with the charged offense.

The Supreme Court of Florida has similarly held that "lesser included" instructions are mandatory. See *State v. Wimberly,* 498 So. 2d 929 (Fla. 1986). However, that court took the more commonly encountered position that the lesser offense must be "*necessarily included*":

> A "necessarily lesser included offense" is, as the name implies, a lesser offense that is always included in the major offense. The trial judge has no discretion in whether to instruct the jury on a necessarily included offense. Once the judge determines that the offense is a necessarily included offense, an instruction must be given.
>
> The requirement that a trial judge must give a requested instruction on a necessarily included offense is bottomed upon a recognition of the jury's right to exercise its "pardon power." [Id. at 932.]

The following is an effective example of an instruction that "shoots for the moon": an invitation to the jury to find the defendant guilty of a minor traffic infraction — here, "weaving" — rather than drunk driving. The author is grateful to Jonathon Artz of Los Angeles, who has used the below instruction with repeated success.

> If you are not satisfied beyond a reasonable doubt that the defendant is guilty of the offenses charged, he may, however, be found guilty of any (lesser) related offense, if the evidence is suf-

ficient to establish his guilt of such lesser related offense beyond a reasonable doubt.

The offense of driving under the influence (Vehicle Code §23152(a)) with which the defendant is charged in Count 1 involves driving. Evidence has been presented which includes the lesser related offense of weaving, in violation of California Vehicle Code §12658(a), which is defined as follows:

> Whenever any roadway has been divided into two or more clearly marked lanes for traffic in one direction, the following rules apply:
>
> (a) A Vehicle shall be driven as nearly as practical entirely within a single lane and shall not be moved from the lane until such movement can be made with reasonable safety.

Finally, of course, defense counsel should be sure that the appropriate definitions and applications of both circumstantial evidence and reasonable doubt are given to the jury. Specifically, the trial judge should be asked to advise the jury that the prosecutor's case regarding whether the defendant was or was not under the influence rests entirely on circumstantial evidence (the only direct evidence would be biochemical observation of brain or motor reflex impairment, a scientific impossibility).

RESOURCES

Obtaining Scientific Articles

Counsel may encounter difficulty in finding many of the scientific articles referred to in the text and listed in the *Bibliography*. If the articles are not obtainable through local university libraries or medical centers, one very helpful source is Dr. Richard Jensen's firm in Minneapolis. Professional Reference Services. The former head of the State of Minnesota's blood-alcohol program, Dr. Jensen is one of the most eminent authorities on blood-alcohol analysis in the country today. He maintains an extensive collection of several thousand scientific articles relating to the subject, and makes them available to counsel for $20 per article by mail or fax. Address: Professional Reference Services, P.O. Box 2793, Loop Station, Minneapolis, MN 55402. Telephone/fax: (612) 349-6777.

NHTSA Manuals

Counsel should seriously consider obtaining the National Highway Traffic Safety Administration's manuals and materials concerning standardized field sobriety tests, DUI driving symptoms, recommended sobriety checkpoint procedures, etc. This can be done by calling the National Technical Information Service's (NTIS) toll-free sales number: 800-553-NTIS (6847). The following are some of NHTSA's more helpful materials:

NHTSA SFST Instructor Manual (PB94-780210)	$57.00
NHTSA SFST Student Manual (PB94-780228)	$36.50
NHTSA SFST Video — Part 1 (PB94-780236)	$25.00
NHTSA SFST Video — Part 2 (PB94-780244)	$25.00
"Psychophysical Tests for DWI Arrest," Burns and Moskowitz (PB 269309)	$27.00
"Development of Field Test of Psychophysical Tests for DWI Arrests," Tharp, Burns and Moskowitz (PB 81203721)	$19.50

"Pilot Test of Selected DWI Protection Procedures for Use At Sobriety Checkpoints," Compton (PB86-170-958) $26.00

In addition, the following materials can be obtained free of charge directly from NHTSA at their technical information number (202-366-2768):

"Improved Sobriety Testing" (DOT-HS-806-512)
"Guide for Detecting Drunk Drivers at Night" (DOT-HS-805-711)

Newsletters

DWI Journal (John Tarantino, ed.). Published monthly by Whitaker Newsletters, 313 South Avenue, P.O. Box 192, Fanwood, NJ 07023 (800-359-6049). Subscription rate: $260/year.

The Drinking/Driving Law Letter (Flem Whited, ed.). Published biweekly by Clark Boardman Callaghan, 155 Pfingzen, Road, Deerfield, IL 60015 (800-221-9428). Subscription rate: $245/year.

For California practitioners: *California DUI Report* (James Scott Bell, ed.). Published monthly by Courtroom Compendiums, P.O. Box 705, Woodland Hills, CA 91365 (818-884-9039). Subscription rate: $99/year.

Organizations

The National College for DUI Defense. Any attorney having a significant practice in the drunk driving field should seriously consider applying for membership in the National College for DUI Defense. The College, headquartered in Atlanta, Georgia (2625 Piedmont Road, Box 56-331, Atlanta, GA 30324-3012), consists of a Board of Regents of 12 of the most prominent DUI attorneys in the country, 100 founding members, and unlimited general membership. The College sponsors the Harvard Summer Session, an intensive three-day seminar/workshop held annually in July at Harvard Law School, as well as an annual one-day scientific seminar in the winter. The College also maintains an Internet website (http://www.ncdd.com/), with access to various resources and listings of members available to the public. The College is in the process of applying for authority from the ABA to certify attorneys as specialists in drunk driving litigation. Information can be obtained from Executive Director Adriana Antelo at (404) 816-3395.

Internet

The website for the National College for DUI Defense is a source of helpful materials for the DUI practitioner, as well as a source of referrals for those seeking counsel. The URL is: http://www.ncdd.com/.

The author of this text maintains a website for DUI practitioners as well as members of the public. The site contains extensive legal and scientific information, free audio seminar lectures, legal research tools, and access to various DUI resources and websites. The URL is: http://www.duicenter.com.

Attorney Josh Dale maintains a website at http://www.dui-help.com, which contains a list of DUI attorneys nationwide for Web "surfers" looking for qualified representation. Attorneys can be listed through links on the site, or by e-mailing Mr. Dale at jdale@jmd-ent.com.

Expert witnesses

Note: Expert blood-alcohol witnesses for the defense can often be found on the faculties of local colleges, commonly in the medical and science departments, and particularly in the fields of analytical chemistry, toxicology, biochemistry, pharmacology, physiology, and forensic science. Individuals who have retired from careers in crime laboratories of law enforcement agencies represent another possible source. Physicians may also be competent to testify about blood-alcohol physiology and, possibly, analysis. Both prosecutors and prosecution witnesses may also be helpful if approached correctly; they have probably encountered a variety of defense experts in their time.

A number of directories exist which may be helpful in locating forensic expert witnesses. These include:

The Forensic Services Directory is published by the National Forensic Center. While most of the experts listed in the Directory would have no application in a drunk driving case, several categories have direct application, including chemistry, biological sciences, pharmacology, toxicology, medicine, and electrical engineering. The Directory does not purport to be a complete listing of all experts, but rather contains only the names of those who have submitted materials to the Center. The price for the 12th edition (1995–1996) is $125.50, plus $5 for shipping, and can be ordered from Forensic Services Directory, Inc., P.O. Box 3161, Princeton, NJ 08540 (800-526-5177). (For those with access to WESTLAW or LEXIS, the Center provides the entire contents of the Directory on those services.)

Directory of Alcohol Related Forensic Experts, published by Whitaker Newsletters, 313 South Avenue, P.O. Box 192, Fanwood, NJ 07023 (800-359-6049), contains a helpful but possibly outdated list. As of this writing (May 1996), the 1990–1991 edition ($49) is the latest version; an update may be published in the future.

The following is a partial list of some of the better-known blood-alcohol experts:

John Castle, Dallas, TX (214-748-5995)

Darrell O. Clardy, Analytical and Forensic Toxicology, Bea, CA (714-993-2220)

Dr. Jonathan D. Cowan, Prospect, KY (502-426-0300)

William Giguiere, Park-Gilman Clinics, Burlingame, CA

Henry S. Greenberg, Forensic Analytical Consultants, Fountain Valley, CA (714-964-5832)

David B. Grossman, Esq., Mineola, NY (516-742-5617)

Phil Hancock, Esq., Decatur, GA (404-378-8158)
Michael P. Hlastala, Ph.D., Department of Medicine, University of Washington, Seattle, WA (206-543-3166)
Dr. Naresh C. Jain, National Toxicology Laboratories, Buena Park, CA (714-521-1891)
Dr. Richard Jensen, Forensic Associates, Minneapolis, MN (612-339-7903)
Wayne Morris, Orlando, FL (407-678-5508)
Oscar Parsons, University of Oklahoma Medical Center
Paul M. Roman, Institute for Behavioral Research, University of Georgia (706-542-6090)
Gil Sapir, Esq., Chicago, IL (312-853-3600)
Dr. David Stafford, Memphis, TN (901-448-6355)
S. Streufert, Pennsylvania State Medical School, Hershey, PA
Richard G. Whalley, Whalley and Associates, San Diego, CA (619-232-6543)
Dr. James Woodford, Atlanta, GA (404-270-1872)

The following are experts on the subject of field sobriety tests:

Dr. Robert J. Belloto, Jr., Ohio State University, Columbus, OH
Dr. Marceline Burns, Southern California Research Institute, Culver City, CA (310-390-8481)
Dr. Spurgeon Cole, Clemson University (803-656-5849)
Dr. L. F. Dell'Osso, Case Western Reserve University, Cleveland, Ohio
Robert Palmer, Prescott, AZ (602-778-2951)
Dr. Russell A. Rockerbie, Victoria, BC, Canada (604-388-0416)
Richard Swope, Davie, FL (305-476-7640)

BIBLIOGRAPHY

The following listing of books, pamphlets, and articles concerned with various aspects of drunk driving litigation may prove helpful to defense counsel, particularly in cross-examination of the adverse expert witness. The list, however, should certainly not be considered exhaustive. (Note: Some of the telephone numbers, prices, etc., of the newsletters and directories listed have been changed. Please see the new "Resources" section preceding this Bibliography for updated information.)

Counsel may encounter difficulty in finding many of these materials, as they involve rather more esoteric subjects than the local library can cover. Consideration should be given to university libraries and laboratories. One very helpful source, however, is a private organization called Professional Reference Services. This organization specializes in scientific articles on alcohol and its measurement and effect on humans, and will forward any such articles for $20 per article by mail or fax. The address of Professional Reference Services is P.O. Box 2793, Loop Station, Minneapolis, MN 55402; telephone (612) 349-6777.

The reader interested in keeping abreast of legal and scientific developments in the field of drunk driving litigation should seriously consider subscribing to a biweekly publication entitled The Drinking/Driving Law Letter. The editor is known by the author to be a knowledgeable attorney, well versed in the intricacies of defending the drunk driving client. The Letter is published biweekly by Clark Boardman Callaghan, 155 Pfingsen Road, Deerfield, IL 60015 (800-221-1423). The subscription rate as of 1996 was $245/year.

Another valuable source of information is the DWI Journal (editor, John Tarantino). The Journal is published monthly by Whitaker Newsletters, 313 South Avenue, P.O. Box 192, Fanwood, NJ 07023 (800-359-6049). Subscription rate: $260/year.

California practitioners should seriously consider the California DUI Report (editor, James Scott Bell). The Report is published monthly by Courtroom Compendiums, P.O. Box 705, Woodland Hills, CA 91365 (818-884-9039). Subscription rate: $99/year.

Finally, counsel wishing to locate a defense blood-alcohol expert should review the Forensic Services Directory. This is produced by the National Forensic Center, which also provides an automated list of expert witnesses through WESTLAW and LEXIS. While a majority of the experts listed in the Directory would have no application to a drinking/driving case, several categories have direct application, including chemistry, biological sciences, pharmacology, toxicology, medicine, and electrical engineering. The Directory does not purport to be a complete listing of all experts, but rather contains only the names of those who have submitted materials to the Center.

The Directory may be obtained from Forensic Services Directory, Inc., P.O. Box 3161, Princeton, NJ 08540 (800-526-5177). The price for the 1995 edition is $125.50, plus $5 shipping.

Another source for locating expert witnesses nationwide is the Directory of Alcohol Related Forensic Experts. Priced at $49, the 1990–1991 edition, which is due for an update, is available from Whitaker Newsletters, 313 South Avenue, P.O. Box 192, Fanwood, NJ 07023 (800-359-6049).

Books and Pamphlets

Allen, R. W., Effects of Alcohol on the Driver's Decision-Making Behavior. Executive Summary and Technical Report 1, NTIS (Springfield, VA) (1978)

American Medical Association, Alcohol and the Impaired Driver: A Manual on the Medicological Aspects of Chemical Tests for Intoxication, AMA (1970)

Bates, D. V., et al., Respiratory Function and Disease, W. B. Saunders (1971)

Borkenstein, R. F., et al., The Role of the Drinking Driver in Traffic Accidents, Indiana University (1964)

Brown, G., Random Tests and Hospital Tests for Blood Alcohol Levels (paper presented at National Road Safety Symposium, Canberra, Australia, Mar. 14–16, 1972). In Proceedings of the National Road Safety Symposium, Commonwealth Department of Shipping and Transportation (Canberra) (1972)

Damkot, D. K., et al., On-the-Road Driving Behavior and Breath Alcohol Concentration, NTIS (Springfield, VA) (1977)

Damm, et al., Handbook of Clinical Laboratory Data, The Chemical Rubber Co. (1965)

Department of Police Administration, Symposium on Alcohol and Road Traffic, Indiana University (1959)

Department of Transportation, National Highway Traffic Safety Administration Forum on Traffic Safety: Alcohol Countermeasures, U.S. Government Printing Office (1971)

Donigan, R. L., Chemical Tests and the Law, Northwestern University (1957)

Dunlop & Associates, Inc., Basic Training Program for Breath Examiner Specialists, U.S. Government Printing Office (1971)

Eckert & Noguchi, Bibliography of Classic and Current References on Alcohol and Alcoholism: The Medical, Legal and Law Enforcement Aspects (2 vol.), Inform (1973)

Erwin, R. E., Defense of Drunk Driving Cases, Matthew Bender (1980)

Fitzgerald, E. F., & Hume, D. H., Intoxication Test Evidence: Criminal and Civil, Clark Boardman Callaghan (Deerfield, Ill.) (1993)

Fonarow, J., Defending Against the Drunk Driving Charge, Sherbourne Press (1973)

Forney, R. B., & Hughes, F. W., Combined Effects of Alcohol and Other Drugs, Charles C. Thomas (1968)

Forrester, G. C., The Use of Chemical Tests for Alcohol in Traffic Law Enforcement, Charles C. Thomas (1950)

Fort, J., Alcohol: Our Biggest Drug Problem, McGraw-Hill (1973)

Garriott, J. C., Medicolegal Aspects of Alcohol, 3d ed, Lawyers and Judges Publishing Co. (Tucson, Ariz.) (1996)

Gibbins, R. J., et al., Research Advances in Alcohol and Drug Problems, John Wiley (1974)

Hendrickson, J. B., et al., Organic Chemistry, McGraw-Hill (3d ed. 1970)

Henry, J. B., et al., Clinical Diagnoses by Laboratory Methods, W. B. Saunders (16th ed. 1979)

Indiana University Law School, Proceedings of the Ad Hoc Committee on Blood-Breath Alcohol Ratio, Indiana University (1972)

Jex, H. R., et al., Alcohol Impairment of Performance on Steering and Discrete Tasks in a Driving Simulator, part I; Effects of Task Loading, part II, Moderate vs. Heavy Drinkers, NTIS (Springfield, VA) (1974)

Joscelyn, K. B., & Maickel, R. P., Drugs and Driving: A Research Review, NTIS (Springfield, VA) (1977)

Kaye, S., & Cardona, E. L., in Proceedings of the Fourth International Conference on Alcohol and Traffic Safety, Center for Studies of Law in Action, Indiana University (1966)

Keiper, Effects of Moderate Blood Alcohol Levels on Driver Alertness, U.S. Government Printing Office

Little, J. W., & Cooper, M., Examination of Tort Liability Issues Connected with Release of Arrested, Intoxicated DWI Offenders, NTIS (Springfield, VA) (1977)

Milner, G., Drugs and Driving: A Survey of the Relationship of Adverse Drug Reactions and Drug-Alcohol Interaction, S. Karger (Basel) (1972)

Moskowitz, H., Effects of Alcohol on Performance in a Driving Simulator of Alcoholics and Social Drinkers, U.S. Department of Transportation (1971)

National Highway Traffic Safety Administration, Guide for Detecting Drunk Drivers at Night, DOT HS-805-711

National Highway Traffic Safety Administration, Pilot Test of Selected DWI Detection Procedures for Use at Sobriety Checkpoints, NHTSA DOT HS-806-724 (1985)

National Highway Traffic Safety Administration, Workshop on In-Vehicle Alcohol Test Devices, DOT HS-807-145 (Sept. 1986)

Nesbitt, M. W., & McGill, D. W., Court Intervention: Pre-Sentence Investigation Techniques for Drinking/Driving Offenses, NTIS (Springfield, VA) (1978)

Nichols, D., Drinking/Driving Litigation, Clark Boardman Callaghan (1991)

Perrine, M. W., & Huntler, M. S., Alcohol Influences on Perceptual-Cognitive Behaviour, University of Vermont Dept. of Psychology

Raymond, A. E., Characteristics of Breathalyzed Drivers (paper presented at National Road Safety Symposium, Canberra, Australia, Mar. 14–16, 1972). In Proceedings of the National Road Safety Symposium. Commonwealth Department of Shipping and Transportation (Canberra) (1972)

Roach, M. K., et al., Biological Aspects of Alcohol, University of Texas (1971)

Sardesai, V. M., Biochemical and Clinical Aspects of Alcohol Metabolism, Charles C. Thomas (1969)

Saunders, D. N., & Pemberton, L. J., Determinants of Police Officers' DUI Activity, NTIS (Springfield, VA) (1977)

Selkurt, E. E., Physiology, Little, Brown & Co. (2d ed. 1966)

Southern California Research Institute, Development and Field Test of Psychophysical Tests for DWI Arrest, National Highway Traffic Safety Administration, PB 81-203721 (1983)

Thompson, G. N., Alcoholism, Charles C. Thomas (1956)

Traffic Institute, Driving Under the Influence of Alcohol or Drugs, Northwestern University (1966)
Traffic Institute, Interpretation of Implied Consent Laws by the Courts, Northwestern University (1972)
Walgren, H., & Barry, Actions of Alcohol (2 vol.), Elsevier (1971)
White, A., et al., Principles of Biochemistry, McGraw-Hill (4th ed. 1965)
Willard, H., et al., Instrumental Methods of Analysis, D. Van Nostrand Co. (4th ed. 1965)
Williams, R. J., Biochemical Individuality, John Wiley (1965)
Winters, et al., Acid Base Physiology in Medicine, The London Co. (1965)

Articles

Al-Lanqawi, et al., Ethanol Kinetics: Extent of Error in Back Extrapolation Procedures, 34 British Journal of Clinical Pharmacology 316 (1992)
Alobaidi, Significance of Variations in Blood: Breath Partition Coefficient of Alcohol, British Medical Journal 1479 (18 December 1976)
Ando, Johanson & Schuster, Effects of Ethanol on Eye Tracking in Rhesus Monkeys and Humans, 26 Pharmacology and Biochemical Behavior 103 (1987)
Aranella, *Schmerber* and the Privilege Against Self Incrimination 20(1) American Criminal Law Review 31 (Summer 1982)
Argeriou, Refusal to Take Breathalyzer Test — Rebutting Adverse Presumption, 11 Criminal Law Bulletin 350 (1975)
Aschan, Different Types of Alcohol Nystagmus, 140 Acta Otolaryngological Supplement 69 (Sweden 1958)
Aschan, et al., Positional Nystagmus in Man During and After Alcohol Intoxication, 17 Quarterly Journal of Studies on Alcohol 381 (Sept. 1956)
Attwood, Effects of Moderate Levels of Blood Alcohol on Responses to Information from Simulated Automobile Rear-Signal Systems, 10(1) Accident Analysis & Prevention 11 (Mar. 1978)
Ball & Lichtenwalner, Ethanol Production in Infected Urine, The New England Journal of Medicine 614 (13 Sept. 1976)
Baloh, Sharma, Moskowitz & Griffith, Effect of Alcohol and Marijuana on Eye Movements, Aviation, Space and Environmental Medicine 18 (Jan. 1979)
Banton, Prosecution of Alcohol Related Traffic Offenses, 23 St. Louis Bar Journal 16 (Winter 1977)
Barni, Alcohol Education: An Alternative for Drinking Drivers 23 St. Louis Bar Journal 44 (Winter 1977)
Barron, et al., The Effect of Ibuprofen on Ethanol Concentration and Elimination Rate, 37 Journal of Forensic Sciences 432 (March 1992)
Bates, Brick & White, The Correspondence Between Saliva and Breath Estimates of Blood Alcohol Concentration: Advantages and Limitations of the Saliva Method, 54 Journal of Studies on Alcohol 17 (1993)
Baylor, Lyane, et al., Effects of Ethanol on Human Fractionated Response Times, 23 Drug and Alcohol Dependence 31 (1989)
Beard, Breath, Alcohol and the Law, 1 British Medical Journal 1033 (1977)
Bell, et al., Diethyl Ether Interference with Infrared Breath Analysis, 16 Journal of Analytical Toxicology (1992)
Beltel, Probability of Arrest While Driving under the Influence of Alcohol, 36(1) Journal of Studies on Alcohol 109 (Jan. 1975)

Berild & Hasselbach, Survival After a Blood Alcohol Concentration of 1127 mg/dl, 2 Lancet 363 (1981)

Biasotti & Valentine, Blood Alcohol Concentration Determined from Urine Samples as a Practical Equivalent or Alternative to Blood and Breath Alcohol Tests, 30 Journal of Forensic Sciences 194 (1985)

Blinder & Kornblum, The Alcoholic Driver, 77 Case and Comment 3 (1972)

Borkenstein, Efficacy of Law Enforcement Procedures Concerning Alcohol, Drugs, and Driving, 11 Modern Problems of Pharmacopsychiatry 1 (1976)

Bradford, Preservation of Blood Samples Containing Alcohol, 11 Journal of Forensic Sciences 244 (1966)

Brick, Diabetes, Breath Acetone and Breathalyzer Accuracy: A Case Study, 9(1) Alcohol, Drugs and Driving (1993)

Brick, et al., Circadian Variations in Behavioral and Biological Sensitivity to Ethanol, 8 Alcoholism: Clinical and Experimental Research 204 (1984)

Brick, et al., Effect of Menstrual Cycle on Blood Alcohol Levels and Behavior, 47 Journal of Studies on Alcohol 472 (1986)

Brick & White, The Correspondence Between Saliva and Breath Estimates of Blood Alcohol Concentration: Advantages and Limitations of the Saliva Method, 54 Journal of Studies on Alcohol 17 (1993)

Brigalia, et al., The Distribution of Ethanol in Postmortem Blood Specimens, 37 Journal of Forensic Sciences 991 (July 1992)

Briggs, Patel, Butterfield & Honeybourne, The Effects of Chronic Obstructive Airways Disease on the Ability to Drive and to Use a Roadside Alcometer, 84 Respiratory Medicine 43 (1990)

Bruno, Iliadis, Trefot, Mariottik, Cano & Jullien, Non-Linear Kinetics of Ethanol Elimination in Man: Medico-Legal Applications of the Terminal Concentration — Time Data Analysis, 21 Forensic Science International 207 (1983)

Budd, Ethanol Levels in Postmortem Body Fluids, 252 Journal of Chromatography 315 (Dec. 1983)

Budd, Postmortem Brain Alcohol Levels, 259 Journal of Chromatography 353 (1983)

Burczynski, Sitar & Wilson, Ethanol Disposition in Man: Comparison of Breathalyzer and Two Methods of Gas-Liquid Chromatography, 20 International Journal of the Addictions 583 (1985)

Burns, Driving Impairment: Blood Alcohol Levels of Alcohol and Other Substances, 1 Alcohol, Drugs and Driving 131 (1985)

Burns, Sobriety Tests for the Presence of Drugs, 3 Alcohol, Drugs and Driving 25 (1987)

Burns & Moskowitz, Gender-Related Differences in Impairment of Performance by Alcohol, 3 Currents in Alcoholism 479 (1978)

Caddy, Sobell & Sobell, Alcohol Breath Tests: Criterion Times for Avoiding Contamination by "Mouth Alcohol," 10(6) Behaviour Research Methods & Instrumentation 814 (1978)

Caiafa & Farnsworth, Under the Influence of California's New Drunk Driving Law: Is the Drunk Driver's Presumption of Innocence on the Rocks?, 10 Pepperdine Law Review 91 (1982)

Calcaterra, Defense of Driving School, 23 St. Louis Bar Journal 40 (Winter 1977)

Campbell, The Problem Drinker in the Traffic Picture, 68 Traffic Safety 6 (1970)

Canfield, Kupiec & Huffine, Postmortem Alcohol Production in Fatal Aircraft Accidents, 38 Journal of Forensic Sciences 914 (1993)

Caplan & Levine, Analysis of Ethanol in Serum, Blood and Urine, 10 Journal of Analytical Toxicology 49 (1986)

Caplan, Yohman & Schaefer, An In Vitro Study of the Accuracy and Precision of Breathalyzer Models 900, 900A, and 1000, 30 Journal of Forensic Sciences 1058 (1985)

Carey, et al., Effects of Moderate Alcohol Intake on Blood Chemistry Values, 216 Journal of American Medical Association 1766 (1971)

Cartlidge & Redmond, Alcohol and Conscious Level, 44 Biomedicine and Pharmacotherapy 205 (1990)

Cary, Whitter & Johnson, Abbott Radiative Energy Attenuation Method for Quantification of Ethanol Evaluated and Compared with Gas-Liquid Chromatography and the DuPont ACA, 30 Clinical Chemistry 1867 (1984)

Casselman, Body Temperature and the Breathalyzer Boobytrap, Michigan Bar Journal 721 (September 1982)

Cater, et al, Statistics and the Virginia Blood Test Statute, 56 Virginia Law Review 349 (1970)

Caughlin, Correlation of Postmortem Blood and Vitreous Humor Alcohol Concentration, 16 Canadian Society of Forensics Journal 61 (1983)

Chambers, et al., Blood Alcohol Levels, 4 Archives of Emergency Medicine 127 (1987)

Chang, Smith, Walkin & Reynolds, The Stability of Ethyl Alcohol in Forensic Blood Specimens, 8 Journal of Analytical Toxicology 66 (1984)

Chesher, Effects of Alcohol and Marijuana in Combination: A Review, 2 Alcohol, Drugs and Driving 105 (1987)

Chiarotti & DeGiovanni, Acetaldehyde Accumulation During Headspace Gas-Chromatographic Determination of Alcohol, 20 Forensic Science International 21 (1982)

Clay & Swenson, Selective Enforcement of Drunken Driving in Phoenix, Arizona, 10(3) Journal of Safety Research 130 (1978)

Cohen, Exposure to Solvents Simulating Ethyl Alcohol Intoxication, 5 Drunk Driving/Liquor Liability Reporter 120 (December 1991)

Cole-Harding & Wilson, Ethanol Metabolism in Men and Women, 48 Journal of Studies on Alcohol 380 (1987)

Cole & Nowaczyk, I May Flunk, but I Ain't Drunk, Clemson University paper

Conkle, Camp & Welch, Trace Composition of Human Respiratory Gas, 30 Archives of Environmental Health 290 (1975)

Considering Measurement Variability When Performing Retrograde Extrapolation of Breath Alcohol Results, 18 Journal of Analytical Toxicology 126 (1994)

Cooper, Infrared Breath Alcohol Analysis Following Inhalation of Gasoline Fumes, 5 Journal of Analytical Toxicology 198 (1981)

Corfitsen, Increased Viso-Motoric Reaction Time of Young Tired Drunk Drivers, 20 Forensic Science International 121 (1982)

Cowan, et al., The Response of the Intoxilyzer 4011AS-A to a Number of Possible Interfering Substances, 35(4) Journal of Forensic Sciences 797 (1990)

Cramton, The Problem of the Drinking Driver, 54 American Bar Association Journal 995 (1968)

Cravey & Jain, Current Status of Blood Alcohol Methods, 12 Journal of Chromatographic Science 209 (1974)

Crockett, et al., Minimum Respiratory Function for Breath Alcohol Testing in South Australia, 32(4) Journal of the Forensic Science Society 333 (1992)

David & Lipson, Central Nervous System Tolerance to High Blood Alcohol Levels, 144 Medical Journal of Australia 9 (1986)

Davis & Dal Cortivo, Endogenous Isopropanol: Forensic and Biochemical Implications, 8 Journal of Analytical Toxicology 209 (1984)

DeLuc, Alcohol Tolerance and Its Significance in Driving, 18 Canadian Society of Forensic Science Journal 1 (1985)

Dergun & Durbar, Alcohol Consumption, Blood Alcohol Level and the Relevance of Body Weight in Experimental Design and Analysis, 51(1) Journal of Studies on Alcohol 24 (1990)

Devgun & Dunbar, Alcohol Consumption, Blood Alcohol Level and the Relevance of Body Weight in Experimental Design and Analysis, 51 Journal for Studies of Alcohol 24 (1990)

DiMaio & Garriott, How Valid Is the 0.10 Percent Alcohol Level as an Indicator of Intoxication?, 39 Pathologist 31 (1985)

Dittmar & Dorian, Ethanol Absorption After Bolus Ingestion of an Alcoholic Beverage: A Medico-Legal Problem (Part I), 15 Canadian Society of Forensics Journal 61 (1982)

Driver, The U.S. Supreme Court and the Chronic Drunkenness Offender, 30 Quarterly Journal of Studies on Alcohol 165 (1969)

Drone & Drone, The DWI: Planned Alternative to Protect the Safety and Security of the Community, 23 St. Louis Bar Journal 48 (Winter 1977)

Dubowski, Absorption, Distribution and Elimination: Highway Safety Aspects, 10 Journal of Studies on Alcohol Supp. 98 (1985)

Dubowski, Alcohol Determination in the Clinical Laboratory, 74 American Journal of Clinical Pathology 747 (1980)

Dubowski, Quality Assurance in Breath-Alcohol Analysis, 18 Journal of Analytical Toxicology 306 (1994)

Dubowski, Studies on Pharmacokinetics of Ethanol in Man, 5 Annals of Clinical & Laboratory Science 309 (1975)

Dubowski, U.S. Department of Transportation Manual for Analysis of Ethanol and Biological Liquids.

Dubowski & Essary, Contamination of Blood Specimens for Alcohol Analysis During Collection, 4 Abstracts & Reviews in Alcohol & Driving 3 (1983)

Dubowski & Essary, Response of Breath-Alcohol Analyzers to Acetone, 7 Journal of Analytical Toxicology 231 (1983)

Dubowski & Essary, Response of Breath-Alcohol Analyzers to Acetone: Further Studies, 8 Journal of Analytical Toxicology 205 (1984)

Eckardt, Industrial Intoxications Which May Simulate Ethyl Alcohol Intake, 40 Industrial Medicine 33 (1971)

Emerson, Hollyhead & Isaacs, The Measurement of Breath Alcohol, 20 Journal of the Forensic Science Society 3 (1980)

Ericksson, Human Acetaldehyde Levels: Aspects of Current Interest, 186 Mutation Research 235 (1987)

Fagen, Tiplady & Scott, Effects of Ethanol on Psychomotor Performance, 59 British Journal of Anaesthesiology 961 (1987)

Feeney, Horne & Williamson, Sobriety Testing: Intoxilyzers and Listerine Antiseptic, 52 Police Chief 70 (1985)

Felby & Olsen, Comparative Studies of Postmortem Ethyl Alcohol in Vitreous Humor, Blood and Muscle, 14 Journal of Forensic Sciences 93 (1969)

Feldman & Cohen, The Questionable Accuracy of Breathalyzer Tests, Trial (June 1983)

Fields & Hricko, Passive Alcohol Sensors: Constitutional Implications, The Prosecutor 45 (Summer 1986)

Fingarette, The Perils of *Powell:* In Search of a Factual Foundation for the Disease Concept of Alcoholism, 83 Harvard Law Review 793 (1970)

Finkel, et al., The Occurrence of Some Drugs and Toxic Agents Encountered in Drinking Driver Investigation, 13 Journal of Forensic Sciences 236 (1968)

Fisher, Simpson & Kapur, Calculation of Blood Alcohol Concentration by Sex, Weight, Number of Drinks and Time, 78 Canadian Journal of Public Health 300 (1987)

Flanagan, et al., Further Observations on the Validity of Urine Alcohol Levels in Road Traffic Offenses, 17(4) Medicine, Science and the Law 269 (1977)

Flanagan, Strike, Rigby & Lochridge, The Effects of Low Doses of Alcohol on Driving Performance, 23 Medicine, Science and the Law 203 (1983)

Flom, Brown, Adams & Jones, Alcohol and Marijuana Effects on Ocular Tracking, 53 American Journal of Optometry & Physiological Optics 764 (1976)

Flores, Results of an Investigation of the Performance of the Smith and Wesson Breathalyzer Model 1000 Breath Alcohol Tester, U.S. DOT, NHTSA (February 1980)

Flores, The State of Compliance of the Smith and Wesson Breathalyzer Model 1000: A Follow-Up Report, U.S. DOT, NHTSA (September 1983)

Food-Induced Lowering of Blood-Ethanol Profiles and Increased Rate of Elimination Immediately after a Meal, 39 Journal of Forensic Sciences 1084 (1994)

Forrester, Diagnostic Breath Testing Equipment, 23 St. Louis Bar Journal 34 (Winter 1977)

Fox & Hayward, Effect of Hypothermia on Breath-Alcohol Analysis, 32 Journal of Forensic Sciences 320 (1987)

Frajola, Blood Alcohol Testing in the Clinical Laboratory: Problems and Suggested Remedies, 39(3) Clinical Chemistry 377 (1993)

Frankvoort, Mulder & Neuteboom, Laboratory Testing of Evidential Breath-Testing Machines, 35 Forensic Science International 27 (1987)

Freed, Radio Frequency Interference with the Model 1000SA Alco-analyzer Gas Chromatograph, 28 Journal of Forensic Sciences 985 (1983)

Fregly, Bergstedt & Graybiel, Relationships Between Blood Alcohol, Positional Alcohol Nystagmus and Postural Equilibrium, 28 Quarterly Journal of Studies on Alcohol 11 (1967)

Frezza & Lieber, High Blood Alcohol Levels in Women: The Role of Decreased Gastric Alcohol Dehydrogenase Activity and First-Pass Metabolism, 322(2) New England Journal of Medicine 95 (1990)

Fukui & Yamamoto, Determination of Breath Alcohol by Infrared Gas Analyzer, 11 Medicine, Science and the Law 182 (1970)

Galex, Police Warning in Drunk Driver Tests, 18 Cleveland-Marshall Law Review 575 (1969)

Gatt, Blood:Breath Ethanol Ratios, 2 Lancet 227 (1984)

Gatt, Effect of Temperature and Blood:Breath Ratio on the Interpretation of Breath Alcohol Results, 134 New Law Journal 249 (1984)

Gaylard, Stambuk & Morgan, Reductions in Breath Ethanol Readings in Normal Male Volunteers Following Mouth Rinsing with Water at Differing Temperatures, 22 Alcohol & Alcoholism 113 (1987)

Gaylard, Stambuk & Morgan, Reductions in Normal Male Volunteers Following Mouth Rinsing with Water at Differing Temperatures, 22 Alcohol and Alcoholism 113 (1987)

Gengo, Gabos, Straley & Manning, Pharmacodynamics of Ethanol: Effects on Performance and Judgment, 30 Journal of Clinical Pharmacology 748 (1990)

Giguiere & Simpson, Medicolegal Alcohol Determination: In Vivo Blood/Breath Ratios as a Function of Time, Proceedings of the 27th Meeting of the International Association of Forensic Toxicologists 494 (Oct. 1990)

Giles, New Instrument Using Gas Sensors for the Quantitative Analysis of Ethanol in Biological Liquids, 10 Alcoholism: Clinical and Experimental Research 521 (1986)

Gilliland & Bost, Alcohol in Decomposed Bodies: Postmortem Synthesis and Distribution, 38 Journal of Forensic Sciences 1266 (1993)

Glendening & Harvey, A Simple Method Using Head-Space Gas for Determination of Blood Alcohol by Gas Chromatography, 14 Journal of Forensic Sciences 136 (1969)

Goding & Dobie, Gaze Nystagmus and Blood Alcohol, 96 Laryngoscope 713 (1986)

Goldberger & Caplan, Infrared Quantitative Evidential Breath Alcohol Analyzer: In Vitro Accuracy and Precision Studies, 31 Journal of Forensic Sciences 16 (1986)

Greenwald, Scientific Evidence in Traffic Cases, 59 Journal of Criminal Law, Criminology and Police Science 57 (1969)

Gullberg, A Concern Associated with Single Breath Alcohol Analysis for Forensic Purposes (Letter to the Editor), 38 Journal of Forensic Sciences 1263 (1993)

Gullberg, The Elimination Rate of Mouth Alcohol. Mathematical Modeling and Implications in Breath Alcohol Analysis, 37 Journal of Forensic Sciences 1363 (September 1992)

Gullberg, Evaluating the Variability of Duplicate Breath Alcohol Analyses as a Function of Subject Age, 33 Medicine, Science & the Law 110 (1993)

Gullberg, Identifying Components of Variability in Breath Alcohol Analysis, 16 Journal of Analytical Toxicology 208 (1992)

Gullberg, Variation in Blood Alcohol Concentration Following the Last Drink, 3 Journal of Police Science and Administration 289 (1982)

Guy, Breath Testing: The Breath of Life, 17 Traffic Digest and Review 7 (1969)

Hahn & Burch, Impaired Ethanol Metabolism with Advancing Age, 7 Alcohol: Clinical and Experimental Research 299 (1983)

Halperin, Is the Driver Drunk? Oculomotor Sobriety Testing, 57 Journal of the American Optometer Association, 654 (1986)

Halperin & Yolton, Is the Driver Drunk? Oculomotor Sobriety Testing, 57 Journal of the American Optometric Association 654 (1986)

Hammond, et al., Blood Ethanol: A Report of Unusually High Levels in Living Patient, 226 Journal of the American Medical Association 63 (1973)

Hansteen, Effects of Cannabis and Alcohol on Automobile Driving and Psychomotor Tracking, 282 Annals of the New York Academy of Science 240 (1976)

Harding, Laessig & Field, Field Performance of the Intoxilyzer 5000: A Comparison of Blood- and Breath-Alcohol Results in Wisconsin Drivers, 35 Journal of Forensic Sciences 1022 (1990)

Hayden, Layden & Hickey, The Stability of Alcohol Content in Samples of Blood and Urine, 146 Irish Journal of Medical Science 48 (1977)

Heise, Concentrations of Alcohol in Samples of Blood and Urine Taken at the Same Time, 12 Journal of Forensic Sciences 454 (1967)

Hesselbrock & Shaskan, Endogenous Breath Acetaldehyde Levels Among Alcoholic and Non-Alcoholic Probands: Effects of Alcohol Use and Smoking, 9 Program of NeuroPsychopharmacology & Biological Psychiatry 259 (1985)

Hindmarch, Kerr & Sherwood, The Effects of Alcohol and Other Drugs on Psychomotor Performance and Cognitive Function, 26 Alcohol and Alcoholism 1 (1991)

Hlastala, Effect of Respiratory Diseases on Alcohol Breath Tests, 7(24) Drinking/Driving Law Letter 1 (1988)

Hlastala, Physiological Errors Associated with Alcohol Breath Testing, 9 The Champion 16 (1985)
Hodgson, Blood Alcohol Testing, 134 Canadian Medical Association Journal 472 (1986)
Hodgson & Shajani, Distribution of Ethanol: Plasma to Whole Blood Ratios, 18 Canadian Society of Forensic Science Journal 73 (1985)
Holt, et al., Alcohol Absorption, Gastric Emptying and a Breathalyzer, 9 British Journal of Clinical Pharmacology 205 (1983)
Holzbecher & Wells, Elimination of Ethanol in Humans, 17 Canadian Society of Forensics Journal (1984)
Honts & Amato-Henderson, Horizontal Gaze Nystagmus Test. The State of the Science in 1995, 71 North Dakota Law Review 671 (1995)
Horowitz, et al., Relationships Between Gastric Emptying of Solid and Caloric Liquid Meals and Alcohol Absorption, 257 American Journal of Physiology 291 (1989)
Howells, Nystagmus as a Physical Sign in Alcohol Intoxication, 1 British Medical Journal 1405 (1956)
Hume & Fitzgerald, Chemical Tests for Intoxication: What Do the Numbers Really Mean?, 57 Annals of Chemistry 876A (1985)
Hunvald & Zimring, Whatever Happened to Implied Consent?, 33 Missouri Law Review 323 (1968)
Issacs & Emerson, Blood: Breath Ethanol Ratios, 2 Lancet 639 (1984)
Jackson, Tucker & Woods, Backtracking Booze with Bayes — The Retrospective Interpretation of Blood Alcohol Data, 31 British Journal of Clinical Pharmacology 55 (1991)
Jain & Cravey, Analysis of Alcohol — A Review of Chemical and Infrared Methods, 10 Journal of Chromatographic Science 263 (1972)
Jain & Cravey, A Review of Breath Alcohol Methods, 12 Journal of Chromatographic Science 214 (1974)
Jaklinska & Tomaszewska, Blood and Urine Alcohol Levels in Cases of Head Injury, 1 Forensic Science 225 (1966)
Jakus, et al., Consumption of Large Doses of Alcohol in a Short Time Span, 56 Forensic Science International 113 (1992)
Jauhonen, Baraona & Miyakawa, Origin of Breath Acetaldehyde During Ethanol Oxidation: Effect of Long-Term Cigarette Smoking, 100 Journal of Laboratory Clinical Medicine 908 (1982)
Johnson, et al., Survival After a Serum Ethanol Concentration of 1½%, 2 Lancet 1394 (1982)
Johnson, Horowitz, Maddox, Wishart & Shearman, Cigarette Smoking and Rate of Gastric Emptying: Effect on Alcohol Absorption, 302 British Medical Journal 20 (1991)
Jollymore, Fraser, Moss & Perry, Comparative Study of Ethyl Alcohol in Blood and Vitreous Humor, 17 Canadian Society of Forensic Science 50 (1984)
Jones, Breath-Acetone Concentrations in Fasting Healthy Men: Response of Infrared Breath-Alcohol Analyzers, 11 Journal of Analytical Toxicology, 67 (1987)
Jones, Circadian Variation in the Effects of Alcohol on Cognitive Performance, 35 Quarterly Journal of Studies on Alcohol 1212 (1974)
Jones, Concentration-Time Profiles of Ethanol in Capillary Blood after Ingestion of Beer, 31 Journal of the Forensic Science Society 429 (1991)
Jones, Detection of Alcohol-Impaired Drivers Using a Passive Alcohol Sensor, 14 Journal of Police Science and Administration 2 (1986)

Jones, Disappearance of Ethanol from the Blood of Human Subjects: Implications in Forensic Toxicology, 38(1) Journal of Forensics 103 (1993)

Jones, Ethanol Distribution Ratios Between Urine and Capillary Blood in Controlled Experiments and in Apprehended Drinking Drivers, 37(1) Journal of Forensic Sciences 21 (1992)

Jones, Evaluation of Breath-Alcohol Instruments, 28 Forensic Science International 147 (1985)

Jones, How Breathing Technique Can Influence the Results of Breath-Alcohol Analysis, 22(4) Medicine, Science and the Law 275 (1982)

Jones, Observations on the Specificity of Breath-Alcohol Analyzers Used for Clinical and Medicolegal Purposes, 34 Journal of Forensic Science 849 (1989)

Jones, Peak Blood-Alcohol Concentration and the Time of its Occurrence After Rapid Drinking on an Empty Stomach, 36(2) Journal of Forensic Sciences 376 (1991)

Jones, Pharmacokinetics of Ethanol in Saliva: Comparison with Blood and Breath Alcohol Profiles, Subjective Feelings of Intoxication, and Diminished Performance, 39 Clinical Chemistry 1837 (1993)

Jones, Physiological Aspects of Breath-Alcohol Measurement, 6(2) Alcohol, Drugs and Driving 1 (1990)

Jones, Role of Rebreathing in Determination of the Blood-Breath Ratio of Expired Ethanol, 55 Journal of Applied Physiology: Respiratory, Environmental and Exercise Physiology 1237 (1983)

Jones, Viability of the Blood: Breath-Alcohol Ratio in Vivo, 39(1) Journal of Studies on Alcohol 1931 (1978)

Jones, A. W., Concentration-Time Profiles of Ethanol in Capillary Blood After Ingestion of Beer, 31 Journal of the Forensic Science Society 429 (1991)

Jones, Hahn & Stalberg, Distribution of Ethanol and Water Between Plasma and Whole Blood; Inter- and Intra-individual Variations after Administration of Ethanol by Intravenous Infusion, 50 Scandinavian Journal of Clinical Laboratory Investigations 775 (1990)

Jones, et al., Measuring Ethanol in Blood and Breath for Legal Purposes: Variability Between Laboratories and Between Breath Instruments, 38 Journal of Clinical Chemistry 743 (1992)

Jones, et al., Peak Blood-Ethanol Concentration and the Time of Its Occurrence After Rapid Drinking on an Empty Stomach, 36(2) Journal of Forensic Sciences 376 (1991)

Jones & Goldberg, Evaluation of Breath Alcohol Instruments I: In Vitro Experiments with Alcolmeter Pocket Model, 12 Forensic Science International 1 (1978)

Jones, Hahn & Stalberg, Pharmacokinetics of Ethanol in Plasma and Whole Blood: Estimation of Total Body Water by the Dilution Principle, 42 European Journal of Clinical Pharmacology 445 (1992)

Jones & Jones, Ethanol Metabolism in Women Taking Oral Contraceptives, 8 Alcoholism: Clinical and Experimental Research 24 (1984)

Jones & Lund, Detection of Alcohol-Impaired Drivers Using a Passive Alcohol Sensor, 14 Journal of Police Science and Administration 153 (1986)

Jones & Neri, Evaluation of Blood-Ethanol Profiles After Consumption of Alcohol Together with a Large Meal, 24(3) Canadian Society of Forensic Science Journal 165 (1991)

Jones & Neri, Reinvestigation of Widmark's Method for Quantitative Evaluation of Blood-Ethanol Profiles: Influence of Alcohol Dose and Mode of Drinking, 33 Clinical Chemistry 1469 (1987)

Jones & Simpson, Reliability of Breath-Alcohol Measurements During the Absorptive Phase, 33 Clinical Chemistry, 2128 (1987)
Jones & Sternebring, Kinetics of Ethanol and Methanol in Alcoholics During Detoxification, 27 Alcohol & Alcoholism 641 (1992)
Jones & Vega, Fast and Slow Drinkers: Blood Alcohol Variables and Cognitive Performance, 34 Quarterly Journal of Studies on Alcohol 797 (1973)
Joye, Drunk Driving: Recommendations for Safer Highways, Trial (June 1983)
Kaji, et al., Intragastrointestinal Alcohol Fermentation Syndrome, 24 Journal of the Forensic Science Society 461 (1984)
Kaplan, Sellers, Hamilton, Naranjo & Dorian, Is There Acute Tolerance to Alcohol at Steady State?, 46 Journal of Studies on Alcohol 253 (1985)
Karabian, California's Implied Consent Statute: An Examination and Evaluation, 1 Loyola (L.A.) Law Review 23 (1968)
Kave & Cardona, Errors of Converting a Urine Alcohol Value into a Blood Alcohol Level, 52 American Journal of Clinical Pathology 577 (1969)
Kaye, Collection and Handling of the Blood Alcohol Specimen, 74 American Journal of Clinical Pathology 743 (1980)
Kelley, Plea Bargaining and Sentencing Alternatives in DWI Cases, 23 St. Louis Bar Journal 24 (Winter 1977)
Kelly & Tarantino, Radio Frequency Interference and the Breathalyzer: A Case Analysis, 31 Rhode Island Bar Journal 6 (June 1983)
Khurana, Gupta & Gupta, Quantitative Relationship Between Blood Alcohol Levels and Positional Alcoholic Nystagmus, 16 Indian Journal of Pharmacology 34 (1984)
Kiger, et al., Passive Alcohol Sensors in Law Enforcement Screenings for Alcohol-impaired Drivers, 9(1) Alcohol, Drugs and Driving (1993)
Knight, Driving and Alcohol: A Case Report of a Biological Impossibility, 24 Medicine, Science and the Law 271 (1984)
Korri, Nuutinen & Salapuro, Increased Blood Acetate, 9 Alcoholism: Clinical and Experimental Research 468 (1985)
Krotosyynski, Gabriel, O'Neill & Claudio, Characterization of Human Expired Air: A Promising Investigation and Diagnostic Technique, 15 Journal of Chromatographic Science 239 (1977)
Labianca, Chemical Basis of the Breathalyzer, 67 Journal of Chemical Education 259 (1990)
Laferty, Ethyl Chloride: Possible Misidentification as Ethanol, 39 Journal of Forensic Sciences 261 (1994)
Landauer & Howat, Low and Moderate Alcohol Doses, Psychomotor Performance, and Perceived Drowsiness, 26 Ergonomics 647 (1983)
Langenbucher & Nathan, Psychology, Public Policy and the Evidence for Alcohol Intoxication, American Psychologist 1070 (October 1983)
Laurell, Effects of Small Doses of Alcohol on Driver Performance in Emergency Traffic Situations, 9(3) Accident Analysis & Prevention 191 (1977)
Lawrence, Herbert & Jeffcoate, Circadian Variation in Effects of Ethanol in Man, 18 Pharmacology Biochemistry & Behaviour 555 (1983)
Lester, Breath Tests for Alcohol, 284 New England Journal of Medicine 1269 (1971)
Lestina & Lund, Laboratory Evaluation of Two Passive Alcohol Sensors, 53 Journal of Studies on Alcohol 328 (1992)
Levine, Smith, Smialek & Caplan, Interpretation of Low Postmortem Concentrations of Ethanol, 38 Journal of Forensic Sciences 663 (1993)
Lindros, Stowell, Pikkarainen & Salaspuro, Elevated Blood Acetaldehyde in Al-

coholics with Accelerated Ethanol Elimination, 13 Pharmacology and Biochemical Behavior 13, 1 Supp 119 (1980)

Little, Control of the Drinking Driver, 54 American Bar Association Journal 555 (1968)

Little, The New Kansas DUI Law: Constitutional Issues and Practical Problems, 22 Washburn Law Journal 340 (1983)

Llaurado, Alcohol Breath Analyzers and Radiofrequency Interference, 16 International Journal of Bio-Medical Computing 3 (1985)

Logan, Gullberg & Elenbaas, Isopropanol Interference with Breath Alcohol Analysis: A Case Report, 39 Journal of Forensic Sciences 1107 (1994)

Lough & Fehn, Efficacy of 1% Sodium Fluoride as a Preservative in Urine Samples Containing Glucose and Candida Albicans, 38 Journal of Forensic Sciences 266 (1993)

Lowrey, The Case for Quickie Breath Tests, 70 Traffic Safety 12 (1970)

Manolis, The Diagnostic Potential of Breath Analysis, 29 Clinical Chemistry 5 (1983)

Marks, Methane and the Infra-Red Breath Alcohol Analyser, The Lancet 50 (7 July 1984)

Marks & MacAvoy, Divided Attention Performance in Cannabis Users and Nonusers Following Alcohol and Cannabis Use Separately and in Combination, 99 Psychopharmacology 3 (1989)

Marraccini, et al., Differences Between Multisite Postmortem Ethanol Concentrations as Related to Agonal Events, 35(6) Journal of Forensic Sciences 1360 (1990)

Marshall, et al., Ethanol Elimination in Males and Females' Relationship to Menstrual Cycle and Body Composition, 3 Hepatology 701 (1983)

Martin, Moll, Schmid & Detti, The Pharmacokinetics of Alcohol In Human Breath, Venous and Arterial Blood After Oral Ingestion, 26 European Journal of Clinical Pharmacology 619 (1984)

Martin & Moss, Measurement of Acute Tolerance to Alcohol in Human Subjects, 17 Alcoholism: Clinical and Experimental Research 211 (1993)

Mason & Dubowski, Breath-Alcohol Analysis: Uses, Methods, and Some Forensic Problems — Review and Opinion, 21 Journal of Forensic Sciences 9 (1976)

Mathews, Chronic Alcohol Addiction and Criminal Responsibility, 7 American Criminal Law Quarterly 2 (1968)

McGuire, Accuracy of Estimating the Sobriety of Drinking Drivers, 17 Journal of Safety Research 81 (1986)

McIvor & Cosbey, Effect of Using Alcoholic and Non-Alcoholic Skin Cleansing Swabs When Sampling Blood for Alcohol Estimation Using Gas Chromatography, 44 British Journal of Clinical Practice 235 (1990)

Mebs, Gerchow & Schmidt, Interference of Acetone with Breath-Alcohol Testing. 21 Blutalkohol 193 (1984)

Minocha, et al., Modulation of Ethanol-Induced Central Nervous System Depression by Ibuprofen, 39 Clinical Pharmacology and Therapeutics 123 (1986)

Money & Landolt, An Unusual Toxicological Property of Alcohol: The Density Effect on the Organ of Balance, Defence and Civil Institute of Environmental Medicine, Advisory Group for Aerospace Research and Development, Neuilly sur Seine, France (1984)

Money, et al., Positional Nystagmus from Ingestion of Alcohol, Heavy Water and Glycerol, 23 Physiologist 73 (1980)

Mulder & Neuteboom, The Effects of Hypo- and Hyperventilation on Breath Alcohol Measurements, 24 Blutalkohol 341 (1987)

Mulholland & Townsend, Bladder Beer — A New Clinical Observation, 95 Transactions of the American Clinical Climatological Association 34 (1983)

Nahas, Pharmacologic and Epidemiologic Aspects of Alcohol and Cannabis, 84 New York State Journal of Medicine 599 (1984)

Nasilowski, Medicolegal Certification of Insobriety, 1 Forensic Science 197 (1966)

Natowicz, Donahue, Gorman, Kane, McKissick & Shaw, Pharmacological Analysis of a Case of Isopropanol Intoxication, 31 Clinical Chemistry 326 (1985)

Neuteboom & Jones, Disappearance Rate of Alcohol from the Blood of Drunk Drivers Calculated from Two Consecutive Samples: What Do the Results Really Mean?, 45 Forensic Science International 107 (1990)

Nichols, Toward a Coordinated Judicial View of the Accuracy of Breath Testing Devices, 59(3) North Dakota Law Review 329 (1983)

Nicholson, et al., Variability in Behavioral Impairment Involved in the Rising and Falling BAC Curve, Journal of Studies on Alcohol 349 (July 1992)

Nine, et al., Serum-Ethanol Determination: Comparison of Lactate and Lactate Dehydrogenase Interference in Three Enzymatic Assays, Journal of Analytical Toxicology 19:192 (1995)

Norris, The Correlation of Angle of Onset of Nystagmus with Blood Alcohol Level: Report of a Field Trial, 25 Journal of the Forensic Science Society 476 (1985)

Odesanmi, The Fatal Blood Alcohol Level in Acute Alcohol Poisoning, 23(1) Medicine, Science and the Law 25 (Jan. 1983)

Ohlsson, Ralph, Mandelkorn, Babb & Hlastala, Accurate Measurement of Blood Alcohol Concentration with Isothermal Rebreathing, 51(1) Journal of Studies on Alcohol 6 (1990)

Oliver & Garriott, Effects of Acetone and Toluene on Breathalyzer Results, 3 Journal of Analytical Toxicology 99 (1979)

O'Malley & Maisto, Factors Affecting the Perception of Intoxication. Dose, Tolerance, and Setting, 9 Addictive Behaviours 111 (1984)

Osborne & Rogers, Interactions of Alcohol and Caffeine on Human Reaction Time, Aviation, Space and Environmental Medicine 523 (June 1983)

Pangman, Horizontal Gaze Nystagmus: The New Drunk Driving Alchemy, The Champion 6 (April 1987)

Papple, The Effect of Non-Ethanolic Volatiles on the Measurement of Blood Ethanol Concentrations with an A.L.E.R.T. Roadside Screening Device, 15 Canadian Society of Forensics Journal 133 (1982)

Papple, The Effect of Oral Contraceptive Steroids (O.C.S.) on the Rate of Post-Absorptive Phase Decline of Blood Alcohol Concentration in the Adult Woman, 15 Canadian Society of Forensics Journal 17 (1982)

Passananti, Wolff & Vessell, Reproducibility of Individual Rates of Ethanol Metabolism in Fasting Subjects, 47 Clinical Pharmacology and Therapy 389 (1990)

Payne, Hill & King, Observations on the Distribution of Alcohol in Blood, Breath and Urine, 1 British Medical Journal 196 (1966)

Penttila, Tenhu & Kataja, Computer Analysis of Clinical Test Correlations with Blood Alcohol and the Physician's Final Evaluation of the State of Intoxication in Cases of Suspected Drunken Driving, 9(2) Blutalkohol 104 (1972)

Perper, Twerski & Wienand, Tolerance at High Blood Alcohol Concentrations: A Study of 110 Cases and Review of the Literature, 31 Journal of Forensic Sciences 212 (1986)

Philips, Breath Tests in Medicine, Scientific American 74 (July 1992)

Philips, Greenberg & Martinez, Endogenous Breath Ethanol Concentrations in Abstinent Alcohol Abusers and Normals, 5(3) Alcohol 263 (1988)
Pishkin, et al., Cognitive and Electrophysiologic Parameters During Ascending and Descending Limbs of the Blood Alcohol Curve, 7 Alcoholism — Clinical and Experimental Research 76 (1983)
Pohereckyk, Brick & Carpenter, Assessment of the Development of Tolerance to Alcohol, 10 Alcoholism: Clinical and Experimental Research 616 (1986)
Pounder & Kuroda, Vitreous Alcohol Is of Limited Value in Predicting Blood Alcohol, 65 Forensic Science International 73 (1994)
Principe, The Vacu-Sampler: A New Device for the Encapsulation of Breath and Other Gaseous Samples, 2 Journal of Police Science and Administration 404 (1974)
Rainey, Relation Between Serum and Whole-Blood Ethanol Concentrations, 39 Clinical Chemistry 2288 (1993)
Randolph & Randolph, Breathalyzer — Statutory and Constitutional Deficiencies, 9 Wake Forest Law Review 331 (1973)
Rauscher, The Law of Defending Driving While Intoxicated Cases, 23 St. Louis Bar Journal 6 (Winter 1977)
Redmond, Alcohol Blood Levels, 16 Annals of Emergency Medicine 374 (1987)
Robertson, et al., Jail Sentences for Driving While Intoxicated in Chicago: A Judicial Action That Failed, 8(1) Law and Society Review 56 (1973)
Roehrenbeck & Russel, Blood Is Thicker Than Water: What You Need to Know to Challenge a Serum Blood Alcohol Result, Criminal Justice (Fall 1993)
Romm & Collins, Body Temperature Influences on Ethanol Elimination Rate, 4 Alcohol 189 (1987)
Rouse, Testing for Legal Intoxication, 39 Pathologist 39 (1985)
Russell & Jones, Breath Ethyl Alcohol Concentration and Analysis in the Presence of Chronic Obstructive Pulmonary Disease, 16 Clinical Biochemistry 182 (June 1983)
Ryan, Alcohol and Blood Sugar Disorders — An Overview, 8 Alcohol Health and Research World 3 (1984)
Saady, Poklis & Dalton, Production of Urinary Ethanol after Sample Collection, 38 Journal of Forensic Sciences 1467 (1993)
Samija, Shajani & Wong, Radio Frequency Interference (RFI): Effects on Evidentiary Breath Testing Using the Breathalyzer Models 900 and 900A. 18 Canadian Society of Forensic Science Journal 211 (1985)
Samuels, Drunk Driving: Challenging the Blood or Urine Analysis, 20(1) Medicine, Science and Law 14 (1980)
Santamaria, Ethanol Ingestion Studies, Department of Transport Office of Road Safety, Department of Community Medicine, St. Vincent's Hospital, Fitzroy, Australia (1979)
Schenker & Speeg, Risk of Alcohol Intake in Men and Women: All May not be Equal, 322 New England Journal of Medicine 127 (1990)
Scherotter, California Vehicle Code Section 23152(b): A Guessing Game for California Drivers, 5 Criminal Justice Journal 249 (1982)
Segal, Bernard & Duffy, Ethanol Elimination Among Different Racial Groups, 9 Alcohol 213 (1992)
Senkowski & Thompson, Accuracy of Blood Alcohol Analysis Using Headspace Gas Chromatography, 35 Journal of Forensic Sciences 176 (1990)
Shajani & Dinn, Blood Alcohol Concentrations Reached in Human Subjects After Consumption of Alcoholic Beverages in a Social Setting, 18 Canadian Society of Forensic Science Journal 38 (1985)

Simpson, Accuracy and Precision of Breath-Alcohol Measurements for a Random Subject in the Postabsorptive State, 33 Clinical Chemistry 261 (1987)

Simpson, Medicolegal Alcohol Determination: Comparison and Consequences of Breath and Blood Analysis, 13(6) Journal of Analytical Toxicology 361 (1989)

Simpson, Medicolegal Alcohol Determination: Implications and Consequences of Irregularities in Blood Alcohol Concentration vs. Time Curves, 16 Journal of Analytical Toxicology 270 (1992)

Smith, Drinking and Driving, 3 Criminal Law Quarterly (1961)

Smith, Constitutional Issues Raised by the Civil-Criminal Dichotomy of the Maine DUI Law, 35 Maine Law Review 385 (1983)

Smith, Science, the Intoxilyzer, and Breath Alcohol Testing, 11 The Champion 8 (1987)

Spector, Alcohol Breath Tests: Gross Errors in Current Methods of Measuring Alveolar Gas Concentrations, 172 Science 57 (1971)

Stapleton, Githrie & Linnoila, Effects of Alcohol and Other Psychotropic Drugs on Eye Movements, 47 Journal of Studies on Alcohol 426 (1986)

Stern, Handling Public Drunkenness: Reforms Despite *Powell,* 55 American Bar Association Journal 656 (1969)

Stowell, Johnson, Aune, Vatne, Ripel & Morland, A Reinvestigation of the Usefulness of Breath Analysis in the Determination of Blood Acetaldehyde Concentrations, 8 Alcoholism: Clinical and Experimental Research 442 (1984)

Studdard, DWI Countermeasure: Testing the Impaired Driver, Police Chief (July 1984)

Sullivan, Hauptman & Bronstein, Lack of Observable Intoxication in Humans with High Plasma Alcohol Concentrations, 32 Journal of Forensic Sciences 1660 (1987)

Sutton, The Effects of Alcohol, Marihuana, and Their Combination on Driving Ability, 44 Journal of Studies on Alcohol 438 (1983)

Tabakoff, Cornell & Hoffman, Alcohol Tolerance, 15 Annals of Emergency Medicine 1005 (1986)

Takase, Yauhara, Takada & Ueshima, Changes in Blood Acetaldehyde Levels After Ethanol Administration in Alcoholics, 7 Alcohol 37 (1990)

Tao, Criminal Drunkenness and the Law, 54 Iowa Law Review 1059 (1969)

Taylor, Blood-Alcohol Presumptions: Guilty Until Proven Innocent, 53 California State Bar Journal 172 (May 1978)

Taylor, Drunk Driving Defense, 7 Criminal Defense 17 (March 1982)

Taylor, Advising the Client Under California's New Drunk Driving Law, 2 California Lawyer 37 (April 1982)

Taylor, Defending the Drunk Driving Client: Initial Considerations, 9 Criminal Defense 3 (Nov. 1982)

Taylor, Drunk Driving Defense, 4 The Defender 11 (Nov. 1982)

Taylor, Blood-Alcohol Evidence and the Fourth Amendment, 10(3) and 10(4) Search and Seizure Law Reports (April and May 1983)

Taylor, Morrow & Yesavage, Acute and 8-Hour Effects of Alcohol (0.08% BAC) on Younger and Older Pilots' Simulator Performance, 65 Aviation, Space and Environmental Medicine 718 (1994)

Taylor, Turrill & Carter, Blood Alcohol Analysis: A Comparison of the Gas-Chromatographic Assay with an Enzymatic Assay, 16 Pathology 157 (1984)

Tharp, Moskowitz & Burns, Circadian Effects on Alcohol Gaze Nystagmus, 18 Psychophysiology 193 (1981)

Thompson, The Constitutionality of Chemical Test Presumptions of Intoxication in Motor Vehicle Statutes, 20 San Diego Law Review 301 (1983)

Tiffany, Optometric Expert Testimony: Foundation for the Horizontal Gaze Nystagmus Test, 57 Journal of Optometry & the Law, 705 (1986)

Trafford & Makin, Breath-Alcohol Concentration May Not Always Reflect the Concentration of Alcohol in Blood, 18 Journal of Analytical Toxicology 225 (1994)

Tsukamoto, et al., Experimental Study on Ethanol Concentration Ratios of Breath to Body Fluid, 25 Nihon University Journal of Medicine 281 (1983)

Tzamaloukas, Jackson & Gallegos, Prediction of Alcohol Blood Levels, 32 Clinical Research 16A (1984)

VanBerkom & Lowell, Chemical Test Evidence in DWI Cases: Some Issues and Challenges, 7 Alcohol, Drugs and Driving 229 (1991)

Voas, Laboratory and Field Tests of a Passive Alcohol Sensing System, 4 Abstracts and Reviews in Alcohol and Driving 3 (1983)

Vogel-Sprott & Barrett, Age, Drinking Habits and the Effects of Alcohol, 45 Journal of Studies on Alcohol 517 (1984)

Watanebe, et al., A Report of Unusually High Blood Ethanol and Acetaldehyde Levels in Two Surviving Patients, 9 Alcoholism: Clinical and Experimental Research 14 (1985)

Watkins & Adler, The Effect of Food on Alcohol Absorption and Elimination Patterns, 38(2) Journal of Forensic Sciences 285 (1993)

Watson, Baton Rouge's Pre-arrest Breath Test and How It's Working, 18 Traffic Digest and Review 7 (1970)

Watson, Watson & Batt, Prediction of Blood Alcohol Concentrations in Human Subjects: Updating the Widmark Equation, 42 Journal of Studies of Alcohol 547 (1981)

Weathermon, McCutcheon & Cowan, Results of Analyses for Alcohol of New Simultaneously Collected Venous Blood and Alveolar Breath Specimens, 9 Alcohol, Drugs and Driving 19 (1993)

Wilbur, Alcoholism: Medical or Legal Problem?, 5 Trial 48a (1969)

Wilinson, Kime & Purnell, Alcohol and Human Eye Movement, 97 Brain 785 (1974)

Wilson, 1982 Amendments to Virginia's Driving While Intoxicated Laws, 17 University of Richmond Law Review 189 (1982)

Wilson & Erwin, Rate of Alcohol Metabolism; Do Not "Correct" the B_{60} Estimates for Comparisons Among Ethnic Groups, 40 Journal of Studies on Alcohol 1093 (1983)

Wilson, Erwin & McClearn, Effects of Ethanol: 1. Acute Metabolic Tolerance and Ethnic Differences, 2 Alcoholism: Clinical and Experimental Research 226 (1984)

Wilson & Niaura, Alcohol and the Disinhibition of Sexual Responsiveness, 45 Journal of Studies on Alcohol 219 (1984)

Wilson, et al., Effect of Age and Chronic Obstructive Pulmonary Disease on the Breathalyzer Estimation of Blood Alcohol Level, 11 Alcoholism: Clinical and Experimental Research 440 (1987)

Winek & Carfagna, Comparison of Plasma, Serum and Whole Blood Ethanol Concentrations, 11 Journal of Analytical Toxicology 267 (1987)

Winek & Murphy, The Rate and Kinetic Order of Ethanol Elimination, 25 Forensic Science International 159 (1984)

Winek, Murphy & Winek, The Unreliability of Using a Urine Ethanol Concentration to a Blood Ethanol Concentration, 25 Forensic Science International 277 (1984)

Wright, Effect of Mouth Temperature on Breath Alcohol Concentration, 163 Journal of Physiology 21P (1962)

Wright & Jones, Breath Alcohol Analysis and the Blood:Breath Ratio, 15 Medicine, Science and the Law 205 (1975)

Yamamoto & Ueda, Studies on Breath Alcohol Analysis for the Estimation of Blood Alcohol Levels, 1 Forensic Science 207 (1966)

Zwahlen, Effect of Alcohol on Driving Skills and Reaction Times, 1(1) Journal of Occupational Accidents 21 (1976)

Text Annotations

Admissibility in criminal cases of blood alcohol test where blood was taken from unconscious driver, 72 A.L.R. 3d 325

Blood tests, 29 Am. Jur. 2d, Evidence §106

Construction of statute or ordinance making it an offense to possess or have alcohol beverages in opened package in motor vehicle, 35 A.L.R.3d 1418

Criminal responsibility of one other than driver, 7 Am. Jur. 2d, Automobiles and Highway Traffic §261

Defense on charge of driving while intoxicated, 19 Am. Jur. Trials 123

Defense to charge of driving under the influence of alcohol, 17 Am. Jur. 2d Proof of Facts 1

Degree of Intoxication, 7 Am. Jur. 2d, Automobiles and Highway Safety §257

Destruction of ampoule used in alcohol breath test as warranting suppression of result of test, 19 A.L.R.4th 509

Discovery and evaluation of medical records, 15 Am. Jur. Trials 373

Dram shop litigation, 12 Am. Jur. Trials 729

Driving under the influence, or when addicted to the use, of drugs as criminal offense, 17 A.L.R.3d 815

Evidence of scientific and mechanical facts, 29 Am. Jur. 2d, Evidence §§103–104

The impaired driver — ascertaining physical condition, 4 Am. Jur., Trials 615

Interviewing the client, 1 Am. Jur. Trials 1

Intoxication by drugs taken for medicinal purposes, 7 Am. Jur. 2d, Automobiles and Highway Traffic §258

Liability based on entrusting automobile to one who is intoxicated or known to be excessive user of intoxicants, 19 A.L.R.3d 1175

Locating scientific and technical experts, 2 Am. Jur. Trials 293

Location of offense as "public"within requirements of enactments against drunkenness, 8 A.L.R.3d 930

Medical or physical examinations or chemical tests, 7 Am. Jur. 2d, Automobiles and Highway Traffic §295

Modern status or rule as to voluntary intoxication as defense to criminal charge, 8 A.L.R.3d 1326

"Motor vehicle" within purview of drunk driving legislation, 7 Am. Jur. 2d, Automobiles and Highway Traffic §255

Nature and intoxicating quality of alcoholic beverages, 29 Am. Jur. 2d, Evidence §§108–109

Necessity and Sufficiency of Proof That Tests of Blood Alcohol Concentration Were Conducted in Conformance with Prescribed Methods, 96 A.L.R.3d 745

Presumptions and inferences as to sobriety or drunkenness, 29 Am. Jur. 2d, Evidence §206

Proof and disproof of alcohol-induced driving impairment through breath alcohol testing, 14 Am Jur. 3d Proof of Facts 229

Proof and disproof of alcohol-induced driving impairment through evidence of observable intoxication and coordination testing, 9 Am. Jur. 3d Proof of Facts 459

Punishment, 7 Am. Jur. 2d, Automobiles and Highway Traffic §262

Qualification as expert to testify as to findings or results of scientific test to determine alcoholic content of blood, 77 A.L.R. 2d 971

Right of person accused of intoxication to have test for alcohol in his system made by own physician, 78 A.L.R.2d 905

Selecting the jury — defense view, 5 Am. Jur. Trials 247

Selecting and preparing expert witnesses, 2 Am. Jur. Trials 585

Statutory provisions as to driving while intoxicated, 7 Am Jur. 2d, Automobiles and Highway Traffic §§253–254

Tests of alcoholic content of blood, 29 Am. Jur. 2d, Evidence §830

Tests of determine alcohol in system, 29 Am. Jur. 2d, Evidence §295

Unreliability of the horizontal gaze nystagmus test, 4 Am. Jur. 3d Proof of Facts 439

Vehicular homicide, 13 Am. Jur. Trials 295

What amounts to violation of drunken-driving statute in officer's "presence" or "view" so as to permit warrantless arrest, 74 A.L.R.3d 1138

What constitutes "driving," "operating," "being in control of," "attempting to operate" motor vehicle under drunk driving statute, 7 Am. Jur. 2d, Automobiles and Highway Traffic §256

Willingness or refusal to submit to examination or test, 29 Am. Jur. 2d. Evidence §294

TABLE OF CASES

References are to sections.

INDEX

References are to sections.